Photographs © Andrea B. Swenson

RHONA SILVERBUSH AND SAMI PLOTKIN

Speak the Speech!

RHONA SILVERBUSH studied theatre and psychology at Brandeis University and holds a law degree from Boston College Law School. She has acted with regional theatre and Shakespeare companies and has directed and taught drama and Shakespeare. Currently, she coaches professional actors, lectures, writes, and is an adjunct faculty member at Columbia University's Teachers College. She and her husband live in New York City with their two aging feline divas.

SAMI PLOTKIN graduated summa cum laude from Brandeis University with a double major in Theatre Arts and English Literature, and honed her stagecraft in London under the tutelage of Royal Shakespeare Company members. She later earned her M.F.A. at Columbia University's School of the Arts. Sami has performed Shakespeare in the United States and on tour in Europe and the former Soviet Union; she now works as an actor, screenwriter, and playwright. During the hours when the New York Public Library is closed, she lives with her husband in Chelsea.

PRAISE FOR

Speak the Speech!

"An enormously useful tool for auditioning actors who are not fully acquainted with the contexts of their audition pieces."

—TINA PACKER, Artistic Director, Shakespeare & Company

"For the actor looking to find in one collection a comprehensive selection of Shakespeare's monologues, *Speak the Speech!* is a rich and comprehensive resource."

—JEFFREY HOROWITZ, Artistic Director, Theatre for a New Audience

Speak the Speech!

SHAKESPEARE'S MONOLOGUES ILLUMINATED

Rhona Silverbush and Sami Plotkin

FABER AND FABER, INC.

AN AFFILIATE OF FARRAR, STRAUS AND GIROUX

NEW YORK

Faber and Faber, Inc.
An affiliate of Farrar, Straus and Giroux
19 Union Square West, New York 10003

Distributed in Canada by Penguin Books of Canada Ltd.
Printed in the United States of America
First edition, 2002

Library of Congress Cataloging-in-Publication Data
Silverbush, Rhona, date.
Speak the speech! : Shakespeare's monologues illuminated / Rhona Silverbush and Sami Plotkin.— 1st ed.
p. cm.
Includes index.
ISBN 0-571-21122-4 (pbk. : alk. paper)
1. Shakespeare, William, 1564–1616—Dramatic production. 2. Shakespeare, William, 1564–1616—Quotations. 3. Shakespeare, William, 1564–1616—Language. 4. Monologues. 5. Acting. I. Plotkin, Sami, date. II. Title.

PR3091 .S45 2002
822.3'3—dc21

2002018877

Designed by Jonathan D. Lippincott

www.fsgbooks.com

3 5 7 9 10 8 6 4

For our husbands

CONTENTS

NOTE: Although the monologues and synopses of the Comedies, Problem Plays, Tragedies, and Romances are grouped by genre and presented alphabetically, the monologues and synopses of the Histories are presented in the chronological order in which the events of the plays actually occurred, because each play is easier to understand in light of the events of the plays that precede it.

PROLOGUE: WHY WE WROTE THIS BOOK xvii

ACKNOWLEDGMENTS xix

THE PLAY'S THE THING xxiii
CHOOSING A MONOLOGUE xxiii

WHAT IS THIS STUFF? xxvii
WHY BOTHER? xxix
CRACKING THE CODE xxxi
VERSE-ATILITY xxxi
A Leg Up on Feet: The Basic Variations xxxi
Additional Variations: Headless Feet and Other Oddities xxxiii
Making the Shoe Fit the Foot xxxvi
We Come to Praise Caesura, Not to Bury It xxxix

RHETORIC—POETIC AND OTHERWISE xli
A Reason to Rhyme xli
Crossing the Sound Barrier xlii
Imagery: "On Your Imaginary Forces Work" xliv
Rhetorically Speaking xlv

THIS EARTH, THIS REALM, THIS ENGLAND: SHAKESPEARE'S LIFE AND TIMES xlix
WHAT'S PAST IS PROLOGUE: ENGLAND IN SHAKESPEARE'S TIME xlix
WITHIN THIS WOODEN O: THEATRE IN SHAKESPEARE'S TIME li
ONE MAN IN HIS TIME PLAYS MANY PARTS: THE BARD'S BIO, IN BRIEF lii

THE LOWDOWN ON PUNCTUATION, SPELLING, ANNOTATION, COMMENTARY, AND LINE NUMBERING lvii

Monologues

THE HISTORIES

KING JOHN
Philip the Bastard (Act I, Scene i) 5
Philip the Bastard (Act II, Scene i) 11
Constance (Act III, Scene i) 17
Constance (Act III, Scene iv) 23
Constance (Act III, Scene iv) 29
Lewis (Act V, Scene ii) 35
Philip the Bastard (Act V, Scene ii) 40

RICHARD II
Duchess of Gloucester (Act I, Scene ii) 46
John of Gaunt (Act II, Scene i) 50
King Richard (Act III, Scene ii) 55
King Richard (Act III, Scene iii) 60
Bishop of Carlisle (Act IV, Scene i) 66

HENRY IV, PART ONE
Hotspur (Act I, Scene iii) 72
Hotspur (Act II, Scene iii) 78
Falstaff (Act V, Scene i) 83

HENRY IV, PART TWO
Mistress Quickly (Act II, Scene i) 87
Lady Percy (Act II, Scene iii) 91
King Henry IV (Act III, Scene i) 98
Falstaff (Act IV, Scene iii) 104
Prince Hal (Act IV, Scene v) 110

HENRY V
Chorus (Prologue) 116
King Henry V (Act I, Scene ii) 122
King Henry V (Act IV, Scene iii) 129
King Henry V (Act V, Scene ii) 137

HENRY VI, PART ONE
Joan la Pucelle (Act V, Scene iii) 143

HENRY VI, PART TWO
Queen Margaret (Act I, Scene iii) 149
Eleanor (Act II, Scene iv) 158

HENRY VI, PART THREE
Queen Margaret (Act I, Scene iv) 164
Richard, Duke of York (Act I, Scene iv) 171
King Henry VI (Act II, Scene v) 179

RICHARD III
Richard (Act I, Scene i) 185
Lady Anne (Act I, Scene ii) 191
Richard (Act I, Scene ii) 197
King Edward IV (Act II, Scene i) 203
Lady Anne (Act IV, Scene i) 208
Margaret (Act IV, Scene iv) 212
King Richard (Act V, Scene iii) 218

HENRY VIII
Queen Katherine (Act II, Scene iv) 223

GENEALOGICAL CHARTS 231

THE COMEDIES

AS YOU LIKE IT
Duke Senior (Act II, Scene i) 243
Jaques (Act II, Scene vii) 248
Phebe (Act III, Scene v) 254
Rosalind (Act III, Scene v) 258
Phebe (Act III, Scene v) 264

THE COMEDY OF ERRORS
Adriana (Act II, Scene ii) 270
Luciana (Act III, Scene ii) 276

LOVE'S LABOUR'S LOST
Berowne (Act V, Scene ii) 282

THE MERCHANT OF VENICE
Shylock (Act I, Scene iii) 285
Launcelot Gobbo (Act II, Scene ii) 291
Shylock (Act III, Scene i) 296
Portia (Act III, Scene iv) 302
Portia (Act IV, Scene i) 308

THE MERRY WIVES OF WINDSOR
Mistress Page (Act II, Scene i) 313
Falstaff (Act III, Scene v) 318

A MIDSUMMER NIGHT'S DREAM
Theseus (Act I, Scene i) 326
Lysander (Act I, Scene i) 330
Helena (Act I, Scene i) 333
Helena (Act I, Scene i) 336
Titania (Act II, Scene i) 342
Oberon (Act II, Scene i) 348
Puck (Act III, Scene ii) 354

Bottom (Act IV, Scene i) 359
Snug (Act V, Scene i) 364

MUCH ADO ABOUT NOTHING
Benedick (Act II, Scene iii) 368
Benedick (Act II, Scene iii) 373

THE TAMING OF THE SHREW
Petruchio (Act IV, Scene i) 377

TWELFTH NIGHT
Orsino (Act I, Scene i) 381
Viola (Act II, Scene ii) 386
Malvolio (Act II, Scene v) 392
Olivia (Act III, Scene i) 401

THE TWO GENTLEMEN OF VERONA
Julia (Act I, Scene ii) 406
Launce (Act II, Scene iii) 413
Launce (Act IV, Scene iv) 420
Julia (Act IV, Scene iv) 425

THE PROBLEM PLAYS

ALL'S WELL THAT ENDS WELL
Helena (Act III, Scene ii) 433

MEASURE FOR MEASURE
Isabella (Act II, Scene ii) 438
Claudio (Act III, Scene i) 443

TROILUS AND CRESSIDA
Ulysses (Act I, Scene iii) 447
Cressida (Act III, Scene ii) 454

THE TRAGEDIES

ANTONY AND CLEOPATRA
Cleopatra (Act I, Scene v) 461
Enobarbus (Act II, Scene ii) 466

Cleopatra (Act IV, Scene xv) 474
Cleopatra (Act V, Scene ii) 481
Cleopatra (Act V, Scene ii) 485
Cleopatra (Act V, Scene ii) 491

CORIOLANUS
Menenius (Act II, Scene i) 497
Coriolanus (Act IV, Scene v) 501
Aufidius (Act IV, Scene v) 506
Volumnia (Act V, Scene iii) 512

HAMLET
Hamlet (Act I, Scene ii) 517
Polonius (Act I, Scene iii) 524
Ophelia (Act II, Scene i) 529
Polonius (Act II, Scene ii) 534
Hamlet (Act II, Scene ii) 542
Hamlet (Act III, Scene i) 552
Ophelia (Act III, Scene i) 559
Hamlet (Act III, Scene ii) 564
King Claudius (Act III, Scene iii) 570
Hamlet (Act III, Scene iii) 576
Gertrude (Act IV, Scene vii) 582

JULIUS CAESAR
Cassius (Act I, Scene ii) 588
Brutus (Act II, Scene i) 597
Portia (Act II, Scene i) 602
Calphurnia (Act II, Scene ii) 610
Antony (Act III, Scene i) 615
Brutus (Act III, Scene ii) 620
Antony (Act III, Scene ii) 625
Antony (Act III, Scene ii) 630

KING LEAR
Edmund (Act I, Scene ii) 637
Edmund (Act I, Scene ii) 642
Goneril (Act I, Scene iv) 648
King Lear (Act II, Scene iv) 654
King Lear (Act III, Scene ii) 660
King Lear (Act III, Scene iv) 665

MACBETH
Lady Macbeth (Act I, Scene v) 671
Lady Macbeth (Act I, Scene v) 677
Macbeth (Act I, Scene vii) 683
Lady Macbeth (Act I, Scene vii) 691
Macbeth (Act II, Scene i) 697
Porter (Act II, Scene iii) 704
Macbeth (Act III, Scene i) 710

OTHELLO
Iago (Act I, Scene i) 717
Othello (Act I, Scene iii) 722
Iago (Act I, Scene iii) 727
Emilia (Act IV, Scene iii) 731

ROMEO AND JULIET
Nurse (Act I, Scene iii) 735
Mercutio (Act I, Scene iv) 742
Mercutio (Act II, Scene i) 749
Romeo (Act II, Scene ii) 756
Juliet (Act II, Scene ii) 762
Juliet (Act II, Scene ii) 766
Juliet (Act II, Scene v) 770
Juliet (Act III, Scene ii) 774
Juliet (Act III, Scene ii) 780
Romeo (Act III, Scene iii) 786
Friar Lawrence (Act III, Scene iii) 791
Lord Capulet (Act III, Scene v) 799
Juliet (Act IV, Scene iii) 806

TIMON OF ATHENS
Timon (Act IV, Scene iii) 812

TITUS ANDRONICUS
Titus Andronicus (Act III, Scene ii) 817
Aaron (Act IV, Scene ii) 822

THE ROMANCES

CYMBELINE
Iachimo (Act II, Scene ii) 829
Imogen (Act III, Scene ii) 837
Imogen (Act III, Scene vi) 843

PERICLES
Dionyza (Act IV, Scene iii) 848

THE TEMPEST
Ariel (Act I, Scene ii) 852
Trinculo (Act II, Scene ii) 859
Caliban (Act III, Scene ii) 864
Prospero (Act IV, Scene i) 868
Prospero (Act V, Scene i) 874

THE WINTER'S TALE
Hermione (Act III, Scene ii) 880
Paulina (Act III, Scene ii) 885
Shepherd (Act III, Scene iii) 891

Synopses

THE HISTORIES
KING JOHN 899
RICHARD II 903
HENRY IV, PART ONE 906
HENRY IV, PART TWO 908
HENRY V 911
HENRY VI, PART ONE 913
HENRY VI, PART TWO 916
HENRY VI, PART THREE 920
RICHARD III 924
HENRY VIII 927

THE COMEDIES
AS YOU LIKE IT 931
THE COMEDY OF ERRORS 935

LOVE'S LABOUR'S LOST 938
THE MERCHANT OF VENICE 942
THE MERRY WIVES OF WINDSOR 946
A MIDSUMMER NIGHT'S DREAM 949
MUCH ADO ABOUT NOTHING 951
THE TAMING OF THE SHREW 954
TWELFTH NIGHT 958
THE TWO GENTLEMEN OF VERONA 960

THE PROBLEM PLAYS
ALL'S WELL THAT ENDS WELL 963
MEASURE FOR MEASURE 966
TROILUS AND CRESSIDA 970

THE TRAGEDIES
ANTONY AND CLEOPATRA 975
CORIOLANUS 978
HAMLET 981
JULIUS CAESAR 985
KING LEAR 988
MACBETH 991
OTHELLO 993
ROMEO AND JULIET 998
TIMON OF ATHENS 1001
TITUS ANDRONICUS 1003

THE ROMANCES
CYMBELINE 1007
PERICLES 1010
THE TEMPEST 1012
THE WINTER'S TALE 1014

GLOSSARY OF COMMON ARCHAIC WORDS, VERB FORMS, ELISIONS, AND CONTRACTIONS 1017

INDEX TO THE MONOLOGUES 1021

PROLOGUE: WHY WE WROTE THIS BOOK

If you've ever had trouble finding a suitable Shakespearean monologue for classwork or auditions—never mind then preparing it—you're not alone. We both remember trying to find an appropriate monologue by searching a volume of Shakespeare's complete works for any block of text with a woman's name attached, and then combing the text of the surrounding scene to try to figure out the woman's age, character, and circumstances. Once we'd found a suitable piece, we were faced with the daunting task of making sense of it. We often commiserated with other actors, who, like us, wished that there were one comprehensive resource that would not only assist an actor in selecting a monologue, but would also annotate it thoroughly; explain the text's references to history, mythology, folklore, and the science of the times; and illuminate acting options presented by Shakespeare's use of meter and other poetic and rhetorical devices. Over the years, we have encountered many actors whose lack of familiarity with these elements deterred them from performing Shakespeare. We hated the thought that actors were missing out on the thrill we've experienced when bringing Shakespeare's words to life, and so we set out to create the resource we and our peers had long wished for. Here it is—we hope that the tools it contains will help you to make confident, creative choices and to revel in the joy of playing Shakespeare.

ACKNOWLEDGMENTS

We are very grateful to a number of people without whom this book would not exist. First and foremost among these is our darling Vincent Virga, our guardian angel and chief champion, who endorsed this book with his characteristic passion, opening doors and wisely stewarding us through the publishing process. Our terrific editor at Faber and Faber, Denise Oswald, has brought her considerable insight, innovation, and commitment to this project, much to its benefit. She was ably assisted by Chandra Wohleber, to whom we also extend our thanks. Jonathan Lippincott, our talented designer, turned a potential design nightmare into the easy-to-use yet beautiful volume you now hold in your hands. Our copy editor, John McGhee, and production editor, Elaine Chubb, deserve not only thanks for their fine work, but also congratulations for surviving the trials this text presented. Heartfelt thanks to our student intern Tom Angiello and our dear friend Sharon Gursen for long days spent proofreading our galleys with us—we'd be cross-eyed without them. We're indebted to Robert Youdelman for his kind counsel and fine legal representation. And our book would not have found its happy home were it not for Margaret Selby, to whom we say, dinner at Gramercy Tavern cannot begin to express our appreciation. We thank Elaine Markson for launching this book on its path to printdom, Peternelle van Arsdale for enthusiastically backing it at Anchor Books, and Alice van Straalen for guiding its development while it resided there. And we owe a great debt of service to the brilliant Siobhan Adcock, our principal editor at Anchor, whose masterful and elegant edits delighted us . . . and proved invaluable.

We stand in awe of her formidable talents both as an editor and as a writer in her own right. Finally, we are grateful to the Ludwig Vogelstein Foundation for lending financial support during the writing of this book.

For their encouragement, support, and professional guidance, we are indebted to Ambassador William J. vanden Heuvel, NYU professor Ralph Buultjens, literary manager Des Gallant of Florida Stage, theatre director Daniel Gidron, and playwright and professor Meir Z. Ribalow. We are also grateful to the theatre professionals who took time to respond to our inquiries and surveys: Michael Kahn of The Shakespeare Theatre, Washington, D.C.; Michael Hall and Ken Kay at the Caldwell Theatre Company in Boca Raton, Florida; Larry Maslon, at NYU's Tisch School of the Arts; Penny Metropulos and Timothy Bond, of the Oregon Shakespeare Festival; Paul Whitworth at Shakespeare Santa Cruz; Joseph Discher of the New Jersey Shakespeare Festival; Louis Tyrrell of Florida Stage; Eve Muson and Sidney J. Friedman of Boston University School for the Arts; Bill Esper at William Esper Studio; Sherron Long of Florida Professional Theatres Association; and Jill Charles, editor, *Regional Theatre Directory*.

It was a pleasure and a privilege to have been able to conduct the bulk of our research at the New York Public Library, an institution that struck us dumb with wonder on a daily basis. The Folger Shakespeare Library generously allowed us access to its archive of visual materials. And for our genealogical research, we relied on the meticulously compiled Directory of Royal Genealogical Data, created by Brian Tompsett, University of Hull, England, and available online at www.dcs.hull.ac.uk/public/genealogy/royal.

To our good friend Alexander Schmidt, with whom we've spent the better part of the past three years, for his painstaking compilation of the *Shakespeare Lexicon and Quotation Dictionary*, first printed 1874, reissued 1971—we extend our heartfelt thanks to the heavens, where he surely must reside. For further exploration of Shakespeare's language, we also turned to: *A Shakespeare Glossary*, by C. T. Onions (revised 1986 by Robert D. Eagleson); *Shakespeare's Language*, by Eugene F. Shewmaker; *Shakespeare's Bawdy*, by Eric Partridge; *A Dictionary of Shakespeare's Sexual Puns and Their Significance*, by Frankie Rubinstein; *Shakespeare's Imagery*, by Caroline Spurgeon; *Pronouncing Shakespeare's Words: A Guide from A to Zounds*, by Dale F. Coye; and, of course, the indispensable *Oxford English Dictionary*. Notable among the many texts we consulted regarding Shakespeare's references, life, and times are *Asimov's Guide to Shakespeare*, by Isaac Asimov; *The Age of Fable*, by Thomas Bulfinch; *Shakespeare A to Z*, by Charles Boyce; *Shakespeare*, by Anthony Burgess; *Shakespeare: A Life in Drama*, by Stanley Wells; *Shakespeare: A Life*, by Park Honan; *Shakespeare ALIVE!*, by Joseph Papp and Elizabeth Kirkland; and *The Age of Shakespeare*, by François

Laroque, translated from the French by Alexandra Campbell. Since there is no single definitive edition of Shakespeare's works, we studied every edition of each play that we could get our hands on before creating this edition of monologues, and we honor their editors all for paving our path. And it goes without saying that we feel lucky beyond measure to have reveled every day in Shakespeare's words.

On a more personal note, we would both be at desk jobs right now were it not for the love and support of our teachers, friends, and family. Glenn and Joy Evans nurtured Sami's early development as an actor and sparked her love of Shakespeare. Joe Niola's willingness to travel hundreds of miles by motorcycle to see Rhona perform, and his unflagging belief in her abilities, move her to tears. And we both feel fortunate to have received the high-caliber training of the gifted and devoted faculty of Brandeis University's Theatre Department.

To our close friends, who forgave our total immersion in our work on this book, we offer not just thanks and apologies but also love, appreciation, and chocolate. This goes double for our fellow OOC, Janet Zipin. We cannot adequately express the gratitude and love we bear our families, who showed their support in myriad ways. Sami's grandparents, Edna and Tod Plotkin, have tried to instill in her a daily appreciation of beauty and of the joy of being alive, and have been a lifelong inspiration to her; her in-laws, Judith and Maxwell Morton, her grandmother-in-law, the late Ruth Rosenblatt, and her brother-in-law, Joshua Morton, have patiently adjusted to her foibles, showing constant interest and support; and her parents, Jon and Gail Plotkin, have been her best friends, trusted confidants, and most ardent advocates since the day she was born—she thanks them all from the bottom of her heart. Rhona feels blessed to have shared the book's progress with her beloved grandparents, Seymour and Elsie Silverbush and Helga and the late Bert Erber; to have been buttressed by the strong, solid love, encouragement, and wisdom of her father and stepmother, Jeffrey and Andrea Silverbush (who also lent us her talent as our photographer), and mother, Aliza Erber (from whom Rhona inherited the "theatre bug"), and her in-laws, Juliet and Gerard Nierenberg; and to have been kept aloft by the overwhelming love and palpable daily support of her treasures, her remarkable siblings Lori, Robert, Tom, and Roddy.

Finally, last but most, we must acknowledge the gift our husbands, George Nierenberg and Keith Morton, have given us during the writing of this book. From the very beginning, they both believed with utter confidence in the value of this project and were certain that we were more than equal to such a mammoth endeavor, and they urged us without a moment's hesitation to undertake it. Though we were all but unavailable to them for over two years, they remained uncomplaining throughout. For the million little kindnesses and understandings, we

Beyond all limit of what else i' th' world
Do love, prize, honor you.

New York City
August 2001

THE PLAY'S THE THING

Actors often approach Shakespeare's plays expecting them to be the most difficult to perform, but once armed with the proper tools they find with delight that his material is actually among the easiest. This is because Shakespeare's text fully supports the actor. In fact, *everything* you need to know in order to perform your monologue is contained in the text. This book will show you how Shakespeare's language reveals a wealth of information about your character's objectives, characteristics, and present state of mind.

CHOOSING A MONOLOGUE

Everyone has his or her own criteria for choosing monologues, but here are a few practical considerations to factor in: first and foremost, if you are going to prepare only one monologue for audition purposes, you should have one piece of verse in your repertoire (we will discuss the difference between verse and prose in "What Is This Stuff?," page xxvii). Auditioners who request classical material usually wish to hear how you handle verse. On the other hand, you may wish to select prose if you are auditioning for a prose play (by Shakespeare or otherwise), or for a role that is written primarily or entirely in prose (for instance, Shakespeare's hilarious clowns or some of Ben Jonson's broadly drawn Londoners). If you do choose prose, be sure to read "Rhetoric—Poetic and Otherwise," page xli, because the elements discussed there may be found in your monologue.

You may also want to consider the time frame in which the monologue was written. As Shakespeare's skills developed, his work became more complex: Shakespeare's late Tragedies, Problem Plays, and Romances contain his most complicated meter, imagery, grammatical structure, and themes, and present the greatest challenge to the actor. If you are working on Shakespeare for the first time, you may want to choose a piece from the earlier Comedies, the Histories, or the early Tragedies. You may also wish to consider whether you prefer to present a standard monologue or a soliloquy (see "Now I Am Alone" and "Some Advice on Auditions," on facing page, for the issues this choice raises).

After polling directors, coaches, professors, and casting directors nationwide, we have designated the frequency with which each monologue in this book is used in auditions (on a scale of 1 to 5, with 5 being the most frequent). You may want to avoid the most frequently used pieces, of which directors are sometimes weary. On the other hand, there is a reason certain monologues are "overused": they're simply the best vehicles with which to convey your ability in an audition setting, and many auditioners understand and appreciate this.

In classroom settings, we urge you to select any monologue that has resonance for you, regardless of the character's gender, age, or ethnicity. (In fact, certain characters such as Rumor, Chorus, and even Ariel or Puck, who are referred to within their plays with male pronouns, are essentially gender neutral.) In auditions, however, you may encounter directors who are not as open to nontradi-

WILL'S WORKS: EARLY, MID, AND LATE

Early Comedies, Tragedies, and Histories:
The Comedy of Errors, *The Two Gentlemen of Verona*, *The Taming of the Shrew*, *Love's Labour's Lost*, *A Midsummer Night's Dream*, *Titus Andronicus*, *Romeo and Juliet*, *Henry VI, Parts One*, *Two*, and *Three*, *Richard III*, *Richard II*, and *King John*

Mid-Career Histories, Comedies, and Tragedies:
Henry IV, Parts One and *Two*, *Henry V*, *The Merry Wives of Windsor*, *The Merchant of Venice*, *Much Ado About Nothing*, *As You Like It*, *Twelfth Night*, *Julius Caesar*, and *Hamlet*

Problem Plays, Late Tragedies, Romances, and one Late History:
Troilus and Cressida, *Measure for Measure*, *All's Well That Ends Well*, *Othello*, *King Lear*, *Timon of Athens*, *Macbeth*, *Coriolanus*, *Antony and Cleopatra*, *Pericles*, *Cymbeline*, *The Winter's Tale*, *The Tempest*, and *Henry VIII*

tional casting as one would wish them to be. If you are concerned that you could occasionally be passed over because of a nontraditional monologue choice, you may wish to present a gender- and age-appropriate piece. Do not, however, concern yourself with ethnicity, since there are very few monologues written specifically for people of non-European descent and Shakespeare's characters are for everybody.

Now I Am Alone: A Note on Soliloquies

Unlike most monologues, which are spoken to other characters, a soliloquy is written to be performed by a character alone on the stage. Soliloquy is a device that allows the actor to break from the convention of realism and communicate openly with the audience. When performing a soliloquy, the actor must first consider whether his or her words are actually being spoken aloud, or whether they are a representation of the character's inner thoughts. Next, if the words are spoken aloud, is the character talking to him- or herself (thinking through a problem, reacting to a situation, etc.) or is he or she addressing the audience directly (seeking help with a problem, trying to gain its sympathy or support, etc.)? Occasionally, a monologue is performed in the manner of a soliloquy, despite the presence of additional characters who are otherwise occupied and do not notice; this is called an "aside."

Some Advice on Auditions

When auditioning, always mentally place the other character(s) in your scene somewhere else onstage or out in the audience behind the auditioner, so she or he will feel comfortable watching you (auditioners find it very annoying when actors address them directly). Even if your piece is a soliloquy and you have decided that your character is speaking to the audience, you should address an imaginary person rather than the very real, very powerful person in front of you, who holds your entire future happiness in the palm of his or her hand.

WHAT IS THIS STUFF?

If you flip through this book, you'll notice that most of the monologues look like poetry, while only a few look like regular paragraphs. That's because most of the plays written in Shakespeare's time were written in poetry. In fact, back then playwrights were not called playwrights, they were called poets.

The monologues in this book that look like regular paragraphs are written in prose, which is ordinary spoken or written language that does not follow any organized rhythmic pattern. Today, most plays are written in prose. In his plays, Shakespeare used prose about 30 percent of the time, to define characters of "lower" social status than his nobles, to create a colloquial, informal, or relaxed tone, or to make a character who usually speaks verse sound particularly genuine and straightforward.

The other 70 percent of the time, Shakespeare wrote in verse. Verse is simply speech or writing that has distinctive patterns of rhythm (think of a nursery rhyme or a song). These patterns are called meter. The building blocks of meter are small groupings of syllables called feet. The foot Shakespeare used predominantly is called an iamb. An iambic foot has two syllables, with the first syllable unaccented, and the second accented.

Presenting Shakespeare's favorite foot, the iamb:

x /
da-**DUM**

Key: / = accented syllable
x = unaccented syllable

Some popular iambs:

x /	x /	x /	x /	x /
escape	Club Med	massage	undress	hot fudge

When you string five iambs together the way Shakespeare often did, you've created a type of meter called iambic pentameter:

x / x / x / x / x /
da-**DUM** da-**DUM** da-**DUM** da-**DUM** da-**DUM**

x / x / x / x / x /
Vacation's over and I've gained ten pounds.

x / x / x / x / x /
That old black magic has me in its spell.

x / x / x / x / x /
Tonight, tonight, I'll see my love tonight.

x / x / x / x / x /
But soft, what light through yonder window breaks?

Of course, not all accented syllables are created equal. When you speak a line of iambic pentameter, you'll find that you naturally stress certain accented syllables more than others.

PUTTING YOUR FOOT IN YOUR MOUTH (EXTRA CREDIT)

There are seven types of feet in this crazy world, each containing two or three syllables. The particular rhythm of each kind of foot depends on which syllable(s) are accented.

The type of meter in a piece of verse is named for the predominant type of foot and predominant number of feet per line. The number of feet per line is referred to using Greek prefixes (*di-* for 2, *tri-* for 3, *tetra-* for 4, *penta-* for 5, *hexa-* for 6, etc.). So, for example, a poem containing predominantly four trochees per line is called trochaic tetrameter. Don't worry—you won't be quizzed on this.

iamb	(x /)	Our book
trochee	(/ x)	helps you
pyrrhic	(x x)	to be
amphibrach	(x / x)	a classi-
anapest	(x x /)	cally trained
dactyl	(/ x x)	thespian.
spondee	(/ /)	Amen.

WHY BOTHER?

Iambic pentameter dominates the plays of Shakespeare and his contemporaries. More specifically, they used unrhymed iambic pentameter, which is commonly known as blank verse, and there were compelling reasons Shakespeare and his cronies bothered to write in it.

Of all the types of meter out there, iambic pentameter is the one that is most similar to the speech patterns of the English language. In fact, our speech often falls naturally into iambic pentameter. And of all the types of meter out there, blank verse is best suited to drama. The sounds of rhymed verse and other types of meter can limit the actor by coloring the content with the author's perspective about it. Blank verse, on the other hand, has a neutral tone, which allows for greater dramatic range because the content alone determines what is expressed.

If the playwrights were so concerned with approximating the natural patterns of spoken English and with having a neutral medium to work in, why did they bother to write in verse at all? Why didn't they just use prose?

Well, since you asked—word for word, verse packs a bigger punch than prose in several interrelated ways:

- Verse is an efficient and compelling means of communication. It enables the author to convey more layers of meaning in fewer words.
- Because verse is an elevated form of language, it elevates the dramatic experience. This is especially appropriate to Shakespeare's plays, because they are concerned with individuals under extraordinary circumstances, making choices with far-reaching consequences. In fact, only one of

Shakespeare's plays, *The Merry Wives of Windsor*, is about small-town, everyday affairs . . . and he wrote that play almost entirely in prose.

- Verse also heightens the experience for the audience by adding musicality. The rhythms of verse add another dimension to a performance much in the same way that a musical score does to a scene in a movie. Furthermore, in Shakespeare's time, basically nonexistent sets, only natural lighting, and cramped audience conditions made theatregoing an aural rather than visual experience. The poetry was therefore the focus of the experience for the audience.
- Verse is a great mnemonic tool. Think of how many song lyrics you know, without having studied them. Not only is this a boon to the actor, but it also helps the audience follow and retain complex ideas and developments. The audience in Shakespeare's day particularly needed this aid, since they lacked the benefit of visual cues. It's a nice perk today, too.

Verse not only served Shakespeare and his audience, it serves today's actor as well. The main reason that Shakespeare's verse warrants examination by us—and you—is that it improves your performance on two levels: Technically, it is a guide to the correct pronunciation of the words in your piece. Artistically, as we explain (repeatedly) in this section, the meter of the verse you speak reveals clues to the characteristics, present state of mind, and objectives of your character.

When Playing a Bear, Disregard the Following

Aside from "Exit, pursued by a bear" in *The Winter's Tale*, Shakespeare rarely put his stage directions between the characters' spoken lines—he most often embedded them directly *into* the lines. This helped his audiences follow the action, since they couldn't all see the stage. It also ensured that the actions he considered most important could not be cut. For example, Richard has given Anne his sword and told her to kill him:

> And humbly beg the death **upon my knee.**
> **Nay, do not pause,** for I did kill King Henry;

You will, however, find extensive stage directions in many editions of Shakespeare's plays. Many of these were added later by editors and should be ignored. Where we have included stage directions with the monologues in this book, they are either Shakespeare's own, or have been carefully and sparingly chosen to clarify the action.

CRACKING THE CODE

First things first. Reminder: if your piece is prose, section A does not apply to you, but you should read section B ("Rhetoric—Poetic and Otherwise," page xli), since most of the elements discussed in that section are applicable to both prose and verse.

VERSE-ATILITY

So your piece is verse. This section will help you recognize the acting clues Shakespeare has put into the text by writing in verse.

Because Shakespeare's verse is almost exclusively iambic pentameter, the verse pieces in this book are all in that meter. This does not mean that every single line consists of five feet, or that every foot is iambic—the meter is considered to be iambic pentameter when the feet are predominantly iambs and almost all the lines contain five feet.

Variations in the meter keep the material from becoming too mechanical or singsong. More important for the actor, they allow a playwright to create a greater range of emotional expression. Shakespeare exploited variations to a far greater extent than had been done before, yielding myriad rich dramatic possibilities. Wherever the meter is varied, you can be sure that Shakespeare deliberately made it so, to achieve a specific result.

SCANSION: NOT SCARY!

Scansion is simply the act of scanning a piece of verse to identify its feet and understand its rhythm. Since the words are linked together in a way that *creates* the meter, you don't need to read the line any differently than you normally would—the meter will naturally emerge. Scanning is just about noticing what Shakespeare did, and exploring how it benefits you as an actor.

A LEG UP ON FEET: THE BASIC VARIATIONS

Here are the two principal variations that appear in Shakespeare's verse:

INVERSION

Sometimes a foot will be inverted, so that the first syllable is accented and the second is unaccented:

/ x
DUM-da

This inverted foot (called a trochee—see "Putting Your Foot in Your Mouth," page xxviii) is always followed by an iamb. It can appear anywhere in a line except at the end, and most often appears in the beginning:

/ x x / x / x / x /
Who are the people in your neighborhood?

/ x x / x / x / x /
These are the forgeries of jealousy!

You'll notice that the inversion starts the line off with a punch, which is a clue to performance. It is a manifestation of the character's state of mind and objective. Perhaps the character is in a hurry, angry, making an important point, interrupting, making a demand, and so on. Wherever in the line this variation falls, noticing it is one way to gain insight into that moment.

DOUBLE ENDING

Very often, you'll find an unstressed extra syllable tacked to the end of a line. This "double ending" used to be called a feminine ending (because it is unstressed, or "weak"—no joke!), but that outmoded term is falling out of favor.

x / x / x / x / x / (x)
da-**DUM** da-**DUM** da-**DUM** da-**DUM** da-**DUM** da

x / x / x / x / x / (x)
Those lazy, hazy, crazy days of summer

x / x / x / x / x / (x)
The slings and arrows of outrageous fortune

Again, a clue: Are there any double endings in your piece? Are there none? If none, is your character intending to punch the end of every single line? If many, does this sound soothing? Does this sound uncertain? Or rambling? Or nervous? Take a look.

Once in a great while you will find a "triple ending," which has two extra unaccented syllables at the end of a line. The two extra syllables do not comprise an extra foot. We point these out wherever they occur to get your creative juices flowing.

O, No! An *O*!

Oh, brother. Oh, boy! Oh my God! Oh, please? Oh, darn! Ooookay. See? We use the word *O* all the time. The English language has incorporated the human impulse to utter certain sounds in certain circumstances (as when a person says "shush" to quiet a crying baby). *O* represents one of those sounds. And yet, somehow, in Shakespeare *O* seems archaic and scary. We feel self-conscious saying it and tend to gloss over it. But consider this:

The word *O* is pronounced as a long O. When you wrap your mouth around it properly, the sound is long in duration. It's naturally big and expressive, and Shakespeare has used it accordingly. An *O* is a clue to what the character is feeling and how the character is responding to the situation at hand. When you pronounce the *O* fully, you will suddenly discover facets of the piece that weren't evident before.

An *O* pronounced properly is, by its very nature, a stressed syllable. When an *O* falls on an unstressed syllable within the meter of the line (especially at the beginning of a line), it delivers additional impact because the ear is surprised to hear a stressed syllable when it expects to hear an unstressed syllable. Pay particular attention to *O*s that you find in your monologue and to where they appear in the meter . . . and don't forget to have fun with them!

ADDITIONAL VARIATIONS: HEADLESS FEET AND OTHER ODDITIES

Other variations you will encounter concern the number of syllables per line.

SIX FEET CRAMMED INTO A LINE

Sometimes you will come across six iambs in one line, which is called hexameter (it's also called an alexandrine).

x / x / x / x / x / x /
What's Hecuba to him, or he to Hecuba

Think Hamlet has a lot on his mind? So much so there isn't enough room in a line for all that's plaguing him?

CROWDED FEET

Once in a while, a line will contain a foot with an extra unaccented syllable before the accented syllable (da-da-**DUM**). (This kind of foot is called an anapest—see "Putting Your Foot in Your Mouth," page xxviii.)

x / x / x / x-x / x /
Strike flat the thick rotundity of the world

You'll find that you will naturally scan the meter properly. Your impulse will be to speed up the two weak syllables, giving the two of them combined the same amount of time you give each one of the other unaccented syllables in the line (like two eighth notes replacing a quarter note).

SILENT FEET

Some lines will appear to have fewer than five feet. These lines actually do contain five feet—the ones you don't see are silent. Shakespeare used the silent feet to build a pause into the material.

x / x / x / x / x /
She should have died hereafter (pause) (pause-pause)

x / x / x / x / x /
There would have been a time for such a word

or:

x / x / x / x / x / (x)
(Pause-pause) (pause-pause) She should have died hereafter

x / x / x / x / x /
There would have been a time for such a word

(Note that in the second instance the first line has a double ending.)

In this example, Macbeth has just been told of his wife's death. Shakespeare understood that the silence would be effective here, and provided it for the actor to work with. Sometimes it is obvious whether the pause comes at the beginning, middle, or end of the line. Sometimes (as it is here), the actor can choose what best expresses his objectives.

HEADLESS FEET

In rare instances, lines are simply missing the first, unstressed syllable of the first iambic foot. These are called headless lines.

x / x / x / x / x /
(pause) Thou hadst been a knave and flatterer

SHARED AND SHEARED LINES

There are two other instances in which your character will speak less than a full line of text:

Shared Lines

Often, a full line will be divided among two or more characters:

x / x / x /
ROMEO: I dreamt a dream tonight.
x / x /
MERCUTIO: And so did I.

This is a good example of the way in which a shared line conveys information about the dynamic or relationship between the characters speaking it. Since it is one line of text, there is no pause in the meter between Romeo's words and Mercutio's. This could reflect their close and comfortable friendship: old friends are often in sync, anticipating each other's thoughts and jumping in on each other's sentences. It could also reflect the high energy level of two young guys letting off steam, or Mercutio's impatience with Romeo's lovesickness. Of course, each shared line you will encounter will reflect the unique dynamics of the characters who share it.

(When extracting a monologue from a scene, it is accepted practice to begin or end the piece with your character's portion of a shared line or to connect two or more short blocks of text by removing other characters' intervening words in order to create a cohesive monologue with a clear beginning, middle, and end.)

Sheared Lines

It is also sometimes necessary to remove segments of your own character's lines that are spoken in response to others, and are part of the scene but not part of the monologue.

In *King John*, Constance has been railing at Salisbury, who interjects, saying:

SALISBURY: I may not go without you to the King.
CONSTANCE: Thou mayst, thou shalt; I will not go with thee.

Salisbury's words and half of Constance's line have been excised from the middle of her monologue, which resumes with "I will not go with thee."

As most monologues are parts of scenes, they will often contain one or more shared or sheared lines. Although you are speaking only part of a shared or sheared line, it is helpful to examine the scene and scan the full line to gain insight into your character's interaction with the other character(s) in the scene. When performing the piece out of context of the play, you may use the pause created by the excised words to advance your own objectives or to make adjustments during transitions.

MAKING THE SHOE FIT THE FOOT

WE SAY, THEY SAID

Sometimes a word won't seem to fit into the meter, even considering any of the variations we've discussed above. This may be because there are certain words that, in Shakespeare's time, were sometimes pronounced with the accent on a different syllable than we hear today. For example, the word *complete*, below, was pronounced with the accent on "com":

x / x / x / x / x /
In complete glory she revealed herself

Although it is preferable, whenever possible, to preserve the meter, sometimes the historic pronunciation is so different from today's that doing so interferes with the audience's ability to comprehend the word. We point out such words when they appear in monologues in this book; though we sometimes offer our opinion on pronunciation, the decision is always yours.

ELISION—SKIMPING ON SYLLABLES

In order to fit the meter, words sometimes need tinkering with. By this we mean short'ning words by elim'nating vow'ls, or by fusing t'gether two adjacent vow'ls. This is called elision, and it takes a few different forms:

Dropping Excess Syll'bles

This involves doing something you do in everyday speech anyway. Many words are spelled as though they have more syllables than we usually pronounce. Shakespeare gen'rally intended them to be pronounced in their more popular, shorter forms. Sometimes elision will be indicated by replacing the letter(s) with an apostrophe, but often the word is spelled normally and the meter will indicate to you which way to pronounce the word. For example:

x / x / x / x / x /
That all is done in reverend care of her (reverend → "rev-rend")

The meter of some lines will require cutting syllables we don't cut in normal speech:

x / x / x / x / x /
To try thy eloquence, now 'tis time—dispatch (eloquence → "el-quence")

x / x / x / x / x /
And kill the innocent gazer with thy sight (innocent → "inn-cent")

Other examples:

dangerous → "daynj-russ"
miraculous → "mirack-less"
natural → "natch-ral"
passionate → "pash-net"
babbling → "babb-ling"
treacherous → "trech-russ"
flattery → "flatt-ry"
shallowest → "shall-west"

Disembow'ling the Vow'ls

A syllable is also sometimes dropped to accommodate the meter when two vowel sounds are adjacent. Sometimes, as above, a vowel sound gets dropped altogether:

diadem → "die-dem"
violent → "vie-lent"

Sometimes the syllable is dropped by "gliding" the two adjacent vowel sounds together:

holier → "hol-yer"
virtuous → "virtch-wuss"
courtier → "court-yer"
Romeo → "Rome-yo"
tedious → "teed-yuss"
mightiest → "might-yest"
perfidious → "perfid-yuss"

And sometimes the last syllable of one word is smooshed with the first syllable of the next word, creating one syllable:

x / x / x / x / x /
I sigh the lack of many a thing I sought (Many a → "men-ya")

Twofers

Two-syllable words are sometimes compressed into one syllable:

hour → "owr"
being → "beeng"
warrant → "warnt"
flower → "flowr"
knowest → "knowst"
spirit → "speert"

*Vis-à-*V *(and Sometimes* Th*)*
In Shakespeare's time, it was common to drop a *v* or a *th* that appeared between two vowels, and to elide the syllables on either side of it into one syllable. Again, sometimes it's noted in the text, but sometimes it's not. (Note: As with all elision, you only do it when the meter requires it!)

e'er or ever → "air"	o'er or over → "ore"
e'en or even → "een"	whe'er or whether → "ware"

Eliding some "v" words will make them awkward to pronounce and difficult for today's audience to understand. For this reason, it is sometimes a good idea to "force" the V sound into the one syllable, or you may wish to keep the two syllables, treating them as a crowded foot (see above). Again, you will choose what to do on a case-by-case basis:

seven or se'en → "sen" or "sevn"	given or gi'n → "gin" or "givn"
devil or dev'l → "del" or "devl"	

CONTRACTION—JUST DO'T
Contractions are sometimes noted in the text, but not always. The meter will indicate that a contraction is necessary, if the spelling hasn't.

Noted in the text:

x / x / x / x / x /
I'll run from thee and hide me in the brakes

Not noted, but the meter instructs us to contract it ourselves (I had → "I'd"):

x / x / x / x / x /
I had thought, sir, to have held my peace until

Shakespeare used many more contractions than we use today. You will see such contractions as:

'tis = it is	i' = in	's = us or is	o' = of
'pon = upon	't = it	wi' = with	th' = the or thou
'em = them	t' = to	'r = your	o' th' = of the

An example of one of these less familiar contractions, not noted in the text:

x / x / x / x / x /
The inaudible and noiseless foot of time (The inaudible → "Th'inaudible")

EXPAN-SI-ON

Just as it is sometimes necessary to elide a word to fit the meter, it is also sometimes necessary to expand a word. No doubt you've come across a word in which the final "ed" is pronounced as a separate syllable—this is the most common example of expansion. Even in Shakespeare's time, expansion was done only where necessary to fit the meter. Some examples:

x / x / x / x / x /
I am too sore empierced with his shaft (empierced → "em-peer-sed")

x / x / x / x /x/
Do botch and bungle up damnation (damnation → "dam-nay-shee-un")

x / x / x / x / x/
To woo a maid in way of marriage (marriage → "ma-ree-age")

x / x / x / x / x/
To be adopted heir to Frederick (Frederick → "Fred-e-rick")

Other examples:

business → "bi-zi-ness"
patient → "pay-shee-ent"
patrician → "pa-tri-shee-an"
licentious → "lie-sen-shee-uss"

YOU SAY "POTATO," I SAY " 'TATER"

Since dialects vary, different actors may pronounce the same word with a different number of syllables. We have included words in our elision and expansion lists that you may not consider elisions or expansions since you already pronounce them that way; we simply wish to ensure that all our readers know which pronunciation fits the meter in each instance.

WE COME TO PRAISE CAESURA, NOT TO BURY IT

We pause here momentarily to discuss the pause that can occur mid-line, which is called a caesura (seh-ZHOOR-uh or seh-ZYOO-ruh). A caesura is usually but not always indicated by punctuation. Since the pause appears mid-line, it's quite brief, suggesting that when a new idea is expressed after a caesura, it has come quickly on the heels of the one that precedes it.

The two basic variations in meter discussed above are frequently found lurking around caesuras.

The inverted foot following a caesura:

x / x / x / / x x /
Be comfort to my age! Here is the gold

The double ending preceding a caesura:

x / x / (x) x / x / x /
Observe my uncle. If his occulted guilt

In addition, you'll sometimes find a line in which the pause you take at a caesura replaces the unstressed syllable of the first foot following the punctuation:

x / x / x / x / x /
To fright them ere destroy. (pause) But come in

BUILD, BREATHE, AND BE QUICK ABOUT IT

We tend to front-load our everyday speech with the information we consider most important, and then let our sentences peter out . . . Lines of verse require that we do just the opposite. A line of verse is usually written to build steadily toward its end, where its key point is usually located.

According to some methods of acting verse, the actor should take a pause at the end of a line only when a thought is completed (usually delineated by punctuation), and continue to the next line without pausing if a thought is continuous. According to other methods, the actor should pause at the end of every line, taking the shortest pause where there is no punctuation and pauses of various lengths depending on the nature of the punctuation where it does appear. We encourage you to pause for a breath at the end of each line and see what you discover; often a pause taken where a thought seems continuous will reveal a new, unexpected meaning.

Actors also tend to slow down verse, to dramatic effect—or so they think. Actually, verse should be spoken *faster* than everyday speech. At the speed of everyday speech, verse would average approximately twelve lines per minute. We suggest that you aim to deliver your monologues at between fifteen and eighteen lines per minute. The timing of monologues in this book is based on this approximation but will obviously vary according to individual delivery.

RHETORIC—POETIC AND OTHERWISE

Poetry is more than the sum of its meter. Understanding the following poetic and rhetorical elements and recognizing them when they occur in your monologue—whether verse or prose—will give you additional clues to the characteristics, present state of mind, and objectives of your character.

A REASON TO RHYME

In his plays, Shakespeare used rhyme sparingly (almost exclusively in verse), to color or enhance the content of certain material. For instance, rhyme can convey a sense of witty repartee; it can lend ethereality to the speech of fairies; or it can poke fun at the speaker by making him or her sound overblown. Furthermore, like meter, rhyme makes the material more memorable.

Shakespeare's rhyme generally appears at the ends of lines, but it can also be found within a line. Sometimes you'll find a whole rhymed passage, but periodically you'll find just one rhymed couplet (two rhymed lines) in what is otherwise blank verse. Often, such a couplet signifies the end of a scene, summing up the scene or carrying the audience into the next.

There are a few variations to look for as well:

HALF RHYME

Shakespeare creates the same effect more subtly by using a half rhyme, in which the two rhyming sounds are very close but not exactly the same:

Earth's increase, foison plenty,
Barns and garners never empty

HISTORIC RHYME

Sometimes you will come across two words that look like a half rhyme, but they're not. That's because pronunciations have changed since Shakespeare's time. In most cases, both words were pronounced slightly differently than they are today, rhyming somewhere in the middle.

When you encounter historic rhymes, you have to decide whether to preserve historical accuracy and rhyme the words, or to give them today's pronunciations so they'll be easier for your audience to understand. In most instances, it makes sense to use modern pronunciations, but there are circumstances under which preserving the rhyme may be preferable (e.g., to create humor).

Examples:

love / prove / Jove
food / good / flood (blood, etc.)

gone / moan
eye / victory (history, melody, etc. . . . all rhymed with "die")

CROSSING THE SOUND BARRIER

While the section on rhyme, above, describes one way in which Shakespeare played with the repetition of sounds, he played with the sounds of words in other ways as well, enriching the material on different levels: like the rhythms of meter, sound repetition heightens the theatregoing experience by adding dimension; the linking of sounds creates an aural through-line; and, most important, the types of sounds found in a particular monologue provide—you guessed it!—yet more clues to the characteristics, present state of mind, and objectives of your character. We discuss the particularities of these clues on a case-by-case basis in the individual monologues' Commentary sections.

ALLITERATION

The repetition of the first sound of two or more neighboring words:

Death, **d**esolation, ruin and **d**ecay

The **h**oney **b**ags steal from the **h**umble **b**ees

For **qu**een, a very **c**aitiff **c**rowned with **c**are

One **h**eaved a-**h**igh, to **b**e **h**urled down **b**elow;
A **m**other only **m**ocked with two sweet **b**abes;
A **d**ream of what thou wert, a **b**reath, a **b**ubble,
A sign of **d**ignity, a garish flag
To be the aim of every **d**angerous shot;
A queen in jest, only to fill the scene.

Where **m**an doth not inhabit, you '**m**ongst **m**en
Being **m**ost unfit to live. I have **m**ade you **m**ad;

ASSONANCE

The repetition of vowel sounds in two or more neighboring words:

Ere **we** will **ea**t our **mea**l in f**ea**r and sl**ee**p

There are three instances of assonance in this one little line:

Barns and garners never empty [quit scanning—it's not in blank verse]

1. Barns / garners
2. garners / never
3. never / empty

CONSONANCE

The repetition of consonant sounds in two or more neighboring words:

> Now **set** the **t**eeth and **st**retch the nos**t**ril wide

> **Wh**en and **wh**ere and how
> **W**e **m**et, **w**e **w**ooed, and **m**ade exchange of vow

> All the infections that the sun sucks up
> From bogs, fens, flats, on Prosper fall, and **m**ake hi**m**
> By inch**m**eal a disease! His spirits hear **m**e,
> And yet I needs **m**ust curse.

ONOMATOPOEIA

The use of a word that sounds like what it means:

> wouldst **gabble** like a thing most brutish

> dance our ringlets to the **whistling** wind

> lovers make **moan**

SEPARATING SUBSEQUENT SOUNDS

Sometimes you'll find two consecutive words in which the first word ends and the second begins with the same sound, such as King Lear's *Blow, winds*, *reason not*, and *is scarce*. These abutting sounds should always be enunciated separately, which will affect the tone of your delivery and give the second word a slight additional emphasis. If they occur in your monologue, separate the sounds and see what you discover.

IMAGERY: "ON YOUR IMAGINARY FORCES WORK"

When it comes to imagery, Shakespeare is the king. He is a marvel at using figures of speech and vivid descriptions to create mental pictures for the audience. He uses several devices to do so; here are the most prevalent:

METAPHOR

The use of a word or phrase denoting one kind of object or action in place of the one actually being described, to imply a likeness or analogy between them:

All the world's a stage,
And all the men and women merely players;

From forth the kennel of thy womb hath crept
A hell-hound that doth hunt us all to death;

SIMILE

A comparison of two essentially unlike things, in which a particular similarity is pointed out by the use of *like* or *as*:

So we grew together
Like to a double cherry, seeming parted,
But yet an union in partition

If I must die,
I will encounter darkness as a bride
And hug it in mine arms.

PERSONIFICATION

The representation of an inanimate object or abstract idea as a personality or as having human attributes:

Grim-visaged war hath smoothed his wrinkled front;

Headstrong liberty is lashed with woe.

SYNECDOCHE

A figure of speech in which a part represents the whole object or idea (as in "bread" for food), or vice versa (as in "the law" for "police"):

Whose words all **ears** took captive

By "ears" the speaker means all listeners.

RHETORICALLY SPEAKING

Rhetoric is the art of writing or speech as a means of communication or persuasion, employing various devices to achieve literary effect. Some devices that Shakespeare used are:

ANTITHESIS

The juxtaposition of opposing or contrasting ideas in balanced or parallel words, phrases, or grammatical structures.

Antithesis is one of the key devices used by Shakespeare. Once you are familiar with it, you'll begin to notice it everywhere—the plays are riddled with it:

To be or not to be, that is the question;

In this most obvious of examples, Hamlet uses antithesis to frame the dilemma he faces.

> Not that I loved Caesar less, but that I loved Rome more. Had you rather Caesar were living, and die all slaves, than that Caesar were dead, to live all free men?

In this prose excerpt, Brutus is using the device to sway the opinion of the crowd. He employs three antithetical pairings in rapid succession, to fuel the crowd's emotional investment in his position before they can think twice about it.

And if King Edward be as true and just
As I am subtle, false and treacherous,
This day should Clarence closely be mew'd up.

Richard III is particularly given to using antithesis. He constantly compares himself to others—his deformity versus the attractiveness of others, his deceitfulness versus the integrity of others, his shrewdness versus their guilelessness, etc.

PUN

A play on words. Sometimes the humor derives from different senses of the same word, and sometimes from the similar sense or sound of different words.

Shakespeare was extremely punny, most often in a bawdy way. Sometimes today's audiences will miss the puns because of changes in word pronunciations or meanings. Where it would be helpful, we point out such puns in our Commentary boxes.

Example:

Horse—a pun for "whores"
Traitor—a pun for "trader" (i.e., pimp)

Diomedes has not only stolen Troilus's former lover, Cressida, but has now also appropriated Troilus's horse. When Troilus meets Diomedes on the battlefield, he says:

> O traitor, Diomed! Turn thy false face, thou traitor!
> And pay the life thou owest me for my horse!

The actor is free to decide whether Troilus puns on purpose or inadvertently (and if inadvertently, whether Troilus even notices that he has punned); the pun is effective whichever way it's played.

DOUBLE ENTENDRE

A word, phrase, or passage having a double meaning, especially when the second meaning is risqué. While this device is related to a pun and might contain a pun or puns, it is subtly different: it plays only on the words themselves, and not on the sounds of words.

Example:

While Oberon, King of the Fairies, is telling a story about Cupid shooting one of his arrows, a second, ribald meaning lies behind his words:

> And loosed his love-shaft smartly from its bow
> As it should pierce a hundred thousand hearts.
> But I might see young Cupid's fiery shaft
> Quenched in the chaste beams of the wat'ry moon

	Literal Meaning	*Double Entendre*
love-shaft	Cupid's arrow	penis
pierce	pierce	penetrate
fiery shaft	flaming arrow	raging hard-on
quenched	extinguished	given a "cold shower"

WHY WHICH WORDS ARE WHERE

A few more elements to consider:

Repetition

Rather than being a "throwaway," repetition of a word or phrase can be an opportunity for an actor to explore the nuance or progression in a character's inward objective or outward action:

A horse! A horse! My kingdom for a horse!

Repetition with a Twist:

When a phrase contains both repeated and new words, the familiar sounds of the repeated words lead the listener to the surprising new word or phrase, with its new sound (which is pleasing to the ear) and new idea (which is pleasing to the mind), naturally highlighting the new idea.

Mad world! Mad kings! Mad composition!

Was ever woman in this humor wooed?
Was ever woman in this humor won?

Word Length

Pay attention to the lengths of the words your character speaks. Does she use particularly long words? Or a series of short, staccato ones? A preponderance of words of one length or the other may suggest that your character is long-winded, supercilious, lovesick, tired, excited, rushed, furious, condescending . . . Again, this is valuable information.

Examples:

Being taken prisoner, Cleopatra defiantly tells her captor,

Sir, I will eat no meat, I'll not drink, sir

. . . Talking between clenched teeth, perhaps?

Don Armado, on the other hand, seeks to impress with his vocabular prowess:

> Sir, it is the King's most sweet pleasure and affection to congratulate the Princess at her pavilion in the posteriors of this day, which the rude multitude call the afternoon.

Most impressive.

THE READINESS IS ALL

The tools explained here and applied throughout this book ready you for—and support—your basic acting work, rather than replacing it. Recognizing the elements contained in the text and knowing how to exploit them will heighten your ability to express your objectives and characterization, whatever method of acting you practice.

THIS EARTH, THIS REALM, THIS ENGLAND: SHAKESPEARE'S LIFE AND TIMES

WHAT'S PAST IS PROLOGUE: ENGLAND IN SHAKESPEARE'S TIME

By the time William Shakespeare was born, Queen Elizabeth I had been on England's throne for six years; she would go on to rule for thirty-nine more. Her long reign spanned an unprecedented period of relative peace (despite the ever-present threat from Spain), during which the English Renaissance flourished. Elizabeth ruled with the interests of her subjects at heart (that is, of course, within the construct of the stratified class system of her time). She encouraged the establishment of free schools for middle-class boys, was a devoted patron of the arts and loved theatre—particularly that of Shakespeare, whose theatrical company, the Chamberlain's Men, was under the patronage of Elizabeth's Lord Chamberlain (the official who managed her personal household). (For additional tidbits on this powerhouse of a Queen, see "Irrelevant History: Tickling the Queen's Fancy," page 352.)

In the eleventh hour, the dying, childless Queen named her cousin James VI of Scotland as her heir. James was crowned James I of England in 1603 and ruled until after Shakespeare's death. He assumed the patronage of Shakespeare's company, henceforth known as the King's Men. A fervent proponent of Protestantism, which had been instituted as England's official religion by King Henry VIII and reinstated under Queen Elizabeth, James persecuted Catholics, even though his own wife, Anne of Denmark, had converted to that faith. He also commissioned the English translation of the Bible now known as the King James Bible. Although James was initially welcomed in England, time proved him a weak and unpopular leader whose errors paved the way for future civil wars. (By the way, it has been said of King James that he *never* bathed or washed. Ever. In his whole life. Oh, except for occasionally dipping his fingertips in rosewater. We're not joking. [For additional dirt on King James, see "Irrelevant History: New King on the Block," page 969, "Wasn't This a Dainty Dish to Put Before the King," page 993, "Buttering Up Banquo's Blood," page 716, and "Explosive Material: The Gunpowder Plays," page 708.])

Thus, Shakespeare's life and plays bridged the Elizabethan and Jacobean eras, as the two monarchs' reigns are called. During that time life in England was short, uncomfortable, and smelly—even for the wealthy. The lack of plumbing meant that sewage was dumped directly into the streets and all water was pumped from wells by hand. Bathing was feared as unhealthy (as was outdoor air, by the nobility). Because the hearth was the chief source of heat and light, winter nights in this chilly, damp country were long, cold, and dark—even for the wealthy. Infant and child mortality was high and the average life expectancy for those lucky enough to survive into adulthood was about forty. The hazards of childbirth (for both mother and child), the bubonic plague, malnutrition, and poor hygiene were common dangers. And so with little time to waste, people matured quickly and were considered adults at about fourteen. Most upper- and middle-class teens were sent away to work as apprentices, maid- or manservants, and the like, while wealthy male adolescents were sent to university or to the Inns of Court, where they were trained in the law. Marriages did not occur at age twelve, as is now commonly believed: noblewomen usually married in their late teens while everyone else commonly married in their early to middle twenties (for information on marriage customs, see "Wedding and Bedding or Betting on Wedding?," page 446). The less-than-wealthy worked like pack mules, their women doing double duty by running the household and earning supplemental income sewing or weaving, etc. A man's home—no matter how modest—was his castle, and he its king (for more on the status of women, see "All Shrews Beshrewed," page 958).

Elizabethans and Jacobeans usually lived and died in their hometowns, and had a morbid fear of "strangers" (as they called any non-English person—for information on attitudes toward Jews and people of color, see "There Are Things in This Comedy . . . That Will Never Please," page 945, and "Renaissance Rationalization of Racism," page 826). And yet the presence of the monarchy was strongly felt in even the most provincial and remote of townships. Official documents permitting travel beyond one's local region were required; traveling without them was considered vagrancy and carried penalties. Taxation was imposed randomly, whenever the monarchy needed funding. And as part of the monarchy's efforts to Protestantize the nation, attendance at Church of England services was made mandatory.

For the vast majority of the population, the existence of God was a given, and the influence of the church on daily life was pervasive. Along with their belief in Heaven and Hell, Elizabethans and Jacobeans fully believed in a host of superstitions and genuinely feared devils, witches, and fairies. Religion, folklore, and astrology explained their universe, while science, still rudimentary, took a backseat. For example, birth defects were believed to be the Devil's work and the croak of a raven signaled the imminent outbreak of the plague. And although it was during Shakespeare's lifetime that Galileo Galilei proposed his theory that the earth and planets revolved around the sun, his ideas would not be widely appreciated for a full century to come. In the meantime, Galileo was in big trouble with Rome while the English persisted in their belief that the sun, moon, and stars revolved about the earth in concentric crystalline spheres, an idea formulated by the Greek astronomer Ptolemy in the second century C.E. Shakespeare's contemporaries saw the design of the universe as a "macrocosm" that paralleled the "microcosm" of the human body and governed its fate (hence the widespread belief in astrology). Coincidentally, the accepted theories of anatomy—and therefore medicine—were those of another second-century Greek, Galen, who believed that the human body was made up of four fluids, called humours, which determined one's health and temperament (for more information, see "Elizabethan Anatomy 101," page 558). Do we wonder why they often died by forty?

WITHIN THIS WOODEN O: THEATRE IN SHAKESPEARE'S TIME

When Elizabeth became Queen in 1558, religious pageants were still England's only form of theatre (for more on this, see "A Cycle Without a Herod Is Like a Miracle Without a Fish," page 568), but these were rapidly losing popularity. Meanwhile, traveling professional acting troupes were appearing throughout the land, performing increasingly secular works in inn yards and town halls. But as their numbers swelled to include swindlers and con artists, the government took sweeping action: in 1572 the Act for the Punishment of Vagabonds was passed, threatening all traveling performers with severe punishment if caught. To circumvent the law, some troupes sought the patronage of noblemen, who employed and protected them. In addition to performing for their patrons, the players traveled to other nobles' homes and to London, where many troupes eventually established permanent theaters. The first structure built solely for the presentation of plays was erected by James Burbage in 1576, and others soon cropped up. They were built just outside official city lines, since London's principally Puritan municipal government prevented theatrical performances in town. The ban was enacted for reasons of religious and political censorship, crowd control, and containment of the plague, which was easily spread in closely packed audiences.

The London theaters were generally three-story, wooden, cylindrical structures similar in style to the inn courtyards in which the troupes had previously performed. The wealthiest patrons enjoyed seating right onstage. Other well-to-do spectators sat in "galleries" in the three tiers around the perimeter, while the poorer "groundlings" stood (unless they'd brought a stool) in the open-air "cockpit" in the center. The stage jutted out into this space and is thought to have contained trapdoors (used as open graves, etc.). The stage was partially covered by a canopy called "the heavens" or "the shadow," and the part of the building behind it housed both the backstage area and two additional playing spaces, a balcony (think Juliet) and a curtained space below it (used as caves, or to suddenly reveal, or "discover," a scene).

In addition to the open-air theaters, there were a few "private" theaters (so called because they were indoors). Indoor performances were more expensive, drawing audiences from the higher social classes and eliciting more sophisticated plays. The mounting of plays indoors advanced theatre craft, because of the need to design lighting (you'd be amazed what could be done with candles) and the opportunity to create more elaborate sets.

Theatre was an old boys' network. All roles, regardless of gender, were played by men or by boy apprentices, a fact that Shakespeare frequently and delightfully exploited, as when he had his boy-women disguise themselves as men, or had his Cleopatra complain that she would one day be whorishly portrayed by "some squeaking Cleopatra." These old boys faced stiff competition from troupes of talented young boys—wildly popular children's companies that had once been boys' choirs and now performed adult plays.

ONE MAN IN HIS TIME PLAYS MANY PARTS: THE BARD'S BIO, IN BRIEF

We cannot here address the debate over the authorship of the Shakespearean canon (principally between the proponents of Shakespeare of Stratford and those of Edward de Vere, Earl of Oxford); there is enough evidence to support both sides, but not enough to conclusively prove either. We will, however, herein state that we are certain that the plays were written by one author, whomever he (or she?) might have been, and that the author's given name is less important than his accomplishment of the glorious and unparalleled body of work he left behind.

Meanwhile, we present here the little that is known about William Shakespeare of Stratford-on-Avon. Unaware of the immortality that awaited him, Shakespeare kept no journal, and only a meager paper trail records the events of his life (circumstances that were not unusual, even for the biggest names of the time).

The eldest son of John Shakespeare, a glove maker, and Mary Arden Shakespeare, the daughter of a wealthy gentleman farmer, William was baptized in the parish church of Stratford-on-Avon on April 26, 1564. His birth date is generally accepted to be April 23 . . . the same day as his death fifty-two years later. Although no records survive to confirm this, it is believed that he attended the well-reputed Stratford grammar school, where he would have studied the Latin and Greek classics (which would have formed the foundation for his wide use of them as source material later on).

Shakespeare would likely have completed grammar school at the age of fifteen. There are few official records of his young adulthood. We do know that at age eighteen he married Anne Hathaway, then twenty-six, and that their daughter Susannah was baptized a mere five months later, on May 26, 1583. A twin boy and girl, Hamnet and Judith, followed, and were baptized on February 22, 1585. Shakespeare's occupation during these years is unknown, but he may have worked for a time with his father, who had once been a respected town alderman but had recently fallen on hard times. He may have been a schoolmaster or a private tutor in a nobleman's household. At some point it is likely that he joined an acting troupe, for we know that by 1592 he was spending much if not all of his time working in the London theatre, while his family remained in Stratford (for Shakespeare's first "review," see "Irrelevant History: Greene's Groatsworth of Gripe," page 178). During these years, he freelanced as an actor and writer with various theatrical companies. The theaters were shut down for much of 1592 and 1593 because of severe outbreaks of the plague; it is believed that Shakespeare wrote his two narrative poems and many if not most of his sonnets during this hiatus. But he was back in the theatre in full force in 1594, when he became a partner in the Chamberlain's Men (the former Strange's Men, which had just come under the patronage of Henry Carey, Baron Hunsdon, Queen Elizabeth's Lord Chamberlain). A shrewd investor of his profits, Shakespeare became quite wealthy and eventually purchased for his family the largest estate in his hometown, called New Place. Fifteen ninety-six started in triumph and ended in tragedy: Shakespeare finally obtained for his father the gentleman's coat of arms the elder Shakespeare had long sought but been denied, but there was to be no heir to carry forward the family's newfound status, due to the untimely death later that year of Shakespeare's eleven-year-old son Hamnet (the cause of death is unrecorded).

In 1599, the Chamberlain's Men built their own open-air theater on the south bank of the Thames. Shakespeare was a one-tenth shareholder in this new theater, which was named the Globe (and which he referred to in the prologue of *Henry V* as "this Wooden O"). Many of Shakespeare's plays publicly debuted in this theater, which burned to the ground when a misfired canon set the roof ablaze during a performance of *Henry VIII* in 1613. It was rebuilt within a year—this time with a tile roof—and functioned until it was torn down in 1644.

When King James succeeded Queen Elizabeth on the throne of England in 1603, he assumed the patronage of Shakespeare's acting company, which was renamed the King's Men. In 1609, the King's Men obtained a venue for the winter season—the indoor Blackfriars Theatre, owned by Richard Burbage, a member of the company. Shakespeare's later plays were written with this more intimate space in mind. The theater's ability to accommodate elaborate sets allowed Shakespeare to incorporate into his plays the fashionable extravagant masques beloved by King James (see "If You Can't Beat 'Em, Join 'Em," page 872). Shakespeare seems to have begun spending more time in Stratford in the early 1610s, and probably fully retired to his estate by 1613. He died three years later, but no one knows of what. His will favored his elder daughter, of whom he seemed quite proud, and had been changed shortly before his death to protect his other daughter from her new husband, an untrustworthy man of whom Shakespeare disapproved. In addition to the traditional rights of dower, Anne was also famously left "the second best bed," probably to ensure that she be permitted to keep her own bed, since in her day the "best bed" was usually reserved for houseguests. Shakespeare's line ended with his grandchildren, but the characters created by the Bard live on.

BARD (BÄRD) *N.*

The first bards were highly venerated members of an ancient order of Celtic poets who composed verses about tribal history, genealogy, tradition, and law, as well as the glory of their warriors and chiefs, which they sang to the accompaniment of harps. By the end of the sixteenth century, the term had come to refer to any poet, including playwrights, who were often identified as the bards of their hometowns (e.g., the "Bard of Epping," or the "Bard of Sleaford"). Shakespeare became known around London (for both his poems and his plays) as the "Bard of Avon." Because of his enduring gifts to the English language, the term "the Bard" is now closely identified with Shakespeare, which has prompted the coining of such terms as *bardolater* and *bardolatry*.

A Firsthand Account of the Globe Fire

From a letter written by one Sir Henry Wotton to his nephew:

> "... certain chambers being shot off at [King Henry's] entry, some of the paper ... did light on the thatch, where being thought at first but an idle smoke, and their eyes more attentive to the show, it kindled inwardly and ran round like a train, consuming within less than an hour the whole house to the very grounds ... [W]herein yet nothing did perish but wood and straw, and a few forsaken cloaks; only one man had his breeches set on fire, that would perhaps have broiled him, if he had not by the benefit of a provident wit put it out with bottle ale."

THE LOWDOWN ON PUNCTUATION, SPELLING, ANNOTATION, COMMENTARY, AND LINE NUMBERING

As there were no standardized rules of punctuation in Shakespeare's day, the punctuation of the Quartos and Folios was used to communicate nuances in delivery (such as a short breath at a comma or an implied "therefore" at a colon). Many later editors of Shakespeare have ignored these acting guides and, as standard rules of punctuation have evolved, have instead simply applied such rules according to their own interpretations of the texts. We have consulted the First Folio (and Quartos where applicable) and have carefully punctuated the material with the goal of preserving the actor's options. As all later editors have done, we have standardized the spelling, with the exception of archaic words.

The monologues contained herein are extensively annotated to provide context as well as meaning. We urge you to use all of the annotation for your piece, rather than just looking up unfamiliar words, for two reasons. First, some seemingly ordinary words had different meanings in Shakespeare's day than they have today (e.g., *humour* usually meant "temperament, mood," and *happy* usually meant "fortunate"); and second, there may be additional contextual information about a word which will enhance your performance. The most commonly used archaic words, verb forms, elisions, and contractions do not appear in annotation, but can be found in the Glossary, page 1017. Any word that does not appear in annotation or the Glossary can readily be found in a desktop dictionary.

In the Commentary section provided for each monologue, we point out various metrical and rhetorical elements within the text, and offer possible interpretations of each. You are free to choose from these, or you may use your understanding of the particular device Shakespeare used in each instance to replace our suggestions with one of your own.

Note: for your convenience, our line numbers correspond in the main to those used in Alexander Schmidt's remarkable *Shakespeare Lexicon and Quotation Dictionary* (1874), which was compiled based on "the great Cambridge edition of Messrs. Clark and Wright" (1864).

Quarto/Folio: Demystifying the Designations

During Shakespeare's lifetime, fourteen of his plays were published as "quartos" (i.e., as books made up of sheets of paper folded in quarters). Five more of Shakespeare's plays were published as quartos in the six years following his death. Among scholars, these twenty-two quartos are classified as either Bad Quartos (unauthorized texts possibly reconstructed by actors from memory for unscrupulous publishers) or Good Quartos (texts drafted from more reliable sources, such as Shakespeare's original manuscripts, known as his Foul Papers). Although some plays were not published in quarto version at all, others exist in one or more different quarto versions.

In 1623, seven years after Shakespeare's death, John Heminge and Henry Condell published a collection of his works as a "folio" (i.e., as a book made up of sheets of paper folded in half) in loving tribute to their colleague. This collection included all of those plays that had previously been published (with the exception of *Pericles*) plus an additional eighteen. It is now known as the First Folio (since three subsequent, less authoritative Folio editions were published in 1632, 1663, and 1685).

Because there are differences between the Quarto and Folio versions of those of Shakespeare's texts for which both exist, we have sometimes had to choose which text to follow. In most cases, the differences are quite small, and we have simply followed what scholars have deemed the most authoritative text. In cases where no single text has emerged as such, we have consulted all of the texts and chosen the version that is most helpful to the actor. In a few cases the variations are more significant, actually affecting interpretation, and in these instances we have provided both texts and suggested possible reasons for choosing each.

Monologues

THE HISTORIES

During the Elizabethan era, the Protestant Reformation took firm hold in England, and nationalistic sentiments rose in response to the constant threat of Counter-Reformation forces in Europe. These feelings fueled a strong interest in English history, which in turn gave rise to the development of a popular new theatrical genre, the history play. For the most part, history plays drew their material from the most authoritative historical sources of the time, Raphael Holinshed's *Chronicles of England, Scotland and Ireland* (second edition, 1587) and Edward Hall's *The Union of the Two Noble and Illustre Families of Lancaster and York* (1548), both of which reflected the trend toward pro-Tudor historical propaganda encouraged by Henry VII, the first monarch in the Tudor dynasty. With their history plays, Elizabethan playwrights carried on this pro-Tudor approach to please Henry VII's granddaughter, Elizabeth I. Although Shakespeare, who is credited with inventing the genre, was not immune to this pressure, his plays were far less propagandistic than those written by his contemporaries. Unlike his colleagues' works, Shakespeare's Histories examined political dilemmas with a depth that makes them still resonant today. Perhaps for this reason, his are the only examples of the genre still widely read and performed.

KING JOHN

ACT I, SCENE i

PHILIP THE BASTARD

GENDER: M
AGE RANGE: adult to mature adult
PROSE/VERSE: blank verse
FREQUENCY OF USE (1–5): 2

Philip the Bastard has just come up in the world: he and his brother Robert sought King John's arbitration of their dispute over their father's inheritance. Dad left all the land to Robert, in a will that Philip, as the older son, naturally contested. Having realized that Philip is actually the bastard son of the late King Richard I, Queen Elinor has made her grandson an offer he can't refuse: she has just invited him to join her in fighting France, if he will relinquish his lands to Robert. Philip has jumped at the chance, and King John has knighted him, then and there, Sir Richard Plantagenet, after his father. The Bastard is delighted at his sudden social advancement. He gladly says goodbye to his brother and his lands, then muses over his new social status:

180 Brother, adieu. Good fortune come to thee,
For thou wast got i' th' way of honesty.
[*Exeunt all but the Bastard*]
A foot of honor better than I was,
But many a many foot of land the worse.
Well, now can I make any Joan a lady.
185 "Good den, Sir Richard!"—"God-a-mercy, fellow!"—
And if his name be George, I'll call him Peter,
For new-made honor doth forget men's names:
'Tis too respective and too sociable
For your conversion. Now your traveler,
190 He and his toothpick at my worship's mess,
And when my knightly stomach is sufficed,
Why then I suck my teeth and catechize
My pickèd man of countries: "My dear Sir,"—
Thus leaning on mine elbow I begin—
195 "I shall beseech you"—that is Question now,
And then comes Answer like an Absey book:
"O Sir," says Answer, "at your best command,
At your employment, at your service, Sir."
"No, Sir," says Question, "I, sweet Sir, at yours."
200 And so, ere Answer knows what Question would,
Saving in dialogue of compliment,
And talking of the Alps and Apennines,
The Pyrenean and the River Po,

180 *adieu* goodbye (French); *Good fortune . . . thee* May good fortune come to you; 181 *got* begotten, fathered; *way of honesty* honest way [*got . . . honesty* conceived within wedlock]; 182 *A foot of honor better* a foot higher in reputation and good name; 183 *many a many foot* a great many feet; 184 *Joan* peasant girl; *lady* common term for a woman of high social standing; 185 *Good den* good evening; *God-a-mercy* God have mercy; may God reward you (a way of saying thank you, used in response to a respectful greeting from an inferior); *fellow* a form of address to a servant or inferior; 188 *respective* respectful; 189 *conversion* change for the better (i.e., change from lower to higher social rank); 190 *my worship's* my (giving himself a title of honor); *mess* dining table (where they dine as befits the Bastard's high rank); 191 *sufficed* satisfied, full; 192 *catechize* teach by means of questions and answers; 193 *pickèd* (1) refined; (2) chosen; *man of countries* traveler [*My pickèd . . . countries* (1) My refined traveler; (2) the traveler I chose (to invite to dinner)]; 195 *I shall beseech you* I ask you (he is being overly solicitious and polite); *Question* referring to the questioner (himself); 196 *Answer* referring to the answerer (the traveler); *Absey book* (AYB-see) ABC book, child's primer (which sometimes included a catechism); 197 *at your best command* I am at your best command; 200 *ere* before; *would* wants; 201 *Saving* except for; *dialogue of compliment* polite conversation, small talk; 202 *Apennines* (A´-puh-NINES) mountains in Italy; 203 *Pyrenean* (PEER-eh-NEE´-an) mountains between France

It draws toward supper in conclusion so.
205 But this is worshipful society,
And fits the mounting spirit like myself;
For he is but a bastard to the time
That doth not smack of observation,
And so am I, whether I smack or no:
210 And not alone in habit and device,
Exterior form, outward accoutrement,
But from the inward motion to deliver
Sweet, sweet, sweet poison for the age's tooth—
Which, though I will not practice to deceive,
215 Yet, to avoid deceit, I mean to learn,
For it shall strew the footsteps of my rising.
But who comes in such haste, in riding-robes?
What woman-post is this? Hath she no husband
That will take pains to blow a horn before her?
220 O me, 'tis my mother. How now, good Lady—
What brings you here to court so hastily?

2 minutes, 30 seconds

and Spain; *River Po* a river in Italy; 204 *It draws toward supper in conclusion so* time passes between dinner and supper in this fashion; 205 *worshipful society* two meanings: (1) the honorable, respectable set (to which he now belongs); and/or (2) reverent, worshipping company (the company of flatterers such as the traveler); 206 *fits* (1) befits, is appropriate for; (2) is pleasing to; *mounting* rising (in social rank); 207 *but* nothing but, only; *bastard to the time* i.e., unfashionable, out-of-date person; 208 *That* who; *smack of* have a taste of, hint of; *observation* experience (knowledge gained by observing); 209 *smack* here, he puns on the word *smoke*; *no* not; 210 *alone* only; *habit* clothing; manner of dressing; *device* the cut and trim of a garment; 211 *accoutrement* accessories; 212 *motion* inclination, impulse; *deliver* speak, serve up; 213 *Sweet, sweet, sweet poison* i.e., extreme flattery; *for the age's tooth* i.e., pleasing to the tastes of this era; 215 *Yet* rather; *to avoid deceit* to avoid being deceived, to avoid being had [*And not alone . . . I mean to learn* I intend to learn not only to dress fashionably and have the outward trappings of a nobleman, but also to develop the impulse to speak in the flattering manner of the time—not to deceive others, but to avoid being taken for a ride by them]; 216 *strew the footsteps* throw petals in the path of (sweeten the path of); *my rising* my advancement in society; 218 *woman-post* female messenger (it would be insulting for a gentlewoman to be mistaken as such); 219 *blow a horn before her* i.e., to announce her arrival, as would befit a woman of stature; 220 *How now* What are you doing here?

COMMENTARY

The conversation that has just taken place before King John, Elinor, and Robert leave the stage provides helpful clues to the opening of this piece: the Bastard has just been elevated to a social status superior to that of his brother. In addition, he has just agreed to join the attack on France. Thus, his *Brother, adieu* may be used to pointedly get in a last jab at Robert, simply to say goodbye to him on equal terms, to rub it in that he is off to France on an important mission, or just to be schmancy now that he's a knight. This leads to interesting possibilities for the second line: Is Philip being sarcastic? Or is he simply reiterating a point he made earlier in the scene to his brother—his illegitimate father gave him honor, while Robert's legitimate father gave him land—i.e., that everything in life is a trade-off?

Another helpful hint from the preceding scene is that Philip has chosen to be the illegitimate son of Richard I rather than the landed son of Sir Robert. This is a good clue to where his priorities lie. Philip obviously has a lot more respect for his biological father than for the one who raised him. When he fantasizes about an inferior wishing him *Good den, Sir Richard*, he is not only relishing his newly bestowed title, but also the identification with his heroic royal father, Richard.

You will notice that if you try to break down the grammatical structure of this monologue, it is not particularly easy to follow: Philip is carried away with excitement over his new status, and uses many run-ons and fragments, which lend the piece a conversational tone. And though it may be impossible to parse in English class, when read aloud it flows beautifully.

The reason it flows so beautifully is that (as one can surmise from this speech) Philip is one smart cookie, and though he may not be familiar with courtly manners, he is witty, sharp, quick with a comeback, and adept at rhetoric: Philip personifies *Question* and *Answer* in the early part of the monologue, using them as characters that represent his and the traveler's roles in their dialogue. Later in the speech, he shifts to antithesis. Just as he earlier countered *Question* with *Answer*, he now compares thesis to antithesis: *not alone in habit and device* versus *But from the inward motion*; *will not practice to deceive* versus *Yet, to avoid deceit*.

Philip also employs rhyme to enhance his speech. The first two lines form a rhyming couplet (*thee / honesty*), which emphasize his farewell to his brother, and also wrap up the group scene, providing a clean transition into the soliloquy. He uses another such couplet at an important transition within the piece: the couplet *The Pyrenean and the River Po, / It draws toward supper in conclusion so* ends Philip's story-style description of the type of company he expects to be keeping, and creates a fresh opening for his cogitations on how he's going to adapt to his new courtly life.

Notice the way sounds are used intermittently to enhance descriptions. In several places, short alliterative phrases punch the important points. For instance, the S sounds in *stomach is sufficed* suggest a stomach stuffed full. The use of two such alliterative phrases in a row (*but a bastard to the time*) draws the listener's attention to Philip's preoccupation with illegitimacy, a preoccupation that is revealed by his use of the word *bastard* in a metaphor for an unrelated concept. And at the end of the piece, the phrases *riding-robes* and *what woman-post* sets up his flippant attitude toward his mother.

The most striking use of sounds is the repetition of the word *Sir*, along with a string of other Servile Ss in Philip's example of *worshipful society*: *Sir* / *beseech* / *Question* / *comes* / *Answer* / *Absey* / *Sir* / *says* / *Question* / *sweet Sir*. The repetition of *sweet* achieves the same effect, subtly reminding the listener of what sort of *sweet poison* he's referring to. For information on exploiting the sound of the word *O*, see "O, No! An *O*!" on page xxxiii.

Philip's favorite linguistic trick seems to be the pun. Notice these: *pickèd man* = the man he picked to dine with him; also, the man who has just used his toothpick; *worshipful* = honorable, respectable; also, worshipping, respectful; *knightly* = knightly; also, nightly (i.e., a man of rank feasts every night, not just on special occasions); *bastard to the time* = out of step with the times (unfashionable); also, illegitimate, as frequently noted by his contemporaries; *smack* = hint, suggest; also, smoke (i.e., he's unfashionable whether he smokes or not); *will* = will; also, sexual desire; *take pains* = bother to; also, have sex; *blow* = blow (as into a musical instrument); also, thrust, during sex; *horn* = musical instrument; also, penis. If you put the last few sexual puns together, Philip is not only saying that his mother has no husband to appropriately accompany her to court, but also implying that her husband did not sexually satisfy her, and thus she has cuckolded him (*horn* is a triple pun: horns were the symbol of the cuckold).

SIGNIFICANT SCANS

Line 220 contains a silent half foot at the first caesura, a double ending before the second caesura, and another double ending at the end of the line:

x / (x) / x / (x) x / x / (x)
O me, (pause) 'tis my mother. How now, good Lady

Don't forget to elide: *Exterior* (Eks-TEER-yor) in line 211;
. . . to contract: *i' th'* (ith') in line 181 and *many a* (MEN-ya) in line 183;

. . . and to expand: *pickèd* (PICK-ehd) in line 193 and *observation* (OB-zer-VAY´-shee-UN) in line 208.

PHILIP THE BASTARD: THREE FOR THE PRICE OF ONE

Shakespeare used not one but three historic sources for the Bastard: first, King Richard I's real-life illegitimate son Philip (hence, Philip the Bastard's first name), about whom very little is known; second, the French general Jean Dunois (known affectionately as the Bastard of Orléans), who is reputed to have said that he would rather be the bastard of a great man than the legitimate heir of a humble one; third, another illegitimate nobleman, William Neville, Lord Falconbridge, who lends to the character his surname and an additional dose of illegitimacy.

IRRELEVANT HISTORY: ABSENCE MADE THE LION-HEART GROW GRANDER

King Richard I, a.k.a. Richard Coeur de Lion, a.k.a. Richard Lion-Heart, has always been a big fave among the British. He was remembered through the centuries as a chivalrous and brave hero, and kept popping up as the protagonist of histories, plays, and romance novels. Perhaps this is because he spent almost his entire reign outside England's borders, fighting first in the crusades and then against King Philip I in France. During the ten years of his rule, Coeur de Lion spent only six months in Merry Old England. All his subjects knew of him was that he was out there fighting in the name of God (theirs), England (theirs), and St. George (also theirs), and that he was doing his country right proud. No wonder Philip is elated to be his son.

KING JOHN

ACT II, SCENE i

PHILIP THE BASTARD

GENDER: M
AGE RANGE: adult to mature adult
PROSE/VERSE: blank verse
FREQUENCY OF USE (1–5): 3

Philip the Bastard has accompanied England's King John to France to fight against King Philip II, who has backed the claim of John's young nephew, Arthur, to the English throne. The Bastard, a newcomer to the world of international diplomacy, has just looked on as the two kings agreed to an eleventh-hour peace treaty, in which King Philip received some lands previously held by the English in return for dropping Arthur's cause. To cement the deal, John's niece, Blanch, is betrothed to King Philip's son and heir, Lewis. As everyone goes off to the wedding ceremony, the Bastard stays behind and reacts to the sudden agreement between the two kings.

Mad world, mad kings, mad composition!
John, to stop Arthur's title in the whole,
Hath willingly departed with a part;
And France, whose armor conscience buckled on,
565 Whom zeal and charity brought to the field
As God's own soldier, rounded in the ear
With that same purpose-changer, that sly devil,
That broker, that still breaks the pate of faith,
That daily break-vow, he that wins of all,
570 Of kings, of beggars, old men, young men, maids,
Who, having no external thing to lose
But the word "maid," cheats the poor maid of that;
That smooth-faced gentleman, tickling Commodity,
Commodity, the bias of the world,
575 The world, who of itself is peisèd well,
Made to run even upon even ground
Till this advantage, this vile-drawing bias,
This sway of motion, this Commodity,
Makes it take head from all indifferency,
580 From all direction, purpose, course, intent.
And this same bias, this Commodity,
This bawd, this broker, this all-changing word,
Clapped on the outward eye of fickle France,
Hath drawn him from his own determined aid,
585 From a resolved and honorable war,
To a most base and vile-concluded peace.
And why rail I on this Commodity?

561 *kings* he refers to King John and King Philip; *composition* agreement; 562 *the whole* i.e., the whole kingdom of England; 563 *departed with* given up; 564 *France* i.e., King Philip (monarchs were often referred to by their countries' names); *whose armor conscience buckled on* i.e., who prepared to fight because he was guided by his conscience; *field* battlefield; 566 *God's own soldier* because he was fighting for Arthur's divine right to the English throne (see "Riding Shotgun with God," page 235); *rounded* whispered; 568 *that still breaks* he who still breaks; *pate* head; 569 *break-vow* vow breaker; *wins of all* conquers all; gets the better of everyone; 570 *maids* unmarried, virginal women; 573 *smooth-faced* having a mild, pleasing appearance; *tickling* flattering; seductive; *Commodity* profit; personal advantage; self-interest (here, personified as a smooth-faced gentleman); 574 *bias* natural inclination, tendency; 575 *who* which; *peisèd* poised, balanced; 577 *vile-drawing* luring or drawing into baseness or evil; 578 *sway of motion* influence on impulses and actions; 579 *it* i.e., the world; *take head from* flee from, rush away from; *indifferency* moderation; impartiality; 582 *bawd* pimp; procurer; 583 *Clapped on* hastily put on; *outward eye* the external view or perspective (as opposed to the "inward eye"—conscience); 584 *drawn* lured; *his own determined aid* assistance he had decided to give; 585 *resolved* decreed; 586 *vile-concluded* despicably settled or agreed upon; 587 *rail I on* do I rail about; do I scold, re-

But for because he hath not wooed me yet.
Not that I have the power to clutch my hand,
590 When his fair angels would salute my palm,
But for my hand, as unattempted yet,
Like a poor beggar, raileth on the rich.
Well, whiles I am a beggar, I will rail
And say there is no sin but to be rich;
595 And being rich, my virtue then shall be
To say there is no vice but beggary.
Since kings break faith upon Commodity,
Gain, be my lord, for I will worship thee.

2 minutes, 15 seconds

proach; 588 ***But for because*** only because; ***wooed*** solicited; courted; 589 ***that*** because; ***power*** strength of character; ***clutch*** clench, close up (in refusal); 590 ***his*** i.e., Commodity's; ***fair*** (1) beautiful; (2) blond, golden-haired; (3) pale, golden; ***angels*** (1) celestial beings; (2) evil spirits, demons; (3) gold coins (nicknamed "angels" because they were stamped with the image of the archangel Michael); ***salute*** (1) greet; come in contact with; (2) a coin from the reign of Henry V; 591 ***for*** because; ***my hand, as unattempted yet*** my hand, which has not yet been "attempted" or "wooed" by Commodity (i.e., my actions, which have not yet been swayed by Commodity); 593 ***whiles*** while; 594 ***but*** except; 597 ***break faith*** break their vows; ***upon*** for the sake of.

COMMENTARY

The legitimacy of the Bastard's birth may have been questionable, but the results of his parents' illegtimate union are not. His native intelligence and insightfulness are unsurpassed by those of his "legitimate" friends and relatives, as this piece proves. The Bastard displays the ability to see both sides of an issue, even under the emotionally charged circumstances of war: despite the fact that he is solidly on King John's side, he understands that King Philip felt he had the moral high ground, and so the Bastard is disgusted rather than pleased to see his enemy abandon the fight. Later in the piece, the Bastard reveals his self-awareness when he admits that the reason for his rant against Commodity is a simple case of sour grapes. Finally, throughout the piece (and throughout the play), the Bastard displays a remarkable facility with language and rhetoric that makes his monologues a delight to explore.

The range of possible interpretations here is very wide. Is he a ranting poet? Is he a calmly logical philosopher? Or perhaps a little of both? Here are a couple of examples (among many) that demonstrate the variety of possible choices:

(1) *Mad world, mad kings, mad composition!* Most editors today punctuate the line thus: "Mad world! mad kings! mad composition!" which might lead one to a quite emphatic interpretation—angry, astonished, or even hysterical with laughter. On the other hand, the First Folio punctuation of this line is "Mad world, mad kings, mad composition:"—which might lead one to think that the Bastard is mulling over what he has just heard, musing at it, or perhaps tsk-tsking to himself. Of course, whatever you choose is valid—just don't miss out on the opportunity to consider the many options. Notice also that, rather than building from least to greatest in this short list of mad things, the Bastard is honing in from the general to the specific.

(2) *And why rail I on this Commodity?* At first glance, this might seem like an obvious tip-off that the Bastard is ranting and railing. But keep in mind that *rail* is different from *rant—rail* simply means "scold" or "reproach." So perhaps the Bastard is not ranting at all. Or, perhaps he is! Or maybe he has just been building to a rant, but now laughs at himself for it. Again, enjoy exploring the range of choices to find your best fit.

Regardless of how you interpret the Bastard, you cannot escape the poet in him. Poetry thoroughly infiltrates his speech, most noticeably in his use of repetition. First, notice the repetition of key words, which has the effect not only of repeating sounds, but also of strengthening and tying together ideas (*mad*; *maid*; *Commodity*; *world*; *vile*; *hand*; *rich*). Next, check out the way in which some of these repetitions create a verbal path leading from one idea to the next: ***maids*** */ Who, having no external thing to lose / But the word "****maid,****" cheats the poor*

maid of that / ***That*** *smooth-faced gentleman, tickling* ***Commodity*** / ***Commodity,*** *the bias of the* ***world*** / *The* ***world,*** *who of itself is peisèd well*; and *whiles I am a* ***beggar,*** *I will rail / And say there is no sin but to be* ***rich*** / *And being* ***rich,*** *my virtue then shall be / To say there is no vice but* ***beggary.***

Notice that the Bastard also uses the repetition of words to develop his personification of *Commodity*. He uses the word *that* repeatedly to build up his introduction of *Commodity* and the word *this* repeatedly to flesh out his descriptions of "him." All of these repetitions cry out for the actor to pay close attention to the use of builds in the monologue. Finally, the repeated use of hyphenated words (*purpose-changer*; *smooth-faced*; *vile-drawing*; *all-changing*; *vile-concluded*) threads similar rhythmic patterns through the piece.

Another aspect of the Bastard's poetry is his delicate use of alliteration and assonance (*departed / part*; *breaks / pate / faith*; *fickle / France*; *raileth / rich*). The most important of these is the rhyming quatrain at the end (*be / beggary / Commodity / thee*) with which he wraps up his own intentions with regard to Commodity, and neatly ties up the soliloqouy, the scene, and the act.

The ease with which the Bastard formulates his arguments is further proof of his intelligence. He uses two types of antithesis. You'll find extended examples, such as comparing the two kings; comparing the *poor maid*'s having nothing to lose with her having something to lose; and comparing King Philip's previous influence—his conscience—with his current one, his *outward eye*. You'll also find more concise, poetic examples of antithesis, each contained within a few lines: *stop Arthur's title in the whole* versus *willingly departed with a part*; *From a resolved and honorable war* versus *To a most base and vile-concluded peace*; *whiles I am a beggar, I will rail / And say there is no sin but to be rich* versus *being rich, my virtue then shall be / To say there is no vice but beggary.*

The Bastard's sharp wit can be seen in his use of puns, metaphor, and personification. The soliloquy is built around the personification of *Commodity*, who becomes a brawling, rakish, yet deceptively ingratiating character through the Bastard's use of metaphor (*breaks the pate of faith*; *cheats the poor maid*; *smooth-faced gentleman*). When he refers to Commodity as a bawd, is it possible he has in the back of his mind Blanch, who has just been as good as sold to King Philip (along with her dowry and some land) in return for peace? Personifying Commodity also provides the opportunity to pun on the meanings of *hath not wooed me yet . . . my hand, as unattempted yet* and *of fair angels . . . salute my palm.*

Another example of the Bastard's wit is the joke he plays on the audience, in which he draws his listeners in to his argument against Commodity, only to surprise them with the punch line in line 598, which reveals his own eagerness to embrace Commodity as soon as he gets the chance.

SIGNIFICANT SCANS

Scanning line 568 clues you in to the use of the word *that*:

x / x / x / x / x /
That broker, that still breaks the pate of faith

Note that the second *that* falls on an accented syllable. This supports a common Shakespearean use of "that" to mean "he who" (rather than "that" in the sense of "who" or "which").

There are two ways to scan line 573. If you pronounce all the syllables, the line is hexameter (a six-footed line). Or, you could elide *gentleman* to give the line the usual five feet (note the double ending before and the inverted foot after the caesura):

x / x / (x) / x x /x/
That smooth-faced gentleman, tickling Commodity *gentleman* (GENL-man)

Don't forget to elide: *power* (POWR) in line 589;

. . . and to expand: *composition* (COM-po-ZIH-shee-UN) in line 561 and *peisèd* (PAY-zehd) or (PEE-zehd) in line 575.

P.S.

For information on the historical origins of Philip, see "Philip the Bastard: Three for the Price of One," page 10.

KING JOHN

ACT III, SCENE i

CONSTANCE

GENDER: F
PROSE/VERSE: blank verse
AGE RANGE: adult to mature adult
FREQUENCY OF USE (1–5): 2

Constance's son, Arthur, is the rightful heir to the English throne, since his father, the late Geoffrey IV, was King John's older brother. Geoffrey was the Duke of Brittany, which, along with other lands in France, is under English rule. When King Richard died and John immediately took the throne, Constance appealed for help to King Philip II of France, who promised to fight the English and put Arthur on the throne (recovering some of France's land in the bargain). Now, instead of fighting, King Philip has accepted a peace agreement with the English, in which he will receive much of the land he was aiming to seize by fighting on Arthur's behalf. The Earl of Salisbury has just told Constance the news of the peace agreement. At first, she can't believe it; then she berates him as if it were all his fault. Finally, little Arthur (who has been standing by quietly) asks his mother to calm down, to which she replies:

If thou that bidst me be content wert grim,
Ugly, and slanderous to thy mother's womb,
45 Full of unpleasing blots and sightless stains,
Lame, foolish, crooked, swart, prodigious,
Patched with foul moles and eye-offending marks,
I would not care, I then would be content;
For then I would not love thee—no, nor thou
50 Become thy great birth, nor deserve a crown.
But thou art fair, and at thy birth, dear boy,
Nature and Fortune joined to make thee great.
Of Nature's gifts thou mayst with lillies boast
And with the half-blown rose; but Fortune, O!
55 She is corrupted, changed and won from thee;
She adulterates hourly with thine Uncle John,
And with her golden hand hath plucked on France
To tread down fair respect of sovereignty,
And made his majesty a bawd to theirs.
60 France is a bawd to Fortune and King John—
That strumpet Fortune, that usurping John!
Tell me, thou fellow, is not France forsworn?
Envenom him with words, or get thee gone
And leave those woes alone which I alone
65 Am bound to under-bear.

43 *that bidst* who asks; *content* calm; *grim* shocking or distressing to look at; 44 *slanderous* disgraceful; 45 *sightless* unsightly; *blots* disfigurements; *stains* blotches; 46 *crooked* having a bent back; deformed; *swart* swarthy; *prodigious* (1) monstrous, deformed; and thus (2) portending evil; 47 *Patched* disfigured; 49 *nor thou* nor would you; 50 *Become* be suitable for, befit; *great birth* high-ranking noble status, due to lineage; 51 *fair* (1) handsome; and thus (2) auspicious, favorable; 52 *Nature* a personification (usually female) of the forces of nature, commonly used in Shakespeare's time; *Fortune* a personification (always female) of the power that decides one's fate, commonly used in Shakespeare's time; *joined* joined together (in partnership); 54 *half-blown* partly blossomed [*Of Nature's . . . rose* You may boast that nature has given you a complexion as delicate and white as lillies, and cheeks as red and perfect as a blossoming rose]; 55 *changed* (1) of another mind or disposition; (2) capriciously fickle in affection or loyalty; *won from thee* lured away from you; 56 *adulterates* commits adultery; 57 *golden* (1) auspicious, favorable to success and happiness; (2) yielding wealth, profitable; *hand* (1) the symbol of power or action; (2) the palm of the hand [*with her golden hand* (1) with her power to bestow success and happiness; (2) with her palm lined with gold, i.e., with bribes]; *plucked on* incited; *France* i.e., King Philip II (monarchs were often referred to by their countries' names); 58 *tread down* trample on; *fair* honorable, just; *of* for; *sovereignty* (1) right to be the sovereign ruler; (2) royal dignity; 59 *his majesty* i.e., King Philip's royalty; *bawd* pimp, procurer; *theirs* i.e., King John's and Fortune's; 62 *fellow* male person or servant (often used contemptuously—Constance's use of it to Salisbury, a nobleman, is extremely insulting); *forsworn* perjured, guilty of breaking his vow; 63 *Envenom* Poison, destroy [*Envenom . . . words* Say something nasty about him]; *get thee gone* get out of here; 65 *bound* destined, forced; *under-bear* endure;

I will not go with thee;
I will instruct my sorrows to be proud,
For grief is proud, and makes his owner stoop.
70 To me, and to the state of my great grief,
Let kings assemble; for my grief's so great
That no supporter but the huge firm earth
Can hold it up. Here I and sorrows sit;
Here is my throne, bid kings come bow to it.

1 minute, 50 seconds

69 *stoop* yield, submit; 70 *state* (1) condition (of grief); (2) greatness, majesty; (3) chair of state, a canopied chair or throne (Constance's grief has made her as proud as a monarch); 71 *Let kings assemble* i.e., let King Philip and King John assemble before Constance, as subjects do before their monarch when he or she sits in state.

COMMENTARY

Take the driving ambition of Lady Macbeth and combine it with the tender but fierce mothering style of a lioness, and what do you get? Constance. When Constance enters a room, everybody knows it—her sheer power and charisma come through in her speech. Notice that her favorite method of communication is grand metaphor.

First, Constance describes the current situation as a sordid love affair: *Fortune* at first loves Arthur, but is wooed away and *won* by King John. King Philip acts as a *bawd* for the *strumpet Fortune* in her adulterous affair with John. What more vulgar metaphor could be devised as an insult to not one, but two kings?

With regard to herself, Constance uses two metaphors. First, briefly, that of a falcon: rather than being owner of her grief, she is its servant. Grief is personified as her master, making her *stoop*, just as the owner trains its falcon to stoop (dive on command) for prey. Finally, Constance's grief becomes a royal presence—one so proud that kings must *come bow* to Constance's *great state*.

These metaphors are often conveyed with the help of antithesis. Using the hawking metaphor, she says *grief is proud, and makes his owner stoop*. The antithetical comparison of what is *Ugly* and *prodigious* with what is *fair* (and thus auspicious) is tied to the metaphor of a *half-blown rose* for her beautiful young son. (If you are working on several Constance pieces, you will find that this metaphor is revisited in III.iv, when she envisions her captured son as a bud eaten away by a cankerworm.)

The larger-than-life scope of her metaphors suggests that Constance is one of those people to whom Something Big is always happening. It is difficult to imagine her in a tranquil emotional state. With Constance, the intensity of the gamma ray is always on HIGH. This comes through in the way she uses words: she doesn't say "Here I and my sorrows sit" or "Here I and sorrow sit," she says *Here I and sorrows sit*, implying that she doesn't just sit there with her own sorrow, but with all the sorrows of the world.

The word *sorrows*, along with many others, appears more than once. Notice which words Constance uses again and again: *fair* (twice); *birth* (twice); *Fortune* (4 times); *John* (3 times); *France* (3 times); *bawd* (twice); *alone* (twice); *grief* (3 times); *proud* (twice); *great* (4 times); *kings* (twice); *sorrows* (twice). Many of Constance's issues stand out in bold relief in this list. Here are some of the things that jump out at us: (1) Fate—Constance is obsessed by the idea that her fate and Arthur's are controlled by an outside force. She rails at *Fortune*; she believes that Arthur's *fair* countenance is an auspicous sign; she feels she is *bound* to endure her hardships. (2) The importance of rank and power—Constance is infuriated by the injustice of Arthur's *birth* being ignored; she feels he will be *great*; she intensely resents the power of the *kings* to usurp and betray. (3) Sorrow and solitude—Constance feels acutely the wrongs done to her and her child. Her *grief* and *sorrows* are of a grand scale; she feels *alone*, and she *is* alone—a widow without companionship or male protection in a patriarchal world.

The repetition of these words not only creates a sort of mantra of what's on Constance's mind, but also contributes to the repetition of sounds in the piece. The use of rhyme, alliteration, and assonance appear in strategic places: the repetition of contemptuous, hiSSing Ss in *sightless stains* is in stark contrast with the line immediately following it, which is made up of motley, disparate sounds (*Lame*, *foolish*, *crooked*, *swart*, *prodigious*). This contrast emphasizes the aural picture of the ugliness she paints. At other moments, little bursts of alliteration highlight important words or ideas in her sentences: *moles* / *marks*; *birth* / *boy*; *fellow* / *France* / *forsworn*; *bound* / *under-bear*; *great* / *grief* / *grief's* / *great*; *sorrows* / *sit*. The assonance in the piece allows Constance to fully express her feelings through the use of moaning Os: *boast* / *blown* / *rose* / *O*; *woes* / *alone* / *alone*. (For more on the word *O*, see "O, No! An *O*!," page xxxiii.)

The most striking sound repetition in the piece is rhyme. There is, of course, the rhyming couplet at the end, in which the sharp, repeated sounds of *sit* and *it* wrap up the piece with spittingly defiant finality. Don't forget to heed the embedded stage direction, *Here I and sorrows sit*. Just before it there's a caesura, providing the perfect pause to do just that. (FYI: another embedded stage direction later in the scene indicates that she has seated herself not in a chair, but on the ground.)

A more unusual series of rhymes and half rhymes is found at the end of the first section: *John* / *John* / *forsworn* / *gone* / *alone*. Notice the strong associations that are formed here among King John, betrayal, and Constance's solitude. This string is followed by a surprisingly abrupt short line. Between the two sections, where Salisbury's half line and the half line of her reply to him have been omitted, there is an opportunity to use the combined four feet of pause to make your transition into the next section of the piece.

It is important to decide whom Constance is addressing with which lines. She is obviously speaking to Arthur at the beginning of the piece, and to Salisbury by the time she says *Tell me, thou fellow*. In between there are many decisions to make: When she speaks to Arthur, has she taken him aside so that they're speaking in semiprivacy? Or does she speak before Salisbury, so that her sentiments are also for his benefit? Or perhaps she thinks so little of Salisbury that she is indifferent to his presence at the beginning of the piece? You must also determine specifically when she shifts her focus, and whether there are transitional sections where she addresses them both. Your decisions will lead you to explore the many delicious ways to use the *France is a bawd to Fortune and King*

John metaphor—perhaps to pounce on Salisbury, to berate him, embarrass him, or shame him, etc.

One thing is sure, Constance is none too pleased with Salisbury, as is evidenced by her use of the familar *thee* and *thou*, which, though appropriate for her son, can be extremely insulting to an adult of equal rank. She also calls him *fellow*, a term applied to servants, and often used contemptuously to those of lower rank.

SIGNIFICANT SCANS

Line 46 is a little tricky to scan. Here's what we think works best: treat it as a headless line, with a silent half foot at the first caesura, and a double ending.

(x) / x / x / x / x / (x)
(pause) Lame, (pause) foolish, crooked, swart, prodigious

Line 50 is also unusual. The third foot (*birth, nor*) is a spondee, i.e., *both* syllables are accented:

x / x / / / x / x /
Become thy great birth, nor deserve a crown

Don't forget to elide: *slanderous* (SLAN-druss) in line 44 and *hourly* (OWR-lee) in line 56;

. . . and to elide and contract: *She adulterates* (sha-DUL-trates) in line 56.

REVISIONIST HISTORY:
CONSTANCE OF BRITTANY, VICTIM OF POETIC LICENSE

Shakespeare altered the facts of Constance's life to suit his fancy (i.e., his needs for the play). Constance was not lonely and miserable as a widow: in fact, she married twice after Geoffrey's death. Her son Arthur was not a little boy at the time of his capture, but a soldier of fifteen (an adult by medieval standards). She was not a helpless, dependent woman, but just the opposite, ruling Brittany for her young son for many years after Geoffrey's death. One thing Shakespeare retained, however, was this Frenchwoman's ambition to see her son on the throne of England.

KING JOHN

ACT III, SCENE iv

CONSTANCE

GENDER: F
AGE RANGE: adult to mature adult
PROSE/VERSE: blank verse
FREQUENCY OF USE (1–5): 3

Constance's young son, Arthur, is the rightful heir to the English throne, which is now held by his usurping uncle, King John. Arthur's claim to the throne was backed by King Philip II of France, who then betrayed him by signing a peace treaty with John. Now the treaty has been broken and, in the fighting between the two countries, little Arthur has been captured by the English. Having just heard this news, Constance has come to King Philip's tent, where she rails at King Philip, his son, Lewis (the Dauphin), and Cardinal Pandulph, the Pope's legate, about her son's capture.

21 Lo, now! Now, see the issue of your peace!

[King Philip: *Patience, good lady! Comfort, gentle Constance!*]

No, I defy all counsel, all redress
But that which ends all counsel, true redress—
25 Death! Death! O, amiable, lovely Death!
Thou odoriferous stench! Sound rottenness!
Arise forth from the couch of lasting night,
Thou hate and terror to prosperity,
And I will kiss thy detestable bones,
30 And put my eyeballs in thy vaulty brows,
And ring these fingers with thy household worms,
And stop this gap of breath with fulsome dust,
And be a carrion monster like thyself.
Come, grin on me, and I will think thou smilest
35 And buss thee as thy wife. Misery's love,
O, come to me!

[King Philip: *O fair affliction, peace!*]

O, that my tongue were in the thunder's mouth!
Then with a passion would I shake the world
40 And rouse from sleep that fell anatomy,
Which cannot hear a lady's feeble voice—
Which scorns a modern invocation.

21 *Lo* Look (used to draw someone's attention); *issue* result, consequence; *your peace* i.e., the peace treaty brokered between King Philip and King John, now broken; 23 *defy* reject; *counsel* advice; *redress* assistance; 24 *But that* Except for the one; *counsel* deliberation, reflection; *odoriferous* fragrant; 27 *Arise forth from* Come up out of; *couch* bed, place of rest; *lasting* everlasting [*the couch of lasting night* either (1) a tomb or (2) Hell]; 28 *Thou hate . . . success* you who are hated and feared by those currently enjoying good fortune; 30 *vaulty* hollow, cavernous; 31 *ring* encircle, as with a ring; *household* under the same government [*thy household worms* the worms you govern]; 32 *stop* fill up; *this gap of breath* i.e., my mouth; *fulsome* physically disgusting, sickening; 33 *carrion* skeleton; 34 *grin* bear one's teeth to express malice, scorn or anguish (a skeleton's natural expression); 35 *buss* kiss; *as* as if I were; 38 *that my tongue were in the thunder's mouth* i.e., if only I could speak as loudly as thunder; 39 *with a passion* violently [*with a passion . . . the world* I would violently shake the world (with my thunderous words)]; 40 *that fell anatomy* that deadly skeleton (i.e., death, which in Shakespeare's day, like today, was often personified as a skeleton); 42 *modern* ordinary;

[PANDULPH: *Lady, you utter madness and not sorrow.*]

45 I am not mad: This hair I tear is mine;
My name is Constance; I was Geoffrey's wife;
Young Arthur is my son, and he is lost.
I am not mad—I would to Heaven I were,
For then 'tis like I should forget myself.
50 O, if I could, what grief should I forget!
Preach some philosophy to make me mad,
And thou shalt be canonized, Cardinal—
For, being not mad but sensible of grief,
My reasonable part produces reason
55 How I may be delivered of these woes,
And teaches me to kill or hang myself.
If I were mad I should forget my son,
Or madly think a babe of clouts were he.
I am not mad: Too well, too well I feel
60 The different plague of each calamity.

1 minute, 15 seconds

46 *Geoffrey* Constance's husband, Geoffrey, Duke of Brittany, was King John's older brother and would have been next in line when King Richard I died had he still been alive at the time; 48 *would* wish; *like* likely; *should* would; *forget myself* forget who I am; forget who I have been; 51 *philosophy* mental exercise; 52 *Cardinal* she speaks to Cardinal Pandulph, the Pope's legate; 53 *sensible of grief* capable of feeling grief [*being not mad . . . grief* not being insane (and therefore unaware of my circumstances), but, rather, being capable of feeling grief]; 54 *reasonable part* that part of me that is endowed with reason (i.e., the mind); 55 *be delivered of* give birth to, have taken out of me; *produces reason / How . . . woes* thinks of a logical way that I might be relieved of these sorrows; 58 *babe of clouts* rag doll [*think a babe of clouts were he* (1) mistake a rag doll for my son; or (2) think he were merely a rag doll]; 59 *too well I feel* I feel too strongly; 60 *The different plague of each calamity* the distinct torment of each disaster.

COMMENTARY

Ironically, Constance the Ranter is a good listener. She wins all of her arguments because she listens to what is said to her and turns it around to prove her own point. She does so three times in this monologue, twice against King Philip and then against Pandulph the Papal legate. She does so because she wants to be heard herself . . . and clearly understood. As emotional as she seems here, she has not relinquished control of herself or of the conversation. Sadly, it is her entire life that she has lost control of. In this scene, Constance has chosen to come meet with King Philip, Pandulph, and the rest (she was not sent for), and, when she has made her point, she will choose to leave. She blames them for Arthur's capture and has come to make them aware of their direct responsibility for his and her impending deaths, for it does seem likely that the little boy will be killed by his captors, if the abject conditions of his imprisonment don't kill him first, and Constance feels she cannot live without him.

Since Constance is wont to rave and rant, you must decide how much of her lamentation is about her own circumstances (she won't be the mother of a king) and how much is about her son's (he's in grave danger); to what extent this lamentation is an expression of pure grief and to what extent (if any) Constance is taking any of her usual delight in melodramatic expression of discontent. Note that Constance uses the word *O* four times in this one passage. (Please check out "O, No! An *O*!," page xxxiii.)

This monologue affords an actor a wonderful opportunity to have fun with varied material and to work on transitions. There are several complete transitions in the piece, from the lines where Constance defiantly answers King Philip to the lines wherein she propositions Death; from her seduction of Death to her wish for thunder's voice; from the thunder imagery to her powerful proof of her sanity and her right to feel grief. To create the monologue, short dialogue has been removed between these segments. Your mission (should you choose to accept it) is to find the thought connections that will smooth these transitions.

After "dissing" King Philip (a bold move—remember, this is the ruler of France! Or maybe not so bold—if she truly wishes to die, she has nothing to lose!), Constance employs horrifyingly sensuous imagery to express her desire to die, personifying Death and trying to rouse him from his dark bedchamber to be her lover/husband. Make the images specific: each builds on those that precede it, leading up to her most horrible image—that of her kissing Death as a wife would. Notice her use of the familiar, intimate *thy* when addressing Death. Constance employs oxymorons throughout this section (*amiable, lovely death*; *odoriferous stench*; *sound rottenness*; *grin on me / I will think thou smilest*) to show that she welcomes those elements of death that frighten most people, since they are preferable to life without her beloved child.

In the final section, Constance asserts her sanity in a well-constructed argument (again using antithesis, contrasting Pandulph's notions of crazy versus sane behavior with her own, and contrasting her living child, worthy of lamentation, with a mere rag doll). She first runs through the same kind of checklist we use to test presence of mind today (I know who I am, who my husband was, who my child is, my home address, what day of the week it is, who the President of the United States is . . .). She very effectively rebuts Pandulph's assertion that she is crazy by asserting that her reaction to her child's imprisonment proves quite the opposite: only one who has lost touch with reality could be tranquil and happy in her situation. Her answer is entirely reasonable—those among us who have had the misfortune of losing a child (or who can empathize with such a loss) can feel their chests constrict in pain as she claims her right to feel, and express, anguish. Constance wraps up this section in the last four lines with three patterns of sound that will reverberate in her listeners' ears—and minds. The first is her repetition of *mad(ly)*. The second is the repetition of the phrase *too well* and its half-rhyme with the phrase *I feel* that follows. The third is the rhyme of the second and fourth of these lines: *a babe of clouts were he / of each calamity*.

Note: if you have the opportunity to present a longer monologue and wish to carry Constance's gorgeous lament to its conclusion, this monologue can be linked with the monologue she delivers next (see page 29).

SIGNIFICANT SCANS

Notice the remarkable evenness of both sections. There are only very occasional variations in meter. In the second section, the meter's nearly perfect unbroken regularity creates an evenness of tone that supports Constance's argument that she is rational and sane.

The line *O, come to me!* is only two feet long (when performed as a scene, the other three feet are spoken by King Philip). When performing this as a monologue, taking the three feet as silent feet gives you a chance to make a transition to the next section.

Notice the pronunciation of *detestable* (DEE-tess-TUH-ble) in line 29. Try it. See how it emphasizes the meaning of the word. Also notice that *canonized* is written to be pronounced ca-NON-ized. You may choose to pronounce it that way to preserve the line's perfect iambic pentameter, or you may prefer to sacrifice the meter in order to pronounce the word in a way more comprehensible to today's audience.

Line 25 is a bit tricky to scan. We suggest that you build in two pauses and then both elide *amiable* (A-mya-ble) and crowd the fourth foot, as follows:

x / x / / / x-x / x /
(pause) Death! (pause) Death! O, amiable, lovely Death!

Or, keeping the pauses, you could choose to pronounce *amiable* with four syllables and treat the line as hexameter:

x / x / / / x / x / x /
(pause) Death! (pause) Death! O, amiable, lovely Death!

In either case, note that the third foot is a spondee (i.e., both syllables are accented). Coupled with the marked repetition of *Death*, the variations in this line give the actor much to play with.

Don't forget to elide: *odoriferous* (O-duh-RIF´-russ) in line 26; *carrion* (CA-ryon) in line 33; *smilest* (SMILST) in line 34; *Heaven* (HEV'N) in line 48; and *being* (BEENG) in line 53;

. . . and to expand: *invocation* (IN-voh-CAY´-shee-UN) in line 42 and *reasonable* (REE´-zon-AH-ble) in line 54.

P.S.

For info on the historical Constance, see "Revisionist History: Constance of Brittany, Victim of Poetic License," page 22.

KING JOHN

ACT III, SCENE iv

CONSTANCE

GENDER: F
AGE RANGE: adult to mature adult
PROSE/VERSE: blank verse
FREQUENCY OF USE (1–5): 3

Note that this monologue immediately follows the piece on page 23, within the same scene and context in the play (we urge you to read that introduction and monologue for full background). Having just heard the news of her son's imprisonment, Constance has entered King Philip's tent with her "hair about her ears," where she rails at King Philip, his son, Lewis (the Dauphin), and Cardinal Pandulph, the Pope's legate, whom she blames for her son's capture. She has just refused to be consoled, invited Death to be her lover, and vehemently defended her reaction as reasonable under the circumstances. When King Philip urges her to "bind up her hairs," she replies:

Yes, that I will; and wherefore will I do it?
70 I tore them from their bonds and cried aloud,
"O that these hands could so redeem my son,
As they have given these hairs their liberty!"
But now I envy at their liberty,
And will again commit them to their bonds,
75 Because my poor child is a prisoner.
And, father Cardinal, I have heard you say
That we shall see and know our friends in Heaven:
If that be true, I shall see my boy again,
For since the birth of Cain, the first male child,
80 To him that did but yesterday suspire,
There was not such a gracious creature born.
But now will canker sorrow eat my bud
And chase the native beauty from his cheek,
And he will look as hollow as a ghost,
85 As dim and meager as an ague's fit,
And so he'll die; and rising so again,
When I shall meet him in the court of Heaven
I shall not know him. Therefore never, never
Must I behold my pretty Arthur more.

Grief fills the room up of my absent child,
Lies in his bed, walks up and down with me,

69 *that I will* I will do that (i.e., I will bind up my hairs); *wherefore* why; 70 *them* i.e., her hairs; *bonds* the cords or bands which held her hairdo in place; 71 *that* I wish that; if only; *so* thus; in the same manner; 73 *envy at* envy (i.e., she feels envy when she compares her hair's liberty with Arthur's captivity); 74 *commit* imprison [*again commit . . . bonds* i.e., tie them (her hairs) up again]; 76 *father Cardinal* she speaks to Cardinal Pandulph; 77 *friends* loved ones; 79 *Cain* the first baby born on earth; 80 *To* Up until; *but* only, just; *suspire* draw breath [*To him . . . suspire* up until the baby that drew its first breath (was born) just yesterday (i.e., the most recent baby born on earth)]; 81 *gracious* (1) lovely, beautiful; (2) righteous, virtuous; 82 *canker* cankerworm, a worm that eats blossoms; *my bud* referring to Arthur [*will canker . . . bud* sorrow will eat away at my son like a cankerworm]; 83 *native* natural; 84 *hollow* sunken; 85 *dim* lusterless, dull; *meager* thin; *ague's fit* fit of chills and shivering caused by a severe fever; 86 *so* thus; in this condition; *rising so again* rising (to Heaven) in this condition; 88 *know* recognize; 89 *never / Must I behold* I will never be able to see; *pretty* pleasing, fine; *more* again; 93 *Grief fills . . . absent child* (1) Grief fills the room with memories of my absent child; and (2) Grief (itself) fills up

95 Puts on his pretty looks, repeats his words,
Remembers me of all his gracious parts,
Stuffs out his vacant garments with his form:
Then have I reason to be fond of grief!
Fare you well. Had you such a loss as I,
100 I could give better comfort than you do.
I will not keep this form upon my head,
When there is such disorder in my wit.
O Lord! My boy, my Arthur, my fair son!
My life, my joy, my food, my all the world!
105 My widow-comfort, and my sorrows' cure!

2 minutes

my absent child's empty room; 95 *repeats* calls to mind the sound of; 96 *Remembers* reminds; *parts* a person's good looks and good character; 97 *Stuffs out* fills; 98 *Then have I reason* therefore I have reason; 101 *this form upon my head* my hair bound up in this manner; 102 *wit* mind [*disorder in my wit* chaos in my mind (not insanity)]; 103 *fair* beautiful.

COMMENTARY

There's no doubt about it—the most difficult thing about this piece is jumping in: your very first line is the answer to a command the audience hasn't heard. Never fear! It is completely possible to use this wonderful piece and get your audience past that little difficulty. First of all, with the first line, don't worry that they don't know what you're agreeing to do in such a defiant manner. If you are invested in your reply, the audience will be lured in—eager to listen and find out what's going on. In the next few lines, Constance explains that she has taken her hair down. If you're still concerned, keep in mind Shakespeare's embedded stage directions: Constance says, *I will again commit them to their bonds*. Doing so will tip the audience off. No problem. Stay tuned for more stage directions later in the piece, when Constance says, *I will not keep this form upon my head* (whereupon she obviously takes her hair back down).

The physicality of putting the hair up and tearing it down allows Constance to act out the ideas she expresses in the monologue. It's a perfect complement to her characteristically melodramatic, overblown words. Constance has behaved in this manner throughout the play: perhaps she gets such a cold response because she is a bit like the boy who cried wolf. That fact, however, does not mitigate her loss one iota. Constance's pain and fear are very real, very intense. Part of the work to be done is discovering what exactly that pain is about. How much of it is true grief at losing her child, versus the grief of losing his birthright? After all, Constance is a woman who would herself have loved to rule: since she couldn't, seeing her son rule would have been the next best thing. How much of Constance's pain has to do with her loss of power? How much with her delight in melodrama? How much with fearing that her child might already be dead?

The power of these emotions makes it more important than ever to clarify your objectives in this scene. One thing that will help you will be to examine the piece and decide to whom Constance is speaking with every line. There are a lot of possible answers: King Philip, Pandulph, Lewis, Attendant, all of them, herself, God.

Constance's unusual mode of attack at the monologue's onset starts it off with intensity: notice that she uses King Philip's own suggestion to "bind up her hairs" against him, and then makes the odd choice to quote herself. Is this for added effect? Is she trying to relive for him the moment when she found out Arthur was gone? Is she driving home her point? Similar questions arise when Constance reminds the Cardinal of his own words to her, that *we shall see and know our friends in Heaven*. Is she being sarcastic with him, throwing his naive statement in his face? Or does she believe that what he has said is true, and fear what that might mean?

Being a drama queen, Constance is prone to using vivid imagery, often contrasting her images: all children ever born on earth versus her son; his *gracious* looks when he was with her versus the *dim and meager* look he'll have in prison; the freedom of her hairs versus her son's imprisonment. Constance also personifies *Grief*, who takes the place of her absent son and imitates him. The personification is another device that expresses her emotions as larger than life, so large that they are physically present.

Constance's dark words are made even darker by the double meanings layered between her lines: (1) *commit them to their bonds*—she will not simply tie up her hair, but will restrain and imprison it, just as her son is restrained and imprisoned; (2) *canker sorrow will eat my bud*—sorrow will eat away at her child, and worms will eat him in his grave; (3) *I will not keep this form upon my head*—Constance sees no reason to keep her hair or her mind in orderly form (this is especially significant if you are combining this piece with the previous monologue, in which Constance has argued that she is *not mad*, i.e., not crazy, but that she wishes she were). For help using the word *O* to its most dramatic effect, see "O, No! An *O*!," page xxiii.

Finally, in the last three lines, Constance delivers a litany of the things Arthur was to her, and it's no mistake that she repeats *my* with every one. This is, after all, about Constance, and what she has lost in losing her son.

Note: if you have the opportunity to present a longer monologue, this piece can be linked with the previous one (see page 23).

SIGNIFICANT SCANS

Note the crowded foot (*I shall see*) in line 78 (or you may contract *I shall* to I'll):

x / x / x - x / x / x /
If that be true, I shall see my boy again

You'll find another crowded foot (*such a*) in line 99, which is also headless:

x / x / x / x - x / x /
(pause) Fare you well. Had you such a loss as I

And notice that line 75 has a dramatic-sounding spondee (a foot with two accented syllables) in it:

x / x / / / x / x /
Because my poor child is a prisoner

Don't forget to elide: *given* (GIV'N) in line 72.

P.S.

For info on the historical Constance, see "Revisionist History: Constance of Brittany, Victim of Poetic License," page 22.

ART(HUR) IMITATING LIFE?

In reality, Arthur was fifteen years old and already leading forces in combat at the time he was captured, but Shakespeare made the character Arthur a young boy. Shakespeare's own son, Hamnet, died in August 1596, at the age of eleven. Is it a coincidence that Shakespeare made Arthur a boy close to Hamnet's age, or is Constance's expression of her loss based on Shakespeare's feelings about his own "absent child"?

KING JOHN

ACT V, SCENE ii

LEWIS

GENDER: M
PROSE/VERSE: blank verse

AGE RANGE: young adult to adult
FREQUENCY OF USE (1–5): 3

Lewis, as the son of King Philip II of France, is the heir to the French throne. At the urging of Pandulph, the Pope's legate, he has gone to war against King John, hoping to claim the English throne through his marriage to John's niece, Blanch. Thus far the war is a great success: Lewis has already taken parts of England. Now John has given in to the Pope's demands, so Pandulph has arrived and told Lewis the war is off. Lewis is outraged, and replies:

Your Grace shall pardon me, I will not back.
I am too highborn to be propertied,
80 To be a secondary at control,
Or useful servingman and instrument
To any sovereign state throughout the world.
Your breath first kindled the dead coal of wars
Between this chastised kingdom and myself,
85 And brought in matter that should feed this fire;
And now 'tis far too huge to be blown out
With that same weak wind which enkindled it.
You taught me how to know the face of right,
Acquainted me with interest to this land,
90 Yea, thrust this enterprise into my heart;
And come ye now to tell me John hath made
His peace with Rome? What is that peace to me?
I, by the honor of my marriage bed,
After young Arthur, claim this land for mine;
95 And now it is half-conquered, must I back
Because that John hath made his peace with Rome?
Am I Rome's slave? What penny hath Rome borne,
What men provided, what munition sent
To underprop this action? Is't not I
100 That undergo this charge? Who else but I,
And such as to my claim are liable,

78 *Your Grace* he speaks to Pandulph; *shall* must (as opposed to "will"); *back* go back; back down; 79 *propertied* used as someone else's property or tool; manipulated; 80 *secondary at control* subordinate or assistant, controlled by a higher authority; 84 *this chastised kingdom* i.e., England; 85 *matter* substance; *that should feed* to feed; 87 *enkindled* kindled; 88 *know the face of right* recognize what is just; recognize a just claim to title or inheritance; 89 *interest to* my interest in; my legal claim to; 90 *enterprise* undertaking; 92 *Rome* i.e., the Pope and the Catholic Church; 93 *honor of* rank that I hold through; 94 *Arthur* King John's nephew, son of John's deceased older brother Geoffrey; 95 *now it is* now that it is; 96 *Because that* because; 99 *underprop* support; *action* military enterprise; 100 *undergo* undertake; take on; endure; *charge* military attack; 101 *liable* (1) allied; (2) subject [*such as to my claim are liable* such people as are allied with

Sweat in this business and maintain this war?
Have I not heard these islanders shout out
Vive le roi! as I have banked their towns?
105 Have I not here the best cards for the game
To win this easy match, played for a crown?
And shall I now give o'er the yielded set?
No, no, on my soul, it never shall be said.

1 minute, 50 seconds

or subject to my claim to the crown]; 103 *islanders* i.e., the English; 104 *Vive le roi!* Long live the King! (French); *banked* (1) landed on the banks of; (2) sailed past the banks of; (3) won [a pun: in card playing, to bank was to win]; 107 *yielded set* game that is as good as won.

COMMENTARY

Who does that Pope think he is, the most powerful man in Europe or something? Sending that bossy legate of his to order kings and princes around! Well, the future King of France will not be dictated to by some Vatican bureaucrat in an oversized hat.

Lewis is a young man, and everything about his speech reflects his youthful, masculine attitude, as well as his background: as the Dauphin, he's not used to being told what to do, and it doesn't suit him well at all. Lewis is a normal, red-blooded male, full of rash self-confidence and further endowed with a sense of royal self-righteousness. So even though the Pope wields enormous power, Lewis has no fear—or if he does, he ignores it and hides it well. Notice that Lewis does not hesitate for a second in his reply to Pandulph. He is polite on the surface (*Your Grace shall pardon me*) but absolutely stubborn and verging on rudeness from the very beginning. He uses hard consonants such as Bs, Ks, Ps, and Ts to forcefully rebuff Pandulph (*back*; *propertied*; *control*), ending each of the first few lines with a punch.

The build in this piece is neatly embedded in its rhythmic structure. The first lines flow along easily, following iambic pentameter with few outstanding variations, until Lewis hits the crux of the matter: The idea in *And come ye now to tell me John hath made / His peace with Rome?* continues past the end of one line and ends abruptly, halfway through the next one. This contrast highlights the first of a series of questions Lewis fires at Pandulph. As the questions begin to flow, fast and furious, they are enhanced by more frequent metric variations. The next question that ends mid-line is another important idea in Lewis's progression, and marks the moment when he starts to get more caustic: *Am I Rome's slave?* Two more questions end mid-line, each setting up a startling jumping-off point for Lewis to get at what's really important—his own sacrifice, and his own rights. He uses *I* many times in the piece, but it receives the most emphasis here, at the ends of these two successive lines, because of the structural setup.

Lewis uses noticeably few repeated sounds in this monologue, making line 87 particularly striking: it has both alliterative Ws (*With / weak / wind / which*) and assonant Is (*With / wind / which / enkindled / it*). What could be the reason for singling out this line? Is Lewis getting extra mileage out of his jab at Pandulph's weakness, especially by using those wimpy W/I combinations?

As we can gather from his avoidance of most poetic devices, Lewis is a pretty straightforward guy. We hate to stereotype, but the fact is, Lewis chooses three of the most stereotypical metaphors a young guy could possibly come up with. First, fire: Pandulph kindled the *dead coal* of wars between England and France; now the fire is raging so *huge* that the *wind* which *enkindled it* is too *weak* to blow it out. (Perhaps Lewis is not quite out of his pyromaniac stage.) Second, games: specifically, a card game. He has *banked* their towns; he has the *best cards for the game*; he's playing an *easy match*, and the prize is the crown; why should he give over the *yielded set*? Lewis's third metaphor is sex. Here's the double (and sometimes not so double) entendre: *too highborn* = two (testicles), borne high; *best cards* = best cods = best scrotum; *the game* = sexual intercourse; *easy* = readily available for sex; *match* = bout of love; *played* = amused oneself sexually; *crown* = genitals; *yielded* = sexually impotent.

The double entendre here is fun to know about, but a bit obscure. Feel free to ignore it or use it, as you choose.

SIGNIFICANT SCANS

For line 104, you must pronounce both syllables of *Vive* (noting the inverted first foot):

/ x x / x / x / x /
Vive le roi! as I have banked their towns *Vive* (VEE-vuh)

Line 108 is a little tricky. Just elide *on my*:

x / x / x /x / x /
No, no, on my soul, it never shall be said *on my* ('nmy)

And don't forget to expand: *liable* (LIE-uh-BLE) in line 101.

REVISIONIST HISTORY: AMBITIOUS FOR ANGLO ACCESSION, PRINCE P.O.S POPE

The things native English-speakers do to the French language . . . Poor Louis the Dauphin was immortalized by Shakespeare as "Lewis the Dolphin." The real Dauphin was encouraged to invade England not by the Pope but by the rebelling English lords, who invited him to invade and become their king. Invade he did, in 1216 at the age of twenty-nine, despite the disapproval of the Pope, who had reconciled with John earlier, and who excommunicated Louis for his action. Louis lost the support of the nobles with the death of John and the accession of Henry III; he withdrew from England shortly thereafter, in 1217. Louis did not succeed his father, King Philip II, until 1223; he reigned as Louis VIII of France until his death three years later.

KING JOHN

ACT V, SCENE ii

PHILIP THE BASTARD

GENDER: M
AGE RANGE: adult to mature adult
PROSE/VERSE: blank verse
FREQUENCY OF USE (1–5): 3

The French, led by Prince Lewis, heir to the French throne, have invaded England with the support of the Pope, who has grievances against England's King John. Since King John has satisfied the Pope, the Pope's legate (ambassador), Pandulph, orders Prince Lewis to withdraw his troops from England. Lewis refuses, insisting that he will fight, whereupon the Bastard, speaking on behalf of King John, tells the Prince in no uncertain terms that King John plans to make the French sorry that they ever even attempted an invasion.

By all the blood that ever fury breathed,
The youth says well. Now hear our English king,
For thus his Royalty doth speak in me:
130 He is prepared—and reason too he should;
This apish and unmannerly approach,
This harnessed masque and unadvisèd revel
This unhaired sauciness and boyish troops
The King doth smile at, and is well prepared
135 To whip this dwarfish war, these pygmy arms,
From out the circle of his territories.
That hand which had the strength, even at your door,
To cudgel you and make you take the hatch,
To dive like buckets in concealèd wells,
140 To crouch in litter of your stable planks,
To lie like pawns locked up in chests and trunks,
To hug with swine, to seek sweet safety out
In vaults and prisons, and to thrill and shake
Even at the crying of your nation's crow,
145 Thinking this voice an armèd Englishman—

127 *that ever fury breathed* that was ever breathed by a storm of rage (i.e., that was ever spilled because of fury); 128 *The youth* i.e., Lewis; *says well* speaks well and to the purpose; 129 *his Royalty* his Majesty (i.e., King John); *in me* through me; 130 *prepared* i.e., prepared to fight; *reason too he should* he has good reason, too; 131 *unmannerly* rude, indecent; *approach* hostile advance, attack; 132 *harnessed* dressed in armor; *masque* elaborately costumed performance (Philip calls Lewis's advance a ridiculous performance of actors costumed as soldiers in armor); *unadvisèd* rash, unwise, imprudent; *revel* festivity, merrymaking; 133 *unhaired* beardless, immature; *boyish* childish, immature; 134 *doth smile at* smiles at (scornfully, indulgently, or with amusement); 135 *whip* drive out by whipping; *these pygmy arms* these tiny (and therefore insignificant) weapons; 136 *From out* out of; *circle* perimeter, boundary; 137 *That hand* i.e., King John's forces; *at your door* i.e., at your own border; 138 *take the hatch* retreat quickly (as if leaping through the hatch of a door); 139 *dive like buckets in concealèd wells* hide by diving down like buckets plunging into hidden wells; 140 *litter* an animal's bed of straw [*crouch in litter . . . planks* crouch down in the straw on the floor of your stable (to hide)]; 141 *pawns* (1) objects taken as security for a loan; (2) chess pieces; 142 *hug with swine* be locked in an embrace with pigs (in order to conceal oneself while hiding in a pigpen); 143 *to thrill* to have a shiver run up the spine, to tremble; 144 *the crying of your nation's crow* (i.e., the sound of the rooster, the traditional symbol of France, contemptuously called a crow by Philip); 145 *Thinking this voice an*

Shall that victorious hand be feebled here
That in your chambers gave you chastisement?
No! Know the gallant monarch is in arms
And like an eagle o'er his aery towers,
150 To souse annoyance that comes near his nest.
And you degenerate, you ingrate revolts,
You bloody Neroes, ripping up the womb
Of your dear mother England, blush for shame;
For your own ladies and pale-visaged maids
155 Like Amazons come tripping after drums,
Their thimbles into armèd gauntlets change,
Their needles to lances, and their gentle hearts
To fierce and bloody inclination.

Indeed, your drums, being beaten, will cry out;
And so shall you, being beaten. Do but start
An echo with the clamor of thy drum,
And even at hand a drum is ready braced
170 That shall reverberate all as loud as thine.
Sound but another, and another shall,

armèd Englishman mistaking the sound of the rooster for the sound of an English soldier; 147 *the gallant monarch* i.e., King John; *in arms* armed; 149 *And like* and is like; *aery* eagle's high nest (also, stronghold built on a height); *towers* flies directly upward before swooping [*And like . . . towers* and soars like an eagle over his high nest before swooping to attack]; 150 *To* prepared to; *souse* swoop down on, pounce on; *annoyance* harm, injury; 151 *ingrate* (in-GRATE) ungrateful; *revolts* deserters, rebels (the Bastard now turns to speak to the three English lords who have defected to the French); 152 *Neroes* Nero was the cruel Roman emperor who set Rome on fire and killed his own mother, ripping open her womb upon her death; 154 *For* because; *pale-visaged* pale-faced; *maids* unmarried, virginal women; 155 *Amazons* in Greek mythology, a nation of fierce female warriors; *tripping after* dancing along behind (also, stumbling morally, by adopting the men's enthusiasm for war); *drums* drums were used to lead troops to battle; 156 *armèd gauntlets* iron gloves used in armed combat [*Their thimbles into armèd gauntlets change* change their thimbles into iron gauntlets]; 158 *inclination* both (1) disposition and (2) the slanting angle of a lance during armed combat; 167 *Do but start* If you even start; 168 *clamor* the sound of the drum [*Do but start . . . drum* If you even dare to begin making the slightest echo of sound with your drums (i.e., if you even begin to hint at making an attack)]; 169 *And* then; *even* (1) likewise; (2) at the same time; *ready braced* prepared and ready [*even at hand . . . braced* our drum is right nearby, just as ready as yours (i.e., our troops are standing by, poised to attack)]; 170 *all as loud as thine* every bit as loudly as yours (by saying that the English drums will be every bit as loud as the French, the Bastard implies that the

As loud as thine, rattle the welkin's ear
And mock the deep-mouthed thunder; for at hand—
Not trusting to this halting legate here,
175 Whom he hath used rather for sport than need—
Is warlike John; and in his forehead sits
A bare-ribbed Death, whose office is this day
To feast upon whole thousands of the French.

2 minutes, 40 seconds

English troops will rush into battle as vigorously); 171 *Sound but another* If you strike another drum (to lead another battalion into battle); *and another* i.e., and another of our drums (leading another English battalion); 172 *the welkin's* the sky's; 173 *deep-mouthed* deep-voiced; 174 *trusting to* having confidence in, placing trust in; *halting* wavering, backsliding; *legate* ambassador of the Pope (here, referring to Pandulph); 175 *hath used rather for sport than need* has used for amusement, rather than out of need; 176 *in his forehead* i.e., in the expression on his face (giving insight into his mood and intention); 177 *A bare-ribbed Death* Death (personified as a skeleton); *office* assignment, task, job; *in his forehead . . . French* i.e., the look on John's face bespeaks his intention to slaughter thousands of the French in battle today.

COMMENTARY

Do you think that the Bastard was sorry to hear Lewis declare that he would not withdraw from England? We don't. There are enough indications throughout the play that the Bastard is itching to fight the French, so he's probably pleased to tell Lewis just where the English will be sending him. Philip is a master of sarcasm, and no doubt enjoys putting it to good use here, in order to belittle Lewis and the French troops.

The Bastard's imagery can be quite menacing. He describes his ruler, King John, as an eagle, with sharp talons and beak, swooping at amazing speed to attack the French in order to protect his nest, England. Many of the Bastard's personifications (*by all the blood that ever fury breathed*; *the deep-mouthed thunder*; *a bare-ribbed Death*) are chilling to imagine.

The Bastard belittles Lewis and his silly little French soldiers, using sarcasm, imagery, punning, double entendre, repetition of ideas, and consonance and assonance in combination to achieve new heights of snide: he is scathing in his vivid descriptions of the cowardice of Lewis's soldiers (*To dive like buckets in concealèd wells / To crouch in litter of your stable planks / To lie like pawns locked up in chests and trunks / To hug with swine, to seek sweet safety out / In vaults and prisons, and to thrill and shake / Even at the crying of your nation's crow / Thinking this voice an armèd Englishman*). Notice that the Bastard, not content with only one depiction, offers *six*, each more ridiculous than the last, to emphasize his contempt for the French troops, and, possibly, to egg Lewis on. The Bastard enjoys repeating words or ideas to heighten their insult (*your drums, being beaten / you, being beaten*; *you degenerate, you ingrate revolts / You bloody Neroes*; *No! Know*).

In calling Lewis a boy and his attack a mere entertainment (*the youth*; *boyish troops*; *unhaired sauciness*; *unadvised*; *dwarfish*; *pygmy*; *the King doth smile at*), Philip implies that Lewis is not a man, with the secondary suggestion that he is effeminate. The following second meanings would have been familiar to an Elizabethan audience: *masque* also means "prostitute"; *boy* also refers to a male who takes the "female" role during homosexual intercourse; *unmannerly* not only means "rude," but also "unmanly," i.e., "effeminate"; *unhaired* not only implies prepubescent, but also, again, girlish; *whip* carries two sexual meanings: (1) castrate; (2) sodomize; *dwarfish war* puns on the word "whore"; *pygmy arms* implies that Lewis has a little penis, since everyone knows that weapons (like cars) are penis substitutes; *swine* also means "bugger" (one who sodomizes): hence, the Bastard's description of Lewis's soldiers embracing pigs to hide from the enemy has the secondary meaning that they are getting screwed. This meaning would not have been at all subtle to the audience in Shakespeare's day; *drum* also means "buttocks."

Note: it is important that you do not play these meanings overtly, since (1) they are *not* the intended primary meaning; and (2) most of these meanings are no longer in use. They can, however, subtly inform your performance.

The sounds of the piece assist the Bastard in presenting bravura and scathing sarcasm. He starts right off with Bold Bs (*By all the blood that ever fury breathed*), uses Cold Cs to describe the punishment King John will mete out to Lewis (*cudgel you*; *make you take the hatch*; *buckets* / *concealed*), uses deriSive Ss when describing the French soldiers' cowardice (*swine* / *seek sweet safety* / *vaults* / *prisons*; *chambers* / *chastisement*), and soaring vowels to describe the eagle (*is in arms*; *like an eagle o'er his aery towers*). He really goes on the offensive in the second section, where DominanT Ds and Ts emerge as the prevailing consonant sounds in the section, with Bs as a close runner-up (*Indeed* / *drums* / *being beaten* / *cry out* / *Do but start* / *drum* / *at hand* / *drum* / *ready braced* / *that* / *reverberate* / *loud* / *sound* / *but* / *loud* / *rattle* / *deep-mouthed thunder* / *at hand* / *not trusting to* / *halting* / *legate* / *forehead* / *bare-ribbed Death* / *day* / *feast* / *thousands*). He also uses onomatopoeia to underscore the violence he describes (*whip*; *thrill*; *ripping*; *rattle*).

SIGNIFICANT SCANS

Notice the remarkably calm and even meter. The Bastard almost never starts new sentences in the middle of lines; where he does (see lines 128 and 167), he wants Lewis to sit up and take notice. The lines are almost all perfectly smoothly iambic—again, the occasional exception is for emphasis. The meter's evenness lends a calmness to the delivery, which creates a far more menacing tone than if the Bastard were erratic and emotional.

Don't forget to elide: *territories* (TERR′-i-TREES) in line 136; *even* = e'en (EEN) in lines 137, 144, and 169; *victorious* (vic-TOR-yuss) in line 146; *degenerate* (dee-JEN-ret) in line 151; *needles* (NEEDLZ) in line 157; *being* (BEENG) in lines 166 and 167; and *reverberate* (re-VER-bret) in line 170;

. . . and to expand: *inclination* (IN-cli-NAY′-shee-UN) in line 158.

P.S.

For information on the historical origins of Philip, see "Philip the Bastard: Three for the Price of One," page 10.

RICHARD II

ACT I, SCENE ii

DUCHESS OF GLOUCESTER

GENDER: F
PROSE/VERSE: blank verse
AGE RANGE: mature adult to older adult
FREQUENCY OF USE (1–5): 3

The Duchess of Gloucester's husband, Prince Thomas of Woodstock, Duke of Gloucester, sixth son of the now-deceased King Edward III of England and uncle of the current king, Richard II, was murdered just prior to the events portrayed in *Richard II*. His widow believes that the murder was committed by Thomas Mowbray, Duke of Norfolk, at the behest of King Richard. She wants blood. To that end, she has gone to the home of her brother-in-law, John of Gaunt, the fourth son of Edward III, to persuade him to avenge his brother's murder.

Finds brotherhood in thee no sharper spur?
10 Hath love in thy old blood no living fire?
Edward's seven sons, whereof thyself art one,
Were as seven vials of his sacred blood,
Or seven fair branches springing from one root:
Some of those seven are dried by nature's course,
15 Some of those branches by the Destinies cut;
But Thomas, my dear lord, my life, my Gloucester,
One vial full of Edward's sacred blood,
One flourishing branch of his most royal root,
Is cracked and all the precious liquor spilt,
20 Is hacked down, and his summer leaves all faded,
By Envy's hand and Murder's bloody axe.
Ah, Gaunt, his blood was thine—that bed, that womb,
That mettle, that self mold that fashioned thee
Made him a man; and though thou livest and breathest,
25 Yet art thou slain in him. Thou dost consent
In some large measure to thy father's death
In that thou seest thy wretched brother die,
Who was the model of thy father's life.
Call it not patience, Gaunt—it is despair.
30 In suffering thus thy brother to be slaughtered,
Thou showest the naked pathway to thy life,
Teaching stern Murder how to butcher thee.
That which in mean men we entitle "patience"
Is pale cold cowardice in noble breasts.
35 What shall I say? To safeguard thine own life,
The best way is to venge my Gloucester's death.

1 minute, 40 seconds

9 *Finds brotherhood . . . spur* Doesn't brotherhood spur you on (to action) any more forcefully than this? 10 *Hath love . . . no living fire* Is the fire of love no longer lit in your blood (i.e., do you no longer feel the heat of love?); 11 *Edward* i.e., King Edward III of England, father of John of Gaunt and Thomas, Duke of Gloucester, as well as of the current king, Richard II; *whereof thyself art one* of which you yourself are one; 12 *as* like; 14 *are dried by nature's course* i.e., died natural deaths; 15 *the Destinies* a.k.a., the Fates: in Greek mythology, the goddesses who spun the thread of one's life, ending it by cutting it at the appointed time [*by the Destinies cut* i.e., cut short by fate]; 16 *lord* husband; 19 *liquor* liquid; 22 *his* i.e., Gloucester's; 23 *mettle* material; *self* same; *fashioned* shaped; 25 *Yet* still, nevertheless; *in him* i.e., through his death; *Thou dost consent* You condone; 26 *In some large measure* to a large degree; 27 *In that* because; *thou seest* i.e., you stand by passively, without taking revenge; 28 *model* a smaller-scale version; *of thy father's life* i.e., of your father; 30 *suffering* permitting; 31 *naked* clear [*Thou showest . . . life* you are clearing the path for the murderers to take your life]; 33 *That* i.e., that attribute; *mean men* ordinary, common men, men of low social status; 34 *in noble breasts* in the hearts of noblemen; 36 *venge* avenge [*To safeguard . . . death* The best way to protect your own life is to avenge the death of my husband (and your brother), Gloucester].

COMMENTARY

There is much room for interpretation of the Duchess of Gloucester's character, but whether you decide that she is inherently a tough cookie or a sweetie pie driven to harsh action by extreme circumstances, there is no mistaking that she is single-minded in her objective in this monologue: she wants her husband's murderer(s) to suffer. Being a woman in medieval England, she must solicit the aid of others (i.e., men) to accomplish this end, and who better to enlist than one who also loved the victim—his older brother, John of Gaunt. But the Duchess knows this is a tough sell, and she must pull out all the persuasive stops.

One notable technique the Duchess employs is repetition. For instance, she repeats the word "seven" in four consecutive lines. Seven is a number often imbued with religious or mystical import—perhaps the Duchess is trying to be hypnotic, or perhaps she seeks to impress upon Gaunt the extent to which the murder is a violation of natural order: the violent excision of one sacred seventh before its proper time. She repeats many other words as well (and enhances them with consonance and assonance, to boot!): ***Some of those seven** / **Some of those** branches*; ***my** dear lord*, ***my** life*, ***my** Gloucester*; ***One** vial* / ***One** flourishing branch*; ***Is** cracked* / ***Is** hacked down*; ***that** bed* / ***that** womb* / ***that** mettle* / ***that** self mold*. In these instances, the Duchess is trying to draw greater attention to the words that *follow* the repeated words. You can have fun with this built-in build.

The Duchess further evokes an ominous mood by personifying the powerful forces of Destiny (*by the Destinies cut*), Envy (*By envy's hand*), and Murder (*Murder's bloody axe*; *Teaching stern Murder how to butcher thee*).

She employs the traditional persuasive technique of antithesis to hammer home her points, contrasting what should have happened with what actually happened; what was with what is; what is with what will be if no action is taken, and what is with what should be: *love* (passionate, hot) versus *no living fire*; *Some of those seven are dried by nature's course* versus *Some of those branches by the Destinies cut*; *full* versus *cracked*; *though thou livest* versus *yet art thou slain*; *patience in mean men* versus *cowardice in noble breasts*.

The Duchess uses consonance and assonance to set a tone that will aid her in convincing Gaunt: meLodic, Lulling Ls and Vs (*Hath **lo**ve* / *no **li**ving*); Sly Ss (*Edward's seven sons* / *as seven vials* / *sacred* / *seven* / *branches* / *springing* / *Some of those seven* / *nature's course* / *Some of those branches* / *Destinies*); deterMined Ms (***mettle*** / ***mold*** / ***Made** him a **man***); and, at the end, a string of crisp, no-nonsense two-and-threesies to finish off the piece (***in mean men** we entitle **patience*** / ***Is pale cold cowardice in noble breasts*** / *What shall I say? To **safeguard thine own life*** / ***The** best way is to **venge** my Gloucester's **death***). Like a grand finale of fireworks, the Duchess is ending on a strong note.

You'll notice that there are many inverted feet at the beginnings of lines—the Duchess is talking about the murder of her husband, after all, and cannot remain dispassionate. By punching the beginnings of these lines, she demonstrates how important it is to her to avenge her husband's death.

The lines are otherwise quite smooth, lending them an almost practiced feeling—perhaps she has given great thought to the arguments she is making with Gaunt.

The Duchess begins a whole new sentence in the middle of a line only twice, doing so each time to nail down an important—and very harsh—point: the new sentence in the middle of line 25 is where she actually tells Gaunt point-blank that his failure to avenge his brother's murder would be tantamount to complicity in the murder. By the way, notice that the meter of this line contains inverted feet both at the beginning of the line and right after the caesura, lending extra emphasis to stressed words, to the whole line, and to the harshness of the point she is making.

The other sentence the Duchess begins in the middle of a line, found on line 35, is where she makes the monologue's second argument: your life is in peril as my husband's was—to protect it, you must avenge my husband's murder.

Don't forget to elide: *seven* (sevn) in lines 11 and 12, (SEVN) in lines 13 and 14; *Destinies* (DEST-neez) in line 15; *flourishing* (FLOR-shing) in line 18; *livest* (LIVST) and *breathest* (BREETHST) in line 24; *seest* (SEEST) in line 27; *suffering* (SUFF-ring) in line 30; *showest* (SHOWST) in line 31;

. . . and to expand: *vials* (VIE-alz) in lines 12 and 17.

Dowager Duchess Debunked

We're very glad that Shakespeare drafted this gem of an older character (as she is generally portrayed), but the actual historical Duchess might not share our enthusiasm for this depiction. In fact, Eleanor de Bohun, Duchess of Gloucester, lived only to the age of thirty-two. No stranger to tragedy, she witnessed the deaths of three of her four daughters (one as an infant, one in childbirth at the age of twelve, and one at the age of seventeen). Her only son, Humphrey, Earl of Buckingham, was taken to Ireland by King Richard in 1399 and imprisoned in the Castle of Trim. When Henry IV took the throne, Humphrey (then about eighteen years old) returned to England only to die of the plague the next month. His mother (who had been living as a nun since her husband's murder two years earlier) died of a broken heart a month later.

RICHARD II

ACT II, SCENE I

JOHN OF GAUNT

GENDER: M
PROSE/VERSE: blank verse
AGE RANGE: mature adult to older adult
FREQUENCY OF USE (1–5): 2

John of Gaunt, uncle to King Richard II and a great warrior in days gone by, is on his deathbed. Gaunt is very worried about the state of the realm under Richard's rule. Richard has squandered the nation's resources and illegally leased out its lands. The dying man has asked for Richard to come to him, and while he awaits the young King's arrival, he tells his brother Edmund, the Duke of York, that he believes that this time the King will heed his advice, since it is given on his deathbed. When York tells him not to waste his dying breath, Gaunt replies:

Methinks I am a prophet new inspired,
And thus expiring do foretell of him:
His rash fierce blaze of riot cannot last,
For violent fires soon burn out themselves;
35 Small showers last long, but sudden storms are short;
He tires betimes that spurs too fast betimes;
With eager feeding, food doth choke the feeder;
Light vanity, insatiate cormorant,
Consuming means, soon preys upon itself.
40 This royal throne of kings, this sceptered isle,
This earth of majesty, this seat of Mars,
This other Eden, demi-paradise,
This fortress built by Nature for herself
Against infection and the hand of war,
45 This happy breed of men, this little world,
This precious stone set in the silver sea,
Which serves it in the office of a wall,
Or as a moat defensive to a house,
Against the envy of less happier lands;
50 This blessed plot, this earth, this realm, this England,
This nurse, this teeming womb of royal kings,
Feared by their breed and famous by their birth,

31 *Methinks* It seems to me; I think; *new* newly, freshly; *inspired* (1) breathed into, infused; and (2) filled with ideas from a higher source (Elizabethans thought of inspiration as the breath of God's spirit, breathed into mankind) [*Methinks . . . inspired* It seems to me that I am newly infused with inspiration from God, as a prophet]; 32 *expiring* (1) literally, breathing out one's last breath; thus (2) dying; *him* he refers to King Richard; 33 *riot* reveling, wild feasting; dissipation, wasteful extravangance; 34 *burn out themselves* burn themselves out; 36 *betimes* soon; *that* who; *spurs* spurs on his horse to ride quickly; *betimes* early in the day [*He tires . . . betimes* he who spurs his horse to ride quickly early in the day will tire himself out quickly]; 37 *eager* ardently desirous; quick; *feeding* eating [*eager feeding* stuffing one's face]; *feeder* eater; 38 *Light* frivolous; careless; *vanity* idle and frivolous behavior; *insatiate* insatiable; unsatisfiably greedy; *cormorant* a seabird (proverbially thought to be greedy, often used as a symbol of gluttony); 39 *Consuming means* Having consumed all its resources or cash; 40 *sceptered* bearing a scepter (i.e., royal); 41 *seat* (1) residence, abode; (2) throne; *Mars* the Roman god of war (i.e., military power) [*seat of Mars* i.e., base of military power]; 42 *other Eden* i.e., second paradise; *demi-paradise* partial paradise; 43 *Nature* the personification of the world around us and the forces that control it; 44 *infection* contagious disease (here it is probably a metaphor for either [1] foreign invasion or [2] the possibility of "catching" something warlike [at the time this play was written, France had been fighting off a terrible case of civil war for thirty years]); *hand of war* war's grip; 45 *happy* fortunate; 47 *in the office of* functioning as; *wall* fortification; 48 *moat defensive to* moat which defends; 49 *envy* malice; *less happier* (1) less happy; (2) less fortunate; 50 *plot* fertile spot of ground for cultivation; 51 *nurse* woman who breastfeeds and cares for an infant and/or raises a child (i.e., the land is "nurse" to the "happy breed" that inhabits it); *teeming* fertile, fruitful; 52 *Feared by* feared because of; *breed* (1) race; (2) lineage; *famous by* famous

Renownèd for their deeds as far from home
For Christian service and true chivalry
55 As is the sepulchre in stubborn Jewry
Of the world's ransom, blessed Mary's son;
This land of such dear souls, this dear, dear land,
Dear for her reputation through the world,
Is now leased out—I die pronouncing it—
60 Like to a tenement or pelting farm.
England, bound in with the triumphant sea,
Whose rocky shore beats back the envious seige
Of watery Neptune, is now bound in with shame,
With inky blots and rotten parchment bonds.
65 That England that was wont to conquer others
Hath made a shameful conquest of itself.
Ah, would the scandal vanish with my life,
How happy then were my ensuing death!

2 minutes, 15 seconds

for; *birth* descent, parentage; 54 *Christian service* specifically, what Gaunt—and medieval Christians, generally—considered the service of bringing Christianity to the heathens through the crusades; *chivalry* (1) bravery and military prowess; (2) knighthood; (3) adherence to the chivalric code of honesty, bravery, courtesy, protection of the weak, etc.; 55 *sepulchre* grave, tomb; *stubborn Jewry* the land of the Jews, then called Judea ("stubborn" because its people refused to accept Christianity and resisted the crusaders); 56 *the world's ransom* Jesus (Timothy 2:5–6, "Christ Jesus; who gave himself [as] a ransom for all") [*Renownèd . . . Mary's son* known for their deeds of Christian service and true chivalry as far from home as Judea, where Mary's son Jesus is entombed]; 60 *Like to* like; *tenement* property leased to a tenant; *pelting* paltry, piddling little; 61 *bound in with* bound by, bordered by; 63 *Neptune* the Roman god of the sea (i.e., the sea); *bound in* legally bonded; under legal obligation; 64 *inky blots and rotten parchment bonds* He refers to the "blank charters" with which King Richard raised money to fund his military excursions in Ireland. The charters were corrupt in two ways: (1) They illegally leased out government lands; and (2) Those leasing the land were bullied into signing them with the amounts to be paid left blank. The King's officers later filled in whatever excessive amount they pleased; 65 *was wont to conquer* was accustomed to conquering; 67 *would the scandal* if only the scandal would; 68 *were my ensuing death* would my ensuing death be [*How happy then . . . death* (1) What a fortunate event my death would be (for England); and (2) How glad I would be to die].

COMMENTARY

Richard II was very popular with Elizabethan audiences, and this speech in particular caught their fancy. It was immediately famous and quoted (it was included in an anthology of poetry as early as 1600) and remains so to this day. That said, this speech is more than just inspiring nationalistic propa— um, poetry. This is a very real, very charged situation in which the stakes are high. It's more important than ever to get past the fame of the words and examine the reality of the moment.

Here's the reality: John of Gaunt is on the brink of death, but rather than cowering in the face of it, he concentrates on using his last moments to their best advantage. He is desperately worried about the fate of his beloved England under a monarch he considers to be irresponsible, corrupt, and incompetent to rule. Fighting off his illness, he puts his last surge of energy into this eloquent speech, which is full of poetic devices.

The structure of Gaunt's argument rests on two series of images, each image conveying his message with increasing force. The first series expresses the idea that violent, sudden actions wear themselves out quickly. His images describe King Richard's flaws and his recent actions, starting with violent fires that burn out quickly; moving on to sudden but short storms; then to the horseman who rides hard only to tire quickly; building to the glutton who eats so fast that he chokes himself; which leads to the final conclusion that vanity (represented by the image of the cormorant, which is so greedy that it soon uses up its resources) ultimately destroys itself. The second series of images describes the majesty of Gaunt's beloved England in increasingly glowing metaphors, concluding with the greatness of its kings, who have enlightened the world through their crusades. This structure makes the contrast with Richard's corruption of his country all the more poignant. These two series of images provide for the actor an internal map of the builds in the piece. All you have to do is follow the map.

Within this structure of builds (called "auxesis"—don't worry, you won't be quizzed on this) Gaunt introduces antithesis: *new inspired* versus *thus expiring*; *Feared by their breed* versus *famous by their birth*; *bound in with the triumphant sea* versus *bound in with shame*; *was wont to conquer others* versus *Hath made a shameful conquest of itself*; *my life* versus *my ensuing death*. The antithesis dramatically illustrates the import of the topic, and in two instances emphasizes the contrast between England's glorious history and England's current wretched state under Richard's reign.

Notice the combined use of alliteration, assonance, and consonance in certain lines to enhance the poetic imagery: the Ss, Ls, and OR sounds in *Small showers last long, but sudden storms are short*; the Fs and EE sounds in *With eager feeding, food doth choke the feeder*; the Ss in *This precious stone set in the silver sea*. The use of parallel structure also enhances the imagery, and lends a sense of ceremonious regality to the descriptions, as in *This earth of majesty, this seat of Mars*. The parallel structure is combined with the alliteration of Fs and Bs in *Feared by their breed and famous by their birth*.

Using the imagery allows you to draw strong mental images for the audience: King Richard as a greedy *cormorant*; England as a *precious stone*; England's God-given royal line of *kings*, who bring the light of their savior to heathens across the world; the *sea*, repeatedly shown as England's powerful protector; finally, the *inky blots and rotten parchment bonds*, which, in Gaunt's depiction, are as physically tainted as they are legally corrupt.

It's incredible and quite telling that despite his condition Gaunt puns throughout the piece. He starts right off in the first two lines: with the intake of his last breath, he is *inspired*; and *expiring* his breath to speak of that inspiration, he dies. He then puns on the word *betimes*, and on the words *bound in*. These puns point to Gaunt's presence of mind.

SIGNIFICANT SCANS

During the ode to England at the center of this piece, you will find no double endings in the build until you hit one on the word "England," which makes it stand out against the background of even flowing rhythm.

Don't forget to elide: *violent* (VI-lent) in line 34; *showers* (SHOWRS) in line 35; *tires* (TYRZ) in line 36; *happier* (HAP-yer) in line 49; and *envious* (EN-vyuss) in line 62.

THEY DIDN'T CALL HIM "WARLIKE GAUNT" FOR NOTHING

They called him "Gaunt" for Ghent, the city in Belgium where he was born; they called him "warlike" for the many years he spent fighting in the Hundred Years' War in France. He was certainly warlike, but the eloquent, poetic side of him that Shakespeare brings out may have had a seed of truth as well: Gaunt was the patron of the poet Geoffrey Chaucer (to whom even Shakespeare pays homage).

RICHARD II

ACT III, SCENE ii

KING RICHARD

GENDER: M
PROSE/VERSE: blank verse
AGE RANGE: adult to mature adult
FREQUENCY OF USE (1–5): 4

King Richard and his cousin Edward York, Duke of Aumerle, have returned from squelching an uprising in Ireland to find that their cousin Henry Bolingbroke, whom Richard had banished, has invaded England. Bolingbroke claims that all he wants is a repeal of his banishment and the return of his late father's confiscated property. But he and his forces have already taken parts of England, and it seems that he is actually after the throne. Richard has just received the news that his people have welcomed Bolingbroke, rushing to fight on his side, and that three of Richard's noble supporters have been executed. When Aumerle asks the whereabouts of his father's troops, Richard cuts him off, saying it doesn't matter where they are.

Of comfort no man speak.
145 Let's talk of graves, of worms, of epitaphs,
Make dust our paper, and with rainy eyes
Write sorrow on the bosom of the earth.
Let's choose executors and talk of wills.
And yet not so, for what can we bequeath
150 Save our deposèd bodies to the ground?
Our land, our lives, and all are Bolingbroke's,
And nothing can we call our own but death
And that small model of the barren earth
Which serves as paste and cover to our bones.
155 For God's sake let us sit upon the ground
And tell sad stories of the death of kings—
How some have been deposed, some slain in war,
Some haunted by the ghosts they have deposed,
Some poisoned by their wives, some sleeping killed;
160 All murdered. For within the hollow crown
That rounds the mortal temples of a king
Keeps Death his court, and there the antic sits,
Scoffing his state and grinning at his pomp,
Allowing him a breath, a little scene,
165 To monarchize, be feared, and kill with looks,
Infusing him with self and vain conceit,

144 *comfort* Aumerle has just mentioned the "comfort" of his father's troops, which at this point are expected to come to their aid [*Of comfort . . . speak* Nobody speak of comfort]; 146 *rainy* tearful [*Make dust our paper . . . bosom of the earth* make the dust of the earth our paper, on which we write our sorrows with the ink of our tears]; 148 *executors* those who are assigned to "execute" or carry out the terms of wills; 150 *Save* except for, other than; *deposèd* (1) dethroned; (2) deprived of life [*our deposèd bodies* my deposed body (Richard uses the royal "we")]; 151 *all are* everything is; *Bolingbroke* (BULL´-ing-BROOK or BOWL´-ing-BROOK) Richard's cousin Henry, Duke of Hereford (named for his birthplace, Bolingbrooke Castle in Lincolnshire); 153 *model of the barren earth* (1) the mound of earth covering the grave ("model": a close outline or covering); (2) the grave, which is the whole world of the dead; (3) the body (Elizabethans saw the body as a microcosm, or small model of the macrocosm, the world); 154 *paste and cover* pastry; pie crust (i.e., covering: this works well with the first definition of model of the barren earth); 157 *deposed* here, dethroned; 158 *ghosts* i.e., the ghosts of kings; *deposed* here, both: (1) dethroned; and (2) deprived of life; 160 *hollow* both: (1) empty, having an open space within; (2) false, superficial; 161 *rounds* surrounds, encircles; *mortal* human (and therefore subject to death); 162 *Keeps Death his court* Death (personified) keeps his court; *antic* jester (since a skull grins like a jester, and Death belittles men, as a jester does with his riddles, Richard personifies Death as a jester); 163 *Scoffing* mocking, ridiculing; *his* i.e., the King's; *state* regal carriage and demeanor; *pomp* (1) magnificence, splendor; (2) ceremonies and processions; 164 *a breath* i.e., a very short time; 165 *monarchize* play at being a king; *kill with looks* kill with just a facial expression or glance; 166 *self and vain conceit* a vain self-conceit;

As if this flesh, which walls about our life,
Were brass impregnable; and humored thus,
Comes at the last, and with a little pin
170 Bores through his castle wall, and farewell king!
Cover your heads, and mock not flesh and blood
With solemn reverence. Throw away respect,
Tradition, form, and ceremonious duty,
For you have but mistook me all this while:
175 I live with bread like you, feel want,
Taste grief, need friends. Subjected thus,
How can you say to me, I am a king?

2 minutes

167 *walls about our life* encloses and defends my life; 168 *brass* A reference to Job 6:12, "Is my strength the strength of stones? Or is my flesh of brass?"; *humored thus* either (1) in this humor, or frame of mind (referring to the King); or (2) having been amused in this manner (referring to Death); 169 *Comes at the last* (Death) comes in the end; *pin* i.e., something trifling as a pin; 170 *his castle wall* (1) the defensive wall surrounding his castle; (2) referring to the walls about our life, i.e., his flesh; 171 *Cover your heads* i.e., put on your hats (which subjects must remove in the presence of the monarch as a sign of respect); 174 *but* merely, simply; 175 *live with* live on; live by eating; *feel want* experience needs; lack a home and means to survive; 176 *Taste* experience, feel; *Subjected thus* (1) Having to endure such human experiences as these; (2) Revealed in this manner to be a subject; 177 *I am* that I am.

COMMENTARY

Richard was born in the wrong place at the wrong time: he may not have been a very good king, but he could have made a very good politician or diplomat, for no one can deny that he's an excellent speaker. It is impossible not to feel for him when he makes this sad, insightful, and gently bitter speech.

The beauty and effectiveness of Richard's speech are partly due to the elegant, moving metaphors he uses (*Make dust our paper, and with rainy eyes / Write sorrow on the bosom of the earth*; *what can we bequeath / Save our deposèd bodies to the ground?*; *within the hollow crown / That rounds the mortal temples of a King / Keeps Death his court*; *with a little pin / Bores through his castle wall, and farewell king!*). The metaphors are complemented by sparing, strategic use of sounds (*land / lives / all / Bolingbroke's*; *with / little / pin*) and repetition of key words (*deposed*—three times; and *king*—four times). Shakespeare uses few devices, relying instead on simplicity of structure and beautiful words to bring out the powerful ideas and emotions in this monologue.

Some directors approach the phrase *farewell king!* as a sort of embedded stage direction, seeing it as an indication that Richard actually removes his crown here. Whether you opt for that physicality or not, the idea itself is clarifying: at this exact moment, Richard feels he is no longer king, which lends added significance to the following line. *Cover your heads* suddenly becomes much more active: Richard is not merely making a sarcastic comment, but actually admonishing those present not to treat a mere subject such as himself like a king. Richard's notion that he is no longer king is also supported by the switch in his form of self-address. Throughout the piece, he has used the royal "we" quite liberally—perhaps to excess, as if trying to make a point. After *farewell king!*, however, he no longer uses the form. Now he says *you have but mistook* me; I *live with bread*; and *How can you say to* me I *am a king?*

SIGNIFICANT SCANS

The scansion of this monologue is telling. There is surprisingly little variation in the meter: there are no extra feet before caesuras, no inverted feet after them, and only one double ending in the entire piece. There are only four inverted feet in the piece, all at the beginnings of lines. You can bet those are there for a reason! The first inverted foot doesn't turn up until halfway through the piece, when Richard introduces Death. After nineteen perfectly iambic lines, Death's *Scoffing* is particularly jarring. The other three times, inverted feet appear in three successive lines. In the second and third instances, Richard is again describing Death's actions (*Comes at the last*; *Bores through his castle wall*). The last instance comes after a big transition (*farewell king!*), when Richard orders the men, *Cover your heads*. This last inverted foot begins the final section, in which Richard comes to his pathetic conclusion (*Subjected thus / How can you say to me, I am a king?*).

The only other variation in the meter occurs in the penultimate two lines, each of which has only four feet, in contrast to the regularity that comes before. This rhythmic contrast underscores the poignant finish, and also gives the actor several options for interpretation. Scanning the two lines, you will see that in each case you can take the extra foot at the beginning or end of the line, or at the caesura. Each choice gives the actor a slightly different focus and emphasis to work with. All of the possible choices are exciting to explore—perhaps he's grasping for the right words, or thinking of what he wants to say next, or overcome by grief . . . The important thing is to make a clear choice and work with it, so that you get the most out of this jewel of a piece.

And don't forget to elide: *ceremonious* (SEH-reh-MO´-nyuss) in line 173.

REVISIONIST RICHARD

Shakespeare shortchanged the real King Richard in the interest of his play (see "The History of a History," page 905), focusing on the last, sad year of an eventful twenty-two-year reign. Richard became king at the age of ten, and was already displaying great agility as a diplomat at the age of fourteen, when he successfully handled a peasant rebellion. His reign was marked by efforts at peacemaking, most importantly in the Hundred Years' War with France. One of the terms of that peace was Richard's marriage to Princess Isabella, then only eight years old. At the time of Richard's downfall, his queen was not a grown woman, as Shakespeare depicts her, but a girl of eleven.

THE STORY OF *SAD STORIES*

Elizabeth audiences would have recognized Richard's reference to *sad stories of the death of kings*—they were familiar with works such as John Lydgate's *Fall of Princes* (a translation in Chaucerian verse of Boccaccio's *On the Fates of Famous Men*, and with the *Mirror for Magistrates*, a collection of verse laments by various authors that were purportedly spoken by participants in the Wars of the Roses and preached the Tudor doctrine of obedience. (For an overview of the Wars of the Roses, see "The Red Rose and the White . . . the Fatal Colors of Our Striving Houses," page 238.)

RICHARD II

ACT III, SCENE iii

KING RICHARD

GENDER: M
PROSE/VERSE: blank verse
AGE RANGE: adult to mature adult
FREQUENCY OF USE (1–5): 3

King Richard has just learned that his cousin Henry Bolingbroke, whom Richard had banished and whose inheritance he had confiscated, has returned to England and is raising troops against him. Richard has further learned that Bolingbroke has executed some of his close friends and supporters, and that other noblemen have defected to Bolingbroke's side. Filled with despair, Richard is holed up in Flint Castle. Bolingbroke, now approaching the castle, has sent Henry Percy, Earl of Northumberland, ahead as a messenger to King Richard, to demand that his inheritance be restored. Northumberland did not bow to the King, which Richard took as a sign that Bolingbroke has returned to England to claim not only his inheritance but also the throne itself. The King has just sent Northumberland back to Bolingbroke to tell him that his inheritance shall be restored, and while he awaits Bolingbroke's reply, Richard says to his cousin and supporter Edward York, Duke of Aumerle:

What must the King do now? Must he submit?
The King shall do it. Must he be deposed?
145 The King shall be contented. Must he lose
The name of King? I' God's name, let it go.
I'll give my jewels for a set of beads,
My gorgeous palace for a hermitage,
My gay apparel for an almsman's gown,
150 My figured goblets for a dish of wood,
My scepter for a palmer's walking-staff,
My subjects for a pair of carvèd saints,
And my large kingdom for a little grave,
A little, little grave, an obscure grave;
155 Or I'll be buried in the King's highway,
Some way of common trade, where subjects' feet
May hourly trample on their sovereign's head;
For on my heart they tread now whilst I live,
And, buried once, why not upon my head?
160 Aumerle, thou weep'st, my tender-hearted cousin.
We'll make foul weather with despisèd tears—
Our sighs and they shall lodge the summer corn,
And make a dearth in this revolting land.
Or shall we play the wantons with our woes
165 And make some pretty match with shedding tears?
As thus, to drop them still upon one place
Till they have fretted us a pair of graves
Within the earth; and, therein laid—"there lies

143 *the King* King Richard is referring to himself; 146 *I'* In; *my jewels* i.e., the crown jewels; 147 *a set of beads* a set of wooden rosary beads; 148 *hermitage* the home of a hermit (one who has gone to a solitary place for a life of religious seclusion); 149 *gay* fine, showy; *almsman* beggar; *gown* long, loose article of clothing (the term was used for clothing worn by both men and women); 150 *figured goblets* fancy drinking glasses, decorated with figures of people; 151 *palmer* pilgrim (who would carry a palm branch to show that he had been to Jerusalem); 152 *carvèd saints* statues of saints carved from wood; 155 *the King's highway* a major public thoroughfare (criminals and suicides were sometimes buried in the highway); 156 *way* road; *trade* traffic [*of common trade* trafficked by ordinary people engaging in ordinary day-to-day activities (as opposed to a cemetery, which is consecrated ground)]; 157 *May hourly trample* may trample hourly; *sovereign* king; 159 *buried once* once I am buried; 161 *despisèd* unnoticed; 162 *they* i.e., our tears; *lodge* flatten, beat down; 163 *dearth* famine and its resulting rise in food prices; *revolting* rebelling; 164 *play the wantons* trifle, dally [*shall we . . . woes* shall we be playful about our problems]; 165 *pretty* clever [*make some pretty match . . . tears* devise some clever game for our crying]; 166 *As thus* For example; *still* continuously, always; 167 *fretted us* eroded for us; 168 *therein*

Two kinsmen digged their graves with weeping eyes."
170 Would not this ill do well? Well, well, I see
I talk but idly, and you laugh at me.
[*Northumberland approaches*]
Most mighty prince, my Lord Northumberland,
What says King Bolingbroke? Will his Majesty
Give Richard leave to live till Richard die?
175 You make a leg, and Bolingbroke says "ay."

2 minutes

laid i.e., once we are laid to rest there (in the graves our tears create); 169 *digged* who dug; 170 *ill* misfortune, unfortunate situation; *do well* be convenient, succeed [*Would not this ill do well* Wouldn't this unfortunate situation conveniently turn out well]; 171 *I talk but idly* I'm only talking foolishly, I'm being cavalier; 173 *King Bolingbroke* sarcastic reference to his cousin Henry Bolingbroke, by which Richard expresses that despite what his cousin says to the contrary, Richard is sure Bolingbroke seeks to usurp his throne; *his Majesty* again, sarcastic reference to Bolingbroke, as though Bolingbroke has assumed the throne; 174 *Richard* again, Richard refers to himself in the third person; *leave* permission; 175 *make a leg* bow (by bending the leg) [*You make a leg . . . "ay"* You're bowing, indicating that Bolingbroke's answer is "yes" (Richard says this sarcastically)].

COMMENTARY

Some people lose control of what they say when upset. Others grow very, very controlled. Some of these latter types have been known to become very, very sarcastic. If you are such a one, or know such a one, this monologue will ring quite true to you. If you've ever wanted to play this sort of character, your search is over.

King Richard is so beside himself that he starts the monologue by referring to himself in the third person. OK, we're joking, but you should decide for yourself why he does so. Perhaps he needs to distance himself to gain perspective on his situation. Or perhaps he keeps calling himself *the King* to emphasize how ridiculous it is that a king should find himself thus compromised.

King Richard's questions (*Must he submit?*, *Must he be deposed?*, and *Must he lose the name of King?*) seem to be redundant, but they're not—Richard gets more specific about what lies ahead of him with each new question. Perhaps, as he thinks aloud, he realizes in increments what lies ahead: submitting to Bolingbroke means being deposed, which, in turn, means losing the name of King, which, in turn, leads Richard to a list comparing all he'll be losing with all he'll be assuming in its place.

Richard's categorical itemization of what he possessed while king versus what he'll have after being deposed range from the incidental (palace, designer duds, etc.) to the items at the heart of the kingdom (scepter, subjects, England itself). Notice the detail with which he describes the items—which perhaps indicates his love for what he has possessed and his loathing for the items that will take their place. Richard could simply have stated that his life would change, but instead he chooses to juxtapose images of the heights of luxury he has enjoyed against those with the most austere ascetic depths of subsistence he imagines will soon be his. He seems in fact to be perversely enjoying the comparison. Painting each item distinctly for your audience will help you decide why this list leads Richard to his ultimate trade-in: his large kingdom for *a little grave*—perhaps suggesting that his losses will be so devastating that death will be the only viable alternative. Or perhaps it dawns on him that even the ascetic life he's describing is a pipe dream, since Bolingbroke will probably have him assassinated to eliminate the threat of a comeback.

Notice how Richard builds on his description of the grave that awaits him. The grave's ignominy increases, from *little grave* to *little, little grave* to *obscure grave* to one located underneath the highway he himself commissioned, beneath the feet of even his lowest subjects.

Richard seems to take some pleasure in what he's putting himself and Aumerle through (he doesn't have to go through such an extensive litany—he chooses to). You must decide the extent to which he is picking at his own scab or simply tormenting Aumerle. Richard's reaction to his cousin's tears could indicate that he enjoys his cousin's distress and decides to needle him, or, conversely, could be played to mean that he realizes that he has upset his cousin and is now trying to cajole a smile from him.

Richard's ironic sense of humor is further evidenced by his wry wordplay: *trade* = traffic (with a play on the similar-sounding *tread*, as in "don't tread on me"); *revolting* = rebelling (with a play on its other meaning, "disgusting"); *fretted* = eroded (with play on its other meaning, "to be upset").

Repetition of words helps give the monologue a sarcastic, self-righteous, and ranting quality. The word *must*, for example, hammers home the insult of being deposed—until now, no one ever told Richard what he "must" do! His repetition of the phrase *The King shall* illustrates his bitterness at having to acquiesce to a mere subject, and also sarcastically asserts his kingly magnanimity. Likewise, the repetition of *My* —— *for* —— in lines 147 through 153 builds in bitterness. Repeating *little* enhances the word's onomatopoeic quality, further underscoring Richard's outrage at his soon-to-be utter disgrace. He repeats *well*—changing its meaning—to segue back to the here-and-now from the little death fantasy with which he was just amusing himself.

The sounds he uses reinforce his caustic tone. Here are only some of the many examples that lace this piece: Richard's repetition of *Must* makes him sound like he is spitting out his first lines. Then you'll find: Gagging Gs (*I' God's name, let it go / I'll give my jewels for a set of beads / My gorgeous palace for a hermitage / My gay apparel for an almsman's gown / My figured goblets*); Dull Ds (*dish of wood*); Peeved, Petulant Ps (*My scepter for a palmer's / pair*); Lamenting Ls, which are later interwoven with Wallowing Ws (*And my large kingdom for a little grave / A little, little grave, an obscure grave / Or I'll be buried . . .* ; *hourly trample*; *whilst I live*; *Aumerle / We'll make foul weather*; *to drop them still / Till they*; *therein laid—there lies*; *Or shall we play the wanton with our woes*; *Would not this ill do well? Well, well*); and other sounds Richard interweaves to enhance the sardonic tone he's adopted (*this ill do well*; *leave to live till*). Nowhere does he sound more mordant than in his well-placed use of rhyme: the poem he constructs for their epitaph (*and, therein laid—"there lies / Two kinsmen digged their graves with weeping eyes"*) is purely mocking. So is his couplet at the end of the piece (*Give Richard leave to live till Richard die? / You make a leg, and Bolingbroke says "ay"*).

At the end of the monologue, he sarcastically addresses Northumberland as *Most mighty prince* (which Northumberland is *not*—he's merely an earl). Convinced that Bolingbroke has effectively deposed him despite Bolingbroke's protestations to the contrary, Richard derisively suggests that by backing a usurper, Northumberland has also just appropriated an undeserved rise in rank.

Remember that although Richard switches from addressing his cousin Aumerle to addressing Northumberland (in lines 172–75), Aumerle is still present, and there is a degree to which anything Richard says to Northumberland is also for Aumerle's benefit. The extent to which Richard intends to affect Aumerle with his words to Northumberland is up to you.

SIGNIFICANT SCANS

There are very few double endings or variations in meter. In the beginning, Richard often starts new sentences in the middles of lines—these sound like outbursts, as though he can't fully rein in his emotions. But then the lines grow eerily smooth (for the most part), in marked contrast to the upsetting nature of their content, indicating that regardless of how distressed the King is, he is able to communicate his frustration, anger, and bitterness in a controlled manner.

Also, notice the pronunciation of *obscure* (OB-scyoor) in line 154. Try it. See how that affects Richard's tone.

Don't forget to elide: *hourly* (OWR-lee) in line 157; and *idly* (IDE-lee) in line 171;

. . . to contract: *Will his* (will'z) in line 173;

. . . and to expand: *jewels* (JEW-ellz) in line 147.

P.S.

For more on the historical Richard II, see "Revisionist Richard," page 59.

RICHARD II

ACT IV, SCENE i

BISHOP OF CARLISLE

GENDER: M
AGE RANGE: mature adult to older adult
PROSE/VERSE: blank verse
FREQUENCY OF USE (1–5): 2

The Bishop of Carlisle is amazed at recent events: Henry Bolingbroke, first cousin to King Richard of England, has returned from banishment with an army to demand his inheritance, which was confiscated by the King. Since his return, Bolingbroke has been increasingly supported by noblemen and commoners alike, who are disgruntled with King Richard's oppressive and irresponsible reign. The King has conceded to Bolingbroke's demands to restore his property and revoke his banishment, but it seems that Bolingbroke seeks more than that. He has now taken over Westminster Hall, where he holds court with the noblemen who have endorsed him. The Bishop of Carlisle is present, and is horrified to hear that those assembled intend to depose the King and replace him with Henry. Outraged, he urges them to reconsider.

115 Worst in this royal presence may I speak,
Yet best beseeming me to speak the truth.
Would God that any in this noble presence
Were enough noble to be upright judge
Of noble Richard—Then true noblesse would
120 Learn him forbearance from so foul a wrong.
What subject can give sentence on his king?
And who sits here that is not Richard's subject?
Thieves are not judged but they are by to hear,
Although apparent guilt be seen in them;
125 And shall the figure of God's majesty,
His captain, steward, deputy elect,
Anointed, crownèd, planted many years,
Be judged by subject and inferior breath,
And he himself not present? O, forfend it God
130 That in a Christian climate souls refined
Should show so heinous, black, obscene a deed!
I speak to subjects, and a subject speaks,
Stirred up by God thus boldly for his king.
My Lord of Hereford here, whom you call King,
135 Is a foul traitor to proud Hereford's king,
And if you crown him, let me prophesy:
The blood of English shall manure the ground
And future ages groan for this foul act,

115 *Worst* least worthy, lowest in rank; *presence* company [*Worst in this . . . speak* I may be the the lowest ranking person amongst the nobles here to speak]; 116 *best beseeming me* I am best suited, i.e., it would make most sense for me (to speak, since I am a bishop, a "man of God"); 117 *Would God* I wish to God; *in this noble presence* amongst the group of nobles present here; 118 *enough noble* noble enough; *upright judge* a righteous, just, and honest judge; 119 *noblesse* nobility; 120 *Learn* teach; *foul* wicked, reprehensible; 121 *give sentence* pass sentence upon, condemn to punishment; 123 *but* unless; *by* present; *to hear* i.e., to hear the sentence being passed down on them; 124 *apparent* obvious; *be seen* is evident [*Although . . . in them* even when they are obviously guilty]; 125 *figure* personification, image; *the figure of God's majesty* the personification of God's grandeur and royalty (i.e., the King—see "Riding Shotgun with God," page 235); 126 *His* i.e., God's; *steward* caretaker, administrator; *deputy elect* selected deputy; 127 *planted* installed (on the throne); *many years* many years ago; 128 *subject* belonging to subjects; *breath* words [*subject and inferior breath* words spoken by subjects, who are inferior]; 129 *And he himself not present* without Richard himself being present; *forfend it God* God forbid; 130 *climate* country; *souls refined* souls that are freed from guilt and redeemed by Jesus' death; 131 *show* do; 132 *a subject speaks* i.e., I who am speaking am myself a subject as well; 133 *Stirred up* impelled; 134 *My Lord of Hereford* i.e., Henry Bolingbroke, Duke of Hereford, King Richard's first cousin, who is taking the throne from Richard; 135 *proud* haughty [*to proud Hereford's king* i.e., to haughty Hereford's own king, King Richard]; 137 *manure* be spread on the ground as fertilizer is spread on a field; 138 *ages* generations; *groan* shall groan;

Peace shall go sleep with Turks and infidels,
140 And in this seat of peace tumultuous wars
Shall kin with kin and kind with kind confound.
Disorder, horror, fear, and mutiny
Shall here inhabit, and this land be called
The field of Golgotha and dead men's skulls.
145 O, if you raise this house against this house,
It will the woefullest division prove
That ever fell upon this cursèd earth!
Prevent it, resist it, let it not be so,
Lest child, child's children, cry against you "woe"!

2 minutes

139 *go sleep with Turks and infidels* the Bishop believes that Turks and other "infidels" (nonbelievers), as non-Christians, are excluded from Heaven and will go to Hell when they "go sleep" (i.e., die) [*Peace shall . . . infidels* peace will go to Hell in a handbasket (i.e., there will be no more peace)]; 140 *seat* residence, abode [*in this seat of peace* in this place where peace resides]; 141 *kind* class, race, ethnic group; *confound* destroy [*Shall kin with kin . . . confound* people will destroy their own relatives and clans]; 143 *Shall here inhabit* will live here; *be called* will be called; 144 *Golgotha* (1) another name for Calvary, where Jesus was crucified; (2) a place of suffering and sacrifice; *dead men's skulls* Golgotha was also known as "the place of dead men's skulls"; 145 *raise* stir up; *this house* i.e., the royal family [*if you raise . . . against this house* i.e., if you stir up one family member (Henry Bolingbroke) and his branch of this family against another member (Henry's first cousin King Richard) and his branch of this family]; 146 *It will the woefullest division prove* it will prove to be the most calamitous schism; 149 *child, child's children* i.e., your children and your children's children; *cry against you "woe"* i.e., denounce you for bringing calamity upon them.

COMMENTARY

Despite his status as a minor character in *Richard II* (Shakespeare didn't provide us with much "backstory" about him), we know this much about the Bishop: he is a man of integrity, religious conviction, and plain old guts. In a time and place rife with the cutting-off of heads, he is not afraid to face down a roomful of future cabinet members of the soon-to-be new King of England and tell them in no uncertain terms that they will all be going straight to Hell (and bringing the entire nation with them) if they depose Richard. In a display of true charity, he places his own safety aside and acts out of concern for everyone else: his king, the souls of the noblemen he's trying to prevent from sinning, the nation, and future generations of sufferers.

To understand what on earth the Bishop is all riled up about, it is essential that you understand the concept of "divine right" to which the medieval English ascribed: they believed (as did Shakespeare's contemporaries) that kings were appointed by God and served as God's deputies on earth (see "Riding Shotgun with God," page 235). They were thus answerable only to God, a concept that is the central premise for the Bishop's monologue.

It is precisely because this piece is delivered by a Bishop citing a theological doctrine that God and the New Testament are invoked so much more here than they are in other monologues by the Bard. In lines 143–44 (*and this land be called / The field of Golgotha and dead men's skulls*), the Bishop refers to Mark 15:22, wherein Golgotha is called "the place of dead men's skulls." In lines 145–47 (*if you raise this house against this house / It will the woefullest division prove / That ever fell upon this cursèd earth*), the Bishop alludes to Matthew 12:25 ("Every kingdom divided against itself shall be brought to naught, and every city or house divided against itself shall not stand").

By repeatedly invoking God and the Scriptures, the Bishop establishes his authority on matters of the soul, subtly creating an aura of mysticism, which lends greater weight to his prophesy of a bloody civil war in England. He happens to be entirely accurate. You get to decide whether his vision is, in fact, divinely inspired or just a product of good common sense and political acumen. FYI: the Bishop is prophesying the Wars of the Roses, depicted in *Henry VI, Parts One, Two,* and *Three* and *Richard III* (see "The Red Rose and the White . . . the Fatal Colors of Our Striving Houses," page 238).

Although clearly upset and very passionate about his topic, the Bishop presents a well-delivered argument to the nobles. Perhaps this is because he is accustomed to public speaking, or because the Bishop is levelheaded in a crisis, or because God speaks through him.

There is a logical progression to the Bishop's argument. First, he modestly sets forth his credentials to speak. He then sets forth three reasons for the noblemen (including Henry Bolingbroke) to reconsider. Each new reason is on behalf of a greater number of people than the one that precedes it: (1) Reconsider on principle, and out of fairness to King Richard: you're not qualified to judge King Richard (only God is qualified to do so); you're compounding sin upon sin by judging Richard in his absence (notice that he tucks into this argument the concept that trial in absentia is a violation of one's rights, a fundamental human right that is unfortunately not yet universally applied even today!); (2) Reconsider for your own sakes: you are committing a sin; and, if the idea of committing sin isn't enough to deter you, you are also committing the crime of treason (for which you could lose your heads); and (3) Reconsider for the sake of your England and all of its inhabitants (including your children and their children): if you persist in this folly, you will be bringing civil war and ruin to the nation.

The Bishop employs the rhetorical device of antithesis to show the nobles the huge discrepancy between the good they believe they are doing to themselves and the evil he believes they are doing themselves, their King, and their country, which, if they persist, will be transformed from a *seat of peace* to *The field of Golgotha and dead men's skulls*. Some examples: *Worst in this royal presence* versus *Yet best beseeming me to speak*; *subjects* versus the divinely appointed *King*; *a Christian climate* versus *so heinous, black, obscene a deed*; *My Lord of Hereford, whom you call King* versus *foul traitor to proud Hereford's king*. And by posing rhetorical questions rather than preaching or lecturing, the Bishop manages to point out the outrageousness of what the nobles propose to do without sounding overly sanctimonious.

As angry as the Bishop is, you'll notice that he is consistently self-effacing, cleverly including himself when reminding the nobles of their lower status (*Worst in this royal presence may I speak*; *I speak to subjects, and a subject speaks / Stirred up by God thus boldly for his king*). He is clearly accustomed to dealing politically with the higher-of-rank. Is the Bishop able to do this with the ease of practice, or is his anger interfering, so that he must force himself to be humble? Your choice.

The Bishop uses repetition of words and sounds to create a moving oration. The repeated words alone give an outline of the whole monologue: (*speak*; *noble*; *subject(s)*; *King*; *God*; *foul*; *Peace*; *kin with kin*; *kind with kind*; *raise this house against this house*; *it* (the deposition of Richard); *child*; *woe*). The repeated vowel and consonant sounds added to the repeated words lend a sweeping, moving feeling to the whole piece. Some of the many examples: ***Yet best beseeming me***; ***Would God***; ***any in this noble presence***; ***forbearance from so foul a wrong***; ***Anointed, crownèd, planted***; ***I speak to subjects and a subject speaks / Stirred***; ***seat of*** *peace*; *Shall* ***kin*** *with* ***kin*** *and* ***kind*** *with* ***kind*** *confound*; ***Prevent*** ***it***, ***resist it***, ***let it not*** / ***lest***, ***child***, ***child's children***, ***cry***). The rhyming couplet at the end of the speech signifies that the Bishop has concluded, ending the piece on a resonant, dread- and awe-inspiring O sound. This echoes his use of the word *O* in lines 129 and 145. For help with using the sound of *O* to its best advantage, check out "O, No! An *O*!" on page xxxiii.

SIGNIFICANT SCANS

The Bishop punches the beginnings of several lines by inverting the first foot, conveying his feelings of urgency, outrage and upset.

Line 129 is a rare six-footed line (hexameter), which draws attention to the impassioned point he makes:

x / x / x / x / x / x /
And he himself not present? O, forfend it God

Don't forget to elide: *inferior* (in-FEER-yur) in line 128; *Hereford* (HEHR-furd) in lines 134 and 135; *tumultuous* (tu-MUHL-chwuss) in line 140;

. . . and to expand: *crownèd* (CRAOW-nehd) in line 127; and *cursèd* (CUR-sehd) in line 147.

REVISIONIST HISTORY: MERKE-Y BACKGROUND

The historical Thomas Merke, Bishop of Carlisle, was indeed a loyal supporter of King Richard, but he never stood up to the roomful of deposing noblemen as Shakespeare depicted. Shakespeare's source, Holinshed's *Chronicles*, reported that the Bishop opposed bringing criminal charges against Richard at a later date, but even this account may be false, since Holinshed's source was unreliable. Although the Bishop did participate in the conspiracy against Bolingbroke, Shakespeare invented his pardon by Henry IV. In actuality, the Bishop was tried and convicted. His life was spared thanks to the intervention of the Pope.

HENRY IV, PART ONE

ACT 1, SCENE iii

HOTSPUR

GENDER: M
AGE RANGE: young adult to adult
PROSE/VERSE: blank verse
FREQUENCY OF USE (1–5): 4

Without the military support of Henry "Hotspur" Percy and his father, Henry Percy, Earl of Northumberland, King Henry could never have deposed Richard II, usurped the throne, and stayed in power all these years. But lately, Hotspur has been feeling snubbed by the King: Henry has not kept the promises he made to them, and has now refused to ransom Hotspur's brother-in-law, Edmund Mortimer (who was fighting against a Welsh rebellion led by Owen Glendower, and has recently been taken prisoner). Now, Hotspur has come to the King's aid once again, by putting down a Scottish rebellion. He has been sent for by the King, who has the gall to ask him why he has refused to turn over his Scottish prisoners. Hotspur explains:

My liege, I did deny no prisoners.
30 But I remember, when the fight was done,
When I was dry with rage and extreme toil,
Breathless and faint, leaning upon my sword,
Came there a certain lord, neat and trimly dressed,
Fresh as a bridegroom, and his chin, new-reaped,
35 Showed like a stubble-land at harvest-home.
He was perfumèd like a milliner,
And 'twixt his finger and his thumb he held
A pouncet-box, which ever and anon
He gave his nose, and took't away again—
40 Who, therewith angry, when it next came there
Took it in snuff—and still he smiled and talked,
And as the soldiers bore dead bodies by,
He called them untaught knaves, unmannerly,
To bring a slovenly unhandsome corse
45 Betwixt the wind and his nobility.
With many holiday and lady terms
He questioned me—amongst the rest demanded
My prisoners in your majesty's behalf.
I then, all smarting, with my wounds being cold,
50 To be so pestered with a popinjay,

29 *liege* sovereign; lord to whom alligeance is owed; 30 *fight* i.e., the battle in which Hotspur and his forces defeated the Scots for King Henry IV; 31 *dry* parched, thirsty; *rage* violence and furiousness of fighting in battle; 32 *leaning upon my sword* i.e., as if it were a cane or crutch; 33 *neat* foppish, dandified, all dolled up in the latest style; *trimly* finely, nicely; 34 *Fresh* lively, vigorous; *his chin, new-reaped* the beard on his chin, having just been closely trimmed (as was fashionable at the time the play was written); 35 *Showed like* looked like; *stubble-land at harvest-home* the land covered with stubbly stalks at the end of the harvest; 36 *milliner* man who sells fancy articles from Milan, such as gloves, ribbons, silks, and lace, which were usually scented with perfume; 37 *'twixt* between (short for *betwixt*); 38 *pouncet-box* small box with a perforated lid, filled with powdered perfume which was sniffed to counteract bad smells; *ever and anon* every now and then; 39 *gave his nose* held up to his nose; 40 *Who* refers to the aforementioned nose; *therewith angry* angry with it (the pouncet box) [*Who, therewith angry* which, angry with the pouncet box (for leaving it to smell the foul odors of the battlefield)]; *when it next came there* i.e., the next time the pouncet box came under his nose; 41 *Took it in snuff* proverbial phrase meaning "took offense"; here it has an additional meaning: the nose either (1) sniffed contemptuously at it; or (2) sniffed it up, as if it were snuff; *still* continually, the whole time; 43 *untaught* ignorant, ill-bred; *knaves* rascals, villains; lowly servants; 44 *To bring* for bringing; *unhandsome* indecent, improper; *corse* corpse; 45 *his nobility* his noble self; 46 *holiday and lady terms* elegant and choice expressions used by ladies (from the proverbial phrase "to speak holiday"); 47 *questioned me* spoke to me, chatted to me; *amongst the rest demanded* amid all the rest of his chatter, he demanded; 48 *in* on; 49 *all smarting* feeling sharp pains all over; *cold* (1) intensely painful; (2) still open to the air, not yet dressed; 50 *with* by; *popinjay* parrot;

Out of my grief and my impatience,
Answered neglectingly I know not what—
He should, or should not—for he made me mad
To see him shine so brisk, and smell so sweet,
55 And talk so like a waiting-gentlewoman
Of guns, of drums, and wounds—God save the mark!—
And telling me the sovereignest thing on earth
Was parmaceti for an inward bruise,
And that it was great pity, so it was,
60 This villainous salt-petre should be digged
Out of the bowels of the harmless earth,
Which many a good tall fellow had destroyed
So cowardly. And but for these vile guns
He would himself have been a soldier.
65 This bald, unjointed chat of his, my lord,
I answered indirectly, as I said,
And I beseech you, let not his report
Come current for an accusation
Betwixt my love and your high majesty.

2 minutes, 30 seconds

51 *grief* in addition to today's meaning, also (1) pain and (2) anger; 52 *neglectingly* (1) carelessly, neglectfully; or (2) slightingly, contemptuously; 54 *shine so brisk* look so smart and trim; 55 *waiting-gentlewoman* high-ranking servant who waits upon a lady in her chamber; 56 *God save the mark!* an expression of impatient scorn; 57 *sovereignest* most excellently medicinal; 58 *parmaceti* (PAR-muh-SEH´-tee) spermaceti, a white, waxlike substance taken from the head of a sperm whale, used to make healing ointments; *inward* internal; 60 *salt-petre* potassium nitrate, the main ingredient in gunpowder; 62 *tall* sturdy; valiant (often, as here, used ironically); *fellow* often, as here, used contemptuously; *had* has; 63 *cowardly* cowardously; *but for* except for; 65 *bald* trivial, inconsequential; *unjointed* incoherent; 66 *indirectly* absentmindedly; ambiguously; 67 *let not* do not let; 68 *Come current* be accepted as currency, i.e., be accepted as valid [*Come current for an accusation* be accepted as a valid accusation]; 69 *my love* the love and allegiance I bear you [*Come current . . . high majesty* be accepted as a valid accusation of wrongdoing, and thus come between my loyalty and your majestic self (by making you doubt my love and allegiance)].

COMMENTARY

Talk about a fish out of water—Hotspur meeting with King Henry at court is like a Jimmy Cagney character sitting in with the Joint Chiefs of Staff in the Oval Office. Hotspur knows he ought to keep his famous temper in check during this audience with the King. The trouble is, keeping things in check is just not his forte. This monologue plays on the tension between Hotspur's anger and his need to pacify the King.

That tension is strongly supported by different elements in the piece. Hotspur's fiery nature comes through in the cadence: the meter is fairly regular, but the piece has a lot of inverted feet at the heads of lines, and several interjections of phrases or switches from one sentence fragment to the next, sometimes even changing syntax. This has the effect of making the piece quite aggressive and yet continuously flowing, as if Hotspur can't wait to get his whole story out, or has one idea after another in quick succession, or perhaps becomes more and more agitated as he relates the story and remembers the irritating details. At the same time, the piece contains many words that must be elided, contracted, or expanded to fit the meter of blank verse (see below). This gives the impression that Hotspur is making an effort to force his impulsive words into a proper and ingratiating form.

Hotspur also tries to ingratiate himself in his form of address. It goes without saying that Hotspur uses only the formal *you* rather than *thee* and *thou*, to show his deference to King Henry. He also goes out of his way to stress the King's sovereignty by frequently injecting the appropriate titles, building from *My liege*, *your majesty*, and *my lord* in the body of the piece up to *your high majesty* at the end. He wraps up the monologue with a little flourish of self-debasement by saying *I beseech you* where he would surely prefer to say "I demand," and by referring to their relationship in terms of *my love* and *your high majesty* rather than simply "me and you," thus stressing his allegiance to his king.

The first line sets up the conflict between such attempts at properly abject behavior and Hotspur's excitable and already aggravated temper: he starts off with *My liege*, but quickly reveals his emotions by combining the emphatic tense with the Defiant Ds of *did deny*. He uses similar hard sounds in combination at particular moments (Bs and Ds: *bore dead bodies by*; Ms and Ds: *made me mad*). You must decide whether he uses them intentionally (to punch the more important or outrageous points?) or unintentionally (losing his grip on his temper?) or a little of each. He also employs different sounds to illustrate the ridiculousness of the emissary, such as Pooh-Poohing Ps and diSguSted Ss (*pestered with a popinjay*; *smell so sweet*). And we can imagine Hotspur using the Affected A sounds in *majesty's behalf* in an exaggerated imitation of the emissary's pretentious manner of speech.

Hotspur often repeats the emissary's words in the piece, offering a great opportunity for the actor to create a caricature as seen through Hotspur's eyes. Note that Hotspur sees the man as someone fashionable, squeamish, and tactless and as a *popinjay* (a parrot or parakeet), a word proverbially used in reference to someone who dresses in a gaudy, ostentatious manner and who chatters on and on about nothing. Keeping in mind Hotspur's own intense passion for war, you can have a lot of fun with the phrases Hotspur repeats: *sovereignest thing on earth / Was parmaceti*; *it was great pity, so it was / This villainous salt-petre should be digged / Out of the bowels of the harmless earth*; *many a good tall fellow had destroyed / So cowardly*; *vile guns*).

Hotspur's expression of disdain for the emissary doesn't stop at caricature. He is disgusted by the emissary's effeminate qualities (*perfumèd*; *smell so sweet*; *talk so like a waiting-gentlewoman*), which, despite his efforts at self-restraint, comes through in double entendre throughout his description: *lady terms* = periods of menstruation; *bald* = hairless, beardless, like a woman; *unjointed* = having no "joint" (penis); *mark* = sexual target (i.e., vagina); *salt-petre* = [in Shakespeare's time, used as a drug to suppress sexual desire].

Hotspur describes everything about the encounter in minute detail: his painful wounds; the sights and smells of the battlefield; his reaction to the outrageous comments of the emissary. We love monologues like this, in which Shakespeare does 90 percent of our sense-memory work for us.

Finally, notice that Hotspur uses the same construction with which he expressed contempt for the emmisary's delicacy (*Betwixt the wind and his nobility*) to impress upon the King his own loyalty as he wraps up this piece (*Betwixt my love and your high majesty*). You may wish to use this to draw a parallel or to contrast the two relationships.

SIGNIFICANT SCANS

In line 31, *extreme* is pronounced with the accent on the first syllable (EKS-treem).

Don't forget to elide: *prisoners* (PRIZ-ners) in line 48 (not in the first line); *being* (beeng) in line 49; and *sovereignest* (SOV-renst) in line 57;

. . . to contract: *neat and* (neet'n) in line 33; and *many a* (MEN-ya) in line 62;

. . . and to expand: *perfumèd* (per-FYOO-mehd) in line 36; *impatience* (im-PAY′-shee-ENCE) in line 51; *soldier* (SOL′-djee-ER) in line 64; and *accusation* (AK-yoo-ZAY′-shee-UN) in line 68.

Hot Stuff

Shakespeare found quite a character in the historical Henry "Hotspur" Percy. It was a safe bet that audiences would flock to see a play about Hotspur, since he was a folk hero of Elizabethans, who admired his chivalry and impetuous acts of bravery.

Although the relationship between the Percy family and King Henry IV is for the the most part historically correct, the real Hotspur was much older than the character Shakespeare developed. Hotspur was actually a year older than King Henry, not the same age as Henry's son Prince Hal. Hotspur had been knighted at the age of eleven and was a seasoned warrior by the time of his death at Shrewsbury. Both the age change and his death at the hands of Hal (we have no record of who actually killed him) were employed by Shakespeare to achieve particular dramatic goals in the play.

One more thing: In *Henry IV, Part Two* (Act II, Scene iii), Lady Percy remembers her late husband as "speaking thick." Although some have interpreted her to mean that Hotspur had a speech impediment, there is no historical evidence to support this. While a few scholars have suggested that Shakespeare may actually have been referring to Hotspur's northern dialect, most scholars interpret the phrase to mean that he spoke extremely quickly, cramming in a lot of words. You may decide to play with any of the above possibilities, but beware—you do not want to sacrifice comprehensibility. You won't want to obscure your acting choices and your ease with classical language by overlaying a funny voice.

HENRY IV, PART ONE

ACT II, SCENE iii

HOTSPUR

GENDER: M
AGE RANGE: young adult to adult
PROSE/VERSE: prose
FREQUENCY OF USE (1–5): 3

Henry "Hotspur" Percy and his father served King Henry IV loyally back in the days when he was just Henry Bolingbroke, cousin to King Richard II. Without the backing and support of the Percy father-and-son team, Bolingbroke would never have managed to depose his cousin and become king. But King Henry quickly forgot all that the Percys did for him, and the disillusioned and disgruntled Percys have been conspiring with other dissatisfied noblemen to overthrow the ingrate. Hotspur, well known as a valiant commander, will lead the military campaign. He has been writing to select nobles, to solicit their support for the rebellion, and has just received a rejection letter from one of those nobles. The hot-tempered Hotspur is beside himself at what he reads in it.

"But for mine own part, my lord, I could be well contented to be there in respect of the love I bear your house—" He could be contented—why is he not then? In respect of the love he bears our house—he
5 shows in this he loves his own barn better than he loves our house. Let me see some more: *"The purpose you undertake is dangerous—"* Why, that's certain—'tis dangerous to take a cold, to sleep, to drink, but I tell you, my lord Fool, out of this
10 nettle, danger, we pluck this flower, safety. *"The purpose you undertake is dangerous, the friends you have named uncertain, the time itself unsorted, and your whole plot too light for the counterpoise of so great an opposition."* Say you so, say you so? I say unto you
15 again, you are a shallow, cowardly hind, and you lie! What a lack-brain is this! By the Lord, our plot is a good plot as ever was laid, our friends true and constant—a good plot, good friends and full of expectation—an excellent plot, very good friends.
20 What a frosty-spirited rogue is this! Why, my lord of York commends the plot and the general course of the action. 'Zounds, an I were now by this rascal I could brain him with his lady's fan. Is there not my father, my uncle, and myself? Lord Edmund

1 *But* only [*But for mine own part* As concerns me only (i.e., if it were only up to me)]; *my lord* a respectful term used to address a nobleman; *be well contented* agree; 2 *in respect of* because of; 3 *house* family; *He* i.e., the author of the letter; 5 *in this* i.e., in what he writes; 6 *our house* Hotspur puns on the word's other meaning, "abode"; *purpose* plan, project; 8 *to take a cold* to catch a cold; 9 *my lord Fool* Hotspur derogatorily addresses the nobleman who wrote the letter as a fool; 10 *nettle* a herb covered with stinging hairs; 11 *friends* people friendly to the cause, coconspirators; 12 *uncertain* unreliable; *unsorted* unsuitable; 13 *light* unweighty, unsubstantial; *for the counterpoise of* to weigh against; *great* mighty; *opposition* opposing power (here, King Henry's forces); 14 *Say you so* Do you say so?; *unto* to; 15 *shallow* stupid; *hind* servant; lowly person (used pejoratively); 16 *lack-brain* fool; 17 *a good plot as ever was laid* as good a plot as was ever devised; 18 *full of expectation* hopeful, promising; 20 *frosty-spirited* cold, dull; *rogue* rascal; *my lord of York* i.e., the Archbishop of York; 21 *commends* praises; *the general course of the action* the whole plan of action; 22 *'Zounds* a mild oath, from contracting "God's wounds"; *an* if; *by* near; 23 *brain him* dash out his brains; *his lady's fan* his wife's fan (i.e., feathers, from which fashionable fans were made at the time); *Is there not* i.e., do we not have on our side; 24 *my father* i.e., Henry Percy, Earl of Northumberland; *my uncle* i.e., Thomas Percy, Earl of Worcester; *Lord Edmund Mortimer* Hotspur's brother-in-law (whose branch of the royal family had a valid

25 Mortimer, my lord of York, and Owen Glendower?
Is there not, besides, the Douglas? Have I not all
their letters to meet me in arms by the ninth of the
next month? And are they not some of them set
forward already? What a pagan rascal is this! An in-
30 fidel! Ha! You shall see now, in very sincerity of fear
and cold heart will he to the King and lay open all
our proceedings. O, I could divide myself and go
to buffets for moving such a dish of skim milk with
so honorable an action! Hang him, let him tell the
35 King—we are prepared. I will set forward tonight.

2 minutes

claim to the throne); 25 *Owen Glendower* Leader of the Welsh forces rebelling against King Henry IV, who aligned with the Percys; 26 *the Douglas* Scottish military leader who joined the Percys' rebellion; 27 *to meet me* pledging to meet me; *in arms* prepared to fight (i.e., with troops, weapons and supplies); 28 *are they not some of them* aren't some of them; *set forward already* on their way already, already setting out; 29 *pagan* i.e., faithless; *infidel* disbeliever, non-Christian; 30 *in very sincerity of fear and cold heart* with very sincere cowardice; 31 *will he* he will go; *lay open* reveal, display; *all our proceedings* all of the actions we are taking; 32 *divide myself and go to buffets* (BUFF-its) split myself in two and fight against myself; 33 *moving* speaking to (about an issue or affair), calling upon; *dish of skim milk* i.e., coward; weak, thin, without substance, like milk that has had the fat removed; 34 *so honorable an action* such an honorable enterprise (as ours); *Hang him* Let him be hanged (for all I care)—i.e., !$@% him.

COMMENTARY

Some people's nicknames are given in jest, because the people themselves are quite the opposite ("Sunshine" for a grumpy guy, etc.), but Hotspur's nickname is apt—his behavior throughout the play reveals a young man who is both hot-tempered and quick to act. Hotspur is clearly angered by the letter he receives, and responds with sarcasm to its contents and its author (*he loves his own barn better than he loves our house*; *'Tis dangerous to take a cold, to sleep, to drink*; *my lord Fool*; *brain him with his lady's fan*; *dish of skim milk*).

Hotspur's imagery communicates precisely what he seeks to express: *out of this nettle, danger, we pluck this flower, safety*; *lack-brain*; *frosty-spirited*; *pagan*; *infidel*; *dish of skim milk*. When he describes actions he would like to take (*brain him with his lady's fan*; *divide myself and go to buffets*) he sounds almost like a Popeye cartoon. Such broad descriptions yield insight into a person who is always ready to jump into the fray—or create a fray to jump into—without a thought to the consequences. In cartoons, a person can be pushed off a cliff and be fine again in the next scene. Hotspur seems to have that adolescent disbelief in his own mortality (or, rather, in death's finality).

Hotspur's repetition of words reveals his agitation at the letter writer's criticism. Whether he takes criticism or rejection well to begin with, the stakes here are unusually high; the nobleman's letter is more than an r.s.v.p. that he can't attend—it's a rejection of Hotspur's ideals and values, as well as his intellect, acumen, and professionalism. Also, Hotspur may need to quickly shoot down what the nobleman writes, lest mulling over the letter weaken his resolve to carry out such a dangerous undertaking.

When he gets upset, Hotspur adds the repetition of words to repetition of sounds in rapid succession, which underscores the sense that the words are rushing out of him: aStonished Ss (*Say / so / say / so / Say*); angrY Ys (*Say you / Say you / I say / you / you*); Loathing Ls (*shallow / lie / lack-brain / Lord / plot / plot / laid*); sPuttering Ps (*plot* is repeated four times in one sentence); Grounded Gs (*good* is repeated four times, followed shortly after by *rogue*); FuRious Fs, Rs, and FRs (*Lord / friends / true / friends / full / friends / frosty-spirited*); as well as strong long-vowel sounds (heY-wAIt-a-minute As: *Say / say / say / again*; accUsatory Us: *you / you / unto / you / you / true*; Oh-nO-you-dOn't Os: *so, so, shallow*; Irate Is: *I / hind / lie*; followed by a chain of sUre OOs; *good / good / good / full / good* and a rapid-fire chain of Emphatic EHs; *friends / friends / expectation / excellent / friends / commends*). Don't forget to look at "O, No! An O!" (page xxxiii) for help with exploiting the O sound to its best advantage.

Hotspur reveals that he is not 100 percent sure of his plot when he has to remind himself that the Archbishop of York—a respected elder—thinks it is sound (lines 20–21). If Hotspur were completely secure in his own judgment, he would not need to bolster it with the assessment of another.

It is characteristic of Hotspur not to entertain even for a moment the validity of the nobleman's concerns (which, if reasonable, could have encouraged Hotspur to work out the bugs in his plan). Rather than giving him pause, the letter spurs him in the opposite direction, to act more quickly than he otherwise might have (*I will set forward tonight*).

Note: this monologue requires that you flip back and forth from reading the letter (someone else's prerecorded thoughts) to commenting on it (your character's own, new thoughts). It also requires a "change of address" from the author of the letter to one of the following: (1) Hotspur himself; (2) something placed on stage for him to address, such as his dog, a mirror, the suit of armor standing stage left, etc.; and/or (3) the audience. You must decide who the *You* is in line 30, and clearly delineate for yourself when Hotspur is talking to the idiot noble who wrote that !@#$% letter, when (if ever) he's talking to himself, or to his favorite hunting dog, etc., and when (again, if ever) he's addressing the audience.

P.S.

For information on the historical Hotspur, see "Hot Stuff" on page 77.

HENRY IV, PART ONE

ACT V, SCENE i

FALSTAFF

GENDER: M
AGE RANGE: older adult
PROSE/VERSE: prose
FREQUENCY OF USE (1–5): 2

Sir John Falstaff has spent the last few years carousing in the company of Prince Hal, heir to the English throne. Now Prince Hal has joined his father's forces to put down rebelling factions in the north and west of England, and he has given Falstaff a command in their army. It is the morning of the first battle. Falstaff has just told Hal he wishes the day were over and everything had come out all right, to which Hal replied, "Thou owest God a death." After Hal departs, Falstaff soliloquizes:

'Tis not due yet—I would be loath to pay him before his day. What need I be so forward with him
130 that calls not on me? Well, 'tis no matter, honor pricks me on. Yea, but how if honor prick me off when I come on? How then? Can honor set to a leg? No. Or an arm? No. Or take away the grief of a wound? No. Honor hath no skill in surgery, then?
135 No. What is honor? A word. What is in that word honor? What is that honor? Air—a trim reckoning! Who hath it? He that died o' Wednesday. Doth he feel it? No. Doth he hear it? No. Is it insensible then? Yea, to the dead. But will it not live with
140 the living? No. Why? Detraction will not suffer it. Therefore I'll none of it. Honor is a mere scutcheon, and so ends my catechism.

1 minute

128 *'Tis* It (my death) is; *be loath to* hate to; *pay him* i.e., pay God the death I owe him by dying; *before his day* i.e., before my debt to him is due; 129 *What need I* Why should I; *forward* willing, ready, taking the initiative; *him* i.e., Death; 130 *calls not on* doesn't call on, doesn't visit; *honor* reputation of military bravery and success; chivalry (which includes today's definition of honor: personal integrity, honesty, etc.); 131 *pricks me on* incites me, spurs me on; *how* what; *prick me off* (1) marks me down, checks my name off (for death)—names on a list were checked off by pricking the paper with a pin; (2) stabs me, kills me; 132 *come on* approach (i.e., approach the battle); *How then*? What shall I do then?; *set to a leg* (1) set a broken leg; (2) graft a severed leg back onto the body; 133 *grief* pain; 136 *Air* i.e., something completely insubstantial, a mere word, spoken on a breath of air; *trim* fine, nice (usually used ironically); *reckoning* accounting, calculation [*a trim reckoning!* a fine total on the balance sheet! (referring ironically to the value of the word *honor*)]; 137 *He that died o' Wednesday* i.e., he who died fighting "honorably" in last Wednesday's battle; 138 *insensible* not able to be perceived by the senses; 139 *will it not live with* can't it be felt or perceived by; 140 *Detraction* Slander, defamation; *suffer* allow [*Detraction will not suffer it* i.e., because the living are always subject to defamation and slander, they cannot enjoy honor]; 141 *I'll none* I'll have none; 141 *scutcheon* escutcheon, a heraldic device, such as a coat of arms, often displayed during funerals of noblemen; 142 *catechism* lesson in the form of questions and answers (usually referring to religious instruction).

COMMENTARY

They say that brevity is the soul of wit. Well then, here is a witty little piece indeed: not only is it brief, but it is also spoken by the wittiest soul in Shakespeare's creation. In fact, wit is quite possibly the only thing Falstaff values above food, wine, and women. It's what he lives for (see Falstaff's monologue about wit, page 104, for more on this).

Falstaff's sense of irony is evident in the structure of this piece, which is delivered in the form of a catechism, a series of questions and answers used to teach a religious lesson. After all, Falstaff is just about the most sacrilegious and un-Christian character you'll find in Shakespeare—aside from outright villains and rogues—and he knows himself well. Falstaff is well versed in religion and gleefully makes use of it throughout the play to rationalize whatever self-indulgent action he intends to take. Here, rather than using biblical quotes, he uses catechism (the most common form of teaching religious precepts) to come to his own conclusions about what he owes God and when he should pay his debts. Notice how frequently he asks questions about *honor* to which his answer is *no*. The repeated juxtaposition of these two words hammers home the theme of this piece. Another aspect of the question-and-answer style is that it is reminiscent of the Socratic method of working out philosophical problems. Falstaff sees himself as something of a philosopher, and would have been amused by the fact that his contempt for the chivalric code of honor, for which he was criticized in his own time, would centuries later be embraced by many.

There are a couple of pitfalls to watch out for with this piece. The first is obvious: since the monologue is a reply to Hal's statement (*thou owest God a death*), it can be difficult for the audience to understand when taken out of context. For this reason, we advise that you use this piece only in classwork, when auditioning for the role of Falstaff (in any of the plays in which he appears), or when auditioning for a director whom you are certain is familiar with the material.

The second pitfall to watch out for is the question-and-answer structure, which can easily become repetitious. In order to keep the piece moving, keep in mind that Falstaff is making up his rationalization as he goes—one of his favorite activities. The progression of Falstaff's logic is just as delightful and surprising to him as it is to the audience. Also, some directors choose to keep Hal on stage to hear the first part of the speech, which gives Falstaff the chance to assert, for Hal's benefit, that *honor pricks* [him] *on*, and then to recant as soon as Hal is out of earshot.

Falstaff is a fun character to play. Enjoy his use of casual, colloquial phrases (*trim reckoning*; *died o' Wednesday*; *be so forward with him that calls not on me*) and his plays on words (*pricks me on*; *pricks me off*). And definitely enjoy his very dry sense of humor, as exhibited in his elegant logic: honor can be enjoyed only by the dead, and they're too dead to appreciate it. Before death, one is constantly subject to defamation, so it is impossible to achieve "honor" without dying in the process. Thus, there is clearly no possible way to enjoy honor, alive or dead—so why bother with it? . . . All you have to do is commit to the roller-coaster logic of Falstaff to have a great ride.

O, Be Some Other Name! or, Cobham Hollered When the Bard Marred His Lollard

The character Falstaff was originally named Oldcastle, after a historical friend of Prince Hal, Sir John Oldcastle, Lord Cobham, whom he met while they were fighting together in Wales. Later, Oldcastle became a Lollard, an adherent to the teachings of Protestant reformer John Wycliffe, who had founded Lollardry in the late 1300s. Lollardry's "poor priests" criticized the Church for amassing great wealth while commoners lived in extreme poverty. As a leader in the Lollard movement, Oldcastle was captured and convicted of heresy during the reign of Henry V, his former friend. Although he escaped from the Tower of London and continued his mission, he was eventually recaptured and executed, in 1417, by hanging over a slow fire. In Shakespeare's time, the Protestant Reformation had already taken hold, having been initiated by Henry VIII (Elizabeth I's father) when he broke with the Pope and created the Church of England. Thus, Shakespeare's audiences would remember Oldcastle as a Protestant martyr.

The character invented by Shakespeare resembled Oldcastle in little other than name. William Brooke, Lord Cobham, one of Oldcastle's descendants, was none too pleased with the slanderous depiction that provoked so much amusement in the theaters at his beloved ancestor's expense. Ironically, around the time the *Henry IV* plays were first being performed, Cobham just happened to be Lord Chamberlain, the Official Personage in Charge of Royal Entertainment. Naturally, it was in Shakespeare's best interests to change the Oldcastle character's name—and fast. What he came up with was the name Falstaff, which some believe is an inside joke: "fall staff" is a nice parallel to "shake spear." Falstaff was, after all, Shakespeare's wittiest and most memorable character—one who even the Queen requested to see again in future plays. Who better to subtly represent the master of complex ideas communicated through witty words?

HENRY IV, PART TWO

ACT II, SCENE i

MISTRESS QUICKLY

GENDER: F | AGE RANGE: mature adult
PROSE/VERSE: prose | FREQUENCY OF USE (1–5): 1.5

Mistress Quickly (also known as the Hostess in *Henry V*), owner of the Boar's Head Tavern in the Eastcheap neighborhood of London, has been taken advantage of by Sir John Falstaff for the last time. He has mooched off her for ages, dodging his ever-growing tab at the Boar's Head and wheedling loans from her when he was short of cash. But now he's gone too far: it seems his promise of marriage was just another such scam. Mistress Quickly wants Falstaff to repay the money he owes her and has enlisted the aid of two officers to arrest him. They have just attempted to do so on a street in Eastcheap, and Falstaff has drawn his sword on them. The Lord Chief Justice (not a fan of Falstaff) has now come upon the scene and demanded to know the cause of the ruckus. Mistress Quickly explains that Falstaff owes her a vast sum of money and "has eaten [her] out of house and home." When Falstaff asks her what he owes her, she replies:

Marry, if thou wert an honest man, thyself and the
money too. Thou didst swear to me upon a parcel-
gilt goblet, sitting in my Dolphin-chamber, at the
95 round table, by a sea-coal fire, upon Wednesday in
Wheeson week, when the Prince broke thy head for
liking his father to a singing-man of Windsor, thou
didst swear to me then, as I was washing thy
wound, to marry me and make me my lady thy
100 wife. Canst thou deny it? Did not goodwife Keech,
the butcher's wife, come in then and call me "gossip
Quickly"? Coming in to borrow a mess of vinegar,
telling us she had a good dish of prawns, whereby
thou didst desire to eat some, whereby I told thee
105 they were ill for a green wound? And didst thou
not, when she was gone downstairs, desire me to
be no more so familiarity with such poor people,
saying that ere long they should call me "madam"?
And didst thou not kiss me and bid me fetch thirty
110 shillings? I put thee now to thy Book-oath: Deny
it, if thou canst.

1 minute

92 *Marry* interjection, short for "By the Virgin Mary"; 93 *parcel-gilt* partly gilded; 94 *Dolphin-chamber* a particular room with that name in Mistress Quickly's tavern and inn (it was customary to give rooms at inns very fancy names); 95 *sea-coal* mineral coal (as opposed to charcoal), brought to London by sea from Newcastle; 96 *Wheeson week* Mistress Quickly mispronounces Whitsuntide, the week commencing on the seventh Sunday after Easter (Whitsunday); *the Prince* i.e., heir to the throne Prince Hal (a good friend of Falstaff's); 97 *liking* likening, comparing; *his father* i.e., King Henry IV; *singing-man* professional singer; 98 *thy wound* i.e., the head wound Falstaff had just received from Prince Hal; 99 *my lady thy wife* as wife of Sir John Falstaff, a knight, Mistress Quickly would be addressed respectfully as "my lady"; 100 *goodwife* an appellation meaning "Mrs."; *Keech* Goodwife Keech's last name, which means "a round lump of cow or ox fat," is a play on her husband's vocation; 101 *gossip* a familiar appellation for a female friend or neighbor (from "god-sib[ling]"); 102 *mess* a small quantity; 104 *desire* want; request; 105 *ill* bad; *green* new, fresh; 106 *desire me . . . familiarity* Mistress Quickly's grammar is uniquely her own; she means "request that I no longer be so intimate"; 108 *ere* before; *should* would; *madam* title of honor given to married ladies of rank; 109 *bid me* order me to; 110 *I put thee now to* I'm putting you to the test of; *Book-oath* swearing on the Bible.

COMMENTARY

Perry Mason, look out! Another fictional character has come to take your place. Mistress Quickly presents a strong and effective case before the Lord Chief Justice: she sets up her premise (*Thou didst swear to me . . . to marry me and make me my lady thy wife*) and then presents leading questions to her recalcitrant witness in cross-examination, laying out the detailed facts that cinch her case (*Canst thou deny it?*, etc.).

This is not to say that Mistress Quickly is being calculating, though—her repeated questioning gives the piece an indignant, and vulnerable, quality. Mistress Quickly seems genuinely hurt and incredulous that Falstaff could deny the tender scene they shared.

Although we have only her account of Falstaff's proposal to her, the speech rings completely true for several reasons, including: (1) she can recount minute details of the events surrounding the marriage proposal (workaday events that may have become memorable to her because they coincided with such an auspicious event); (2) she asks him to swear on a Bible, implying that she is willing to do the same (which could damn her soul for eternity were she to lie); (3) we've seen Falstaff in action, and this account comports with behavior we could expect from him on a good day.

Note the wonderful string of Ws (*Wednesday* / *Wheeson week, when* / *Windsor* / *was washing thy wound* / *wife*). They give the piece a slightly out-of-breath and out-of-control feel. Aside from which, they're just funny.

While you should certainly enjoy her malapropisms and wacky grammar (*Wheeson week*; *to be no more so familiarity*), do not condescend toward her. Also, notice—but be careful not to comment on—the grand airs she affects: the *parcel-gilt goblet* Falstaff used in her tavern, the *Dolphin-chamber* (very fancy!); *sea-coal* (no plain ol' charcoal to heat her establishment!); her eagerness to be called *my lady* and *madam* and to have *no more such familiarity* with a common butcher's wife (who will no longer be addressing her by the familiar *gossip*). The monologue juxtaposes these grand airs against the commonplace conduct that she can't shed: she uses a mild oath to start the piece (*Marry*); she reports matter-of-factly that Falstaff was smacked in the head; she is called *gossip* by her neighbor, the butcher's wife; she uses indelicate phrases like *a mess of vinegar*. The detail with which she can recall the mundane moments surrounding the "proposal of marriage" is also endearing and humorous. Mistress Quickly herself, however, is attempting to be anything but. She is completely earnest. Be sincere and the comical elements Shakespeare has written into the piece will do their work all by themselves.

What's in a Name?

Sometimes, a lot. Shakespeare wanted to convey a lot of information about Mistress Quickly, the bawdy owner of a tavern and inn in a slummy London neighborhood, who fraternizes with prostitutes. So he gave her the name Quickly, which his contemporaries would have considered a pun on the phrase "a quick lay." 'Nuff said.

HENRY IV, PART TWO

ACT II, SCENE iii

LADY PERCY

GENDER: F
PROSE/VERSE: blank verse
AGE RANGE: young adult to adult
FREQUENCY OF USE (1–5): 5

Young Lady Percy adored her husband, Henry "Harry" Percy (also nicknamed "Hotspur" for his renowned quickness to act). Hotspur and his father, Henry Percy, Earl of Northumberland (Northumberland, for short), had been loyal friends to King Henry IV back in the days before he was king, and were instrumental in helping him usurp the throne from his cousin, King Richard II (in *Richard II*). But King Henry did not return the friendship after he became king, and so the Percys and others formed a rebellion. The rebels gathered to fight King Henry's army at Shrewsbury, but Hotspur's father failed to arrive with his troops, claiming he was ill. Outnumbered by the King's forces, the rebels were soundly defeated in the battle, and Hotspur was killed by King Henry's son, Prince Hal (in *Henry IV, Part One*). Now the rebels are planning their next battle, and Northumberland is preparing to join them. His wife and Lady Percy have begged him not to go, but he insists that his honor requires him to keep his promise to join the other rebels. Lady Percy, still reeling from the news of her husband's death, is outraged by her father-in-law's chutzpah, and turns his argument to go into a reason he should stay.

O yet, for God's sake, go not to these wars!
10 The time was, Father, that you broke your word
When you were more endeared to it than now;
When your own Percy, when my heart's dear Harry,
Threw many a northward look to see his father
Bring up his powers, but he did long in vain.
15 Who then persuaded you to stay at home?
There were two honors lost, yours and your son's.
For yours, the God of Heaven brighten it!
For his, it stuck upon him as the sun
In the grey vault of Heaven, and by his light
20 Did all the chivalry of England move
To do brave acts. He was indeed the glass
Wherein the noble youth did dress themselves.
He had no legs that practiced not his gait;
And speaking thick, which nature made his blemish,
25 Became the accents of the valiant,
For those that could speak low and tardily
Would turn their own perfection to abuse
To seem like him: so that in speech, in gait,
In diet, in affections of delight,
30 In military rules, humours of blood,
He was the mark and glass, copy and book,

9 *yet* still, even so; *these wars* i.e., the upcoming battle between the rebel forces and those of King Henry IV; 11 *endeared* bound, obliged (with play on "dear," because she speaks of Northumberland's promise to his dear son) [*When you were more endeared to it than now* when you were more bound to it (were more required to uphold it) than you are now]; 13 *Threw many a northward look* kept looking northward; 14 *Bring up* advance; *his powers* his troops; *long* wish (for his father's troops to arrive to back up his own); 15 *then* i.e., at the time of the battle of Shrewsbury, when Northumberland failed to show up, his son's troops were defeated, and his son was killed; 17 *For yours* As for yours (i.e., your honor); *the God of Heaven brighten it* may the God of Heaven make it more illustrious; 18 *For his* As for his (i.e., Hotspur's honor); *stuck upon him* was set into him (like a gem); 19 *vault of Heaven* i.e., the sky; *by his light* i.e., guided by the light his honor shed; 20 *the chivalry* the knights; 21 *glass* mirror; 22 *Wherein . . . dress themselves* in which the young noblemen looked when dressing themselves (i.e., they imitated his fashion choices); 23 *He had no legs . . . his gait* There were no young noblemen following him who did not emulate his walk and run; 24 *speaking thick* speaking quickly (sometimes also defined as [1] speaking with a dialect of northern England, or [2] speaking with a speech impediment); *nature* the controlling forces of the world, i.e., God [*which nature . . . blemish* which God gave him as a blemish]; 26 *low* quietly; *tardily* slowly; 27 *turn* change; *their own perfection* their own perfect ways of speaking; *abuse* misuse; fault [*Would turn . . . abuse* would change their perfect way of speaking into his faulty way of speaking (would mimic his flawed speech patterns)]; 29 *affections of delight* inclinations toward pleasure, i.e., favorite pastimes; 30 *military rules* i.e., the military principles to which Hotspur adhered; *humours of blood* caprices, whims; 31 *mark* guide; beacon; *copy* example; *book* i.e., object full of

That fashioned others. And him—O wondrous him!
O miracle of men!—him did you leave,
Second to none, unseconded by you,
35 To look upon the hideous god of war
In disadvantage, to abide a field
Where nothing but the sound of Hotspur's name
Did seem defensible. So you left him.
Never, O never do his ghost the wrong
40 To hold your honor more precise and nice
With others than with him. Let them alone.
The Marshal and the Archbishop are strong.
Had my sweet Harry had but half their numbers,
Today might I, hanging on Hotspur's neck,
45 Have talked of Monmouth's grave.

2 minutes

matter to be studied; 32 *fashioned* shaped, formed; 33 *did you leave* you left; 34 *unseconded* unsupported; 35 *To look upon . . . war* To face battle; 36 *In* at a; *abide* meet in combat; *a field* in battle [*abide a field* face a battle]; 38 *defensible* able to make a defense [*Where nothing . . . defensible* where it seems that nothing (no one) but Hotspur was competent to mount a defense]; *So* In this manner; 40 *precise* conscientiously, exactingly, punctiliously; *nice* synonymous with *precise*: Lady Percy is repeating for emphasis [*never do his ghost the wrong . . . than with him* never wrong your son's ghost by being more conscientious about preserving your honor (by keeping your word) with other people than you were with him]; 41 *Let them alone* i.e., let them fight this battle without you; 42 *The Marshal* i.e., Lord Mowbray, Earl Marshall of England; *the Archbishop* i.e., Richard Scroop, the Archbishop of York [*The Marshal and the Archbishop* the other rebel leaders with whom Northumberland plotted to overthrow King Henry, who are currently awaiting his aid in battle]; 43 *their numbers* their troops; 45 *Monmouth* surname of Prince Hal, who was born in Monmouth, Wales (Prince Hal killed Hotspur in hand-to-hand combat at the battle of Shrewsbury).

COMMENTARY

Salt has just been rubbed in Lady Percy's wounds. If her father-in-law had kept his promise to his son and brought his troops to fight at Shrewsbury, her husband might still be alive. It must be excruciating to hear her father-in-law say that he must keep his promise to the other rebels, after he broke this same promise to his own son. And yet Lady Percy's anger at her father-in-law coexists with her love for him (or, perhaps, for her mother-in-law, who fears losing her husband after having just lost her son)—she is clearly committed to trying to save him by persuading him not to join the other rebels. As you know, it is important to understand and address Lady Percy's objectives, obstacles to objectives, and many conflicting emotions, and to decide what Lady Percy is experiencing and doing at each moment of the monologue.

Notice that Lady Percy is a master of the well-placed, direct, brutally short phrase or sentence, which she usually juxtaposes against longer, more descriptive segments. She starts with the very first line: composed of short words full of hard sounds, it packs a punch (*O yet, for God's sake, go not to these wars!*). Other short sharp phrases that stand out in contrast to their surrounding segments to make strong points include: *but he did long in vain*; *To do brave acts*; *To seem like him*; *him did you leave*; *So you left him* (more on this one below); *Let them alone*.

On the other hand, she is never short or sharp in describing her beloved Harry. Like her husband, Lady Percy is a rather direct communicator, not given to imagery, and yet well versed in the art of description. When she does use imagery, it is to illustrate her belief that her husband was a young god among men. She compares Hotspur's honor to the *sun*, the mightiest and strongest power in the cosmos (and notice that in making this analogy she calls Hotspur himself *the grey vault of Heaven*). The knights that followed him are like inferior stars, moved by his magnificent, awe-inspiring force.

Her choice of the phrase *all the chivalry of England* to mean "the knights of England" is another example of her use of superlatives. Here, her choice serves to heighten her homage to Hotspur: all the knights that emulate him are already chivalry personified, and yet Hotspur surpasses even them. Similarly, by calling him the mirror in which the chivalrous knights look, Lady Percy complements her late husband by emphasizing that he was himself chivalrous perfection, as well as a tremendous leader, capable of inspiring these noble men to acts of heroism. In fact, when she comments on her husband's speech patterns, *which nature made his blemish*, she suggests that she considered his speech the *only* little blemish in an otherwise divine being.

Beware the pitfall of listing his attributes (lines 28–30) without differentiating them from one another. It helps to notice that there is a progression in the list, from those characteristics of his that were easiest for the young knights of England to emulate (his speech patterns and his walk) to those that would take serious effort and dedication to emulate (affections of delight, military rules) to Hotspur's intangible whims. The young noblemen of England worshipped Hotspur enough even to try to anticipate and emulate his random fancies and impulses.

The shape of this monologue is gorgeous. Lady Percy lulls her audience into thinking that she has gone on a wild tangent in eulogizing her husband, when, in fact, she has done so entirely to a purpose: the greater the heights to which she so splendidly and movingly builds him, the lower seem the depths of his betrayal at the hands of his father. Lady Percy has crafted so piercingly lovely a view of Hotspur that it is then agonizing to hear her say *And him—O wondrous him! / O miracle of men!—him did you leave* . . . She has, all along, been building her case that Northumberland should now abandon the rebellion.

The horror of Hotspur's last hours haunts her, and she describes them to her father-in-law to shame him for betraying his promise to his son, and to dissuade him from joining the fighting now. She invokes the image of Hotspur standing on the battlefield of Shrewsbury to face alone *the hideous god of war*—she imagines aloud how abandoned he must have felt: *unseconded by you*; *To look upon the hideous god of war in disadvantage*; *to abide a field / Where nothing but the sound of Hotspur's name / Did seem defensible*.

Notice the repetition of concepts for emphasis (sometimes using the same word, sometimes using synonyms instead of actual word repetition): *For yours / For his*; *mark and glass, copy and book*; *him / O wondrous him / him*; *Never, O never*; *precise and nice*). Furthermore, notice the rhyme of *precise and nice*: she is making fun of her father-in-law's show of honor—the tone created by the rhyme expresses exactly what she thinks of it.

Lady Percy uses other sounds to express her sentiments. For example, there are many angRy, aRguing Rs and Warring Ws in the first few lines: *wars / was / Father / broke your word / When / were more endeared / now / When your own Percy / when / heart's dear Harry / Threw / northward / father / Bring / powers*. The Hs at the end create a sense of Heavy breathing: *Had / Harry had but half / hanging / Hotspur's / Have*. Perhaps she is trying not to cry. Or perhaps she is being defiant (Ha!). Certainly, the half rhyme and Vehement Vs at the very end (*Have / grave*) reinforce this possibility. (Be sure to check out "O, No! An *O*!" on page xxxiii for help with using the sound of the word *O* to its best advantage.)

Lady Percy cannot completely avoid sarcasm: she plays with the different meanings of *second* to dig at her father-in-law for deserting his son (*second to none, unseconded by you*), and she refers to her husband's nemesis as *Monmouth*, a contemptuous way to refer to the Crown Prince. Note, though, that however angry she might be toward her father-in-law, she still addresses him at all times with the respectful, deferential *you* instead of *thou*.

SIGNIFICANT SCANS

Scanning the meter of this monologue reveals ample evidence that Lady Percy is quite emotional about her subject matter. There are frequent caesuras, interrupting the natural flow of the lines. On line 12, for example, she interrupts herself because she cannot help but personalize what she is saying: *When your own Percy, when my heart's dear Harry*. She likewise changes gears in the middle of line 21 to begin describing her late husband's remarkable attributes.

Furthermore, there are many inverted feet, both at the beginnings of lines and at caesuras. It seems that sometimes she cannot help but blurt things out, while at other times she punches the first syllable to emphasize the point she is making. There are also some double endings at ends of lines and before caesuras, further emphasizing her agitation and the urgency with which she speaks.

What is arguably the most dramatic moment in the monologue is set up by building in a silent syllable right before it. Line 38 has a pause at the caesura (as well as a double ending at the end of the line):

x / x / x / x / x / (x)
Did seem defensible. (pause) So you left him

Thus the pointed *So you left him* is simply devastating. The abruptness of the last, three-footed line (*Have talked of Monmouth's grave*) is similarly striking and harsh.

Don't forget to elide: *powers* (POWRZ) in line 14; *Heaven* (HEV'N) in line 19 (but *not* in line 17!); *hideous* (HID-yuss) in line 35;

. . . to contract: *many a* (MEN-ya) in line 13;

. . . and to expand: *valiant* (VAL´-ee-ENT) in line 25.

POOR LADY P.

We don't know much about the historical Lady Percy, but we do know this: although her husband, Hotspur, calls her Kate in *Henry IV, Part One* (Act II, Scene iii), her name was really Elizabeth. And while we can't attribute the real Hotspur's death at Shrewsbury to Prince Hal, the real Lady Percy did have reason to hate King Henry and his brood: he snatched the throne right out from under her loved ones' bottoms. King Henry IV was the grandson of King Edward III (through his *fourth* son, John of Gaunt). Lady Percy was

Edward III's great-granddaughter (through his *third* son, Lionel, Duke of Clarence). This makes her King Henry's first cousin once removed (and Prince Hal's second cousin) to be exact (see "Genealogical Chart—the Wars of the Roses," pages 236–37). If King Henry hadn't seized the throne from the childless Richard II, the throne would have passed over to Lady Percy's branch of the family (to her brother's son, to be exact). And you wouldn't be preparing this particular monologue at this particular time (or ever, to be exact).

HENRY IV, PART TWO

ACT III, SCENE i

KING HENRY IV

GENDER: M
PROSE/VERSE: blank verse
AGE RANGE: mature adult
FREQUENCY OF USE (1–5): 2

King Henry can't sleep, and it's no wonder: he's got the threat of a French invasion from the east, the Welsh leader Owen Glendower causing problems along the border to the west, and worst of all, his own English nobles rebelling against him in the north! Henry has amassed his troops, and he's ready to fight the rebels, but the responsibility weighs heavily on him. Since he can't get to sleep, he has rolled out of bed in the middle of the night and sent for his closest supporters, the Earls of Surrey and Warwick. While he awaits their arrival, he soliloquizes:

How many thousand of my poorest subjects
5 Are at this hour asleep? O sleep, O gentle sleep,
Nature's soft nurse, how have I frighted thee,
That thou no more will weigh my eyelids down,
And steep my senses in forgetfulness?
Why rather, sleep, liest thou in smoky cribs,
10 Upon uneasy pallets stretching thee,
And hushed with buzzing night-flies to thy slumber,
Than in the perfumed chambers of the great,
Under the canopies of costly state,
And lulled with sound of sweetest melody?
15 O thou dull god, why liest thou with the vile
In loathsome beds, and leav'st the kingly couch
A watch-case or a common 'larum bell?
Wilt thou upon the high and giddy mast
Seal up the ship-boy's eyes and rock his brains
20 In cradle of the rude imperious surge,
And in the visitation of the winds,
Who take the ruffian billows by the top,
Curling their monstrous heads and hanging them

6 *soft* gentle, tender; *nurse* one who takes motherly care of; *frighted thee* scared you off; 7 *That* so that; *no more will* will no longer; 8 *steep* soak; 9 *smoky cribs* smoky hovels (the poor lived in cramped huts, which often had no chimney to ventilate smoke from the fire); 10 *uneasy* hard, uncomfortable; *pallets* rough beds made of straw [*Why rather, sleep . . . to thy slumber* Sleep, why would you rather lie in smoky hovels, stretching yourself out on uncomfortable straw beds, being lulled to sleep by buzzing night insects]; 12 *perfumed* wealthy Elizabethans thought too much fresh air was unhealthy, and used perfume to mask the musty odors of rooms that were rarely aired; *chambers* bedrooms; 13 *state* pomp and splendour; 15 *dull* sleepy, weary [*dull god* Morpheus, god of sleep]; *the vile* those who are "low-born," "common"; 16 *couch* bed; 17 *watch-case* ornate gold or silver case in which a watch is kept; *'larum* alarm [*watch-case or a common 'larum bell* [Henry compares himself (lying in his elaborate bed) to a watch, which ticks away the hours ceaselessly while lying in its beautiful case, and then to a bell-man who must remain awake in his bell tower, in order to ring the alarm in case of danger]; 18 *giddy* causing the sensation of dizziness or vertigo; 19 *Seal up* close (also "seel up," a hawking term: the hawk's eyes are sewn shut in early training); *ship-boy* i.e., the boy who serves as the ship's lookout; *rock his brains* i.e., rock him to sleep; put his thoughts to rest; 20 *In cradle* in the cradle; *rude* harsh, rough, turbulent; *imperious* tyrannical; 21 *visitation* violent assault; 22 *ruffian* boisterous, raging; *billows* huge waves; 23 *monstrous* huge [*Curling their monstrous . . . slippery clouds* i.e., curling the huge peaks of the waves, and crashing them down with a deafening noise,

With deafening clamor in the slippery clouds,
25 That with the hurly, Death itself awakes?
Canst thou—O partial sleep—give thy repose
To the wet sea-boy in an hour so rude,
And in the calmest and most stillest night
With all appliances and means to boot
30 Deny it to a king? Then happy low, lie down.
Uneasy lies the head that wears the crown.

1 minute, 40 seconds

creating "clouds" of slippery white foam]; 25 *hurly* tumult, confusion, uproar; *Death* i.e., the personification of death; 26 *Canst thou* Can you; *partial* favoring one party more than another; 27 *in an hour so rude* at such a turbulent, distressing moment; 28 *And* and yet; and at the same time; *most stillest* stillest; most quiet and tranquil; 29 *appliances* devices, accessories (i.e., furnishings designed to make one comfortable); *to boot* in addition; to one's advantage; 30 *happy* fortunate; *low* commoners.

COMMENTARY

If you've ever had insomnia, you know there's only one thing you can do about it. Instead of tossing and turning in wakeful anguish while challenging your math skills with the numeration of imaginary sheep, you have to get out of bed and *do something*. At the moment of this soliloquy, King Henry is making the painful transition from his tantalizing but restless bed to tackling the problems that are keeping him awake. While he waits for his friends to arrive and help him through his crisis, Henry gets caught up in the irony of his sleepless situation.

And we mean caught up in: the imagery here just carries him away. This piece is so full of imagery, it's almost as if Henry is restlessly creating for himself the dreams that elude him. First, there are the vivid images of sleep coming to the poor in their smoky hovels, then the contrasting images of Henry's royal bed, enhanced by the metaphors of the *watch-case* and the *'larum bell*, places where sleep never visits. Finally, there is the extended and detailed image of the ship boy who is able to sleep in the crow's nest of his ship, in the middle of a storm. All of these images are extremely helpful to the actor; they are so real to Henry that they can't help but be real for you. If you are specific in your visualizations, the imagery will turn what could be a one-note complaint into a story or an exploration of the variation in experiences gleaned from different walks of life. Don't forget that you can use the powerful storm imagery in your work on the character: it may be used as a metaphor for the storm that is raging in Henry's mind, or for the battle he is about to fight.

The imagery in this piece is strongly supported by the use of consonance and assonance, the most noticeable example of which is the plethora of Ss saturating the soliloquy: *thousands / poorest / subjects / asleep / sleep / sleep / soft / steep / senses / forgetfulness / sleep / liest / smoky / cribs / uneasy / pallets / stretching / sound / sweetest*). But don't let that distract you from the other examples of consonance: Nurturing Ns (*Nature's / nurse*); Weary Ws (*wilt / weigh*); Lulling Ls (*lulled / melody / dull / liest / vile / loathsome / leav'st / kingly / low / lie*). Taken together, these gentle sounds can form a lullaby in themselves; a soft plea for sleep; or a gentle resignation to wakefulness. The assonance in the piece flows right along in the same soft vein: there are drOWsy OWs (*How / thousand / hour*); whining Is (*I / frighted*; *my / eyelids*; *why / liest / vile*); Exhausted EHs (*senses / forgetfulness*); plEAding EEs (*uneasy / thee*); and frUstrated UHs (*uneasy / hushed / buzzing / slumber*; *lulled / dull*). Also, make use of the onomatopoeic sounds in the piece: *hushed / buzzing / slumber / lulled / melody / 'larum bell / clamor / slippery*.

Because so many of these are soft, gentle sounds, it is particularly striking when harder sounds are used. Only when King Henry refers to himself (in his sleepless state) or to his own bedchamber do the soft consonants and assonant vowels disappear, to be replaced by many hard consonants: *canopy / costly*; *kingly couch / A watch-case or a common 'larum bell*; *Deny it to a king*. The contrast in sounds can be used to underscore the heavy burden Henry feels he carries as compared to the carefree existence of his subjects.

King Henry describes his own bed with the formality of a rhyming couplet (*Than in the perfumed chambers of the great, / Under the canopies of costly state*). In contrast, he describes the night flies' lullaby to the poor using the informality of onomatopoeia (*hushed*; *buzzing*). In this way, the relaxation of the poor and the constraints on such relaxation for the rich are communicated by means of the sounds in the piece. Also, the word *O* appears *four* times in this piece. For help with exploiting the sound of *O*, see "O, No! An *O*!," page xxxiii.

SIGNIFICANT SCANS

Notice that there are *two* of those very rare lines with six feet (hexameter) in this relatively short piece! The first is in the second line:

x / x / x / x / x / x /
Are at this hour asleep? O sleep. O gentle sleep

You may choose to use the length of this line to express the tedious passage of the night hours, or perhaps you will interpret its crowdedness as resulting from the desperation and panic that seizes you when you really need to sleep but can't. However you interpret the line, its unusual length combined with the repetition of *asleep* and *sleep* perfectly evokes the misery that insomnia brings with it in the wee hours of the night.

The second example of hexameter appears in the second to last line:

x / x / x / x / x / x /
Deny it to a king? Then happy low, lie down

Notice that the above line has a similar structure to the previous hexametric line (the first three feet forming the end of a question begun on the previous line; the next three starting a new idea). You can use this to link the end of the piece back to the beginning aurally, and to highlight this line and the next, which together form a beautiful and memorable rhyming couplet that poetically summarizes the soliloquy.

Finally, don't forget to elide: *hour* (OWR) in line 25 and line 27; *liest* (lyst) in line 9 and (LYST) in line 15; *imperious* (im-PEER-yus) in line 20; *ruffian* (RUFF-yan) in line 22; *deafening* (DEF-ning) and *slippery* (SLIP-ree) in line 24.

Whatever Was Ailing Him, It Wasn't Pretty

Although Henry is portrayed in this play as ailing throughout most of his reign, in reality he did not become ill until the last two years. He developed epilepsy and another illness which his doctors believed to be leprosy, but which may actually have been syphilis. Many of his subjects perceived Henry's illness as God's punishment for having executed an archbishop—Richard Le Scrope (Scroop in the play). Henry was unable to rule during his illness, and England's government was controlled by his son, Prince Hal (the future Henry V).

HENRY IV, PART TWO

ACT IV, SCENE iii

FALSTAFF

GENDER: M
PROSE/VERSE: prose
AGE RANGE: older adult
FREQUENCY OF USE (1–5): 1

Now that the rebel leaders have been captured and the battle between the rebels and King Henry IV's troops has been called off, both armies have been disbanded and soldiers are making their ways home. Sir John Falstaff has just encountered a rebel officer, Sir John Coleville of the Dale, who, mistakenly assuming Falstaff to be courageous, surrendered to him on the spot; whereupon Prince John appeared and angrily accused Falstaff of having hidden until the threat of battle had safely passed (which he most likely did). Prince John was unimpressed when Falstaff handed over his prisoner, and remained surly despite Falstaff's best efforts at humor. As the Prince was departing for the royal court, Falstaff asked him to deliver a good report of him there and John has just replied that he will speak better of Falstaff than he deserves. Now that the Prince is safely out of earshot, Falstaff retorts:

I would you had but the wit—'twere better than
your dukedom. Good faith, this same young sober-
blooded boy doth not love me, nor a man cannot
95 make him laugh—but that's no marvel, he drinks
no wine. There's never any of these demure boys
come to any proof, for thin drink doth so overcool
their blood, and making many fish meals, that they
fall into a kind of male greensickness, and then
100 when they marry they get wenches. They are generally fools and cowards, which some of us should be
too, but for inflammation. A good sherris sack hath
a twofold operation in it: it ascends me into the
brain; dries me there all the foolish and dull and
105 crudy vapors which environ it; makes it apprehensive, quick, forgetive, full of nimble, fiery, and de-
lectable shapes, which, delivered o'er to the voice,
the tongue, which is the birth, becomes excellent
wit. The second property of your excellent sherris is

92 *would* wish; *wit* intelligence [*I would . . . wit* I only wish you had the intelligence]; *'twere better* it would be better; 93 *your dukedom* Shakespeare believed that Prince John also held the title (and the property) of Duke of Lancaster; in fact, the title was held by Prince Hal. John was the Duke of Bedford. [*'twere better . . . dukedom* it (i.e., a little intelligence) would be better for you (worth more to you) than your dukedom]; *Good faith* in all truth, indeed (from "in good faith"); *same* used to point out a particular person or thing, often with contempt; *sober-blooded* calm, cool, and collected (with pun on "not drunk") [*this same young sober-blooded boy* i.e., Prince John]; 94 *nor a man cannot* nor can any man; 95 *that's no marvel* that's nothing strange; 96 *There's never* There has never been; *demure* solemn, grave; 97 *come to any proof* prove themselves; come to any good [*There's never . . . proof* None of these serious types has ever amounted to anything]; *thin drink* unsubstantial drink, i.e., one with little alcohol (with a lower alcohol content than "sack"); *overcool* make excessively cold [*for thin drink . . . their blood* because less (or non-) alcoholic beverages make their blood so excessively cool]; 98 *making many fish meals* they eat too much fish (and not enough hearty meat)—also implying that they are too religious (adhering to the Christian practice of eating fish on Fridays and during Lent); 99 *male greensickness* a male version of "greensickness," a disease, like anemia, principally afflicting young women, and characterized by a pale complexion; 100 *get* beget, father [*for thin drink . . . wenches* because drinking beverages that are not alcoholic enough, and eating too much fish, gives them a male version of greensickness, so that when they marry they beget only girls]; 101 *should* would; 102 *inflammation* heating of the blood from drinking [*but for inflammation* if our blood were not warmed up by drinking]; *sherris* sherry; *sack* generic name for a light, dry wine from Spain and the Canary Islands, imported into England in the sixteenth and seventeenth centuries; 103 *operation* effect; *ascends me into the brain* rises up (from my stomach) into my brain; 104 *dries me* dries up for me; 105 *crudy* (CROO-dee) curdled; *vapors* "exhalations" emanating from bodily organs (especially the stomach) believed in Shakespeare's time to be mentally or physically harmful; *environ* surround; *apprehensive* quick to learn or understand, perceptive; 106 *forgetive* (FOR-je-tive) capable of imagining or inventing; 107 *shapes* things emerging from the imagination; *delivered* transferred (with pun on "birthed"); 108 *which is the*

110 the warming of the blood, which before (cold and settled) left the liver white and pale, which is the badge of pusillanimity and cowardice. But the sherris warms it and makes it course from the inwards to the parts extreme. It illumineth the face, which
115 (as a beacon), gives warning to all the rest of this little kingdom (man), to arm; and then the vital commoners and inland petty spirits muster me all to their captain—the heart—who, great and puffed up with this retinue, doth any deed of courage;
120 and this valor comes of sherris. So that skill in the weapon is nothing without sack, for that sets it a-work; and learning a mere hoard of gold kept by a devil, till sack commences it and sets it in act and use. Hereof comes it that Prince Harry is valiant,
125 for the cold blood he did naturally inherit of his father he hath, like lean, sterile, and bare land, ma-

birth Falstaff applies the analogy of giving birth to his creative process: he "conceives" his witty ideas when he drinks; he is in delivery while the thought travels from brain to tongue, and the brilliant words are "born" when they are finally uttered aloud. This analogy follows in the same vein as his previous statement that men who do not drink enough alcohol are less virile and therefore beget only girls.; 111 *settled* stagnant; *liver* the liver was believed by Elizabethans to be the source of courage; 112 *pusillanimity* lack of courage; 113 *course* circulate; *the inwards* the inner parts of the body; the bowels; 114 *the parts extreme* outermost extremeties, i.e., fingers and toes; 116 *to arm* to take up weapons; *vital* life-giving; 117 *inland* people living inland were characterized as gentle and refined (in contrast to coastal dwellers, who were considered more barbaric); *spirits* people [*vital commoners . . . spirits* "vital spirits" was a phrase used in Shakespeare's time for fluids of the body; Falstaff analogizes the body's life-giving fluids as lively, lusty common folk and its other, more benign bodily fluids as the more refined inland dwellers]; *muster* assemble [*muster me all to their captain* all gather and rally for me at their captain]; 119 *retinue* a body of people waiting upon an important personage; *doth any deed of courage* does all sorts of courageous deeds; 120 *So that* So; *skill in the weapon* skill at using a weapon, skill at armed combat; 121 *that* i.e., sack; *sets it a-work* puts it (the skill) to work; 122 *learning* education; *a mere hoard of gold kept by a devil* i.e., merely stored (unused) wealth; this refers to the Elizabethan superstition that gold mines were guarded by devils; 123 *commences it* gets it started; *sets it in act and use* puts it into action and makes it useful; 124 *Hereof comes it* This is the reason that; *Prince Harry* Falstaff's friend, a.k.a. Prince Hal, heir to the English throne; 125 *did naturally inherit of* inherited genetically from; 126 *manured* fertilized;

FALSTAFF

nured, husbanded, and tilled with excellent endeavor of drinking good and good store of fertile sherris, that he is become very hot and valiant. If I
130 had a thousand sons, the first humane principle I would teach them should be to forswear thin potations and to addict themselves to sack.

2 minutes, 30 seconds

127 *husbanded* cultivated; *with excellent endeavor of* with the very worthwhile effort of; 128 *good and good store of* good quality, and a good amount of; *fertile* both (1) abundant and (2) conducive to creativity; 129 *is become* has become; 130 *the first humane principle* the first rule of being a human being; 131 *forswear* refuse, renounce; *potations* beverages [*thin potations* (see *thin drinks*, above)].

COMMENTARY

Somebody once wrote, "What a piece of work is a man." Though the line is spoken by Hamlet, it certainly applies to our friend Falstaff. Whole Ph.D. theses have been written about this character. He's been called a coward and a jester, but to play him as either of these would be doing yourself and your character a great disservice.

Falstaff lives by a code that differs from the chivalric code of his contemporaries. He is a man of about seventy who has honed his opinions and his lifestyle to his complete satisfaction over the years. He loves to expound, and will share his worldview with whoever will listen . . . even if that person is only himself. While this monologue seems to be a treatise extolling the multiple virtues of wine, it is also a look at the attributes that Falstaff most prizes. While honor is esteemed by most men of his day, Falstaff most respects intelligence . . . and the sense of humor that intelligence affords a person (see monologue, page 83, for Falstaff's opinions on honor). This is apparent right at the beginning of this monologue, where he disparages Prince John for his lack of both.

Falstaff's own superb intelligence is evidenced in two ways: what he says and how he says it. This monologue is an example of prose at its finest. Falstaff's relish of language mirrors that of his creator, in that he not only excels at wordplay, but also has a great love for it. He amuses himself with simultaneously gorgeous and hilarious descriptions, and entertaining personifications of the body's composite parts. This piece is a lovely homage to the art of rhetoric, to the creation of witty speech. Falstaff is supremely proud of his ability to string together words and ideas to manipulate others, usually by making them laugh and/or by tying them into a logical knot. He believes that drink yields this ability and thus hones his skill at circumventing danger.

Falstaff clearly delights in the art of circumvention—it brings him joy to be faced with trouble and to blithely wriggle his way out of and around it. For him, trouble is merely an opportunity to engage in his favorite mental exercise . . . one that never proves too strenuous. He is a genius at defending seemingly indefensible positions. His success here with Prince John was less stunning than usual; perhaps this explains his grumbling dig aimed at the Prince's departing back.

And yet you'll notice that Falstaff is not self-doubting (not here, and not ever). He blames his inability to charm Prince John on the Prince immediately, and forges happily forward. This extremely brilliant fellow is oddly naïve about the political world in which he is caught up and about the complexities of the situations in which he finds himself. Maybe he is just that sure of his ability to talk his way out of anything. Remember that although the audience knows he is cruising for disaster, Falstaff himself is blissfully unaware of the fact until the moment of his rejection by the newly crowned Hal at the end of this play. This is important: because the audience is aware of his impending fall, your commitment to this character's blithe advance through life makes bittersweet the audience's enjoyment of his wit.

Your goal is to have the audience enjoy Falstaff for—not despite—his shortcomings. To that end, notice how pleased Falstaff is with himself, and how self-centered. Falstaff relates everything to himself. He uses *me* four times, *I* three times, and goes on at length about the workings of *his* own magnificent body and mind. Never mind that Prince John is preoccupied with putting down a powerful insurrection—Falstaff focuses on the fact that John doesn't seem to like *him*; Falstaff describes wine's marvelous effect on *him*; if *he* had boys, he'd teach them to drink, etc.

While this monologue reveals Falstaff's high opinion of his best attribute—his keen intelligence—the piece is also certainly what it promises to be: a delightful treatise on the subject of wine. Ahh, wine. Falstaff's play on the meaning of *sober*—both (1) serious-minded and (2) not drunk—shows his contempt for the state of sobriety right from the beginning. Falstaff further condemns sobriety (it gives one anemia and leads—oh, horror!—to the fathering of girls) before leaving discussion of the negatives of sobriety to laud the benefits of drunkenness.

While sobriety stifles virility, drinking accomplishes the opposite: it creates the ultimate in virility by yielding—not boys, better than boys—wit! Falstaff, like other creative types through the ages, attributes his creative output to the intake of substances. It is interesting that Falstaff defines true virility in terms of intellectual rather than sexual output. Falstaff may engage in whatever pastimes he enjoys with Mistress Quickly or the prostitute Doll Tearsheet, but these are mere diversions. Falstaff derives his feeling of virility by creating verbal gems—they are his children.

At the close of this monologue, Falstaff proves the piece's own content: he has not forgotten why he is waxing prosaic about wine, and neatly brings his argument around full circle to its first topic, Prince John. Falstaff concludes with his assessment of how Prince Hal achieved superiority over his brother John—unlike the dour John, Hal has worked hard to overcome the coldness he and his brother inherited from his father, and has applied himself dutifully and diligently to drinking. He's done Falstaff proud . . . or so Falstaff thinks . . .

P.S.

For the origin of Falstaff's character, see "O, Be Some Other Name! or, Cobham Hollered When the Bard Marred His Lollard," page 86.

HENRY IV, PART TWO

ACT IV, SCENE v

PRINCE HAL

GENDER: M
AGE RANGE: young adult to adult
PROSE/VERSE: blank verse
FREQUENCY OF USE (1–5): 2

Hearing that his father, King Henry IV, was on his deathbed, Prince Hal rushed to the palace, only to find his father unconscious. The Prince saw the crown lying beside King Henry and blamed the heavy burden it placed on the King for his illness. Detecting no breath from his father, Prince Hal believed he'd just died, and, crying, left the room with the crown. King Henry was not dead, however; when he awoke and found his son and crown missing, he was furious! He ordered Prince Hal brought back to him and has just berated him, accusing him of delighting in his father's death (*dig my grave thyself*) and of being eager to assume the throne. Prince Hal, devastated, replies:

PRINCE HAL

O pardon me, my liege! But for my tears,
140 The moist impediments unto my speech,
I had forestalled this dear and deep rebuke
Ere you with grief had spoke and I had heard
The course of it so far. There is your crown,
And He that wears the crown immortally
145 Long guard it yours! If I affect it more
Than as your honor and as your renown,
Let me no more from this obedience rise,
Which my most inward true and duteous spirit
Teacheth, this prostrate and exterior bending.
150 God witness with me, when I here came in,
And found no course of breath within your Majesty,
How cold it struck my heart! If I do feign,
O let me in my present wildness die
And never live to show the incredulous world
155 The noble change that I have purposèd!
Coming to look on you, thinking you dead—
And dead almost, my liege, to think you were—
I spake unto this crown as having sense,
And thus upbraided it: "The care on thee depending
160 Hath fed upon the body of my father;
Therefore thou best of gold art worst of gold;
Other, less fine in carat, is more precious,
Preserving life in medicine potable;

139 *my liege* my sovereign, my ruler; *But for* If not for; 140 *the moist impediments . . . speech* which are moist obstacles making it difficult for me to speak; 141 *had* would have; *dear* both (1) earnest and (2) grievous; *deep* intense, heartfelt; 142 *Ere* before; 144 *He that wears the crown immortally* i.e., God; 145 *Long guard it yours* keep it (i.e., the crown) yours for a long time; *affect* aspire to [*If I affect it more . . . renown* If I aspire to be king, expecting to do anything more than to continue ruling as honorably and renownedly as you have]; 147 *from this obedience* from this kneeling or lying flat position (of obedience) [*Let me no more from this obedience rise* may I never again get up from this kneeling (or lying flat) position (i.e., may I be struck down right now)]; 148 *my most inward* my innermost (coming from my soul); 149 *exterior* outward; *bending* bowing down; 150 *God witness with me* God is my witness; *when I here came in* when I came in here; 151 *course* current of air [*no course of breath* i.e., no breathing]; 153 *in my present wildness* in the dissolute lifestyle I'm currently living; 155 *The noble change* the change to noble behavior; *purposèd* intended; 157 *dead almost* (I was) almost dead; *to think you were* thinking that you were (dead); 158 *as having sense* as though it had senses (and could hear); 159 *on thee depending* connected with you [*the care . . . depending* the anxiety that comes with wearing you]; 161 *thou best of gold* you, which are the finest gold object; *worst of gold* the worst gold object; 162 *less fine in carat* of poorer quality gold; 163 *in medicine potable* in liquid medicine (in Shakespeare's time, gold was believed to have curative qualities and its liquid form was used as an ingredient in

But thou, most fine, most honored, most renowned,
165 Hast eat thy bearer up." Thus, my most royal liege,
Accusing it, I put it on my head,
To try with it, as with an enemy
That had before my face murdered my father,
The quarrel of a true inheritor.
170 But if it did infect my blood with joy,
Or swell my thoughts to any strain of pride,
If any rebel or vain spirit of mine
Did with the least affection of a welcome
Give entertainment to the might of it,
175 Let God forever keep it from my head,
And make me as the poorest vassal is
That doth with awe and terror kneel to it!

2 minutes, 20 seconds

medicines); 165 *eat* consumed; *thy bearer* your wearer; *Thus* In this manner; 167 *try with it* to combat it; 169 *quarrel* dispute that cannot be settled with words; *a true inheritor* a faithful heir; 170 *infect my blood* contaminate me, affect me adversely; 171 *swell my thoughts to* swell my head with; *strain* impulse, feeling, motion of the mind; 173 *affection* bent of mind, disposition; 174 *Give entertainment to* give hospitable reception to (i.e., consider positively); *the might of it* the power of the crown; 176 *as* like; *vassal* subject (under a monarch's rule); 177 *That doth . . . kneel* who . . . kneels.

COMMENTARY

Let's assess Prince Hal's situation at this moment in the play: not only did he think his father had died and begin grieving, only to learn that his father is still alive (but minutes from death); and not only did his dying father just vehemently attack him; and not only is his father about to go to his grave mistakenly believing the absolute worst about him, but Prince Hal is about to assume the throne of a nation that collectively believes him to be a dissolute hedonist. We think it's a fair assumption that Hal is in turmoil right now.

This may account for the many references to God in this monologue. It is common to think about higher powers when a loved one is facing death. Also, Prince Hal believed his father was already dead—his living and breathing (and screaming) may seem to Hal to be a miracle wrought by God. Furthermore, Prince Hal would have believed his accession to the throne to be divinely ordained (see "Riding Shotgun with God," page 235). Finally (and most important), Prince Hal must convince his father quickly of his good intentions, before his father goes to the grave with harsh misconceptions about him. Invoking God as a witness and inviting God's wrath upon him should he be lying are powerful ways to assure the King of his earnestness.

And so this monologue is full of oaths: Prince Hal repeatedly puts himself at the mercy of the higher authority (*If I affect it more / Than as your honor and as your renown, / Let me no more from this obedience rise . . .*; *God witness with me*; *If I do feign, / O let me in my present wildness die . . .*; *But if it did infect my blood with joy . . . Let God forever keep it from my head, / And make me as the poorest vassal is / That doth with awe and terror kneel to it!*). Don't forget to look at "O, No! An *O*!" on page xxxiii for help with using the word *O* to its best advantage.

Another effective technique Hal uses in forging his argument is that of antithesis: *best of gold* versus *worst of gold*; *less fine in carat* versus *more precious*; *preserving life* versus *eat thy bearer up*. The oaths, the antithesis, the expressions of humility, and the many expressions of respect and love for his father (*your honor and as your renown*; *my most royal liege*; *dead almost to think you were* [dead]) combine to create a beautiful, heartfelt, and convincing answer that completely assuages his father's fury and soothes him in his dying moments.

Notice that Shakespeare has embedded stage directions in the monologue: (1) either Prince Hal has just stopped crying or is still crying (he says right at the beginning of the piece that his crying prevented him from speaking and explaining to his father why he took the crown); and (2) Prince Hal gets down on the ground to show his obedience to the King, his father. He is either bowing, bending onto his knees, or lying prostate on the ground. The language supports all three—perhaps he does only one of them, or perhaps he shifts from one to another. You decide what works for you.

True to form, the meter gets chockful of variations in places where Prince Hal would logically get most emotional about what he is saying. There are several double endings, which may suggest that Prince Hal is almost stammering to convince his father of his good intentions. There are also several inverted feet at beginnings of lines and after caesuras, showing where he is being emphatic—perhaps to be persuasive, or perhaps because he is blurting something out, or both. Some of these inverted feet happen when the Prince is making a proclamation of some sort, i.e., *Long guard it yours!* at the beginning of line 145. One falls on *murdered*, in line 168 (where the caesura is not marked by punctuation), giving extra force to this potent word.

In line 151, the Prince recounts the moment he first thought his father was dead. No wonder the line has a meter variation—a triple ending—to set it apart from other lines.

x / x / x / x / x / (x)(x)
And found no course of breath within your Majesty

Or you may elide *Majesty* (MAJ-stee) and make it a regular five-foot line with a double ending:

x / x / x / x / x / (x)
And found no course of breath within your Majesty

Notably, there are two rare hexameters (lines with six feet) in this one monologue. The first hexameter (line 159) has a double ending:

x / x / x / x / x / x / (x)
And thus upbraided it: "The care on thee depending

The second hexameter (line 165) has an inverted foot after the caesura:

x / x / x / / x x / x /
Hast eat thy bearer up." Thus, my most royal liege

And line 150, in which Hal jumps feet first into his explanation to his father, is important enough to get a spondee (a foot with both syllables accented) at the beginning of the line:

/ / x / x / x / x /
God witness with me, when I here came in

Don't forget to elide: *obedience* (o-BEE-dyence) in line 147; *duteous* (DYOO-tyuss) in line 148; *exterior* (ex-TEER-yur) in line 149; *medicine* (MED-sin) in line 163; and *spirit* (SPEERT) in line 172 (but not necessarily in line 148, which can be read as a double ending);

... to contract and elide: *the incredulous* (th'in-CREDJ-luss) in line 154;

... and to expand: *purposèd* (PUR´-poh-SEHD) in line 155.

FROM HELL-RAISING HAL TO HALLOWED HARRY

The historical Hal was indeed the party animal Shakespeare made him out to be. However, the real Hal's escapades and drunken carousing were most likely limited to special occasions. Most of his time was probably spent in military training, as Hal was an accomplished warrior at a very early age. He was knighted at twelve, fought with Henry Percy against Owen Glendower at fourteen, and commanded his father's forces to their victory at Shrewsbury two years later. When he succeeded his father on the throne at twenty-five, he stemmed civil war and restored a sense of national pride by devoting most of his reign to his campaign in France. His military successes, combined with his charisma, just rule, and compassionate regard for the poor, made him a hero in the eyes of his subjects and the generations of English that followed. Henry fell ill during his third invasion of France and died shortly upon returning to English soil, never having seen the infant son his wife bore him while he was abroad.

HENRY V

PROLOGUE

CHORUS

GENDER: F/M
PROSE/VERSE: blank verse
AGE RANGE: any age
FREQUENCY OF USE (1–5): 4

Shakespeare took on a daunting task in tackling the life of Henry V. Henry was a beloved national hero to the Elizabethans, and any retelling of Henry's military campaign against France would have to meet some high expectations. In the prologue, Shakespeare uses the Chorus to apologize for the inadequacy of the stage in presenting such grand events, and to urge the audience to use their imaginations to enhance the play.

O for a Muse of fire, that would ascend
The brightest heaven of invention:
A kingdom for a stage, princes to act,
And monarchs to behold the swelling scene.
5 Then should the warlike Harry, like himself,
Assume the port of Mars, and at his heels,
Leashed in like hounds, should famine, sword, and fire
Crouch for employment. But pardon, gentles all,
The flat unraisèd spirits that hath dared
10 On this unworthy scaffold to bring forth
So great an object. Can this cockpit hold
The vasty fields of France? Or may we cram
Within this wooden O the very casques
That did affright the air at Agincourt?
15 O, pardon, since a crooked figure may
Attest in little place a million,
And let us, ciphers to this great accompt,

1 *Muse* personification of inspiration (according to Greek mythology, the Muses, nine sisters, were the goddesses who inspired the arts) [*Muse of fire* inspiration as bright and soaring as fire (Elizabethans believed that fire was the most buoyant of the four elements, rising above earth, water, and air)]; *ascend* rise up to; 2 *invention* creativity, inventiveness; 3 *princes* kings, monarchs [*princes . . . scene* i.e., the kings of England and France to duke it out, and the monarchs of Europe to watch the battle]; 4 *swelling* magnificent, grand; 5 *warlike* having the qualities of a good warrior; *Harry* i.e., King Henry V [*Then should the warlike Harry* Then the warlike Harry would]; *like himself* this is a note to the Elizabethan audience: in this play Henry will be the heroic Harry you expect, not the juvenile delinquent he was in his younger days, as presented in *Henry IV, Parts One and Two*; 6 *port* bearing, stately appearance; *Mars* the Roman god of war; 7 *famine, sword, and fire* Bellona, the Roman goddess of war, had three "handmaidens" at her service: famine, blood, and fire. Shakespeare replaces "blood" with the sword that will draw the blood; 8 *Crouch for employment* hunch or squat down close to the ground, ready to be of service; *But pardon* i.e., Since there is no muse of fire, please excuse . . . ; *gentles all* all you gentlemen and gentlewomen (i.e., you audience members); 9 *flat* dull, uninteresting; *unraisèd* earthbound, not lofty; *spirits* actors (and their playwright); 10 *scaffold* platform, stage; 11 *So great an object* i.e., the history of King Henry V [*The flat . . . object* the dull, unlofty actors who have dared to bring forth such a lofty subject on such an unworthy stage]; *cockpit* a small arena used for cockfights (here, a metaphor for the performance area on the floor of a theater); 12 *vasty* vast; *may* can; 13 *wooden O* Elizabethan theaters were generally round wooden structures with covered seating around the perimeter, with the main portion of the stage at the center, in the open air—for this reason, Shakespeare's company, the Chamberlain's Men, named their theater the Globe; *the very casques* (1) the very same helmets; (2) the very same number of soldiers in helmets; (3) even the helmets; 14 *did affright the air* filled the air with terror; *Agincourt* the site, in northern France, of Henry V's most famous victory; 15 *crooked* bent, rounded [*a crooked figure* a zero]; 16 *a crooked figure . . . a million* a zero, placed in the lowest position, can change the value of 100,000 to 1,000,000; 17 *ciphers* (1) zeros; (2) decipherers; *accompt* (1) sum, account; (2) account, retelling. (Note: in Shakespeare's time *accompt*

On your imaginary forces work.
Suppose within the girdle of these walls
20 Are now confined two mighty monarchies,
Whose high uprearèd and abutting fronts
The perilous narrow ocean parts asunder.
Piece out our imperfections with your thoughts:
Into a thousand parts divide one man,
25 And make imaginary puissance.
Think, when we talk of horses, that you see them
Printing their proud hoofs i' th' receiving earth:
For 'tis your thoughts that now must deck our kings,
Carry them here and there, jumping o'er times;
30 Turning th' accomplishment of many years
Into an hour-glass. For the which supply,
Admit me Chorus to this history,
Who, prologue-like, your humble patience pray,
Gently to hear, kindly to judge, our play.

2 minutes

was pronounced "a-COWNT," but today's most common pronunciation is "a-COMPT." Either is acceptable.) [*ciphers to this great accompt* a play on words: (1) nothing compared to this great sum; and (2) decipherers of this great story]; 18 *On your imaginary forces work* affect your imaginations; 19 *Suppose* Imagine; *girdle* a belt worn around the waist; 20 *two mighty monarchies* i.e., the monarchies of King Henry V of England and King Charles VI of France; 21 *high uprearèd* highly raised; *fronts* frontiers, borders [*high uprearèd and abutting fronts* i.e., the cliffs of Dover in England and Calais in France]; 22 *narrow ocean* i.e., the English Channel [*Whose high uprearèd . . . asunder* whose borders, the high cliffs of Dover and Calais, are kept apart by the narrow, dangerous English Channel]; 23 *Piece out* Fill in, make complete; 24 *Into a thousand parts . . . man* turn each actor into a thousand; 25 *make* create (in your mind); *puissance* military power; armies, troops; 27 *Printing* making footprints with; *proud* vigorous, full of spirit; *receiving* accepting, taking into; 28 *deck* dress, adorn; 29 *jumping o'er times* skipping periods of time; 31 *hour-glass* i.e., a short period of time [*Turning . . . hour-glass* condensing events that took place over many years into a short period of time (the actual events of the play took place between 1414 and 1420)]; *For the which supply* For this function; to support this (i.e., to supply the help and information to feed your imaginations); 32 *Admit me* allow me to act as; *Chorus* interpreter or commentator to a dumb show or play (an ancient Greek dramatic convention: originally a group of singing, dancing commentators); 33 *Who* Chorus refers to herself; *prologue-like* prologues were often used in Elizabethan plays to introduce the action, to ingratiate the players to and to flatter the audience; *humble* refers to herself, not to the audience; 34 *Gently* mildly, kindly; *hear* Elizabethans went to hear, rather than to see, a play (see "Why Bother?," page xxix).

COMMENTARY

At first it may appear that playing the Chorus is completely different from playing a "normal" role, and in some ways it is. Rather than taking part in the play, the Chorus comments on it; rather than communicating mostly with the other characters and placing a "fourth wall" between herself and the audience, the Chorus communicates solely with the audience, and rarely crosses to the players' side of the "wall." In preparing to play the Chorus, however, you must do the same work you would for any other role: you must still define your objectives, and develop tactics or actions to those objectives. The only difference is that you are now using your tactics on the audience rather than on another character, and the objectives you seek to achieve are generally concerned with the audience's reception of the play, instead of the events that take place within it.

That said, these differences are an important factor in your decision whether or not to use this piece, as is the fact that this material (like most chorus pieces) is more stylized and less realistic than most nonchorus material. This piece is a good choice if you are interested in demonstrating or developing a facility with verse and with highly poetic, rhetorical language. (Or, of course, if you are auditioning for a chorus part!) On the other hand, if you are auditioning for a nonchorus role, you may want to choose a less formal piece. If you *do* choose to use this piece in an audition, make sure that you target an imaginary audience rather than the director. (For more on this, see "Now I Am Alone: A Note on Soliloquies" and "Some Advice on Auditions," page xxv.)

Shakespeare uses the Chorus to build up the audience's anticipation. Because the audience is already so eager to witness the well-known feats of the beloved hero, the Chorus can tease it with tantalizing tidbits. Shakespeare has provided some excellent devices to support your attempts to engage the audience. Most notably, the piece is jam-packed with imagery so dramatic and exciting it's almost impossible for the audience members to resist bringing the imagery to life in their imaginations. The two major themes that the Chorus attempts, through imagery, to meld into a grand spectacle for the audience are theatre and war. Notice the way she interweaves the two themes throughout the piece. Notice also that her references to the theatre are always derogatory: she calls it an *unworthy scaffold*, a *cockpit*, and a *wooden O*; she calls the players zeros and speaks of their imperfections. What is the reason for all this self-deprecation? As an actor, you face an important choice here—is the Chorus sincerely apologizing for the players' inadequacy? Is she trying to lower the audience's expectations so that the play will be sure to surpass them? Is she being politely humble, all the while brimming over with pride? Is she being smug, because she is confident that the play will sweep the audience off its collective feet? Or maybe she's putting down the theatre in order to build up the glory of Henry himself in comparison?

The Chorus uses metaphor to create resounding images. For instance, creative inspiration takes the form of the bright, intense, and buoyant element of fire, and inventiveness becomes a heaven. *Warlike Harry* is painted as the god of war, with the tools of war—famine, sword, and fire—leashed at his feet, waiting to spring on his enemy. The *fronts*, or high cliffs of Dover and Calais, *abutting* at the English Channel are a powerful metaphor for the military fronts of the two countries, which will soon be "abutting" (i.e., coming up against each other) in battle. The Chorus puts these metaphors to work, persuasively contrasting the great spectacle of a Muse of fire with the inadequacies of the wooden O in the first two sections, and also making individual contrasts within that structure (*Muse of fire, that would ascend* with *flat unraisèd spirits*; *unworthy scaffold* with *So great an object*; *cockpit* with *vasty fields*).

The way you, as the Chorus, use these metaphors will depend partly on what you think about the issues they represent: is the Chorus full of nationalistic fervor, responding to the heroism of Henry? Or does she think that it's all pointless bloodshed, and react with irony and sarcasm? Or is she ambivalent? Or resigned . . . ? Don't assume that the Chorus has no character traits or opinions of her own. Deciding whether to approach the role from the mind-set of an Elizabethan or from a modern-day perspective will influence your choices.

Whatever her feelings about the topic at hand, and to whatever degree she imparts them to the audience, as a diplomat of sorts between audience and play, the Chorus certainly knows her job, and she fulfills it. She is unfailingly polite with the audience, using the formal *you*, calling them *gentles*, begging their pardon twice, and humbly praying for their patience and kindness at the end. Her last line plays on *Gently* and *kindly*, subtly reminding audience members that they are "kind gentlemen" and "kind gentlewomen" (as they would often be addressed in Elizabethan times), and while the actors are up on stage working they should behave as such (which, in Elizabethan times, they didn't).

The Chorus's politeness is part of her stylized and formal manner, which is also evident in the unusual number of words that must be expanded to fit the meter (see below). Also notice that throughout the piece Shakespeare makes frequent use of complicated and unusual grammatical structures, making the material much less realistic than regular characters' speeches, and that he wraps up with a formal rhyming couplet (*pray / play*). (The two preceding lines were also a rhyming couplet in Shakespeare's day, with the historic rhyme of *supply / history*, but we suggest you don't rhyme them, since the rhyme adds humor when humor isn't intended.)

Some other poetic devices to note and make use of: groups of sound repetition are scattered throughout, most of which pinpoint important words or phrases (*ascend / heaven / invention*; *swelling scene*; *fields of France*; *affright / air / Agincourt*; *mighty monarchies*; *man / make / imaginary*; *Printing / proud*. Notice the chain of phrases directing the audience members to use their minds (*imaginary forces work*; *Piece out our imperfections with your thoughts*; *make imaginary*; *Think*; *'tis your thoughts*), with which you can connect one tactic to the next. There is also the extended play on *O*: the theater is the *wooden O*; the actors are compared to *ciphers* (crooked figures, zeros) and amount to little in comparison to the great sum of the *account* of history. The other possible meaning, though, is more respectful: actors are the decipherers of this great account, or history. You may choose to focus on the first meaning (the Chorus is humbled by the greatness of Harry), the second (the Chorus is proud to be an actor relaying this great tale), or *both* (perhaps the Chorus feigns humility, while cleverly conveying her real feelings . . .). On top of all this, the many *O*s spoken in the piece provide another layer of meaning and sound to play with. Speaking of *O*s, if you decide that the Chorus is the tongue-in-cheek type, you may wish to play with the sexual double entendre of *O*, which in Shakespeare's time was a euphemism for "vagina." The Chorus is suggesting that the audience has entered the "O" for pleasure, which they can achieve if they put their fantasies to work. For more on O, be sure to see "O, No! An *O*!" on page xxxiii.

Don't forget to elide: *fire* (FYR) in line 1; *perilous* (PEHR-lus) in line 22; *o'er* (ore) in line 29; *hour-glass* (OWR-glass) in line 31;

. . . to contract: i' th' (ITH) in line 27; *th' accomplishment* (thuh-COM′-plish-MENT) in line 30;

. . . and to expand: *invention* (in-VEN′-shee-UN) in line 2; *unraisèd* (un-RAY-zehd) in line 9; *million* (MIL′-ee-UN) in line 16; *uprearèd* (up-REER-ehd) in line 21; and *puissance* (PWEE′-ih-SANCE) in line 25.

The Ruin of Rouen

According to Shakespeare's main source for *Henry V*, Holinshed's *Chronicles of England, Scotland, and Ireland*, Henry told the people of Rouen, France, that Bellona (the Roman goddess of war) had three "handmaidens" at her service, famine, blood, and fire, and that he was using the mildest of these—famine—in besieging them (nice of him, wasn't it?). Shakespeare's Chorus alludes to these three as the dogs that are leashed in at Henry's heels, waiting to do him service. Rouen was the final stronghold Henry conquered in France before Charles VI handed over the crown. Although in *Henry V* Shakespeare glosses over Henry's entire second campaign in France (fast-forwarding to the treaty and Henry's betrothal to Katherine), the fall of Rouen was a big deal, and Shakespeare's audience would have been quite familiar with the allusion, which the Chorus uses as another way to build up Henry's heroism.

HENRY V

ACT I, SCENE ii

KING HENRY V

GENDER: M
AGE RANGE: adult
PROSE/VERSE: blank verse
FREQUENCY OF USE (1–5): 5

The two previous plays in the tetralogy (*Henry IV, Parts One* and *Two*) told the story of Prince Hal's transformation from degenerate youth (slumming with a bunch of commoners) to hero (fighting valiantly against rebels in northern England). After Henry IV's death at the end of *Part Two*, Prince Hal became King Henry V, and renounced his old ways. At the start of *Henry V* he has been the King only a very short while. He holds a formal gathering at court, to ascertain whether the French throne is his by right, which the Bishop of Canterbury affirms. Just as Henry resolves to take what is rightfully his, the French Ambassador arrives, with a "gift" from Lewis the Dauphin (heir to the French throne). The gift is a chest full of tennis balls. Henry responds to the insult:

We are glad the Dauphin is so pleasant with us.
260 His present and your pains we thank you for:
When we have matched our rackets with these balls,
We will in France, by God's grace, play a set
Shall strike his father's crown into the hazard.
Tell him he hath made a match with such a wrangler
265 That all the courts of France will be disturbed
With chases. And we understand him well,
How he comes o'er us with our wilder days,
Not measuring what use we made of them.
We never valued this poor seat of England,
270 And therefore living hence, did give ourself
To barbarous license, as 'tis ever common
That men are merriest when they are from home.
But tell the Dauphin I will keep my state,
Be like a king, and show my sail of greatness
275 When I do rouse me in my throne of France.
For that I have laid by my majesty
And plodded like a man for working-days:

259 *We* Henry refers to himself with the royal "we"; *pleasant* merry, facetious; 261 *matched* (1) matched up, paired; and (2) met in combat; 263 *Shall* that shall; *his father's* i.e., France's King Charles VI's; *hazard* (1) hole in the wall of a royal tennis court, having a similar function to a goal, in that points were scored when a ball was driven into it; and (2) danger, jeopardy; 264 *hath made a match* has arranged to play a tennis match; *wrangler* contentious opponent; 265 *courts* (1) tennis courts (royal tennis was played in a walled court); and (2) royal courts; 266 *chases* (1) in tennis, the second bounce of the ball on one side of the court, which results in points for the opponent (as a metaphor for the cannonballs that will rain down on France); and (2) hunts (as a metaphor for the English military pursuit of the French); 267 *comes o'er us with* three possible meanings: (1) reminds me of; (2) puts me down by mentioning; (3) taunts me with; *wilder days* refers to Henry's days as Prince Hal, juvenile delinquent (see *Henry IV, Parts One* and *Two*, pages 906 and 908); 268 *measuring* considering; *use we made of* advantage or profit we gained from; 269 *poor* worthy of pity (because of having been neglected); *seat* (1) throne; (2) place of residence; (3) land held as property (i.e., England); 270 *hence* away from (i.e., away from court and the throne); *did give ourself* gave myself over to; 271 *license* unrestrained lawlessness and immorality; 272 *merriest* both (1) most fun-loving and (2) most self-indulgent; *from* away from; 273 *keep my state* (1) behave with the pomp and dignity appropriate to my kingship; and (2) guard and attend to my throne (with play on *state* to mean "country"); 274 *sail* (1) that which powers a ship; and/or (2) fleet of ships [*show my sail of greatness* i.e., display my full power]; 275 *do rouse me in* raise myself up on; elevate myself to; 276 *For that* i.e., in order to attain the throne of France; *laid by* put aside; *majesty* royal status; 277 *man for working-days* a man made for working days, i.e., a common working man [*laid by . . . working-days* another reference to Henry's youth, spent in the company of commoners];

But I will rise there with so full a glory
That I will dazzle all the eyes of France,
280 Yea, strike the Dauphin blind to look on us.
And tell the pleasant prince this mock of his
Hath turned his balls to gun-stones, and his soul
Shall stand sore-chargèd for the wasteful vengeance
That shall fly with them; for many a thousand widows
285 Shall this his mock mock out of their dear husbands,
Mock mothers from their sons, mock castles down;
And some are yet ungotten and unborn
That shall have cause to curse the Dauphin's scorn.
But this lies all within the will of God,
290 To whom I do appeal, and in whose name,
Tell you the Dauphin, I am coming on
To venge me as I may, and to put forth
My rightful hand in a well-hallowed cause.
So get you hence in peace. And tell the Dauphin
295 His jest will savor but of shallow wit,
When thousands weep more than did laugh at it.
Convey them with safe conduct. Fare you well.

2 minutes, 20 seconds

278 *rise* like the sun, a symbol Shakespeare frequently used to evoke royal majesty; *there* i.e., in France; 280 *Yea* indeed; *strike the Dauphin blind* cause the Dauphin to go blind (with a play on *strike* as in "deliver a blow," or "attack militarily"); *to look on us* just by looking at me; 282 *gun-stones* cannonballs (which were originally made of stone); 283 *Shall stand sore-chargèd* will be heavily burdened; *wasteful* ruinous, destructive; 284 *for many a thousand . . . dear husbands* for this tennis-ball gag of his shall "mock" many thousands of widows out of their dear husbands (by causing them to die in battle); 287 *yet ungotten* not yet begotten (i.e., not even conceived yet); 289 *this lies all within* (1) all of this is subject to; or (2) this is entirely subject to; 291 *Tell you* tell; *coming on* advancing, approaching; 292 *venge me as I may* avenge myself as well as I am able; 293 *rightful* lawful, legitimate; *well-hallowed* thoroughly sanctified and holy (the French throne is Henry's divine right—see "Riding Shotgun with God," page 235); 294 *get you hence* get on your way; 295 *savor* give off a smell; give the impression; *but* only; *shallow* (1) not deep, having a small amount; and (2) silly, stupid; *wit* (1) mental capacity: intellect, understanding, judgment, imagination; and therefore: (2) sense of humor [*savor but of shallow wit* (1) give the impression of a limited mental capacity; and therefore: (2) give the impression of a silly, stupid sense of humor]; 297 *Convey them* Lead them away (refers to the French Ambassador and his party); *safe conduct* an escort or guard (to guarantee their safety).

COMMENTARY

That little smart aleck of a Dauphin thinks that just because Henry has spent his youth goofing off with his buddies, he hasn't got the know-how or the you-know-whats to take the offensive in anything more serious than tennis. Well, Mr. Dauphin, you've got another think coming. Your little insult is about to backfire—literally.

Background is extremely important to this piece. First, there is Henry's family history, of which he is acutely aware: since Henry's father, King Henry IV, usurped the throne, Henry believes that God is pretty miffed (see "Riding Shotgun with God," page 235), and only by righting his father's wrong can he hope to stop God's punishment—the civil wars that plagued England throughout his father's reign. Henry's claim to the French throne, however, is quite valid (see "Genealogy of French Monarchs . . . ," page 232). Henry is thus convinced that if he fulfills his divine right by taking France, God will forgive him for the sins of his father and let him reign happily ever after over the two countries. It may sound ludicrous to us, but it made perfect sense to the English in Henry's time as well as in Shakespeare's. It's necessary to enter that mind-set to understand Henry.

Second, consider the more immediate circumstances. Henry is in court, surrounded by all of his advisers, where he is not only a new and untried monarch, but also one with a spotty reputation. The moves he makes here are critical in asserting his power over the high-ranking officials and the Church, and in gaining their support and respect. Henry has already resolved to go to war by the time the Ambassador arrives, and his decision was not rash, but carefully considered. In replying to the Dauphin's jest, there are many pressures to consider: the impression he makes on the Ambassador will be carried back to the French, and may affect their view of him; the impression he makes on his own officials and advisers is equally important, especially if they are going to war. Furthermore, given recent history, Henry may wish to assert his power as a king in order to nip in the bud any possibility of a coup.

In light of all this, it comes as no surprise to see the remarkable care with which Henry's reply is constructed. It is extremely revealing to note that he is able to pull off such a calculated and effective response, completely impromptu. How does he do it?

First, he asserts his own superiority. He makes ample use of the royal "we," repeating the words *we*, *us*, and *our* a dozen times in the first half of the piece. At the same time, Henry deflates the Dauphin's insulting prank by speaking as though he were amused, communicating that he is not troubled by his old reputation, and not the least bit threatened by the Dauphin's piddling pranks (notice the Pooh-Poohing Ps: *pleasant / present / pains*). Henry is sardonically polite, thanking the Ambassador for the balls, and—under the pretense of accepting an invitation to play a tennis match—he coldly and casually proposes his invasion of France in an extended tennis metaphor. Take note of the small sound groupings that enhance the pointed formality of his sarcasm (*have / matched / rackets*; *set / shall / strike*; *made / match*).

This monologue progresses through five sections, the divisions being clearly delineated. In the first transition, Henry drops the tennis metaphor mid-line, and begins a completely new idea with the chilling phrase *And we understand him well*. This abrupt change signals a change in tactic. Henry has dropped the sardonic humor and moved on to serious business, revealing to the Ambassador that he can see past the Dauphin's jest. In this second section, Henry makes a general antithetical comparison between the way he was as Prince Hal and the way he will be as King Henry. This comparison is supported by smaller-scale antitheses (*never valued this poor seat of England* versus *I will keep my state*; *plodded* versus *will rise*; *dazzle all the eyes of France* versus *strike the Dauphin blind*). Henry intentionally evokes his own sordid past, since the image of his new, re-created self is all the more powerful in contrast to his former self. Henry repeats his intention to prove his power and worth three times in a row, and concludes with the metaphor of the immeasurably powerful sun, which can *dazzle* as well as *blind*. Henry places the *eyes of France* under his mercilessly bright glare, using synecdoche to turn the French from men into mere receptors of his intensity and might. With this manipulative speech, Henry is already doing what the speech promises—displaying his strength. To that end, notice that an important change takes place within this second section: having asserted his sovereignty by stressing the royal "we" earlier, he now asserts his personal power by switching to "I."

Again, we come to a clear change in direction: after a full stop, the third section starts with *And tell the pleasant prince*. By now a pattern has started to emerge. As soon as Henry completes one tactic, he hits the Ambassador with another before the man can reply or take his leave. Henry apparently can't resist revisiting the tennis-ball joke, and here is where he gets across his most potent message for the Dauphin, returning the Dauphin's derisive jest, but with a more violent purpose. Here, *mock* is a euphemism for the carnage and destruction that the Dauphin has unleashed on his own country with his careless jest. Henry highlights his important points with alliteration: the foolishness of the Dauphin (*pleasant / prince*); the burden on his soul (*soul / stand / sore*); the fact that he will be cursed (*cause / curse*). A memorable rhyming couplet (*unborn / scorn*) underscores Henry's most salient point at the end of the section. Finally, Henry seizes the opportunity to turn the Dauphin's jest back on him, calling the Dauphin's virility into direct question—the *balls* he thought he showed in making the jest are exposed as rash bravado, which provokes the *gun-stones* that will punish him and his people. Henry further attacks the Dauphin's manhood with the common Elizabethan double entendre of *shallow wit* (small genitals). Although Henry's wrath is crystal clear in his sarcasm and in the harshness of his threats, he never loses his cool! The meter remains quite regular, even when he is at his most cutting.

Henry transitions to the fourth section with *But this lies all within the will of God*. Here, he puts forth in a simple, straightforward manner the fact that divine right is the true motivation for the destruction he plans. His synecdoche (*put forth / My rightful hand*) and casual language (*venge me as I may*) have the effect of downplaying his statement, perhaps to imply that divine right leaves no room for argument. Or perhaps he is being purposely casual in order to have a more menacing effect. Maybe he is being straightforward to make sure the message doesn't get garbled in transit to the Dauphin. But make no mistake—in the end, he punches the message: the inverted foot combined with the strong consonant (T) in *Tell you the Dauphin* is a strong contrast to the soft sounds of this section.

Henry concludes with a combination of the rhetorical tactics he has used throughout the piece. While being meticulously polite, seeing to the Ambassador's safety and wishing him a proper farewell, he makes sure to get in a final, memorable rhyming couplet (*shallow wit / laugh at it*) that sums up his response to the Dauphin's little jest.

SIGNIFICANT SCANS

Here are two scansion options for line 284, both of which require the contraction of *many a* (MEN-ya). (Also note the double ending at the end of the line in both cases.)

(1) You may treat *That shall fly* as a crowded foot:

x - x / x / x / x / x / (x)
That shall fly with them; for many a thousand widows

(2) You may treat *them* as a double ending before the caesura:

x / x / (x) x / x / x / (x)
That shall fly with them; for many a thousand widows

There are an unusual number of contractions in this piece, which contribute to Henry's off-the-cuff manner and menacing faux jocularity: *We are* (We're) in line 259; *he hath* (hyath) in line 264; and *many a* (MEN-ya) in line 284.

Finally, don't forget to elide: *pleasant* (PLESNT) in line 259 (but *not* in line 281); *barbarous* (BAR-brus) in line 271; and *merriest* (MER-yest) in line 272.

P.S.

For information on the historical Henry V, see "From Hell-Raising Hal to Hallowed Harry," page 115.

HENRY V

ACT IV, SCENE iii

KING HENRY V

GENDER: M
PROSE/VERSE: blank verse
AGE RANGE: adult
FREQUENCY OF USE (1–5): 4

King Henry V of England's rightful claim to the French throne has recently been confirmed (to understand the basis of his claim, see "Genealogy of French Monarchs . . . ," page 232), and he has launched a campaign to claim *le trône*. The French city of Harfleur has already surrendered, and the opposing English and French armies have now gathered at the battlefield outside the town of Agincourt. The English are weary, sick, and hungry from travel . . . and outnumbered by the French three to one. It is minutes before the battle and the English troops are assembled to fight. As King Henry arrives, the Earl of Westmoreland wishes aloud that even one ten-thousandth of the men still back in England were here in France to fight. King Henry replies:

What's he that wishes so?
My cousin Westmoreland? No, my fair cousin.
20 If we are marked to die, we are enough
To do our country loss; and if to live,
The fewer men, the greater share of honor.
God's will, I pray thee wish not one man more.
By Jove, I am not covetous for gold,
25 Nor care I who doth feed upon my cost;
It yearns me not if men my garments wear—
Such outward things dwell not in my desires.
But if it be a sin to covet honor
I am the most offending soul alive.
30 No, 'faith, my coz, wish not a man from England.
God's peace, I would not lose so great an honor
As one man more, methinks, would share from me
For the best hope I have. O do not wish one more!
Rather proclaim it, Westmoreland, through my host,
35 That he which hath no stomach to this fight,
Let him depart—His passport shall be made
And crowns for convoy put into his purse.
We would not die in that man's company
That fears his fellowship to die with us.

18 *What's he* Who is it; *that* who; 19 *Westmoreland* Ralph Neville, Earl of Westmoreland, Henry's cousin by marriage; *fair* good; 20 *marked* designated, specifically chosen, i.e., by God; *we are enough / To do our country loss* both (1) we are a large enough group of soldiers to be a loss to our country and (2) we are valuable enough to be a loss to our country; 22 *honor* in Shakespeare's time, specifically a reputation of military bravery and success; 23 *God's will* By God's will; *pray* ask of, entreat; 24 *By Jove* By God (although Jove is the supreme god of the Romans, Elizabethans often substituted his name for the word *God*); 25 *doth feed* eats; *upon my cost* at my expense; 26 *yearns me not* doesn't bother me; 27 *outward* exterior, surface; *dwell not in my desires* I do not desire; 29 *the most offending soul alive* the biggest sinner alive; 30 *'faith* in faith, i.e., in truth, truthfully; *coz* cousin, kinsman (a term of familiarity); *wish not a man from England* do not wish we had even one more English soldier; 31 *God's peace* By the order in the universe created by God; *so great an* even as much; 32 *would share from me* would take from me by taking his proportionate share (of the honor and glory of fighting); 33 *For* in exchange for; *the best hope I have* i.e., my hope of salvation; 34 *through my host* throughout my army; 35 *hath no stomach* i.e., doesn't have the guts; *to this fight* to fight in this battle; 36 *passport* written permission to travel (in Shakespeare's time, written permission was required to travel anywhere, even between towns within England); 37 *crowns* coins, money; *convoy* means of transportation; 38 *We* both (1) the royal "we" and (2) we who will be fighting together today; *fellowship* equality of fortune, companionship in adversity [*That fears his fellowship to die with us* who is afraid to

40 This day is called the feast of Crispian.
He that outlives this day and comes safe home
Will stand a-tiptoe when this day is named
And rouse him at the name of Crispian.
He that shall see this day and live old age
45 Will yearly on the vigil feast his neighbors
And say "Tomorrow is Saint Crispian."
Then will he strip his sleeve and show his scars,
And say "These wounds I had on Crispin's day."
Old men forget; yet all shall be forgot,
50 But he'll remember—with advantages—
What feats he did that day. Then shall our names,
Familiar in his mouth as household words—
Harry the King, Bedford and Exeter,
Warwick and Talbot, Salisbury and Gloucester—
55 Be in their flowing cups freshly remembered.
This story shall the good man teach his son,
And Crispin Crispian shall ne'er go by
From this day to the ending of the world
But we in it shall be rememberèd:
60 We few, we happy few, we band of brothers—
For he today that sheds his blood with me
Shall be my brother; be he ne'er so vile,

cast his lot in with ours and possibly die with us]; 40 *feast of Crispian* (CRIS´-pee-AN) October 25, the feast day of the martyred Roman brothers Crispinus and Crispianus, who became the patron saints of shoemakers; 42 *stand a-tiptoe* i.e., stand tall, feel exalted; *named* mentioned; 43 *rouse him* raise himself to his full height, straighten himself up with pride; 44 *see this day* experience this day (i.e., fight in today's battle); *and live old age* and live to old age; 45 *on the vigil* i.e., on the evening before the feast of St. Crispian; *feast his neighbors* entertain his neighbors, treat his neighbors to a feast; 48 *These wounds I had* I received these wounds; 49 *yet* i.e., by that time; 50 *advantages* embellishments; 53 *Harry* one of King Henry's nicknames; *Bedford* King Henry's younger brother, Prince John Plantagenet of Lancaster, Duke of Bedford; *Exeter* King Henry's uncle, Thomas Beaufort, Duke of Exeter, illegitimate brother of King Henry IV, military commander under both kings; 54 *Warwick* (WAR-ick) Richard Beauchamp, Earl of Warwick; *Talbot* Lord John Talbot; *Salisbury* (SAWLZ´-bur-REE) Thomas Montague, Earl of Salisbury, diplomat, administrator, and general; *Gloucester* (GLAW-ster) King Henry's youngest brother, Prince Humphrey, Duke of Gloucester; 55 *Be in their flowing cups freshly remembered* be toasted anew; 56 *the good man* i.e., the good veteran of today's battle; 57 *Crispin Crispian* i.e., the feast of St. Crispian; 59 *But we in it shall be rememberèd* without those of us who fought here today being remembered; 62 *be he ne'er so vile* no

This day shall gentle his condition;
And gentlemen in England now abed
65 Shall think themselves accursed they were not here,
And hold their manhoods cheap whiles any speaks
That fought with us upon Saint Crispin's day.

3 minutes

matter how lowborn he may be; 63 *This day shall gentle his condition* i.e., fighting on this day shall make him into a gentleman; 64 *now abed* in their beds right now; 65 *Shall think themselves accursed they were not here* will consider themselves cursed for not being here; 66 *hold their manhoods cheap* not consider their manhoods worth much (i.e., consider themselves weak and womanish); *whiles any* whenever anyone.

COMMENTARY

Like the high school principal scheduling the mandatory-attendance pep rally before the Big Game, the medieval European commander in times of war was expected to deliver a go-get-'em speech to his troops, to inspire them to go into battle and get their limbs hacked off. No one does this better than King Henry V does in this most famous of rallying speeches.

We'll never know what (if anything) King Henry might have prepared in advance to say to his men, since instead he seizes the opportunity presented by Westmoreland's grumbling and proceeds to build upon it brilliantly. Although he delivers the speech extempore—and quite passionately—Henry cleverly constructs each component of the speech to motivate his listeners as persuasively as the most effective evangelist. (And don't worry that the first line's reference is not immediately clear out of context—all is explained in the five lines that follow, and the speech moves forward quite clearly from there.)

Remember that although the King seems at first to be answering Westmoreland alone, he is really publicly addressing all the troops from the moment he utters his first word. He quickly establishes a friendly, accessible tone by demonstrating that he understands Westmoreland's gripe (whereas other kings may have considered the Earl's plaintive comment seditious)—and further extends generosity (both of spirit and means) toward any soldier who might wish to back out of the fight. But Henry also makes it clear right up front that he himself intends to stay, putting his own neck on the line, doing every bit as much as he asks of his soldiers. This, of course, makes it a little bit difficult for anyone to take him up on his offer to pay their way home.

The King knows full well that he has only these few moments before battle in which to convince his men that it's not suicidal to engage the larger French army. Although he starts out by saying that he would not want to die in the company of one who is afraid to die with him, he deftly—and immediately—changes the subject, replacing the mental picture of dead English soldiers with that of one English soldier who survives the battle and lives to a comfortable old age, an image each listening soldier would happily embrace.

Henry encourages his soldiers' dreams of honor and glory, appealing to nobles and peasants alike: by naming the nobles individually, he makes each one feel important, and personally accountable for the English army's success. He appeals to the peasants by calling them his brothers (and who wouldn't want to be brother to the heroic young King?), and by suggesting that fighting in the day's battle will make gentlemen of them (how many of them never fantasized about that?). Henry's language builds and reinforces the camaraderie between himself and the troops. Notice the repetition of *we* (*We few, we happy few, we band of brothers*). With each repetition of the word, Henry increases the payoff for his soldiers incrementally, from good (we're a team) to better (we're a lucky, winning team) to best (we're not just teammates, but brothers). And by calling himself *Harry the King*, King Henry subtly encourages the idea that he is no loftier than the men he addresses—in fact, they are each familiar enough with him to call him Harry.

King Henry bolsters the soldiers' confidence by promoting glorious fantasies of the future. Who wouldn't want to be a hero among his community, not just upon his victorious return home, but *annually*?: *He that shall see this day and live old age / Will yearly on the vigil feast his neighbors / And say "Tomorrow is Saint Crispian." / Then will he strip his sleeve and show his scars, / And say "These wounds I had on Crispin's day."* And who wouldn't want to be immortalized?—*Crispin Crispian shall ne'er go by / From this day to the ending of the world / But we in it shall be rememberèd*. The King further fuels his soldiers' motivation by conferring upon all who stay and fight the official title of "More Macho Than" (*gentlemen in England now abed / Shall think themselves accursed they were not here / And hold their manhoods cheap whiles any speaks / That fought with us upon Saint Crispin's day.*). Even the horses must be chomping at their bits to get into the fray by now.

By mentioning repeatedly that the battle falls on St. Crispin's Day, King Henry names the battle, giving it historical moment before it even occurs. Furthermore, since Crispinus and Crispianus were beatified shoemakers, Henry implies that commoners who fight on their day may attain similar heights of glory. King Henry concludes his stirring speech with one final mention of St. Crispin's Day, which serves to remind us that this is, above all, a saint's day—a holy day, a day to do God's work. Henry thus subtly links the battle at hand to all those of biblical lore in which the righteous few defeated the heathen mighty . . . because they had God as their secret weapon. Who among the soldiers could possibly break ranks now? It would be more than cowardly, more than unheroic, more than unbrotherly, more than unmasculine, it would be downright *sacrilegious*.

Notice how Henry heightens the effectiveness of his arguments through antithesis: *If we are marked to die . . .* versus *and if to live . . .*; *The fewer men* versus *the greater share of honor*; *I am not covetous for gold* versus *I do commit the sin of coveting honor*; *Old men forget* versus *But he'll remember*; *be he ne'er so vile* versus *This day shall gentle his condition*.

SIGNIFICANT SCANS

The first line has only three feet of spoken text, because it is the second half of a line he shares with Westmoreland, but since you are preparing this monologue outside of the scene, you can use the extra silent feet, if you like: maybe King Henry would pause to seek an answer to the question he poses in his first line, or maybe he needs time to decide how to respond publicly to Westmoreland's very legitimate concern without letting its demoralizing nature infect the troops right before battle.

You'll notice that there are many lines with double endings at first, and far fewer later on in the monologue. Perhaps the King is trying to cram a lot of inspiration into his words at first, before his listeners all defect, and lightens up when he realizes his audience is responding well. Or perhaps he is nervous at first, gaining confidence as he goes. Or perhaps at first he is stalling for time while he thinks up the next thing he is going to say.

Line 33 is one of those rare hexameters (six-footed lines). This one has an inverted beginning and extra accent on *O* (be sure to see "O, No! An *O*!," page xxxiii):

/ x x / x / / / x / x /
For the best hope I have. O do not wish one more!

The line can also be read as pentameter, by contracting *the best* (TH'BEST) and crowding *hope I have*:

x / x - x / / / x / x /
For the best hope I have. O do not wish one more!

Notice that *O do not wish one more!* starts in the middle of the line, which enhances the feeling that the sentence is an interjection, blurted out.

Similarly, notice that line 55 contains an inverted foot in the middle of the line (FRESH-ly), after a caesura that is not marked by punctuation (also note the double ending):

x / x / x / / x x / (x)
Be in their flowing cups freshly remembered

Don't forget to contract: *proclaim it* (pro-CLAIMT) in line 34;
. . . and to expand: *condition* (con-DISH ′-ee-YUN) in line 63.

Medieval Maccabees

It is historical fact that King Henry and his meager forces did battle the French at Agincourt on St. Crispin's Day, October 25, 1415. Although Henry's ragged, exhausted, and starving troops were outnumbered by the well-fed and well-rested French by approximately three to one (Shakespeare exaggerated), they defeated them soundly. The English owed their victory to the latest in technological advances, the longbow, against which the obsolete medieval methods of warfare of the French were doomed to fail.

Agincourt was a great victory for the English, but not the one by which they ultimately conquered France. There was more bloodshed and mayhem to come before King Henry could ultimately settle down with Catherine of Valois to rule over both England and France (see "The Ruin of Rouen," page 121).

P.S.

For information on the historical Henry V, see "From Hell-Raising Hal to Hallowed Harry," page 115.

HENRY V

ACT V, SCENE ii

KING HENRY V

GENDER: M | AGE RANGE: adult

PROSE/VERSE: mostly prose | FREQUENCY OF USE (1–5): 3

After long, hard years of fighting, Henry V of England has finally prevailed in France. He has presented his terms to King Charles the VI, and all that remains is the formality of signing the treaty. One thing, however, must still be settled: Henry would like to marry King Charles's daughter, Katherine of Valois, which would cement his right and the right of his heirs to rule France (not to mention, she's beautiful). While King Charles looks over the treaty before relinquishing his crown, Henry has a few minutes to win the love of Katherine—who, by the way, speaks almost no English.

Fair Katherine, and most fair,
Will you vouchsafe to teach a soldier terms
100 Such as will enter at a lady's ear
And plead his love-suit to her gentle heart?

125 I' faith, Kate, my wooing is fit for thy understanding; I am glad thou canst speak no better English, for if thou couldst, thou wouldst find me such a plain king that thou wouldst think I had sold my farm to buy my crown. I know no ways to
130 mince it in love but directly to say, "I love you." Then, if you urge me farther than to say, "Do you in faith?" I wear out my suit. Give me your answer, i' faith do, and so clap hands and a bargain. How say you, lady? Marry, if you would put me to verses
135 or to dance for your sake, Kate, why, you undid me: for the one, I have neither words nor measure; and for the other, I have no strength in measure, yet a reasonable measure in strength. If I could win a lady at leapfrog, or by vaulting into my saddle
140 with my armor on my back, under the correction of

98 *Fair* Beautiful; good, accomplished; 99 *vouchsafe* condescend; *soldier* refers to himself; 100 *enter at* enter; 101 *love-suit* courtship; petition of love; *gentle* (1) soft, tender; (2) kind; (3) of noble descent; 125 *I' faith* In good faith, in truth; 130 *mince* speak or act with affectation [*mince it in love* speak flowery love talk]; 132 *wear out my suit* exhaust my strategies for courting you; 133 *clap hands* shake hands [*clap hands and a bargain* i.e., let's shake on it]; *How say you* What do you say; 134 *Marry* Indeed (an interjection derived from "by the Virgin Mary"); *put me to verses or to dance* make me recite verses or dance; 135 *for your sake* in order to win your love; *you undid me* you would undo me; you would ruin me (i.e., you would ruin my attempts at courting you); 136 *one* i.e., reciting verses; *neither words nor measure* neither poetic ability nor a sense of meter or poetic rhythm; 137 *other* i.e., dancing; *measure* a slow stately dance [*strength in measure* talent for dancing a measure]; 138 *measure in strength* amount of physical strength; 139 *at* in the game of; *vaulting into my saddle with my armor on my back* leaping onto my horse wearing all my armor (a full set of armor was very heavy; this would be a feat of great strength); 140 *under the correction . . . be it spoken* although my saying so may be reproached as

bragging be it spoken, I should quickly leap into a
wife; or if I might buffet for my love, or bound my
horse for her favors, I could lay on like a butcher
and sit like a jackanapes, never off. But before God,
145 Kate, I cannot look greenly, nor gasp out my eloquence, nor I have no cunning in protestation;
only downright oaths which I never use till urged,
nor never break for urging. If thou canst love a fellow of this temper, Kate, whose face is not worth
150 sunburning, that never looks in his glass for love of
anything he sees there, let thine eye be thy cook. I
speak to thee plain soldier. If thou canst love me for
this, take me; if not, to say to thee that I shall die is
true—but for thy love, by the Lord, no. Yet I love
155 thee too. And while thou liv'st, dear Kate, take a
fellow of plain and uncoined constancy, for he perforce must do thee right, because he hath not the
gift to woo in other places; for these fellows of infinite tongue that can rhyme themselves into ladies'
160 favors, they do always reason themselves out again.

bragging (i.e., if you will excuse me for saying so); 141 *should* would; 142 *might* could; *buffet* box, fight with the fists; *bound my horse* make my horse leap; 143 *favors* affection, kind regards; *lay on* strike hard blows; 144 *sit* sit on my horse; *jackanapes* trained ape or monkey (monkeys trained to ride horseback were a common feature in the entertainment at Elizabethan fairs); *never off* never falling off; 145 *look greenly* gaze at you like an immature and lovesick youth; 146 *nor I have no* Shakespeare often used the double negative for emphasis; *cunning in protestation* skill in making solemn vows of love; 147 *downright* blunt, undisguised; *never use till urged* i.e., never use lightly; never use until it is required of me; 148 *for urging* however much I am urged to do so; 149 *temper* temperament, disposition; *face is not worth sunburning* i.e., sunburning can't make it uglier because it is already so ugly (in Shakespeare's time a pale complexion was considered beautiful); 150 *that* who; *glass* looking-glass, mirror; 151 *be thy cook* i.e., dress the dish to your own liking (proverbial); 152 *plain soldier* plainly, like a soldier; 155 *while thou liv'st* a common Elizabethan expression used when giving advice; 156 *uncoined* Referring to metal be-fore it has been minted. Thus, two possible meanings: (1) in its natural state, i.e., innocent, un-practiced in love; or (2) not good as currency, unfit for circulation, i.e., unfit to woo other women; *constancy* faithfulness; *perforce* necessarily; 158 *in other places* i.e., other women; *infinite*

What! A speaker is but a prater; a rhyme is but a
ballad. A good leg will fall, a straight back will
stoop, a black beard will turn white, a curled pate
will grow bald, a fair face will wither, a full eye will
165 wax hollow; but a good heart, Kate, is the sun and
the moon—or rather, the sun and not the moon,
for it shines bright and never changes but keeps his
course truly. If thou would have such a one, take
me; and take me, take a soldier; take a soldier, take
170 a king. And what say'st thou then to my love?
Speak, my fair, and fairly, I pray thee.

3 minutes

tongue boundless speaking ability; 161 *What!* i.e., after all, when it comes right down to it; *but* nothing but; *prater* chatterer (derogatory); 162 *ballad* popular song or poem (which Henry contemptuously considers a low art form); *fall* waste away, decay; 163 *stoop* become bent; *curled pate* head of curly hair; 164 *full* lively, bright; 165 *wax* grow, become (often used in reference to the moon); *hollow* sunken and dim; *sun and the moon* i.e., that which gives light to the world, that which makes the world bright; 167 *his* its (a common usage in Shakespeare's time); 168 *would have* would like to have, or would accept, as a husband; 171 *fairly* kindly, gently; propitiously; *pray thee* ask you, entreat you.

COMMENTARY

You've just spent the last four years of your life traipsing all over northern France on horseback, living in grimy tents and fighting gory battles. To say you're a little out of touch with civilized society might be a bit of an understatement. Now you've got about four minutes to court this ultra-refined, sweet-smelling Princess of France, and you don't speak a word of French. Winning the war was a snap by comparison.

Henry first tries a conventional wooing tactic; he doesn't have flowers or chocolate, but he speaks to Katherine in verse. Needless to say this is a dismal failure. Henry is extremely uncomfortable adopting a courtly persona, as one can see in this sad, stilted attempt. He repeats the word *fair*, but not to very poetic effect—it seems more likely that he is too nervous to think of another complimentary word. He makes elementary attempts at using poetic sounds (*teach / terms*; *enter / ear*), and employs an awkward metaphor (*enter at a lady's ear*) that is goofy rather than elegant. (Never mind the fact that it's a bit indelicate to speak of entering any part of a lady when first approaching her.) Luckily, Katherine's English is so limited that she has no idea what he's saying anyway. So it's no surprise when, after only four lines, Henry abandons the poetry and switches to prose.

Once Henry switches to prose, it's a whole different ball game. Although the entire speech is an extended discussion of his lack of courtship skills, he is actually rather charming. Even though Katherine doesn't know what he's saying, one can imagine that she might find Henry rather sweet (not to mention, he's about to become King of France). Earlier in the play, Henry proved himself to be a great speaker (see monologue, page 129), and he uses several devices here that make him quite persuasive. One of these is antithesis (*for the one* versus *for the other*; *never use till urged* versus *never break for urging*; *to say to thee that I shall die is true* versus *but for thy love, by the Lord, no*; *rhyme themselves into ladies' favors* versus *reason themselves out again*, etc.). Antithesis is one of the most persuasive rhetorical devices, and one that—because it is so illustrative and is often accompanied by tonal shifts and physical gestures—might be helpful in communicating with someone who speaks a different language.

Henry also makes strategic use of the repetition of ideas and structures—which is also a good way to communicate with someone with limited understanding of a language. And at the end of the speech, he uses repetition to eloquently sum up for her exactly who he is (*take me, take a soldier; take a soldier, take a king*) and state honestly what kind of husband she would be getting. His words illustrate that he cannot separate himself from what he is, a soldier and a king; these things define him. Notice that at the very end of the piece he once more repeats the word *fair* (*fairly*); this time he is sure of himself—he is in his own element—and now his repetition is elegant and poetic.

Henry uses builds to complement the repetition in the piece, the most prominent example of which comes toward the end, when he lists all the external attributes of a man that will not last. He builds these up (*A good leg will fall, a straight back will / stoop . . .*) to create a strong contrast with *the sun and the moon*, a metaphor for the good, constant heart he has to offer her.

Henry speaks in a colloquial manner throughout (*sold my farm to buy my crown*; *mince it in love*; *put me to verses*; *speak to you plain soldier*; etc.), creating the impression that he's honest and sincere (whether he really is or not is up to you). Although his style of speech is simple and straightforward, Henry's intelligence and humor come through in his use of puns. Most notable is the pun on *strength* to mean both "skill" and "physical strength," coupled with the triple pun on *measure* to mean "poetic rhythm," "dance," and "amount." Henry also lets some double entendre slip in (such as *lay on . . .* ; *leap into a wife*; *fellows of infinite* [*fin* is French for "end," thus "in" the "end," or buttocks] *tongue* [penis] . . . *into ladies' favors*; and the riding metaphors), but keep in mind that he knows this will go right over Katherine's head—perhaps he's just amusing himself, or maybe the years of hanging out in the trenches with sex-starved soldiers has gotten him into the habit of bawdy talk, and he has to make a concerted effort to clean up his act.

Finally, notice when Henry switches from the formal *you* to the more familiar *thee* and *thou*. He starts out using *you*, switches to *thee* when he drops the verse, then uses the two forms intermittently for a while. By the end of the piece, he's firmly ensconced in the familiar form. Perhaps he's trying to accustom her to a more familiar relationship. Or perhaps she has shown him some encouraging sign?

SIGNIFICANT SCANS

Since there are only three and a half lines to scan, you don't have much to worry about. Notice that the first line has only three feet. That is because the first two feet were spoken by another character. All you have to do is imagine two silent feet before you start to speak, and your scansion will come out right. It might be helpful to decide that Henry needs the time to summon up his courage to speak, or that he's rehearsing in his head what to say in verse.

Note: this scene is quite long, and has lots of monologue material for Henry. We've chosen what we think works best without a partner, but if you'd like to perform a longer piece, there's more for the taking.

P.S.

For information on the historical Henry V, see "From Hell-Raising Hal to Hallowed Harry," page 115.

HENRY VI, PART ONE

ACT V, SCENE iii

JOAN LA PUCELLE

GENDER: F
AGE RANGE: young adult to adult
PROSE/VERSE: blank verse
FREQUENCY OF USE (1–5): 3

The Hundred Years' War has been raging between England and France on French soil for almost a century now. Recently, Joan la Pucelle (a.k.a. Joan of Arc), a young French maiden of common birth, came to Charles the Dauphin (heir to the throne of France), claiming that she had had a vision from Heaven instructing her to help her country. After proving her ability in hand-to-hand combat with the Dauphin, Joan was welcomed as a military leader, and she helped the French win many victories. Now she is in the midst of a battle at Angiers, in which the English seem to have the upper hand. In a moment alone, she appeals to fiends from Hell—the true source of her powers—to help her win the day.

The Regent conquers, and the Frenchmen fly.
Now help, ye charming spells and periapts,
And ye choice spirits that admonish me,
And give me signs of future accidents.
5 You speedy helpers, that are substitutes
Under the lordly monarch of the North,
Appear, and aid me in this enterprise.
[*Enter fiends*]
This speedy and quick appearance argues proof
Of your accustomed diligence to me.
10 Now ye familiar spirits, that are culled
Out of the powerful regions under earth,
Help me this once, that France may get the field.
[*They walk, and speak not.*]
O, hold me not with silence over-long—
Where I was wont to feed you with my blood,
15 I'll lop a member off and give it you
In earnest of a further benefit,
So you do condescend to help me now.
[*They hang their heads.*]
No hope to have redress? My body shall
Pay recompense, if you will grant my suit.
[*They shake their heads.*]
20 Cannot my body nor blood-sacrifice
Entreat you to your wonted furtherance?
Then take my soul—my body, soul, and all,
Before that England give the French the foil.

1 *Regent* i.e., the Duke of York (in the play, appointed Regent of France [one appointed to rule on behalf of a sovereign] by England's Henry VI [although historically, Bedford was still the Regent at the time of this battle]); *fly* flee; 2 *charming* using the power of magical charms; *periapts* amulets; 3 *choice* excellent; *admonish* (1) instruct, guide; (2) inform or warn of danger; 4 *accidents* events, occurrences; 5 *substitutes / Under* deputies of; delegates who act for; 6 *monarch of the North* ruler of all evil spirits (probably Lucifer, whom the Bible describes as sitting on his throne "toward the north"); 8 *quick* both: (1) swift; and (2) in living form; 9 *diligence* careful and diligent service; 10 *familiar* having a supernatural and/or serviceable relationship to humans; 12 *get the field* win the battle; 13 *hold me not* do not make me wait; 14 *Where* whereas; *was wont to feed* was accustomed to feeding [*was wont . . . blood* witches were believed to have attendant spirits who drank their blood and gave them magical powers and service in exchange]; 15 *member* part of the body; 16 *In earnest* as a pledge, a down payment; *benefit* profit, payment; 17 *So* if; *condescend* consent, agree; 18 *redress* help, assistance; 19 *Pay recompense* serve as payment; 21 *wonted furtherance* customary assistance; 23 *Before that England . . . the foil* rather than

[*They depart*]
See, they forsake me. Now the time is come
25 That France must vail her lofty plumèd crest
And let her head fall into England's lap.
My ancient incantations are too weak,
And Hell too strong for me to buckle with.
Now, France, thy glory droopeth to the dust.

1 minute, 50 seconds

allow the English to defeat the French; 25 *vail* lower, let fall; *lofty plumèd crest* high-plumed helmet; 27 *ancient* former; 28 *buckle with* fight with in close single combat; wrestle with.

COMMENTARY

Don't expect an Elizabethan to be on time for dinner if a black cat is in her path—Elizabethans were an extremely superstitious bunch. Having relatively little science to explain the physical world around them, Shakespeare's audience firmly believed in the existence of meddlesome ghosts, fairies, demons, and other supernatural beings. Presenting these beings onstage then must have made quite an impression, and it still can. Not only do we retain some of those superstitions and beliefs, but thanks to our knowledge of modern psychology, today's audiences will also find it creepy to contemplate the mysterious psychological phenomena that might cause a character to imagine such spirits. This is good news for anyone playing Joan, as it is another tool to work with. Whatever their origin, though, the fiends are very real to Joan.

Although the fiends will probably not be represented onstage when you perform this monologue, the images Joan uses help the audience see what she sees: *speedy helpers, that are substitutes / Under the lordly monarch of the North*; *speedy and quick appearance*; *familiar spirits, that are culled / Out of the powerful regions under earth*. Whether the fiends are physically represented or not, these images, combined with Joan's description of the horrible actions her witchcraft entails (*your accustomed diligence to me*; *Where I was wont to feed you with my blood, / I'll lop a member off and give it you*; *My body shall / Pay recompense*), influence the audience's perception of the fiends' hideousness. Note that the phrase *My body shall / Pay recompense* may have a sexual second meaning in addition to its literal one. Joan's final imagery (*France must vail her lofty plumèd crest / And let her head fall into England's lap*) stands out in stark contrast to the others she has built up in the piece: it is no coincidence that the image of France personified as a proud female wearing a plumed warrior's helmet is reminiscent of Joan herself. The plumed helmet falling into the lap of England is symbolic of Joan's as well as France's shame—for her the two are inseparable. The word *lap* functions in its physical definition within the metaphor, but also means "control" or "charge." Thus it has the second literal meaning of France falling under England's rule when the battle is lost.

All of this imagery is supported and intensified by Joan's manner of speech. Most of the monologue is an incantation. The meter flows very smoothly, encouraging a flowing, chanting, or singsongy style, befitting a ritual conjuring. The few variations are carefully placed inverted first feet on lines 6, 11, and 12, which occur when she is urgently calling on her spirits to come to her (*Under*; *Out*; *Help*).

There are many sound repetitions that add to this rhythmic effect. Notice the frequent chantable vowel sounds (*Appear, and aid*; *in this enterprise*; *appear-*

ance argues / accustomed; *O, hold / over-long*), as well as the witchy-sounding consonant combinations (*Frenchmen fly*; *charming spells / choice spirits*; *Where I was wont*; *French the foil*; *droopeth to the dust*). In addition, there is the constant repetition of words or parts of words—a timeworn element of weaving magic spells (*Frenchmen fly / French the foil*; *speedy helpers / speedy and quick*; *Appear / appearance*; *wont / wonted*; *further / furtherance*; *Now help / Now ye / Help me / help me now / Now the time / Now, France*).

Also, notice that the couplet at the climax of the monologue, the moment in which Joan is ready to give every part of herself to the evil spirits to save France (*Then take my soul—my body, soul, and all, / Before that England give the French the foil*), is accentuated by the half-rhyme *all / foil* (which in Shakespeare's day may well have been a full rhyme, since pronunciations have changed).

Joan employs the most ancient usage of the word *ye* (the nominative plural), which may have already sounded more archaic than "you" even to Shakespeare's audience. This usage, as well as the pun on *ancient* (whose primary meaning here is "former"), lends her incantation a sense of being a magical formula passed down through the ages. The other archaic form she uses is the familiar pronoun *thy*. She calls her spirits using the more formal, respectful *you*, but when she refers to her beloved France, she feels intimate enough to say *thy glory*.

There are several important transitions to make in this piece. At the start of the monologue, although Joan is distressed at the course of the battle so far, she is fairly certain that her fiends will come to her aid as they have in the past. Her main worry is probably that she is about to commit an act of heresy in the midst of battle—she needs to be sure that no one sees her. There are several indicators in the text that hint at the progression of Joan's realization that she has another problem on her hands—her fiends are deserting her. The first step in this progression is indicated by the embedded stage direction, *O, hold me not with silence over-long*; the next, by her queries to the fiends after the increasingly excessive offers she makes to them. Obviously, she is watching their responses and responding to them in turn. You must make specific choices as to what Joan sees and hears the fiends do—whether they are still and silent, make gestures, or even speak to her. This will aid your performance and clarify your transitions for the audience.

When reading this monologue for the first time, you will most likely be shocked by what seems like an egregious misinterpretation of a great heroine (see "Revisionist History: Misinterpreting the Maid," page 148). In order to use the piece successfully, however, it will be necessary to get past those feelings and interpret this material in a way that makes sense to you. Was Joan initially the holy "maid" she claimed to be, who was somehow lured to the dark side over the course of years in battle? Or was she merely using that image to conceal the real, heretical source of her power all along? Or maybe there is some mysterious way in which she is both saint and sinner at once . . . There are many possible interpretations. The important thing is to make sure your backstory works with the material Shakespeare has written. In order for that to happen you may have to let go of a lot of preconceived ideas about who Joan is.

Don't forget to elide: *powerful* (POWR-ful) in line 11;

. . . and to contract: *speedy and* (SPEED-yand) in line 8.

Revisionist History: Misinterpreting the Maid

She has a small army of names: Joan of Arc, the Maid of Orleans, Saint Joan, la Pucelle (which means "virgin"). For most of us, these names evoke a fairly standard image—a virginal, divinely inspired, powerful teenage heroine. Although Shakespeare may have been aware of this slant on Joan, that image of her was not marketable on his side of the Channel, nor was it the image his sources described. The English historians Holinshed and Hall, on whose works Shakespeare based his Histories, portrayed Joan as a slutty sorceress. Taking into consideration the extreme anti-French sentiment felt by the English, the omnipresent discrimination against women, and the astounding, perhaps threatening fact that a young girl was so powerful and successful in leading troops to battle, this portrayal is not surprising. Shakespeare chose to name his character Pucelle for a reason: *Pucelle* plays on the Elizabethan word *pussel* or *puzzel*, which means "slut." How could he go wrong giving his audience such a despicable figure on whom to vent their anti-French feelings?

It has been suggested that the real Joan may not have been a saint or a sinner, but a schizophrenic. The descriptions of the voices she claimed to hear, and the fervor with which she adhered to their call, are consistent with the type of symptoms the disorder sometimes causes.

HENRY VI, PART TWO

ACT I, SCENE iii

QUEEN MARGARET

GENDER: F
AGE RANGE: young adult to adult
PROSE/VERSE: blank verse
FREQUENCY OF USE (1–5): 1

Margaret of Anjou first met William de la Pole, Duke of Suffolk, when he was fighting in her home country of France. Suffolk was instantly smitten, and, already married himself, he arranged for her to be married to the weak King Henry VI of England, personally escorting her to his country. Now ensconced in the royal palace (as well as in Suffolk's bed), Margaret is learning that being Queen of England is not the glamorous power trip she had envisioned. After hearing tedious and troubling petitions from the commoners and dismissing the petitioners in anger, Margaret complains to her lover:

45 My Lord of Suffolk, say, is this the guise,
Is this the fashions in the court of England?
Is this the government of Britain's isle,
And this the royalty of Albion's King?
What—shall King Henry be a pupil still
50 Under the surly Gloucester's governance?
Am I a queen in title and in style,
And must be made a subject to a duke?
I tell thee, Pole, when in the city Tours
Thou rannest a tilt in honor of my love
55 And stolest away the ladies' hearts of France,
I thought King Henry had resembled thee
In courage, courtship and proportion.
But all his mind is bent to holiness,
To number Ave-Maries on his beads;
60 His champions are the prophets and apostles,
His weapons, holy saws of sacred writ,

45 *My Lord of Suffolk* Noblemen and -women frequently addressed each other as "my lord" or "my lady"; *say* tell me; *guise* customary, accepted practice of a country; 46 *fashions* prevailing custom, accepted practice (Margaret uses the plural—see Commentary); *court of England* England's royal court; the King and his retinue; 47 *the government of Britain's isle* i.e., the way England's government operates; 48 *the royalty* the office and dignity of a king; *Albion* England (a poetic name); 49 *What* an exclamation, here expressing contempt and impatience; *be a pupil still* still be a ward, under the care of a guardian (implying one who is underage); 50 *Gloucester* i.e., Humphrey, Duke of Gloucester (King Henry's uncle, who was appointed Protector of the Realm and of the King [see definition, below] when King Henry was crowned at the age of nine months, and who is still Protector, despite the fact that King Henry is an adult) [*shall King Henry be . . . Gloucester's governance* is King Henry still a ward being directed and controlled by his surly uncle Gloucester?]; 51 *in style* in name (with a play on the meaning "how I am dressed," i.e., in outward appearance); 52 *must be made a subject to a duke* i.e., despite the fact that the Duke is actually her subject; 53 *Pole* Queen Margaret addresses the Duke of Suffolk by his last name; *Tours* (TOOR) a town in France; 54 *rannest a tilt* competed in a jousting tournament; *in honor of my love* i.e., in honor of the occasion of my marriage to King Henry (with secondary meaning, referring to the love affair between herself and Suffolk) [*when in the city Tours . . . my love* Historically, when Margaret was betrothed to King Henry, and Suffolk traveled to France to escort her back to England, nuptial celebrations were held in the city of Tours, which included jousting competitions, in which Suffolk participated]; 56 *had resembled* would resemble; 57 *courtship* courtliness (with a play on the secondary meaning, "wooing"); *proportion* bodily shape, physique; 58 *all his mind* his whole mind; *is bent to* is inclined towards; *holiness* religious matters; 59 *number* count; *Ave-Maries* (AH-vay MAIR-eez) in English, Hail Marys, repetitions of a particular Catholic prayer, counted off on rosary beads; 60 *champions* warriors who fight for a particular cause or person (Margaret refers to the King's Champions, chosen to joust on behalf of the King, with a play on the concept of the Christian as God's champion [a reference to Ephesians 6]); 61 *saws* maxims, moral sayings; *of sacred writ* from

His study is his tilt-yard, and his loves
Are brazen images of canonized saints.
I would the College of the Cardinals
65 Would choose him Pope, and carry him to Rome,
And set the triple crown upon his head—
That were a state fit for "his Holiness."

71 Beside the haughty Protector have we Beaufort
The imperious churchman, Somerset, Buckingham,
And grumbling York; and not the least of these
But can do more in England than the King.

Not all these lords do vex me half so much
As that proud dame, the Lord Protector's wife:
80 She sweeps it through the court with troops of ladies—
More like an empress than Duke Humphrey's wife.
Strangers in court do take her for the Queen!
She bears a duke's revenues on her back,

Scripture; 62 *study* i.e., place of study; *tilt-yard* a place where jousts take place; *loves* in keeping with Margaret's jousting analogy: those for whom he'd be jousting, were he not such a wimp; also, literally, the things he cherishes; 63 *brazen* brass; *images* statues; 64 *would* wish; *College of the Cardinals* the highest council of the Catholic Church of Rome, which elects the Pope from among its own members; 65 *choose him* select him to be; 66 *the triple crown* the crown of the Pope (to replace the crown Henry currently wears, of the King of England); 67 *were* would be; *state* status, rank; 71 *Beside* Aside from; *Protector* one who exercises the ruling power in a kingdom while its ruler is either a minor or is disabled (here, Margaret refers to the King's uncle Humphrey, Duke of Gloucester); *Beaufort / The imperious churchman* i.e., Cardinal Henry Beaufort (the King's half-great-uncle); 72 *Somerset* i.e., Edmund Beaufort, Duke of Somerset (a cousin of the King, and nephew of Cardinal Beaufort); *Buckingham* i.e., Sir Humphrey Stafford, Duke of Buckingham (a cousin of the King); 73 *York* i.e., Richard Plantagenet, Duke of York (a cousin of the King, and contender to the throne); *not the least . . . than the King* even the lowliest of these can accomplish more (i.e., has more power) in England than the King does; 78 *Not all* None of; 79 *the Lord Protector's wife* i.e., Eleanor, Duchess of Gloucester; 80 *sweeps it* passes by strongly and pompously; 83 *bears* wears; *revenues* income [*She bears . . . on her back* i.e., she wears extraordinarily expensive clothing, costing the equivalent of a duke's in-

And in her heart she scorns our poverty.
85 Shall I not live to be avenged on her?
Contemptuous, base-born callet as she is,
She vaunted 'mongst her minions t' other day,
The very train of her worst wearing gown
Was better worth than all my father's lands
90 Till Suffolk gave two dukedoms for his daughter.

2 minutes, 20 seconds

come]; 84 *our* my (Margaret uses the royal "we"); 86 *base-born* of low birth (low class)—Margaret refers to the historically true fact that the Duchess of Gloucester was of "lower birth" than the rest of the nobles and many had disapproved of Duke Humphrey's marrying her; *callet* a woman of bad character; a prostitute; 87 *vaunted* boasted, exulted; *minions* spoiled favorites of a royal person; *t' other* the other; 88 *The very* the mere; *train* the elongated part of a skirt or gown which trails behind; *worst wearing* oldest, most ragged and most worn out; 89 *better worth* worth more money; 90 *Till Suffolk gave two dukedoms for his daughter* The Duke of Suffolk brokered a deal between King Henry and Margaret's father, the Duke of Anjou, in which the Duke of Anjou received the French regions of Anjou and Maine, formerly occupied by the English, in exchange for marrying his daughter to King Henry.

COMMENTARY

Here is a fun piece to choose if you wish to dish, if you've an urge to purge, if you're out to pout . . . and shout. Margaret feels she's been had: *nothing* about being the Queen is as she imagined it—her king is a dud, she has bothersome responsibilities such as listening to the complaints of grubby commoners, and, worst of all, despite being Queen of England she must still answer to others! She could have stayed at home in France to do that! In this delightfully varied monologue, Margaret very expressively conveys her feelings of disappointment, frustration, aggravation, humiliation, and bitterness.

Margaret begins the monologue with a series of mock questions about King Henry and about the customs of English courtly life (questions to which she already knows the answers). By so doing, she is playing up the "ignorant foreigner" routine to sarcastically reveal her contempt for the King and his royal court. The repetition of *Is this* heightens the sense of Margaret's frustration. She is a pressure cooker waiting to blow, building closer to that moment with each rhetorical *Is this* . . . question, until she reaches the ultimate insult: *Am I a queen in title and in style / And must be made a subject to a duke?*

Shakespeare has fun with the fact that Margaret is French, using the repeated sounds of *is this*, coupled with other S and Z sounds (*Suffolk / say / guise / Is this / fashions / Is this / Britain's / And this / Albion's*). There are even more Zs when you realize that the French pronounce all THs as Zs as well. This preponderance of Zs, coupled with Margaret's grammatically incorrect *Is this the fashions*, start the piece off with a bit of a French flavor—<u>not</u> that we are recommending that you adopt a phony French accent for this piece! If your French accent is up to snuff, go for it, but it is far more important that you be true to Margaret's intentions than to the historical Margaret's dialect. Shakespeare has built in sounds that are suggestive of the French accent to do the job for you.

The young Margaret's values are on display in this piece: she is obviously quite taken with chivalric behavior (whether or not it is reflective of true chivalric honor and integrity). In an extended jousting metaphor, Margaret holds up the trappings of chivalry as the model against which she compares King Henry's genuine religious devotion. By making the comparison, the Queen reveals to the audience her love for Suffolk and her utter contempt for her husband. No doubt she really has fantasized that the College of the Cardinals would take Henry away to Rome to be Pope (clearly not a position for which she has any reverence!), leaving her to ably rule England in his stead, aided by her trusty "adviser," her hero (in its truest meaning—he jousted for her, after all!), Suffolk.

Beware of sounding expository: Shakespeare uses this speech to explain to the audience that Suffolk jousted in the Queen's honor in the city of Tours and that King Henry has not proved the romantic giant she expected. Likewise, Margaret is describing for the audience the scene at the royal court, painting a picture of daily life among the King's ridiculous retinue. Suffolk already knows all this . . . she is surely not saying it for his edification. You must justify Margaret's expositing, and to do so, Shakespeare has given you her palpable anger and frustration—perhaps she needs to vent her frustration to the only one she trusts. Also, Margaret may want Suffolk's support and assistance in bringing down all who keep her from assuming her rightful position of authority. This is a strong and active choice to make (in fact, one that the scene supports, since Suffolk is about to assure her that such plots have already been hatched). Luckily for you, Shakespeare has given you enough variation in the structure of the piece to prevent the monologue from sounding like static exposition, beginning with a series of questions, moving into a memory of Suffolk's glory in France, then to an extended comparison of Suffolk and the King, then on to a list of the nobles who really rule England when her husband should be doing so, and finally to a bitter anecdote about that !@#$% Duchess.

Notice Margaret's use of double meanings: when she reminds Suffolk of his joust in Tours (*in honor of my love*), she means both in honor of her marriage to the King and in honor of her love of Suffolk himself. When she says that the King's *loves* are *brazen images of canonized saints*, she is using *loves* to mean both what Henry would joust for were he chivalrous like Suffolk, and, literally, the things he cares for in the world (which all relate to his religious devotion). You may decide that by conspicuously leaving herself off the list of Henry's loves, she also intends to express that he doesn't love her.

Work with the many colorful words and phrases Margaret uses when discussing her nemesis, the Duchess of Gloucester, and the way in which her descriptions are supported by the sounds of the words. Savor the roundness of the vowels in *proud*, and the string of three one-syllable words (*that proud dame*). The sarcasm—and her enjoyment of it—can't help but roll off her tongue. Likewise, savor the sound of the onomatopoeic *sweeps it*: one instantly envisions the swishing of the many layers of heavy fabric in the skirts of the Duchess's fabulous gowns (as Margaret cattily informs Suffolk, the Duchess *bears a duke's revenues on her back*) as the Duchess whips through the royal palace, acting as though she owns the place, *More like an empress than Duke Humphrey's wife*. You can employ the sound of *sweeps it* to convey precisely what Margaret thinks of her doing so. Margaret's uncharitable description of the Duchess's entourage (*troops of ladies*; *minions*) gives you much to work with. Is she implying that these women are a tough bunch? Or that they are ugly and ungraceful, and hence masculine and soldierlike? Or that they serve as a human shield, protecting the Duchess from Margaret? You decide.

Enjoy her spontaneous outbursts (*Strangers in court do take her for the Queen!* and *Shall I not live to be avenged on her?*). As Margaret herself acknowledges, nobody pushes her buttons like the Duchess does. Margaret just can't contain herself while talking about her. You can vent with the wonderful vicious Vs in *live to be avenged* and spit out the words *Contemptuous* and *callet*. The sounds of the words communicate how Margaret feels and what she wishes to say about it.

By going on the offensive about the Duchess, Margaret unwittingly reveals that she is feeling quite defensive. Being the object of the Duchess's cattiness is especially painful to her since Margaret's acceptance in court, as the daughter of an impoverished French noble, was so hard won. Notice that Margaret so hates to be upstaged by a mere Duchess (particularly one of "lower birth") that she slips in the royal "we" to regain some footing (*she scorns our poverty*).

Margaret finishes off the piece by weaving together a gorgeous string of consonance and assonance: Vs (*live to be avenged*); Cs, Ns, Bs, and Ts (*Contemptuous base-born callet*); Ss and SHs (*as she is / She*); Bs and Us (*bears a duke's revenues on her back*); Ms, Ns, Ss, Ts, and Rs (*'mongst her minions; t'other / train*); Ws, Rs, and URs (*worst wearing gown / Was better worth*); and ending with another UR and a trio of Defiant Ds (*dukedoms / daughter*).

You may find it interesting to know that the compilers of the First Folio studded this piece with commas—far more than make grammatical sense. If you were to do nothing but take a breath at each of these commas, the piece would automatically take on a tone of agitation—the commas in the First Folio were placed there to alert the actor that Queen Margaret is getting quite worked up about her subject matter (no pun intended!).

SIGNIFICANT SCANS

Line 63 is tricky. Here are three possibilities for you to choose from: The line could be delivered as one of those rare, six-footed lines (hexameter) [canonized (CA'-noh-NIE-zehd)]:

x / x / x / x / x / x /
Are brazen images of canonized saints

. . . or as pentameter [images (IM-jiz); canonized (ca-NON-ized)]:

x / x / x / x / x /
Are brazen images of canonized saints

. . . or pentameter, with a crowded fifth foot:

x / x / x / x / x - x /
Are brazen images of canonized saints

Note that line 67 has two inverted feet, the second of which falls after a caesura that is not marked by punctuation (also note the inverted foot at the start of the line):

/ x x / / x x / x /
That were a state fit for "his Holiness"

The two inversions draw attention to the line, highlighting its sarcasm.

Line 71 has a crowded foot (—*ty Protec*—) plus a double ending:

x / x / x - x / x / x / (x)
Beside the haughty Protector have we Beaufort

Notice the historic pronunciation of *revenues* (reh-VEN-yooz) in line 83. You may prefer to sacrifice the meter for the more familiar pronunciation. Try it both ways and then decide.

Don't forget to elide: *Albion's* (AL-byonz) in line 48; *rannest* (RANST) in line 54; *stolest* (STOLST) in line 55; *champions* (CHAMP-yunz) in line 60; *Somerset* (SUM'R-set) in line 72; and *Contemptuous* (con-TEMP-chwuss) in line 86;

. . . to contract: *The imperious* (th'im-PEER-yuss) in line 72;

. . . and to expand: *proportion* (pro-PORE´-shee-UN) in line 57.

Revisionist History: She-Wolf's Heart, Wrapped in a French Tiger's Hide

It is the rare Shakespearean character who actually lives out the span of her life over the course of one or more plays. Margaret of Anjou is such a one (appearing as a young woman in *Henry VI, Parts One* and *Two*, a middle-aged woman in *Henry VI, Part Three*, and an old dowager in *Richard III*) and the audience has the pleasure of watching her flower (read: grow more brutal, cruel, and vindictive) from play to play. Called a *She-wolf of France* and a *Tiger's heart wrapped in a woman's hide*, Margaret is arguably one of Shakespeare's most cold-blooded creations.

The historical Margaret of Anjou lived from 1430 to 1482 and, while outspoken and courageous, was not the figure of malice suggested by her stage counterpart. She was a mere girl of fourteen when she arrived in England to be King Henry's bride. She never hated the Duchess of Gloucester because she never knew the Duchess, who had been exiled a number of years before the vessel carrying Margaret ever banked on England's shores. Nor is there any evidence that Margaret had an affair with the middle-aged Suffolk, although she probably had little love for her husband, who was declared insane in 1453, suffering from what historians believe was either catatonic schizophrenia or a depressive stupor for about a year (he lost his memory, ability to speak, and motor coordination, and barely moved). Margaret put in a bid to be appointed Protector during Henry's period of incompetency, but was passed over in favor of the English—and male—York. Isaac Asimov aptly observed that given the temperaments of the royal couple, all would have been bliss had the tough, politically minded Margaret been permitted to be king and the gentler, milder Henry permitted to perform the duties of queen.

Later, during the Wars of the Roses, Margaret did lead her husband's forces for sixteen years against those of the Yorkists, but unlike the scenes in *Henry VI, Part Three*, she was not present at either York's death at the Battle of Wakefield or at that of her own son at the Battle of Tewkesbury. She was captured a few days after that battle and imprisoned for approximately six years. Eventually ransomed by the French King Louis XI, she returned to France to live out the brief remainder of her life. Having long departed not only from England but also from life itself, Margaret was not present in England for the goings-on in the royal court so loosely (and deliciously) depicted by Shakespeare in *Richard III*.

HENRY VI, PART TWO

ACT II, SCENE iv

ELEANOR

GENDER: F
AGE RANGE: adult to mature adult
PROSE/VERSE: blank verse
FREQUENCY OF USE (1–5): 2

Eleanor, Duchess of Gloucester, who has long aspired to be Queen of England, has been convicted of the treasonous act of conducting a seance to determine whether her husband, Humphrey (the King's uncle), would become king himself someday. She has been sentenced to three days public penance followed by lifetime banishment to the Isle of Man. She is now being paraded through the streets dressed in a white sheet, barefoot, and with papers pinned to her back on which her crimes are written for all to read. Crowds have assembled to witness the public humiliation of this important royal personage. The Duchess's husband has arrived at the designated spot to watch her pass by. She has just approached him there, and is permitted to speak with him briefly.

Come you, my lord, to see my open shame?
20 Now thou dost penance, too. Look how they gaze!
See how the giddy multitude do point
And nod their heads and throw their eyes on thee.
Ah, Gloucester, hide thee from their hateful looks,
And in thy closet pent up, rue my shame
25 And ban thine enemies, both mine and thine.

[GLOUCESTER: *Be patient, gentle Nell; forget this grief.*]

Ah, Gloucester, teach me to forget myself;
For whilst I think I am thy married wife,
And thou a prince, Protector of this land,
30 Methinks I should not thus be led along,
Mailed up in shame, with papers on my back,
And followed with a rabble that rejoice
To see my tears and hear my deep-fet groans.
The ruthless flint doth cut my tender feet,
35 And when I start, the envious people laugh
And bid me be advisèd how I tread.
Ah, Humphrey, can I bear this shameful yoke?
Trowest thou that e'er I'll look upon the world,
Or count them happy that enjoys the sun?

19 *my lord* my husband; *my open shame* my public humiliation; 21 *giddy* thoughtless; *multitude* crowd (with the connotation "crowd of commoners"); 22 *throw their eyes* i.e., turn to stare; *on* at; 23 *Gloucester* the Duchess addresses her husband, Humphrey, Duke of Gloucester, by his title; *hide thee* hide yourself; 24 *closet* private bedroom or study [*in thy closet pent up* shut away in your bedroom/study]; *rue* regret; grieve for, lament; 25 *ban* curse; 29 *a prince* the Duchess's husband was the youngest son of King Henry IV, the brother of Henry V, and the uncle of Henry VI; *Protector of this land* because Henry became king at the age of nine months, his uncle Humphrey was appointed Protector of the baby King and of England (a.k.a. Regent), effectively ruling on behalf of the King; 31 *Mailed up* wrapped up, enveloped (a term used in falconry: one technique used to tame a falcon was to wrap her in a cloth so that she could not struggle by moving her wings); *papers on my back* criminals undergoing punishment usually had papers affixed to the backs of their clothing, on which their offenses were written; 32 *with* by; *rabble* crowd; 33 *deep-fet* from deep within; 34 *flint* a particularly hard stone; 35 *start* i.e., twitch from pain; *envious* spiteful, malicious; 36 *bid me* order me to; *be advisèd* be careful; 37 *yoke* a curved wooden device placed on the necks of draft animals (usually oxen), by which they are kept together when pulling a load (often, as here, used figuratively to mean "suffering"); 38 *Trowest thou* Do you suppose; *look upon* take notice of, care for; *the world* society, the people among whom I live; 39 *happy* lucky; *that enjoys* who possess with pleasure [*Trowest thou . . . the sun* ambiguous meaning—two possible interpretations: (1) Do you think I'll ever care for society or think that those who enjoy the world are fortunate?; (2) Do you suppose I'll ever

40 No, dark shall be my light, and night my day;
To think upon my pomp shall be my hell.
Sometime I'll say I am Duke Humphrey's wife,
And he a prince and ruler of the land;
Yet so he ruled and such a prince he was
45 As he stood by whilst I, his forlorn duchess,
Was made a wonder and a pointing-stock
To every idle rascal follower.
But be thou mild and blush not at my shame,
Nor stir at nothing till the axe of death
50 Hang over thee, as sure it shortly will;
For Suffolk, he that can do all in all
With her that hateth thee and hates us all,
And York, and impious Beaufort, that false priest,
Have all limed bushes to betray thy wings;
55 And fly thou how thou canst, they'll tangle thee.
But fear not thou until thy foot be snared,
Nor never seek prevention of thy foes.

2 minutes, 15 seconds

care about society or be able to enjoy life again?]; 41 *pomp* i.e., the Duchess's former greatness or power; 42 *Sometime* from time to time, now and then; 44 *so he ruled and such a prince he was* he ruled in such a way and was such a prince; 45 *As* that; 46 *wonder* object of surprise, object to be marveled at; *pointing-stock* someone to be pointed at and ridiculed, a butt of ridicule; 47 *rascal* both (1) inferior, worthless and (2) belonging to the rabble; *follower* pursuer (i.e., one of the rabble chasing after the Duchess to ridicule her); 48 *mild* calm, gentle; *blush not . . . shame* do not feel shame yourself because of my shame; 49 *stir at* get roused by, get agitated over; 51 *Suffolk* i.e., William de la Pole, Duke of Suffolk (a powerful noble, currently having an affair with Queen Margaret, who hates Gloucester and, as the Duchess has surmised, is plotting his downfall); *he that can do all in all* i.e., Suffolk (he who can do whatever he wants in all situations); 52 *her that hateth thee and hates us all* i.e., Queen Margaret (who has not disguised her hatred for the Duke and Duchess of Gloucester or the rest of their cronies); 53 *York* Richard Plantagenet, Duke of York (who asserts his own claim to the throne [see "Genealogical Chart—the Wars of the Roses," pages 236–37] and Suffolk's plot against Gloucester); *impious Beaufort, that false priest* the irreligious political operative, Cardinal Henry Beaufort (who has long been Gloucester's nemesis in the royal court) (note: Eleanor's hunch is right—Beaufort and Suffolk are plotting his downfall and will eventually have him murdered); 54 *limed bushes* smeared bushes with birdlime (a sticky material made of holly, mistletoe, or other plants, which is smeared onto the limb of a bush or a tree to catch the birds that land on it); 55 *fly thou how thou canst* no matter how you try to fly (with a play on its second meaning, "flee"); *tangle* ensnare, entrap; 56 *fear not thou* don't you worry; 57 *Nor never* Shakespeare often used double negatives for emphasis; *seek prevention of* take action to safeguard against and to forestall.

COMMENTARY

If only we could turn back the hands of time, reconsider a decision, not make that left turn . . . Eleanor, Duchess of Gloucester's husband, Humphrey, Duke of Gloucester, has been Protector of the Realm and of the King since King Henry was crowned at the tender age of nine months. This means that Gloucester has been ruling England on his nephew the King's behalf for decades. But being the wife of the second most powerful man in England wasn't enough for Eleanor—she felt that "Queen Eleanor" had quite a nice ring to it. And by acting on her ambition (and getting caught), the Duchess has brought her entire world crashing down. As the piece makes clear, the Duchess feels no remorse for her actions, but simply frustration and bitterness at being caught and brought down. It is clear that she is in anguish as she suffers her public humiliation on the very streets she used to ride through in triumph, paraded before the very rabble she used to command.

Plumbing the text of Eleanor's monologue yields much information about her mental state. Notice that she begins by addressing her husband with the very formal *you*, and then quickly switches to *thee* for the rest of the piece. Remember that she and her husband are not alone, but are on a public street, surrounded by hostile hordes who have turned out to mock the Duchess. She is also flanked by the Sheriff and officers, who lead her through the streets as their prisoner. Maybe Eleanor's first words to her husband are more public (and hence more formal) and then she draws closer to him and speaks to him more privately. Or maybe Eleanor has not seen her husband since her sentencing and is so mortified when he first sees her in her shamed condition that she bashfully resorts to formality, but then reverts to the familiar form of address when she realizes that Gloucester hasn't changed toward her—he is her same, loving husband. Similarly, it is interesting to note that while the Duchess's first line is about her own shame, she quickly switches her focus to the shame her husband must be experiencing. In the first few lines, she jumps back and forth between utter mortification and concern for her husband's mental well-being. This comports with how overwhelming the entire experience must be for her.

The Duchess is an articulate person. She uses the rhetorical devices of contrast and antithesis to richly illustrate the agony of her descent from the heights of power, contrasting, for instance, her lofty position with her shameful downfall; Her husband's royalty and power with his inability to prevent her punishment; *rabble that rejoice* with *my tears . . . my deep-fet groans*; *ruthless flint* with *tender feet*; *dark* with *light*; *night* with *day*; *my pomp* with *my hell*; *duchess* with *idle rascal follower*; *fly thou how thou canst* with *they'll tangle thee*.

Eleanor's frustration and exhaustion—as well as perhaps the sense that she is trying not to cry in public—come across with the breathiness of all the THs that inundate the first eleven lines: (*thou / they / the / their / throw / their / thee / thee / their / thy / thine / thine / think / thy / thou / thus*). Lines 22–26 all begin with complAIning, Acrid As, complemented by the whIny-sounding *mine / thine*. Other sound pairings or groupings weave a path through the piece, pulling it together aurally, and giving the Duchess a clever and biting tone. Some examples: Ts, EEs, Ms, and Ps (*teach me to forget myself; a prince / Protector; Methinks / Mailed up*); As and Rs (*a rabble that rejoice*); EEs, Fs, and Ts (*deep-fet / flint / feet*); SHs, OOR/ORs, and Ts (*as sure / it shortly*); Hs, As, THATs, Ts, Ss, ALLs, and HATEs (*he that can do all in all / With her that hateth thee and hates us all*); Bs and Ts (*bushes to betray*); and THs, OWs, EYs/EEs, and Ls (*fly thou how thou canst, they'll tangle thee*).

The monologue provides insight into the Duchess's conflicted relationship with her husband. She urges him to leave the site and avoid ridicule because she cares for him, but she also shows some contempt for him, and one gets the sense that she feels that they would be far better off had she been allowed to wear the pants in the family. If Gloucester had pursued his wife's kingly aspirations for him, perhaps she would not be in her current predicament. Over the course of the monologue, the Duchess apparently recovers her sense of self enough to be caustic toward her husband at the close. Her warning to him about his imminent danger is laced with the sarcasm and anger she can't overcome—she is saying, in effect, "Don't learn from my downfall or bother to take any action to protect yourself (you certainly didn't take any to protect me!). Just blithely continue on your oblivious way until it's too late." In a way that is totally consistent with human nature, she distances herself from her husband in their final moments together by lashing out at him, making it easier to say goodbye forever.

SIGNIFICANT SCANS

The very first foot in the very first line is inverted, giving the sense that the Duchess is blurting out her first words to her husband. Perhaps she is startled at seeing him suddenly. Perhaps being seen by him is harder than being seen by anonymous strangers, and she is wailing. Aside from this, there are only very occasional inverted feet at starts of lines and after caesuras (for example, line 20: *Look how they gaze!*). For the most part, the monologue is made up of very even iambic pentameter, which gives it a resigned feeling. Since Eleanor probably wishes she could disappear altogether, and variations call attention to themselves, the Duchess may be avoiding them. Perhaps she is weary from three days of being paraded through the streets, or perhaps she is trying very hard to stay emotionally controlled . . . Or some or all of the above.

Note that the accent falls on the first syllable of *forlorn* (FOR-lorn) in line 45.

Don't forget to elide: *envious* (EN-vyuss) in line 35 and *Trowest* (TROE'ST) in line 38;

. . . to contract: *and impious* (n'im-PIE-uss) in line 53;

. . . and to expand: *advisèd* (ad-VIE-zehd) in line 36.

Have Ouija Board, Will Travel

Shakespeare didn't have to take any liberties to create a dramatic story line about Eleanor Cobham, Duchess of Gloucester—the historical figure delivered all the drama he could hope for. The real Duchess was Gloucester's mistress before becoming his second wife, and was not considered high class enough for the royal son, brother, and uncle of kings. She dabbled openly in sorcery and did, in fact, conduct a seance to learn when King Henry would die. As in the play, she was tried for sorcery, sentenced to public humiliation (normally a punishment meted out to prostitutes), and exiled. All this occurred, however, several years before Queen Margaret burst onto the English royal scene. Shakespeare altered the dates to create the hatred between the two women and to imply that the Duchess's banishment was one of the events that hastened her husband's downfall and death.

HENRY VI, PART THREE

ACT I, SCENE iv

QUEEN MARGARET

GENDER: F
AGE RANGE: adult to mature adult
PROSE/VERSE: blank verse
FREQUENCY OF USE (1–5): 4

Queen Margaret's wimp of a husband, King Henry VI, just isn't good king material. When Richard Plantagenet, Duke of York, marched on London claiming that he was the rightful heir to the English throne, Henry buckled and signed an act of Parliament making York the Protector of the Realm, and heir to the crown after Henry's death. In return, York vowed to put aside his arms and allow Henry to live out his reign unmolested. Margaret was outraged—the agreement disinherited her son, Prince Edward. She took up arms on her own and went out to fight York, supported by the armies of the northern lords—most notably Lord Clifford and the Earl of Northumberland. Together, they have finally defeated York's forces. During the battle, Clifford captured and killed York's young son Rutland. Now they have captured the Duke himself, and Margaret can't wait to exact her revenge. When Northumberland asks what she would like to have done with him, she replies:

Brave warriors, Clifford and Northumberland,
Come, make him stand upon a molehill here
That raught at mountains with outstretchèd arms,
Yet parted but the shadow with his hand.
70 What, was it you who would be England's king?
Was't you that reveled in our Parliament
And made a preachment of your high descent?
Where are your mess of sons to back you now,
The wanton Edward and the lusty George?
75 And where's that valiant crook-back prodigy,
Dicky your boy, that with his grumbling voice
Was wont to cheer his dad in mutinies?
Or, with the rest, where is your darling Rutland?
Look, York: I stained this napkin with the blood
80 That valiant Clifford with his rapier's point
Made issue from the bosom of the boy;
And if thine eyes can water for his death,
I give thee this to dry your cheeks withal.
Alas, poor York! But that I hate thee deadly,
85 I should lament thy miserable state.
I prithee, grieve, to make me merry, York.
What, hath thy fiery heart so parched thine entrails
That not a tear can fall for Rutland's death?

66 *Clifford* i.e., Lord John Clifford (who has sworn revenge on the Yorks for killing his father); *Northumberland* i.e., Henry Percy, Earl of Northumberland (son of the Northumberland who died at St. Albans fighting for Henry VI, and grandson of Hotspur, who died fighting against Henry IV); 68 *raught* reached; 69 *parted but the shadow* divided and took as his share only the shadow (of the mountain); 70 *would be* claims to be; desires to be; 71 *reveled* (1) indulged yourself (by taking the throne illegally); and/or (2) feasted and partied noisily, as if at a masquerade party; 72 *preachment* sermon (although he did not include it in the play, Shakespeare refers to an incident mentioned in his source material: York gave a formal speech to the members of Parliament, in which he outlined his claim to the throne); *high descent* i.e., his descent from the third son of Edward III, as opposed to King Henry's descent from the fourth son (see "Genealogical Chart—the Wars of the Roses," pages 236–37); 73 *mess* a set or group of four (usually referring to groups of people arranged at a dinner table for a large party); 74 *wanton* (1) capricious, frivolous; (2) lewd, lasciviously playful; *Edward* i.e., York's oldest son, Edward Plantagenet, Earl of March (later King Edward IV); *lusty* (1) lustful; (2) vigorous, strong, energetic; *George* i.e., York's third son, George Plantagenet of York; 75 *crook-back* hunchbacked; *prodigy* (1) monster; (2) portent, bad omen; 76 *Dicky* i.e., York's fourth son, Richard Plantagenet of York (later King Richard III); 77 *Was wont to* used to; *cheer* incite, encourage; 78 *Rutland* i.e., York's second son, Edmund Plantagenet, Earl of Rutland; 79 *napkin* handkerchief; 80 *rapier* a slender, two-edged sword used mainly for thrusting; 81 *issue* flow out; *bosom* chest (i.e., heart); 83 *withal* with; 84 *Alas* an interjection expressing sorrow or pity, used here sarcastically; *But* Except; *deadly* implacably; to the death; 85 *should* would; 86 *I prithee* ask you, entreat you (from "I pray thee"); 87 *fiery* ardent, spirited; *entrails* bowels (thought by Elizabethans to be

Why art thou patient, man? Thou shouldst be mad;
90 And I to make thee mad do mock thee thus.
Stamp, rave and fret, that I may sing and dance.
Thou wouldst be fee'd, I see, to make me sport.
York cannot speak unless he wear a crown.
A crown for York! And lords, bow low to him.
95 Hold you his hands whilst I do set it on.
[*She places a paper crown or a garland on his head*]
Ay, marry, sir, now he looks like a king!
Ay, this is he that took King Henry's chair,
And this is he was his adopted heir.
But how is it that great Plantagenet
100 Is crowned so soon and broke his solemn oath?
As I bethink me, you should not be king
Till our King Henry had shook hands with Death.
And will you pale your head in Henry's glory,
And rob his temples of the diadem,
105 Now, in his life, against your holy oath?
O, 'tis a fault too too unpardonable!
Off with the crown, and with the crown, his head;
And whilst we breathe, take time to do him dead.

2 minutes, 30 seconds

the source of sympathetic emotions); 89 *patient* calm, composed; *mad* both stark-raving and hopping; 91 *fret* express anger and vexation; *that* so that; 92 *fee'd* paid; *to make me sport* to amuse me; 96 *marry* indeed (an interjection originating from the phrase, "by the Virgin Mary"); 97 *chair* throne; 98 *he was* he who was; 99 *Plantagenet* i.e., York; 100 *his solemn oath* i.e., York's oath not to seize the throne before Henry's death; 101 *bethink me* remember; 102 *shook hands with Death* i.e., died; 103 *pale* encircle; *glory* splendor, magnificence (i.e., the crown); 104 *diadem* crown; 108 *take time* seize the opportunity; *do him dead* i.e., kill him.

COMMENTARY

Queen Margaret has finally caught the rat that has been living it up in her pantry, and she's eager to teach him a lesson before exterminating him. This piece is fairly dripping with the loathing she bears the would-be usurper of her husband's (and more important, one day her son's) crown.

There are several excellent clues to interpretation in the meter. You'll notice the rhythm flows along with overall ease, and yet there are several variations in key positions. Notice which words fall on inverted feet, punching the beginnings of the lines in these carefully chosen spots (*Where are your mess of sons to back you now*; *Dicky your boy*; *Stamp, rave and fret, that I may sing and dance*; *Off with the crown*). Double endings also fall on particularly important points (*where is your darling Rutland?*; *I hate thee deadly*; *hath thy fiery heart so parched thine entrails*; *will you pale your head in Henry's glory*. In two places, words must be expanded to fit the meter (see below). Both are useful in performance. The first, *outstretchèd*, emphasizes the ridiculous lengths to which York was trying to extend his reach—far beyond his pathetic little grasp. The second, *miserable,* allows Margaret to really drag out the mental torture she's inflicting with her mockery.

That mockery is greatly enhanced by paying close attention to the meter. For instance, the natural tendency would be to say the line *York cannot speak unless he wear a crown* with emphasis on *York*. But if you read it according to the meter, it has a much more caustic effect:

x / x / x / x / x /
York cannot speak unless he wear a crown

Similarly, the line *Ay, marry, sir, now he looks like a king* seems as though it should have emphasis on *now*, since she has just placed the crown on his head, but if you read the line according to the meter, emphasizing *he*, you get a much more sarcastic result:

x / x / x / x / x /
Ay, marry, sir, now he looks like a king

Working in tandem with the meter, the sounds in this piece contribute significantly to Margaret's torment of York. Most manifest are the many Marvelous Ms (*make / him / molehill / mountains*; *make me merry*), which can be used to merrily mock or malevolently menace. Sometimes the Ms are intertwined with other sound repetitions. The best example is the phrase *to make thee mad do mock thee thus*, which has Ms in combination with *to / do* and *thee / thee / thus*, as well as the Ks in *make* and *mock*. Notice Margaret's Badgering Bs (*bosom of the boy*) and Huffy Hs (*Henry had shook hands / head in Henry's*), as well as other little sound bites such as *thy fiery* and *heart so parched*. And for help with exploiting the sound of the word *O* to its best advantage, see "O, No! An *O*!," page xxxiii.

Sometimes these combinations of sounds become somewhat singsongy. The line *What, was it you who would be England's king?* with its alliterative Ws, assonant AHs and OOs, and the rhyme in *England's king*, becomes almost a mocking schoolyard song when followed by the rhyming couplet *Was't you that reveled in our Parliament / And made a preachment of your high descent?* Margaret carries the mockery through, using another couplet (*chair / heir*) after she places the paper crown on York's head. Here, the sense of the singsongy children's rhyme is enhanced by the repetition of *Ay* and *this is he*. Finally, Margaret closes the piece with another of these couplets (*head / dead*), creating an eerie contrast between the whimsy of the rhyme and the seriousness of the death sentence she pronounces for York.

Keeping in mind that most lines in iambic pentameter build to the last word, it is helpful to take note of the string of words Shakespeare has used at the ends of the five lines in the cruelest section of the piece—the moment when Margaret tells York of his young son's death. These lines build to the words *Rutland*, *blood*, *point*, *boy*, and *death*, driving home the horrible story's important points. This is where Margaret is really pulling out all the stops to hurt York. She relishes the gory details of the boy's death, then gives York a handkerchief stained with his son's blood with which to dry his tears.

Margaret chooses her words carefully—they are her best weapons. Even her repetitions of small words can be used to good advantage. First, look at the phrase *too too unpardonable*. Is she repeating this simple word for added force? Is she struggling for exactly the perfect word with which to follow it? Whatever your interpretation, you can make use of the juxtaposition of the repeated short jab of *too* and the single long word, *unpardonable*. Second, rather than simply saying "Parliament" or "King Henry," Margaret pointedly says *our Parliament* and *our King Henry*. Although you may decide that the character uses *our* to represent herself as fighting for all England's good, or to emphasize the fact that she's got all the northern lords on her side against York, it is clear that at the very least she uses it to imply the royal "we" (usually used only by the sovereign). Or, you may decide that Margaret feels justified using the royal "we" outright, either because she is married to Henry, or because she considers herself to have taken Henry's place, since he gave up the crown, and it was she who fought to keep it.

Another example of careful word choice is Margaret's frequent ironic use of endearments (*Dicky*; *darling Rutland*; *lusty George*; *Alas, poor York!*) or casual, chatty phrases (*cheer his dad*; *Ay, marry, sir*; *As I bethink me*). These are the most nasty aspects of the piece, by virtue of the extreme contrast between the words she speaks and the meanings she implies. Another key element of Margaret's biting sarcasm is her use of double entendre. For instance, she calls George *lusty* as if praising a colleague's son for his energy, but she implies her real meaning, that he is lustful. She uses the word *reveled* to describe York's takeover of Parliament with his supporters. Whether she actually means that he and his friends partied there or not, using that particular word has a second meaning: *reveling* was the term used in connection with maskers (those taking part in a masquerade party). Thus, Margaret implies that York and his supporters were merely playing at being king and nobles, and are not really worthy of those titles.

Margaret is not satisfied, however, with cruel words, but augments her taunts by physicalizing them. By standing York on a *molehill*, she makes reference to the old saying "king of the molehill," a common expression of contempt. She further belittles him by instructing the lords to *bow low* to him, and by "crowning" him. Next, she strikes right to the heart—she physicalizes the fact of Rutland's savage murder by offering York the bloody handkerchief with which to wipe his tears. Because of the physicality in this scene, there are many embedded stage directions in Margaret's speech that help you figure out what she is doing, what the others in the scene are doing, and to whom she is speaking in different parts of the piece (examples: lines 67, 79, 83, 87–88, and 94–95).

Don't forget to elide: *warriors* (WAR-yerz) in line 66; *valiant* (VAL-yint) in lines 75 and 80; *rapier's* (RAYP-yerz) in line 80; and *unpardonable* (un-PARD´-nuh-BL) in line 106;

. . . and to expand: *outstretchèd* (out-STRETCH-ehd) in line 68 and *miserable* (MIZ´-er-UH-bl) in line 85.

P.S.

For background on the historical Margaret, see "Revisionist History: She-Wolf's Heart, Wrapped in a French Tiger's Hide," page 156.

A MOUNTAIN OUT OF A MOLEHILL

Perhaps Margaret would not have selected this particular manner of tormenting her captive had she been more familiar with her Scriptures. The spectacle of York's ordeal echoes the mocking of Jesus before his Crucifixion: the molehill is a miniature Calvary (a.k.a. Golgotha), the hill outside Jerusalem on which Jesus was crucified; York's garland or paper crown is reminiscent of

Jesus' crown of thorns; Pilate's soldiers "bowed the knee before [Jesus], and mocked him," just as Margaret's soldiers are ordered to do to York. Shakespeare borrowed this parallel from his source material, Holinshed's *Chronicles*.

Here's what really happened: York was found dead on the field, and his head was put up on the walls of York, adorned with a paper crown. Yes, it's gruesome, but heads on city walls were all the rage in Shakespeare's time. The gates of London featured an ongoing exhibit of the latest heads off the chopping block and gallows.

REVISIONIST HISTORY: NOT THE NATURAL ORDER OF THINGS

Yet again, Shakespeare has revised history to suit his needs: In 1460 *darling Rutland* was seventeen, several years an adult by medieval standards. He was killed while fighting in the Battle of Wakefield rather than fleeing from it, and it is not known who killed him. The Yorkists tweaked Rutland's age to gain sympathy for their cause by playing on the extreme hatred the English bore toward Margaret, and far be it from Shakespeare to correct such a juicy, dramatic story. Rutland's brothers, the *lusty George* and *that valiant crook-back prodigy*, Richard, were eleven and eight years old respectively at this time. By changing their ages, Shakespeare was able to include these pivotal characters in the plot of the Wars of the Roses well before their time.

HENRY VI, PART THREE

ACT I, SCENE iv

RICHARD, DUKE OF YORK

GENDER: M
AGE RANGE: mature adult
PROSE/VERSE: blank verse
FREQUENCY OF USE (1–5): 2

Richard Plantagenet, Duke of York, has a valid claim to the throne of England (see "Genealogical Chart—the Wars of the Roses," pages 236–37). He raised armed forces to support him, and marched on London, where the weak-willed King Henry made him heir to the throne through an Act of Parliament. York's sons, however, convinced him not to wait for Henry's death, but to take the throne right away, by force. And so York has been at war with the forces of Queen Margaret, who is fighting for her son's right to inherit the throne. York has now been captured by Margaret and two of the northern lords who support her, Lord Clifford and the Earl of Northumberland. Margaret has just cruelly tormented York with his failure to complete the coup and with the death of his second son, Rutland (see Margaret's monologue, page 164). York replies:

She-wolf of France, but worse than wolves of France,
Whose tongue more poisons than the adder's tooth—
How ill-beseeming is it in thy sex
To triumph like an Amazonian trull
115 Upon their woes whom Fortune captivates.
But that thy face is vizard-like, unchanging,
Made impudent with use of evil deeds,
I would assay, proud queen, to make thee blush.
To tell thee whence thou cam'st, of whom derived,
120 Were shame enough to shame thee, wert not shameless.
Thy father bears the type of King of Naples,
Of both the Sicils and Jerusalem.
Yet not so wealthy as an English yeoman.
Hath that poor monarch taught thee to insult?
125 It needs not, nor it boots thee not, proud queen,
Unless the adage must be verified,
That beggars mounted run their horse to death.
'Tis beauty that doth oft make women proud;
But God he knows thy share thereof is small.
130 'Tis virtue that doth make them most admired;
The contrary doth make thee wondered at.
'Tis government that makes them seem divine;

111 *She-wolf of France* Before her marriage to King Henry, Margaret was an impoverished French noblewoman; 112 *more poisons* is more poisonous than; *adder* the common European viper, a small venomous snake; *tooth* the bite of; 113 *ill-beseeming* unbecoming [*How ill-beseeming . . . sex* how unbecoming it is for someone of your gender]; 114 *triumph* exult or rejoice triumphantly; *Amazonian* of the Amazons (a race of fierce female warriors in Greek mythology); *trull* (1) lewd or promiscuous woman; (2) prostitute; 115 *Fortune* fate (personified as a capricious goddess who determines human destiny); *captivates* makes a captive; subdues [*Upon their woes whom Fortune captivates* i.e., over the sorrows of those whose fate it is to be imprisoned or subdued]; 116 *vizard-like* masklike, having a fixed expression; 117 *use of evil deeds* habitual practice of doing evil acts; 118 *assay* try; 119 *whence* from where; *of whom derived* from whom you are descended; 120 *Were* would be; *wert not shameless* if you were not impudent and insensible to shame; 121 *Thy father* i.e., Reignier, King of Naples and Duke of Anjou; *bears the type* carries the title; *King of Naples* the kingdom of Naples at that time included most of southern Italy; 122 *the Sicils* the kingdoms of Naples and Sicily; 123 *Yet* i.e., yet he is; *yeoman* freeholder; independent, landowning farmer, of lower rank than gentleman; 124 *poor* (1) having little material wealth; and (2) insignificant, worthless; 125 *It needs not* It is not necessary; *nor it boots thee not* nor does it help you; *proud* haughty; cold, unkind; 127 *run* ride at a gallop [*beggars mounted . . . death* with this adage, York suggests that Margaret, like the beggar suddenly in possession of a horse, has abused her queenship]; 128 *proud* exalted, lofty; 129 *God he knows* God knows; 130 *most* very much; 131 *contrary* (CON´-truh-REE) opposite (of virtue); *wondered at* i.e., the subject of surprise and astonishment; 132 *government* self-discipline, self-

The want thereof makes thee abominable.
Thou art as opposite to every good
135 As the Antipodes are unto us,
Or as the South to the Septentrion.
O tiger's heart wrapped in a woman's hide,
How could'st thou drain the life-blood of the child,
To bid the father wipe his eyes withal,
140 And yet be seen to bear a woman's face?
Women are soft, mild, pitiful and flexible;
Thou stern, obdurate, flinty, rough, remorseless.
Bid'st thou me rage? Why now thou hast thy wish.
Would'st have me weep? Why, now thou hast thy will;
145 For raging wind blows up incessant showers,
And when the rage allays, the rain begins.
These tears are my sweet Rutland's obsequies,
And every drop cries vengeance for his death
'Gainst thee, fell Clifford, and thee, false Frenchwoman.

That face of his the hungry cannibals
Would not have touched, would not have stained with blood;
But you are more inhuman, more inexorable—
155 O, ten times more—than tigers of Hyrcania.
See, ruthless queen, a hapless father's tears.
This cloth thou dipped'st in blood of my sweet boy
And I with tears do wash the blood away.

control; 133 *want thereof* lack of it; 135 *Antipodes* (an-TIH´-puh-DEEZ) people inhabiting the opposite side of the globe (*antipodes* means "opposed feet," referring to the feet of the people standing on the other side of the globe, which are opposite ours); 136 *Septentrion* The north (from "septentriones," the seven stars of Ursa Major, or the Big Dipper); 139 *withal* with it; 141 *pitiful* compassionate, having pity; *flexible* soft, docile; 142 *stern* fierce; cruel; severe; *flinty* hard-hearted; 143 *Bid'st thou me* Do you ask me to; 146 *the rage* i.e., the furious wind of the storm; *allays* abates, decreases (from the proverbs "after wind comes rain" and "a little rain allays a great wind"); 147 *Rutland* i.e., Edmund Plantagenet, Earl of Rutland (York's youngest son, murdered by Margaret); *obsequies* (OB´-seh-KWEEZ) (1) expressions of love and piety owed to the deceased; (2) funeral rites; 149 *fell* cruel; savage; *false* untrustworthy; dishonest; 155 *Hyrcania* (Her-KAY´-nee-UH) a region of ancient Persia, on the Caspian Sea [*tigers of Hyrcania* Hyrcanian tigers were first mentioned in Virgil's *Aeneid*, and by Elizabethan times had become proverbially fierce]; 156 *hapless* both (1) unfortunate and (2) unhappy; 157 *This cloth* in her preceding monologue, Margaret handed York a handkerchief stained with Rutland's

Keep thou the napkin and go boast of this,
160 And if thou tell the heavy story right,
Upon my soul the hearers will shed tears;
Yea, even my foes will shed fast-falling tears,
And say "Alas! It was a piteous deed."
There, take the crown, and with the crown, my curse;
165 And in thy need, such comfort come to thee
As now I reap at thy too cruel hand.
Hard-hearted Clifford, take me from the world,
My soul to Heaven, my blood upon your heads.

3 minutes, 15 seconds

blood, with which to wipe the tears he sheds for the boy; 159 ***napkin*** handkerchief; 160 ***heavy*** serious, sorrowful; 163 ***piteous*** contemptible, miserable (not "pitiful," as defined today); 164 ***the crown*** he refers to the paper crown that Margaret has mockingly put on his head; 165 ***in thy need such comfort*** when you are in need may the same type of comfort; 167 ***take me from the world*** i.e., kill me; 168 ***My soul to Heaven, my blood upon your heads*** i.e., my soul will rise to Heaven, and the sin of my murder will be on your heads.

COMMENTARY

This piece is spoken in reply to Margaret's monologue on page 164, in which she cruelly and sarcastically torments her prisoner. In light of her viciousness, York's reaction is remarkable: he has silently endured her taunts, and refused to give her the satisfaction of seeing him cry and rant over his failed try for the crown or the violent death of his young son. Margaret has kept Clifford from slaying York immediately in order to enjoy her foe's last words, which she supposes will be a lament over his dead child or a cowardly entreaty for his life. York does not oblige. Instead, he delivers a surprisingly complex and formal repudiation of everything that is Margaret—her character, looks, descent, and womanhood are all characterized as rotten. And York makes it clear that it is her deeds, rather than his words, that will yield her infamy. History will remember her for those deeds, so although she may kill York now, she has already done him the favor of setting his revenge in motion all by herself.

How is York able to accomplish this turning of tables? Well, besides being courageous and determined, he is also a well-educated man. He exhibits a talent for the use of rhetoric, as well as knowledge of Latin. One of York's favorite rhetorical devices is double entendre. With the opening words *She-wolf of France* he is not only calling Margaret a vicious feral animal, but also using a play on the Latin word for wolf, *lupa*, which also means "lewd woman" or "prostitute." This is no random insult: in *Henry VI, Part Two*, Margaret had a long-term adulterous affair with the Duke of Suffolk and now that he's out of the picture the nature of her relationship with the "northern lords" (exactly how many of them are there, anyway?) is suspect. York puns on this subject again with *false Frenchwoman*: while the primary meaning of *false* in this context is "untrustworthy" or "dishonest," the word was also commonly used in Shakespeare's time to mean "adulterous." York's most complex play on words is his use of *rain*. He concludes the first section of this speech with the metaphor of wind and rain (often used as symbols of God's wrath) for his raging and tears. Rather than the hysterical, ranting rage that Margaret hoped for, York shows her the rage of righteous anger; rather than pathetic tears, this anger brings on the rain—tears for the wronged Rutland—of which every drop cries out vengeance. Thus, with *rain* he alludes to the vengeance that will be brought to bear on Margaret after his death, when his heirs eventually "reign"—remember that York believes in his (and his heirs') divine right to rule (see "Riding Shotgun with God," page 235). He is sure that God will intercede and his cause will ultimately prevail.

The storm of anger and tears is one of many images York employs. He is quite fond of comparing Margaret with savage beasts. In addition to the *wolves of France*, he compares her to an adder—which her tongue outpoisons—and calls her more inhuman than *tigers of Hyrcania* (a reference to Virgil's *Aeneid*, further evidence of his knowledge of Latin). York has a metaphor or simile for each despicable aspect of Margaret: she triumphs over him like an *Amazonian trull*; her face is *vizard-like*; taking after her lowly father, she misuses her power the way a beggar who is given a horse runs it to death.

The most important rhetorical device in this monologue, however, is antithesis, on which the whole denunciation of Margaret is structured. There are examples of antithesis in many of the beginning lines (*She-wolf of France* versus *worse than wolves of France*; *Were shame enough* versus *wert not shameless*; *Thy father* versus *an English yeoman*). Later in this section of the piece, the antithesis becomes more structured. There are two groupings of these antitheses. The first group uses the word *'Tis* to introduce each thesis (the ideal woman's attributes), which is then followed by a line describing its antithesis (Margaret). The second of these groupings is a laundry list of a respectable woman's pure qualities (*Women are soft, mild, pitiful and flexible*), followed by a pile of Margaret's dirty ones (*Thou stern, obdurate, flinty, rough, remorseless*). Even the storm metaphor at the end of the first section contains an antithesis (*rage allays* versus *rain begins*). In the second section, the antithesis continues (*This cloth thou dipped'st in blood* versus *I with tears do wash the blood away*), and finally drives home the damning conclusion of York's speech (*My soul to Heaven* versus *my blood upon your heads*). Complementing this antithesis is the parallel construction of the two consecutive lines in which a question is asked and immediately answered (*Bid'st thou me rage?* with *Why now thou hast thy wish*; *Would'st have me weep?* with *Why, now thou hast thy will*).

The meter in this piece is also a significant source of information. Most noticeably, there are many lines with inverted first feet, beginning with *She-wolf*, which starts off the piece with a bang. There are also many elisions and many double endings, both at the ends of lines and around caesuras, including a couple of triple endings (see the difficult-to-scan examples, below). You must decide what causes the resulting sense of urgency. Is York rushing to get his whole repudiation out before they kill him? Are the words simply tumbling out because he is so incensed? Is it because he has held back all throughout her torments, and now he's letting loose?

York intersperses different assonant vowels thoroughout the piece, which are very handy for using the voice to its fullest advantage (*ill-beseeming is it in*; *rage / allays / rain*; *every / vengeance / death / 'Gainst / fell*; *go boast*; *hearers / tears*). York weaves his condemnation of Margaret almost like a spell, using lots of alliteration to bind his words into a powerful pronouncement (*worse than wolves*; *triumph / trull*; *As the Antipodes*; *South / Septentrion*; *Would'st / weep / Why / will / wind*; *fell / false / Frenchwoman*; *ten / times / tigers*). Many of the repeated sounds are concentrated in the final few cursing lines of the piece: Examples include

Cursing Cs (*crown* / *crown* / *curse* / *comfort* / *come* / *cruel* / *Clifford*), Relentless Rs (*There* / *crown* / *crown* / *curse* / *comfort* / *reap* / *cruel* / *Hard-hearted* / *Clifford* / *world*), and Hostile Hs (*hand* / *Hard-hearted* / *Heaven* / *heads*).

Notice which words York chooses to repeat: *proud queen* / *proud*; *shame* / *shame* / *shameless*; *rage* / *raging* / *rage*. These repetitions drive home his main points: Margaret is proud without justification; she is shameful and shameless; York does rage, but not in the way she has just commanded him to do for her pleasure (see Margaret's monologue, page 164)—just the opposite, his rage will bring vengeance on her.

SIGNIFICANT SCANS

Line 141 can be scanned several ways, all of which require that you invert the first foot. We think it then scans most naturally with a silent, unaccented half foot at the first caesura, another inverted foot after the second caesura, an elision (*pitiful* [PIT-ful]), and a triple ending (phew!):

/ x x / x / / x x / (x-x)
Women are soft, (pause) mild, pitiful and flexible

Note that to scan line 142 properly, you must use the archaic pronunciation of the word *obdurate* (ob-DYOOR-eht).

Line 154 can be scanned two ways:

With a triple ending, and eliding *inexorable* (in-EGGS-ra-bl)—

x / x / x / x / x / (x-x)
But you are more inhuman, more inexorable

Or, with a crowded foot and contracting *you are* (YOU'RE) and *inexorable* (in-EGGS-ra-BL)—

x / x - x / x / x / x /
But you are more inhuman, more inexorable

Lines 120 and 152 are scanned by most editors as we have shown them here, but the First Folio has them distributed somewhat differently. This may have to do with transcription errors, or space restrictions on the page, but it is also possible that they were written that way. Here is how they appear in the Folio:

Were shame enough to shame thee,
Wert thou not shameless.

That face of his
The hungry cannibals would not have touched,
would not have stained with blood;

You may choose to perform them either way, but if you use the Folio version, you must decide whether York pauses at the beginnings or ends of the short lines, and why. For example, after saying *That face of his* he may be so overcome by the recollection of his child's face that he needs a moment to compose himself before he continues.

Don't forget to elide: *Amazonian* (AM´-uh-ZO-nyan) in line 114; *abominable* (a-BOM´-na-BL) in line 133; *pitiful* (PIT-ful) in line 141; *inexorable* (in-EGGS-ra-bl) in line 154; *even* (E'EN) in line 162; *piteous* (PIH-tyuss) in line 163; and *Heaven* (HEV'N) in line 168 (or you may choose to scan *Heaven* as a double ending before the caesura);

. . . and to expand: *cruel* (CROO-el) in line 166.

IRRELEVANT HISTORY: GREENE'S GROATSWORTH OF GRIPE

The line *O tiger's heart wrapped in a woman's hide* has enjoyed its own celebrity outside the context of *Henry VI, Part Three*, as the object of the earliest literary reference to Shakespeare and his work. In 1592, playwright Robert Greene languished on his deathbed, scribbling his last words. One of these short autobiographical writings contained a warning to his fellow playwrights: beware the players (actors) who threaten to displace you—you, the very men who make them famous. Greene singled out one player in particular: "an upstart crow, beautified with our feathers, that with his *tiger's heart wrapped in a player's hide* supposes he is as well able to bombast out a blank verse as the best of you; and . . . is in his own conceit the only Shake-scene in the country." Whether Greene simply chose this particular line in this particular play to exemplify Shakespeare's bold and popular style or had reason to resent Shakespeare for taking the credit after merely rewriting someone else's work, we'll never know (see "*The Contention* and *The Whole Contention*: A Lot to Contend With, and No One Is Content," page 920). Greene most likely never intended to publish these writings, but the lack of anything approaching copyright law in the 1590s allowed his publisher, Henry Chettle, to print them and keep all the profit. Chettle entitled the collection *A Groatsworth of Wit Bought with a Million of Repentance*. Ironically, Greene's last few bitter scribblings about the fledgling writer Shakespeare are his most remembered and most repeated words.

HENRY VI, PART THREE

ACT II, SCENE v

KING HENRY VI

GENDER: M
PROSE/VERSE: blank verse
AGE RANGE: mature adult
FREQUENCY OF USE (1–5): 1

The armed forces of sweet, gentle, ineffectual King Henry VI are fighting the forces of his cousins, the Yorks, who seek the throne for themselves. His troops are led by his wife, Queen Margaret, along with Lord Clifford and the Earl of Northumberland. As Henry is a liability on the battlefield (he's no warrior, and he's the other side's prime target), he has been sent away from the fighting by his wife and Clifford. He meanders to a nearby hilltop, to ponder his life.

This battle fares like to the morning's war,
When dying clouds contend with growing light,
What time the shepherd, blowing of his nails,
Can neither call it perfect day nor night.
5 Now sways it this way, like a mighty sea
Forced by the tide to combat with the wind;
Now sways it that way, like the selfsame sea
Forced to retire by fury of the wind.
Sometime the flood prevails, and then the wind;
10 Now one the better, then another best;
Both tugging to be victors, breast to breast,
Yet neither conqueror nor conquerèd.
So is the equal poise of this fell war.
Here on this molehill will I sit me down.
15 To whom God will, there be the victory.
For Margaret my queen, and Clifford, too,
Have chid me from the battle, swearing both
They prosper best of all when I am thence.
Would I were dead, if God's good will were so,
20 For what is in this world but grief and woe?
O God! Methinks it were a happy life
To be no better than a homely swain;
To sit upon a hill, as I do now,
To carve out dials quaintly, point by point,
25 Thereby to see the minutes how they run—
How many makes the hour full complete,
How many hours brings about the day,
How many days will finish up the year,
How many years a mortal man may live;

1 *fares like to* is playing itself out like; 2 *contend with* battle against; 3 *What time* the time when; *blowing of his nails* i.e., blowing on his fingers, to warm them; 4 *Can neither call it perfect* can't pinpoint it as either being exactly; 8 *fury* angry storm; 9 *Sometime* At one moment; 10 *the better* is proving the better (of the two); *then another best* i.e., then the other takes the lead; 12 *Yet neither conqueror nor conquerèd* Yet neither side is emerging as the clear victor or the clear loser; 13 *equal poise* equal weight of the two sides (as in the two balanced sides of a scale); *fell* cruel; 15 *To whom God will, there be the victory* The victory will be granted to whomever God wishes; 16 *Clifford* i.e., Lord John Clifford (a virulently pro-Lancastrian noble, because his father was killed by Richard, Duke of York); 17 *chid me from* scoldingly shooed me away from; 18 *prosper best of all* are the most successful; *thence* not there, elsewhere; 19 *Would* I wish; 21 *were* would be; 22 *homely* simple, humble; *swain* shepherd; 24 *dials* sundials (shepherds would often carve out sundials in the turf of hillsides); *quaintly* neatly; skillfully; artfully; *point by point* one point on the sundial at a time (i.e., one bit at a time); 25 *to see the minutes how they run* to see how

30 When this is known, then to divide the times—
So many hours must I tend my flock,
So many hours must I take my rest,
So many hours must I contemplate,
So many hours must I sport myself;
35 So many days my ewes have been with young,
So many weeks ere the poor fools will ean,
So many years ere I shall shear the fleece:
So minutes, hours, days, months, and years,
Passed over to the end they were created,
40 Would bring white hairs unto a quiet grave.
Ah, what a life were this! How sweet! How lovely!
Gives not the hawthorn bush a sweeter shade
To shepherds looking on their silly sheep
Than doth a rich embroidered canopy
45 To kings that fear their subjects' treachery?
O yes, it doth—a thousand-fold, it doth!
And to conclude, the shepherd's homely curds,
His cold thin drink out of his leather bottle,
His wonted sleep under a fresh tree's shade,
50 All which secure and sweetly he enjoys,
Is far beyond a prince's delicates,
His viands sparkling in a golden cup,
His body couchèd in a curious bed,
When care, mistrust, and treason waits on him.

3 minutes

quickly the minutes pass; 31 *So many* this many; 34 *sport myself* amuse myself, play; 36 *ere* before; *fools* a term of endearment; *ean* give birth; 38 *So* in this manner; 39 *Passed over to* spent in accordance with; *the end they were created* the purpose for which they were made; 40 *Would bring white hairs unto a quiet grave* i.e., would allow one to reach old age and to die peacefully; 43 *looking on* watching over; *silly* innocent, helpless; 47 *curds* a dish made from coagulated milk, eaten by peasants; 48 *thin drink* beverage with a low alcohol content; 49 *wonted* customary; 50 *All which* all of which; *secure* free from worries; 51 *Is far beyond* far surpasses; *delicates* delicacies; 52 *viands* (VIE-undz) food (especially dressed meats); *cup* a sort of plate (probably like a shallow soup bowl); 53 *couchèd* laid down; *curious* gorgeous; 54 *care* grief, sorrow; *waits on* attends, serves.

COMMENTARY

We tend to think that kings, as sovereign rulers of others, must surely be masters of their own destinies. Not so—at least not if you're King Henry. His life has been determined by others since he became King of England at the age of nine months. We finally hear how he feels about it in this piece.

As you can see, Henry uses imagery to describe the battle between his forces and those of the Yorks. It is interesting to note that the similes he chooses (*This battle fares like to the morning's war, / When dying clouds contend with growing light; Now sways it this way, like a mighty sea / fury of the wind / the flood*) are of forces of nature, beyond the control of mere mortals. As cruel (*fell*) as he considers the war, the meek Henry believes that he can do nothing to prevent the battle or to affect its outcome—all he can do is get out of the storm. He will not even go so far as to hope that his troops prevail, saying instead, *To whom God will, there be the victory*. It is important to know that King Henry is a devoutly religious man—he may not wish to anger God by substituting his judgment for God's. Also, he has expressed elsewhere in the play that he believes the Yorks do have a valid claim to the throne. He may very well be feeling torn between his loyalty to his wife, son, and followers and his sense of justice.

It can't feel good to be the most powerful man in England and, simultaneously, the most ineffectual. And, in fact, we know from his outburst (*Would I were dead, if God's good will were so, / For what is in this world but grief and woe? / O God!*) that King Henry is despondent. It comports with his devoutness that he would qualify his death wish with *if God's will be so*—remember that he would consider suicide a sin. No matter how sincerely King Henry wishes to be dead, he will not imply (even to himself!) that he would interfere with God's master plan and seek out death a moment before God bestows it upon him.

Since King Henry can't take his own life—having no choice but to remain on earth until he's called (or, as it turns out, is sent) to his Maker—he must continue to concern himself with earthly matters. But the matters on his own plate have proved too unbearable to think about. And so Henry turns his mind to what he imagines to be a perfect earthly existence—that of a shepherd. We have a clue that Henry has thought about the shepherd's life before, because he randomly mentions shepherds right at the onset of this monologue, when he's comparing the battle to the early-morning contest between night and day, *What time the shepherd, blowing of his nails, / Can neither call it perfect day nor night*. Henry wishes desperately that he were a shepherd. Notice the detail with which he describes the life he'd lead. If there were mail-order catalogues in his day, you know he'd have pored over the shepherd-supply ones.

Henry lets himself get carried off by his reverie. The rhythms created by the unusual number of repetitions of phrases, words, and sounds give the piece a chanting quality, which can be interpreted as liturgical in nature (which would soothe his spirit, given his religious bent). The lulling quality of these repetitions suggests that he is trying to calm himself. In the first section, notice the repetition of words and sounds at the ends of lines (*sea*, *wind*, and the rhyming *night* and *light*). The very notable sound combination of Soothing Ss and SHuSHing SHs throughout the shepherd section of the piece also support this idea, and stand in contrast with the Woeful Ws and Grief-stricken Gs (*Would / were / God's good will were / what / world / grief / woe*), as well as against a string of Curt Cs at the end, which bring Henry back out of the reverie and into the cruel reality of his existence (*conclude / curds / cold / delicates / cup / couchèd / curious / care*). Also notice the rhymes (*light / night*; *best / breast*; *so / woe*; *canopy / treachery*), which alert the listener's ear to (1) the futility of military posturing; (2) the fact that Henry wants to kill himself; and (3) the important point Henry is making about the richness of the poor peasant's existence versus the bankrupt nature of the King's. And, for help exploiting the word *O* to its best advantage, see "O, No! An *O*!," page xxxiii.

Be careful not to throw away a wonderful opportunity: the repetition of phrases (such as *How many* . . . and *So many* . . .) affords you the challenge of finding the nuances that will differentiate each phrase repetition from the ones that preceded it and will create a build among them.

Notice the embedded stage direction in the monologue (*Here on this molehill will I sit me down*), but keep in mind that you don't have to sit at that moment (or may change your mind) and you don't have to be seated for the whole monologue. FYI: this is the selfsame molehill upon which, one act earlier, Margaret and Clifford tormented, tortured, and killed the Duke of York. Of course, Henry doesn't know this chilling fact, but the audience does, which heightens the pathos of the piece with no effort on your part!

SIGNIFICANT SCANS

There are a few interesting scansion variations to notice. The first is that this piece contains an unusual number of inverted (trochaic) feet in the middle of lines following caesuras that are not indicated by punctuation: *like to* in line 1; *ere the* in line 36; *ere I* in line 37; *unto* in line 40; *out of* in line 48; *under* in line 49. All but the first of these occur when King Henry is talking about the shepherd's life. This lends an air of enthusiasm to this section that is missing from the rest of the monologue, indicating that Henry is excited about his topic. He also inverts the first foot of lines 25–29 and 31–37 (beginning with *Thereby* . . . , *How many* . . . , and *So many* . . .). These lines make up the bulk of Henry's fantasy about being a shepherd.

Line 38 is tricky—give a silent half foot to the caesura after *days*, and the meter will fall into place:

x / x /x / x / x /
So minutes, hours, days, (pause) months and years

Don't forget to elide: *curious* (KYOOR-yuss) in line 53;
. . . and to expand: *conquerèd* (CON´-kur-EHD) in line 12; *Margaret* (MAR´-ga-RET) in line 16; and *couchèd* (COW-chehd) in line 53.

IMPOTENT POTENTATE

Poor, poor Henry VI would have been a wonderfully happy shepherd, or monk, even. Instead, he was put to work as King of England at the age of nine months. Henry was not cut out to reign. The pressures of the monarchy caused him to suffer a mental breakdown in 1453, shortly after his son was born, and he was declared insane, suffering from what historians believe was either catatonic schizophrenia or a depressive stupor for about a year (he lost his memory, ability to speak, and motor coordination, and barely moved). Following his recovery, he "ruled" through the Wars of the Roses until he was deposed in 1461 by the Yorkist Edward IV. He spent four years hiding out in Scotland and another five as a prisoner in the Tower of London until the Lancastrian forces restored him to the throne in 1470. His second reign was brief, however. He was captured by the Yorks at the Battle of Barnet, reinterned in the Tower, and murdered there—supposedly while at prayer—in 1471. During his reign (such as it was) he was a patron of the arts and literature, and founded Eton College. His subjects loved him, revering him as a saint, and after his death made pilgrimages to his grave, where miracles were said to occur. This made King Edward so uncomfortable that he tried to prevent the pilgrimages, which only heightened the fervor of Henry's devotees. When Richard III succeeded Edward he reversed tactics, moving Henry's body to the Chapel of St. George at Windsor, his birthplace, amid a show of great honor, but the gesture did little to increase Richard's popularity with his subjects.

RICHARD III

ACT I, SCENE i

RICHARD

GENDER: M | AGE RANGE: adult to mature adult
PROSE/VERSE: blank verse | FREQUENCY OF USE (1–5): 4

Richard Plantagenet of York, Duke of Gloucester, is the younger brother of King Edward IV, who has recently ascended England's throne as a result of the Yorks' triumph over their cousins, the Lancasters, in the Wars of the Roses (for an overview, see "The Red Rose and the White . . . the Fatal Colors of Our Striving Houses," page 238). Richard wants to be king. As *Richard III* opens, Richard (who has been biding his time and helping his father's and brother's military efforts in *Henry VI, Parts Two* and *Three*) reveals his intentions for the course of the play with this soliloquy.

Now is the winter of our discontent
Made glorious summer by this son of York;
And all the clouds that loured upon our house
In the deep bosom of the ocean buried.
5 Now are our brows bound with victorious wreaths,
Our bruisèd arms set up for monuments,
Our stern alarums changed to merry meetings,
Our dreadful marches to delightful measures.
Grim-visaged War hath smoothed his wrinkled front,
10 And now, instead of mounting barbèd steeds
To fright the souls of fearful adversaries,
He capers nimbly in a lady's chamber
To the lascivious pleasing of a lute.
But I, that am not shaped for sportive tricks
15 Nor made to court an amorous looking-glass;
I, that am rudely stamped, and want love's majesty
To strut before a wanton ambling nymph;
I, that am curtailed of this fair proportion,

1 *winter of our discontent* i.e., the time of discontent for the York branch of the royal family, during which the usurping Lancastrian branch held the throne; 2 *son of York* (1) i.e., Edward IV (son of Richard, Duke of York, whose valid claim to the English throne [see "Genealogical Chart—the Wars of the Roses," pages 236–37] sparked the Wars of the Roses); and (2) the York family, as represented by the emblem of the blazing "sun," adopted by King Edward IV after he saw a vision of three suns during the Battle of Mortimer's Cross, in which he defeated the Lancastrian forces; 3 *loured* (rhymes with "soured") looked dark and threatening; frowned; *house* i.e., the house of York, the branch of the royal family to which Richard belongs; 4 *buried* are buried; 5 *brows* heads; *bound* crowned; 6 *bruisèd arms* battered armor; *monuments* memorials [*bruisèd arms set up for monuments* battered armor hung up as monuments (in medieval times, the armor of royalty who died in battle was sometimes hung over their tombs)]; 7 *stern* severe; gloomy; *alarums* (1) calls to arms (from "all arm"); (2) military attacks; *meetings* gatherings; 8 *dreadful* (1) fearful; and/or (2) inspiring fear; *measures* dance steps; 9 *Grim-visaged* Grim-faced; *War* war, personified; *wrinkled front* frowning forehead; 10 *barbèd* wearing horse armor (from the French *barde*, the covering that protected the chest and sides of a horse); 11 *fearful* (1) fearful; and/or (2) inspiring fear; 12 *He* i.e., war personified (but audiences of Shakespeare's time would have recognized this as an allusion to the victorious warrior King Edward IV—a notorious adulterer); *capers* (1) dances; (2) lecherously cavorts; 13 *lascivious pleasing* pleasingly lascivious music; *lute* stringed, wooden musical instrument (popular from the fourteenth to seventeenth centuries); 14 *shaped for* made for; *sportive tricks* sexual games; 15 *court* attempt to please, woo [*court an amorous looking-glass* i.e., try to love what I see in the mirror; or, pose for a mirror that will not reflect a positive image back at me]; 16 *rudely* crudely, roughly; *stamped* formed by being imprinted or pressed [*rudely stamped* badly made; or, marked with a rough appearance]; *want* lack [*want love's majesty / To strut* lack the grandeur love inspires, which gives one the confidence to strut]; 17 *ambling* moving or walking affectedly; *nymph* beautiful young woman; 18 *fair* favorable, attractive; *proportion* shape, form [*curtailed of this fair proportion* (CUR-tayld) i.e., badly cut out of the attractively proportioned pattern his brother was properly cut from]; 19 *feature* good looks; *Nature* nature, personified [*Cheated . . . Nature*

Cheated of feature by dissembling Nature,
20 Deformed, unfinished, sent before my time
Into the breathing world, scarce half made up—
And that so lamely and unfashionable
That dogs bark at me as I halt by them—
Why, I, in this weak piping time of peace,
25 Have no delight to pass away the time
Unless to spy my shadow in the sun
And descant on mine own deformity.
And therefore, since I cannot prove a lover
To entertain these fair well-spoken days,
30 I am determinèd to prove a villain
And hate the idle pleasures of these days.
Plots have I laid, inductions dangerous,
By drunken prophecies, libels and dreams,
To set my brother Clarence and the King
35 In deadly hate the one against the other;
And if King Edward be as true and just
As I am subtle, false, and treacherous,
This day should Clarence closely be mewed up
About a prophecy, which says that G
40 Of Edward's heirs the murderer shall be.
Dive, thoughts, down to my soul—here Clarence comes.

2 minutes, 20 seconds

(1) given this poor outward appearance by Nature, who thus disguises my greatness; or (2) cheated of the advantage of handsome appearance, which Nature usually grants to evil men]; 21 *breathing* living [*sent before . . . world* i.e., born prematurely]; *scarce* scarcely, hardly; *half made up* half finished ("made up" is a tailor's term); 22 *And that* i.e., and at that, made up; *lamely* (1) haltingly; (2) imperfectly, defectively; *unfashionable* deformed, badly made; 23 *halt* limp; 24 *Why* an interjection used for emphasis, like an expletive; *weak piping time of peace* time of peace, characterized by the soft sound of pipes (associated with shepherds and dancing), rather than shrill fifes and angry drums (associated with time of war); 25 *delight* i.e., delightful activity; 26 *Unless* except; 27 *descant on* (DESS-kant) discourse or comment on; 28 *prove* prove to be, turn out to be; 29 *entertain* i.e., entertain myself during; *fair* (1) not cloudy or dim (referring to good weather); (2) in a good state, in order; *well-spoken days* (1) days in which soft, eloquent words are spoken; or (2) days in which slick speech-making is popular; 30 *determinèd* (1) resolved; (2) fated; 32 *inductions dangerous* dangerous first steps or preparations; 33 *By drunken prophecies* by means of prophecies spoken to drunken revelers, and/or spoken under the influence of drink; 35 *In deadly . . . other* in murderous, hateful opposition to each other; 37 *false* deceitful, untrustworthy, and unfaithful; *treacherous* treasonous, disloyal; 38 *closely* in narrow confinement; *mewed up* confined, caged (a hawking term) [*should . . . mewed up* will be caged in narrow confinement]; 39 *About* because of; *G* The *G* has been interpreted by the King as referring to his brother, the Duke of Clarence, whose first name is George. Keep in mind, however, that Richard's title is Duke of Gloucester. Hmm . . . ; 40 *Edward's heirs* the prophecy is not about King Edward IV's heirs, but about the descendants of Edward III: Edward IV and his brothers, Clarence and Richard [*Of Edward's . . . be* shall be the murderer of Edward's heirs].

COMMENTARY

What is it about Richard that makes his evil machinations so seductive? One has only to glance at these first few lines of *Richard III* to realize it is his spellbinding way with words, combined with his keen, intelligent, and witty take on the world (and on himself!) that fascinates both his audience and his victims.

Richard keeps his listeners' ears pricked and alert in many ways. For instance, you will find a lot of variation in the meter of this speech. There are many double endings and many inverted first feet—including one in the opening line, which starts the play off with an urgent bang, commanding the audience's attention. (In Elizabethan times there was no overture, dimming lights, or curtain to raise: the *Now* broadcasts these introductory peripherals with a single word.) Several of the inverted feet fall on the word *I*—Richard may be purposely asserting himself, or perhaps this is his usual self-centered style, or maybe he's still trying to convince himself of his own power to get what he wants, depending on your interpretation. These variations make the piece dynamic, railing against the established meter the way Richard rails against his allotted fate. And yet Richard uses many elisions that force regularity of meter and two formal expansions, which evoke the feeling that he is speaking with precision—you may decide to use this precision to convey the fact that you know what you want and intend to get it, or to carefully convince yourself that you do.

Despite all the variations, the words and ideas in this piece are tightly bound to each other through the use of sounds. First, notice the astounding assonance: hOWling OWs (*Now / our / clouds / loured / house / Now / brows / bound / Our / Our / Our / now / mounting*)—wow!; Irritated IHs (*is / winter / discontent / this*); AggrIEved EEs (*Cheated / feature*); hAteful As (*capers / lady's / chamber*); whIning Is (*Why / I / piping / time*); and many more examples woven throughout the piece. Also, admire the adroit alliteration: Spitting Ss (*summer / son*); Bitter Bs (*bosom / buried / brows / bound / bruisèd*); Manipulative Ms accented by Determined and Deceitful Ds (*monuments / merry meetings / dreadful marches / delightful measures / mounted*); Festering Fs (*fright / fearful*); Leering Ls (*lady's / lascivious / lute*, complemented by the Ls in *nimbly* and *pleasing*); additional Determined Ds (*days / dangerous / drunken / dreams*); and many other such expressive sounds. In contrast to all these tightly connected sounds and meanings, though, notice the four blunt words that encapsulate Richard's description of himself: *scarce half made up*.

Richard wraps up his soliloquy with a rhyming couplet (*G / be*) before the last line of the piece (in which he sees Clarence coming, escorted by guards—Richard's plan is already in motion). Although you are free to cut this last line, we feel it provides a good opportunity to showcase your ability to transition smoothly from soliloquy to scene.

Certain words are frequently repeated to accent important aspects of the speech. For instance, repetition of *Now* promotes a sense of urgency, while the often-used *Our* highlights Richard's ironic bitterness—although he is a York, he does not really belong, and does not feel part of the good fortune the others are enjoying. Likewise, *I, that am* emphasizes Richard's dual sense of himself—he feels he is singled out as a freak on one hand, and as an ingenious future ruler on the other. All of these repetitions contribute to the built-in build in the piece, of which you must be aware; make sure to begin the monologue at a level that leaves room for the build.

The rhetorical device in which Richard takes the most pleasure is the pun, of which there is a plethora in this piece: *son* = (1) Edward, the son of Richard, Duke of York; and a play on (2) the house of York, as represented by Edward's emblem of the blazing sun; *mounting* = (1) getting on (a horse) in order to ride; and an indirect play on the idea of (2) "mounting" a woman to engage in sexual intercourse; *curtailed* = (1) cut short; and a play on (2) "curtal," an animal that has lost its tail; *Plots* = (1) secret plans or schemes to achieve an evil purpose; and a play on (2) the central narratives of stage plays; *inductions* = (1) first steps or preparations; with a play on (2) in Elizabethan theatre, an introduction or prologue to a stage play.

What is even more remarkable is that the puns are part of a series of metaphors that reveal the complexity of Richard's thoughts. Like the use of *Plots* and *inductions* in one line to pun on the same set of meanings, there are several instances where Richard extends a pun into a longer metaphor. For example, he refers to himself as *half made up,* a term a tailor would commonly apply to a half-finished garment, and then extends the reference by using the word *unfashionable* in the next line. The word *descant* describes how Richard discourses or comments on his own deformity, but also puns on the word's original meaning—to sing a melody or counterpoint against a simple musical theme. Thus, *descant* completes an extended musical metaphor (*delightful measures*; *pleasing of a lute*; *weak piping time*) with the idea that he will *descant* over all this peaceful music—his voice will stand out and become the melody, just as he intends to become king.

Richard's metaphors make use of antitheses and other contrasting images that also have deeper secondary meanings: the words *winter of our discontent / Made glorious summer* not only illustrate the difference between the Yorks' state pre- and postvictory, but also refer to the actual seasons of the events—the last battles of the Wars of the Roses took place over the winter of 1471, ending with the Battle of Tewkesbury in May, so it was in fact a pretty *glorious summer* for the Yorks. Richard also personifies a *Grim-visaged War*, living it up around the castle and making time with the ladies during peacetime, an image in which Shakespeare's audiences would have recognized King Edward, who fought furiously to secure the throne but later became a notorious lecher, and whose barroom and bedroom preoccupations may eventually have killed him. The antithetical phrasing of *cannot prove a lover* versus *determinèd to prove a villain* and *King Edward be as true and just* versus *I am subtle, false, and treacherous* emphasizes Richard's villainy to chilling effect by setting it in stark relief to his brother's benevolence.

Although this piece is the very first moment of *Richard III*, you can learn a lot about Richard's backstory by reading the two preceding plays in the tetralogy, *Henry VI, Parts Two* and *Three*.

Don't forget to elide: *glorious* (GLO-ryuss) in line 2; *victorious* (vik-TOR-yuss) in line 5; *lascivious* (luh-SIH-vyuss) in line 13; *amorous* (AM-russ) in line 15; and *unfashionable* (un-FA´-shnuh-BL) in line 22;

. . . and to expand: *bruisèd* (BROO-zehd) in line 6 and *determinèd* (de-TER´-mih-NEHD) in line 30.

REVISIONIST *RICHARD*: WE DO MISTAKE HIS PERSON ALL THIS WHILE

Although he may not have been any more of a Dudley Do-Right than his fellow English monarchs, Richard III was no worse than most of them, and certainly not the archvillain that history and Shakespeare have made him out to be. Rather than plotting to remove all his nearest and dearest relatives from his pathway to the throne, Richard loyally supported his brother Edward IV throughout his twenty-two-year reign and pleaded for the life of their traitorous brother George, Duke of Clarence. Richard was not responsible for his wife's death, nor did he ever intend to marry his niece—in fact, he was horrified by the idea. Richard did seize Edward IV's two young princes after Edward's death and place them in the Tower. It is not known whether he had them killed, but this is the one atrocity historians generally believe he did commit. It is probably because of this one awful (but for a medieval monarch, certainly not unprecedented) deed that Tudor supporters were able to start a myriad of rumors to justify the Earl of Richmond's usurpation of the throne. Such rumors evolved into the legend of Richard's evil, and became recorded "history" through Shakespeare's sources, the Renaissance historians Holinshed and Hall. H and H relied heavily upon the writings of Sir Thomas More, who, in the service of Henry VII's son, Henry VIII, was likely to be disposed toward the Tudor point of view. Oh, and one more thing—as we know from contemporary portraits as well as from Richard's recorded prowess in battle, he was not hunchbacked, clubfooted, withered in the arm, or ugly . . . nor as far as we know was he born feet first with a full set of teeth.

RICHARD III

ACT I, SCENE ii

LADY ANNE

GENDER: F
AGE RANGE: young adult to adult
PROSE/VERSE: blank verse
FREQUENCY OF USE (1–5): 4

In *Henry VI, Part Three*, Lady Anne Neville's father-in-law, King Henry VI of England, was overthrown and imprisoned by his cousins, the Yorks. In the process, Lady Anne's husband, Crown Prince Edward, was captured in battle and killed by his Yorkist cousin Richard, and Richard's brothers. Richard then murdered King Henry VI while the latter was at prayer in his prison cell. Richard's eldest brother, Edward, is now King of England. At the moment, Lady Anne is on a London street, accompanying the remains of her father-in-law from St. Paul's Cathedral to the monastery at Chertsey, where he will be laid to rest.

Set down, set down your honorable load
(If honor may be shrouded in a hearse),
Whilst I awhile obsequiously lament
The untimely fall of virtuous Lancaster.
5 Poor key-cold figure of a holy king,
Pale ashes of the House of Lancaster,
Thou bloodless remnant of that royal blood,
Be it lawful that I invocate thy ghost
To hear the lamentations of poor Anne,
10 Wife to thy Edward, to thy slaughtered son,
Stabbed by the selfsame hand that made these wounds.
Lo, in these windows that let forth thy life
I pour the helpless balm of my poor eyes.
O, cursèd be the hand that made these holes!
15 Cursèd the heart that had the heart to do it!
Cursèd the blood that let this blood from hence!
More direful hap betide that hated wretch
That makes us wretched by the death of thee
Than I can wish to adders, spiders, toads,
20 Or any creeping venomed thing that lives!
If ever he have child, abortive be it,
Prodigious and untimely brought to light,
Whose ugly and unnatural aspect
May fright the hopeful mother at the view;

1 *your honorable load* i.e., the coffin; 2 *shrouded* both (1) wrapped in a shroud and (2) hidden, sheltered; *hearse* coffin on a bier (a frame with handles); 3 *obsequiously* mournfully, in a manner befitting a funeral; 4 *fall* death (i.e., murder); *Lancaster* i.e., King Henry (who was descended from the Lancastrian branch of the royal family [see "Genealogical Chart—the Wars of the Roses," pages 236–37]); 5 *key-cold* deathly cold (as cold as a metal key); *a holy king* kings were believed to be chosen by God—see "Riding Shotgun with God," page 235; Henry, in particular, was reknowned for his piety; 7 *bloodless* (1) devoid of blood; (2) pale, ashen; *blood* bloodline; 8 *Be it lawful* let it be permissible under law (one explanation for this statement is that it was illegal to commit acts of witchcraft—summoning a dead spirit, however saintly, would be perceived as a crime); *invocate* conjure; 10 *Wife to thy Edward* i.e., widow of your son, Edward; 12 *Lo* Look (a word used to draw a listener's attention); *windows* i.e., the wounds where Richard stabbed King Henry; *let forth* let out, released; 13 *helpless* unhelpful; *the helpless balm . . . eyes* i.e., my unhelpful tears; 16 *let* let out; *this blood* i.e., King Henry's blood; *from hence* from here (i.e., from King Henry's body); 17 *More direful* way more horrible; *hap* fortune; *betide* befall; *wretch* here, a term of abhorrence; 18 *by the death of thee* i.e., by killing you; 19 *adders* common European vipers, small venomous snakes found in England; 21 *abortive* monstrous, unnatural, deformed; 22 *Prodigious* abnormal, monstrous; portending evil (because of its abnormality); *untimely brought to light* born prematurely; 24 *the hopeful mother* the child's mother, who is waiting hopefully for the first glance of her newborn child; *at the view* i.e., at the sight

25 And that be heir to his unhappiness!
If ever he have wife, let her be made
More miserable by the death of him
Than I am made by my young lord, and thee!
Come now towards Chertsey with your holy load,
30 Taken from Paul's to be interrèd there.
And still, as you are weary of the weight,
Rest you, whiles I lament King Henry's corse.

1 minute, 50 seconds

of the monstrous baby; 25 ***that*** i.e., the monstrous child; ***unhappiness*** misfortune; evil; 28 ***lord*** husband; 29 ***Chertsey*** (CHUR-zee) a monastery along the Thames River west of London; ***your holy load*** i.e., King Henry's coffin; 30 ***Paul's*** St. Paul's Cathedral in London; 31 ***still, as*** whenever; 32 ***corse*** archaic version of "corpse."

COMMENTARY

Lady Anne has witnessed the destruction of everyone and everything important to her. Her father, Sir Richard Neville, Earl of Warwick, was killed in battle at about the same time that her young husband, Prince Edward, heir to the throne, and her kind and loving father-in-law, King Henry VI, were both murdered. She is no longer a member of England's ruling family. With the Yorks now in power, it seems that no one but herself continues to pay homage to the man who used to rule the entire country.

Shakespeare starts the monologue by embedding a stage direction to the coffin bearers in Lady Anne's lines: *Set down, set down your honorable load*. You must decide why Lady Anne repeats herself. An obvious choice is that the pallbearers didn't hear or obey her right away. Or perhaps she's buying time while she fishes for the right term for the coffin and its contents (stopping herself from blurting out something indelicate). Choose something specific that works for you. Also notice the other embedded stage direction: *I pour the helpless balm of my poor eyes*. Shakespeare wanted Lady Anne to cry, and he wasn't about to leave it to the actor's discretion. Remember that Lady Anne is not alone—she is on a public street in London, in the presence of a whole funeral procession. It is up to you to decide how much of the piece she delivers to others and how much she says to herself—which raises another question: how much of what she says is genuine and how much is being said for the benefit of her listeners?

Lady Anne begins her lamentation with imagery befitting a mournful tribute to a monarch (*Pale ashes of the House of Lancaster*) and to a wronged loved one (*windows that let forth thy life*; *the helpless balm of my poor eyes*). But midway through, her clever wordplay (*bloodless remnant of that royal blood*; *the heart that had the heart*; *the blood that let this blood*; *that hated wretch / That makes us wretched*) marks the point at which this piece becomes straightforward invective. For all that Anne may have believed she would allow herself to lament only awhile, her elegy cannot help but devolve into a curse. Like family members of murder victims since time began, Anne can't mourn the victims without wishing revenge upon the perpetrator. And once she begins, the curses increase in proportion to the losses she has suffered at his hands. Once she begins, she just can't stop.

You'll notice that there are builds within Anne's curses—she uses *cursèd* three times, first cursing the murderer's hand, then his heart, and then his blood (working her way inward toward his soul, perhaps?). She grows increasingly imaginative and specific as she describes the exact fates she wishes him to suffer. As an actor, it is important that you recognize and work with the builds you've been given, so that the monologue does not become a static list of curses.

It is useful for your character development to note that Anne's curses reflect clearly what would horrify *her*. She is obviously even more afraid of poisonous spiders and toads than she is of adders (since they "trump" the snakes in her progression of curses). She wishes upon Richard that he have a deformed child (so deformed that it would frighten its own *mother*), and—the ultimate curse she can imagine—she wishes that Richard's *wife* be made even more miserable by his death than she herself has been made by Richard's murder of her husband. (This curse would have made Elizabethan audiences squirm, since they knew as they heard it that she was shortly to become his wife.) Cursing doesn't seem like Anne's forte—these seem to be the best she can come up with given her lack of practice. Her guileless curses reveal her vulnerability under these circumstances . . . she's ripe for the manipulation by Richard that is about to ensue.

The monologue is peppered with consonance and assonance that support its content. For example: Spitting Ss (*thy slaughtered son / Stabbed by the self-same hand . . .*); Horrified—and Heaving—Hs (*the helpless balm / the hand that made these holes / the heart that had the heart / from hence / More direful hap betide that hated wretch . . .*); and Mad Ms in Anne's final curse (*let her be made / More miserable by the death of him / Than I am made by my . . .*). And for help with using the sound of the word *O* to its best advantage, see "O, No! An *O*!" on page xxxiii.

SIGNIFICANT SCANS

Although the meter of the monologue is quite regular at the beginning, as Anne gets worked up there are several lines in which she inverts the first foot of the line, punching the first syllable (*Wife / Stabbed / Lo* then *Cursèd / Cursèd*). These inversions emphasize the angry words she's speaking—their presence in three consecutive lines and in two consecutive lines shortly thereafter creates a natural build.

In order to scan line 23 properly, you must pronounce *aspect* with the stress on the second syllable (a-SPECT), as it is always pronounced in Shakespeare's verse.

Don't forget to elide: *obsequiously* (ob-SEE´-queess-LEE) in line 3 and *virtuous* (VIR-chwuss) in line 4;

. . . to contract: *The untimely* (th'un-TIME-lee) in line 4; *Be it* (beet) in lines 8 and 21; and *do it* (DOOT) in line 15;

. . . and to expand: *honorable* (HON´-o-RAH-ble) in line 1; *cursèd* (CUR-sehd) in lines 14, 15, and 16; *miserable* (MIZ´-er-UH-bl) in line 27; and *interrèd* (in-TER-rehd) in line 30. Notice that expanding these particular words helps Anne emphasize the points she is making.

REVISIONIST *RICHARD*:
LADY ANNE NEVILLE—NEVER TEMPTED BY THE DEVIL

Lady Anne Beauchamp Neville was only fifteen years old when Prince Edward died, and it is not certain what their "marriage" consisted of at the time, since it had been arranged for political reasons. In addition, Edward died in battle at Tewkesbury, not at Richard's hand. Thus the reasons for Anne's loathing of her second husband are all invented. She may even have found the real circumstances of their union romantic and exciting. After Prince Edward's death, Anne was hidden away by Richard's brother the Duke of Clarence. Clarence had married Anne's sister, Isabella, and wanted to keep Anne from remarrying, so that he would have control of the entire estate of their father, the powerful Earl of Warwick. Richard didn't let this stop him. He snuck into his brother's estate, kidnapped Lady Anne, carried her off, and married her. Anne was all of eighteen years old at the time. Richard ruled their portion of the Warwick estate admirably for many years, during which he was loyal to his brother King Edward IV. We hope those were good years for Anne, because she died at the age of twenty-nine—probably from tuberculosis rather than any treachery of Richard's.

RICHARD III

ACT I, SCENE ii

RICHARD

GENDER: M
AGE RANGE: adult to mature adult
PROSE/VERSE: blank verse
FREQUENCY OF USE (1–5): 4

Richard has just intercepted Lady Anne Neville, the young widow of the late Crown Prince Edward (whom Richard and his brothers murdered), as she accompanied the corpse of her late father-in-law, the former King Henry VI (whom Richard and his brothers deposed, and whom Richard then murdered), to its final resting place. Despite Anne's loathing of Richard, he has actually succeeded in using his compelling, persuasive powers to convince her to consider his suit for her hand in marriage! He can't believe it! Richard intends to become king by whatever means necessary. Marrying the widow of the former crown prince would strengthen his claim to the throne; getting her to agree is proving an easier task than he'd ever imagined! Richard has just persuaded Anne to leave the coffin with him—he will inter King Henry. As soon as Anne leaves, Richard crows over his success with her.

Was ever woman in this humor wooed?
Was ever woman in this humor won?
230 I'll have her, but I'll not keep her long.
What—I that killed her husband and his father,
To take her in her heart's extremest hate,
With curses in her mouth, tears in her eyes,
The bleeding witness of my hatred by,
235 Having God, her conscience, and these bars against me,
And I no friends to back my suit at all
But the plain devil and dissembling looks?
And yet to win her, all the world to nothing!
Ha!
240 Hath she forgot already that brave prince,
Edward, her lord, whom I some three months since
Stabbed in my angry mood at Tewkesbury?
A sweeter and a lovelier gentleman,
Framed in the prodigality of nature,
245 Young, valiant, wise, and, no doubt, right royal,
The spacious world cannot again afford.
And will she yet abase her eyes on me,
That cropped the golden prime of this sweet prince
And made her widow to a woeful bed?
250 On me, whose all not equals Edward's moiety?
On me, that halts and am misshapen thus?
My dukedom to a beggarly denier,
I do mistake my person all this while!

228 *humor* temporary state of mind, mood [*Was ever woman in this humor wooed* Was any woman in such a state of mind ever wooed]; 231 *What* an exclamation, used here to express incredulity; 234 *The bleeding witness of my hatred* i.e., the corpse of King Henry VI: in Shakespeare's time, it was believed that the corpse of a murder victim would bleed anew when in the presence of its murderer; *by* right nearby; 235 *bars* impediments; 236 *I no friends to back my suit* I, with no allies to support me in my suit (for Anne's hand in marriage); 237 *dissembling* assuming a false appearance; 238 *all the world to nothing* i.e., against huge odds; 241 *lord* husband; *some three months since* about three months ago; 242 *Tewkesbury* site of the Battle of Tewkesbury, in which the Lancasters were defeated by the Yorks, and Prince Edward was killed by Richard and his brothers; 244 *Framed* shaped, formed; *prodigality* wasteful extravagance, lavish abundance [*Framed . . . of nature* shaped by nature at its most lavish and extravagant (i.e., extraordinarily handsome)]; 245 *right* very; 246 *The spacious world* i.e., the whole wide world; *cannot again afford* will never provide again; 247 *yet* nevertheless; *abase* make base, lower [*abase her eyes on me* i.e., lower her sights by considering me for her next spouse]; 248 *golden* precious, excellent; 250 *all* i.e., whole self; *not equals* doesn't equal; *moiety* half; 251 *halts* limps; 252 *denier* (duh-NEER) a copper coin worth one twelfth of a penny [*My dukedom to a beggarly denier* I'd bet my whole dukedom against a nearly worthless denier]; 253 *I do mistake my person*

Upon my life, she finds (although I cannot)
255 Myself to be a marvelous proper man.
I'll be at charges for a looking glass
And entertain a score or two of tailors
To study fashions to adorn my body:
Since I am crept in favor with myself,
260 I will maintain it with some little cost.
But first I'll turn yon fellow in his grave,
And then return, lamenting, to my love.
Shine out, fair sun, till I have bought a glass,
That I may see my shadow as I pass.

2 minutes

all this while I've been mistaking (i.e., underestimating) my appearance this whole time; 254 *finds . . . / Myself* considers me; 255 *marvelous proper* marvelously handsome; 256 *be at charges* incur some expense; 257 *entertain* hire, retain; *a score* twenty; 258 *study* devise; 259 *am crept in favor with myself* unexpectedly find myself handsome; 260 *it* i.e., my newfound handsomeness; *with some little cost* by spending a bit; 261 *yon* over there [*turn . . . in* put . . . into]; 263 *fair* bright; auspicious; *glass* mirror (short for "looking glass"); 264 *That* So that.

COMMENTARY

Richard wants to be king, has a strategy, and is setting it in place as a chess champion does, always thinking several steps ahead. Anne is an important piece on the chessboard: formerly his opponent's pawn, she must now be Richard's queen to maneuver strategically about the board until she can be sacrificed (once he's king). Richard is amazed—and delighted—to find that his successful manipulation of her was far easier than anticipated. This bodes well for the rest of his plans for obtaining the throne. Various elements of this piece reflect Richard's elation, his smug self-satisfaction, and his sardonic sense of humor, including his use of consonance and assonance. For example, the Whooping Ws in the first two lines (*Was ever woman in this humor wooed? / Was ever woman in this humor won?*) start off the piece by conveying his euphoria. Likewise, the SMug and SMarmy Ms and Ss in line 255 (*Myself to be a marvelous proper man*) reinforce Richard's sarcasm.

Notice where Richard chooses to use repetition. The first two lines are nearly identical, but for the final word of each line. Here, the repetition highlights the changed word, focusing the listener's attention on the new information. This creates a build from *wooed* to *won*—at first Richard can't believe he wooed a woman under these circumstances. Then it occurs to him: he not only can't believe that he *wooed* her, but also that he did so *successfully*, i.e., that he has basically *won* her! Similarly, you must decide why Richard repeats the mocking *on me* (on li'l ol' me!) in lines 247, 250, and 251, to create nuance in meaning and a build in intensity.

Speaking of Richard's mocking tone, you'll notice other ways in which he pokes fun at his subject matter. One example is his description of Anne's late husband, which can be interpreted as derisive in its glowing effusiveness. Another is his sardonic delight at discovering that he himself must have become a handsome prince when he wasn't looking, rather than the toad he was when he looked in the mirror that morning. Richard knows he's actually still a toad inside and out—he loves the idea that he managed to seduce Anne warts and all (which doesn't preclude the interpretation that he also believes she found something sexy in him). Richard's mocking tone is also evident in the foppish air he adopts while planning for a whole new wardrobe . . . before remembering that—oh, yeah—first he's got to bury this guy, and in the fact that he tucks the word *lamenting* into line 262. He murdered Henry, he's not sorry, and he will not truly be lamenting anytime soon. Richard is enjoying the irony of the situation to the fullest.

As you cannot help but notice, line 239 has only one syllable in it (*Ha!*), which leaves you with four and a half feet of silence to play with. You may take the pause before or after the exclamation, or you may take some of it before and some after. Perhaps Richard does a little happy dance. Or "admires" his reflection in a shop window. Or just reflects in amazement. Wherever and however you decide to take the pause(s), Shakespeare clearly wanted to give Richard time to savor his accomplishment. And savor it he does. Also notice Richard's repeated use of *I*, which increases in frequency toward the end of the piece, as he overcomes his incredulity and begins to play.

Note the rhymes in the last four lines of the piece. The first pair (*grave / love*) may have been a historic rhyme—even today's half rhyme juxtaposes the words' meanings, emphasizing the levity with which he approaches both tasks at hand. Enjoy the deliciously gleeful rhyming couplet at the end (*a glass / I pass*)—it's not random or inadvertent that the sound being rhymed is "ass." Richard delights in making asses of everyone around him.

SIGNIFICANT SCANS

The many inverted (trochaic) feet and double endings give the meter a varied and syncopated feel, which supports the notion that Richard is both shocked and euphoric at his success. The inverted feet at the beginnings of lines show high bursts of energy, and the double endings suggest that he is babbling with elation.

Line 230 has a silent half foot at the caesura. Taking the brief pause sets up the very shocking thing he's about to say:

x / x / x / x / x /
I'll have her, (pause) but I'll not keep her long

There is a crowded foot at the beginning of line 235 (which also has a double ending):

x - x / x / x / x / x / (x)
Having God, her conscience, and these bars against me

In line 254, you have the choice of either eliding *although* ('LTHOUGH) or contracting *cannot* (CAN'T).

Line 245 is chockful of variations, which, while difficult to decipher, will enable you to deliver the line naturally. It is headless, with another pause after the first caesura, a crowded fourth foot (*and, no doubt*), and a double ending. Try it this way (eliding *valiant* [VAL-yent]):

x / x / x / x - x / x / (x)
(pause) Young, (pause) valiant, wise, and, no doubt, right royal

And don't forget to elide: *lovelier* (LUV-lyer) in line 243; *valiant* (VAL-yent) in line 245; and *marvelous* (MAR-vluss) in line 255.

P.S.

For information on the historical Richard III, see "Revisionist *Richard*: We Do Mistake His Person All This While," page 190.

RICHARD III

ACT II, SCENE i

KING EDWARD IV

GENDER: M
AGE RANGE: adult to mature adult
PROSE/VERSE: blank verse
FREQUENCY OF USE (1–5): 2

King Edward IV is dying. He has gone to great lengths to reconcile his bickering relatives, so that there will be peace in the royal family when he is gone. Just as he completes this difficult undertaking and all the cousins have shaken hands and professed their love to one another, Edward's youngest brother, Richard, arrives and announces that their middle brother, George, Duke of Clarence, is dead. King Edward is shocked. Although he had imprisoned Clarence and sentenced him to death over an incriminating prophecy, Edward had then rescinded the execution order. Unfortunately (as Richard has just explained), that second order arrived too late (a lie—actually, unbeknownst to Edward, Richard had Clarence murdered). Lord Thomas Stanley, Earl of Derby, has chosen this moment to arrive and beg the King's pardon for his servant, who has been sentenced to death for killing a gentleman. Edward responds to the request:

Have I a tongue to doom my brother's death,
And shall that tongue give pardon to a slave?
My brother killed no man—his fault was thought,
105 And yet his punishment was bitter death.
Who sued to me for him? Who, in my wrath,
Kneeled at my feet and bid me be advised?
Who spoke of brotherhood? Who spoke of love?
Who told me how the poor soul did forsake
110 The mighty Warwick and did fight for me?
Who told me, in the field at Tewkesbury,
When Oxford had me down, he rescued me
And said, "Dear brother, live, and be a king"?
Who told me, when we both lay in the field
115 Frozen almost to death, how he did lap me
Even in his garments, and did give himself
All thin and naked, to the numb-cold night?
All this from my remembrance brutish wrath
Sinfully plucked, and not a man of you
120 Had so much grace to put it in my mind.
But when your carters or your waiting vassals
Have done a drunken slaughter and defaced
The precious image of our dear Redeemer,
You straight are on your knees for pardon, pardon,
125 And I, unjustly too, must grant it you.
But for my brother not a man would speak,

102 *to doom* which is capable of decreeing; 103 *slave* here, used contemptuously to mean "wretched servant"; 104 *fault* offense, crime; 106 *sued* entreated, begged; *for him* on his behalf; *in my wrath* when I was angry; 107 *be advised* be persuaded, reconsider; 110 *Warwick* Richard Neville, Earl of Warwick, the most powerful noble in England, was known as "the King-maker" (Warwick was Clarence's father-in-law, yet Clarence deserted him and fought against him on behalf of his brother Edward); 111 *Who told me* i.e., who reminded me that; *Tewkesbury* site of the final, decisive battle in which Edward and the Yorkists defeated the Lancastrian forces in the Wars of the Roses; 112 *Oxford* John de Vere, Earl of Oxford, a Lancastrian supporter; *had me down* i.e., had struck him down in battle, and was ready to kill him; 113 *live, and be a king* the implication is that Clarence could easily have let Edward die, and then become king himself; 115 *lap* wrap; 116 *Even* used here for emphasis; *did give* surrendered, exposed; 117 *All* used here for emphasis; *thin* thinly clothed; 119 *plucked* took away; *not a man of you* not a single one of you; 120 *so much* enough; *grace* virtue, godliness; 121 *carters* cart drivers; *waiting vassals* attendants, servants; 122 *done a drunken slaughter* i.e., murdered someone while drunk; *defaced / The precious . . . Redeemer* Edward believes that God created man in God's own image; thus, murdering a man is disfiguring or obliterating the image of God; 124 *straight* immedi-

Nor I, ungracious, speak unto myself
For him, poor soul! The proudest of you all
Have been beholding to him in his life
130 Yet none of you would once beg for his life.
O God! I fear thy justice will take hold
On me and you, and mine and yours, for this.
Come, Hastings, help me to my closet. Ah, poor Clarence!

1 minute, 50 seconds

ately; 128 *proudest* loftiest, haughtiest; 129 *beholding* beholden, indebted; 132 *you* he addresses all those present; *mine and yours* my family members and yours; 133 *Hastings* William Hastings, the Lord Chamberlain; *closet* private chamber [*help me to my closet* one of the many duties of the Lord Chamberlain].

COMMENTARY

The most noticable aspect of King Edward's monologue is its simplicity. He avoids complex poetic devices, and uses common, superfluous words (*Even in his garments*; *All thin and naked*) for emphasis. He uses the emphatic form of verbs to highlight the noble actions of his brother (*did forsake / The mighty Warwick*; *did fight for me*; *did lap me / Even in his garments*; *did give himself / All thin and naked*). This simplicity is an important factor in deciding how you want to interpret the character. Keep in mind that Edward is deathly ill. He has had to drag himself out of bed to make peace among his loved ones, and needs help returning to it after the news of Clarence's death arrives—in the very next scene, in fact, we learn of his death. The simplicity of the monologue may therefore be due to the fact that Edward has very little energy left in him. On the other hand, he has never been known to be a great orator. His career as renowned warrior, notorious adulterer, and relatively inactive king has not required much speech making—maybe he's just a plain-spoken kind of guy. The one prominent rhetorical device he uses is synecdoche, when he says *Have I a tongue to doom* and *shall that tongue give pardon*—but even this usage seems to be completely uncalculated. It's simply a way to soften the fact that it was not his tongue at all, but he himself, who gave the death sentence.

Though simple, Edward's style is nonetheless effective. Note his repetition at the end of line 124 (*pardon, pardon*). Shakespeare never repeats words without reason. You must decide what that reason is here: Is he firing it off accusingly at two different people in a row? Is the first matter of fact and the second incredulous? Is the first angry and the second resigned? As you can see, the possibilities cover a wide range of interpretations. Edward also asks the same rephrased question over and over, harping on the question of *who* is to be blamed, which makes it clear that Edward is eager to find someone else with whom to share (or on whom to dump altogether) his massive guilt over Clarence's death. Note the progression in the monologue from these accusing questions to Edward's acceptance that he, too, was at fault. Paying close attention to this progression is the key to building a solid arc into your performance.

Another dead giveaway (no pun intended) to the course of this build can be found in the meter, which reflects Edward's increasing agitation. The meter is completely free of variation until halfway through the piece, where an inverted first foot appears with *Frozen* in line 115. There's another on the following line with *Even*, and a third three lines later with *Sinfully*. The first double ending also appears on line 115, followed by several more farther on. Finally, with the last line, Edward's perfectly regular meter falls apart completely, with a rare six-footed line (an alexandrine) and a double ending:

x / x / x / x / x / x / (x)
Come, Hastings, help me to my closet. Ah, poor Clarence!

This piece contains several interesting clues to Edward's motivation for shifting the blame away from himself: notice that Edward uses the intimate *thy* when addressing God, which implies that he feels a close relationship with his Maker, a relationship that is of course crucial to Edward on his deathbed. Furthermore, as the king, Edward has a special relationship with God, whom he believes has granted him the divine right to rule (see "Riding Shotgun with God," page 235). Edward often frames an action in religious terms (*Sinfully plucked*; *so much grace*; *defaced / The precious image of our dear Redeemer*). His final exclamation, *O God! I fear thy justice will take hold*, underscores his anguish: since the King is so near death, the fear that God will punish his soul, his country, and his family takes on enormous proportions. The stakes here are very high. For help with using the sound of the word *O* to its best advantage, see "O, No! An *O*!," page xxxiii.

Make sure you know whom you are addressing, when—Lord Stanley, a particular family member, the group as a whole, etc. This is particularly important in the last three lines, when Edward begins by addressing God (*I fear thy justice will take hold / On me*), then switches mid-sentence to one or more of the people present (*and you, and mine and yours*), then homes in on Hastings to help him escape to privacy.

Don't forget to elide: *Even* (E'EN) in line 116.

Revisionist *Richard*: Now It's Apparent—Clarence Was Arrant

Shakespeare invented the touching story about Clarence and Edward in the field at Tewkesbury to underscore Clarence's saintliness in contrast with Richard's malice. Due to the misinformation provided in his sources, Shakespeare believed he was simply elaborating on the accurate facts of Clarence's death and Richard's villainy. He couldn't have been more wrong. As it turns out, Clarence *did* plot repeatedly against King Edward and Richard *did* plead sincerely for his brother's life. After forgiving Clarence many times, Edward finally had him tried, convicted, and executed for treason—the murder and the rescinded sentence were all just rumor (presented as truth by Shakespeare's sources). It is true, however, that from that time forward, whenever he granted a pardon, King Edward lamented that no one had pleaded to him for Clarence's life.

RICHARD III

ACT IV, SCENE i

LADY ANNE

GENDER: F
AGE RANGE: young adult to adult
PROSE/VERSE: blank verse
FREQUENCY OF USE (1–5): 3

If only the Lancaster branch of the royal family had stayed in power, Lady Anne would be sitting pretty right now. She had just married the Lancastrian heir to the throne, Edward, Prince of Wales, when the last battles of the Wars of the Roses broke out. Her new husband and her father-in-law, King Henry VI, were both killed at the hands of Richard Plantagenet of York, Duke of Gloucester. Soon after, Richard convinced her to marry him—a move she has regretted every moment since. Now Anne, Queen Elizabeth, and the old Duchess of York (Richard's mum) have come to the Tower of London to try to visit Elizabeth's sons, who are being held there. A messenger arrives: Richard has been declared king, and Anne is summoned to be crowned his queen. As they part, Elizabeth asks Anne to *wish* [*herself*] *no harm*, to which Anne replies:

No? Why? When he that is my husband now
Came to me as I followed Henry's corse,
When scarce the blood was well washed from his hands
Which issued from my other angel husband
70 And that dear saint which I then weeping followed—
O when, I say, I looked on Richard's face,
This was my wish: "Be thou," quoth I, "accursed
For making me, so young, so old a widow;
And when thou wed'st, let sorrow haunt thy bed,
75 And be thy wife—if any be so mad—
More miserable by the life of thee
Than thou hast made me by my dear lord's death."
Lo, ere I can repeat this curse again,
Within so small a time, my woman's heart
80 Grossly grew captive to his honey words,
And proved the subject of mine own soul's curse,
Which hitherto hath held mine eyes from rest;
For never yet one hour in his bed
Did I enjoy the golden dew of sleep,
85 But with his timorous dreams was still awaked.
Besides, he hates me for my father, Warwick,
And will, no doubt, shortly be rid of me.

1 minute, 20 seconds

67 *Henry's corse* the body of King Henry VI (Lady Anne's former father-in-law, the Lancastrian king of England deposed by the Yorks and murdered by Richard [see "Genealogical Chart—the Wars of the Roses," pages 236–37]); 69 *my other angel husband* i.e., Anne's first husband, Edward, Prince of Wales (King Henry VI's son and heir), also murdered by Richard; *his hands* i.e., Richard's hands; 70 *that dear saint* i.e., the devout King Henry, who was revered by the people as saintly; 72 *quoth I* I said; 73 *so young* at such a young age; *so old a widow* (1) so long a widow (Anne felt this way because time had passed so slowly since her husband's death); or possibly (2) such a weary, worn-out widow (because the trauma of her husband's murder has aged her); 75 *if any be so mad* i.e., if anyone is so insane as to marry you; 76 *by the life of thee* by your existence; and, by the life you lead; 78 *Lo* Look, behold; *ere* before; *can* could; 80 *Grossly* stupidly; *grew captive* became captivated; 81 *subject of* one who is subjected to; 82 *hitherto* ever since; *hath held mine eyes from rest* i.e., has kept me from sleeping; 84 *golden* precious, excellent; *dew* i.e., refreshing quality [*golden dew of sleep* precious, refreshing sleep]; 85 *timorous dreams* in Shakespeare's sources, usurping rulers were commonly depicted as being plagued by insomnia and nightmares; *still* continuously [*For never yet . . . awaked* for I have not yet enjoyed a single hour of peaceful sleep without being constantly awakened by his nightmares]; 86 *Warwick* (WAR-ick) Richard Neville, Earl of Warwick (known as "the Kingmaker" for his loyalty to the Yorkist cause and his part in putting Edward on the throne, Warwick later deserted to the Lancastrians, and was thus an enemy to Richard).

COMMENTARY

Lady Anne is having a much-overdue reality check. Suddenly the uncomplaining Anne has just had too much: here she is, trying to visit the princes her own husband has locked away in the Tower, when word arrives that he has been made king. She is about to be dragged away from her friend Elizabeth, the rightful queen, to be made queen in her place, which is the last thing she wants. Anne snaps: the situation is just too awful. When Elizabeth says something nice to let her know there are no hard feelings, Anne does not simply make a polite reply, but delves into her innermost thoughts. So it's not necessary to worry that the audience will be confused by the *No? Why?* spoken in reply to Elizabeth. The reply ends there, and the rest of the piece stands on its own.

Anne takes six whole lines to set up the memory she is about to relate, repeating the word *when* with each more detailed element of the setup. Why? Has this horrible memory been repressed so long that it takes a while to emerge now? Or, conversely, has Anne been obsessing over it daily, creating a huge backlog of details to be voiced? Or is it difficult to bring herself to retell the unthinkable story of her own folly? You will want to think through these kinds of questions carefully. They are particularly important in this piece, which features a whole series of emotions (and thus actions) that Anne goes through in a very short period of time. First, there is the fact that she just found out she is to be queen; next, there are all the emotions brought on by her regrettable actions; and finally, at the end, there is cold resignation to her fate. Each stage of the piece must be a choice, and it will be a challenge to find the right action to combat the temptation to "emote." You may find it helpful to refer to the scene in which Anne's curse and capitulation actually take place, or at least to the monologue in which she curses Richard (page 191).

Notice that Anne's use of the powerful rhetorical device of antithesis echoes and supports the nature of what she's saying. The antithesis in this piece is appropriate to her state of mind—she is comparing her past with her present; what is with what could have been (*he that is my husband now* versus *my other angel husband*; *so young* versus *so old*; *the life of thee* versus *my dear lord's death*; *Did I enjoy the golden dew of sleep* versus *with his timorous dreams was still awaked*).

Take advantage of the small, well-placed groupings of alliteration and assonance to discover which words and ideas Anne wants to emphasize (*when thou wed'st*; *so small*; *Grossly grew*; *own soul's*; *hitherto hath held*; *with his timorous*). And for help with using the sound of the word *O* to its best advantage, see "O, No! An *O*!," page xxxiii.

Finally, notice that throughout the piece the grammatical construction is quite complex—until the last two lines, which are very direct. This juxtaposition makes the end of the monologue, in which she anticipates her own impending death, all the more harsh and threatening.

Don't forget to elide: *timorous* (TIM-russ) in line 85;

. . . and to expand: *miserable* (MI′-zer-UH-bl) in line 76 (this expansion emphasizes how truly miserable Anne had hoped Richard's wife would be).

P.S.

For information on the historical Anne, see "Revisionist *Richard*: Lady Anne Neville—Never Tempted by the Devil," page 196.

RICHARD III

ACT IV, SCENE iv

MARGARET

GENDER: F
PROSE/VERSE: blank verse
AGE RANGE: mature adult to older adult
FREQUENCY OF USE (1–5): 3

Margaret's late husband, Henry IV (of the Lancastrian branch of the royal family), was King of England and she was queen (see "Genealogical Chart—the Wars of the Roses," pages 236–37) until the York branch deposed her husband in the Wars of the Roses and Edward Plantagenet became king. In *Henry VI, Part Three*, Edward and his brothers George (a.k.a. Clarence) and Richard stabbed to death Margaret's son (also named Edward), and Richard murdered poor Henry. Now that King Edward has died of illness, Margaret has been delighted to see that Richard—in his drive to become king himself—has been murdering his own immediate family and cronies. Margaret is about to retire to her native France to live out the remainder of her days in comfort, but first she pays a farewell visit to the grieving Elizabeth (whose brother, eldest son, and two youngest sons have all recently been murdered by Richard) and the Duchess of York (mother of Richard and of the late Edward and Clarence, and grandmother of the murdered princes). During her visit, she gloats over the suffering of Elizabeth and the Duchess at the hands of Richard.

35 If ancient sorrow be most reverend,
Give mine the benefit of seniory,
And let my griefs frown on the upper hand.
If sorrow can admit society,
Tell o'er your woes again by viewing mine:
40 I had an Edward till a Richard killed him;
I had a husband till a Richard killed him.
Thou hadst an Edward till a Richard killed him;
Thou hadst a Richard till a Richard killed him.
Thou hadst a Clarence too, and Richard killed him.
45 From forth the kennel of thy womb hath crept
A hellhound that doth hunt us all to death:
That dog, that had his teeth before his eyes,
To worry lambs and lap their gentle blood;
That excellent grand tyrant of the earth,
50 That reigns in gallèd eyes of weeping souls;
That foul defacer of God's handiwork,
Thy womb let loose to chase us to our graves.
O upright, just, and true-disposing God,
How do I thank thee that this carnal cur
55 Preys on the issue of his mother's body
And makes her pew-fellow with others' moan!

35 *ancient* long-standing; *most reverend* worthy of the most respect; 36 *the benefit* the right; *seniory* both (1) seniority and (2) sovereignty, supremacy; 37 *on the upper hand* from a position of superiority; 38 *admit* tolerate, suffer; *society* company; 39 *Tell o'er* review; 40 *an Edward* i.e., the late Lancastrian Prince Edward (Margaret's son, heir to the throne, who was murdered by Richard and his brothers Edward and Clarence); *a Richard* i.e., Richard, Duke of Gloucester, now King Richard III; 41 *a husband* i.e., the late King Henry VI; 42 *an Edward* i.e., Elizabeth's young son, Edward IV's heir, the Yorkist Prince Edward (whom Richard imprisoned in the Tower with Edward's younger brother and then had assassinated so that they would not stand in his path to the throne); 43 *Thou hadst a Richard* i.e., Elizabeth's youngest son, Richard, Duke of York (murdered along with his older brother in the Tower)—this is the only use of the name Richard that does not refer to Richard III; 44 *Thou hadst a Clarence* Margaret now addresses Richard's mother, the elderly Duchess of York; 45 *From forth* Out of; 47 *that had his teeth before his eyes* legend had it that Richard was born with teeth; since a newborn's eyes do not focus well at first, Margaret says that Richard had his teeth first; 48 *worry* pull to pieces with one's teeth; 49 *excellent* unequaled, supreme (in Shakespeare's day, the word could, as here, carry a negative connotation it no longer has); *grand* principal, chief; 50 *reigns in gallèd eyes of weeping souls* is supreme at creating sore eyes in weeping people (whom Richard has victimized)—with a play on Richard's reign, which has brought on such suffering; 53 *true-disposing* righteous, justly ordaining; 54 *carnal* carnivorous; *cur* dog (a term of contempt); 56 *pew-fellow*

Bear with me—I am hungry for revenge,
And now I cloy me with beholding it.
Thy Edward he is dead, that killed my Edward;
Thy other Edward dead, to quit my Edward;
65 Young York he is but boot, because both they
Matched not the high perfection of my loss.
Thy Clarence he is dead that stabbed my Edward,
And the beholders of this frantic play,
The adulterate Hastings, Rivers, Vaughan, Grey,
70 Untimely smothered in their dusky graves.
Richard yet lives—Hell's black intelligencer,
Only reserved their factor to buy souls
And send them thither. But at hand, at hand
Ensues his piteous and unpitied end.
75 Earth gapes, Hell burns, fiends roar, saints pray,
To have him suddenly conveyed from hence.
Cancel his bond of life, dear God, I pray,
That I may live and say "The dog is dead!"

2 minutes, 20 seconds

with others' moan i.e., companion to other mourners; 62 *I cloy me* I am satiating myself (stuffing myself until I'm full) [*I cloy me with beholding it* i.e., I can't get enough of the sight of it]; 63 *Thy Edward* i.e., Elizabeth's husband, King Edward IV; 64 *Thy other Edward* i.e., Elizabeth's son, Prince Edward (mentioned in line 42); *to quit* to pay for, in exchange for; 65 *Young York* i.e., young Richard of York, Elizabeth's youngest son (mentioned in line 43); *but boot* merely thrown into the bargain (to make up the difference in value between the two Yorkist Edwards [King Edward IV and his son] and her perfect Edward); 66 *Matched not* were not equal to; *the high perfection of my loss* i.e., both (1) Margaret's loss of her exquisitely perfect son; and (2) the supremacy of Margaret's loss; 68 *beholders* witnesses (who didn't intercede); *frantic* frenzied, insane; *play* act (with a play on the word's primary meaning, suggesting that the murder was committed with no more compunction that if it were a game); 69 *adulterate* adulterous [*adulterate Hastings* i.e., the Lord Chamberlain, Lord William Hastings—falsely accused of treason and executed by Richard—whose affair with one Mistress Jane Shore had been the subject of scandal]; *Rivers* i.e., Elizabeth's brother, Anthony Woodville, Earl of Rivers (whom Richard executed to prevent him from protecting his nephews, Edward and York); *Vaughan* (VAW-un) i.e., Sir Thomas Vaughan (an ally of Elizabeth, executed by Richard for no other reason); *Grey* i.e., Sir Richard Grey (adult son of Elizabeth from her first marriage, executed by Richard to prevent him from protecting his young half brothers, Edward and York); 70 *Untimely smothered* stifled in an untimely fashion, i.e., killed young; *dusky* gloomy; 71 *yet* still; *black* evil; *intelligencer* agent, spy; 72 *reserved* preserved, i.e., kept alive; *factor* agent [*Only reserved . . . factor* only being kept alive in order to be their (the devils') agent]; 73 *thither* to that place, i.e., to Hell; *at hand* very soon; 74 *Ensues* is about to happen; *piteous* miserable; *unpitied* unmourned; *end* death; 75 *gapes* opens its mouth wide; *fiends* devils from Hell; 76 *suddenly* immediately; *conveyed* carried or led away (here meaning "carted off to Hell"); *from hence* from here; 77 *bond* lease [*Cancel his bond of life* i.e., end his life]; 78 *That* so that; *live and say* i.e., live long enough to say.

COMMENTARY

Ex-Queen Margaret has waited a long time to see the usurping Yorks suffer as she did. That day has finally come, and Margaret exults in the grief of Elizabeth and the Duchess of York, who mourn the death of King Edward from illness, as well as the subsequent violent murders of the little princes in the Tower, Elizabeth's oldest son and her brother, and the Duchess's son Clarence . . . all by Richard's design. But why content oneself with merely knowing from afar that one's enemies suffer, when one can have much more fun by paying a little visit and personally rubbing their noses in it?

Since Margaret experienced her losses several years ago, you must find your own balance between exultation and grief. Margaret's language suggests that she relishes taunting the two women. The piece's most striking language element, the pervasive use of repetition, conveys her bitter tone, as she cleverly plays on the names and relationships her dead have in common with that of the York women. Her use of repetition builds, as she begins lines with *I had a . . .* twice in a row, *thou hadst a . . .* three times in a row, *that* three times in a row (with a fourth just preceding it), and the most shocking *till a Richard killed him*, which becomes humorous in an outrageous and warped way when repeated five times in a row. She repeats whole phrases and sentences with only minor changes, to ironic effect: her words sound increasingly singsongy and become maddening to listen to . . . which is just what she intends. A note of caution, however: with each repetition, Margaret changes the phrase slightly to include a different fact (such as the name of another person killed by Richard or of a member of her own family revenged by the death of a member of Richard's, etc.); be sure to clearly communicate what that new bit of information is, so that instead of becoming an unfathomable laundry list of the deceased, the monologue will build in horror. You must also decide why Margaret repeats *at hand* in line 73: she may be admonishing the two women, or gleefully anticipating the day Richard finally rots in Hell, etc.

The repetition of sounds (much of which derives from the repetition of words) is the other prominent feature of this monologue. We recommend you read this piece aloud early in the process of preparing it, just to wrap your mouth around these sounds and see what you discover; they are wondrously expressive of Margaret's intentions. Examples include: THrEAtening THs and EHs (*from forth / thy / hath / doth / death* and *the kennel / crept / hellhound / death*); Harsh Hs (*hath / hellhound / hunt*); Lacerating Ls, sometimes combined with hiSSing Ss, spiTTing Ts, crUel OOs, and Ripping Rs (*lambs / lap / gentle blood* and *let loose to chase us to our graves*); pOIsonous Ys (*I cloy me* and *Young York*); and aBrasive Bs (*but boot, because both*). The sounds and meanings of the final words of many lines (in the position where they are to receive the most prominence) are marvelously malevolent, while others are pointedly powerful, such as *killed him*, *crept*, *death*, *blood*, *earth*, *souls*, *graves*, *God*, *cur*, *moan*, *revenge*, *end*, *hence*, *dead*. Margaret is relentlessly hammering her two foes, feeding on her own words, deriving increasing power from them and building to a strong finish . . . Did those York women think for a second Margaret would leave for France without an "I told you so," would just fade away? Oh, no, not she.

Margaret employes antithesis throughout the monologue, both to liken the fates of the Yorks and the Lancasters at Richard's hands, and to contrast the general unworthiness of the Yorks' losses with *the high perfection of* her own: *your woes* versus *mine*; *I had* versus *Thou hadst*; Margaret's *Edward* versus Elizabeth's *Edward*; Margaret's *husband* versus Elizabeth's husband; Margaret's child versus Elizabeth's children. She also uses antithesis to call upon resources from both good and evil to assist her in cursing Richard: *piteous* versus *unpitied*; *Earth* versus *Hell*; *fiends roar* versus *saints pray*; *Cancel his bond of life* versus *that I may live*. And her lengthy list of Richard's victims in *their dusky graves* makes sinister her three short words: *Richard yet lives*.

Obviously, Margaret couldn't care less that she is addressing members of the current ruling family, to whom she supposedly owes loyalty and is supposed to exhibit obeisance. But a queen to the end, she will never defer to these usurpers. She uses the formal, respectful *your* once before discarding it in favor of the familiar *thou* and *thy*. Although they are not onstage with you when you perform this monologue in audition, be specific about when you are addressing Elizabeth, when the elderly Duchess, and when you are speaking to both of them.

Margaret's imagery is menacing throughout the monologue. Her extended metaphor of Richard as a dog paints a vivid picture of him while managing both to blame and insult his mother (*From forth the kennel of thy womb hath crept / A hellhound*; *That dog*, *that had his teeth . . . To worry lambs*; *Thy womb let loose . . .* ; *this carnal cur*; *The dog is dead*). Margaret's other images, some of them personifications of grim emotions, are no less unsettling (*my griefs frown*; *If sorrow can admit society*; *That reigns in gallèd eyes of weeping souls*; *Hell's black intelligencer*; *Earth gapes, Hell burns, fiends roar, saints pray*). One senses from her description that Richard has left only the sights of blood and fire and the sound of wailing in his wake. Margaret rather shamelessly puts herself in the company of saints when she follows *saints pray* with *I pray*, considering that her own actions have occasionally smacked of Richard's in her day (in *Henry VI, Parts One* and *Two*; see monologue, page 164), and that she does not show much loving kindness toward the bereaved here. But remember that Margaret firmly believes the crown was rightfully the property of her husband and son and was usurped by their murderers, and that the Yorks deserve the horrors that have at long last befallen them. Over the many years she's had to endure Yorkist reign, her bitterness has compounded. It finally has an outlet in the climactic call to the heavens in lines 75–79 (ending with the weighty Ds and Gs of *dear God / dog / dead* and the "Amen"-provoking rhyme of *pray / say*).

SIGNIFICANT SCANS

The monologue's meter is very even, with most sentences beginning new lines (making those rare exceptions, such as *But at hand, at hand* in line 73 jump out as more impetuous than their more calculated counterparts). This evenness suggests that Margaret is in complete control of herself and her speech; long awaiting this opportunity, she has probably given thought in advance to what she wishes to say. The most common variation is the double ending at line ends. Perhaps Margaret has too much to say and not enough time in which to say it all. Or perhaps they belie her excitement at finally speaking her mind. Or both. There are also occasional inverted feet, punching the beginnings of lines, as well as two inverted feet in the middle of lines 37 and 56 that do not follow caesuras as such mid-line inversions normally do:

x / x / / x x / x /
And let my griefs frown on the upper hand
x / x / / x x / x /
And makes her pew-fellow with others' moan

Don't forget to elide: *o'er* (ORE) in line 39; *foul* (FOWL) in line 51; *our* (owr) in line 52; and *piteous* (PIH-tyuss) in line 74;

. . . to elide and contract: *The adulterate* (Th'u-DULL-trut) in line 69;

. . . to expand: *gallèd* (GALL-ehd) in line 50; and *Vaughan* (VAW-un) in line 69;

. . . and not to elide: *reverend* (REH-vur-END) in line 35 (normally elided in today's speech).

P.S.

For background on the historical Margaret, see "Revisionist History: She-Wolf's Heart, Wrapped in a French Tiger's Hide," page 156.

RICHARD III

ACT V, SCENE iii

KING RICHARD

GENDER: M
PROSE/VERSE: blank verse
AGE RANGE: adult to mature adult
FREQUENCY OF USE (1–5): 2

After his branch of the royal family, the Yorks, finally won the Wars of the Roses (see "Genealogical Chart—the Wars of Roses," pages 236–37), ousted the Lancasters, and gained control of the English throne, King Richard III clawed his way to the top by any nasty means necessary (you know—lies, deceit, fratricide, killing small children—the usual). Now his sovereignty is being challenged by the Lancastrian heir, Henry Tudor, Earl of Richmond, who has raised an army and invaded England to reclaim the throne. Both armies are camped out in Bosworth Field on the night before the big battle. Richard's sleep is disturbed by foreboding dreams. One after another, the ghosts of those he has murdered appear and condemn him to "despair and die." Toward the end, Richard dreams of the next day's battle, then awakes.

Give me another horse! Bind up my wounds!
Have mercy, Jesu!—Soft, I did but dream.
O coward conscience, how dost thou afflict me!
180 The lights burn blue. It is now dead midnight.
Cold fearful drops stand on my trembling flesh.
What do I fear? Myself? There's none else by.
Richard loves Richard; that is, I am I.
Is there a murderer here? No. Yes, I am.
185 Then fly. What, from myself? Great reason why,
Lest I revenge. What, myself upon myself?
Alack, I love myself. Wherefore? For any good
That I myself have done unto myself?
O no. Alas, I rather hate myself
190 For hateful deeds committed by myself.
I am a villain—yet I lie, I am not!
Fool, of thyself speak well! Fool, do not flatter.
My conscience hath a thousand several tongues,
And every tongue brings in a several tale,
195 And every tale condemns me for a villain:
Perjury, perjury, in the highest degree;
Murder, stern murder, in the direst degree;
All several sins, all used in each degree,
Throng to the bar, crying all, "Guilty, guilty!"
200 I shall despair—there is no creature loves me,
And if I die, no soul will pity me.
Nay, wherefore should they, since that I myself
Find in myself no pity to myself?
Methought the souls of all that I had murdered
205 Came to my tent, and every one did threat
Tomorrow's vengeance on the head of Richard.

1 minute, 45 seconds

178 *Jesu* Jesus; *Soft* Stop; wait [*Soft . . . dream* Wait, I was only dreaming]; 179 *how dost thou* how much you; 180 *lights burn blue* Shakespeare's contemporaries believed that candles, lamps, or fires burning blue were signs of the presence of ghosts; *dead* deathlike; as still as death; 181 *Cold fearful drops* i.e., of sweat; 182 *by* present; 185 *fly* flee, run away; *Great reason why* There's good reason I should flee; 186 *revenge* take revenge; *myself upon myself* i.e., me, take revenge upon myself; 187 *Wherefore* Why; 189 *I rather hate* on the contrary, I hate; 192 *do not flatter* i.e., flattery will not work on yourself; 193 *several* separate, different [*My conscience . . . tongues* refers to the proverb "A man's conscience is a thousand witnesses"]; 195 *for* as; 197 *stern* cruel; pitiless; 198 *All several sins* every different sin; *used* committed; *in each degree* at every level of criminality; 199 *bar* place of judgment (referring to the railing that encloses the judge in a court of law, which one approaches to plead a case); 202 *Nay* used to amplify what has been said before; *since that* since; 203 *to* for; 205 *did threat / Tomorrow's vengeance* i.e., threatened that in tomorrow's battle, vengeance will be done for the wrongs I have committed.

COMMENTARY

Have you ever awakened from a dream with the creepy feeling that it either will or already has come true, and you just *have* to call your aunt Irene to make sure she's OK? Well, Richard just had that dream in spades. And, as everyone knows, he will very soon be calling desperately for that replacement horse—in fact, he will offer his kingdom for it!

In this piece there is a definite progression of different thought processes. In the first two lines, Richard is clearly still asleep, dreaming of the next day's battle. Notice that just before he awakes, he calls out, *Have mercy, Jesu!*—the first sign that at least subconsciously he is not as secure in his wicked and godless attitude toward life as he seems. In preparing for the moment of waking from this dream, and for the lines to follow, be aware that as with real dreams, what Richard remembers at first is only the *last* part of the dream—losing his horse and being wounded—not the dire condemnations of the ghosts.

In the next section of the piece, we meet both sides of the true Richard at once: the devil-may-care (or, shall we say, "devil-I-am") villain he professes himself to be throughout the play, and the troubled, nightmare-plagued conscience he has repressed for so long. This dichotomy is expressed through the dialogue he has with himself: almost all the lines are broken up by caesuras, with ideas beginning and ending mid-line. This gives the piece a chopped-up, confused feeling, which works well both because Richard has just awakened from a terrible dream and because he is torn between his two selves, and arguing between them. He often seems to be interrupting himself with his next thought. The meter is full of irregularities, including this awkward crowded foot (*What, myself*):

/ x x /   x - x / x / x /
Lest I revenge. What, myself upon myself?

and one of those rare six-footed lines (hexameter):

x / x / x / x / x /x /
Alack, I love myself. Wherefore? For any good

Note that Richard uses *myself* twelve times in this piece. Twelve—that's no accident! At this moment, Richard is having a serious identity crisis, caused by his emerging conscience, which, for the moment, wins out. The major focus of the second section of the piece is the build leading to that victory—which, as Richard sees it, is a defeat. This build is created by the repetition of words—such as *several*, *tongue*, *every*, *tale*, *degree*—and of cadences, as in these lines:

/ x / x / x / x /
Perjury, perjury, in the highest degree — perjury (PER-jree); highest (HIGH'ST)

/ x x / x / x / x /
Murder, stern murder, in the direst degree — direst (DIRE'ST)

The poetic elements assist the buildup of actual, increasingly egregious crimes Richard has committed. Pay attention to the repetition and rhyme of words like *degree*, *guilty*, and *me* in the incriminating lines 196–201. For help with using the sound of the word *O* to its best advantage, see "O, No! An *O*!," page xxxiii.

There are many references in this piece to other scenes in the play. Although your audience will miss out on those references if they don't know the play, you can still greatly benefit from them in your character development. First, note that in the opening monologue of the play, Richard was "determined to prove a villain" (see monologue, page 185). Now he finds he *is* one. What was that progression like for him? How does he feel about it now? Second, note that in that very same monologue, as well as in all of his speeches throughout the play, he uses extremely complex language, even in soliloquy, when he is ostensibly alone. Here, in contrast, he speaks fairly honest, plain English (within the realm of verse). What does that tell you about the personality he has constructed for the world and for himself versus the person he might really have been? Finally, remember that his late wife, Lady Anne, has spoken of his nightly "timorous dreams" (see monologue, page 208). That lets us know these nightmares are a regular occurrence. How does that inform this moment? In tonight's dream, the ghosts have all told him to "despair and die." Even before he remembers that part of the dream, he says, *I shall despair*, which lets us know that his subconscious self is having great effect on his conscious existence. All of this is helpful in developing a character with enough depth to achieve the intense self-examination and honesty this piece requires.

Don't forget to elide: *murderer* (MUR-drer) in line 184; *several* (SEV-ruhl) in lines 193 and 198; *perjury* (PER-jry) and *highest* (HIGH'ST) in line 196; *direst* (DIRE'ST) in line 197; and *crying* (CRY'NG) in line 199;

. . . and to contract: *I am* (I'm) at the end of line 191, but *not* at the beginning of that line or in lines 183 or 184.

P.S.

For information on the historical Richard, see "Revisionist *Richard*: We Do Mistake His Person All This While," page 190.

HENRY VIII

ACT II, SCENE iv

QUEEN KATHERINE

GENDER: F
AGE RANGE: mature adult
PROSE/VERSE: blank verse
FREQUENCY OF USE (1–5): 2

Katherine of Aragon, Queen of England, has been an exemplary wife to King Henry VIII for over twenty years, bearing his children and lovingly supporting his endeavors. But he has misplaced his confidence in the corrupt Cardinal Wolsey, who has convinced him to divorce her, claiming that their marriage violates church law because Katherine was previously married to Henry's late brother. The divorce is under way and Katherine has just kneeled at the King's feet and passionately pleaded with him to stay the proceedings until she can receive legal advice from her royal family in Spain. Cardinal Wolsey has interjected, saying that there are enough men present to plead Katherine's case for her and the hearing should go ahead. Katherine replies:

Lord Cardinal,
To you I speak.

[WOLSEY: *Your pleasure, Madam.*]

Sir,
70 I am about to weep, but thinking that
We are a queen, or long have dreamed so, certain
The daughter of a king, my drops of tears
I'll turn to sparks of fire.

75 I do believe,
Induced by potent circumstances, that
You are mine enemy, and make my challenge
You shall not be my judge. For it is you
Have blown this coal betwixt my lord and me,
80 Which God's dew quench! Therefore I say again,
I utterly abhor, yea, from my soul
Refuse you for my judge, whom yet once more
I hold my most malicious foe, and think not
At all a friend to truth.

105 My lord, my lord,
I am a simple woman, much too weak
T' oppose your cunning. Y' are meek and humble-mouthed,
You sign your place and calling, in full seeming,
With meekness and humility; but your heart
110 Is crammed with arrogancy, spleen and pride.

71 *We* I (Queen Katherine is using the royal "we"); *certain* certainly; 72 *The daughter of a king* Katherine was the daughter of King Ferdinand and Queen Isabella of Spain (see "Keeping Her Head Under Pressure," page 228); 77 *challenge* a legal term for an objection especially to a particular jury member; 78 *You* that you; 79 *blown this coal* a proverbial expression in Shakespeare's day, meaning "stirred up strife"; *betwixt* between; *my lord* i.e., my husband; 80 *God's dew quench* i.e., may God extinguish; 81 *abhor* both (1) detest and (2) reject (a legal term); 82 *Refuse you for my judge* reject you as my judge; 83 *hold* consider; *think not / At all a friend to truth* i.e., do not think (you) care about the truth; 107 *humble-mouthed* mild in speech; 108 *sign* display; *place* both (1) station in life and (2) official position, profession; *calling* vocation in the ecclesiastical profession [*sign your place and calling* give an outward show of your high religious position (with a possible additional double meaning, "make the sign of the cross")]; *in full seeming* to all outward appearances; 110 *arrogancy* presumption; *spleen* here, malice (the spleen was be-

You have by Fortune, and his Highness' favors,
Gone slightly o'er low steps, and now are mounted
Where powers are your retainers, and your words,
Domestics to you, serve your will as 't please
115 Yourself pronounce their office. I must tell you,
You tender more your person's honor than
Your high profession spiritual; that again
I do refuse you for my judge, and here
Before you all, appeal unto the Pope,
120 To bring my whole cause 'fore his Holiness,
And to be judged by him.
[*She curtsies to the King and offers to depart*]

1 minute, 45 seconds

lieved to be the body's source of powerful emotions such as malice); *pride* arrogance; 111 *Fortune* i.e., good fortune (personified as a capricious goddess, who assigned people's lots in life according to her whim); *favors* benevolence, kindly regard; 112 *slightly* easily; *o'er low steps* i.e., over the lower rungs of the ladder (of success); 113 *powers* those in positions of power (such as King Henry)—also, possibly, the powers you now wield; *retainers* attendants, servants; 114 *Domestics to you* (1) your domestic servants; (2) vassals, directly dependent on you; 115 *office* function [*your words . . . office* your words, like servants, carry out your will in whatever way you wish of them]; 116 *tender* cherish; *your person's* your own; *honor* high rank, eminence; 117 *Your high profession spiritual* i.e., your lofty holy profession; 120 *whole* (1) substantial; (2) entire; *cause* court case [*To bring my whole cause 'fore his Holiness* i.e., either (1) to bring my very substantial case before the Pope or (2) to bring my whole case before the Pope (removing it entirely from your jurisdiction)].

COMMENTARY

Katherine is taking a huge risk: her husband reveres and trusts Cardinal Wolsey; in fact, recently the Duke of Buckingham was wrongly executed for treason because Wolsey had convinced the King of his guilt. Wolsey has orchestrated this divorce, and since he has the ear of the King and she no longer does, angering him could prove likewise fatal. Katherine could have expressed her intention to appeal to the Pope directly to the King. You must decide whether Katherine's confrontation of Wolsey is intentional or whether she just can't keep her hostility and outrage toward Wolsey to herself anymore. Embedded stage directions not only guide you to subvert your grief and frustration into anger at the source of your misery, Wolsey, but even provide your motivation for doing so—namely, that you are too royal to weep before him (*I am about to weep . . . my drops of tears / I'll turn to sparks of fire*).

There is little imagery in the monologue, but those images Katherine does use, such as the dangerous *sparks of fire* and *this coal betwixt my lord and me* convey the heat of her fury. The King's blindness to the truth of Katherine's words makes the accuracy of her imagery in lines 113–15 all the more chilling. But however grim her prospects, she will not permit this injustice to be visited on her without a fight.

Katherine uses the royal *We* in line 71 to remind Wolsey that she is his queen. She then switches to *I* for the remainder of the monologue, which makes the speech deeply personal: she wants Wolsey to feel the sting of her words and to know who has stung him. She makes sure to point out that he has achieved his position only thanks to fortune and King Henry's largesse (as opposed his own merit and God), implying that he is an irreligious usurper of power who has no right to serve as a judge in the holy matter of her marriage.

Katherine's message is important enough that she repeats each section of it, saying at the onset that Wolsey is her *enemy* and then again that he is her *most malicious foe*, stating twice that she does not accept him as her judge, calling him *meek and humble-mouthed* and then reiterating that he fakes *meekness and humility*, and saying both that his heart is *crammed with arrogancy, spleen and pride* and that he cares more about his own *honor* than his *high profession spiritual*. She uses the rhetorical device of antithesis to emphasize her points: *drops of tears* versus *sparks of fire*; *foe* versus *friend*; *You sign . . . meekness and humility* versus *Your heart . . . arrogancy, spleen and pride*; *your person's honor* versus *Your high profession spiritual*; and *refuse you* versus *appeal unto the Pope*.

In line 105, Katherine repeats *My lord* to shut Wolsey up; in addition, she follows the repetition of this respectful term of address with the mock humbleness of *I am a simple woman*, which suggests that the repetition is a mocking show of faux respect intended to convey the utter contempt with which she actually regards him. She then reverts from sarcasm to blunt, straightforward honesty, castigating him soundly and bringing this travesty of a trial to an end . . . at least for the time being.

Finally, consider that Katherine, who is originally from Spain, is quite articulate in her adopted tongue, but would obviously feel at a disadvantage in a legal setting, where difficult religious and legal jargon will be bandied about. Although she is a foreigner, we urge you not to adopt an accent for auditions, as doing so may interfere with your comprehensibility. Also don't forget that although Katherine is speaking to Wolsey, the two are not alone: she is in the quasi-public forum of the court. You must decide whether Katherine ever forgets about the others in her rage toward Wolsey or is cognizant of their presence at all times and uses the forum to inform them of his corruption and malice.

SIGNIFICANT SCANS

The monologue contains several double endings, both at line ends and mid-line before caesuras, reflecting that Katherine has much to say quickly—she may be trying to speak her mind before she is ordered to be still. The first two thirds of the monologue is free of elisions, further proof that she wants Wolsey to understand her in no uncertain terms. This lack of elision may also reflect Katherine's initial self-consciousness at speaking before the court, and may suggest the careful way in which she speaks the language that she learned in adulthood. Katherine then uses many elisions in the remainder of the monologue, as she can no longer suppress a stream of anger and bitterness toward Wolsey. This sense that Katherine is on the offensive is reinforced by the considerable length of her sentences and by the fact that they start and end mid-line, where little pause is taken between them. The few inverted feet place stress on the words *I*, *We*, and *You* (highlighting the disparity she feels between them), and on *Therefore* in line 80 (which attracts attention to her forceful restatement of the monologue's most important point, that she refuses to grant Wolsey jurisdiction over her).

Line 69 is shared with Cardinal Wolsey. The pause created where his words have been excised is of course used to choke back tears, since Katherine herself next says that she is holding them back, but may also be used to decide how to word what you wish to say, to gather your courage before lacing into him or to try to restrain yourself from doing so:

x / x / x / x / x /
To you I speak (pause-pause) (pause-pause) (pause) Sir

But you may disregard the pause created between lines 73 and 75 (where lines have been excised to create this monologue) and simply combine *I'll turn to sparks of fire* and *I do believe* into one line of regular iambic pentameter, creating momentum appropriate to your attack on Wolsey:

x / x / x / x / x /
I'll turn to sparks of fire. I do believe

Similarly, lines spoken by Wolsey (mid-84 to mid-105) have been excised, and lines 84 and 105 combine to form one line of perfect iambic pentameter. To transition between them, you need only notice that Wolsey is about to speak before cutting him off with *My lord, my lord*.

x / x / x / x / x /
At all a friend to truth. My lord, my lord

Line 83 may simply be treated as regular pentameter with a double ending, or you may crowd the final foot (*and think not*), placing the stress on *not* instead of *think*:

x / x / x / x / x - x /
I hold my most malicious foe, and think not

Don't forget to elide: *fire* (FYR) in line 73; *humility* (hyoo-MILL-tee) in line 109; *Highness'* (HIE-ness, *not* HIE-nessez) in line 111; *o'er* (ORE) in line 112; *powers* (POWRZ) in line 113; *spiritual* (SPEER-tchwull) in line 117; and *'fore* (FOR) in line 120;

. . . and to contract: *T' oppose* (tuh-POSE) and *Y' are* (yar) in line 107; *as't* (ast) in line 114.

One final note: this monologue is the culmination of a scene full of rich material for Katherine. If you're lucky enough to have occasion to prepare an unusually long monologue, her preceding speech to King Henry in this scene is terrific and can be tacked on to the beginning of this one.

Keeping Her Head Under Pressure

The historical Katherine of Aragon was the daughter of King Ferdinand II and Queen Isabella of Spain, who married her off at the age of sixteen to Prince Arthur, heir apparent to the English throne, to cement ties between the two nations. Poor Arthur died the next year, but his younger brother,

Henry, saw a good thing in Katherine and married her himself just after being crowned King Henry VIII. This required a papal dispensation, as Church law proscribed the marriage of a man to his brother's widow as incest. Katherine didn't disappoint in most ways: while Henry waged a military campaign in France, she ruled as regent in England and masterminded its successful defense against a Scottish invasion. She did disappoint by failing to produce a male heir; of six offspring, only one daughter survived infancy. Desperate for an heir, the King sought to have the marriage annulled. When the Pope refused to do so, Henry split from Rome, married Anne Boleyn, and declared himself head of the English Church, precipitating the English Reformation. Katherine never acknowledged her new title, Princess Dowager, or that her marriage was invalid, but Henry was "lenient" with her: unlike two of his five subsequent wives, who met their ends on the chopping block when they failed to produce male heirs, Katherine was permitted to live out the remainder of her life in modest comfort, if not the dignity she'd earned.

THE CARDINAL'S COMEUPPANCE BY KATHERINE CONFIRMED

When writing this scene, Shakespeare did not stray far from his source, the historian Raphael Holinshed, who states in his *Chronicles* that at the actual hearing "the queen . . . openlie protested, that she did utterlie abhorre, refuse, and forsake such a judge, as was not onlie a most malicious enimie to hir, but also a manifest adversarie to all right and justice."

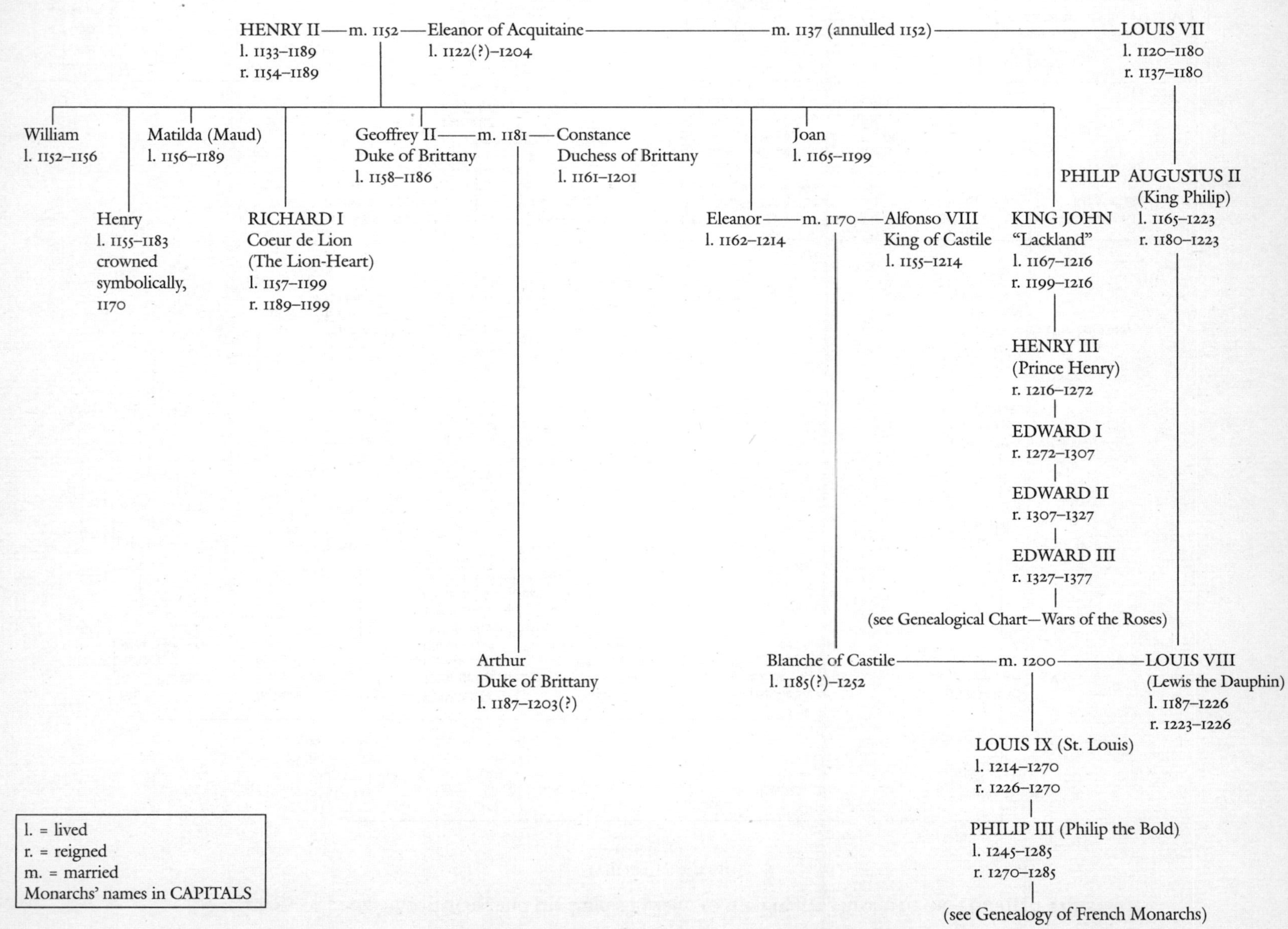
Genealogical Chart for *King John*
HENRY II—m. 1152—Eleanor of Acquitaine—m. 1137 (annulled 1152)—LOUIS VII
l. 1133–1189
r. 1154–1189
l. 1122(?)–1204
l. 1120–1180
r. 1137–1180
William
l. 1152–1156
Matilda (Maud)
l. 1156–1189
Geoffrey II—m. 1181—Constance
Duke of Brittany
l. 1158–1186
Duchess of Brittany
l. 1161–1201
Joan
l. 1165–1199
PHILIP AUGUSTUS II
(King Philip)
l. 1165–1223
r. 1180–1223
Henry
l. 1155–1183
crowned
symbolically,
1170
RICHARD I
Coeur de Lion
(The Lion-Heart)
l. 1157–1199
r. 1189–1199
Eleanor—m. 1170—Alfonso VIII
l. 1162–1214
King of Castile
l. 1155–1214
KING JOHN
"Lackland"
l. 1167–1216
r. 1199–1216
HENRY III
(Prince Henry)
r. 1216–1272
EDWARD I
r. 1272–1307
EDWARD II
r. 1307–1327
EDWARD III
r. 1327–1377
(see Genealogical Chart—Wars of the Roses)
Arthur
Duke of Brittany
l. 1187–1203(?)
Blanche of Castile—m. 1200—LOUIS VIII
l. 1185(?)–1252
(Lewis the Dauphin)
l. 1187–1226
r. 1223–1226
LOUIS IX (St. Louis)
l. 1214–1270
r. 1226–1270
PHILIP III (Philip the Bold)
l. 1245–1285
r. 1270–1285
(see Genealogy of French Monarchs)
l. = lived
r. = reigned
m. = married
Monarchs' names in CAPITALS

Genealogy of French Monarchs, and the English Claim to the French Throne in the Hundred Years' War

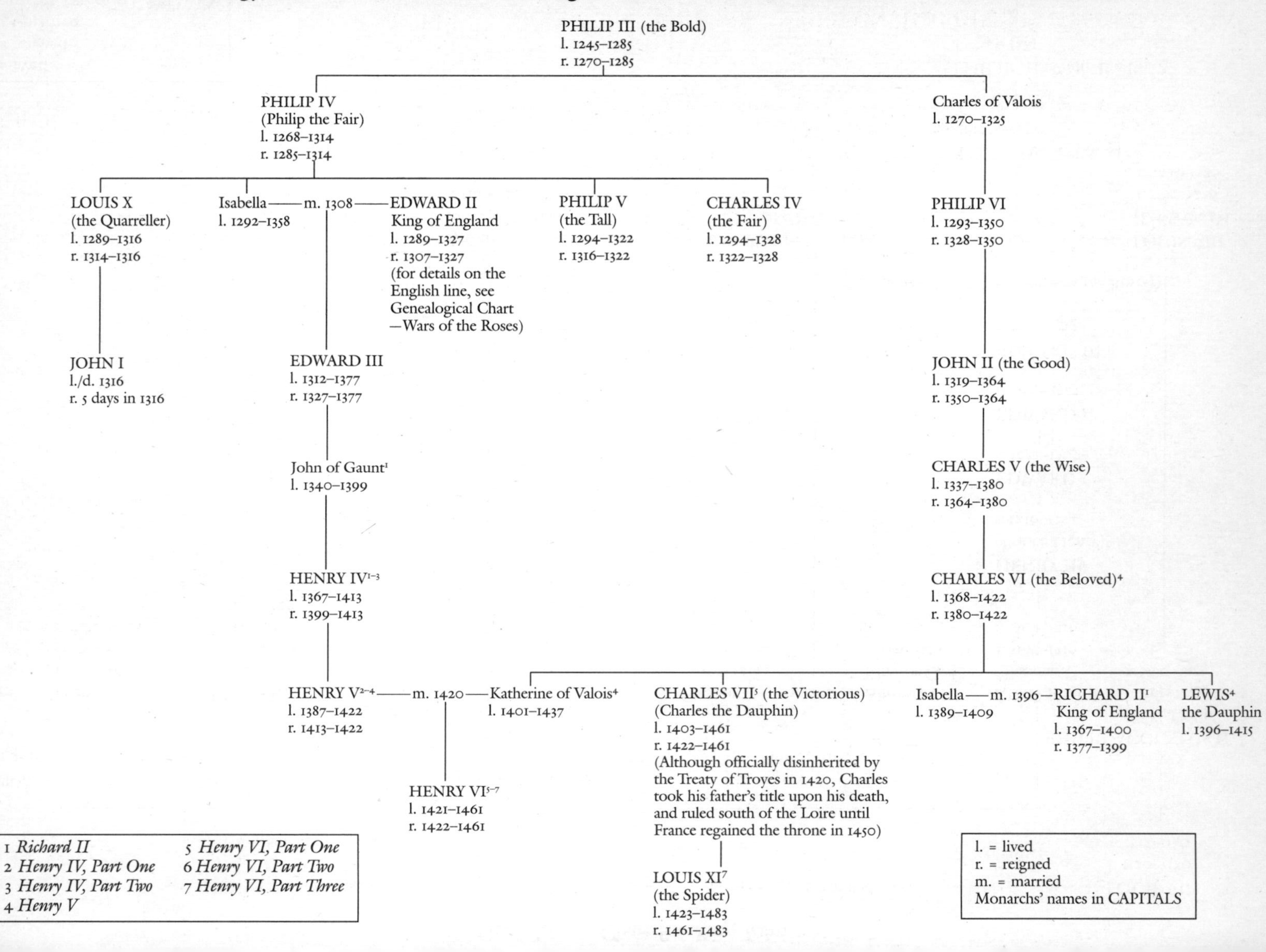

Inconvenient Illness and Insanity Ignored

Throughout the last thirty years of his forty-two-year reign, Charles VI of France was plagued by bouts of insanity that produced violent rages and dementia. This accounts for the authority wielded by the character of his son the Dauphin in *Henry V*, as well as the debilitating insanity of Charles's grandson Henry VI of England, who almost certainly inherited the illness through his mother, Katherine of Valois. Shakespeare never directly addresses the insanity of grandfather or grandson in his History plays. It seems the Bard was reluctant to risk insulting his patroness Queen Elizabeth I, who was, after all, their direct descendant.

Leaning on the Loi Salique

When Charles IV died in 1328 leaving no direct heir to the French throne, the French chose his cousin Philip VI as his successor. Edward III of England objected, asserting his own claim to the French throne through his mother, Isabella, Charles IV's sister. The French rejected Edward's claim, citing the Loi Salique (Salic Law), which prohibited the French crown from passing to, or through, a woman. Daunted by the powerful French forces that backed Philip VI's claim, Edward III, then only sixteen, reluctantly backed down and recognized Philip as the French king. But the question of sovereignty stirred up differences between the two countries concerning the status of certain lands in northern France that Edward had inherited and now claimed for England; in 1337 these differences erupted into the long, intermittent conflict that would come to be known as the Hundred Years' War. The war reached its height during the reign of Henry V, who was determined to secure the French crown. Shakespeare summed up Henry's attitude by having him declare that he was "No King of England, if not King of France!" Ironically, Henry V was part of the Lancastrian branch of the English royal family, which asserted its right to rule on the grounds that the Yorks' claim was invalid because it passed through a woman, Philippa, Countess of Ulster (see "Genealogical Chart—the Wars of the Roses," pages 236–37).

Dauphin, Dolphin, Same Thing

"Dauphin" is simply the title of the French heir apparent, whoever he may be. Charles VI was fortunate to have a pool of twelve children to draw from, as four of his dauphins predeceased him. The first two died in childhood and were succeeded by their younger brother Louis, Lewis the Dauphin of *Henry V*. Louis died at the age of nineteen, not in the Battle of Agincourt as depicted in the play, but two months later, of syphilis, which had made him too sick even to fight in the battle. Shakespeare omits mention of the fourth dauphin, John, who died in 1417 at the age of twenty, and introduces us instead to number five, Charles the Dauphin, in *Henry VI, Part One*. Although the French had already crowned Charles by the time of the events of the play, Shakespeare's reference to him as "the Dauphin" reflects the English position that their own Henry VI ruled France at the time. Each of Shakespeare's dauphins is referred to in the First Folio as "Dolphin," an archaic English variant of the word.

ARISTOCRATIC SELF-AGGRANDIZEMENT RUN AMOK

RIDING SHOTGUN WITH GOD

The monarchs in Shakespeare's plays and those who ruled in his lifetime based their absolute authority on the convenient doctrine of "divine right," which held that a sovereign's right to rule derived directly from God. The right was inherited from a ruler's ancestors, whom God had ordained, and was believed to be reaffirmed by God for each legitimate successor. A ruler was therefore responsible not to the people, but to his or her Maker. Because royal actions were thought to manifest God's will, resistance to a ruler was considered both treasonous and sinful. By the same token, anyone who believed he or she held the valid claim to the throne felt not only justified in trying to seize the crown, but also obligated by God to do so.

IMAGINE BEING KNOWN AS "415 SOUTH STREET"

In medieval and Renaissance times, kings and landed royalty were often referred to by the names of their territories. Hence, throughout Shakespeare's plays, characters address or refer to one another by such pithy appellations as "France," "England," "Austria," "York," "Salisbury," "Warwick," and so on.

Genealogical Chart—

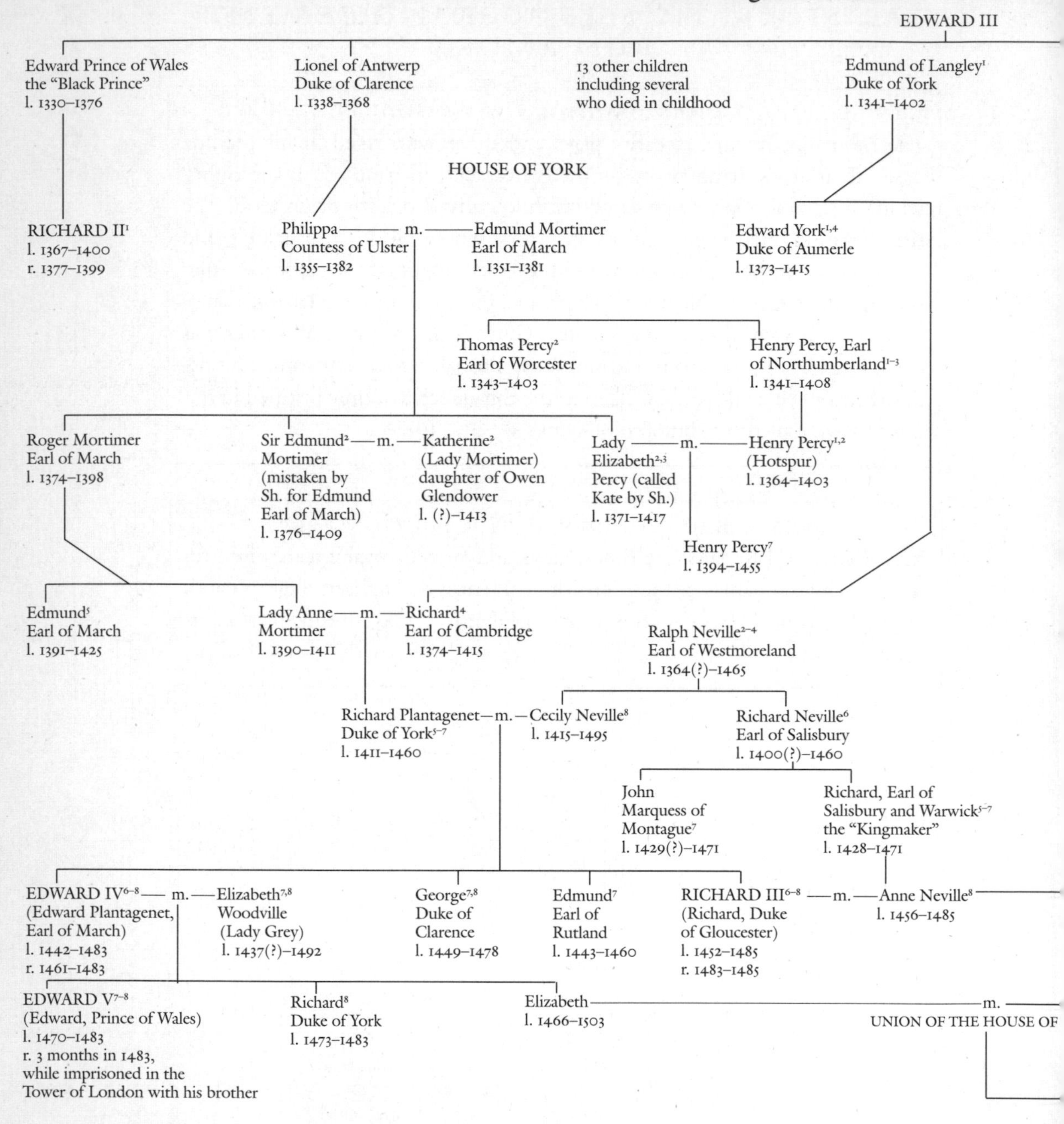

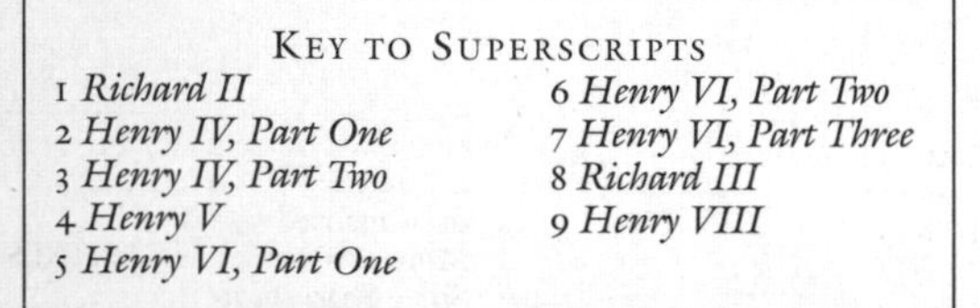

KEY TO SUPERSCRIPTS
1 *Richard II*
2 *Henry IV, Part One*
3 *Henry IV, Part Two*
4 *Henry V*
5 *Henry VI, Part One*
6 *Henry VI, Part Two*
7 *Henry VI, Part Three*
8 *Richard III*
9 *Henry VIII*

the Wars of the Roses

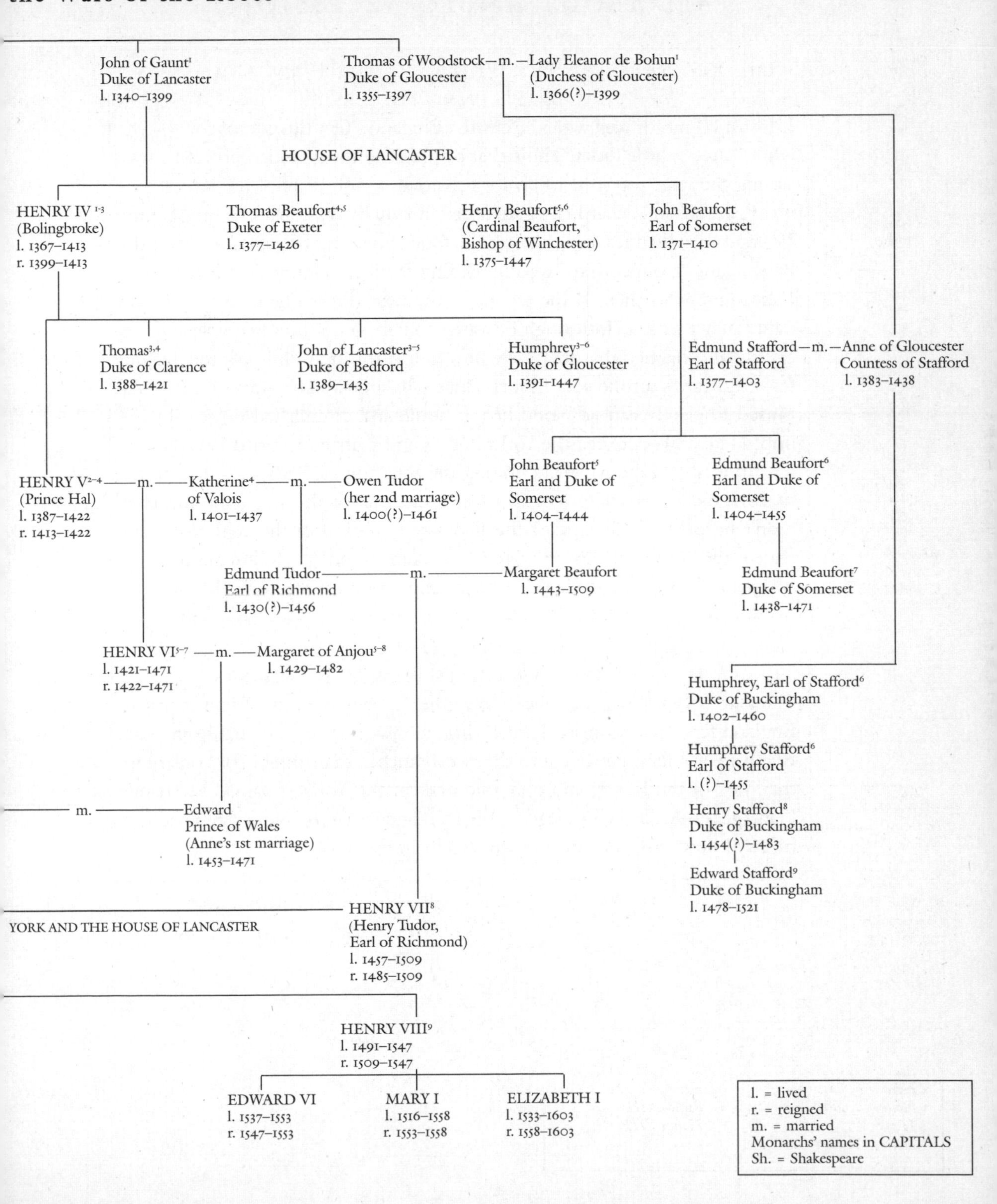

John of Gaunt[1]
Duke of Lancaster
l. 1340–1399
Thomas of Woodstock—m.—Lady Eleanor de Bohun[1]
Duke of Gloucester
l. 1355–1397
(Duchess of Gloucester)
l. 1366(?)–1399
HOUSE OF LANCASTER
HENRY IV [1-3]
(Bolingbroke)
l. 1367–1413
r. 1399–1413
Thomas Beaufort[4,5]
Duke of Exeter
l. 1377–1426
Henry Beaufort[5,6]
(Cardinal Beaufort,
Bishop of Winchester)
l. 1375–1447
John Beaufort
Earl of Somerset
l. 1371–1410
Thomas[3,4]
Duke of Clarence
l. 1388–1421
John of Lancaster[3-5]
Duke of Bedford
l. 1389–1435
Humphrey[3-6]
Duke of Gloucester
l. 1391–1447
Edmund Stafford—m.—Anne of Gloucester
Earl of Stafford
l. 1377–1403
Countess of Stafford
l. 1383–1438
HENRY V[2-4]—m.—Katherine[4]—m.—Owen Tudor
(Prince Hal)
l. 1387–1422
r. 1413–1422
of Valois
l. 1401–1437
(her 2nd marriage)
l. 1400(?)–1461
John Beaufort[5]
Earl and Duke of
Somerset
l. 1404–1444
Edmund Beaufort[6]
Earl and Duke of
Somerset
l. 1404–1455
Edmund Tudor—m.—Margaret Beaufort
Earl of Richmond
l. 1430(?)–1456
l. 1443–1509
Edmund Beaufort[7]
Duke of Somerset
l. 1438–1471
HENRY VI[5-7]—m.—Margaret of Anjou[5-8]
l. 1421–1471
r. 1422–1471
l. 1429–1482
Humphrey, Earl of Stafford[6]
Duke of Buckingham
l. 1402–1460
Humphrey Stafford[6]
Earl of Stafford
l. (?)–1455
Henry Stafford[8]
Duke of Buckingham
l. 1454(?)–1483
Edward Stafford[9]
Duke of Buckingham
l. 1478–1521
m.—Edward
Prince of Wales
(Anne's 1st marriage)
l. 1453–1471
HENRY VII[8]
(Henry Tudor,
Earl of Richmond)
l. 1457–1509
r. 1485–1509
YORK AND THE HOUSE OF LANCASTER
HENRY VIII[9]
l. 1491–1547
r. 1509–1547
EDWARD VI
l. 1537–1553
r. 1547–1553
MARY I
l. 1516–1558
r. 1553–1558
ELIZABETH I
l. 1533–1603
r. 1558–1603
l. = lived
r. = reigned
m. = married
Monarchs' names in CAPITALS
Sh. = Shakespeare

ALL ABOUT ANGLO ACCESSIONS

THE RED ROSE AND THE WHITE . . . THE FATAL COLORS OF OUR STRIVING HOUSES

Edward III meant well when he created England's first dukedoms for his five adult sons . . . little did he know that by granting them landed power he was setting the stage for years of civil war, known as the Wars of the Roses. Edward's grandson Richard II was deposed in 1399 by his cousin Henry (Henry IV) and then died leaving no son. The four remaining branches of Edward's descendants grouped into two contending families: Henry IV's branch, the Lancasters, who claimed the throne as the next direct line of male descendants after Richard II, through Edward's fourth son, John of Gaunt; and the Yorks, who claimed that they were next in line through Philippa, the daughter of Edward's second son, Lionel, Duke of Clarence. The Wars of the Roses caused England years of bloodshed at home and diminished power abroad until Henry VII defeated the Yorks in 1485 and married Edward IV's daughter, Princess Elizabeth, finally uniting the two houses. Although the House of York did use a white rose as its emblem during the wars, the red rose didn't become emblematic of the Lancasters until after the civil strife had ended; the Wars of the Roses were not so named until the following century, when writers such as Shakespeare began exploiting the roses' symbolism.

DYNASTY DEEMED THE DEVIL'S DESCENDANTS

The Plantagenet kings, descended from the Angevin dynasty of France, ruled England from 1154 until Richard II was deposed in 1399. At that point, the English royal family broke into the two branches that fought for control in the Wars of the Roses, and only one branch, the Yorks, retained the name Plantagenet. According to legend, the Plantagenet kings—who often had red hair and fiery tempers—were descended from the devil.

A Pawn Queened and Checkmated

Although this chart seems to indicate that England had only two monarchs between the reign of Henry VIII and that of his daughter Elizabeth I, there was actually a third. While young Edward VI was king, the Duke of Northumberland persuaded Edward to name his cousin Lady Jane Grey as his successor rather than his sister Mary. Upon Edward's death, Jane, Northumberland's daughter-in-law and a pawn in his bid for power, was crowned. She reigned for nine days, until Mary's supporters put their candidate on the throne and imprisoned "Queen Jane," who was beheaded seven months later.

O, What a Tangled Web They Wove

You'll often find rich material for character development by delving into historical records. Not only did many of the actual historical figures live eventful lives, but their families also constantly intermarried. Thus, as the two branches of the royal family struggled for power and the different players switched loyalties, individual family members often found that a close relative had become a bitter enemy. For example, Henry Stafford, Duke of Buckingham, supported Richard III in imprisoning the young Edward V and seizing the throne despite the fact that the child was his nephew by marriage: Buckingham's wife was Katherine Woodville, sister of Elizabeth Woodville (Edward V's mother), and as the two eldest of sixteen Woodville children, the sisters may have been quite close.

Because European royal and noble families have long handed down their given names as well as their titles, the same names appear from one generation to the next. When researching your character, be careful to check her dates of birth or accession, to be sure you're not accidentally studying the life of her mother, aunt, or cousin.

THE COMEDIES

The roots of Elizabethan and Jacobean comedy are found in the ancient Roman plays of Plautus and Terence, which were revived and performed in the mid-1500s and then imitated in the years that followed. Playwrights were also influenced by Italian *novelle*, short romantic novels from which they drew many of their story lines. Although there are several categories of Elizabethan and Jacobean comedy, Shakespeare's Comedies all belong to the most popular of these, the romantic comedy. Romantic comedies revolve around the trials of young lovers who are thwarted but eventually triumph in their efforts to live together happily ever after. Each play sends its characters through an obstacle course of improbable circumstances involving such conventional devices as mistaken identities, twins separated at birth, and so on; the young women frequently disguise themselves as boys, and their lovers consistently fail to recognize them. Eventually, the misunderstandings are unraveled: romantic comedies always end in marriage or the promise of marriage, affirming that Love conquers all. Shakespeare's "early" Comedies, written before 1599, are his simplest, and conform more closely to the parameters of the genre than those that followed; his "mature" Comedies, written right around the turn of the century, reveal greater depth and are thought by many to be his best work in the genre; his later works, written in the early seventeenth century and influenced by his intense concentration on his great Tragedies, are now considered a separate subgenre called the Problem Plays.

AS YOU LIKE IT

ACT II, SCENE i

DUKE SENIOR

GENDER: M
PROSE/VERSE: blank verse
AGE RANGE: mature adult
FREQUENCY OF USE (1–5): 2.5

Duke Senior's brother has usurped his dukedom and banished him from his own lands. The Duke and his loyal followers now live, as another character puts it, "like the old Robin Hood of England" in the Forest of Arden, where the Duke is essentially holding court, and young men from across the land flock to join him.

Now, my co-mates and brothers in exile,
Hath not old custom made this life more sweet
Than that of painted pomp? Are not these woods
More free from peril than the envious court?
5 Here feel we not the penalty of Adam,
The seasons' difference, as the icy fang
And churlish chiding of the winter's wind,
Which when it bites and blows upon my body
Even till I shrink with cold, I smile and say
10 "This is no flattery: these are counselors
That feelingly persuade me what I am . . ."?
Sweet are the uses of adversity,
Which, like the toad, ugly and venomous,
Wears yet a precious jewel in his head;
15 And this our life, exempt from public haunt,
Finds tongues in trees, books in the running brooks,
Sermons in stones, and good in every thing.
I would not change it.

1 minute

1 *co-mates* companions; 2 *old custom* (1) the custom of ancient times (of praising the simple country life) and/or (2) long-continuing habit (it was proverbial that "custom" made all things easy)—choice of definition relates to the play's double time: see Commentary; 3 *painted* i.e., artificial; *pomp* (1) magnificence, splendor; (2) greatness, power; 4 *envious* malignant, breeding spite and hatred; 5 *feel we not* do we not feel; 6 *difference* both (1) change and (2) dissension, discord [*the penalty of Adam, / The seasons' difference* in the Garden of Eden, it was perpetually spring: the change of seasons was one of Adam's punishments for eating the forbidden fruit]; *as* for example; 7 *churlish* rough, brutal; 10 *This is no flattery . . . what I am* the Duke compares the sincere counsel he receives from the winds to the sycophantic "yessing" of his counselors at court; *these* i.e., the winds; 11 *feelingly* both (1) by means of my senses and (2) earnestly, in a heartfelt manner; *persuade me* convince me; counsel me as to; 12 *uses of* (1) profits of, benefits of; (2) ways of life associated with; 13 *venomous* according to popular lore originating in ancient Roman times, toads were poisonous; 14 *yet* nevertheless [*Wears yet a precious jewel in his head* Elizabethans believed that the toad's head contained the "toadstone," which was thought to be an antidote against poison. If set in a ring, the stone was also said to warn against the presence of poison by changing color; *jewel in his head* possibly also refers to the toad's eye, beautiful in contrast with his head]; 15 *public haunt* frequent contact with many people.

COMMENTARY

Duke Senior's speech is full of the techniques most often used in *As You Like It*: alliteration, puns, and the communicating-forest motif explained below. In the first half of the piece, for example, you will find a build in the three rhetorical questions he poses. The first two are each a line and a half long, and have relatively obvious, easily assumed answers. These build to a longer, more complicated question, which is less likely to immediately elicit the response he desires. The Duke, however, an experienced ruler well versed in the methods of oratory, knows that he is steering his band of followers toward the conclusion he wishes them to reach. He steeps this build (and another at the end of the piece) in powerfully poetic and persuasive alliteration: *painted pomp*; *churlish chiding*; *winter's*; *wind / Which when*; *bites / blows / body*; *smile / say*; *tongues / trees*; *books / brooks*; *Sermons / stones*. He also uses many inverted feet throughout the speech, punching each important point.

Which raises the question: why all the effort? If the Duke is to flourish in exile, his *co-mates* must be content. Does he feel a responsibility to keep up his followers' morale, to convince them that this truly is a better life than the comfortable existence they knew at court? Has there been grumbling in the ranks? Or does the Duke feel the need to convince himself of the value of this forest life, to keep from becoming bitter over his lost dukedom?

If there are any visions of his former greatness dancing in his head, he hides them well, replacing them with images from nature. The Duke wields imagery easily and effectively. His reference to *the penalty of Adam* refers to Adam's banishment from Eden and subsequent experience of the changes of season. Although the Duke's banishment parallels Adam's, it also contrasts with it since the Duke feels that despite experiencing the seasons' changes, he has returned to a kind of Eden. He presents the popular Elizabethan view of pastoral existence as idyllic, far preferable to life at court or in the cities. The Duke means to convince his friends that feeling *the penalty of Adam* is a good thing: they have reconnected with truthful nature and escaped from the deceitful court. Much of the Duke's alliteration enhances the imagery of the biting *fang* and *churlish chiding* of winter, thus increasing the effect of his surprising conclusion that this is a benefit. The imagery used to describe adversity in lines 13–14 is enhanced by a string of assonant EHs: *venomous / yet / precious / jewel / head*. Like the biblical reference, this simile has two meanings: even something ugly contains something beautiful; and, what seems to be harmful may actually be even more beneficial. Thus, the *toad* is an example of the idea expressed in the Duke's final group of images (*tongues in trees, books in the running brooks, / Sermons in stones*), that the forest possesses and communicates knowledge. A startling string of alliteration builds through the last two lines but ceases in the last phrase, setting up a pattern that the ear expects to hear continued. The unexpected break in the pattern increases the impact of the Duke's closing thought.

One of the two meanings of *old custom* in line 2 implies that the Duke and his followers have been in exile for a long period of time. His niece Celia's reference to her having been young when her uncle was exiled (in Act I, Scene iii) supports this. But at the opening of the play, characters report the Duke's banishment as a recent event, and his daughter Rosalind grieves over it as though it has just occurred. The use of two simultaneous time frames is an example of double time, one of Shakespeare's favorite devices. Do not let it confuse you: choose the time frame that best serves your development of the character, and go with it (for more on double time, see "Double Double Time and Trouble," page 998).

SIGNIFICANT SCANS

Line 1 is tricky. The traditional way to scan it would be with a simple inverted first foot, using the historic pronunciations of *co-mates* (co-MAYTZ) and *exile* (ex-ILE) with the accent on the second syllable:

/ x x / x / x / x /
Now, my co-mates and brothers in exile

If this works for you, great! It has the advantage of being unexpected, causing the listener to pay attention right at the start of the piece. It also emphasizes the fact that the Duke and his followers are not just companions, but are linked by their fraternity *in exile*.

On the other hand, if you are uncomfortable with a line so different from today's normal speech or feel your audience won't understand you, try this variation:

/ x x / x - x / x x /(x)
Now, (pause) my co-mates and brothers in exile

(Invert the first foot, but take its second syllable as a silent pause after the caesura; crowd the third foot [*-mates and*]; invert the fourth foot; and use today's pronunciation of *co-mates* and *exile*).

The last line of the piece (*I would not change it*) appears in the First Folio as the first half of a line ascribed to Amiens, the next speaker, who continues with "Happy is your grace . . ." Many editors, however, believe that the Folio is in error and that the line was intended to be shared, *I would not change it* finishing

Duke Senior's speech and "Happy is your grace" beginning Amiens's reply. If you are performing this role in the play or a scene thereof, your director will obviously have provided the chosen text, but if you are working on the monologue on your own, feel free to keep or drop the half-line as it suits you.

Don't forget to elide: *envious* (EN-vyuss) in line 4; *difference* (DIFF-renss) in line 6; *Even* (EEN) in line 9; and *flattery* (FLAT-ree) in line 10.

AS YOU LIKE IT

ACT II, SCENE vii

JAQUES

GENDER: M
PROSE/VERSE: blank verse
AGE RANGE: adult to mature adult
FREQUENCY OF USE (1–5): 4

Jaques (JAY-kweez) is a loyal follower of Duke Senior, who has been banished from his dukedom by his usurping brother. Jaques and several other courtiers left with the Duke and have been living with him in the Forest of Arden. When the Duke points out to his friends that "This wide and universal theater / Presents more woeful pageants" than their own, Jaques takes up the theme:

JAQUES

All the world's a stage,
140 And all the men and women merely players;
They have their exits and their entrances,
And one man in his time plays many parts,
His acts being seven ages. At first the infant,
Mewling and puking in his nurse's arms.
145 Then the whining school-boy with his satchel
And shining morning face, creeping like snail
Unwillingly to school. And then the lover,
Sighing like furnace, with a woeful ballad
Made to his mistress' eyebrow. Then a soldier,
150 Full of strange oaths and bearded like the pard,
Jealous in honor, sudden, and quick in quarrel,
Seeking the bubble reputation
Even in the cannon's mouth. And then the justice,
In fair round belly, with good capon lined,
155 With eyes severe and beard of formal cut,
Full of wise saws and modern instances,
And so he plays his part. The sixth age shifts
Into the lean and slippered pantaloon,
With spectacles on nose and pouch on side,

139 *All the world's a stage* a common observation of long standing, popular among Elizabethans; *As You Like It* may have been written for the opening season of the Globe Theatre, and this speech could be an allusion to the new theater's motto: *Totus mundus agit histrionem*; 143 *His acts* i.e., the acts in the play of his life; *seven ages* seven stages of life (the concept of the "seven ages of man" [that human life was divided into seven distinct periods] originated with the ancient Greeks, and was described by both Proclus and Hippocrates; the idea was still common in Shakespeare's day); 144 *Mewling* mewing like a cat; 146 *like snail* a common form in Shakespeare's time, halfway between "like a snail" and "snail-like"; 149 *Made* written and/or sung; *his mistress'* i.e., the woman he is wooing; 150 *strange* (1) foreign and/or (2) extraordinary [*strange oaths* (1) i.e., swearwords learned while fighting in another country and/or (2) extraordinary words or phrases for swearing to something]; *pard* leopard [*bearded like the pard* Elizabethans were generally not familiar with leopards, but often saw the heraldic emblem of "lions leopardé," which, though lions, were casually called "leopards"; since the word *beard* could refer to any type of facial hair, Jaques's reference may have suggested hair and a beard resembling a lion's mane]; 151 *Jealous in honor* i.e., touchy about matters concerning his honor; *sudden* (1) hasty, rash; (2) impetuous, passionate; *in* to; 152 *bubble* i.e., empty, insubstantial thing; *reputation* i.e., good name ("reputation" was an important goal for military men); 153 *justice* judge; 154 *fair* (1) appropriate; (2) handsome; *capon* a small rooster that has been castrated to make its meat more tender [*with good capon lined* alluding to the "capon-justice," a common term for the judge who was easily bribed with a capon]; 156 *saws* maxims; *modern* commonplace, trite; *instances* illustrations or proofs (of his opinions); 157 *shifts* "shift" was a technical term for changing scene in Elizabethan theatre; 158 *pantaloon* a stock "foolish old man" character from *commedia dell'arte* (Italian comedy of the sixteenth to eighteenth centuries) and with

160 His youthful hose well saved, a world too wide
For his shrunk shank, and his big manly voice,
Turning again toward childish treble, pipes
And whistles in his sound. Last scene of all,
That ends this strange eventful history,
165 Is second childishness and mere oblivion,
Sans teeth, sans eyes, sans taste, sans everything.

1 minute, 40 seconds

which Elizabethan theatregoers were familiar; 160 *youthful hose* the breeches he wore when he was young; 161 *shank* the part of the leg from the knee to the ankle; 163 *his* its; 164 *strange* (1) extraordinary, remarkable; (2) odd, surprising; *history* history play; 165 *second childishness* i.e., a return to the helplessness of infancy; *mere* absolute, utter; *oblivion* loss of memory; 166 *Sans* (English pronunciation: SAHNZ) French for "without."

COMMENTARY

This monologue is famous for its brilliant development of a popular metaphor into an expression of Jaques's pessimistic philosophy that life is essentially a meaningless series of mundane events (often mistakenly touted as Shakespeare's own philosophy). But it is also a great example of one of Shakespeare's best gifts to the actor: his talent for taking a shallow convention or stereotype and giving it depth without sacrificing its humorous or satirical qualities. Shakespeare wrote Jaques as a parody of a fashionable attitude at court in Elizabethan times: world-weary, melancholic cynicism. But Shakespeare allows his character to transcend the type, as is evident in this passage. Here, Jaques speaks too eloquently for the audience to laugh at him, and instead makes the audience laugh—or at least knowingly smile—with him, even if they don't agree with his philosophy.

Although the Elizabethan fashion may have been merely to affect such ideas, it is important to keep in mind that Jaques actually ascribes to them. He spends many hours wandering the Forest of Arden in isolation, contemplating them. Perhaps that is why this monologue is so poetically removed from everyday speech. Jaques may just now be giving voice to thoughts that he's been ruminating on for days. Maybe the Duke's comment prompted his scattered thoughts to suddenly "click." Or maybe Jaques has composed this piece of poetry in advance, and seizes the Duke's remark as the perfect moment to recite it to his friends. Because this piece is often viewed as a "set piece" rather than an active, plot-advancing part of the play, it is particularly important to make it active by pinning down your motivation in delivering it.

Jaques lines up the parallels between human life and staged action with a barrage of stage terms (*stage*; *players*; *exits*; *entrances*; *plays many parts*; *acts*). He extends the metaphor throughout the monologue by continuing to make theatrical references throughout: *bearded* and *In fair round belly* are worded to sound as though they are costume elements; *plays his part* brings us back to the stage metaphor directly; *shifts* was a technical term meaning "changes scene"; *pantaloon* makes the old man a stock *commedia dell'arte* character, for whom *spectacles*, *pouch*, *hose* that are too big, and a *childish treble* were all conventional characteristics; finally he mentions the *Last scene*, and the *history* at the monologue's close. Comparisons between human life and stage plays usually ended with the observation that life amounts to either a comedy or a tragedy, depending on the commentator's personal philosophy. Jaques avoids the debate altogether, making it a *history*. He may feel that the usual argument over life's nature is pointless, since life itself is meaningless. A *history* is the right category for Jaques's nihilistic staging of human life, as it comes closest to merely recording the facts that occur, rather than ascribing a particular meaning to them.

Thankfully, Jaques's pessimism does not preclude a wry sense of humor. This piece is packed with sardonic words and phrases; be sure to explore their use. For example, the term *woeful ballad* is not complimentary; Elizabethans often used the word *ballad* with contempt for its trite sentimentalism. The phrase *mistress' eyebrow* derides the ballad maker's trivial subject matter and tendency to catalogue ad nauseam the minutiae of the beloved's qualities. In the phrase *bubble reputation*, Jaques uses the disparaging word *bubble* and the expanded pronunciation of *reputation* to ridicule the soldier's obsession with military honors. Also, *fair round belly* sarcastically praises the bloated belly of the judge, who has grown fat off bribes. Jaques twice mentions the cut of the man's beard, making fun of the particularity with which the many possible cuts were differentiated, and the habit of judging a man by the cut.

These detailed depictions bring each stage of this everyman's existence vividly to life, and even if your audience does not agree with your implied theory of life's meaning(lessness), they will be right with you along the journey. Even when Jaques is not being sarcastic, he is elegantly expressive, choosing exactly the right words for each idea. For instance, *shifts* not only carries through the stage theme, but also perfectly echoes the slow, gentle shift from middle age to old age, as we experience it in life. And notice his choice for the final word of the final sentence. One might expect to hear "Sans teeth, sans eyes, sans taste, sans <u>anything</u>," implying that the man is without any of the things he once had (all, as we have seen, trivial in any case). Instead, Jaques ends with *sans* everything, changing the scope of the sentence. In this case, man is without everything that exists, or could exist. In other words, he is not only without his former trivial possessions or pleasures, but also without any possible meaning in his life, without the abstract comforts of hope, love, or faith. Powerful stuff, brought in on the waves of the soft repeated sound of *sans*.

Jaques accents his thoughts with sound repetitions (particularly alliteration) throughout. Some examples: *exits / entrances*; *Mewling / puking*; *whining / shining*; *Made / mistress*; *quick / quarrel*; *severe / beard*; *play / part*; *world / wide*; *shrunk shank*; and *ends / eventful*. Also, make use of the lovely onomatopoeic description of the pantaloon's voice with the words *pipes* and *whistles*.

SIGNIFICANT SCANS

This piece is full of metric variation, with many inverted first feet and double endings, as well as several mid-line variations of both kinds. If you examine the placement of these variations, however, you will notice that the majority of them are concentrated in the descriptions of the first four ages of the man's life. They ease off with middle age, and by the time the pantaloon is introduced, aggressive first-foot inversions disappear altogether. In this way the meter of the speech seems to imitate the rhythm of the man's life. The perfect iambic rhythm of the last line, with each foot separated by a caesura, feels like the slowing heartbeat of the old man approaching death.

Six of the seven stages are introduced mid-line after a caesura, encouraging a steady flow from one stage to the next (again, just like in life). Jaques seems to take more time discussing the sixth stage than all the others. Does it hold more interest for him somehow? Is Jaques in middle age and contemplating the next stage of his own life? Or does he merely focus on this stage because the pantaloon best fulfills his metaphor?

Note that the monologue starts mid-line and mid-foot. If you have trouble scanning the meter, count out two and a half feet in your head before you speak and the words will scan correctly. Also, line 145 is headless (and has a double ending), giving it the same complaining tone Jaques ascribes to the boy:

x / x / x / x / x / (x)
(pause) Then the whining school-boy with his satchel

Here are two of the most difficult scans:

Line 143 has two double endings (one before the caesura and one at the end) and requires the elision of *being* (beeng):

x / x / x / (x) x / x / (x)
His acts being seven ages. At first the infant

Line 151 has inverted feet at both the beginning and after the first caesura, and double endings both before the first caesura and at the end of the line, mimicking the impetuosity of the hot-tempered young man:

/ x x / (x) / x x / x / (x)
Jealous in honor, sudden, and quick in quarrel

Don't forget to elide: *players* (PLAYRZ) in line 140 (optional); *being* (beeng) in line 143; *mistress'* (MISS-tress, *not* MISS-tress-z) in line 149; *Even* (EEN) in line 153; and *oblivion* (o-BLIV-yun) in line 165;

. . . and to expand: *reputation* (RE-pyoo-TAY′-shee-UN) in line 152.

AS YOU LIKE IT

ACT III, SCENE V

PHEBE

GENDER: F
AGE RANGE: young adult
PROSE/VERSE: blank verse
FREQUENCY OF USE (1–5): 5

Try as she might, the shepherdess Phebe has not been able to ditch her unwanted suitor, the shepherd Silvius, who follows her everywhere, whining incessantly about his undying love for her. He has just accused her of being more cruel than a common executioner, who at least begs his victim's pardon before lopping off his or her head. At the end of her tether, Phebe replies:

PHEBE

I would not be thy executioner.
I fly thee, for I would not injure thee.
10 Thou tell'st me there is murder in mine eye;
'Tis pretty, sure, and very probable
That eyes, that are the frail'st and softest things,
Who shut their coward gates on atomies,
Should be called tyrants, butchers, murderers.
15 Now I do frown on thee with all my heart,
And if mine eyes can wound, now let them kill thee.
Now counterfeit to swoon, why now, fall down,
Or if thou canst not, O for shame, for shame,
Lie not, to say mine eyes are murderers.
20 Now show the wound mine eye hath made in thee.
Scratch thee but with a pin, and there remains
Some scar of it; lean upon a rush,
The cicatrice and capable impressure
Thy palm a moment keeps; but now mine eyes,
25 Which I have darted at thee, hurt thee not.
Nor, I am sure, there is no force in eyes
That can do hurt.

1 minute

8 *would not be* do not wish to be; 9 *fly* flee, run away from; 11 *pretty* admirable, fine (may refer either to *mine eye* or *That eyes . . . murderers*, or punningly to both); *sure* surely; 13 *shut their coward gates* i.e., blink; *on* against, to ward off; *atomies* tiny atoms, i.e., specks of dust; 17 *counterfeit* pretend; 19 *Lie not, to say* Do not lie by saying; 22 *rush* long-stemmed marsh grass (an emblem of weakness); 23 *cicatrice* (SIK′-uh-TRISS) scarlike mark; *capable impressure* receptive impression; 26 *Nor . . . there is no* Nor . . . is there any (the double negative is often used for emphasis in Shakespeare).

COMMENTARY

Phebe shares her name with the famously chaste and cold goddess of the moon (a.k.a. Diana), and she certainly lives up to her namesake. In her harsh rejection of Silvius's love, Phebe fulfills her role as the scornful shepherdess often seen in the Pastoral, a popular genre during the English Renaissance. But although Phebe may only be a stereotype to some, she must be a fully developed character for you.

It is therefore important to decide why Phebe chooses this moment to dissect Silvius's metaphor as if it were a literal statement. Is she exasperated with him and thus being as cruel as she can in hopes of getting rid of him? Does she enjoy toying with him and watching his frustration as she purposely misses the point of what he has said? Does his sentimentality make her sick? Is she tired of having to play the stereotypical role of coldhearted love object?

SIGNIFICANT SCANS

Whatever motivation you choose, the conviction with which Phebe argues her point requires that you make the choice decisively. The monologue's language and meter are simple and direct, suiting her personality, her lack of education, and her desire to convey her message in no uncertain terms. The meter flows regularly, with only two elisions and a few simple variations. The most notable of these variations occurs when Phebe "attacks" Silvius with her allegedly murderous eyes. She begins the attack in line 15 with an aggressive inverted first foot, and continues it in line 16, which has an inverted foot mid-line after the caesura, as well as a double ending.

Line 22 has a pause after the caesura, during the first syllable of the third foot:

x / x / x / x / x /
Some scar of it; (pause) lean upon a rush

You might use this small pause to think of the next example in Phebe's argument; perhaps she is wracking her brain for something that will add an implied insult to her proof, and then hits on the image of the weak *rush*. Or she may be pausing to check whether this is all sinking in yet for poor Silvius (this possibility is supported by the next line: the frustrated, rapid-fire diction that follows, as well as the hissing *cicatrice*, suggest he's still not getting her meaning and she's impatiently illustrating her point <u>again</u>).

Line 27 is short, leaving three feet of silence where the ear expects the line to continue. This gives the piece a surprisingly blunt and effective end, and holds the audience's attention, allowing you to play with that moment of unexpected silence.

Some of Phebe's word choices are particularly interesting. Most notable is her frequent use of the familiar *thee* and *thy* throughout the piece. It is probable that she and Silvius have known each other for many years, tending their sheep together since childhood, and that they long ago became accustomed to using the familiar form with each other. Or perhaps Phebe uses the intimate form teasingly, to torment the poor fellow. Perhaps she uses the form to subtly string him along, despite her protestations, because she's addicted to his flattery. Or maybe the words slip out because she subconsciously cares for him to some degree (which would be nice when performing the play, since she marries him at the end).

Also notice that Phebe says she *darted* her eyes at Silvius. She could be referring to the preceding moment, when she "assaulted" him with her eyes to prove that it would do no damage. On the other hand, she may be referring to having glanced at him when he spoke to her . . . or even to having flirted with him. Your choice will depend on how you see Phebe. It is even possible that Phebe uses *darted* with intentional double entendre. In Shakespeare's time, *dart* was sometimes used to carry the secondary meaning, "copulate." Likewise, *eye* could be taken to mean any of the human orifices, and *wound* to mean "vagina." The phrases *fall down* and *Lie not* can also be interpreted to have sexual second meanings. Taken in context of the monologue, Phebe could be using these double meanings to convey the idea that as a woman she could not and has not assaulted him sexually. Perhaps Phebe herself has been the object of unwanted advances in a more physical sense, and resents Silvius's speaking of her rejection of him as though it were more harmful than the abuse she herself has experienced. Each time Phebe uses double entendre, she may do so unwittingly, or she may do so intentionally, to taunt Silvius, to tease him, or even to disgust him and hopefully break him of his blind love for her, or for the reasons mentioned above. Finally, for help with using the word *O* to its best advantage, see "O, No! An *O*!," page xxxiii.

AS YOU LIKE IT

ACT III, SCENE V

ROSALIND

GENDER: F
AGE RANGE: young adult
PROSE/VERSE: blank verse
FREQUENCY OF USE (1–5): 5

Since her recent banishment from the dukedom by her uncle the Duke, Rosalind and her cousin Celia have been hiding out in the Forest of Arden, posing as a young man named Ganymede and his sister, Aliena. Rosalind has discovered that the guy she loves, Orlando, is also now hiding out in the forest, and—posing to him as Ganymede—she has been testing his love before revealing her true identity. Orlando has failed to arrive for a scheduled visit with "Ganymede" and Rosalind is upset. While waiting for him, she and "Aliena" have just witnessed a scene between a young shepherd named Silvius and Phebe, the shepherdess he loves—who does not return his feelings. Phebe has just berated Silvius cruelly, telling him to leave her alone and insisting that she does not pity him. "Ganymede" has seen enough and jumps into the conversation, saying:

ROSALIND

35 And why, I pray you? Who might be your mother,
That you insult, exult, and all at once,
Over the wretched? What though you have no beauty—
As, by my faith, I see no more in you
Than without candle may go dark to bed—
40 Must you be therefore proud and pitiless?
Why, what means this? Why do you look on me?
I see no more in you than in the ordinary
Of Nature's sale-work. 'Od's my little life,
I think she means to tangle my eyes too!
45 No, faith, proud mistress, hope not after it.
'Tis not your inky brows, your black silk hair,
Your bugle eyeballs, nor your cheek of cream
That can entame my spirits to your worship.
You foolish shepherd, wherefore do you follow her,
50 Like foggy South, puffing with wind and rain?
You are a thousand times a properer man
Than she a woman. 'Tis such fools as you
That makes the world full of ill-favored children.

35 *I pray you* I ask you; *Who might be your mother* In Shakespeare's time it was believed that women inherited from their mothers those "feminine" virtues of tenderness and compassion that Phebe evidently lacks; 36 *and all at once* i.e., both at the same time; 37 *the wretched* the miserable, the unhappy (with possible second meaning: the pathetic); *What though* Though; 38 *by my faith* i.e., I swear; *I see no more in you* i.e., I see no more beauty in you [*I see no more . . . dark to bed* Two possible meanings: (1) Phebe is so unattractive that there is no hope of someone taking her to bed as long as there is enough candlelight to see her by; (2) Phebe's beauty is not bright enough to light up a room]; 40 *therefore* The use of this word here confuses scholars, but it fits with "Ganymede's" overall use of inverted logic throughout this monologue in which she calls the beautiful Phebe ugly, and then proceeds to praise and put down Phebe's features simultaneously. One suggested meaning for the whole sentence: "Being physically ugly . . . must you therefore also exhibit the unattractive qualities of pride and pitilessness."; *proud* arrogant; 41 *Why* an exclamation of surprise; *this* "Ganymede" refers to the fact that Phebe is noticeably falling for "him"; *on* at; 42 *the ordinary / Of Nature's sale-work* Nature's run-of-the-mill, ready-made goods (which are inferior to custom-made)—"Ganymede" personifies Nature as a merchant; 43 *'Od's* short for "May God save" [*'Od's my little life* Here, an exclamation of mortification]; 44 *tangle* ensnare [*tangle my eyes* i.e., cause me to fall in love with her]; 45 *faith* truly, really (short for "in faith"); *mistress* miss (here, used with contempt, to distance herself from Phebe); *hope not after it* don't hold out hope for it (i.e., that I'll fall in love with you); 47 *bugle* a black, tube-shaped glass bead [*bugle eyeballs* shining black eyes]; 48 *That can entame my spirits to your worship* That can tame my feelings to worship you (i.e., that can make me fall in love with you); 49 *You foolish shepherd* now addressing Silvius; *wherefore* why; 50 *South* the wind that blows from the south; 51 *properer* better looking; 53 *ill-favored* ugly;

'Tis not her glass but you that flatters her,
55 And out of you she sees herself more proper
Than any of her lineaments can show her.
But, mistress, know yourself. Down on your knees,
And thank Heaven, fasting, for a good man's love;
For I must tell you friendly in your ear,
60 Sell when you can—you are not for all markets.
Cry the man mercy, love him, take his offer;
Foul is most foul, being foul to be a scoffer.
So take her to thee, shepherd. Fare you well.

1 minute, 40 seconds

54 *glass* looking glass, mirror; 56 *lineaments* (LIN´-yuh-MUNTS) features; 57 *mistress* "Ganymede" turns her attention back to Phebe; *Down* Get down; 59 *friendly* as a friend; *in your ear* i.e., quietly, secretly, just between you and me; 61 *Cry the man mercy* Beg the man's mercy; 62 *Foul* ugly (with second meaning, "wicked"); *scoffer* one who mocks another [*Foul is most foul, being foul to be a scoffer* i.e., ugliness is at its absolute ugliest when it is enhanced by the added ugliness of being a scoffer].

COMMENTARY

Scholars, directors, actors, and theatregoers agree that Rosalind is one of the wittiest, most spirited, most charming and winsome, most sensitive and human of all Shakespeare's characters. So to do this monologue you must grapple with the obvious question: why is Rosalind so uncharacteristically harsh here?

To understand her sudden vitriol, you must place this scene in its greater context. Rosalind has just been stood up by Orlando. Now she is confronted with a couple in which the man loves with the same constancy with which she loves the seemingly lackadaisical Orlando. Phebe's cruelty toward Silvius is thus highly personal to Rosalind—it reminds her of Orlando's seeming insensitivity toward her love, and wounds her as surely as it wounds Silvius. Hence her anger, which actually reflects her frustration with Orlando, though it is directed at Phebe. And her lack of pity for Silvius reflects her frustration with herself—she has let herself be vulnerable with someone who doesn't hold her in high enough regard even to show up on time . . . if he shows up at all.

Perhaps Rosalind also seeks to match Phebe's cruelty in order to give Phebe a dose of her own medicine. Furthermore, remember that Rosalind is posing as a young man. Perhaps—especially in the wake of her disappointment by Orlando—she perceives young men as insensitive and strives to play that role convincingly. The tough, direct language sounds particularly male; Rosalind has become adept at impersonating a young, cheeky guy. And, of course, Rosalind wants love to prevail. On paper, the shepherds Phebe and Silvius are a perfect match. If only Phebe would see Silvius's good qualities and get with the program, the couple could enjoy what Rosalind herself longs for.

Since Rosalind is trying hard to denigrate Phebe's looks, she capitalizes on the fact that Phebe has dark hair and eyes, which in Elizabethan times were not prized as highly as their lighter counterparts. But despite Rosalind's insistence to the contrary, her imagery proves that Phebe is quite lovely; when actually describing her, the truthful Rosalind can't help but use terms that illustrate Phebe's beauty (*black silk hair*; *bugle eyeballs*; *cheek of cream*). The rest of Rosalind's imagery is purposely workaday and unlovely (for example, *the ordinary / Of Nature's sale-work*; *foggy South, puffing with wind and rain*; *you are not for all markets*), further supporting her guise as a brash and macho country guy.

Rosalind uses consonance and assonance to bolster her bravura. Examples include: *insult / exult*; *proud / pitiless*; *Why / what / Why*; *Why / Why / me / I / ordinary*; *ordinary / Of / 'Od's*; *little life*; *brows / black / bugle eyeballs*; *cheek of cream*; *foolish / follow / foggy / puffing / fools / ill-favored / flatters*; *fasting / For / for / friendly*. Also note the repetition of such words as *proper(er)*; *fool(ish)*; and *Foul*, which highlight the contrast between Silvius's good and bad qualities, and the contrast between Silvius and Phebe.

SIGNIFICANT SCANS

The meter of this monologue also supports Rosalind's ruse that she is a young man. It is chockful of variations (many double endings and several inverted feet), as well as sentences that begin and end mid-line. This combination gives the piece a syncopation, abruptness, and quickness of pace. The frequent full stops mid-line (where you do not pause as long as you would at a full stop at a line's end) suggest that Rosalind is thinking on her feet and that her thoughts are coming to her quickly. And doubtless, she doesn't want to give Phebe a chance to interject. The double endings' extra syllables and the inverted feet's unexpected punched words help create Rosalind's indignant tone.

Three lines go so far as to contain twelve syllables:

(1) Line 37 is pentameter with two double endings, one before the caesura and the other at the line's end (also note the inverted first foot):

/ x x / (x) / x x / x / (x)
Over the wretched? What though you have no beauty

(2) Line 42 is hexameter (a rare six-footed line), and the word *ordinary* is elided (OR′-dun-REE):

x / x / x / x / x / x /
I see no more in you than in the ordinary

(3) Line 49 also has twelve syllables. It can be scanned as hexameter, which underscores Rosalind's frustration with Silvius:

x / x / x / x / x / x /
You foolish shepherd, wherefore do you follow her

Or it can be scanned as pentameter with a crowded fourth foot, in which *do you* is elided (d'you) (—fore do you fol—), which makes Rosalind sound tougher, helping her pass as Ganymede:

x / x / x / x - x / x /
You foolish shepherd, wherefore do you follow her

Line 53 has an inverted third foot following a caesura which is not marked by punctuation (as well as a double ending):

x / x / / x x / x / (x)
That makes the world full of ill-favored children

Notice that the monologue builds naturally to its crescendo in lines 60–62, three lines in a row that each begin with an inverted foot and end with a double ending, drawing attention to Rosalind's hilariously worded main message to Phebe: get over your nasty little self and love Silvius. She wraps up this point with a bow, the rhyming couplet in lines 61–62 (*offer* / *scoffer*), and takes her leave.

Don't forget to elide: *ordinary* (OR′-dun-REE) in line 42; *properer* (PROP-rer) in line 51; *lineaments* (LIN′-yuh-MUNTS) in line 56; and *being* (BEENG) and all three instances of *Foul* (FOWL) in line 62;

to contract: *do you* (d'yoo) in line 49 (optional);

and to either contract *And thank* ('nd thank) or elide *Heaven* (Hev'n) in line 58.

WHAT'S IN A NAME?
Rosalind deliberately adopted the name Ganymede, telling Celia "I'll have no worse a name than Jove's own page." But the name also serves a second purpose: according to Greek mythology, Zeus, King of the Gods (later named Jove by the Romans), fell in lust with a beautiful young Trojan prince named Ganymede. He swept down in the form of an eagle and carried the youth to Mount Olympus to serve as his cupbearer. The choice of this name for Rosalind's male alter ego is apt for the somewhat effeminate "young man" (despite Rosalind's best attempts at machismo) who is ardently wooed by Orlando.

AS YOU LIKE IT

ACT III, SCENE v

PHEBE

GENDER: F
AGE RANGE: young adult
PROSE/VERSE: blank verse
FREQUENCY OF USE (1–5): 5

Phebe, a shepherdess, is not the least bit in love with Silvius, the wimpy young shepherd who follows her everywhere like a puppy dog, imploring her to be his. A few minutes ago, she was scolding Silvius for following her (see monologue, page 254) when suddenly a young man appeared and soundly rebuked her, telling her that she should jump at Silvius's marriage proposal since she is not attractive enough to elicit a better one (see monologue, page 258). The stranger then departed as suddenly as he had arrived. Phebe (who doesn't realize that the youth is actually a young woman in disguise) has fallen in love with the newcomer and hopes to use Silvius as her messenger to him. She asks Silvius if he knows the youth, he replies that he does, and then, lest Silvius read too much into her inquiry, she adds:

PHEBE

Think not I love him, though I ask for him.
110 'Tis but a peevish boy—yet he talks well.
But what care I for words? Yet words do well
When he that speaks them pleases those that hear.
It is a pretty youth—not very pretty;
But sure he's proud—and yet his pride becomes him;
115 He'll make a proper man. The best thing in him
Is his complexion; and faster than his tongue
Did make offense, his eye did heal it up.
He is not very tall—yet for his years he's tall.
His leg is but so-so—and yet 'tis well.
120 There was a pretty redness in his lip,
A little riper and more lusty red
Than that mixed in his cheek; 'twas just the difference
Betwixt the constant red and mingled damask.
There be some women, Silvius, had they marked him
125 In parcels as I did, would have gone near
To fall in love with him, but, for my part,
I love him not nor hate him not—and yet
I have more cause to hate him than to love him,

109 *Think not I love him* Do not think that I'm in love with him; 110 *'Tis but* He's just; *peevish* silly; cross, wrangling; 111 *do well* i.e., are quite effective; 113 *It* He (*it* was often used in place of *he* or *she* in Shakespeare's day); *pretty* good looking, fine; 114 *sure he's proud* he's certainly arrogant; 116 *complexion* one's whole external appearance (not, as today, merely that of the face); *faster than . . . offense* before he had even said something offending; 117 *his eye* (1) his beautiful eyes; and/or (2) the look in his eye; 119 *but* merely [*His leg . . . so-so* Elizabethan men wore hose, and men's clearly delineated legs were considered one of their attractive features, much as women's are in many Western cultures today]; 121 *riper* both fuller and redder; *lusty* luxuriant (with intended or unintended sexual double entendre); 122 *that mixed in his cheek* i.e., the shades of red visible in his cheeks; *just* exactly; 123 *Betwixt* between; *constant* uniform; *mingled damask* (DAM-usk) this may refer to one or both of the following: (1) unlike the "constant" red of a red rose, the "damask" rose had various hues in it—the term is also applied to a pink rose (which "mingled" white and red); (2) "damask silk" (so named because it came from Damascus) was multihued. Both references illustrate that "Ganymede's" lips were a deeper and more uniformly red color than his also-rosy cheeks; 124 *had they marked him* if they had observed him; 125 *In parcels* feature by feature; *would have gone near / To fall* (who) would have

For what had he to do to chide at me?
130 He said mine eyes were black and my hair black;
And, now I am remembered, scorned at me;
I marvel why I answered not again.
But that's all one: omittance is no quittance.
I'll write to him a very taunting letter,
135 And thou shalt bear it—wilt thou, Silvius?

1 minute, 40 seconds

come close to falling; 129 ***what had he to do*** i.e., what reason did he have; 130 ***He said . . . hair black*** Elizabethans considered fair skin, eyes, and hair more beautiful than dark skin, eyes, and hair; 131 ***now I am remembered*** i.e., now that I think of it; ***scorned at*** mocked; 132 ***I marvel why I answered not again*** i.e., I'm amazed that I didn't answer back; 133 ***that's all one*** i.e., that's neither here nor there; never mind; ***omittance is no quittance*** a proverb meaning "failure to do something at the time is not a discharge from the responsibility of doing it in the long run." Phebe refers to her failure to speak back to "Ganymede."

COMMENTARY

Phebe the shepherdess knows these woods like the back of her hand, but as of five minutes ago she can no longer tell you which end is up and which is down. She has fallen in love with "Ganymede," the saucy young lad who appeared out of nowhere, yelled at her, and left as suddenly as he arrived. It was a whirlwind experience, and Phebe has yet to sort out what happened, never mind how she feels about it or about the youth who has turned her world upside down. She has been deeply insulted by this youth, yet she is oddly attracted to him, which is confusing to her. Although it is evident to the audience that Phebe is in love with "Ganymede," you must decide whether Phebe herself realizes she is in love with him before she commences the monologue and, if so, merely pretends otherwise so as to persuade Silvius to be her messenger to him (this choice does not preclude her being confused about her feelings—after all, he treated her horribly). Alternatively, Phebe may be coming to the realization that she is in love over the course of the monologue, or may not yet have admitted it to herself by the monologue's end. And you have another decision to make: is Phebe excited about being in love or does she wish to convince herself as well as Silvius that she is not in love with the insulting youth? The most obvious evidence of Phebe's tumultuous frame of mind is the way she repeatedly states a disparaging opinion about one of "Ganymede's" features, and then immediately contradicts herself, asserting her true opinion about it.

Phebe's rattled composure is communicated through the monologue's meter: she begins the piece with an inverted foot, punching the first word of the first line, as though she is nervously hastening to assure Silvius—and perhaps herself—that she is not in love with "Ganymede." Her abruptness is also consistent with her habitually strident tone toward Silvius, even though she has softened it somewhat now that she, too, is in love. From the first line, almost every statement is interrupted mid-line at the caesura by its opposite, or by mention of some new fabulous feature of "Ganymede's" that Phebe has just thought of, taking the monologue on a breathless, breakneck, zigzaggy race to the finish line, where Phebe enlists Silvius to deliver her letter. Phebe is clearly thinking on her feet, trying to make sense of her stirred-up thoughts as she goes. She also may not wish to give Silvius a chance to interrupt her. The pace is emphasized by another metrical device: the pervasive use of double endings (and even an optional triple ending in line 122, depending on whether you choose to elide *difference*). The double endings appear both at line endings and mid-line before caesuras, and create the sense that Phebe is breathlessly babbling with excitement, trepidation, longing, bewilderment, or a combination thereof. Her quick, short words further compound this effect: she is not choosing them carefully—they are tumbling out of her. Also notice the dearth of elisions and contractions in this monologue. The only mandatory elision is *Silvius*, in line 124—he is the only thing she belittles, as though she disdains to pronounce his name fully. This is in marked contrast to her exaltation of "Ganymede's" features, which she enunciates to their fullest. Similarly, her use of Relishing Rs (*pretty redness / riper / red*) to describe the lips she wants to kiss perfectly conveys that desiRe.

Phebe's expressions are very conversational (for example: *but so-so*; *for my part*; *now I am remembered*; *I marvel . . . answered not again*; *that's all one*; *omittance is no quittance*). Such phrases help establish Phebe's youth and her lack of education.

You must decide how much of the monologue Phebe delivers directly to Silvius and how much is delivered more to herself (as though soliloquizing). Don't forget for a moment that Silvius is right there throughout the piece (particularly as Phebe attempts to diminish "Ganymede"). In fact, remember that no matter how selfish Phebe may be, she may also experience a twinge of guilt at gushing about the dreamy "Ganymede" to a man who is in love with her—this could account in part for her attempts at deprecation.

As a final note, it is interesting that Phebe rhapsodizes about the very qualities of "Ganymede" that point to the fact that "he" is actually female, such as the *pretty redness in his lip*; "his" rosy cheeks, "his" eyes . . . even denigrating his lack of height and *so-so* legs, without putting the pieces of the puzzle together. Phebe doesn't even use male pronouns to refer to "Ganymede" at first, she uses the word *it*. Although this was a common usage of the word in Shakespeare's time, his choice of *it* here is a delightful wink from the Bard to his audience behind Phebe's back. And yet, that said, it is critical not to play Phebe as though she knows anything about "Ganymede's" true identity! Phebe's conscious mind is unaware that "Ganymede" is a woman. In fact, she later expresses a wish to marry "him," but discovers "his" true identity in the final scene along with everyone else.

SIGNIFICANT SCANS

Line 118 can be scanned as a rare six-footed line (hexameter), enhancing the sense of babbling mentioned above:

x / x /x / x / x / x /
He is not very tall—yet for his years he's tall

Or, you may contract *He is* (He's) and treat *very tall* as a crowded foot, making the line pentameter:

```
x  /  x-x  /     x  /  x    /   x    /
He is not very tall—yet for his years he's tall
```

The advantage to scanning the line this way is that you emphasize *not* rather than *is*.

Don't forget to elide: *difference* (DIF-renss) in line 122 (optional) and *Silvius* (SIL-vyuss) in line 124;

. . . and to contract: *He is* (He's) in line 118 (optional).

THE COMEDY OF ERRORS

ACT II, SCENE ii

ADRIANA

GENDER: F
AGE RANGE: adult
PROSE/VERSE: blank verse
FREQUENCY OF USE (1–5): 4.5

Adriana's husband, Antipholus, failed to return home for lunch today. The servant she sent to fetch him returned alone, reporting that his master denied knowing him or even having a wife or a home in Ephesus. Believing that Antipholus has been spending his time with another woman, Adriana, accompanied by her sister, Luciana, has tracked him down herself (or so she believes—little does she know the man they've confronted is really her husband's long-lost twin by the same name, who has recently arrived from Syracuse with his servant), and berates him for his infidelity.

Ay, ay, Antipholus, look strange and frown,
Some other mistress hath thy sweet aspects;
I am not Adriana, nor thy wife.
115 The time was once when thou unurged wouldst vow
That never words were music to thine ear,
That never object pleasing in thine eye,
That never touch well welcome to thy hand,
That never meat sweet-savored in thy taste,
120 Unless I spake, or looked, or touched, or carved to thee.
How comes it now, my husband, O, how comes it,
That thou art then estrangèd from thyself?
Thyself I call it, being strange to me,
That undividable, incorporate,
125 Am better than thy dear self's better part.
Ah, do not tear away thyself from me;
For know, my love, as easy mayst thou fall
A drop of water in the breaking gulf,
And take unmingled thence that drop again
130 Without addition or diminishing,
As take from me thyself, and not me too.
How dearly would it touch thee to the quick,
Shouldst thou but hear I were licentious?
And that this body, consecrate to thee,

112 *look strange* i.e., act as though we were strangers and/or look at me as though we were strangers; 113 *sweet aspects* (a-SPECTS) looks, glances; 114 *not . . . nor* Shakespeare often used double negatives for emphasis; 117 *That never object pleasing in thine eye* That no object in your range of vision was ever pleasing (Shakespeare plays on the biblical phrase "pleasing in thine eye," meaning "pleasing to you"; Adriana uses the phrase "in thine eye" literally. In the construction of line 118, the verb *was* is similarly understood.); 118 *well* much, greatly; 119 *sweet-savored* sweet-tasting; 120 *carved to thee* carved the meat for you; 122 *then* i.e., even with all this having been so; *estrangèd from thyself* (1) acting estranged from (i.e., unlike) yourself; (2) acting estranged from me (because I am "your other half"); 123 *being strange to* acting estranged from; 124 *That* who; *undividable* i.e., undividable from you (because we're married); *incorporate* i.e., one with you in body; 125 *better than* i.e., more essential to you than; *better part* (1) soul; (2) best and most essential qualities (with play on sexual double meaning: "genitals") [*Thyself I call it . . . better part* I call it estrangement from yourself that you are estranged from me, who am indivisibly one with you, and am closer to you than your own most essential parts (Adriana plays on the idea that Antipholus is at once estranged from her, from himself, and from his own best and most essential qualities)]; 127 *as easy mayst thou fall* you may as easily let fall (with a possible play on "you may as easily fall from grace"); 128 *in* into; *breaking gulf* i.e., whirlpool or undertow created by breaking waves; 129 *thence* from there; 131 *As take from me thyself, and not me too* as take yourself away from me without taking away part of me as well; 132 *dearly* intensely, grievously (a uniquely Shakespearean definition of the word); *touch thee to the quick* cause you pain; 133 *Shouldst thou but hear* if you were merely to hear; 134 *conse-*

135 By ruffian lust should be contaminate!
Wouldst thou not spit at me, and spurn at me,
And hurl the name of husband in my face,
And tear the stained skin off my harlot brow,
And from my false hand cut the wedding ring,
140 And break it with a deep-divorcing vow?
I know thou canst, and therefore see thou do it.
I am possessed with an adulterate blot—
My blood is mingled with the crime of lust;
For if we two be one, and thou play false,
145 I do digest the poison of thy flesh,
Being strumpeted by thy contagion.
Keep then fair league and truce with thy true bed,
I live unstained, thou undishonorèd.

2 minutes

crate consecrated; 135 *ruffian* coarse, vulgar; pimplike; *should be contaminate* was contaminated; 136 *spurn at* (1) kick; (2) treat with contempt; 138 *stained skin off my harlot brow* The forehead was considered an indicator of character, as in the proverb "In the forehead and in the eye, the lecture of the heart doth lie"; this may also be an allusion to branding, a punishment for prostitution in Shakespeare's time; 139 *false* (1) deceitful; (2) adulterous; 140 *break it* (1) i.e., destroy our marriage; or (2) break the ring, to symbolize the destruction of our marriage; 141 *I know thou canst, and therefore see thou do it* either (1) I know you have the right, so go right ahead and do so: (a) since I am, as your other half, made guilty by your adultery; or, (b) if I ever commit adultery; or (2) I know you have it in you, so I visualize you doing so (if I were to commit adultery); 142 *possessed with an adulterate blot* permeated with the disgracing stain of adultery; 143 *crime* both (1) sin and (2) crime; 144 *play false* commit adultery; 146 *strumpeted by thy contagion* made a whore by your contagious, poisoned flesh; 147 *fair league* peace, amity, friendship; *truce* peace; *true* lawful, rightful [*Keep then fair league and truce with thy true bed* i.e., If you are faithful to our marriage]; 148 *I live unstained, thou undishonorèd* i.e., I will be free of disgrace, and you free of dishonor.

COMMENTARY

Adriana's entire well-being depends on her marriage, which is her world. Her husband's recent behavior is jeopardizing their marriage, her personal happiness, and her good standing in the community. Adriana takes the concept of being united in spirit and body through marriage literally. Since she also genuinely loves her husband and is a zealous adherent to the mores of her society, Antipholus's antics have injured her on two fronts: she is hurt by the loss of their intimacy, and she is disgraced by the dishonor that comes to her through association with him.

Adriana's deep love for her husband and the importance she places on their marriage are revealed in her manner of addressing him. She calls him *my husband*, *thy dear self*, and *my love* and uses the intimate *thy* and *thou* throughout, even though they are in public space. In lines 116–19, Adriana uses anaphora (a rhetorical device in which words or phrases are repeated at the beginning of successive clauses) to remind her husband of their old way of life together. The repeated echoes of *That never* . . . convey the poetic haze of affectionate reminiscence through which she views their early love.

In contrast, Adriana uses harsh words and images to describe adultery and its effects (*ruffian lust*; *crime of lust*; *digest the poison*; *strumpeted by thy contagion*) and to envision Antipholus's actions toward her if the situation were reversed (*spit at me, and spurn at me*; *hurl the name of husband in my face*; *tear the stained skin off my harlot brow*; *cut the wedding ring*; *break it with a deep-divorcing vow*). She pleads with him not to *tear away* himself and sets the metaphor for their union amid a *breaking gulf*. The contrast between these harsh words and the sweetness with which Adriana addresses Antipholus and describes his former devotion communicates the violence she feels Antipholus is doing to the sacred and fragile construct of their marriage. Several of the words that convey Adriana's distress are emphasized through repeated use in the course of the monologue (*strange* / *estrangèd*; *husband*; *tear*; *break* / *breaking*; *false*; *stained* / *unstained*). Note that the phrase *tear away thyself from me* in line 126 may be used figuratively, in keeping with the indivisible nature of the union which Adriana is about to describe. It may also be taken more literally, as an embedded stage direction indicating that Adriana has taken Antipholus's arm or hand, and that he has just broken away from her.

Antipholus's behavior earlier today elicited such similarly harsh words from Adriana that her sister, Luciana, saw fit to lecture her (as the Abbess will later) on proper wifely obedience (for the source material of said lectures, see "*Errors'* Escapades in Ephesus Emanate from Ephesians," page 938). Adriana is accused of speaking shrewishly, an act that threatened the patriarchal status quo of Elizabethan society, and for which women were often criminally prosecuted (for more on "shrews," see "All Shrews Beshrewed," page 958). It is up to you to decide whether to give Adriana a twenty-first-century perspective on these issues, to retain the Elizabethan mind-set Shakespeare gave her, or to adopt some intermediate perspective. Antipholus and Dromio of Syracuse attribute Adriana's bewildering behavior toward them to supernatural forces. This would have made perfect sense to the Elizabethan audience, who saw fairies and demons as very real threats, and for whom a "shrewish" woman such as Adriana was as dangerous as a witch, a fiend, or a person possessed.

Adriana's use of proverbial concepts (*A drop of water in the breaking gulf*; *touch thee to the quick*; *my harlot brow*) reinforces her connection to societal norms and mores; she uses ideas that have developed through social consensus to shore up her argument. (Also, FYI: the metaphor of a drop of water in the sea is a motif in the play: Antipholus of Syracuse, the man Adriana addresses, referred to himself earlier as a "drop of water" in the ocean, seeking another drop—his long-lost twin, Adriana's husband—and will use the metaphor again later in the play, when he declares his love for Luciana.) Although Adriana desires a sin-free life, she is probably not a prude. In fact, the double entendre of *thy dear self's better part* may suggest that she sees her husband's sexuality as one of his essential qualities. If so, it would be precisely because she values their sexual relationship that she sees his extramarital dallying as such a devastating betrayal. Furthermore, the words *that this body . . . By ruffian lust should be contaminate* are sexually provocative. Adriana may be attempting to appeal to her husband's he-man sense of sexual ownership to get her point across.

Adriana repeats the word *Ay* consecutively in the first line and *How comes it* almost consecutively in line 121. Be sure to choose a reason for repeating each phrase, in order to differentiate between the first and second uses. Perhaps Antipholus is not listening and/or turns away. Or maybe Adriana is searching for her next phrase or stalling to regain her composure, etc. Adriana also uses an unusual number of expansions, drawing attention to certain words (*estrangèd*; *licentious*; *contagion*; *undishonorèd*). Note the relationship among the words: the first three describe Antipholus's current unpleasant and sinful condition, and the last describes his state after he has reformed his behavior. Viewed as a series, these words mark the progression of the major points of the monologue. In the final line, the expansion of *undishonorèd* completes the rhyming couplet (*bed* / *undishonorèd*) and works in concert with the inverted feet found both at the beginning of the line and after the caesura to emphasize Adriana's urgent wish to live an upright life, and to wrap up her sermon to her husband on a convincingly strong and memorable note.

This piece contains two words that are debated by editors. The first is *crime* in line 143, which some editors change to "grime." We feel the change is unnecessary (to Elizabethans, adultery was both a crime by law and a crime against God), but you may choose whichever you prefer, as both are generally accepted. The second word, *unstained* in line 148, appears in the First Folio as "distained" and may or may not have been what Shakespeare intended (the word usually meant "dishonored" or "defiled," but some editors have suggested that he intended it here in the sense of "dis-stained," i.e., unstained). Although we normally retain the words of the most authoritative text (which, for *Comedy*, is the First Folio), in this case today's understanding of "distained" would interfere with the intended meaning of the sentence, so we have joined the majority of editors in making the change.

SIGNIFICANT SCANS

The meter of this piece contains only a couple of inversions and double endings, and is notably free of less common variations, with two exceptions. As noted above, the two inversions in the final line emphasize Adriana's final point. In addition, line 120 is hexameter (a rare six-footed line) with a spondaic second foot:

x / / / x / x / x / x /
Unless I spake, or looked, or touched, or carved to thee

The extra syllables in this line emphasize the extent to which Antipholus was devoted to his wife. The line draws attention to itself, providing an elegant, emphatic climax to the build in the lines leading up to it.

The monologue's meter reveals Adriana's tone through the words it stresses. For instance, the accent on *sweet* in line 113 underscores Adriana's jealous reproach. Similarly, the accent on *hear* in 133 pointedly reminds Antipholus how angry he would be were he merely to *hear* that she had been unfaithful to him. And you have a choice in line 142: you may invert the first foot, which aggressively punches the word *I*, emphasizing the point Adriana has been leading to throughout the piece—that *she* is tainted by Antipholus's behavior; or you may keep the foot iambic, stressing the word *am*, which, in tandem with interpretation 1a of line 141 (see Annotation), insists that he may as well punish her as an adulterer already, since because of his behavior she *is* one.

Don't forget to elide: *ruffian* (RUFF-yan) in line 135; *adulterate* (a-DUL-tret) in line 142; and *Being* (beeng) in line 146;

. . . and to expand: *estrangèd* (eh-STRAIN-jehd) in line 122; *licentious* (lie-SEN´-shee-USS) in line 133; *contagion* (con-TAY´-jee-UN) in line 146; and *undishonorèd* (UN-dis-HON´-or-EHD) in line 148.

THE COMEDY OF ERRORS

ACT III, SCENE ii

LUCIANA

GENDER: F
PROSE/VERSE: rhymed iambic pentameter
AGE RANGE: young adult to adult
FREQUENCY OF USE (1–5): 4

Luciana's sister, Adriana, is distraught: her husband Antipholus has denied that he is married to her . . . or that he even knows her at all. Adriana is convinced that he has tired of her and has found a new, younger love (little do she and Luciana realize that the man they're dealing with does *not* know them—he is Antipholus's long-lost identical twin brother, also called Antipholus, who does not know that he's found his brother's town and encountered his brother's wife and sister-in-law, and who can't figure out how on earth these strange women know his name). Observing Antipholus, Luciana is now convinced that Adriana is correct: he must be acting so cold because he has found a new love. When she has a moment alone with him, she urges him not to break her sister's heart.

And may it be that you have quite forgot
A husband's office? Shall, Antipholus,
Even in the spring of love thy love-springs rot?
Shall love, in building, grow so ruinous?
5 If you did wed my sister for her wealth,
Then for her wealth's sake use her with more kindness;
Or if you like elsewhere, do it by stealth.
Muffle your false love with some show of blindness;
Let not my sister read it in your eye.
10 Be not thy tongue thy own shame's orator.
Look sweet, speak fair, become disloyalty;
Apparel vice like virtue's harbinger.
Bear a fair presence, though your heart be tainted;
Teach sin the carriage of a holy saint.
15 Be secret-false—what need she be acquainted?
What simple thief brags of his own attaint?
'Tis double wrong to truant with your bed

2 *office* particular duty, specific responsibility; 3 *Even in the spring of love* i.e., while your love for Adriana is still in its earliest stages; *love-springs* the tender young sprigs and buds of love [*Shall, Antipholus . . . rot?* i.e., Antipholus, Will you let your love for Adriana rot while it is still in its earliest stages?]; 4 *in building* i.e., while it is still growing; *grow so ruinous* become so decayed; 6 *use* treat; 7 *if you like elsewhere* i.e., if you love someone else; *by stealth* clandestinely; 8 *Muffle* Hide, cloak; *your false love* i.e., your unfaithfulness; *some show of blindness* i.e., with some blinding show; 9 *read it* i.e., perceive it, detect it; 10 *orator* advocate [*Be not thy tongue thy own shame's orator* Luciana adapts the proverbs "It is an ill thing to be wicked, but a worse to boast of it" and "Keep your tongue within your teeth"]; 11 *fair* kindly, gently; *become disloyalty* be gracious in your disloyalty, put a good front on your disloyalty; 12 *Apparel* dress up, clothe; *vice* immoral conduct, personified; *virtue's* moral rightness, personified; *harbinger* forerunner (one who bears word of another's approach) [*Apparel vice like virtue's harbinger* Luciana adapts the proverbs "Vice is often clothed in Virtue's habit (clothing)" and "Fine words dress ill deeds"]; 13 *Bear a fair presence* i.e., put on a good face; *tainted* corrupted [*though your heart be tainted* i.e., by love for another] [*Bear a fair . . . tainted* Luciana adapts the adage "Fair face, foul heart"]; 14 *sin* sin, personified; *carriage* bearing, manners [*Teach sin the carriage of a holy saint* i.e., teach yourself (a person who is sinning) to bear yourself as though you were a saint (i.e., one who is the model of virtue)]; 15 *secret-false* faithless in secret; *what need she be acquainted?* why does she need to be informed?; 16 *What simple thief brags* What thief is simple (stupid) enough to brag; *attaint* disgrace, crime; 17 *double* doubly; *truant with* wander from,

And let her read it in thy looks at board.
Shame hath a bastard fame, well managèd;
20 Ill deeds is doubled with an evil word.
Alas, poor women!—make us but believe,
Being compact of credit, that you love us:
Though others have the arm, show us the sleeve.
We in your motion turn, and you may move us.
25 Then, gentle brother, get you in again;
Comfort my sister, cheer her, call her wife.
'Tis holy sport to be a little vain
When the sweet breath of flattery conquers strife.

1 minute, 40 seconds

i.e., be unfaithful to; 18 *at board* at the table, i.e., at mealtime [*bed . . . board* the term "bed and board" was used to refer to marriage]; 19 *a bastard fame* spurious honor [*Shame hath . . . managèd* Shameful behavior can have a certain (though spurious) honor if it is handled properly]; 20 *is doubled* i.e., are made twice as evil [*Ill deeds is doubled . . . word* Luciana adapts the proverb "To do evil and then brag of it is a double wickedness"]; 21 *but* just, merely; 22 *compact* (comPACT) composed of [*Being compact of credit* Since we are made up entirely of trust, i.e., designed to believe anything]; 24 *motion* orbit; *you may move us* i.e., (1) you may prevail upon us; and/or (2) your actions determine ours (with play on *motion* in the same line); 25 *brother* i.e., brother-in-law; *get you in again* i.e., go back into the room where Adriana is; 26 *Comfort* console; *cheer* all of the following: (1) comfort; (2) encourage; and (3) cheer up; 27 *sport* jest; *vain* false [*be a little vain* falsely flatter a little] ['*Tis holy sport to be a little vain* i.e., it is actually a holy jest (rather than a sinful outright lie) to offer a little false flattery].

COMMENTARY

Luciana finds herself caught in the middle of her sister's marital struggles. Having earlier given her sister advice on forbearance, patience, and gentle acceptance (all the expected Elizabethan wifely behavior), she now has the opportunity to counsel the other half of the couple, and her exhortation is heartfelt.

The meter contains many inverted feet at the beginnings of lines, as well as mid-line following caesuras, giving the piece an emphatic tone that comports with Luciana's conviction in what she says and her strong desire to impress her message upon her brother-in-law. The inversions also suggest that Luciana is frustrated or angry with him, that she's been holding back her feelings while Adriana was around, just waiting for this moment to let them burst forth. Notice the inverted foot after the caesura in line 7: it stresses the word *do* in *do it*, emphasizing the phrase. This is a surprising twist—one would expect Luciana to tell her brother-in-law to abandon his lover, but she surprises the audience by urging instead to *do it* (have your extramarital affair) covertly so as not to hurt Adriana's feelings . . . quite the practical approach. The word preceding the caesura, *elsewhere*, is pronounced with the accent on the second syllable (else-WHERE). The use of this historic pronunciation today surprises the listeners' ears, catching their attention and preparing them for the delightful surprise that follows.

The monologue's several double endings underscore Luciana's key points (*kindness*; *blindness*; *tainted*; *acquainted*; *love us*; *move us*). The expansion of *managèd* in line 19 also emphasizes Luciana's ironic exhortation that Antipholus manage his affair *with . . . fame* ("honor") by preserving his wife's feelings.

The scarcity of elisions and contractions also indicates that Luciana wants to be clearly understood; as does Shakespeare's use of consecutive words in which the last letter of the first word is the same as the first letter of the second word (such as *building, grow*; *wealth's sake*; *sister read*). Be sure to enunciate each word in these pairs separately rather than slurring the two words together as we do in everyday speech—see how doing so affects your delivery.

Antithesis is one of the principal elements of this monologue, as Luciana contrasts the actual love she believes Antipholus feels for another woman with the show of love she'd have him present Adriana (*vice* versus *virtue*; *fair presence* versus *tainted heart*; *sin* versus *holy saint*; *the arm* versus *the sleeve*). Other examples of antithesis include *spring* (blooming) versus *rot* and *building* versus *ruinous*.

Although Luciana uses imagery frequently (for example, personifying virtue, vice, sin, and flattery), the imagery is usually not her own: she borrows liberally from proverbs. In fact, part of the monologue's humor stems from her adaptations of well-worn adages, which could suggest that Luciana is not the most original thinker on the block. After all, Luciana has made it clear to Adriana and now makes it clear to Antipholus that women are inferior to men in the natural order of the universe, even suggesting with *motion* that women orbit men as all the stars and planets orbit the earth (as the Elizabethan populace believed). You may decide that Luciana is somewhat simpleminded and blithely accepts the precepts of her elders, parroting the platitudes they've taught her . . . or at least the gist of them; or you may decide that she is sharper than she appears, and uses a tactic that she thinks will be effective in persuading Antipholus—a macho type whom *she* may not consider the most original thinker on the block.

Similarly, the phrase *Though others have the arm, show us the sleeve* echoes her sister's words in Act II, when Adriana said that she would attach herself to her husband's *sleeve* as a "vine" attaches to a mighty "elm" and would derive strength from him. Here, Luciana adapts her sister's imagery, changing her sister's view of the *sleeve* as a solid source of support to her own perception of it as a hollow show of affection. Depending on which interpretation of her character you wish to develop, you may decide that this use of her sister's words reveals a lack of originality, or, quite the opposite, that it exhibits her originality in adapting the imagery of others.

Consonance and assonance abound in this monologue, and are often woven together (some examples: ***building***; ***grow so***; ***wed / wealth***; ***Muffle / false love / blindness***; ***Let not / it / not / tongue / orator***; ***sweet / speak***; ***vice / virtue / harbinger***; ***Bear / fair***; ***sin / saint / false***; ***need she***; ***bed / board / bastard***; ***Shame / fame***; ***Ill deeds / doubled / evil***; ***compact / credit***; ***love us***; ***motion / may / move***; ***in / again***). But the most important sound element in this monologue is its rhyme! Don't play this up; the rhyme will make its presence felt and will work its magic, lending humor to a piece that Luciana could not be delivering more earnestly or desperately. The joke is that she's lecturing the wrong guy; her passion is for naught. Also, since Antipholus is falling in love with her as she speaks, it's likely that Luciana is lecturing the guy she'll one day marry, and her advice might then be applied to her own marriage—another joke on her. Shakespeare's use of the rhyme pokes gentle fun at Luciana, indicating to the audience that it need not be upset along with Luciana . . . all will be well—and she will be appeased—soon enough.

SIGNIFICANT SCANS

Line 16 contains an inverted third foot following a caesura that is not marked by punctuation:

x / x / / x x / x /
What simple thief brags of his own attaint?

Don't forget to elide: *Even* (E'EN) in line 3 and *flattery* (FLAT-ree) in line 28;

. . . and to expand: *managèd* (MA´-na-JEHD) in line 19.

LOVE'S LABOUR'S LOST

ACT V, SCENE ii

BEROWNE

GENDER: M
PROSE/VERSE: rhymed iambic pentameter
AGE RANGE: young adult to adult
FREQUENCY OF USE (1–5): 3

The King and his courtiers (Berowne, Dumaine, and Longaville) have been wooing the visiting Princess of France and her ladies-in-waiting (Rosaline, Katherine, and Maria) in a flowery manner perceived by the women as being disingenuous. The Princess has berated them for it, and Rosaline, whom Berowne loves, has just chimed in as well. Berowne replies:

Thus pour the stars down plagues for perjury.
395 Can any face of brass hold longer out?
Here stand I—lady, dart thy skill at me.
Bruise me with scorn, confound me with a flout,
Thrust thy sharp wit quite through my ignorance,
Cut me to pieces with thy keen conceit,
400 And I will wish thee nevermore to dance,
Nor nevermore in Russian habit wait;
O, never will I trust to speeches penned,
Nor to the motion of a schoolboy's tongue,
Nor never come in vizard to my friend,
405 Nor woo in rhyme, like a blind harper's song.
Taffeta phrases, silken terms precise,
Three-piled hyperboles, spruce affectation,
Figures pedantical—these summer flies
Have blown me full of maggot ostentation.
410 I do forswear them, and I here protest
By this white glove (how white the hand God knows)
Henceforth my wooing mind shall be expressed
In russet yeas and honest kersey noes.
And to begin, wench—so God help me, la!—
415 My love to thee is sound, sans crack or flaw.

1 minute, 15 seconds

394 *pour the stars down* the stars pour down, i.e., destiny or fate hands down (Elizabethans believed that the stars determined human destiny); *for* in return for; 395 *face of brass* surface made of brass (and therefore hardened, unchangeable, not feeling shame); *hold longer out* hold out longer; 396 *lady* a courteous term of address for a woman of high social rank; *dart* shoot, throw (as an arrow); *skill* wit, cunning; 397 *confound* ruin, destroy; *flout* a mock, a gibe; 398 *quite* completely; 399 *keen* bitter, acrimonious (with a play on second meaning, "sharp"); *conceit* mental capacity; 400 *wish* ask, invite; *wish thee nevermore to dance* never again ask you to dance; 401 *habit* garb, clothing; *wait* be in attendance [*in Russian habit wait* wait (upon you) wearing Russian clothing]; 402 *never will I trust to speeches penned* I will never trust in written speeches; 404 *vizard* mask; *friend* lover, sweetheart; 405 *blind harper's song* ballad, love song (harpists were proverbially blind); 407 *Three-piled* i.e., the thickest (three-piled velvet was the thickest and most expensive kind); *hyperboles* exaggerations; *spruce* foppish, dapper; 408 *Figures* figures of speech; *pedantical* pedantic, making an excessive or tedious show of learning; 409 *maggot* maggotlike; 410 *forswear* swear to reject; *protest* vow; 413 *russet* simple, homespun; *yeas* yesses (plural of *yea*); *kersey* plain, made of coarse cloth; *noes* plural of *no*; 414 *wench* a familiar way of addressing a woman (can vary in tone from affectionate to contemptuous; here, used affectionately); *la!* an exclamation used to add emphasis to an earnest affirmation; 415 *to* for; *sans* (English pronunciation: SAHNZ) French for "without."

COMMENTARY

Berowne (Bih-ROHN, also sometimes Bih-ROON or Bih-ROWN) has had the rug pulled out from under him: Rosaline has mocked his posturing and affected method of wooing her. For the first time he must differentiate between genuine art and hollow artifice.

Part of the charm of this piece is that Berowne uses poetry to renounce Poetry. Berowne rhymes throughout the monologue, as he does throughout the play. The rhyme is a manifestation of his education, his courtly manners, and his extraordinary wit. It establishes a humorous tone, which signals the audience that it's OK to enjoy Berowne's distress: it will be resolved. But do not "play" the rhyme; let it work for you while you work on other things. Berowne also uses poetic imagery to illustrate his intention to simplify. He starts off by personifying the stars as inflicting dire punishment for his offense. He uses the metaphor of sword fighting to describe Rosaline's assault on him (*dart thy skill*; *Thrust thy sharp wit*; *Cut me to pieces*). He wraps up with an antithetical metaphor, in which he compares the fine fabric of the poetry he will give up with the simple, homespun cloth of the plain language he will adopt from now on.

Berowne's emotional state is evident in the use of trochaic variations (i.e., inverted feet) of line openings throughout the piece. Notice where he punches the first syllable of a line and where he doesn't. When he does, is he blurting something out in anger? Is he driving home a point? Also consider the overall flow of the piece. Aside from trochaic variations, the meter is notably regular: there are only two double endings, there are a great many lines without caesuras, and almost no changes of idea mid-line. This may reflect the degree to which Berowne has internalized his poetic sensibilities, how truly second-nature his refined use of language has become.

The couplet at the end concludes Berowne's oration with a delightful surprise. Though you could interpret Berowne as calmly contrite in this monologue, his wry tone throughout the play suggests that this piece is more of the same; that Berowne is still upset and uses his new candid method of speech to tell Rosaline exactly what he thinks of her criticism. The fact that a candid declaration of love is what follows is charming and unexpected . . . although his highfalutin linguistics creep back in with *sans*—he's not completely cured yet! Or you may decide that *sans*, as a shortcut for "without," is proof of Berowne's pledge to speak in brief, unadorned words. Note that Berowne emphasizes the surprise of his declaration by surprising the listener's ear with the same trick used in the sonnet form: a switch in rhyme scheme from a series of quatrains (ABAB, CDCD, etc.) to the closing couplet (KK).

Finally, for help with using the word *O* to its best advantage, see "O, No! An *O*!" on page xxxiii.

THE MERCHANT OF VENICE

ACT 1, SCENE iii

SHYLOCK

GENDER: M
PROSE/VERSE: blank verse
AGE RANGE: mature adult to older adult
FREQUENCY OF USE (1–5): 2

Shylock, a Jewish moneylender, has been approached by a merchant, Antonio, who has asked that Shylock lend him three thousand ducats. Shylock is incredulous: not only has Antonio lent money to his friends interest-free in the past, which has brought down interest rates and hurt Shylock's business, but more important, Antonio has never made an attempt to hide his anti-Semitism and disdain for usury, hurling racial and religious slurs at Shylock and even kicking him and spitting in his face on numerous occasions. And now he comes to Shylock for help! Shylock replies:

Signor Antonio, many a time and oft
In the Rialto you have rated me
About my moneys and my usances.
110 Still I have borne it with a patient shrug,
For suff'rance is the badge of all our tribe.
You call me misbeliever, cut-throat dog,
And spet upon my Jewish gaberdine,
And all for use of that which is mine own.
115 Well then, it now appears you need my help:
Go to then, you come to me and you say,
"Shylock, we would have moneys." You say so—
You that did void your rheum upon my beard
And foot me as you spurn a stranger cur
120 Over your threshold: Moneys is your suit.
What should I say to you? Should I not say,
"Hath a dog money? Is it possible
A cur can lend three thousand ducats?" Or
Shall I bend low, and in a bondman's key,
125 With bated breath and whisp'ring humbleness,

108 *the Rialto* Venice's business center; also the building of the same name where Venice's merchant exchange was housed; *rated* berated, railed at, reviled (with allusion to the fact that Antonio's interest-free moneylending lowers the interest rate); 109 *moneys* sums of money (the term was not commonly used, and it is often suggested that Shylock's repeated use of the word indicates that he is not speaking his native tongue); *usances* interest paid for money; 111 *suff'rance* patient endurance (with play on "suffering"); *all our tribe* i.e., the Jewish people; 112 *misbeliever* infidel (one who believes a false religion); 113 *spet* spit; *gaberdine* a long and loose outer garment [*my Jewish gaberdine* Jews in Venice were required to wear a long cloak similar to those worn by penitent pilgrims, to show their "inherent sinfulness"; furthermore, they were required to affix a yellow *O* to their garments and then (because they became adept at concealing it) a yellow hat as well]; 114 *use* making use of (with secondary allusion to usury) [*use of that . . . own* a reference to Matthew 20:15, where the master of the house says, "Is it not lawful for me to do what I will with mine own?"]; 116 *Go to then* an exclamation of reproof, such as "Come on, then"; 117 *would have* want (i.e., want to borrow); 118 *rheum* phlegm [*void your rheum* spit]; *my beard* Shakespeare's original audience would have been presented with a Shylock sporting the stereotypical long red beard believed typical of the devil-descended Jew; 119 *foot* kick; *spurn* kick; *stranger* unfamiliar; *cur* dog [*spurn . . . threshold* kick a stray dog that is on your threshold]; 120 *suit* formal request; 124 *bondman's* slave; *key* tone of voice; 125 *bated*

Say this:
"Fair sir, you spet on me on Wednesday last;
You spurned me such a day; another time
You called me dog; and for these courtesies
130 I'll lend you thus much moneys"?

1 minute, 30 seconds

weakened [*bated breath* i.e., a weak voice]; 127 *Fair* good (a courteous term of address); *spet* spat; 128 *such a day* i.e., on such and such a day; 130 *thus much moneys* used colloquially to denote an indefinite amount, i.e., "such and such an amount of money."

COMMENTARY

Unlike most "villains" in Shakespeare's plays (who enjoy committing evil for its own sake), and unlike most Jewish characters in Elizabethan English theatre (who were almost exclusively such villains), Shylock is a complex character, who acts villainously in response to the habitual, state-sanctioned villainy of those against whom he now seeks revenge. In this monologue, Shylock sets forth the motivation for his actions throughout the play: Antonio's persecution of him has been perfectly legal; Shylock must find an equally legal means of redress. Not that he expects in his wildest dreams to be able to collect his "pound of flesh"; Antonio's collateral is sound and Shylock no doubt intends to be repaid the three thousand ducats. But one can fantasize . . . The phrase *For suff'rance is the badge of all our tribe* may be a clue that Shylock desires revenge both for himself and for the greater wrongs perpetrated against his people. The unrelenting, recurrent nature of the abuses Shylock has suffered at Antonio's hands is conveyed through the intentionally redundant phrase *many a time and oft* and by the repeated mention of Antonio's specific acts of battery against him (such as spitting and kicking) as well as the merchant's verbal insults (such as calling him a *dog*) and anti-Jewish epithets. Shylock's repeated mention of these abuses indicates how deeply they have wounded him over time, and how acutely aggrieved he is still. Note that he has not fabricated any of Antonio's offenses; indeed, Antonio will confirm them all in his next lines.

In this monologue, Shylock describes scenes for us that don't occur onstage but that are critical backstory, and he does so quite vividly. He is specific about the nature and cause of the abuse he has suffered at Antonio's hands (and feet . . . and mouth); Shakespeare has done most of your homework for you by supplying these details. The more specifically you paint these past scenes for yourself and your audience, the clearer your actions and objectives will become.

Shylock's intentional double meaning with the word *rated* points to the frustration he feels at being hated by Christians for something they have cornered him into doing: as commerce-based economy replaced land-based economy in medieval Europe and usury (forbidden to Christians by religious law) became a necessity, Jews were barred by law from pursuing most professions and were forced into moneylending . . . and yet they were then considered immoral for making their living in this way. It heaps injury on insult for Shylock to be discriminatorily denied other means of supporting himself and then persecuted for doing what his Christian neighbors actually want—and need—him to do (for more information about Jews and usury, see "There Are Things in This Comedy . . . That Will Never Please," page 945).

In processing Antonio's audacious request and determining how best to handle it, Shylock finds an outlet in sarcasm and irony, which define the tone of this piece. The language indicates Shylock's incredulity that his nemesis would be asking him for money after treating him like garbage. He alludes to the New Testament with line 114 (see Annotation), perhaps to shame Antonio, and perhaps to preclude any rebuttal from him—for how can Antonio negate his own scripture? In lines 115–17, Shylock turns Antonio's request over in his mind, repeating it as though trying to get used to the idea of it. This sets up the string of sarcasms that carries Shylock through to the grand finale of lines 127–30.

Take advantage of the expressive sounds of this piece, such as the onomatopoeic *spet* in lines 113 and 127, and the gorgeous assonance—particularly the marked use of the O sound. Jews in Venice were required to wear yellow *O*s on their garments, which, as has oft been noted, visually mimics the vocal cry of the oppressed. Also note the Bitter-Sounding combinations of assonance and consonance, such as *spurn a stranger cur / Over your . . .*; *bend low / bondman's / bated breath / humbleness / Say this*; and *thus much moneys*.

Shylock's language is a bit formal, incorporating repeated words and phrases (e.g., in line 116, *you come to me and you say* and in line 121, *What should I say to you? Should I not say . . .*), and some slightly strange words and phrases, such as *moneys*, *a stranger cur*, and *thus much*. The overall effect is that of the careful speech of a foreigner. While some actors have performed this role with an accent, we recommend that you do not overlay one for audition purposes; the language of the text will create all the "foreignness" you need.

SIGNIFICANT SCANS

The many inverted first feet punch the beginnings of lines, creating a tone of indignation. Aside from these inversions, however, and the very occasional double ending, the meter is fairly smooth through line 116, after which many sentences begin and end mid-line. Some of these sentences are short, and the frequency of mid-line full stops increases, quickening the pace and the urgency, and creating a sense of increasing ire as Shylock works himself up.

Though you could scan line 116 as regular iambic pentameter, the stresses would fall on strange syllables (which you may prefer, as it may add to the sense that Shylock is not speaking his native tongue). We recommend, instead, that you take a one-syllable pause at the caesura and contract *to me* (t'mee):

x / x / x / x / x /
Go to then, (pause) you come to me and you say

Shakespeare wrote line 126 with only one foot of spoken text and a built-in four-foot pause: This gives Shylock time to do what he has just suggested (*bend low*), and prepare what he will say with his mock-*bated breath and whisp'ring humbleness*. Furthermore, it creates a moment of tense anticipation, before Shylock delivers his most cuttingly ironic comment of all. This final line is likewise intentionally short, leaving one and a half feet of silence at the end, which allows Shylock's bitterness to resonate in his listeners' minds.

Don't forget to elide: *Antonio* (An-TONE-yo) in line 107; *suff'rance* (SUFF-rinss) in line 111; and *whisp'ring* (WISS-pring) in line 125;

. . . and to contract: *many a* (MEN-ya) in line 107 and *to me* (t'mee) in line 116.

. . . But Names Can Ever Hurt Thee

While Shylock's name is infamous, and its dubious career since the character's creation has been well documented, the name's origin is still the subject of debate. Shakespeare's inspiration may have been all, some, or none of the following sources:

- *Shallach* is the Hebrew word for "cormorant," which in Shakespeare's time was often used derogatorily to describe usurers (the bird was at that time proverbially thought of as greedy).
- A 1606 pamphlet, *News from Rome* (believed to have been printed much earlier and then reissued), referred to "certain prophesies of a Jew called Caleb Shillocke."
- In the list of Noah's descendants in Genesis, one finds the name Shalach, as well as Tubal and Iscah (Jessica).
- *Shycock*, a word used in cockfighting, was also applied to wary or cowardly persons, especially those who kept themselves hidden for fear of officials in medieval and Renaissance Europe (an apt word for a Jew, who had plenty to fear from officials in Elizabethan England).
- *Shullock* or *shallock* was a sixteenth-century English word meaning "contemptible idler."
- A book by the Jewish historian Josephus (translated from the Latin to English by Peter Morwyng) became so popular that it was reprinted ten times between 1558 and 1615. In it, a city of Jews was besieged and three leaders were chosen to parley with a Roman captain called Antonius. One of these three was called Shiloch.

THE MERCHANT OF VENICE

ACT II, SCENE II

LAUNCELOT GOBBO

GENDER: M
PROSE/VERSE: prose
AGE RANGE: young adult to adult
FREQUENCY OF USE (1–5): 5

Launcelot Gobbo is the servant of Shylock, a Jewish moneylender. Though contracted to work for the Jew, Launcelot debates whether to honor the contract and remain in Shylock's service, or to break it and flee:

Certainly my conscience will serve me to run from
this Jew my master. The fiend is at mine elbow and
tempts me, saying to me, "Gobbo, Launcelot
Gobbo, good Launcelot," or "good Gobbo," or
5 "good Launcelot Gobbo—use your legs, take the
start, run away." My conscience says "No: take
heed, honest Launcelot, take heed, honest
Gobbo"—or (as aforesaid)—"honest Launcelot
Gobbo—do not run; scorn running with thy
10 heels." Well, the most courageous fiend bids me
pack. "Via!" says the fiend, "away!" says the fiend.
"For the Heavens, rouse up a brave mind," says the
fiend, "and run!" Well, my conscience, hanging
about the neck of my heart, says very wisely to me,
15 "My honest friend Launcelot,"—being an honest
man's son, or rather, an honest woman's son, for indeed my father did something smack, something
grow to; he had a kind of taste—well, my conscience says "Launcelot, budge not." "Budge!" says
20 the fiend. "Budge not," says my conscience. "Conscience," say I, "you counsel well." "Fiend," say I,

1 *will serve me to* i.e., will not only permit, but will encourage me (with a play on "be sub-servient to," i.e., doing whatever I tell it to do instead of vice versa); 2 *The fiend* i.e., the little devil in one that is the opposite of the conscience; what Freud later deemed the "id"—the fiend and the conscience were two well-known characters in medieval morality plays (see Commentary); 5 *take the start* break out, set forth suddenly and swiftly; 8 *aforesaid* mentioned before (a word used by only three of Shakespeare's characters, in attempts to sound impres-sive); 9 *scorn* refuse, disdain [*scorn . . . with thy heels* (1) run away from; (2) kick aside] [*scorn running with thy / heels* (1) run away from running away; (2) kick aside the notion of running away (either option means "reject the notion of running away")]; 10 *courageous* both (1) brave and (2) encouraging; *bids me* commands me to; 11 *pack* be gone; *Via* (VIE-uh) An expression of encouragement, loosely from the Italian "Go!," used to urge on horses, oarsmen, and troops; *away!* Begone! Run away from here!; 12 *For the Heavens* a mild oath, similar to "For Heaven's sake," or "By Heaven"; *rouse up* excite to action [*rouse up a brave mind* i.e., stir up your courage to act]; 13 *hanging about the neck of* i.e., like a woman clinging to a man (thus pre-venting him from acting valorously); 14 *my heart* i.e., the seat of courage; 15 *honest* all of the following: (1) truthful; (2) law-abiding; and (3) chaste; 17 *something* to some degree, a little; *smack* have a taste (two possible meanings: [1] was an unsavory character; and/or [2] had a taste for the ladies [i.e., was habitually unfaithful]); *something grow to* Unclear meaning. One suggested meaning: "he was unsavory" ("growing" to the pot like burnt milk, which tasted disagreeable); another: develop a little (liking for women); 18 *he had a kind of taste* again, i.e.,

"you counsel well." To be ruled by my conscience, I
should stay with the Jew my master, who—God
bless the mark—is a kind of devil; and to run away
25 from the Jew, I should be ruled by the fiend,
who—saving your reverence—is the devil himself.
Certainly the Jew is the very devil incarnation; and,
in my conscience, my conscience is but a kind of
hard conscience to offer to counsel me to stay with
30 the Jew. The fiend gives the more friendly counsel:
I will run, fiend; my heels are at your commandment. I will run.

2 minutes

(1) he was unsavory; and/or (2) he had a taste for women; 22 *To be* i.e., If I let myself be; 23 *God bless the mark* an expression used to apologize for using coarse language or being profane; 24 *is a kind of devil* Elizabethans believed that Jews were descendants of Satan—see "There Are Things in This Comedy . . . That Will Never Please" [page 945]; 26 *saving your reverence* an affected-sounding expression used to apologize for using coarse language or being profane, similar to "if you'll pardon the expression"; *is the devil himself* i.e., is an actual devil; 27 *incarnation* incarnate; 28 *in my conscience* an expression similar to "in good conscience," used here for emphasis; 29 *hard* severe, overly rigorous; *offer* presume; 30 *friendly* kind, benevolent; 31 *commandment* command (a malapropism).

COMMENTARY

Although many are inclined to dismiss Launcelot Gobbo's speech as more filling than matter, they are quite wrong—while it is humorous in tone, the monologue's subject matter is of the gravest nature: Launcelot must make a potentially life-altering decision, one that also distresses him because his decision could compromise his integrity and the state of his immortal soul.

Shakespeare parodies two well-known conventions in this monologue. The antithetical *fiend* and *conscience* parody a morality play: Elizabethans were familiar with the late-medieval morality-play convention of the "battle for the soul" of the "everyman." Launcelot, of course, has cast himself as the central character. In an interesting twist, however, he argues that obeying his conscience will keep him aligned with the *devil incarnation* (Shylock the Jew), while obeying the fiend and immorally violating his contract will free him from the devil's clutches. Notice the jokes in lines 12–13: Launcelot puts the mild oath *For the Heavens* into the mouth of the fiend, and has the fiend say, essentially, "be brave enough to be cowardly and flee." This parallels the syntax of the moral and linguistic paradox in lines 9–10: "run away from running away," and his ultimate paradoxical alignment with the actual devil, in order to avoid the quasi-devil, his master.

Launcelot also initially pretends to be a lawyer arguing a case, parodying the English barrister's legal argumentation familiar to Elizabethan audiences. His lawyer routine includes the precision with which he recalls the fiend's exact salutation of him, and use of such highfalutin phrases as *as aforesaid* and *saving your reverence*. Here, he combines parodies of the civil law of the land and the divine law of the Morality Play to weigh the propriety of fleeing from his present master. But note that Launcelot ultimately rejects the conclusion to which his own logic leads him, in favor of the conclusion he happens to prefer. The monologue's very first sentence reveals that Launcelot wants the debate to favor his defection from Shylock. When it doesn't (because Launcelot is truly an honest guy, uncomfortable with flouting his conscience), he finds an alternate logic to support the outcome he desires. Launcelot is too honest to allow an expression to stand that isn't entirely truthful: *being an honest man's son*. He is compelled to correct it . . . and to amend the correction . . . and to augment the emendation . . . until he's finally satisfied that he's stated the plain truth of the matter . . . even though the matter is off point.

In lines 16–18, Launcelot says the same thing in three different ways. Perhaps he's fishing for a delicate way to explain his father's lechery and only unwittingly says increasingly indelicate things. Or perhaps he knows exactly what he is saying, enjoys the joke, and is fishing for ever-bigger laughs. The sexual innuendo is already quite clear when he speaks of his father's poor character and philandering, but the words he uses have even coarser sexual double meanings, which would have been apparent to Elizabethan audiences: *something* = entire female genitalia [as opposed to the vagina, for which the slang term was "nothing," and the penis, which was given the slang term "thing"]; *smack* = (verb) to kiss noisily; *grow to* = get an erection; *taste* = enjoy sexually; *hard* = erect; *Conscience* = "cunnus" (female genitalia) + "science" (knowledge . . . in the biblical sense); Launcelot's misuse of the word *incarnation*, which suggests "in carnation," i.e., "in the flesh," is another double entendre, perhaps harkening to Launcelot's discussion of his father's lechery, or, more generally, to sinful behavior, befitting a *devil incarnate*.

It is impossible to ignore the anti-Semitic references to Shylock, such as *a kind of devil* and *the very devil incarnation*, as well as the fact that he calls him, simply, *the Jew*. These references reflect the pervasive anti-Semitism of Shakespeare's times (see "There Are Things . . . ," page 945)—the principal reason Launcelot wishes to leave Shylock's employ is that Shylock is Jewish. It is a sign of Gobbo's deep-seated dislike for Shylock that he ultimately chooses the actual devil over the *kind of devil*. But Launcelot's hatred of Shylock may not be merely anti-Semitic; it may also reflect his master's mistreatment of him—Jessica will later call her father's household "hell." Remember that masters—regardless of their religion—habitually mistreated their servants. Elizabethans found this a source of amusement when depicted on stage.

Launcelot Gobbo is called "Clown" in the stage directions, but although he often acts as Shakespeare's "clown" characters do, some scholars argue that he does not behave as one consistently, particularly since his duties later, when in Bassanio's employ, include acting as Bassanio's fool. The "fool" in Shakespeare's day (and in his plays) was a skilled professional with a keen wit and a highly developed sense of irony, who would comment trenchantly on issues of the day, offering insightful criticism with the objectivity of an outsider and the bitingly targeted humor of an insider. In this monologue, however, Launcelot is pure clown: he is simple (the many repetitions of words, phrases, and phrasal structure help establish this), uses malapropisms, and presents such funny material as this monologue, which does not impact upon the principal story lines of the play.

Or, Good Anachronism Gobbo

Not knowing much about Jews generally—or about Jewish life in Venice specifically—Shakespeare made many mistakes in *The Merchant of Venice*, not the least of which was having a Jew of Venice's Jewish ghetto employ a Christian servant, which was not permitted in sixteenth-century Venice. Had Launcelot been a real live servant, he would have been receiving his paycheck—and his beatings—from some other guy.

THE MERCHANT OF VENICE

ACT III, SCENE I

SHYLOCK

GENDER: M
AGE RANGE: mature adult to older adult
PROSE/VERSE: prose
FREQUENCY OF USE (1–5): 3

Recently Shylock, a Jewish moneylender, was approached by Antonio, a Venetian nobleman who had often insulted, kicked, and spat on him in the past, who requested a loan to aid his friend Bassanio. Shylock agreed to the loan and even waived the interest, on the condition that Antonio put up a pound of his flesh as collateral. Then these same two ungrateful Venetians helped their friend elope with Shylock's daughter, Jessica, and convert her to Christianity! Now Shylock has learned that some of the trading expeditions in which Antonio invested his money have failed, and it seems as though Antonio will have to forfeit his debt. Shylock has run into two of Antonio's friends, who are surprised when Shylock threatens to collect his pound of flesh. One of the men asks him, "What's that good for?" and Shylock replies:

55 To bait fish withal;—if it will feed nothing else, it
will feed my revenge. He hath disgraced me,
and hindered me half a million; laughed at
my losses, mocked at my gains, scorned my
nation, thwarted my bargains, cooled my friends,
60 heated mine enemies—and what's his reason?
I am a Jew. Hath not a Jew eyes? Hath not a
Jew hands, organs, dimensions, senses, affections,
passions? Fed with the same food, hurt with the
same weapons, subject to the same diseases,
65 healed by the same means, warmed and cooled
by the same winter and summer as a Christian is?
If you prick us, do we not bleed? If you tickle us,
do we not laugh? If you poison us, do we not
die? And if you wrong us, shall we not revenge?
70 If we are like you in the rest, we shall resemble
you in that. If a Jew wrong a Christian, what is
his humility? Revenge. If a Christian wrong a
Jew, what should his sufferance be by Christian
example? Why, revenge. The villainy you teach
75 me I will execute, and it shall go hard but I will
better the instruction.

1 minute, 30 seconds

55 *bait* i.e., use as bait for; *withal* with it; *if it will feed nothing else* Shylock may be referring to an old superstition that Jews ate Christian flesh; 57 *hindered me half a million* both (1) prevented me from earning half a million ducats and (2) got in my way half a million times; 58 *my nation* i.e., my people, the Jews; 59 *bargains* i.e., business deals; *cooled* alienated; 60 *heated mine enemies* fired up my enemies (against me); 62 *dimensions* (1) bodily form; (2) limbs; *affections* inclinations, desires; 63 *passions* strong emotions; *Fed* i.e., are we not fed; 69 *revenge* i.e., seek revenge; take revenge; 71 *what is his humility* i.e., how does the Christian manifest the humility (humble submission to suffering) that is taught in his religion (Shylock judges Christians by their own teachings, alluding to passages found in Matthew 5: "whosoever shall smite thee on thy right cheek, turn to him the other also" and "Love your enemies . . . do good to them that hate you"); 73 *his sufferance* i.e., the Jew's manner of enduring injury or suffering; *by* i.e., as shown by; 74 *The villainy you teach me* i.e., the evil behavior that you Christians teach me by example; 75 *execute* practice, perform (with a play on the more lethal definition; Shylock implies that he will kill Antonio by demanding that his bond be fulfilled); *go hard but* be difficult for it not to happen that [*it shall go hard but I will* i.e., I will most certainly]; 76 *better the instruction* i.e., provide an even better example of villainy than the Christians have.

COMMENTARY

Probably more than any other character name in Shakespeare's canon, *Shylock* immediately calls to mind a vivid stereotype that encompasses physical characteristics, voice, dress, and even movements. When you approach this piece, it will be necessary to clear your mind of these images and to start fresh, making your own choices.

In tandem with these choices, you will need to decide whether Shylock initially intended the bond as a means to entrap his enemy or merely as a joke; when he proposed it, he called it a "merry sport" and responded to Bassanio's suspicions by saying, "what should I gain / By the exaction of the forfeiture?" (As the "pound of flesh" fable was so common, it has been suggested that its use could seem to the characters in the play no more literal than the words "For the sum of one dollar and other considerations" do today.) Although it is legitimate to decide that Shylock sets the bond as a trap from the outset, this seems less likely when one considers that Antonio's prospects for financial success at the time the bond was signed were excellent; betting on the forfeiture of the bond would be a rather poor attempt at revenge on the part of such a shrewd businessman as Shylock. The truth may lie in the middle, with Shylock viewing the clause as more of a fantasy than a joke—like a lottery ticket, something to enjoy imagining, despite the near impossibility of its ever coming to pass. Many actors choose the scene in which this monologue takes place as the turning point in Shylock's intent. Just before this monologue, Shylock complains to Antonio's friends that the recent loss of several of Antonio's ships will probably force him to default on his loan. Perhaps the possibility of actually enacting the bond comes to Shylock just as he tells Antonio's friends, "Let him look to his bond." Maybe the building fury of this monologue prompts him to make the decision as he reaches its last few, highly embittered lines. Or perhaps this entire monologue is just bluster (and/or Shylock is merely thinking of terrifying Antonio with the threat of the bond at this point), and it is not until later in the scene or the play that he resolves literally to take his pound of flesh.

The view that Shylock did not initially intend evil in proposing the bond comports with the obvious fact that Shylock is not your everyday, run-of-the-mill villain. Although he shares the humor, intelligence, and cynicism of the Machiavel (the Elizabethan character type that Shakespeare so deftly realized in such paragons of evil as Iago, Edmund, and Richard III), Shylock differs from the type in its most essential aspect: he does not, as all Machiavels do, delight in evil for its own sake. Rather, he has been driven to it by a lifetime of scorn, derision, discrimination, and cruelty heaped on him by the Christian world—and by Antonio in particular—simply because of his "race" and religion (see monologue, page 285). Shylock's monologue is paradoxical—his eloquent plea for tolerance also serves as a rationalization for the vengeful murder he himself wishes to commit, an act that is expressly forbidden by the very religion for which he has suffered oppression. This paradox has led scholars to takes sides over Shylock's mind-set at this moment—some seeing him as completely coldhearted and manipulative, without concern for the inherent evil of his plan, while others all but dismiss his desire to kill, focusing entirely on the moving pathos of his plea. Keep in mind that your interpretation may lean toward either of these two views, or may recognize truths in both—paradoxical complexity of character is innately human.

When performed on stage, this speech transcends both its place in the play and the character who speaks it. As he does with all of his stock characters, Shakespeare has here humanized the stereotype. Whether he did so intuitively or in a deliberate attempt to preach tolerance we will never know. (For more information on Elizabethan attitudes toward Jews and Shakespeare's intent in *Merchant*, see "There Are Things in This Comedy . . . That Will Never Please," page 945.) What we do know is that in its eloquent simplicity this speech cannot help but stir compassion in anyone who hears it. The fact that it has been embraced and reutilized by some (such as Ernst Lubitsch, in his masterpiece *To Be or Not to Be*) and avoided by others (for example, Nazi propagandists, who used this play to excite anti-Semitic sentiment and carefully excised Shylock's persuasive speeches) is testament to its power. With this in mind, you could lift the piece out of its context and create any character you choose, from a victim of the Spanish Inquisition to a Holocaust survivor to a schoolkid being bullied by skinheads.

Shakespeare assigned prose passages predominantly to his comedic characters and speeches. In *Merchant*, and particularly in this piece, he used it for the first time to serious ends. As prose feels less artificial than verse, its use here allows Shylock to be realistic and sincere. It enhances the impression that Shylock's eloquent plea for understanding, and the enraged expression of his desire for revenge, are spontaneous rather than calculated.

Although this prose is spoken impromptu and in a casual setting, Shakespeare has managed to make it (as we have said) one of the most eloquent passages in his plays. Shylock uses simple, effective techniques to make his points clear. His principal device is antithesis, which serves in this piece to equate, rather than differentiate between, two things (as is more common). First, Shylock uses it to convey the comprehensiveness of Antonio's hate, outlining the ways that Antonio has injured him on both sides of every issue: *laughed at my losses* versus *mocked at my gains*; *scorned my nation* versus *thwarted my bargains* (i.e., thwarted me personally); *cooled my friends* versus *heated mine enemies*. Later, he uses antithesis to build to his conclusion about the sameness of Jews and

Christians (*we are like you*) *in the rest* versus (*we shall resemble you*) *in that* and *If a Jew wrong a Christian . . . Revenge* versus *If a Christian wrong a Jew . . . revenge.* Shylock also puts to use the simple, undeniable proof of a detailed list: he lists the ways Antonio has wronged him; he lists the human qualities that Jews share with other humans; and he asks a series of rhetorical questions that amount to a list of ways in which a Jew reacts just as a Christian would to outside forces. Notice that both the second list and the series of questions build from the physical to the psychological. The list in lines 61–63 is carefully constructed to move from the most physically evident similarities between Jews and Christians (*eyes*; *hands, organs, dimensions*) to the sensations that are the natural result of possessing those physical attributes (*senses, affections*) and finally to the emotional result of those sensations (*passions*). Thus Shylock conveys his (and other Jews') humanity in a manner that utilizes logic but is ultimately even more powerful than logic, leading to intuitive and emotional connections via simply intellectual ones. His use of word repetition, another effective technique, hammers home his key ideas with the word *same* (used five times) and the word *revenge* (used three times).

Perhaps most important, after *To bait fish withal* (which answers the question he has just been asked) Shylock uses parallel phrasing throughout the piece. Notice that the structure he uses in lines 55–56 (*if it will feed nothing else, it will feed my revenge*) is repeated in 70–71 (*If we are like you . . . we shall resemble you . . .*). Structure and phrasing are repeated in series for the remainder of the piece: *Hath not . . .* ; *If you . . . do we . . .* ; and finally, the antithesis in lines 70–74, mentioned above, in which the same words and phrasing are repeated, with only the words *Christian* and *Jew* switched, emphasizing the sameness of said *Christian* and *Jew*. All of these parallel structures, repetitions, and antitheses form a build of sameness that leads to and emphasizes the one difference Shylock introduces at the end: [*he*] *will better the instruction*. How chilling those simple words are when juxtaposed with the elaborate build of parallels, during which the full extent of Shylock's fury has been unleashed.

Shylock's language is also subtly sarcastic—so subtly it can easily be missed. In line 55 (*if it will feed nothing else*), in which he refers to Antonio's flesh, Shylock alludes to the Christian superstition that Jews ate Christian flesh. This idea would seem particularly outrageous to Shylock, who won't even eat the same meat that Christians eat, due to the dietary restrictions of his religion. Leaving aside the notion that Christians would think themselves worthy of gracing a Jew's Sabbath table, it would deeply offend Shylock that Christians would think Jews so barbaric in the religious practices he holds sacred. In the last sentence of the piece, Shylock plays on the word *execute*, which is more meaningful than the men he addresses suspect. In Shylock's culture, teaching is revered while murder is reviled. His ironic suggestion that Christians have taught him to kill is the highest insult he could fling at Christianity and its followers.

Shylock's expert use of language reveals that despite the hardships he has faced, he is an educated man. It is for you to discover the source of that education: long nights of study and discussion with his fellow Jews? Conscientious parents who saw to it that he was taught either at a Jewish school or at home? Self-education gleaned in dribs and drabs while fending for himself in an alien country? . . .

A technical note: when performing this piece solo for someone unfamiliar with the text, you may want to cut the first phrase, *To bait fish withal*, and simply begin with *if it will feed nothing else, it will feed my revenge*. The latter statement is so basic that the listener need not know what the "it" is: right away he or she understands that at issue is the simple question of whether it is acceptable to commit a wrong in order to avenge a wrong.

P.S.

For information on possible origins of Shylock's name, see ". . . But Names Can Ever Hurt Thee," page 290.

THE MERCHANT OF VENICE

ACT III, SCENE iv

PORTIA

GENDER: F
PROSE/VERSE: blank verse
AGE RANGE: young adult to adult
FREQUENCY OF USE (1–5): 2

Portia and her waiting-gentlewoman Nerissa have just been married to Bassanio and Gratiano, but immediately after the wedding their husbands departed for Venice, where they hope to save the life of their friend Antonio. Antonio had used his credit to secure a loan for Bassanio. News arrived just before the double wedding that Antonio's fortune was lost, and that since he was unable to repay the loan his creditor is now suing to exact his bond—the pound of Antonio's flesh closest to his heart. Portia sent Bassanio off to Venice with enough money to repay the debt twenty times over, but she has now decided to travel to Venice, and to play a more direct role in rescuing her husband's generous friend.

PORTIA

Come on Nerissa, I have work in hand
That you yet know not of. We'll see our husbands
Before they think of us—
60 —but in such a habit
That they shall think we are accomplishèd
With that we lack. I'll hold thee any wager,
When we are both accoutered like young men,
I'll prove the prettier fellow of the two,
65 And wear my dagger with a braver grace,
And speak between the change of man and boy
With a reed voice, and turn two mincing steps
Into a manly stride; and speak of frays
Like a fine bragging youth; and tell quaint lies
70 How honorable ladies sought my love
Which I denying, they fell sick and died—
I could not do withal. Then I'll repent,
And wish for all that, that I had not killed them.
And twenty of these puny lies I'll tell,
75 That men shall swear I have discontinued school
Above a twelvemonth. I have within my mind

60 *habit* mode of dress, costume; 61 *accomplishèd / With* possessed of, equipped with; 62 *that we lack* that which we lack, i.e., penises [*they shall think . . . that we lack* i.e., they'll think we're men]; *hold thee any wager* make you any bet; 63 *accoutered* clothed; 64 *prettier* more pleasing, more handsome; 65 *wear* both wear and wield; *braver grace* i.e., finer and more graceful skill; 66 *speak between the change of man and boy* i.e., speak as a young man does when his voice is changing; 67 *reed* reedy, squeaky (like a reed pipe); *turn two mincing steps / Into a manly stride* i.e., turn two of my small, dainty steps into one long, manly stride; 68 *frays* bouts of single combat, whether with swords, words, or fists; 69 *quaint* clever, ingenious; 71 *Which I denying* i.e., and when I denied to give it (my love) to them; 72 *could not do withal* i.e., could not do anything about it; could not help it (a common expression in Shakespeare's time); *repent* i.e., regret my callousness; 73 *for all that* i.e., despite the fact that I could not prevent their deaths; *killed them* i.e., been the cause of their deaths; 74 *puny* childish, petty; 75 *That* so that; *I have*

A thousand raw tricks of these bragging Jacks,
Which I will practice.

81 But come, I'll tell thee all my whole device
When I am in my coach, which stays for us
At the park gate; and therefore haste away,
For we must measure twenty miles today.

1 minute, 30 seconds

discontinued school / Above a twelvemonth I finished going to school over a year ago; 77 *raw* crude, immature; *tricks* (1) character traits; (2) pranks, jokes; *Jacks* fellows, knaves (in Shakespeare's time, used contemptuously); 78 *practice* use, put into practice; 81 *device* plan; 82 *stays* waits; 83 *park* i.e., an enclosed tract of land adjoining Portia's mansion; *haste away* hurry up and get ready to leave; 84 *measure* cover, travel.

COMMENTARY

During the last few months, Portia has been subjected to her late father's absolute power over her fate; his will stipulated that her suitors chose from among three caskets to discover whether they had won his consent to marry her. Portia was powerless and frustrated by her inability to participate in choosing her own husband. Luckily, the numerous undesirable suitors who tried their luck all chose incorrectly, and Portia's favorite, Bassanio, chose correctly (with a few subtle hints from her). Since that moment, Portia has been reclaiming her own power: she instructed her own husband in how to save his friend, and she is now planning to take matters into her own hands even further by dressing up as a man and traveling to Venice to try to save him herself. Portia is enjoying the prospect wholeheartedly. After being controlled by her late father, she relishes the idea of becoming a man herself and seizing some of men's power.

Portia's delight at this prospect and her energetic initiative in bringing it to fruition are evident in the meter and punctuation of the piece. Most of Portia's ideas spill over from one line into the next, so that breaks occur mid-line, where an actor does not pause for long, rather than at the ends of lines, where an actor takes a slightly longer pause. This, combined with several double endings, creates the impression that Portia is on a roll, bursting with ideas. There are no full stops between *I'll hold thee any wager* in line 62 and *could not do withal* in line 72, creating an energetic pace and a continuous flow across eleven lines as Portia comes up with one idea after another for her brilliant performance as a man. And, at the heart of this section, Portia begins three consecutive lines (67–69)—in which she focuses on the male characteristics she will portray—with "masculinely" aggressive inverted feet.

The energy produced by these elements in the monologue as well as its content naturally lend themselves to an animated physicality in performance. It will be up to you to decide to what degree Portia is already trying out her ideas on Nerissa. While experimenting with *the fine bragging youth*'s walk, stance, gestures, voice, and expressions (all as portrayed via the viewpoint and physicality of Portia), you will discover that you are expanding your repertoire with a funny and active monologue that showcases your comedic talent.

Notice Portia's switch from the more formal *you* in the second line to the familiar *thee* in the rest of the piece. As the piece begins, she has just been seeing to the affairs of her estate during her upcoming absence—when she begins speaking with Nerissa she is still in the mode of mistress of a great country estate. She soon becomes much more relaxed and intimate, as indicated not only in the change in her term of address, but also in her casual, chatty manner with Nerissa, her frequent use of contractions—*We'll*; *I'll* (five times) and *I've* (twice)—and her casual expressions (*I could not do withal*; *I have within my mind*; *these bragging Jacks*; *all my whole*). The tone that emerges from this language also conveys Portia's absolute confidence in her ability to imitate and fool men: she's got them pegged.

As she herself says, one of the masculine attributes she intends to mimic is the male tendency to focus on and brag about sex. She has already begun to do so: Portia's use of double entendre in this piece demonstates her ability to bandy bawdy words with any man she comes across. For instance, she explains to Nerissa her plan to travel in disguise by alluding to the male genitalia they lack (note that the expansion of the word *accomplishèd* is like a verbal wink at Nerissa over the joke), and she puns on the common expression *I could not do withal*, using the words' more literal meaning (*withal* means "with it") to refer to her lack of the necessary equipment with which to have *killed them* (i.e., given them orgasms). Portia also uses sexual double entendre that was understood in Shakespeare's time: with the word *dagger* she refers to her imaginary penis; with *frays* she alludes not only to single combat with men, but also to a different type of "combat," performed in bed; and by telling "*quaint*" *lies* she will be telling lies about "women's genitalia." Although these words are too obscure for today's audience to understand, awareness of their original use affords you a clearer understanding of Portia's character: no prim and prissy maiden would use such language, much less find it funny. This language also reveals the trust, intimacy, and shared sense of humor between Portia and Nerissa.

You will find sound repetitions scattered throughout the piece (mostly rhymed pairs of words) that enhance Portia's dramatizations and her good-natured devaluation of men (e.g., *prove / prettier*; *braver grace*; *speak between*; *I denying / died*; *bragging Jacks*). Don't forget to separate the back-to-back Ds in *and died*, which will emphasize the melodrama of *died*. Also note the lovely rhyming couplet that neatly wraps up the monologue and the scene (*away / today*) and marks the women's imminent departure.

SIGNIFICANT SCANS

Portions of lines 59 and 60 have been excised to create this piece (they are a brief exchange between Portia and Nerissa). Since the subject matter of the two half lines flows seamlessly, we suggest that you create one line of regular iambic pentameter with a double ending. To do so, simply treat *but in such* as a crowded foot:

x / x / x / x - x / x / (x)
Before they think of us—but in such a habit

Line 77 contains an inverted third foot following a caesura which is not marked by punctuation:

x / x / / x x / x /
A thousand raw tricks of these bragging Jacks

Half of line 78 and all of 79–80 have been excised (another exchange between Portia and Nerissa). We suggest that you use the resulting two and a half silent feet at the end of line 78 to transition from your excitement over your upcoming adventure to your realization of the immediate need to set out quickly for Venice. You may even decide to take a moment before rushing Nerissa off to the waiting coach to try out one of the *raw tricks* she will *practice* when dressed as a man.

Don't forget to elide: *our* (owr) in line 58 and *prettier* (PRIH-tyer) in line 64;
. . . to contract: *I have* (I've) in lines 75 and 76;
. . . and to expand: *accomplishèd* (a-COM´-plih-SHED) in line 61.

THE MERCHANT OF VENICE

ACT IV, SCENE i

PORTIA

GENDER: F
PROSE/VERSE: blank verse
AGE RANGE: young adult to adult
FREQUENCY OF USE (1–5): 3

Portia, a wealthy young heiress, has just married Bassanio, whose friend Antonio is in grave peril on Bassanio's account: Antonio borrowed from a Jewish moneylender, Shylock, to supply Bassanio with money he needed. The loan was interest-free, but with a catch: if Antonio failed to pay in time, Shylock could collect a pound of his flesh, to be taken from the area closest to his heart (obviously killing Antonio). Antonio's investments have since failed, forcing him to default on the loan. Portia sent Bassanio to the Duke's court in Venice with money to pay Antonio's debt twenty times over, but, fearing that this would not placate Shylock, Portia has traveled to the court herself, disguised as a young male lawyer, with a letter of recommendation from her good friend, a well-respected elderly lawyer. Antonio has admitted that the contract is indeed binding, and Portia has concluded that Shylock must then be merciful. Shylock has just retorted, "On what compulsion must I? Tell me that." Portia replies:

The quality of mercy is not strained;
185 It droppeth as the gentle rain from Heaven
Upon the place beneath. It is twice blest—
It blesseth him that gives and him that takes.
'Tis mightiest in the mightiest—it becomes
The thronèd monarch better than his crown.
190 His scepter shows the force of temporal power,
The attribute to awe and majesty
Wherein doth sit the dread and fear of kings;
But mercy is above this sceptered sway:
It is enthronèd in the hearts of kings;
195 It is an attribute to God Himself;
And earthly power doth then show likest God's
When mercy seasons justice. Therefore, Jew,
Though justice be thy plea, consider this:
That in the course of justice none of us
200 Should see salvation. We do pray for mercy,
And that same prayer doth teach us all to render
The deeds of mercy. I have spoke thus much
To mitigate the justice of thy plea,
Which if thou follow, this strict court of Venice
205 Must needs give sentence 'gainst the merchant there.

1 minute, 15 seconds

184 *strained* constrained, forced, compelled (with secondary meaning referring to rain metaphor of line 185: "filtered, squeezed out"); 185 *gentle rain* a reference to Ecclesiasticus 35:19, "Oh, how fair a thing is mercy in the time of anguish and trouble! It is like a cloud of rain, that cometh in the time of a drought"; 186 *the place beneath* i.e., Earth; *is twice blest* i.e., gives a double blessing; 187 *that gives* i.e., who bestows mercy upon another; *that takes* i.e., who is the recipient of the mercy; 188 *it becomes / The thronèd monarch better* i.e., mercy is a more fitting, attractive, and important attribute of a ruler; 190 *shows* represents; *temporal* pertaining to this world, i.e., not spiritual or eternal; 191 *attribute to* symbol of; 192 *Wherein doth sit . . . of kings* in which the power of kings to command awe and fear symbolically resides; 193 *sway* power, authority, rule; 194 *enthronèd* i.e., seated, lodged; 195 *an attribute to* a characteristic that pertains to; 196 *show likest* most resemble; 197 *seasons* tempers; 198 *thy plea* your suit (i.e., the remedy you are suing in court for); 199 *in the course of justice* i.e., if justice were administered strictly; 200 *Should* would [*none of us . . . salvation* an allusion to the doctrine of original sin and the correlative concept that because humans are born with sin, salvation cannot be achieved through good works or through justice, but only through God's mercy]; 201 *render* give in return; 202 *I have spoke thus much* i.e., I have said all of this; 203 *mitigate the justice of thy plea* i.e., to urge you to soften your suit for strict justice; 205 *Must needs give sentence 'gainst* must rule against; *the merchant there* i.e., Antonio.

COMMENTARY

This is one of the most famously moving monologues in Shakespeare's canon (ironically, another monologue that makes the list is that of Shylock—see monologue, page 296). Portia, who espouses the belief—commonly held in medieval and Renaissance times—that *the quality of mercy* sets Christianity apart from all false faiths, strives to instill this critical virtue in Shylock to save Antonio's life.

It is important to place the first sentence in context. Portia has just been stumped and needs to recover: she has just said that Shylock *must . . . be merciful* and Shylock has retorted *On what compulsion must I? Tell me that*. The answer is, honestly, "on no compulsion"—Shylock cannot be forced to be merciful. He can only be *persuaded*, and so Portia must do her best to persuade him. Although she may have anticipated his attitude, she may alternatively be taken aback and/or shocked by his question: she has probably never before encountered someone who doesn't take for granted that mercy should temper justice. How can she even begin to explain a concept that has always been a given for her and every other person she knows? This is a helluva first case for a fledgling lawyer (not to mention one without any actual legal training) to argue. Here is where Portia's strength of conviction comes to the rescue.

This conviction stems from Shakespeare's—and therefore Portia's—erroneous understanding of the relationship between the Old Testament and the New Testament, a dichotomy invented and perpetuated by the medieval Church, which pits the Old Testament God of harsh justice (i.e., the God of the Jews) against the New Testament God of mercy and loving kindness (i.e., the God of the Christians). It is important to note that, knowing nothing of Judaism beyond the anti-Semitic fallacies about its tenets and its people, Shakespeare didn't understand that Judaism, like most religions, is predicated on mercy: for example, though lines 197–202 invoked for Shakespeare's audience the Lord's Prayer ("Forgive us our trespasses as we forgive those who trespass against us"), they are also reminiscent of Psalm 143:2 ("Enter not into judgment with thy servants, O Lord, for no flesh is righteous in thy sight"), and Ecclesiasticus 28:2 ("Forgive thy neighbor the hurt that he hath done thee, so shall thy sins be forgiven thee also, when thou prayest"). But Portia, being a creature of Shakespeare's times, believes that mercy is the sole domain of Christianity, and is wholeheartedly committed to enlightening Shylock with her point of view.

Though this is considered a "set speech" with formal structure, take care not to deliver it in a rigid manner. The monologue is structured using antithesis, which highlights the contrast between *justice* (which provides only earthly returns) and *mercy* (which yields salvation); *strained* and *droppeth as the gentle rain . . .* ; *him that gives* and *him that takes*; *scepter* and *mercy*; *temporal power* and

God Himself. It also has a clearly logical progression, setting out a thesis, expanding the thesis in general terms, and then specifically applying it to the situation at hand. And though you want to fight against rigid delivery, you can use the monologue's structure to fit Portia's demeanor to the formal courtroom setting, in order to convince the court that she is really a young male lawyer, well versed in legal argument. What will help you move beyond the monologue's formula is Portia's passionate desire to convince Shylock. Portia acknowledges in lines 202–5 that she has no real legal argument against Shylock's position: he has a valid contract with Antonio that the merchant has violated. Portia's objective in this monologue is therefore clear: she *must* convince him of the critical quality of mercy or Antonio will die. She is thus arguing from both her deep-rooted beliefs and her mission to save a life. Her belief and her mission make dynamic the rigidity of structure of this "set speech."

Portia's imagery is likewise a powerful persuasive tool, conveying her passionate spiritual commitment to her position. For example, the phrase *as the gentle rain from Heaven*, aside from being a biblical reference (see Annotation), also suggests that mercy is a nourishing gift from God. Further, all of the *monarch* imagery—as well as the added emphasis on the words *thronèd* and *enthronèd* created by expanding them—reminds Shylock that exhibiting mercy would put him squarely in the category of monarchs (whom Elizabethans believed were ordained by God to rule on God's behalf—see "Riding Shotgun with God," page 235), and of the Almighty ruler, the King of Kings.

Portia's repetition of words, phrases, and phrasal structure help make this monologue a powerful and moving piece of oratory. Examples include: *blest / blesseth*; *him that gives and him that takes*; *mightiest in the mightiest*; *scepter / sceptered*; *thronèd / enthronèd*; *God / God's*; *justice* (four times); *mercy* (five times). Other language elements color the monologue as well. For example, Portia's refusal to call Shylock by name (*Therefore, Jew*) is direct evidence of her anti-Semitism (exhibited to an even greater degree by all the other Christians in the play). Portia's conviction in her "one true faith" is what compells her at once to revile Shylock and try, in essence, to proselytize him. So you could make the choice that she uses the term more gently here, simply as an acknowledgment that she speaks to an outsider, for whom she assumes the concept she explains is likewise foreign. Also, *the merchant there* can be interpreted as an embedded stage direction to gesture in some manner toward Antonio.

Ironically, Portia delivers a gorgeous and compelling argument for the necessity of mercy right before she throws the full weight of "justice" at Shylock without a shred of mercy, reminding the court of an old law by which, as a foreigner who has attempted to take a Venetian citizen's life, Shylock must forfeit half of his estate to his victim and the other half to the state; furthermore, his life is at the mercy of the Duke. It is the Duke and then Antonio who ultimately temper Portia's justice with mercy, the Duke by sparing Shylock's life and Antonio by pledging his half of the estate to Shylock's daughter.

SIGNIFICANT SCANS

The meter is very even, with only a few double endings, and the occasional sentence beginning mid-line. Look at the few words that create double endings at the ends of lines: *Heaven*; *power*; *mercy*; *render*; *Venice*. These words highlight Portia's point that true heavenly power is shown through the rendering of mercy here on earth. Portia most often changes gears in those few sentences that begin mid-line (where the pause between sentences is kept quite brief), indicating that her thoughts are coming to her quickly and with surety. Portia clearly feels powerful in men's clothing, in her role as brilliant young lawyer. Here, her talents can flourish—she is out from under the thumb of her deceased father and her new lord and master, and is in her element, taking her own bold steps on behalf of mercy, her husband, womankind, and her religion.

Don't forget to elide: *mightiest* (MITE-yest) twice in line 188; *temporal* (TEMP-rull) in line 190; *power* (POWR) in line 196 (but not in line 190, which has a double ending); and *prayer* (PRARE) in line 201;

. . . and to expand: *thronèd* (THROW-nehd) in line 189 and *enthronèd* (en-THROW-nehd) in line 194.

Mercy Me!

Shakespeare didn't invent the argument for mercy over justice—as usual, he took an existing idea and embellished it: in a medieval allegory, the devil appeared and claimed mankind on the grounds of justice, but the Virgin Mary saved mankind by advocating mercy. This allegory translated beautifully, given that Elizabethan lore made reference to Jews being the devil's spawn.

THE MERRY WIVES OF WINDSOR

ACT II, SCENE i

MISTRESS PAGE

GENDER: F
AGE RANGE: mature adult
PROSE/VERSE: prose
FREQUENCY OF USE (1–5): 3.5

Mistress Margaret Page has just received a letter from Sir John Falstaff, a local (and rather disreputable) knight whom her husband has recently entertained in their home. She reads the letter aloud and soliloquizes in response to it.

What, have I 'scaped love-letters in the holiday-time of my beauty, and am I now a subject for them? Let me see!

[*she reads:*]

Ask me no reason why I love you, for though Love use
5 *Reason for his precisian, he admits not for his counselor.*
You are not young, nor am I: go then, there's sympathy.
You are merry, so am I: ha, ha! then there's more sympathy. You love sack, and so do I: would you desire better sympathy? Let it suffice thee, Mistress Page, at least
10 *if the love of a soldier can suffice, that I love thee. I will not say, pity me—'tis not a soldier-like phrase; but I say, love me. By me,*
Thine own true knight,
By day or night,
15 *Or any kind of light,*
With all his might
For thee to fight. —*John Falstaff.*

What a Herod of Jewry is this! O wicked, wicked world! One that is well-nigh worn to pieces with
20 age to show himself a young gallant! What an unweighed behavior hath this Flemish drunkard

1 *'scaped* escaped, avoided; *holiday-time* gay and festive time, hey-day [*the holiday-time of my beauty* i.e., my youth, when I was beautiful]; 5 *precisian* (pre-SIH-zhun) strict adviser (such as a Puritan minister); *counselor* here: confidant [*though Love use . . . his counselor* i.e., although Love uses Reason as his adviser, he does not turn to him as a confidant (Love is like a king with both a court chaplain and a privy council, each serving in a different capacity)]; 6 *go then* i.e., there you have it (with sexual double entendre: "[Let's] go to it, then"); *sympathy* conformity; agreement of disposition; 7 *merry* in Shakespeare's time, the word *merry* carried a secondary connotation, "sexually wanton"; 8 *sack* generic name for a light, dry wine from Spain and the Canary Islands, imported into England in the sixteenth and seventeenth centuries; 11 *soldier-like phrase* phrase befitting a soldier; 17 *For thee to fight* to fight for thee (in Shakespeare's time, the word *fight* was used interchangeably with *contend*, which carried the sexual double meaning "wrestle with sexually," i.e., "have sex with"; thus, *For thee to fight* also implies "To have sex with you"); 18 *Herod of Jewry* Herod of Judea (i.e., Herod the Great, Tetrarch [ruler of a region under the ancient Roman Empire] of Judea 37 B.C.E.–4 C.E., who was "exceeding wroth" when the three wise men failed to notify him of their visit to the baby Jesus, and who then ordered the deaths of all the babies in Bethlehem; Herod was represented in the old mystery plays as a bombastic, ranting tyrant [see "A Cycle Without a Herod Is Like a Miracle Without a Fish," page 568]); 19 *well-nigh* just about; 20 *show himself* offer himself as if he were; *gallant* (GAL-unt; or, guh-LAHNT) ladies' man; 21 *unweighed* not carefully considered; done lightly; *Flemish* i.e., drunken (Falstaff is only "Flemish" in the sense that the word is a slur: Elizabethans considered the Flemish [the people of Flanders, formerly a country, now a

picked (with the devil's name!) out of my conversation, that he dares in this manner assay me? Why he hath not been thrice in my company! What should
25 I say to him? I was then frugal of my mirth—Heaven forgive me! Why, I'll exhibit a bill in the parliament for the putting down of men. How shall I be revenged on him? For revenged I will be, as sure as his guts are made of puddings.

1 minute, 50 seconds

region in Belgium, France, and the Netherlands] notorious drunkards); 22 *picked* understood; *with the devil's name* either (1) with the help of the devil or (2) in the devil's name (possibly a mild oath); *conversation* conduct; 23 *assay* (a-SAY) approach or accost with a particular purpose in mind (with sexual double entendre: "attempt sexual intercourse with"); 24 *thrice* three times; *What should I say* either (1) what could I have said (that would have led him on in any way)? or (2) what could he possibly expect me to say (in response to this letter); 25 *frugal of my mirth* i.e., careful not to be too friendly with him; 26 *exhibit* submit for consideration; 27 *putting down* suppression, destruction (with sexual double entendre in which Mistress Page turns the tables on the usual meaning: forcing or laying down a woman for sexual intercourse); 29 *puddings* sausages made of an animal's stomach or entrails stuffed with a mixture of minced meat, suet, oatmeal, and seasoning, and then boiled (with sexual double entendre: "pudding" is Elizabethan slang for "penis").

COMMENTARY

If Mistress Page had been born in another era, she would have made a perfect suffragette: her unshakable adherence to traditional values is no obstacle to her forthright and energetic determination to avenge herself and her sex for wrongs done by men—or, in this case, *a* man: Falstaff.

Ask yourself exactly what Mistress Page is thinking at the start of the scene. She may already have opened the letter. If so, has she read only the salutation and opening lines, and is she now about to continue reading? Or has she already read the whole letter, and is she rereading it now to dispel her utter disbelief at the letter's contents? On the other hand, Mistress Page may not have opened the letter yet. Perhaps the envelope is covered in little hearts pierced with arrows, giving its nature away, or maybe Falstaff behaved so inappropriately when he dined with the Pages that she suspects the letter's intent. It is also possible that Mistress Page does not even remotely suspect the nature of Falstaff's communication. Perhaps she thinks it is only a thank-you note for the lovely dinner she served, and she is shocked to find that words she said completely in jest (*have I 'scaped love-letters . . . a subject for them*) are true. Your decision about what stage in the process of discovering Falstaff's advances Mistress Page has reached by the time she begins the monologue will shape your reaction to the letter as you read it aloud.

The prose of *Merry Wives* is well suited to the straightforward and honest Mistress Page. She uses common expressions and small-town colloquialisms to express herself (*holiday-time of my beauty*; *What a Herod of Jewry is this*; *O wicked, wicked world*; *well-nigh worn to pieces*; *Flemish drunkard*; *with the devil's name*; *Heaven forgive me*). Though she speaks plainly, the clever Mistress Page is no babe in the woods; Falstaff's vulgar double entendre does not escape her. She views Falstaff as both outlandishly amusing and disgustingly sinful, and is both amused and angry, as is neatly conveyed by her choice of metaphor for him: *Herod of Jewry*. For Mistress P. (and her Elizabethan audience), this name conjures up both the stock character from the old mystery plays, a raging, absurd, bombastic figure, and the actual Herod of the New Testament whom that character represents, an evil, baby-killing egomaniac. It is up to you to find your own balance between Mistress Page's outrage and amusement, and to decide specifically where she expresses each.

Mistress Page is justifiably angry at the insult to her honor that is implicit in Falstaff's proposal. To make it worse, the letter's double entendre slanders her with the assumption that she is already *merry*, a word that in Shakespeare's time also meant "sexually wanton." Furthermore, the final line of his love poem (such as it is) takes the insult another step, by suggesting that he is ready to take a roll in the hay with her. Mistress Page responds to Falstaff's subtle and not-so-subtle suggestions with some double entendres of her own. Using the expression *putting down*, she turns the tables on Falstaff's intention to "put her down" with a joke ("put her down" was Elizabethan double entendre for "have sex with her," sometimes implying the use of force). Her claim that she'll introduce a bill in parliament for the *putting down of men* deflates Falstaff's sexual power with laughter and with the implication that he and his erection will be suppressed.

Mistress Page closes the piece with another joke. When she says *his guts are made of puddings*, she denigrates him in several ways. There is the simple use of repetition of meaning (*puddings*, used in the plural, was in Shakespeare's time synonomous with *guts*), which emphasizes her assessment of him as a pile of slimy guts. In addition, an already clever play on words is enhanced with yet a third idea by the sexual double meaning of *pudding* (penis): *puddings*, or sausages, are stuffed into the *guts* of those who eat them; *puddings* themselves are stuffed intestines, or *guts*; and *puddings* (penises) are stuffed into someone else's "guts" during sex.

Mistress Page's use of double entendre reveals her ability to laugh at Falstaff, hinting at the manner in which she might read his letter. And there is much to laugh at: Falstaff's sheer audacity; his airs; his complete, obtuse misreading of her attitude toward him; his reference to the worn-out cliché that love is without reason; and of course the utter doggerel he submits in place of romantic poetry to close his letter. Go ahead and revel in it!

THE MERRY WIVES OF WINDSOR

ACT III, SCENE v

FALSTAFF

GENDER: M | AGE RANGE: older adult

PROSE/VERSE: prose | FREQUENCY OF USE (1–5): 2

Sir John Falstaff, old, dissolute, and ever short of cash, fancies that two of the town of Windsor's financially comfortable matrons, Mistress Ford and Mistress Page, are enamored of him, and believes that he can extort money from them. He sent each a faux love letter, not realizing that the two good friends would share their letters with each other and quickly figure him out. They have decided to turn the tables on him: by pretending to respond to his advances, they will make a fool of him and force him to squander the remainder of his own funds. Falstaff also doesn't realize that his cronies have alerted both Mr. Ford and Mr. Page that he intends to woo their wives. Ford, a jealous man unsure of his wife's chastity, disguised himself as one "Master Brooke" who wished to seduce Mistress Ford. "Master Brooke" hired Falstaff (who eagerly pounced on this additional source of money) to pave the way for his love suit by first seducing her himself. "Master Brooke" then resumed his original identity as Mr. Ford and returned home at the time of the rendezvous with a posse of friends, certain he'd catch his wife and Falstaff in a clinch. Forewarned of his approach, Mrs. Ford smuggled Falstaff out of the house in a laundry hamper. Falstaff now relates the close encounter to "Master Brooke":

62 Now, Master Brooke, you come to know what hath passed between me and Ford's wife?

65 Master Brooke, I will not lie to you. I was at her house the hour she appointed me.

But the peaking cornuto her husband, Master Brooke, dwelling in a continual 'larum of jealousy, comes me in the instant of our encounter, after we had embraced,
75 kissed, protested, and, as it were, spoke the prologue of our comedy; and at his heels a rabble of his companions, thither provoked and instigated by his distemper, and, forsooth, to search his house for his wife's love.

You shall hear. As good luck would have
85 it, comes in one Mistress Page, gives intelligence of Ford's approach; and, in her invention and Ford's wife's distraction, they conveyed me into a buck-basket—

90 Yes, a buck-basket!—rammed me in with foul shirts and smocks, socks, foul stockings, greasy

FALSTAFF

63 *hath passed* has transpired; 66 *appointed* fixed, determined [*the hour she appointed me* at the time she set for me to arrive]; 71 *peaking* sneaking (a term used with contempt); *cornuto* cuckold (man whose wife has been sexually unfaithful), from the Latin word meaning "horned"; 72 *dwelling* existing; 73 *'larum* call to arms [*dwelling in a continual 'larum of jealousy* being in a constant state of jealous agitation (in which he rouses other men to assist him)]; *comes me* comes; *in the instant of our encounter* i.e., at the moment we were to begin our actual sexual encounter; 75 *protested* declared our love; 76 *comedy* merry (as opposed to "humorous") play [*spoke the prologue of our comedy* i.e., had declared our intentions and were about to act on them, as the prologue of a play establishes what will occur onstage before the scenes unfold for the audience]; *rabble* crowd (a term of contempt); 77 *thither* to that place (i.e., to Ford's home); *provoked* impelled; *instigated* incited; 78 *distemper* mental derangement, perturbation; *forsooth* an exclamation earnestly meaning "in truth" when used by people of lesser education, but implying contempt when used—as by Falstaff—by people of higher social rank; 79 *love* lover; 86 *invention* skill in contriving a solution to a difficulty; 87 *distraction* perturbation, despair; *conveyed me* carried me secretly, i.e., placed me secretly; *buck-basket* portable laundry hamper; 91 *foul* filthy; *smocks* women's undergarments, shifts; *greasy* both filthy and

napkins, that, Master Brooke, there was the rankest compound of villainous smell that ever offended nostril.

Nay, you shall hear, Master Brooke, what I have suffered to bring this woman to evil for your good. Being thus crammed in the basket, a couple
100 of Ford's knaves, his hinds, were called forth by their mistress to carry me in the name of foul clothes to Datchet Lane. They took me on their shoulders; met the jealous knave their master in the door, who asked them once or twice what they had
105 in their basket. I quaked for fear lest the lunatic knave would have searched it; but Fate, ordaining he should be a cuckold, held his hand. Well, on went he for a search, and away went I for foul clothes. But mark the sequel, Master Brooke. —I
110 suffered the pangs of three several deaths: first, an intolerable fright, to be detected with a jealous, rotten bell-wether; next, to be compassed, like a good bilbo in the circumference of a peck, hilt to point, heel to head; and then, to be stopped in, like a
115 strong distillation, with stinking clothes that fretted

smeared in grease; 92 *napkins* handkerchiefs; *that* so that; 93 *villainous* vile; 98 *bring this woman to evil* i.e., corrupt this woman (through adultery); 100 *knaves* here meaning menial servants (with secondary connotation, "rascals"); *hinds* menial servants (with connotation of contempt); 101 *in the name of* i.e., under the guise of being; 102 *Datchet Lane* a street in the town of Windsor on the banks of the Thames River, where laundry could be washed; 103 *knave* here: villain 104 *door* doorway; 106 *Fate* the goddess Fate, who, according to classical mythology, controls the destinies of humans [*Fate, ordaining he should be a cuckold* Falstaff refers to the maxim "cuckolds come by destiny"]; 107 *held* stopped [*held his hand* i.e., stopped him from acting]; 108 *for foul clothes* i.e., taken for (assumed to be) dirty laundry; 109 *mark* listen to, pay attention to; *the sequel* what happened next; 110 *several* separate, distinct; 111 *with* by; 112 *bell-wether* the male sheep—often castrated—that leads the flock, around whose neck a bell is usually affixed; *compassed* curved; *a good bilbo* a well-tempered Spanish Bilboa sword (part of the test of the quality of a blade was to bend it from the tip to the handle to make sure it did not snap in two); 113 *circumference* periphery; *peck* a container that held a quarter of a bushel (a dry measure of eight quarts) [*in the circumference of a peck* i.e., curled up around the inside edges of a container no bigger than a peck]; *hilt* the handle of a sword; 114 *stopped in* shut in (with play on the "stopper" of a bottle); 115 *distillation* the substance extracted by distilling (here, a potion with a potent odor, distilled from the stewing laundry); *fretted* rotted, fermented [*fretted . . . grease* Falstaff adapts the proverbial phrase "frying or stewing in one's own grease," which

in their own grease. Think of that—a man of my kidney—think of that—that am as subject to heat as butter, a man of continual dissolution and thaw.—It was a miracle to 'scape suffocation. And in the
120 height of this bath, when I was more than half stewed in grease, like a Dutch dish, to be thrown into the Thames and cooled, glowing hot, in that surge, like a horseshoe! Think of that—hissing hot!—think of that, Master Brooke!

Master Brooke, I will be thrown into Aetna, as I have been into Thames, ere I will leave
130 her thus. Her husband is this morning gone a-birding. I have received from her another embassy of meeting: 'twixt eight and nine is the hour, Master Brooke.

3 minutes, 15 seconds

refers to behaving wickedly]; 117 *kidney* constitution; *subject* susceptible; 118 *continual* incessant, chronic; *dissolution* dissolving, turning into liquid (possibly a reference to sweating); *thaw* melting; 119 *to 'scape* to be saved from, to avoid; 120 *bath* i.e., heat like that of a bath; 121 *a Dutch dish* the Dutch were proverbially addicted to butter and their food was famously greasy; 122 *the Thames* (Temz) the principal river of England, flowing eastward from the country's southwest through London to the North Sea—Windsor is located in the river's lower valley; 123 *surge* violently moving water; *hissing hot* i.e., hot enough to make a hissing sound upon contact with the cold water; 129 *Aetna* Mount Etna, an active volcano located in eastern Sicily; *ere* before [*ere I will leave her thus* i.e., before I will leave Mrs. Ford still faithful to her husband]; 131 *a-birding* bird shooting; *embassy* message [*another embassy of meeting* i.e., message setting up another tryst]; 132 *'twixt* between; *the hour* i.e., the hour set for the next rendezvous.

COMMENTARY

It is said that *The Merry Wives of Windsor* was commissioned by the Queen for a particular event, that she specifically requested (read: commanded) that it portray Falstaff in love, and that Shakespeare had approximately fourteen days to accomplish the job. If so, this would have created a bit of a quandary for the Bard, for to have Falstaff truly fall in love would be to deny Falstaff's personality altogether. Shakespeare solved this by having Falstaff feign love and attempt romantic liaisons in order to swindle his love interests, a scheme often undertaken by the Falstaff of the History plays. But to permit Falstaff to seduce Mistress Ford would have bucked the moral conventions of the day, so Shakespeare was compelled to have Falstaff fail stunningly, becoming the butt of the predominant joke of the play. And so, although the Falstaff of *Merry Wives* is as dissipated, as conniving, as gloriously self-important as is the Falstaff of the Histories, he lacks the original Falstaff's wittiness par excellence. In this monologue, Shakespeare presents the new-and-impaired Falstaff in all his self-perceived glory.

The imagery in this monologue—Falstaff's principal device—is intended both to show his valor and to express how aggrieved he is at his undeserved ill treatment. In this manner he hopes to impress "Master Brooke" with his heroics and dedication, so that although the first attempt at seducing Mistress Ford was an utter fiasco, "Master Brooke" will continue to finance Falstaff in this most noble undertaking. Falstaff the spin doctor recounts what was ultimately a humiliating event with self-aggrandizing metaphors and similes to characterize himself as valorous, chivalrous, and macho throughout the experience. For example, of all the images he could choose to describe his curled-up position in the basket of dirty laundry, he chooses the dashing image of a *bilbo*, the finest of Spanish blades. To explain how hot and sweaty he was amid the filthy laundry, he uses the term *glowing hot*—a beautiful image (not befitting him), as well as a gross exaggeration, even though he probably never felt as hot in his life as he did in that basket. The term *surge* is bald overstatement when applied to the placid Thames, which, though slightly displaced when Falstaff was thrown in, was scarcely roiling. Words and phrases such as *a distillation*, *bath*, and *a Dutch dish* creatively express his indignation at being made filthy and greasy and then being dumped unceremoniously into the Thames (his frustration and indignation are further indicated by his use of the phrase *comes me*, which is an antiquated tense known as the "ethical dative," often used by Shakespeare's characters to express such sentiments). The terms he uses when describing his "mission," such as *gives intelligence* and *conveyed me*, give it the tone of a spy's delicate and expert covert operation. And with his phrase *I will be thrown into Aetna, as I have been into*

Thames, ere I will leave her thus, as though he's rescuing Mrs. Ford from some terrible fate, Falstaff is saying that he is so dedicated to the cause that he'd go through fire and water to accomplish it—a heroic sentiment. Falstaff doesn't want his tale of hardship to backfire, causing "Master Brooke" to deem the enterprise too dangerous to be continued. Quite the contrary, he wants to be perceived as dedicated and thus to keep "Master Brooke" invested for the long haul. Most of this imagery (however mixed the metaphors and similes), as well as the clever euphemistic antithesis of *to bring this woman to evil for your good*, shows Falstaff to be intelligent and facile with words, if not graced with the brilliant wit of the Falstaff of the History plays.

Despite his often clever and apt use of imagery, Falstaff also occasionally evokes images with meanings he did not intend, with the result that he inadvertently makes himself the butt of jokes. For example, he uses the word *dissolution*, which instantly reminds the reader that Falstaff is "dissolute." He uses the phrase *a man of my kidney* to mean "a man of my constitution," but the word choice raises the image of Falstaff as a quivering mass of flesh (and, for today's audience, perhaps that of his assuredly ruinously cirrhotic liver as well). When mentioned on the heels of the images of the greasy *Dutch dish* and Falstaff's particular *kidney*, the second meaning of the term *hissing* ("farting") gives the sentence a hilarious double meaning. Since Falstaff has an entirely different double entendre in mind for *hissing* (discussed below), this indelicate scatological meaning is surely unintentional. Furthermore, Falstaff addresses "Master Brooke" by name a full nine times in this monologue, which, cumulatively, is funny because it continuously reminds the listener that Falstaff is actually addressing Mr. Ford and is shooting himself in the foot. You must decide specifically why Falstaff keeps repeating the name: is he trying to seem deferential? To create a sense of intimacy between them? To get "Master Brooke's" attention? (We can imagine that "Master Brooke" is growing increasingly angry and distracted as he listens and realizes that he's been duped himself. Though he doesn't know why, Falstaff may notice this reaction.)

And, of course, Falstaff has no idea of the extent to which he is fueling "Master Brooke's" fire with the double entendre he fully intends. Notice all the "cuckold" double entendre: since horns were symbolic of cuckoldry, Falstaff no doubt thinks his several references to horned animals (particularly rams) are terribly clever: *cornuto*; *rammed*; *buck* (*-basket*); *bell-wether* (this one is a particularly harsh metaphor to apply to Ford, since it implies that he is old, castrated, a cuckold, and as stupid as a sheep, and that the mob he led to the house was equally dim-witted). Falstaff has no idea that with each additional witticism, "Master Brooke's" apoplexy is increasing in direct proportion to his own self-satisfaction. Falstaff's other uses of double entendre would endear him no further to "Master

Brooke." Elizabethans would have understood the double meanings of the following words (but be careful not to play them overtly, as they are intended as secondary—not primary—meanings, and as their archaic sexual meanings are lost on today's audiences): Mention of a sword of any kind would have been interpreted as "penis"—Elizabethans would have understood Falstaff's likening himself to a *bilbo* (one of the finest of swords) to be quite audacious on his part. Furthermore, *compassed* meant "involved in the sex act"; *circumference*, a circular periphery, would be construed as a "vagina"; *peck*, as today, meant "to strike with quick, repeated movements": *compassed, like a good bilbo in the circumference of a peck* meant "involved in the sex act, like a virile penis thrusting in a vagina." This would conjure images for Ford of his wife and Falstaff that he'd rather not consider. The word *hinds* had the additional meaning "asses," which would have insulted Mr. Ford, as the term was applied to his household servants. The term *horseshoe* was a pun for a "whore's shoe," which meant a "whore's vagina"; when this image was coupled (so to speak) with the image of the motion of the *surge* Falstaff was cast into (which is reminiscent of the movement of copulation), it would have reminded the jealous Mr. Ford of what Falstaff intended to do with his wife (and would have insulted said wife at the same time). Similarly, *hour* was a common pun for "whore." It would have further infuriated Ford to hear that Falstaff's ardor was *cooled* when he was *hissing hot* with lust (or so Mr. Ford believed) for Mr. Ford's wife.

"Master Brooke's" lines, which have been excised to create the monologue, are merely responses to Falstaff's story, urging him onward in the telling of it; the transitions between segments are very smooth even without them. Falstaff's use of prose is appropriate to his colloquial storytelling manner—the manner of a person who has just been through a trying experience and is still in the throes of it as he relates the tale, and yet who has also sufficiently recovered to be thinking on his feet as he manipulates the story to his best advantage.

Finally, keep in mind that Falstaff has just recently returned from his adventure in the Thames, and could even still be cold and wet. This creates "business" possibilities for you to explore in the piece: are you wringing yourself dry, shivering, changing your clothes, trying to get warm, pouring water out of your shoes, sneezing with the cold you caught, drinking heavily to warm and comfort yourself, etc.?

"BROOKE": WATER UNDER THE BRIDGE

It is thought that when Shakespeare wrote *Merry Wives* in or about 1597, he chose Brooke as Ford's pseudonym for three reasons. First, "Brooke"—a water reference—cleverly parallels that of "Ford." Second, Shakespeare's audience would have been familiar with the word's bawdy second meaning, "pimp," a befitting term for Ford, who, as "Brooke" arranges trysts between Falstaff and his own wife. Third, the name pokes fun at the gentleman who had just recently required that Shakespeare change the name originally given to his character in the *Henry IV* plays from Oldcastle to another name (Shakespeare chose Falstaff): that gentleman was William *Brooke*, Lord Cobham (whose martyred ancestor was named Oldcastle [see "O, Be Some Other Name! . . . ," page 86]). Though Brooke is the name used in the 1602 Quarto (indicating that it was also the name used in performance at that time), it was changed to "Broome" in the 1623 First Folio. This may have been at the behest of the humorless Lord Cobham. Or the name may have been changed because King James had put down rebellions by two brothers named Brooke in 1604, and the compilers of the Folio didn't want to remind the King of unpleasant events, lest he plan similarly unpleasant events for *them* . . . Happily, editors later restored Shakespeare's subtle joke.

A MIDSUMMER NIGHT'S DREAM

ACT I, SCENE i

THESEUS

GENDER: M
AGE RANGE: adult to mature adult
PROSE/VERSE: blank verse
FREQUENCY OF USE (1–5): 1

At his palace, Theseus, Duke of Athens, and his bride-to-be, Hippolyta, have been discussing their upcoming wedding. Egeus, an Athenian nobleman, has just barged in with his daughter, Hermia. With them are Demetrius, whom Egeus wants Hermia to marry, and Lysander, whom Hermia wishes to marry. Egeus has asked Theseus to enforce the Athenian law under which Hermia must obey his wishes or be put to death. Theseus's interpretation of the law is slightly different. He explains Hermia's options to her and warns her to weigh the consequences of her choice carefully.

65 Either to die the death, or to abjure
Forever the society of men.
Therefore, fair Hermia, question your desires,
Know of your youth, examine well your blood,
Whether (if you yield not to your father's choice)
70 You can endure the livery of a nun,
For aye to be in shady cloister mewed,
To live a barren sister all your life,
Chanting faint hymns to the cold fruitless moon.
Thrice blessèd they that master so their blood
75 To undergo such maiden pilgrimage;
But earthlier happy is the rose distilled
Than that which, withering on the virgin thorn,
Grows, lives, and dies in single blessedness.

Take time to pause, and by the next new moon—
The sealing day betwixt my love and me
85 For everlasting bond of fellowship—
Upon that day either prepare to die
For disobedience to your father's will,
Or else to wed Demetrius, as he would,
Or on Diana's altar to protest
90 For aye austerity and single life.

1 minute, 20 seconds

65 *die the death* i.e., be put to death; *abjure* renounce; 66 *society of men* both (1) life within Athenian society and (2) literally, the presence of men; 68 *Know of* be aware of, understand; *blood* passions and feelings; 70 *the livery of a nun* a nun's habit, i.e., the life of a nun; 71 *For aye* forever; *cloister* convent; *mewed* confined [*in shady cloister mewed* confined in a dark convent]; 72 *To live* to live as; 73 *faint* unenthusiastic; *cold fruitless moon* Athenian nuns served Diana, goddess of the moon, who was chaste and therefore referred to by Theseus as "cold" (i.e., frigid, sexless) and "fruitless" (i.e., childless); 74 *Thrice blessèd they . . . maiden pilgrimage* those who control their passions to live in celibate seclusion will be blessed three times over; 76 *earthlier happy* happier on earth; *the rose distilled* the rose that gets plucked and made into perfume [*But earthlier happy . . . in single blessedness* Theseus uses this analogy to impress upon Hermia that she will be happier married to Demetrius than alone in the convent]; 84 *sealing day* wedding day; *betwixt* between; 85 *For* of; 88 *as he would* as he wishes (the *he* refers to Hermia's father, Egeus); 89 *protest* take a vow; 90 *austerity and single life* poverty and celibacy.

COMMENTARY

This speech reveals Theseus's characteristics. The language is that of a highly educated statesman who is accustomed to public speaking. Although impromptu, the speech is logically structured, measured, and judicious. Aware of the political import of his every word, Theseus acknowledges Egeus's absolute authority over Hermia yet benevolently offers Hermia options and the time to consider them. It is unclear why Theseus interprets the Athenian law differently than Egeus does. You may decide that he is better versed in the fine points of the law, or that as a kind ruler he does not wish to see Hermia die and is using his royal discretion to modify the law without disregarding it. The choice you make will influence your development of the character and your interpretation of the monologue.

Although this monologue demonstrates his public persona, signs of Theseus's private persona also peek through. He betrays excitement about his upcoming wedding and bride-to-be . . . and his opinion of a celibate life is clear. Theseus's private life parallels his public statement: a chivalrous chauvinist, he kidnaps his bride (see "Monster Slayer–cum–Statesman," on facing page), but then treats her with kindness and a modicum of respect; he likewise approves of the deal between Egeus and Demetrius, but then shows Hermia kindness and limited respect by allowing her to choose her fate.

SIGNIFICANT SCANS

There is a concentration of inverted first feet at the beginning of this piece (four in the first five lines!), which suggests that Theseus is sterner and more aggressive at the start and softens (slightly) in the second half. There is also a complete absence of softening double endings (with an optional exception in line 67), supporting Theseus's self-assured and authoritative tone.

In addition to its inverted first foot, line 73 contains a phyrric third foot (two unaccented syllables) followed by a spondaic fourth foot (two accented syllables), which emphasize the frightening bleakness of young Hermia's long, desolate future should she disobey her father:

/ x x / x x / / x /
Chanting faint hymns to the cold fruitless moon

Line 86 contains an inverted foot mid-line following a caesura that is not marked by punctuation:

x / x / /x x / x /
Upon that day either prepare to die

Don't forget to elide: *Hermia* (HER-mya) in line 67; *desires* (de-ZIERZ) in line 67 (optional); *livery* (LIV-ree) in line 70; *earthlier* (ERTH-lyer) in line 76; *withering* (WITH-ring) in line 77; *disobedience* (DIS´-o-BEED-yenss) in line 87; and *Demetrius* (Dih-MEE-tryuss) in line 88;

. . . to contract: *to your* (tyore) in line 69;

. . . and to expand: *blessèd* (BLEH-sehd) in line 74.

Monster Slayer–cum–Statesman

Theseus is a prominent character in Greek mythology who is probably based on a historical figure. He began his career as a monster slayer while still a teen, bringing down such notorious monsters as Periphetes and Procrustes the Stretcher. But Theseus would secure his tenure in mythology for his most famous slay, that human with the head of a bull, the Minotaur of Crete. The untimely death of his father, King Aegeus of Athens, launched Theseus's long and prosperous rule of that city-state, during which he was well loved and venerated. Not content to be a stay-at-home king, however, he continued his exploits, which included an invasion of the land of the Amazons. There he first met his wife, Hippolyta (a.k.a. Antiope), the Amazon Queen, whom he promptly abducted. He carried her back to Athens to be his queen, and it is at this point in his story that our play is set.

A MIDSUMMER NIGHT'S DREAM

ACT I, SCENE I

LYSANDER

GENDER: M
AGE RANGE: young adult
PROSE/VERSE: blank verse
FREQUENCY OF USE (1–5): 2.5

Lysander and Hermia, who are in love, have just been told that Hermia must obey her father's wishes and marry Demetrius; otherwise, she must either become a nun or be put to death. Lysander feels very sorry for himself and Hermia, and is disillusioned by the many obstacles to love.

LYSANDER

135 Ay me! For aught that I could ever read,
Could ever hear by tale or history,
The course of true love never did run smooth;
But either it was different in blood,
Or else misgraffèd in respect of years,
140 Or else it stood upon the choice of friends.
Or, if there were a sympathy in choice,
War, death or sickness did lay siege to it,
Making it momentany as a sound,
Swift as a shadow, short as any dream,
145 Brief as the lightning in the collied night
That in a spleen unfolds both heaven and earth,
And ere a man hath power to say, "Behold!"
The jaws of darkness do devour it up:
So quick bright things come to confusion.

1 minute

135 *Ay me!* an interjection of dismay; *For aught* from anything; 137 *smooth* smoothly; 138 *different in blood* of different social classes (can also mean "of incompatible temperaments"—see "Elizabethan Anatomy 101," page 558); 139 *misgraffèd in respect of years* mismatched in age; 140 *stood upon* depended on; *friends* family members; 141 *Or, if there were a sympathy in choice* or, if the lovers were well matched (i.e. they have none of the above problems); 143 *momentany* momentary; 145 *collied* black as coal; 146 *in a spleen* in a fit (i.e., in a sudden motion); *unfolds* reveals (by lighting up); 147 *ere* before; *hath power* i.e., is able; 148 *it* i.e., the lightning; 149 *So quick bright things come to confusion* that's how quickly things of splendid beauty (such as love) are ruined.

COMMENTARY

This monologue provides our only insight into Lysander's character (he cannot be held accountable for his erratic behavior later, when he is under the spell of Cupid's flower). Lysander is "singing the blues." This reaction to his predicament suggests a philosophical nature. It reveals a maturity of feeling toward Hermia, and a thoughtful and sensitive disposition (in contrast to that of Demetrius, whose fickle behavior indicates infatuation, not love).

The poetic language of this piece sets its tone. Note the elegance of the monologue's construction. The build in Lysander's lament is supported by the repetition of *Or* in three consecutive lines (139–41) (FYI: a device called anaphora), followed by the repeated use of inverted first feet in three consecutive lines (143–45). In addition, none of the monologue's lines are broken by the introduction of new thoughts and most do not violate the natural meter of blank verse, including Lysander's exclamation at the start of the piece (where one might expect an inverted foot). Notice that when iambic pentameter is uninterrupted, it imitates the rhythm of the human heartbeat . . . the perfect medium for a lovesick swain. Art, by its nature, glorifies its subject; by creating an elegy to their love, for which he has already begun grieving, Lysander elevates that love to heroic proportions.

Note: we have deleted three of Hermia's lines to create an uninterrupted monologue. Since her lines are interjections in response to Lysander's comments and do not interfere with his thought process, they do not affect the progression of this piece. His lines, therefore, flow smoothly with hers removed.

SIGNIFICANT SCANS

Don't forget to elide: *heaven* (HEV'N) in line 146; *power* (POWR) in line 147; *devour* (de-VOWR) in line 148 (note the OW sound echoed in *power* and *devour*, which effectively expresses Lysander's pain at losing his love);

. . . and to expand: *different* (DIFF´-er-ENT) in line 138; and *misgraffèd* (miss-GRA-fehd) in line 139.

Although the meter of the piece seems to call for the expansion of *confusion* in the final line, we suggest that you *not* expand the word, leaving the final, usually accented syllable silent. This will allow you to avoid an awkward expansion at the end of a beautiful piece of poetry. Furthermore, by ending the piece slightly sooner than expected, you will aurally mimic the *brief*ness of *lightning*, thus paralleling the *confusion* Lysander speaks of by slightly "ruining" the *bright thing* that is this little piece of verse.

A MIDSUMMER'S NIGHT DREAM

ACT 1, SCENE 1

HELENA

GENDER: F
AGE RANGE: young adult
PROSE/VERSE: rhymed iambic pentameter
FREQUENCY OF USE (1–5): 4

Helena has recently been jilted by her fiancé, Demetrius. She is still bereft. Demetrius now professes love for Helena's best friend, Hermia, and has obtained her father's consent to marry her. Hermia does not love him, however; she and Lysander are in love. At this point in the play, Helena has just come upon Hermia and Lysander. When Hermia greets her with "God speed, fair Helena," Helena replies:

Call you me fair? That fair again unsay.
Demetrius loves your fair. O happy fair!
Your eyes are lodestars and your tongue's sweet air
More tuneable than lark to shepherd's ear
185 When wheat is green, when hawthorn buds appear.
Sickness is catching: O were favour so,
Yours would I catch, fair Hermia, ere I go;
My ear should catch your voice, my eye your eye,
My tongue should catch your tongue's sweet melody.
190 Were the world mine, Demetrius being bated,
The rest I'd give to be to you translated.
O teach me how you look, and with what art
You sway the motion of Demetrius' heart.

45 seconds

181 *Call you me fair?* Are you calling me beautiful?; *That fair again unsay* i.e., take back that compliment; 182 *your fair* your beauty; *happy* lucky; 183 *lodestars* stars that sailors used to guide them, believed to have magnetic powers; *air* tune, melody; 184 *tuneable* melodious; *than lark to shepherd's ear* than a lark is to a shepherd's ear (i.e., to the shepherd who hears it); 185 *When wheat . . . appear* i.e., in springtime; 186 *favour* physical appearance; *so* that way; 187 *Yours would I catch* I would catch yours (i.e., your looks); *ere* before [*ere I go* the meaning of this phrase in this context is unclear, but we suggest "before I do anything else" or "before I die"]; 188 *should* would; 190 *bated* excepted; 191 *translated* transformed [*Were the world mine . . . translated* If the world were mine, I'd give it all away—except for Demetrius—to become you]; 192 *art* skill (with play on second meaning, "magic").

COMMENTARY

Have you ever noticed how, when a person gets dumped, he or she relates *everything* to the breakup? Although Hermia has merely greeted Helena with a common phrase, Helena latches on to the one word in it—*fair*—that relates to her predicament, and she's off and running.

Helena isolates Hermia's best features and cites romantic imagery for each one. This mini-ode to Hermia's attributes suggests that she has been sitting at her mirror and comparing herself to Hermia, feature by feature, to determine which of Hermia's qualities won Demetrius over. Helena's tone with Hermia is informal and intimate, as befits their long-standing close friendship.

Note how often Helena uses the exclamation *O* (see "O, No! An *O*!," page xxxiii). Since she is only human, it is natural that a little piece of Helena enjoys being a drama queen. Shakespeare uses rhyming couplets throughout the monologue (including the historic rhyme of *eye* with *melody*, which we do not recommend; forcing *melody* to rhyme with *eye* will make you sound as though you are fishing for a laugh). By rhyming the monologue, Shakespeare highlights the melodrama, poking fun at Helena's angst and sharing a laugh with the audience at her expense. Be aware of this, but do not succumb to the temptation to play the melodrama. The more sincere Helena is, the better the joke.

SIGNIFICANT SCANS

Four of the thirteen lines in this short piece begin with inverted feet, which are a clue to Helena's exasperation. There are only two softening double endings (in lines 190 and 191) and the meter flows quite regularly, in keeping with Helena's candid assertion of her envy of Hermia. But notice that the word *your* in line 182 is stressed, even though it falls in an unstressed position in the line. This draws extra attention to it, since it comes as a surprise to your listeners.

Don't forget to elide: *Demetrius* (De-MEE-tryuss) in lines 182 and 190; *Hermia* (HER-mya) in line 187; and *Demetrius'* (De-MEE-tryuss, *not* De-MEE-tryuss-ez) in line 193.

A MIDSUMMER NIGHT'S DREAM

ACT I, SCENE i

HELENA

GENDER: F
AGE RANGE: young adult
PROSE/VERSE: rhymed iambic pentameter
FREQUENCY OF USE (1–5): 5

Helena is miserable. She was engaged to Demetrius, with whom she was—and still is—deeply in love. Demetrius, however, has fallen in love with Helena's oldest and dearest friend, Hermia. He recently broke off his engagement to Helena and obtained Hermia's father's consent to marry her, despite the fact that Hermia is in love with Lysander and the two wish to be married. The Duke of Athens has warned Hermia that she must obey her father or she will either be killed or forced to live as a nun. She and Lysander have just confided in Helena that they plan to flee and will be navigating the thick forest outside Athens tomorrow night. They've just wished Helena the best of luck with Demetrius and gone off to pack. Helena says:

How happy some o'er other some can be!
Through Athens I am thought as fair as she.
But what of that? Demetrius thinks not so;
He will not know what all but he do know.
230 And as he errs, doting on Hermia's eyes,
So I, admiring of his qualities.
Things base and vile, holding no quantity,
Love can transpose to form and dignity:
Love looks not with the eyes, but with the mind,
235 And therefore is winged Cupid painted blind.
Nor hath Love's mind of any judgment taste;
Wings and no eyes figure unheedy haste.
And therefore is Love said to be a child,
Because in choice he is so oft beguiled.
240 As waggish boys in game themselves forswear,
So the boy Love is perjured everywhere:
For ere Demetrius looked on Hermia's eyne
He hailed down oaths that he was only mine.
And when this hail some heat from Hermia felt,

226 *happy* both (1) lucky and (2) happy; *o'er other some* over others, more than others [*How happy . . . can be!* How much luckier and happier some people are than others!]; 227 *fair* beautiful; 229 *will not know* refuses to see; *what all but he do know* what everyone sees except for him (i.e., that Helena is as beautiful as Hermia); 230 *errs* goes astray; *doting on* being excessively in love with; 231 *So I* So do I (I'm also making a mistake); *admiring of his qualities* i.e., by considering his attributes worthy of love; 232 *base* (1) lowly; (2) of inferior quality; *holding no quantity* out of proportion (to the value love makes them seem to have); 233 *Love* both (1) the emotion and (2) a name for Cupid, the god of Love in classical mythology; *transpose* transform; *form and dignity* good appearance and worth; 235 *therefore is winged Cupid painted blind* Cupid has often been depicted as a blind boy with wings who shot arrows of love at random—hence the term "love is blind"; 236 *of any judgment taste* even the slightest bit (taste) of judgment; 237 *figure* symbolize; *unheedy* reckless, inconsiderate; 239 *beguiled* deceived [*in choice he is so oft beguiled* i.e., Cupid is so often deceived into shooting arrows at, and causing love to strike, the wrong people]; 240 *waggish* playful; *in game* playing a sport; *themselves forswear* perjure themselves; swear falsely; 241 *is perjured* his oaths (of love) are broken, i.e., oaths made in his name are broken; 242 *ere* before; *eyne* (INE) eyes (an archaic plural form, used to maintain

245 So he dissolved, and showers of oaths did melt.
I will go tell him of fair Hermia's flight;
Then to the wood will he tomorrow night
Pursue her; and for this intelligence
If I have thanks, it is a dear expense.
250 But herein mean I to enrich my pain,
To have his sight thither and back again.

1 minute, 30 seconds

the rhyme); 245 *he dissolved* his emotions disintegrated; 246 *flight* i.e., secret escape; 247 *the wood* the forest; 249 *a dear expense* (1) at great cost; (2) a worthwhile expenditure [*for this intelligence . . . a dear expense* two possible meanings: (1a) if Demetrius even bothers to thank me for this information, it will seem as though it cost him (pained him) to do so; (1b) if Demetrius thanks me for this information, it is at great cost to me (because I will have led him to Hermia); or (2) this information is an expense worth making, because it may elicit thanks from Demetrius]; 250 *herein* in this; *mean I* I intend; *to enrich my pain* i.e., to make my pain pay off (with a possible play on "make my pain greater"); 251 *To have his sight thither and back again* three possible meanings: (1) to have Demetrius's sight fall upon Hermia's devotion to another ("thither") and then return to see Helena's loyalty ("back again"); (2) to be able to see Demetrius (to have him within her sight) throughout the trek into the woods and back; or (3) to be in Demetrius's sight (to have his sight upon her) throughout the trek there and back.

COMMENTARY

Alas, poor Helena. We know her, Horatio . . . as does every woman who has ever pined away for love of some undeserving, Camel-smoking, bass-playin' bad boy driving an '87 Pinto . . .

Ahem, anyway, Helena's in pain, but she's not one to let it get the best of her. She's almost done complaining about it, and then she's really going to take control of matters. Her monologue has a clear progression from griping about her plight, to trying to understand it in a way that soothes her wounded ego, to planning action in the hope of improving the situation. It is only in the middle section of the piece, in which Helena ponders Love, that her imagery takes center stage. In the first and last sections, Helena favors simple language, which helps create her youthful and plaintive tone. Simple language calls for simple delivery, for two reasons: the impact will be greater than if the simple material is unduly overdramatized; and both the simple material and the more complex imagery will be more effective for the contrast between them. Notice in particular Helena's exclusive use of single-syllable words in line 229 (*He will not know . . .*), which gives the line a staccato cadence that expresses her frustration at his inability to recognize an obvious fact.

Even Helena's imagery (concentrated in lines 233–45) is rather unsophisticated and clichéd, adding to the monologue's charming adolescent tone. Her predominant image is an extended *Cupid* metaphor, on which she elaborates with several well-worn adages. Clearly, *Love* commands Helena's attention these days. Baffled by Demetrius's senseless and abrupt abandonment of her, Helena is trying to make sense of the situation, to figure out how love works, and simultaneously to salvage what is left of her self-esteem following a brutal rejection. Her only consolation lies in her conclusion that there is neither rhyme nor reason to the whole business; if Love were logical, Demetrius clearly would not have jilted Helena to pursue someone whom she equals, as *all but he do know*. Love's *blind*ness allows Helena to take comfort in the notion that she was not rejected because of any flaw of her own. Similarly, Helena likens Demetrius's betrayal to a hailstorm: *hailed down oaths*; *dissolved*; *showers of oaths did melt*. His rejection of her was a natural disaster, beyond human prevention and as arbitrary as the weather. And in fact, Helena's rationalization that *Love* is *perjured everywhere* and that it is readily transferable is 100 percent correct in the world of this play, in which such emotions—as well as the weather—are governed by supernatural forces, as Helena will discover when all four lovers take to the woods.

At line 245, Helena abruptly concludes her commentary about Love's (and Demetrius's) capriciousness. Maybe it's too painful to continue reminding herself of it, or maybe she's cheered herself up by acquitting her own attributes of any responsibility for the breakup. Perhaps she just becomes aware of the time. Whatever reason you choose for Helena's transition, it's now time to get practical, in Helena's unique sense of the word; she switches gears and mobilizes. To prepare this final section of the piece, you must make some specific choices: you must decide whether Helena first hits on the idea to inform Demetrius of Hermia and Lysander's escape to the woods when she mentions it in line 246, or whether she decided to tell him earlier, as soon as the couple told her. This decision will inform your delivery of lines 246–51. You must also decide precisely what Helena hopes to accomplish: Does she aspire only to a kind word of thanks from Demetrius, thinking that with even that small wish she is setting her sights too high? Or does she hope that while Demetrius pursues the other couple and she pursues him, she and he will have the "togetherness time" needed for his love to be rekindled? Or does she hope that when he witnesses Hermia's love for another and sees how loyal Helena has remained in contrast, Demetrius will shift his affections back to her? Your specific choice regarding what Helena thinks she can accomplish, as well as what her wishful thinking will allow her to fantasize about accomplishing, will make your objectives and actions in the last section of this monologue clear.

You surely can't help but notice the rhyme, one of the key devices in the monologue. Its couplets create a sense of melodrama, which suggests that Helena is enjoying her pain a wee bit. The couplets include the historic rhymes of *eyes* with *qualities* in lines 230–31 and *pain* with *again* in lines 250–51. You can maintain them if you want an easy laugh, but we urge you to test them out first; it may not be worth compromising Helena's earnestness. The other rhymes lend the piece plenty of humor, which assures your audience that although Helena is distraught now, she will triumph in the end. The "built-in" humor frees you to play the monologue with complete sincerity; in fact, the more truthful you are, the better the joke.

SIGNIFICANT SCANS

The meter is fairly regular, but has several inverted first feet, punching the first words of lines 233 (*Love*), 236 (*Nor*—optional), 237 (*Wings*), 241 (*So*), 245 (*So*), 246 (*I*), and 247 (*Then*), which point to Helena's distress.

Although it is rare for inverted feet to follow caesuras that are not marked by punctuation, this monologue contains two such instances:

Line 237 contains an inverted first foot in addition to its mid-line inversion—

/ x x / / x x / x /
Wings and no eyes figure unheedy haste

And the use of the variation in the final line of the piece ends it with a jolt of energy—

x / x / / x x / x /
To have his sight thither and back again

Helena consistently begins new thoughts at the beginnings of lines, except in lines 228 and 248. In both of these instances, she ends a thought mid-line and quickly follows it up with a self-pitying remark about Demetrius's mistreatment of her. But each time, Helena bounces back; and although she begins the monologue despairingly, she ends it on an optimistic note.

Don't forget to elide: *o'er* (ore) in line 226; *Demetrius* (Dih-MEE-tryuss) in lines 228 and 242; *Hermia's* (HER-myahz) in lines 230, 242, and 246, and *Hermia* (HER-myah) in line 244; and *showers* (SHOWRZ [rhymes with "sours"]) in line 245.

A MIDSUMMER NIGHT'S DREAM

ACT II, SCENE i

TITANIA

GENDER: F
AGE RANGE: adult
PROSE/VERSE: blank verse
FREQUENCY OF USE (1–5): 3.5

Oberon, King of the Fairies, and Titania, the Fairy Queen, have been having marital difficulties that stem from a dispute over a little human boy Titania has been raising, whom Oberon wants for himself. They have just met inadvertently in the forest and have resumed fighting. Titania has confronted Oberon with his affair with Hippolyta, the Amazon Queen. Oberon, in response, has just accused Titania of an affair with Theseus, Duke of Athens. Titania replies:

TITANIA

These are the forgeries of jealousy:
And never since the middle summer's spring
Met we on hill, in dale, forest or mead,
By pavèd fountain or by rushy brook,
85 Or in the beachèd margent of the sea
To dance our ringlets to the whistling wind,
But with thy brawls thou hast disturbed our sport.
Therefore the winds, piping to us in vain,
As in revenge have sucked up from the sea
90 Contagious fogs—which, falling in the land,
Hath every pelting river made so proud
That they have overborne their continents.
The ox hath therefore stretched his yoke in vain,
The plowman lost his sweat, and the green corn
95 Hath rotted ere his youth attained a beard.
The fold stands empty in the drownèd field,
And crows are fatted with the murrion flock.
The nine-men's-morris is filled up with mud,
And the quaint mazes in the wanton green,
100 For lack of tread, are undistinguishable.
The human mortals want their winter cheer—
No night is now with hymn or carol blessed.
Therefore the moon, the governess of floods,

81 *the forgeries of jealousy* i.e., lies provoked by jealousy; 82 *middle summer's spring* beginning of the midsummer season; 83 *mead* meadow; 84 *pavèd* pebbly; *rushy* full of rushes; 85 *beachèd margent* (MAR-junt) flat strip of seashore; 86 *ringlets* circle dances; *whistling wind* Titania is being literal: the whistling of the wind was the music to which the fairies danced; 87 *sport* fun, pleasure (can also mean "sensual enjoyment of love"; since Oberon has just accused Titania of having an affair with Theseus, you may choose to interpret her use of the word as a way of denying the affair without technically lying); 88 *piping* playing its music (on reeds, as though on flutes [most flutes in Shakespeare's time were made from reeds]); 89 *As in* In; 90 *Therefore the winds . . . Contagious fogs* Because of Oberon's repeated disturbances, Titania's company could not dance to the wind's music. Insulted and infuriated, the winds took revenge by creating an infectious fog out of water from the sea (with disastrous results, described next); 91 *pelting* piddling little; *proud* pumped up (both with water and with pride); 92 *overborne their continents* flooded over their banks; 93 *stretched his yoke* i.e., while pulling the plow; 94 *lost his sweat* i.e., wasted his efforts; *green* unripe, immature; *corn* grain from which bread is made (refers to wheat, not maize); 95 *ere* before; *attained a beard* matured; developed bristly, beard-like shoots; 96 *fold* sheep pen; *drownèd* flooded; 97 *fatted* made fat by eating; *murrion* infected with murrain, a disease of sheep and cattle; 98 *nine-men's-morris* a gameboard carved out of the turf, on which men played a game by the same name; 99 *the quaint mazes . . . are undistinguishable* the intricate series of paths in the luxuriant grass of the village green have become overgrown from lack of use and can't be made out from the rest of the grass; 101 *want* lack; 103 *moon* Diana, the goddess of the moon, to whom the hymns and carols should have been sung;

Pale in her anger, washes all the air
105 That rheumatic diseases do abound.
And thorough this distemperature we see
The seasons alter, hoary-headed frosts
Fall in the fresh lap of the crimson rose,
And on old Hiems' thin and icy crown
110 An odorous chaplet of sweet summer buds
Is, as in mockery, set. The spring, the summer
The childing autumn, angry winter change
Their wonted liveries; and the mazèd world
By their increase now knows not which is which.
115 And this same progeny of evils comes
From our debate, from our dissension:
We are their parents and original.

2 minutes

the governess of floods so called because the moon affects the tides, and could cause floods; 104 *washes all the air* fills the air with humidity (the moon was believed to shed moisture upon the earth); 105 *That* so that; *rheumatic diseases* (ROO´-muh-TIK) diseases that cause the eyes and nose to run; *do abound* are epidemic; 106 *thorough* through; *distemperature* can mean disorder of the body, the mind, or the weather: all three apply here; 107 *hoary-headed* white-headed (like the white-haired head of an elderly person) [*hoary-headed frosts . . . the crimson rose* a metaphor describing the chaotic untimely changes of season: the frosts of winter suddenly appear in the midst ("lap") of summer's blooms]; 109 *Hiems'* (HIE-umz, *not* HIE-umz-ez) Hiems is the elderly personification of winter; *crown* head; 110 *odorous* fragrant; *chaplet* wreath worn on the head; 111 *set* placed; 112 *childing* fruitful (since autumn is the season of harvest); 113 *wonted* usual; *liveries* garments; *mazèd* bewildered; 114 *By their increase* (in-KREESS) i.e., by what each season produces; 117 *original* source.

COMMENTARY

Don't be daunted by the density of this piece. If you break it down, you will see that Titania is telling a story with a natural progression of events—events that cause her great distress. As Queen of the Fairies, Titania is integrally connected to nature: as this monologue shows, the mental states of the Fairy King and Queen are physically manifested on earth, and the elements of nature communicate with Titania as they do not with mere mortals. These elements have faces and personalities. Thus, the personification used by Shakespeare as a literary device is for Titania a literal description of her friends in the natural world. The *whistling winds*, the *pelting* (and *proud*) *river*, the *green corn*, the *moon*, *Hiems'*, the *mazèd world*; all of these are actual beings in Titania's universe, who play roles in the story she tells. This story is told through vivid imagery: Titania describes the consequences of Oberon's bad behavior in graphic detail. Use her powerful images to your advantage—here is a perfect opportunity to use your visualization techniques to bring to life the chaos depicted in this piece.

Titania's outrage at Oberon is expressed in the meter, which contains many inverted feet, both at beginnings of lines and mid-line following caesuras; one such example is the very first word she speaks, which starts the piece off forcefully. Other examples include *Therefore*; *And the quaint*; *Pale in her anger*; *We are their parents*; etc. A first-foot inversion creates the illusion of more than usual stress on the fourth syllable in the line, because the two preceding syllables are both unstressed. A good example is the word *brawls*, which fairly leaps out of line 87. The line also contains an inverted foot mid-line, following a caesura that is not marked by punctuation, placing accusatory emphasis on the word *thou*:

/ x x / / x x / x /
But with thy brawls thou hast disturbed our sport

These variations naturally highlight the key words that express Titania's point: Oberon's aggression is to blame for their *dissension* and the earth's disasters. Be sure to pronounce the TH sounds of *with* and *thy* separately and distinctly, rather than slurring them together as they are in everyday speech, which will enhance Titania's defiant delivery.

With her emphatic use of the familiar forms *thee* and *thou* rather than the respectful "you," which a king might expect his wife to use in public, Titania asserts that, as Oberon's wife and Queen, she is his equal; her use of the form may even be intended as a put-down.

Music making and dance are among the chief pursuits of the fairies in this play. Titania's way of speaking reflects her musicality; her phrases have a melodic feel. Notice her extensive use of alliteration (e.g., *summer's spring*; *whistling wind*; *sucked up from the sea*; *pelting / proud*; *fold / field / fatted / flock*; *want their winter*; *No night is now*; *hoary-headed*; *sweet summer / set / spring / summer*; *now knows not*), as well as consonance and assonance (*forgeries of jealousy*; *beachèd margent*; *whistling wind*; *nine-men's-morris*; *quaint mazes*; *is as*; *which is which*; etc.). The many elisions in this piece also contribute to its smoothly flowing musicality, while the complete absence of casual contractions keeps the piece formal and powerful. Also note words which are either onomatopoeic or near onomatopoeic: e.g., *whistling*; *piping*; *proud* (in the sense of swollen).

Although the abundant description in this lengthy piece puts it in danger of becoming a "laundry list," staying invested in and advancing the story will keep the monologue active and the stakes high.

SIGNIFICANT SCANS

Line 116 traditionally requires the elision of both *our*s and the expansion of *dissension*, thus scanning as shown:

x / x / x / x / x /
From our debate, from our dissension

The expansion of *dissension* gives you the opportunity to express your scorn for it. But if you feel that this expansion will create unintended humor or go over the heads of your audience, you could choose instead to place a one-foot pause at the caesura (note the resultant double ending):

x / x / x / x / x / (x)
From our debate, (pause-pause) from our dissension

Don't forget to elide: *our* (owr) in lines 86 and 87, and (OWR) in both instances in line 116; *whistling* (WHISS-ling) in line 86; *murrion* (MUR-yun) in line 97; *undistinguishable* (UN-dis-TING′-gwish-BL) in line 100; *distemperature* (dis-TEMP′-ruh-CHUR) in line 106; *Hiems'* (HIE-umz, *not* HIE-umz-ez) in line 109; *odorous* (ODE-russ) in line 110; *mockery* (MOK-ree) in line 111; and *liveries* (LIV-reez) in line 113;

. . . and to expand: *pavèd* (PAY-vehd) in line 84; *beachèd* (BEE-chehd) in line 85; *drownèd* (DROW-nehd) in line 96; *mazèd* (MAY-zehd) in line 113; and *dissension* (diss-EN′-shee-UN) in line 116 (optional).

Also note the historic pronunciations of *rheumatic* (ROO′-muh-TIK) and *increase* (in-KREESS), which allow the proper scansion of lines 105 and 114.

Midsummer Madness

What is Midsummer Night, anyway? It is the eve of Midsummer, the summer solstice, or longest day of the year, when the sun is highest in the sky (June 21, by our present calendar). According to English tradition, however, Midsummer Day is celebrated on June 24, the feast day of St. John the Baptist, which places Midsummer Night on the twenty-third. A folk belief arose that the heat at Midsummer caused temporary madness. There was some truth to the belief: the height and duration of the sun at summer solstice produces extreme heat, increasing the possibility of sunstroke, which can sometimes cause hallucinations. Elizabethans labeled the erratic behavior arising from such hallucinations and the fantastic experiences reported by its sufferers "Midsummer madness."

Meteorological Madness

Since it is generally accepted that *Midsummer* was written in 1595 or 1596, Titania's description of terrible flooding, extended foul weather, and disordered seasons is probably a reference to the freak weather patterns that hit England in the years 1594–96, when Elizabethans found themselves huddled by the fire in mid-July and devastated by floods at Christmastime.

A MIDSUMMER NIGHT'S DREAM

ACT II, SCENE i

OBERON

GENDER: M
AGE RANGE: adult
PROSE/VERSE: blank verse
FREQUENCY OF USE (1–5): 3.5

Oberon, King of the Fairies, is angry that Titania, the Fairy Queen, will not give him the little human boy she has been raising. He has devised a plan to take revenge for her disobedience and to get the boy from her in the process. He sends Puck for the magical flower he will need to carry out this plan.

OBERON

My gentle Puck, come hither. Thou rememberest
Since once I sat upon a promontory,
150 And heard a mermaid on a dolphin's back
Uttering such dulcet and harmonious breath
That the rude sea grew civil at her song,
And certain stars shot madly from their spheres
To hear the sea-maid's music?

[PUCK: *I remember.*]

155 That very time I saw (but thou couldst not),
Flying between the cold moon and the earth,
Cupid all armed. A certain aim he took
At a fair vestal thronèd by the west,
And loosed his love-shaft smartly from his bow
160 As it should pierce a hundred thousand hearts.
But I might see young Cupid's fiery shaft
Quenched in the chaste beams of the watery moon,
And the imperial votress passèd on,
In maiden meditation, fancy free.
165 Yet marked I where the bolt of Cupid fell:
It fell upon a little western flower,
Before milk-white, now purple with love's wound;

148 *hither* here; *Thou rememberest* Do you remember; 149 *Since once* that time when; 151 *dulcet* gently melodious; *breath* singing; 152 *the rude sea grew civil at her song* the sea, which was acting impolite by being rough and choppy, improved its deportment and became calm when it heard her song; 153 *spheres* In Ptolemaic astronomy, the moon and stars were fixed in concentric crystalline spheres that carried them around the earth. What mortals would have seen as shooting stars, Oberon knew were stars shooting out of their spheres down to earth to hear the mermaid's alluring music; 156 *cold moon* Diana, goddess of the moon, was chaste and therefore referred to by Oberon as "cold" (i.e., frigid, sexless); 157 *A certain aim he took* He fixed his aim; 158 *fair* beautiful; *vestal* woman who has taken a vow of chastity; *thronèd by the west* seated with the western sky behind her, so that she seemed to be sitting on a throne made up of the light of the setting sun; 159 *loosed* let loose from his bow, shot; *love-shaft* arrow; *smartly* deftly; also, in a manner calculated to cause the sharpest love-pangs; 160 *As it should* as if it could; 161 *might* was able to; 162 *Quenched in the chaste beams of the watery moon* in Elizabethan times, the moon was believed to shed moisture upon the earth; to protect her devotee (the "vestal," above), Diana, goddess of the moon, shed misty moonbeams that diverted Cupid's arrow from its target; 163 *votress* woman who takes an oath (here the "vestal" mentioned above, who had taken an oath of chastity) [*imperial votress* see "Irrelevant History: Tickling the Queen's Fancy," page 352]; 164 *In maiden meditation* (1) in the reflection required by her religious order; also (2) thinking virginal thoughts; *fancy free* with no thoughts of love; 165 *marked I* I saw and made note of; *the bolt of Cupid* i.e., Cupid's arrow; 167 *Before* i.e., before being pierced by

And maidens call it "love-in-idleness."
Fetch me that flower—the herb I showed thee once.
170 The juice of it on sleeping eyelids laid
Will make or man or woman madly dote
Upon the next live creature that it sees.
Fetch me this herb, and be thou here again
Ere the leviathan can swim a league.

1 minute, 30 seconds

175 [PUCK: *I'll put a girdle round about the earth*
In forty minutes.] [*He exits*]

Having once this juice,
I'll watch Titania when she is asleep
And drop the liquor of it in her eyes.
The next thing then she, waking, looks upon—
180 Be it on lion, bear, or wolf or bull,
On meddling monkey or on busy ape—
She shall pursue it with the soul of love.
And ere I take this charm from off her sight
(As I can take it with another herb),
185 I'll make her render up her page to me.
But who comes here? I am invisible,
And I will overhear their conference.

2 minutes, 15 seconds

Cupid's arrow; *now purple with love's wound* the flower turned purple (as if entirely stained with blood) when pierced by the arrow; 168 *maidens* young, unmarried (and, of course, virginal) women; *love-in-idleness* a purple, white, or purple-and-white-streaked English pansy; 170 *on sleeping eyelids laid* when dropped upon the eyelids of a sleeping person; 171 *or man or woman* either a man or a woman; 174 *Ere* before; *leviathan* whale; also, a large sea monster; *league* a nautical unit of measurement equivalent to three miles; 176 *Having once* Once I have; 178 *liquor* liquid (with a play on "liquor's" intoxicating qualities); 182 *soul* quintessence; 183 *take this charm from off her sight* remove this spell from her eyes (returning her perception to normal); 185 *render up* hand over; *page* a young boy waiting on a person of distinction (in this case, the changeling boy whom Titania will not give to Oberon); 186 *I am invisible* with these words, Oberon makes himself invisible; 187 *conference* conversation.

COMMENTARY

Oberon's world is a place we would love to visit. His acquaintances include not only mortals, but also gods and goddesses, monsters and sea creatures. He is not speaking figuratively of seeing *Cupid* in action or of hearing the mermaid sing; nor does he consider these events to be out of the ordinary. His mention of a *dolphin*, *leviathan*, *lion*, *bear*, *wolf*, *bull*, *monkey*, and *ape* in this single monologue suggests that his interaction with the animal kingdom is an everyday occurrence. Similarly, his relationship to the elements of the cosmos is personal: the personification of the moon, stars, and sea used by Shakespeare as a literary device is for Oberon a literal description of his celestial and watery colleagues.

Fairies are not necessarily the innocent sprites they are reputed to be. In fact, in Elizabethan times they were thought of as malevolent creatures who reveled in tricking and tormenting humans. The fairies in *Midsummer*, however, have been toned down by Shakespeare and enjoy fairly harmless mischief and lechery. Oberon reveals his penchant for lewdness in the second segment of this piece, which is laced with double entendre. He uses suggestive language to recount the otherwise innocent story of Cupid's attempt to bring love into a nun's life, indicating that he sees the incident on a more base and physical level. As Oberon tells it, Cupid was on a mission: he did not want that vestal virgin to remain a virgin for long. He *loosed his love-shaft* (need we explain *love-shaft*?) with such virility *[a]s it should pierce a hundred thousand hearts* (or whatever other body parts might interest him). Sadly for Cupid, his *fiery shaft* was given a cold shower by Diana, the chaste goddess of the moon. Although he didn't score with the young beauty, *the bolt of Cupid* nevertheless ravaged the *little western flower*, which was *Before milk-white* with virginity, but is *now purple with love's wound*.

Oberon gleefully tells Puck how he discovered the flower's magical power. His excitement in relating the story and his eagerness to set his plan in motion are borne out in the verse. Every time Oberon introduces an important development in the story or wants to emphasize an element in it, the meter reflects the fact in one of two ways: (1) the first (normally unstressed) foot of a line is stressed (e.g., *Cupid all armed* in line 157 introduces Cupid; *Fetch* is so important to Oberon that he punches it twice, etc.); or (2) a new sentence begins in the middle of a line (e.g., *A certain aim he took* begins the central action of the tale; *I am invisible* accompanies an act of magic, etc.).

The Fairies' speech is more melodic than that of the mortals, reflecting their musical nature—dancing and music making are habitual and ritual activities. With its variations in meter, including extra feet in several lines—double endings both at line ends and mid-line before caesuras—this piece has an aggressive, sometimes syncopated, masculine cadence and musicality. This tone is enhanced by the hard-edged consonants throughout the monologue and the use of sound repetition. Notice the use of alliteration (e.g., *certains stars*; *all armed*; *loosed his love-shaft*; *maiden meditation*; *fancy free*; *meddling monkey*; etc.); consonance (e.g., *Since once I sat*; *rude sea grew civil*; *Quenched / chaste*; etc.); and assonance (e.g., *heard a mermaid*; *rude sea grew civil*; *or man or woman*; *make her render up her page*; etc.). And Oberon clearly relishes using near-onomatopoeic words, such as *dulcet*; *smartly*; *Quenched*; *wound*; *madly dote*; and *soul of love*.

SIGNIFICANT SCANS

Lines 154 and 176 are both shared with Puck, whose lines have been excised to create the monologue. We suggest that you use the resulting foot and a half of silence at the end of line 154 and the two and a half feet of silence at the beginning of line 176 to make your two key transitions in the piece. Both pauses are perfectly placed: the first as Oberon prepares to tell his story; and the second as he ushers Puck off on his errand and begins to formulate his plan.

Don't get hung up on line 163. Just elide *imperial* and expand *passèd* (and note the inversion of the first foot) and you're all set:

/ x x / x / x / x /
And the imperial votress passèd on

By expanding *passèd*, Oberon emphasizes the stunning failure of Cupid's plan.

Don't forget to elide: *rememberest* (re-MEM-brest) in line 148; *Uttering* (UTT-ring) and *harmonious* (har-MOE-nyuss) in line 151; *fiery* (FIE-ree) in line 161; *watery* (WA-tree) in line 162; and *imperial* (im-PEER-yal) in line 163;

. . . and to expand: *thronèd* (THROW-nehd) in line 158; *passèd* (PASS-ehd) in line 163; and *conference* (CON´-fer-ENCE) in line 187.

IRRELEVANT HISTORY: TICKLING THE QUEEN'S FANCY

Shakespeare knew which side his bread was buttered on: the "fair vestal" in this piece alludes to his patroness, Queen Elizabeth I, who was, at sixty-five—as her loyal subjects would (often and loudly) attest—still as lovely as a budding English rose. Woe unto the hapless courtier who failed to rein in his laughter at the notion of her floating by *[i]n maiden meditation, fancy free*. Throughout her long reign, the never-married Elizabeth enjoyed many close friendships with nobles of the opposite sex, but her PR campaign promoted her as the Virgin Queen, and her subjects accepted her as such with pride.

This monologue also would have tickled the Queen's fancy with its topical reference to the spectacular pageants frequently presented to entertain her, two of which are known to have included elements similar to those Oberon describes in the opening section of the piece.

A MIDSUMMER NIGHT'S DREAM

ACT III, SCENE ii

PUCK

GENDER: M
AGE RANGE: young adult to adult
PROSE/VERSE: rhymed iambic pentameter
FREQUENCY OF USE (1–5): 4

Puck has just been on an errand for his master, Oberon, King of the Fairies, which turned out better than he ever could have hoped: as instructed, he put a potion on the eyes of Oberon's sleeping queen, Titania, which makes the victim madly love the first thing she sees on waking (in this state, she will easily surrender to Oberon the little changeling boy she has adopted, whom Oberon wants as a page). Puck then had some fun at the expense of six bungling Athenians, sticking a donkey's head on one of them, which frightened the others out of their wits. Just then Titania waked, and immediately fell deeply in love with the monster Puck had created. Puck joyfully reports of his success to Oberon:

My mistress with a monster is in love!
Near to her close and consecrated bower,
While she was in her dull and sleeping hour,
A crew of patches, rude mechanicals
10 That work for bread upon Athenian stalls
Were met together to rehearse a play
Intended for great Theseus' nuptial day.
The shallowest thick-skin of that barren sort,
Who Pyramus presented in their sport,
15 Forsook his scene and entered in a brake,
When I did him at his advantage take:
An ass's nole I fixèd on his head.
Anon his Thisbe must be answerèd,
And forth my mimic comes. When they him spy—
20 As wild geese that the creeping fowler eye,
Or russet-pated choughs, many in sort,
Rising and cawing at the gun's report,
Sever themselves and madly sweep the sky—
So at his sight away his fellows fly;

6 *My mistress* i.e., my master's wife; 7 *close* enclosed, hidden, private; *consecrated* sacred; *bower* arbor; shelter of leaves and flowers (which serves as Titania's boudoir); 8 *in her dull and sleeping hour* i.e., fast asleep; 9 *patches* people who behave foolishly (a popular name for court fools or jesters, perhaps due to their multicolored clothing; here, Puck applies the term to a group of goofy laborers); *rude* crude, unrefined; *mechanicals* workmen; 10 *work for bread* i.e., earn their living; *upon* at; *stalls* small sheds in which occupations were carried out (such as carpentry, tailoring, weaving, etc.); 11 *Were met together* were meeting; had gathered together; 12 *Theseus'* Duke of Athens, and hero of ancient Greek mythology (see "Monster Slayer–cum–Statesman," page 329); *nuptial day* wedding day (Theseus is soon to be married to Hippolyta, Queen of the Amazons); 13 *shallowest* silliest, most stupid; *thick-skin* blockhead; person incapable of sensitive feeling (Puck insults the Athenian workmen by applying to them this common term for a stupid country bumpkin); *barren sort* stupid group; 14 *Pyramus* a young lover of classical legend, who killed himself when he mistakenly believed his beloved Thisbe was dead; she then woke to find him truly dead, and killed herself [*Who Pyramus presented* who played the role of Pyramus]; *sport* entertainment (in this case, the play they are rehearsing); 15 *Forsook his scene* left the area they used as a stage; *brake* clump of bushes; 16 *I did him at his advantage take* I took advantage of him; 17 *nole* head ("noodle"); *fixèd* attached; 18 *Anon* Soon, presently; *Thisbe* i.e., the workman who played the role of Thisbe, Pyramus's beloved; 19 *mimic* actor, player; *him spy* see him; 20 *As wild geese that the creeping fowler eye* like wild geese that see the creeping bird hunter; 21 *russet-pated* gray-headed (In Shakespeare's day, *russet* was applied to various shades of both gray and brown); *choughs* (CHUFFS) small Eurasian crows with glossy black feathers and red beaks and feet; *many in sort* i.e., in a large flock; 22 *Rising* i.e., flying up and away; 23 *Sever themselves* i.e., split up; 24 *So* i.e., just like the

25 And at our stamp, here o'er and o'er one falls;
He "murder" cries, and "help from Athens" calls.
Their sense thus weak, lost with their fears thus strong,
Made senseless things begin to do them wrong:
For briars and thorns at their apparel snatch;
30 Some sleeves, some hats—from yielders all things catch.
I led them on in this distracted fear
And left sweet Pyramus translated there;
When in that moment, so it came to pass,
Titania waked, and straightway loved an ass!

2 minutes

birds; *at his sight* when they see him; *his fellows* his fellow workmen; *fly* flee, run away; 25 *our stamp* the stamping of my foot; *here* now; *o'er* (ORE) over; *one* i.e., one of the men; 27 *Their sense thus weak* Their power of reasoning weakened in this manner; *lost with their fears thus strong* i.e., and overwhelmed because their fears are so strong; 28 *senseless things* inanimate things (things that are not sentient); *Made senseless things . . . wrong* i.e., their fear and the loss of their power to reason made inanimate things seem to harm them; 30 *from yielders all things catch* i.e., anything (e.g., briars, thorns, etc.) can steal from cowards who give up easily; 31 *distracted* maddening; 32 *translated* (tranz-LAY-ted) transformed; 34 *straightway* immediately; *an ass* i.e., Bottom, whose head has been replaced with that of an ass.

COMMENTARY

A hilarious story is never as much fun when you're alone as when you share it with a friend. Puck can't wait to share a laugh with Oberon over the practical joke he has just played. Even more to the point, he hopes to please his master with the wonderful, unexpected outcome of his prank. So Puck draws out the story, savoring all the colorful details, bringing them to life for Oberon, and proudly boasting of his own unbelievable success . . . Puck is sure to get extra credit for this one.

The meter is quite regular, and Puck elides and expands a number of words to make it so. And after the first line, with its alliterative Ms (*My mistress / monster*), the entire monologue falls into neat rhyming couplets. (If you're working on the piece within the context of the whole scene, notice that Puck's first line actually completes a rhyming couplet begun by Oberon.) The meter and rhyme combine to create an energetic yet incantatory feel that perfectly befits the mischievous, spell-casting Hobgoblin. These elements give the piece a bright and clever tone that perfectly embodies Puck's light and tricksy mood and personality—Puck is a fast thinker who can rhyme on his or her feet.

Puck is not only Oberon's right-hand fairy, but also his court jester. A seasoned storyteller, he sets the scene and weaves his tale easily, keeping the listener riveted by creating a build in the action. He reserves the use of imagery to describe the story's climax—the pandemonium Puck incited among the mechanicals. Notice that Puck uses inverted feet at the point in the story when all hell breaks loose (at the beginnings of lines 22–24 and after the caesura in line 25). These contrast with the piece's otherwise regular iambic pentameter, enhancing the atmosphere of hysteria. Afterward, Puck deftly creates a decrescendo in the story (with an accompanying cessation of inversions), preparing the way for a second build, which brings the story full circle and surprises Oberon with its punch line. You couldn't ask for a better arc in a monologue, so take advantage of it!

The phrase *our stamp* is much debated by scholars. Since Puck refers to the *stamp* as the action with which he set off all this pandemonium, the consensus among editors is that *our* is either his way of referring to an action he and Oberon customarily use in their magic, or is used jokingly in the sense of the royal "we." It has also been suggested that *our stamp* is a transcription error, and should be replaced with "a stump" (the man falls over a tree stump) or "one stamp" (shorthand for "at one stamp" which means "all at once"). We suggest you stick with *our stamp*, which is funny and right in line with the rest of the story, since Puck repeatedly highlights his own part in the action. Of course, you are free to use one of the alternative readings if it works for you.

And, of course, don't forget to address Puck's physical characteristics: body, movement, and voice. This is one of the most exciting aspects of playing a supernatural creature: there is no limit to where your imagination can take you. Notice that Puck tells the entire story in the present tense, a sure sign that she or he is fully involved in and actively conveying its progression—most likely reenacting it for Oberon to some degree. Have fun illustrating the story for Oberon as seen through Puck's eyes. Relating it with Puck's mischievous callousness and impish delight will give your performance color and depth.

Don't forget to elide: *bower* (BOWR) in line 7; *hour* (OWR) in line 8; *Athenian* (uh-THEEN-yun) in line 10; *Theseus'* (THEES-yuss, *not* THEES-yuss-ez) in line 12; *shallowest* (SHALL-west) in line 13; *our* (OWR) in line 25; and *briars* (BRYRZ) in line 29;

. . . and to expand: *fixèd* (FIX-ed) in line 17 and *answerèd* (AN´-ser-ED) in line 18.

A PUCK CONFORMABLE, AS OTHER HOUSEHOLD PUCKS

To Elizabethans, fairies and other supernatural beings were very real and not to be taken lightly. They were seen as generally malevolent creatures who emerged at night and harmed humans just for the fun of it, pinching them black and blue, playing tricks on them, or driving them mad. They would sometimes even steal human babies, leaving in their cradles fairy babes, or "changelings." A puck was one of the worst of these small but dangerous beings. A figure of folklore, the puck was identified in different European countries as an evil goblin, elf, or demon. Shakespeare's Puck combines this character with that of a mischievous sprite known as Robin Goodfellow, who had evolved from a devilish creature of Celtic folklore into a household spirit who swept out the house with his broom while its human inhabitants slept. Robin insisted on tidiness, and punished or played tricks on slovenly housewives. He could be an asset to the household if appeased with respectful treatment: he liked to be flattered and addressed by his given name, Robin, preferably in combination with the euphemism Goodfellow, but equally approved of the nickname Hobgoblin (Hob is the diminutive of Robin). Despite his benevolent side, Robin was still seen by Elizabethans as a frightening, malicious trickster. Shakespeare veered away from the devilish aspects of both of the characters he drew from, creating in Puck a fun-loving sprite who was mischievous rather than evil, who suited the playwright's own needs in *Midsummer* and who ensured that Robin Goodfellow would be playing his tricks for generations to come.

A MIDSUMMER NIGHT'S DREAM

ACT IV, SCENE i

BOTTOM

GENDER: M
AGE RANGE: adult to mature adult
PROSE/VERSE: prose
FREQUENCY OF USE (1–5): 3

The last thing he knew, Nick Bottom and his friends were in the forest outside Athens rehearsing a play to be performed for the Duke on his upcoming wedding day. Bottom had hoped to be amply rewarded for his moving performance in the important role of Pyramus, but now he finds that his fellow players have disappeared: he must have fallen asleep while waiting for his cue. As Bottom wakes, he recalls that he has had a most extraordinary dream, in which he had the head of an ass and was the pampered lover of Titania, the Fairy Queen (little does he know this was no dream . . .). Confused and excited, he soliloquizes:

205 When my cue comes, call me and I will answer. My next is "Most fair Pyramus—" Heigh-ho! Peter Quince! Flute the bellows-mender! Snout the tinker! Starveling! God's my life—stolen hence and left me asleep! I have had a most rare vision. I have
210 had a dream past the wit of man to say what dream it was. Man is but an ass if he go about to expound this dream. Methought I was—there is no man can tell what. Methought I was—and methought I had—but man is but a patched fool if he will offer
215 to say what methought I had. The eye of man hath not heard, the ear of man hath not seen, man's hand is not able to taste, his tongue to conceive, nor his heart to report what my dream was. I will get Peter Quince to write a ballad of this dream. It
220 shall be called "Bottom's Dream," because it hath no bottom; and I will sing it in the latter end of a play, before the Duke. Peradventure, to make it the more gracious, I shall sing it at her death.

1 minute, 30 seconds

206 *next* next cue; *fair* (1) handsome; (2) good; accomplished; *Pyramus* (PEER´-uh-MUSS) the romantic lead of the play Bottom was rehearsing (see "Never Was a Story Mangled Thus . . . ," page 363); *Heigh-ho!* two possible interpretations: (1) an exclamation used to call to a person at a distance; (2) a big yawn (since Bottom is just waking up); 208 *God's my life* a mild oath: possibly "God save my life" or "God bless my life"; *stolen hence* sneaked away; 209 *rare* extraordinary; *vision* triple meaning: (1) dream; (2) supernatural apparition (i.e., Titania); (3) a person of extraordinary beauty (again, Titania); 210 *past the wit of man* beyond the ability of the human mind; 211 *but* nothing but; *go about to expound* to take on the task of explaining in detail; 212 *Methought* It seemed to me; *can tell* who can tell; 214 *patched* wearing the many-colored clothing of a jester or fool; *offer* attempt; 215 *The eye . . . to report* a botched allusion to I Corinthians 2:9—see Commentary; 217 *conceive* understand; 218 *report* tell; 219 *of* about; 220 *hath no bottom* Bottom uses this phrase to mean "is deeply profound," unintentionally and unwittingly conveying the near-opposite meaning: has no foundation in reality; 221 *end* extremity [*the latter end* the last part]; 222 *the Duke* Theseus, Duke of Athens (see "Monster Slayer–cum–Statesman," page 329); *Peradventure* Perhaps; 223 *gracious* appealing, lovely; *her* refers to Thisbe, Pyramus's love interest.

COMMENTARY

The line between sleeping and waking often blurs, producing eerie experiences. We have all at some time awakened in a unfamiliar place and had a moment of utter confusion; most of us have also had the experience of waking from a dream so vivid and so moving that it haunts us. No wonder Bottom is overwhelmed—he believes that he is experiencing both of these disorienting phenomena at once!

Bottom's fragmented prose and his fits and starts at explaining his dream convey his confusion. His talent for botching language is exaggerated in this monologue, especially in the dramatic build of lines 215–18, where he alludes—intentionally or otherwise—to I Corinthians 2:9, but completely jumbles the word order. The passage to which he refers reads: "The eye hath not seen, and the ear hath not heard, neither have entered into the heart of man, the things which God hath prepared for them that love him. But God hath revealed them unto us by His spirit; for the spirit searcheth all things, yea the deep things of God!" The reference is relevant to Bottom's "dream" in that it, like God's gifts in the passage, cannot be expressed with words or felt by the senses, but has been communicated supernaturally. A 1557 version of the Bible translates the last phrase of the passage as "the Spirit searcheth . . . the bottom of God's secrets"—perhaps prompting Shakespeare to relate "God's secrets" to Bottom's dream, which *has no bottom*—i.e., is deeply profound. Although the events that Bottom remembers as a dream may seem frivolous, they are just the opposite. It would have been a rare and exciting experience for a commoner like Bottom to be treated as a special and valuable individual by anyone of higher rank, not to mention Titania, who is both a queen and a supernatural being. Despite his confusion, Bottom understands that he has had a profoundly meaningful experience, whether he perceives this extraordinary dream as a once-in-a-lifetime event or as yet another dramatic episode in the fascinating progression of the Life of Bottom. In any case, Bottom is a doer by nature, so he is not interested in sitting around analyzing his dream, but immediately hits on a plan to use it to enhance his performance before the Duke.

Although Bottom's unintentional play on words with the phrase *has no bottom* causes him to state unwittingly that his dream is without foundation in reality, his intended meaning also resonates with the audience, perhaps simply because he takes it so seriously himself. This monologue is particularly striking in that the laughter it provokes is tempered by a genuine pathos that arises from Bottom's utter sincerity and his poignant desire for achievement and affirmation. Bottom's aspirations are reflected in what he thinks of as refined, educated speech, with such impressive words as *expound* and *Peradventure*, and with technically correct but redundant-sounding phrases such as *offer to say* and *latter end of a play*.

Eighteenth-century editors suggested that the words *at her* in line 223 were a transcriber's error for "after," which would lead to the hilarious conclusion that in his role as Pyramus, Bottom intends to rise to his feet after his own death to sing the ballad. When the play is finally presented in Act V, Bottom's performance supports this idea. His protracted enactment of the suicide scene demonstrates that he is eager to extend his stage time. Although you could get away with the eighteenth-century change in the text, virtually all of today's editors retain the reading of the First Folio, as we have done. The words *at her* reveal a more layered intent for the passage. Upon waking, Bottom was confused by his belief that he was still at rehearsal and by the lingering *vision* in his mind. Whatever he recalls of the vision, he surely remembers his beautiful love interest and feels some pain at the loss of her, which would give him insight into Pyramus's pain at the loss of Thisbe. Perhaps his bewilderment has not completely dissipated by the end of the piece, and he has merged Thisbe and Titania in his mind. This idea is supported by his use of *a play* rather than "the play" in lines 221–22 and the vague *her death* in line 223. Thus it seems appropriate to Bottom that he will sing a ballad about Titania to commemorate the death of Thisbe.

Appellations Apropos to Aspiring Actors' Actual Avocations

In Act III, Scene ii, Puck refers to Bottom and his cohorts as a "crew of patches, rude mechanicals," meaning a paltry group of vulgar artisans and handicraftsmen. Although the term is now archaic, these characters are referred to as "the Mechanicals" by theatre folk to this day. Each of the Mechanicals' names alludes to his vocation. Nick Bottom is a weaver (in Shakespeare's day, the word *bottom* referred to the reel on which a skein of thread was wound). Peter Quince's name derives from *quines* or *quoins*, the wooden wedges he uses as a carpenter. Tom Snout is a tinker, who repairs kitchen and household utensils, particularly the "snouts," or spouts, of kettles. Francis Flute's name refers not only to his flutelike treble voice, which allows him to play a woman's role, but also to the fluted sides of the bellows and church organs he mends as a bellows mender. Robin Starveling, as his name implies, is extremely slim; tailors such as Starveling were proverbially thin (hence the Elizabethan saying "Nine tailors make a man"). And Snug's name refers to the tight, close-fitting joints in the furniture he makes as a joiner, or furniture maker.

Never Was a Story Mangled Thus, As This of Thisbe and Her Pyramus

Bottom and his friends have selected as their theme a romantic tragedy that first appeared in Ovid's *Metamorphoses* and that was well known to Shakespeare's audience. Pyramus and Thisbe were young lovers of ancient Babylon whose parents were sworn enemies. They arranged to meet in secret one night, and when Thisbe arrived first, she was frightened away by a lion. She dropped her veil as she fled. As it happened, the lion had just finished off a large, bloody ox. Finding the veil, he munched on it a bit, found it rather bland, and left it behind. Arriving on the scene moments later, Pyramus found the bloodied veil and, assuming Thisbe was done for, promptly killed himself. When Thisbe returned and found him, she followed suit. Story line sound familiar? *A Midsummer Night's Dream* and *Romeo and Juliet* were written during the same period. Although there is evidence that seems to suggest *Midsummer* was written on the heels of *R&J*, it is not conclusive. Whether the comedy inspired or parodied the tragedy, we'll never know.

A MIDSUMMER NIGHT'S DREAM

ACT V, SCENE i

SNUG

GENDER: M
AGE RANGE: any age
PROSE/VERSE: rhymed iambic pentameter
FREQUENCY OF USE (1–5): 1

A group of goofy laborers (a.k.a. "the Mechanicals"—see "Appellations Apropos to Aspiring Actors' Actual Avocations," page 362) have prepared a play, which they now present at the nuptial celebration of Theseus, Duke of Athens, and Hippolyta, the Amazon Queen. With this monologue, Snug earnestly seeks to reassure the ladies in the audience that he is only an actor portraying the character of Lion and not an actual beast.

You, ladies, you whose gentle hearts do fear
The smallest monstrous mouse that creeps on floor,
May now, perchance, both quake and tremble here,
225 When Lion rough in wildest rage doth roar.
Then know that I, one Snug the joiner, am
A lion-fell, nor else no lion's dam;
For if I should as Lion come in strife
Into this place, 'twere pity on my life.

30 seconds

223 *monstrous* shocking, horrible (with an unintended play on another common meaning for the word in Shakespeare's time, "enormous"); 224 *perchance* perhaps, maybe; *quake* tremble (Snug is unwittingly redundant); 226 *joiner* maker of wooden furniture; 227 *lion-fell* lion skin [*I, one Snug . . . lion-fell* Snug is explaining that he is merely draped in lion skin, but is just Snug the furniture maker underneath]; *dam* mother [*nor else no lion's dam* Shakespeare has made Snug so inarticulate that it is now unclear exactly what this means. Two possibilities: (1) nor is any lion's mother my mother (my mother is not a lion, so neither am I); (2) nor am I any lion's mother (and therefore am not a lion)]; 228 *as Lion come* come before you as a real lion; *in strife* intending violence; 229 *'twere pity on my life* (1) I would have to beg for pity, to spare my life (from the punishment I would receive if I were to frighten you); or (2) I would be unworthy of life (if I were to frighten you that way).

COMMENTARY

It is never specified whether Quince, the director, wrote this introduction for Snug, whether Snug says it "extempore"—as he was instructed to do (in Act III) when the play calls for him to roar—or whether Snug's speech lies somewhere between these two possibilities. We feel that the more active choice is that Snug speaks for himself, following guidelines laid out for him by his fellow actor, Bottom, in Act III, Scene i:

> . . . he himself must speak through, saying thus . . . "Ladies," or "Fair ladies—I would wish you," or "I would request you," or "I would entreat you—not to fear, not to tremble. My life for yours: if you think I come hither as a lion, it were pity of my life. No, I am no such thing. I am a man, as other men are"—and there indeed let him name his name, and tell them plainly he is Snug the joiner.

This choice allows you to have more fun with the content. For example, notice Snug's buildup, which culminates in the dramatic *When Lion rough in wildest rage doth roar*: perhaps Snug can't resist being just the teensiest bit scary before he reveals his identity in line 226. Also note how earnestly he makes Bottom's words his own, especially at the end.

Notice Snug's poetic flair in lines 223 (*smallest monstrous mouse*) and 224 (*both quake and tremble here*), and in his sudden change in rhyme scheme (probably unconscious) halfway through the piece. The simplicity of the rhymes, coupled with the simplicity of the meter, lends this piece a singsongy, almost childlike cadence, which befits Snug's self-described "slow[ness] of study."

The delightful liony irony of this piece is that Snug is terribly afraid that he will create too much dramatic effect with his performance (causing terror), when he actually creates too little (causing laughter). The absurdity is heightened by the fact that he delivers his speech principally to Hippolyta, Queen of the Amazons, who could probably bring a lion to its knees with one hand tied behind her back. Nevertheless, it is exactly the fact that Snug is oblivious to this irony that makes the piece so hilarious, so be sure not to play it.

IRRELEVANT HISTORY: WHO WAS THE KING OF BEASTS?
This monologue is a joke. One that was tailor-made for Queen Elizabeth's court, that is: in 1594, King James VI of Scotland proudly announced that at his infant son's christening the baptismal chariot would be drawn into the feast by nothing less than the king of beasts, an actual lion. As the great day

neared, however, the King realized that lions eat people, and that the lion might find his well-fed royal personage to be the choicest morsel in the banquet hall. Explaining that the ladies in the hall might be frightened by the sight of a real lion, King James, we are horrified to report, substituted a "Moor" (as Elizabethans referred to people of African descent).

Ladies, indeed. News of the King's chicken-heartedness traveled fast. The Elizabethan audience would have roared with laughter at this monologue's satire of their queen's timid Scottish counterpart. They knew that Queen Elizabeth could've eaten King James for breakfast.

P.S.

For information about the origin of our gentle friend's name, see "Appellations Apropos to Aspiring Actors' Actual Avocations," page 362.

MUCH ADO ABOUT NOTHING

ACT II, SCENE iii

BENEDICK

GENDER: M
AGE RANGE: young adult to adult
PROSE/VERSE: prose
FREQUENCY OF USE (1–5): 4.5

Benedick, a gentleman of the court of Don Pedro, Prince of Aragon, has long decried amorous relationships and the swift debilitation they visit on otherwise promising young men (though it is apparent to all but him that he himself is actually in love with Beatrice). In the orchard at the estate of Leonato, Governor of Messina, whom the Prince and his courtiers are visiting, Benedick bemoans love's hold on its latest victim, his close friend and comrade-in-arms Claudio.

I do much wonder that one man, seeing how much another man is a fool when he dedicates his behaviors to
10 love, will, after he hath laughed at such shallow follies in others, become the argument of his own scorn by falling in love—and such a man is Claudio. I have known when there was no music with him but the drum and the fife, and now had he
15 rather hear the tabor and the pipe. I have known when he would have walked ten mile afoot to see a good armor, and now will he lie ten nights awake carving the fashion of a new doublet. He was wont to speak plain and to the purpose, like an honest
20 man and a soldier, and now is he turned orthography; his words are a very fantastical banquet—just so many strange dishes. May I be so converted and see with these eyes? I cannot tell; I think not. I will not be sworn but love may transform me to an oys-
25 ter; but I'll take my oath on it, till he have made an oyster of me, he shall never make me such a fool.

7 *I do much wonder* I am amazed; 9 *dedicates his behaviors to love* i.e., devoting his attention to love, thereby displaying the various outward manifestations of being in love; 10 *shallow* silly, stupid; 11 *argument* subject; *of his own scorn* i.e., of the very thing he had derided in others; 13 *with* for; 14 *the drum and the fife* the musical instruments used for military music; *had he rather* he would rather; 15 *tabor* small handheld drum [*the tabor and the pipe* the musical instruments played during festivities and festivals, associated with merrymaking and dancing]; 16 *mile* miles; *afoot* on foot; *a good armor* a good suit of armor; 18 *carving* designing; *doublet* the short, tight-fitting jacket with or without sleeves that was the principal article of clothing of a Jacobean man; *was wont to* used to; 19 *to the purpose* to the point; 20 *is he turned* he has become an; *orthography* technically, the term means "the art of writing words with the proper letters, according to accepted usage" (considered an affectation, since spelling was not yet standardized in Shakespeare's time); here, Benedick means one who has become overelaborate in his choice and pronunciation of words; 21 *fantastical* full of fanciful notions or ideas; 22 *May I be so converted* Could I be transformed in this way? 23 *these eyes* i.e., the eyes of a lover; *I will not be sworn but love may* I can't swear that love won't; *oyster* Benedick may be referring to the moody silence of a lover, who has "clammed up"; 25 *I'll take my oath on it* I swear; *he* i.e., Love (possibly making metaphoric reference to Cupid, the mischevious god of love often referred

One woman is fair, yet I am well; another is wise, yet I am well; another virtuous, yet I am well; but till all graces be in one woman, one woman shall
30 not come in my grace. Rich she shall be, that's certain; wise, or I'll none; virtuous, or I'll never cheapen her; fair, or I'll never look on her; mild, or come not near me; noble, or not I for an angel; of good discourse, an excellent musician, and her hair
35 shall be of what color it please God. Ha! The Prince and Monsieur Love! I will hide me in the arbor.

1 minute, 50 seconds

to, simply, as Love); 27 *fair* beautiful; *well* healthy (i.e., not sick with love); 29 *graces* lovely and pleasing attributes (according to ancient Greek mythology, the three Graces were the goddesses who bestowed all beauty, charm, and gracefulness upon humanity); *one woman shall not* no one particular woman shall; 30 *my grace* my good will (punning on "graces," above); 31 *I'll none* I'll have none of her (i.e., I won't have her); 32 *cheapen her* bargain for her (with double meaning: "cheapen her virtue" [by sleeping with her]); *on* at; *mild* mild-mannered, gentle; 33 *noble* of a socially high-ranking family (with a pun on "noble": a gold coin worth one third of a pound); *not I for* I wouldn't have her even if she were; *angel* the heavenly variety (with a pun on "angel": a gold coin worth one half of a pound, i.e., I wouldn't pay an angel for her); *of good discourse* skilled at the art of conversation; 35 *of what color it please God* whatever color God wants it to be, i.e., I don't care what color her hair is, as long as it is the color God made it (rather than dyed); *Ha!* Benedick expresses surprise upon seeing the approach of Don Pedro and Claudio; *The Prince* i.e., Don Pedro; 36 *Monsieur Love* a sarcastic reference to Claudio; *me* myself.

COMMENTARY

Benedick is currently in the mental state affectionately referred to by Freudian theorists as "denial": in love with a woman who purports to loathe him, he won't admit his feelings for her, even to himself. He takes every opportunity to distance himself from the whole sordid business of love as well as from the entire female gender. Benedick probably also blames love for taking his good friend from him. A pang of jealousy is understandable: Claudio's focus is now elsewhere, and Benedick can no longer count on him for the same brotherhood they had previously enjoyed. It's not surprising that Benedick vents his frustration on love and women.

But Benedick is not a misogynist, despite his best attempts to prove himself one. It is important to know more about the plot in order to develop Benedick's character: once he finally does acknowledge his love for Beatrice (which happens later in this scene; see monologue, page 373), he shows rock-solid respect for her judgment, intellect, and integrity—as well as for Hero's character and virtue—and proves that he considers Beatrice his peer in every way. Furthermore, Benedick's own integrity is displayed more than once in the play. For example, he confronts the Prince when he thinks the Prince has wooed Hero for himself instead of for Claudio, a stance that could have proved dangerous had the Prince, in fact, done so. And he challenges Claudio to a duel for shaming Hero at their wedding, which severs his ties with both his Prince and his close friend. In both instances, it would have been simpler, more politically expedient, and less risky to stay uninvolved, but he chose to act unselfishly and honorably on behalf of others. Benedick is not one to take the easy road if it diverges from the ethical one. And, finally, his sense of humor reveals a keen intelligence. Note his witty puns (*grace . . . graces*; *noble . . . angel*), the first of which is combined with the rhetorical device of chiasmus (the inversion of the second of two parallel phrases or clauses); double entendre (*cheapen her*); and such phrases as *now is he turned orthography . . .* , *her hair shall be of what color it please God*, and *The Prince and Monsieur Love!*

Benedick's use of prose helps illustrate his disdain for Claudio's *orthography*, and emphasizes his own determination to *speak plain*, as he believes a bachelor should. He uses the effective device of antithesis to show himself how far Claudio has fallen: *one man* versus *another man*; *laughed at such . . . follies* versus *become the argument of his own scorn*; *the drum and the fife* versus *the tabor and the pipe*; *walked ten miles afoot* versus *lie ten nights awake*; *armor* versus *doublet*; *speak plain and to the purpose* versus *orthography*. He then uses repetition of words and phrases (examples include: *One woman*; *another*; *yet I am well*; *I'll never*) to prove his bionic immunity to love. Although Benedick is ostensibly using these devices to illustrate the monologue's overarching antithetical contrast of Claudio's weakness and his own invulnerability, they actually reveal a very different sentiment: his protestations permit him to fantasize about his dream woman . . . a clue that he secretly longs for exactly what Claudio has obtained.

What's in a Name?

Shakespeare chose the names of his contentious couple carefully: The name Benedick derives from the Latin *benedictus*, meaning "blessed"; Beatrice from the Latin *beatrix*, meaning "she who blesses." The play has contributed to the English lexicon as well: over time, a man who remains a bachelor has come to be referred to as a "Benedick."

MUCH ADO ABOUT NOTHING

ACT II, SCENE III

BENEDICK

GENDER: M
PROSE/VERSE: prose
AGE RANGE: young adult to adult
FREQUENCY OF USE (1–5): 4

After a resounding military triumph, Benedick and several of his friends have arrived at the home of Leonato, Governor of Messina, for a well-deserved rest. Among the lovely noblewomen residing here is Leonato's niece Beatrice, with whom Benedick once had an ill-fated romance. Beatrice and Benedick express their residual rancor through a long-standing verbal rivalry, and upon Benedick's arrival, the two picked up right where they left off, exchanging scathingly witty barbs at the expense of love and marriage in general, and each other in particular. Benedick is now in the orchard, where he has been marveling to himself that his friend Claudio has become a fool for love of Leonato's daughter Hero (see monologue, page 368). Spying his friends approaching, he hid in the bushes and was astonished to overhear that Beatrice is pining away with love for him but refuses to admit it, knowing of his disdain for love and for her (little does he know that they are staging this conversation as part of a plot to bring him and Beatrice together). Benedick's attitude toward love—and Beatrice—is almost instantaneously transformed. As his friends walk off, he soliloquizes:

This can be no trick: the conference was sadly
230 borne; they have the truth of this from Hero. They
seem to pity the lady; it seems her affections have
their full bent. Love me? Why, it must be requited.
I hear how I am censured: they say I will bear myself proudly if I perceive the love come from her;
235 they say, too, that she will rather die than give any
sign of affection. I did never think to marry. —I
must not seem proud. —Happy are they that hear
their detractions, and can put them to mending.
They say the lady is fair—'tis a truth, I can bear
240 them witness; and virtuous—'tis so, I cannot reprove it; and wise, but for loving me—by my troth
it is no addition to her wit, nor no great argument
of her folly, for I will be horribly in love with her. I
may chance have some odd quirks and remnants of
245 wit broken on me, because I have railed so long
against marriage, but doth not the appetite alter? A
man loves the meat in his youth that he cannot endure in his age. Shall quips and sentences and these

229 *conference* conversation; *sadly borne* seriously conducted; 230 *have the truth of this from* have been told that this is true by; 231 *the lady* i.e., Beatrice; *have their full bent* are strained to their limit (in archery, a bow has "full bent" when the string is drawn until the head of the arrow touches the bow); 233 *censured* judged (in Shakespeare's day, the word did not carry a negative connotation); 238 *their detractions* criticisms of themselves; *put them to mending* go about remedying them; 239 *fair* beautiful; 240 *reprove* (1) disprove; and/or (2) refute; 241 *but* except; *by my troth* (1) by my faith; (2) by my truth (a mild oath, or an assertion of one's honesty; with a possible allusion to pledging his troth [faithfulness] to Beatrice); 242 *wit* here, wisdom [*it is no addition to her wit* i.e., it is no credit to her intelligence]; *argument* evidence; 244 *chance* possibly; *odd* out of their proper context, leftover (i.e., no longer relevant); *quirks* witty expressions or puns; 245 *wit* here: humor [*odd quirks . . . broken on me* irrelevant witticisms and scraps of jokes told at my expense]; 247 *meat* food; 248 *quips* sharp, sarcastic remarks; *sentences* wise sayings, maxims; *these paper bullets of the brain* i.e., mere words taken from the pages of books and shot at the jokester's victim (as mere "paper bullets," the words will do him no real injury);

paper bullets of the brain awe a man from the
250 career of his humor? No—the world must be peopled. When I said I would die a bachelor, I did not think I should live till I were married. —Here comes Beatrice. By this day, she's a fair lady. I do spy some marks of love in her.

1 minute, 40 seconds

249 *awe* frighten; 250 *career* (1) short gallop at full speed; (2) course (as in a race); *humor* inclination (for a particular thing)—human inclinations and temperaments were thought by Elizabethans to be governed by one's physiological makeup (for further information, see "Elizabethan Anatomy 101," page 558) [*from the career of his humor* from galloping full speed ahead on the course toward the thing he desires]; 252 *should* would; 254 *marks* signs.

COMMENTARY

Having just soliloquized his disdain for Claudio's having fallen so easily and so headlong into love with Hero, Benedick now trips into an identical freefall for Beatrice. This is an extremely intelligent man—a war hero and verbal ace. We can only assume that deep down Benedick has been waiting for that nudge.

This former disparager of love now throws himself wholeheartedly into the melodrama and love talk he so recently derided: he recounts his love's beauty, virtue, and wisdom, uses an overwrought phrase to state that he *will be horribly in love with her*, and heroically declares that *the world must be peopled* (which is also a rationalization for doing so quick an about-face). Immediately after this monologue, he will greet Beatrice with a courtly line of verse, though he has just been speaking in (and she addresses him with) more mundane prose.

Benedick jumps haphazardly from one thought to the next as he juggles his previous disdain for love, his newfound affection for Beatrice, his compassion for her, his own pride, and his well-founded worry that he will be the butt of numerous jokes once his change of heart becomes public knowledge. Clearly, Benedick is more than a bit flustered and excited by the news he has just heard. In the First Folio, there are only four full stops in the entire piece, and even as we have punctuated it here there are noticeably fewer than usual, encouraging a quick pace and continuous flow that convey Benedick's state of mind.

Benedick's language in this monologue belies his discomfiture. Elsewhere in the play, his modus operandi is to deftly and coolly craft linguistic barbs intended to sting to the quick. Here, he does just the opposite. His simple speech could reveal that his previous verbal feats did not come to him naturally, but were part of a carefully constructed front, or that the recognition of his love for Beatrice makes him flustered, interfering with his natural talents. In this soliloquy, Benedick has let down his guard. His vulnerability, however, is tempered by the pride he still harbors. Notice that Benedick admonishes himself not to *seem proud*. He is willing to humble himself with Beatrice, but he is still the same self-confident Benedick, sure that he has not been tricked, and ready to rescue Beatrice from her current heartbreak, people the world, and dismiss his old attitudes with a number of clever rationalizations. Benedick's use of prose befits his candor and his spontaneous acknowledgment of his true feelings; it allows his earnestness and genuine concern for Beatrice (*Love me? Why, it must be requited*) to outshine his pride.

P.S.

Impress your friends with Benedick trivia: see "What's in a Name?," page 372.

THE TAMING OF THE SHREW

ACT IV, SCENE i

PETRUCHIO

GENDER: M
AGE RANGE: adult
PROSE/VERSE: blank verse
FREQUENCY OF USE (1–5): 4

Petruchio accomplished both of his goals while visiting in Padua: he had a lovely time with his good friend Hortensio, and found himself a rich wife, Katherina. The fact that she is a renowned shrew doesn't worry him. He has just brought her home to his country house and has begun the process of taming her. So far, so good. He shares his game plan in a soliloquy.

Thus have I politicly begun my reign,
And 'tis my hope to end successfully.
My falcon now is sharp and passing empty,
And till she stoop she must not be full-gorged,
195 For then she never looks upon her lure.
Another way I have to man my haggard,
To make her come and know her keeper's call:
That is to watch her, as we watch these kites
That bate and beat and will not be obedient.
200 She ate no meat today, nor none shall eat;
Last night she slept not, nor tonight she shall not—
As with the meat, some undeservèd fault
I'll find about the making of the bed,
And here I'll fling the pillow, there the bolster,
205 This way the coverlet, another way the sheets.
Ay, and amid this hurly I intend
That all is done in reverend care of her.
And in conclusion, she shall watch all night,
And if she chance to nod I'll rail and brawl
210 And with the clamor keep her still awake.
This is a way to kill a wife with kindness,
And thus I'll curb her mad and headstrong humor.
He that knows better how to tame a shrew,
Now let him speak—'tis charity to show.

1 minute, 30 seconds

191 *politicly* shrewdly or wisely, with the skill of a ruler; 193 *falcon* type of hawk, often trained for use in hunting (here, Petruchio refers to Katherina); *sharp* hungry, eager; *passing* extremely; *empty* hungry; 194 *stoop* descend quickly on its prey, as trained to do; *full-gorged* fully fed, sated; 195 *never looks upon* would never look at; *lure* decoy, device used in training falcons; 196 *Another way I have* I have another way; *man* tame, make accustomed to men; *haggard* wild adult hawk, usually female; 198 *watch* here, keep awake (in falconry, hawks were kept awake as an integral part of their training); *kites* falcons (also a term of contempt; may also be a pun on "Kate"); 199 *bate* flutter the wings; attempt to escape a falconer's wrist; *beat* flap the wings with force, possibly in anger; 200 *nor none shall eat* nor shall she eat any; 204 *bolster* a long, decorative pillow; 205 *coverlet* bedspread; 206 *hurly* commotion, tumult; *intend* pretend; 207 *reverend* reverent, humble, showing every respect; 208 *watch* here, stay awake; 209 *chance* happens; *nod* nod off; *rail* complain vehemently; *brawl* make noise, create a disturbance; 210 *still* continually, constantly; 212 *humor* temperament, disposition; 214 *charity* a kind act, a good deed; *shrew* a sharp-tongued, scolding woman (see "All Shrews Beshrewed," page 958); *show* reveal (it).

COMMENTARY

Tame Your Shrew in Two Days or Less . . . or Your Money Back! Petruchio has developed a surefire method for breaking the will of his sharp-tongued and headstrong new wife. As he explains, it's just like taming a falcon. A wild falcon's will was traditionally broken using hunger and sleep-deprivation techniques.

Petruchio's cute little falconry metaphor also contains not-so-cute double entendre. While the sexual overtone is still evident today, the extent and specificity of the entendre is revealed only when the archaic bawdy meanings of certain words are understood. We'll interpret some words, and you take it from there: *stoop* = bend over (for sex); *full-gorged* = fully filled; *haggard* = whore; *come* = [you know this one]; *keeper* = pimp; *to man* = to possess sexually; *watch* = keep awake (by having sex); *bate and beat* = put up a fight.

This piece is also crowded with consonance: most instances contain hard, manly consonants, such as Tough Ts (*That / bate / beat / not / obedient / ate / meat / today*), Brawling Bs (*bate and beat and will not be obedient*), Cruel Ks and hard Cs (*make / come / keeper's call / kites*; *kill / kindness / curb*), Nasty, Negative Ns (*no / nor / none / night / not / nor / tonight / not*), and Churlish CHs (*watch / chance*). As he begins to sum up, relishing his certain conquest, Petruchio lolls about in pLeasurabLe Ls (*I'll / rail / brawl / clamor / still / kill*), and harps on Hearty Hs (*headstrong humor / He*). He also uses a bit of swaggering assonance (*man / haggard*; *beat / be / obedient*). And you have a choice to make regarding the final two lines, which form a historic rhyme: in Shakespeare's day, the words *shrew* and *show* rhymed. While a rhyming couplet is a stylish way to end a piece, you risk losing the audience's comprehension. Also, they may think you are making a joke when you don't mean to.

Notice the orderly, no-nonsense parallel phrase structure Petruchio employs. This is boot camp, after all: *She ate no meat today, nor none shall eat*; / *Last night she slept not, nor tonight she shall not*; *And here I'll fling the pillow, here the bolster, / This way the coverlet, another way the sheets.*

SIGNIFICANT SCANS

In the first line, the word *politicly* is pronounced PAW´-li-tik-LEE and contains a crowded foot (—*liticly*) in addition to its inverted first foot:

/ x x /x-x/ x / x /
Thus have I politicly begun my reign

The frequency of aggressive-sounding inverted feet such as this one increases as the monologue progresses, suggesting that his enthusiasm for the plan grows as he describes it.

Line 205 contains a rare triple ending mid-line before the caesura (in addition to its inverted first foot):

/ x x / x-x x / x / x /
This way the coverlet, another way the sheets

And don't forget to elide: *obedient* (oh-BEE-dyent) in line 199.

TWELFTH NIGHT

ACT 1, SCENE 1

ORSINO

GENDER: M
AGE RANGE: adult
PROSE/VERSE: blank verse
FREQUENCY OF USE (1–5): 3

Orsino, Duke of Illyria, is madly in love with the idea of being in love . . . um, we mean, with Olivia, a countess living nearby. The feeling is not mutual, and she consistently rejects his advances, driving him to distraction. He has sent one of his gentlemen-in-waiting to plead his love suit once more, and languishes in agony while awaiting the man's return.

If music be the food of love, play on—
Give me excess of it, that, surfeiting,
The appetite may sicken, and so die.
That strain again! It had a dying fall;
5 O, it came o'er my ear like the sweet sound
That breathes upon a bank of violets,
Stealing and giving odor. Enough; no more! –
'Tis not so sweet now as it was before.
O spirit of love, how quick and fresh art thou,
10 That, notwithstanding thy capacity,
Receiveth as the sea: nought enters there
Of what validity and pitch soe'er,
But falls into abatement and low price.
Even in a minute. So full of shapes is fancy,
15 That it alone is high fantastical.

O, when mine eyes did see Olivia first,
20 Methought she purged the air of pestilence!
That instant was I turned into a hart;
And my desires, like fell and cruel hounds,
E'er since pursue me.
[*Enter Valentine*]
How now! What news from her?

1 minute, 15 seconds

2 *excess* (ek-SESS) too much; *surfeiting* feeling sick as a result of excess; 4 *That strain again* i.e., play that passage of music again; *dying fall* a musical device in which the melody moves upward to a peak, only to plummet suddenly to one of its lowest tones; 5 *the sweet sound . . . bank of violets* i.e., the wind; 8 *so* as; 9 *quick and fresh* alive and energetic; 10 *That* in that; *capacity* here, meaning the outer limit of its power to contain; 11 *Receiveth as the sea* i.e., receive without limit; *nought* nothing; *there* the sea (i.e., that sea of love); 12 *validity and pitch* high value and superiority (in falconry, the "pitch" was the highest point of a bird's flight) [*Of what validity and pitch soe'er* of any high value and superiority whatsoever]; 13 *abatement* diminished regard; *price* estimation; 14 *Even in a minute* In just a minute [*notwithstanding . . . in a minute* disregarding its actual capacity, the lover's spirit takes in everything without limit, like the sea, but whatever enters there, regardless of its high value, quickly loses its worth]; *shapes* fantasies; *fancy* love; 15 *alone* without a parallel; *high* highly; *fantastical* imaginative (Shakespeare's use of the word carried a negative connotation) [*it alone is high fantastical* i.e., it is unparalleled in its imaginative ability]; 19 *mine* my; *did see Olivia first* first saw Olivia; 20 *Methought* It seemed to me; 21 *hart* a male deer; 22 *fell* fierce, savage, cruel [*That instant was I . . . pursue me* Orsino refers to the myth of Acteon, a hunter who inadvertently stumbled upon the chaste goddess Diana while she bathed and was caught admiring her. The furious goddess turned him into a stag, and his own hunting dogs turned on him and killed him]; 24 *How now!* an exclamation of surprise; *from her* i.e., do you bring from Olivia.

COMMENTARY

These are the opening lines of the play, and they establish the atmosphere of dis-ease that pervades Illyria. Their inherent melodrama—Orsino's angst, expressed in lofty imagery, far outweighs its cause—also introduces humor, which assures the audience that although Orsino suffers now, he will eventually live happily ever after. This frees you to commit fully to Orsino's languor and malaise without playing the humor—it will emerge from the context on its own. Similarly, though you-the-actor may realize that Orsino is in love with the agony of being in love, you-the-character have no idea that this is so. Orsino genuinely believes Olivia to be the object of his tormented passion, and your performance must not comment on him; rather, you must invest in this belief. This monologue establishes elements of Orsino's character: his cultured poetic and musical nature; his obsession with his unrequited love; and his royalty and the resultant unfamiliarity with being denied his every wish.

The monologue contains three discrete sections. In lines 1–8, Orsino focuses on the role music plays for one in love, and his desire to be stuffed with it so that it might quell his appetite for love. When performed in production, the first part of this monologue is actually accompanied by music, so it is fitting that the section's meter (mostly smooth iambic pentameter, with the occasional inverted foot and only one mid-line double ending) and its sounds combine to lend it a lyrical quality. Notice the staccato effect of *it, that, surfeiting*, the rise and fall of *so die* and *dying fall* (which mimics the *dying fall* Orsino mentions—see Annotation), the conjuring up of woodwind instruments with *sweet sound / breathes / Stealing*, and the operatically sweeping and emotive Os of *so / O / o'er / odor / no / more / so / before*. Also note that Orsino uses the word *O* three times in this short piece (for more on this, see "O, No! An *O*!," page xxiii). All of these musical elements suggest that Orsino loves the operatic melodrama of being lovesick. In fact, Orsino does not take even the slightest pause to listen to the music he's just ordered his musicians to repeat. He talks right through it and then moodily and abruptly orders it halted in lines 6–8. He reinforces the order's finality with a rhyming couplet—often used to signal the end of a soliloquy or scene—in lines 7–8 (*no more / before*), which is amplified by *odor*, in line 7.

In the next section of the monologue (lines 9–15) Orsino tackles the *spirit of love* itself: being in love with the pain of unrequited love rather than with an actual reciprocating person (in exemplary Petrarchan fashion), Orsino has come to believe that love encompasses more than it is capable of absorbing and thereby devalues its own love object, as well as anything that satisfies the lover's desire (such as the music he's been listening to, which is *not so sweet now as it was before*). Orsino's simile of love absorbing endlessly like the sea, swallowing up more than it can accommodate, subtly suggests the idea of overeating to the point of nausea, as well as the nausea of seasickness. The implications complement his earlier image of bingeing on *the food of love* to the point of nausea in order to lose all taste for love. Also notice that for all Orsino decries love as something that *alone is high fantastical*, it is actually he himself who is being so.

Only in the final section (lines 19–24) does Orsino acknowledge the alleged object of his desire. But after dedicating a mere two lines to her, he quickly returns to his main topic . . . the effect of love upon himself—and discusses the pain he has felt since being struck by love. Of course, it is possible to decide that Orsino avoids thinking of Olivia directly because her rejection of him has been too painful to bear. But this interpretation does not negate the fact that Orsino is devoting all of his energy to being as fully lovesick as possible.

Orsino's grand imagery is the primary tool with which he picks the scabs of his love wounds. The imagery engages all the senses. It reveals a person with finely honed aesthetic sensibilities, who notices and loves the beauty of nature but who also probes at nature's ugly side (for example, in Orsino's references to the sickness brought on by gluttony, and the vicious killing of a deer by hounds). Orsino's allusion to classical mythology is consistent with the classical education he would have received as a member of royalty. Orsino's royalty is also manifested in his use of several imperatives (*play on*; *Give me*; *That strain again*; *Enough*); as a duke, he is accustomed to commanding others to satisfy his slightest whim. These impatient imperatives, combined with Orsino's self-pity, compound the sense of his moodiness.

SIGNIFICANT SCANS

This moodiness is reinforced by the meter, in which the flow of the regular iambic pentameter is broken by several inverted feet at the beginnings of lines, punching the first words of those lines and creating the sense that Orsino is agitated, as well as emphatic about what he is saying. In addition to the inverted foot at the beginning of line 5, another appears unexpectedly mid-line, following a caesura that is not marked by punctuation (a rare occurrence):

/ x x / x / / x x /
O, it came o'er my ear like the sweet sound

There are also a sprinkling of double endings, both at ends of lines and mid-line before caesuras, usually at the end of a protracted image, suggesting that Orsino is running on about his obsession. An example is line 7, which has both an inverted first foot and a double ending before the caesura.

Line 14 is even trickier to scan, with an inverted first foot (in which *Even* is elided [EEN]), and double endings both before the caesura and at the line's end:

/ x x / (x) x / x / x /(x)
Even in a minute. So full of shapes is fancy

Don't forget to elide: *spirit* (SPEERT) in line 9; *Even* (EEN) in line 14; *Olivia* (o-LIV-ya) in line 19; and *desires* (de-ZIRES) in line 22;

. . . to contract: *o'er* (ORE) in line 5; *soe'er* (so-AIR) in line 12; and *e'er* (AIR) in line 23;

. . . and to expand: *cruel* (CROO-ell) in line 22—though Orsino is ostensibly discussing his desires (describing them as *cruel hounds*), this expansion emphasizes the cruelty of Olivia's rejection, which keeps his desires from being sated.

TWELFTH NIGHT

ACT II, SCENE ii

VIOLA

GENDER: F
AGE RANGE: young adult
PROSE/VERSE: blank verse
FREQUENCY OF USE (1–5): 5

Shipwrecked and helpless on the shores of Illyria, Viola disguised herself as a young man and sought out employment with the local ruler, Duke Orsino. Orsino has been pining away for the Countess Olivia, who repeatedly rejects him. En route home after an unsuccessful attempt at winning Olivia's love for her master (which was difficult, since she herself has fallen desperately in love with him), Viola (dressed as "Cesario") has just been accosted by Olivia's steward Malvolio, who rudely "returned" a ring Viola supposedly left with her. Malvolio told "Cesario" that Olivia "will have none of [his] lord's ring," threw the ring on the ground, and left. Viola soliloquizes:

I left no ring with her. What means this lady?
Fortune forbid my outside hath not charmed her.
20 She made good view of me—indeed so much
That methought her eyes had lost her tongue,
For she did speak in starts distractedly.
She loves me sure; the cunning of her passion
Invites me in this churlish messenger.
25 None of my lord's ring? Why, he sent her none;
I am the man. If it be so, as 'tis,
Poor lady, she were better love a dream.
Disguise, I see thou art a wickedness
Wherein the pregnant enemy does much.
30 How easy is it for the proper false
In women's waxen hearts to set their forms.
Alas, our frailty is the cause, not we,
For such as we are made of, such we be.
How will this fadge? My master loves her dearly;
35 And I, poor monster, fond as much on him;
And she, mistaken, seems to dote on me.
What will become of this? As I am man,
My state is desperate for my master's love.
As I am woman—now alas the day!—
40 What thriftless sighs shall poor Olivia breathe?
O time, thou must untangle this, not I,
'Tis too hard a knot for me t'untie.

1 minute, 30 seconds

19 *Fortune* i.e., the goddess Fortune (who determines human destiny) [*Fortune forbid* an expression similar to "God forbid"]; *outside* appearance; 20 *made good view of* (1) took a good look at; and/or (2) looked favorably at; 21 *her eyes had lost* what she saw had made her lose; 22 *in starts* disjointedly; 23 *sure* for sure; *cunning* craftiness; 24 *in* by means of; *churlish* rude [*churlish messenger* i.e., Malvolio] [*Invites me in this churlish messenger* uses this churlish messenger to allure me]; 26 *the man* i.e., the man whom she loves; *'tis* i.e., it seems to be; 27 *were better love* would be better off loving; 29 *pregnant* clever, artful [*the pregnant enemy* i.e., Satan]; 30 *proper* fine, handsome (used of men) [*the proper false* good-looking, deceitful men]; 31 *waxen* i.e., malleable, impressionable; *set their forms* imprint their images [*In women's waxen hearts . . . forms* to embed themselves firmly in women's hearts]; 34 *fadge* succeed, i.e., work itself out; 35 *monster* unnatural creature (because she is, at the moment, both man and woman); *fond as much on him* (1) love him as deeply (here, *fond* is a verb); or (2) am as deeply in love with him (here, *fond* is an adjective); 36 *dote on* love excessively (a different meaning than it has today, here emphasizing feelings rather than actions); 38 *desperate* hopeless [*As I am man . . . my master's love* i.e., dressed as a man, my desire for my master's love is hopeless (with secondary meaning: in my current state—shipwrecked with no resources and dressed as a man—I am desperately in need of my master's good favor, so I must go on wooing Olivia)]; 40 *thriftless* unprofitable, i.e., having no hope of success.

COMMENTARY

There is a good reason directors have heard the "ring speech" so many times that it now causes them to roll their eyes or cringe: it's a great audition piece! It's simple, straightforward, and easily understood, and provides an interesting and active progression for the actor. Viola's best qualities shine through in its lines: her optimism, her empathy, her open self-reflection, her willingness to let go of troubles she cannot solve today—everything audiences love her for. We suggest that you go ahead and use this monologue when you are doing class-work or performing in or auditioning for *Twelfth Night*, but that you think twice before making it your principal audition piece. These days directors will take points off just for having to sit through it for the sixty-seventh time that day.

When approaching this soliloquy, the first decision you must make is to whom it is addressed. Is Viola working the problem out for herself (retaining the fourth wall), or is she sharing her thoughts with the audience? Or is it a combination of the two? If you decide to engage the audience when performing this piece in an audition, just remember not to use the director or her assistant as your target. Place an imaginary audience member elsewhere in the room.

This monologue has an absolutely divine, defined progression, which is accented by variations in meter and sound repetition. For instance, in the first line Viola establishes the truth about the ring (*I left no ring with her*) and the question it raises (*What means this lady?*), clearly delineating the two steps with the caesura, and drawing attention to the question with the double ending. In the following line, Viola's new thought is emphasized by an inverted foot (*Fortune*), another double ending, and the alliteration and assonance of *Fortune forbid*. The next important step is Viola's conclusion in line 23 that Olivia is definitely in love with her. Here we find another double ending, as well as the SHs and Es of *She loves me sure*. In lines 25–26, Viola's realization that Olivia has sent the ring as a message to her rather than Orsino is emphasized by three aggressive inverted feet (one beginning each line, and the third after the caesura in line 26).

Notice that Viola's language complements the tone set by the meter: line 25 is made up of direct, single-syllable words, and line 26 is even more pointed, containing only single-syllable words with no compound consonants. The sound repetitions in line 26 of As and Ms (*am / man*) and IHs (*If it / 'tis*) emphasize her startling statement of the problem at hand.

In the lines that follow, the metrical variations cease as Viola begins to think about Olivia's fate, the complicated consequences of her disguise, and the unfortunate inability of women (including herself) to keep from falling for the Mr. Wrongs of the world. When Viola finally returns to the matter at hand, her new line of thought (*How will this fadge?*) is kicked off by the inverted first foot and the double ending in line 34, contributing to her I-can't-believe-the-mess-I'm-in-ish tone. Be careful not to anticipate ideas before their time. Use the cues in meter and sound repetition to help you delineate each step in Viola's thought process.

Keep your ears open for additional sound repetition in the piece. Some examples are: Ss (*speak / starts*); EHs (*pregnant enemy*); Z sounds and IHs (*easy is it*); Ws and ENs (*women's waxen*); Ts and Ss (*hearts to set*). Notice the effect of the one-syllable string full of hard consonants (R, Ds, K, Ts) that imitate Olivia's tongue-tied speech: *For she did speak in starts*. The rhyming couplet in lines 32–33 (*we / be*) neatly wraps up the first large section of the monologue before Viola launches into her concluding lines. Another rhyming couplet (*I / t'untie*) ties up the loose ends in lines 41–42 (no pun intended), finishing the piece in an upbeat manner that perfectly expresses Viola's optimistic attitude. And for help using the word *O* to its best advantage, see "O, No! An *O*!," page xxxiii.

Sound repetition isn't the only repetition that provides clues to Viola's attempts to make sense of her conundrum. Repetition of words, phrases, and sentence structure is the tool with which she seeks to *untangle* this complex *knot*. Notice the similarity in structure among the lines that introduce the three major sections of the monologue: lines 18, 25, and 34 all contain caesuras with full stops. Line 18 begins with a statement, then continues with a question. In line 25, this order is reversed, but there is the added similarity of the *ring* being mentioned in the first part of both lines. Line 34 follows line 25 exactly in structure: a question; full stop; a phrase setting up the next argument.

In lines 25 and 33 the repetition of the words *None* and *such* (respectively) clarify and emphasize Viola's meaning. The repetition of similar phrasing in lines 35–36 (*And I . . . on him / And she . . . on me*) combined with the identical structure of the two lines helps Viola express the differences among Orsino's infatuation, Olivia's, and her own. The repetition of phrasing in lines 37 and 39 (*As I am man / As I am woman*) lays out clearly the antithesis between Viola's problems as a man vs. as a woman.

Viola's choice of imagery reveals her vulnerability and her strength: she sees her heart (and those of all women) as made of wax, in which men easily imprint their images. This image makes her next statement (*our frailty is the cause, not we*) less repugnant to today's sensibilities than the proverbial idea it relates to (women as the weaker sex), in that the *frailty* Viola describes is not a weakness, but simply the human tendency to fall in love without reason or control. The imagery also contains an allusion to Satan (*the pregnant enemy*) disguising himself as a snake and tempting Eve. Thus Viola reveals a rational ability to face her own faults with aplomb.

Although there are no actual embedded stage directions, there are two important aspects of the situation to consider and make physical. First, remember that Malvolio has just thrown the ring into the dirt. You have the option of picking it up and using it as you wish during the piece. It can be a helpful prop, prompting your thoughts at moments in the speech. You will then have to consider whether to wear the ring (what sign would that send Olivia?), put it away in a pocket, or leave it on the ground. Considering that but for her disguise Viola would be homeless and destitute in Illyria, it seems unlikely that she would leave such a valuable item behind. Second, remember that Viola's clothing is part of her current identity, and she examines it directly in this piece. If you are performing in a production of the play, you will have costume items to play with. But even if you are doing classwork or auditioning, your clothing is important. As always, you'll want to wear regular clothing that works well with the role you are playing—i.e., in this case, slacks, not a skirt. Since Viola suddenly sees her own disguise as wicked during this monologue, you may want to consider wearing something you can work with, such as a hat, jacket, or vest. When experimenting with such an item, think about what it means to Viola: her disguise is simultaneously her protector (providing her livelihood and keeping her safe from rape), a handicap (preventing her from revealing her love to the Duke), and a harmless influence (encouraging Olivia to love "Cesario"). Viola may feel torn between throwing off her disguise for good and hiding even more securely under it.

SIGNIFICANT SCANS

Notice that line 21, as it appears above (and in the First Folio), requires a pause during the second syllable of the first foot:

x / x / x / x / x /
That (pause) methought her eyes had lost her tongue

You could use the pause to remember that moment at Olivia's home, to think of a good way to express Olivia's reaction when she looked at you, or perhaps to imitate Olivia's hesitation. Alternatively, some editors fill out the line's meter by adding the word *sure* (following the Second Folio), making the line regular iambic pentameter:

x / x / x / x / x /
That sure methought her eyes had lost her tongue

This choice allows the thought to flow more smoothly. Choose whichever version best suits your interpretation.

Line 42 is also headless (with no alternatives) and contains the contraction *t'untie* (tun-TIE):

x / x / x / x / x /
(pause) 'Tis too hard a knot for me t'untie

In the First Folio, lines 32–33 read:

Alas, O, frailty is the cause, not we,
For such as we are made, if such we be.

Almost without exception, editors have amended this passage as it appears in the monologue, above. We have kept the change because it is now so commonly used that the original may sound like an error to someone not intimately familiar with the text. Nevertheless, feel free to use the First Folio version, which makes sense if understood to mean "Alas, O, frailty is the cause, not we women, for this is how we must naturally behave, since we are women."

Don't forget to elide: *Olivia* (o-LIV-ya) in line 40.

TWELFTH NIGHT

ACT II, SCENE v

MALVOLIO

GENDER: M
AGE RANGE: adult to mature adult
PROSE/VERSE: prose (with some verse)
FREQUENCY OF USE (1–5): 3

Malvolio has a difficult job as steward of the Countess Olivia's household, what with her waiting-gentlewoman Maria, her drunken uncle Sir Toby Belch and their friends carousing at all hours of the night, and the lady of the house herself in mourning. If only the Countess would get over her brother's death and take notice of her handsome and capable steward, the situation would be vastly improved. Malvolio has just been fantasizing about marrying Olivia and becoming the count, when he comes upon a rather interesting letter (which, unbeknownst to him, was forged by Maria and planted for him to find).

91 What employment have we here?
[*he picks up a letter from the ground*]

95 By my life, it is my lady's hand: these be her very
Cs, her Us, her Ts, and thus makes she her great Ps.
It is in contempt of question her hand.

[*he reads*]
To the Unknown Beloved this, and my Good Wishes.
Her very phrases! By your leave, wax. —Soft, and
the impressure her Lucrece, with which she uses to
105 seal. 'Tis my lady. —To whom should this be?

[*he reads*]
Jove knows I love,
but who?
Lips, do not move;
110 *No man must know.*
—"No man must know." What follows? The
numbers altered. "No man must know." If this
should be thee, Malvolio!

[*he reads*]
115 *I may command where I adore,*
But silence, like a Lucrece knife,

91 *employment* business; 95 *my lady* term of address for a woman of high rank; here, my employer, the Countess Olivia; *hand* handwriting; 96 *great* capital; 97 *in contempt of question* i.e., without a doubt; 102 *Unknown* unconscious, unaware (that he is beloved); *this* i.e., the letter itself; 103 *By your leave, wax* a conventional expression by which the reader begs pardon of the wax seal on a letter before breaking it; in Shakespeare's day, the letter would simply be folded over and sealed, rather than sent in an envelope; *Soft* Wait a minute; 104 *the impressure her Lucrece* (in this line, pronounced loo-CREESS) the impression (in the wax seal) is her Lucrece. (The seal that Olivia uses on her letters is apparently a picture of Lucretia, a beautiful Roman noblewoman who was famed for her virtue. After being raped [and thus dishonored], Lucretia became a symbol of chastity for centuries to follow; she is also the subject of Shakespeare's narrative poem *The Rape of Lucrece*); *uses to seal* customarily seals; 107 *Jove* Jupiter, king of the gods in ancient Roman mythology (often used interchangeably with the Judeo-Christian God in Shakespeare); 111 *The numbers altered* The meter (of the poetry) is altered; 116 *Lucrece knife*

With bloodless stroke my heart doth gore;
M.O.A.I. doth sway my life.

121 "M.O.A.I. doth sway my life." Nay, but first, let me see, let me see, let me see.

"I may command where I adore." Why, she may command me; I serve her, she is my lady. Why, this is evident to any formal capacity. There is no ob-
130 struction in this. And the end—what should that alphabetical position portend? If I could make that resemble something in me! Softly, "M.O.A.I."—

137 "M" . . . Malvolio. "M"—why, that begins my name!

141 "M" . . . But there is no consonancy in the sequel; that suffers under probation: "A" should follow, but "O" does.

147 And then "I" comes behind.

"M.O.A.I." This simulation is not as the former, and yet to crush this a little, it would bow to me, for every one of those letters are in my name. Soft, here follows prose:
[*He reads*]
155 *If this fall into thy hand, revolve. In my stars I am above thee, but be not afraid of greatness. Some are born great, some achieve greatness, and some have greatness*

(here LOO-creess) Lucretia committed suicide by stabbing herself; 118 *sway* rule; 129 *formal capacity* normal intellect; sane mind; *obstruction* difficulty, obstacle; 130 *should* could; 131 *position* positioning, placement; *portend* signify; 132 *Softly* Gently, carefully; 141 *consonancy* agreement, consistency; *the sequel* that which follows; 142 *suffers under probation* i.e., becomes strained under close examination; 151 *simulation* disguise, i.e., hidden message; *as the former* like the preceding one; 152 *to crush* i.e., if I force; *bow to me* accommodate me; 155 *revolve* think, consider;

thrust upon 'em. Thy Fates open their hands. Let thy blood and spirit embrace them. And, to inure thyself to
160 *what thou art like to be, cast thy humble slough and appear fresh. Be opposite with a kinsman, surly with servants. Let thy tongue tang arguments of state. Put thyself into the trick of singularity. She thus advises thee that sighs for thee. Remember who commended thy yel-*
165 *low stockings and wished to see thee ever cross-gartered. I say, remember. Go to, thou art made, if thou desir'st to be so. If not, let me see thee a steward still, the fellow of servants, and not worthy to touch Fortune's fingers. Farewell. She that would alter services with thee,*
170 *—The Fortunate-Unhappy.*

Daylight and champian discovers not more! This is open. I will be proud, I will read politic authors, I will baffle Sir Toby, I will wash off gross acquain-

stars i.e., destiny; 158 *Fates* in classical mythology, the three goddesses who control human destiny [*Thy Fates open their hands* i.e., your Fates are reaching out to you]; 159 *blood* passion, emotions; *spirit* courage; *inure* accustom; 160 *like* likely; *cast* shed, throw off; *slough* (pronounced sluff) skin of a snake, i.e., accustomed humble demeanor; 161 *opposite with* hostile to; contrary with; *kinsman* i.e., Olivia's uncle, Sir Toby Belch; 162 *tang arguments of state* twang loudly with political opinions; 163 *trick* particular habit; *singularity* peculiarity [*Put thyself into the trick of singularity* Get into the habit of acting peculiar]; 165 *ever* always; *cross-gartered* wearing garters made of ribbon that cross behind the knee and tie in a large bow in front, above the knee (a fashion popular from 1560 until c. 1600, cross-gartering may have been a sign of a hopeful lover, in contrast to the despairing lover, who went "ungartered"); 166 *Go to* a phrase used for emphasis, here meaning approximately "I'm telling you"; *made* (1) fortunate; (2) wealthy (with a play on the idea that Olivia will "make" Malvolio fortunate and wealthy); 167 *steward* one who manages an estate [*let me see thee a steward still* i.e., continue behaving like a steward in front of me (with implied second meaning, I'll see to it that you remain a lowly steward)]; *fellow* equal; comrade; 168 *Fortune* the power that determines human destiny, personified; 169 *alter services with thee* exchange positions with you, i.e., be servant of you who serve me (as your obedient wife), playing on both (1) marry you in an "altar service" at church and (2) have sexual intercourse with you (*alter* and *serve* were common Elizabethan slang terms for "copulate"); 171 *champian* (CHAM-pee-un) flat, open country (a variant of *champaign*); *discovers* reveals; 172 *open* evident, perfectly clear; *proud* arrogant; *politic authors* writers who are experts in politics; 173 *baffle* publicly humiliate (a play on words, since Sir Toby is a

tance, I will be point-devise the very man. I do not
175 now fool myself, to let imagination jade me; for
every reason excites to this, that my lady loves me.
She did commend my yellow stockings of late, she
did praise my leg being cross-gartered, and in this
she manifests herself to my love and, with a kind of
180 injunction, drives me to these habits of her liking. I
thank my stars, I am happy. I will be strange, stout,
in yellow stockings, and cross-gartered, even with
the swiftness of putting-on. Jove and my stars be
praised! Here is yet a postscript:
185 [*he reads*]
Thou canst not choose but know who I am. If thou entertain'st my love, let it appear in thy smiling; thy smiles become thee well. Therefore in my presence still smile, dear my sweet, I prithee.
190 Jove, I thank thee! I will smile. I will do everything
thou wilt have me.

5 minutes

knight: *baffle* is a technical term from chivalry, denoting a punishment by which a perjured knight was publicly disgraced, and which included being hung up by the heels); *gross* crude, base; 174 *point-devise* (POYNT´-dih-VICE´) precisely (from the French *à point devis*, arranged to a point); *the very man* i.e., exactly the man the letter describes; 175 *jade me* trick me; make me appear ridiculous and contemptible (a "jade" is an unruly horse: Malvolio means he does not intend to be tricked or made to look foolish like a confident rider who either [1] is suddenly thrown from his horse or [2] suddenly finds that his horse has slipped its head out of the collar and escaped, leaving him stranded); 176 *excites to this* urges this conclusion; 179 *manifests herself to my love* reveals her desire for my love; 180 *these habits* this attire; 181 *happy* lucky, fortunate; *strange* aloof; *stout* arrogant, haughty; 182 *even with the swiftness of putting-on* i.e., just as quickly as I can put them on; 186 *Thou canst not choose but know* i.e., you must know; *entertain'st* accept; 188 *still* continually; 189 *prithee* entreat you (from "pray thee"); 191 *wilt have me* want me to do.

COMMENTARY

Although Malvolio shares a few characteristics with the conventional Elizabethan "stage steward" and "stage Puritan," he is far more complex than either of those stock characters. Malvolio has many human elements that inspire sympathy and even a little respect in addition to the usual disdain and ridicule. If you play Malvolio as a well-rounded character rather than a caricature—especially if you are working on this monologue in the context of the whole play—you will be well rewarded with a performance that is not only funny, but richly meaningful as well.

Malvolio has no idea that the letter he finds is a forgery planted by Maria to trick him. As the son of a yeoman (a servant one class below a gentleman), Malvolio is less educated and less sophisticated than Maria, who as a waiting-gentlewoman is probably an impoverished relative or friend-of-a-friend of Olivia's. Maria has the advantage of being a gentlewoman familiar with the ways of the upper class, knows her mistress's handwriting well enough to mimic it, and, most important, is sharp as a tack. She has played directly to Malvolio's dearest wish, and he is easily taken in by the letter: he is delighted by the simplistic and sentimental poetry, which Olivia would never have been caught dead writing; he is swayed by the repeated use of the familiar *thee* and *thou*, which is appropriate between lovers; and he is probably impressed by the elegant use of assonance and consonance in the prose section of the letter (*surly with servants*; *tongue tang*; *She thus advises thee that sighs for thee*), perhaps even accentuating the sounds as he reads, savoring them.

For the audience, one of the most delightful aspects of this monologue is watching Malvolio fall for the letter hook, line, and sinker, despite his determination to decipher its meaning meticulously. Malvolio is well aware of the possibility of making an error in interpreting the letter, so he analyzes it step by step until he is convinced, and able to state, *I do not now fool myself, to let imagination jade me*. Be sure to break the piece down and pay close attention to each adjustment as Malvolio goes through this process. The many embedded stage directions within the piece will help to guide you: *What employment have we here?* (he sees the letter); *By my life, it is my lady's hand* (he examines the outside of the letter); *By your leave, wax* (he prepares to open the letter); *Soft, and the impressure her Lucrece* (he stops himself from opening the letter, and examines its seal). Another way to trace Malvolio's thought process is to discover or decide when he is reading; when he is speaking to himself, to the letter, to *Jove*, etc.; and when he is rereading part of the letter or simply repeating to himself something he has read. Notice that it is not until the very last sentence in the piece that Malvolio addresses Olivia herself (or the letter itself). Malvolio now feels fully confident, and ready to face his love as an equal. He even addresses her as she addresses him in the letter, with the intimate *thou* (which Malvolio the steward could never do with the countess he works for). Keep in mind that Malvolio is seeing the letter for the first time: he is surprised, delighted, and excited by what he finds there. Keep your reactions fresh by controlling the impulse to anticipate the letter's contents.

The final step in Malvolio's analysis of the letter contains a long build, which starts in line 171, when he concludes that he has clearly understood the letter's meaning (with *This is open*), and runs all the way to *Jove and my stars be praised* in line 183. The build starts with the repetition of *I will* in five consecutive phrases, confirming that he will follow all the instructions in the letter. The build continues as Malvolio enumerates all the ways in which the letter refers to him, and then lists additional specific behaviors with which he will meet the letter's requests, again starting with *I will*. This is a long build, and although it may have a few dips in it, it is nevertheless continuous. Plan ahead, and leave room for an escalation in energy and pace. At the end of the monologue take advantage of the final *I will*, which now resonates with the excitement of the previous build.

Just before he discovered the letter, Malvolio was fantasizing that he was the Count, married to and dallying with Olivia. He has been practicing the lofty speeches he, as the Count, would use to address Olivia's servants and kinsman Toby Belch. Malvolio continues to use elevated language throughout the monologue (*What employment have we here?*; *evident to any formal capacity*; *what should that alphabetical position portend?*; *there is no consonancy in the sequel*; *This simulation is not as the former*; *point-devise the very man*; *she manifests herself to my love*). He is practicing these phrases in earnest, since this is exactly the sort of speech he believes befits a count. The attempt itself is evidence of Malvolio's humble origins: he does not feel that his own speech is appropriate to a person of higher rank. Indeed, Malvolio is correct in his analysis, for his language and allusions are notably unsophisticated. He speaks in inelegant prose, uses unnecessarily overblown words, and frequently mentions his *stars* and his fate in a superstitious rather than philosophical manner. Malvolio sounds most genuine and unaffected toward the end of the monologue when he earnestly exclaims *Jove and my stars be praised!* and *Jove, I thank thee!* Perhaps in his excitement he has dropped his high-class pretensions. Be sure to experiment with possible deliveries of the word *smile* for the customarily dour Malvolio. The word is conducive to an awkward, exaggerated grin. Or perhaps Malvolio even tries out a few different facial expressions Olivia might like. Either way, you're sure to come up with something hilarious!

You will notice that two of the four letters Malvolio examines on the outside of the note do not actually appear in the words he reads there. It has been suggested that the full address might read "To the Unknown Beloved, this, and my good wishes, with Care Present," which was one of the customary ways of addressing a letter in Shakespeare's day. In any case, the letters Malvolio picks out are not chosen at random by Shakespeare. Hearing the first three letters, Elizabethan audience members would have spelled out in their minds the word *cut*, which in their time had a much less innocent second meaning: for the word's contemporary equivalent, add an *n*. Accordingly, Elizabethans would have interpreted *thus makes she her great Ps* to mean "thus she urinates (pees) abundantly." Nevertheless, Malvolio is oblivious to these bawdy jokes, and you should most certainly not play them overtly. There is one sexual double entendre, however, that you may decide Malvolio intends. The phrase *She that would alter services with thee* has two secondary meanings, as the annotation indicates. Depending on your interpretation of Malvolio's character, you may choose to have him react only to the primary meaning, or to one or both of the secondary meanings.

One last note: the ambiguous punctuation of this material in the First Folio allows lines 141–42 to be read two different ways. We have chosen the reading that is more accessible to today's audience, but you may prefer to change the punctuation and read the word as follows: ". . . But there is no consonancy in the sequel that suffers under probation." With this punctuation, the word *suffers* means "bears up under." The two possible readings give *suffers* almost exactly opposite meanings!

Malvolio: Named in the Name of Jesting

Malvolio is so much more complex than the stock steward and, as many believe, Puritan characters from which he is drawn that many scholars believe he must have been invented to lampoon a specific person. The chief suspect is one Sir William Knollys, Queen Elizabeth's Comptroller of the Royal Household (an office analogous to Malvolio's position as Olivia's steward). Knollys was notoriously infatuated with a much younger woman, Mary Fitton, who was one of the Queen's Maids of Honor. It has been proposed that Malvolio's name is a threefold mockery of Knollys: the name, broken down to its Italian roots (*mal* = ill; bad; evil; and *voglia* = will; desire) means both "ill-will," playing on the Comptroller's intolerance for fun and laughter; and "evil desire," ridiculing the old, married man's lecherous desire for young Mary Fitton. Even more pointedly, "Malvolio" plays on the nickname by which everyone knew Mary Fitton: Mall. To Elizabethans of the royal court, where the play was performed at least once, Malvolio's name repeated again and again throughout the play would have sounded much like a repetition of the Italian phrase *Mall voglio*, or "I want Mall." Poor old humorless Knollys—Malvolio's humiliation in the play would have paled in comparison with his.

Why the Punishment Fit the "Crime"

For Elizabethans, Malvolio's situation reflected the complex societal changes they were experiencing. As the feudal system broke down, wealthy landowners had less need for the protection of—and less money to support—"retainers" (such as Sir Toby, Fabian, Sir Andrew, and Feste). Meanwhile, services and comfort were becoming more important and, as a result, people of lower classes (such as Malvolio) were seen to be edging out people who ranked above them. Also distressing to those higher up the ladder was the emerging pattern of people improving their societal rank by marrying above their birth. Malvolio's ambition to do so would have outraged the many gentry in Shakespeare's audiences during public performances. This explains why Elizabethan theatregoers accepted and even enjoyed Malvolio's humiliating punishment, which seems vastly out of proportion today.

TWELFTH NIGHT

ACT III, SCENE i

OLIVIA

GENDER: F
PROSE/VERSE: blank verse
AGE RANGE: young adult to adult
FREQUENCY OF USE (1–5): 2

The Countess Olivia has secluded herself from the world to mourn the recent death of her brother. She is being wooed relentlessly by Duke Orsino of Illyria but does not return his affection and has consistently turned away the messengers he has been sending to plead his love suit . . . until the arrival of his new page, "Cesario"—who, unbeknownst to Olivia, is actually a woman in disguise. The witty, charming, and attractive page talked his way into her home and into her heart. After he left, bearing away another rejection message to Orsino, Olivia planted the seeds for a return visit: she sent her steward after "the youth" with a ring she professed he'd just left with her from the Duke, though "Cesario" never gave her any such ring. "Cesario" has now returned and begins to woo her again on Orsino's behalf, but Olivia interrupts him with:

O by your leave I pray you,
I bade you never speak again of him;
But would you undertake another suit,
120 I had rather hear you to solicit that
Than music from the spheres.

[VIOLA: *Dear lady—*]

Give me leave, beseech you. I did send,
After the last enchantment you did here,
A ring in chase of you. So did I abuse
125 Myself, my servant, and, I fear me, you.
Under your hard construction must I sit,
To force that on you in a shameful cunning
Which you knew none of yours. What might you think?
Have you not set mine honor at the stake
130 And baited it with all th' unmuzzled thoughts
That tyrannous heart can think? To one of your receiving
Enough is shown; a cypress, not a bosom,
Hides my heart. So, let me hear you speak.

1 minute

117 *by your leave* with your permission; *pray* ask earnestly; 118 *bade* (BAD or BAID) commanded; 119 *would you* if you would; *suit* i.e., love suit [*would you . . . another suit* implying: if you would undertake to woo me on your own behalf]; 120 *had rather* would rather; 121 *from the spheres* i.e., from the heavens (in Shakespeare's time, the English still believed the concepts of Ptolemaic astronomy, according to which the sun, moon, and stars circled the earth in crystalline spheres, each of which produced a musical tone, harmonious with the others but inaudible to the human ear); 122 *Give me leave* i.e., please allow me to continue; *beseech you* I urgently implore you; 123 *enchantment* charm [*the last enchantment you did here* i.e., "Cesario's" last visit to Olivia, during which Olivia became enchanted with "him"]; 124 *I did send . . . A ring in chase of you* i.e., I sent . . . a servant chasing after you to give you a ring; *So* In this manner; *abuse* both (1) deceive and (2) disgrace; 125 *my servant* i.e., her steward, Malvolio, whom Olivia sent chasing after the departing "Cesario" to give "him" the ring; *I fear me* I am afraid; 126 *hard* harsh; *construction* manner of construing something [*Under your hard construction must I sit* i.e., you surely must judge my action harshly]; 127 *that* a thing (i.e., the ring); *cunning* falseness [*in a shameful cunning* by means of a disgraceful trick]; 128 *knew none of yours* knew was not yours; 129 *honor* good reputation (in Elizabethan times, a woman who was as forward with a man as Olivia has been with "Cesario" was often perceived as wanton, lewd, unchaste, etc.) [*set mine honor at the stake . . . heart can think* Olivia uses the metaphor of "bear-baiting," a form of popular entertainment in Shakespeare's time in which a bear was tied to a stake and set upon by vicious and hungry dogs, who ripped it to shreds while it did its best to defend itself. Olivia likens her honor to the bear and "Cesario's" thoughts to the attacking dogs]; 131 *receiving* intelligence, perception; 132 *Enough is shown* i.e., I have revealed enough (about my feelings); *cypress* a thin, sheer fabric similar to crepe, often in Shakespeare's time dyed black and used for mourning garments, originally purchased from Cyprus [*a cypress . . . my heart* i.e., my love for you is only thinly veiled].

COMMENTARY

We often hear that bravery entails confronting known danger despite one's fear of it. Olivia's delivery of this monologue, in which she is painfully honest to "Cesario" about her shameful ring ruse and her feelings for him, and risks censure by the person she loves, is just such an act of bravery.

Olivia is accustomed to giving orders to underlings; she immediately follows her initial solicitous overture toward Orsino's page (*O by your leave I pray you*) with the authoritarian *I bade you never speak again of him*, but then quickly remembers herself and reverts to language of parity with *But would you . . .* From that moment on, she ceases to treat "Cesario" as a page and becomes simply a woman in love with a man (well, at least as far as *she* knows). Note the progression in her solicitousness toward "Cesario," as she moves from simple courtesy in line 117 to downright entreaty in line 122.

And then comes the heart of Olivia's speech (lines 122–28), in which she is honest and remorseful about her prior subterfuge. The simple and straightforward language of this section supports its confessional tone. It is important not to imbue simple language with undue "emotionality"; simple words call for simple delivery of the lines. Perhaps Olivia has rehearsed these lines over and over in her head ever since she sent Malvolio chasing after "Cesario" with the ring. Or you may decide that Olivia feels relief at finally "coming clean" to Cesario, or that although she is fighting internal turmoil, she manages to maintain her calm outward demeanor. You may decide that at different moments she is feeling aspects of each. Olivia keeps a lid on her inner turmoil until she can do so no longer: the outburst *What might you think?* that follows, and the reversion to complex language with the extended bearbaiting metaphor, are clues that she has been entertaining complex thoughts and emotions which have finally surfaced. Your interpretation of the contrast Olivia makes between "Cesario's" *tyrannous heart* and her own vulnerable one, protected by no more than a mere *cypress*, will inform these choices.

As the monologue progresses, Olivia grows increasingly less subtle in expressing her love for "Cesario": she first hints at wanting Cesario to plead *another suit* (meaning, but not saying, "your own"); then uses the simple word *that* (again, meaning "your love suit"); then calls his last visit *the last enchantment you did here* (now saying that "he" enchanted her . . . charming, but still ambiguous); then says that "Cesario" knows her drift (*To one of your receiving / Enough is shown*) and that it is not necessary to state how she feels (although to encourage his reciprocity, she uses subtly sexually suggestive words to make this point—*a cypress, not a bosom, / Hides my heart*). These examples reveal her shyness or nervousness with "Cesario" and/or her inherent "feminine virtue" and modesty. It can also be argued that although indirect in her language, Olivia is actually being quite bold by advancing her feelings at all (particularly as many times as she does in one short monologue), rather than waiting to be wooed by the man she loves, as was expected in her day.

There are a few well-placed instances of assonance and consonance to play with, such as the plEAding EEs of *me / leave / beseech* and the Heaving Hs of *heart / Hides / heart / hear*. And for help using the sound of the word *O* to its best advantage, see "O, No! An *O*!," page xxxiii.

SIGNIFICANT SCANS

The first, excised portion of line 117 (spoken by "Cesario") is two feet long, creating two silent feet at the start of Olivia's first line and indicating that Olivia's three final feet have a double ending (note that the first of these feet is inverted):

/ x x / x / (x)
O by your leave I pray you

There are two silent feet at the end of line 121 (one is intentional; the other is due to "Cesario's" excised dialogue). During this pause, Olivia prepares to bite the bullet and acknowledge her trickery as well as her love for "Cesario," so you can use the silent feet (plus the silent half foot at the beginning of line 122) to make this transition.

Do not belabor this pause, however, since the next line (the headless line 122) is used to cut off "Cesario" before "he" can prevent Olivia from saying what she needs to say:

x / x / x / x / x /
(pause) Give me leave, beseech you. I did send

When scanning line 124, take just a one-syllable pause at the caesura and treat the line as a hexameter (a rare six-footed line):

x / x / x / x / x /x /
A ring in chase of you. (pause) So did I abuse

Even after you elide *tyrannous*, line 131 has a surprising thirteen syllables—it is a hexameter with a double ending:

x / x / x / x / x / x / (x)
That tyrannous heart can think? To one of your receiving

The line's unexpected length is the crescendo of the monologue: in this line Olivia is at her most anguished and most vulnerable, and she courageously discloses her feelings of love for "Cesario." Of course, you are free to buck tradition and decide that Olivia used the bear-baiting metaphor manipulatively, to establish to "Cesario" that she is vulnerable and then proclaim her love, perhaps counting on "his" chivalry to prevent "him" from wounding her further by rejecting her.

Note that line 133 is also headless, but the double ending from the line before creates the illusion that it is not. Don't fall into that trap: be sure to take your natural pause at the end of line 132 and your one-syllable pause at the head of 133, and see what this does for your delivery. Perhaps Olivia is flustered by having used the word *bosom*, or perhaps she struggles to bring her words back into line and stop babbling before she embarrasses herself further.

Don't forget to elide: *tyrannous* (TIR-nuss) in line 131;

. . . and to contract: *I had* (I'd) in line 120; and *th' unmuzzled* (thun-MUZ-zld) in line 130.

THE TWO GENTLEMEN OF VERONA

ACT I, SCENE ii

JULIA

GENDER: F
PROSE/VERSE: blank verse
AGE RANGE: young adult
FREQUENCY OF USE (1–5): 5

Julia's waiting-woman, Lucetta, has been teasing her mercilessly about Proteus, one of Julia's many suitors. Lucetta has possession of a love letter for Julia from Proteus that Julia has pretended not to care about, wishing that her maid would intuit her desire to read it and would force her to do so. Julia has just angrily dismissed Lucetta, but she instantly regretted doing so, and has now called her back. Lucetta has escalated her taunts, causing Julia to lose patience and exclaim:

JULIA

This babble shall not henceforth trouble me.
Here is a coil with protestation!
[*She tears the letter*]
100 Go get you gone, and let the papers lie—
You would be fingering them to anger me.
[*Lucetta exits*]

105 O hateful hands, to tear such loving words!
Injurious wasps, to feed on such sweet honey
And kill the bees that yield it with your stings!
I'll kiss each several paper for amends.
Look, here is writ, "kind Julia"—unkind Julia!
110 As in revenge of thy ingratitude,
I throw thy name against the bruising stones,
Trampling contemptuously on thy disdain.
And here is writ, "love-wounded Proteus."
Poor wounded name, my bosom as a bed
115 Shall lodge thee till thy wound be throughly healed;
And thus I search it with a sovereign kiss.
But twice or thrice was "Proteus" written down.
Be calm, good wind, blow not a word away,
Till I have found each letter in the letter—

97 *coil* commotion, fuss; 98 *protestation* solemn promises or declarations of love (i.e., the love letter) [*Here is a coil with protestation* two possible meanings: (1) I'll show you a big to-do about protestations of love (referring to what she is doing or about to do to the letter); or (2) This is a big fuss made up of protestations of love (referring to the letter itself)]; 101 *You would be* i.e., (1) You only want to pick them up so you can be; (2) If you pick them up, you would only be; *fingering* (1) touching, fidgeting with; or (2) pilfering; 106 *wasps* i.e., her fingers; 108 *several* separate; *for* to make; 109 *Unkind* (UN-kind) Inhuman; cruel; 110 *As* As if; 115 *throughly* thoroughly; 116 *search* probe (as when cleansing a wound), i.e., cleanse; *sovereign*

120 Except mine own name; that some whirlwind bear
Unto a ragged, fearful, hanging rock
And throw it thence into the raging sea!
Lo, here in one line is his name twice writ,
"Poor forlorn Proteus, passionate Proteus,
125 To the sweet Julia"—that I'll tear away.
And yet I will not, sith so prettily
He couples it with his complaining names.
Thus will I fold them one upon another:
Now, kiss, embrace, contend, do what you will.

2 minutes

healing (i.e., having supreme healing powers); 120 *that* i.e., Julia's name (any scrap of the letter on which her name is written); 121 *ragged* rugged; *fearful* dreadful; terrifying; *hanging rock* i.e., overhanging cliff; 123 *Lo* Look; 124 *passionate* grief-stricken (i.e., for lack of Julia's love); 126 *sith* since; 127 *complaining* lamenting, bewailing; 129 *contend* quarrel, fight, struggle (with play on sexual double meaning: "struggle" in a sexual embrace).

COMMENTARY

The moments leading up to this monologue provide more than the usual insight into Julia's present state of mind. She asked Lucetta to evaluate her many suitors, and when Lucetta revealed that she preferred Proteus over all the others, Julia pretended to like him the least; when Lucetta offered Proteus's letter, Julia pretended not to care a whit about it. She then became fed up with Lucetta's teasing and rudely dismissed her. The next moment, Julia regretted her mean words and her lost chance to see Proteus's letter. She called Lucetta back, but rather than apologizing, she became embarrassed and angry once again and entered a second round of confrontational banter, which ends, as we see at the start of this piece, with yet another rude dismissal of her maid. Through her erratic behavior, Julia displays all the signs of a young person who has fallen headlong into love, but who is not yet ready to go public with the fact.

Julia's constant and extreme emotional swings, her ever-shifting focus, and her surprisingly harsh tone with Lucetta in the first two lines are the primary evidence in the monologue of her preoccupation. It will be important to decide why Julia acts this way before you delve into the piece. If you are playing the role within the context of the Elizabethan era, consider the culture and mores of the time. For instance, young Elizabethan women were expected to be unenthusiastic about love, and to insist on being "won"; Julia may fear that Lucetta will gossip, and that word will get back to Proteus and possibly cool his ardor. Or, since a young woman of Julia's social class would probably have had little knowledge about (or experience of) sex, she may just be horribly embarrassed by Lucetta's insinuations about her and Proteus. Even if you choose to set this monologue in a completely different era, there are many other possible explanations for her behavior. Julia may simply be reacting to the overwhelming rush of emotion that accompanies first love; perhaps she's afraid that confessing her love will jinx it; or, having had little intimate conversation with Proteus, maybe she wants to keep her attraction to him in check until she's sure about him . . .

Once you've decided why Julia keeps shifting her focus and her emotions, notice that these shifts are beautifully expressed through her use of antithesis, for example: *hateful hands* versus *loving words*; *feed on such sweet honey* versus *kill the bees that yield it*; *I throw thy name against the bruising stones* versus *I search it with a sovereign kiss*. As the monologue progresses, Julia's imagery reflects the swell of her emotions. Her metaphors change from simple images with which she is quite familiar (the *wasps* that represent her fingers, feeding on *honey* and yet killing *the bees that yield it*; and the tears in Proteus's letter, which she treats as a *wound* that can be healed with her *kiss*) to much more dramatic images that reveal an active imagination and an ability to visualize (the frightening cliff from which a *whirlwind* is to fling her name into the *raging sea*).

This is one of the most physically active monologues in Shakespeare, which makes it a lot of fun to work with. The embedded stage directions will help you pin down Julia's actions. For instance, *Go get you gone, and let the papers lie* indicates that she has not only torn up the letter, but has also dropped the pieces to the ground (perhaps flinging them emphatically, or calmly but defiantly allowing them to flutter to the ground before Lucetta's face) and that Lucetta has moved to pick them up. Almost every line in the monologue provides similar information for you to interpret as you block your movements. Inverted first feet underscore several of these actions: in line 98, Julia is probably grabbing, tearing, or making some gesture with Proteus's letter just as she says *Here is a coil*; in line 112, she is *Trampling* on her own written name as she verbally punches the word that describes her action; in line 125, she notices with displeasure that her own name is mentioned as she reads the words *To the sweet Julia*; and in line 128, she daringly and suggestively folds her own name against Proteus's as she says *Thus will I fold them*. These inverted feet, as well as several double endings scattered throughout the piece, enhance Julia's agitated and excited tone.

There are several word choices that require special attention. The word *throughly* was historically pronounced "THROO-lee," but some actors choose to make it more accessible by saying "THOR-lee," as if it were an elision of *thoroughly*, of which *throughly* is an archaic form. Also, notice the historic pronunciation of *unkind* (UN-kind), which sounds perfectly normal as it is used here, since we frequently change the emphasis to the first syllable of "un" words in order to do just what Julia is doing here—negate the positive form of the word (*kind*), which she has just mentioned. Finally, the choice of the word *babble* is debated by editors. Although it appears as "babble" in the First Folio, scholars agree that this could be a Shakespearean spelling of the word *bauble*, which in his time meant an insignificant thing, often a love token. The word is used elsewhere in Shakespeare to refer to a letter, and could easily have been intended here. Since we'll never know Shakespeare's intent, feel free to choose either word for your own use. If you do choose *bauble*, be aware that for Elizabethans it also carried a sexual double meaning, "penis."

While we're on the subject of sexual double entendre, a factor that may have exacerbated Julia's embarrassment (and may have fueled her excitement over Proteus) is the bawdy double entendre in her banter with Lucetta just before the monologue, in which they discussed Proteus's letter as if it were his genitals. In this monologue, the sexual references continue. While the following meanings would have been familiar to Elizabethans, most are too obscure for today's audience. They can, however, serve as a guide to your character's state of mind:

coil = penis; *fingering* = touching intimately; *wound* = genitals (male or female); *lodge* = enter sexually; *contend* = "struggle" amorously. Of these, the only word Julia imbues with an overtly sexual meaning to any degree is *contend*—it's up to you to decide how to play it . . .

This monologue is studded with sound repetitions that help Julia express her varied emotions. Julia dismisses Lucetta with Gruff Gs (*Go get / gone*) and Lashes out at her with Ls (*let / lie*); she repeats the NGER sound, perhaps liNGERing on its guttural tone to leer at or scold Lucetta (*fingering / anger*); she Hurls self-Hating Hs at her own Hands (*hateful hands*); she comforts Proteus's name with Babying Bs (*bosom / bed*); she Soothes it with Soft Ss (*search / sovereign / kiss*); she reMoNstrates with herself using MeaN Ms and Ns (*mine own name*); she OOs over Proteus, and resounds the P, R, T, and O sounds of his name when reading aloud his poetry (*Poor forlorn Proteus, passionate Proteus*); she forgIves her own name with dIsmIssing IH sounds (*will / sith / prettily / it with his*); and she vocalizes Proteus's pAIn with AY sounds (*complaining names*). For help with Julia's *O*, see "O, No! An *O*!," page xxxiii.

SIGNIFICANT SCANS

Line 123 has an inverted fifth foot, which doesn't follow a caesura as it normally would:

x / x / x / x / / x
Lo, here in one line is his name twice writ

You may also feel the impulse to invert the third foot, to accent *Lo*, and/or to make the last syllable a spondee (two accented syllables)—don't get your knickers in a twist about the meter of this line, just say the line as it seems most natural to you, and it will naturally reflect the meter's variations. The meter is intentionally irregular, expressing Julia's excitement and agitation as she pieces the letter together.

Line 124 is not as complicated as it seems. It has a double ending before the caesura and an inverted foot after it (don't forget to elide the first *Proteus* [PRO-tyuss] but not the second):

x / x /(x) / x x / x/
Poor forlorn Proteus, passionate Proteus

We have shown line 124 as you would scan it using the historic pronunciation of the word *forlorn* (FOR-lorn). If you prefer, you may use today's pronunciation, and invert the first foot of the line. Notice that Julia pronounces Proteus's name two different ways in this line, first with two syllables, then with three. If you try out these pronunciations within the meter, you will find that the second use of his name feels as though it is being dragged out, or perhaps moaned or wailed, as if Julia's pity for her suitor grows into a lament for him as she reads the line.

Don't forget to elide: *fingering* (FING-ring) in line 101; *Injurious* (in-JYOOR-yuss) in line 106; *several* (SEV-ral) in line 108; *Julia* (JOOL-yuh) in lines 109 (twice) and 125 (Julia always elides her own name, diminishing it in keeping with her self-admonishing tone); *contemptuously* (con-TEMP′-tchwuss-LEE) in line 112; and *Proteus* (PRO-tyuss) in line 117 and in its first occurrence in line 124, but not in line 113, or in its second occurrence in line 124;

. . . and to expand: *protestation* (PRO-tess-TAY′-shee-UN) in line 98; this expansion is a good opportunity to mock Proteus's love letter by stretching out the word until it sounds ridiculous (perhaps it is not accidental that the word is reminiscent of her suitor's name). However, if the expansion doesn't work for you, simply pronounce the word as you would normally, but be aware of the silent, one-syllable pause that results at the end of the line. You might choose to take advantage of the fact that the listener expects to hear this syllable (usually accented), which normally gets an additional slight emphasis since iambic lines naturally build in emphasis from beginning to end. For instance, you could fill the silent beat with a gesture or action, such as snatching the letter from Lucetta, scooping it up off the floor, making your first tear in it, or even stomping your foot in a fit of pique.

THE TWO GENTLEMEN OF VERONA

ACT II, SCENE iii

LAUNCE

GENDER: M
PROSE/VERSE: prose
AGE RANGE: young adult to adult
FREQUENCY OF USE (1–5): 5

Launce is soon to travel to the imperial court in Milan with his employer, a young gentleman named Proteus. Launce has no idea how long he'll be gone, and is terribly distressed to leave his family, to whom he and his dog, Crab, have just said their goodbyes. Launce shares with the audience his dismay at his dog's nonchalant reaction to the sad parting that has just taken place.

Nay, 'twill be this hour ere I have done weeping; all
the kind of the Launces have this very fault. I have
received my proportion like the prodigious son and
am going with Sir Proteus to the Imperial's court. I
5 think Crab, my dog, be the sourest-natured dog
that lives: my mother weeping, my father wailing,
my sister crying, our maid howling, our cat wringing her hands, and all our house in great perplexity;
yet did not this cruel-hearted cur shed one tear. He
10 is a stone, a very pebble-stone, and has no more
pity in him than a dog. A Jew would have wept to
have seen our parting. Why, my grandam, having
no eyes, look you, wept herself blind at my parting.
Nay, I'll show you the manner of it. [*Taking off his*
15 *shoes*] This shoe is my father. No, this left shoe is my
father—no, no, this left shoe is my mother. Nay
that cannot be so neither. Yes, it is so, it is so: it
hath the worser sole; this shoe with the hole in it is
my mother—and this is my father. A vengeance
20 on't, there 'tis! Now, sir, this staff is my sister, for,

1 *Nay* here, used to amplify what is about to be said; *this hour* an hour; *ere* before; *have done* am finished; 2 *kind* kindred, family; *this very fault* i.e., the fault of excessive crying; 3 *proportion* a malapropism for "portion," i.e., assigned role; *prodigious* a malapropism for "prodigal" (Launce intends to refer to the Prodigal Son, of the New Testament parable—see Commentary; its actual meaning is "monstrous, abnormal"); 4 *Sir Proteus* although the word *sir* was used to address or refer to gentlemen such as Proteus, its use as a title before his proper name is incorrect, implying that he is a knight or baronet; *Imperial's court* he combines "Emperor's court" and "imperial court"; 5 *Crab* Crab's name implies (as it would today) that he is crabby and sour-tempered—see "What's in a Name?" (page 424); 9 *yet did not this cruel-hearted cur* yet this cruel-hearted cur did not; 10 *very* often used by Shakespeare to emphasize the exact quality of the thing it describes; 11 *A Jew would have wept* anti-Semitism was the norm for Elizabethans, for whom the idea that Jews lacked pity was proverbial; 12 *grandam* (GRAN-dam) grandmother; 13 *look you* an expression used to stress what one is about to say or show; 14 *Nay* here, used to amplify what has gone before; 16 *Nay* here, simply used in place of "No" [*Nay . . . cannot . . . neither* Shakespeare often used double (and sometimes, as here, triple) negatives for emphasis]; 18 *worser* worse [*worser sole* used with a pun on "worser soul": a reference to the ongoing debate in Shakespeare's time as to whether a woman's soul was "inferior" to a man's (misogyny being right up there with anti-Semitism as a norm among Elizabethans)]; *this shoe with the hole in it is my mother* a bawdy reference, likening the hole in his shoe to his mother's genitalia; 19 *A vengeance on't* a mild curse; 20 *there 'tis* i.e., there you have it; *staff* walking stick;

look you, she is as white as a lily and as small as a
wand. This hat is Nan, our maid. I am the dog. No,
the dog is himself and I am the dog. O, the dog is
me, and I am myself. Ay, so, so. Now I come to my
25 father; [*He kneels*] "Father, your blessing." Now
should not the shoe speak a word for weeping.
Now should I kiss my father; [*He kisses the shoe*]
well, he weeps on. Now come I to my mother. O
that she could speak now, like a wood woman!
30 Well, I kiss her. [*He kisses the other shoe*] Why, there
'tis. Here's my mother's breath up and down. Now
come I to my sister; mark the moan she makes.
Now the dog all this while sheds not a tear nor
speaks a word. But see how I lay the dust with my
35 tears.

2 minutes, 40 seconds

21 *small* slender; 22 *wand* twig; stick; 26 *should not the shoe speak* either (1) the shoe should not speak (in order to correctly portray my father's response) or (2) the shoe (i.e., my father) does not speak; 29 *wood* mad, frenzied (with a play on "wooden," in reference to the wooden shoe that he has used to represent his mother); 31 *Here's* i.e., this is; *up and down* exactly; 32 *mark* listen to; 34 *lay* prevent from rising.

COMMENTARY

Launce's conspicuous lack of involvement with the central plot of *Two Gents* has led some scholars to propose that he may have been a belated addition to a script that was too short. H. B. Charlton commented that Launce "has no real right within the play, except that gentlemen must have servants, and Elizabethan audiences must have clowns." Charlton was referring to a character type that was ubiquitous in Elizabethan theatre. The Elizabethan clown was generally a rustic fellow, often a caricature of a peasant, whose humor was based on his buffoonish awkwardness and misuse of language, but who was nevertheless oddly astute. Today's audiences must also have their clowns, and few fill the role as well as Shakespeare's. Launce's hilarious yet poignant little one-man play-within-a-play is one of our favorite delights in the canon. Like several of Shakespeare's clowns, Launce is an unusual example of the type in that he is of higher social rank than a peasant (he serves a gentleman, and his family even has a maid). He does, however, embody all of the clown's humorous characteristics, as this monologue demonstrates.

Launce's lack of sophistication is evident in his earnest and naïve misunderstanding of the world around him: he fully expects his dog to understand the concept of their imminent departure and to feel compassion for him as a result; he also demonstrates the simple departure scene for his audience using whatever props he has at hand, expecting that his careful reenactment will clear everything up for minds he assumes to be as simple as his own.

Launce's use of language is the key to this monologue's humor. You can't miss his ridiculous malapropisms (*proportion*; *prodigious*), or the phrases he simply gets wrong, such as *Imperial's court* (he has probably heard Proteus mention the "imperial court" and the "Emperor's court," and has combined the two) and, possibly, *kind of the Launces* (assuming that *Launce* is his given name rather than his surname). With no intentional irony, Launce mentions that his grandmother, who has lost her eyesight, *wept herself blind*. These words and phrases result in puns and jokes that Launce does not intend and is not even aware of. All you have to do is play Launce's intended meaning with sincerity, and Shakespeare's language gets the laughs for you! Take advantage of Launce's repeated use of colloquial words and phrases, such as *Nay*; *look you*; *there 'tis*; *Now should*; and *Now come I*. Are these phrases repeated with the same cadence or tone of voice every time? Are they perhaps accompanied by some specific gesture or tick? Are these examples of his storytelling technique, building as the story progresses? Be sure to consider all the possible reasons (conscious or unconscious) for Launce's repetitions.

Don't be fooled by Launce's preference for what might appear to be insignificant, "throwaway" phrases—there's often humorous potential in them for "business." For instance, his mild curse *A vengeance on't* (which might seem quite bold to him) could express his frustration with his final casting decision, but it might also have some unexpected cause—perhaps he has been inspecting and then removing the shoes while discussing them, and now has trouble removing the second shoe for use in the "scene." Likewise, Launce's simple "little" words offer rich possibilities. For example, with *Ay, so, so* in line 24, Launce may be taking special care to make sure the audience is with him thus far, asking them, "So?" and then reaffirming to himself, "So." Or perhaps he is reviewing his setup and checking off the placement of each "character" with an "ay" or a "so." Maybe the whole scenario of the reenactment is just too confusing, and he's trying to get it all straight in his head. The possible interpretations of Launce's plain words are infinite. For this reason we have punctuated the monologue as simply as possible, which allows you to repunctuate in your mind to suit your interpretation. The First Folio punctuates this entire monologue without a single full stop until the end, suggesting that all of the ideas are somewhat interconnected and that the relationship of one sentence or phrase to the next is flexible.

The sexual double entendre in reference to Launce's mother would have been clear to Elizabethans and is likely to be understood by today's audience members as well. It is not meant as a vulgar swipe at his mother, but is made inadvertently in the course of casting his shoes as his parents. That he even frames a debate over which shoe should represent which parent is absurd; add to that the fact that he earnestly makes the decision based on one shoe's apparent sex and the state of its "soul," and it becomes hilarious. But what ultimately sets this monologue apart from schtick is the sweet poignancy of Launce's ability to cast the worn shoe as his mother without at all diminishing her. Launce's devotion to his shoe parents attests to the sweetness of his own soul, and it enriches the monologue: in addition to broad hilarity, we have the more substantial humor that stems from character.

Launce reveals his social rank and cultural influences through his choice of references: the lowbrow, bawdy humor of public taverns (as seen in his unwitting entendre) and poorly understood religious concepts. In Elizabethan times, Church liturgies were still delivered in Latin; only the sermon was in English, and even that might have been difficult for the average congregant to understand. Hence, Launce's botched reference to the parable of the prodigal son. Not only does he get the words wrong, but he also chooses a poor analogy: the prodigal son leaves his family callously, while Launce is torn reluctantly away; the prodigal son demands his "portion" from his father, while Launce receives his "portion"—his assignment to travel to Milan—from his employer; the prodigal son has shoes put on his feet by the joyful father upon his return, while

Launce removes his own shoes just as he is departing. The reference could not be more inept!

The monologue is full of clues that will encourage you to discover its possibilities for physical humor. First, there is the simple presence of Crab to be considered. Perhaps you have a talented canine friend with his own thespian aspirations (who knows the commands "sit" and "stay"). If not, you will have to come up with an appropriate scene partner. Under certain circumstances, you may be creative in your casting (e.g., another actor, a stuffed animal, a sock puppet). If you are auditioning for the role of Launce, however, we suggest a very specific and carefully thought-out imaginary dog, since the director will already have in mind a concept for Crab. Be sure to consider how to juxtapose your imaginary dog with the tangible props you will be using in your "parting scene" reenactment. These props are essential to the piece: each suggests myriad possibilities for physical comedy. Examine the text for embedded stage directions and possible physical interpretations. For instance, one obvious interpretation of *Here's my mother's breath up and down* is that the smell of Launce's mother's shoe reminds him of his mother's bad breath. It has also been suggested that when mentioning his *mother's breath* Launce refers to her weeping voice, and that he makes the wooden shoe squeak or creak to imitate her weeping sounds. You must ask yourself how Launce handles and places the objects that represent his family. Does he create a relationship with or among them using movements or sounds? How does the father shoe "bless" him? How does the walking-stick sister *moan*? Ask yourself as many questions of this sort as you can think of, and you will find hilarious actions with which to answer them. Choose or fabricate your props carefully, working with them as early in the rehearsal process as possible. They will spark your imagination as you work.

This piece provides a great opportunity to work on your comic timing, to tap into your inventiveness, and to interact with the audience. But if you choose this monologue as an audition piece, avoid annoying the director or her assistant by playing directly to them. Instead, place some imaginary audience members elsewhere in the room.

IRRELEVANT HISTORY: A CLOWN OF RENOWN

It is believed that the role of Launce was originated by none other than Will Kemp, the most famous portrayer of Elizabethan clowns, who was notorious for monopolizing the stage with improvisations on and expansions of his lines, to the delight of his audiences and the chargin of his fellow players. A master of self-promotion, Kemp once performed a morris dance (a traditional English costumed dance) along the nearly hundred-mile stretch of road from London to Norwich, a stunt that took him nine days. And, of course, he followed up with a book about his feat, entitled *Kemps Nine Daies Wonder*. In *Two Gents*, Kemp would have performed the role of Launce alongside his own trained dog, who was almost as talented a performer as his master. However, we can be sure that Kemp, unlike many actors in centuries to come, did not allow the dog to steal the show.

THE TWO GENTLEMEN OF VERONA

ACT IV, SCENE iv

LAUNCE

GENDER: M
AGE RANGE: young adult to adult
PROSE/VERSE: prose
FREQUENCY OF USE (1–5): 4.5

Launce is the manservant of Proteus, a young gentleman, and as such must accompany his young master wheresoe'er he goes. When Proteus—and, therefore, Launce—had to leave Verona for the court of the Duke of Milan, Launce tearfully bid his loving family adieu (see monologue, page 413), but hoped to find comfort so far from home in the presence of his loyal dog, Crab. The mangy ingrate, however, has had different ideas.

When a man's servant shall play
the cur with him, look you, it goes hard: one that I
brought up of a puppy; one that I saved from
drowning, when three or four of his blind brothers
5 and sisters went to it! I have taught him, even as
one would say, precisely, "Thus I would teach a
dog." I was sent to deliver him as a present to Mistress Silvia from my master; and I came no sooner
into the dining-chamber but he steps me to her
10 trencher and steals her capon's leg. O, 'tis a foul
thing when a cur cannot keep himself in all companies! I would have, as one should say, one that
takes upon him to be a dog indeed—to be, as it
were, a dog at all things. If I had not had more wit
15 than he, to take a fault upon me that he did, I think
verily he had been hanged for't; sure as I live he had
suffered for't. You shall judge: he thrusts me himself into the company of three or four gentleman-
like dogs under the Duke's table. He had not been
20 there—bless the mark!—a pissing while, but all the

1 *a man's servant* Launce refers to his dog, Crab; 2 *cur* dog [*play the cur* since the word *cur* had the connotation of "rascal," *play the cur* was understood to parallel the phrase "play the devil"]; *look you* an expression equivalent to "you can be sure of it" or just "look" (used for emphasis, to mean "pay attention"); *goes hard* is very serious business; 3 *brought up of a puppy* raised since he was a puppy; 4 *blind* because they were newborn; 5 *went to it* went to their deaths, i.e., were drowned; 6 *precisely* a term mimicking the overly academic speech of the pedagogue, misapplied by Launce in his attempt to express that he has taught Crab, through example, the finest of etiquette [*even as one . . . a dog* in exactly one's ideal method of canine instruction]; 7 *Mistress Silvia* i.e., the daughter of the Duke of Milan, with whom Launce's employer is in love; 8 *my master* i.e., Proteus (who, incidentally, had sent him to deliver a cute little puppy; Launce delivered Crab because the puppy was stolen); 9 *dining-chamber* dining room; *steps me* takes steps, walks; 10 *trencher* plate; *capon's* a rooster that has been castrated to make its meat more tender; *foul* bad; 11 *keep himself* restrain himself, behave well; *in all companies* in all kinds of company; 12 *I would have* i.e., I expect that he behave as; 13 *takes upon him* undertakes; *to be a dog indeed* i.e., to behave with proper dog etiquette; 14 *a dog at all things* a common expression meaning "well-versed at all things"; *wit* intelligence, common sense; 15 *to take a fault upon me that he did* to take the responsibility for a wrongdoing he (Crab) committed; 16 *verily* in truth, really; *had been* would have been; *hanged* in Elizabethan England, dogs were sometimes punished with hanging; *had suffered* would have been killed; 17 *thrusts me himself* imposes himself, obtrudes; 20 *bless the mark!* an expression used to apologize for using coarse language;

chamber smelt him. "Out with the dog!" says one;
"What cur is that?" says another; "Whip him out,"
says the third; "Hang him up," says the Duke. I,
having been acquainted with the smell before,
25 knew it was Crab and goes me to the fellow that
whips the dogs. "Friend," quoth I, "you mean to
whip the dog?" "Ay, marry, do I," quoth he. "You
do him the more wrong," quoth I, " 'twas I did the
thing you wot of." He makes me no more ado but
30 whips me out of the chamber. How many masters
would do this for his servant? Nay, I'll be sworn, I
have sat in the stocks for puddings he hath stol'n,
otherwise he had been executed. I have stood on
the pillory for geese he hath killed, otherwise he
35 had suffered for't. Thou thinkst not of this now.
Nay, I remember the trick you served me when I
took my leave of Madam Silvia: did I not bid thee
still mark me and do as I do? When didst thou see
me heave up my leg and make water against a gen-
40 tlewoman's farthingale? Didst thou ever see me do
such a trick?

2 minutes, 15 seconds

a pissing while proverbial for "a very short while," but here it is also given its literal meaning, "just long enough to urinate"; *all the chamber smelt him* (1) everyone in the room smelled him; (2) the whole room smelled like/of him; 22 *Whip him out* Drive him out of the room by whipping him; 25 *goes me* goes; 26 *quoth I* I said; 27 *marry* an exclamation used here to mean "to be sure" (short for "By the Virgin Mary"); 28 *the more wrong* the greater offense (i.e., of the wrong he's done to you versus the wrong you'd be doing to him, yours would be the greater, because he hasn't wronged you at all); 29 *wot* know (often, as here, used by a person of lower social status attempting to sound cultured when speaking to a person of higher social status); *He makes me no more ado but* Without further ado, he; 31 *Nay* here, used to amplify what has just been said; *I'll be sworn* I swear; 32 *the stocks* in Elizabethan times, an instrument of punishment made of wood, set in a public place, with holes for the ankles and sometimes also the wrists of an offender, in which he or she was secured to undergo public scrutiny, derision, and sometimes physical abuse; *puddings* sausages made of an animal's stomach or entrails stuffed with a mixture of minced meat, suet, oatmeal, and seasoning, and then boiled; 34 *the pillory* in Elizabethan times, a wooden instrument of punishment, erected on a post, with holes for the head and wrists of an offender (requiring that he or she stand), set in a public place to expose the offender to public derision, etc.; 35 *Thou* Launce now addresses Crab directly; 36 *trick* here, a mischievous prank [*the trick you served me* the trick you played on me]; *I took my leave of* I said farewell to; 37 *bid* order, command; 38 *still* continuously; *mark me* observe me; 39 *make water* urinate; *gentlewoman* a woman of high social rank; 40 *farthingale* a hoop skirt worn by women in Europe in the sixteenth and seveteenth centuries; 41 *trick* here, foolish action.

COMMENTARY

Launce has been having a rough time navigating among the beau monde of Milan, and Crab has been no help at all . . . so much for man's best friend. Luckily for you, Launce's minidrama is in no way integral to the play's primary plot lines, so you can pour out your indignant tale of Crab's betrayal—and your triage thereof—without needing your viewer to understand any larger context; this monologue stands well on its own.

Launce is a delightful example of Shakespeare's clown, the simple, unsophisticated and bumbling, yet also oddly astute type who inadvertently draws laughs through his mishaps, malapropisms, and charmingly candid and funny asides. This monologue is just such an aside, in which the audience is given a chance to enjoy this complex and touching individual. Ironically, this "social inferior" exhibits character far superior to that of most of his noble counterparts: he shows more steadfast loyalty and deeper love than Proteus, more common sense and ingenuity than Valentine, and more paternal affection toward his canine ward than the Duke exhibits toward his own daughter. Launce proves himself sensitive, sincere, and big-hearted, with a mature sense of responsibility, taking his obligation as master quite seriously.

This is a good monologue to select if you wish to try your hand at storytelling. Here is one of those stories told right after the event it recounts: an event in which the stakes were high and only Launce's quick thinking prevented utter catastrophe. Perhaps he has just made his getaway (Crab in tow) and is still out of breath, or perhaps he has had a moment or three to compose himself, but either way, Launce is still aggrieved, as is evident from his many exclamations (for help using the sound of the exclamatory *O* to its best advantage, see "O, No! An *O*!," page xxxiii). Launce can't even begin to tell the story until he has exclaimed at length about being undermined by someone he's raised since puppyhood; he only gets through the first sentence of the story before he can't help but exclaim again, and it takes eight lines of complaining before Launce can resume his anecdote.

In true storytelling style, Launce tries his hand at imitating the lords and the Duke. He may be attempting to comment on these important personages, which could result in a hilariously pointed piece of parody, or in a failed attempt that humorously reveals more about himself than it does about the lords. Launce also shifts from addressing the audience to addressing Crab directly, which enables you to switch from Launce's manner of speaking with people to the way he speaks to his dog. Given that he expects Crab to have a human's understanding of protocol (and of human emotions—see monologue, page 413), does he also speak to Crab as though the dog were a human being? Or does he speak to Crab in one of those voices that people with pets use with their four-legged friends? Experiment for yourself, but whatever you do, do not forget that Crab is present while you deliver this monologue.

Furthermore, Shakespeare has humorously played on Launce's perception of Crab by having Launce apply to his dog—whom he treats as a person—dog-related expressions commonly applied to people (it's not unlike Shakespeare's casting an adolescent boy to play a young woman disguised as an adolescent boy . . .). Examples include *play the cur* and *a dog at all things*.

Notice the ample evidence that Launce is a fish out of water in the Duke's court: he tries very hard to elevate his speech, using such terms as *precisely* and *wot*, and the delicately euphemistic *did the thing you wot of* instead of "urinated under the table." Yet his workaday speech pervades the monologue in several ways. First, he speaks in unstructured prose. He uses bad grammar (such as *How many masters would do this for his servant?*). He also uses an archaic grammatical form known as the ethical dative (i.e., the recurring use of the word *me* where it no longer belongs: *steps me*; *thrusts me*; *goes me*; *makes me no further ado*), a form that is used here to reflect his indignation at Crab's behavior and its effect on him. Though the monologue is in prose, he often contracts and elides words, such as *for't* and *stol'n*. And finally, the monologue is rife with short colloquial phrases—many of them interjections—such as *look you*; *it goes hard*; *as one should say*; *verily*; *bless the mark!*; *a pissing while*; and *I'll be sworn*. Similarly, he twice uses *Nay* to emphasize points he is making. And, while we're on the subject of repetition, notice the two well-placed uses of the word *cur*, a derogatory term for "dog," which expresses Launce's frustration, and the verbs with which Launce describes Crab's actions: *steps me*; *steals*; *thrusts me himself*; *hath stol'n*; *hath killed*; *trick you served me*; *heave up my leg and make water*. Mischevious little scamp, that Crab. Wouldn't part with him for the world.

What's in a Name?

The name Crab is short for "Crab Apple." When casting Crab, therefore, directors through the ages have generally typed him as a small, scrappy, and puckered-looking mutt with a face only his human could love.

P.S.

So you're to be the latest in a long line of Launces? For information on the original Launce, see "Irrelevant History: A Clown of Renown," page 418.

THE TWO GENTLEMEN OF VERONA

ACT IV, SCENE iv

JULIA

GENDER: F
AGE RANGE: young adult
PROSE/VERSE: blank verse
FREQUENCY OF USE (1–5): 3

Julia is in love with Proteus; the two pledged eternal love before Proteus was shipped off to join his friend Valentine at the court of the Duke of Milan. Julia missed Proteus so terribly that she disguised herself as a page named Sebastian and traveled to Milan to see him. There, she was shocked to discover that he has shifted his affections to the Duke's daughter, Silvia, who, in turn, loves Valentine. Proteus employs "Sebastian" and sends "him" to deliver a ring to Silvia in exchange for her portrait. "Sebastian" runs the errand and speaks with Silvia of "his mistress" back home, eliciting Silvia's pity for the woman Proteus has ditched. After Silvia leaves, Julia assesses the woman Proteus now pursues.

185 A virtuous gentlewoman, mild and beautiful!
I hope my master's suit will be but cold,
Since she respects my mistress' love so much.
Alas, how love can trifle with itself!
Here is her picture: Let me see . . . I think,
190 If I had such a tire, this face of mine
Were full as lovely as is this of hers;
And yet the painter flattered her a little,
Unless I flatter with myself too much.
Her hair is auburn, mine is perfect yellow:
195 If that be all the difference in his love,
I'll get me such a colored periwig.
Her eyes are grey as glass, and so are mine;
Ay, but her forehead's low, and mine's as high.
What should it be that he respects in her
200 But I can make respective in myself,
If this fond Love were not a blinded god?
Come, shadow, come, and take this shadow up,

185 *gentlewoman* a woman of high social rank; *mild* tender, gentle; 186 *my master's* i.e., Proteus (both [1] my betrothed ["my master" and "my mistress" were common terms for romantic partners] and [2] my employer [since Julia poses as "Sebastian" and, as such, is employed as Proteus's page]); *suit* i.e., love suit to Silvia; *be but cold* be (1) unwelcome (and hence, [2] ineffectual and unsuccessful); 187 *my mistress'* i.e., Julia herself (as Proteus's servant, "Sebastian" would have referred to his master's beloved as "my mistress"; here, she wryly continues the fiction she employed with Silvia); 188 *trifle with itself* (1) make light of itself (by being easily transferable) or (2) play with itself (by creating this messy love quadrangle); 189 *see* Julia examines the portrait of Silvia; 190 *tire* headdress (from the word *attire*); 191 *Were* would be; *full as* every bit as, just as; 193 *flatter with* flatter; 194 *auburn* in Elizabethan England, *auburn* meant white-blond (nearly white); *perfect* (1) completely; (2) perfect; *yellow* a deeper blond than "auburn" [*perfect yellow* the color of Queen Elizabeth's hair, blond was the preferred hair color in Shakespeare's England]; 196 *such a colored periwig* a wig of that color; 198 *low* Elizabethans considered a high forehead attractive, possibly because Queen Elizabeth herself had a high forehead; *as high* i.e., as hers is low; 199 *should* could [*What should it be* i.e., what is it]; *respects* cares for; takes notice of; 200 *But I can* that I couldn't; *make respective* both (1) make worthy of being cared for and (2) find the equal of; 201 *fond* foolish; *Love* i.e., Cupid (the god of love); *a blinded god* Cupid is traditionally depicted as a blind boy, who shoots his arrows and causes love to strike randomly and indiscriminately (hence the phrase "Love is blind"); 202 *Come, shadow* Julia speaks to herself (*shadow* was a pejorative term for a person, suggesting that he or she was scarcely worth being called a person); *take this shadow up* all of the following: (1) pick

For 'tis thy rival. O thou senseless form,
Thou shalt be worshipped, kissed, loved and adored!
205 And, were there sense in his idolatry,
My substance should be statue in thy stead.
I'll use thee kindly for thy mistress' sake,
That used me so; or else, by Jove I vow,
I should have scratched out your unseeing eyes
210 To make my master out of love with thee!

1 minute, 30 seconds

up this portrait; (2) rebuke this portrait, scold this portrait; and (3) oppose this portrait, defeat this portrait in battle; 203 *senseless* incapable of sensing, feeling, or perceiving; *form* image, portrait; 205 *idolatry* the choice of word connotes both (1) the intensity of Proteus's feelings and (2) the sacrilege of directing them to a false love instead of to his one true love; *were there sense in* if there were any logic to; 206 *statue* idol; *substance* i.e., flesh and blood [*My substance should be statue in thy stead* i.e., it would be my actual self he would be worshipping instead of a representation of yours]; 207 *use thee* treat you; *thy mistress'* i.e., Silvia (the woman you serve by being her portrait); 208 *so* in such a manner; *Jove* a.k.a. Jupiter, the Roman ruler of the gods (the counterpart of the Greek god Zeus); 209 *should* would; *unseeing eyes* i.e., because they are those of a portrait, instead of the real-life Silvia's actual eyes.

COMMENTARY

If you would like to perform a monologue in the vein of Viola's famous "ring speech," but would prefer one less frequently, as it were, enjoyed by auditioners, this charming speech might fit the bill. Like Viola, Julia finds herself in men's attire, wooing another woman on behalf of the man she herself loves. And, like Viola, Julia has great spirit and pluck. After all, Julia missed Proteus so much that she left the safety of her home and identity and trekked far to be near him. When she discovered him in hot pursuit of another woman, Julia chose to stay and forge onward in the hope of salvaging her love, rather than return home to lick her wounds. What a woman. This monologue is straightforward and utterly human. Though Julia's situation is frankly ridiculous, everyone can identify with the contradictory feelings she experiences, now that she's faced her rival for Proteus's affections and has found an attractive and terrific woman who, under better circumstances and had she not been wearing pants, Julia would have wished to befriend.

The meter of the monologue supports the idea that Julia is initially rattled. The first line has several extra syllables, giving it a triple ending and requiring the elision of *virtuous* (VIR-tchwuss):

x / x / x / x / x /(x-x)
A virtuous gentlewoman, mild and beautiful!

All of these extra syllables suggest that Julia has been unnerved by Silvia's qualities—it is natural to want to be able to hate her rival for Proteus's affections, and yet she finds that she cannot, in all fairness, hate this kind, compassionate, and quite attractive person.

There are a few inverted feet at the beginnings of lines, first in line 189 (where Julia summons the courage to look at the portrait she will be giving to Proteus), an optional one in line 198 (where, after admitting that their eyes are equally beautiful, she seizes on the fact that her forehead is more attractive than her rival's), and then two more in lines 202 and 204 (where Julia expresses frustration that Proteus has transferred his affections from her to Silvia). The monologue contains a triple ending in the line in which Julia acknowledges Silvia's beauty, and two double endings in the two lines in which Julia diminishes Silvia's beauty. Perhaps the extra syllables merely reflect her upset at losing Proteus's love to a woman no lovelier than she herself, but perhaps they also reflect her discomfort at disparaging a person who has spoken kindly about her. Generally, however, the meter is regular, causing these few variations to stand out in contrast.

Julia's language is spare and direct. Her use of imagery is sparse; what little there is refers to Roman gods (*Love*; *Jove*) and idol worship. The imagery hints at the tension between Julia's idealistic belief that love is sacred and exalted and her more realistic feeling that love is random and, like the impetuous gods of Roman lore, fickle and arbitrary. Remember that simple, unadorned language requires simple, clean delivery—emotionalizing would fit neither the language nor Julia's character. She has shown that she rolls with the punches courageously. She doesn't waste much time bemoaning her fate, but takes action to combat it (although she does express her frustration with a well-placed *O*—see "O, No! An *O*!," page xxxiii. She keeps her spirits up by amusing herself with wordplay, such as *respects* / *respective* and the three meanings of *take this shadow up*. Even in this monologue, where she concludes that she will be kind to Silvia's portrait in return for the kindness Silvia has shown her, she spunkily adds that if not for that, she would have readily defaced the portrait to dissuade Proteus from loving her rival.

Be specific about why Julia continues the fiction of "my mistress" in the third line of the monologue: Is she simply expressing her wry sense of humor to keep her spirits up? Does doing so help her stay in character? Or is she being protective: would it be too painful to let down her guard and acknowledge that it is she herself for whom Silvia has just expressed pity?

Notice Shakespeare's nod to Queen Elizabeth: each time Julia mentions a difference between her looks and Silvia's, Julia's "more attractive" features are the ones that resemble Queen Elizabeth's. As the Queen's features defined beauty during her reign, Julia is pointing out in frustration that she is the more attractive of the two. Love must be blind if Proteus prefers Silvia's less-fashionable look.

Don't forget to elide: *virtuous* (VIR-tchwuss) in line 185; *mistress'* (MISS-tress not MISS-tress-ez) in lines 187 and 207; and *difference* (DIFF-renss) in line 195.

THE PROBLEM PLAYS

Shakespeare's Problem Plays were written in the first few years of the seventeenth century, the same period in which he wrote his greatest Tragedies, which clearly influenced the Problem Plays' development. Although they are structured like comedies and have some characteristics of comedy, the Problem Plays contain tragic elements as well. The term *Problem Play* was coined in the 1890s and referred to works of the time that intentionally sparked public discourse on social problems. Thus, its use with regard to Shakespeare's work implies that he likewise intended to make the audience examine certain social issues. His Problem Plays are so called because of their disturbing nature: they raise difficult issues and their ambiguous endings intentionally leave the audience feeling uncomfortable. They also reflect the popular trend toward satire that emerged during the Jacobean era. But Shakespeare's audiences still wanted their satires to have happy endings: the Problem Plays were all box office flops when first produced. They remained out of favor for centuries, and it was not until the late 1800s that they began to be reassessed and appreciated. In the progression of Shakespeare's development as a playwright, these plays can be seen as a sort of bridge between his mature Comedies and the Romances, which were still to come.

ALL'S WELL THAT ENDS WELL

ACT III, SCENE ii

HELENA

GENDER: F
PROSE/VERSE: blank verse
AGE RANGE: young adult to adult
FREQUENCY OF USE (1–5): 4

Helena is married to Bertram, Count of Rossillion, and is completely in love with him. He wants nothing to do with her, has refused to consummate their marriage, and has run off to fight in Italy, sending Helena to live with his mother. Helena has just received a horrible letter from Bertram, stating that he will never live with her as husband and wife, and will not return home to France as long as she is there. After reading his letter, she soliloquizes:

"Till I have no wife I have nothing in France."
Nothing in France until he has no wife!
Thou shalt have none, Rossillion, none in France;
105 Then hast thou all again. Poor Lord, is't I
That chase thee from thy country and expose
Those tender limbs of thine to the event
Of the none-sparing war? And is it I
That drive thee from the sportive court, where thou
110 Wast shot at with fair eyes, to be the mark
Of smoky muskets? O you leaden messengers,
That ride upon the violent speed of fire,
Fly with false aim, move the still 'pearing air
That sings with piercing, do not touch my lord;
115 Whoever shoots at him, I set him there;
Whoever charges on his forward breast,
I am the caitiff that do hold him to't;
And though I kill him not, I am the cause
His death was so effected. Better 'twere
120 I met the ravin lion when he roared
With sharp constraint of hunger; better 'twere
That all the miseries which nature owes
Were mine at once. No, come thou home, Rossillion,
Whence honor but of danger wins a scar,
125 As oft it loses all. I will be gone;

105 *all again* i.e., everything you had before once again; 107 *event* possible consequences; 109 *sportive* merry, pleasure-filled; *court* i.e., of the King of France; 110 *fair* beautiful; *mark* target; 111 *leaden messengers* i.e., lead bullets; 112 *fire* i.e., gunfire; 113 *false* not right; erroneous; *still 'pearing* appearing motionless; 114 *sings with piercing* i.e., produces a sound like singing, as the bullet passes through it; 115 *I set him there* I put him there (i.e., I am the reason he is there); 116 *forward* situated at the front (of the line of battle); 117 *caitiff* despicable wretch; *do hold him to't* i.e., keeps him fighting; 119 *was so effected* would happen that way [*I am the cause . . . effected* i.e., it will be my fault if he gets killed]; *Better 'twere* It would be better; 120 *ravin* (RAY-vin) ravenous; 121 *constraint* compulsion, force; 122 *owes* owns, has; 124 *Whence* from the place where; *honor but of danger wins a scar* i.e., being honorable in this dangerous situation will only get you a scar; 125 *As oft it loses all* as often as it (i.e., being honorable) loses everything (i.e.,

1 minute, 50 seconds

My being here it is that holds thee hence.
Shall I stay here to do't? No, no, although
The air of paradise did fan the house
And angels officed all. I will be gone,
130 That pitiful Rumor may report my flight
To consolate thine ear. Come, night—end, day,
For with the dark (poor thief) I'll steal away.

one's life); 126 *My being here it is* it is my presence here; *holds thee hence* keeps you there; 127 *although* even if; 128 *did fan* i.e., wafted through; 129 *officed all* performed all the household chores; 130 *pitiful* having pity, compassionate; *Rumor* Helena is personifying rumor; 131 *consolate* console; 132 *poor thief* Helena refers to herself.

COMMENTARY

One of the greatest challenges in playing Shakespeare's comedic heroines is justifying passionate love for clearly inferior love interests. Of all the comedic heroines, Helena offers you the biggest workout of your suspension-of-disbelief muscle. Bertram's a worm; committing to Helena's love for him is nevertheless critical to playing her. So . . . if his beauty is only skin deep, make it big beauty. Cast (fill in your favorite screen idol here). Think about ice cream. Substitute your puppy. Do what you have to do.

Helena is a remarkably thoughtful person. Instead of freaking out and running away, she carefully thinks through her situation and arrives at a well-thought-out plan to . . . run away. She draws a straight line of logic from the monologue's beginning to its end: (1) Bertram won't return to France while I am here; (2) Have I therefore caused him to put himself in danger on the battlefield?; (3) He is in danger; (4) This danger is my fault: even if someone else inflicts the wound, it's my fault for sending him there; (5) Since it's my fault, I deserve to be hurt instead of him; (6) Therefore, I must go out into the dangerous world, so he can come home to safety.

Helena uses contrasts to organize the progression of her arguments: the *nothing* Bertram has by having a wife versus the *all* he will regain when he has *none*; her presence in France versus his absence; the flirtatious looks shot in his direction at court versus the deadly bullets now shot at him in battle; her preference for her own brutal death versus her fervent wish for his safety; and the images of *paradise* and *angels* at home versus images of darkness and thievery as she *steal[s] away*. These contrasts are augmented by her use of antithesis: *I kill him not* versus *I am the cause*; and *night* versus *day*.

Helena laces her logic with active imagery to convince herself that she must go. She creates vivid pictures of the battlefield (*smoky muskets*; *violent speed of fire*); the *ravin lion* roaring in acute hunger; *angels* doing housework; and Helena herself as a *poor thief* stealing away in the dark. She also uses many personifications: the singing *air*; the *leaden messengers* of death; compassionate *Rumor*; *honor* risking his life.

Repetition of sounds and words enhances the emotional impact of Helena's heartache and self-reproach: the piece is packed with assonance (*leaden messengers*; *sportive court*; *ride / violent / fire*; *death / effected / better*) and alliteration (*holds / hence*; *thou / then / that / thee / thy / thine*; *no / nothing / none*). Word and phrase repetitions abound: *no / nothing / none*; *is't I / is it I*; *Whoever shoots . . . / Whoever charges*; *better 'twere* (twice); *I will be gone* (twice). Helena summarizes the conclusion she's reached with a rhyming couplet at the end (*day / away*). And Helena's repeated use of the familiar terms *thee*, *thou*, *thy*, and *thine* convey the intimacy she feels toward Bertram.

Note: for help using the sound of the word *O* to its best advantage, see "O, No! An *O*!," page xxxiii.

SIGNIFICANT SCANS

The very first line is a tricky one. Here are two options (in both cases, *—thing in France* is read as a crowded foot):

```
    x       /  x    /   x    /   x          /    x - x      /
(pause) Till I have no wife I have nothing in France
```
[contracting the second *I have* (I've)]

```
x    /       x    /  x          /  x - x      /          x     /
Till I have no wife I have nothing in France (pause-pause)
```
[contracting both *I haves*]

Line 111 is a rare six-footed line (hexameter), drawing attention to Helena's terror at the prospect of Bertram being shot:

```
 x     / x    /   x     /  x    /  x    /    x  /
Of smoky muskets? O you leaden messengers
```

Don't forget to elide: *Rossillion* (Ruh-SIL-yun) in lines 104 and 123; *violent* (VIE-lent) in line 112; and *pitiful* (PIT-ful) in line 130;

. . . and to contract: *is't* (ist) in line 105; *to't* (TOOT) in line 117; and *do't* (DOOT) in line 127.

P.S.

For information about Helena's integrity and her actions later in the play, see "Bed-Tricking Bertram," page 965.

MEASURE FOR MEASURE

ACT II, SCENE ii

ISABELLA

GENDER: F
PROSE/VERSE: blank verse

AGE RANGE: young adult to adult
FREQUENCY OF USE (1–5): 3.5

Isabella's brother, Claudio, has just been sentenced to death for impregnating his fiancée in violation of a long-unenforced statute that criminalizes sex out of wedlock. Duke Vincentio, ruler of Vienna, is away from the city and the law has been revived in his absence by his deputy, Angelo. Isabella has come to Angelo from the convent where she is a novitiate to plead with him for her brother's life. Angelo has just stated unequivocally that Claudio will die tomorrow. An anguished Isabella replies:

So you must be the first that gives this sentence,
And he, that suffers. O, it is excellent
To have a giant's strength, but it is tyrannous
To use it like a giant.

[LUCIO, aside to Isabella: *That's well said.*]

110 Could great men thunder
As Jove himself does, Jove would ne'er be quiet,
For every pelting, petty officer
Would use his Heaven for thunder,
Nothing but thunder. Merciful Heaven,
115 Thou rather with thy sharp and sulphurous bolt
Splits the unwedgeable and gnarled oak
Than the soft myrtle. But man, proud man,
Dressed in a little brief authority,
Most ignorant of what he's most assured—
120 His glassy essence—like an angry ape
Plays such fantastic tricks before high Heaven
As makes the angels weep, who, with our spleens,
Would all themselves laugh mortal.

1 minute

106 *this sentence* i.e., the death sentence handed down for engaging in sexual activity before marriage; 107 *he* i.e., Isabella's brother, Claudio; *that suffers* i.e., the first to be executed; *excellent* often used ironically in Shakespeare's time; 110 *great men* men in positions of power; *thunder* make the sound of thunder [*Could . . . thunder* If powerful men could make thunder]; 111 *Jove* a.k.a. Zeus (to the Greeks) or Jupiter (to the Romans), Greco-Roman king of the gods (considered the god of thunderbolts and known, among other things, for throwing them); *quiet* free from disturbance, tranquil; 112 *pelting* paltry, piddling little; 113 *his Heaven* i.e., Jove's sky, where he hangs out; 115 *Thou* refers to Heaven, or to Jove in Heaven; *sulphurous* made of or impregnated with brimstone—believed in Shakespeare's time to be a quality of thunder and lightning; 116 *Splits* split; *unwedgeable* unsplittable (as with a wedge); 117 *proud* haughty, overly proud; 118 *Dressed in* (1) equipped with; (2) wearing; 119 *Most ignorant of what he's most assured* knowing the least about the thing in which he places the most confidence; 120 *glassy* as fragile as glass; *essence* soul; 121 *such* the kind of; *fantastic* any or all of the following: ludicrous; grotesque; capricious, irrational; *before* in front of; in full view of; 122 *As* that; *makes* make; *spleens* Elizabethans believed the spleen to be the organ that produced strong emotions and laughter—for more on obsolete human physiology, see "Elizabethan Anatomy 101," page 558; 123 *mortal* to death [*who, with our spleens . . . mortal* who, if they had spleens (and could laugh), would all laugh themselves to death].

COMMENTARY

Isabella is in a very precarious situation: she is responding emotionally to Angelo's unjust decision to execute her brother the next day. And yet she cannot say exactly what she'd like to say, since Angelo is, after all, her ruler while the Duke is away. She has come to convince him to spare her brother's life, and perhaps she can still soften him. If she is too blunt, she will anger Angelo and the last shred of hope will be lost. The opening section is full of perSuaSive Ss, many of which are coupled with Tense Ts that lend the lines the angry tone she tries to keep in check: *So*; *must*; *first*; *gives*; *this*; *sentence*; *suffers*; *it is excellent*; *giant's strength*; *tyrannous*; *use*.

Rather than call Angelo names, Isabella uses the safe generalization of *man* (i.e., humans in general and men in positions of power specifically). She uses antithesis to introduce the concept that the great must wield their power with care (*it is excellent . . . a giant's strength* versus *it is tyrannous . . . like a giant*). This paves the way for the many contrasts with which she implies that Angelo is a *pelting, petty officer* and an *ape* for handing down a much too severe punishment against the powerless Claudio. She contrasts sizes (*excellent*, *giant*, *great* versus *pelting*, *petty*, *little brief*) to emphasize this point and suggests with the antithetical pairing *most ignorant* versus *most assured* that Angelo look to his own soul a bit further before taking a man's life.

She reminds Angelo that he's not actually the Duke with the biting (yet veiled and indirect) line *Dressed in a little brief authority*. While she is still generalizing when she speaks of men and their short life spans, she is also pointedly reminding Angelo that his tenure as Acting Duke of Vienna is short, like a briefly borrowed article of clothing that he must return to its rightful owner. As his position is temporary, he should beware condemning her brother to the permanent fate of death.

Isabella personifies *Heaven*, speaking directly to it. Remember: Isabella was about to join a convent; she's religious and has no doubt forged a personal relationship with her God. In addressing Heaven, she uses the intimate *thee* and *thy*; in addressing Angelo, the deputy to the Duke, she uses the formal, deferential *you*. She also uses *Heaven* three times in this short monologue, imbuing her *little brief* moment in the spotlight with moral authority.

SIGNIFICANT SCANS

The meter of this short piece is irregular and uneven: it has some lines containing double endings and several lines containing fewer than five feet of spoken text. It also has many inverted (trochaic) feet at the beginnings of lines, reflecting Isabella's indignation and passion about what she is saying, and creating the emphatic tone in which she attempts to persuade Angelo to abandon his folly and let Claudio live.

Lucio's words in line 109 have been excised to create this monologue, resulting in a one-and-a-half-foot pause at the end of the line:

x / x / x / x / x /
To use it like a giant (pause) (pause-pause)

Furthermore, line 110 has only two and a half feet of spoken text, incorporating an intentional two-and-a-half-foot pause, which may be used either at the line's beginning (combining it with the pause in line 109), in which case the line has a double ending, or at the line's end:

x / x / x / x / x / (x)
(pause-pause) (pause-pause) (pause-pause) Could great men thunder

x / x / x / x / x /
Could great men thunder (pause) (pause-pause) (pause-pause)

Shakespeare has written another intentional pause into this short monologue, at the end of line 113 (notice that *Heaven* is elided [HEV'N]):

x / x / x / x / x /
Would use his Heaven for thunder (pause) (pause-pause)

The extra feet of silence give Isabella a chance to think about what she's just said. She will then confirm it in the next line (*Nothing but thunder*).

Line 114 is difficult to scan. There is another built-in pause at the caesura (another chance for Isabella to be thinking and making a tactical shift). The first and fourth feet are inverted, and there are two double endings, emphasizing the vehemence with which she concludes one point and begins the next.

/ x x / (x) x / / x x / (x)
Nothing but thunder. (pause-pause) Merciful Heaven

Similarly, you must take a half-foot pause at the caesura in line 117 (which also has an inverted first foot):

/ x x / x / x / x /
Than the soft myrtle. (pause) But man, proud man

As with line 109, the last foot and a half of the final line have been excised. We recommend that you take the pause to let your words sink in:

x / x / x / x / x /
Would all themselves laugh mortal (pause) (pause-pause)

Though you could elide *tyrannous* (TEER-nuss) in line 108, we recommend that you treat it as a triple ending (TEER-uh-nuss), so that you don't deemphasize this important word.

Don't forget to elide: *Heaven* (HEV'N) in line 113 and *sulphurous* (SUL-fruss) in line 115;

. . . to contract: *it is* (IT'S) or ('TIZ) in line 107;

. . . and to expand: *gnarled* (NAR-uld) or (NAR-ledd) in line 116.

P.S.

For information about Isabella's integrity and her actions later in the play, see "The Bed-Trick Shtick," page 969.

MEASURE FOR MEASURE

ACT III, SCENE i

CLAUDIO

GENDER: M
PROSE/VERSE: blank verse
AGE RANGE: young adult to adult
FREQUENCY OF USE (1–5): 4

Claudio has been arrested and imprisoned by Angelo, the acting ruler of Vienna, who has reinstituted enforcement of an old law forbidding premarital sex. Claudio had broken the law by impregnating his fiancée, Julietta (see "Wedding and Bedding or Betting on Wedding?," page 446). Claudio's sister, Isabella, visits him in prison with the bad news that he will have to die. Angelo refuses to pardon Claudio unless Isabella sleeps with him, which of course she cannot do without losing her good name and damning her soul. Claudio at first agrees with her that he will have to die, but once the reality of the sentence sinks in, he rethinks the situation.

Ay, but to die, and go we know not where,
To lie in cold obstruction and to rot,
120 This sensible warm motion to become
A kneaded clod; and the delighted spirit
To bathe in fiery floods, or to reside
In thrilling region of thick-ribbèd ice;
To be imprisoned in the viewless winds
125 And blown with restless violence round about
The pendent world; or to be worse than worst
Of those that lawless and incertain thought
Imagine howling—'tis too horrible.
The weariest and most loathèd worldly life
130 That age, ache, penury, and imprisonment
Can lay on nature is a paradise
To what we fear of death.

[ISABELLA: *Alas, alas!*]

Sweet sister, let me live.
What sin you do to save a brother's life,
135 Nature dispenses with the deed so far
That it becomes a virtue.

1 minute

119 *obstruction* (1) cessation of vital functions, such as the flow of blood, or (2) state of being blocked or hindered [*lie in cold obstruction* (1) be cold, with no vital functions, as a corpse, or (2) lie buried, trapped in the cold ground]; 120 *sensible* capable of feeling, sentient; *warm* alive; *motion* the body, controlled by the soul (in Shakespeare's time, the word *motion* meant "puppet show," and sometimes "puppet"; here, the body is a puppet, inanimate without its puppet master, the soul) [*sensible warm motion* sentient, living body]; 121 *clod* lump of earth; *delighted* delightful [*delighted spirit* the soul, which had given the body delight]; 123 *thrilling* piercingly cold; *thick-ribbèd* having strong ribs (i.e., so strongly enclosing that it cannot be broken through) [*thrilling . . . ice* extreme cold was one of the common concepts of Hell in Shakespeare's time; Virgil had introduced the concept in the *Aeneid*, and Dante elaborated on it in the *Divine Comedy*, describing the ninth circle of Hell as a frozen region where sinners were "shrined in ice"]; 124 *viewless* invisible; 126 *pendent* hanging, suspended [*pendent world* the earth, suspended in space]; *worst* the most tortured or afflicted souls in Hell; 127 *that* who; *lawless* unruly; *thought* thoughts; 128 *howling* i.e., as the tortured souls do in Hell [*those that lawless . . . howling* those souls that one's unruly and uncertain thoughts imagine to be howling in Hell]; 129 *worldly* earthly; 130 *penury* extreme poverty; 131 *lay on* inflict on, impose on; *nature* the physical constitution of a human being; 132 *To* compared to; 134 *What* Whatever; 135 *Nature* (1) the force that controls the universe; (2) natural feeling, common to all human beings; *dispenses with* excuses, pardons; *so far* to such a degree.

COMMENTARY

If you're fascinated by Shakespeare's poetic plunge into the fear and awe of death in *Hamlet*, but you have your own fear and awe of tackling the "To be, or not to be" speech, here's a less overused, less intimidating piece that explores the same themes.

Claudio shares Hamlet's terror of the undiscovered country (but not his preoccupation with it). Claudio, however, does not have the same luxury as Hamlet; Claudio's life is in someone else's hands. And, although Hamlet has only his own psyche to grapple with, Claudio must confront something more specific and far more rigid: his sister's morality. Keep in mind that throughout this piece Claudio is desperately trying to make his sister feel his fears, to convince her to save his life.

Claudio's emotional state is evident in the meter of his speech: his ideas frequently flow past the end of one line and continue to the middle of the next one, where a new thought begins. Is he running on due to nervousness? Are the horrible possibilities just tumbling out of him? Perhaps he's hurrying to get everything in before his sister cuts him off. The outpouring continues without stop until the key word *death*, which is underscored by a little "death" in the speech—a pause. The line *To what we fear of death* has only three feet of spoken text (where Isabella's words have been excised), as does the next line, where the pause is built in by Shakespeare. You must decide whether you prefer to take all four feet of pause between the two lines, or to pause for two feet after *death*, and another two feet after *live*. The pause may seem minor, but silence is very powerful. In this case, it provides time for Claudio's transition from the body to its conclusion.

Claudio can't help but use the imagery of the afterlife that his religion and his culture have ingrained in him. These images appear in antithetical pairs (*sensible warm motion* versus *kneaded clod*; *bathe in fiery floods* versus *reside / In thrilling region of thick-ribbèd ice*). The pairs culminate in the striking contrast between the summation of Claudio's argument (*fear of death*) and his final appeal to his sister (*let me live*), which is further enhanced by the pause between the two lines.

The imagery is delicately spiced with alliteration and assonance (*fiery / floods*; *thick-ribbèd*; *worse / worst*; *howling / horrible*; *weariest / worldly*; *age / ache*; *penury / imprisonment*; *lay / nature*). Alliteration and assonance also emerge in pairs in lines 118 (*Ay / die*; *go / know*; *know not*) and 133 (*Sweet sister*; *let / live*). The first is the opening line of the piece, and the second is the first line of Claudio's final plea for his life. In both cases, the sound combinations focus the listener more intently on what is being said.

Don't forget to elide: *fiery* (FIE-ree) in line 122; *violence* (VIE-lence) in line 125; and *weariest* (WEER-yest) in line 129;

. . . to contract: *and imprisonment* ('ndim-PRI´-zn-MENT) in line 130;

. . . and to expand: *thick-ribbèd* (thick-RIH-behd) in line 123 and *loathèd* (LOW-thehd) in line 129.

WEDDING AND BEDDING OR BETTING ON WEDDING?

In Shakespeare's day, getting married was a process, not an event. The many steps to wedded bliss took months to complete, and it wasn't clear at exactly what point in the process a couple was actually married (although according to the Church, the final grain of rice had to hit the ground before the bride and groom could hit the sack). The customary steps of marriage were: a couple checked each other out and decided they'd like to wed (or their families decided for them)—at this stage they were not even slightly married; the couple then made a private commitment to wed—now they were slightly married, and some couples felt they were married enough to get it on; they next engaged in a betrothal ceremony, called "handfasting," in which they held hands and exchanged vows, usually in public and before formal witnesses—this was a binding contract, and the couple was now too married to wriggle out of it, thus it was not uncommon for a couple to consider themselves wed and to act accordingly; the couple's wedding banns (public pronouncements of their wedding) were then read three Sundays in a row at their parish church—they were in the homestretch now (almost completely married); finally, the couple was actually married in a church ceremony and given a wedding feast. Now they were 100 percent married.

Claudio and Juliet had conducted the handfasting ceremony, but in private, which unfortunately for Claudio was insufficient to get him off the hook. Angelo and Mariana were much further along in the process—they had completed all but the final wedding ceremony before Angelo abandoned Mariana. Since their marriage contract was binding, Mariana was left in a state of marital limbo, unwed to Angelo but not free to marry anyone else. Lucio and the mother of his child had taken step two, although Lucio never intended to reach step three: he promised marriage only in order to bed the woman. At the close of the play, the Duke and Isabella are just embarking on step number one.

TROILUS AND CRESSIDA

ACT I, SCENE iii

ULYSSES

GENDER: M
AGE RANGE: mature adult
PROSE/VERSE: blank verse
FREQUENCY OF USE (1–5): 1

Trojan War: War Room (or, rather, war tent) Strategy Meeting of the Greek Commanders. Achilles is not present—nor is Patroclus. Ulysses has just been saying that the Greeks' failure to defeat Troy (after seven years of fighting) is due to disorder and lack of respect for authority in the ranks. He faults Achilles for setting a bad example: after all, there's a war going on and Achilles won't come out of his damn tent. Ulysses is fed up with Achilles' and Patroclus's childish and insubordinate behavior. He relates a galling scene he caught sight of:

The great Achilles, whom opinion crowns
The sinew and the forehand of our host,
Having his ear full of his airy fame,
145 Grows dainty of his worth, and in his tent
Lies mocking our designs. With him Patroclus,
Upon a lazy bed, the livelong day
Breaks scurril jests,
And with ridiculous and silly action
150 (Which, slanderer, he imitation calls)
He pageants us. Sometime, great Agamemnon,
Thy topless deputation he puts on,
And like a strutting player, whose conceit
Lies in his hamstring, and doth think it rich
155 To hear the wooden dialogue and sound
'Twixt his stretched footing and the scaffoldage,
Such to-be-pitied and o'er-wrested seeming
He acts thy greatness in; and when he speaks,
'Tis like a chime a-mending, with terms unsquared,
160 Which from the tongue of roaring Typhon dropped
Would seem hyperboles. At this fusty stuff
The large Achilles, on his pressed bed lolling,
From his deep chest laughs out a loud applause,
Cries "Excellent! 'Tis Agamemnon right!
165 Now play me Nestor—hem, and stroke thy beard

142 *opinion* i.e., public opinion; *crowns* glorifies; 143 *sinew* strength, main source of support; *forehand* one who is preferred above others or who holds the front position; mainstay; *host* army; 144 *Having his ear full of* constantly hearing about; *airy* lofty; 145 *dainty of* overly concerned with; 146 *designs* enterprises; 148 *Breaks scurril jests* cracks vulgar jokes; 149 *action* actions, gestures; 150 *he imitation calls* he calls imitation; 151 *pageants* mimics, as in the theatre; 152 *topless deputation* supreme authority; 153 *player* actor; *conceit* imagination, wit, skill; 154 *hamstring* tendon at the back of the knee [*whose conceit . . . hamstring* whose wit and acting skill amount to no more than strutting (i.e., he's a witless ham)]; *doth think it rich* thinks it is delightful; 155 *wooden dialogue* sounds produced by shoes striking wood (with double meaning, "stilted dialogue"); 156 *'Twixt* between; *stretched footing* exaggerated stride; *scaffoldage* wooden stage; 157 *o'er-wrested* wildly misinterpreted, distorted; *seeming* presentation [*Such to-be-pitied . . . thy greatness in* he performs his imitation of your greatness in such a pathetic and distorted presentation, as just described]; 159 *chime a-mending* a set of bells that is out of tune; *unsquared* inappropriate, not suited to the purpose; 160 *Typhon* the biggest, scariest monster in all of mythology, which had one hundred serpents' heads whose eyes shot fire, who breathed out fiery rocks, and (most important) who had a roaring voice [*from the tongue . . . Typhon dropped* even if spoken by the roaring monster Typhon]; 161 *seem hyperboles* seem like gross exaggerations; *fusty* stale; trite, hackneyed; 162 *pressed* weighed down; 164 *right* exactly; 165 *play me Nestor* i.e., do your imitation of Nestor for me; *hem* make the sound of clearing the throat;

As he, being dressed to some oration."
That's done, as near as the extremest ends
Of parallels, as like as Vulcan and his wife.
Yet god Achilles still cries "Excellent!
170 'Tis Nestor right! Now play him me, Patroclus,
Arming to answer in a night alarm."
And then, forsooth, the faint defects of age
Must be the scene of mirth: to cough and spit,
And, with a palsy fumbling on his gorget,
175 Shake in and out the rivet. And at this sport
Sir Valor dies; cries "O, enough Patroclus,
Or give me ribs of steel—I shall split all
In pleasure of my spleen!" And in this fashion
All our abilities, gifts, natures, shapes,
180 Severals and generals of grace exact,
Achievements, plots, orders, preventions,
Excitements to the field or speech for truce,
Success or loss, what is or is not, serves
As stuff for these two to make paradoxes.

2 minutes, 30 seconds

166 *As he* as he does; *being dressed to* when he is being prepared for; *oration* speech; 167 *near* i.e., as close an impersonation; 168 *as like as* as much alike as; *Vulcan and his wife* Vulcan, the ugliest of the gods, was married to Venus, the most beautiful goddess; 169 *god Achilles* Ulysses is being sarcastic; 170 *Now play him me* Now portray him for me; 171 *Arming* putting on his armor; *answer in* respond to; *alarm* a call to arms, a notice of approaching danger; 172 *forsooth* in truth, certainly (used here with contempt); *faint* feeble, weak; 173 *Must be the scene of mirth* become the subject of laughter; 174 *palsy* palsied (trembling from palsy); *on* with; *gorget* (GOR-jet) the piece of armor that protects the throat; 175 *rivet* an iron pin used to fasten pieces of armor together [*Shake in and out the rivet* shake the rivet in and out (of its hole in the gorget)]; *sport* entertainment; 176 *Sir Valor* i.e., Achilles; *dies* i.e., dies with laughter; 178 *pleasure of my spleen* laughter (the spleen was considered the source of human emotions); 179 *our* i.e., the Greek commanders'; 180 *Severals and generals* individual and collective qualities; *of grace* of excellence; *exact* particular, minute [*Severals . . . exact* the particular excellent qualities of the individual commanders and of the group as a whole]; 181 *preventions* defensive strategies; 182 *Excitements to the field* encouragements to fight, pep talks; 184 *stuff* material, fodder; *paradoxes* absurdities, objects of ridicule.

COMMENTARY

If you enjoy telling a story and fleshing it out by doing imitations of the people in it, this piece is for you. It is delightfully layered: you get to portray an indignant Ulysses, who is portraying both Achilles and Patroclus, who, in turn, is portraying both Agamemnon and Nestor.

To make this challenging monologue shine, it is essential that you have a clear mental picture of each image. A thorough consideration of the annotation will help you understand the vivid imagery and how it represents what Ulysses saw, which will enable you to project effectively to your audience a detailed recollection of the event.

Ulysses uses imagery to comment on the story as he tells it. He "chain-smokes" imagery, lighting each image off the butt of the one before. He often uses sardonic similes (*like a strutting player*; *like a chime a-mending*; *as near as the extremest end*; *as like as Vulcan and his wife*). He also likes synecdoche (*The sinew and the forehand of our host*; *Having his ear full*), and he wraps up the piece with antithesis (*Excitements to the field* versus *speech for truce*; *Success* versus *loss*; *what is* versus *is not*). Pay attention to the lavish descriptions of sights and sounds that Ulysses employs to inflame the commanders against Achilles.

There are some wonderful consonance and assonance combinations (*Having his ear full of his airy fame*; *Arming to answer in a night alarm*; *stretched footing and the scaffoldage*; *tongue of / Typhon*; *fusty stuff*; *pressed bed*; *dies / Cries*) that help Ulysses act the part of Patroclus, as well as vent his own frustration. Also note where two consecutive words end and begin with the same sound (*Breaks scurril* in line 148; *doth think* in line 154; *this sport* in line 175; *As stuff* in line 184). Be sure to enunciate the end of one word and the beginning of the next separately, rather than slurring them together as we do in everyday speech. This will emphasize the second word of each pair, as well as support Ulysses's tone of disgust.

The fact that Achilles and his good friend Patroclus spend so much time alone together in Achilles' tent is lost on no one in the Greek camp. In fact, one of the other Greeks calls Patroclus Achilles' "male varlot," a combination of *varlet* (meaning both valet and rascal) and *harlot*. Throughout his speech, Ulysses uses double entendre to express his contempt for Achilles and Patroclus. He may believe they are having a sexual relationship, or he may merely be insulting them with homophobic wordplay. The following second meanings would have been easily understood—and enjoyed—by the audience of Shakespeare's time: *pressed* = pressed down during sex; *arming to answer*: arm = penis; answer = a thrust during sex [*arming to answer* = preparing the penis to penetrate]; *Shake in and out the rivet*: since a rivet is phallic, you can figure this one out for yourself;

sport = "rolling in the hay"; *dies* = has an orgasm; *spleen* = penis or semen. In light of these definitions, phrases such as *O, enough Patroclus / I shall split all in pleasure of my spleen* take on new meaning.

SIGNIFICANT SCANS

The monologue contains many lines with extra syllables, most notably double endings both at line ends and mid-line before caesuras. All these extra syllables in Ulysses' speech add to its density, which you are free to interpret: Does he sound like a stammerer? Is he a fast talker? Does he sound wordy? Is he packing the words in because he has a lot to communicate? Is he the kind of guy who can't keep it brief? And so on.

Line 161 can be scanned in two ways. You may crowd the fourth foot (*At this fus*—):

x / x / x / x - x / x /
Would seem hyperboles. At this fusty stuff

Or you may elide *hyperboles* (hie-PER-bleez):

x / x / x / x / x /
Would seem hyperboles. At this fusty stuff

Another example of extra syllables is line 168, which is hexameter (a rare, six-footed line):

x /x / x /x /x / x /
Of parallels, as like as Vulcan and his wife

Line 148's two feet of spoken text stand out by contrast with these hypersyllabic lines. While you have the option of placing the line's three silent feet at the front of the line or some before and some after the words, we recommend that you use the pause at the end of the line to make the shift in which Ulysses decides to illustrate what he has just said.

You may scan line 166 in either of two ways: you may elide *being* (beeng) and expand *oration* (or-RAY´-shee-UN), which emphasizes the portrayal of Nestor's pomposity—

x / x / x / x /x/
As he, being dressed to some oration

Or, if you are uncomfortable with the expansion, you may take a one-syllable pause at the caesura, which eliminates the elision and the expansion, and creates a double ending—

x / x /x / x / x / (x)
As he, (pause) being dressed to some oration

Don't forget to elide: *our* (owr) in lines 143, 146, and 179; *hyperboles* (hie-PER-bleez) in line 161 (optional); *being* (beeng) in line 166 (optional); *fumbling* (FUM-bling) in line 174; *enough* (nuff) in line 176; and *Severals* (SEV-rulz) in line 180;

. . . to contract: *With him* (With'm) in line 146 and *play him* (play'm) in line 170;

. . . and to expand: *oration* (or-RAY′-shee-UN) in line 166 (optional) and *preventions* (pre-VEN′-shee-UNZ) in line 181.

ULYSSES: KING; WAR HERO; ACCIDENTAL TOURIST

Later dubbed Ulysses by the Romans, our hero was known as Odysseus to his fellow Greeks. King of the Greek island Ithaca, newly married to the remarkable Penelope, and proud father of Telemachus, a bouncing baby boy, the last thing Ulysses wanted was to haul off to Troy and fight someone else's ten-year war (see "The Trojan War: Back to Haunt You," page 973). But once on Trojan soil, Ulysses proved a brilliant strategist and brave warrior. His coup de grace, the Trojan Horse ploy, finally secured the Greeks' victory.

Subsequent generations of Greeks passed down the tale of the war and its aftermath, 'til it grew like that fish your pappy caught in '42. Ulysses was one of the favorites in the saga, even worshipped as a demigod in some parts. But it was the blind poet Homer who launched Ulysses into posterity by giving him a featured role in his epic poem the *Iliad*.

Building on the *Iliad*'s runaway success, Homer made Ulysses a star in the eponymously titled spinoff, the *Odyssey*, which has made the Epic Bestseller List 140,400 weeks running. An immediate hit, the *Odyssey* recounted Ulysses' protracted voyage home to his beloved wife and child. All he did was take one wrong turn and poke a cyclops in the eye, and he was screwed: the cyclops's god-of-the-sea dad, Neptune, turned what should have been a short hop home into an eleven-year megillah, during which Ulysses had to rescue his crew-turned-pigs from the enchantment of the daughter of the sun, resist the irresistible Sirens' song, escape a six-headed monster and a deadly whirlpool, pass up the chance for immortality with a beautiful sea nymph, swim for miles in deadly waters, beg for food and clothing, and prove his valor in Olympic sports.

And that's not all. Ulysses arrived home to find that his wife and son had effectively been held captive in their own castle for the last twenty years by the hundred or so suitors who assumed him dead and wanted to marry his wife. The resourceful Penelope had managed to hold them off this long, but the suitors were tired of feasting, partying, and using up Ulysses' land and possessions, and were nearing the end of their patience. Ulysses arrived just in time to trick the evil suitors, kill them all in revenge, and live happily ever after with his family.

TROILUS AND CRESSIDA

ACT III, SCENE ii

CRESSIDA

GENDER: F
PROSE/VERSE: blank verse
AGE RANGE: young adult
FREQUENCY OF USE (1–5): 4

Prince Troilus is totally sweet on Cressida. Cressida is *totally* sweet on Troilus. Troilus has laid his cards on the table. Cressida has played hers close to the chest because, as everyone knows, no Trojan prince worth his salt will buy the cow unless it plays hard to get. Troilus has been groveling for months. Cressida's uncle has finally arranged a tryst at her home: pheromones fill the air. Troilus swears his everlasting love. Cressida finally confesses hers, as well. Troilus has just asked his love why she was so hard to win. She replies:

125 Hard to seem won; but I was won, my lord,
With the first glance that ever—pardon me:
If I confess too much, you will play the tyrant.
I love you now, but till now not so much
But I might master it. In faith, I lie:
130 My thoughts were like unbridled children grown
Too headstrong for their mother. See, we fools!
Why have I blabbed? Who shall be true to us
When we are so unsecret to ourselves?
But though I loved you well, I wooed you not—
135 And yet, good faith, I wished myself a man,
Or that we women had men's privilege
Of speaking first. Sweet, bid me hold my tongue,
For in this rapture I shall surely speak
The thing I shall repent. See, see—your silence,
140 Cunning in dumbness, from my weakness draws
My very soul of counsel—stop my mouth!

1 minute

125 *Hard to seem won* I seemed hard to win; *my lord* a common term of address for a nobleman; 128 *not so much / But I might master it* not so much that I couldn't control it; 129 *In faith* Truly, indeed; 130 *unbridled* unruly; 131 *we fools* referring to women; 132 *us* referring, again, to women; 133 *unsecret to ourselves* betraying our own secrets (and therefore untrue to ourselves); 135 *good faith* in good faith, truly; *wished myself* wished I were; 137 *speaking first* i.e., making the overtures in courtship; *Sweet* Sweetheart; 138 *rapture* lovesick delirium; *speak* say; 139 *The thing* a thing, something; *repent* regret; 140 *Cunning in dumbness* strategically mute; *draws* draws out, extracts; 141 *very soul of counsel* innermost secrets [*from my weakness . . . of counsel* extracts my innermost secrets (i.e., my love for you) out of my weakness]; *Stop my mouth* (1) Stop up (plug up) my mouth; and thereby (2) Stop my mouth from talking.

COMMENTARY

Cressida is completely nuts for Troilus, and she doesn't want to mess it up. She's *this* close to clinching the deal, and she has got to play her cards right: as every young Trojan gentlewoman knows, lesson number one in husband catching is "Don't chase them, make them chase you." It was easy to be coy when they were just pen pals, but now that he's standing here, plopping his heart in her lap, it's hard to not jump him, never mind keep her feelings to herself. But that would ruin everything and stop Troilus in his tracks faster than a Grecian arrow.

There's no room for trifling emotionalism in a transaction as important as a love match. For generations, Trojan women have secured their mates through the tactical deployment of aloofness and reserve. Cressida uses antithesis in an attempt to implement this method by discussing love in a businesslike manner. She uses the device to be both forthright (because she wants to be) and deceitful (because she thinks she has to be): *seem won* versus *was won*; *I confess* versus *you will play*; *love you now* versus *till now not so much*; *true to us* versus *unsecret to ourselves*; *I loved you well* versus *I wooed you not*; and *wished myself a man* versus *that we women had men's privilege / Of speaking first*.

In addition to antithesis, Cressida also uses words and phrases that have more than one meaning. When Cressida says that Troilus will *play the tyrant*, she means two related things: (1) as soon as he knows he has won her, he will no longer need to woo her, and will begin to act like her lord and master (as he will when they are married); (2) if his wooing succeeds too easily, he will not value the prize, and will be a tyrannical lord and master, rather than a loving one. There are many meanings in the question *Who shall be true to us / When we are so unsecret to ourselves?*, the primary one being "What men will be true to us women if we can't even be true to ourselves?" In specific terms, her question asks how Cressida could expect Troilus to love and commit to her if she reveals her love for him. In general, it asks, "Who will ever fall in love with us again if we reveal our game plan for snaring men?"—a blunder Cressida can't stop herself from making in this piece. And with *us*, *we*, and *ourselves* Cressida may be using the royal "we," which, while not her primary intent, could either help her restore her dignity and distance from Troilus, or betray her desire to wed Prince Troilus and thus become a royal personage.

In Cressida's opening line, *seem* and *was* naturally receive emphasis even though they fall on unaccented syllables within the meter of the line. Simply speak the line as you would in normal speech, giving them the stress they merit. Because the stress is unexpected, the words will have the heightened emphasis they need to set up the rest of the monologue.

The frequent inverted (trochaic) feet at the beginnings of lines and following caesuras enhance the sense that Cressida speaks in fits and starts as she blurts out her feelings and then quickly tries to recant and regain control. The infrequent occurrence of double endings or elisions and expansions keeps the meter rolling and fosters the sense that she's nervously babbling.

Don't forget to elide: *you will* (Yool) in line 127;

. . . and to expand: *privilege* (PRI´-vi-LEDJ) in line 136.

THE TRAGEDIES

Elizabethan and Jacobean tragedy began to take shape in the middle of the sixteenth century, when English playwrights turned for inspiration to ancient Greek and Roman tragedy, which centered on a hero whose fatal flaws cause social upheaval and whose downfall is necessary to restore social order, producing catharsis for the audience. The most influential classical tragedian was Seneca, from whom Shakespeare and his contemporaries adopted the five-act structure, the use of *sententiae* (pithy statements), and bloody topics often involving portents and supernatural events. The main subgenres of tragedy that emerged were the domestic tragedy (of which *Othello* is Shakespeare's only example), which focuses on events with personal rather than societal consequences; the villain tragedy, in which an aggressive individual is at once villainous and heroic (as in *Macbeth*); and the revenge tragedy, the most popular category (to which *Titus Andronicus* conforms closely, and which *Hamlet* stems from but surpasses). Shakespeare conformed to these subgenres but usually far transcended them, especially during his "tragic period," roughly 1601–1608, the years in which he concentrated intensely on the genre. Four plays from this period (*Hamlet*, *Othello*, *King Lear*, and *Macbeth*) are considered to be the masterpieces of Shakespeare's canon.

ANTONY AND CLEOPATRA

ACT I, SCENE v

CLEOPATRA

GENDER: F
PROSE/VERSE: blank verse
AGE RANGE: adult to mature adult
FREQUENCY OF USE (1–5): 3

Egypt's Queen Cleopatra is having an affair with Mark Antony, one of the Triumvirs who rule the Roman Empire. As Egypt is part of Antony's third of the empire, Cleo hopes to keep a firm hold on her power through her relationship with him. She has masterfully manipulated the besotted Antony with her well-practiced courtesan's wiles, but in the process she has also fallen head over heels in love with him. Antony has dallied too long in Egypt; his third of the empire is in a shambles due to his neglect, and he has just returned to Rome to straighten things out. Cleopatra can't stand it! She shares her feelings with her waiting-women and her eunuch, addressing her favorite attendant, Charmian:

O Charmian!
Where think'st thou he is now? Stands he, or sits he?
20 Or does he walk? Or is he on his horse?
O happy horse to bear the weight of Antony!
Do bravely, horse, for wot'st thou whom thou mov'st?
The demi-Atlas of the earth, the arm
And burgonet of men. He's speaking now,
25 Or murmuring, "Where's my serpent of old Nile?"
For so he calls me. Now I feed myself
With most delicious poison. Think on me,
That am with Phoebus' amorous pinches black,
And wrinkled deep in time. Broad-fronted Caesar,
30 When thou wast here above the ground, I was
A morsel for a monarch; and great Pompey
Would stand and make his eyes grow in my brow,
There would he anchor his aspect, and die
With looking on his life.

1 minute

18 *Charmian* (KAR´-mee-AN is preferred, but SHAR´— and CHAR´— are also acceptable); 21 *happy* lucky, fortunate; 22 *bravely* splendidly; in a manner worthy of the cry "bravo"; *wot'st thou* do you know; 23 *demi-Atlas* half-Atlas (In classical mythology, the Titan Atlas was condemned by Zeus to support the heavens on his shoulders [later, the world replaced the heavens as his burden]. Here, Antony and Caesar each bear the weight of half the Roman world—the third member of the Triumvirate, Lepidus, is of no consequence); *arm* i.e., the strong arm, armor or weapons of a soldier (symbolizing offensive strength); 24 *burgonet* (BUR´-guh-NET) helmet (of the particular style invented in the 1400s by Burgundians [to Jacobeans, a symbol of defensive strength]) [*the arm and burgonet* i.e., the model soldier]; 25 *serpent of old Nile* Egyptian cobra (a highly venomous snake, the asp, which Egyptians held in reverence and used as a symbol of royalty); 27 *on* of; 28 *Phoebus'* (FEE-buss) the sun, personified as Phoebus Apollo, god of the sun in classical mythology [*with Phoebus' amorous pinches black* i.e., darkly tanned by the loving "pinches" of the sun's rays]; 29 *wrinkled deep in time* deeply wrinkled by time; *Broad-fronted* Having a broad forehead or face (may refer to his receding hairline); *Caesar* Julius Caesar (who helped Cleopatra wrest control of Egypt from her brother-husband, Ptolemy XII, when she was only twenty-one years old; Caesar was her lover from then until his death); 30 *here above the ground* i.e., alive; 31 *Pompey* Gnaius Pompeius (another of Cleopatra's past lovers; older brother of the Pompey in the play, and son of Julius Caesar's enemy Pompey the Great—Shakespeare may have used the word *great* to confuse the two, intentionally padding Cleopatra's résumé of romantic conquests); 32 *make his eyes grow in my brow* i.e., fix his gaze on my face; 33 *aspect* (a-SPECT) gaze; *die* i.e., pine away from love and passion; 34 *on* at; *his life* i.e., Cleopatra (a common term of endearment in Shakespeare's work).

COMMENTARY

Good news! The giddy, infatuated schoolgirl in us doesn't die with the first signs of cellulite, she just hibernates until we come across a monologue like this one (or a cute, brooding, poverty-stricken saxophone player). While feeding herself *delicious poison*, Cleopatra feeds us delicious material. Cleo combines the charm of an excited schoolgirl with the sensuality of an experienced lover and the sexual savvy of a courtesan. No wonder so many powerful men found her fascinating.

These layers of Cleopatra's personality are revealed in both the monologue's meter and rhetorical devices. At the start of the piece, she crams four interrogatives into two lines, jumping in on herself with adolescent animation, and giving Charmian no time to reply. Yet in the very next line she begins to use some very adult sexual double entendre. Note the second meanings of these words, with which Jacobeans would have been familiar: *horse* = "whores"; *bear the weight* = take the underneath position in missionary-style sexual intercourse (*happy horse to bear the weight of Antony*: aside from Cleo's obvious meaning, this is also a reference to the political "whores" [Caesar's sycophants] back in Rome who have borne the "weight" of his duties while he was away, and must "wait" for Antony to arrive, when they will "bear his weight" [be nailed by him]—these are plays on earlier uses of the word in the play); *do* = "do the deed," i.e., have sex; *mov'st* = move, i.e., sexually arouse; *pinches* = sexual caresses; *wrinkle* = act of sex [*wrinkled deep* = having often been the receiver of sexual acts]; *morsel* = sexually tasty tidbit; *stand* = have an erection; *eyes* = genitals [here, penis]; *brow* = pubis [the mound over the genitals, as the eyebrow is over the eye]; *die* = experience an orgasm. In light of these meanings, and within the context of the last few lines, *his eyes grow in my brow* and *anchor his aspect, and die* take on interesting new meanings.

This is one of the few times when one of Shakespeare's characters uses double entendre overtly. Perhaps Cleopatra is evoking for herself the enjoyable memories of her dalliances with Antony, or is tantalizing herself in anticipation of his eventual return. Or maybe she's amusing herself by scandalizing her attendants. Or all of the above. Some of the double meanings will still be clear for today's audiences. If you enjoy them, feel free to play actively whichever words and phrases you think best, noting the others for your private understanding of the character. Cleopatra's deliberate use of double entendre reveals that she perceives herself as an irresistible lover—even the sun god is attracted to her! Later in the play she will also see Death as a lover.

The several double endings and inverted feet combine with the many sentences that begin and end mid-line to give Cleopatra's speech a jumpy cadence, in which one thought rushes upon the next and transitions occur quickly. This creates an energy that propels her on a rapid path through the monologue.

Although the piece is short, it does have a fairly important transition midway through. In the first lines, Cleopatra seems caught up in her emotions. Then, in the middle of line 26, she changes gears; she becomes more self-aware, switching her focus from Antony to herself (after all, how long can such a self-involved queen concentrate on something other than herself?) and examining her reactions. Two possible interpretations have been suggested for the next phrase (another new thought beginning mid-line with *Think on me . . .*). *Think* may refer to Antony, as in "How could Antony possibly be thinking (i.e., lovingly/lustily) about me?" Or Cleopatra could be saying, "Let's take an honest look at me . . ." In either case, you must decide whether Cleopatra is examining her beauty (and, as seen above, sexual experience) seriously, perhaps fearing that her age has marred her beauty, or whether she is doing it humorously, perhaps fishing for compliments from her attendants, or simply trying to make them (and herself) laugh. Her actual age (about twenty-nine) could support either interpretation: in Shakespeare's time a woman of twenty-nine, although by no means old, was also no spring chicken. On the other hand, ancient Roman standards (and life expectancy) were quite different from Jacobean ones, and Plutarch wrote that Cleopatra met Antony "at the age when a woman's beauty is at the prime, and she is also of best judgment." It has become customary to cast Antony and Cleopatra as older lovers, and to portray Cleo as well past twenty-nine, yet stunning. So it is entirely valid to play her as an older woman who is completely confident of her sexual attraction.

Cleopatra's confidence is evident in her use of the familiar *thou* throughout the piece. This is not unusual, since she is speaking to close confidants, as well as figuratively to (and of) men who were her lovers—yet one wonders if there is *anyone* with whom Egypt's Queen uses the respectful "you"! Also, you must decide when Cleopatra is addressing her attendants, and when and to what extent she is talking to herself.

Keep an eye out for the little sound bites of assonance and consonance in the piece, which Cleopatra uses like a spice to enhance her often flippant, humorous comments (for example: *happy horse*; *morsel for a monarch*; *anchor his aspect*). And for help using the sound of the word *O* to its best advantage, see "O, No! An O!," page xxxiii.

You probably caught Cleopatra's foreshadowing reference to her eventual suicide in the phrases *serpent of old Nile* and *feed myself with most delicious poison*; it's a thrilling device with which Shakespeare takes advantage of his audience's familiarity with the story. Cleopatra, however, has no idea she's doing it. That's what makes it work, so don't play it. You should also be aware that earlier in this scene, Cleopatra asked Charmian for a dose of mandragora, a sleeping potion made from the mandrake plant, which contains a strong narcotic. It has been suggested that the words *Now I feed myself / With most delicious poison* are an embedded stage direction indicating that Cleopatra now receives and drinks the potion. But there is no actual stage direction to this effect, and the words in question work quite well in reference to her thoughts alone, especially as the idea of love as a "sweet poison" was proverbial. We suggest that you not muddy your performance and sap your energy level by playing this monologue as though you were drugged, particularly in an audition.

Don't forget to elide: *Antony* (ANT-nee) in line 21 (or make it a triple ending [ANT-uh-nee]); *murmuring* (MUR-mring) in line 25; *Phoebus'* (FEE-buss, *not* FEE-buss-ez) and *amorous* (AM-russ) in line 28.

ATHENIAN ARROGATOR/EGYPTIAN EMPRESS/DRAMA QUEEN

The most famous Egyptian of all time was actually Greek. Cleopatra VII's ancestor the first Ptolemy, a leading general in the Greek army of Alexander the Great, seized Egypt for himself after Alexander's death. Ptolemy made himself king, and his descendants—considered demigods by their subjects—reigned after him in a long line of succession leading directly to Cleopatra. Following the Ptolemaic custom of marriage between siblings, Cleopatra was married at seventeen to her twelve-year-old brother, Ptolemy XII, and they ruled jointly. With the help of Julius Caesar, Cleopatra wrested control of Egypt from her brother-husband. After Ptolemy XII accidentally drowned in the Nile, Cleopatra married the next brother in line, Ptolemy XIII (then age eleven). Her second marriage didn't stop her from having an affair with Julius Caesar (whose son Caesarion would become Ptolemy XIV, the last in the dynasty), and she soon had her second husband-brother poisoned. By some accounts, Cleopatra found true passion with Antony. Though it's not mentioned in the play, Cleopatra and Antony were married in 36 B.C.E., but as Antony was already married to Octavia, the marriage was not recognized by Rome (or by straitlaced Jacobean theatregoers). Antony treated Cleopatra as his wife, recognized their three children as his legitimate heirs, and eventually divorced Octavia for Cleopatra. Although Cleopatra did fight alongside Antony against Caesar, Shakespeare attributes to her rather more of the blame for Antony's defeat than is her due (see "Antony A-Go-Go," page 619). Furthermore, though Cleopatra was renowned for her appeal to men, it was her intelligence and mesmerizing charisma that drew them: her beauty was Shakespeare's invention. Likewise (as far as we know) her peevishness, her self-centered nature, and her penchant for dramatics.

ANTONY AND CLEOPATRA

ACT II, SCENE ii

ENOBARBUS

GENDER: M
PROSE/VERSE: blank verse
AGE RANGE: mature adult
FREQUENCY OF USE (1–5): 4

Mark Antony's loyal chief lieutenant, Enobarbus, is worried about him: Antony has foolishly fallen for Egypt's Queen Cleopatra and has ignored his responsibilities to his fellow rulers of Rome, Caesar and Lepidus. Furthermore, the two wrongly suspect Antony of wishing to depose them and rule solo. The three rulers and their followers have just held a summit meeting in Rome, at which it has been decided that the newly widowed Antony will marry Caesar's sister, Octavia. After the meeting, some of the followers have expressed relief that Antony and Caesar have thus mended their friendship, but Enobarbus is sure that Antony will eventually desert Caesar's sister for Cleopatra, and explains:

ENOBARBUS

195 I will tell you—
The barge she sat in, like a burnished throne,
Burned on the water: the poop was beaten gold;
Purple the sails, and so perfumèd that
The winds were lovesick with them; the oars were silver,
200 Which to the tune of flutes kept stroke, and made
The water which they beat to follow faster,
As amorous of their strokes. For her own person,
It beggared all description: she did lie
In her pavilion—cloth of gold, of tissue—
205 O'erpicturing that Venus where we see
The fancy outwork Nature. On each side her
Stood pretty dimpled boys, like smiling Cupids,
With divers-colored fans, whose wind did seem
To glow the delicate cheeks which they did cool,
210 And what they undid did.

Her gentlewomen, like the Nereides,
So many mermaids, tended her i' th' eyes,
And made their bends adornings. At the helm

196 *barge* pleasure boat; *burnished* bright, shining; 197 *poop* the raised deck on the aftermost part of a ship; *was beaten gold* i.e., was made of gold (*beaten gold* could mean either [1] completely covered in gold leaf or [2] made entirely of gold that has been forged into shape); 200 *to the tune of flutes kept stroke* rowed to the rhythm of music played on flutes; 202 *As amorous of* as though in love with; *For her own person* As for Cleopatra's own external appearance; 203 *beggared all description* exhausted the resources of description, i.e., was beyond one's ability to describe; 204 *pavilion* tent [*In her pavilion* under the shade of a canopy]; *cloth of gold, of tissue* Generally believed to mean a rich silk interwoven with threads of gold. *Tissue* meant that the threads of gold were twisted rather than plain, which created a thicker, more luxurious texture; 205 *O'erpicturing* outdepicting, surpassing the picture of; *that Venus* scholars are not sure whether Shakespeare refers to a particular painting or sculpture of Venus, such as Apelles' *Venus Anadyomene* (in which Venus rises from the sea); 206 *fancy* imagination (of the painter); *outwork Nature* outperform nature (i.e., create a more beautiful image of woman than nature is capable of creating); *On each side her* On each side of her; 207 *like* in the guise of (as opposed to merely "resembling"); 208 *divers-colored* of different colors; 209 *glow* make hot, flush; 210 *And what they undid did* (UN-did) And redo what they undid [*fans, whose wind . . . undid did* i.e., fans, the breeze from which seemed to make Cleopatra's delicate cheeks even more hot and flushed, thereby undoing the cooling that they were assigned to do]; 211 *Her gentlewomen* i.e., Cleopatra's ladies-in-waiting; *the Nereides* (NEER´-ee-IDZ) In ancient Greek mythology, fifty beautiful sea nymphs, completely human in form, the daughters of the minor sea deities Doris and Nereus (who was also known as "the old man of the sea"); 212 *So many* as if they were that many; *tended her i' th' eyes* several possible meanings: (1) waited on her within her sight (as opposed to in the background); (2) waited on her every glance (i.e., anticipated her every need); (3) actually attended to her eyes (perhaps shading them, or making them beautiful, or, with second definition of line 213, "tended to what she looked at"); 213 *made their bends*

A seeming mermaid steers—the silken tackle
215 Swell with the touches of those flower-soft hands
That yarely frame the office. From the barge
A strange invisible perfume hits the sense
Of the adjacent wharfs. The city cast
Her people out upon her; and Antony,
220 Enthroned i' th' market place, did sit alone,
Whistling to the air, which, but for vacancy,
Had gone to gaze on Cleopatra too,
And made a gap in nature.
Upon her landing, Antony sent to her,
225 Invited her to supper. She replied,
It should be better he became her guest,
Which she entreated. Our courteous Antony,
Whom ne'er the word of "No" woman heard speak,
Being barbered ten times o'er, goes to the feast,
230 And for his ordinary pays his heart
For what his eyes eat only.

2 minutes

adornings two possible meanings: (1) made their bowing (to Cleopatra) graceful and lovely to behold; (2) made what her eyes looked at (bended upon) lovely to see (with third definition of line 212); 214 *A seeming mermaid* i.e., a lady-in-waiting in the guise of a mermaid; *tackle* a ship's ropes and sails; 216 *yarely* (YAHR-lee or YAIR-lee) readily, nimbly, skillfully (a sailing term); *frame the office* perform the job; 217 *hits the sense / Of the adjacent wharfs* struck the senses of (was detected by) the people on nearby wharfs; 218 *The city cast . . . upon her* i.e., the people of the city all rushed out to greet her; 220 *Enthroned i' th' market place* seated upon his throne in the market place (as was the custom of Roman rulers); 221 *but for vacancy* but for the fact that nature abhors a vacuum; 222 *Had gone* would have gone; 223 *And made* and would have made; 226 *should* might; 228 *Whom ne'er the word of "No" woman heard speak* primarily, whom no woman ever heard speak the word "No"; but also implying, who never heard a woman speak the word "No"; 230 *ordinary* meal ("ordinary" actually meant a public dinner in a tavern; Enobarbus uses the word to be amusing).

COMMENTARY

Leave it to Shakespeare to put some of the most sensuous descriptive poetry in all of his plays into the mouth of one of his gruffest, least romantically inclined, most sardonic characters. This paradox offers an actor the opportunity to produce a wonderfully layered monologue, in which a character goes against type to accomplish a desired end. The extent to which this is uncomfortable for Enobarbus (if at all) is up to you.

So why does Enobarbus deliver this speech? He has a compelling reason to lay it on thick: he must disabuse his colleagues of the notion that Antony's marriage to Caesar's sister, Octavia, will smooth over the tensions between the two rulers and stave off civil war. Enobarbus knows that Antony is addicted to Cleopatra and will be incapable of giving her up . . . and who would be? As Enobarbus has seen firsthand, she is an erotic fantasy come true. He needs to make his listeners understand that because of Cleopatra's hypnotic effect on Antony, more trouble lies ahead . . . despite the positive timbre of the meeting they've just conducted and despite whether Antony intends to stray or not. So as not to be dismissed out of hand by the other men, Enobarbus must fully describe the erotic spell Cleopatra has cast on Antony.

To say that imagery (most often simile) is Enobarbus's primary technique would be an understatement. This monologue is renowned for it. Enobarbus not only paints a vivid picture of Cleopatra's splendor, he also fully engages almost all the senses of his listeners. And yet to prevent this piece from becoming a laundry list of descriptors, you must realize that Enobarbus uses these descriptions to tell a story with a beginning, middle, and end: he progresses from the first sighting of Cleopatra upriver to the heartstopping effect she produced on those ashore as the boat progressed toward Antony, to the insulting (albeit humorous) abandonment of Antony by his supplicants in the marketplace upon her arrival, to the invitations he and she exchanged, to Antony's nervous preparation for their meeting, to the inevitable outcome of that first feast.

Be sure to clearly visualize for yourself each of the many details that combined to create what must have been a spectacular and memorable event for those who experienced it. In effect, Enobarbus is acknowledging Cleopatra as one of the earliest special-effects experts. As his painting references suggest, Cleopatra is both the painter and the subject of her painting (portraying herself as a goddess, just as an artist has created the supernaturally beautiful *Venus* Enobarbus mentions); she is at once the director (as well as the set, costume, and lighting designer) of her own pageant, and its celebrated and worshipped theme. You may interpret this monologue as either a thunderstruck homage to her splendor (despite Enobarbus's disapproval of Antony's affair with her) or a shrewd assessment of her cunning artistry and manipulation . . . or both.

Enobarbus uses hyperbole to impress upon his colleagues Cleopatra's presence and power. Whether to express awe of Cleopatra or to point out her calculated artistry, Enobarbus heaps image upon image, elaborately overdescribing each element of the spectacle (*The winds were lovesick with them*; *O'erpicturing that Venus where we see / The fancy outwork Nature*; *So many mermaids*; *Being barbered ten times o'er*—to point out a few). Also notice the humorous picture of Antony presiding over an empty marketplace, thoroughly upstaged by the arrival of the luscious-looking, -smelling, and -sounding queen. As with his initial descriptions, you must decide whether this extravagant imagery stems from a frank appreciation of a remarkable experience and/or whether it is intended to be deprecating, since Enobarbus has made it clear elsewhere in the play that he does not approve of Antony's dallying with Cleopatra at the expense of his political responsibilities. Notice that after setting the scene for the Egyptian Queen, Enobarbus uses the emphatic form when introducing his listeners to her for the first time in line 203 (*she did lie*), which literally helps her make a grand entrance.

Enobarbus's imagery of sailors tying intricate knots has a subtle double meaning: *tended her i' th' eyes, / And made their bends adornings*—an *eye* is the loop of a cord and a *bend* is the knot. Is he suggesting that Cleopatra's servants helped her tie her viewers in knots? Is this part of a sexual double entendre, suggestive either of sadomasochism (bondage) or of sex generally ("tuck length of rope through loop . . .")? Enobarbus uses sexual innuendo (with such words as the oars' ever-quickening *strokes* and the mermaid-clad servants' *bends*, the phrases *she did lie* and *what they undid did* or the sentence *the silken tackle / Swell with the touches of those flower-soft hands* . . .), as well as extensive sexual and bodily function double entendre in describing this scene to "the guys." The double meanings of the following words and phrases would have been familiar to audiences in Shakespeare's time: *barge* is synonymous with *foist*, which means "fart"; *burnished* / *burned* = suffered from venereal disease; *throne* = (1) toilet; (2) "thrown" (sexually tumbled); *poop* = (1) syphilis; (2) a man's buttocks; *gold* = excrement; *winds* = farts; *lovesick* = sick with venereal disease; *fancy* = sexual desire; *lie* = recline for sexual intercourse; *Cupids* = pimps; *fans* = buttocks; *eye* = vagina; *yare* = sexually ready, well-endowed; *perfume* = whore; *sense* = "scents" (incense used to cure venereal disease); *cast* = vomited; *Enthroned* = on the toilet; *Whistling* = (1) farting (*Enthroned / Whistling* = farting on the toilet); (2) "Siffling" (having syphilis); *barber* = whore.

Though substituting the double meanings does not give the whole passage a coherent second meaning (although it does give occasional lines vivid second meanings, such as lines 208–9), the pervasive double entendre creates a general tone of bawdiness, as well as a suggestion of filth, disease, and moral decay that conveys Enobarbus's feelings about Antony's affair with the Egyptian Queen.

Notice how the sounds express both Enobarbus's character and the delicious scene he portrays. When juxtaposed with the sensuousness of the scene, the Brusque and aBruPt Bs and Ps at the start of this monologue (*barge / burnished / Burned / poop / beaten / Purple / perfumèd*) help establish Enobarbus's gruff personality. Enobarbus then uses sounds to heighten the sensuality of the imagery, with hypnotic assonance such as *tune of flutes* and *faster, / As amorous* (here, the build of assonance does seem to quicken the pace) and with even more sensuous consonance, such as the pleaSing Ss, yuMMy Ms, and Flowery Fs (*follow faster, / As amorous of their strokes*; *gentlewomen / So many mermaids / eyes / made / bends adornings / helm / seeming mermaid steers / silken / Swell / touches of those flower-soft hands / frame the office. From*). Enobarbus's gruffness reasserts itself in the Graceless Gs toward the end of the piece (*gone to gaze / gap*).

Despite his elegant descriptions, Enobarbus often uses colloquial expressions such as *For her own person, / It beggared all description*; the casual and humorous *Our courteous Antony, / Whom ne'er the word of "No" woman heard speak, / Being barbered ten times o'er*; and the lowbrow term *ordinary*. He also casually alternates between past and present tense in a colloquial manner. These touches create an anecdotal tone, which may suggest that grim as his overall message is, Enobarbus enjoys relating the event to the guys.

SIGNIFICANT SCANS

In the first line, you can either contract *I will* (I'll) and give the line one and a half feet of spoken text:

x / x
I will tell you

Or treat the line as headless with two feet of spoken text:

x / x / x
(pause) I will tell you

Either way, most of the line is silent. Perhaps Enobarbus uses the pause to build anticipation in his listeners. Or perhaps he is trying to decide which magnificent detail to re-create first.

This monologue has many double endings at the ends of lines, as well as mid-line at caesuras (and, in line 199, at both). These double endings soften line endings, which, along with the many elisions, adds to the sensuous quality of the piece.

There are several lines that contain fewer than five feet of spoken text. Line 210 has only three spoken feet (the remainder of the line, spoken by one of Caesar's followers, has been excised to create the monologue), which gives you a two-foot pause . . . perhaps to gauge the effect of your description on the guys, or to collect yourself, if you've been getting a bit too hot yourself at the memory . . . (You'll notice that the stress falls on "un" in *undid*, which helps clarify the meaning of the line.) Line 223 has only three and a half feet of spoken text, providing a transitional pause in which to fast-forward the story from the boat trip to Cleopatra's landing. Finally, the last line is also only three feet (with a double ending): we suggest you use the last two silent feet—perhaps to hammer home your final point (that Antony is lost) with some physical action, perhaps to assess whether your words have had their desired effect, or perhaps to enjoy a laugh at your own witticism.

Don't forget to elide: *amorous* (AM-russ) in line 202; *O'erpicturing* (ore-PIC′-chur-ING) in line 205; *smiling* (SMIE-ling) in line 207; *delicate* (DEL-kit) in line 209; *flower-soft* (FLOWR-soft) in line 215; *invisible* (in-VIZ-bl) in line 217; *Antony* (ANT-nee) in line 224 (but not in lines 219 and 227); *Our* (owr) and *courteous* (KUR-tyuss) in line 227; *ne'er* (NAIR) in line 228; *Being* (beeng) and *o'er* (ORE) in line 229;

. . . and to contract: *I will* (I'll) in line 195 (optional); *i' th' eyes* (ith-EYES) in line 212; *i' th' market* (ith-MAR-ket) in line 220; and *the air* (TH'AIR) in line 221.

GENERALLY SIDED WITH THE WINNER

The historical Enobarbus, Imperatorial General Gnaeus Domitius Ahenobarbus, was a real swashbuckler. A talented military commander, he fought for Pompey the Great against Julius Caesar, but was pardoned after Caesar's victory. He repaid the kindness by aligning with Caesar's assassins, Brutus and Cassius. He won an important battle for them at Philippi, for which he was made imperator (supreme commander). After Brutus and Cassius were defeated by Antony, Octavius Caesar, and Lepidus, Ahenobarbus took to the seas as a pirate, controlling the Adriatic with his own fleet and issuing coins bearing his own image. Eventually pardoned by Antony and made governor of Bithynia, he returned that favor with loyal support for eight years . . . but deserted Antony when the going got tough, before the battle of Actium (rather than after, as in the play), and died shortly thereafter. Shakespeare's source (North's translation of Plutarch) listed the cause of death as a broken heart, but illness seems a more likely culprit.

Stranger Than Fiction

Shakespeare didn't invent the details of Cleopatra's grand entrance into Antony's life. The silver oars, purple sails, golden poop, costumed attendants, and Cleopatra's own appearance in the guise of the love goddess were described by Plutarch in his *Life of Marcus Antonius*, and read by Shakespeare in Sir Thomas North's 1579 translation. Relying on the crusty Enobarbus to do the spectacle justice is the monologue's only dramatic leap.

ANTONY AND CLEOPATRA

ACT IV, SCENE xv

CLEOPATRA

GENDER: F
AGE RANGE: adult to mature adult
PROSE/VERSE: blank verse
FREQUENCY OF USE (1–5): 2

Cleopatra, Queen of Egypt, is holed up in her burial monument to avoid capture by Caesar's approaching forces. Meanwhile, her lover Antony, thinking her dead, has fatally wounded himself. Near death, he has been brought to Cleopatra on a litter. Fearing to unlock the gates lest she be captured, she and her attendants (Iras and Charmian) hoisted the dying Antony up into the monument. With his last words, Antony has told her to save her own life if possible, and to be proud of his past achievements and of his honorable death. As he dies, she laments:

Noblest of men, woo't die?

60 Hast thou no care of me? Shall I abide
In this dull world, which in thy absence is
No better than a sty? O, see, my women— [*Antony dies*]
The crown o' the earth doth melt. My lord?
O, withered is the garland of the war,

65 The soldier's pole is fallen; young boys and girls
Are level now with men; the odds is gone,
And there is nothing left remarkable
Beneath the visiting moon!

No more but e'en a woman, and commanded
By such poor passion as the maid that milks

75 And does the meanest chares. It were for me
To throw my scepter at the injurious gods,
To tell them that this world did equal theirs,
Till they had stol'n our jewel. All's but naught—
Patience is sottish, and impatience does

80 Become a dog that's mad; then is it sin
To rush into the secret house of death
Ere death dare come to us? How do you, women?
What, what, good cheer! Why how now, Charmian?

59 *woo't* wilt thou; 60 *care of* concern for; 62 *sty* filthy and imprisoning enclosure for swine (stronger meaning than today—not used colloquially to mean "a messy place"); 64 *the garland of the war* (1) the flower of all soldiers; (2) the crowning glory of the war; 65 *pole* several possible meanings, none exclusive of the others: (1) battle standard; (2) polestar (the North Star), i.e., the soldier all other soldiers looked to for guidance; (3) maypole (the maypole, a symbol of the phallus, was first used in pagan rituals of spring—in Shakespeare's time, maypoles were still entwined in garlands in every village on May Day); 66 *the odds is gone* there is no longer any distinction or difference between things (i.e., Antony's death has leveled the rest of the world to mediocrity; also, there is now no one to place odds on in the pursuit of glory); 67 *remarkable* marvelous (a new word in Shakespeare's time, with a stronger meaning than it has today); 68 *visiting* (1) i.e., regularly returning in its different phases; (2) afflicting; punishing (the goddess of the moon, Diana [a.k.a. Artemis], had several personalities, one of which was that of huntress and destroyer) [*Beneath the visiting moon* Jacobeans believed that everything above the moon was the realm of "permanence," while everything below it was the world of "mutability" (change), thus the reference to the moon, as opposed to today's "everything under the sun"]; 73 *No more but e'en* Nothing more than; 74 *such poor passion* the same contemptible passion (Jacobeans believed that women were prone to an ailment called "hysterica passio" [also called "the mother"]; it was thought to be brought on by strong emotions, and its symptoms included swooning, a sensation of choking, and seizures); 75 *the meanest chares* (CHAIRZ) the most menial chores; *It were for me* It would be right for me; 78 *All's but naught* i.e., everything is useless; 79 *sottish* foolish, doltishly stupid; *does / Become* suits; is fitting behavior for; 80 *mad* rabid; 82 *Ere* before; *dare* ventures to; *How do you* How are you doing; 83 *What* often, as here, used as a word of exclamation to express surprise, impatience, exulta-

My noble girls! Ah, women, women. Look!
85 Our lamp is spent, it's out! Good sirs, take heart.
We'll bury him; and then, what's brave, what's noble,
Let's do it after the high Roman fashion
And make death proud to take us. Come, away—
This case of that huge spirit now is cold.
90 Ah, women, women! Come, we have no friend
But resolution and the briefest end.

1 minute, 45 seconds

tion, etc.; *Why* often, as here, used to express (or pretend) surprise or a new perception; *how now* what is the matter; *Charmian* (KAR′-mee-AN is preferred, but SHAR′— and CHAR′— are also acceptable); 85 *lamp is spent* our torch is extinguished, i.e., Antony, our guiding light, is gone; *Good sirs* used in Shakespeare's time for both men and women; 86 *what's brave, what's noble* the act that's brave and noble (suicide); 87 *after* in, following; *high* dignified, exalted; deserving of respect and reverence; 88 *Come, away* i.e., come with me, and bring the body away with us; 89 *This case* i.e., Antony's corpse; 91 *resolution* i.e., the resolve to commit suicide; *briefest* swiftest.

COMMENTARY

There's no denying that Cleopatra loves her theatrics, and at the moment she couldn't ask for better material. There's also no denying the Queen's selfish nature, even at her beloved's deathbed. Most lovers' impulse would be to run out to the dying man, but she, fearing for her own safety, hoisted him up to her, which surely wasted precious minutes, and couldn't have been too comfortable for him. In the moment before this monologue, Cleopatra is so busy railing against Fortune that she almost doesn't let Antony say his last words. Even Antony's death is all about her: only about one third of this monologue mourns the great Antony—the rest focuses on Cleopatra's fate.

And yet it is impossible not to empathize with Cleopatra. Her lament over Antony, though brief, is gorgeous and heartfelt. Her flair for the dramatic may be vain, but it also expresses a deep appreciation of life. Cleopatra lives every moment with an exhilarating intensity that is hard to resist. Her combined qualities of youthful exuberance and worldly experience, of self-involvement and intense love of others, are what make her a complex and fascinating character to play, a woman who one moment uses her (and her servants') own brute strength to haul a dying man up to her on a litter, and the next is swooning over his death.

Such complexity creates great poignancy in the role. For instance, throughout the play Cleopatra has pouted and has cajoled Antony. Now, with *Hast thou no care of me*, she may be reacting in her usual fashion, or she may be tenderly teasing, recalling their old dynamic in a bittersweet way. However you play the monologue's opening lines, they reveal the coexistence of selfishness and love that sets its tone.

There are only three inverted (trochaic) feet in the piece, and two of them fall in the first two lines. Notice that this happens in the moment before Antony dies, so that the inversions add a feeling of urgency to Cleopatra's attempt to convince him not to die. The fact that the piece starts out mid-line also adds to the abruptness of her words. When Antony does die, Cleopatra's next line (63) has an interesting variation (in addition to the contraction of *o' the*). It contains a silent foot, which could be either the fourth or fifth foot in the line. We think it works best as the fourth:

x / x / x / x / x /
The crown o' the earth doth melt. (pause-pause) My lord?

The pause gives you time to take in Antony's death. The First Folio punctuates *My lord* as shown, with a question mark, which was most often intended as interrogative, but was sometimes used in place of an exclamation point. This leaves the phrase open to many interesting uses. Wherever you place the pause, your character must understand that Antony is dead by the time you utter the lamenting *O* at the start of the next line. For more on the effective use of *O*, be sure to see "O, No! An *O*!," page xxxiii. The only other trochaic inversion appears in the second half of the piece, which otherwise has fairly regular meter and several soft double endings. In contrast, the inversion in line 79 emphasizes the contempt and frustration with which Cleopatra spits out the word *Patience*.

Between the two sections of the speech, Cleopatra swoons and then recovers. Iras calls out "Empress" when she sees Cleopatra revive. The beginning of the second section, *No more but e'en a woman*, is often played as a direct response to Iras, but it is not necessary to approach the line this way. Cleopatra's great power as Empress is of no use now: Antony's death reduces her to the level of other women, the irony of which would surely strike her whether Iras speaks or not. It is a legitimate choice not to enact the swoon—you may simply use the two silent feet at the end of line 68 to allow this irony to occur to your character, and to make the transition from lamenting Antony to thinking of her own fate. If you do choose something physical, we suggest that you tone it down to a head rush, or a near faint, rather than a full swoon, as you will not have the conversation of the women to fill the awkward moment when you are "unconscious." Also, if you are using this as an audition piece, you will not want to waste precious time lying inert on the floor!

Given Cleopatra's penchant for the dramatic, her extensive use of imagery is not surprising. In the first section, she creates a build in imagery that elevates Antony first to the greatest of soldiers, then to the guiding example for all soldiers, then to the standard without which value cannot be measured, and finally to the only thing of value on the earth. Notice that assonance and consonance enhance this imagery (*withered / war*; *soldier's pole*; *odds / gone*), while the final image is intentionally stark in comparison, free of sound repetitions and ending mid-line, communicating the barrenness of the image. Cleopatra uses double entendre in two of her images of Antony: *The crown o' the earth doth melt* and *The soldier's pole is fallen* both express the loss of her favorite of Antony's attributes—his sexual prowess (in Shakespeare's day *crown* was a familiar euphemism for "genitals"; *pole* needs no explanation). In the second section, antithetical images reveal the turmoil in Cleopatra's mind: one moment she sees herself as no better than the common *maid that milks*, the next she imagines defying *the injurious gods*; *Patience is sottish*, while *impatience* is fitting for a rabid dog. Other images extend her exaltation of Antony (*our jewel*; *Our lamp*; *that huge spirit*). Still others help her imagine the deed she proposes, making it a tangible option (*rush into the secret house of death / Ere death dare come to us*) and securing the decision firmly in her mind (*make death proud to take us*).

Several sound repetitions in the second section emphasize Cleopatra's points. Pooh-Poohing Ps (*poor / passion*) and conteMptuous Ms (*maid / milks / meanest*) accentuate her feelings about her loss of stature; the assonance of *is it sin* highlights the moment she conceives a solution to her problem; the Defiant Ds (*death / death / dare*) express her bold overtures to death. The last two lines form a rhyming couplet (*friend / end*) that adds weight to Cleopatra's resolution and memorably wraps up monologue, scene, and act.

Be sure to pin down whom Cleopatra addresses at all times (her women, Antony, Antony's guards waiting below, or herself). Some of her comments to her women are unexpected (*What, what, good cheer! Why how now, Charmian?*): How are the women reacting to Antony's death and Cleopatra's words? Are they truly saddened for their Queen? Are they grieving for Antony? Are they fearful for themselves? Horrified by Cleo's theatrics? Cleopatra may feel brief elation at the thought of joining Antony in death (not to mention the sheer drama of it), which could explain her urging them to have *good cheer*. Perhaps it's all an act of bravura to help herself overcome her fear of committing suicide. Or maybe she's being sarcastic, or is crying through her words, and using them to cheer herself. Explore your options, and then specify for yourself the dynamic among the three women at every moment.

Notice how frequently Cleopatra calls out to her women. She is never alone, and has no soliloquies in the play. Her women are both her audience and her support system, and her frequent appeals to them here (at a moment when many would wish to be alone with the dying or dead loved one) give one the impression that she sees them as an extension of herself. Indeed, she assumes they will die with her. She calls Antony *our jewel* and *Our lamp*, and goes on to include the women in her suicide plans. Why? While she certainly assumes that, as is customary for an Egyptian ruler, her servants will die and be buried with her, there are additional factors to consider: Cleopatra may assume that her women feel the same loss of a great man that she does. She may not be quite as unafraid of death as her bravado suggests, so the thought of her women joining her may be comforting. And, given her larger-than-life persona, perhaps she does see the women as extensions of herself—when a massive star dies, the black hole it creates sucks the surrounding smaller stars into it. Though Cleopatra ascribes this quality to Antony, it is really a projection of herself.

Note that *Good sirs* is most likely intended toward the women (a common usage in Shakespeare's time), but can also be addressed to Antony's men (possibly still waiting below), to assure them that she will bury Antony with the appropriate splendor. Choose the interpretation that best suits your circumstances and your audience.

Don't forget to elide: *visiting* (VIZ-ting) in line 68 and *Our* (owr) in line 85;
. . . to contract: *o' the earth* (uh-THYERTH) in line 63;
. . . and to contract and elide: *the injurious* (th'in-JOOR-yuss) in line 76.

P.S.

For info on the historical Cleopatra, see "Athenian Arrogator/Egyptian Empress/Drama Queen," page 465.

ANTONY AND CLEOPATRA

ACT V, SCENE ii

CLEOPATRA

GENDER: F
AGE RANGE: adult to mature adult
PROSE/VERSE: blank verse
FREQUENCY OF USE (1–5): 3

Cleopatra's lover, Antony, has been defeated by Caesar and has nobly committed suicide. Caesar has taken Cleopatra prisoner and intends to bring her back to Rome, to be paraded through the streets in his triumphal march. Cleopatra has just tried to stab herself with her dagger, but was disarmed. One of Caesar's military leaders, Proculeius, then urged her to relax, falsely promising that Caesar would treat her kindly. After calling for death to take her and being told to calm down, the furious Cleopatra retorts:

Sir, I will eat no meat, I'll not drink, sir—
50 If idle talk will once be necessary—
I'll not sleep neither. This mortal house I'll ruin,
Do Caesar what he can. Know, sir, that I
Will not wait pinioned at your master's court
Nor once be chastised with the sober eye
55 Of dull Octavia. Shall they hoist me up
And show me to the shouting varletry
Of censuring Rome? Rather a ditch in Egypt
Be gentle grave unto me! Rather on Nilus' mud
Lay me stark-naked and let the waterflies
60 Blow me into abhorring! Rather make
My country's high pyramides my gibbet
And hang me up in chains!

50 seconds

49 *meat* food; 50 *If idle talk will once be necessary* i.e., if I really must waste time now in useless talking; 51 *This mortal house* i.e., my body (also, perhaps, her royal lineage, the House of Ptolemy); 53 *wait* pay attendance, do service, act as a servant; *pinioned* (1) with one's arms tied behind one's back; (2) with clipped wings; 54 *once* ever; *sober* modest; demure; chaste; 55 *dull* both (1) tedious and (2) irksome; *Octavia* Caesar's sister, whom Antony married in an attempt to cement peace and friendship between himself and Caesar, but whom he abandoned soon thereafter to return to Cleopatra; 56 *varletry* rabble, mob comprised of "lower-class" people (from the word *varlet*, which means [1] servant and [2] knave, rascal); 57 *censuring* judging (used in Shakespeare's time without today's negative connotation); 58 *gentle* noble, high-ranking (with pun on second meaning, "maggot"); *Nilus'* the Nile River [*on Nilus' mud* for a certain time period each autumn, the Nile rises and deposits silt from the highlands of Ethiopia on its banks, which replenishes the fertility of Egypt's soil]; 60 *Blow* deposit their larvae (maggots) on; *into abhorring* making me abhorrent [*Blow . . . abhorring* make me abhorrent by swelling my dead body with their larvae]; 61 *pyramides* (pih-RAM´-ih-DEEZ) the archaic form of *pyramids*; *gibbet* (JIH-bit) post from which corpses were displayed after hanging.

COMMENTARY

We love this little monologue, in which Cleopatra tells the Roman military leader exactly who rules over whom in Egypt. Not only will Caesar's minion not tell her when to calm down, but Caesar himself will not prevail over her. Egypt may be a colony of Rome for the time being, but Cleopatra is still its queen, descended from a long line of Ptolemies; ultimately, Caesar cannot control her. As she says so passionately here, she will die on her beloved soil and will not be degraded by captivity in Rome. A ditch in Egypt would more nobly befit its queen than would the most generous treatment Caesar could offer her in Rome. Even if the Romans kill her in Egypt, Cleopatra will have prevailed.

The meter of this piece sets Cleopatra's defiant and angry tone. The frequent inverted feet (most often in the middle of lines at caesuras, but occasionally punching the beginnings of lines as well) convey her indignation, and the frequent double endings suggest that she is upset. Furthermore, the fact that most of her sentences begin and end mid-line (where the actor does not pause as long as she would at the end of a line) keeps the monologue moving at a steady clip. Cleopatra's use of the word *Rather* to begin three successive sentences further accelerates her pace.

The sounds Cleopatra uses also convey her defiance, her fury, and her intentions from the very first line. She spits out a string of predominantly short, sharp words ending (and occasionally beginning) in crisp Ts, Ks, and Ps. The first section of the monologue has a string of defiant variations on *no*, including a homonymous *Know* in line 52 (*no / not / not / Know / not / Nor*). Her chain of SH/CH/Js (*Shall / show / shouting / censuring / ditch / Egypt / gentle*) sound menacing whether Cleopatra is shouting or whispering. Play with the expressive *abhorring* and *gibbet* (which, like the earlier short words, can be spit out), and the near-onomatopoeic *hoist* (which neatly communicates the humiliation she would feel) and *Blow*, all of which are designed to make Proculeius cringe. And Cleopatra economically expresses her contempt for Antony's politically expedient wife, Octavia, with the plodding words *sober* and *dull*, which describe traits that the sexy, charismatic Cleopatra would consider pathetic in a woman.

With her proud mention of her country's magnificent assets, such as the Nile and the pyramids, Cleopatra asserts her superiority over Proculeius, trying to intimidate him with whatever awe-inspiring means are at her disposal. He'd best think twice before condescending to her again.

And finally, Cleopatra is too sensual to avoid coupling death with sex, which she does with sexual innuendo (*Lay me stark-naked and let the waterflies / Blow me into abhorring*—a sexual pun on "whoring"). It is up to you to decide whether she does so intentionally, to unnerve Proculeius, or inadvertently, because she is an inherently sexual person.

You may scan the first line several different ways, depending on where you wish the emphases to fall: the first foot (*Sir, I*) can be iambic or trochaic (inverted); the final two feet can either be scanned as straight iambic pentameter (I'll NOT drink, SIR), *or* you can take a half-foot pause at the caesura and treat the last syllable as a double ending:

x / x / (x)
(pause) I'll not drink, sir

Line 58 is hexameter, a rare six-footed line (note its elisions, below).

Don't forget to elide: *Octavia* (Oc-TAVE-ya) in line 55; *censuring* (SEN-shring) in line 57; and *unto* ('ntoo) and *Nilus'* (NIE-luss, *not* NIE-luss-ez) in line 58;

. . . to either elide *stark-naked* (stark-NAY´KD) or contract *the waterflies* (TH'WA´-ter-FLIZE) in line 59;

. . . and to contract: *into abhorring* (IN-t'ab-HOR´-ing) in line 60.

P.S.

For information on the historical Cleopatra, see "Athenian Arrogator/Egyptian Empress/Drama Queen," page 465.

ANTONY AND CLEOPATRA

ACT V, SCENE ii

CLEOPATRA

GENDER: F

PROSE/VERSE: blank verse

AGE RANGE: adult to mature adult

FREQUENCY OF USE (1–5): 2.5

Queen Cleopatra and her lover, Mark Antony, have been at war with Octavius Caesar over control of the Eastern Empire. Now their forces have been defeated and Antony has committed suicide. Caesar's men have arrived at the monument where Cleopatra has been hiding. Fearing that Caesar would cart her off to Rome and parade her through the streets, she immediately tried to stab herself, but was quickly disarmed. Cleopatra now tries to win over Caesar's representative, Dolabella, hoping to get information about Caesar's intentions, or perhaps gain an ally.

No matter, sir, what I have heard or known. —
You laugh when boys or women tell their dreams,
75 Is't not your trick?

I dreamt there was an Emperor Antony.
O, such another sleep, that I might see
But such another man.

His face was as the heavens, and therein stuck
80 A sun and moon which kept their course and lighted
The little o' the earth.

His legs bestrid the ocean; his rear'd arm
Crested the world; his voice was propertied
As all the tunèd spheres, and that to friends;
85 But when he meant to quail and shake the orb,
He was as rattling thunder. For his bounty,
There was no winter in't. An Antony it was
That grew the more by reaping. His delights
Were dolphin-like: they showed his back above
90 The element they lived in; in his livery
Walked crowns and crownets—realms and islands were

75 *trick* particular habit or custom; 78 *But* only; 79 *stuck* were fixed (Jacobeans still believed in Ptolemaic astronomy, according to which the heavenly bodies were fixed in concentric, crystalline "spheres" that moved around the earth); 81 *The little o' the earth* i.e., the tiny humans of the earth; 82 *bestrid* stood or walked with the legs extended across (an allusion to the Colossus of Rhodes, a statue that was said to have stood astride the harbor of ancient Rhodes, with ships passing between its legs); *rear'd* upraised; 83 *Crested* topped; surmounted [*his rear'd arm / Crested the world* i.e., his might dominated the world (alluding to heraldry: a warrior's raised arm was a common "crest," or image above the shield on a coat of arms)]; *propertied / As* had the same properties as; 84 *all the tunèd spheres* all the harmonious music of the spheres (Pythagoras hypothesized that each heavenly body, as a result of its movement, must produce a particular tone; together the tones would form a beautiful harmony, which the human ear was not capable of detecting); *and* often, as here, used simply for emphasis; *that to friends* i.e., that voice, or such a voice, he used to friends; 85 *quail* (1) quell, overpower; or (2) make quail, terrify; *orb* i.e., the earth; 86 *For* as for; *bounty* (1) generosity, munificence; (2) virtue, active benevolence; 87 *winter* i.e., coldness and barrenness; 88 *His delights . . . element they lived in* i.e., he rose above (or remained master of) the pleasures he reveled in just as the dolphin shows its back above the water as it plays (the dolphin was a popular Renaissance symbol representing several concepts: sensuality, divine kingship, and [in heraldry] charity, swiftness, diligence, and love); 90 *in his livery* (1) among those wearing his livery (distinctive uniform); (2) in his possession; under his guardianship (a legal term); 91 *crownets* coronets [*crowns and crownets* i.e.,

As plates dropped from his pocket.

93 Think you there was, or might be, such a man
As this I dreamed of?

But if there be, or ever were one such
It's past the size of dreaming—nature wants stuff
To vie strange forms with fancy; yet to imagine
An Antony, were nature's piece 'gainst fancy,

100 Condemning shadows quite.

1 minute, 30 seconds

kings and princes]; 92 *plates* silver coins; 96 *one such* i.e., a man such as Antony; 97 *It's past the size of dreaming* i.e., no mere dream or imagination could invent something so great as Antony; *wants* lacks; *stuff* materials; 98 *strange* wonderful, extraordinary; *fancy* imagination; *forms* i.e., things formed by nature (with play on second meaning, "external appearance") [*To vie strange forms with fancy* to compete with imagination in the creation of wonderful, extraordinary forms]; 99 *piece* person of supreme excellence [*yet to imagine / An Antony, were nature's piece 'gainst fancy* i.e., yet when nature creates an Antony it has a supremely excellent product to pit against imagination]; 100 *shadows* images produced by the imagination [*Condemning shadows quite* i.e., completely surpassing imagination's best images, thereby proving them defective].

COMMENTARY

Cleopatra's strength of character truly shines in this scene. Most people in her untenable situation would be reduced to quivering Jell-O, but not Cleopatra! She keeps her cool, remains regally defiant, and uses all the tactics that have worked for her in the past. (You might want to look at the preceding monologue, page 481, in which Cleopatra responds to Proculeius, her initial captor, whom Dolabella has just replaced.) This monologue is meant to challenge and to persuade Dolabella, and Cleopatra uses both of her best negotiating techniques: seduction and absolute self-possession.

By calling Dolabella on one of his personal characteristics, Cleopatra immediately puts their relationship on a more intimate level, and asserts the upper hand. Although her description of Antony builds to a direct challenge to Dolabella to recognize the enormity of her loss, Cleopatra seeks empathy, not pity. Although she is a helpless captive, Cleopatra maintains her own dignity, keeping herself at, or even above, his level. At the same time, the eulogy is full of sexual double entendre, and although it describes another man, it can be used to imply future similar appreciation (and perhaps similar pleasures?) for Dolabella. She starts right off using the word *matter*, which to Shakespeare's audience also referred to female genitalia. Cleopatra then describes Antony's *delights* (a word often used to refer specifically to sexual pleasures) as *dolphin-like*, unabashedly getting to the point about her favorite aspect of Antony's greatness: dolphins were thought in Shakespeare's time to be highly sensual creatures. She uses the phrase *shake the orb*, exploiting the double meaning of the word *shake* (engage in the sex act) and the phrase *grew the more by reaping*, which doesn't require much translation. In her two uses of *fancy*, she implies not only the word's primary meaning, "imagination," but also its second one, "amorous inclination."

Cleopatra constructs a pedestal for Antony using two poetic devices, imagery and sound repetition. The synecdochic images she chooses make Antony larger than life: she need merely describe *His legs* bestriding the ocean to communicate his wide-ranging influence; *his rear'd arm* cresting the world to convey his military might; *his voice* as heavenly music to friends and thunder to enemies to get across the enormous effect of his pleasure or displeasure with those around him. Reducing the kings and princes in his service to *crowns and crownets* raises him even higher in comparison. These images and others portray Antony as a powerful giant, his bounty as a never-ending harvest season, and his creation as nature's triumph over imagination. (It's fun to notice that Cleopatra's frequent heraldic imagery is completely anachronistic—a habit of Shakespeare's that is particularly amusing here, amid the pyramids!)

Cleopatra's seductive and poetic speech is strongly supported by sounds. She repeats phrases with variations that echo her key thoughts (*such another sleep*; *such another man*; *such a man*; and *one such*), using the repetitions of *An Antony* and *an Emperor Antony* to compound the sense of Antony's greatness those phrases imply. She also weaves Seductive Ss throughout the piece, starting off with a Striking String of them: *such* / *sleep* / *see* / *such* / *His face was as* / *heavens* / *stuck* / *sun*. You'll find plenty of assonance and consonance, such as *kept* / *course*, *lighted* / *little*, and *dropped from* / *pocket*, so look for them and use them. And for help exploiting the sound of the word *O* to its best advantage, see "O, No! An *O*!," page xxxiii.

In the end, Cleopatra is enormously successful in her efforts. Although Dolabella does not agree with Cleopatra's view of Antony, the eulogy does humanize her and her grief to such a degree that in the few lines which follow this speech Dolabella reveals Caesar's plans for her, putting his own security at risk.

Note: there are two textual disputes about this piece that you may want to consider. Some editors believe that the word *autumn* was intended in line 87 in place of *Antony*. We think that's unlikely, since Cleopatra is speaking metaphorically, and since such a transcription error would have been unusual. This change reduces the effect of the repetition of *An Antony*, but if you prefer the more literal description that "an autumn" produces, you are free to use the phrase: there are pages of tedious discourse that back up either choice! A second, more interesting dispute concerns the reading of *little o' the earth* in line 81: some scholars prefer "little O, the earth." Shakespeare was fond of punning on the word *O*, referring to the "wooden O"—the Globe Theatre, where most of his audiences watched his later plays. "Little O" is a joke that many bardolaters (and some lay folk) will get and like, and it plays on the *O* sound, which Cleopatra has just used four lines earlier. It also adds another double entendre to the piece, since *O* was common slang for "vagina." On the other hand, with this version Cleopatra refers only to the tiny earth rather than the little tiny creatures on it, which sacrifices Cleopatra's lovely point about Antony's benevolence toward all the little people. There is no way to know which reading Shakespeare intended, so take your pick.

SIGNIFICANT SCANS

In the monologue's first line, *I* is stressed. Is Cleopatra sarcastic, self-deprecating, or resigned? Does she overtly reveal her anger, or is she veiling it in politeness? Notice that after delivering this barb, she proceeds to control the conversation. Likewise, scanning line 82 as regular iambic pentameter emphasizes the words *his* and *arm*, aggressively pointing out that it was Antony's arm (not Caesar's) that *Crested the world*.

Although the meter in this piece is fairly regular, many ideas begin and end mid-line, creating a continuous flow of ideas from one to the next, especially during Cleopatra's description of her "dream." The first inverted (trochaic) foot appears in this section, emphasizing Antony's power by punching *Crested* in line 83 (and, optionally, *He* in line 86). Another inversion accentuates Cleopatra's challenge to Dolabella in line 93, and two mid-line inversions following the caesuras in lines 97 and 98 heighten the build in Cleopatra's final statement.

This monologue is interspersed with bits of dialogue for Dolabella, which are mostly interjections and do not affect the content of the piece. They are, however, often lines shared with Cleopatra, which leaves this monologue with six sheared lines (75—two feet of spoken text; 78, 81, 92, and 100—three feet each; 94—two and a half feet). Happily, these lines all fall before new ideas are introduced. It makes the most sense to use the silent feet to transition to Cleopatra's next thought, or, if appropriate, her next tactic with Dolabella. The short last line will surprise the listener's ear, leaving a poignant silence in which your last words will resound.

Don't forget to elide: *Emperor* (EMP-ror) in line 76; *heavens* (HEV'NZ) in line 79; *Antony* (ANT-nee) in line 87 (but *not* in lines 76 or 99); and *livery* (LIV-ree) in line 90;

. . . to contract: *it was* (TWUHZ) line 87;

. . . and to expand: *tunèd* (TYOO-nehd) in line 84.

P.S.
For information on the historical Cleopatra, see "Athenian Arrogator/Egyptian Empress/Drama Queen," page 465.

ANTONY AND CLEOPATRA

ACT V, SCENE ii

CLEOPATRA

GENDER: F
PROSE/VERSE: blank verse
AGE RANGE: adult to mature adult
FREQUENCY OF USE (1–5): 3.5

Queen Cleopatra's lover, the Roman Triumvir Antony, was defeated by Caesar and has nobly killed himself; the captive Cleopatra is determined to do the same rather than permit herself to be carted to Rome and paraded through the streets in disgrace. She has already attempted suicide once, but was disarmed. She has now sent for asps, which have just been smuggled to her in a basket of figs. Her waiting-women, Charmian and Iras, have now brought her finest gown, crown, and other regalia, to help her prepare to meet Antony in the afterlife in splendor.

Give me my robe, put on my crown—I have
Immortal longings in me. Now no more
285 The juice of Egypt's grape shall moist this lip.
Yare, yare, good Iras, quick—methinks I hear
Antony call; I see him rouse himself
To praise my noble act; I hear him mock
The luck of Caesar, which the gods give men
290 To excuse their after wrath. Husband, I come!
Now to that name my courage prove my title!
I am fire and air—my other elements
I give to baser life. So, have you done?
Come then and take the last warmth of my lips.
295 Farewell, kind Charmian; Iras, long farewell.
[*Kisses them. Iras falls and dies*]
Have I the aspic in my lips? Dost fall?
If thou and nature can so gently part,
The stroke of death is as a lover's pinch,
Which hurts and is desired. Dost thou lie still?
300 If thus thou vanishest, thou tellst the world
It is not worth leave-taking.

284 *Immortal longings* longings for immortality (primarily the "afterlife," but also "lasting fame"); *no more / The juice of Egypt's grape shall moist this lip* i.e., I shall never again taste Egypt's wines; 286 *Yare* (YAHR or YAIR) Be quick and deft (a sailing term); 288 *my noble act* i.e., my suicide (considered noble under certain circumstances by ancient Romans); 289 *The luck of Caesar* Octavius Caesar was noted for his good fortune, which Cleopatra mocks here as undeserved; 290 *after* subsequent [*The luck of Caesar, which . . . after wrath* ancient Romans believed that when the gods gave good fortune to particular humans, they'd later grow jealous of them and punish them for enjoying it]; *Husband* i.e., Antony—see "Athenian Arrogator/Egyptian Empress/Drama Queen," page 465; 291 *Now to that name my courage prove my title* i.e., may I now show the courage (by killing myself) that would prove I've got the right ("title") to that name ("Husband"); 292 *I am fire and air—my other elements* According to Aristotle, humans were composed of four elements: the two "higher" elements of fire and air, and the two "lower" elements of earth and water; men were thought to have a greater proportion of hot, dry air and fire, rendering them more moral, while women's supposed preponderance of cold, moist earth and water somehow accounted for their fickle and deceptive natures. Cleopatra's maintenance of her higher elements and abandonment of her lower ones symbolizes her imminent separation of soul (*fire and air*) and body (*my other elements*); 293 *I give to baser life* either (1) I leave here amongst mortal life (lowly compared to that of the afterlife) or (2) I leave here for lowlier life-forms (i.e. for worms to eat); *have you done* i.e., are you finished dressing me in my gown and crown; 295 *long farewell* farewell for a long time; 296 *aspic* asp (the small, highly venomous Egyptian cobra, the bite of which was believed to guarantee entry into the afterlife); *fall* both (1) fall to the ground and (2) die; 297 *nature* i.e., life; 300 *If thus thou van-*

This proves me base.
If she first meet the curlèd Antony,
305 He'll make demand of her, and spend that kiss
Which is my heaven to have. Come, thou mortal wretch,
[*To an asp which she applies to her breast*]
With thy sharp teeth this knot intrinsicate
Of life at once untie. Poor venomous fool,
Be angry, and dispatch. O, couldst thou speak,
310 That I might hear thee call great Caesar ass
Unpolicied!

1 minute, 50 seconds

ishest i.e., if you die in this manner; 303 *This . . . base* i.e., Iras's dying before I do does not make me look good; 304 *curlèd* curly-haired; 305 *He'll make demand . . . my heaven to have* Antony will ask her about me, and for her information will reward her with that kiss which is rightfully my heavenly reward/which is heavenly to me; *wretch* lowly creature (sometimes, as here, used as a term of endearment) [*thou mortal wretch* i.e., the asp, whose bite inflicts a mortal wound]; 307 *intrinsicate* (1) intricate; and/or (2) internal, deep-rooted [*this knot intrinsicate / Of life* this intricate, deep-rooted knot of life]; 309 *dispatch* make haste (with play on second and third meanings, "put to death" and "finish up the business at hand"); 311 *Unpolicied* proved lacking in statecraft; proved stupid [*ass / Unpolicied* an ass who has been proved to be lacking in statecraft and/or is stupid].

COMMENTARY

Cleopatra is at the end of the line . . . but she is also at the beginning . . . of an eternity shared with her beloved Antony. And Cleopatra intends to make as grand an exit from life and entrance into eternity as she has ever made anywhere. Here, just as at her very first meeting with Antony (described by Enobarbus: see monologue, page 466), Cleopatra carefully sets her scene and directs it (*Give me my robe*, etc.), then stars in it. Notice how peeved she is in line 303 to be upstaged by one of her "supporting actors" . . . much as she may have loved her.

She begins the monologue with a line that has at least one and possibly two inverted feet (the first at the start of the line and the second, which is optional, mid-line following the caesura) as she issues two rapid-fire commands. Cleopatra has not been humbled by Caesar; ever the Queen, she will seize attention and start her final speech strongly. The dearth of elisions and contractions throughout this piece emphasize Cleopatra's precision and clarity of purpose.

In true diva style, Cleopatra issues the order to dress her, then proclaims the grandiose and gorgeous *I have immortal longings in me*. Her other proclamations in the first section of the monologue are similarly grand and self-important. Cleopatra shows her eagerness to meet Antony in the afterlife by indicating that she is already en route: she already feels her soul parting from her body and can hear and see Antony. For help using the dramatic sound of the word *O* to its best advantage, see "O, No! An *O*!," page xxxiii.

The quick pace of the monologue supports this eagerness. Many sentences end and begin mid-line, where you do not take as long a pause as you would at a line's end. Cleopatra also hurries because time is of the essence. She has already been prevented from stabbing herself and must act before a guard returns to foil this suicide attempt as well. Also, whether she acknowledges it to herself or not, she may be a bit afraid and must act while she has the nerve. Cleopatra frames the monologue with exhortations of haste, pushing her waiting-woman to hurry at the beginning of the monologue with *Yare, yare, good Iras, quick*, and, at the end of the monologue, bidding the asp to *dispatch*, which furthers the sense of urgency.

This active monologue contains many embedded stage directions, which indicate that Cleopatra permits herself to be dressed and bejeweled by her waiting-women (*Give me my robe . . .*), that she kisses them goodbye when they have finished (*So, have you done? / Come then and take the last warmth of my lips*), that Iras falls to the ground, lies still, and dies (*Dost fall?*; *Dost thou lie still? / If thus thou vanishest . . .*), and that Cleopatra picks up the asp to be bitten and killed by it (*Come, thou mortal wretch*). Scholars debate the cause of Iras's death. Some believe she is bitten by an asp while moving the basket, others that she intentionally picks up an asp while Cleopatra is primping and arranging her robe, and others maintain that she dies of a broken heart at the loss of her mistress (paralleling Enobarbus's death for love of Antony). Your decision will inform your response to her death. If Iras is bitten by an asp, for example, Cleopatra might very well examine her to see how badly death by snakebite will hurt. If she dies of a broken heart, Cleopatra might be doubly moved by her death. Since lines 301 and 303 are sheared (due to excised dialogue), you may take the five intervening silent feet as pauses, which will give you time to comtemplate Iras's body. Or you may combine the two lines into one line of iambic pentameter.

Even in death, Cleopatra is ever the sensualist. Despite professing to have left earthly matters behind, she uses terms that evoke taste, sound, sight, smell, and touch. For example, she expresses that she has finished living by saying that her lip will never again be moistened by wine, thus evoking not just the taste of wine, but also the feeling of the slightly sticky, cool moisture on one's lips (also note her national pride: the Queen of Egypt wouldn't drink an import!). Likewise, in place of the perfunctory "kiss me goodbye" she tells her waiting-women to *take the last warmth of* [*her*] *lips*. Lips figure prominently in this monologue—they are mentioned three times, and kissing is mentioned twice. Cleopatra likens *The stroke of death* to *a lover's pinch, / Which hurts and is desired*. She refers to her lover as *the curlèd Antony*, suggesting how often she has run her fingers through his curls (and reminding the audience that Enobarbus said Antony was *barbered ten times o'er* in preparation for his first meeting with Cleopatra). And she welcomes, rather than avoids, the asp's *sharp teeth*.

Cleopatra uses sexual double entendre to suggest that death is, to her, the ultimate sensual experience, coupling death with sex. Examples include: *robe* and *crown* = vagina; *yare* = sexually ready; Antony *rouses* himself for her *act* and she *comes*; *stroke* = (1) sexual thrust; (2) tender amorous caress. Remember, however, that these words are merely intended to be sexually suggestive—their double meanings should not be played too overtly (particularly as some of their double meanings have been lost over the centuries).

SIGNIFICANT SCANS

Line 306, a rare six-footed line, is tricky to scan. It has a pyrrhic first foot (two unaccented syllables), a spondaic second foot (two accented syllables, emphasizing the two most important words in the line), and a half-foot pause at the caesura, in which to make the momentous transition to picking up the asp and committing suicide:

x x / / x / x / x / x /

Which is my heaven to have. (pause) Come, thou mortal wretch [HEV'N]

With its extra syllables, this important line draws attention to itself.

The final line has only two feet of spoken text (the rest of the line, shared by Charmian and Cleopatra, has been excised). This gives you a final three-foot pause in which to enjoy cheating Caesar. Cleopatra relishes duping him through death; it is the second-sweetest part (after rejoining Antony) of her grand exit. Or you can use the pause to feel the effects of the poison now coursing through your veins. (Note, however, that Cleopatra has two more brief exchanges with Charmian before finally dying.)

By the way, when dying of a snakebite (which in real life takes several hours), one experiences nausea, vomiting, sweating, fever, weakness, prickling and itching, muscle twitches, an altered mental state, hypotension (sudden drop in blood pressure), and shock. Though you will not want to enact most of these symptoms toward the end of this monologue, some of them might inform your performance.

A note of caution: although this is a wonderful piece for showcasing your talents, it is difficult to use in auditions, because of Cleopatra's complex interaction with Charmian and Iras.

Don't forget to elide: *Charmian* (KAR-myan or SHAR-myan) in line 295; *desired* (de-ZIERD) in line 299; *heaven* (HEV'N) in line 306; and *venomous* (VEN-muss) in line 308;

. . . to contract: *To excuse* (T'ex-KYOOZ) in line 290; *I am* (I'm) in line 292; and *It is* (It's or 'Tiz) in line 301;

. . . and to expand: *curlèd* (KUR-lehd) in line 304.

P.S.

For information on the historical Cleopatra, see "Athenian Arrogator/ Egyptian Empress/Drama Queen," page 465.

CORIOLANUS

ACT II, SCENE i

MENENIUS

GENDER: M
AGE RANGE: mature adult to older adult
PROSE/VERSE: prose
FREQUENCY OF USE (1–5): 1

Like most of the patricians (nobles of Rome), Menenius Agrippa has little use for the commoners, but he endures them (since they're not going anywhere). He just wishes that they hadn't been granted the right to elect their own tribunes (judges), since they are unsophisticated in matters of government and can't possibly make educated decisions. Proof positive: the fools have elected two tribunes, Sicinius Velutus and Junius Brutus, whom Menenius suspects have been inciting the commoners against the mighty warrior Caius Martius Coriolanus (to whose many military victories the commoners owe their very lives). Menenius encounters the two tribunes and is angered by their negative comments about Coriolanus. When he insults them, they retort that he "is known well enough, too," implying that he's known around town to have his own bad qualities. He says to them:

I am known to be a humourous patrician, and one
that loves a cup of hot wine with not a drop of allaying Tiber in 't; said to be something imperfect in
favoring the first complaint, hasty and tinder-like
55 upon too trivial motion; one that converses more
with the buttock of night than with the forehead of
the morning. What I think I utter, and spend my
malice in my breath. Meeting two such wealsmen
as you are—I cannot call you Lycurgeses—if the
60 drink you give me touch my palate adversely, I
make a crooked face at it. I cannot say your worships have delivered the matter well when I find the
ass in compound with the major part of your syllables; and though I must be content to bear with
65 those that say you are reverend grave men, yet they
lie deadly that tell you you have good faces. If you
see this in the map of my microcosm, follows it
that I am known well enough too? What harm can
your bisson conspectuities glean out of this charac-
70 ter, if I be known well enough too?

1 minute

You know neither me, yourselves, nor anything.
You are ambitious for poor knaves' caps and
legs: you wear out a good wholesome forenoon in
75 hearing a cause between an orange-wife and a
faucet-seller, and then rejourn the controversy of

51 *humourous* whimsical, capricious, moody; *patrician* a nobleman of Rome; 52 *allaying* dilut-ing; 53 *Tiber* the Tiber River (i.e., water); *something* somewhat; *in favoring* in that I tend to give preference to; 54 *the first complaint* whichever side presents their argument first; *tinder-like* quick to anger, easily ignitable (like a tinderbox); 55 *too trivial motion* the slightest provocation; *converses* associates; 58 *my breath* what I speak; *wealsmen* statesmen; 59 *Lycurgeses* (Lie-KUR′-ga-SEEZ) lawmakers (Lycurges was the legendary wise creator of Sparta's constitution); 60 *touch my palate adversely* tastes bad; 61 *your worships* title of respect by which the tribunes are ad-dressed; 62 *delivered* reported; 63 *in compound with* mixed in with; *your syllables* your words [*I find the ass . . . your syllables* I find most of what you said to be assinine (Menenius puns on the "as[s]" in judges' frequent use of the compound word *whereas*)]; 65 *grave* venerated, respected; 66 *deadly* wickedly (with a play on "grave," used just before) [*they lie deadly . . . faces* those who tell you that you have good faces are lying shamelessly]; 67 *the map of my microcosm* i.e., my face (the world was conceived of as a "macrocosm" and humans "microcosms"—one's face was considered one's "map"); *follows it* doesn't it follow; 69 *bisson conspectuities* blinded sight (i.e., false perceptions); *character* the outward signs of inner qualities (i.e., the face, facial expres-sions); 73 *knaves'* servants'; *caps and legs* i.e., deference (removing caps and bowing legs to show respect); 74 *forenoon* the part of the morning during which business is usually transacted; 75 *hearing a cause* adjudicating a case; *orange-wife* woman who sells oranges; 76 *faucet-seller*

three-pence to a second day of audience. When you
are hearing a matter between party and party, if you
chance to be pinched with the colic, you make faces
80 like mummers, set up the bloody flag against all patience, and, in roaring for a chamber-pot, dismiss
the controversy bleeding, the more entangled by
your hearing. All the peace you make in their cause
is calling both the parties knaves. You are a pair of
85 strange ones.

Our very priests become mockers if they shall encounter such ridiculous subjects as you are. When
you speak best unto the purpose, it is not worth the
90 wagging of your beards; and your beards deserve
not so honorable a grave as to stuff a botcher's
cushion or to be entombed in an ass's packsaddle.
Yet you must be saying Martius is proud, who, in a
cheap estimation, is worth all your predecessors
95 since Deucalion, though peradventure some of the
best of 'em were hereditary hangmen. God-den to
your worships: more of your conversation would
infect my brain, being the herdsmen of the beastly
plebians. I will be bold to take my leave of you.

2 minutes, 30 seconds

seller of taps for wine barrels; *rejourn* put off, adjourn; *controversy of three-pence* lawsuit over (a mere) threepence; 77 *day of audience* day in court; 79 *pinched* pained; *the colic* bowel or intestinal pain; 80 *mummers* pantomime actors; *bloody flag* standard (flag of war) [*set up the bloody flag against* declare war against]; 82 *bleeding* still unhealed, still unresolved; 88 *subjects* creatures, beings [*Our very priests . . . as you are* Even our priests (who are solemn, serious, and compassionate) will become mockers if they encounter creatures as ridiculous as you are]; 89 *speak best unto the purpose* speak to the best of your ability about the subject before you; 91 *botcher* mender of old clothes, patcher; 92 *packsaddle* a stuffed saddle, specially designed to support the load on a pack animal; 93 *Yet you must be saying* i.e., yet you (of all people) have the nerve to be saying; *in a cheap estimation* even giving a conservative estimate of his worth; 94 *predecessors* ancestors; 95 *Deucalion* character in ancient Greek mythology who survived the worldwide flood and then repopulated the earth by throwing stones on the ground that turned into people; *peradventure* perhaps, perchance; 96 *hereditary hangmen* Professions were often handed down from father to son. Execution was, as you can imagine, not a reputable profession. To accuse a person of descending from hangmen was to insult him by implying that he was of low and disreputable origin; *God-den* Good evening; 98 *being* you being; 99 *plebians* commoners of ancient Rome; *be bold to* be so bold as to.

COMMENTARY

Menenius knew that this business of the commoners electing their own tribunes would spell trouble, and sure enough, it has. The nitwits have gone and elected these two self-serving rabble-rousers, who are now sticking their noses where they don't belong. You've got to give Menenius credit for being rather self-aware: he describes his quick temper and his habit of speaking his mind, as he proceeds to lose his temper and speak his mind to them. Menenius obviously has a large vocabulary at his disposal, evidence of his high level of education. He chooses big, pompous words to assert his superiority over the tribunes, which, coupled with his sarcastic gibes and nasty imagery, gives the piece its overall caustic tone.

Said nasty imagery is quite colorful and is peppered throughout the piece: in reference to himself (*buttock of night / forehead of the morning*; *spend my malice in my breath*; *the map of my microcosm*); to the tribunes' effect on him (*if the drink . . . face at it*; *I find the ass . . . syllables*); and to the tribunes themselves (*cannot call you Lycurgeses*; *pinched with the colic*; *faces like mummers*; *the bloody flag*; *your beards deserve not . . . packsaddle*; *Deucalion*; *hereditary hangmen*; *herdsmen of the beastly plebians*). And isn't it interesting that he returns more than once to ass metaphors (*buttock of night*; *the ass in compound with . . . syllables*; *ass's packsaddle*). Last but certainly not least, you've surely realized by now that Menenius is speaking in prose, rather than verse. He tends to prefer this mode of communication, using it anytime he is emotionally invested in the point he's making. As he says in this piece, "what he thinks, he utters"—perhaps the directness of prose best enables him to do so.

MENENIUS AGRIPPA: A LEGEND IN HIS OWN TIME

Ol' Menenius didn't appear in your Roman history books because he's only a legendary character, and an insignificant one at that. He appears in Livy's *Early History of Rome* and Plutarch's *Lives* as the orator of "the belly speech" (incorporated by Shakespeare into Act I, Scene i), in which he tells the rioters that the aristocrats are the "belly" of Rome, who do all the hard work of digesting so that the rest of the body can have nutrition, while the commoners are the "great toe"—the lowliest part of the body that benefits from the belly's work without having to do much, and that runs away first when the body is attacked. Shakespeare took this minor little nothing of a guy (after all, he only saved Rome once) and fleshed him out into the curmudgeonly close friend and father figure of Coriolanus.

CORIOLANUS

ACT IV, SCENE v

CORIOLANUS

GENDER: M
PROSE/VERSE: blank verse
AGE RANGE: adult to mature adult
FREQUENCY OF USE (1–5): 3

Caius Martius Coriolanus, who has defeated the Volscians at least five times (and who, in fact, was given the surname Coriolanus to honor his recent capture of the Volscian city Corioles), has just been exiled from his native Rome as punishment for his contemptuous behavior toward the Roman common people. Furious at being exiled, he has come to Antium, to the home of his archnemesis, the Volscian general, Tullus Aufidius, where he offers to help Aufidius capture and decimate Rome.

My name is Caius Martius, who hath done
To thee particularly, and to all the Volsces,
Great hurt and mischief; thereto witness may
My surname, Coriolanus. The painful service,
75 The extreme dangers, and the drops of blood
Shed for my thankless country, are requited
But with that surname—a good memory
And witness of the malice and displeasure
Which thou shouldst bear me. Only that name remains:
80 The cruelty and envy of the people,
Permitted by our dastard nobles who
Have all forsook me, hath devoured the rest,
And suffered me by th' voice of slaves to be
Whooped out of Rome. Now this extremity
85 Hath brought me to thy hearth; not out of hope
(Mistake me not) to save my life—for if
I had feared death, of all the men i' th' world
I would have 'voided thee—but in mere spite,
To be full quit of those my banishers
90 Stand I before thee here. Then if thou hast
A heart of wreak in thee, that wilt revenge
Thine own particular wrongs and stop those maims
Of shame seen through thy country, speed thee straight
And make my misery serve thy turn. So use it
95 That my revengeful services may prove
As benefits to thee, for I will fight
Against my cankered country with the spleen

71 *Caius Martius* (KIE-uss MAR-shuss); 72 *Volsces* (VOL-seez or VOL-skeez); 73 *witness may* you may witness; 74 *service* i.e., military service; 76 *requited* repaid; 77 *But* only; *memory* reminder, memorial; 81 *dastard* cowardly; 83 *suffered me* allowed me (i.e., sat back and didn't prevent me); *voice* both (1) sound and (2) vote, decision; *slaves* here, Coriolanus refers derogatorily to the common people; 84 *Whooped out* driven out with jeering and shouting [*suffered me . . . of Rome* stood by and permitted me to be driven out of Rome (as per the vote of the commoners), to the sounds of jeering and shouting]; *extremity* most distressing or dangerous situation; calamity; 85 *thy hearth* i.e., your home; 88 *'voided* avoided; *in mere spite* solely out of malice; 89 *To be full quit of* to be fully revenged on, to get completely even with; *those my banishers* those who have banished me; 91 *wreak* vengeance; 92 *maims / Of shame* deep crippling injuries, desecrations (could refer to land taken by the Romans; to property they desecrated; or to their vicious maimings and killings of the Volscian people themselves); 93 *speed thee straight* make haste, take action right away; 94 *serve thy turn* serve your purpose, be of help to you; *So use it / That* Take advantage of it in such a way that; 95 *may prove / As* may prove to be; 97 *cankered* infected, corrupted, evil; *spleen* malice, hatred (the spleen was believed to be

Of all the under fiends. But if so be
Thou dar'st not this, and that to prove more fortunes
100 Th'art tired, then, in a word, I also am
Longer to live most weary, and present
My throat to thee and to thy ancient malice;
Which not to cut would show thee but a fool,
Since I have ever followed thee with hate,
105 Drawn tuns of blood out of thy country's breast,
And cannot live but to thy shame, unless
It be to do thee service.

2 minutes, 15 seconds

the organ from which emotions [especially anger] emanated); 98 *under fiends* devils of the underworld (i.e., devils from Hell); *if so be / Thou dar'st not this* if the situation is that you do not dare to undertake this; 99 *to prove more fortunes / Th'art tired* you're too fed up to try your luck again; 100 *I also am / Longer to live most weary* I'm also very weary of living any longer; 102 *thy ancient malice* your long-standing enmity; 103 *Which not to cut* which, if you do not cut it; *show thee* make you appear to be; 104 *ever* always; 105 *tuns* large casks or barrels for holding liquids; very large units of measurement for liquids; *thy country's breast* i.e., the Volscian soldiers and civilians killed by Romans; thus, the Volscian people themselves; 106 *but to thy shame* without causing you shame; *unless / It be to do thee service* unless it be to help you (to attack the Romans).

COMMENTARY

The army: it's not just a career, it's a way of life. Just ask Coriolanus. As almost every character expressly states at least once during the play, Coriolanus is a military man through and through, and damn proud of it. His martial aspect so suffuses his whole demeanor that he cannot speak like a civilian—he doesn't know what one sounds like. This entire speech to Aufidius is built on short, sharp, curt, militaristic, one-syllable words, with several two-syllable words but only a smattering of longer ones. In fact, as indicated below, some of the longer ones are elided to fit the meter, giving them a more clipped sound than normal.

Coriolanus uses the familiar *thee* to address Aufidius. Perhaps he feels that having fought each other so often has bred a familiarity between them. Or maybe he is asserting his superiority over Aufidius, since he has bested him in battle repeatedly.

While not poetically inclined, Coriolanus conveys the humiliation he felt at his banishment from Rome with the onomatopoeic *Whooped out of Rome*. In the single word *Whooped* one can hear the jeering and hollering that chased the former superstar warrior as he was thrown out of town. Coriolanus also employs a bit of synecdoche (*voice of slaves* = the consensus of all the commoners; *heart of wreak* = vengeful nature; *thy country's breast* = the hearts and bodies of the nation's people).

Notice the stage direction tucked into the monologue: Coriolanus tells Aufidius that he is baring his throat to him. Never fear: although he bares his throat to his nemesis, Coriolanus doesn't really give Aufidius the option of killing him. Rather, he presents his enemy with two options: Aufidius can kill him if he no longer has a warrior's vengeful heart, no longer desires to avenge the wrongs wrought on him and his nation, doesn't dare to attack Rome, and is washed up—or Aufidius can take Coriolanus up on his offer of aid against Rome. Some choice. Coriolanus has framed the question so that Aufidius's honor requires that they team up.

The double entendre in this piece is extremely subtle but present, and paves the way for the much more overt sexual tone of Aufidius's reply (see Aufidius's monologue, page 506): *service* = both military and sexual (Coriolanus uses the term or a permutation thereof several times throughout the monologue); *turn* = a sexual encounter; *serve thy turn* = service you sexually; *maims of shame* = castration (figurative, not literal, resulting from Coriolanus's repeated victories over Aufidius in battle).

You'll notice that there are many double endings in this piece, both at the ends of lines and at caesuras. Why all the extra syllables? Does Coriolanus know that Aufidius will be keenly interested in whatever he has to say, no matter how long? Does he like keeping Aufidius on his toes by not speaking in a predictable manner? Are the extra syllables also a sign, perhaps, that he is weary after his long journey from Rome?

Don't forget to elide: *particularly* (par-TICK-lee) or *to all* (TWALL) in line 72; *Coriolanus* (COR-yo-LA´-nus) in line 74; *particular* (par-TICK-lar) in line 92; *misery* (MIZ-ree) in line 94; and *tired* (TIE'RD) in line 100;

. . . to contract: *th' voice* in line 83 becomes one syllable, as does *i' th' world* in line 87;

. . . and to expand *cruelty* (CRU´-el-TY) in line 80.

Also note that *extreme* in line 75 is pronounced EK-streem.

Last but not least, the final line is divided between Coriolanus and Aufidius—Coriolanus speaks only three and a half of its feet. If you are lifting this monologue out of the scene and presenting it on its own, you can use the very brief silence at the end, if it serves you to do so.

ANGRY YOUNG (RO)MAN

Around C.E. 100, the Greek historian Plutarch wrote his collection of Greek and Roman biographies, *Parallel Lives*. Coriolanus (born circa 526 B.C.E.) was one of the Romans who made the cut, although it's debatable whether Plutarch's tales about him actually happened or were merely legends. Plutarch's *Lives* was translated into English in 1579 by Sir Thomas North.

North's translation of the *Lives* proved a gold mine of dramatic material. Shakespeare probably figured he'd hit the mother lode when he read about Coriolanus: descendant of an early Roman king; hostile, arrogant, and hopelessly unsocialized elitist; one-man battalion; Rome's Greatest Hero–turned–Rome's Greatest Enemy; and pseudosocial egocentric with a terminal mother fixation. What more could a playwright ask for?

CORIOLANUS

ACT IV, SCENE v

AUFIDIUS

GENDER: M
AGE RANGE: adult to mature adult
PROSE/VERSE: blank verse
FREQUENCY OF USE (1–5): 1

The Volscian general Tellus Aufidius has never once defeated his archnemesis, Caius Martius Coriolanus of Rome. After his most recent defeat by Coriolanus at the city of Corioles, Aufidius vowed that he would take down Coriolanus the next time they met on the battlefield, even if he had to resort to less-than-honorable methods to do so. Aufidius has been raising a new army with which to attack Rome, and tonight is feasting the Volscian senators to gain their consent to attack. A stranger dressed as a poor man has crashed the feast, and reveals himself to be Coriolanus. He explains that he has been wrongfully banished from Rome, and he wants revenge. He offers his services to the Volscians, volunteering to help Aufidius decimate the city that has repeatedly conquered and ravaged Aufidius's people. Aufidius, ecstatic, replies:

O, Martius, Martius!

Each word thou hast spoke hath weeded from my heart
A root of ancient envy. If Jupiter
110 Should from yond cloud speak divine things,
And say, " 'Tis true," I'd not believe them more
Than thee, all noble Martius. Let me twine
Mine arms about that body, where against
My grainèd ash an hundred times hath broke
115 And scarred the moon with splinters; here I clip
The anvil of my sword, and do contest
As hotly and as nobly with thy love
As ever in ambitious strength I did
Contend against thy valor. Know thou first,
120 I loved the maid I married—never man
Sighed truer breath—but that I see thee here,
Thou noble thing, more dances my rapt heart
Than when I first my wedded mistress saw
Bestride my threshold. Why, thou Mars, I tell thee,
125 We have a power on foot, and I had purpose
Once more to hew thy target from they brawn
Or lose mine arm for't. Thou hast beat me out
Twelve several times, and I have nightly since
Dreamt of encounters 'twixt thyself and me—
130 We have been down together in my sleep
Unbuckling helms, fisting each other's throat—

AUFIDIUS

109 *ancient* long-standing; *envy* resentment, hatred, malice; *Jupiter* the supreme god of the Romans; 110 *Should* would; *yond cloud* that cloud over there; 113 *where against* against which; 114 *grainèd ash* spear made of ash wood; *an hundred times hath broke* has broken a hundred times; 115 *clip* embrace; 116 *anvil of my sword* an anvil is used in blacksmithing—a sword is struck against it; here, refers to Coriolanus's body; *do contest* come to grips; 118 *I did / Contend against thy valor* I fought against your bravery (your brave fighting) [*As ever . . . valor* As I ever fought with ambitious strength against your valor]; 119 *Know thou first* First of all, I want you to know that; 120 *maid* unmarried (and therefore, of course, virginal) woman; *never man / Sighed truer breath* never did a man emit more genuine and faithful sighs (of love); 122 *rapt* ecstatic, joyous; 123 *Than when . . . saw* than when I first saw my wedded wife; 124 *Bestride* military term for standing over a fallen soldier; Aufidius uses it here to describe his bride standing over the threshold of his home; *Mars* the Roman god of war (here, referring to Coriolanus); 125 *We* i.e., the Volscians; *power* armed force [*a power on foot* i.e., troops of foot soldiers]; *had purpose* intended; 126 *hew* chop, hack; *target* shield; *brawn* muscular arm; 127 *for't* i.e., in the attempt; 128 *several* separate, different; 129 *'twixt* between; 130 *down* i.e., on the ground; 131 *Un-*

And waked half dead with nothing. Worthy Martius,
Had we no other quarrel else to Rome but that
Thou art thence banished, we would muster all
135 From twelve to seventy, and pouring war
Into the bowels of ungrateful Rome,
Like a bold flood o'erbeat. O, come, go in,
And take our friendly senators by the hands,
Who now are here, taking their leaves of me
140 Who am prepared against your territories,
Though not for Rome itself.

[CORIOLANUS: *You bless me, gods!*]

Therefore, most absolute sir, if thou wilt have
The leading of thine own revenges, take
The one half of my commission and set down—
145 As best thou art experienced, since thou knowst
Thy country's strength and weakness—thine own ways
Whether to knock against the gates of Rome,
Or rudely visit them in parts remote
To fright them ere destroy. But come in:
150 Let me commend thee first to those that shall
Say yea to thy desires. A thousand welcomes!
And more a friend than e'er an enemy;
Yet, Martius, that was much. Your hand; most welcome!

2 minutes, 45 seconds

buckling tearing off (in a fight); *helms* helmets; *fisting* grabbing, trying to throttle; 132 *with* from; 133 *no other quarrel . . . banished* no other cause for a dispute with Rome except the fact that you've been banished from there; *muster* assemble (troops); 134 *all / From twelve to seventy* i.e., all the able-bodied men between the ages of twelve and seventy; 137 *o'erbeat* overflow, overwhelm the land (i.e., overpower Rome) [*Like a bold flood o'erbeat* overflow like a bold flood]; 140 *prepared against your territories* prepared to attack your outlying territories (the outlying territories of Rome); 141 *Though not for Rome itself* though not yet prepared to attack the city of Rome itself; 142 *absolute* perfect, peerless; 143 *leading* leadership, command, generalship [*if thou wilt . . . revenges* if you will take command of the troops that will help you revenge yourself against Rome]; 144 *The one half of my commission* one half of the soldiers under my command; *set down* determine; 145 *As best thou art experienced* since you are the more experienced of the two of us; 148 *rudely* brutally, with violence; *visit* punish; *in parts remote* in the outlying Roman provinces; 149 *ere destroy* before destroying (them); 150 *those* i.e., the Volscian senators; 152 *more a friend than e'er an enemy* you are now more of a friend (to me and the Volscian people) than you ever were an enemy; 153 *that was much* i.e., the enmity was great—you were once a huge enemy; *Your hand* Give me your hand.

COMMENTARY

Could this guy be tougher? Aufidius's language (like that of his nemesis, Coriolanus, whose monologue directly precedes this one in the play [see page 501]) is composed chiefly of crisp, curt, one-syllable words, reinforcing his military-man background. Granted, much of this monologue is specifically about fighting and waging war, but even when Aufidius discusses other matters, he consistently chooses military imagery to illustrate his points (he describes Coriolanus as an *anvil*, describes love as a fight, even ascribes soldierly meanings to his lovely wife's benign actions). And when he *is* discussing fighting and warfare, Aufidius is descriptive and emphatic—he clearly relishes the topic. For example, he doesn't just state that he intended to fight Coriolanus again, he states that he planned to seek him out and rip his shield from his muscular arm or lose his own arm trying. Other "tough-guy lingo" includes: *My grainèd ash an hundred times hath broke and scarred the moon with splinters*; *thou Mars*; *Unbuckling helms, fisting each other's throat*; *half dead*; *pouring war . . . bold flood o'erbeat*; *rudely visit them*; *fright them ere destroy*; *revenges*.

Aufidius is extremely complimentary of Coriolanus throughout the monologue, referring to him as *Mars* (the god of war), *noble*, perfect, and peerless. He cites Coriolanus's valor, his brawn, his superior strategic prowess regarding an attack on Rome. Perhaps Aufidius is in awe of his nemesis and we're witnessing hero worship. Or perhaps he is employing a tactic to disarm him. Or both . . .

Aufidius uses antithesis, usually (but not exclusively) to contrast the two warriors' past enmity with their newly forged amity (*twine mine arms about that body* versus *where against my grainèd ash an hundred times hath broke . . .* ; *I . . . contest . . . with thy love* versus *I did contend against thy valor*; *knock against the gates* versus *rudely visit*; *friend* versus *enemy*). And, like Coriolanus, Aufidius employs the familiar *thee* toward his rival. Like Coriolanus, he may feel that having fought each other so often has bred an intimacy between them (the content of the speech would certainly suggest that Aufidius feels this way). Also, having just been addressed in the familiar *thee* by Coriolanus (used either toward a peer or an underling, but never toward a superior), Aufidius would have to use the same form of address, or suggest that Coriolanus is his social better.

The blatant sexual overtones of this monologue are self-evident even to today's English speaker. They're yours to play with, if you choose.

And finally, see "O, No! An *O*!," page xxxiii, for help with exploiting the sound of the word *O* to its best advantage.

SIGNIFICANT SCANS

Aufidius can't believe it! His archnemesis, of whom he dreams *nightly*, is standing in his foyer, a mere arm's length away, baring his throat to Aufidius and offering to help him (to help him!) bring to its knees the city-state that has brutally conquered his nation. Aufidius is clearly excited (the content supports this), perhaps even nervous or overwhelmed. Perhaps he's thinking a mile a minute. He's certainly going through some sort of emotional upheaval, as evidenced by the meter, which is chockful of interesting variations. In addition to the more common double endings and trochaic inversions, the piece contains several less frequently seen variations:

Line 110 is a four-footed line (with an inverted first foot):

/ x x / x / x / x /
Should from yond cloud speak divine things (pause-pause) [DIH-vine]

Note: although we have placed the extra foot at the end of the line, you can place it either at the front or the end. Furthermore, you may elect to invert the third foot (*speak div*—) and pronounce *divine* as we do today.

Line 133 is a six-footed line (hexameter), with a trochaic first foot:

/ x x / x / x / x / x /
Had we no other quarrel else to Rome but that

Line 149 has a caesura at which the pause stands in for a silent half foot:

x / x / x / x / x /
To fright them ere destroy. (pause) But come in

Don't forget to elide: *power* (POWR) in line 125; *senators* (SEN-tors) in line 138; *absolute* (AB-sloot) in line 142; and *experienced* (ex-PEER-yenced) in line 145;

. . . and to contract: *thou hast* in line 108 becomes *th'hast* (THAST) (or you can crowd the two words into a crowded foot if you think *th'hast* is too hard for an audience to comprehend); and *The one* in line 144 becomes *Th'one* (THWUN).

TULLUS AUFIDIUS: A GLUTTON FOR PUNISHMENT

Around C.E. 100, the Greek historian Plutarch wrote his collection of Greek and Roman biographies, *Parallel Lives*. Coriolanus (born circa 526 B.C.E.) was one of the Romans who made the cut, although it's debatable whether Plutarch's tales about him actually happened or were merely legends. Plutarch's *Lives* was translated into English in 1579 by Sir Thomas North.

The *Lives* describes Aufidius as having "wealth, bravery, and conspicuous lineage" as well as "a certain grandeur of spirit." Plutarch briefly mentions the rivalry between Coriolanus and the Volscian general, but Shakespeare developed it into the intense relationship between the two found in the play, and thought up Aufidius's unsinkable "tomorrow is another day" philosophy. Legend has it that after Coriolanus's death, Aufidius continued to fight against Rome and was eventually killed in battle.

CORIOLANUS

ACT V, SCENE iii

VOLUMNIA

GENDER: F
AGE RANGE: mature adult to older adult
PROSE/VERSE: blank verse
FREQUENCY OF USE (1–5): 2

Volumnia has raised her son, Caius Martius Coriolanus, to be the fiercest, most fearless, and most noble warrior in Rome, and on that front he's done his momma proud: he's just led the Romans to victory over the Volscian city Corioles (he conquered the place nearly singlehandedly), and in appreciation Rome bestowed upon Volumnia's boy the surname Coriolanus. But Coriolanus has a little problem with pride, which has gotten him banished from Rome. He's mad. And now he's getting even. He's defected to the Volscians and has pledged to help them decimate Rome. He is now camped with them just outside Rome, preparing to attack. Coriolanus has refused to meet with either his close friend General Cominius or the noble Menenius, who is like a father to him. It's time to send in the big guns: Momma Volumnia, dragging with her Coriolanus's wife, Virgilia, his son, little Martius Jr., and a friend, Valeria. The battle of wills between mother and son is drawing to a close. Volumnia has been trying all her artillery, with no apparent success. As Coriolanus moves to leave, saying "I've sat too long," she stops him with:

VOLUMNIA

Nay, go not from us thus.
If it were so that our request did tend
To save the Romans, thereby to destroy
The Volsces whom you serve, you might condemn us
135 As poisonous to your honor. No, our suit
Is that you reconcile them: While the Volsces
May say "This mercy we have showed," the Romans
"This we received," and each in either side
Give the all-hail to thee and cry "Be blessed
140 For making up this peace!" Thou knowst, great son,
The end of war's uncertain; but this certain:
That if thou conquer Rome, the benefit
Which thou shalt thereby reap is such a name
Whose repetition will be dogged with curses;
145 Whose chronicle thus writ: "The man was noble,
But with his last attempt he wiped it out,
Destroyed his country, and his name remains
To the ensuing age abhorred." Speak to me, son.
Thou hast affected the fine strains of honor
150 To imitate the graces of the gods—
To tear with thunder the wide cheeks o' the air,
And yet to charge thy sulphur with a bolt
That should but rive an oak. Why dost not speak?
Thinkst thou it honorable for a noble man
155 Still to remember wrongs? Daughter, speak you—
He cares not for your weeping. Speak thou, boy—
Perhaps thy childishness will move him more
Than can our reasons. There's no man in the world
More bound to's mother, yet here he lets me prate
160 Like one i' th' stocks. Thou hast never in thy life

132 *did tend* aimed at; 134 *serve* both (1) help and (2) do military service for; *you might* then you could; 136 *While* so that the; 140 *making up* forging, creating; 144 *dogged* harassed; 145 *chronicle* historical record; *thus writ* will be written as follows; 146 *attempt* enterprise; 148 *To the ensuing age abhorred* detested by those in times to come; 149 *affected* aimed for, strived to attain; *fine strains of honor* refinements of honor; 152 *yet* now; *charge* to load (a weapon); *sulphur* brimstone, believed by Elizabethans to be what lightning bolts were made of; 153 *rive* split [*a bolt / That should but rive an oak* a lightning bolt that would be powerful enough to split a whole oak in two]; 155 *Still* continually, always; *Daughter* she refers to her daughter-in-law, Virgilia; 156 *boy* she refers to her grandson, Martius Jr.; 157 *childishness* qualities of a child; 158 *reasons* good arguments; 159 *bound* owing gratitude; *prate* babble; 160 *stocks* a large wooden device erected in a public place, into which the legs of a person convicted of an offense were locked as a form of punishment (as a person could not move until released, he would have ample time

Showed thy dear mother any courtesy,
When she (poor hen), fond of no second brood,
Has clucked thee to the wars, and safely home
Loaden with honor. Say my request's unjust,
165 And spurn me back; but if it be not so,
Thou art not honest, and the gods will plague thee
That thou restrainst from me the duty which
To a mother's part belongs. He turns away.
Down ladies, let us shame him with our knees.
170 To his surname Coriolanus 'longs more pride
Than pity to our prayers. Down. An end—
This is the last. So we will home to Rome
And die among our neighbors. Nay, behold's:
This boy, that cannot tell what he would have
175 But kneels and holds up hands for fellowship,
Does reason our petition with more strength
Than thou hast to deny't. Come, let us go—
This fellow had a Volscian to his mother,
His wife is in Corioli, and his child
180 Like him by chance. Yet give us our dispatch.
I am hushed until our city be afire,
And then I'll speak a little.

3 minutes

to idly "prate"); 162 *fond of* loving, doting on; *brood* batch of chickens all hatched at once [*no second brood* Volumnia means that she has no other children]; 163 *clucked thee* called you; 164 *Loaden* loaded down with, supplied in excess, rewarded; 165 *spurn* kick; 167 *restrainst* withholds [*That thou restrainst . . . belongs* for keeping from me the reverence and respect that is a mother's rightful share]; 169 *with our knees* i.e., by getting down on our knees; 170 *'longs* belongs; 171 *prayers* entreaty, urgent request [*To his surname . . . our prayers* i.e., his new surname, Coriolanus, makes him more arrogant than compassionate toward our urgent pleas]; 173 *behold's* either (1) behold us, look at us, or (2) let us behold; 174 *would have* wants; 175 *But* nevertheless; *for fellowship* to keep us company; 176 *Does reason our petition* articulates our plea; 178 *to* for; 179 *Corioli* (kuh-RYE-lee) the Volscian city conquered by Coriolanus for the Romans (for which he now fights against the Romans); *his child / Like him* this child resembles him; 180 *dispatch* permission to leave, dismissal.

COMMENTARY

Volumnia had the bad luck of being born a woman in ancient Rome; she was thus precluded from going to battle and ripping men's heads off. So she did the next best thing: she produced a boy and raised him to take her place. Well, Volumnia, you've created a monster, and thanks to him, the city of Rome will soon be rubble. You'd better fix this . . . and fast. In this scene, Volumnia puts to use the various methods with which she has always controlled her son. But while Coriolanus has always buckled quickly in the past, this time he's not knuckling under. Volumnia recognizes this and keeps shifting tactics—you'll notice how the frequent caesuras and changes of direction in the middle of lines emphasize her abrupt abandonment of one tactic in favor of a new one.

Volumnia is unaccustomed to such defiance from Coriolanus, and it clearly rattles her. She issues directives to those around her, and her increasingly agitated reactions serve as embedded stage directions which indicate that her directives are not being obeyed. For example, in line 148, she orders Coriolanus, *Speak to me*. She continues talking, and five lines later she says, *Why dost not speak?* (which is a stage direction to Coriolanus not to attempt to speak during those five lines). When he persists in his silence, Volumnia turns (in the middle of a line) to Virgilia (who is also usually a pushover) with *Daughter, speak you— / He cares not for your weeping* (a stage direction to Virgilia to continue crying). Volumnia turns to her last hope, little Martius Jr., saying, *Speak thou, boy.* Obviously, Virgilia has not spoken.

It gets worse. Volumnia shifts tactics, ordering the other women down on their knees: *Down ladies, let us shame him with our knees*. Clearly, at least one (if not both) does not obey, because she must repeat the command two lines later: *Down*. Finally someone obeys her—the boy (and possibly the women as well) kneels obediently, for three lines later Volumnia says, *This boy, that cannot tell what he would have / But kneels and holds up hands for fellowship*.

Volumnia tries one argument after another, often using antithesis to make her points (*While the Volsces / May say "This mercy we have showed"* versus *the Romans / "This we received"*; *The end of war's uncertain* versus *but this certain*; *"The man was noble"* versus *"his name remains / To the ensuing age abhorred"*). You'll also discover some wonderful besEEching EE sounds in the beginning of the piece (before she gets good and mad): *received / each / either / thee / be / peace*.

We are finally seeing a vulnerable Volumnia. Her world is no longer on firm ground. She may find this disconcerting, or infuriating, or ironic and somehow funny . . . That she finds it humiliating is apparent in the imagery she employs (*he lets me prate / Like one i' th' stocks*; *When she (poor hen), fond of no second brood, / Has clucked thee to the wars*).

The short first line is actually the second half of a full line: Coriolanus uses the first half to announce that he's leaving, and Volumnia jumps in to entreat him to stay.

There are extra syllables littering this monologue, with double endings abounding, both at ends of lines and before caesuras: Volumnia must speak fast and be convincing, and grows increasingly agitated, to boot. She is also emphatic and/or emotional, punching the beginnings of phrases and sentences, as evidenced by the many inverted (trochaic) beginnings and trochaic feet following caesuras.

Line 151 has a crowded third foot (—*der the wide*) and an inverted foot after a caesura that is not marked by punctuation:

x / x / x - x / / x x /
To tear with thunder the wide cheeks o' the air

Line 148 can be either hexameter (a rare six-footed line) or regular pentameter, depending on whether or not you choose to contract the first three words, *To the ensuing* (t'th'en-SOO-ing). Either way, you must invert the foot immediately following the caesura (for hexameter, invert the first foot as well):

/ x x /x / x / / x x /
"To the ensuing age abhorred." Speak to me, son

x /x / x / / x x /
"To the ensuing age abhorred." Speak to me, son

Don't forget to elide: *Poisonous* (POY-znuss) in line 135; *honorable* (HON´-ra-BLE) in line 154; *Coriolanus* (COR-yo-LA´-nus) in line 170; and *Corioli* (kuh-RYE-lee) in line 179;

. . . and to contract: *for a* (fra) in line 154; *Thou hast* (THAST) in line 160; *To a* (T'A) in line 168; *To his* (T'IZ); and *I am hushed* (I'm HUSHED) in line 181.

Finally, the last line is short. Shakespeare follows it with one of his few stage directions, a profound one for Coriolanus: *Holds her by the hand, silent*. Obviously, Volumnia was effective.

Note: this monologue is the culmination of a sceneful of persuasion by Volumnia. It stands beautifully on its own, but if you're interested in performing an even longer piece, more material is there for the taking.

HAMLET

ACT 1, SCENE ii

HAMLET

GENDER: M
PROSE/VERSE: blank verse
AGE RANGE: young adult to adult
FREQUENCY OF USE (1–5): 4

Hamlet, Prince of Denmark, lost his father about two months ago. Within a month of the King's death, Hamlet's uncle Claudius became king and married Hamlet's mother. Hamlet's grief is now exacerbated by disgust. His father's body is practically still warm in the grave, and his mother is already off enjoying marriage with her brother-in-law (considered incestuous by Elizabethans and forbidden by Church law). Hamlet would like to go back to the university at Wittenberg, where he has been studying—at least that would be an escape from this place—but he has just been denied permission by Claudius. Hamlet soliloquizes his anguish:

O that this too too sullied flesh would melt,
130 Thaw, and resolve itself into a dew,
Or that the Everlasting had not fixed
His canon 'gainst self-slaughter. O God, God!
How weary, stale, flat, and unprofitable
Seem to me all the uses of this world!
135 Fie on't, ah fie! 'Tis an unweeded garden
That grows to seed—things rank and gross in nature
Possess it merely. That it should come to this!
But two months dead—nay, not so much, not two—
So excellent a king, that was to this
140 Hyperion to a satyr; so loving to my mother
That he might not beteem the winds of heaven
Visit her face too roughly. Heaven and earth,
Must I remember? Why, she would hang on him
As if increase of appetite had grown
145 By what it fed on, and yet within a month—
Let me not think on't. Frailty, thy name is woman.—

129 *that* often, as here, used to express a wish for the phrase that follows; i.e., if only; I wish; *sullied* blemished, soiled, defiled [*this too too sullied flesh* i.e., my body]; 130 *Thaw* dissolve; *resolve* convert by breaking into elementary parts; *dew* moisture [*flesh would . . . dew* Elizabethans would have been familiar with St. Paul's comments on the desire to "dissolve" and be with God in 2 Corinthians 5]; 131 *the Everlasting* God; *fixed* set permanently in place (often used with an implied moral sense); 132 *canon* religious law [*fixed / His canon* permanently set down his law]; *self-slaughter* suicide; 133 *weary* irksome, dissatisfying, tiresome; *stale* vapid, trite; *flat* insipid, dull; *unprofitable* useless, serving no purpose; 134 *uses* customs; goings-on [*Seem . . . world* all the things we do in this world seem to me]; 135 *Fie on't* an exclamation expressing contempt or dislike; *'Tis* i.e., the world is; *garden* a popular Elizabethan metaphor for the world; 136 *grows to seed* matures to the stage of yielding seeds (i.e., deteriorates like an uncultivated garden, in which the unpicked fruit rots on the tree or vine, and produces seeds); *rank* (1) foul, disgusting; (2) overgrown; *gross* coarse, unrefined; 137 *Possess* fill, take up; *merely* entirely, completely [*things rank . . . Possess it merely* things that are inherently foul, overgrown, and coarse fill it completely]; 138 *But* Only; *nay* often, as here, used to correct what has just been said; *not so much* i.e., not even that many; 139 *So excellent a king* Hamlet refers to his father; *to this* i.e., to this king (Claudius); 140 *Hyperion* in ancient Greek mythology, the sun god (considered an ideal of male beauty, and sometimes seen as the sun itself, Hyperion was one of the Titans, a race of early deities of gigantic size and enormous strength); *satyr* (SAY-tr) in ancient Greek mythology, a lecherous woodland creature that is half man, half goat [*that was to this / Hyperion to a satyr* who was to this king as Hyperion is to a satyr]; 141 *might not beteem* would not allow; *winds* both (1) currents of air and (2) breaths; sighs [*winds of heaven* the wind, envisioned as God's breath or sighs]; 142 *Visit* i.e., blow against; 144 *As if increase of appetite had grown / By what it fed on* (in-CREESS) As if (her) appetite had been increased by feeding on the very thing it was hungry for (i.e., as if her appetite for her husband was only increased, rather than sated, by the time she spent with him); 146 *on't* i.e., about it; *Frailty* Weakness (in both a physical and moral sense) [*Frailty, thy name is woman* i.e., women are the

A little month—or ere those shoes were old
With which she followed my poor father's body
Like Niobe, all tears—why she—
150 O God, a beast that wants discourse of reason
Would have mourned longer—married with my uncle,
My father's brother—but no more like my father
Than I to Hercules. Within a month,
Ere yet the salt of most unrighteous tears
155 Had left the flushing in her gallèd eyes,
She married. O, most wicked speed, to post
With such dexterity to incestuous sheets!
It is not, nor it cannot come to good.
But break, my heart, for I must hold my tongue.

1 minute, 50 seconds

epitome of moral and physical weakness]; 147 *little* brief [*A little month* i.e., only a month]; *or ere* before [*or ere those shoes . . . father's body* before the shoes she wore while following my father's body (in his funeral procession) had grown old]; 149 *Niobe* (NIE´-uh-BEE) In ancient Greek mythology, Niobe, Queen of Thebes, boasted of her seven sons and seven daughters that they far surpassed the children of the goddess Leto, and urged the people of Thebes to worship her rather than Leto. Leto's two children, Artemis and Apollo, punished Niobe by killing all of her children. Niobe's inconsolable grief turned her into a stone that continually shed tears; *all tears* entirely overcome with tears; 150 *wants* lacks; *discourse of reason* (diss-KORSS) the faculty of rational thought (a common term in Shakespeare's time: "discourse of reason" was thought to be the main difference between humans and animals); 153 *Hercules* the greatest hero in ancient Greek mythology, who performed many superhuman tasks [*Than I to Hercules* i.e., than I am like Hercules]; 154 *Ere yet* even before; *unrighteous* insincere, dishonest; 155 *left* (1) stopped; or (2) left behind; *flushing* redness; *gallèd* irritated (from crying) [*Ere yet . . . gallèd eyes* (1) even before the salt of her insincere tears had stopped reddening her irritated eyes; or (2) even before the salt of her insincere tears had had time to redden and irritate her eyes]; 156 *post* hasten, hurry; 158 *nor it cannot come to good* and it cannot result in anything good (Shakespeare often used the double negative for emphasis).

Mix-and-Match *Hamlet*

Since there is no single authoritative text of *Hamlet*, editors often disagree on which version to use in certain passages. While in most cases we have selected the text that clearly works best in performance, here there are two instances in which we thought the choices were best left up to you. Choose the text that works best with your own interpretation of the piece.

Line 129 contains one of the most debated words in Shakespeare's canon. We have chosen *sullied* because the meaning is more relevant to Hamlet's main focus in the monologue (and the play), but you may replace it with *solid*, a more literal choice with respect to the line itself. Whichever word Shakespeare actually intended, it is not hard to imagine that he used the near homonym purposefully. We suggest that, for today's audience, *sullied* is more likely to evoke the dual meaning.

Line 149 may alternatively be read, "Like Niobe, all tears—why she, even she—" In this version, the meter of the line is completed by adding "even she." If you choose this reading, don't forget to elide *even* (e'en), which is used here for emphasis. We prefer the short version of the line, which allows more choices for interpretation without losing any content. It also avoids the use of *even*, which, in this context, is unfamiliar to today's audiences, and requires an elision that is slightly awkward to today's ear. Since line 149 continues from 148, you will not want to take the one-foot pause at the head of the line. That leaves two options: (1) you may take the silent foot at the caesura, which provides a pause at a good transition point and still forces Hamlet to interrupt himself abruptly (since Hamlet comes back to the sentence he interrupted with no pause in line 151, it seems as though the interruption was intended to be abrupt); (2) you may take the pause at the end of the line, perhaps choking up or cringing at the thought that has come to mind, etc.

COMMENTARY

Hamlet is so miserable with grief over his father's recent death, and feels so defiled by his mother's incestuous marriage, that he wishes he could just melt away to nothing. Shakespeare has imbued Hamlet with an Elizabethan understanding of the world, which shapes the imagery with which Hamlet envisions his escape. Elizabethans believed that all physical and mental ailments were caused by an imbalance in the four elements, or "humours," which made up the human body (see "Elizabethan Anatomy 101," page 558). Hamlet speaks literally of the physical causes of his grief. According to Elizabethan medicine, "melancholia," from which Hamlet is suffering, is caused by an excess of black bile, which if it were to *melt* and *resolve* would release him. At the same time, Hamlet speaks metaphorically: the black bile of which he has an overload is the humour related to earth—he goes on to describe the earth as *an unweeded garden*. Perhaps Hamlet would like to escape earth, which disgusts him, and become *dew*, which was believed to be moisture shed by the moon—he would be escaping to the pure realm of the heavens. Since Hamlet is obsessed with his mother's breach of chastity, it is understandable that he would be attracted to the moon, the domain of the classical goddess Diana, known for her chastity.

This oblique reference to Diana is in keeping with Hamlet's repeated use of imagery from classical mythology in this piece (*Hyperion to a satyr*; *Like Niobe, all tears*; *Than I to Hercules*). Perhaps these characters and stories are vivid in his mind due to his recent studies at Wittenberg, where he would have been studying Virgil, Ovid, Homer, and the like in their original Latin and Greek. No doubt both Wittenberg and the subjects he studied there would represent an escape to Hamlet. In addition, the ancient myths provide a construct in which all acts of God (such as death) are explained in literal terms, and immoral or dishonorable behavior is promptly punished on a grand scale—a scenario preferable to Hamlet's murky, muddied existence in Denmark, where he sees wrongs, but must *hold* [*his*] *tongue*. Hamlet's contrast of himself with Hercules is particularly painful—unlike Hercules (whose greatest heroic actions were performed to redeem the murder of his own wife and children, committed while temporarily insane), Hamlet feels powerless to cleanse his *sullied* state through action.

As much as Hamlet is attracted to his secular studies at school (Wittenberg was famous as the birthplace of Martin Luther's religious reforms), God is still quite a prominent character in his world. Hamlet calls out to God repeatedly throughout the piece, using the word *God* three times, the word *heaven* twice, and referring to *the Everlasting*. Since Hamlet is clearly earnest in his wish to obey God's law when he rejects suicide as an option, it seems possible that all of these outcries are sincere. Or you may decide that Hamlet is simply afraid of death and pain, is using God's law against suicide as a face-saving excuse, and uses God's name as an expletive rather than an appeal. Or perhaps Hamlet's beliefs—and thus his references and approaches to God—vary from one moment to the next, like those of many people.

Keep an eye out for unusual word uses. For instance, in the first line Hamlet repeats the word *too*, creating strong emphasis on the word *sullied*, which is the key to his deliberation: he feels absolutely filthy with his mother's sin. This sets up the main conflict Hamlet faces in the piece. Another example is the word *gallèd*, which is emphasized by its expanded pronunciation, and which carries a second meaning: hurt, or injured. Perhaps the implication is that Gertrude's own eyes are injured by her actions; certainly Hamlet's eyes are. Finally, notice the abundance of *O*s in the piece—a whopping four of them! Be sure to see "O, No! An *O*!," page xxxiii, for help with using them to their best advantage.

SIGNIFICANT SCANS

The meter of this piece is packed with information about its performance. Notice that almost one third of all the lines begin with an inverted first foot! Hamlet's anger, frustration, and disgust seem to burst out of him as he punches the first words of so many lines. Three of these inversions appear in the first three consecutive lines, starting the piece off with a sense of urgency and drive. Take note of the three lines in the piece that have not only one but two inversions, one in the first foot and one after a caesura (lines 135, 142, and 146). In line 135, the variations underscore Hamlet's absolute disgust with the world. In line 142, they reveal his outrage and anguish at the memory of his father's tenderness toward his mother. The emphasis on the words *Visit* and *face* suggests an angrily ironic view of his father's naive protectiveness toward his undeserving wife. Line 146 has two double endings in addition to the two inversions, powerfully emphasizing Hamlet's denunciation of women.

The piece is riddled with stops and starts mid-line, sentence fragments, and interruptions, which are symptomatic of Hamlet's extreme agitation. In the last seven lines, however, the scansion becomes much more regular. Although Hamlet is still very upset, he has now moved past his initial impulse toward suicide and the enraging comparison between the two brothers. Toward the end of the piece he reluctantly faces the reality of the present, and comes to the conclusion that he can—or will—say nothing. The change in meter reflects that resignation, as well as Hamlet's "melancholic" state of mind: Elizabethans believed that melancholia caused one to deliberate doubtfully and at length before taking any action.

When Hamlet reaches the crux of what is bothering him he gets out the big guns: in addition to the imagery and antithesis he uses to compare the two kings, he uses even more extreme and layered variations in meter. Line 140 is a rare six-footed line (hexameter), and it has double endings after the caesura and at the end of the line, for a grand total of fourteen syllables—all leading accusingly to the word *mother*:

x / x / x /(x) x / x / x / (x)
Hyperion to a satyr; so loving to my mother

The scansion of line 151 (which has an inverted first foot and a double ending) elicits the outraged, pointed emphasis on *with*:

/ x x / x / x / x / (x)
Would have mourned longer—married with my uncle

Notice the mid-line inversion of *flat, and* necessary to correctly scan line 133, as well as the crowded foot (——*fitable*):

x /x / / x x /x-x /
How weary, stale, flat, and unprofitable

Finally, note the historic pronunciation of the words *increase* (in-CREESS) in line 144 and *discourse* (diss-KORSS) in line 150. And, for discussion of line 149 and its scansion, see "Mix-and-Match *Hamlet*," page 520.

Don't forget to elide: *Hyperion* (Hie-PEER-yun) in line 140;

. . . to contract *and* elide: *to incestuous* (t'in-SESS-tchwuss) in line 157;

. . . and to expand: *gallèd* (GAWL-ehd) in line 155.

HAMLET

ACT I, SCENE iii

POLONIUS

GENDER: M
PROSE/VERSE: blank verse
AGE RANGE: mature adult to older adult
FREQUENCY OF USE (1–5): 3

Polonius's only son, Laertes, is about to set sail for Paris, where he is a university student. Polonius thought that Laertes had already boarded the ship and is surprised to find him still ashore. Seizing the opportunity to guide his son, Polonius says:

55 Yet here, Laertes? Aboard, aboard for shame!
The wind sits in the shoulder of your sail,
And you are stayed for. There—my blessing with thee!
And these few precepts in thy memory
Look thou character: Give thy thoughts no tongue,
60 Nor any unproportioned thought his act.
Be thou familiar, but by no means vulgar.
Those friends thou hast, and their adoption tried,
Grapple them to thy soul with hoops of steel,
But do not dull thy palm with entertainment
65 Of each new-hatched, unfledgèd courage. Beware
Of entrance to a quarrel; but, being in,
Bear't that th'opposèd may beware of thee.
Give every man thy ear, but few thy voice;
Take each man's censure, but reserve thy judgment.
70 Costly thy habit as thy purse can buy,
But not expressed in fancy—rich, not gaudy—
For the apparel oft proclaims the man,
And they in France of the best rank and station
Are of a most select and generous chief in that.

55 *Yet* still; *Aboard* i.e., board your ship; 56 *The wind sits in the shoulder of your sail* i.e., the wind is favorable (for sailing toward France); 57 *stayed* waited; *my blessing with thee* i.e., I send my blessing with you; 59 *Look thou* see to it that you; *character* (ka-RAK-tur) inscribe [*these few precepts . . . character* see to it that you inscribe these few precepts in your memory]; *Give thy thoughts no tongue* i.e., do not speak your thoughts; 60 *unproportioned* unsuitable, unruly [*Nor any . . . his act* i.e., nor should you act upon any unsuitable thoughts]; 61 *familiar* kind, friendly; *vulgar* i.e., by being indiscriminate about whom you select as friends; 62 *and their adoption tried* once your choice of them as friends has been successfully tested; 63 *Grapple* clasp; 64 *dull thy palm* i.e., wear out your handshake, making it meaningless and valueless; *entertainment* hospitable reception; 65 *unfledgèd* young, unripe; *courage* young man of spirit, young gallant, young swashbuckler; 66 *to* into; *being in* i.e., once you're already in a fight; 67 *Bear't* i.e., carry it out; *that* in such a manner that; *th'opposèd* the opponent; *may beware of thee* will forever after beware you; 68 *Give every man thy ear, but few thy voice* i.e., listen to everyone, but speak very rarely yourself; 69 *Take* i.e., listen to; *censure* judgment; 70 *habit* clothing; *purse* in Shakespeare's time, a small moneybag, used by both men and women [*Costly thy habit as thy purse can buy* Your clothing should be as expensive as you can afford]; 71 *expressed in fancy* shown by ostentatiously fancy clothing; 72 *the apparel oft proclaims the man* the clothing often sets forth the characteristics of the man; 73 *best rank and station* highest social class; 74 *select* choice, excellent; *generous* noble, of noble birth; *chief* principally [*Are of a most . . . that* Scholars generally believe that this line has survived erroneously. Suggested meanings: (1) show their high-class stature by dressing well, but not gaudily; or (2) are most distinguished by their richness (but not gaudiness) of dress; or (3) show their excellent and high-class taste principally through

75 Neither a borrower nor a lender be,
For loan oft loses both itself and friend,
And borrowing dulls the edge of husbandry.
This above all: to thine own self be true,
And it must follow, as the night the day,
80 Thou canst not then be false to any man.
Farewell. My blessing season this in thee.

1 minute, 40 seconds

their choice of dress]; 76 *loan oft loses both itself and friend* i.e., by lending, one often loses both the item (or money) lent as well as the friend to whom the loan was extended; 77 *husbandry* thrift, economy [*borrowing dulls the edge of husbandry* borrowing makes one less thrifty and economical]; 78 *This* i.e., remember this; 81 *season* ripen, mature [*My blessing season this in thee* May my blessing make my advice blossom in you (i.e., may my blessing enable you to fully understand and implement all of this advice)].

MIX-AND-MATCH *HAMLET*

Since there is no single authoritative text of *Hamlet*, editors often disagree on which version to use in certain passages. While in most cases we have selected the text that clearly works best in performance, here there is one choice we thought best left up to you: the First Folio has the word *comrade* in place of *courage* in line 65. While we prefer *courage* for the image it conveys of a young swashbuckler, you may prefer *comrade* for its comprehensibility to today's audience.

COMMENTARY

Want to utter a couple of Shakespeare's best-known lines? They're in here, just waiting for you to bring them to life. Shakespeare gave them to the hilariously long-winded Polonius to impart, making his prosaic precepts delightfully palatable to everyone (except Laertes).

Polonius places great store in his own advice. Notice that he urges Laertes to rush, but then keeps Laertes standing there for ages while he talks his ear off. It is clear that Polonius considers his own wisdom well worth holding up the ship. It also seems likely that he doesn't realize just how long-winded he is (in fact, he advises his son to be frugal with his utterings). Perhaps he also wishes to keep his son with him just a bit longer before the young man departs on the treacherous seas for a faraway place. It's funny that Polonius advises Laertes to *Give every man thy ear, but few thy voice; / Take each man's censure, but reserve thy judgment*—he clearly doesn't heed his own advice on this point!

There is ample additional evidence that Polonius thinks highly of his own wisdom. For example, the meter of the monologue draws attention to what Polonius considers his most important pearls, by inverting the first foot of each line in which he introduces a key instruction (*Look thou*; *Be thou familiar*; *Grapple them to thy*; *Costly thy habit*; *Neither a borrower*; *This above all*). Polonius's choice of words also suggests his high opinion of his own advice. For example, in line 81, he states *My blessing season this in thee*. By choosing the word *season* (ripen, mature), he expresses not the wish that his blessing might make the advice easier to tolerate, but rather that his blessing make his advice take better hold in Laertes and fully blossom in him.

Shakespeare pokes gentle fun at pedantic Polonius. He includes several rhymes, historic rhymes, and half rhymes (*thee / memory*; *buy / gaudy*; *be / husbandry*; *day / thee*) that create a tone reminiscent of Sunday-school aphorisms, which makes him sound amusingly simplistic. By building humor into the piece, Shakespeare has freed you of the need to play it for laughs. You can busy yourself with exploring Polonius's intentions. It is particularly important that you decide why he gives each new bit of advice, and why he does so in this particular order (he seems to be building in order of importance). This will prevent the monologue from becoming a laundry list of maxims.

In line 57, the word *There* is ambiguous: most editors have punctuated the line as we have, since it seems most likely to be an embedded stage direction (indicating that Polonius either places his hand upon Laertes' head to bless him, or gives him an embrace, etc.). But you may decide to follow the First Folio's interpretation of the line as *And you are stayed for there. My blessing with thee*, and deliver the word *there* to mean that Polonius is gesturing in the direction of the ship. Note: if you choose the First Folio version, you have two scansion choices—(1) normal iambic pentameter with a double ending, which places an interesting emphasis on the word *with* (perhaps he wishes to highlight that the blessing will travel with his son, or perhaps his son was departing, and he uses the word to stop him in his tracks—not so fast, sonny, I've got twenty-four more lines to say to you!); or (2) iambic pentameter with a crowded fifth foot (—*sing with thee*), which may also imply that his son is leaving and Polonius rushes to prevent him.

You can have fun with line 65, in which a new sentence begins unexpectedly at the end of line with the word *Beware*. Lest Laertes think his father has finished preaching and dare to reply, Polonius cuts in quickly to continue waxing eloquent with a new directive.

Line 74 is believed by most scholars to have been recorded for posterity incorrectly, which accounts for both its excessive length (a hexameter, or six-footed line) and its unclear meaning. Commit fully to whatever meaning you give it (see annotation for suggestions), and that meaning will be clear to your listeners. Note that you must also elide *generous* (JEN-russ) to scan the line correctly:

x /x / x/ x / x / x /
Are of a most select and generous chief in that

Don't forget that *character*, in line 59, is pronounced with the accent on the second syllable (ka-RAK-tur).

Also don't forget to elide: *courage* (KURJ) in line 65; *generous* (JEN-russ) in line 74; *borrower* (BAR-wur) in line 75; and *borrowing* (BAR-wing) in line 77;

. . . to contract: *Bear't* (BEART) in line 67;

. . . to expand: *unfledgèd* (un-FLEH-jehd) in line 65;

. . . and to contract *and* expand: *th'opposèd* (thu-POSE-ehd) in line 67.

HAMLET

ACT II, SCENE i

OPHELIA

GENDER: F
PROSE/VERSE: blank verse
AGE RANGE: young adult
FREQUENCY OF USE (1–5): 3

Ophelia, daughter to King Claudius's chief adviser, Polonius, has been courted quite seriously by Prince Hamlet, and was dismayed when her father ordered her to reject all further advances on the grounds that Hamlet would never be permitted to wed a nonroyal. A dutiful daughter, however, she obeyed, returning all of Hamlet's love letters and gifts, and refusing to see him. Barred doors notwithstanding, Hamlet has just barged into her private quarters and behaved most strangely. Terrified, Ophelia has run to her father to tell him of it.

75 O, my lord, my lord, I have been so affrighted!

My lord, as I was sewing in my closet,
Lord Hamlet, with his doublet all unbraced,
No hat upon his head, his stockings fouled,
80 Ungartered, and down-gyvèd to his ankles,
Pale as his shirt, his knees knocking each other,
And with a look so piteous in purport
As if he had been loosèd out of Hell
To speak of horrors—he comes before me.

He took me by the wrist and held me hard.
Then goes he to the length of all his arm,
And, with his other hand thus o'er his brow,
90 He falls to such perusal of my face
As he would draw it. Long stayed he so.
At last, a little shaking of mine arm,
And thrice his head thus waving up and down,
He raised a sigh so piteous and profound
95 As it did seem to shatter all his bulk
And end his being. That done, he lets me go,
And, with his head over his shoulder turned,
He seemed to find his way without his eyes,
For out o' doors he went without their helps,
100 And, to the last, bended their light on me.

1 minute, 20 seconds

75 *my lord* an address of respect used toward a nobleman; 77 *closet* private room; 78 *doublet* a close-fitting jacket with a small skirt, which was the primary article of clothing of the Elizabethan male; *unbraced* unbuttoned (it was considered unseemly to appear in public with one's doublet unbuttoned); 79 *fouled* dirtied, soiled; 80 *Ungartered* without garters (worn by Elizabethan men to hold up their stockings); *down-gyvèd to his ankles* (down-JIE-vehd or down-GUY-vehd) fallen down around his ankles like a prisoner's gyves (leg shackles); 82 *piteous* eliciting compassion; *purport* meaning; expression; 83 *loosèd* let loose, set free; 88 *all his arm* his whole arm [*goes he . . . his arm* i.e., he extends his arm to hold me at arm's length from him]; 89 *thus* like so; 90 *falls to* begins; applies himself to; *perusal* careful examination; 91 *As* as if; *Long* For a long time; 92 *a little . . . arm* shaking my arm a little; 93 *his head thus waving up and down* moving his head up and down like this; 94 *raised a sigh* heaved a sigh; 95 *As* that; *all his bulk* his whole body; 97 *with his head over his shoulder turned* with his head turned to look back over his shoulder; 100 *to the last* i.e., until Hamlet was completely gone from view; *bended* turned [*bended their light on me* i.e., kept them focused on me].

COMMENTARY

Here is a wonderful opportunity to do sense-memory work in order to realize for yourself and then for the audience a scene that does not occur onstage. Shakespeare has provided all the raw material, by detailing in the monologue what Hamlet looked like when he accosted Ophelia, exactly how he acted, and how she felt about it.

It is important to consider Ophelia's upbringing and past in order to understand the full impact of Hamlet's visit upon her. As the daughter of a high-ranking member of the Danish royal court, raised to be a modest, virtuous noblewoman, Ophelia has been extremely sheltered. She has probably experienced firsthand very little that would be deemed unsuitable for young ladies; and as books were scarce and her education no doubt carefully monitored by her father, she has probably read little that would shock her innocent sensibilities. We can safely assume that she has been taught to be devout, and believes wholeheartedly in Heaven and Hell. In short, Hamlet's visit must have scared the living daylights out of her.

The very first line bears this out: for one thing, she says so outright (*I have been so affrighted*); second, she repeats the phrase *my lord*, which may indicate that she is babbling with fear (more on that repetition below); also, the very first word is *O* (see "O, No! An *O*!," page xxiii). Furthermore, the line is full of variations in meter—it's headless, has a contraction (*I have* [I've]), a crowded foot (*so affright*——), and a double ending:

x / x / x / x / x - x / (x)
(pause) O, my lord, my lord, I have been so affrighted!

All of these variations in one line create a feeling of upheaval, agitation, and panic, as if Ophelia had just seen the work of the devil himself, and, indeed, she says she just may have (*As if he had been loosèd out of Hell / To speak of horrors*). Ophelia means this literally. To her, Hell is a very real place. For all she knows, a demon has overtaken Hamlet and inhabited his body. Ophelia's belief system (shared by Elizabethans), which includes evil spirits, demons, and goblins, renders the possible reasons for Hamlet's behavior absolutely terrifying. In the First Folio edition, this piece is littered with commas—a signal to the actor to be breathing more rapidly than normal, which would create the sense of being out of breath from agitation and fright. And perhaps Ophelia is unwittingly clairvoyant in lines 82–84, since this is the first event in a chain reaction that will lead to the horror of her own madness and death.

While Ophelia may repeat *my lord* because she is babbling with fear, another possibility is that she wishes to reassure herself that she is really in the presence of her dad (who will surely protect her from evil). Or perhaps she wants to be sure she's gotten his attention (we can imagine that the very busy and important statesman Polonius often listens to Ophelia with half an ear). The choice is yours, but be specific and clear so that the second *my lord* is repeated for a distinct reason (and so that the third *my lord*, in line 77, is altogether different from either of its predecessors).

The sounds of this monologue underscore Ophelia's fright and upset, helping her describe the terrifying spectacle. For example, the piece is laced with Horrified, Heaving Hs (*Hamlet / hat / head*; *he / Hell / horrors / he*; *He / held / hard / he / hand / he*; *he / his head / He / he / helps*). It contains onomatopoeic words, such as *knocking*, *sigh*, and *shatter*. There are many more such helpful sounds in both sections of this monologue for you to explore.

In the first section Ophelia sets the scene, and in the second she acts it out. She does a thorough job of both. We know that she's frightened, but don't forget that she also loves Hamlet—no doubt some of that fear is for <u>his</u> well-being too. Perhaps Ophelia hopes that the more detailed she makes her description to Polonius, the greater the likelihood that her dad can fix the problem.

It may be helpful to know that Elizabethans typically wore hats at all times, even indoors, making the fact that Hamlet had *No hat upon his head* a cause for alarm. And an Elizabethan man would never present himself to a woman (other than his wife) with his doublet unbuttoned or his legs uncovered. Elizabethans considered such disarray evidence of potentially fatal lovesickness. However, Hamlet's behavior transcended mere lovesickness, and it was reasonable of Ophelia to fear the worst.

Ophelia's progression from hysterical to, well, slightly less hysterical is borne out in the meter: the first section contains many double endings, conveying the sense that she is babbling a bit. Line 84 contains an extra silent foot at the caesura, as well as a double ending:

x / x / x / x / x / (x)
To speak of horrors—(pause) he comes before me

Perhaps Ophelia needs to collect her thoughts (which have run away with her a bit). Or perhaps she needs a moment to see if she's forgotten to describe anything.

The relative absence of these double endings in the second section (there is one in line 96, before the caesura) suggests that her hysteria eases somewhat—at least enough to demonstrate Hamlet's actions to her father (as indicated by the word *thus* in lines 89 and 93, both embedded stage directions instructing you to do so). Ophelia is still sufficiently agitated, though, to finish sentences and begin new ones in the middles of lines 91 and 96 (which both contain variations), creating a sense of jumpiness.

There is another silent foot at a caesura in line 91:

x / x / x / x / x /
As he would draw it. (pause) Long stayed he so

Perhaps Ophelia is pausing for a moment to gauge Polonius's reaction to this bizarre behavior. Or perhaps she pauses to demonstrate how Hamlet stared at her.

While there are some inverted feet at the beginnings of lines and after caesuras (which are fairly standard variations), there are also two instances in which Ophelia inverts a foot after a caesura that is not marked by punctuation: in line 81 (*knocking*) and in line 97 (*over*). Again, with these unexpected inversions she emphasizes his frightening demeanor.

Don't forget to elide: *piteous* (PIT-yuss) in lines 82 and 94 and *o'er* (ORE) in line 89;

. . . to contract: *I have* (I've) in line 75;

. . . and to expand: *down-gyvèd* (down-JIE-vehd or down-GUY-vehd) in line 80 and *loosèd* (LOO-sehd) in line 83.

HAMLET

ACT II, SCENE II

POLONIUS

GENDER: M AGE RANGE: mature adult to older adult
PROSE/VERSE: blank verse (with prose) FREQUENCY OF USE (1–5): 3

When Polonius, the trusted adviser to King Claudius, discovered that Queen Gertrude's son, Prince Hamlet, was courting his daughter, Ophelia, he put a stop to it right away, forbidding her to accept communications of any kind from the Prince. Meanwhile, to the consternation of all, Hamlet has been acting insane lately. No one has been able to ascertain why . . . until now. Ophelia has just come to Polonius, quite distraught. It seems that Hamlet has just visited her acting maniacal, his clothing in complete disarray. (For more information, see Ophelia's monologue, page 529.) Polonius is convinced that Hamlet's madness must be caused by his unrequited love for Ophelia and rushes with Ophelia to the royal court to share this insight. There, he presents his discovery to the King and Queen.

My liege, and madam, to expostulate
What majesty should be, what duty is,
Why day is day, night night, and time is time,
Were nothing but to waste night, day, and time.
90 Therefore, since brevity is the soul of wit,
And tediousness the limbs and outward flourishes,
I will be brief. Your noble son is mad.
"Mad" call I it, for to define true madness,
What is't but to be nothing else but mad?
95 But let that go.

[QUEEN: *More matter, with less art.*]

Madam, I swear I use no art at all.
That he is mad 'tis true; 'tis true, 'tis pity;
And pity 'tis 'tis true—a foolish figure,
But farewell it, for I will use no art.
100 Mad let us grant him then. And now remains
That we find out the cause of this effect—
Or rather say the cause of this defect,
For this effect defective comes by cause.
Thus it remains, and the remainder thus—
105 Perpend:
I have a daughter—have while she is mine—

86 *My liege* My sovereign (a respectful term used to address a ruler); *madam* a respectful term used to address a woman of high social rank; *expostulate* discuss (a grandiloquent term); 89 *Were* would be; 90 *wit* intelligence, wisdom, comprehension; 91 *tediousness* boringly excessive wordiness, prolixity; *limbs* body; *flourishes* decoration, ostentatious embellishment [*tediousness . . . flourishes* i.e., prolixity is the "body" and earthly trappings (as opposed to the essence) of wit]; 93 *it* i.e., Hamlet's condition; *for* because; *for to define . . . nothing else but mad* Polonius intends to say, "It is insane to try to define insanity." What he inadvertently says is, "I define insanity as, simply, insanity."; 95 *But let that go* i.e., umm, never mind (Polonius is embarrassed by his dopey misstatement); 96 *art* both (1) rhetorical ornamentations and (2) artifice; 97 *'tis true, 'tis pity* of course it's a pity; 98 *pity 'tis 'tis true* what a pity it is that it is true; *figure* figure of speech, rhetorical device; 99 *farewell it* goodbye to it (the rhetorical wordplay in which he just indulged); 100 *Mad let us grant him then* Then let us acknowledge that he (Hamlet) is insane; *now remains* i.e., what now remains for us to do; 102 *Or rather say* or, rather, I should say; *defect* i.e., Hamlet's mental defect, his insanity; 103 *this effect defective* i.e., the effect of mental deficiency that Hamlet is manifesting; *comes by cause* has a cause, is caused by something; 104 *Thus it remains, and the remainder thus* Polonius intends to say, "This is the situation as it now stands, and here is the solution"; he actually just repeats himself, tying himself in a knot; 105 *Perpend* consider (a pompously ornate word that Shakespeare gave to only three characters, all of whom affect grandiose airs); 106 *while she is mine* i.e., until she is mar-

Who in her duty and obedience, mark,
Hath given me this. Now gather and surmise.
[Reads:] *To the celestial and my soul's idol,*
110 *the most beautified Ophelia—*
That's an ill phrase, a vile phrase; "beautified"
is a vile phrase. But you shall hear
[Reads:]—*these; in her excellent white bosom,*
these, et cetera.

Doubt thou the stars are fire,
Doubt that the sun doth move,
Doubt truth to be a liar,
But never doubt I love.
120 *O dear Ophelia, I am ill at these numbers. I have not art to*
reckon my groans. But that I love thee best, O most best,
believe it. Adieu.
Thine evermore, most dear lady, whilst this
machine is to him, Hamlet.
125 This in obedience hath my daughter shown me,
And, more above, hath his solicitings,
As they fell out by time, by means, and place,
All given to mine ear.

But what might you think
When I had seen this hot love on the wing

ried; 107 *mark* heed, pay attention; 108 *gather* (1) gain information; (2) draw inferences from the information gained; 110 *beautified* rendered beautiful; graced with beauty (see "Irrelevant History: Bitter or Bemused by 'Beautified'?," page 541); 113 *these* i.e., these letters, meaning "this letter"—in Shakespeare's day, a single written correspondence was called either "a letter" or "letters"; *in her excellent white bosom* i.e., in the pocket sewn into Elizabethan women's clothing at the bosom, in which they kept handkerchiefs, letters, small coin purses, etc.; 118 *Doubt truth to be a liar* suspect that truth might be a liar (i.e., as in lines 116 and 117; doubt the seemingly undoubtable); 119 *never doubt I love* i.e., never doubt that I love you; 120 *numbers* poetry (because it was written in meter, which is measurable) [*ill at these numbers* bad at this poetry]; 121 *reckon* sum up (a play on the traditional meaning of "numbers"); *groans* i.e., of lovesickness [*have not art . . . my groans* (1) do not have the talent or skill to sum up my lovesickness through poetry; (2) can't possibly count how lovesick I am (because it's too huge an amount)]; 124 *machine* body; *to him* his [*whilst this machine is to him* i.e., while he (Hamlet) is still in this body]; 126 *more above* furthermore, moreover; *hath . . . given to mine ear* has . . . told me; *solicitings* entreaties, urgings; 127 *As* the manner in which; *fell out* took place; *by* according to [*more above, hath his solicitings . . . all given to mine ear* furthermore, (she) has told me about all of his overtures, detailing the time, the means of communication, and the place of each];

POLONIUS

(As I perceived it, I must tell you that,
Before my daughter told me)—what might you
135 Or my dear Majesty your queen here think,
If I had played the desk or table-book,
Or given my heart a winking, mute and dumb,
Or looked upon this love with idle sight?—
What might you think? No, I went round to work,
140 And my young mistress thus I did bespeak:
"Lord Hamlet is a prince out of thy star.
This must not be." And then I prescripts gave her,
That she should lock herself from his resort,
Admit no messengers, receive no tokens;
145 Which done, she took the fruits of my advice,
And he, repellèd—a short tale to make—
Fell into a sadness, then into a fast,
Thence to a watch, thence into a weakness,
Thence to a lightness, and, by this declension,
150 Into the madness wherein now he raves,
And we all mourn for.

3 minutes, 40 seconds

133 *As* since; 136 *table-book* notebook [*If I had played . . . table-book* (1) If I had passively and silently taken note of the information; and/or, since both desks and table-books gave support to the writer; (2) If I had unwittingly helped transmit the communications]; 137 *given my heart a winking* closed the eyes of my heart (i.e., not cared); *mute and dumb* Polonius is being redundant; 138 *idle* careless [*looked upon . . . idle sight* observed this wooing without caring]; 139 *round* roundly, straightforwardly, without beating around the bush; 140 *my young mistress* my young lady (i.e., Ophelia—here, used contemptuously and condescendingly); *did bespeak* spoke to; 141 *out of thy star* beyond your destiny (stars were thought to influence and determine people's affairs, destinies, fortunes, social positions, etc.); 142 *prescripts* instructions, directions; 143 *lock herself from* withhold herself from; *resort* visits; 144 *tokens* love tokens, gifts given as mementos of love; 145 *Which done* i.e., once these instructions were given; *she took the fruits of my advice* i.e., she obeyed my advice; 146 *repellèd* turned away, rejected; *a short tale to make* to make a long story short; 147 *a sadness* a depression (carrying a stronger meaning than it does today); *a fast* a loss of appetite; 148 *a watch* insomnia; 149 *a lightness* light-headedness; *declension* decline, deterioration; 150 *wherein* in which.

COMMENTARY

Polonius is eager to score brownie points with the royal couple, and here's his chance: he believes he has proof of the cause of Prince Hamlet's recent onset of madness—unrequited love for Polonius's daughter, Ophelia. Polonius must wonder what rewards he will reap for this invaluable information . . . as long as he makes an effective presentation. We'd like to say he gets off to a good start, but he doesn't. You surely can't help but notice (and hopefully enjoy!) that in describing the tediousness he wishes to avoid, Polonius himself is rambling tediously. You must decide why this is so: Is he nervous about his presentation? Or is he confidently and proudly setting up the revelation with an introduction, for maximum impact? Notice that it is not until the seventh line of this monologue that Polonius finally says *I will be brief*. And line 91, in which he describes *tediousness* as something to avoid, is a tedious six feet long (a.k.a. hexameter)! If you wish to build on this, consider the First Folio's version of lines 104–5, which it combines into one line of hexameter (which also has two inverted feet):

/ x x / / x x / x / x /
Thus it remains, and the remainder thus—Perpend

Similarly, notice that at the very end of this very long-winded monologue, Polonius sums up with the words *a short tale to make* when he has made it anything but!

You can play with the contrast between the lengthy setup and the short, concise *Your noble son is mad* (although even there Polonius feels compelled to flatter with *your noble son* rather than opting for, simply, "Hamlet"). He then reverts to his accustomed prolixity. This verbosity tends to get Polonius into trouble, as he weaves and wends his way into making statements he didn't necessarily intend (see Annotation, lines 93–94 and 104, for examples).

And yet, although he knows he is irritating the Queen, perhaps he is incapable of abandoning it and we see here his best efforts to do so, which fall short (as when he says *a foolish figure, / But farewell it, for I will use no art*, and then leaps right back into rhetoric). Or perhaps he is merely making a show of trying to curtail himself for the Queen, because it is only the King he cares to impress.

Polonius's verbosity is also expressed through his excessively ornate and elaborate verbiage: the ridiculously magniloquent *expostulate* in line 86 and *Perpend* in line 105; the grand *gather and surmise* (which actually undermines his airtight case, since *surmise* suggests that his evidence is flimsy); the redundant *mute and dumb* in line 137; and the condescending *my young mistress*. Notice that Polonius feels he must formally introduce (and then expand upon) every detail, including the obvious (i.e., *Your noble son is mad*; *I have a daughter*). Finally, scanning the meter of the piece reveals many double endings, which emphasize its rambling tone.

Polonius's many smug, self-important comments make it impossible to ignore the bumptious character that emerges: he goes to great lengths to flex his muscles before the King and Queen, making a big show of Ophelia's obedience to him (*I have a daughter . . . Who in her duty and obedience, mark, / Hath given me this*; *This in obedience hath my daughter shown me*; *she took the fruits of my advice*). He also falsely takes credit for having noticed Hamlet's love for Ophelia (*As I perceived it, I must tell you that, / Before my daughter told me*), when in fact he didn't—he freely admitted to Ophelia in Act I, Scene iii, that he was informed of it. And he makes a big show of his devotion to the court (*What might you think? No, I went round to work*). Polonius is also quite self-congratulatory about his own wisdom (*she took the fruits of my advice*). His advice yields fruit! There are truly valuable gems among the rubble of Polonius's blatherings (e.g., "Neither a borrower nor a lender be" and "This above all: to thine own self be true" [see monologue, page 524]); and, in this monologue, *brevity is the soul of wit*), but they must be mined, whereas Polonius believes that everything he utters is already polished and set. Very shortly after Polonius says *Perpend*, he says *mark*—this could indicate that he is not receiving the absolutely rapt attention from the King and/or the Queen that he feels he deserves.

You can have lots of fun with Polonius's distasteful reaction to the love poetry Hamlet has composed for his daughter. After reading Hamlet's poetry aloud, Polonius breaks into imagery himself (*hot love on the wing*; *If I had played the desk or table-book*; *Or given my heart a winking*; *idle sight*; *the fruits of my advice*). Perhaps he feels a Freudian rivalry toward his daughter's suitor and subconsciously tries to show up Hamlet with his superior poetic ability. Or perhaps he uses his imagery to mock Hamlet's (which he clearly hates).

One word of caution: it is important to remember that while this mono logue is quite humorous at Polonius's expense, Polonius himself is completely unaware of the joke. While you, the actor, may very well consider Polonius a blowhard, you must also be fully invested in his intentions and find it in your heart to understand why he adopts his methods—the elements discussed above will establish the humor.

SIGNIFICANT SCANS

Do not be alarmed by the quick shifts from blank verse to prose to the iambic trimeter (with trochaic inversions) found in lines 116–19. Just go with the flow. Speak each as you normally would, and the monologue will take its proper shape. The different meters serve two purposes: (1) they distinguish Polonius's disingenuous, formal courtly manner from his regular speech (when he lets down his guard for a moment because he's caught up in annoyance at the word *beautified*); and (2) they set the stiffness and impersonal tone of Hamlet's love poetry apart from the candor and intimacy of the prose that follows in his letter to Ophelia.

Line 95 contains only two feet of spoken text: *But let that go*. Use the silent feet (the Queen's interjection) to make the transition to your next line.

The historic pronounciation of the word *defect* in line 102 (dih-FECT) fits the meter. The contemporary pronounciation, however, creates a useful departure from meter: it places extra emphasis exactly where you want it (on *de*——), contrasting the word with *effect* on the previous line, as Polonius intends.

Lines have been excised from the middle of line 128 to the middle of line 131: We suggest that you combine the two to create one line of iambic pentameter, with a crowded fifth foot (*might you think*):

x / x / x / x / x - x /
All given to mine ear. But what might you think

While the monologue contains several instances of inverted feet at the beginnings of lines or after caesuras (which are fairly common variations), line 141 contains an inverted foot after a caesura that is not marked by punctuation (which is relatively rare in Shakespeare's plays, although frequent in *Hamlet*):

x / x / x / / x x /
Lord Hamlet is a prince out of thy star

Line 148 contains a silent half foot at the caesura (as well as an inverted first foot and a double ending):

/ x x / x / x / x / (x)
Thence to a watch, (pause) thence into a weakness

The shortness of the final line (*And we all mourn for*) lets you take the silent final feet to bask in the adulation that Polonius surely expects to receive for his brilliant deduction.

Don't forget to elide: *brevity* (BREV-tee) in line 90; *tediousness* (TEED′-yuss-NESS) in line 91; *obedience* (o-BEE-dyinss) in lines 107 and 125; and *given* (GIV'N or GI'N) in lines 108 and 137 (but not in line 128);

. . . to contract: *into a* (IN-twa) in line 147 (the first into, *not* the second!);

. . . and to expand: *repellèd* (re-PEH-lehd) in line 146—this expansion draws attention to the word, which emphasizes Polonius's point (finally!) that *this* is the reason Hamlet has gone mad.

IRRELEVANT HISTORY: BITTER OR BEMUSED BY "BEAUTIFIED"? They say you never forget your first review. Shakespeare didn't either: the earliest surviving reference to Shakespeare's writing is found in a 1592 deathbed essay by a disgruntled fellow playwright, Robert Greene, who referred to Shakespeare as "an upstart crow, *beautified* with our feathers . . ." (for more on this, see "Irrelevant History: Greene's Groatsworth of Gripe," page 178). Was the use of the word *beautified* in this monologue just a random word choice, or was Shakespeare exacting revenge on Greene years later by putting his words in pompous Polonius's mouth?

HAMLET

ACT II, SCENE ii

HAMLET

GENDER: M
PROSE/VERSE: blank verse
AGE RANGE: young adult to adult
FREQUENCY OF USE (1–5): 5

Hamlet, Prince of Denmark, is in mourning—his father died about two months ago, and to his horror his mother then married her late husband's brother, Claudius, who assumed the throne (such a marriage was considered incest by Elizabethans and was forbidden by Church law). Furthermore, Hamlet recently saw what he believes to be his father's ghost, which claimed that Claudius murdered him in his sleep, and demanded that Hamlet take revenge. Hamlet swore to do so, but has not yet taken action. Now he is not only disgusted with his mother and his uncle but with himself as well. Meanwhile, a troupe of players has arrived at Elsinore Castle, and one of them has just performed a monologue about the sacking of Troy. As the player described Queen Hecuba's distress at seeing the Greek warrior Pyrrhus hack her husband to death, tears came to his eyes and his voice broke with emotion. After dismissing the players, Hamlet soliloquizes:

575 Now I am alone.
O what a rogue and peasant slave am I!
Is it not monstrous that this player here,
But in a fiction, in a dream of passion,
Could force his soul so to his own conceit
580 That from her working all his visage wanned,
Tears in his eyes, distraction in his aspect,
A broken voice, and his whole function suiting
With forms to his conceit? And all for nothing—
For Hecuba?
585 What's Hecuba to him, or he to her,
That he should weep for her? What would he do,
Had he the motive and the cue of passion
That I have? He would drown the stage with tears,
And cleave the general ear with horrid speech,
590 Make mad the guilty and appal the free,
Confound the ignorant, and amaze indeed
The very faculties of eyes and ears.
Yet I,
A dull and muddy-mettled rascal, peak
595 Like John-a-dreams, unpregnant of my cause,

576 *rogue* unprincipled person, rascal (often, as here, used as a reproach); *peasant* low, base (like a peasant)—here, used reproachfully or derogatorily; *slave* often, as here, a term of contempt; 577 *monstrous* (1) shocking, horrible; (2) unnatural; 578 *But* merely, only; *dream of passion* an imaginary event in which violent emotion is experienced; 579 *conceit* imaginative concept [*force his soul so to his own conceit* make his inner essence come into such perfect accord with his imaginative concept of the role he played]; 580 *her* i.e., his soul's; *working* work, activity; *all his visage* his whole face; *wanned* turned pale; 581 *distraction* despair, emotional disturbance; *aspect* (a-SPECT) countenance, mien; 582 *function* mental activity; *suiting* fitting, adapting appropriately; 583 *forms* bodily expressions, physical gestures [*his whole function suiting / With forms to his conceit* all of his mental activity creating the appropriate bodily expressions of his concept of the character]; 584 *Hecuba* Queen of Troy (who, in the player's speech, witnessed Pyrrhus's slaying of her husband, King Priam); 587 *cue* stimulus (with a play on the theatrical meaning); 589 *cleave* penetrate, pierce; *the general ear* the ears of the public; 590 *mad* (1) insane; (2) without self-control, acting rashly [*Make mad the guilty* make the guilty insane and/or rash in action]; *appal* cause extreme fear in; *free* innocent; 591 *amaze* bewilder, utterly astound and confuse (used in Shakespeare's time with a stronger meaning than it has today); 592 *very* denotes that the word it modifies is to be understood in its full, unrestricted sense; *faculties* natures, essential qualities; 594 *dull* (1) slow, indolent; (2) spiritless; (3) unfeeling; *muddy-mettled* dull-spirited (with a play on the origin of *mettle*, "metal," likening Hamlet to metal once bright and now dulled); *rascal* scoundrel (with a play on the second meaning, a young, lean deer not worth hunting); *peak* mope about (with a play on second meaning, to complement *rascal*: languish, grow lean); 595 *John-a-dreams* a dreamy fellow; *unpregnant of* in-

And can say nothing—no, not for a king,
Upon whose property and most dear life
A damned defeat was made. Am I a coward?
Who calls me villain, breaks my pate across,
600 Plucks off my beard and blows it in my face,
Tweaks me by the nose, gives me the lie i' th' throat
As deep as to the lungs? Who does me this?
Ha!
'Swounds, I should take it—for it cannot be
605 But I am pigeon-livered, and lack gall
To make oppression bitter, or ere this
I should have fatted all the region kites
With this slave's offal. Bloody, bawdy villain!
Remorseless, treacherous, lecherous, kindless villain!
610 O, vengeance!
Why, what an ass am I! This is most brave,
That I, the son of a dear father murdered,
Prompted to my revenge by Heaven and Hell,
Must like a whore unpack my heart with words,
615 And fall a-cursing like a very drab,

different to, not spurred to action by; 596 *a king* i.e., Hamlet's murdered father; 597 *property and most dear life* (1) most valuable possession, his life; or (2) possessions (his crown and queen) and very valuable life; 598 *defeat* destruction [*damned defeat was made* act of destruction deserving damnation was perpetrated]; 599 *pate* head [*breaks my pate across* strikes me across the head, breaking the skin]; 600 *Plucks off my beard and blows it in my face* tugs out the hairs of my beard and blows them at my face; 601 *the lie i' th' throat* a lie that was intentionally told and could not have been a slip of the tongue [*gives me the lie i' th' throat* accuses me of being an outright liar]; 602 *As deep as to the lungs* i.e., reprehensibly deep (the deeper the origin of the lie, the more reprehensible it is); *Who does me this?* Who does this to me?; 604 *'Swounds* (SWOONDZ) short for "By God's wounds"; used as an expletive; *should* would; *it cannot be / But I am* i.e., I must be (Shakespeare often used double negatives for emphasis); 605 *pigeon-livered* meek, overly mild-tempered (in Shakespeare's time, the pigeon was a symbol of meekness, as it was believed to have no gall [see *gall*, below]—emotions [particularly passionate emotions] were believed to originate in the liver); *gall* Elizabethans believed that the body was composed of four fluids called "humours," which were believed to determine temperament (see "Elizabethan Anatomy 101," page 558). Gall, more commonly know as "yellow bile" or "choler," was the source of bitterness and rancor; 606 *To make oppression bitter* to make tyranny seem bitter to me; *or ere this* or else before now; 607 *fatted* fattened up; *region* from the upper air; *kites* hawks (any of several varieties, both birds of prey and scavengers) [*all the region kites* all the birds of prey and scavengers of the sky]; 608 *offal* the parts of a butchered animal not fit for use [*this slave's offal* i.e., King Claudius's worthless body]; *Bloody* (1) Cruel, bloodthirsty; (2) Stained with blood; 609 *kindless* unnatural, inhuman; 611 *most brave* extremely becoming; extremely admirable; 613 *Prompted to my revenge by Heaven and Hell* dual meanings: (1) prompted to my revenge by the "good" motive of meting out true justice and the "bad" motive of personal hatred—both are elements of human "nature" to which the ghost appeals; (2) prompted to my revenge by a ghost that might be either an angel or a devil; 615 *drab*

A scullion! Fie upon't, foh!
About, my brains. Hum—I have heard
That guilty creatures sitting at a play
Have, by the very cunning of the scene,
620 Been struck so to the soul that presently
They have proclaimed their malefactions.
For murder, though it have no tongue, will speak
With most miraculous organ. I'll have these players
Play something like the murder of my father
625 Before mine uncle. I'll observe his looks—
I'll tent him to the quick. If he do blench,
I know my course. The spirit I have seen
May be a devil, and the devil hath power
T'assume a pleasing shape. Yea, and perhaps,
630 Out of my weakness and my melancholy,
As he is very potent with such spirits,
Abuses me to damn me. I'll have grounds
More relative than this. The play's the thing
Wherein I'll catch the conscience of the King.

3 minutes, 30 seconds

strumpet, lewd woman; 616 *scullion* domestic servant of the lowest rank, who washes pots and kettles in the kitchen (commonly used as a term of contempt); *Fie upon't* an exclamation expressing contempt or dislike; *foh* an exclamation expressing contempt or hatred; 617 *About, my brains* Get to work, brains; *Hum* an interjection used when deliberating over something; 618 *creatures* i.e., people; 619 *very* mere; *cunning* art, skill; *scene* theatrical performance; 620 *presently* immediately; 623 *miraculous organ* voice; means of communication [*will speak / With most miraculous organ* will make itself known by the most miraculous means of communication]; 624 *Play* perform; *something like* i.e., a play that is similar to; 625 *Before mine uncle* in my uncle's presence; 626 *tent* probe (a tent was a roll of lint or gauze used to examine, keep open, or cleanse a wound); *quick* (1) living, alive; (2) sharp, piercing [*to the quick* (1) to the living flesh, i.e., until he feels pain; (2) sharply, piercingly]; *do blench* flinches; 627 *my course* i.e., the course of action I will take; *spirit* i.e., the thing that has claimed to be his father's ghost; 629 *Yea* often, as here, used to affirm what has just been said; 630 *melancholy* depression, gloominess, sadness (The term *melancholy* was used to describe a whole range of conditions, from simple sadness or moodiness to chronic disease. Melancholy was believed to result from the excretion of too much black bile, one of the four "humours" [see "Elizabethan Anatomy 101," page 558]); 631 *As* since; *is very potent with* has great power to exploit; *spirits* states of mind; 632 *Abuses* deludes, deceives [*perhaps, / Out of . . . to damn me* perhaps, since he (the devil) has great power to exploit such states of mind, he is taking advantage of my weakness and melancholy, and is deceiving me in order to damn me (by getting me to murder Claudius)—Elizabethans believed that people with melancholy temperaments were prone to hallucinations and were highly susceptible to the devil's tricks]; *I'll have grounds* i.e., before I kill Claudius, I want grounds; 633 *relative* (1) directly related, conclusive; (2) relatable, easily told [*More relative than this* i.e., (1) more conclusive than the ghost's claims; (2) more easily explained to others than the fact that I spoke to my father's ghost]; 634 *catch* seize, in order to perceive.

Mix-and-Match *Hamlet*

Since there is no single authoritative text of *Hamlet*, editors often disagree on which version to use in certain passages. While in most cases we have selected the text that clearly works best in performance, here there are three instances in which we thought the choices were best left up to you. Choose the text that works best with your own interpretation of the piece.

Line 585 may alternatively be read, *What's Hecuba to him, or he to Hecuba*—in this version, the line scans as hexameter, a rare six-footed line. With this choice, the unusual length of the line and the repetition of Hecuba's name emphasize Hamlet's distress that the player has exhibited more emotion than he, with much less motive.

Line 610, *O, vengeance!* is believed by some to be an ad-lib inserted by an actor. Some editors choose to leave it out, but we like the contrast between this short, climactic line and the dense, heavily elided line that precedes it, as well as the contrast within the line between the fullness of *O, vengeance!* and the emptiness of the silent feet. In addition, this line gives you more time to make one of the major transitions in the piece. However, you may choose to leave the line out, which directly juxtaposes Hamlet's cursing of Claudius with his cursing of himself, and allows the pace of the cursing to continue unbroken, which may work well for you.

In line 616, *A scullion!* could instead be read, *A stallion!*—in Shakespeare's time, *stallion* also meant prostitute (male or female). We have chosen *scullion* because it is slightly more accessible to today's audience, but you may decide to use *stallion*, especially if your Hamlet is obsessively focused on Claudius's incestuous behavior.

COMMENTARY

Hamlet fits the Elizabethan profile of a melancholic temperament to a T: he is moody, extremely witty, full of doubts and suspicions, fearful, prone to nightmares and visions, and although he is deeply passionate, he deliberates at length before acting on his passions (see "Elizabethan Anatomy 101," page 558). But the fact that Hamlet is a textbook example of melancholia still leaves most questions about him unanswered, because in Shakespeare's time that diagnosis covered a wide range of problems. It may have meant Hamlet was simply still grieving over his father's death, or it may have meant he was stark raving mad—or something else in between. Thus it is up to you to determine Hamlet's state of mind, and the nature of his "weakness."

One thing is certain about Hamlet's mind—it's moving a mile a minute. This piece is extremely active, and has a great progression, meaning you can use it effectively to showcase your versatility. Two major aspects of the meter in this piece will help you chart its progression. The first is the extraordinary number of short lines. They're all deliberately placed, and each one can be used to make a transition to Hamlet's next line of thinking.

- Line 584 (*For Hecuba?*) divides Hamlet's reflection on the player into two separate builds: first there is the build in his description of the player's performance. Then, line 584 provides three silent feet in which to transition to the next build, which focuses on the actions Hamlet imagines the player would have taken in Hamlet's circumstances. You may choose to place all three silent feet at the beginning or end of the line, or to break them up.
- The four feet of silence in line 593 give you the chance to move thoughtfully from the detailed image you have painted of the player to the comparison with your own sorry self. You may choose to put the four silent feet at the start of the line, and linger over the fantasy of the player you've just described, or to put the pause at the end of the line—perhaps Hamlet is reluctant to examine his own behavior in the same circumstances. Or perhaps you will place some of the silent feet before *Yet I*, and some after.
- Although you may choose to leave out line 610 (see "Mix-and-Match *Hamlet*," on facing page), we recommend that you keep it. Notice how nicely Hamlet's cursing builds up to this dramatic—or perhaps melodramatic?—climax. If you scan the line as follows . . .

  x / x / (x)
  (pause) O, (pause) vengeance!

  . . . you then get three silent feet in which to make the transition to the next beat. The pause is a nice contrast to what has gone before, and gives you time to transition to laughing at and/or deriding yourself in the lines to come.
- Line 603 has only one syllable! You may choose to place the four and a half feet of silence before the *Ha!* (perhaps Hamlet is really looking for some supernatural response to his rhetorical question, or maybe he takes the time to imagine how he would respond if someone <u>did</u> offend and challenge him in the ways he has just listed). Or, you may put them after the *Ha!* (perhaps Hamlet says *Ha!* as if to answer his own question—"No one!"—or perhaps he says it as a challenge to the pow-

ers that be, and then waits for a response during the silence that follows). As with the lines above, you may also choose to break up the pause.

- Line 616 is short by two feet, and line 617 by one. We suggest that you place the two-foot pause in line 616 at the end of the line, where it provides a nice transition from Hamlet's self-abasement to his decision to commit to a suitable action to solve his problem. The pause in line 617 works nicely at the caesura, where it provides transition time—this time from cogitation over the problem to conception of a solution. Read this way, the lines would scan as follows (note the double ending before the caesura and the inverted foot after it in line 616):

x / (x) / x x / x / x /
A scullion! Fie upon't, foh! (pause-pause) (pause-pause)
x / x / x / x / x /
About, my brains. (pause-pause) Hum—I have heard

- And, of course, the first line of the soliloquy (*Now I am alone*) also contains silent feet, since we have sheared the first half of it (which was unrelated to the piece). You have the option of placing the resultant pause either at the beginning or the end of the line. Although the scansion of the line as a whole requires the contraction of *I am* to "I'm," there is no need to use the contraction if you are performing this monologue independent from the play.

The second prominent feature in the meter is the frequent use of sentences that end and begin mid-line. Notice that in every single case, the meter is continuous across the caesura. This creates a feeling that the words are tumbling out of Hamlet, and that one thought leads him right to the next. A perfect example of this is line 588, in which Hamlet doesn't pause at all after his own question, but goes on to answer it immediately. If you use this element of the meter in conjunction with the contrasting pauses described above, moving fluidly from one idea to the next in most of the lines, and using pauses to make the major transitions at the short lines Shakespeare has provided, the shape and progression of the entire piece will simply jump out at you! Try it—you'll get effective and dynamic results that will guide your interpretation of Hamlet's thought progression as he finally decides to takes action.

Hamlet's imagery provides insight into his perspectives on his uncle and on himself. He envisions Claudius as *offal*—bloody animal waste fit only to be eaten by scavenger birds; this bloody image connects easily to the later one, in which Claudius is a wound Hamlet intends to *tent*. Hamlet also sees Claudius as *bawdy* and *lecherous*, and, if you choose to use the word *stallion* rather than *scullion* in line 616, he calls him a male prostitute, which relates his disgust with Claudius to his disgust with himself, since Hamlet goes on to compare himself to a *whore* or a *drab* who *fall*[*s*] (i.e., falls from virtue) *a-cursing*. Thus, Hamlet has chosen to apply imagery in this piece only to the two main characters in his conflict, himself and Claudius, and in so doing, he has likened them to each other, rather than differentiating between them. The only other character or thing in the piece to which he applies imagery is that which stands between them: murder. Hamlet personifies *murder*, with a poetic twist on the old saying that "murder will out," saying that *murder . . . will speak / With most miraculous organ*. Surely he is thinking not only of the crime he believes Claudius has committed, but also of the one he intends to commit.

Be aware that although Hamlet is a well-educated and highly intelligent prince (which is evident in his use of imagery, sounds, and complex ideas), he makes extensive use of casual contractions and elisions, as well as crude curses and colloquialisms. Perhaps Hamlet is trying to sound tough; maybe he's accentuating his wit and sarcasm; maybe this base language suits his mood. The repeated use of elisions and contractions in particular provides a great contrast for the one expansion in the piece, *malefactions*. Does Hamlet stretch out the word as the idea to set a trap for Claudius takes shape in his mind? Or has the idea come at the beginning of the line, after which he pronounces each syllable of the last word in triumph? Explore your options.

There are many wonderful uses of sounds in this piece. First, notice the simple groupings of consonance, assonance, and alliteration: *O* / *rogue*; *working* / *wanned*; *cleave* / *ear* / *speech*; *damned defeat*; *it* / *pigeon-livered* / *bitter* / *this*; *Bloody, bawdy*; *treacherous* / *lecherous*; *dear* / *father* / *murdered*; *whore* / *heart*; *Fie* / *foh*; *Hum* / *have* / *heard*; *most miraculous*. Next, note lines and phrases in which one sound repetition leads into the next, often overlapping, or ending with the same sound the phrase began with: Morose UHs, Ms, and Ls (*dull and muddy-mettled rascal*); Ns and INGs (*nothing—no, not for a king*); long A sounds that combine with as well as bracket a harsh string of Bs and Ps (*breaks my pate across, / Plucks off my beard and blows it in my face*); Ws leading to flat As, leading back to *I*, which echoes *Why* (*Why, what an ass am I*). Hamlet's description of the player's response, had he Hamlet's motive, is heightened by a string of kEEning EE sounds at the ends of lines 588–92 (*tears* / *speech* / *free* / *indeed* / *ears*).

Also, look for whole phrases or lines saturated by certain sounds or combinations of sounds: Ss and Ts (*Tears in his eyes, distraction in his aspect* and *struck so to the soul*); Hs combined with EE and ER sounds, in a string of one-syllable words after *Hecuba* (*Hecuba to him, or he to her, / That he should weep for her*);

EHs (*Prompted to my revenge by Heaven and Hell*); and Soft Cs and Ss with long Os (*force his soul so to his own conceit*). The long Os echo the sound of the word *O*, which is used in two key positions in the piece. For help with using *O* to its best advantage, see "O, No! An *O*!," page xxxiii.

The repetition of sound is the most striking poetic element in this soliloquy. The sound patterns generate momentum and heighten the intensity, expressing and thereby reinforcing Hamlet's emotions. Sound patterns also elevate Hamlet's language, investing the listener in the outcome of his dilemma. In contrast, note that when Hamlet formulates his plan, his speech becomes more prosaic and pragmatic: the sound repetitions and the images disappear. They do not resurface until the last two lines, which form a rhyming couplet (*thing* / *King*) and which conclude with the alliteration of decisively crisp C and K sounds (*catch* / *conscience* / *King*).

Finally, notice the sexual puns in lines 627–32. Shakespeare's audiences would have been familiar with these second meanings: *course* = a session of sexual intercourse; *devil* = Elizabethans believed in hermaphroditic or bisexual devils who copulated with men, women, children, and especially witches; *shape* = sexual organs; *potent* = sexually potent; *such* = sick, morally decayed; *spirits* = penis or semen; *Abuses* = copulates with or sodomizes; *damn* = dam, i.e., make a woman of.

The double entendre in these lines reinforces Hamlet's description of himself as an *ass*, a *whore*, and a *drab*. For the most part, this double entendre will be lost on today's audience, but it gives you valuable insight, revealing the extent to which Hamlet's fears about the nature of the Ghost and its intentions are tangible obstacles to taking action.

SIGNIFICANT SCANS

In line 601, which has inverted feet both at the head of the line and after the caesura, you will also find two contractions—*the nose* (TH'NOSE) and *i' th'* (ith'):

/ x x / / x x / x /
Tweaks me by the nose, gives me the lie i' th' throat

Line 623 seems hard to scan, due to its elision (see below) and its two double endings, but it's actually quite simple:

x / x / x / (x) x / x / (x)
With most miraculous organ. I'll have these players

Don't forget to elide: *monstrous* (MON-struss) in line 577; *general* (JEN-rl) in line 589; *ignorant* (IG-nrant) in line 591; *treacherous* (TRETCH-russ) and *lecherous* (LETCH-russ) in line 609; *Heaven* (HEV'N) in line 613; *miraculous* (mih-RACK-luss) in line 623; and the second instance of *devil* (DEV'L) in line 628 (but not the first);

. . . to expand: *malefactions* (MAL-eh-FAC´-shee-UNZ) in line 621;

. . . and to contract: *in his* (INZ) in line 581; *the nose* (TH'NOSE) in line 601; and *i' th'* (ith') in line 601.

HAMLET

ACT III, SCENE i

HAMLET

GENDER: M
AGE RANGE: young adult to adult
PROSE/VERSE: blank verse
FREQUENCY OF USE (1–5): 5

Prince Hamlet of Denmark was visited by the spirit of his recently deceased father. The Ghost claimed he was murdered by Hamlet's uncle Claudius (who married Hamlet's mother only a month after the late King's death, and assumed the throne), and demanded that Hamlet avenge his death. Hamlet was already mourning the loss of his father and distressed by his mother's hasty and (by Elizabethan standards) incestuous marriage to her brother-in-law, as well as by his uncle's power grab. Now he is in a quandary: he is plagued by the injustice to his father and honor-bound to avenge it, but is aware of the many dire consequences (in life and in the afterlife) of exacting revenge. Tormented, he soliloquizes:

To be, or not to be—that is the question:
Whether 'tis nobler in the mind to suffer
The slings and arrows of outrageous fortune,
Or to take arms against a sea of troubles
60 And by opposing end them. To die—to sleep,
No more; and by a sleep to say we end
The heartache and the thousand natural shocks
That flesh is heir to. 'Tis a consummation
Devoutly to be wished. To die—to sleep;
65 To sleep, perchance to dream. —Ay, there's the rub,
For in that sleep of death what dreams may come,
When we have shuffled off this mortal coil,
Must give us pause. There's the respect
That makes calamity of so long life:
70 For who would bear the whips and scorns of time,
The oppressor's wrong, the proud man's contumely,
The pangs of disprized love, the law's delay,
The insolence of office, and the spurns
That patient merit of the unworthy takes,
75 When he himself might his quietus make

56 *To be* to exist, to live; 57 *nobler in the mind to suffer* It is debated whether *in the mind* modifies *nobler* or *to suffer*. If you choose the former, the phrase *nobler in the mind* = "heroic" (having either the fortitude to endure life or the courage to end it) and *suffer* = "endure." If you choose the latter, the word *nobler* = "more honorable" and the phrase *in the mind to suffer* = "to suffer mentally from"; 58 *slings* weapons composed of a looped strap in which a stone is whirled and then flung; *outrageous* violent, atrocious; *fortune* fate; chance; 59 *take arms against* take up arms against, battle against; 60 *opposing* i.e., opposing the *sea of troubles*; 61 *No more* i.e., nothing more than to sleep; *to say* to suppose; 62 *shocks* armed clashes (i.e., painful conflicts); 63 *flesh* mortals [*That flesh is heir to* that mortals inherit (i.e., that are part and parcel of the human experience)]; *consummation* ultimate end (a secondary meaning, "a dissolving into nothingness," echoes Hamlet's previously stated desire to "melt, / Thaw, and resolve . . . into a dew" [see monologue, page 517], and alludes to Montaigne's *Essays* and possibly to 2 Corinthians 5); 64 *Devoutly to be wished* to be earnestly wished for; 65 *rub* obstruction that alters the course of an argument, chain of thought, or action; 67 *shuffled off* got rid of, cast aside; *coil* both (1) a length of rope wound around something and (2) turmoil of activity, tumult [*mortal coil* i.e., both the human body (which encompasses the soul) and the worldly activities and troubles encountered while in the human body]; 68 *give us pause* make us stop and think; *respect* consideration; 69 *calamity* i.e., human life (which is by nature calamitous); *of so long life* so long-lived [*That makes . . . life* that makes calamity last so long, i.e., that makes people put up with such long, calamitous lives]; 70 *scorns* mockeries; *time* i.e., the world we live in; 71 *oppressor's wrong* injury or injustice perpetrated by an oppressor; *contumely* contemptuous treatment, taunts; 72 *disprized* (DIS-prized) unvalued; *the law's delay* i.e., the excessive lengthiness of the judicial process (a common complaint in Elizabethan times); 73 *office* public officials; *spurns* insults; kicks; 74 *That patient merit of the unworthy takes* i.e., that meritorious people must patiently accept from worthless people; 75 *quietus* (kwie-EE-tuss) final settlement of an

With a bare bodkin? Who would fardels bear,
To grunt and sweat under a weary life,
But that the dread of something after death—
The undiscovered country, from whose bourn
80 No traveler returns—puzzles the will,
And makes us rather bear those ills we have
Than fly to others that we know not of?
Thus conscience does make cowards of us all,
And thus the native hue of resolution
85 Is sicklied o'er with the pale cast of thought,
And enterprises of great pitch and moment
With this regard their currents turn awry
And lose the name of action. —Soft you now,
The fair Ophelia. —Nymph, in thy orisons
90 Be all my sins remembered.

2 minutes

account [*might his quietus make* could settle his account]; 76 *bare* mere; *bodkin* scholars disagree on which of the following definitions is intended here: (1) a sharp instrument for making holes in cloth or leather; (2) a long, ornamental hairpin; or (3) a dagger or stiletto; *fardels* packs, bundles, burdens; 77 *weary* tiresome, irksome [*under a weary life* i.e., under the burden of a tiresome life]; 78 *But that* if it were not for; 79 *bourn* territory; 80 *puzzles* confounds, rendering incapable of action; *the will* the part of the mind governing desire and intention to act; 81 *rather* more willingly; 82 *fly* both (1) move rapidly and eagerly; (2) flee; *know not of* know nothing about; 83 *conscience* (1) thought, rumination (here, thinking about the uncertainty of the afterlife, which causes fear and, consequently, inaction); or (2) moral judgment (here, the belief that suicide and murder are sins, which causes fear of retribution in the afterlife, and, consequently, action); 84 *native* natural, genuine; *resolution* resoluteness, undaunted courage [*the native hue of resolution* the ruddy complexion that Elizabethans believed characteristic of resolute people (see "Elizabethan Anatomy 101," page 558)]; 85 *sicklied o'er* covered over with a pale, sickly color; *cast* coloring, tinge [*pale cast of thought* pale complexion of a thoughtful, melancholic person (see "Elizabethan Anatomy 101," page 558)]; 86 *pitch* height, high aspiration (a term from falconry: the highest point in a falcon's flight before it swoops to attack its prey); *moment* consequence, importance; 87 *With this regard* because this is thought about; *currents* course, progress [*their currents* i.e., the progress of these enterprises]; *awry* away from the correct course; 88 *lose* forfeit, abandon (because you've lost the zeal for); *name* (1) honor; (2) title [*And lose the name of action* (1) and lose the honor that action would have won; (2) i.e., and can no longer be called "action" (because they are now passive)]; *Soft you* Be quiet; 89 *fair* beautiful; good; virtuous; *Nymph* minor divinity of nature, represented as a beautiful young maiden (often used to refer to or address a beautiful young woman); *orisons* (OR´-ih-ZUNZ) prayers; 90 *Be all my sins* may all my sins be; *remembered* (1) mentioned; (2) considered.

COMMENTARY

So, you've decided to tackle the most exhaustively discussed soliloquy in the English language—we don't blame you. Its ideas have resonated with people and its complexities have intrigued them since the play was first presented. A quick skim will reveal that the soliloquy is written in general terms—Hamlet never uses *I* and speaks generally about the human condition rather than speaking specifically about his particular circumstances. This has fueled a heated, centuries-long debate about the soliloquy's meaning. Some scholars maintain that the soliloquy is merely what it seems at face value, an academic discussion about the pros and cons of living, but this is not a strong choice for an actor to make.

Of the more active and personal choices, the most common interpretation is that Hamlet is debating the pros and cons of suicide. Another possibility is that Hamlet is debating whether or not to take action and kill Claudius, with the full awareness that this action will ultimately result in his own undoing and death—either he will die in the commission of the murder, or he will be executed for it subsequently. Since both suicide and murder are sins, either interpretation carries with it the specter of punishment in the afterlife, which inhibits action. As for why Hamlet speaks in general terms about the human condition, perhaps he finds it too painful to articulate his present quandary and feelings specifically. And perhaps he uses the words *we* and *us* rather than "I" to assert his right to the throne that was stolen from him by Claudius (employing the royal "we," which only reigning monarchs used).

In keeping with the impersonal tone of the piece, its structure is based on the stylistically formal device of antithesis. Perhaps Hamlet chooses this device consciously, to keep his thoughts at arm's length where he can handle them, or perhaps he turns to it unconsciously, as an automatic defense mechanism; perhaps the antithesis is a manifestation of the numb detachment of depression, or evidence of an inherent tendency to overthink his problems. Antithesis is established in the first line with *To be, or not to be*. It continues with an extended consideration of the two polar-opposite options: *suffer / The slings and arrows of outrageous fortune* or *take arms against a sea of troubles / And by opposing end them*. After stating the pros (ending life's troubles) and cons (an uncertain fate: *what dreams may come*) of *taking arms against a sea of troubles*, he uses antithesis again in his conclusion that fear of what comes after death *makes us rather bear those ills we have / Than fly to others that we know not of*. Following this train of thought, antithesis is then used to ironically contrast the question as it is loftily framed in the beginning of the piece (*Whether 'tis nobler in the mind to suffer . . .*), with its cynical answer stated toward the end (*Thus conscience does make cowards of us all*)—that the choice is not based on honor, but rather on cowardice.

To best explain the lose-lose proposition he has set forth, Hamlet employs very apt imagery. Do not take points off for his mixed metaphor in line 59 (*to take arms against a sea of troubles*)—it perfectly expresses the futility of attacking a boundless and overpowering force . . . with weapons and tactics that are useless against it, to boot. Shakespeare's audience would have been familiar with this imagery, since they knew of ancient Celtic warriors who jumped in and attacked the incoming tide with their swords, rather than show fear by retreating from the waves (said warriors, of course, perished).

The central metaphor that envelops this monologue is the common Renaissance concept of death as a dreamless sleep, which Shakespeare takes to the next step by imagining the afterlife as a dream. This metaphor is laced through the piece using repetition of both sounds and phrasing: *To die / to sleep / by a sleep / to say / heir to / to be wished / To die / to sleep / To sleep / to dream / sleep of death what dreams*. The repetition keeps Hamlet and his listeners focused on the problem at hand: our inadequate knowledge and amorphous images of the afterlife. Furthermore, the repetition is one clue to Hamlet's state of mind. The repeating loop of sounds, phrasing, and images perfectly captures the cyclical, obsessive thought patterns of a depressed person, who ruminates fixatedly about the source of his misery and anxiety. Notice Hamlet's foregone conclusion that troubles and living are coexistent, which is consistent with a depressed person's negative perceptions of his world.

There are many more sound repetitions (consonance and assonance) that further underscore Hamlet's state of mind. This chain of sound links conveys Hamlet along the path of his torturous thought process. Some examples (there are more for you to find!): Ts/Bs/OOs/EEs (*To be / not to be / 'tis nobler*); Ss (*suffer / slings*); Rs/ORs/Os/Ss/Ts (*arrows / outrageous / fortune / Or to take / against / troubles / opposing / no more*); As/Ss/Ts (*arms against a sea / troubles*); SHs (*shocks / flesh / consummation / wished*); Ds (*Devoutly / die / dream / death / dreams*); UHs (*rub / come / shuffled / us*); Rs (*For / bear / scorn / oppressor / wrong / proud / disprized*); Ps/Bs (*sleep / sleep / perchance / rub / sleep*); Ps/Rs (*oppressor / proud / pangs / disprized*); Ls (*contumely / love / law's delay / insolence*); Os and UH sounds/Ss/Fs and V sounds (*insolence of office / of / unworthy*); Ms (*himself might / make*); Bs/AIRs (*bare bodkin / bear*); Ts (*grunt / sweat / But / that*); EHs (*sweat / dread / death*); UHs/Ns (*undiscovered county / bourn / returns / puzzles / us / others / know not of / Thus / conscience*); Cs (*conscience / cowards*); UHs/Ss (*Thus / does / of us / thus / of / resolution*); OOs (*hue / resolution*); Ts/URs/ENTs (*cast / thought / enterprises / great pitch / moment / currents / turn*); Ns/Fs (*Soft / now / fair Ophelia / Nymph / orisons / sins*).

Don't forget that when the same sound appears at the end of one word and the beginning of the next, you should separate them and pronounce each one distinctly. See what effect this has on your delivery. Examples: line 65 (*sleep, per-*

chance); line 80 (*traveler returns*); line 87 (*With this*). Also notice the onomatopoeia of such words as *shocks*, *shuffled*, *whips*, *grunt*, *fly*, and *Soft*.

Another factor contributing to the obsessive tone of the piece is its meter, which contains agitated variations and mid-line beginnings and endings of sentences, but not many full stops, creating an incessant, unremitting progression from one idea to the next—these thoughts won't let him be! The soliloquy is chockful of double endings, both at the ends of lines and before caesuras. In fact, the first five lines contain double endings (line 5 in the middle of the line, before the caesura). There are many inverted feet, both at the heads of lines and after caesuras. Two of these follow caesuras that are not marked by punctuation (lines 75 and 77), which is unusual:

x / x / / x x/x /
When he himself might his quietus make

x / x / / x x / x /
To grunt and sweat under a weary life

Line 85 contains a pyrrhic foot (a foot that contains two unaccented syllables) and a spondaic foot (a foot that contains two accented syllables):

x / x / x x / / x /
Is sicklied o'er with the pale cast of thought

The inverted and spondaic feet punch unexpected syllables, contributing to Hamlet's intensity.

Notice that line 68 contains only four spoken feet. We suggest that you take the one silent foot at the caesura, right after Hamlet himself says that the uncertainty of the afterlife *Must give us pause*. Notice that at this point in the soliloquy he's thought about the concept enough for it to give him pause; by the end of the piece, after further consideration, it stops him altogether.

You may opt to drop the final two and a half lines (*Soft you now . . . remembered*), which is the transition into Hamlet's scene with Ophelia. If you decide to keep the lines, notice the crowded foot in line 89 (*in thy or*——):

x / x /x / x - x / x /
The fair Ophelia. —Nymph, in thy orisons

Don't forget to elide: *natural* (NATCH-rul) in line 62 and *Ophelia* (o-PHEEL-yuh) in line 89;

. . . to contract: *The oppressor's* (thu-PRESS-erz) in line 71 and *the unworthy* (thun-WOR-thee) in line 74;

. . . and to expand: *traveler* (TRA´-ve-LER) in line 80.

ELIZABETHAN ANATOMY 101

Elizabethans believed that the human body was made up of four fluids called "humours": blood, yellow bile (a.k.a. choler or gall), phlegm, and black bile. These fluids were thought to determine a person's temperament and physical constitution. An even balance of the humours produced a person of "good humour." However, most people appeared to have one dominant humour, so Elizabethans divided human temperaments and physical characteristics into four categories: (1) The "sanguine" person had an excess of blood, which was defined as warm and humid, like air. A sanguine temperament was thought of as passionate, cheerful, confident, and courageous, and was of sturdy build and ruddy complexion. (2) The "choleric" person had an excess of choler (a.k.a. yellow bile or gall), thought of as hot and dry, like fire. He or she was hot-tempered, bitter, resentful, and foolish, and had a tendency to babble. Although cholerics were swift to anger and to act, their energy was quickly spent. (3) The "phlegmatic" person was thought to have an excess of phlegm. Phlegm was defined as cold and wet in nature, like water, and produced a person who was sluggish, apathetic, fond of bodily pleasures, and able to keep a cool head in an emergency. Phlegmatics were thought to be delicate and of slim build. (4) The "melancholic" person had an excess of black bile, which was thought of as cold and dry, like earth. The melancholic was characterized as gloomy, serious, thoughtful, and pale-complected. Melancholics were likely to be witty and of quick intelligence. Although slow to anger, they were most likely to focus on feelings of fear, sadness, and jealousy, which tended to simmer quietly, becoming extremely fervent and long-lasting. A melancholic would deliberate at length, was suspicious and distrustful, and was prone to nightmares and visions. In a word: Hamlet!

HAMLET

ACT III, SCENE i

OPHELIA

GENDER: F
PROSE/VERSE: blank verse
AGE RANGE: young adult
FREQUENCY OF USE (1–5): 4

Because her father is the King's adviser, Ophelia has grown up at the Danish court, and has come to know Prince Hamlet quite well. He has been courting her for a while now, and despite her father's warnings to stay away from him, Ophelia is head over heels for the smart, handsome, romantic, and princely guy. Recently, though, at her father's insistence, Ophelia obediently returned all of Hamlet's little gifts and love notes, and refused to see him again. Hamlet has begun acting crazy, which Ophelia's father attributes to her sudden rejection of him. Her father and the King just made her talk with Hamlet while they spied on the encounter. Hamlet acted crazier than ever, speaking to her crudely and telling her to get herself to a nunnery—which even *she* knows is slang for a brothel! Hamlet has just left, and the heartbroken Ophelia soliloquizes:

O what a noble mind is here o'erthrown!
The courtier's, soldier's, scholar's, eye, tongue, sword,
160 Th' expectancy and rose of the fair state,
The glass of fashion and the mold of form,
Th' observed of all observers—quite, quite down.
And I, of ladies most deject and wretched,
That sucked the honey of his music vows,
165 Now see that noble and most sovereign reason
Like sweet bells jangled out of tune and harsh;
That unmatched form and feature of blown youth
Blasted with ecstacy. O woe is me
T' have seen what I have seen, see what I see.

45 seconds

158 *noble* (1) magnanimous, dignified; (2) magnificent; (3) of noble ancestry; *o'erthrown* brought to nothing (with play on second meaning, "deposed"); 159 *eye* i.e., perceptiveness; *tongue* i.e., manner of speaking; skill with language; *sword* i.e., skill with a sword; military prowess; 160 *expectancy* hope, expectation; *rose* an Elizabethan symbol of youth and beauty; *fair* honorable; well-ordered; in its best form; *state* nation [*expectancy and rose of the fair state* young, beautiful hope of the good nation of Denmark, i.e., young, beautiful, eagerly anticipated heir of Denmark]; 161 *glass* mirror; *fashion* the tastes and habits of those with good breeding [*glass of fashion* i.e., the perfect image of good breeding]; *mold* model; *form* proper behavior; 162 *observed* looked up to [*Th' observed of all observers* i.e., the one looked up to by all who observe him]; *quite* completely; *down* fallen or struck from a high place to a low one; 163 *most* the most; 164 *music* pleasing to the ear; *vows* i.e., vows of love; 165 *sovereign* a combination of (1) princely; (2) supreme, excellent; (3) having the right and ability to rule (his mind); *reason* the power of the mind that distinguishes right from wrong, good from bad, etc., and which correctly perceives the world; 166 *jangled* (1) rung discordantly; (2) put out of tune; 167 *unmatched* (UN-matched) unequaled; *feature* shape of the whole body; physical appearance; *blown* in full bloom [*unmatched form and feature of blown youth* unequaled behavior and physical appearance of youth in full bloom]; 168 *Blasted* blighted, withered; *ecstacy* madness.

MIX-AND-MATCH *HAMLET*

Since there is no single authoritative text of *Hamlet*, editors often disagree on which version to use in certain passages. While in most cases we have selected the text that clearly works best in performance, here there is one choice we thought best left up to you: line 166 (*Like sweet bells jangled out of tune and harsh*) may alternatively be read *Like sweet bells jangled out of time and harsh*. As you can see, the two readings have similar but slightly different meanings, which are also affected by which definition you prefer for *jangled* (see Annotation) and by how the word is used in the sentence (i.e., whether you mentally place a comma after *bells* or after *jangled*). Your interpretation of the line will convey Ophelia's perception of Hamlet's madness.

COMMENTARY

Ophelia fell in love with the ideal Renaissance prince, and since the greatest ideal of the Renaissance is reason, the very core of what she loved is now—as far as she can discern—destroyed. Although she loves him, Ophelia is unable to read what lies below the surface of Hamlet's madness. Perhaps this is because Ophelia has been taught by her overbearing father that seeing is believing. Notice that Ophelia's brief eulogy to her beloved's sanity speaks almost exclusively of his externally evident qualities, and that Ophelia repeatedly glorifies what she has *seen*, and laments what she now *see*[*s*].

Ophelia uses the words *noble* (twice), *sovereign*, and *o'erthrown*, all of which have meanings both related and unrelated to royalty. She is not punning lightly, but rather fully intends all the meanings of each word. Her use of these words reveals Ophelia's sense that their dual and triple meanings are interconnected and interdependent—for her, Hamlet's royalty and his fine qualities go hand in hand. Note the use of these words in the build from line 159 to line 162. The rhythm of line 159 (see Significant Scans, below), the repetition of words (*noble*; *form*; *observed / observers*; *quite*), and the repetiton of structures all contribute to this build. Ophelia is verbally reconstructing her beloved's pedestal, and finally brings it crashing *quite, quite down*, just as her illusion of his princeliness has been destroyed. Make sure you start at a level that will allow room for the build to crescendo. Also, notice the juxtaposition of her elegant description of the former Hamlet with her simplistic statement of his downfall. Is she simply at a loss for words to describe such a thing—either because of her youth or because of the enormity of the horror? Or is she actually aware that this simple repetition is quite effective in illustrating just how low Hamlet has fallen?

Ophelia uses quite a bit of assonance, perhaps choosing vowels because they so effectively express extreme emotion (she's also thrown in a bit of consonance), such as: *O* / *noble* / *o'erthrown*; *glass* / *fashion*; *mold* / *form*; *deject* / *wretched*; *sucked* / *honey* / *of*; *noble* / *most*; *form* / *feature*; *O* / *woe*. The most frequently sounded vowel you'll find is the long O, which echoes Ophelia's lamenting *O*s throughout the piece. In twelve short lines, Ophelia says *O* twice, so be sure to see "O, No! An *O*!," page xxxiii, for more on getting the most out of the word. Finally, notice the wonderful string of sounds in the last line (*seen* / *seen* / *see* / *see*), all of which fall on accented syllables, forcefully underscoring Ophelia's summation of her lament, and carrying the sound of the rhyming couplet (*me* / *see*) all the way through the last line.

Ophelia also expresses herself through sound with onomatopoeia, which is concentrated at the end of the piece (*jangled*; *harsh*; *Blasted*). Notice that the inversion of the first foot in line 168 makes *Blasted* almost blast off. The onomatopoeic use of *jangled* is, as far as we're concerned, one of the most perfect word placements in all of Shakespeare—enjoy it!

Ophelia uses quite a bit of imagery in this brief piece. She describes Hamlet as a *rose* from which she (the bee?) *sucked the honey* of his love vows, then returns to the image with *blown* and *Blasted*. Perhaps the most striking line of the piece contains the simile in which Hamlet's previously ideal reason is *Like sweet bells jangled out of tune and harsh*, a line that hearkens back to his *music vows*. Line 159 is a powerful use of synecdoche, in which the *courtier's, soldier's, scholar's, eye, tongue, sword* represent Hamlet's fine qualities, which are exactly those qualities required of a great ruler. You have certainly noticed that the second series of words is out of order in relation to the first. What does that tell you about Ophelia's state of mind?

SIGNIFICANT SCANS

Several of the variations in this piece result in spondaic feet (two accented syllables) at the ends of lines. This unusual variation appearing so many times in these short lines has a jarring effect that complements the onomatopoeia mentioned above and mimics Ophelia's own jarred state. For instance, the last foot of line 159 is a spondee:

x / x / x / x / / /
The courtier's, soldier's, scholar's, eye, tongue, sword

Alternately, this line can be considered hexameter:

x / x / x / x / x / x /
The courtier's, soldier's, scholar's, eye, (pause) tongue, (pause) sword

Lines 160 and 167 each end in a pyrrhic foot (two unaccented syllables) followed by a spondee (note the historic pronunciation of *unmatched* [UN-matched] in 167):

x / x / x / x x / /
Th' expectancy and rose of the fair state

x / x / x / x x / /
That unmatched form and feature of blown youth

These variations, combined with the inverted first feet in lines 158, 165, and 168, and after the caesuras in lines 168 and 169, express through the meter the upheaval Ophelia is experiencing.

Don't forget to elide: *courtier's* (KOR-tyerz) in line 159;

. . . and to contract: *Th' expectancy* (Th'ex-PEC´-tan-SEE) in line 160; *Th' observed* (Th'ob-ZERVD) in line 162; and *T' have* (T'av) in line 169.

HAMLET

ACT III, SCENE ii

HAMLET

GENDER: M
PROSE/VERSE: prose
AGE RANGE: young adult to adult
FREQUENCY OF USE (1–5): 3

Hamlet, Prince of Denmark, is in mourning—his father died about two months ago, and to his horror his mother then married her late husband's brother, Claudius, who assumed the throne (such a marriage was considered incest by Elizabethans and was forbidden by Church law). Furthermore, Hamlet recently saw what he believes to be his father's ghost, which claimed that Claudius murdered him in his sleep, and demanded that Hamlet take revenge. A troupe of players has arrived at Elsinore Castle, and Hamlet has asked them to perform a play that is similar in circumstance to his father's murder as described by the Ghost—he hopes it will spark some reaction from Claudius that will reveal his guilt and verify that the Ghost was speaking the truth. Hamlet has written some lines to be inserted into the play to make the comparison even more pointed. It is imperative that the lines be performed properly in order for his scheme to work, so before the performance begins, Hamlet lectures three of the players about acting technique:

Speak the speech, I pray you, as I pronounced it to
you, trippingly on the tongue; but if you mouth it,
as many of your players do, I had as lief the town-
crier had spoke my lines. Nor do not saw the air
5 too much with your hand, thus, but use all gently;
for in the very torrent, tempest, and, as I may say,
whirlwind of your passion, you must acquire and
beget a temperance that may give it smoothness.
O, it offends me to the soul to hear a robustious
10 periwig-pated fellow tear a passion to tatters, to
very rags, to split the ears of the groundlings, who
for the most part are capable of nothing but inexplicable dumb-shows and noise. I would have such
a fellow whipped for o'erdoing Termagant. It out-
15 Herods Herod. Pray you avoid it.

50 seconds

Be not too tame neither, but let your own discretion be your tutor. Suit the action to the word, the
word to the action, with this special observance:
20 that you o'erstep not the modesty of nature. For

1 *pray* ask, entreat; 2 *trippingly* with words flowing lightly and nimbly; *mouth* recite in a loud, affected voice; 3 *your* not making reference to the person addressed, but to the general existence of the thing indicated [*many of your players* i.e., many actors in general]; *had as lief* (LEEF) would just as soon; would have been just as happy if; 4 *my lines* i.e., the lines I wrote; 5 *use all* treat everything; *gently* (1) softly, with moderation; (2) in the manner of a gentleman; 6 *for in the very* for even in the; *as I may say* i.e., so to speak; 7 *passion* passionate speech; 8 *beget* get, obtain; 9 *robustious* (1) stout; (2) boisterous; 10 *periwig-pated* wig-headed; 11 *groundlings* audience members standing or sitting on the ground in the pit of the theater (the "cheap seats") (see "Within This Wooden O: Theatre in Shakespeare's Time," page li); 12 *capable* able to understand and appreciate; 12 *inexplicable* unintelligible; 13 *dumb-shows* pantomimes (in Shakespeare's time a play, act, or scene was often prefaced by a brief pantomime of the story that was about to be presented); *noise* (1) voices or sounds causing a disturbance; (2) music; *I would have such a fellow whipped* i.e., as far as I'm concerned, a fellow like that should be whipped; 14 *Termagant* (TER´-muh-GANT) a god invented by western Europeans in the Middle Ages, and believed to be worshipped by Muslims (represented as a violent, ranting character in medieval mystery plays [see "A Cycle Without a Herod Is Like a Miracle Without a Fish," page 568]); 15 *Herod* Herod the Great, tetrarch (ruler of a region under the ancient Roman Empire) of Judea, 37 B.C.E.–4 C.E., who was "exceeding wroth" when the three wise men failed to report back to him after seeking out the baby Jesus at his birthplace, and who then ordered the death of all the babies in Bethlehem (Herod was represented in the mystery plays as a ranting tyrant [see "A Cycle Without a Herod . . . ," page 568]); 19 *special* particular; *observance* strict adherence to something (especially to truth and reality); 20 *modesty of nature* nature's inherent moderation; 21 *from* contrary to; *playing* acting on the stage;

anything so o'erdone is from the purpose of playing, whose end, both at the first and now, was and is to hold as 'twere the mirror up to nature; to show virtue her feature, scorn her own image, and
25 the very age and body of the time his form and pressure. Now, this overdone or come tardy off, though it makes the unskillful laugh, cannot but make the judicious grieve, the censure of the which one must in your allowance o'erweigh a whole the-
30 ater of others. O, there be players that I have seen play—and heard others praise, and that highly—not to speak it profanely, that neither having th' accent of Christians, nor the gait of Christian, pagan, nor man, have so strutted and bellowed that I have
35 thought some of Nature's journeymen had made men, and not made them well, they imitated humanity so abominably.

1 minute, 50 seconds

24 *virtue* virtue, personified (representing those who are virtuous); *feature* bodily shape, external appearance; *scorn* that which deserves scorn, i.e., folly and sin, personified (representing those who are foolish or sinful); 25 *very* veritable, true; *body of the time* essential quality of the era [*the very age and body of the time* the true state of things as they are in our present time]; *his* i.e., their; *form* image, portrait; 26 *pressure* impression made in wax or other substance (i.e., likeness); *come tardy off* brought off (performed) inadequately; 27 *the unskillful* the uneducated and thus undiscerning; *cannot but* must, will undoubtably; 28 *make the judicious grieve* offend those who are discerning; *censure* judgment (used in Shakespeare's time without a negative connotation); *of the which one* of even one of whom (i.e., of even one of the judicious); 29 *must in your allowance* you must acknowledge does; *o'erweigh* outweigh; 31 *that* i.e., praise; 32 *not to speak it profanely* i.e., I don't mean to offend God with what I am about to say, but; *th' accent* the pronunciation; 33 *Christians* i.e., ordinary, decent human beings (from Hamlet's perspective, and that of most Elizabethan theatregoers); *of Christian* of a Christian; *pagan* one who is not of the Christian religion (thought of in Shakespeare's time as an uncivilized and damned heathen); 34 *nor man* nor of any human being; 35 *Nature's* nature, personified; *journeymen* hired workmen, usually day workers (rather than master craftsmen)—used pejoratively; 37 *abominably* detestably; brutishly (Shakespeare spelled the word "abhominably," reflecting the Elizabethan belief that the word was derived from the Latin *ab homine*, meaning "away from man, inhuman, beastly," a definition that fits perfectly here).

COMMENTARY

This piece is often referred to as a message from Shakespeare presenting his views on acting in general, or perhaps a complaint about the way his lines had been performed by a particular actor in his troupe, but these and other ideas about Shakespeare's intent in writing this monologue—while interesting—are only conjecture. As an actor, to perform this piece well and have fun with it, you need only consider one person's objectives—your character's.

Hamlet has been to university in the big city, and has probably seen many performances, good and bad. He may very well have strong opinions about acting techniques, but this is a rather odd time to be focusing so intently on them. Why does Hamlet get so worked up, and go on at such length when instructing the players? Perhaps this is how Hamlet deals with his nerves—after all, his plan is about to be put into action, and could produce serious consequences. Or maybe Hamlet has been holding in his frustration with his mother and uncle too long, and is taking it out on the players (or maybe Hamlet harbors a secret wish to direct?) . . . of course, Hamlet's strongest motivation is his need for the performance to be flawless if his plan is to succeed.

The material itself presents several questions about Hamlet's intent and manner that will help you develop your interpretation of the piece. First, notice that although this is a prose piece, it has poetic elements. For instance, Hamlet uses imagery to convey his main idea. The Renaissance concept of theatre's function was quite familiar to Shakespeare's audience, as was the metaphor of theatre holding a *mirror up to nature*. The concept derives from the idea that comedy is "an imitation of life, a mirror of custom, and an image of truth," which is attributed to Cicero. Although today's audiences are certainly not as familiar with this concept, the metaphor itself simply and beautifully expresses it—the audience will easily make the backward leap from the more recent cliché of life imitating art. Shakespeare uses a similarly familiar reference with his allusions to *Termagant* and *Herod*: many of his audience members would vividly remember viewing such performances. Since today's audience is not familiar with that experience it is especially important that you envision the images as specifically as possible, to convey the gist of the idea.

Hamlet also uses the powerful rhetorical tool of antithesis to explain his views to the players (*Speak the speech . . . trippingly* versus *mouth it*; *do not saw the air* versus *use all gently*; *torrent, tempest . . . whirlwind* versus *temperance . . . smoothness*; *at the first* versus *now*; *was* versus *is*; *show virtue her feature* versus *scorn her own image*; *makes the unskillful laugh* versus *cannot but make the judicious grieve*; *the which one* versus *a whole theater of others*). The comparisons carry you from point to point through the piece, creating a logical structure on which

Hamlet builds his argument. You may decide that Hamlet demonstrates for the players the difference between good acting and bad. This choice would be supported by the presence of the embedded stage direction *do not saw the air too much with your hand, thus*, which indictates that Hamlet is showing the player what *not* to do with his hands on stage. Hamlet uses the double negative several times for emphasis (*Nor do not*; *Be not too tame neither*; *cannot but make*).

The repetition of sounds in this piece beautifully enhances the words' meanings. Notice how well the alliteration of *Speak the speech* and *trippingly on the tongue* illustrate the instruction Hamlet is giving to the player; how perfectly the Pooh-Poohing Ps of *periwig-pated* express Hamlet's disdain; how well suited the assonant vowels in *passion to tatters* are to the imitation of such bad acting. Look for sound clues such as these and ask yourself how Hamlet is using them in each instance. He also uses the word *O* twice. For help with using *O* to its full potential, see "O, No! An *O*!," page xxxiii. Also notice how many times the O sound is echoed in words that begin with *o'er* (*o'erdoing*; *o'erstep*; *o'erdone*; *o'erweigh*).

Hamlet almost always chooses the elided form *o'er* rather than "over" in this piece. The resulting casual tone coupled with other aspects of the material brings up interesting questions. For example, Hamlet is unusually verbose with the players, frequently using cliché and superfluous phrases (*as I may say*; *as 'twere*; *not to speak it profanely*; *in your allowance*). Hamlet is also uncharacteristically redundant throughout, sprinkling the piece with minibuilds (*torrent, tempest . . . whirlwind*; *tear a passion to tatters, to very rags*; *heard others praise, and that highly*; and so on). Why does he alter his manner of speech in this monologue? Is he simply trying to speak in a casual, colloquial, or thorough and instructional way that he thinks the players will understand? Is he putting on a bit of the pompous air that he has heard from his professors at Wittenberg? Or is he simply anxious and excited about the trap he has set for Claudius, and thus running on nervously? Your answers to questions like these will guide your performance.

Note: this monologue is one of the rare few that can be performed entirely outside the context of the play. Instead of Hamlet, you could create any character in any context that works for you . . . from a frustrated director of a small theater in the Galápagos Islands to a smug nineteenth-century schoolmaster directing his boys in the annual Christmas pageant.

A Cycle Without a Herod Is Like a Miracle Without a Fish

English drama originated with religious presentations performed by clergymen in Latin. In 1210, the Church forbade its clergy to participate in such activities, and the lay people took their places in the ever-evolving performances. Out of this tradition emerged the mystery plays (a.k.a. the cycle plays or miracle plays). Mysteries were whole series or "cycles" of plays dramatizing biblical highlights from Creation right up to Judgment Day. The plays were performed on wagons called "pageants," each of which carried a stage and props. After one play was finished, the next pageant would be wheeled in. The wagons traveled from one town to the next in their respective regions, usually once a year to celebrate a religious feast day. One of the most popular figures in these plays was Herod, who was always portrayed as ranting and tyrannical. One surviving play even contains the stage direction "Herod rages in the pageant, and in the street also." Shakespeare may have seen this very play—or one like it—when he was young, or may have been told of them. The mystery plays died out during the second half of the sixteenth century, as audiences turned to secular works by Shakespeare and his contemporaries.

HAMLET

ACT III, SCENE iii

KING CLAUDIUS

GENDER: M
PROSE/VERSE: blank verse
AGE RANGE: mature adult
FREQUENCY OF USE (1–5): 3

King Claudius has been keeping a terrible secret: about two months ago, he killed his own brother (the previous king). He then married his brother's widow, Gertrude—an incestuous act (according to Elizabethan mores), but one that would ensure his accession to the throne rather than his nephew Hamlet's. Claudius has just had a very disturbing experience. While watching the performance of a play arranged by Hamlet, he suddenly realized he was seeing a reenactment of that crime. Claudius was so upset by what he saw that he interrupted the whole performance, creating quite a scene. Fearing that tonight's performance means that Hamlet had discovered his secret, Claudius has arranged to send his nephew away to England immediately. Now that he is finally alone, Claudius's sinful deed weighs heavily on his mind. He soliloquizes:

O, my offense is rank, it smells to Heaven.
It hath the primal eldest curse upon't—
A brother's murder. Pray can I not,
Though inclination be as sharp as will,
40 My stronger guilt defeats my strong intent,
And, like a man to double business bound,
I stand in pause where I shall first begin,
And both neglect. What if this cursèd hand
Were thicker than itself with brother's blood?
45 Is there not rain enough in the sweet heavens
To wash it white as snow? Whereto serves mercy
But to confront the visage of Offense?
And what's in prayer but this twofold force,
To be forestallèd ere we come to fall,
50 Or pardoned being down? Then I'll look up,
My fault is past. But O, what form of prayer
Can serve my turn? "Forgive my foul murder"?
That cannot be, since I am still possessed
Of those effects for which I did the murder:
55 My crown, mine own ambition, and my queen.
May one be pardoned and retain the offense?
In the corrupted currents of this world
Offense's gilded hand may shove by justice,
And oft 'tis seen the wicked prize itself
60 Buys out the law. But 'tis not so above;

36 *offense* both (1) crime and (2) sin; *rank* (1) having a strong, offensive smell, putrid; (2) foul, disgusting, morally offensive; 37 *primal eldest curse* the curse God put on Cain for slaying his brother, Abel (Genesis 4:11); 39 *Though inclination be as sharp as will* though my natural impulse (to pray) is as keen as my determination to do so; 41 *bound* (1) obligated; (2) intending to set out for a particular destination [*to double business bound* obligated to set out for each of two different destinations, to attend to two different matters]; 42 *stand in pause* stand still in reflection; *where I shall first begin* (1) on the spot from which I am to begin my intended action; and/or (2) in doubt as to which action to begin first; 44 *thicker than itself with brother's blood* covered with a layer of my brother's blood thicker than my hand itself; 45 *rain enough* i.e., enough mercy; 46 *Whereto serves mercy* What purpose does mercy serve; 47 *the visage of Offense* the face of offense personified; 49 *ere* before; *come to fall* fall from grace, sin; 50 *being down* i.e., once we have already "fallen," or sinned; *look up* take heart, cheer up (with a play on "look up toward Heaven" [in prayer]); 51 *My fault is past* my sin has already been committed; 52 *serve my turn* be appropriate to my situation; satisfy the requirements of my circumstance; 53 *am still possessed / Of* still possess; 54 *effects* things, acquisitions; 56 *and retain* while one still retains; *the offense* i.e., the fruits of my sin (the continued enjoyment of which perpetuates the sin itself); 57 *currents* courses, ways (with a play on *currency*); 58 *gilded hand* hand holding gold (with a play on *guilt*); *shove by* elbow past, thrust aside; 59 *the wicked prize . . . the law* the goods gained by wicked crimes are used to bribe one's way out of the laws against those very crimes; *above*

There is no shuffling, there the action lies
In his true nature, and we ourselves compelled
Even to the teeth and foreheads of our faults
To give in evidence. What then? What rests?
65 Try what repentance can. What can it not?
Yet what can it, when one cannot repent?
O wretched state! O bosom black as death!
O limèd soul, that struggling to be free
Art more engaged! Help, angels! —Make assay.
70 Bow, stubborn knees; and heart with strings of steel,
Be soft as sinews of the new-born babe.
All may be well.
[*He kneels and tries to pray*]

97 My words fly up, my thoughts remain below.
Words without thoughts never to Heaven go.

2 minutes, 20 seconds

i.e., in Heaven; 61 *There* i.e., up there, in Heaven; *is* there is; *shuffling* evasion through trickery, double-dealing, or sleight of hand; *the action* both (1) the deed (i.e., the crime) and (2) a legal action; 62 *his* its [*the action lies / In his true nature* (1) the crime is revealed in its essence; and (2) a legal action proceeds as it is intended to]; 63 *Even* used here for emphasis; *to the teeth and foreheads of* i.e., face-to-face in confrontation with [*Even to the teeth . . . give in evidence* to provide evidence (against ourselves), confronting our sins face to face]; 64 *What rests?* What remains? (i.e., what else can I do?); 65 *Try what repentance can* (I must) try to gain the forgiveness that repentance is capable of acquiring; *What can it not?* i.e., what is repentance not capable of?; 67 *state* (1) situation, circumstances; (2) pomp, splendor, appearance of dignity and greatness that attends royalty; (3) condition of the mind and soul; *bosom* heart; 68 *limèd* caught (as with birdlime, a sticky substance spread on twigs or branches to trap birds)—in many traditions, including Christianity, birds represent the embodiment of the soul; *struggling . . . engaged* while struggling to free itself, the limed bird became more thoroughly covered with the birdlime, and thus more securely entangled; 69 *Make assay* Make an attempt (he addresses either the angels or himself); 70 *strings* heartstrings, tendons of the heart (which Elizabethans believed held it in place); 71 *sinews* tendons (believed by Elizabethans to be the source of strength in the body); 98 *Words without thoughts* i.e. prayer uttered without true repentance; *never to Heaven go* i.e., never achieve a state of grace for the person who prays.

COMMENTARY

According to Claudius's deeply ingrained Christian belief system, he has gotten himself into quite a bad situation. In this monologue he carefully explores how to escape the eternal consequences of his crimes. Because Claudius has such a good understanding of Christian doctrine, the imagery he uses to describe his guilt—and Heaven's view of it—is quite clear-cut. Of course, the most important thing described is his *offense*. First, he imagines that the smell of it is so *rank* that it reaches Heaven; then he personifies *Offense*: it meets face to face with mercy, and has a hand laden with gold, with which it is able to *shove by justice*. In his imagery, as in life, Claudius's *Offense* and its effect on him have become things he cannot control. Claudius also has vivid imagery for the state of his soul, the saving of which is the key objective in this piece. Although Claudius killed his brother with poison, he describes his own guilt in biblical terms: Claudius's *cursèd hand* is *thicker than itself with brother's blood*. His hope of being cleansed by God's forgiveness is also a biblical reference. He refers to Heaven's mercy as *rain* that will *wash* his hand *white as snow*. Perhaps Claudius has been reading Psalm 51 ("wash me until I am white as snow") or Isaiah ("Your hands are covered with blood . . . Though your sins are like scarlet, they shall be white as snow"). The soul Claudius hopes to save is presented as a bird that struggles to free itself from birdlime, but only gets more entangled, suggesting that since he actually recognizes his sin but still cannot repent, he feels his sin is all the more serious. Finally, Claudius sees his own heart as *black as death* and as having heartstrings as hard as *steel*. Once again, he uses imagery that envisions the state of his heart and soul as something separate from himself, which he can only attempt—unsuccessfully—to control.

Claudius uses one image unlike those mentioned above: he says he is like a *man to double business bound*, who cannot choose between two actions, and thus does nothing, an image that stands out because it is so much more mundane than the others, and because it is the only simile in a piece full of metaphor. It represents the heart of his problem: faced with a choice between continuing his sinful behavior (and ensuring damnation) or renouncing the fruits of his crimes (and saving his soul), Claudius is unable to do either. Claudius wishes there were a third path that would combine the benefits of each choice and avoid the downsides. Perhaps he chooses this workaday simile to downplay the magnitude of his crimes and indecision or the prospect of eons in Hell? The audience may also notice that with this metaphor Claudius unwittingly likens his state to Hamlet's.

Take note of the many double meanings and puns Claudius uses: *rank*; *bound*; *look up*; *currents*; *gilded*; *action lies in his true nature* (see Annotation).

These fall quite naturally into place in the monologue, suggesting a facility with language that reveals Claudius's quick intelligence.

Another notable word choice is *offense*, which appears four times in the monologue, driving home at once the fact of Claudius's guilt and the dilemma of his perspective: he does not regret the crime because of its outcome or its nature, but because it is an *offense* to God, and as such will condemn him to damnation. The word *offense* echoes another much-repeated word, *O*, which appears five times. To make sure you take full advantage of all these expressive *O*s, see "O, No! An *O*!," page xxxiii.

One of those expressive *O*s begins the monologue, its sound echoed by the first appearance of the word *offense*. This *O* is further emphasized because it is the first syllable of an inverted foot. This metric variation is one of many in the piece, which has a good number of trochaic inversions both at the beginnings of lines and after caesuras. It also has many double endings, both at the ends of lines and before caesuras. And of course, there are the caesuras themselves, which are often caused by new sentences ending and beginning mid-line. All of these elements (especially when combined with the flow of sounds mentioned below) contribute to the sense that Claudius's thoughts move along continuously from one idea to the next. You'll also notice the small number of elisions and contractions, in comparison with several noticeable expansions, which give the piece the deliberate tone of someone carefully thinking something through.

The monologue's consonance carries you straight through from beginning to end. There are several recurring sound combinations, most of which interweave with one another—most prominently Fs, Ss, and STs in different combinations (*offense / smells / eldest / curse*; *stronger / defeats / strong / intent*; *stand / first*; *serves / mercy*; *Offense / this / twofold force / forestallèd / fall / fault / past / form*; *Forgive / foul*; *since / still / possessed / effects*; *Offense's / justice*; *'tis seen / prize itself*; *foreheads / faults*; *soul / struggling / free*; *stubborn / strings / steel*; *soft / sinews*); also, Bs combined with Ds (*double business bound*; *begin / both*; *brother's blood*; *being down*; *bosom black / death*; *Bow / new-born babe*); and smaller groupings found throughout, such as Ws (*wash / white / snow / Whereto*), Cs and Rs (*corrupted / currents*), and Ls (*All / well*). Be sure to look for more!

Notice the assonance woven in with this consonance, particularly the EH sounds (*possessed / effects*; *ourselves compelled*; *evidence / then / rests / repentance / repent*); but also others, such as ERs (*serve / turn*) and EEs (*Even / teeth*). Some of the sound combinations you'll find are extremely complex. For instance, notice that the repeated sounds in *this twofold force / To be forestallèd ere we come to fall* (F, OR, ST, ALL) echo the important word in the sentence, *forestallèd*. And in lines 65–66 the sound repetitions stem from the repetition of the same words in different orders (*what / can / What can it not / what can it / cannot*).

Finally, the last two lines of this piece are actually said later in the scene, after Claudius has tried to pray (during one of Hamlet's soliloquies). You may choose to end the piece at line 73, or to use the three silent feet at the end of line 73 to attempt to pray, and then include lines 97–98. These last two lines add a final transition for the actor; they also wrap the piece up with a nice twist as well as a rhyming couplet (*below / go*).

Note: the punctuation we have chosen for line 39 allows for two possible readings (as does the text of the Second Quarto, considered the most authoritative of the texts). The idea may refer to the line before it, or lead into the line that follows.

SIGNIFICANT SCANS

Line 45 has an unusual pyrrhic fourth foot (two unaccented syllables), followed by a spondaic fifth foot (two accented syllables) in addition to its trochaic first foot and its double ending:

/ x x / x / x x / / (x)
Is there not rain enough in the sweet heavens

Notice that the two resulting unstressed syllables highlight the next two stressed ones, which fall on *sweet heavens*. The words also receive additional attention due to the double ending.

Line 66 is headless, and has a double ending before the caesura:

x / x / (x) x / x / x /
(pause) Yet what can it, when one cannot repent?

Don't forget to elide: *Even* (E'EN) in line 63 and *struggling* (STRUG-ling) in line 68;

. . . to contract: *the offense* (th'off-ENSS) in line 56;

. . . and to expand: *cursèd* (KER-sehd) in line 43; *prayer* (PRAY-er) in line 48; *forestallèd* (for-STAWL-ehd) in line 49; and *limèd* (LIE-mehd) in line 68.

HAMLET

ACT III, SCENE iii

HAMLET

GENDER: M
PROSE/VERSE: blank verse
AGE RANGE: young adult to adult
FREQUENCY OF USE (1–5): 3.5

Prince Hamlet's uncle Claudius has just unwittingly walked right into a plot that Hamlet laid to determine whether Claudius murdered Hamlet's father, the late King of Denmark, before marrying Hamlet's mother and assuming the throne. Claudius's actions have revealed that he did, indeed, murder his brother, and Hamlet now feels ready to exact revenge. He comes upon Claudius, who is kneeling, seemingly deep in prayer. Here's his chance! Hamlet says:

Now I might do it pat, now he is a-praying,
And now I'll do't. [*Draws his sword*]
And so he goes to Heaven,
75 And so am I revenged. That would be scanned:
A villain kills my father, and for that,
I, his sole son, do this same villain send
To Heaven.
Why, this is hire and salary, not revenge.
80 He took my father grossly, full of bread,
With all his crimes broad blown, as flush as May;
And how his audit stands, who knows save Heaven?
But in our circumstance and course of thought
'Tis heavy with him. And am I then revenged
85 To take him in the purging of his soul,
When he is fit and seasoned for his passage?
No.
Up, sword, and know thou a more horrid hent:
When he is drunk asleep, or in his rage,

72 *pat* quite to the purpose, exactly; 74 *so* i.e., by my doing so; *he goes to Heaven* Hamlet believes that Claudius's soul is at this moment being cleansed by prayer and repentance and that killing him now would therefore send him directly to Heaven; 75 *would be* must be; *scanned* carefully examined; 79 *hire and salary* i.e., something Claudius should hire and pay me to do for him; 80 *grossly* coarsely (i.e., while my father was in a state of coarse sensuality); *full of bread* i.e., in a sinful state (a reference to Ezekiel 16:49, "the iniquity of thy sister Sodom, pride, fullness of bread, and abundance of idleness") [*grossly, full of bread* i.e., unfit to enter Heaven because he was in the midst of enjoying earthly pleasures and was unconfessed of his sins]; 81 *crimes* i.e., sins; *broad blown* in full bloom; *flush* vigorous, in their prime; 82 *audit* final account (with God) [*how his audit stands* i.e., how he is being judged by God]; *save* except for; 83 *in our circumstance* to our mortal senses; 84 *heavy* severe, hard ['*Tis heavy with him* i.e., his fate is in grave condition]; 85 *take him* i.e., take his life, kill him; *in the purging of his soul* as he is confessing his sins and his soul is being cleansed of them; 86 *fit* prepared; *seasoned* matured, ripened; *for his passage* i.e., for his passage to Heaven; 88 *Up* Back into your scabbard; *know thou* i.e., wait and you'll experience; *hent* hold, grasp [*know thou a more horrid hent* wait and you'll experience a grasp by me that will cause more horror (i.e., when I will grasp you and use

90 Or in th' incestuous pleasure of his bed,
At game a-swearing, or about some act
That has no relish of salvation in't—
Then trip him, that his heels may kick at Heaven,
And that his soul may be as damned and black
95 As Hell, whereto it goes. My mother stays.
This physic but prolongs thy sickly days.

1 minute, 30 seconds

you to kill Claudius at a time that will send him to Hell)]; 90 *th' incestuous pleasure of his bed* in Shakespeare's time, it was considered incest to marry and have sexual intercourse with a brother's widow; 91 *At game* playing some game involving gambling (cards, etc.); *about* in the commission; 92 *relish* tincture, slight taste [*no relish of salvation in't* not even the slightest taste of salvation in it]; 93 *that* so that [*that his heels may kick at Heaven* i.e., because he will be heading toward Hell]; 95 *whereto it goes* to which it will go; *stays* waits; 96 *physic* remedy for a disease (here, the reprieve from murder that Hamlet grants Claudius); *but* merely.

COMMENTARY

Hamlet was elated (momentarily) at the success of his plot to reveal Claudius's guilt. Until now, while devastated by the notion of the murder and by his mother's hasty marriage to Claudius, Hamlet felt incapable of taking action against his uncle . . . yet he berated himself for procrastinating. At this point in the play's action, however, Hamlet is finally intent on wreaking revenge on his uncle, and it is legitimate to focus on what he is experiencing at this moment and to decide that he stops himself from killing Claudius solely for the reason he claims in this monologue. On the other hand, it is likely that some of his prior ambivalence still inhibits him. You can add into the mix the fact that it must be hard to go through with taking the life of another human being, however you might loathe him or her.

Regardless of how much backstory you concern yourself with, it is important to set the immediate scene for yourself with as much detail as possible. For example, remember where you are! If you are close enough to kill the King, you are close enough to be discovered by him with your sword drawn. Speed is of the essence—Hamlet is not ruminating languidly here! The sounds Hamlet uses in the first two lines of the monologue suggest a burst of energy: the word *now* is spoken three times in the first line and a half—perhaps Hamlet is egging himself on. Also, the repeated acTive, Tense T and exPlosive P sounds create a tone of determined action: *might do it pat / a-praying / do't*. The meter of the first line also helps: the first foot is inverted, so that the very first syllable of the monologue is punched, giving the sense that Hamlet is blurting it out. The last three words are contracted <u>and</u> elided: *he is a-praying* (HE'S a-PRAING), which, combined with the elision of "do it" into *do't*, creates a sense that Hamlet is rushing to action.

And then it occurs to Hamlet that by killing Claudius while he's at prayer, he would be sending him to Heaven. Notice the meter of line 74—Hamlet realizes mid-line (only one and a half lines into the monologue) that killing Claudius now would achieve the opposite of revenge. No sooner does Hamlet decide to do the deed than he backpedals. Also notice Hamlet's self-deprecating sarcasm, mocking his own half-hatched bravura (*And so am I revenged*; *That would be scanned*; *Why, this is hire and salary, not revenge*). Hamlet has a firm belief in the Christian God and some form of an afterlife (with which he has been grappling—see monologues, pages 517 and 552). Although he doesn't know exactly what awaits humans after death, Hamlet is not about to take chances now—he can only truly exact revenge by ensuring that Claudius's soul is damned, as was his father's. This makes the task of revenge that much more difficult to execute. You may also wish to explore the less sympathetic sides of Hamlet that are revealed by his desire to send Claudius to Hell: (1) it takes a degree of coldness to calculate when best to commit a murder so as to obtain optimal revenge; and (2) it is a bit audacious to play God by presuming that you can determine where a person's soul will go after death.

Hamlet clearly expresses his motivation for ensuring that Claudius's soul goes south: in the space of only two lines (80–81), Hamlet uses four different expressions to describe his father's unconfessed state at the time of his murder. Hamlet is obviously tormented by the insult-upon-injury visited on his beloved father, who was not only murdered and replaced, but whose soul was sent to Hell. Hamlet is therefore determined that Claudius's soul not meet with a kinder fate.

Note the use of the familiar *thou* when Hamlet speaks to his sword. We know that Hamlet is a decent fencer, but has Hamlet ever used this weapon in actual combat in the past? Or has he forged an intimate relationship with the sword just recently, while planning the murder of his uncle and reviewing possible scenarios (most, if not all, involving the sword) in his mind? Notice the embedded stage direction (*Up, sword*), instructing you to, well, put up your sword.

It is interesting to see how easily his uncle's vices roll off Hamlet's tongue—while the relationship with Hamlet's mother is new, Hamlet may have already known of his uncle's other reprehensible pastimes. Or they may have come to Hamlet's attention only in the brief time since Claudius married Hamlet's mother. The decision is yours—these specific descriptions of Claudius's loathesome behavior help to further ground your character's hatred of him.

SIGNIFICANT SCANS

Lines 78 and 87 are short, leaving several feet of silence for you to play with. In line 78, perhaps the silent feet at the end of the line give Hamlet a moment to recover from the close call—he almost made a colossal blunder! Perhaps he takes a moment to think about the effects of sending Claudius to Heaven. Or perhaps he's afraid he was just too loud, and checks to make sure he was not detected by Claudius . . . In line 87, you may decide where to place the extra feet. Wherever you place them—at the beginning of the line, at the end, or divided—the word *No* lands with great resonance and finality because it is juxtaposed with silence. Hamlet is about to change gears and put away his sword. The four and a half feet of silence give you time to come to terms with passing up the opportunity to exact revenge.

Although there are several ways to scan line 84, we feel it makes the most sense to treat *——vy with him* as a crowded foot:

x /x-x / x / x / x /
'Tis heavy with him. And am I then revenged

Don't forget to elide: *a-praying* (a-PRAING) in line 72 (or pronounce as three syllables, giving the line a double ending) and *salary* (SAL-ree) in line 79;

. . . to contract: *he is* (HE'S) in line 72; *'Tis* (TIZ) in line 84; and *in't* (INT) in line 92;

. . . and to both contract and elide: *th' incestuous* (th'in-SESS-tchwuss) in line 90.

HAMLET

ACT IV, SCENE vii

GERTRUDE

GENDER: F
AGE RANGE: mature adult
PROSE/VERSE: blank verse
FREQUENCY OF USE (1–5): 4

About two months ago, Queen Gertrude's husband died, and soon after, she married his brother, who assumed the throne (such a marriage was considered incestuous by Elizabethans, by the way). The wedding was the last nice thing that happened to her. Since then, her son, Hamlet, has gone insane—he recently railed wildly at her about her marriage and then began talking to the air and claiming that a ghost was in the room. He then killed Polonius, the most trusted adviser to her husband, King Claudius. Claudius sent Hamlet away to England to keep him out of any further trouble, and then Ophelia, Polonius's lovely daughter—whom Gertrude had hoped her son might marry—went mad as well, presumably from grief over her father's death at the hand of the man she loved. Gertrude has just come from witnessing Ophelia's death, which she describes to King Claudius and Laertes, Ophelia's brother.

GERTRUDE

One woe doth tread upon another's heel,
165 So fast they follow. Your sister's drowned, Laertes.

There is a willow grows askant the brook
That shows his hoary leaves in the glassy stream.
Therewith fantastic garlands did she make,
170 Of crow-flowers, nettles, daisies, and long purples,
That liberal shepherds give a grosser name,
But our cold maids do dead men's fingers call them.
There on the pendent boughs her crownet weeds
Clambering to hang, an envious sliver broke,
175 When down her weedy trophies and herself
Fell in the weeping brook. Her clothes spread wide,
And mermaid-like awhile they bore her up,
Which time she chanted snatches of old lauds

165 *So fast they follow* they follow one another so quickly; 167 *willow* to Elizabethans, the willow tree was an emblem of lost or unrequited love; a man or woman traditionally made a garland of willow, which was either worn or hung on the tree; *askant* slanting across, leaning over (a willow planted on a riverbank often leans toward the water); 168 *hoary* grayish-white (the color of the underside of the leaf of a common willow); *glassy* glasslike, mirrorlike [*That shows his hoary leaves in the glassy stream* i.e., whose leaves' grayish-white undersides are mirrored in the stream]; 169 *Therewith* i.e., with its twigs; *fantastic* fanciful; produced by an unrestrained imagination; 170 *crow-flowers* the identity of this flower is disputed: possibly (1) buttercups, but more likely (2) ragged robins, flowers whose petals are cut into narrow sections (a symbol of dejection in Shakespeare's time); *nettles* poisonous weeds, covered with stinging hairs and bearing white or purple flowers (associated with betrayal in Shakespeare's time); *daisies* for Elizabethans, an emblem of love's deceived victims; *long purples* probably a wild orchis, a type of orchid that blooms in a long purple spike; 171 *liberal* free-spoken; foul-mouthed; *grosser* coarser, more vulgar [*grosser name* Shakespeare may have had in mind one of these nicknames for the orchis: priest's pintle, dog's cods, fool's ballocks, bull's pizzle, or goat's cullions; or any of a number of similar terms which derived from the testiclelike tubers that form the plant's roots]; 172 *cold* chaste; *maids* virginal young women; *dead men's fingers* i.e., a more innocent description of the orchis's pale, tuberous roots; 173 *pendent* hanging; *crownet weeds* weeds woven into a coronet; 174 *envious* malicious, spiteful; *sliver* small branch [*There on . . . broke* As she climbed on the hanging boughs to drape her garlands of weeds there, a spiteful branch broke]; 175 *trophies* monuments or memorials, often hung over graves or tombs to honor the dead [*weedy trophies* i.e., the garlands she had made] [*When down . . . Fell* At which time she and her garlands fell down into]; *Her clothes spread wide . . . bore her up* i.e., her skirts spread out across the surface of the water, and for a while they held her up like a mermaid; 178 *Which time* dur-

As one incapable of her own distress,
180 Or like a creature native and indued
Unto that element. But long it could not be
Till that her garments, heavy with their drink,
Pulled the poor wretch from her melodious lay
To muddy death.

1 minute, 10 seconds

ing which time; *lauds* hymns praising God; 179 *incapable of* insensible to; unaware of; unable to perceive and comprehend; 180 *indued / Unto* having the qualities required for; suited for; 181 *that element* i.e., water; 182 *Till that* until; *their drink* i.e., the water that they had absorbed; 183 *wretch* miserable creature (sometimes, as here, used to express pity); *lay* song.

COMMENTARY

With this monologue, Gertrude makes her audience believe it has seen an additional scene—one impossible to stage. The material is really one continuous piece of imagery, through which Gertrude vividly conveys the simultaneous horror and beauty of Ophelia's death. The detailed description is full of emblems that would have had specific meanings to an Elizabethan audience. Although today's audience generally will not make the same connections, your understanding of the meanings implied by the symbolism will help you communicate them.

The material itself is quite unusual. Gertrude's poetic wording and complex grammatical construction seems out of character in comparison to her material in the rest of the play. The elevated language in this piece indicates that Gertrude has been profoundly affected by what she has just seen. Which raises the question: exactly *how* was she affected? How is it that she saw the accident in such detail (as if in close proximity) and watched so long, and yet Ophelia was not saved? Most likely Gertrude cannot swim, and tried to call for help, but was out of earshot. Maybe she was so shocked by what she saw that she was unable to move, or was close enough to see the tragedy, but too far to get there in time. Or maybe Gertrude believes that poor, mad Ophelia, with both parents dead and the man she loves gone, is better off drowned. Then again, perhaps Gertrude actually waded into the brook and tried to save Ophelia but was not able to do so . . . it is possible that she enters the room with her skirts sopping wet. Gertrude may also be protecting Ophelia's reputation, fabricating these details to cover up having witnessed a different scene—a damning suicide. There are many options, and the question will certainly be central in the minds of the audience, so be sure to make a choice you can feel grounded in. And, of course, doing this background work is essential to bringing the scene to life for yourself and your audience.

The meter of the piece is both illuminating and thought-provoking. Notice that almost half of the lines begin with inverted first feet. The piece is made up of only a few long sentences, which often carry over the line endings to end mid-line. These elements give the piece a strong, flowing feel, which seems to imitate the current of the brook she describes. At the same time, there is a notable absence in the speech of exclamations, laments, sentence fragments, self-interruptions, or the use of the word *O*, which one might expect from a character who has just watched helplessly as an innocent young woman drowned. The piece is strangely calm, and almost choruslike, which prompts one to examine Gertrude's state of mind. Is she simply in a state of shock over the tragedy, and/or over the fact that she was unable to prevent it? Is she numbed by the fear that her own actions have set into motion the chain of events culminating in Ophelia's death? Does she feel a mother's guilt for her son's seemingly cruel rejection of Ophelia? Is it possible that she knew all along about the murder of her first husband—or has since surmised it—and is now pointedly accusing Claudius with this detailed description of the long-range consequences of his crime? Or perhaps she is trying, in a strange fashion, to make Ophelia's death poetic and thus noble—and peaceful—for her devastated brother. Again, there are many complicated possible motivations for this speech, and it is up to you to choose one or more that you will enjoy exploring. Notice that the long final sentence of the monologue ends mid-line, finishing the piece abruptly. Take advantage of the remaining three feet of silence, which will take the listener's ear by surprise, and use the moment to end the monologue—silence is a powerful echo of death.

There is no escaping the blatant sexual double entendre in this piece. A look at all of the words that had second meanings in Shakespeare's time reveals the extent of this: *willow* = a symbol of lechery; *brook* = pimp; *hoary* = a homonym for "whorey"; *fantastic* = sexually desirous; *fingers* = penises; *broke* = defiled or violated sexually; *down* = lying down, for intercourse (used in reference to prostitutes); *Fell* = sinned by copulation (i.e., fell from virtue); *weeping* = whoring (alludes to Mary Magdalene, who wept with repentance for her prostitution); *clothes* = a play on the word *close*, "lechery"; *spread wide* = to open for intercourse; *mermaid-like* = like a prostitute; *snatches* = sexual acts, copulations; *old* = a reference to *hoary*, above; *creature* = harlot (sometimes refers to one who practices sodomy or bestiality); *indued* = (*due* means testicles; your inference is as good as ours for *indue*); *heavy* = pregnant; *lay* = act of sexual intercourse; *muddy* = filthy with excrement; *death* = orgasm.

This undeniably pervasive use of double entendre, combined with Gertrude's reference to the coarser names for long purples, naturally prompts the important question of why she uses such language. It's a difficult question, but its answer provides a clue to Gertrude's objective in the piece. Gertrude may consciously choose to use language that violates the chaste Ophelia (the *cold maid*) in order to drive home the violence done to her purity by the *hoary* willow and the *muddy* stream. She may be using the vulgar references to imply that Ophelia was *not* chaste and brought her own death upon herself, or it may be a way for Gertrude to accuse herself or Claudius for their own immoral sexual behavior. On the other hand, Gertrude may be using this language only subconsciously, perhaps out of guilt. Or, since the subconscious commonly responds to close encounters with death by seeking the life-affirming antidote of sex, Gertrude's language may merely be a manifestation of that response. Gertrude's sexual double entendre surrounds and submerges Ophelia, engulfing her just as the water did.

Perhaps the most interesting use of wordplay in this piece is the emblematic "picture-writing" of line 170, in which Shakespeare embedded a coded message to his audience (unfortunately lost today): *crow-flowers* were also called "fair maids of France"; *nettles* meant "stung to the quick"; *daisies* were known as the "virgin bloom" of spring; *long purples* were also called "dead men's fingers." Thus, *crow-flowers, nettles, daisies, and long purples* meant, to the horticulturally savvy, "A fair maid stung to the quick, her virgin bloom under the cold hand of death."

SIGNIFICANT SCANS

Lines 168 and 179 scan most intelligibly with crowded feet, rather than contractions:

x / x / x / x - x / x /
That shows his hoary leaves in the glassy stream

x / x / x / x - x / x /
As one incapable of her own distress

Line 181 is an unusual six-footed line (hexameter), with an inverted first foot:

/ x x /x / x / x / x /
Unto that element. But long it could not be

Or you could elide *element* (EL-ment), creating iambic pentameter with a double ending before the caesura.

Don't forget to elide: *crow-flowers* (CROW-flowrz) in line 170; *liberal* (LIB-ral) in line 171; *Clambering* (CLAM-bring) and *envious* (EN-vyuss) in line 174; and *melodious* (mel-OH-dyuss) in line 183.

ART IMITATING DEATH: *HAMLET* INSPIRED BY HAMLETT?

Ophelia's death by drowning may have been inspired by an event that took place in Tippington, a village near Stratford, in 1579, when Shakespeare was fifteen years old. A young woman named Katherine Hamlett (coincidence?) went to fetch water from the Avon River with a pail. She slipped and fell in (accidentally?) and was drowned. The coroner's jury deliberated over her death for two months, finally deciding that it was not a suicide. As with Ophelia, we'll never know for sure.

JULIUS CAESAR

ACT I, SCENE II

CASSIUS

GENDER: M
PROSE/VERSE: blank verse
AGE RANGE: mature adult
FREQUENCY OF USE (1–5): 5

Military generals have been fighting for control of Rome and its territories for years. The most recent disputes have been between Julius Caesar and Gnaeus Pompeius (a.k.a. Pompey), who at first ruled together but were soon vying for control. Cassius originally supported Pompey, but once it looked as though Caesar was going to prevail, he switched sides. Cassius has just returned from Spain (part of Rome's territory), where he and his forces helped defeat Pompey's sons, the last holdouts against Caesar. Cassius is disturbed to see Caesar's increasing power. Caesar is already Rome's dictator, and now the people want to crown him emperor. Cassius, a dyed-in-the-wool republican, can't bear to see the long-standing government of Rome—in which all noble families share power—destroyed. If that were to happen, he and the entire nobility would be no better than slaves. He intends to stop Caesar, but to pull it off he must enlist the support of Brutus, who is revered by patricians and plebeians alike. Cassius sets out to win Brutus over.

90 I know that virtue to be in you, Brutus,
As well as I do know your outward favor.
Well, honor is the subject of my story.
I cannot tell what you and other men
Think of this life, but for my single self,
95 I had as lief not be as live to be
In awe of such a thing as I myself.
I was born free as Caesar; so were you.
We both have fed as well, and we can both
Endure the winter's cold as well as he.
100 For once, upon a raw and gusty day,
The troubled Tiber chafing with her shores,
Caesar said to me, "Dar'st thou, Cassius, now
Leap in with me into this angry flood
And swim to yonder point?" Upon the word,
105 Accoutred as I was, I plungèd in
And bade him follow; so indeed he did.
The torrent roared, and we did buffet it
With lusty sinews, throwing it aside
And stemming it with hearts of controversy.
110 But ere we could arrive the point proposed,
Caesar cried, "Help me, Cassius, or I sink!"
I, as Aeneas, our great ancestor,
Did from the flames of Troy upon his shoulder
The old Anchises bear, so from the waves of Tiber
115 Did I the tired Caesar. And this man
Is now become a god, and Cassius is
A wretched creature, and must bend his body

90 *that virtue* i.e., honor; 91 *outward favor* (1) outward appearance; (2) kind demeanor; 94 *for my single self* as for myself in particular; 95 *I had as lief not be* (LEEF) I would just as soon not exist; 96 *such a thing as I myself* a thing like myself (i.e., a mere mortal); 97 *free as Caesar* as legitimately a free man as Caesar (in ancient Rome, "freemen" enjoyed particular personal, civil, and political freedoms of citizenship not granted to slaves, women, etc.); 101 *Tiber* Rome's river, which frequently overflows its banks; *chafing with* raging against; 104 *point* promontory; peninsula; *Upon the word* The moment he said it; 105 *Accoutred* fully dressed and/or wearing a full suit of armor; 108 *lusty* strong, vigorous; *sinews* tendons (considered, in Shakespeare's time, to be the source of physical strength); *it* i.e., the river's strong current; 109 *stemming* making headway against; *hearts of controversy* hearts eager for competition (both with the waves and with each other); 110 *ere* before; *arrive* arrive at; 111 *sink* i.e., drown; 112 *Aeneas, our great ancestor* Aeneas, the hero of Virgil's *Aeneid*, was the legendary founder of Rome; 114 *Anchises* Aeneas's father [*Did from the flames . . . old Anchises bear* carried the old Anchises away from the burning Troy on his shoulders]; *so from . . . tired Caesar* in that same manner I carried Caesar from the waves of the Tiber; 116 *Is now become* i.e., is now seen as; 117 *wretched* paltry,

If Caesar carelessly but nod on him.
He had a fever when he was in Spain,
120 And when the fit was on him, I did mark
How he did shake—'tis true, this god did shake;
His coward lips did from their color fly,
And that same eye whose bend doth awe the world
Did lose his luster. I did hear him groan;
125 Ay, and that tongue of his that bade the Romans
Mark him and write his speeches in their books,
"Alas," it cried, "give me some drink, Titinius,"
As a sick girl. Ye gods, it doth amaze me
A man of such a feeble temper should
130 So get the start of the majestic world
And bear the palm alone.

2 minutes, 30 seconds

135 Why, man, he doth bestride the narrow world
Like a Colossus, and we petty men
Walk under his huge legs and peep about
To find ourselves dishonorable graves.
Men at some time are masters of their fates.
140 The fault, dear Brutus, is not in our stars,
But in ourselves, that we are underlings.

contemptible; *bend his body* bow; 118 *carelessly* both (1) offhandedly and (2) uncaringly; *on* at; 119 *Spain* Caesar and his army have just returned, triumphant, from civil war in Spain, which was then Roman territory. Cassius had fought with Pompey against Caesar in an earlier contest for control of Rome, but Caesar forgave him, and Cassius fought for Caesar in Spain, against Pompey's sons; 120 *fit* attack of chills that accompany a high fever [*when the fit was on him* when he suffered an attack of chills during his fever]; *did mark* noticed; 122 *coward* cowardly; *did from their color fly* fled from their color (as cowardly soldiers flee, deserting their "colors" [their flag]); 123 *bend* glance; gaze; 126 *Mark* pay attention to; 127 *Titinius* close friend of Cassius and officer in his forces, who was also present at the recent conflict in Spain; 128 *As* like; 129 *temper* temperament; constitution [*feeble temper* physical and emotional weakness]; 130 *get the start of* outdistance; 131 *bear* (1) win; (2) carry away; *the palm* a palm frond, the traditional prize for the victor in a race (the palm symbolized glory and superiority); 135 *doth bestride* straddles; 136 *Colossus* a bronze statue of Apollo over one hundred feet tall, which overlooked the harbor of Rhodes. Although it toppled in the earthquake of 224 B.C.E., only fifty-six years after it was built, the Colossus made history as one of the Seven Wonders of the ancient world. By Cassius's time (two centuries later) popular legend had increased its size so that it stood straddling the harbor, while ships passed under its legs; 138 *dishonorable graves* graves devoid of honor and good reputation (such as slaves would be buried in) [*peep about . . . dishonorable graves* furtively look forward to dying a debased, dishonorable death]; 139 *at some time* i.e., at some particular moment in their lives; 140 *in our stars* i.e., in our fates (in Shakespeare's time, people's fates were widely believed to be determined by astrology) [*The fault . . . that we are underlings* either: (1) The fact that we are underlings is not due to fate, dear Brutus, but due to our own actions; or (2) The problem (that we are little, dishonorable men compared to Caesar) is not in our fates, dear Brutus, but in the fact that we have chosen to act

Brutus and Caesar: What should be in that "Caesar"?
Why should that name be sounded more than yours?
Write them together, yours is as fair a name;
145 Sound them, it doth become the mouth as well;
Weigh them, it is as heavy; conjure with 'em,
"Brutus" will start a spirit as soon as "Caesar."
Now, in the names of all the gods at once,
Upon what meat doth this our Caesar feed,
150 That he is grown so great? Age, thou art shamed!
Rome, thou hast lost the breed of noble bloods!
When went there by an age, since the great flood,
But it was famed with more than with one man?
When could they say, 'til now, that talked of Rome
155 That her wide walks encompassed but one man?
Now is it Rome indeed, and room enough,
When there is in it but one only man.
O, you and I have heard our fathers say
There was a Brutus once that would have brooked
160 Th' eternal devil to keep his state in Rome
As easily as a king.

1 minute, 30 seconds

4 minutes

like underlings]; 142 *What should be in that "Caesar"* What special qualities should be attributed to that name, "Caesar"; 143 *sounded* (1) spoken; with a play on both (2) measured for depth and (3) proclaimed (trumpets were "sounded" before proclamations were made); 144 *Write them together* i.e., write them down side by side; *fair* handsome, beautiful; 145 *Sound* pronounce; *it* i.e., your name; *doth become the mouth as well* is as well suited to the mouth; 146 *conjure with 'em* use them in magic spells to raise spirits from the dead; 147 *start a spirit* raise a spirit from the dead (with a play on *start*, to mean "startle" [out of its grave]); *as soon as* as easily as; 149 *meat* i.e., food of any kind [*Upon what meat . . . Caesar feed* what kind of food does our guy Caesar eat]; 150 *is grown so great* has grown so huge and powerful; *Age* Cassius addresses the era in which he lives; 151 *breed* (1) profit, benefit; (2) art of breeding; *bloods* spirited, courageous young men [*lost the breed of noble bloods* (1) lost the benefit of spirited, courageous nobles; (2) lost the ability to breed spirited, courageous, nobly descended young men]; 152 *went there by an age* has an era gone by; *great flood* although today's audiences, like those in Shakespeare's time, will probably think of the biblical flood in the story of Noah, Cassius actually refers to a similar story from Greek and Roman mythology, in which Zeus sent a deluge to destroy all of the human race, with the exception of two goody-goodies, Deucalion and Pyrrah, the King and Queen of Pithia; 153 *But it was famed . . . one man* without it (the age) being made famous by more than one man; 154 *When could they say, 'til now, that talked of Rome* until now, when could those who talked of Rome say; 155 *walks* parks, gardens, and tracts of land (that surrounded ancient Rome); 156 *Now is it Rome indeed* now this is indeed Rome; 157 *but one only* only one single; 159 *a Brutus* a man named Brutus (Cassius refers to the legendary Lucius Junius Brutus, who ousted the tyrannical Tarquins from Rome and founded the Roman republic in 509 B.C.E., assumed to be Brutus's ancestor); *brooked* tolerated, allowed; 160 *eternal* eternally damned (perhaps from confusion with *infernal*; used to express extreme abhorrence); *keep his state* participate in the pomp and ceremony befitting his high position [*brooked / Th' eternal devil . . . easily as a king* allowed the devil himself to rule Rome as easily as he would allow a human monarch to do so].

COMMENTARY

Cassius's whole way of life is at stake: for centuries, the noble families of Rome have each had an equal vote in the Senate, and as a group they have been free to wield unlimited power over the commoners. It's been a cushy lifestyle, and Cassius is loath to see it end. On top of that, it is sickening to see Caesar eating up so much publicity and attention, when other people (himself, for instance) are just as deserving. Cassius is eager to take action, and Brutus is the only man who can help.

Cassius employs several different tactics to persuade Brutus that something must be done. In the first section, he uses the arguments that are most poignant to *him*: Caesar—who is no better than any of the other nobles—is lording it over everyone, and Cassius fears he will wrest all power from the Senate. Who is he to do that? Cassius cites examples from his own experience, which he tries to make as vivid for Brutus as they are in his mind, first telling the story of the swimming contest, then that of Caesar's illness. In the process, Cassius reveals his own competitive, resentful feelings toward Caesar: he likens himself to the great *Aeneas*, and Caesar to the feeble old *Anchises*. He sarcastically portrays Caesar as a *god* who *carelessly but nod*[*s*] *on him*, and himself as a *wretched creature* who *must bend his body*. In the last few lines of the section, he states outright his annoyance that the undeserving Caesar is winning in this political race. Cassius may be starting with this strategy because he thinks that Brutus will respond to the same personal affronts that got his own dander up. Perhaps he simply needs to unload a bit before he can straighten out his thoughts. Or is he, in a calculated way, trying to engage Brutus's emotions, to add urgency to the more rational arguments that follow? There are many possibilities . . . It is especially important to make a specific choice of action in this first, highly charged section, to prevent it from becoming a big rant or whine. You also have to decide how honest Cassius is. Are his stories true? Shakespeare's source material tells of a swimming incident very different from the one Cassius relates: according to Plutarch's *Lives*, Caesar evaded Egyptians who were shooting arrows at him by swimming almost a quarter of a mile to safety, all the while holding some books aloft to keep them dry. Plutarch also writes of Caesar's epilepsy, but he makes it clear that Caesar handled his illness courageously. You must decide whether Cassius's stories are a pack of clever lies, or whether Shakespeare's Cassius knew some things about Caesar that Plutarch left out of his account . . . or whether perhaps Cassius believes he speaks the truth, but his perception of Caesar is warped by outrage or envy.

Your transition between the two sections of the monologue is facilitated by the two silent feet in line 131, where Brutus's words have been excised. Notice the change in strategy, as well as the change in tone. Cassius starts off with *Why, man*, indicating that perhaps Brutus is distracted by the sounds (and possibly sights) of Caesar's triumphal festivities, and Cassius needs to grab his attention. Or he may be using the words to set apart his next tactic, or in an attempt to be a little more casual or familiar with Brutus. In any case, the words introduce the more carefully thought-out strategies that follow. First, Cassius shifts from comparing Caesar with himself to comparing Caesar with all men. At the same time he shifts his imagery from descriptions that relate to his personal experience to one that is familiar to everyone: the *Colossus*. He then takes the shift a step further, comparing Caesar to Brutus by equating the qualities of their names. There is a repetition of phrasing in these lines that creates a natural build. The conclusion of the build ends memorably with a sentence that begins mid-line (*conjure with 'em*), which surprises your listeners' ears with its abruptness and unexpected content. With his next shift of tactic, Cassius appeals to Brutus's pride in and sense of personal obligation toward Rome and its noble families (of which Brutus's is the noblest of all). Here he begins another build, which plays on subtle changes in the repeated use of a phrase (*with one man / but one man / but one only man*), each more pointed than the next. As always, make sure you start at a level that will allow room for your builds. In the last lines of the piece, Cassius refines his appeal to Brutus's personal interest in the future government of Rome by evoking the memory of his ancestor, Lucius Junius *Brutus*, the founder of the Roman republic.

The first section of the monologue provides the context for the second, although either section can be performed on its own. And, although Cassius is often portrayed as a villain, the material actually permits a broader interpretation: you could choose to balance his personal competitiveness with a geniune desire to protect the age-old Roman system of government. What is Cassius's intent when he gets carried away in the second section? Your answer to this question rests in your interpretation of the language: for example, it was believed that a *spirit* could be roused only in the name of a god, so the words *start a spirit* could be used seriously, to put Brutus on par with Caesar (as Cassius did for himself in the first section) by suggesting that Brutus is as godlike as Caesar; or it could be an example of an ironic sense of humor in Cassius. Likewise, Cassius's direct addresses to *Age* and *Rome* could be an attempt to elevate the stakes in Brutus's mind, or a sarcastic put-down of the current state of his time and his nation.

You'll find many helpful clues to Cassius's character in his word choices. Notice when he chooses to use *thou* in contrast to the formal, respectful *you* with which he addresses Brutus. The first time he says *thou* (in line 102), he is quoting Caesar. Caesar's use of the word *thou* to one who should be considered an equal is a sign of disrespect and an affront to the person addressed. The next time Cassius uses *thou* is in addressing his *Age* and *Rome*. Since the familiar form is used without disrespect in intimate relationships, Cassius could be addressing *Age* and *Rome* with affection, or his use of the form could be a sign of contempt for their current deplorable state. It could also be a combination of the two . . . it depends on who *your* Cassius is.

Cassius uses the emphatic form extensively to drive his points home to Brutus: *do know*; *did buffet*; *Did . . . the old Anchises bear*; *did mark*; *did . . . fly*; *Did lose*; *doth amaze*; *doth bestride*; *doth become*. It appears in conjunction with repetition in line 121 (*How he did shake—'tis true, this god did shake*), assertively underscoring Caesar's weakness. Other word repetitions achieve a similar effect: the word *Caesar* appears nine times, and the words *man* or *men* appear eight times, helping Cassius communicate his point that Caesar is merely a man like other men, and not a god.

Cassius also repeats sounds. Notice the many small chunks of assonance throughout, which emphasize attributes of the three men that he is intent on comparing: *virtue / to / you / Brutus*; *I / myself*; *free / Caesar*; *fed / well*; *I / tired*; *nod / on*; *petty / men*; *more / yours*; *meat / Caesar / feed*. There are many similar chunks of alliteration, which enhance the main points of the stories he tells in the first part of his speech: *subject / story*; *single / self*; *troubled / Tiber*; *point / proposed*; *from the flames*; *bend / body*; *lose / luster*; *Brutus / brooked*. Here and there consonance contributes to the flow from one sound group to the next, for example: *wretched / creature*; *Brutus / start / spirit / as / soon / Caesar / names / gods / once*; *breed / noble / bloods*. Perhaps the most memorable sounds in the piece are the ones that combine with others to create striking little sound bites, which Cassius surely hopes will echo in Brutus's mind: As, Ls, and EEs in *had as lief not be as live to be*; soft Cs and Ss, hard Cs and Ks, EEs, and Is in *Caesar cried, "Help me Cassius, or I sink!"*; hard Cs, Ls, short Is, Fs, and Rs in *coward lips did from their color fly*; GRs and Os in *grown so great*; short As, Ws, and UH sounds in *That her wide walks encompassed but one man*. For help exploiting the sound of the word *O* to its best advantage, see "O, No! An *O*!," page xxxiii. Finally, note the homonym in line 156 (*Rome / room*). In Shakespeare's day, these two words were sometimes pronounced alike (scholars suggest that *Rome* was interchangeably rhymed with both *roam* and *room*). Even in contemporary English, the sounds are similar enough to make the clever pun clear, exemplifying Cassius's sarcastic, pointed, even funny tone.

SIGNIFICANT SCANS

This piece starts with three lines that have double endings, which soften your delivery, suggesting that Cassius is easing gently into his appeal to Brutus. During the story that follows, most of the lines do not have double endings: this is not a pretty tale, and Cassius is getting down to the matters at hand more directly. In the second section, the double endings fall on the word *Caesar*, making his name stand out against the regular flow of the meter.

Line 102 is headless and has an elision (CA-syuss or CA-shuss) and two contractions (*to me* and *Dar'st*):

x / x / x / x / x /
(pause) Caesar said to me, "Dar'st thou, Cassius, now

Line 114 is a rare six-footed line (hexameter), made even longer by its double ending:

x / x /x / x / x / x /(x)
The old Anchises bear, so from the waves of Tiber

There are many lines that have inverted first feet or inverted feet after caesuras, and many lines that have double endings before caesuras or at the end of lines. Several lines have some combination of these variations. Line 142 has all four!

/ x x / (x) / x x / x / (x)
Brutus and Caesar: What should be in that "Caesar"?

These variations create an overwrought tone—perhaps this is where Cassius's indignation reaches its peak, or perhaps he's laying it on thick to make Brutus feel indignant too.

Don't forget to elide: *Cassius* (CA-syuss or CA-shuss) in lines 102, 111, and 116; *Titinius* (tie-TIN-yuss) in line 127; *spirit* (SPEERT) in line 147; *devil* (DEV'L) in line 160; and *easily* (EEZ-lee) in line 161;

. . . to expand: *plungèd* (PLUN-jehd) in line 105 and *dishonorable* (dis-ON´-er-UH-bl) in line 138 (notice the extra emphasis these expansions place on two important points: Cassius's bravery in plunging into the Tiber without hesitation, and the level to which men like Cassius have been degraded by Caesar's disproportionate power);

. . . and to contract: *to me* (t'mee) and *Dar'st* (DAIRST) in line 102; and *Th' eternal* (Thee-TER-nal) in line 160.

Curt Comments on Cassius, Confessedly Critical

The historical Cassius was an accomplished general, but lacked people skills; he was known for his sarcasm and hot temper. A flagrant opportunist, he initially sided with Caesar's enemy, the more manipulable Pompey, but pledged eternal devotion to Caesar after Pompey's decisive defeat. He was made peregrine praetor, and fought with Caesar against Pompey's sons in Spain, from whence they have just returned when the events of this play begin. Shakespeare's account of the rest of Cassius's malcontented life is fairly accurate.

JULIUS CAESAR

ACT II, SCENE i

BRUTUS

GENDER: M
PROSE/VERSE: blank verse
AGE RANGE: mature adult
FREQUENCY OF USE (1–5): 2

Marcus Brutus, respected and honorable member of Rome's oldest noble family, has just been convinced by Caius Cassius to lead a group of conspirators—all nobles—in a plot to kill Julius Caesar, the dictator of Rome. Brutus has been grappling with this decision all night long. He loves and respects Caesar as a person, but he feels that Caesar is too powerful. He has concluded that Caesar must die to preserve the government of the Roman republic (founded by Brutus's own ancestor), in which all noble families share power by voting in the Senate. Cassius has just suggested that the conspirators kill Caesar's right-hand man, Mark Antony, as well. Brutus warns Cassius against such an action:

Our course will seem too bloody, Caius Cassius,
To cut the head off and then hack the limbs—
Like wrath in death and envy afterwards;
165 For Antony is but a limb of Caesar.
Let's be sacrificers, but not butchers, Caius.
We all stand up against the spirit of Caesar,
And in the spirit of men there is no blood.
O, that we then could come by Caesar's spirit
170 And not dismember Caesar! But, alas,
Caesar must bleed for it. And, gentle friends,
Let's kill him boldly, but not wrathfully;
Let's carve him as a dish fit for the gods,
Not hew him as a carcass fit for hounds.
175 And let our hearts, as subtle masters do,
Stir up their servants to an act of rage
And after seem to chide 'em. This shall make
Our purpose necessary, and not envious;
Which so appearing to the common eyes
180 We shall be called purgers, not murderers.
And for Mark Antony, think not of him,
For he can do no more than Caesar's arm
When Caesar's head is off.

1 minute, 20 seconds

162 *course* proceeding, course of action (with a play on *corse*, the archaic version of *corpse*; Brutus may be punning on the corpse of Caesar and/or the "body politic" of Rome); 163 *To cut* i.e., if we cut; *hack* hack off; 164 *envy* malice [*Like wrath in death and envy afterwards* i.e., it will seem as though we killed him in anger and hacked him up afterwards out of personal malice]; 167 *stand up* make a stand, rise up; *spirit of Caesar* basic principles that inspire Caesar; 168 *spirit of men* souls of humans; 169 *that we then could* if only we could, if that is so; 171 *bleed* i.e., die (with a play on the idea of bloodletting, a common cure in which patients were "purged" of "bad blood"); *for it* i.e., in order for us to eradicate his spirit (and thus protect the republic); *gentle* both (1) nobly descended and (2) not violent; 172 *wrathfully* angrily; 173 *carve him . . . gods* either (1) carve him as a priest would carve up a sacrifice to the gods or (2) carve him up as a delicacy fit to serve to the gods; 174 *hew him . . . hounds* after a hunt, the deer was ceremoniously carved up and shared among the participants, unlike other animals, whose carcasses were hacked up and tossed to the dogs; 175 *subtle* sly, cunning; 176 *their servants* i.e., their hearts' servants: their passions and their hands [*And let our hearts . . . chide 'em* editors suggest two different meanings: (1) let our hearts remain uninvolved while urging our hands to commit an act of rage, and afterwards let our hearts reproach our hands for their violent acts; (2) let our hearts slyly encourage our hands to commit this act of rage, but afterwards let us pretend to regret that the violence was necessary]; 178 *envious* malicious [*make / Our purpose necessary, and not envious* make our cause seem necessary (to protect the republic) and not motivated by personal malice]; 179 *Which so appearing to the common eyes* our cause thus appearing necessary to the common people; 180 *purgers* purifiers, healers (alluding to surgeons, who "cured" their patients by bloodletting in Shakespeare's day); 183 *is off* i.e., has been cut off.

COMMENTARY

Cassius's suggestion that the conspirators kill Mark Antony as well as Caesar is just the sort of thing Brutus has been worrying about. The last thing he wants is to be involved in a vile, dishonorable bloodbath. If Brutus is going to participate in the assassination, he must convince Cassius (who controls the others) to do it the right way.

Brutus uses antithesis, distinguishing between the honorable act he hopes to commit and a greedy act of savage violence, to impress upon Cassius and the others the importance of committing murder honorably: *sacrificers* versus *butchers*; *boldly* versus *wrathfully*; *carve him as a dish fit for the gods* versus *hew him as a carcass fit for hounds*; *necessary* versus *envious*; *purgers* versus *murderers*. And Brutus uses metaphors to make his comparisons vivid in the minds of his listeners. He urges his *gentle friends* to be like priests making a solemn ritual sacrifice; like hunters ceremoniously carving up their respected prey; and like surgeons purging their patients of disease. Why does Brutus repeat the same idea in so many different terms? Your answer to that question will define how you interpret Brutus. If you believe he is honestly trying to do the honorable and patriotic thing, and has no selfish motives, then perhaps he is rallying the others to the same noble cause. Or maybe he loves Caesar and is trying to make the murder seem ritualistic so that he can keep his emotions in check. Or, if you think he is basically honest but has some sublimated selfish motives, perhaps he is trying to convince himself as well as the others that they are not butchers. If you think Brutus is downright crafty and is just hiding behind a mask of respectability, you may decide that he is purely concerned with appearances, and is trying to restrain the others from actions that could sway the people's opinion against them.

However you envision Brutus, there is one motif in this monologue you must squarely confront: its brutal and bloody imagery. The unrelenting outpouring of gory words and ideas overpowers all other aspects of the piece: *bloody*; *cut the head off*; *hack the limbs*; *butchers*; *dismember Caesar*; *Caesar must bleed for it*; *kill him*; *carve him*; *hew him as a carcass*; *act of rage*; *murderers*; *Caesar's arm / When Caesar's head is off*. While Brutus seems to be using these images to convince the conspirators to spare Antony and kill Caesar *boldly, but not wrathfully*, the profusion of gore suggests that he is plagued by the images and must fight against them even to speak of committing the act he has reluctantly undertaken.

Brutus emphasizes several important points with sound repetition. The key words in a line are often alliterative (*head / hack*), assonant (*death / envy*; *Caesar / bleed*; *gentle friends*), or consonant (*wrath / death*). Also note the hard, Cutting Cs (*course / Caius / Cassius / cut / hack*; *carve / carcass*; *could / come*), which contrast with the Civilized, Soft Ss and Cs thoughout (the most striking strings: *Let's* / *sacrificers* / *butchers* / *Caius* / *stand* / *against* / *spirit* / *Caesar's spirit* / *dismember Caesar* / *alas*; and *hearts* / *subtle masters* / *Stir* / *servants* / *seem*). The hard and soft sounds echo the contrast between the honorable and savage ways of killing he describes. And for help exploiting the sound of the word *O* to its best advantage, see "O, No! An *O*!," page xxxiii.

Brutus also uses several puns, and you'll have to decide to what degree he intends them and to what end he uses them. As you'll find in the annotation, Brutus plays on *course will seem too bloody*; *spirit*; *Caesar must bleed for it*; and *purgers*.

SIGNIFICANT SCANS

Two lines in this piece have tricky metrical variations that make the lines stand out. Both are lines in which Brutus emphasizes his main point to Cassius—that they must be *sacrificers* not *butchers*, *purgers* not *murderers*.

Line 166, in which Brutus sets forth his argument, is headless hexameter (a rare six-footed line), with a pyrrhic fourth foot (two unaccented syllables) and a spondaic fifth foot (two accented syllables), as well as a double ending:

x / x / x / x x / / x / (x)
(pause) Let's be sacrificers, but not butchers, Caius

You may also choose (as some editors have suggested) to expand *Let's* (LET-uss), changing the headless first foot to an inverted one:

/ x x / x / x x / / x / (x)
Let 's be sacrificers, but not butchers, Caius

Line 180 requires the contraction of *We shall* (WE'LL) in its inverted first foot, and has a half-foot pause at the caesura:

/ x x / x / x / x /
We shall be called purgers, (pause) not murderers

Line 183 (*When Caesar's head is off*) is short. This abrupt mid-line ending to the monologue is jarring. The scansion of lines 182–83 effectively suggests the image of a flailing arm jerking around on a suddenly headless body.

Don't forget to elide: *Cassius* (CA-shuss or CA-syuss) in line 162; *spirit* (SPEERT) in lines 167, 168, and 169; and *envious* (EN-vyuss) in line 178;

. . . and to contract: *We shall* (WE'LL) in line 180.

Revisionist History: Brutus in Brief

Brutus fans have long portayed him as upstanding and morally superior, but historical evidence presents a more self-serving, less judicious fellow. Originally allied with Caesar's enemy, Pompey, Brutus fought against Caesar until Pompey's defeat, whereupon he was taken prisoner by Caesar, who pardoned him and made him governor of Cisalpine Gaul (now northern Italy), and later, urban praetor of Rome. Although Caesar favored him, Brutus expressed opposition by supporting his uncle Cato—one of Caesar's longtime foes—and marrying Cato's daughter Porcia (yes, his first cousin). Brutus's assassination of Caesar was not in the interest of Rome, but of its ruling class: Caesar had been instigating reforms that diminished their powers. For a Stoic, Brutus was remarkably impatient. During the final confrontation at Philippi, his forces held a strategic position in the hills, which Antony and Octavius were unable to attack. Had Brutus merely waited them out rather than initiating a second battle, their forces would have died of starvation and disease in the marshy lowlands.

JULIUS CAESAR

ACT II, SCENE i

PORTIA

GENDER: F
AGE RANGE: mature adult
PROSE/VERSE: blank verse
FREQUENCY OF USE (1–5): 5

Portia is very concerned about her husband, Brutus. He's been preoccupied with some distressing matter and won't speak with her about it, dismissing her inquiries in an uncharacteristically unkind way. He hasn't slept all night, and snuck out of bed to pace in the garden. Around dawn, six or seven men came to meet secretly with him. They didn't stay long; they've just left and he's resumed his pacing. Enough is enough. Portia can't bear to see Brutus suffering alone. She is his wife and should know what's troubling him. Portia goes to the garden and confronts Brutus.

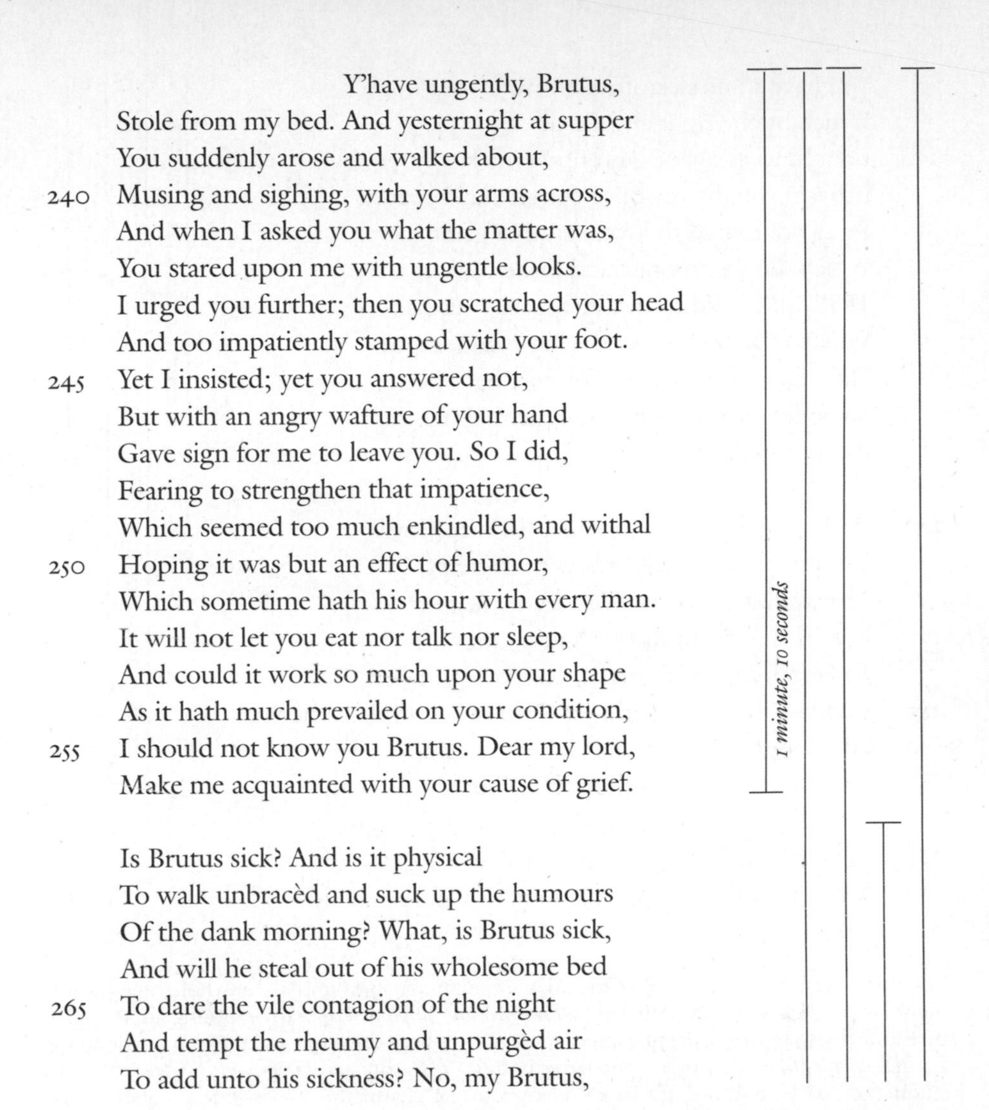

Y'have ungently, Brutus,
Stole from my bed. And yesternight at supper
You suddenly arose and walked about,
240 Musing and sighing, with your arms across,
And when I asked you what the matter was,
You stared upon me with ungentle looks.
I urged you further; then you scratched your head
And too impatiently stamped with your foot.
245 Yet I insisted; yet you answered not,
But with an angry wafture of your hand
Gave sign for me to leave you. So I did,
Fearing to strengthen that impatience,
Which seemed too much enkindled, and withal
250 Hoping it was but an effect of humor,
Which sometime hath his hour with every man.
It will not let you eat nor talk nor sleep,
And could it work so much upon your shape
As it hath much prevailed on your condition,
255 I should not know you Brutus. Dear my lord,
Make me acquainted with your cause of grief.

Is Brutus sick? And is it physical
To walk unbracèd and suck up the humours
Of the dank morning? What, is Brutus sick,
And will he steal out of his wholesome bed
265 To dare the vile contagion of the night
And tempt the rheumy and unpurgèd air
To add unto his sickness? No, my Brutus,

237 *ungently* discourteously; 238 *Stole* snuck away; *yesternight* last night, yesterday evening; 240 *Musing* thinking deeply about unpleasant thoughts; *across* i.e., crossed, folded; 241 *what the matter was* both (1) what was the subject of your thoughts and (2) what was wrong; 243 *urged you further* i.e., pressed you further to tell me what was troubling you; 245 *Yet I insisted* I continued to insist; 246 *wafture* impatient, dismissive wave; 249 *too much enkindled* too inflamed; *withal* yet, at the same time; 250 *but an effect of humor* merely a result of a temporary bad mood; 251 *sometime* from time to time [*sometime . . . with every man* spends an hour from time to time with every man, i.e., that strikes every man briefly from time to time]; 253 *could it* if it could; *work so much upon* i.e., have as much of an effect upon; *shape* i.e., outward appearance; 254 *As it . . . prevailed on* as it has greatly influenced, as it has overtaken; *condition* mental disposition; 255 *should not* wouldn't; *know you Brutus* recognize you as Brutus, know you to be Brutus; *my lord* my husband; 256 *your cause of grief* i.e., the cause of your worrying; 261 *physical* healthy; 262 *unbracèd* with unbuttoned or loosened clothing; *humours* moisture; 265 *vile . . . night* repulsive or evil contagiousness inherent to night; 266 *rheumy* causing rheumatic diseases (any of a group of diseases such as pneumonia and tuberculosis, which Elizabethans be-

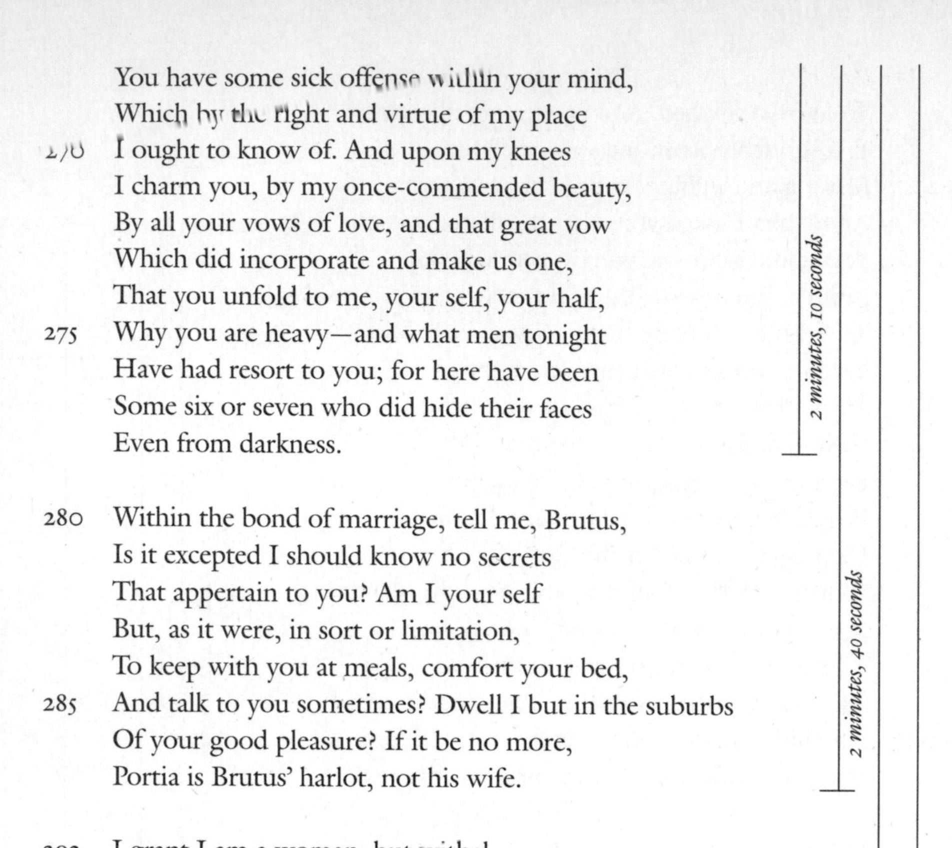

You have some sick offense within your mind,
Which by the right and virtue of my place
270 I ought to know of. And upon my knees
I charm you, by my once-commended beauty,
By all your vows of love, and that great vow
Which did incorporate and make us one,
That you unfold to me, your self, your half,
275 Why you are heavy—and what men tonight
Have had resort to you; for here have been
Some six or seven who did hide their faces
Even from darkness.

280 Within the bond of marriage, tell me, Brutus,
Is it excepted I should know no secrets
That appertain to you? Am I your self
But, as it were, in sort or limitation,
To keep with you at meals, comfort your bed,
285 And talk to you sometimes? Dwell I but in the suburbs
Of your good pleasure? If it be no more,
Portia is Brutus' harlot, not his wife.

292 I grant I am a woman, but withal
A woman that Lord Brutus took to wife.

2 minutes, 10 seconds

2 minutes, 40 seconds

lieved were caused by a buildup of the body's fluids); *unpurgèd* impure, unwholesome (moist night air was believed to be impure) [*the rheumy and unpurgèd air* early morning air, thought by Elizabethans to still be damp because it has not yet been dried out and purified by the sun]; 268 *sick offense* harmful disorder; 269 *virtue* both (1) authority and (2) power; *my place* my position (i.e., as your wife); 271 *charm* place a magic charm that forces one to obey; *once-commended* once-praised; 272 *great* powerful; divine; 273 *did incorporate* united; combined into one body (Elizabethans were well acquainted with the passages from Genesis 2:24, Matthew 19:5, and Ephesians 5:30–32, which referred to a husband and wife as "one flesh") [*that great vow / Which did incorporate and make us one* i.e., our marriage]; 274 *unfold* reveal; *your self, your half* i.e., your wife (the other part of your self, your other half, ever since marriage made us "one flesh"); 275 *heavy* sad; 276 *resort* visits paid (*resort* has the sexual double meaning of "brothel," which paves the way for lines 285–87) [*Have had resort to you* have visited you]; *here have been / Some six or seven* approximately six or seven (men) have been here; 281 *Is it excepted* a legal term: is there a reservation or a restriction [*Within the bond of marriage . . . / Is it excepted* Within the marriage contract is there a clause containing a reservation that]; 282 *appertain* belong; 283 *But* only, except; *in sort or limitation* legal terms: in a certain manner or with restrictions; 284 *keep with you* converse with you; *comfort* give pleasure to [*comfort your bed* i.e., have sexual intercourse with you]; 285 *the suburbs* the outskirts (the suburbs of Elizabethan London were where the brothels were located); 286 *your good pleasure* your will, your wishes; *If it be no more* If it is no more (than that), i.e., if I am of no more importance to you than that; 292 *withal* nevertheless; 295 *Cato* i.e., Marcus Porcius Cato (95–46 B.C.E.), who led anti-Caesar

I grant I am a woman, but withal
295 A woman well reputed, Cato's daughter.
Think you I am no stronger than my sex,
Being so fathered and so husbanded?
Tell me your counsels—I will not disclose 'em.
I have made strong proof of my constancy,
300 Giving myself a voluntary wound
Here, in the thigh. Can I bear that with patience,
And not my husband's secrets?

2 minutes, 10 seconds

3 minutes, 10 seconds

forces in Africa and who committed suicide to avoid being taken captive by Caesar, was renowned for his integrity; 296 *my sex* my gender, women; 297 *Being so fathered and so husbanded* having such a father (as Cato) and such a husband (as yourself); 298 *counsels* secrets; 299 *have made strong proof* have given strong proof, have given a strong demonstration; *constancy* self-control; resolve; faithfulness; 301 *patience* calmness and composure during suffering.

COMMENTARY

Portia is on a mission: she must convince Brutus to tell her what is troubling him. No doubt she wishes to be helpful to him. She is also hurt that she's been shut out from his important affairs. Perhaps she is imagining the worst and wishes to put her mind at rest by knowing the truth. It is up to you to decide exactly why Portia is so determined to know.

There are clues from the onset of the monologue that Portia is upset at Brutus's dismissive treatment of her. Her repetition of words and phrases is one such indication. For example, Portia did not like Brutus's impatience toward her: not only does she mention it twice (lines 244 and 248), but the first time, she emphasizes it with the word *too* and describes its manifestation (*And too impatiently stamped with your foot*), and the second time, she highlights the word itself with an expanded pronunciation (im-PAY´-shee-ENCE). Notice that the stresses in meter in the last two feet of line 244 fall on *with* and *foot*. When the line is pronounced accordingly, you'll notice that Portia's description of Brutus's action very naturally takes on an aggrieved tone.

Even with Brutus's lines excised, it is clear that he persists in withholding his secret. In each section of the monologue save the last, Portia tries to elicit the information and fails. She then switches tactics in the following section. Although the first section seems like rote exposition, it actually serves two purposes. It enables Portia to air her grievance with Brutus: she is not accustomed to being dismissed as though she were some run-of-the-mill, ordinary woman; nor is she accustomed to being treated unkindly. Alerting him to the fact that he's misbehaved should make him wish to remedy the fact. It also asserts that Portia has evidence of Brutus's preoccupation with some matter, which will hopefully prompt him to reveal it—after all, theirs is not a marriage in which secrets are kept.

But Brutus declines to reveal his secret, telling her he's out of bed because he's not feeling well. Portia then switches tactics, asking rhetorical questions to point out the absurdity of his feeble reply. These interrogatives reveal the flimsiness of his excuse in a way that simple declarative sentences would not. When performing this monologue, don't worry that the audience hasn't heard Brutus's line. Your lines make abundantly clear what he has said. In addition, line 264 contains an inverted foot (*out of*) in the middle of the line, after a caesura not marked by punctuation (which is rare):

x / x / / x x / x /
And will he steal out of his wholesome bed

By emphasizing *out* when the listener's ear wasn't expecting it, Portia further highlights the absurdity of Brutus's notion that being sick would prompt a person to get out of, rather than into, bed (and, if you want to give line 244 a different reading than we suggest above, you can invert *stamped with*, as well).

Portia then switches tactics again, "conjuring" Brutus to elicit his secret through the "magic" of her *beauty* (which she self-deprecatingly mocks)—a strong choice for the actor is that she is using humor to lighten him up and connect with him, while simultaneously begging him by getting on her knees (note the embedded stage direction in line 270, instructing the actor to kneel: *And upon my knees / I charm you . . .*). Portia begins this new tactic in the middle of a line, as though she thinks up the idea on the spot and jumps to implement it. She also plays her ace card, revealing that she knows Brutus has just been visited secretly by *some six or seven* men. He can no longer deny that something is going on.

When this tactic doesn't work, Portia shows Brutus her anger and frustration—in addition to withholding from her, Brutus has permitted her to grovel before him to no avail. The meter helps create her angry tone: Portia starts new sentences mid-line in lines 282, 285, and 286, cutting her own lines short, which suggests that her words are pouring out of her. Line 285 is a rare six-footed line (an alexandrine) with a double ending (and an inverted foot after the caesura):

x / x / x / / x x / x / (x)
And talk to you sometimes? Dwell I but in the suburbs

This extra-long line draws attention to itself, focusing the listener on this dramatic crescendo, and on the surprisingly crass way in which this consummate lady is about to express herself: *Dwell I but in the suburbs / Of your good pleasure?* The primary meaning of the image ("Am I only of peripheral importance to you?") is clear, but its secondary sexual image makes the point even more bitingly: *suburbs* were where the brothels were located; *your good pleasure* means "your wishes, your will," but also implies sexual pleasure. Portia is saying, "Am I no more to you than a good lay?" This double entendre is not inadvertent: she confirms her meaning when she then says, *If it be no more, / Portia is Brutus' harlot, not his wife*.

This train of thought leads quite naturally to the next, in which she intends to prove that although she is a woman, she has value outside the bedroom. Notice how she uses alliteration (and repetition) to support her intention: *woman / withal / woman / wife / woman / withal / woman / well reputed / wound*. Does she use these Warrior Ws to sound strong to Brutus? To bolster her own courage as she goes for broke? You must decide why she repeats the phrase *I grant I am a woman, but withal* . . . Perhaps she repeats it to replace an argument that has thus far failed to persuade him (i.e., that she is his wife) with one that has greater impact (i.e., that she is Cato's daughter). Perhaps she repeats it in fury, shocked or betrayed that Brutus is dismissing her because she's a woman. Does Portia believe that women are the "weaker sex" but consider herself the exception, or is she being sardonic by using and repeating that phrase? Whatever you decide, notice the build created by the repetition.

Since she failed to move him by comparing herself to a prostitute, Portia now decides to remind him just exactly who it is that he's diminishing. Notice the progression in her self-definition as Portia seeks the best way to prove herself Brutus's equal, despite her gender. First she bases her worth on the fact that Brutus considered her a worthy choice of spouse. Then she bases it on her powerful and stoic father, Cato (a step closer to self-actualization: at least she's now in her own gene pool, although she still defines her worth through her affiliation with a man). It is only when she proffers an accomplishment of her own (her courageous bearing of her voluntary wound) that she achieves her goal. Portia is every inch the stoic her father was. Remember that the whole time she's been speaking, Portia has been suffering from a serious wound she's inflicted on her own thigh . . . without letting on to her husband until now (note the embedded stage direction that Portia point out her wound: *Here, on the thigh*). She has wounded herself to prove that she can withstand torture with composure and that Brutus can trust her with his secrets. This is the tactic that finally works. Impressed, Brutus promises to tell all.

Imagery is used sparingly in this straightforward monologue, and only to support logical points Portia is making (the personification of *humor*; Portia as a sorceress: *I charm you*; Portia as Brutus's *self* and *half*; *the suburbs of your good pleasure*; *Portia is Brutus' harlot*). The meter provides insight into Portia's character and her state of mind. It is noteworthy that this very long monologue with its very long lines contains almost no elisions of words to shorten the lines. Most of Shakespeare's characters speak with a great many elisions, giving them a naturalistic speaking style. Portia's, on the other hand, is measured and precise, conveying the sense that despite her anger, she manages to remain in control of her feelings (she is the perfect match for her husband!) . . . or at least strives to do so. The scarcity of elisions also gives the listener the impression that Portia is a highly educated and well-spoken woman.

There are double endings galore throughout the monologue, suggesting that Portia has much to say, that she is trying to say it before Brutus waves her away again (as he did at supper last night), and that she is agitated. Other indications of her inner turmoil are the numerous inverted (trochaic) feet at the beginnings of lines, giving them a blurted or emphatic tone, as well as some inverted feet located in the middles of lines at caesuras.

Don't forget to elide: *hour* (OWR) in line 251; *Even* (E'EN) in line 277; and *Brutus'* (BROO-tuss, *not* BROO-tuss-ez) in line 287;

. . . and to expand: *impatience* (im-PAY´-shee-ENCE) in line 248; *unbracèd* (un-BRAY-sehd) in line 262; and *unpurgèd* (un-PUR-jehd) in line 266.

Plutarch's Portia

The historical Portia (spelled "Porcia") was the daughter of the great statesman Marcus Porcius Cato ("Cato the Younger"), and she seems to have inherited many of his best qualities: honesty, integrity, and courage. She was well educated and described by the historian Plutarch as being "addicted to philosophy." Had she had the opportunity, she might have made a great statesperson herself. Porcia was married at a young age to Marcus Calpurnius Bibulus, who died leaving her with one son. That son, Bibulus, later wrote the *Memoirs of Brutus*, a brief account of the life of Porcia's second husband (and first cousin), Brutus, whom she married in 46 B.C.E., only two years before Caesar's murder. Plutarch portrays their marriage as mutually loving and respectful, recording that Brutus said of Portia that she "had a mind as valiant and as active for the good of her country as the best of us." The scene in which this monologue appears closely follows Plutarch's account of the events and the conversation it depicts. Shakespeare adheres to the lore that upon hearing of her husband's imminent defeat, Porcia committed suicide by swallowing hot coals. But historians believe that she chose to die by breathing in the fumes of burning coals rather than languish indefinitely with a chronic illness.

JULIUS CAESAR

ACT II, SCENE II

CALPHURNIA

GENDER: F
AGE RANGE: adult to mature adult
PROSE/VERSE: blank verse
FREQUENCY OF USE (1–5): 3

Calphurnia has had a hell of a night. She kept dreaming that her husband, Julius Caesar, dictator of Rome, was being murdered. While she tossed and turned in bed, a violent storm raged outside. When she got up to pace she saw and heard strange things, and was told of even more bizarre events seen by the night watchmen. Calphurnia is not one to believe superstitious mumbo-jumbo, but the things she saw and dreamed last night were completely abnormal, and she's terrified that something horrible will happen to her husband if he goes to the Senate today as planned. When she finds him preparing to go out, she attempts to stop him.

8 What mean you, Caesar? Think you to walk forth?
You shall not stir out of your house today.

Caesar, I never stood on ceremonies,
Yet now they fright me. There is one within,
15 Besides the things that we have heard and seen,
Recounts most horrid sights seen by the watch.
A lioness hath whelpèd in the streets,
And graves have yawned and yielded up their dead;
Fierce fiery warriors fight upon the clouds
20 In ranks and squadrons and right form of war,
Which drizzled blood upon the Capitol;
The noise of battle hurtled in the air,
Horses did neigh, and dying men did groan,
And ghosts did shriek and squeal about the streets.
25 O Caesar, these things are beyond all use,
And I do fear them.

30 When beggars die, there are no comets seen;
The heavens themselves blaze forth the death of princes.

1 minute

8 *mean you* do you intend; *Think you to walk forth* Do you intend to go out; 13 *stood on* made much of, attached importance to; *ceremonies* the ceremonial interpretation of omens or portents; 14 *one* someone; *within* in the next room; 16 *Recounts* who recounts; *watch* night watchmen; 17 *hath whelpèd* has given birth to cubs; 20 *ranks* rows of troops; *squadrons* groups of soldiers fighting in square formations; *right form of war* regular military formation [*Fierce . . . war* Calphurnia's imagery refers to either (1) lightning or (2) the aurora borealis, or northern lights]; 21 *clouds . . . Which drizzled blood* the blood that drizzles from the storm clouds is probably a reference to the "blood-rain" or "red rain" occurring in southern Europe, which is caused by sands from the Sahara Desert, which are whipped up into the atmosphere in sandstorms; *Capitol* the ancient Roman building in which the Senate assembled (also refers to the hill on which the Capitol building and the temple of Jupiter stood); 22 *hurtled* clashed, clattered; 24 *did shriek and squeal about* in Homer, Virgil, and Horace, ghosts make sounds similar to the squeals of bats; 25 *use* usual, normal experience [*beyond all use* completely abnormal]; 31 *blaze forth* both (1) proclaim (as with a trumpet) and (2) literally, flame forth [*When beggars die . . . princes* Calphurnia refers to the superstition that comets portended the deaths of great ones. Plutarch's *Lives*, Shakespeare's main source for *Julius Caesar*, reports a bright comet appearing after Caesar's death].

COMMENTARY

Calphurnia has a gut feeling that something is about to go disastrously wrong for Caesar. In this short piece, she uses every method she can think of to persuade her husband to stay home.

Calphurnia addresses Caesar with the formal and respectful *you* rather than the intimate "thou" that a wife might use. Nevertheless, she is clearly not cowed by him, as she starts off in the first two lines by giving her dictator husband a direct order not to *stir out of* [*his*] *house today*. Caesar is not shocked by her order, but simply states in the intervening lines that he *does* intend to go out. This gives us helpful information about Calphurnia's status in their relationship: she is accustomed to speaking her mind freely to him. Unfortunately, he is accustomed to ignoring her, so Calphurnia must find a new tactic in the next section, as her lines continue. We suggest that you treat lines 9 and 13 as contiguous, pausing only as long as you normally would at the end of a line and making a quick transition in that time. Since she believes this is a life-or-death situation, Calphurnia has to keep Caesar listening to keep him from leaving.

Calphurnia now assures Caesar that she has never been superstitious before, and she goes on to describe the previous night's events, trying to make him see that today's situation is unique. She uses several devices to stress the import of her words. For instance, she uses the emphatic form (*did neigh*; *did groan*; *did shriek*) to highlight some of the frightening sounds they heard during the night. Elsewhere, she uses pairs of words in which the first ends and the second begins with the same letter (*sights seen*; *and dying*; *comets seen*). When you separate the sounds, rather than slurring them as we do in everyday speech, the second word receives additional emphasis. This happens twice with the word *seen*, emphasizing the fact that these omens have actually been witnessed.

Omens are a major motif in the world Shakespeare created for the play. Although she has dismissed the validity of omens in the past, Calphurnia must take them seriously now that she's experiencing them firsthand and in such abundance. Shakespeare has begun your acting homework for you by providing detailed descriptions that engage most of the senses. Calphurnia's description of the night's events is thick with imagery, which builds toward a cacophony of frightening sounds. In addition, many of her words are either onomatopoeic or particularly expressive of their meanings, bringing her imagery to life (*yawned*; *Fierce*; *drizzled*; *neigh*; *groan*; *shriek*). The build may be subconscious or intentional: Calphurnia may simply be so frightened that the build happens as her fear feeds on itself. Or she may be deliberately using expressive sounds and imagery to impress upon Caesar the grave danger the omens portend. The sound of the word *O* is also quite expressive. For help with its delivery, see "O, No! An *O*!," page xxxiii.

The sound sequences in Calphurnia's plea to her husband aurally connect the piece from beginning to end. Collectively, they support the build and enhance Calphurnia's argument. Here are the predominant sound connections (you will find more!): EEs (*mean / Caesar*); soft Cs combined with Rs (*Caesar / never / stood / ceremonies*); Ss and Ts combined with EE and I sounds (*Recounts / most / sights / seen / lioness / streets*); Ys combined with Ns and Ds (*And / yawned and yielded / dead*); Fs and Rs combined with EE and I sounds (*Fierce / fiery / warriors / fight*); Rs and Ds (*ranks / squadrons and right form / war*); IHs (*Which / drizzled*); TLs (*battle / hurtled*); Rs and Ds again, combined with Ns (*Horses did neigh, and dying men did groan*); Ss and Ts again, combined with Ks (*ghosts / shriek / squeal / about / streets*); EEs again (*Caesar / these / beyond / fear*); EHs (*When / beggars / comets / heavens / themselves / death / princes*).

Within each line or phrase, the repeated sounds often lead to or echo the important word or words. For example, in lines 25–26 the EE sounds lead to the word *fear*, and in the last two lines the EH sounds resonate in the key words: *comets*, *death*, *princes*. In the piece as a whole, the repeated sounds are most often soft, mysterious Ss, Cs, or Fs, alternated or combined with hard driving Rs, Ns, and Ds, which help communicate both the eerie, supernatural quality of the events described and the dangerous, urgent nature of their message.

In line 26, two and a half feet of Caesar's dialogue have been excised to create this monologue. We suggest that you use the resulting silent feet to make the transition into your last two lines. Caesar has refused to believe that the night's portents have anything to do with him. Calphurnia must take her best shot to convince him that they do. You can take this moment to decide how: you may be appealing subtly to his ego; or simply revealing the logical conclusion based on your evidence; or blurting out a last-ditch attempt to stop him—your choice.

SIGNIFICANT SCANS

The third foot of line 9 (*out of*) is inverted, even though it follows a caesura that is not marked by punctuation (which is rare), making Calphurnia's command more forceful.

Line 25 is slightly tricky to scan. It is headless and has a silent half foot after *O*, as well as a double ending before the caesura and a crowded foot (*are beyond*):

```
        x    /    x     / (x)  x    /    x - x   /    x   /
(pause) O (pause) Caesar, these things are beyond all use
```

Don't forget to elide: *fiery* (FIE-ree) and *warriors* (WOR-yerz) in line 19; and *heavens* (HEV'NZ) in line 31;

. . . and to expand: *whelpèd* (WHEL-pehd) in line 17.

How Would He Like It If We Called Him "Shakespheare"?

Shakespeare and his contemporaries all spelled Calpurnia's name with the extra *h* found in their source, North's translation of Plutarch's *Lives*. This misspelling would have been irksome not only to the lady in question but to her father as well: he was a patriarch of the distinguished Piso family, of the renowned *Calpurnia* clan. He was also a powerful Roman general who had fought with Pompey against Caesar. You can guess where this is leading . . . Caesar's marriage to Calpurnia was arranged purely for political ends. So it is not surprising that it was not the model of wedded bliss. Not much more is known about Calpurnia, except that she was loyal and devoted to her philandering husband, and dutifully helped Antony's cause after Caesar was murdered, even though Antony's ally Octavius was merely her husband's appointed heir, and not their son.

JULIUS CAESAR

ACT III, SCENE i

ANTONY

GENDER: M
AGE RANGE: adult to mature adult
PROSE/VERSE: blank verse
FREQUENCY OF USE (1–5): 4

A group of patricians led by Marcus Brutus has just assassinated the dictator Julius Caesar, Mark Antony's close friend and mentor. Antony himself has been spared. Summoned to the scene of the murder minutes after it occurred, Antony has just pledged allegiance to Brutus in exchange for an explanation of the conspirators' motives and has shaken the bloody hand of each conspirator. Brutus has granted him permission to speak at Caesar's public funeral, and the conspirators have departed. Left alone with the still-bleeding corpse, Antony reveals his true intentions:

O pardon me, thou bleeding piece of earth,
255 That I am meek and gentle with these butchers!
Thou art the ruins of the noblest man
That ever livèd in the tide of times.
Woe to the hand that shed this costly blood!
Over thy wounds now do I prophesy—
260 Which like dumb mouths do ope their ruby lips
To beg the voice and utterance of my tongue—
A curse shall light upon the limbs of men;
Domestic fury and fierce civil strife
Shall cumber all the parts of Italy;
265 Blood and destruction shall be so in use,
And dreadful objects so familiar,
That mothers shall but smile when they behold
Their infants quartered with the hands of war,
All pity choked with custom of fell deeds;
270 And Caesar's spirit, ranging for revenge,
With Ate by his side come hot from hell,
Shall in these confines with a monarch's voice
Cry "Havoc" and let slip the dogs of war,
That this foul deed shall smell above the earth
275 With carrion men groaning for burial.

1 minute, 20 seconds

255 *gentle* (1) not violent; (2) behaving with civility (like a nobleman); 257 *the tide of times* the course of history, the course of time; 258 *costly* both (1) valuable and (2) expensive to the murderers; 260 *ope* open; 261 *To beg the voice and utterance of my tongue* i.e., to beg me to speak on their behalf; 262 *light upon* come down on, strike; 263 *Domestic fury* i.e., a storm of rage within the nation; *civil strife* civil war; 264 *cumber* overwhelm; harass, trouble; 265 *in use* commonplace, habitual; 266 *objects* sights; 267 *but* merely; 268 *quartered with* cut to pieces by, slaughtered by; 269 *custom* habituation to; *fell* cruel, savage [*All pity choked with custom of fell deeds* all normal pity having been ended by their habituation to cruel acts]; 270 *ranging* roaming, roving; 271 *Ate* (AH-tay) Greek goddess of discord and retribution; *hot* full of fury; violent; 272 *confines* territories; 273 *"Havoc"* a war cry shouted by monarchs, ordering their soldiers to commit indiscriminate, unrestrained mass slaughter, destruction, and pillage; *let slip* unleash (a "slip" was a leash from which racing greyhounds could be easily released); 274 *That* so that; 275 *carrion* dead and rotting.

COMMENTARY

If you're looking for high drama in a monologue, look no further. Just imagine the situation: Antony's close friend and mentor, Julius Caesar, has just been viciously murdered. As Caesar's right-hand man, Antony fully expected that his life would be taken as well, but oddly, he's been spared. He has just had to act conciliatory toward Caesar's killers, all the while confronted by the sight of his beloved friend's mutilated corpse, still lying in a pool of its own blood. We can imagine that it has taken every ounce of willpower to hold back his grief and rage.

Now that Antony is alone with Caesar's body, he can finally pour out his true thoughts and feelings. And he does. You'll notice that the sounds in this monologue hold the key that unlocks Antony's state of mind. He starts right out with a woeful *O* (followed and reinforced a bit later with the O sounds in *noblest / Woe / Over*)—for help exploiting the sound of the word *O* to its best advantage, see "O, No! An *O*!," page xxxiii. As soon as he gives vent to his first *O*, he immediately blurts out exPlosive Ps and Bs (*pardon / bleeding piece / butchers*). These sounds support the idea that he's been choking back his real thoughts while making nice with the enemy, and has wanted to burst. Notice the grIEving, wEEping EEs (*me / bleeding piece / meek*). Some of the sounds are onomatopoeic and bolster Antony's imagery (*meek*; *Cry*; *slip*; *groaning*). The consonance and assonance woven through the piece create a sense of continuity and a natural escalation of intensity. Some examples: Ts and Vs (*That ever livèd in the tide of times*); Ds (*livèd / tide / hand / shed / blood*); Fs and Ss (*Domestic fury and fierce civil strife*); ORs (*quartered / war*); Rs and Js (*ranging for revenge*); UMs and Hs (*come hot from hell*); AHs and Ks (*hot / confines / monarch's / Cry "Havoc"*); and Ns (*carrion men groaning*).

Antony often ends one word and starts the next with the same consonant. It is important that you enunciate each separately rather than slurring them together. (Examples: lines 254–55 [*earth / That*; *am meek*]; line 260 [*dumb mouths*]; line 262 [*shall light*]; line 263 [*fierce civil*]; line 265 [*and destruction*]; line 266 [*And dreadful*; *objects so*]; line 268 [*with the*]; line 269 [*of fell*]; line 270 [*Caesar's spirit*]; line 271 [*his side*].) Listen to the effect that separating these sounds has on the timbre of the piece. Antony sounds like he is spitting out his words—his loathing for the conspirators, bitterness at the murder of his beloved friend, and fierce determination to wreak revenge become, literally, pronounced.

Antony uses imagery throughout the monologue, first to express his most sincere apology to Caesar for making nice with his murderers, then to vow revenge in the most graphic, horrifying detail—even upon the innocent. Notice that he specifically mentions Caesar's wounds, calling them *dumb mouths*, that *do ope their ruby lips / To beg the voice and utterance of my tongue*. Antony will not let himself or the audience forget for a minute that Caesar died a violent and horrible death. He then describes the effects of the civil war he will launch, using imagery that suggests his relish of the wholesale, indiscriminate carnage to ensue. Or perhaps he considers it the inevitable result of such a traitorous act or hopes the war will turn the masses against the conspirators whose assassination of Caesar sparked it.

The prophecy grows more specific in detail and imagery as it progresses, from the vague *A curse shall light upon the limbs of men* to the more specific *civil strife* to the shockingly vivid *Blood and destruction shall be so in use . . . That mothers shall but smile when they behold / Their infants quartered with the hands of war* and the equally detailed image of Caesar's ghost, with the goddess of discord at his side, shouting "*Havoc*" and releasing *the dogs of war*, who will leave corpses begging to be buried. Remember that Shakespeare's contemporaries believed in ghosts; the image of Caesar's ghost was a bone-chillingly real possibility. Also notice that Antony's imagery calls upon most of the senses: the sights of blood and bloodshed, the sounds of war cries, the tactile feeling of being choked, the smell of rotting human carcasses.

SIGNIFICANT SCANS

In scanning this monologue, you'll notice that there are no mid-line stops, suggesting that in a measured, controlled, and calculating way Antony is setting forth the punishment he will exact for Caesar's murder. As his images become more vivid and horrific, his sentences grow longer; although he is in control of his thoughts, he gives himself increasing license to enjoy visualizing his revenge.

Antony inverts the first foot in each of three consecutive lines (lines 258–60), punching the first syllable of each. These are the lines in which he commences his curse of Caesar's killers, and the emphatic variation in meter makes the curse sound all the more venomous. He also inverts the first foot of line 265, which startles the audience by emphasizing the word *Blood*, paving the way for the more horrifying images to come. Lines 259 and 275 have inverted feet mid-line, following caesuras that are not marked by punctuation (a rare occurence):

/ x x / / x x / x /
Over thy wounds now do I prophesy

x / x / / x x / x /
With carrion men groaning for burial

Line 259 grabs the listeners' attention, prepping them to listen with anticipation to Antony's "prophecy." Its echo in line 275, the final line, wraps up the piece on a strong, aggressive note.

Don't forget to elide: *utterance* (UTT-rance) in line 261 and *carrion* (CA-ryun) in line 275;

. . . and to expand: *familiar* (fa-MIL´-ee-ER) in line 266.

Antony A-Go-Go

Historians may quibble about particular details of the life of Marcus Antonius, but all agree that he was the life of the toga party. After a dissipated youth, Antony became a cavalry commander. He joined his cousin Julius Caesar in conquering parts of Gaul for the Roman Empire, and served him with dedication throughout the subsequent civil war against Pompey the Great. He proved instrumental to Caesar's defeat of Pompey when he and Caesar launched a successful two-pronged attack, each leading part of their forces and attacking simultaneously from opposite directions. Antony was a competent but not outstanding general, and became Caesar's right-hand man principally because of his unswerving loyalty. Shakespeare's depiction of Antony follows Plutarch's *Life of Antony* fairly closely. After Caesar's murder, Antony did in fact deliver a moving oration that incited the commoners to drive the conspirators from Rome. In *Antony and Cleopatra*, Shakespeare exploits Antony's reputation as a party animal, going so far as to imply that his love of the good life and his relationship with Cleopatra were to blame for his downfall. Nevertheless, the playwright portrays Antony more evenhandedly than did Plutarch, who scorned Antony's hedonism as moral weakness. The real cause of Antony's downfall was a complex combination of political and military factors, including Octavius's shrewd use of propaganda against him (which caused a loss of support within the Roman population and his own ranks), Antony's poor strategic planning, and the diminished and inferior resources he had with which to fight the civil war. Antony's retreat in the Battle of Actium was merely the final straw in his defeat.

JULIUS CAESAR

ACT III, SCENE ii

BRUTUS

GENDER: M | AGE RANGE: mature adult
PROSE/VERSE: prose | FREQUENCY OF USE (1–5): 3

Marcus Brutus has just led a conspiracy to assassinate Julius Caesar to prevent him from becoming emperor and to protect Rome's republican form of government (in which all nobles were represented). Now, at Caesar's funeral, Brutus must address an angry crowd of commoners. Caesar was popular, and the common people are not inclined to accept Brutus's claim that the assassination was justified.

Romans, countrymen and lovers, hear me for my
15 cause, and be silent that you may hear. Believe me
for mine honor, and have respect to mine honor
that you may believe. Censure me in your wisdom,
and awake your senses that you may the better
judge. If there be any in this assembly, any dear
20 friend of Caesar's, to him I say that Brutus' love to
Caesar was no less than his. If then that friend demand
why Brutus rose against Caesar, this is my
answer: Not that I loved Caesar less, but that I
loved Rome more. Had you rather Caesar were living,
25 and die all slaves, than that Caesar were dead,
to live all freemen? As Caesar loved me, I weep for
him; as he was fortunate, I rejoice at it; as he was
valiant, I honor him; but, as he was ambitious, I
slew him. There is tears for his love, joy for his
30 fortune, honor for his valor, and death for his
ambition. Who is here so base that would be a
bondman? If any, speak—for him have I offended.
Who is here so rude that would not be a Roman? If
any, speak—for him have I offended. Who is here
35 so vile that will not love his country? If any,
speak—for him have I offended. I pause for a reply.

[PLEBEIANS: *None, Brutus, none.*]

14 *lovers* friends; well-wishers; *hear me for my cause* (1) hear out the reason I assassinated Caesar; (2) hear out the cause I supported; (3) hear the case I shall present before you (here *cause* means a cause of action in law); 16 *for* for the sake of; *have respect to mine honor* bear in mind that I am a man of honor; 17 *Censure* Judge (without today's negative connotation); *in* i.e., using; 18 *senses* minds, mental powers, faculties of thinking; *the better judge* judge more discriminately; 26 *to live all* so that you all may live as; *freemen* Roman men with the status of "freemen" enjoyed particular personal, civil, and political freedoms of citizenship not granted to slaves; 27 *fortunate* here, successful, prosperous; 31 *base* lowly; low-minded; *that would be* that he would choose to be, that he wouldn't mind being; 32 *bondman* a slave; *him* i.e., that person; 33 *rude* uncivilized, barbarous; *that would not be a Roman* i.e., that chooses not to participate in Rome's highly advanced, progressive, and civilized society; 35 *vile* wretched, lowly, menial; *that will not love his country* i.e., that he does not love his country enough to sacrifice the ambitious Caesar to preserve the greater good; 39 *than you shall do to Brutus* i.e., than I'd expect you to do to me under similar circumstances; *The question / of his death* the considera-

Then none have I offended. I have done no more
to Caesar than you shall do to Brutus. The question
40 of his death is enrolled in the Capitol: his glory not
extenuated, wherein he was worthy; nor his offenses enforced, for which he suffered death.
[*Enter Mark Antony (and others) with Caesar's body*]
Here comes his body, mourned by Mark Antony,
45 who, though he had no hand in his death, shall receive the benefit of his dying: a place in the Commonwealth—as which of you shall not? With this I
depart: that, as I slew my best lover for the good of
Rome, I have the same dagger for myself when it
50 shall please my country to need my death.

2 minutes, 20 seconds

tions that led to the decision to assassinate him; 40 *enrolled* recorded (written on rolls of parchment) and registered; *the Capitol* the fort or castle adjacent to the temple of Jupiter (the supreme Roman god), atop a hill in Rome, where the ancient Roman Senate assembled; 41 *extenuated* diminished, undervalued; *wherein* for which (referring to Caesar's glory); 42 *enforced* overly emphasized; 46 *a place in the Commonwealth* a place in the body politic (i.e., citizenship with all the rights of a freeman); 50 *need* consider necessary, call for.

COMMENTARY

Brutus is faced with a daunting task: Caesar was beloved by the commoners of Rome. They demand to know why he was killed, and Brutus must answer them. He realizes that he is, in effect, on trial and must sway the jury—the commoners. This may explain the quick progression in his first words to the crowd; these terms of address increase in familiarity from *Romans* (which does not directly establish a relationship between himself and the crowd) to *countrymen* (which establishes the bond of shared nationality, and hence shared purpose, background, identity, heritage, culture, etc.—but still not necessarily intimacy) to *lovers* (dear friends of his). It is yours to decide whether he has chosen this progression of appellations in advance to draw the people in, or is amending his greeting impromptu, based on the chilly reception he receives from the crowd. The embedded stage direction in his follow-up phrase—*and be silent that you may hear*—suggests that the crowd may not yet have piped down for his speech, prompting an admonition from Brutus.

Brutus adopts a rational, straightforward, and logical style and approach. To persuade the crowd, he relies most heavily on two rhetorical devices: The first is chiasmus, the inversion of the second of two parallel phrases or clauses (for example, *Believe me for mine honor, and have respect to mine honor that you may believe*). In lines 14–19 he uses chiasmus to tell the crowd that he respects its judgment and trusts that the group will soberly consider all the factors (the chief one being his own inherently honorable nature). He is also subtly reminding them to act accordingly. The second device is antithesis, which Brutus uses to sway the opinion of the crowd, setting up a stark "either/or" scenario: either support my killing of Caesar or publicly proclaim yourself a barbarous, traitorous slave. By firing off three antithetical pairings in rapid succession, he fuels the crowd's emotional investment in his position before they can think twice about it (*Not that I loved Caesar less, but that I loved Rome more. Had you rather Caesar were living, and die all slaves, than that Caesar were dead, to live all freemen?*). And by choosing the interrogatory format (and asking questions with foregone conclusions), Brutus forces the people of Rome to voice their support of his position.

In lines 26–36 Brutus uses repetition of phrases and ideas to create a build in the monologue. Lines 29–31 repeat in a kind of shorthand what he has just said in lines 26–29, building his pace and intensity and helping him carry his listeners away in the current of his rationalization. Perhaps he also feels that the people will not comprehend unless he "dumbs it down" and spells it out for them. In addition, notice his use of consonance to tie his thoughts together (*base / bondman*; *rude / Roman*; *vile / love*) and his use of repetition to tie the whole segment together (*Who is here so . . . If any, speak—for him have I offended*). The repetition of words, phrases, and structure forms a crescendo, bolstered by the build in adjectives from *base* to *rude* (worse) to *vile* (worst).

Dropping the rhetorical devices, Brutus then tries to legitimize the murder by likening it to a governmental procedure, mentioning that the issues concerning Caesar's assassination are *enrolled in the Capitol*, where affairs of state are conducted and law is both created and enforced. He is also suggesting that the crowd not condemn him too hastily, before reviewing the record, possibly hoping that even if he hasn't completely convinced the crowd, he might at least avert an immediate riot.

When Antony arrives with Caesar's coffin, Brutus introduces him. He uses Antony's participation in the funeral to demonstrate that Caesar's right-hand man is in his camp. Brutus may feel entirely confident of Antony's loyalty, since they did shake hands over Caesar's bloody body. Or he may suspect Antony's motives and seek to undermine Antony's speech by implying that Antony's innocence of the murder is shameful: although Antony *had no hand in* Caesar's death, he—like all Romans—benefits from it. When Brutus reiterates that he selflessly killed his best friend for the good of Rome, he may also be subtly suggesting that Antony placed his friendship with Caesar (and the attendant power he enjoyed) above the needs of the people. Moreover, Brutus is fully prepared to commit the ultimate act of selflessness—suicide—should the people demand it of him. (Would Antony do the same?)

P.S.

For information on the historical Brutus, see "Revisionist History: Brutus in Brief," page 601.

JULIUS CAESAR

ACT III, SCENE ii

ANTONY

GENDER: M
PROSE/VERSE: blank verse
AGE RANGE: adult to mature adult
FREQUENCY OF USE (1–5): 4

Until a few days ago, Mark Antony was right-hand man to Julius Caesar, the dictator of Rome. Now everything has changed. Caesar has been murdered by a group of patricians led by Brutus, the most respected patrician in Rome, and Cassius, an influential Roman general. Antony has pretended to make peace with the conspirators, and has persuaded Brutus to allow him to speak here at Caesar's funeral. Brutus has just delivered his speech, explaining that Caesar was ambitious and had to be sacrificed to protect the Roman republic. Now it's Antony's turn. This is his chance to sway the people through subtle manipulation, and to put the conspirators on the defensive while he and his ally, Octavius Caesar (Julius Caesar's heir), prepare to fight them. If he can get the people riled up, they may even run the murderers out of town. With this goal in mind, Antony addresses the crowd:

Friends, Romans, countrymen, lend me your ears.
I come to bury Caesar, not to praise him.
80 The evil that men do lives after them,
The good is oft interrèd with their bones;
So let it be with Caesar. The noble Brutus
Hath told you Caesar was ambitious;
If it were so, it was a grievous fault,
85 And grievously hath Caesar answered it.
Here, under leave of Brutus and the rest
(For Brutus is an honorable man,
So are they all; all honorable men)
Come I to speak in Caesar's funeral.
90 He was my friend, faithful and just to me,
But Brutus says he was ambitious,
And Brutus is an honorable man.
He hath brought many captives home to Rome,
Whose ransoms did the general coffers fill;
95 Did this in Caesar seem ambitious?
When that the poor have cried, Caesar hath wept;
Ambition should be made of sterner stuff—
Yet Brutus says he was ambitious,
And Brutus is an honorable man.
100 You all did see that on the Lupercal
I thrice presented him a kingly crown
Which he did thrice refuse. Was this ambition?
Yet Brutus says he was ambitious,
And sure he is an honorable man.
105 I speak not to disprove what Brutus spoke,
But here I am to speak what I do know:
You all did love him once, not without cause.

81 *interrèd* buried (Shakespeare was fully aware that the ancient Romans cremated their dead, and makes reference to it later in the play. He often used contemporary references [such as the custom of burial, here] that made his ideas more accessible to his Elizabethan audience); 82 *noble* (1) of noble birth; and possibly (2) dignified, magnanimous, lofty; 84 *If it were so* i.e., if he was ambitious; *grievous* criminal; deserving censure and punishment; 85 *grievously* at a terrible, high price (with a play on the word *grievance*, implying that Caesar's punishment was unjust); *hath Caesar answered it* Caesar has paid the penalty for it; 86 *under leave* with the permission; *the rest* i.e., the other conspirators who murdered Caesar; 93 *He* i.e., Caesar; 94 *coffers* chests holding money [*general coffers* the public treasury]; 96 *When that* When; *cried* cried out; 97 *sterner* more hard-hearted, less compassionate; 100 *the Lupercal* February 15, the day of Lupercalia, an ancient Roman festival celebrated to ensure the fertility of people, fields, and

What cause withholds you then to mourn for him?
O judgment! Thou art fled to brutish beasts,
110 And men have lost their reason. —Bear with me.
My heart is in the coffin there with Caesar,
And I must pause till it come back to me.
[*He weeps*]

But yesterday the word of Caesar might
Have stood against the world; now lies he there,
125 And none so poor to do him reverence.
O masters, if I were disposed to stir
Your hearts and minds to mutiny and rage
I should do Brutus wrong and Cassius wrong,
Who, you all know, are honorable men.
130 I will not do them wrong; I rather choose
To wrong the dead, to wrong myself and you,
Than I will wrong such honorable men.
But here's a parchment with the seal of Caesar;
I found it in his closet—'tis his will.
135 Let but the commons hear this testament—
Which, pardon me, I do not mean to read—
And they would go and kiss dead Caesar's wounds
And dip their napkins in his sacred blood,
Yea, beg a hair of him for memory
140 And, dying, mention it within their wills,
Bequeathing it as a rich legacy
Unto their issue.

2 minutes

3 minutes, 15 seconds

flocks; 104 *sure* assuredly, certainly; 108 *withholds . . . to mourn for* i.e., keeps you from mourning for him; 109 *judgment* judgment, personified; *Thou art fled* You have run away; *brutish* bestial (with a play on Brutus's name, and on the Latin adjective *brutus*, which means "dull," "stupid," or "irrational"); 123 *But* Only; *word* command; 124 *stood against* withstood, resisted; 125 *none so poor to do him reverence* no one is so low in rank as to be lower than he, and thus owe him reverence; 126 *masters* a common, respectful title used to address men; 128 *should* would; 131 *the dead* i.e., Caesar; 133 *parchment* document written on sheepskin; *seal* impression made in wax to seal a document; 134 *closet* either (1) locked box, cabinet, or storage space or (2) private study; 135 *Let but the commons* Just let the common people; 136 *mean* intend, plan; 138 *napkins* handkerchiefs; 139 *Yea* often, as here, used to affirm what has just been said; *beg a hair of him* beg him for one of his hairs; *for memory* as a remembrance; 140 *dying* i.e., when they die; 142 *issue* children; descendants (i.e., heirs).

COMMENTARY

Antony is a talented orator who has his audience pegged. This speech is full of techniques with which he wraps the uneducated plebeians around his clever little pinky. Antony tailors this speech to his audience, using simple words, simple grammar, and simple ideas, and appealing to basic emotions such as anger, self-righteousness, and greed. He uses reverse psychology and takes advantage of mob mentality. Yet Antony's own complex intelligence is evident in his method. He intersperses simple statements of fact with rhetorical questions to make his argument sound Socratic, so that his listeners believe they are responding to logic; in fact he is manipulating his listeners, leading them to make erroneous leaps of logic. This illusion of logical progression is supported by the repetition of certain words used in successive statements that sound logical, but which in reality neither prove nor disprove Brutus's claims against Caesar (*spoke / speak*—105–6; *cause*—107–8; *wrong*—130–32). This "logic" stirs up anger over Caesar's death with recollections that rekindle their positive emotions toward him.

Irony is Antony's core technique for manipulating the crowd: by repeating the phrase *Brutus is an honorable man*, Antony slowly builds doubt as to the truth of the statement. In the same way, he casts doubt on the truth of Brutus's claim that Caesar was *ambitious*, without overtly seeming to do so. In both cases, he consistently expands *honorable* and *ambitious* to fit the meter, creating a sarcastic tone around *honorable* and making *ambitious* sound trumped-up and ridiculous. When Antony uses the word *ambition* to question Brutus's claim, he does not expand the word, which makes his portrayal of Caesar seem sensible in contrast to Brutus's distorted one.

As the ironic repetitions continue, Antony creates a build in the ironic tension. Some examples: in lines 84–85, he puns on *grievous* and *grievously* (see Annotation); in line 104, he adds torque to the irony of *Brutus is an honorable man*, making it *sure he is an honorable man*; and in 109, he puns on *Brutus* with *brutish*. But remember that what makes the speech so effective is the fact that Antony is not presenting his irony outright to the crowd. Like an actor, he is "playing" just the opposite—utter sincerity, sorrow, and perplexity at the situation.

The meter of the piece reveals that Antony is also a master of oratory vocal technique. There are several inverted (trochaic) feet, both at the beginnings of lines and after caesuras, which makes your delivery forceful and thus persuasive.

The very first line of the piece is headless and has a silent syllable after the first caesura, as well as two crowded feet (—*trymen lend* and *me your ears*). Although technically iambic, the line sounds as though its first four feet are trochaic, which helps Antony grab the attention of the crowd:

```
    x      /       x      / x      / x - x    /   x - x    /
(pause) Friends, (pause) Romans, countrymen, lend me your ears
```

After its unusual first line, the monologue's meter is extremely regular, with very few double endings and very little variation around caesuras. Because sentences frequently begin and end mid-line, there is a briefer pause between them than there would be if they began and ended at line breaks. The combination of these factors creates a continuous movement through the piece, suggesting that Antony keeps the energy flowing in his attempt to rile up the crowd.

Little bursts of assonance and consonance throughout the piece make it more persuasive and memorable, especially as the first section builds toward the pause in which he weeps (*home* / *Rome*; *Did this in* / *ambitious*; *sterner stuff*; *kingly crown*; *speak* / *disprove* / *spoke* / *speak*; *love* / *once*; *brutish beasts*). In the second section, small sound groupings (*were* / *stir*; *minds* / *mutiny*) give way to richer combinations of assonance and consonance in many phrases, as Antony works the crowd into a frenzy over Caesar's will: (kiss / dip / napkins in his; it in his closet—'tis his will; pardon me, I do not mean to read; hair of him for memory; it within their wills). Also note that when you pronounce both of the abutting Ds in *And dying*, rather than slurring them as we do in everyday speech, the second word receives extra emphasis, increasing the resonance of the final idea of the piece. And for help exploiting the sound of the word *O* to its best advantage, see "O, No! An *O*!," page xxxiii.

There is an obvious embedded stage direction between the two sections (*I must pause . . .*); here, Antony pauses while the plebeians converse. If you're using both sections of this piece as a continuous monologue, you'll have to build in a short pause in which to weep and recover. This brings up the most important question for an actor preparing this piece: how much of Antony's emotion is honest and how much is for show? Did he intend to weep? He genuinely loved Caesar; perhaps he has unintentionally aroused his own grief. He may also have been manipulating not only the crowd but also his own honest emotions to achieve an effect, as actors often do.

Don't forget to elide: *general* (JEN-rul) in line 94 and *Cassius* (CA-syuss or CA-shuss) in line 128;

. . . and to expand: *interrèd* (in-TER-ehd) in line 81; *ambitious* (am-BIH´-shee-USS) in lines 83, 91, 95, 98, and 103 (but <u>not</u> *Ambition* in lines 97 and 102); *honorable* (ON´-er-UH-bl) in lines 87, 88, 92, 99, 104, 129, and 132; *reverence* (REH´-ver-ENSS) in line 125; and *memory* (MEH´-muh-REE) in line 139.

One final note: if you have the opportunity to present a longer monologue, this piece can be linked with the following one (see page 630).

P.S.

For information about the historical Antony, see "Antony A-Go-Go," page 619.

JULIUS CAESAR

ACT III, SCENE ii

ANTONY

GENDER: M
PROSE/VERSE: blank verse
AGE RANGE: adult to mature adult
FREQUENCY OF USE (1–5): 4

Antony, Julius Caesar's right-hand man, geniunely loved the mighty general/dictator, whose recent assassination caused him enormous grief. Antony pretended to pledge allegiance to Caesar's assassins, but secretly vowed to wage a bloody civil war against them. Marcus Brutus, the leader of the conspiracy against Caesar, granted Antony permission to speak at Caesar's funeral, which is now under way. Brutus was first to address the people of Rome, explaining that Caesar was slain to protect their liberty from his greedy ambition to rule. Easily persuaded by Brutus, the people called for him to be crowned. Antony has just brought Caesar's body before the people and has refuted Brutus's claim that Caesar was ambitious, "insisting" all the while that Brutus is an honorable person who must have had good reason for his actions (see monologue, page 625). Having easily swayed the people away from Brutus, he now descends from the pulpit into the crowd, where Caesar's casket rests, shows them the toga in which Caesar was murdered, and says:

ANTONY

If you have tears, prepare to shed them now.
You all do know this mantle. I remember
175 The first time ever Caesar put it on:
'Twas on a summer's evening in his tent,
That day he overcame the Nervii.
Look, in this place ran Cassius' dagger through;
See what a rent the envious Casca made;
180 Through this the well-belovèd Brutus stabbed,
And, as he plucked his cursèd steel away,
Mark how the blood of Caesar followed it,
As rushing out of doors to be resolved
If Brutus so unkindly knocked or no,
185 For Brutus, as you know, was Caesar's angel.
Judge, O you gods, how dearly Caesar loved him!
This was the most unkindest cut of all,
For when the noble Caesar saw him stab,
Ingratitude, more strong than traitors' arms,
190 Quite vanquished him. Then burst his mighty heart,
And, in his mantle muffling up his face,
Even at the base of Pompey's statue—
Which all the while ran blood—great Caesar fell.
O, what a fall was there, my countrymen!
195 Then I, and you, and all of us fell down,

174 *mantle* cloak [here, toga]; 177 *the Nervii* (NUR´-vee-IE) a fierce tribe of ancient Gaul (from a region now in Belgium), conquered by Caesar in a decisive and celebrated victory in 57 B.C.E. Antony was not actually present at that battle; 178 *Cassius'* i.e., Caius Cassius Longinus, who originated the plot to assassinate Caesar [*in this place ran Cassius' dagger through* this is the spot on the toga where Cassius's dagger ran through it]; 179 *rent* slit, tear, gash; *envious* malicious, spiteful; *Casca* i.e., Publius Servius Casca, one of the coconspirators against Caesar; 180 *well-belovèd* i.e., by Caesar; 181 *plucked* pulled, tugged; *steel* weapon; 182 *Mark* see, perceive; 183 *As* as though; *to be resolved* to be freed from uncertainty, to be sure, to be informed; 184 *unkindly* cruelly; *knocked* rapped at the door (with a play on another meaning of *knocked*, "struck down"); *or no* or not; 185 *angel* favorite; 187 *the most unkindest* the most hard-hearted (with a second meaning, "unnatural," which could refer to the outside possibility that Brutus committed patricide [since it was rumored that his mother had had an affair with Caesar around the time of his birth]); 189 *traitors' arms* the weapons of traitors [*Ingratitude . . . traitor's arms* i.e., the ingratitude of friends, which has a stronger impact than the weapons of enemy traitors]; 191 *muffling up* covering up; 192 *Even* here used as a term of emphasis; *Pompey's* i.e., Gnaius Pompeius Magnus, a.k.a. Pompey the Great, Roman general and statesman, enemy of Caesar defeated and killed by him in 48 B.C.E.; 193 *ran* spouted [*Pompey's statue . . . ran blood* i.e., even Caesar's enemy felt empathy for him. (In Shakespeare's time it was believed that the corpse [here, the statue] of a murdered man would bleed in the presence of his murderer. Antony suggests that even someone Caesar killed felt that Caesar's assassination was unjust)]; *fell* both

Whilst bloody treason flourished over us.
O, now you weep, and I perceive you feel
The dint of pity. These are gracious drops.
Kind souls, what, weep you when you but behold
200 Our Caesar's vesture wounded? Look you here—
Here is himself, marred, as you see, with traitors.

1 minute, 45 seconds

Good friends, sweet friends, let me not stir you up
215 To such a sudden flood of mutiny.
They that have done this deed are honorable.
What private griefs they have, alas, I know not,
That made them do it. They are wise and honorable,
And will no doubt with reasons answer you.
220 I come not, friends, to steal away your hearts.
I am no orator, as Brutus is,
But—as you know me all—a plain blunt man
That love my friend; and that they know full well
That gave me public leave to speak of him.
225 For I have neither wit, nor words, nor worth,
Action, nor utterance, nor the power of speech
To stir men's blood; I only speak right on.
I tell you that which you yourselves do know,
Show you sweet Caesar's wounds, poor poor dumb mouths,
230 And bid them speak for me. But were I Brutus,
And Brutus Antony, there were an Antony
Would ruffle up your spirits and put a tongue
In every wound of Caesar that should move
The stones of Rome to rise and mutiny.

3 minutes

(1) died and (2) was overthrown; 196 *flourished over us* both (1) brandished a sword over us and (2) sounded a trumpet in triumph; 198 *dint* impression, dent (i.e., slight effect); *gracious* benevolent; virtuous; *drops* i.e., teardrops; 199 *what* here, an expression of mock surprise; *but* merely; 200 *vesture* garment; 201 *himself* i.e., Caesar himself; *marred* destroyed, disfigured, defaced; *with* by; 217 *private griefs* personal grievances [*What private griefs they have, alas, I know not, / That made them do it* I don't know what personal grievances they have that made them do it]; 219 *with reasons answer you* i.e., explain their motives to you; 222 *as you know me all* as you all know me to be; 223 *That love* who loves, or who loved; 224 *public leave to speak of him* permission to speak publicly about him; 225 *wit* intelligence; *worth* merit, deservedness; 226 *Action* the knack for gestures (accompanying spoken words); *utterance* skill at elocution; *the power of speech* the power to speak persuasively or movingly; 227 *To stir men's blood* to rouse people's passions and emotions; *right on* straightforwardly, directly; 228 *that* i.e., those facts; 230 *bid them speak for me* ask them to speak for me (i.e., let them speak for me); 231 *there were* that would be; 232 *Would* who would; *ruffle up* stir up into a rage; 233 *should* would.

COMMENTARY

In Mark Antony, Shakespeare has created a character rife with paradox. He is at once a sympathetic character who displays integrity and a manipulative schemer. Upon Caesar's death, for example, Antony's outpouring of love and grief for Caesar makes him a sympathetic character, while the relish with which he plots the destruction of innocent lives to avenge Caesar's murder makes him anything but (see monologue, page 615). Likewise, in this monologue (which continues Antony's oration to the people of Rome at Caesar's funeral; see monologue, page 625) Antony's shrewd and calculated manipulation of Rome's commoners is of questionable integrity. Yet it is clear that, though manipulative, the speech is not false; Antony passionately believes everything he says.

Like a prosecutor delivering his closing argument to the jury, Antony wants his listeners to experience the assassination as though they'd been there themselves, to feel the full impact of the brutality, and to "convict" the conspirators. And so he re-creates the crime in detail, painting the perps as vicious traitors, illustrating the victim's agony (both physical and mental), and describing the scene in all its violent horror. Antony purposely names the three conspirators most responsible for the bloody act. He walks his listeners through the deed one stab at a time, so that they will realize how long it took for Caesar to fall. He lingers over the moment that Caesar realized that his favorite had betrayed him: according to Antony, it was not the multiple stab wounds that stopped Caesar's heart, but the realization that Brutus was among his murderers.

Of course, Antony doesn't actually know which conspirator made which rip in Caesar's cloak—he wasn't there when Caesar was stabbed. And Antony doesn't know whether the toga he presents to the crowd is the very one Caesar wore when he defeated the Nervii (it probably wasn't; he defeated them thirteen years earlier!), but by saying it was, Antony reminds the Romans of Caesar's long history of bravery on their behalf. Does Antony make all of this up to manipulate the crowd? Or, in his torment over Caesar's death, has he imagined the murder scene over and over, so that the version he presents to the crowd feels completely real to him? After all, knowing Caesar as well as he does, he has correctly intuited Caesar's response to Brutus at the time of the attack. The answer probably lies somewhere between these two options . . . the decision is yours.

Antony uses his description of the assassination to lay the groundwork for his argument: we all fell with Caesar, because *bloody treason* triumphed. *Treason* is a powerful word, made all the more vile by the modifier *bloody*. Notice the different ways in which Antony uses blood imagery. Even the statue of Caesar's enemy Pompey abhors Caesar's murder and spouts sympathetic blood (making these images specific for yourself will help you convey their horror to your audience). Mentioning Pompey further serves to remind the people of Caesar's valiant acts in their service. Antony is deliberately stirring up the people of Rome to riot against the conspirators while disclaiming that he is doing so; the riot must seem like the people's own idea. Antony knows that Brutus has just convinced the crowd of his justification for killing Caesar, and they have just called for him to be crowned. One wrong move, and this crowd could rip Antony limb from limb. He *must* appear conciliatory, and let the people think that they are drawing their own conclusions. Notice the ways in which Antony undermines Brutus:

- Every time he seems to compliment Brutus, Antony actually points out the extent of Brutus's betrayal of Caesar (*well-belovèd Brutus*; *Brutus . . . was Caesar's angel*; *They that have done this deed are honorable*; *They are wise and honorable*; *I am no orator, as Brutus is*). Notice how he amends his description of the assassins, building from *honorable* to *wise and honorable*. Who could accuse him of slandering them when he praises them so extravagantly?
- Of all the stab wounds Caesar received, that of Brutus was *the most unkindest cut*. Note the double superlative he employs for emphasis;
- He calls Brutus's act merely *Ingratitude* (but notes that it is *more strong than traitors' arms*).
- He contrasts himself—*a plain blunt man*—with Brutus, with the implication that Brutus is a "sharp" man, who has just used cunning to sway the populace.

Antony's speaking style backs up his claim to be *a plain blunt man*. Note the preponderance of one-syllable words in this monologue (for example, *But—as you know me all—a plain blunt man that love my friend*, all plain, blunt words). He even elides *utterance* in line 226, illustrating his point that elocution is not his strong suit. Antony's longer words stand out in contrast. And notice the two he lengthens on purpose: *belovèd* and *cursèd*. The juxtaposition of these two expanded words in sequential lines expresses the enormity of Brutus's betrayal with just two words. Be careful with the simple words: you do not want to imbue them with undue "emotionality." Ironically, simple words pack their biggest punches when delivered simply. Save the grander delivery for the grander material, which is also here. By contrast with the simpler stuff, it, in turn, will have a bigger impact.

Antony is not as artless a speaker as he professes to be. He ties his oratory together with the help of assonance and consonance, which weave through the piece, creating a sense of unification, motion, and intensity, and sweeping up the listener: Some examples (there are more): *remember / ever / tent / rent / envious; ran Cassius' dagger / Casca / stabbed / And, as; unkindly knocked or no; no / know / O; stab / Ingratitude / than / vanquished; mighty / mantle muffling; over / O; weep / perceive / feel; dint of pity; what, weep you when you but behold / wounded; here / Here / himself; friends / friends; up / such / sudden flood; They that have done this deed; neither wit, nor words, nor worth / Action, nor utterance, nor the power;* etc. And for help exploiting the sound of the word *O* to its best advantage, see "O, No! An *O*!," page xxxiii.

The images Antony chooses seem simple—they are not flowery and are always employed to make direct points. His use of them, however, is actually quite sophisticated. His detailed images of the murder portray not only its violence but also its implicit betrayal and degeneracy (*the blood of Caesar followed it / As rushing out of doors to be resolved / If Brutus so unkindly knocked or no*; *Ingratitude . . . Quite vanquished him*; *Pompey's statue . . . ran blood*; *poor poor dumb mouths*; *the stones of Rome would rise and mutiny*).

SIGNIFICANT SCANS

Antony varies his meter quite a bit. There are many inverted feet at the beginnings of lines or mid-line following caesuras. In addition to these commonly found inversions, you'll also notice the occasional word that falls on a normally unaccented syllable but that seems to demand a stress (such as *this* in line 178, or both *Judge* and *O* in line 186). Punching these feet against the meter creates the sense that Antony is being emphatic, is trying to be persuasive, or is emotional about what he is saying. Many of the lines have double endings, which could indicate that Antony is trying to express a thought quickly, before he is interrupted by anyone; or, when he is "praising" the conspirators, that he is not sincere in his praise and can't deliver this praise with strength and conviction. Some of the lines have both inverted feet and double endings, giving the whole monologue a spirited energy—this is one of the most important performances of Antony's life, and he is in high gear.

Line 217 contains a crowded fifth foot (*I know not*).

And line 218 can be scanned either of two ways. You can contract *They are* (They're) and elide *honorable* (ON´-ra-BL). In this reading, you may either contract *do it* (DOOT) or treat it as a double ending:

x / x / (x) x / x / x /
That made them do it. They are wise and honorable

Or you can leave *They are* as is, making the elided *honorable* a triple ending:

x / x / x / x / x / (x-x)
That made them do it. They are wise and honorable

Line 231 can also be read in two ways. You may scan it as hexameter (a rare six-footed line), with an inverted foot following the caesura:

x / x / x / / x x / x /
And Brutus Antony, there were an Antony

Notice that the last syllable of *Antony*—unaccented in normal speech—falls on stressed syllables both times it occurs. While it need not receive as much stress as other stressed syllables, giving it some stress encourages a dynamic reading in which Antony creates anticipation for what he says next. The line's extra foot creates a crescendo in his conclusion. Or, you may choose to elide the first *Antony* (ANT-nee) and scan the line as pentameter with a double ending before the caesura and the same inverted foot following the caesura:

x / x / (x) / x x / x /
And Brutus Antony, there were an Antony

This reading creates a longer build to the variation (the accent on the last syllable of *Antony* at the end of the line).

Don't forget to elide: *Cassius'* (CA-shuss or CA-syuss, not CA-shu-sez or CA-syuh-sez) in line 178; *envious* (EN-vyuss) in line 179; *muffling* (MUFF-ling) in line 191; *Even* (e'en) in line 192; *honorable* (ON´-ra-BL) in lines 216 and 218; *utterance* (UTT-rance) and *power* (POWR) in line 226; and *spirits* (SPEERTS) in line 232;

. . . to contract: *do it* (DOOT)—optional; and *They are* (They're) in line 218;

. . . and to expand: *Nervii* (NUR´-vee-IE) in line 177; *belovèd* (be-LUH-vehd) in line 180; *cursèd* (CUR-sehd) in line 181; and *statue* (STA´-tchoo-UH) in line 192.

One final note: if you have the opportunity to present a longer monologue, this piece can be linked with the previous one (see page 625).

P.S.

For information about the historical Antony, see "Antony A-Go-Go," page 619.

KING LEAR

ACT I, SCENE ii

EDMUND

GENDER: M
AGE RANGE: young adult to adult
PROSE/VERSE: blank verse
FREQUENCY OF USE (1–5): 5

Edmund is the illegitimate younger son of the Earl of Gloucester. While Gloucester has asserted that he loves Edmund and has grudgingly acknowledged him as his own, he has also made disparaging comments about Edmund's bastardy. The conventions of the time prevent Edmund from inheriting from his father, partially because he is the younger son but principally because he was conceived out of wedlock. Not one to take discrimination lying down, Edmund has devised a plan to acquire his brother's inheritance, which he will launch with the help of a letter. He soliloquizes:

Thou, Nature, art my goddess; to thy law
My services are bound. Wherefore should I
Stand in the plague of custom and permit
The curiosity of nations to deprive me?
5 For that I am some twelve or fourteen moonshines
Lag of a brother? Why "bastard"? Wherefore "base,"
When my dimensions are as well compact,
My mind as generous and my shape as true
As honest madam's issue? Why brand they us
10 With "base," with "baseness," "bastardy," "base," "base,"
Who, in the lusty stealth of nature, take
More composition and fierce quality
Than doth within a dull, stale, tired bed
Go to the creating a whole tribe of fops
15 Got 'tween a sleep and wake? —Well then,
Legitimate Edgar, I must have your land.
Our father's love is to the bastard Edmund
As to th' legitimate. Fine word, "legitimate"!
Well, my legitimate, if this letter speed
20 And my invention thrive, Edmund the base
Shall top th' legitimate. I grow; I prosper.
Now, gods, stand up for bastards!

1 minute, 15 seconds

1 *Nature* An important word (and thematic subject) in this play, it means different things to different people. Edmund uses it to mean that which precedes and is the opposite of civilized law; *goddess* Edmund personifies nature as Mother Nature, a pagan goddess of fertility—*King Lear* takes place in pre-Christian Britain and the play's characters are pagan [*Thou, Nature . . . bound* since Edmund is a bastard (also known as a "natural child" in Shakespeare's time), he is pledging to worship Nature and follow her dictates]; 2 *Wherefore* why; 3 *Stand in* submit to, be subject to; *the plague of custom* the evil of convention (which, whether enacted as law or not, carries the same weight)—here, the denial of inheritance to an illegitimate (and younger) son; 4 *curiosity* fastidiousness, capricious overrefinement [*The curiosity of nations* i.e., the capricious, overly refined customary laws created by mere humans]; 5 *For that* because; *moonshines* months; 6 *Lag of* lagging behind (i.e., younger than); *base* both (1) illegitimate and (2) lowly, vile, despicable, inferior; 7 *my dimensions are as well compact* my body parts are as well formed; 8 *generous* noble, honorable, courageous; *as true* i.e., as true to my father's image; 9 *honest* chaste [*honest madam's issue* the offspring of a married woman]; *Why brand they us* why do they brand us; 11 *lusty* having a sexual appetite (with play on second meaning; vigorous, energetic, active) [*lusty stealth of nature* i.e., stealthy yet vigorous enjoyment of sex (between adulterers)]; *take* derive; *composition* completeness, robustness; *fierce* energetic [*take / More composition and fierce quality* derive more physical and mental strength and vigor]; 13 *a dull, stale, tired bed* i.e., a marriage bed (in which boredom has set in); 14 *Go to the creating a* get busy creating a; *fops* fools; 15 *Got* begot, conceived; *'tween a sleep and wake* i.e., in the state of being half asleep [*Than doth within a dull . . . sleep and wake* i.e., than goes into the creating of a whole tribe of fools conceived halfheartedly by snoozing people in a boring marital bed (Edmund compares the vitality inherited by illegitimate children with the dullness of legitimate offspring)]; 17 *is to the bastard Edmund / As to th' legitimate* i.e., belongs to illegitimate ol' me as much as it belongs to my legitimate brother; 19 *speed* succeeds; 20 *invention* (1) scheme, plan; (2) inventiveness.

COMMENTARY

When Edmund first appears, he seems like the nicest of guys. Throughout the rest of the play, however, he proves that he isn't. But why isn't he? What went wrong in his formative years? He tells us here. In this monologue, Edmund sets out both the larger motivation for his actions in the play and his umbrella objective in this scene. He is very bitter at being treated unfairly his whole life because of an accident of birth, and he will take through villainy what should have been given him by right.

To justify his position, Edmund makes one of the earliest arguments on record favoring natural law over positivism (the theory that there is no law apart from man-made law). He asserts that certain rights predate and transcend those laws created by people, and that rules should be broken if they violate natural law. Edmund deliberately rejects the meaning of the word *Nature* as held by Lear and Gloucester: the natural bonds between parents and children. Instead, Edmund defines *Nature* as natural law.

Edmund's intelligence, humor, charisma, and sheer energy are assets he consciously uses to engage the audience and gain its support. His rapid-fire question format builds rapport and create collusion with the audience. Perhaps he is also trying to psych himself up to take action. He is not rationalizing—there is no need for that, as Edmund has, in fact, been grievously wronged. He need only remind himself of that wrong to shore up his anger so that he can carry out his plan (FYI: in the beginning of Act I, Gloucester explains that Edmund "hath been out nine years, and away he shall again"—perhaps to be raised in a strange house, or perhaps to military service; he then disparages Edmund publicly for being illegitimate: "the whoreson must be acknowledged").

Edmund's argument has an intelligent, logical structure, which is based on the monologue's overarching contrast of the two principal words he plays with: the underrated, underappreciated *bastard* versus the overrated *legitimate*. In this monologue, Edmund acts like Shakespeare the writer, exploring the etymology and the poetic value of *bastard* and *bastardy* in lines 6 and 10, and thoroughly exploiting the poetic sound elements of *legitimate*. Edmund is irked by what he believes to be the origin of the word *bastard*: the word *base* (in fact, the words' similarity is coincidental—the two do not share etymological roots)—why should his parents' marital status have so completely affected his own status in society?

Edmund's repetition of *bastard* / *base* and *legitimate* is the most striking element of this monologue. Since Shakespeare never repeats words without cause, it is your job to imbue each subsequent use of *bastard* / *base* / *baseness* / *bastardy*—and, later, *legitimate*—with its own purpose to communicate clearly to your audience why Edmund repeats himself. Perhaps his insistent repetition allows him to vent the deep bitterness and frustration that have been on a slow boil for years. This bitterness is made palpable by his repetition of the similar-sounding words in line 10 (take advantage of the Barbed Bs!), as well as by the contemptuous way in which he repeats the word *legitimate*—play with the word . . . it begs to be spit out. Perhaps, too, Edmund seeks to diminish the impact of both words by repeating them until they have lost their power (as Lenny Bruce did with "obscene" words).

Edmund's utter disdain for legitimate offspring emerges in his oh-so-snide phrase *honest madam's issue* in line 9, and in lines 13–15: the Dull Ds in *Than doth within a dull, stale, tired bed*; his sarcastic *Go to the creating a whole tribe of fops / Got 'tween a sleep and wake*; and his references to his brother as *Legitimate Edgar* and *my legitimate*.

Edmund's double entendres make his contempt even more plain. The double meanings of the following words would have been familiar to a Jacobean audience: *Nature* = the sexual organs (also, *natural child* was a term used in Shakespeare's time for "bastard"); *stale* = sexually unappealing; *Go to the creating* = "Go to it," have sex; *top* = mount; *grow* = become erect; *stand up for* (give power to) = give sexual power (i.e., an erection) to. Beware, however, that the double meanings of these words are secondary and should not be played overtly, particularly since some of their meanings have been lost over time and will not resonate for today's audience.

At the end of the monologue, Edmund divulges his intention (hinted at by his subversive definition of *Nature* at the beginning of the piece) to turn matters upside down: the *base* shall *top* the *legitimate* and make the legitimate son appear to be a bastard in his father's eyes (and, in fact, Edmund shall succeed, for Gloucester will fall for Edmund's plot and believe that Edgar intends him harm, and will call Edgar *abhorred*—"hated," but also "son of a whore").

Note the embedded stage direction in line 19 (*if this letter speed* . . .), which obviously refers to a specific letter that Edmund has either been holding throughout the entire monologue or has just now produced from a pocket.

SIGNIFICANT SCANS

There are many full stops mid-line, suggesting that Edmund's thoughts are following fast upon one anothers' heels. There are also several double endings in this piece, both at the ends of lines and mid-line before caesuras, as well as several inverted feet, both at the beginnings of lines and in the middle, immediately following caesuras. Together, these variations contribute to the monologue's tone of emphatic indignation.

Notice that line 15 has only four feet of spoken text—Shakespeare clearly intended that you take a one-foot pause. It makes sense to take that pause at the full stop following *wake*, since Edmund is mid-thought at both the beginning and the end of the line (and thus can't take the pause at either of those places); and since the full stop is where Edmund shifts from griping about discrimination against bastards in general to articulating his intention to right the specific discrimination against him by conning his father. Similarly, the final line of the monologue has only three and a half feet of spoken text, in which Edmund peremptorily rallies the gods to action, rather than asking them for help. We think the pause is better taken at the end of the line, so you don't break your momentum.

Don't forget to elide: *generous* (JEN-russ) in line 8;

. . . to contract: *the creating* (th´cree-AY-ting) in line 14;

. . . to both elide and contract: *The curiosity* (Th'kyoor-YOH´-sih-TEE) in line 4.

A note about eliding/contracting *Legitimate* and *th' legitimate*: elide in lines 16 and 19 (leh-JIT-mit); elide and contract *th' legitimate* in line 18 (thleh-JIT-mit); do not elide *legitimate* in line 18; just contract *th' legitimate* in line 21 (but do *not* elide *legitimate*).

Irrelevant History: Bastard Chic

It seems that witty treatises discussing (but not overtly endorsing) infidelity were all the rage in the mid- to late sixteenth and early seventeenth centuries. This monologue's argument in defense of the illegitimate was not introduced by Edmund; it was first posited by Ortensio Landi in *Paradossi* (1543), is believed to have been recapped in Anthony Munday's *The Defense of Contraries* (1602)—parts of which are lost—and was further explored in an essay entitled "A paradox in the defence of bastardy, approving that the bastard is more worthy to be esteemed than he that is lawfully born," in *A Treasury of Ancient and Modern Times* by Thomas Milles (1613). Less titillating but no less interesting is Edmund's argument about the moral supremacy of nature over the laws of men, an argument Shakespeare may have encountered in Montaigne's *Essays* (in John Florio's English translation, 1603), in an essay that contrasted nature and custom.

KING LEAR

ACT I, SCENE ii

EDMUND

GENDER: M
AGE RANGE: young adult to adult
PROSE/VERSE: prose
FREQUENCY OF USE (1–5): 4

Edmund, illegitimate son of the Earl of Gloucester, has hatched a plan to become his father's heir by turning his father against his legitimate half brother Edgar. Edmund has just shown Gloucester a forged letter in which Edgar supposedly asks Edmund to help him get rid of their father in return for half of his estate. Gloucester easily fell for the trick, and then blamed all his problems on astrology. Gloucester has just left, and Edmund soliloquizes:

EDMUND

This is the excellent foppery of the world, that
when we are sick in fortune—often the surfeits of
130 our own behavior—we make guilty of our disasters
the sun, the moon, and stars, as if we were villains
on necessity, fools by heavenly compulsion, knaves,
thieves, and treachers by spherical predominance;
drunkards, liars, and adulterers by an enforced obe-
135 dience of planetary influence; and all that we are
evil in, by a divine thrusting on. An admirable
evasion of whoremaster man, to lay his goatish
disposition to the charge of a star! My father
compounded with my mother under the dragon's
140 tail, and my nativity was under Ursa Major, so
that it follows I am rough and lecherous. Fut! I

128 *foppery* folly; 129 *sick in* in a bad state with regard to [*when we are sick in fortune* i.e., when bad things happen to us]; *surfeits* the natural results of excesses; 130 *disasters* used here as a pun: in Elizabethan times, the word *disasters* carried two meanings: (1) catastrophic destruction (as today); and (2) misfortunes caused by cosmic forces ("disasters" derived from ancient astrology, and referred to malevolent influences of the sun, stars, and planets; Jacobeans still believed that their fates were determined by the stars) [*we make guilty of our disasters the sun, the moon, and stars* we make the sun, moon, and stars guilty of the disasters we have brought on ourselves]; 132 *on* by; *compulsion* constraint, coercion; *knaves* rascals, villains; 133 *treachers* traitors; *spherical* planetary [*spherical predominance* the superior influence of a particular planet (i.e., the influence of the particular planet that was most powerful at the moment of a person's birth)]; 135 *of* to; 136 *by* is caused by; *divine* supernatural; *thrusting on* forcing onward, incitement; 137 *whoremaster* one who has dealings with whores, i.e., lecher, fornicator [*whoremaster man* lecherous, fornicating mankind]; *goatish* lustful, lascivious; 138 *charge* responsibility [*lay his goatish disposition to the charge of a star* lay the responsibility for his lasciviousness on astrology]; 139 *compounded with my mother* both (1) mixed with my mother (through intercourse) and (2) made (me), with my mother; *under the dragon's tail* i.e., under the northern constellation Draco; 140 *nativity* birth; *Ursa Major* the Great Bear (a.k.a. the Big Dipper), the most prominent northern constellation; 141 *rough* (1) unfeeling, cruel; (2) rude, coarse; *Fut!* (rhymes with *foot* and *put*) an exclamation of dismissive contempt (derived from "God's

should have been that I am had the maidenliest star in
the firmament twinkled on my bastardizing. —Edgar—
[*Enter Edgar*]
Pat he comes, like the catastrophe of an old com-
145 edy. My cue is villainous melancholy, with a sigh
like Tom o' Bedlam. O, these eclipses do portend
these divisions! Fa, sol, la, mi.

1 minute, 10 seconds

foot!"); 142 *should* would; *that* what; *maidenliest* most chaste, most virginal; 143 *firmament* sky; *twinkled on* i.e., been dominant at the time of; *my bastardizing* my extramarital conception; 144 *Pat* fittingly, exactly suited to the purpose; *catastrophe* that which produces the final resolution in a play (here, a specific reference to the conventional character who arrives toward the end of the play and resolves all its conflicts); 145 *cue* a combination of (1) the role a person is to play; (2) necessary course of action; (3) mood, frame of mind; *villainous* (1) wicked, vile; (2) wretched, pitiful; 146 *Tom o' Bedlam* an insane but harmless wandering beggar (Tom was a common English name often used to represent men of lower-than-average intelligence. *Bedlam* is a corruption of *Bethlehem*, which refers to the hospital of St. Mary of Bethlehem, a London insane asylum, which sometimes released nonviolent inmates to fend for themselves on the streets. Due to the hospital's notoriously chaotic conditions, the word *bedlam* became a colloquial term for a wild, noisy disturbance); *these eclipses* a topical reference alluding to an eclipse of the moon seen by Londoners in September 1605 and an eclipse of the sun just two weeks later; Jacobeans believed eclipses to be omens of disaster; *do portend* are omens of; 147 *divisions* discords, differences (with a play on another meaning: "musical variations," specifically, short, complicated passages made up of many notes that are variations on a longer, simpler theme).

COMMENTARY

Edmund is the perfect example of a Machiavel, a standard character type who delights in evil for its own sake. The Machiavel is cynical, clever, lewd, and humorous, and uses reason and intelligence to achieve selfish ends. Although Edmund's contempt for astrology is not uncommon today, Shakespeare's audience would have found such disregard for commonly held beliefs to be troubling evidence of Edmund's atheism and evil nature. Today, actors interpret Edmund as a more complex character, fleshing him out with real motives and objectives.

You may decide that Edmund is bitter about society's (and particularly his father's) unjust rejection of him as an illegitimate child (for more on this, see monologue, page 637), and/or that now that his plan is under way, he is cool as a cucumber and bemused by the ease with which he manipulates those around him. However you envision him, you must consider the determination with which Edmund goes about getting what he wants: Edmund doesn't just sit around complaining about his misfortune, he takes action, and that active energy animates his speech. Be sure to start the piece at a level that leaves room for the build in Edmund's description of the way people blame their faults on astrology. He could have said so once in simple terms, but instead he builds an eloquent, impassioned list of specific faults that people chalk up to "the stars." If you are as specific in visualizing these faults as Edmund is in enumerating them, you'll make quite clear to your audience that Edmund doesn't exactly see humanity through rose-colored glasses. The build maximizes the impact of such ironical phrases as *heavenly compulsion* and *spherical predominance*, with which Edmund mocks "astrology-speak."

Edmund uses plain, unpoetic, yet elegant prose, which creates the sense that he is being candid with the listener, an impression supported by the fact that Edmund is as honest about his own failings as he is about others'. In fact, Edmund delivers most of the speech in the second person plural, including himself with the rest of foolish humankind. He even makes fun of astrology by using himself as an example, stating ironically: *My father compounded with my mother under the dragon's tail, and my nativity was under Ursa Major, so that it follows I am rough and lecherous*. The constellations he claims to be born under are actually meaningless, since they are not part of the zodiac. Perhaps he is rejecting any outside influence on his *rough*, *lecherous* nature (to which he openly—perhaps even gleefully—admits). Or perhaps he uses this faux jargon irreverently to subtly place the responsibility for his nature on his illegitimacy—he is *rough* because the world has treated him roughly for being a bastard.

Such subtleties in Edmund's speech reveal his calculating intelligence, as does his use of puns. Edmund puns mockingly on *disasters* (see Annotation), with the effect of speaking the word as if it were in derisive quotation marks. After using *divisions* with its primary meaning in line 147, he sings a few notes, amusing himself by pointing out the word's musical definition. Edmund also amuses himself with sexual double entendre, which confirms his roughness and lechery. He puns on the phrase *a divine thrusting on* and on the word *compounded* (with reference to his own parents, no less!), and he refers to being born under the constellation Draco with the phrase *under the dragon's tail* (in Shakespeare's day, *tail* was colloquially used to refer to male or female genitals, depending on context). This wordplay creates a background of frank sexuality for Edmund's more straightforward insults: humanity is *goatish* and a *whoremaster* and his own parents *bastardiz*[*ers*].

Edmund also cleverly juxtaposes words not often used in conjunction with each other, surprising and delighting the listener's ear while brilliantly expressing his thoughts. Such combinations as *excellent foppery* and *villainous melancholy* illustrate Edmund's sharp sarcasm while creating layers of meaning and humor. For instance, one gets the sense that by *excellent foppery* Edmund means not only foppery in the highest degree, but also foppery that is excellent for the humor it provides, or for the opportunities it gives him to deceive others. By *villainous melancholy*, it seems as though he means not only a false appearance of melancholy, with which he can deceive Edgar, but also perhaps that the tendency of those who are melancholy to avoid action is villainous, or that melancholy itself leads to villainous behavior (an established Jacobean construct).

Be sure to make the appropriate transition when Edgar approaches. The words *O, these eclipses do portend these divisions! Fa, sol, la, mi* are intended for Edgar's benefit. *O* is usually used to express thoughts or emotions of great import, and can be used quite effectively to do so (see "O, No! An *O*!," page xxxiii). In this case, Edmund is simultaneously invoking (for Edgar) and mocking (for himself or the audience) the dramatic meaning of *O*. Edmund is not afraid of overdoing it with Edgar, since he clearly believes his brother isn't the brightest candle in the chandelier. Notice Shakespeare's insertion of musical notes (*Fa, sol, la, mi*): Edmund is putting on an innocent, I'm-not-doing-much, just-humming-to-myself sort of air as Edgar arrives.

Who Do Those Jacobeans Think They Are, the Center of the Universe?

Actually, they did. Although Copernicus developed the theories on which modern astronomy is based several years before Shakespeare's birth, his ideas were still known only to and accepted by a select few scholars and scientists. In Shakespeare's day, the prevailing belief was still that the earth was the center of a universe that existed solely for the use and benefit of humankind. This view was based on the ideas of Ptolemy, an Alexandrian astronomer of the second century C.E., who claimed that the sun and planets were fixed in concentric "spheres" that revolved around the earth. The stars were attached in the outermost sphere. So it is no surprise that Jacobeans believed so strongly in astrology—it was only logical. The cosmos was thought of as a "macrocosm" and the human body as a "microcosm." The two systems had parallels on every level, and thus human fate could be read in the macrocosm of the stars.

KING LEAR

ACT I, SCENE iv

GONERIL

GENDER: F
PROSE/VERSE: blank verse
AGE RANGE: young adult to adult
FREQUENCY OF USE (1–5): 2

When Goneril's father, King Lear of Britain, wished to retire and divide the kingdom among his three daughters, he commanded each to declare her love for him. Vying for the largest portion, Goneril gushed convincingly. Her sister Regan was effusive as well, but the youngest, Cordelia, refused to participate, and Lear divided her portion between the others. Now sovereign over half of Britain, Goneril has no further use for her father. But the doddering old fool has just taken up residence in her palace with a retinue of a hundred rowdy younger knights. Not wanting him to get too comfortable, Goneril refused to see her father, and commanded her servant to be surly with him . . . and the servant was struck for his pains! Furthermore, Lear's thugs have not stopped carousing since they arrived and have vandalized her beautiful home. Furious, Goneril confronts Lear:

GONERIL

220 Not only, sir, this your all-licensed fool,
But other of your insolent retinue
Do hourly carp and quarrel, breaking forth
In rank and not-to-be-endurèd riots. Sir,
I had thought by making this well known unto you
225 To have found a safe redress, but now grow fearful,
By what yourself too late have spoke and done,
That you protect this course and put it on
By your allowance; which if you should, the fault
Would not 'scape censure, nor the redresses sleep,
230 Which in the tender of a wholesome weal
Might in their working do you that offense
Which else were shame, that then necessity
Will call discreet proceeding.

This admiration, sir, is much o' th' savor
Of other your new pranks. I do beseech you
260 To understand my purposes aright:
As you are old and reverend, should be wise.
Here do you keep a hundred knights and squires,
Men so disordered, so debauched and bold,
That this our court, infected with their manners,
265 Shows like a riotous inn—epicurism and lust
Makes it more like a tavern or a brothel

220 *all-licensed* privileged to do or say anything; *fool* jester (she probably also intends the second meaning, idiot) [*this your all-licensed fool* this fool of yours, whom you permit to do or say whatever he wishes]; 221 *other* i.e., other members; 222 *quarrel* i.e., seek an opportunity for a fray; 223 *rank* gross; 225 *safe redress* sure remedy; 226 *yourself* i.e., you yourself; *too late* only too recently; 227 *course* course of action, conduct; *put it on* encourage it; 228 *By your allowance* with your permission; *if you should* i.e., if you were to do so; 229 *censure* blame; *nor* nor would; *redresses* corrective measures; *sleep* i.e., be neglected, fail to be implemented; 230 *tender of* i.e., tender care for; *wholesome weal* healthy state, well-ordered society; 231 *in their working* i.e., in the application of such care; *do you that offense / Which else were shame* i.e., take action that would under other circumstances cause you embarrassment; 232 *that then necessity / Will call discreet proceeding* which, in that case, the necessity of the circumstances would deem appropriate [*if you should . . . discreet proceeding* Goneril's language here is a bit abstract, but she says, in essence, "if you encourage your knights to continue their riotous, destructive behavior, your behavior will require that I take corrective measures for the good of society that under other circumstances might shame you, but which here would be necessary and be considered only appropriate"]; 258 *admiration* air of wonderment; *savor* (1) smell; (2) have a particular characteristic [*is much o' th' savor* smells like, i.e., is similar to]; 259 *other your* your other; 260 *purposes* meaning; *aright* rightly, without mistake; 261 *should be* you should be; 263 *disordered* ill-behaved; 264 *this our court* this royal court of mine; *manners* behavior; 265 *Shows like* looks like;

Than a graced palace. The shame itself doth speak
For instant remedy. Be then desired,
By her that else will take the thing she begs,
270 A little to disquantity your train,
And the remainders that shall still depend
To be such men as may besort your age,
Which know themselves and you.

1 minute, 45 seconds

inn in Shakespeare's day, inns not only housed travelers, they also contained taverns and were known to be rowdy; *epicurism* (eh-PIH´-kyoo-RIZM) gluttony; 267 *graced* (1) dignified; (2) i.e., graced by the presence of royalty; 268 *Be then desired* therefore, be requested; 269 *her that else will take the thing she begs* she who otherwise will take what she requests (she refers to herself); 270 *disquantity* diminish [*A little to disquantity your train* to diminish the size of your train (i.e., the number of your followers) a little]; 271 *the remainders that shall still depend* i.e., the men that shall still remain dependent on you; 272 *such men as* the sort of men who; *besort* (bih-SORT) befit, suit (Shakespeare coined this word); 273 *Which know themselves and you* i.e., who know how to conduct themselves as befits their positions and yours.

COMMENTARY

Want to act out some aggression without wrecking your real-life relationships? Play Goneril. Goneril learned from the best. Here, she is probably behaving as her role-model dad did while king, capriciously meting out decrees. But the former king has never been on the receiving end of such decrees. Newly retired, he's just not used to it yet and needs to learn his rightful place. Keep in mind that Goneril absolutely detests her husband, the Duke of Albany—was hers an arranged marriage of Lear's making? Perhaps Goneril harbors anger at her father for the absolute power he has wielded over her life until now. And, if Goneril is to be believed, Lear's men have caroused so riotously that they have turned her castle upside down (although you could decide that they have done no such thing, and that Goneril is fabricating an excuse to humiliate her father). If the knights have indeed been destructive, Goneril has ample immediate justification for her fury.

You've surely noticed that the language is challenging, containing, for example, many unusually long sentences with meandering clauses. In lines 228–33 the syntax is especially hard to follow and the imagery is scant, making Goneril's message somewhat obscure: is she trying to hide a bit of residual nervousness about speaking to her father, the ex-king, so rudely? Is she attempting to befuddle Lear so that he will feel old and senile? Is she trying to be highfalutin and officious? The choice is yours. She uses formal speech throughout the piece in her attempt to establish her power: She has wasted no time in adopting the royal "we" (*our* in line 264) to point out her sovereign status (although she does not do so elsewhere), and she addresses her father with the aloof *sir*, as she did when he was king, which suggests that they were never close. Does she continue to do so out of habit or intentionally, to retain her distance?

Certain phrases convey Goneril's sharp tongue: *this your all-licensed fool*; *rank and not-to-be-endurèd riots*; *understand my purposes aright*; *As you are old and reverend, should be wise*; *this our court . . . Shows like a riotous inn*; *The shame itself doth speak / For instant remedy*; *By her that else will take the thing she begs*; *disquantity*; *such men as may besort your age*. Many of these phrases—as well as some others—have the further effect of infantilizing Lear, turning the tables on him and coopting his power: *your insolent retinue*; *not-to-be-endurèd riots*; *the fault / Would not 'scape censure*; *other your new pranks*; *understand . . . aright*; *As you are old . . . wise*; *By her that . . . begs*.

Goneril boldly proclaims lines 267–68 (*the shame itself doth speak / For instant remedy*) as fact, not opinion. Her scandalous imagery (of her castle as a *brothel*, *infected* by Lear's knights' debauchery) is unspeakably insulting to the elderly former king. And in the same breath in which she "requests" that Lear dismiss a number of his men, she establishes that this "request" is in fact a command, and that she will execute the order if he does not. Her deliberate fluctuation between entreating false humility and contemptuous chastisement make her debasement of Lear all the more sharp-edged. Goneril concludes with an emasculating final insult: by reducing his retinue to only *such men as may besort* [his] *age*, she links Lear's diminished power with his advanced age—"power" in this case meaning the number and median age of his knights; and, therefore, his total amount of testosterone, i.e., his virility and machismo.

While there are many examples of consonance and assonance in the piece (such as *fool* / *retinue*; *found* / *safe* / *fearful*; *protect* / *put*; *Which* / *weal* / *working*; *brothel* / *Be* / *By* / *begs*), the overwhelming sound woven throughout is the hiSSing S (reinforced by Z and SH) (*sir* / *licensed* / *insolent* / *Sir* / *safe* / *redress* / *spoke* / *course* / *allowance* / *should* / *'scape censure* / *redresses sleep* / *offense* / *shame* / *necessity* / *discreet*; *sir* / *savor* / *pranks* / *beseech* / *purposes* / *should* / *wise* / *squires* / *so disordered* / *so* / *this* / *manners* / *Shows* / *riotous* / *epicurism* / *lust* / *Makes* / *graced palace* / *shame itself* / *speak* / *desired* / *begs* / *disquantity* / *remainders* / *shall still* / *such* / *as* / *besort* / *themselves*), which helps create Goneril's venomous tone.

SIGNIFICANT SCANS

You may have noticed by now that the meter of this piece is markedly irregular, most notably in its many lines containing extra syllables. Goneril uses more double endings than most characters, both at the ends of lines and in the middles of lines before caesuras, as well as hexameter (rare six-footed lines) and lines that require elisions and contractions to fit pentameter. Line 223 is hexameter, but can be delivered as pentameter with a double ending by contracting *not-to-be-endurèd* (NOT-t'bee'n-DYOO-rehd), if you prefer.

Line 233 has only three and a half feet of spoken text. When the whole scene is performed, the line is pentameter and is shared with the Fool. Here, however, you may take the extra feet to make your transition to your next tactic: attacking Lear himself rather than his men.

Goneril uses her frequent double endings to drive home her message to Lear. For example, the regular ending of line 260 is juxtaposed against the two consecutive double endings in lines 258–59; line 260's abrupt ending on the word *aright* sounds particularly stem in contrast to the softer endings of the previous two lines, making its chastisement sting all the more.

Hexameter makes a second appearance in line 265. For the meter to scan correctly, you must pronounce *epicurism* with the accent on the second syllable (eh-PIH´-kyoo-RIZM), as it was pronounced in Shakespeare's time. The first foot of the line is inverted and the word *riotous* is elided (RIE-tuss), as well:

/ x x / x / x /x/ x /
Shows like a riotous inn—epicurism and lust

Three consecutive lines have inverted first feet (265–67). These are the lines in which Goneril explains the shameful effect of the knights' behavior on her dignified, elegant home, and the cluster of punched line beginnings shows that she is upset. Perhaps she takes great pride in the beauty of her home. Perhaps the knights have destroyed beloved knickknacks or furniture. But notice that Goneril never directly addresses Lear's effect on her personally; perhaps discussing the damage to her home is as close as Goneril can comfortably come to expressing the damage to her equilibrium.

Don't forget to elide: *insolent* (IN-slint) in line 221; *hourly* (OWR-lee) in line 222; *unto* ('nto) in line 224; *allowance* (a-LOUNCE) in line 228; *reverend* (REV-rend) in line 261; and *riotous* (RIE-tuss) and *epicurism* (eh-PIH´-kyoo-RIZM) in line 265;

. . . to contract: *I had* (I'd) in line 224; *To have* (T'have) in line 225; *the redresses* (th'ree-DREH-sez) in line 229; and *o' th' savor* (oth-SAY-vor) in line 258;

. . . and to expand: *endurèd* (en-DYOO-rehd) in line 223—this expansion heightens Goneril's imperious and strident tone, and suggests the extended agony she's had to endure, thank-you-very-much-Dad.

KING LEAR

ACT II, SCENE iv

KING LEAR

GENDER: M
AGE RANGE: older adult
PROSE/VERSE: blank verse
FREQUENCY OF USE (1–5): 3

Wishing to retire, King Lear recently divided up his kingdom between two of his daughters, Goneril and Regan. (He disinherited his third daughter, Cordelia, when she refused to proclaim publicly, on demand, her great love for her father.) Lear had intended to spend alternating months at the residences of Goneril and Regan, living in a style befitting his status as king emeritus. Now his two daughters are refusing to house his train of one hundred knights, demeaning him by whittling down the number they will accept to fifty, and then to twenty-five. Now they ask why he should need any of them! Lear is outraged! He replies:

O reason not the need! Our basest beggars
Are in the poorest thing superfluous;
Allow not nature more than nature needs,
270 Man's life is cheap as beast's. Thou art a lady;
If only to go warm were gorgeous,
Why nature needs not what thou gorgeous wear'st,
Which scarcely keeps thee warm. But, for true need, —
You heavens, give me that patience, patience I need!
275 You see me here, you gods, a poor old man,
As full of grief as age, wretched in both!
If it be you that stirs these daughters' hearts
Against their father, fool me not so much
To bear it tamely. Touch me with noble anger,
280 And let not women's weapons, water-drops,
Stain my man's cheeks! No, you unnatural hags,
I will have such revenges on you both

267 *reason not* do not debate, do not argue about; *basest* of the lowest social rank; 268 *superfluous* possessed of more than is necessary [*Are in the poorest thing superfluous* (1) have something that is not absolutely necessary, no matter how little they possess; or (2) have something, however poor and insignificant it may be, that is not absolutely necessary]; 269 *Allow not* i.e., if one does not allow; *nature* i.e., human nature [*Allow not . . . needs* If human nature is not allowed more than just what animal nature needs to sustain life]; 270 *Man's life is cheap as beast's* i.e., then a person's life is of as little value as an animal's; *lady* a woman of high social rank; 271 *only* merely; *to go warm* to be dressed warmly; 272 *Why* an interjection used for emphasis, especially when something new comes to mind or is being pointed out; *nature needs not* (your) human nature would not require [*If only to go . . . keeps thee warm* if you looked gorgeous merely by dressing warmly, your nature would not require that you wear the gorgeous clothes you are dressed in right now, which scarcely keep you warm]; 275 *poor* (1) deserving of pity; and (2) weak (perhaps with plays on [3] insignificant, worthless and [4] destitute of riches and property); 276 *wretched in* made miserable by; 277 *that* who; 278 *fool me not so much / To bear* do not make me such a fool as to make me bear; 279 *Touch me* Move me; imbue me; *noble anger* i.e., righteous anger; 280 *water-drops* i.e., tears; 281 *Stain* (1) mark, spot; (2) disgrace; *my man's cheeks* i.e., my cheeks, which are those of a man (and hence should not be stained with tears);

That all the world shall—I will do such things,
What they are, yet I know not, but they shall be
285 The terrors of the earth. You think I'll weep,
No, I'll not weep—
[*Storm and tempest*]
I have full cause of weeping, but this heart
Shall break into a hundred thousand flaws
Or ere I'll weep. O Fool, I shall go mad.

1 minute, 20 seconds

unnatural here, inhuman in the highest degree; 284 *yet I know not* I don't know yet; 287 *full cause of weeping* abundant reason to weep; 288 *flaws* fragments (with a possible play on [1] sudden, brief bursts of wind and/or [2] sudden outbursts of emotion); 289 *Or ere* before; *Fool* he addresses his jester.

COMMENTARY

During this monologue, a storm is brewing . . . both literally and figuratively. Keep in mind that as the monologue begins, an actual storm is moving in, and by the end, the rain is starting to fall and the wind to blow. Lear is either oblivious to, or completely unconcerned by, the weather; his own internal storm is brewing. His daughters, recently so effusive in their love for him, are now showing him utter disrespect.

Lear's agitation is evident in the monologue's meter: nine of the twenty-three lines contain inverted (trochaic) feet, and a couple of those lines have two such inversions. There are also several sentences that begin and end mid-line. These elements give the piece an agitated feel, and create a sense of driven, forceful movement from one idea to the next. In contrast to the frequency of these variations, there are only three double endings, which tend to soften line endings. The absence of more double endings keeps the tone appropriately aggressive and hard. The variations are concentrated in the middle of the piece: only one inversion appears in the first six lines, and one in the last five. This has the effect of emphasizing Lear's agitation as the piece progresses, as well as his drop in energy as his tirade draws to a close.

Sound repetition, predominantly alliteration and assonance, further enhances Lear's tone. There are two dominant sound elements in the piece. First, there are NEEdling, Nettled EEs and Ns (*reason not* / *need*; *not nature* / *nature needs*; *cheap* / *beast's*; *nature* / *needs* / *not*; *need* / *see me here* / *grief*). Second, there are Wailing, Warring, What-the-heck?!ing Ws (*warm* / *Why* / *what* / *thou* / *wear'st* / *Which* / *warm*; *women's weapons* / *water-drops*). The repetition of the same few sounds throughout the piece is a powerful factor contributing to the build as well as to the intensity of the monologue. Keep an eye out for other small groupings of assonance, such as OR sounds (*warm* / *gorgeous*) and short As (*unnatural hags* / *have*). Also watch for small pairings of alliteration, like these Bs (*basest beggars*); Fs (*father* / *fool*); and Ts (*tamely* / *Touch*). Notice that the Ws are employed again toward the end, complemented by the repetition of similar phrasing (*I'll weep* / *I'll not weep* / *weeping* / *I'll weep*). And for help with using Lear's *O*s to their best effect, see "O, No! An *O*!," page xxxiii.

Many of the major transitions in this monologue can be pinpointed by noting whom Lear is addressing at each moment. At the start of the monologue, he speaks to one of his two daughters, either Regan, who spoke last, or—since Regan was really just chiming in—Goneril. Note that in line 273, Lear is about to go on about *true need* when he cuts himself off. He then addresses the gods—or, if you like, you may direct this "plea to the gods" to yourself, the audience, the Fool, or, pointedly, the daughters. In the middle of line 281, Lear changes focus again, addressing both daughters. Then, in the last line, Lear addresses the Fool. Be specific about your focus at all times, especially if you are using this piece in an audition, without the benefit of other actors on stage. Also, notice that each change of focus signals a change in tactics, which, of course, must be equally specific.

This piece is full of helpful hints about Lear's character and present state of mind. For instance, in the opening line, Lear's use of the word *our* could simply mean "England's" or "mankind's," but it also (either directly or by implication) carries the weight of the royal "we," which Lear may now be regretting having relinquished the right to use. In line 271, the meter requires the expansion of the word *gorgeous*, which creates the sense that Lear is mocking his daughter, while repudiating her logic (notice, though, that Lear does *not* expand *gorgeous* in line 272). Lear is clearly skilled at debate, using complex chiasmus to make his point (*If only to go warm . . . scarcely keeps thee warm*), but he believes the issue of need should not be subject to debate, and thus soon switches tactics.

In lines 282–85, Lear, so articulate only a few lines before, is at a loss for words. Having worked himself into a state, perhaps he is so overcome by anger that he finds himself speechless; maybe he is suddenly aware of his own powerlessness and is left sputtering; or perhaps he realizes that his threats are ineffectual, and tries to reassert an imposing presence with *The terrors of the earth* to mask his humiliation. Whatever you choose, recognize the vulnerability he tries to mask with bravura, and be sure to take advantage of these telling lines.

Some editors punctuate the last line with an exclamation mark (*O Fool, I shall go mad!*). The difference among editions is a tip-off that there is a wide range of possible interpretations for the last moment of the piece: perhaps Lear is still angrily raging about his daughters; or maybe he turns helplessly or hopelessly to the Fool after his encounter with them, looking for consolation, an explanation, or just a symphatetic ear. With *I shall go mad*, is Lear being colloquial, indirectly threatening his daughters, experiencing a portent, or perhaps recognizing the first effects of the madness that will soon fully grip him?

SIGNIFICANT SCANS

Line 274 seems difficult to scan, but it's quite simple—just elide *heavens* (HEV'NZ) (or read it as having a double ending) and note the inverted (trochaic) feet after both caesuras, as well as the double ending before the second caesura:

x / / x x / (x) / x x /
You heavens, give me that patience, patience I need!

Line 284 has a crowded first foot (*What they are*) and an inverted foot after the first caesura:

x - x / / x x / x / x /
What they are, yet I know not, but they shall be

Finally, Shakespeare has intentionally given line 286 only two feet of text. Although you may use the three remaining silent feet to whatever purpose you choose, we suggest that their placement is directly related to the content of the line (*No, I'll not weep*). Either Lear is, in fact, weeping, or he is desperately holding back tears and is unable to speak at that moment without losing control and breaking down. You may use the silent feet either before or after (or some before and some after) in support of whichever interpretation you choose, as well as to respond to the storm's noise, wind, and rain. Keep in mind that although you may not have the benefit of sound or lighting cues to react to, the storm would certainly have an effect on Lear, even if only to exacerbate subconsciously his emotional distress.

Don't forget to elide: *heavens* (HEV'NZ) in line 274 and *unnatural* (un-NA-tchrul) in line 281;

. . . and to expand: *gorgeous* (GORE´-jee-USS) in line 271, but *not* in line 272.

KING LEAR

ACT III, SCENE ii

KING LEAR

GENDER: M
PROSE/VERSE: blank verse
AGE RANGE: older adult
FREQUENCY OF USE (1–5): 3

Wishing to retire, King Lear recently commanded his three daughters to proclaim their love for him publicly, and divided up his kingdom between the two who fawningly complied. He intended to spend alternating months living with each daughter in a style befitting his status as king emeritus. But these daughters have both just refused to take him in unless he gives up his train of one hundred knights—an unacceptable humiliation. Lear is outraged. Rather than humbly acquiesce, he has now wandered out onto the health with the Fool in tow, despite the fact that a terrible hurricane has begun. Lear rants at the storm:

Blow, winds, and crack your cheeks! Rage! Blow!
You cataracts and hurricanoes, spout
Till you have drenched our steeples, drowned the cocks!
You sulphurous and thought-executing fires,
5 Vaunt-couriers of oak-cleaving thunderbolts,
Singe my white head! And thou, all-shaking thunder,
Strike flat the thick rotundity of the world!
Crack Nature's molds, all germens spill at once
That make ingrateful man!

Rumble thy bellyful! Spit, fire! Spout, rain!
15 Nor rain, wind, thunder, fire are my daughters.
I tax not you, you elements, with unkindness;
I never gave you kingdom, called you children,
You owe me no subscription. Then let fall
Your horrible pleasure. Here I stand, your slave,
20 A poor, infirm, weak, and despised old man.
But yet I call you servile ministers,
That will with two pernicious daughters join
Your high-engendered battles 'gainst a head
So old and white as this. O, ho! 'Tis foul.

1 minute, 30 seconds

1 *crack your cheeks* on old maps, the winds are often drawn as faces with cheeks that bulge as they blow; 2 *cataracts* great downpours of water (usually used in plural and usually refers to the floodgates of Heaven); *hurricanoes* waterspouts (tornadoes over water); 3 *our steeples* i.e., the church steeples of our kingdom; *drowned* submerged in water; *cocks* weathervanes (traditionally shaped like roosters); 4 *sulphurous* made of brimstone (in Shakespeare's time, thunder and lightning were thought to contain brimstone); *thought-executing* three possible meanings: (1) executing an action the moment it is thought of, or at the speed of thought; (2) carrying out someone's thoughts (in this case, carrying out the thoughts of Jove [a.k.a. Jupiter], ruler of the ancient Roman gods, who wielded thunderbolts); (3) thought-destroying; *fires* i.e., lightning; 5 *Vaunt-couriers* advance messengers, forerunners (originally, the foremost scouts in an army); *oak-cleaving* oak-tree-splitting; 6 *white* i.e., white-haired; 8 *germens* seeds; *spill* destroy; 9 *ingrateful* ungrateful [*all germens spill . . . ingrateful man* immediately destroy all the seeds that bring forth ungrateful humans]; 14 *Rumble thy bellyful* i.e., rumble to your heart's content; 16 *tax not you . . . with* do not accuse you of . . . ; 17 *children* i.e., my children; 18 *subscription* submission, obedience; *Then let fall / Your horrible pleasure* i.e., so do whatever horrible thing you please; 21 *ministers* agents, underlings; 22 *That will* in that you are willing to; 23 *high-engendered* born of the Heavens (both literally, referring to the lightning and thunder themselves, and figuratively, referring to their cause—Jove's [or God's] wrath); *battles* battalions; 24 *foul* here, (1) wicked; (2) disgraceful.

COMMENTARY

In this monologue, Lear's perspective on the world and the forces that govern it has begun to warp—evidence that he is already headed down the path toward the full-fledged madness that is to come.

Lear's imagery reveals that he perceives the storm that is raging around him as an expression of God's wrath, and its elements—wind, lightning, thunder, and rain—as agents of God (Shakespeare often anachronistically incorporated such elements of his own era as the Christian concept of God into his pre-Christian plays, and vice versa). Lear refers to the lightning as *sulphurous*, meaning "made of brimstone," thus likening it to Hellfire; he speaks of *Vaunt-couriers* wielding *thunderbolts*, the weapons of Jove, whose name and image were often used in place of the Judeo-Christian God in Shakespeare's time; and he speaks of *high-engendered battles*, meaning battalions created in the sky by a divine hand.

Lear exhorts these agents of God to destroy the human world (*spout / Till you have drenched our steeples, drowned the cocks!*). It may seem vain of Lear to wish or expect the destruction of the world simply because of his own ruin, but in his day—as in Shakespeare's—the fortunes of the state were intricately entwined with those of its ruler (and indeed, now that Lear is out of power, his kingdom is about to suffer a civil war). And since in Shakespeare's time rulers were believed to be the selected representatives of God, the injustices done to Lear subvert the natural order, and chaos *should* ensue (see "Riding Shotgun with God," page 235).

As the monologue progresses and Lear urges the storm on to further destruction, he employs images that are contradictory to his perception of the world: although the storm's elements are actually elements of nature, Lear does not perceive these "agents of God" as part of—or even related to—the natural world. Instead, he sees God and Nature as two separate entities, and he encourages God's agents to act <u>against</u> *Nature*, whom he sees as having created the world and its evil inhabitants, humans. In addition to seeking the destruction of the world humans have built, Lear desires the destruction of the natural world (*Strike flat the thick rotundity of the world! / Crack Nature's molds, all germens spill at once / That make ingrateful man!*), which he sees as inherently female (nature is usually personifed as female) and thus a breeder of evil. An underlying layer of sexual references (familiar to Jacobeans) reveals Lear's bitter resentment against sex, femaleness, and reproduction: *cocks* = penises [as today]; *rotundity* = roundness of pregnancy; *Crack Nature's molds* = break open Nature's womb [*mold* = womb]; *germens* = semen; *bellyful* = contents of the womb [belly = womb]; *let fall* = let yourself fall from virtue by having sex; *pleasure* = sexual pleasure; *foul* = obscene.

There are also several "farting" double meanings (*Blow, winds*; *crack your cheeks*; *sulphurous*; *all-shaking thunder*; *Rumble thy bellyful*). These dare the storm to show disrespect for ("fart on") Lear as his daughters have. Remember that double entendre is just that—hidden meaning, which usually is not played overtly. It can, however, inform your development of the character and your performance.

The sounds in Lear's speech express his anger in several ways. There are many onomatopoeic words (*crack*; *spout*; *Strike*; *Rumble*; *Spit*), which not only draw aural pictures of Lear's images, but also contain the same hard consonants that are repeated throughout the piece—Bullying Bs, Spitting Ss, Ps, and Ts, Damning Ds, Raging Rs, and Clobbering Ks and hard Cs. Also, where two consecutive words begin and end with the same letter (*Blow, winds*; *hurricanoes, spout*), be sure to separate the sounds; notice how this affects your performance.

Three of the four double endings in this monologue occur when Lear is speaking specifically about his daughters (lines 15–17). The double endings provide a slightly softer delivery in a piece full of hard line endings and hard sounds. Perhaps Lear is less in control when speaking of his daughters, due to the intensity of his wrath and pain. These lines begin a decline in Lear's energy. You must decide why he loses steam as the monologue draws to a close. Factors may include his advanced age, his encroaching madness, emotional distress, frustration, and resignation.

SIGNIFICANT SCANS

You can't miss the powerful, aggressive running start in this piece, where *Blow* (with its Bursting B) falls on the first spoken, accented syllable of the line. The piece continues to build until it tapers off in the second half, so make sure you start at a level that leaves room for the increase in intensity.

Line 1 may be scanned three ways, depending on your interpretation of it. You may choose to read it as hexameter (a rare six-footed line):

x / x / x / x / x / x /
(pause) Blow, (pause) winds, and crack your cheeks! (pause) Rage! (pause) Blow!

Or you may choose to read the line as iambic pentameter with a spondee as the first foot:

/ / x / x / x / x /
Blow, winds, and crack your cheeks! (pause) Rage! (pause) Blow!

Punching the first two syllables in rapid succession hits the listener with the storm from the first moment. Or, you may choose to read the line as iambic pentameter with a spondee as the last foot:

x / x / x / x / / /
(pause) Blow, (pause) winds, and crack your cheeks! Rage! Blow!

Notice that this choice builds to a more agitated, quick delivery at the end of the line, since the words *Rage! Blow!*, spoken as one foot rather than two, eliminate the pauses.

Line 4 can be scanned two ways: You can simply elide *sulphurous* (SUL-fruss) and stress the second and fourth syllables of *thought-executing* (thought-EX′-eh-CYOO-ting), or you can choose not to elide *sulphurous* and create a crowded fourth foot (—*execu*—):

x / x / x / x-x / x /
You sulphurous and thought-executing fires

Line 7 can be read several ways, but we suggest simply crowding —*dity of*:

x / x / x / x-x / x /
Strike flat the thick rotundity of the world!

Line 14 ends with two spondees:

/ x x / x / / / / /
Rumble thy bellyful! Spit, fire! Spout, rain!

Also, notice that line 9 is short. Be sure to decide specifically how you wish to use the two silent feet at the end of the line. Perhaps the storm is rumbling loudly, provoking Lear's comment in his next line. Or maybe this is where Lear begins his transition into the second half of the piece, in which he is more subdued. Or maybe he's just stopped to catch his breath—remember, Lear is an octogenarian out on the open heath in a raging hurricane!

Don't forget to elide: *sulphurous* (SUL-fruss) in line 4 (optional); *Vaunt-couriers* (Vawnt-KER-yerz) in line 5; *elements* (EL-ments) in line 16; and *horrible* (HOR-bl) in line 19;

. . . and to expand: *fire* (FIE-er) in line 15.

KING LEAR

ACT III, SCENE iv

KING LEAR

GENDER: M
PROSE/VERSE: blank verse
AGE RANGE: older adult
FREQUENCY OF USE (1–5): 3

Wishing to retire, King Lear of Britain divided his kingdom between his two elder daughters, Goneril and Regan, disinheriting his youngest daughter, Cordelia, for failing to overstate her love for him publicly as her sisters had done (banished, she married the King of France). After divesting himself of his kingdom, Lear was shocked to find that Goneril and Regan cared nothing for him but had flattered him only to get his lands and power. They have cruelly humiliated him, ultimately barring him from the home of his friend Gloucester and driving him out into the wilderness in a torrential storm, accompanied only by his court fool. He has encountered his trusty servant, Kent (in disguise), and the three have just come upon a hovel. Still outside the hovel in the tempest, Lear struggles to keep his sanity in the face of the enormous outrage he has just endured.

Thou think'st 'tis much that this contentious storm
Invades us to the skin; So 'tis to thee,
But where the greater malady is fixed,
The lesser is scarce felt. Thou'dst shun a bear,
10 But if thy flight lay toward the roaring sea,
Thoud'st meet the bear i' th' mouth. When the mind's free,
The body's delicate: this tempest in my mind
Doth from my senses take all feeling else,
Save what beats there—filial ingratitude.
15 Is it not as this mouth should tear this hand
For lifting food to 't? But I will punish home;
No, I will weep no more. In such a night
To shut me out? Pour on—I will endure.
In such a night as this? O Regan, Goneril,
20 Your old kind father whose frank heart gave all!
O, that way madness lies; let me shun that;
No more of that.

[KENT: *Good my lord, enter here.*]

Prithee go in thyself; Seek thine own ease.
This tempest will not give me leave to ponder
25 On things would hurt me more. But I'll go in.
In, boy—go first. You houseless poverty—
Nay, get thee in. I'll pray, and then I'll sleep.

6 *'tis much* i.e., it's a big deal; *contentious* eager for combat; 7 *Invades* penetrates (with play on military term); 8 *fixed* lodged, rooted (here, in the mind); 9 *scarce* hardly, barely; *shun* avoid; flee from; 10 *flight* escape; 11 *meet the bear i' th' mouth* i.e., confront the bear face-to-face; *free* i.e., free from worry, at peace [*When the mind's free, / The body's delicate* i.e., when the mind is not preoccupied with troubles, the body's problems become noticeable]; 13 *Doth from my senses take all feeling else* i.e., makes me incapable of feeling anything beside my mental anguish; 14 *Save* except for; *beats* hammers at [*Save what beats there* i.e., except what won't stop pounding away at my mind]; *filial ingratitude* the ingratitude of offspring; 15 *it* i.e., filial ingratitude; *as* as if, like; *tear* lacerate, hurt or destroy in a savage manner [*Is it not . . . food to 't* i.e., isn't my daughters' ingratitude just the same as if my own mouth were to rip apart my hand for bringing food up to it]; 16 *home* completely, to my complete satisfaction [*punish home* i.e., thoroughly punish my daughters]; 18 *Pour on* this is addressed to the storm, but could additionally be used to defy his daughters; 20 *frank* generous, bountiful; 21 *that way* in that direction [*that way madness lies* i.e., I'll go mad if I think about that]; 23 *Prithee* Please (a corruption of the phrase *pray thee*, meaning, "I ask of you"); *ease* means of relief; freedom from pain [*Seek thine own ease* i.e., go get out of the storm]; 24 *give me leave* allow me; 25 *would* that would; 26 *boy* Lear addresses the Fool; *poverty* people who suffer from poverty; 27 *Nay* used here to empha-

[*Exit Fool*]

Poor naked wretches, wheresoe'er you are,
That bide the pelting of this pitiless storm,
30 How shall your houseless heads and unfed sides,
Your looped and windowed raggedness, defend you
From seasons such as these? O, I have ta'en
Too little care of this! Take physic, pomp—
Expose thyself to feel what wretches feel,
35 That thou may'st shake the superflux to them
And show the heavens more just.

1 minute, 50 seconds

size what he said before; *get thee in* i.e., go inside; 28 *wretches* miserable creatures (here, used to express pity); *wheresoe'er* in whatever places; 29 *bide* endure, bear; 30 *sides* bodies; 31 *looped* full of holes; *windowed* full of holes (full of "windows," thus letting in the elements); 32 *seasons* (1) times of the year; (2) weather conditions; *I have ta'en / Too little care of this* i.e. when I was king, I did not take adequate care of the poor; 33 *physic* remedy for a disease (in Shakespeare's day, this usually involved a purge of some kind) [*Take physic* cure yourself]; *pomp* (1) the magnificence of lavish living; (2) a magnificent display of grandeur, such as a pageant or procession (here, used to mean wealthy and powerful people in general); 35 *That* so that; *shake* cast off, allow to trickle down; *superflux* overflow, wealth above one's needs (the word was coined by Shakespeare, and plays on *flux*, meaning "discharge from the bowels"); 36 *show the heavens more just* prove the higher powers to be more fair and equitable.

COMMENTARY

Lear's world has just been turned upside down, and not by the storm! His devastating mistreatment at the hands of his two daughters is more than the elderly Lear can bear. This is the scene in the play in which Lear grapples with madness, and every line of this monologue bears evidence of that struggle.

Lear's tormented battle to retain his sanity is borne out by the meter of the monologue: it is chockful of variations such as inverted feet at the beginnings of lines and following caesuras (or, as in line 21, in both places), and double endings preceding caesuras and at the ends of lines (there is even a potential triple ending at the end of line 19—see Significant Scans). Even more important, Lear continuously begins new sentences in the middle of lines, which creates the sense that he truly has a *tempest in [his] mind*, which churns up his thoughts so that they are flying at high velocity and landing atop one another. His thoughts switch back and forth between topics with unusual frequency. Lear puts up a valiant fight, yet it takes several bouts before he can banish his daughters' betrayal from his thoughts . . . and although he seems to finally push it from the forefront of his mind, thoughts of it most certainly lurk just out of reach, ready to resurface if he lets down his guard for even a moment. Lear seems frustrated at how difficult it is to assert control over his own mind, as though his daughters are getting the best of him even there. (By the way, in support of this interpretation of Lear's mental state, the monologue's punctuation in the First Folio almost never contains a full stop, emphasizing its rambling quality.) For help exploiting the tormented sound of the word *O* to its best advantage, see "O, No! An *O*!," page xxxiii.

Even after Lear seems to have controlled the thoughts of his daughters' cruelty, his mind continues to jump between those thoughts connected to the here and now and those that carry him to other matters (*In, boy—go first. You houseless poverty— / Nay, get thee in*), giving the listener the sense that he is still warring between the real world and the troubled one of his tormented mind. Alternatively, you could decide that *You houseless poverty* refers to Kent and the Fool, now homeless due to Lear's daughters' cruelty . . . and that it is their state that prompts Lear to think of his other homeless subjects.

Notice that Lear articulates the sub-issue that his daughters would shut the doors against him on such a night as this, rather than the larger issue that if they are capable of such actions, they clearly do not love him. Perhaps naming the larger issue would put Lear entirely over the edge, in which case this self-protective move could be considered perfectly sane. Also notice that he makes the illogical logical: because the storm's assault helps him block out his internal torment, it is quite reasonable that he wishes to remain in it. So you must ask yourself the obvious question: at this moment in the play, is Lear losing or still holding his own in the battle for his sanity? Is he behaving irrationally or is he actually being quite sane under insane circumstances? It is important that you make a clear choice. In doing so, you should also consider the monologue's clear three-step progression from Lear's concern only for himself, to his concern for the well-being of one he knows and cares for (the Fool), to his concern for the well-being of strangers (the destitute among his subjects). Although Lear does lose his sanity at some point in this scene, this monologue may be a brief interval of complete lucidity before it happens. The decision is yours.

Lear knows that the Fool is too devoted to enter the hovel unless his master promises to follow. Does he say *I'll pray, and then I'll sleep* as a tactic to remain in the storm (how can the Fool argue with a wish to pray)? Or is he sincerely desirous of prayer as an attempt to displace his anguish with soothing, redemptive thoughts? What follows is not a conventional prayer, but in a strange way Lear truly captures the spirit of prayer: he expresses sincere repentance and seeks blessings not for himself but for the unfortunate *Poor naked wretches*, those who have suffered from his neglect while he was king. Although scholars have written treatises about the "Christian" sentiments he expresses here, his prayers are actually universal, which is fitting since Lear is a pre-Christian king. In fact, Lear ultimately does not appeal to a divine higher power, but to the higher power that has control over the poor, i.e., the powerful wealthy.

Many editions have the stage direction "kneels" at the beginning of line 28, but since it is not in either the original Quarto or Folio editions, we have left it out. It is a commonly accepted stage direction because actors have often had the impulse to kneel at this point in the monologue, as Lear begins to move toward humility (partway between his mocking kneel to Regan, earlier in the play, and his sincerely apologetic kneel before Cordelia toward the play's end). Of course, since this action is not indicated by an embedded stage direction, nor is it attributable to Shakespeare, you should follow your own impulse.

Lear's imagery paints the raging storm as an attacking enemy force (*contentious*; *Invades us*); his thoughts as howling, raging, and violent (*tempest in my mind*; *what beats there*); his daughters' ingratitude as beastly (likened to a mouth attacking the hand that has fed it); his generosity as heartfelt (in synecdoche: *whose frank heart gave all*); *madness* as a travel destination (*O, that way madness lies*); poor people in reference to their condition (*You houseless poverty*); and powerful people in reference to their condition (*pomp*, which he addresses with the familiar *thou*—Lear, as the former king, clearly feels intimate with both powerful people and the condition of *pomp*).

To make sense of the world's harsh realities, Lear underscores its injustices with contrasts (*filial ingratitude* versus *Your old kind father*; *wretches* versus *pomp*; *looped and windowed raggedness* versus *superflux*) and tries to bring a sense of order to his own thoughts using antitheses (*this contentious storm* versus *this tempest in my mind*; *the greater malady* versus *The lesser*; *Thou'dst shun a bear* versus *Thou'dst meet the bear i' th' mouth*; *the mind's free* versus *The body's delicate*).

SIGNIFICANT SCANS

Line 12 can scanned two ways: It can be hexameter (a rare six-footed line):

x / x /x/ x / x / x /
The body's delicate: this tempest in my mind

Or you can deliver it as pentameter (with a double ending before the caesura), if you elide *delicate* (DEL-kit):

x / x / (x) x / x / x /
The body's delicate: this tempest in my mind

Line 14 is headless and has a crowded foot (—*ial ingra*—); note the elision of *filial* (FIL-yull):

x / x / x /x - x / x /
(pause) Save what beats there—filial ingratitude

Depending on whether you slightly stress the last syllable or not, line 19 may be read either as iambic pentameter with a triple ending (GON-uh-rl) or as another hexameter (GON´-uh-RIL).

When presenting this monologue solo, you must take Kent's partial line (in line 22) as three silent feet. You may use this brief pause to make your transition to your next line, finally banishing the thoughts of your daughters and changing your focus to the storm's effects on you and on others. Also note that the last two feet of the monologue are silent, permitting your last words to resonate.

Line 29 also has a crowded foot (—*tiless storm*):

x / x / x / x /x - x /
That bide the pelting of this pitiless storm

Or you could just elide *pitiless* (PIT-less), making the foot a regular ol' iamb.

Line 30: *unfed* should be pronounced with the accent on the first syllable (UN-fed).

Don't forget to elide: *delicate* (DEL-kit) in line 12 (optional—see above); *filial* (FIL-yull) in line 14; *ta'en* (TAIN) in line 32; *heavens* (HEV'NZ) in line 36;

. . . and to contract: *i' th' mouth* (ith-MOUTH) in line 11.

MACBETH

ACT 1, SCENE v

LADY MACBETH

GENDER: F AGE RANGE: adult to mature adult
PROSE/VERSE: prose and blank verse FREQUENCY OF USE (1–5): 4

Lady Macbeth's husband has been away putting down rebellions and has just valiantly defeated the forces of the traitorous Thane of Cawdor. Lady M. has now received a letter from Macbeth, explaining that after the battle he encountered three witches who addressed him by his title of Thane of Glamis, but also by the title Thane of Cawdor, and as future King of Scotland. One of their prophesies has already come to pass—as soon as they disappeared, he received a message from his kinsman King Duncan, granting him the title Thane of Cawdor as reward for his valor. Lady Macbeth enters, in the middle of reading the letter aloud.

[*Reads*:]

. . . They met me in the day of success, and I have learned by the perfect'st report they have more in them than mortal knowledge. When I burned in desire to question them further, they made themselves air, into
5 *which they vanished. Whiles I stood rapt in the wonder of it came missives from the King, who all-hailed me "Thane of Cawdor," by which title, before, these Weird Sisters saluted me and referred me to the coming on of time with "Hail, King-that-shalt-be." This have*
10 *I thought good to deliver thee, my dearest partner of greatness, that thou might'st not lose the dues of rejoicing by being ignorant of what greatness is promised thee. Lay it to thy heart, and farewell.*

Glamis thou art, and Cawdor, and shalt be
15 What thou art promised. Yet do I fear thy nature—
It is too full o' th' milk of human kindness
To catch the nearest way. Thou wouldst be great,
Art not without ambition, but without
The illness should attend it. What thou wouldst highly,

1 *They* i.e., the three witches; *in the day of success* i.e., on the day Macbeth defeated the Thane of Cawdor; 2 *perfect'st* best-informed, most reliable; *they have . . . mortal knowledge* i.e., the witches have greater powers of knowledge, perception, and clairvoyance than do mere mortals; 5 *in the wonder of it* with astonishment at it; 6 *missives* messengers; *all-hailed* greeted me with "all-hail" (a salutation expressing a wish of health and happiness); 7 *Thane* an old Scottish title of honor, roughly equivalent to the English title earl; 8 *Weird* both (1) concerned with fate or destiny and (2) involving the supernatural, unearthly (from the Anglo-Saxon *wyrd*, meaning "fate" [the word's contemporary meaning, "strange," has evolved in large part due to the grotesque and odd characterization of the witches in this play]) [*Weird Sisters* a term used to refer to the three Fates of both Norse and Greek mythology, female deities who controlled human destiny—here the term is applied to the three witches]; *the coming on of time* i.e., the future; 10 *deliver thee* i.e., tell to you; 11 *that* so that; *the dues of rejoicing* the rejoicing that is yours by right; 13 *Lay it to thy heart* Consider it; 14 *Glamis* i.e., Thane of Glamis (a title of nobility already long held by Macbeth); 16 *shalt be / What thou art promised* i.e., will become King of Scotland; *fear* worry about; 16 *human kindness* human nature (from "humankind-ness") [*th' milk of human kindness* human nature passed down through a mother's milk (in Shakespeare's time it was believed that human traits were transmitted through nursing)] [*too full o' th' milk of human kindness* too full of tender human nature (to commit the unnatural act of murder)]; 17 *catch the nearest way* take the fastest route (to the throne), i.e., kill the present king; 18 *but without* but you lack; 19 *illness* evil (*illness* did not mean "sickness" in Shakespeare's time); *should attend it* that should accompany it (*it* meaning "ambition"); *What thou wouldst highly*

20 That wouldst thou holily; wouldst not play false
And yet wouldst wrongly win. Thou'dst have, great Glamis,
That which cries "Thus thou must do," if thou have it,
And that which rather thou dost fear to do
Than wishest should be undone. Hie thee hither,
25 That I may pour my spirits in thine ear
And chastise with the valor of my tongue
All that impedes thee from the golden round,
Which fate and metaphysical aid doth seem
To have thee crowned withal.

1 minute, 40 seconds

What you strongly desire; 20 *That* i.e., that thing (which you strongly desire); *wouldst thou holily* you would like to come by in a saintly way; *wouldst not play false* you don't want to act wrongly; 21 *And yet wouldst wrongly win* and yet you'd like to win undeservedly; 22 *Thus thou must do* You must commit this act [i.e., you must kill the King]; *if thou have it* if you have that ambition [*Thou'dst have . . . should be undone* You'd have the thing that cries out "You must do this" (i.e., the crown), if you have it (i.e., the ambition), and if you'll do the deed despite your fear of doing it, rather than wish the deed to remain undone]; 24 *Hie thee hither* Hurry here; 25 *spirits* sentiments (with a play on a second meaning, "courage"); 27 *the golden round* i.e., the crown; 28 *metaphysical* supernatural; 29 *withal* with it.

COMMENTARY

This monologue marks Lady Macbeth's first entrance in the play—this is the moment in which she establishes herself. The piece therefore contains much information about her character, her worldview, her ambition, and her relationship with her husband. So you must be very specific: why does she read her letter aloud? Is this her first read-through of the letter or is she rereading it? If she rereads it, why? Perhaps she can't believe her eyes and wonders if she misread it. Perhaps she loved what she read and wants to hear it again . . . How does she react to each part of the letter's contents? At what exact moment does it actually dawn on her that this news means her husband must kill the King?

Macbeth's endearment *my dearest partner of greatness* is information about his view of their relationship, and your Lady Macbeth may or may not share his conception of their marriage. There are clues that even if she adores her husband, she perceives flaws in him: for example, there is her contemptuous overstatement in line 20 of Macbeth's annoying little tendency to be decent and moral (*holily*). Although you may decide that Lady M. manipulates her husband's love for her, seeing him merely as her ticket to the good life, a far more nuanced and interesting performance results from acknowledging that she may love her husband passionately and yet not be blind to his "faults."

Lady Macbeth frets that Macbeth is too tender, his nature *too full o' th' milk of human kindness*. She herself has been a mother and nursed an infant (see "Dial Lady M. for Murder," page 676) and yet she is not afflicted with this malady (or so she convinces herself). Much has been made of Lady Macbeth's desire to be "unsexed," to divest herself of the "female" traits of compassion and tenderness (see monologue on page 677). And yet her frequent references to female physical characteristics (here, a mother's milk describing compassion) suggest that she does not wish to shed her femininity, but merely the "weak" aspects of it. She seems quite interested in keeping her sexuality intact . . . and using it to her advantage.

Lady Macbeth uses antithesis in several ways: she contrasts Macbeth's attributes with his shortcomings (*Art not without ambition* versus *but without / The illness should attend it*); she contrasts what he rightfully wants with how he wrongfully approaches it (*What thou wouldst highly* versus *That wouldst thou holily*; and *wouldst not play falsely* versus *And yet wouldst wrongly win*); she contrasts how she hopes he will respond to the witches' prophecy with how she fears he might respond (*that which rather thou dost fear to do* versus *Than wishest should be undone*). Along with these antitheses, she contrasts her husband's weaknesses with her own courage (*thy nature . . . too full o' th' milk of human kindness* versus *my spirits* and *the valor of my tongue*).

Notice that in lines 14–15, Lady M. does not bring herself to say the word *king*. Why does she stop short and substitute the somewhat clumsy *What thou art promised*? Is she afraid to "jinx" Macbeth (in keeping with her superstitious nature—she doesn't doubt the witches for a moment)? Is she trying to contain her excitement so she can begin planning, or to keep her hopes in check? Does the term *king* conjure up guilty images of King Duncan, who must be sacrificed to their ambition? Likewise, instead of saying "to kill King Duncan in order to become king" she uses the euphemism *To catch the nearest way*. She then proceeds (in lines 18–24) to twist her language into a knot in order to avoid articulating the deed. This circumlocution is consistent with her character throughout the play. Though she steels herself against the ethical implications of her actions, her subconscious is bothered nonetheless: she will state later that she could have killed the King herself if he hadn't resembled her father; and she will go mad, hallucinating that she cannot wipe the King's blood off her hands and ultimately killing herself. The euphemistic phrases here provide you with the opportunity to establish this complex element of her character.

Although Lady Macbeth means no harm to Macbeth when she urges him to hurry home so that she might *pour* [*her*] *spirits in* [*his*] *ear*, be aware that the line has a sinister double meaning: in *Hamlet*, King Claudius murdered his elder brother by pouring poison in his ear. This method of murder was—and still is—familiar to Shakespeare's audience and the line will cause a shiver to run up its collective spine. She will pour "poison" in his ear later in the play, when she exhorts him to set aside his misgivings and kill the King.

Notice that Lady Macbeth's language becomes absolutely straightforward (and that the verse becomes even and perfectly iambic) in her final run-on sentence, as though she's making a quick beeline for the crown now that her mind is set on it. But being a woman, Lady Macbeth must rely on her husband to commit the act that she is resolved to see done . . . hence her impatient *Hie thee hither*.

SIGNIFICANT SCANS

As you can see, lines 1–13 are in prose and the remainder are in blank verse. As a result, this monologue affords you the opportunity to show the ease with which you glide from one form to the other. The change from prose to verse marks an important shift in tone. You can use the switch to show the difference between Macbeth's relaxed confidence in his wife, and his wife's take-charge approach. Lady Macbeth's use of verse helps show that she is approaching the situation from a place of confidence, strength, and clarity of purpose. Later in the play, when she loses her mind, she will also lose her ability to versify and will speak in the less precise form of prose.

This monologue is studded with double endings at line ends and, in lines 15 and 20, both at line ends and mid-line before the caesuras. These double endings help give the piece its jumpy, excited feeling. Note that the stress falls on *must* in line 22; Lady M. is determined that the King be killed! Similarly, the stress falls on *un* in *undone* in line 24, which highlights the antithesis, illuminating her meaning in a difficult passage.

The last line has only three spoken feet (we've sheared her final two, which are spoken to an arriving messenger). This gives you two final feet of silence, in which to revel in the image of your husband wearing the crown (which surely comes in his-n-hers . . .).

Don't forget to elide: *metaphysical* (MEH-ta-FIZZ′-kl) in line 28;

. . . and to contract: *o' th' milk* (oth-MILK) in line 16.

DIAL LADY M. FOR MURDER

Though the historical Lady Macbeth (whose given name was Gruoch—no wonder Shakespeare stuck with "Lady"!) did not conspire to kill her king, she had good reason to be ambitious for the throne . . . it had been grabbed from her grampa. The historical Macbeth's claim was based not only on his relationship to Duncan (they were both descendants of Kenneth II), but also on his wife's direct descent from King Kenneth III, from whom Duncan's grandfather, Malcolm II, usurped the throne. Also, this was Lady Macbeth's second marriage; in fact, her son Lulach (Macbeth's stepson, alluded to in the play) ruled for a short time after Macbeth's death until he himself was defeated and killed by Malcolm III. Poor Gruoch—despite her innocence, she will be forever remembered for madly trying to wash Duncan's blood from her hands.

MACBETH

ACT I, SCENE v

LADY MACBETH

GENDER: F
PROSE/VERSE: blank verse
AGE RANGE: adult to mature adult
FREQUENCY OF USE (1–5): 5

Lady Macbeth has just received a letter from her husband, informing her that he has met three witches with clairvoyant powers, who hailed him as the future King of Scotland (see her previous monologue, page 671). Lady Macbeth believes that if their words are to prove true, she and Macbeth must murder the present King Duncan, Macbeth's kinsman, who will be visiting them shortly. She conjures demonic spirits to give her the cruelty she will need to carry out the deed:

The raven himself is hoarse
40 That croaks the fatal entrance of Duncan
Under my battlements. Come, you spirits
That tend on mortal thoughts, unsex me here,
And fill me from the crown to the toe top-full
Of direst cruelty. Make thick my blood,
45 Stop up th' access and passage to remorse,
That no compunctious visitings of nature
Shake my fell purpose, nor keep peace between
Th' effect and it. Come to my woman's breasts
And take my milk for gall, you murdering ministers,
50 Wherever in your sightless substances
You wait on nature's mischief. Come, thick night,
And pall thee in the dunnest smoke of Hell,
That my keen knife see not the wound it makes,
Nor Heaven peep through the blanket of the dark
55 To cry "Hold, hold!"

1 minute

39 *The raven himself* In Shakespeare's time, the raven was considered a bad omen, often signifying impending death; 40 *That croaks* i.e., that announces by croaking; *fatal* both (1) directed by fate and (2) resulting in death; 41 *battlements* parapets built atop the outer walls of a castle, fort, or walled city, with window- or door-size openings through which the building or city could be defended; *you spirits* she calls on demonic spirits from Hell (with a play on the second and third meanings "courage" and "mental power"); 42 *tend* wait on, serve; *mortal thoughts* deadly designs; *unsex me* take away my feminine qualities; 44 *direst* most dreadful; 45 *remorse* compassion, tenderness [*Make thick my blood, / Stop up . . . remorse* i.e., so that pity is blocked and cannot travel through my veins to my heart]; 46 *compunctious* pricking the conscience; *visitings* attacks, fits; *nature* natural human feelings; 47 *fell* fierce, cruel; *keep peace between / Th' effect and it* i.e., make peaceful restraint interfere between my intentions (*it*) and my actions (*Th' effect*); 49 *gall* bile (secreted by the liver and believed in Shakespeare's time to foster ill temper [see "Elizabethan Anatomy 101," page 558]) [*take my milk for gall* (1) replace my milk with gall; or (2) nourish yourselves with my milk, which has become gall]; *murdering ministers* i.e., the demonic spirits Lady M. is conjuring [*Come . . . murdering ministers* It was believed that such demonic spirits would assist a human in the commission of the Devil's work in exchange for nourishment from the human, which they would take by sucking at a "mark" on the human's body. Here, Lady Macbeth invites them to use her breast as their mark]; 50 *sightless* invisible; *substances* beings; 51 *nature's mischief* i.e., either (1) mischief done to nature, violation of nature's order committed by wickedness or (2) both injury engendered in human nature and done to it; 52 *pall thee* wrap you up (as in a cloak); *dunnest* darkest; 53 *That* so that; 55 *Hold* refrain, stop.

COMMENTARY

This brief soliloquy is highly concentrated . . . but please do not dilute: it fairly begs to be acted, containing more than enough guidelines to help an actor give a complex, multidimensional performance that goes far beyond a simple incantation. As her prior monologue indicates (see page 671), Lady M. is ambitious to become queen, excited at the prospect of seeing her husband become king, nervous about his ability to bring it about, and eager to provide the necessary support.

Lady Macbeth makes it clear from the first line that she is thoroughly committed to killing King Duncan. Her use of the phrase *my battlements* confirms how ingrained the decision already is: she now thinks of her castle not as a home, but as a fort. The first decision you must make, however, is whether this commitment is still subconscious (and the phrase merely a "Freudian slip") or quite conscious. And if you decide that she believes she is still grappling reluctantly with the concept and will commit to it only with the help of evil spirits, you must then decide at what point in the monologue she finally does consciously commit to the murder. Do not take this commitment lightly: Shakespeare's England believed firmly in the existence of Heaven and Hell, demons and sorcerers. Regardless of whether you, the actor, decide that your Lady M. ever sees the demons (in reality or in her mind), with this speech Lady Macbeth is pledging herself to the forces of evil—a horrific act.

You must next decide how comfortable Lady Macbeth is with summoning demonic *spirits*. Is she already acquainted with them, or is this her first time trying to establish a connection with them? How confident is she at this moment in her role as murderer, and how much courage does she still need to summon from them? Exploring Lady M.'s use of the word *visitings* in line 46 with its contemptuous-sounding modifier, *compunctious*, may help you answer that question: she seems to consider human feelings of compassion involuntary fits of weakness to ride out—as with the hiccups, just sit tight for a minute and they'll pass. Lady M. clearly wishes to disassociate herself from normal human nature. You must decide how far along in that process she is at each step of this soliloquy.

Once she begins conjuring the spirits, Lady Macbeth doesn't let up: notice that the first word of each sentence invokes their presence (*Come*; *Make*; *Stop*; *Come*; *Come*). Her dark conjuring and creepily descriptive instruction promote the ominous atmosphere first created by the Witches at the start of the play, which will hover over the remainder of the action. Lady M. is truly inviting evil to enter the room and remain there throughout. Her conjuring has the effect of imbuing her with the wicked characteristics of the spirits she summons, successfully distancing her from the human emotions she sets out to destroy in herself.

Much has been made of Lady Macbeth's sexuality, partly because she makes such explicit reference to it herself. As in her previous monologue, she draws attention to her own womanly qualities, ostensibly to cast them off . . . Yet her specific reference to her breasts and the act of nursing, in which she chooses her breast to be the "mark" from which the spirits feed (see Annotation), suggests that she does not actually wish to be "unsexed," but, rather, to lose only the "weak" aspects of her gender and incorporate the "strong" aspects of the male while retaining her very female sexuality. Marks to feed demon spirits were traditionally on the arm, not the breast: perhaps she chooses a sexual body part as her mark because she feels that this will help recast her breast as a nonfeminine object. Or perhaps she is aware of the power of her sexuality, considers it the source of her power over her husband, and wishes to augment its strength, so that she will be sure to bend him to her will. Or perhaps, since she has been a mother (as she explains elsewhere in the play), she turns to the method of nourishment to which she is accustomed. You need to find a motivation that makes sense to you.

Lady Macbeth uses antithesis to contrast what she is (a woman with natural human compassion) with what she wishes to be (a ruthless, supernaturally guided murderer): *remorse . . . compunctious visitings of nature* versus *my fell purpose*; *my milk* versus *gall*; *Hell* versus *Heaven*.

Notice that Lady M. says it is *my . . . knife* (as opposed to her husband's) that shall make the wound. In her earlier monologue she expressed uncertainty that Macbeth had the toughness to carry it off. She may also feel it would be unfair to expect him to do something she's not wholeheartedly willing to do herself. Her ability to specify details of the crime (*knife*, *wound*) indicates that she understands the gruesome nature of the act. She does not sugar-coat her actions to make them more palatable. Though she will go crazy *after* the murder, she certainly could not argue insanity or non compos mentis at the time of the murder as a defense.

The soliloquy contains a built-in build in intensity, culminating in the moment when Lady Macbeth, now in the realm of the supernatural, can freely command *night* to come serve as accomplice to her crime. She is not content to settle for the darkest that night alone has to offer. Rather, she requires that it give her added insurance by *palling* its darkness (*Macbeth* is full of clothing imagery) in *the dunnest smoke of Hell*. The lady wants it blacker than black. Why?

Well, for all her toughness, wethinks the lady doth protest too much: her desire to shield the deed from *Heaven*'s view indicates that the spirits have not completed their work yet—she is not wholly impervious to morality. Or perhaps her own self-interest makes her worry about her eternal soul. She therefore plans to circumvent Heaven's influence by committing the murder at night, with the added security of a screen of smoke from Hell.

Enjoy the consonance and assonance, which help to create a tone of necromantic incantation. Examples include Murderous Ms (*Come* / *my woman's* / *my milk* / *murdering ministers*) and Nefarious Ns (*nature's* / *night* / *in the dunnest* / *keen knife see not* / *Nor*) as well as smaller sound-groupings (such as *himself is hoarse*; *to the toe top-full*; *Make thick*; *Stop up*; *th' access and passage to remorse*; *nature* / *Shake*; *keep peace between*; *sightless substances*). Also, Lady Macbeth often ends one word and begins another with the same sound (*That tend*; *keep peace*; *sightless substances*; *keen knife*, and, sort of, *dunnest smoke*). You'll hear the increased power in your delivery when you distinctly separate the words rather than slurring them together.

Lady Macbeth's long sentences add to the incantatory tone, and pull her smoothly through the monologue. You must decide whether she is eager to begin, or is frightened and speaks quickly to keep from losing her nerve. Or, in the process of psyching herself up, she may get carried away. The lengthy final sentence creates an acceleration to the final exclamation, helping you finish on a powerful note.

SIGNIFICANT SCANS

There are several inverted feet, both at the beginnings of lines and mid-line after caesuras, as well as several double endings, creating an emphatic and urgent tone that suggests Lady M. seeks to command her spirits both forcefully and quickly.

Line 39 has only three feet of spoken text, one of which (*—en himself*) is crowded. This gives you the opportunity to collect your scattered thoughts before you plunge into your conjuring, or to check that no servants are loitering within earshot, etc. Similarly, the pause at the caesura before *Come* in line 41 (which also has an inverted first foot) gives you a chance to take a deep breath before embarking on a path from which there can be no return. Remember, not only does she risk eternal damnation, but if she is caught conjuring Lady M. could face burning at the stake.

/ x x / x / x / x /
Under my battlements. (pause) Come, you spirits

Note that this scansion of the line requires the elision of the word *spirits* (SPEERTS). Alternatively, you may pronounce the word as we do today and treat the extra syllable as a double ending.

Line 44 can be scanned two ways: you can pronounce all three syllables

(CROO′-ell-TEE) or you can elide *cruelty* (CROOL-tee) and take a pause at the caesura before *Make* (as in line 44). In line 45, *th' access* is given its historical pronunciation, with the accent on the second syllable (th'ak-SESS). And the last line has only two feet of spoken text, giving you three silent feet at the end in which to await the demonic spirits, welcome them into your soul, gather strength from your own words, grow fearful, etc.

Don't forget to elide: *spirits* (SPEERTS) in line 41 (optional); *murdering* (MUR-dring) and *ministers* (MIN-sters) in line 49; and *Heaven* (HEV'N) in line 54;

. . . to contract: *the toe* (TH'TOE) in line 43 and *Th' effect* (Th'e-FECT) in line 48;

. . . and to expand: *entrance* (EN′-ter-ENSS) in line 40—this expansion emphasizes that Duncan's crucial *entrance* will be his last.

P.S.

For information on the historical Lady M., see "Dial Lady M. for Murder," page 676.

MACBETH

ACT 1, SCENE vii

MACBETH

GENDER: M
AGE RANGE: mature adult
PROSE/VERSE: blank verse
FREQUENCY OF USE (1–5): 4

Macbeth has encountered three witches who prophesied that he would become King of Scotland. To bring this to pass, Macbeth and his wife have agreed to kill his kinsman King Duncan and seize the Scottish crown. But now that Duncan has arrived as a guest at his castle, Macbeth is having second thoughts about committing the murder. He soliloquizes:

If it were done, when 'tis done, then 'twere well
It were done quickly; if th' assassination
Could trammel up the consequence, and catch,
With his surcease, success; that but this blow
5 Might be the be-all and the end-all . . . here,
But here upon this bank and shoal of time,
We'd jump the life to come. But in these cases
We still have judgment here; that we but teach
Bloody instructions, which being taught, return
10 To plague th' inventor. This even-handed justice
Commends th' ingredience of our poisoned chalice
To our own lips. He's here in double trust:
First, as I am his kinsman and his subject,
Strong both against the deed; then, as his host,
15 Who should against his murderer shut the door,
Not bear the knife myself. Besides, this Duncan
Hath borne his faculties so meek, hath been
So clear in his great office, that his virtues
Will plead like angels, trumpet-tongued against
20 The deep damnation of his taking-off;
And Pity, like a naked new-born babe
Striding the blast, or Heaven's cherubin, horsed

1 *If it were done . . . quickly* perhaps playing on the proverb "The thing done has an end"; 3 *trammel up* (1) entangle, as in a net (*trammel* meaning a long net used to catch partridges or fish; this metaphor seems to be continued with the word *catch* at the end of the line); and/or (2) tie up (*trammel* meaning a device used to control horses; this metaphor is connected with the references to horses later in the speech); 4 *surcease* cessation, stopping (a legal term) [*his surcease* either (1) Duncan's death or (2) the cessation of the consequences (Shakespeare commonly uses *his* in place of "its")]; *success* used with a play on "succession" to the throne; *that but* if only; *this blow* i.e., the assassination; 5 *the be-all and the end-all* the entirety of the action and that which completes and contains it; 6 *bank* riverbank (or "bench"—see Commentary); *shoal* shallow; sandbar (or replace with "school"—see Commentary); 7 *We'd jump the life to come* (1) We'd risk the fates of our souls in the afterlife; or (2) We'd evade the issue of what will become of our souls in the afterlife; *these cases* i.e., murder cases; 8 *still* always; *have judgment here* receive judgment and punishment in this life; *that* in that; *but* only; 9 *instructions* lessons; 11 *Commends* recommends; offers; *ingredience* mixture of ingredients; *chalice* cup, goblet (symbol of sacredness and trust, as the chalice used at the Last Supper, and in Christian worship); 14 *Strong both* both strong arguments; 17 *borne his faculties* wielded his powers; *meek* (1) humbly; (2) gently, compassionately; 18 *clear* blameless, irreproachable; *his great office* i.e., his reign; 19 *plead . . . against* testify . . . against; 20 *taking-off* murder; 21 *Pity* pity, personified; 22 *Striding the blast* mounting the cold, violent gusts of wind (i.e., riding the storm of indignation from the heavens)—with a play on *blast* to mean the blowing of a trumpet; *cherubin* cherub (singular)—possibly Gabriel, God's avenging archangel, and the head of the Cheru-

Upon the sightless couriers of the air,
Shall blow the horrid deed in every eye,
25 That tears shall drown the wind. I have no spur
To prick the sides of my intent, but only
Vaulting ambition, which o'erleaps itself
And falls on th' other—
[*Enter Lady Macbeth*]
How now, what news?

1 minute, 40 seconds

bim; also, the winds were often depicted as cherubs on Renaissance maps; 23 *sightless* invisible [*horsed / Upon . . . couriers of the air* riding on the winds as on horses]; 24 *blow* both (1) sound an announcement, as with a trumpet, and (2) propel (as dust blown into the eye); 25 *That* so that; *tears shall drown the wind* i.e., tears will become as abundant as rain, and calm the wind (alluding to the proverbial idea that rain caused wind to abate); 26 *but only* except; 27 *Vaulting* leaping [*Vaulting ambition* a reference to the Gunpowder Plot of 1605, in which kegs of gunpowder were stockpiled in a vault beneath Parliament, with the intention of blowing it, the King, and the entire government sky-high (see "Explosive Material: The Gunpowder Plays," page 708)]; *o'erleaps itself* leaps too far; 28 *other* i.e., other side [*Vaulting . . . other* i.e., ambition, which is like a rider, vaulting into the saddle, who leaps too far and falls on the other side of the horse]; 29 *How now* a common exclamation meaning "What is the matter?" or "What are you doing here?"

COMMENTARY

This piece is quite well known but not always well understood. Don't let the ongoing debate among scholars deter you from choosing this powerful soliloquy. The questions that arise in preparing it will yield interesting choices and elicit varied and unique interpretations.

Some editors have placed a period after *quickly* in line 2, which alters the meaning of the very first sentence. In contrast, we have punctuated the first *three* sentences without any full stops, taking a cue from the First Folio (the only surviving source for the text). This punctuation makes it clear that Macbeth is not saying "If it's going to be done, then when it *is* done, it's best it was done quickly," but rather, that he is playing on different meanings of the word *done* in the first line and a half, saying "If the deed were completely finished with when it is accomplished, then it would be best to go ahead and perform it quickly." He then repeats this sentiment twice more in other terms. The repetition emphasizes Macbeth's fervent wish that he could do the deed and be done with it, safe from the consequences of punishment in this life or the next one. He repeats not only the idea, but also the key word, *done*. With all of this in mind, the following scansion of the first line makes the most sense:

```
/x  x    /       /  x   x     /      x    /
If it were done, when 'tis done, then 'twere well
```

Or, alternatively, you could scan it this way, crowding *then 'twere well*:

```
/x  x    /       x        /  x    /     x - x     /
If it were done, (pause) when 'tis done, then 'twere well
```

Of course, you are free to agree with editors who separate the meaning of the first statement from that of the second and third, in which case this scansion of line 1 will work well for you:

```
/x  x    /     x   /   x    /     x    /
If it were done, when 'tis done, then 'twere well
```

That said, most of the debate over this monologue centers on the *next* idea (*here upon this bank and shoal of time, / We'd jump the life to come*)—in which Macbeth imagines how one might behave if it were possible to commit an act that is complete in itself. There are two possible interpretations of these lines. According to the first of these, the phrase *bank and shoal of time* is meant to evoke an island, i.e., a frozen moment, in the river of time (Shakespeare often depicts time as a flowing river), which provides the opportunity to commit an act free of consequences. On the other hand, in the First Folio the word *school* appears in place of the word *shoal*. Most traditional editors, knowing that *school* was a common spelling of *shoal* in Shakespeare's time, have assumed that he intended the word *shoal*. Others, however, claim that *school* itself is intended here, and that *bank* means "bench" (as was also common in Shakespeare's time)—particularly a schoolhouse bench. Read this way, the phrase *bank and school of time* refers to a "school of thought," i.e., a way of thinking, according to which acts may be committed outside of time and consequences. The use of *bank* to mean "bench" and the replacement of *shoal* with *school* in the text allows you to create a through-line with the words *teach*, *instructions*, and *taught*, which appear a few lines later. We recommend the first interpretation, because it will probably be more comprehensible to today's audience, but since no one has had the opportunity to take up the matter with the Bard himself in recent years, you should feel comfortable interpreting this section either way.

And that's not all the literary ambiguity in this piece. The two generally accepted possible meanings of *We'd jump the life to come* are shown in the Annotation. There is also debate about the word *cherubin*: as you can see in the Annotation, we chose to interpret it as singular, which seems to fit best in context. Some editors have argued, however, that Shakespeare intended the plural *cherubim* or *cherubins*, or thought that *cherubin* was plural (reasonable, since the word in its original Hebrew is a plural of *cherub*). Again, feel free to adopt the form and meaning that works best for you.

Once you have pinned down your interpretion of the text, you are ready to delve into the richness of its poetry, the most striking element of which is its relentless imagery. Now this is a man with an active imagination! In fact, Macbeth is famous for it, and this monologue is a prime example of his excitable mind at work.

Throughout the play, Macbeth attempts to trick time, to live outside it, and this has a very disturbing effect on him: for Macbeth, time is out of joint and his mind is awash with frightening imagery, putting him in a state of perpetual nightmare. He is plagued by what may happen if he continues his course: the assassination will catch up *consequence* as if in a net, or tied like horses; men are like teachers, instructing others to emulate their bloody actions; and *justice*, personified, will cordially offer the bloody deeds of the teacher back to him in a poisoned *chalice*. The chalice and other religious references subtly equate the enormity of the betrayal Macbeth is contemplating with Judas's betrayal of Jesus. Duncan, like Jesus, had "almost supped" when Macbeth left the table, just as Judas did before his betrayal. Likewise, Macbeth's comment that *'twere well /*

It were done quickly recalls Jesus' words to Judas at the last supper, "That thou doest, do quickly." No wonder Macbeth has a change of heart! There are powerful images dancing in his head. As the piece—and Macbeth's fear—build, the images intensify: Duncan's virtues will *plead like angels, trumpet-tongued*; *Pity* personified as a *naked new-born babe* will ride in on the winds; then, re-created as Heaven's avenging angel, Pity will ride in on the winds and *blow the horrid deed in every eye*, after which *tears shall drown the wind*.

Macbeth's visualizations of these consequences bring him to the conclusion that he should abandon his murderous plan, as he will suggest to Lady Macbeth in the next scene. Nevertheless, many interpret the last two lines to indicate that deep down Macbeth fears that his *Vaulting ambition* will urge him forward on the course toward self-destruction; just as we are often unable to wake ourselves from our nightmares, Macbeth may be unable to alter the fated course that causes his nightmarish visions.

In these last few lines, Macbeth also hints at his own impotence and sterility through double entendre. The second meanings of the words below would have been familiar to audiences of Shakespeare's time: *spur* = erect penis; *prick* = to engage in sexual intercourse; *Vaulting* = engaging energetically in sexual intercourse [*vaulting ambition* = the ambition to engage in sex]. In Shakespeare's time the word *ride* and the image of horseback riding often had sexual double meanings. Here, Macbeth comments on his own impotence: since he has no *spur* to *prick* with, his *Vaulting ambition* is not successful—he's either missing his mark, or shooting blanks, or both.

Since Macbeth aspires to be king, his use of the words *we* in lines 7–8 and *our* in lines 11–12 may be seen as an anticipation of his right to use the royal "we." It may also be a tactic in which Macbeth explores his own dilemma less personally, as if disinterestedly considering the human condition in general. Macbeth also distances himself from the horror of the deed he proposes by objectifying his kinsman (whom he certainly knows quite well), calling him *this Duncan*.

Another phrase that carries a lot of baggage is *double trust*—notice he says double, but names three and then adds a fourth reason he should not betray Duncan's trust. These reasons are stronger to him than they seem to us today. Of course, being Duncan's kinsman and the King's subject are powerful reasons not to do him harm. But Macbeth's responsibility as a host may be an even greater obstacle. This responsibility, which dated back to prehistory, when travelers were completely dependent on strangers for hospitality, was considered sacred. According to the strict conventions that developed over time, a host was responsible for the well-being of his guests and was required not only to refrain from doing them harm, but also to protect them against harm from others. In addition, the words *double trust* may allude to an act of 1597, by which the commission of a murder under the "trust, credit, assurance and power of the slayer" became treason—making Macbeth's crime seem doubly treasonous to Elizabethans. One can imagine that Macbeth's fourth argument—that Duncan's goodness will make Macbeth's crime even more damnable—is right on target.

The combination of meter and sound repetitions drive the monologue forward like a powerful freight train. The incredible chain of sound repetitions and Macbeth's continuous chain of thoughts beginning and ending mid-line join together in a powerful mélange of rhythm, momentum, and connectedness. This is particularly powerful in the first five lines: note the phrase and sound repetition in the first sentence, soon followed by *consequence* / *catch*; *surcease* / *success*; *that but this blow*; *be the be-all and the end-all*. Though not as pronounced in the remainder of the piece, the sound repetitions persist, with hard Ds, Ts, Ns, and Bs (*double trust*; *trumpet-tongued*; *deep damnation*; *naked new-born babe*). The many double endings at line ends and before caesuras contribute to the continuity of sound and thought, and subtly evoke Macbeth's rattled nerves.

SIGNIFICANT SCANS

Line 14 has a spondaic first foot (i.e., both syllables are stressed), as well as a trochaic (inverted) foot after the caesura:

/ / x / x / / x x /
Strong both against the deed; then, as his host

Here are two different ways to scan line 22: you could invert the first and third feet, and crowd the fifth (—*ubin, horsed*)—

/ x x / / x x / x-x /
Striding the blast, or Heaven's cherubin, horsed

Notice that this places a stress on the word *or*: Macbeth is trumping his first metaphor with a more ominous one (i.e., the naked newborn, *Pity*, replaced by the avenging *cherubin*, who, if interpreted as the archangel Gabriel, would have been an imposing figure with 140 pairs of wings).

Alternatively, you could invert the first foot and crowd the fifth (as above), but keep the third foot iambic—

/ x x / x / x / x-x /
Striding the blast, or Heaven's cherubin, horsed

This reading emphasizes *Heaven's cherubin* himself.

In line 28, Macbeth cuts himself off as he sees his wife entering. Notice that the second syllable of the third foot is silent—it is easy to imagine that Macbeth was about to say "side," to complete his idea, but was distracted by his wife's entrance, and thus left off mid-sentence to ask her *what news?*:

x / x / x / x / x /
And falls on th' other—(pause) How now, what news?

Don't forget to elide: *being* (BEENG) in line 9; *murderer* (MER-drer) in line 15; *couriers* (KER-yerz) in line 23; and *o'erleaps* (ore-LEEPS) in line 27.

. . . to contract: all the occurrences of *th'* with the words that follow them in lines 2, 10, 11, and 28 (consider the effect this frequent contraction has on your delivery—is Macbeth rushing, or is it a way for Shakespeare to subtly indicate Macbeth's Scottish dialect without your having to adopt one?);

. . . and to contract *and* elide: *th' ingredience* (th'in-GREED-yenss) in line 11.

REVISIONIST HISTORY: MUCH-MALIGNED MACBETH

Shakespeare took more than a few liberties with the historical Macbeth's life, both for dramatic effect and to please his monarch (see "Wasn't This a Dainty Dish to Put Before the King," page 993). To start with, he ascribed to the poor guy a murder he did not commit! Thumbing through Holinshed's dense *Scottish Chronicles*, Shakespeare read about a noble named Donwald, who—at the urging of his wife—murdered the early Scottish ruler King Dubh (Duff to Holinshed) in his sleep. Shakespeare promptly reassigned the dishonorable deed to his Macbeth. The historical Macbeth did take the throne from King Duncan, but under perfectly legitimate circumstances: Macbeth had a claim to the throne through his wife, the granddaughter of Kenneth III, from whom Duncan's grandfather usurped the throne. Furthermore, both he and Duncan were descendants of King Kenneth II at a time when the strongest and most competent member of the royal family was supposed to hold the throne, since in eleventh-century Scotland the throne was not passed down through primogeniture. When a weak and ineffectual king such as the historical Duncan ruled, a stronger kinsman was expected to take the throne—by force if necessary—to bring stability to the nation. Macbeth took the throne honorably on the battlefield, where Duncan was slain. Macbeth then ruled peaceably and well for fifteen years. Because King James was believed to be a direct descendant of Duncan, however, it behooved Shakespeare to present Macbeth as a usurping, malignant traitor.

MACBETH

ACT 1, SCENE vii

LADY MACBETH

GENDER: F
PROSE/VERSE: blank verse
AGE RANGE: adult to mature adult
FREQUENCY OF USE (1–5): 4

Lady Macbeth's husband encountered three witches who prophesied that he would become king of Scotland. To bring this to pass, she and Macbeth agreed on a plan to kill his kinsman King Duncan and seize the Scottish crown. But now that Duncan has arrived as a guest at their castle, Macbeth is having second thoughts about committing the murder. Lady Macbeth convinces him to go through with the deed:

35 Was the hope drunk,
Wherein you dressed yourself? Hath it slept since?
And wakes it now, to look so green and pale
At what it did so freely? From this time
Such I account thy love. Art thou afeard
40 To be the same in thine own act and valor,
As thou art in desire? Wouldst thou have that
Which thou esteem'st the ornament of life,
And live a coward in thine own esteem,
Letting "I dare not" wait upon "I would,"
45 Like the poor cat i' th' adage?

When you durst do it, then you were a man;
50 And, to be more than what you were, you would
Be so much more the man. Nor time, nor place
Did then adhere, and yet you would make both:
They have made themselves, and that their fitness now
Does unmake you. I have given suck, and know
55 How tender 'tis to love the babe that milks me:
I would, while it was smiling in my face,
Have plucked my nipple from his boneless gums,

37 *green and pale* i.e., with nausea, as from a hangover; 38 *what it did* i.e., having resolved and plotted to murder Duncan; *From this time . . . thy love* i.e., from now on I will consider your love for me as fickle and contemptible as your lack of resolve; 40 *act* actions; 41 *that / Which . . . ornament of life* that which you believe makes life beautiful, i.e., the crown, and all its attendant power and glory (with a play on *ornament* to mean a decorative piece of jewelry or clothing) [*Wouldst thou have . . . thine own esteem* i.e., do you desire the crown and yet choose to live like a self-acknowledged coward]; 44 *wait upon* follow after; 45 *cat i' th' adage* refers to the adage "The cat wishes to eat fish, but she will not wet her feet"; 49 *durst* dared; 50 *to be more . . . more the man* i.e., if you'd act like more than what you were when you proposed the deed (by actually committing it), you'd be that much more a man (with an implied second meaning: to become king, you were willing to act so much more manly); 51 *Nor* Neither; 52 *Did then adhere* was then suitable; *would make both* wanted to make both time and place suitable; 53 *and that their fitness now* and the very fact that they are suitable now; 54 *Does unmake you* (UN-make) (1) unnerves you; and/or (2) makes you incapable of taking action; 57 *boneless*

And dashed the brains out, had I so sworn as you
Have done to this.

60 But screw your courage to the sticking-place,
And we'll not fail. When Duncan is asleep
(Whereto the rather shall his day's hard journey
Soundly invite him), his two chamberlains
Will I with wine and wassail so convince,
65 That memory, the warder of the brain,
Shall be a fume, and the receipt of reason
A limbeck only. When in swinish sleep
Their drenchèd natures lie, as in a death,
What cannot you and I perform upon
70 Th' unguarded Duncan? What not put upon
His spongy officers, who shall bear the guilt
Of our great quell?

77 Who dares receive it other,
As we shall make our griefs and clamor roar
Upon his death?

2 minutes, 10 seconds

toothless; 58 *the* frequently used by Shakespeare in place of "his"; 60 *But* Simply, only; *sticking-place* place in which a thing stops and holds tightly (referring to either [1] the point to which the peg on a stringed instrument must be tightened to achieve the correct pitch or [2] the point to which the cord of a crossbow must be tightened to correctly propel the arrow—with a possible play on *sticking-place* to mean "stab wound") [*screw your courage to the sticking-place* i.e., screw up your courage until it holds]; 62 *Whereto the rather* to which all the sooner; 63 *Soundly invite him* invite him to sleep soundly (with an ironic play on the "sound," or "strong and healthy," sleep of death); *chamberlains* officers who manage the king's private chambers; 64 *wassail* (WOSS-ll) drunken carousing; *convince* overcome, overpower (with a play on "persuade," a less common meaning of the word in Shakespeare's work); 65 *warder* guard, keeper; 66 *fume* anything that hinders the brain's function (delusion, drunkenness, etc.); *receipt of reason* receptacle of reason, i.e., the brain; 67 *limbeck* alembic, still (an apparatus used for distillation; here, either [1] the part of the still into which fumes rise [in this case the fumes rise into the brain, clouding it] or [2] the part of the still that holds the crude, undistilled liquids [in this case, the brain, which should be the receptacle in which the final refined thought is gathered, acts merely as a container for undistilled, clouded thought]); *swinish* (1) beastly, gross; (2) drunken; 68 *drenchèd* drowned (in liquor), perhaps with a play on "drench," a dose of medicine given to animals; *natures* selves; 71 *spongy* i.e., soaked with liquor, like sponges; 72 *quell* killing (both words have the same root); 77 *receive it other* understand or believe it to be otherwise.

COMMENTARY

One of the most enticing things about this role and this monologue in particular is that Lady Macbeth can be interpreted in so many different ways. Over the centuries, she has been played as a heartless villain and an irresistible siren; as an ambitious naïf and as a savvy sorceress. The choices you make about what kind of person Lady Macbeth is will determine your choices in this monologue.

Time is of the essence for the Macbeths. Tonight is their only opportunity to kill Duncan, since he plans to depart in the morning. Also, Duncan is eating dinner as she speaks, unaccompanied by either his host or hostess; just prior to this monologue, Lady M. expressed concern that their rude absence will arouse his suspicion, so she is eager to get Macbeth on board and then get back to the dining room a.s.a.p. She wastes no time, jumping right in with a first line that starts with an inverted first foot, setting an aggressive tone (note that she speaks only the last two feet of the line; the first three are Macbeth's). She then tries one tactic after another until she hits on one that works. By repeatedly beginning new sentences and new tactics mid-line, she enhances the sense of urgency.

In the first section, Lady Macbeth twice uses imagery to compare her husband's former murderous ambition with his present cowardice (he dressed himself in a drunken *hope*, which now awakens with a hangover and causes him to waver; he falters like the *cat i' th' adage*). Lady Macbeth obviously knows her husband well; perhaps she uses imagery here to engage his unusually active imagination. She tries to shame him into action by calling him a coward, and uses her love as leverage, threatening to withdraw it if he doesn't fulfill his promise to make her queen (after all, how can she love a fickle backpedaler?). Perhaps she's also trying to make Macbeth angry in the hope that his anger will spur him on. Lady Macbeth frequently and pointedly uses the familiar *thee* and *thou* in this section: perhaps she is simply addressing him as a wife would normally address her husband in private, using the repetition to emphasize either their partnership in the plot or her love for him. Her later switch to the formal *you*, however, may suggest that she uses the familiar form to degrade him, as this usage is also appropriate from an adult to a child, or a superior to one of lower rank.

The last two lines of the first section (44 and 45) and the first two lines of the next (49 and 50) all begin with inverted (trochaic) feet, and line 49 has one after the caesura as well. These create an aggressive build from the end of Lady Macbeth's first persuasive tactic to her second, in which she takes a more conciliatory tone. In this section the forceful trochaic inversions disappear, and double endings soften Lady Macbeth's speech. She switches her form of address to the respectful *you* while describing Macbeth's opportunity to become a real man, a manly man. You get to decide whether she's playing on his desire to be manly or tempting him with the love and favors he'll receive from her if he proves his courage. Conversely, if you decide that her earlier use of *thee* was intimate, not condescending, here the shift to *you* may be a sign of distance and disgust at his cowardice.

In the middle of this second section (lines 49–59), Lady Macbeth switches tactics yet again, comparing her husband's courage and honor to her own. Actors have approached these lines in many different ways. Your interpretation will depend completely on your view of Lady M. If you feel that she is cold, calculating, and/or blinded by ambition, you may interpret as hard, cruel, and literal her claim that she would have *dashed the brains out* of her nursing child. Alternatively, you might decide that Lady M. describes a mother violently killing her child *despite* her love for it, to show Macbeth just how seriously she takes her vows. This second interpretation, which seems better supported by the material, allows you to portray her as a more complex person; one who so passionately loves those close to her that she is willing to commit treason and murder to benefit them. Consider, too, the identity of the baby in question. Since Macbeth has no heirs, there are two possible explanations. This may have been a baby of Macbeth's that, as was all too common at the time, died in infancy or childhood. Or Lady Macbeth may be referring to her son by her first marriage (see "Dial Lady M. for Murder," page 676). The last line of this section (59) has only two feet of spoken text (the remainder, a brief exchange between Macbeth and Lady Macbeth, has been excised to create this monologue). The three silent feet fall at an opportune moment, allowing you to make the transition to your next action. Perhaps Lady M. is running out of ideas and needs to think for a moment—or maybe her arguments are having an effect and she's watching Macbeth, allowing *him* to think.

Lady Macbeth finally succeeds in persuading her husband with her third tactic. In the last section (lines 60–72 and 77–79) she lays out the plan for Macbeth in detail, to make it seem real and plausible. She exhorts him, *screw your courage to the sticking-place*, using imagery to help Macbeth visualize his courage and begin summoning it. To convince him of the ease with which they will trick Duncan's chamberlains, she makes distilleries of their very *brain*[*s*], which she will cloud with a *fume* of drunkenness. This is particularly powerful, because she has used the image of drunkenness earlier in the piece as a way of ridiculing Macbeth. With this image, and with words such as *swinish* and *spongy*, she paints the chamberlains as rather despicable and deserving of their fate. Notice that metrically inverted feet appear again, enhancing Lady M.'s efforts to urge her husband on (lines 63, 66, and 69). Lines 72 and 77 are both short, due to excised dialogue, but they happen to fit together perfectly, creating a line of normal iambic pentameter with a double ending. Line 79 is also short, providing three silent feet in which to wait (hopefully? confidently? desperately?) for Macbeth's reply.

The irony that infuses this piece is enhanced by wordplay (see Annotation): Lady Macbeth is one smart (and manipulative) cookie! Also, repeated sounds enhance her arguments, such as these small groupings of assonance and consonance: *slept since*; *act and valor / As*; *durst do*; *tender 'tis*; *milks me*; *while / smiling*; *receipt of reason*; *swinish sleep*. There are also wonderful sound strings, such as Ws and THs (*Wouldst thou have that / Which thou*) and Ws, IHs, IEs, leading to Ss (*Will I with wine and wassail so convince*). Lady Macbeth weaves a web of words from which Macbeth finally cannot withdraw.

Don't forget to elide: *desire* (de-ZIRE) in line 41 (optional) and *our* (OWR) in line 72;

. . . to contract: *They have* (They've) in line 53; *I have* (I've) in line 54; *Th' unguarded* (thun-GAR-ded) in line 70; and *who shall* (who'll) in line 71;

. . . and to expand: *memory* (MEH´-muh-REE) in line 65 and *drenchèd* (DREN-chehd) in line 68.

P.S.

For information about the historical Lady Macbeth, see "Dial Lady M. for Murder," page 676.

MACBETH

ACT II, SCENE I

MACBETH

GENDER: M
PROSE/VERSE: blank verse
AGE RANGE: mature adult
FREQUENCY OF USE (1–5): 5

Macbeth encountered three witches who prophesied that he would be King of Scotland. To that end, Macbeth and the missus planned to kill their kinsman, the present King Duncan, who is currently visiting them. When Macbeth's resolve wavered, his wife mocked his cowardice and presented a plan of action—late at night, she'll ply the King's servants with wine and will ring a bell to notify Macbeth once they've passed out. Macbeth shall then kill the sleeping King and leave the bloody dagger with the unconscious servants, framing them. Now the time has come. Everyone has gone off to sleep. Alone outside the King's chambers waiting for the bell to ring, Macbeth suddenly sees an apparition—a levitating dagger.

Is this a dagger which I see before me,
The handle toward my hand? Come, let me clutch thee. —
35 I have thee not, and yet I see thee still.
Art thou not, fatal vision, sensible
To feeling as to sight? Or art thou but
A dagger of the mind, a false creation
Proceeding from the heat-oppressèd brain?
40 I see thee yet, in form as palpable
As this which now I draw.
[*He draws his dagger*]
Thou marshal'st me the way that I was going,
And such an instrument I was to use. —
Mine eyes are made the fools o' th' other senses
45 Or else worth all the rest. —I see thee still,
And, on thy blade and dudgeon, gouts of blood,
Which was not so before. —There's no such thing.
It is the bloody business which informs
Thus to mine eyes. —Now o'er the one-half world
50 Nature seems dead, and wicked dreams abuse
The curtained sleep: witchcraft celebrates
Pale Hecate's offerings; and withered murder,
Alarumed by his sentinel, the wolf,

36 *fatal vision* both (1) an apparition of death and (2) a vision of what is fated; *sensible* capable of being sensed [*sensible / To feeling* capable of being felt when touched]; 39 *heat-oppressèd* feverishly excited; 40 *yet* still; *palpable* touchable, i.e., tangible, manifest; 42 *marshal'st* lead, direct [*Thou marshal'st me . . . going* (1) You are leading me in the direction I was already heading (i.e., toward Duncan's room); and/or (2) You urge me toward the commission of the murder I already intended to commit]; 43 *such an instrument I was to use* I was planning to use the same kind of weapon; 44 *Mine eyes are made . . . all the rest* Either my other senses are playing tricks on my eyes (i.e., the dagger is an apparition), or my eyes are worth more than my other senses (i.e., they can perceive what my other senses cannot); 46 *dudgeon* handle of a dagger; *gouts* drops; 48 *the bloody business* i.e., the murder; *informs / Thus* takes this shape; gives this false impression; 49 *the one-half world* i.e., this hemisphere; 50 *Nature seems dead* the natural world seems dead (because everything is asleep)—with play on another meaning of *nature*, natural tender human emotions, which seem dead in Macbeth; *abuse* all of the following: (1) deceive; (2) put to wrong use; and (3) pervert, corrupt; 51 *curtained* (1) enclosed by bed curtains; (2) hidden away from consciousness; *witchcraft* i.e., witches practicing withcraft; 52 *Pale Hecate's* in Greek mythology, Hecate was the goddess of the underworld and one of the goddesses of the moon (hence *Pale Hecate*, although to the Greeks she was the goddess of the dark side of the moon). Because of her association with the underground, she came to be considered the queen of withcraft by medieval Europeans [*witchcraft . . . offerings* witches are offering sacrifices to celebrate their pale queen, Hecate]; *withered* gaunt and ghostlike; 53 *Alarumed*

Whose howl's his watch, thus with his stealthy pace,
55 With Tarquin's ravishing strides, towards his design
Moves like a ghost. —Thou sure and firm-set earth,
Hear not my steps, which way they walk, for fear
Thy very stones prate of my whereabouts
And take the present horror from the time
60 Which now suits with it. —Whiles I threat, he lives;
Words to the heat of deeds too cold breath gives.
[*A bell rings.*]
I go, and it is done; the bell invites me.
Hear it not, Duncan, for it is a knell
That summons thee to Heaven or to Hell.

1 minute, 50 seconds

summoned to action (from the call to arms, "all armed!"); 54 *his watch* depending on whether you interpret *his* to mean "the murderer's" or "the wolf's": (1) the murderer's way of marking the passage of the night; or (2) the wolf's watchword (the signal he calls out when keeping the watch); 55 *Tarquin* an early Roman prince, whose rape and mutilation of his cousin's wife, Lucrece, is the subject of Shakespeare's narrative poem *The Rape of Lucrece* [*Tarquin's ravishing strides* the stealthy steps Tarquin took when moving toward Lucrece to rape her]; *design* enterprise, work in hand; 56 *sure* stable, steady; 58 *prate of* tattle about (possibly a reference to Luke 19:40, ". . . if these should hold their peace, the stones would cry"); 59 *take the present horror from the time* take away (with his footsteps) the horror of the moment's total silence, i.e., break the horrific silence; 60 *suits* is fitting, agrees; *Whiles I threat* i.e., while I stand here merely threatening to act (instead of acting); 61 *Words to the heat of deeds too cold breath gives* i.e., words cool off the heat of action; 62 *it is done* i.e., the murder is as good as committed; 63 *knell* the tolling of a bell rung at a funeral.

COMMENTARY

Macbeth is a mass of contradictions: brave, yet afraid to commit this murder; principled, yet ambitious enough to override his own ethics in order to become king. Here he finds himself waiting to carry out an act he does not wish to commit, to obtain a prize he badly wants.

To deliver this piece successfully, it is important to chart what Macbeth experiences and what actions he takes in response, from moment to moment. He establishes a relationship with the *dagger*, speaking directly to it as he might to another character. You must decide why his first impulse is to clutch it: it may not be floating at first (though it is commonly interpreted as floating at some point). Perhaps he sees the dagger lying on a table and takes it for a real dagger—maybe left for him by Lady Macbeth?—until his first unsuccessful attempt to clutch it. Or perhaps it floats from the onset, and he clutches it to determine whether it is real, or in the hope that doing so will make it vanish. You must make specific choices if you are to convince your audience that you actually believe you *see* a dagger before you. Macbeth wonders whether his own anxious imagination (which he himself knows is quite vivid) has created the dagger, or whether the dagger is supernatural, sent from below to guide his way. His flip-flopping between the two possibilities parallels his own ambivalence about committing the murder. Macbeth's incredulity gives way to acceptance and, finally, to a grim interpretation of the dagger's presence (it is a manifestation of the murder he is about to commit). It is up to you to decide whether this means the dagger is a hallucination or a spirit guide from hell . . . or whether its origin is no longer important to Macbeth.

Macbeth's normally active imagination is in overdrive here, creating ominous imagery to paint a picture of supernatural forces of evil at work. The dagger itself is vividly depicted, down to its whereabouts (*before me*), the direction in which its handle is pointing, and the droplets of blood that suddenly appear not only on its blade but its handle as well (reminding the audience that murder is a messy business). Witches, wolves, and rapists make guest appearances in this monologue, and the very stones are moved by horror to squawk. Lady Macbeth's bell (probably an ordinary little household object, and certainly quiet enough not to rouse the sleeping King) takes on the awesome timbre of a death toll. Notice the many references to motion and direction: *before me*; *handle toward my hand*; *Come*; *Proceeding from*; *Thou marshal'st me the way that I was going*; *with his stealthy pace*; *Tarquin's ravishing strides*; *towards his design / Moves like a ghost*; *my steps, which way they walk*; *I go*; *the bell invites me*; *That summons thee to Heaven or to Hell*. With these references, Macbeth suggests that he is being pulled toward Duncan's bedroom by a force beyond himself—he himself is not responsible for the murder he is about to commit. Remember, he has convinced himself that his future kingship, and therefore Duncan's death, is fated: Macbeth, an extension of his dagger, is merely the instrument that will fulfill the Witches' prophecy (and yet, because Macbeth believes wholeheartedly in eternal damnation, he knows full well that by murdering the good-hearted Duncan he is compacting with the Devil as firmly as the worshipping witches he describes).

The monologue's imagery also depicts the impending murder in all its chilling horror. With the *dagger*, *gouts of blood*, *bloody business*, *abuse*, *witchcraft / Pale Hecate's offerings*, *withered murder*, [howling] *wolf*, *stealthy pace*, *Tarquin's ravishing strides*, *horror*, and *knell*, Macbeth lives the murder in his mind by describing it aloud (thereby giving the audience the opportunity to experience it, even though the actual murder will take place offstage). You must decide why he does so. How much of the imagery is a conscious attempt to rationalize the murder and ready himself, as though preparing for battle, and how much emerges unconsciously from his moral agony? Note that the monologue begins with a question but progresses to a definitive statement of intent: *I go, and it is done*. Macbeth's use of the present tense reveals that by the end of the piece Duncan doesn't stand a chance. He has already been murdered in Macbeth's mind before Macbeth has even entered his room to do the deed. It is for you to decide whether Macbeth has come to peace with the idea by now or whether he is rushing to act before he can think himself out of it.

Macbeth uses antithesis to figure out the floating dagger (*Is this a dagger which I see before me* versus *Or art thou but a dagger of the mind . . .* ; *I have thee not* versus *and yet I see thee still*; *sensible to feeling* versus *as to sight*) and to spur himself to action (*Whiles I threat, he lives* versus *I go, and it is done*).

Consonance and assonance help create the air of mysticism . . . and general creepiness. Examples include: *handle / hand*; *Come / clutch*; *thee / thee / see thee*; *not / yet / not / fatal / sight / but*; *Proceeding / heat-oppressèd*; *o' th' other*; *see thee still*; *And / blade and dudgeon / dreams*; *witchcraft / Hecate's*; *withered murder / Alarumed*; *the wolf / Whose howl's his watch, thus with his stealthy pace / With*; *which way they walk*; *for fear*; *take / time*; *heat of deeds*; *lives / gives*; *Heaven / Hell*; *bell / knell / Hell*).

There are many embedded stage directions:

- In line 34, *Come, let me clutch thee* sets up an unsuccessful attempt to do so.
- In line 41, *As this which now I draw* necessitates that you draw your own dagger. You are given two feet of silence at the end of the line in which to do so. Macbeth tries throughout this piece to banish the floating dagger and to repudiate its existence: here, he may be drawing his own dagger against the apparition.

- In line 42, *Thou marshal'st me the way that I was going* suggests that Macbeth follows the dagger . . . (though you may also interpret this as metaphor: see Annotation).
- *Hear not my steps* in line 57 suggests that Macbeth attempts to walk silently.
- With line 62's *I go* . . . , Macbeth prepares to depart; he will do so two lines later.

This soliloquy merits not one but two rhyming couplets to wrap it up (lines 60–61: *lives* / *gives*; and lines 63–64: *knell* / *Hell*). The first indicates Macbeth's resolve to commit the murder. The second, following the sounding of the bell (and rhyming with Macbeth's use of the word *bell* in line 62), confirms this sense of resolve and infuses it with an additional burst of energy, as though Macbeth is charging into battle.

SIGNIFICANT SCANS

The many double endings at the ends of lines give the monologue a sense of urgency, as though Macbeth has much to say in little time, as well as the sense that he is babbling a bit, perhaps in nervousness, or in confusion at the sight of the apparition. The piece also contains many inverted feet, at the beginnings of lines as well as mid-line following caesuras, heightening the tension.

Even more notably, the monologue is full of mid-line sentence endings, where you do not pause as long as you would if the sentences ended at the ends of the lines. These quicken the pace of the whole piece, further augmenting the sense of urgency. These mid-line shifts of focus also lend an anxious and erratic quality to Macbeth's quickly changing thoughts.

Line 51 has a one-half foot pause at the caesura:

x / x / x / x /x /
The curtained sleep: (pause) witchcraft celebrates

Line 58 has an unexpected inverted foot mid-line, following a caesura that is not marked by punctuation:

x /x / / x x / x /
Thy very stones prate of my whereabouts

All of the above variations, in the aggregate, help you create Macbeth's trapped-in-a-bad-dream, edge-of-hysteria tone.

Don't forget to elide: *marshal'st* (MAR-shalst) in line 42; *o'er* (ORE) in line 49; and *ravishing* (RAV-shing) in line 55;

... to contract: *o' th' other* (uth-UH-ther) in line 44;

... and to expand: *oppressèd* (o-PREH-sehd) in line 39.

P.S.

For information on the historical Macbeth, see "Revisionist History: Much-Maligned Macbeth," page 690.

MACBETH

ACT II, SCENE iii

PORTER

GENDER: M
PROSE/VERSE: prose
AGE RANGE: mature adult to older adult
FREQUENCY OF USE (1–5): 2

The sun is about to rise on the Macbeth household. King Duncan has come to visit, and there was great feasting in his honor last night. Too much feasting, in fact, by nobles and servants alike. The Porter (doorkeeper) had a few (OK, several) too many, and is profoundly drunk. Someone is knocking at the front door. Before opening the door, the Porter says:

PORTER

Here's a knocking, indeed! If a man were Porter
of Hell-Gate, he should have old turning the key.
[*Knocking heard at door*] Knock, knock, knock.
Who's there, in the name of Beelzebub? Here's a
5 farmer, that hanged himself on the expectation of
plenty. Come in time! Have napkins enough about
you; here you'll sweat for 't. [*Knocking*] Knock,
knock. Who's there, i' th' other devil's name? Faith,
here's an equivocator, that could swear in both the
10 scales against either scale, who committed treason
enough for God's sake, yet could not equivocate
to Heaven. O, come in, equivocator. [*Knocking*]
Knock, knock, knock. Who's there? Faith, here's an

1 *Porter* Doorkeeper; 2 *Hell-Gate* the front gate of Hell, through which it was believed damned souls were first admitted [*Porter of Hell-Gate* a stock figure in medieval drama, who served as St. Peter's evil counterpart]; *old* plenty of, too much of (colloquial term) [*old turning the key* too much key turning (i.e., he'd be too busy letting everyone into Hell)]; 4 *Beelzebub* (Bee-EL´-zi-BUB or BEL´-zi-BUB) the prince of devils (from Matthew 12:24, from the Hebrew *Ba-al Z´voov*, meaning "Lord of the Flies"); 5 *farmer* a reference to Father Henry Garnet, tried for treason—see "Explosive Material: The Gunpowder Plays," page 708; *on the expectation of plenty* i.e., having hoarded grain only to find that an unexpectedly good harvest ("plenty") is anticipated, which will bring low prices and, hence, financial ruin; 6 *Come in time* either (1) I'll come to the door in good time or (2) (to the farmer) you've arrived right on time; *napkins* handkerchiefs; *about you* on your person; 7 *here you'll sweat for 't* i.e., here in Hell you'll be punished for committing the sin of suicide; 8 *i' th' other devil's name* the Porter wishes to name a devil besides Beelzebub, but can't recall its name; *Faith* short for *in faith*, meaning "indeed"; 9 *equivocator* one who uses ambiguous language in order to deceive (another reference to Father Garnet—see "Explosive Material . . . ," page 708); *the scales* i.e., the scales of justice [*that could swear . . . either scale* i.e., who could as easily "swear" in a court of law on behalf of one side as the other]; 11 *for God's sake* an expletive that takes God's name in vain but also plays on "for the sake of religion" (see "Explosive Material . . . ," page 708); *yet could not equivocate to Heaven* i.e.,

English tailor come hither for stealing out of a
15 French hose. Come in, tailor. Here you may roast
your goose. [*Knocking*] Knock, knock. Never at
quiet! What are you? —But this place is too cold
for Hell. I'll devil-porter it no further. I had
thought to have let in some of all professions, that
20 go the primrose way to th' everlasting bonfire.
[*Knocking*] Anon, anon! I pray you, remember the
Porter.

1 minute, 20 seconds

yet could not get away with equivocating before God; 14 *tailor* another reference to Father Garnet—see "Explosive Material . . . ," page 708; *hither* to this place (i.e., to Hell); 15 *French hose* a tight-fitting style of men's breeches, recently come into fashion [*stealing out of a French hose* Tailors were notorious for stealing by using less fabric than promised when making breeches. Once the fashion changed from loose, billowing breeches to tight-fitting "French" ones, the imaginary tailor's theft of fabric became noticeable and he was caught]; 16 *goose* tailor's iron (colloquial term) [*you may roast your goose* you may heat your iron (with possible reference to killing the goose that laid the golden eggs [just as the tailor ruined himself by trying to get rich too quickly], and, possibly, to the phrase *cook your goose*, i.e., undo yourself)]; *Never at quiet* either "It's never quiet around here" or "I never get any peace and quiet"; 18 *devil-porter it* i.e., pretend to be the porter of Hell-Gate; 20 *go the primrose way* take the broad and pleasurable path (from Matthew 7:13); *th' everlasting bonfire* i.e., Hell; 21 *Anon* Right away; *I pray you* I entreat you; please; *remember the Porter* this is a request for a tip.

COMMENTARY

What can we tell you about the Porter? Not too much, because this is his one and only scene in the play, which can be exciting for an actor with a good imagination who enjoys filling in the gaps. We know that he is the Macbeths' doorkeeper and that he's sleepy and very, very drunk; the soliloquy's prose, which is chockful of colloquial expressions (suggesting little education) as well as contractions (read: slurred words), supports these facts. We also know that the Porter has a vivid imagination, that he's a tad cynical, and that he's got a bawdy sense of humor. Beyond that, you get to invent him to your specifications. He may be entering to open the door, or he may have been "on duty" and already stationed in its vicinity. He may be less than pleased to be roused by the knocking, or he may take it in stride. He may be an alcoholic, or he may be a teetotaler who got drunk last night for the first time.

The Porter hurls himself into his imaginary job, location, and company, and seems to be amusing himself heartily, regardless of how objectively amusing he actually is. Your commitment to this fantasy may help you answer an important question: why doesn't the Porter answer the door sooner than he does? Besides relishing his make-believe scenario, perhaps the door is clear across the stage and he is too drunk to get there quickly or even to find it; or perhaps he finds it but is too drunk to remember that he needs to open it. He may be annoyed at this disruption of his drunken slumber and therefore taking his sweet time, or he may be too hungover to care that he is being remiss. Perhaps he cannot find his keys, or is too drunk to handle the intricate business of unlocking and bolting the door's many, heavy locks. Or perhaps he needs to get dressed or urinate or vomit, and attends to his needs during the monologue, before answering the door. Similarly, you must decide whether to busy yourself with the business of unlocking the door during the monologue at all; perhaps the Porter does so afterward.

Though the Porter may seem at first glance like simple comic relief, he is anything but. Although the Porter has no knowledge of the Macbeths' murder of King Duncan, he unwittingly makes biting comments about the deed. By evoking Hell, he points out that the Macbeths have just made of their home—and their world—a hell. The Porter also inadvertently moralizes about Macbeth: he discusses treason (Macbeth has killed his king), equivocation (akin to Macbeth's rationalizing his murder of Duncan), a cooked goose (Macbeth has undone himself by overreaching), execution (Macbeth will be killed by Macduff for his crimes), and Hell (where Macbeth's soul will presumably reside). All three of the people the Porter welcomes to Hell have committed sins of overreaching: the greedy *Farmer* by hoarding grain to corner a market; the *equivoca-*

tor by trying to testify in a manner that will save his skin both here and in the afterlife; and the *tailor* by cheating his client out of fabric one time too many.

The Porter entertains himself (and his Jacobean audience) with double entendre. The second meanings of the following words and phrases would have been obvious to an audience in Shakespeare's day: *knocking* = lechery; sex; *Gate* = vulva; *turning the key* = having sex; *Come* = orgasm, ejaculate; *sweat* = sitting in a "sweat tub" was prescribed to treat venereal disease; *devil* = a bisexual or hermaphrodite; *treason* = a "traitor" was a pun on the word *trader*, meaning a pimp, prostitute, or brothel customer; *Heaven* = homosexual love; *hose* = penis; *goose* = prostitute; *cold* = frigid, sexually chaste; house of *profession* = brothel.

Though the Porter is drunk and sleepy, there is some built-in escalation in pace, as though the guests arrive at Hell on one another's heels; the Porter can barely keep up. His fantasy aside, the escalation of pace also suggests that the incessant knocking gradually pulls him out of his slumber . . . much to his chagrin. Hence his *Never at quiet!*

Finally, since this is a soliloquy, you must decide whether you are speaking to yourself or to the audience, including them in the fun (or switching between the two). Certain lines, however, are addressed to the men waiting at the gate (some are obvious, such as *Anon, anon*; others are optional, such as *Who's there?*). As for the last line, however, you must make a clear decision whether you have admitted the men and seek a tip from them for your efforts, or are directly addressing the audience, whom you hope you've delighted with your clever little performance.

Explosive Material: The Gunpowder Plays

England was rocked to its core (figuratively) in November 1605, when its Parliament was almost rocked to its core (literally). A group of radical Catholics, directed from papal Rome and reacting to continued persecution by the Reformationist King James, stockpiled thirty-six kegs of gunpowder in a vault under Parliament, intending to blow up the King, his heir, and the entire government. The plot was leaked in a letter containing rather obvious clues. The letter found its way to King James, who later claimed to have decoded it with God's help. Munitions expert Guy "Guido" Fawkes was caught red-handed in the eleventh hour, about to light the fuse. The conspirators were swiftly caught, tried, and torturously executed for treason. King James instantly disseminated his official version of the affair, in which he claimed that God revealed the plot to him as a sign of God's support for both the Reformation as the one true faith and King James as the legitimate ruler of England (which James touted as the Reformation's bulwark). During this time, the normally stringent censorship of political allusions in literature of all forms was relaxed to permit the arts to advance James's version of events. The year 1606 therefore yielded a crop of "Gunpowder Plays" such as *Macbeth*, all of which contained the following elements: (1) indirect but obvious references to the Gunpowder Plot; (2) attempted or actual cataclysmic destruction of a kingdom, through plotting, equivocation, and witchcraft; (3) exploration of the use of deception to test loyalty; and (4) experimentation with the equivocal nature of language.

Blowing the Lid Off the Porter's Speech

A Jesuit priest who was aware of but not directly involved in the plot became the fall guy for all clergy involved in the Gunpowder Plot. Though the Porter never mentions Father Henry Garnet, a large segment of his speech is a grim joke at the priest's expense. Father Garnet was arrested and tried in 1606. Though accused of giving false testimony at his trial, Father Garnet, alias "Farmer" (aha!), argued that he merely "equivocated" (the long-persecuted Jesuits permitted themselves to avoid self-incrimination by evading truthful answers to political questions with ambiguous doublespeak). This argument particularly angered King James, who encouraged the populace to ridicule Garnet and thoroughly enjoy his subsequent execution. With all three of the men he welcomes to Hell, the Porter is referring to Father Garnet: the farmer (Garnet's alias), the equivocator (Garnet's infamous defense), and the tailor (in a notorious follow-up news item, a tailor was questioned for possession of a relic containing the executed Garnet's blood). The many other references to the Gunpowder Plot in the Porter's speech are far too complex to explain here in full, and would, in any case, be incomprehensible to your audience. But if we have whetted your appetite, there are volumes available on the topic.

MACBETH

ACT III, SCENE i

MACBETH

GENDER: M
PROSE/VERSE: blank verse
AGE RANGE: mature adult
FREQUENCY OF USE (1–5): 3

Macbeth murdered his kinsman, King Duncan, and then assumed the throne, fulfilling a prophecy made by three witches that he would be King of Scotland. But now Macbeth is troubled by the fact that those same witches also prophesied that his friend Banquo would father kings. He ruminates over the situation in soliloquy.

To be thus is nothing, but to be safely thus.
Our fears in Banquo
50 Stick deep, and in his royalty of nature
Reigns that which would be feared. 'Tis much he dares
And to that dauntless temper of his mind
He hath a wisdom that doth guide his valor
To act in safety. There is none but he
55 Whose being I do fear; and under him
My genius is rebuked, as it is said
Mark Antony's was by Caesar. He chid the sisters
When first they put the name of king upon me
And bade them speak to him. Then, prophet-like,
60 They hailed him father to a line of kings.
Upon my head they placed a fruitless crown
And put a barren scepter in my grip,
Thence to be wrenched with an unlineal hand,

48 *To be thus is nothing, but to be safely thus* i.e., to be king is nothing, unless one is safely king; 49 *Our fears in Banquo / Stick deep* (1) My fears about Banquo stick deep into my flesh, like thorns; and/or (2) My fears about Banquo are well grounded (with a subtle second reading: "My fears will soon cause me to stick deep [as with a dagger] in Banquo"); *royalty of nature* regal temperament (also alluding to the royalty of Banquo's descendants, as predicted by the witches); 51 *Reigns* prevails (with a play on "rules as king"); *would be* should be; *'Tis much he dares* i.e., he is very courageous; 52 *to* in addition to; *dauntless temper* fearless temperament; 55 *being* existence; 56 *genius* guiding and guardian spirit; *rebuked* restrained, checked; *as it is said / Mark Antony's was by Caesar* a reference to Plutarch's *Life of Antony*, according to which an Egyptian soothsayer told Antony "your genius . . . dreads his; when absent from him yours is proud and brave, but in his presence, unmanly and dejected"; 57 *the sisters* the Weird Sisters, a.k.a. the three witches; 58 *put the name of king upon me* (1) conferred upon me the title of king; and (2) imposed upon me the responsibility of kingship (through their prophecy); 61 *fruitless* having no offspring; 62 *scepter* the staff or baton which, along with the crown, is an official symbol of kingship (with double entendre: Jacobeans were familiar with *scepter* as representing the penis) [*barren scepter* kingship devoid of heirs (with a play on: impotent and sterile penis)]; 63 *unlineal* not directly descended; not hereditary [*with an unlineal hand* i.e., by a ruler not de-

No son of mine succeeding. If 't be so,
65 For Banquo's issue have I filed my mind;
For them the gracious Duncan have I murdered,
Put rancors in the vessel of my peace
Only for them, and mine eternal jewel
Given to the common enemy of man
70 To make them kings—the seeds of Banquo kings.
Rather than so, come fate into the list,
And champion me to th' utterance. —Who's there?

1 minute, 30 seconds

scended from Macbeth]; 64 *succeeding* i.e., succeeding to my throne; 65 *filed* defiled; 67 *rancors* (1) bitter ill feelings; (2) acids, i.e., poisons [*Put rancors in the vessel of my peace* i.e., either (1) acted as my own bitter enemy; poisoned myself (in an earlier monologue [see page 683], Macbeth equates murdering Duncan with drinking from a poisoned chalice) or (2) destroyed my state of grace ("vessel" alluding to the chalice used in Christian worship)]; 68 *mine eternal jewel* i.e., my immortal soul; 69 *common enemy of man* i.e., Satan; 70 *seeds* (1) offspring; (2) sons; 71 *come fate* let fate come; *list* tilt yards (the enclosed spaces where knights competed in tournaments or settled disputes in one-on-one trial by combat); 72 *champion* (1) fight on behalf of; or (2) challenge to a contest; *to th' utterance* to the utmost extremity, i.e., to the death (from the French *à outrance*) [*come fate . . . to th' utterance* editors propose two possible (and opposite) meanings: (1) let fate come into the yard and fight for me to the death; or (2) let fate come and challenge me—I will fight to the death]; *Who's there* phrase commonly used to summon a servant.

COMMENTARY

In this monologue, Macbeth is on the brink of having his best friend murdered. Obviously, getting your backstory straight is key! Banquo does indeed suspect Macbeth of Duncan's murder and wonder about his own descendants' prospects. Nevertheless, Banquo has remained outwardly loyal to Macbeth, showing no signs that he either mistrusts or intends evil toward him. Which raises the question, what specifically prompts Macbeth's worry? Is it the fact that thus far all of the Witches' prophecies have come true? He and Banquo are (or were) quite close; has Macbeth intuited his friend's true feelings? Or, considering Macbeth's famously active imagination, has he perhaps projected the ambitions and intentions he felt toward Duncan onto Banquo? Your choice.

The arrangement of lines 48–51 in the First Folio (our only surviving source) is corrupt. Since editors have suggested many different arrangements, we reviewed all of the possibilities and chose the one that seems to work best for actors. With this arrangement, the scansion of line 48 has a crowded foot (*To be thus*) as well as a double ending before the caesura and an inverted foot after it:

x - x / x / (x) / x x / x /
To be thus is nothing, but to be safely thus

The repetition of rhythm created by the crowding enhances the repetition of phrasing in the line, throwing into relief the important added word in the second phrase—*safely*. The crowding also contrasts nicely with what follows. Line 49 has three silent feet at the beginning, which give you time to ruminate: Macbeth may have just remembered the prophecy about Banquo's heirs, and uses the pause to reach the conclusion that Banquo is a threat; or perhaps he has been troubled by the prophecy from the onset, and now pauses to consider whether he's ready to confront it. In either case, notice how the powerful first line resonates in the pause.

Line 49 initiates a pattern in which ideas begin and end mid-line, creating steady movement from one idea to the next, as though once begun, Macbeth's thoughts flood his mind in a continuous current. Line 49 also contains one of the many double endings in this piece, which soften line endings and support the feeling of an uninterrupted flow.

When you hit line 52, your first inclination may be to invert the first foot of the line, but upon further examination you will notice that using regular iambic rhythm will help you convey the meaning of the word *to* (here, "in addition to") by stressing it. Try it and see how your delivery is affected.

Line 57 is not as tricky as it seems. It contains two double endings, and requires the elision of *Antony's* (ANT-neez):

x / x / x / (x) x / x / (x)
Mark Antony's was by Caesar. He chid the sisters

Aside from the subtle implications of the phrase *Stick deep* (see Annotation), line 57 contains the first use of imagery in the monologue. From here on, the monologue is almost nothing but imagery (*vessel of my peace*; *eternal jewel*; *come fate into the list and champion me*; etc.). This may be unusual for most characters, but it is typical of Macbeth, who is noted for having the most vivid imagination of all Shakespearean characters. Several of these images are synecdoche (*unlineal hand*; *fruitless crown*; *barren scepter*), lending them an unnatural, sinister quality: Macbeth's use of disembodied parts to represent the whole suggests that he believes he and Banquo are only the sum of their composite parts, propelled and affected by fate.

One example of synecdoche appears in line 63, where it joins with other devices to drive the line. First, notice the striking use of inverted feet: after a single inversion in the opening line (following the caesura), there are none in the next thirteen lines, and here, suddenly, there are two! And the second of these follows a caesura not marked by punctuation—a rare occurrence. This gives the line its angrily emphatic tone (don't forget to elide *unlineal* [un-LIN-yal]):

/ x x / / x x / x /
Thence to be wrenched with an unlineal hand

Next, the assonance of *Thence to be wrenched* also contributes to the line's power, as does the near-onomatopoeic *wrenched*. Keep your eye out for other strings of expressive assonance and consonance scattered through the piece, such as *chid / sisters*; *son / succeeding / so*; and *filed my mind*. With its trochaic inversions, line 63 marks a change in the monologue's meter. During the first half of the piece, there are quite a few double endings, which soften line endings and give the verse a more agitated or hesitant feel. In contrast, the trochaic inversions toward the end of the piece (four in the last five lines) create a more determined, aggressive tone. These metric variations support the monologue's progression from Macbeth's indecision to his conviction that Banquo must be killed. Regardless of which meaning you choose for the last two lines (see Annotation), Macbeth is clearly determined to fight to the death, a determination that is reflected in the monologue's aggressive tone and meter.

In line 70, the word *them* is used for the third time in reference to Banquo's descendants. The line reads quite well as regular blank verse, but its meaning invites you to accent *them* at least slightly. Notice that in the previous uses of *them* (lines 66 and 68) the word fell naturally on accented syllables, while this one falls on an unaccented syllable. Stressing the word here works against the meter, building on the previous two iterations and giving *them* additional emphasis in the third.

Macbeth makes a few other telling word choices. He starts off the monologue using the royal "we" (*Our fears*) but quickly shifts to "I," which may result simply from the transition between speaking to his servant and speaking in soliloquy. Or perhaps Macbeth still does not feel comfortable with the royal "we," knowing he wrongfully acquired the right to use it, and attempts to assert his royalty with the formal address. Macbeth also uses the word *put* in this piece three times—he is clearly feeling put-upon (pun intended), complaining not only of the mixed blessing of the Witches' prophecies, but also of the evils he has put on himself in making those prophecies come true.

Keep in mind that just after this soliloquy Macbeth will convince two men that Banquo was responsible for their misfortunes and will offer them a hefty sum to kill Banquo and his son. It has been proposed that these are either desperately poor men whose land has been repossessed by a greedy landowner, or soldiers who have been wronged, presumably while fighting under Banquo, who was a commander for Macbeth. Macbeth's manipulation of these men reveals just how far his character has degenerated by this point in the play, and that he meant what he said in lines 68–69: he believes that his soul is already damned, so he might as well do whatever it takes to keep the prize he sold it for.

Finally, the last phrase may be read as a response to the sound of the servant approaching with the assassins who will murder Banquo, but it may be used just as legitimately to summon a servant, now that Macbeth has made up his mind to take action against Banquo. In Jacobean drama *Who's there* was often used to mean "Whichever servant is nearby, get in here!"

Don't forget to elide: *Antony's* (ANT-neez) in line 57; *unlineal* (un-LIN-yal) in line 63; *Given* (GIV'N) in line 69; and *champion* (CHAMP-yun) in line 72;

. . . and to contract: *If 't* (IFT) in line 64 and *th' utterance* (TH'UT′-er-ANCE) in line 72.

P.S.

For information about the historical Macbeth, see "Revisionist History: Much-Maligned Macbeth," page 690.

Buttering Up Banquo's Blood

Macbeth's extensive praise for Banquo in this piece and the honorable depiction of him in the play were for the benefit of King James I. The truth is that Banquo was a political invention based on an ancient chieftain: he was created in the 1400s to give King James's house, the Stuarts, a male ancestor who was an early ruler in Scotland, since the Stuarts' reign didn't begin until 1371. By the time Shakespeare's source—the historian Holinshed—wrote about Banquo, he was accepted as fact. But Holinshed wrote during Queen Elizabeth's reign, and had no reason to make Banquo look particularly good; in his account Banquo is Macbeth's collaborator. Shakespeare, on the other hand, had good reason to please the monarch who reigned when he created his Banquo—and he made sure the King could bask in the reflected glory of his ancestor's depiction here.

OTHELLO

ACT I, SCENE i

IAGO

GENDER: M
PROSE/VERSE: blank verse
AGE RANGE: adult to mature adult
FREQUENCY OF USE (1–5): 3

Late night on a Venetian street: Iago, ensign to Othello, the famous Venetian general and war hero, has met up with Roderigo, a gentleman. Iago has been passed over for promotion to lieutenant. He is angry and offended, and explains to his "friend" Roderigo (whom he is planning to dupe into helping him get revenge) why he continues to serve Othello.

O, sir, content you.
I follow him to serve my turn upon him.
We cannot all be masters, nor all masters
Cannot be truly followed. You shall mark
45 Many a duteous and knee-crooking knave
That, doting on his own obsequious bondage,
Wears out his time much like his master's ass,
For naught but provender, and when he's old, cashiered.
Whip me such honest knaves. Others there are
50 Who, trimmed in forms and visages of duty,
Keep yet their hearts attending on themselves;
And throwing but shows of service on their lords,
Do well thrive by them, and when they have lined their coats
Do themselves homage. These fellows have some soul;
55 And such a one do I profess myself. For, sir,
It is as sure as you are Roderigo,
Were I the Moor, I would not be Iago.
In following him, I follow but myself.
Heaven is my judge, not I for love and duty,

41 *content you* be content; 42 *serve my turn upon him* to serve my purpose (of getting revenge) on him; 43 *nor all masters / Cannot* nor can all masters (the double negative was commonly used in Shakespeare's time for emphasis); 44 *mark* notice; 45 *knee-crooking* curtsying (common show of respect by men or women in Shakespeare's time); *knave* (1) menial servant; (2) rascal; 46 *That* i.e., who; 47 *Wears out* wastes; *much like his master's ass* the same way his master's donkey does; 48 *provender* fodder, dry food for livestock; *cashiered* dismissed; discarded from service; 49 *Whip me* (1) Spare me from; or (2) Whip for me (i.e., whip, [as you would a donkey] for all I care); 50 *trimmed in* dressed up in; *forms* (1) ceremonies; (2) manners, modes of behavior; *visages* appearances [*trimmed . . . of duty* putting on the manners and appearance of obedient respect due to a superior]; 51 *Keep yet* nevertheless, keep; *attending on* serving; 52 *but* only; 53 *Do well thrive* thrive well; *lined their coats* filled their pockets; 54 *homage* formal promise of loyalty and service to a feudal lord [*Do themselves homage* serve themselves; are their own masters]; 55 *profess myself* declare myself to be; 57 *the Moor* i.e., Othello, who was a Moor (technically, a native of northwest Africa, although in Shakespeare's day the term was applied to anyone of darker complexion than a western European) [*Were I the Moor* if I were Othello]; 58 *following* serving; 59 *Heaven is my judge* As Heaven is my witness (i.e., the irreverent Iago is

60 But seeming so, for my peculiar end;
For when my outward action doth demonstrate
The native act and figure of my heart
In complement extern, 'tis not long after
But I will wear my heart upon my sleeve
65 For daws to peck at—I am not what I am.

1 minute, 30 seconds

swearing by Heaven [i.e., God], taking the name of Heaven in vain); *not I for* I am not for; 60 *peculiar* own particular, private; *end* goal [*not I for . . . peculiar end* I am not one for giving my master real love and duty, but rather for appearing that way in order to achieve my own private goals]; 62 *native* natural; *act* operation, action; *figure* written character [*figure of my heart* what is written in my heart]; 63 *complement extern* external show or appearance; 64 *But* that; 65 *daws* jackdaws (small crows); *I am not what I am* I am not what I appear to be.

COMMENTARY

This is a unique moment for Iago. Throughout the play he alternates between clever deceitfulness with others and candid revelations in soliloquy. In this speech, the two modes are combined: Iago uses the truth about himself and his desires to convince Roderigo that they are both on the same side, all in order to dupe him into serving Iago's purposes.

Iago's smooth-talking manner is well served by the wonderfully manipulable vowels Shakespeare provides through the frequent use of assonance in this piece (*sir* / *serve* / *turn*; *follow* / *upon* / *cannot* / *all* / *Cannot* / *followed*; *cannot* / *master* / *masters* / *Cannot*; *doting* / *own*; *obsequious* / *bondage* / *naught* / *provender* / *honest*; *master's* / *ass* / *cashiered*; *yet* / *attending* / *themselves*; *throwing* / *shows* / *coats* / *soul*). It is up to you to decide what he does with all these vowels. Lull his victim into a trance, perhaps? Use them as a showpiece for his honey-tongued persuasion? Or create a false sense of ease and security for the listener? Iago complements these sounds with the powerful rhetorical tool of antithesis, beginning with a simple comparison between what servants lack (*We cannot all be masters*) and what the masters lack (*all masters* / *Cannot be truly followed*). He then moves on to more contrast, outlining first the type of true and loyal servant he despises, then the type of self-serving knave he professes to be. Finally, just in case Roderigo is too stupid to get it, Iago uses antithesis to explain his show of duty to Othello: *Were I the Moor, I would not be Iago*; *In following him, I follow but myself*; *not I for love and duty,* / *But seeming so*.

Wethinks Iago doth protest too much. He puts on a devil-may-care attitude, but if he is really not affected by his low station, then where does all his resentment and hatred come from? Could it be that his anger (and thus his scheming) stems from the reality that he is indeed one of those fawning, doting servants he despises?

Certainly, if you consider the double entendre revealed in the second meanings ascribed to certain words in Shakespeare's time, it seems that Iago is tired of being screwed, and wishes to "serve his turn" and become the one who does the screwing: *serve* = mount sexually (in reference to a stallion with a mare); *mark* = sexual target; *master's ass* = master's buttocks (as today); *but*[*t*] *shows of service* and *follow but*[*t*] *myself* = additional buttocks references; *peculiar* = private; *end* = penis.

SIGNIFICANT SCANS

This piece has a few striking variations in meter, beginning with the obvious short first line. It will take careful attention to pull off two and a half feet of silence at the end of the very first line. Perhaps Iago has interrupted or even snapped at Roderigo with *O, sir, content you,* and takes the beats to compose himself. Maybe he has "earnestly" appealed to him and pauses for effect before going on. Or maybe he has implied, in hushed tones, that he's about to share a secret, and then makes a show of checking to see if anyone's listening during the pause.

The second major metrical variation provides a great contrast with the shortness of the first line: There are two alexandrines (lines with six feet) in this piece (lines 48 and 55), which is unusual:

x / x / x / x / x / x /
For naught but provender, and when he's old, cashiered

x / x / x / x / x / x /
And such a one do I profess myself. For, sir

Don't forget to elide: *duteous* (DYOO-tyuss) in line 45; *obsequious* (ob-SEE-kwyuss) in line 46; *throwing* (THROING) in line 52; *following* (FOLL-wing) in line 58; and *Heaven* (HEV'N) in line 59;

. . . and to contract: *by them* (BY'EM) and *they have* (they've) in line 53.

And one last note: the meter calls for the historic pronunciation of *demonstrate* (dem-ON-strayt) in line 61, so you'll have to choose between meter that's slightly off and a pronunciation that's slightly off to today's listener.

OTHELLO

ACT I, SCENE iii

OTHELLO

GENDER: M
PROSE/VERSE: blank verse
AGE RANGE: adult to mature adult
FREQUENCY OF USE (1–5): 4

Othello, war hero and respected general in the powerful Venetian fleet, has eloped with Desdemona, a gentlewoman. Late the same night, the Duke of Venice has called an emergency council to discuss Othello's imminent naval expedition to defend Cyprus from the Turks. At the council, Desdemona's father, Brabantio, accuses Othello (before the Duke and all the senators) of using magic to seduce his daughter. Othello defends his courtship of Desdemona as honorable and honest.

Her father loved me, oft invited me;
Still questioned me the story of my life
130 From year to year—the battles, sieges, fortunes
That I have passed.
I ran it through, even from my boyish days
To the very moment that he bade me tell it,
Wherein I spake of most disastrous chances:
135 Of moving accidents by flood and field;
Of hairbreath scapes i' th' imminent deadly breach;
Of being taken by the insolent foe
And sold to slavery; of my redemption thence,
And portance in my traveler's history.
140 Wherein of antres vast and deserts idle,
Rough quarries, rocks, and hills whose heads touch heaven
It was my hint to speak—such was my process;
And of the cannibals that each other eat,
The Anthropophagi, and men whose heads
145 Do grow below their shoulders. This to hear
Would Desdemona seriously incline,
But still the house affairs would draw her thence,

128 *invited me* i.e., to his home; 129 *Still* always, continually; 130 *fortunes* good or bad accidents of fate; 131 *passed* lived through, experienced; 132 *even* used here for emphasis; 134 *chances* events; 135 *moving* emotionally stirring; *accidents* misfortunes; *by* in; 136 *scapes* escapes; *imminent* threatening; *breach* gap in a fortification; 138 *redemption* ransom; 139 *portance* (1) conduct, behavior; (2) attitude, demeanor; 140 *antres* (ANT-erz) caverns; *idle* barren; 142 *hint* occasion, opportunity; *process* story, tale; 144 *Anthropophagi* (AN-throh-POFF´-uh-GIE or AN-throh-POFF´-uh-JIE; both rhyme with "pie") the Greek name for the cannibals; 145 *This to hear / Would Desdemona seriously incline* i.e., Desdemona would be earnestly eager to hear this;

Which ever as she could with haste dispatch
She'd come again, and with a greedy ear
150 Devour up my discourse. Which I observing,
Took once a pliant hour, and found good means
To draw from her a prayer of earnest heart
That I would all my pilgrimage dilate,
Whereof by parcels she had something heard,
155 But not intentively. I did consent,
And often did beguile her of her tears
When I did speak of some distressful stroke
That my youth suffered. My story being done,
She gave me for my pains a world of sighs.
160 She swore, in faith, 'twas strange, 'twas passing strange;
'Twas pitiful, 'twas wondrous pitiful.
She wished she had not heard it, yet she wished
That Heaven had made her such a man. She thanked me,
And bade me, if I had a friend that loved her,
165 I should but teach him how to tell my story,
And that would woo her. Upon this hint I spake.
She loved me for the dangers I had passed,
And I loved her that she did pity them.
This is the only witchcraft I have used.
170 Here comes the lady; let her witness it.

2 minutes, 30 seconds

148 *ever as* as soon as; *with haste dispatch* quickly finish up; 151 *Took* chose; *pliant* convenient; suitable; *good means* a good opportunity; a good way; 152 *prayer* entreaty, request; 153 *dilate* relate fully [*all my pilgrimage dilate* tell the whole tale of my long journey]; 154 *Whereof* of which; *by parcels* in pieces [*Whereof . . . something heard* some of which she had heard, in bits and pieces]; 155 *intentively* with full attention; 156 *did beguile* drew from, in an agreeable way; 157 *stroke* (1) any stroke of bad luck; (2) the stroke of a weapon; 158 *my youth suffered* I suffered in my youth; 160 *passing* surpassingly, exceedingly; 161 *pitiful* inspiring compassion; *wondrous* wonderfully, admirably; 163 *made her such a man* made such a man for her (with possible second meaning: had made her a man, like him [so she could have such adventures]); 165 *I should but* I only had to; 166 *hint* occasion, opportunity (i.e., not a hint or cue from Desdemona, as a more recent definition would indicate); 168 *that* for the fact that; *did pity* had compassion for; 170 *witness* attest to.

COMMENTARY

Who is Othello? Nobody knows. Although we learn quite a bit about his character (he's virtuous, respected, a great warrior, honorable, even-tempered), we know almost nothing about his past. Where is he from? What's his native language? What race is he? What religion? Othello could be from just about anywhere in Asia or Africa (although, over time, the role has come to be interpreted most often as a man of West African descent). Shakespeare and his contemporaries applied the term *Moor* to anybody with darker skin than theirs, sporting a pair of exotic pantaloons. In fact, this may account for our lack of background on Othello. Even in this monologue, which purportedly tells some of his story, Othello merely does a lot of name-dropping and bragging, while leaving out the important bits, such as why he was on such a crazy journey to begin with. Was he fighting, and if so, for whom? Who rescued him from slavery? How did he end up as a Venetian general? And more important, what did he bring us? Anyway, playing Othello is a great opportunity to go wild inventing your backstory, and you'll need it to make this monologue work.

Othello is a great storyteller (he's told those darn war stories so many times that even his horse knows 'em by heart) and saves his best rhetorical devices for use in relating his epic: notice where his choices of assonance (*disastrous chances*; *i' th' imminent*; *redemption thence*; *each / eat*; *men / heads*) and consonance (*flood and field*; *sold to slavery*; *hills / whose / heads / heaven / hint*) are concentrated. He also has a habit of using extra words for emphasis (***even*** *from my boyish days*; ***very*** *moment*; ***most*** *disastrous*; ***ever*** *as she could*; *Took* ***once*** *a pliant hour*) and similarly, he repeatedly uses the past emphatic tense: *did consent*; *did beguile*; *did speak*. Consider though that perhaps this tendency reflects the carefully formal speech of a non-native speaker of a language (if you choose to play Othello as an immigrant to Venice). Othello uses antithesis to emphasize the point of the story he tells the court here: *She loved me for the dangers I had passed* versus *And I loved her that she did pity them*. You can use the telling of this story to demonstrate the storytelling gifts that so mesmerized Desdemona.

SIGNIFICANT SCANS

Notice that the meter is quite regular, creating a fluid, storytelling rhythm. In most of the places where the flow is interrupted, there is a specific change in the direction of the story: you'll find caesuras where he leaves off the story of his adventures, to speak of Desdemona's interest in it; where he begins telling how he approached Desdemona; where he moves on to his repetition of the story just for her; where he tells of her reaction to the story; and where he wraps up with his proposal to her—all instances where he mentions his beloved.

Of course, you will have noticed that in line 131 Shakespeare gives you three feet of silence to play with. Is Othello musing over his past? Does he hesitate to talk about it because he's modest? Is he pausing for dramatic effect before impressing the senators and Governor of Venice? Pick something that works for you.

Line 150 is a regular iambic line with a double ending. You have to elide *devour* (de-VOWR) and use the archaic pronunciation of *discourse* (dis-KORSS) to get it right:

x / x / x / x / x / (x)
Devour up my discourse. Which I observing

Don't forget to elide: *even* (e'en) in line 132; *insolent* (IN-slent) in line 137; *slavery* (SLAY-vree) in line 138; *traveler's* (TRAV-lerz) in line 139; *cannibals* (CAN-blz) in line 143; *seriously* (SEER´-yuss-LEE) in line 146; *Devour* (de-VOWR) in line 150; *hour* (OWR) in line 151; *prayer* (PRARE) in line 152; and *Heaven* (HEV'N) in line 163;

. . . and to contract: *To the* (T'the) in line 133.

Notice that almost all of the elisions and the contraction fall in the first half of the piece. What does this tell you about Othello's state of mind? Is he angry at the false accusation that he has used magic? Is he anxious about how his story will be received? Why do the elisions abate? Does he gain confidence? Does the memory of his courtship of Desdemona soothe or bolster him? The answers to these questions go to the heart of your interpretation of Othello.

P.S.

For more information about Elizabethan and Jacobean attitudes toward people of color, see "Renaissance Rationalization of Racism," page 826.

OTHELLO

ACT I, SCENE iii

IAGO

GENDER: M
AGE RANGE: adult to mature adult
PROSE/VERSE: blank verse
FREQUENCY OF USE (1–5): 4

Iago, ensign to the great Venetian general Othello, will soon be traveling to Cyprus on an expedition with his master. Iago has just convinced his "friend" Roderigo to go along with them (bringing all the cash he can muster up) by promising that he will help Roderigo become the lover of Othello's new wife, Desdemona. After Roderigo leaves, Iago reflects on how easy and enjoyable it is to dupe him. He then comes up with a plan to get revenge on Othello, who has passed him over for promotion and (Iago believes) has slept with his wife. At the same time, he will get revenge on Cassio, who received the lieutenant's position that should have been his.

Thus do I ever make my fool my purse;
390 For I mine own gained knowledge should profane
If I would time expend with such a snipe,
But for my sport and profit. I hate the Moor,
And it is thought abroad that 'twixt my sheets
He's done my office. I know not if't be true,
395 But I, for mere suspicion of that kind,
Will do as if for surety. He holds me well;
The better shall my purpose work on him.
Cassio's a proper man. Let me see now;
To get his place, and to plume up my will
400 In double knavery. How? How? Let's see . . .
After some time, to abuse Othello's ears
That he is too familiar with his wife.
He hath a person and a smooth dispose
To be suspected—framed to make women false.
405 The Moor is of a free and open nature
That thinks men honest that but seem to be so,
And will as tenderly be led by th' nose
As asses are.
I have it; it is engendered. Hell and night
410 Must bring this monstrous birth to the world's light.

1 minute, 20 seconds

389 *do I ever* I always; *purse* a small money bag, carried by both men and women in Shakespeare's time [*make my fool my purse* use my latest dupe as a source of profit]; 390 *I mine own gained knowledge should profane* I would waste the knowledge I have earned by experience; 391 *would time expend* would spend time [*I mine own . . . time expend* it would be a waste of my time and an insult to my own intelligence]; *snipe* simpleton, fool (the snipe, a common shorebird, is easily trapped); 392 *But* except; *sport* amusement, entertainment; *the Moor* i.e., Othello, who was a Moor (technically, a native of northwest Africa, although in Shakespeare's day the term was applied to anyone of darker complexion than a western European—see "Renaissance Rationalization of Racism," page 826); 393 *thought abroad* rumored; *'twixt* between; 394 *done my office* i.e., slept with my wife (a husband's job); 396 *do as if for surety* act as if it were certain; *holds me well* thinks well of me; 397 *purpose* plan; 398 *proper* (1) handsome; (2) admirable, virtuous; 399 *his place* Cassio's position as Othello's lieutenant; *plume up* glorify, give triumph to; *will* wish, desire [*plume . . . will* give triumphant victory to my hopes]; 400 *In* by using; *knavery* trickery; 401 *abuse* deceive; 402 *he* i.e., Cassio; *his* i.e., Othello's; 403 *person* external appearance; *smooth* mild, gentle, agreeable; *dispose* manner; 404 *framed* molded, fashioned; *false* unfaithful [*He hath . . . false* He has the good looks and mild manners that are easy to suspect—just the kind of guy women would cheat with]; 406 *that* who; *but* only; 407 *tenderly* gently, tamely; *by th' nose* i.e., like a donkey wearing a bridle; 409 *engendered* conceived; 410 *monstrous* unnatural, abnormal; *birth* plan I am hatching.

COMMENTARY

If you're in the market for a very active piece and you enjoy getting into the mind-set of someone truly despicable, you've found what you're looking for. You can't get more despicable than Iago, who is an example of the "Machiavel," the cynical, clever, lewd, and humorous Elizabethan character type who delights in evil for its own sake, and uses reason and intelligence to achieve his selfish ends. In this monologue you actually get to develop your fiendish scheme to destroy both Othello and Cassio.

Iago has a native intelligence and facility with language that not only makes it easy for him to snow his victims, but also illuminates his private moments: Even when Iago is alone, his speech is poetic, from his first lyrical line onward. Throughout the piece, discrete clumps of consonance (*mine own gained knowledge*; *expend with such a snipe*; *with his wife*; *Must bring this monstrous birth*) and, especially, assonance (*thought abroad*; *purpose work*; *me see*; *seem to be so*; *tenderly be led*; *As asses are*; *engendered. Hell*) contribute to this lyricism. As Iago develops his plan, these small sound groupings help bind up each idea, strengthen it, and individuate it from the next one.

Notice that when Iago begins to talk about the Moor, the hosTile Ts come out in full force (*hate* / *thought* / *that* / *'twixt* / *sheets*), and likewise, when he gets into his plan to frame Cassio, the Sneaky Ss and Foxy Fs are predominant (*smooth* / *dispose* / *suspected*; *framed* / *false*). Iago brings the whole plan to a neat and satisfying conclusion with a rhyming couplet (*night* / *light*).

Iago, ever duplicitous and two-faced, even puns on his deception of others through outward appearances, using second meanings of the words *knavery* (tricks of dress or adornment) and *plume up* (dress up, adorn with feathers). And, like Iago himself, this piece has a less easily discernible, more scurrilous side. Iago is obsessed with the idea that Othello has slept with his wife, although there is no evidence or even suggestion in the play that this is true . . . which could lead one to suspect that Iago has an overactive and rather dirty mind. That would explain the double entendre hidden in this piece, which echoes the more delicately phrased way Iago makes his accusation: he refers to Othello as having *done* [*his*] *office*, which would have been understood by the audience in Shakespeare's time. Here's some help finding the good parts: *kind* = the sex act (from a common expression, "do the deed of kind" = do the deed); *get* = beget (and that's accomplished by . . .); *place* = vagina or anus, depending on your gender; *plume* = penis (*plume up*—well, you know . . .); *will* = sexual desire; penis (Shakespeare often used the sexual pun on his own name); *double* = testicles; *abuse* = have sex with; masturbate.

All of this leads quite naturally to Iago's scheme being *engendered*, or conceived, and then being born, the product of this *birth* being Iago's increase in rank, which is *monstrous* or unnatural, since station and "birth" (social standing) are usually only inherited.

SIGNIFICANT SCANS

The most important (and certainly most noticable!) variation is in line 408. Shakespeare gives you three whole feet of silence to work with. In context, it really only makes sense to take them at the end of the line, which is the perfect place for Iago to be thinking over all the details of the plan before he commits to it with the rhyming couplet at the end.

Don't forget to elide: *surety* (SHER-tee) in line 396;

. . . and to contract: *to abuse* (tuh-BYOOZ) in line 401 and *it is* (ITS or TIZ) in line 409.

OTHELLO

ACT IV, SCENE iii

EMILIA

GENDER: F
PROSE/VERSE: blank verse
AGE RANGE: adult to mature adult
FREQUENCY OF USE (1–5): 5

Iago's wife, Emilia, attendant to Desdemona, helps her mistress prepare for bed. Desdemona's husband, Othello, presently the Governor of Cyprus, has recently been in a jealous rage, which neither of the women can understand, since Desdemona's behavior is so clearly beyond reproof. Othello has ordered Desdemona to go to bed and to dismiss Emilia, for he will return shortly. Desdemona is bewildered, and has just asked Emilia if she believes there are women who would commit such a horrible sin as adultery. Emilia believes there are many such women, and defends them in this speech.

But I do think it is their husbands' faults
If wives do fall. Say that they slack their duties
And pour our treasures into foreign laps;
90 Or else break out in peevish jealousies,
Throwing restraint upon us; or say they strike us;
Or scant our former having in despite—
Why, we have galls, and though we have some grace,
Yet have we some revenge. Let husbands know
95 Their wives have sense like them. They see, and smell,
And have their palates both for sweet and sour,
As husbands have. What is it that they do
When they change us for others? Is it sport?
I think it is. And doth affection breed it?
100 I think it doth. Is't frailty that thus errs?
It is so, too. And have not we affections,
Desires for sport, and frailty, as men have?
Then let them use us well, else let them know,
The ills we do, their ills instruct us so.

1 minute

88 *do fall* i.e., leave the path of virtue, commit sin; *slack* neglect; *duties* i.e., their husbandly duties, in the bedroom; 89 *foreign laps* the laps of other women; 92 *scant* reduce; *having* allowance for expenses; *in despite* to spite us; 93 *galls* tempers; abilities to feel resentment; *grace* virtue; 94 *revenge* i.e., desire for revenge; 95 *sense* senses; both physical perception and emotions; 96 *palates* i.e., the ability to taste; 98 *sport* (1) pleasure, amusement; (2) amorous dalliance; (3) sexual intercourse; 99 *affection* natural impulse; passion; instinct; 100 *frailty* moral weakness; also, weakness for sex; 103 *use* treat; 104 *so* i.e., to do them.

COMMENTARY

Although Emilia speaks of women in general, this piece is extremely personal: she's clearly speaking about her own experience. Over the course of the play we witness several instances in which Iago verbally or physically abuses Emilia—such maltreatment is probably recurrent. The ease with which a long list of spousal abuses rolls off her tongue supports the idea that she is well acquainted with such oppressions.

Emilia has already admitted to Desdemona that she *would* commit adultery, and it would not be a stretch to imagine that she has at least entertained the thought, if not an actual man. Desdemona has just declared that she would not commit such a sin "for the whole world." The play has given us ample evidence that Emilia loves and respects Desdemona. You may decide that Emilia is therefore fiercely invested in rationalizing for herself the behavior that her mistress so abhors, and/or in convincing Desdemona that there are circumstances in which such an act is excusable. Or you may decide that as a hard-bitten woman of experience, Emilia finds Desdemona's naïveté amusing (or alarming), and wants her to understand the ways of the world. All of these objectives are supported by Emilia's sudden, lengthy answer to her mistress in a scene made up of otherwise simple exchanges.

This monologue walks a fine line in its approach to the main subject, sex. Emilia consciously uses double entendre to point out to Desdemona that women have a right to get sexual satisfaction elsewhere if their husbands don't give it to them. Although she certainly would have the vocabulary at her disposal to be more direct, Emilia is delicate in her references to sex. Perhaps she is being protective of her noble mistress's sensibilities; perhaps she herself is too modest to be vulgar; perhaps she fears making a bad impression, or simply enjoys being clever. Whatever reason(s) you choose for her, Emilia's use of double entendre and her direct references to sexual infidelity complement one another in the piece: *pour our treasures into foreign laps* (give gifts and their attention to other women) = put the "family jewels" in other women's "laps"; *sweet* (the flavor, sweetness) = sexual intimacy; *palates both for sweet and sour* (tastebuds that enjoy both sweet and sour flavors) = a taste for both loving sex and hot sex; *Desires for sport, and frailty* (desires for amusement, and moral weakness) = sexual desires and weakness of the flesh; *use* (treat) = copulate; *use us well* (treat us well) = satisfy us sexually.

Emilia has a simple and elegant rhetorical style (notice there are no difficult lines to scan!). She uses a series of rhetorical questions with parallel structure to compare men with women, and complements this with antithesis (*grace* versus *revenge*; *The ills we do* versus *their ills*). Her ask-and-immediately-answer method creates a barbed and caustic tone that captures her bitterness about the indignities women suffer at men's hands. Her strategic placement of alliteration in the speech is very helpful: the first example emphasizes the thesis of her speech (*faults* / *fall*); the Ss combined with hard Cs, Ks, and Ts (*say* / *strike* / *us* / *scant* / *despite*) further emphasize how she feels about men's treatment of women—she'd like to spit on them! The hard Gs (*galls* / *grace*) enforce the idea that women have the same qualities as men; the soft Ss, now combined with vowels, appear when she speaks of the women's feelings (*sense* / *see* / *smell* / *sweet* / *sour*); and then give way to contemptuous H sounds when she brings up the men again (*husbands* / *have*).

Finally, several elements combine to reinforce Emilia's conviction in her concluding statement: the repetition of words (*let them* / *let them*; *ills* / *ills*); the strong use of assonance (*Then* / *let* / *them* / *well* / *else* / *let* / *them*; *ills* / *ills* / *instruct*); and the fact that the last two lines form a rhyming couplet (*know* / *so*).

SIGNIFICANT SCANS

There are several double endings, both at line ends and mid-line before caesuras (line 91 has both, as well as an inverted first foot), suggesting that Emilia has much to say on this topic.

Don't forget to elide: *frailty* (FRALE-tee) in lines 100 and 102 and *Desires* (De-ZIRES) in line 102;

. . . and to contract: *Is't* (ist) in line 100.

ROMEO AND JULIET

ACT 1, SCENE iii

NURSE

GENDER: F
PROSE/VERSE: blank verse
AGE RANGE: mature adult
FREQUENCY OF USE (1–5): 3

Nurse has taken care of Juliet since she was a baby. Now that Juliet is a young woman, Nurse looks forward with bittersweet pride to seeing her charge married off to some rich, handsome young man. When Lady Capulet comes to Juliet's chamber looking for her daughter, Nurse is only too pleased to reminisce about her favorite little girl. When the subject of Juliet's age comes up, Nurse declares:

Faith, I can tell her age unto an hour;
I'll lay fourteen of my teeth—
And yet to my teen be it spoken, I have but four—
She's not fourteen. How long is it now
15 To Lammastide?

Come Lammas Eve at night shall she be fourteen.
Susan and she—God rest all Christian souls!—
Were of an age. Well, Susan is with God;
20 She was too good for me. But as I said,
On Lammas Eve at night shall she be fourteen,
That shall she. Marry, I remember it well.
'Tis since the earthquake now eleven years,
And she was weaned—I never shall forget it—
25 Of all the days in the year, upon that day.
For I had then laid wormwood to my dug,
Sitting in the sun, under the dovehouse wall.
My lord and you were then at Mantua.
Nay, I do bear a brain! But as I said,

11 *Faith* In faith, in truth; *tell* count, tell you the number of; 12 *lay* lay down (in a bet), wager; 13 *teen* sorrow; affliction [or, *to my teen* may be a contraction of the colloquial expression "to my teeth," meaning "to my face," i.e., openly]; *be it spoken* i.e., I say it; *I have but four* I have only four (teeth); 15 *Lammastide* (LAM´-uss-TIDE) August 1, on which the early English Church celebrated a harvest festival for the first ripe wheat. Hlafmasse loaves were made from the wheat and consecrated in a religious service (*hlafmasse = loaf + mass*)—*Lammastide* was also used to refer to the time around the festival; 17 *Lammas Eve* July 31, the eve of the Lammastide festival; 18 *Susan* the Nurse's daughter, who died in childhood; *God rest all Christian souls!* an expression commonly used in Shakespeare's time when the dead were mentioned; 19 *of an age* the same age; 22 *Marry* an interjection deriving from "By the Virgin Mary," used here to affirm what has just been said; 23 *'Tis* i.e., it has been; *the earthquake* Verona lies in a region of northern Italy where serious earthquakes take place periodically. There has been much speculation by scholars over which quake in particular the Nurse refers to, all inconclusive; 26 *wormwood* a proverbially bitter-tasting and medicinal herb, used by Elizabethans in the form of wormwood oil [*laid wormwood to* put wormwood oil on]; *dug* breast; 27 *under the dovehouse wall* by the wall of the dovehouse; 28 *My lord* she refers to Capulet, Juliet's father; *Mantua* the nearest large town, about twenty miles from the Capulets' hometown of Verona; 29 *Nay* No (used here to amplify what she is saying); *do bear* am endowed with [*Nay, I do bear a brain* i.e.,

30 When it did taste the wormwood on the nipple
Of my dug and felt it bitter, pretty fool,
To see it tetchy and fall out with the dug!
"Shake," quoth the dovehouse—'twas no need I trow,
To bid me trudge—
35 And since that time it is eleven years.
For then she could stand high-lone. Nay, by th' rood,
She could have run and waddled all about,
For even the day before she broke her brow,
And then my husband—God be with his soul,
40 He was a merry man—took up the child.
"Yea," quoth he, "dost thou fall upon thy face?
Thou wilt fall backward when thou hast more wit,
Wilt thou not, Jule?" And, by my holidam,
The pretty wretch left crying and said, "Ay."
45 To see now how a jest shall come about!
I warrant, an I should live a thousand years,
I never should forget it. "Wilt thou not, Jule?," quoth he,
And, pretty fool, it stinted and said, "Ay."

50 Yes, madam, but I cannot choose but laugh
To think it should leave crying and say, "Ay."
And yet I warrant it had upon it brow
A bump as big as a young cockerel's stone.
A perilous knock, and it cried bitterly.

wow, have I got a good memory]; 30 *it* i.e., the baby, Juliet; 31 *felt it bitter* perceived its bitter taste; *fool* In Elizabethan times, often a term of endearment; 32 *tetchy* irritable, fretful [*To see it tetchy* to see her become fretful]; *fall out with* become irritated with; quarrel with; 33 *quoth* said ["*Shake," quoth the dovehouse* i.e., the dovehouse shook]; *I trow* (rhymes with *know*) I dare say, I assure you [*'twas . . . trudge* i.e., I assure you, there was need to tell me to get out of the way]; 36 *then* by then; *stand high-lone* stand up all by herself; *Nay* No (often, as here, used to introduce a correction of what has just been said); *by th' rood* by the cross (i.e., the crucifix); 38 *even* just; *broke her brow* cut or bruised her forehead; 41 *Yea* Yes (sometimes, as here, used to introduce a question that expresses surprise or amusement); 42 *wit* understanding, judgment; 43 *holidam* (HOL´-ih-DUM) holiness, salvation; holy relic [*by my holidam* a common oath in Shakespeare's time]; 44 *wretch* miserable creature (sometimes, as here, used as a pitying term of endearment); *left* stopped; 45 *a jest shall come about* i.e., Juliet is now of marrying age, and will soon be "falling backward" into bed with her husband, as the Nurse's husband predicted; 46 *an I should live* if I live; 47 *should* will; 48 *stinted* stopped (crying); 51 *leave* stop; 52 *it* its (i.e., her) [*upon it brow* on her forehead]; 53 *cockerel's* young rooster's; *stone* testicle; 54 *perilous* dread-

55 "Yea," quoth my husband, "fall'st upon thy face?
Thou wilt fall backward when thou comest to age
Wilt thou not, Jule?" It stinted and said, "Ay."

Peace, I have done. God mark thee to his grace!
60 Thou wast the prettiest babe that e'er I nursed.
An I might live to see thee married once,
I have my wish.

3 minutes

ful, alarming; *knock* injury, blow; 56 *comest to age* come of age; 59 *Peace* i.e., take it easy, relax; *have* am; *God mark thee to his grace* (1) May God count you as one of those who deserve salvation; or (2) God can count you as one of his best works; 61 *An I might* If I could; *once* one day.

COMMENTARY

Despite Nurse's hard life, she has always kept her good spirits. As a wet nurse, she has breast-fed and cared for other people's children since the birth of her own child made her eligible for the job. Nurse's daughter, Susan, was born near the time of Juliet's birth. Like many children of wet nurses, Susan died in childhood. Her death could have been due to many causes (child mortality was very high, due to smallpox, the plague, open fireplaces, etc.), but it surely didn't help that Nurse breast-fed Juliet with milk that was meant for Susan, so Susan may have been weaned early or received less milk than she needed. Whatever the cause, Susan's death was a great loss to Nurse, who turned to little Juliet as her consolation. There is no doubt that Nurse loves Juliet as a daughter. Since the deaths of her husband and her own child, Nurse has had no family but Juliet to love and look after. Thus, Nurse's jokes and teasing are done in the most loving way, and her enjoyment of the memories is sincere.

Nurse has a good sense of humor. She puns well (*fourteen / to my teen / teeth*) and tells a good (though admittedly long) story. Yet much of the laughter she provokes is character driven, and it is easy to find the elements in her manner of speech that make her funny. First, there is her tendency to go on—at length, and in a jolly manner—and to be unaware that her audience has had enough. Note that after she tells the anecdote of Juliet falling on her face, she repeats the punch line (Juliet ceasing her crying and saying "*Ay*") three times, finding each telling just as amusing as the first.

Nurse's speech is utterly colloquial in nature: notice her frequent use of common words and expressions (such as *Nay*; *Marry*; *I warrant*; *To see it*) and her provincial-sounding idiom ("*Shake*," *quoth the dovehouse*; *by th' rood*; *by my holidam*; and so on). Nurse likes to call Juliet by teasing nicknames (*pretty fool*; *pretty wretch*; *Jule*), which reveal her affection for and intimacy with Juliet. Whether out of habit, superstition, fondness, or just adherence to local custom, Nurse calls on God to bless the dead (her husband and daughter) when she mentions them.

Nurse is clearly comfortable with her body, calling her own nipple by the colloquial *dug*, and speaking about it with no more delicacy than if it were her earlobe—not surprising from someone whose breasts were the tools of her trade. One also can't help noticing, as evidenced by her choice of anecdotal material, that Nurse has a rather bawdy sense of humor, and that she thinks of sex as something Juliet will enjoy. In addition, although the sexual double meanings of the following words are lost on today's audiences, your understanding of them will inform your development of the character: *brow* = pubic mound; *broke* = devirginated [*broke her brow* = lost her virginity]; *merry* = sexually wanton;

face = genital area or buttocks; *fall backward* = fall and lie on one's back for sexual intercourse; *wit* = male or female genitals (here, male); *Jule* = a homonym for *jewel*, which means "maidenhead"; *Ay* = homonym for *eye*, slang for a human orifice, i.e., vagina; *jest* = an act of sexual intercourse; *come* = experience an orgasm; *about* = "a bout" of sexual intercourse; *knock* = an act of sexual intercourse (*knocking house* meant "brothel"). Although today's audiences will miss most of these references (which were commonly understood by Elizabethans), the gist of the double entendre will be clear, especially since it is heard in the context of a bawdy story. A full understanding of Nurse's double entendre will help you define her character and her actions more clearly for yourself and for your audience.

SIGNIFICANT SCANS

This piece may seem difficult to scan. It has an unusual number of elisions and contractions (see below). It also has quite a few variations. These metrical elements combine with the language elements above to give Nurse the informal, colloquial, and inelegant tone that defines her character.

There are several lines in this monologue that are short, some because they were written that way and others because they are shared with another character when performing the entire scene. In line 12, there are two silent feet at the front of the line. You could use that time to calculate how many years have passed since Juliet's birth. In line 15, there are three silent feet at the end of the line. You might choose to use the time to figure out how long it is 'til Lammastide (two weeks). Since line 34 is a continuation of the sentence in the previous line, we suggest you take its three silent feet at the end of the line. You might use them to muse over how quickly the eleven years have passed, or to savor a fond memory of nursing Susan or Juliet—there are plenty of things for Nurse to think over. Line 62 is another short line that continues from the line before. Since you are speaking verse, the audience will expect another three feet of meter and will keep watching you, even though this line falls at the end of the piece. You could use the last three feet to think about Juliet's marriage. Is Nurse glad for her? Or is she sad to be losing her charge after all these years? Probably a bit of both.

Line 13 has not one but two contractions (*to my* [t'my] and *be it* [beet]) as well as a double ending before the caesura:

x / x / x / (x) x / x /
And yet to my teen be it spoken, I have but four

Line 14 has a silent half-foot pause at the caesura:

x / x / x / x / x /
She's not fourteen. (pause) How long is it now

Line 47 is hexameter (a rare, six-footed line), with an inverted (trochaic) foot after the first caesura and a double ending before the second caesura:

x / x / x / x / x / (x) x /
I never should forget it. "Wilt thou not, Jule?," quoth he

Line 57 is headless, and has a double ending before the caesura:

x / x / (x) x / x / x /
(pause) "Wilt thou not, Jule?" It stinted and said "Ay."

Don't forget to elide: *even* (E'EN) in line 38; *warrant* (WARNT) in line 52; *perilous* (PEHR-luss) in line 54 (some editors prefer the archiac "parlous" (PAR-luss); *comest* (KUMST) in line 56; and *prettiest* (PRIT-yest) in line 60;

. . . to contract: *of my* ('vmy) in lines 12 and 31; *to my* (t'my) and *be it* (beet) in line 13; *she be* (SH'BEE) in line 21; *remember it* (re-MEM-brit) in line 22; *the year* (TH'YEER) in line 25; *the sun* (TH'SUN) in line 27; *with the* (with') in line 32; and *she could* (sh'cood) in line 36;

. . . and in line 46, to *either* elide *warrant* (WARNT) *or* contract *an I* (NIE).

What's in a Name?

Juliet is named for the month of her birth, July—and the month of her birth was no accident. Shakespeare set Juliet's birthday on Lammastide, the feast of the early harvest, to associate her with early ripening. In fact, Shakespeare went out of his way to emphasize Juliet's youth, changing her age from sixteen (in the source material) to not quite fourteen. Although Lady Capulet insists that young women of Juliet's age are marrying and having babies right and left in Verona, fourteen would have seemed young to Elizabethans, who expected women to marry between their late teens and mid-twenties.

P.S. Like many Elizabethans, Nurse no doubt misunderstands the origin of the word *Lammas*, believing it comes from *lamb* + *mass*, which may be why she often calls Juliet "Lamb."

ROMEO AND JULIET

ACT I, SCENE iv

MERCUTIO

GENDER: M
AGE RANGE: young adult to adult
PROSE/VERSE: blank verse
FREQUENCY OF USE (1–5): 4

Mercutio is on his way to the Capulets' masked ball with his buddies, Romeo and Benvolio. Romeo is wallowing in lovesickness for some young thing named Rosaline and is moping and dragging his feet. He's cramping their style. Mercutio, who has no use for love (but plenty of use for sex), is exasperated and pokes fun at Romeo, trying to kid him out of his malaise. When Romeo says that he's had an ominous dream, Mercutio replies:

MERCUTIO

O then I see Queen Mab hath been with you.
She is the fairies' midwife, and she comes
55 In shape no bigger than an agate-stone
On the forefinger of an alderman,
Drawn with a team of little atomies
Athwart men's noses as they lie asleep.
Her chariot is an empty hazelnut,
60 Made by the joiner squirrel or old grub—
Time out o' mind the fairies' coachmakers.
Her wagon-spokes made of long spinners' legs;
The cover, of the wings of grasshoppers;
The traces, of the smallest spider's web;
65 The collars, of the moonshine's watery beams;
Her whip, of cricket's bone; the lash, of film;
Her wagoner, a small gray-coated gnat,
Not half so big as a round little worm
Pricked from the lazy finger of a maid.
70 And in this state she gallops night by night
Through lovers' brains, and then they dream of love;

53 *Queen Mab* the dream fairy (Shakespeare either invented or was the first to introduce into literature this character from folklore, who, it seems, is derived from the ancient Irish goddess Mabh, ruler of a tribe of "little people," and from a Warwickshire colloquial term, *Mab-led*, meaning "led astray by a fairy or elf"); 54 *midwife* here, the fairy who delivers the dreams of humans; 55 *In shape* i.e., in size; *agate-stone* a quartz crystal, usually carved with tiny figures and set in a seal ring; 57 *with* by; *atomies* little atoms (i.e., the teensiest of creatures); 58 *Athwart* across; 60 *joiner* maker of wooden furniture [*joiner squirrel* furniture-making squirrel]; *grub* an insect that bores into wood; 61 *Time out o' mind* for longer than anyone can remember; 62 *spinners'* spiders'; 63 *cover* i.e., chariot cover; 64 *traces* harness straps; 65 *watery* in Elizabethan times, the moon was believed to shed moisture upon the earth; 66 *whip* i.e., the handle of the whip; *lash* the cord of the whip; *film* (1) gossamer: the fine film of a cobweb often seen floating through the air or caught on bushes or grass; or (2) the thin membrane that separates seeds in pods; 67 *wagoner* driver of the chariot; 69 *Pricked* removed; *maid* unmarried virginal woman [*a round little worm / Pricked from the lazy finger of a maid* Mercutio refers to the proverbial warning that maggots will breed in the idle fingers of lazy maidens]; 70 *state* splen-

O'er courtiers' knees, that dream on curtsies straight;
O'er lawyers' fingers, who straight dream on fees;
O'er ladies' lips, who straight on kisses dream,
75 Which oft the angry Mab with blisters plagues
Because their breaths with sweetmeats tainted are.
Sometime she gallops o'er a courtier's nose,
And then dreams he of smelling out a suit;
And sometime comes she with a tithe-pig's tail,
80 Tickling a parson's nose as he lies asleep,
Then dreams he of another benefice;
Sometime she driveth o'er a soldier's neck,
And then dreams he of cutting foreign throats,
Of breaches, ambuscadoes, Spanish blades,
85 Of healths five-fathom deep; and then anon
Drums in his ear, at which he starts and wakes,
And being thus frighted, swears a prayer or two
And sleeps again. This is that very Mab
That plaits the manes of horses in the night
90 And bakes the elf-locks in foul sluttish hairs,
Which once untangled, much misfortune bodes.
This is the hag, when maids lie on their backs,
That presses them and learns them first to bear,

did, grand procession; 72 *straight* immediately; 76 *sweetmeats* candied fruit, especially plums; *tainted* slightly tinged; 77 *Sometime* From time to time; 78 *smelling out a suit* sniffing out a petition he'll be paid to present to the King; 79 *tithe-pig* pig given to a parson as part of a parishioner's tithe (yearly 10 percent tax to the Church, often paid in kind with produce, livestock, goods, etc.); 81 *benefice* (BEN´-uh-FISS) a church position, to which specific property, assets, and/or a salary are attached [*another benefice* i.e., a more profitable church position than he has now]; 84 *breaches* gaps in the castle or city walls of enemies; *ambuscadoes* ambushes; *Spanish blades* i.e., swords made of Toledo steel, which were famous throughout Europe for their strength; 85 *healths* toasts to one's health; *fathom* a depth of six feet [*five-fathom* i.e., very deep] [*healths of five-fathom* toasts made with large steins of ale]; *anon* immediately; 86 *Drums* she drums; 87 *swears a prayer* the startled soldier impulsively blurts out a curse, when he should be uttering a prayer; 90 *bakes* to harden and paste together; *elf-locks* matted hair (believed to be clumped together by elves); *foul* dirty (also, diseased; disgraceful); *sluttish* (1) unclean, nasty; and (2) sexually loose, slutty (elves were believed to hate and punish slovenly and/or slutty women); 91 *much misfortune bodes* is an omen of much upcoming bad fortune (because it was believed that the elves grew angry and retaliated when the hair they'd matted was untangled); 93 *presses them* (1) uses pressure to pin them down; and (2) presses them down during the sexual act (Elizabethans believed that sexual dreams were brought by evil spirits who took the form of a life-size sexual partner); *learns* teaches [*learns them first* i.e., is the first to teach them]; *to bear* (1) to carry and give birth to a child; and (2) to bear the weight of a man during sex; and, possible choice: (3) to bear suffering (which Mercutio considers to be the lot of

Making them women of good carriage.
95 This is she—

[ROMEO: *Peace, peace, Mercutio, peace.*
Thou talk'st of nothing.]

True, I talk of dreams,
Which are the children of an idle brain,
Begot of nothing but vain fantasy,
Which is as thin of substance as the air
100 And more inconstant than the wind, who woos
Even now the frozen bosom of the North,
And, being angered, puffs away from thence,
Turning his face to the dew-dropping South.

2 minutes, 50 seconds

women in life); 94 ***women of good carriage*** Mercutio plays on three meanings of *carriage*: (1) good posture; (2) bearing the weight of a sexual partner; (3) carrying children during pregnancy; 98 ***nothing*** Romeo plays on the Elizabethan slang term for (1) *vagina* (a woman has no penis, or "no thing"); and (2) sexual intercourse (a pun on *noting*: the word *prick* was a synonym for a musical "note." Since *prick* was a slang term for a penis, *pricking* was slang for "having sex," as was its synonym, *noting*); ***vain*** empty, frivolous; ***fantasy*** imagination; 100 ***inconstant*** fickle, changeable; ***who woos / Even now the frozen bosom of the North*** who, right now as we speak, is wooing the North's frigid heart (but she gives him the cold shoulder); 103 ***dew-dropping*** rainy.

COMMENTARY

Mercutio is a rationalist. There is no room in his modern philosophy for Romeo's romantic fatalism, and he jumps in to debunk the superstitious drivel that has Romeo in its clutches. Mercutio has no respect for the power of dreams, and at the start of the monologue he facetiously pooh-poohs dreams by lampooning their folkloric purveyors in minute detail, literally belittling them almost out of existence (even making atoms smaller than they are by adding the diminutive *ies* to create the word *atomies*).

But his rhetorical strategy backfires somewhat: in an effort to dispel their hold on Romeo, Mercutio unleashes the power of dreams, which takes firm hold of him. Mercutio very quickly becomes carried away with the dream forces he was at first simply describing. The speech has a dreamlike quality, which is expressed through the astonishing use of imagery in every single line. These images become free-associative, as dreams often do, and soon transform from innocent dream to menacing nightmare (in fact, the First Folio and Quarto versions of this speech are printed mostly as free-flowing, unstructured prose, although the metrical nature of the verse is evident). This transformation from the benign to the malignant is supported by a parallel transformation of Mab's whole persona: she changes in size from *no bigger than an agate-stone* to the size of a full-grown man; she changes in disposition from harmless dream fairy to malevolent incubus (a male spirit or demon which, in medieval and Renaissance times, was believed to descend upon sleeping people and to try to copulate with women). Mab's initial charm heightens the impact of her later grotesqueness. The built-in acceleration in the pace of the piece intensifies Mercutio's spiraling descent into nightmare.

Using the build created by these integral components is critical to prevent this from being a static list of images. So is using all your senses to make each image as specific and detailed for yourself as possible. Although you can stage this monologue successfully in many ways, we believe that of all Shakespeare's monologues this one particularly benefits from the use of physical action. The physicality will help you be specific and will support the build.

Although Mercutio may seem out of control, he is very much in control of his language. He uses a profusion of double entendre in the monologue to debase Romeo's romantic notions, which he believes are just the trappings of sexual desire. Elizabethan audiences would have been familiar with the sexual meanings listed for each of the words and phrases below: *Queen*: a play on *quean* = slut, harlot; *Mab* = common name for a slut; *been with you* = slept with you; *stone* = testicle; *forefinger* = penis [*an agate-stone / On the forefinger of an alderman* = an alderman's testicle]; *noses* = penises; *hazelnut*: the pun on *nuts* is self-evident; *joiner* = copulating; *squirrel* = harlot [*joiner squirrel* (who makes her living hollowing out hazelnuts) = copulating harlot (who makes her living emptying men's nuts)]; *wings* = genitals; *worm* = syphilis; *Pricked* = copulated; *finger* = penis [*worm / Pricked from the lazy finger* = syphilis contracted through contact with a penis during sexual intercourse (the First Quarto has the word *man* in place of *maid*, though *maid* has long been the more common choice among editors)]; *brains* = excrement [*lovers' brains* also = romantic crap]; *lips* = the labia; *angry* = having an erection; *blisters* = herpes; *sweetmeats*: prunes were considered a prevention or cure for venereal disease; *tail* = male or female genitalia; *breaches* = vaginas or anuses; *blades*: another word for "sword," which also = penis; *prayer* = fart; *presses* = presses down during the sexual act; *idle* = sexually wanton; *Begot of* = fathered by (in keeping with sexual sense of rest of the piece); *vain* = penis; *fantasy* = sexual desire; *puffs* = fornicates; *Turning . . . to* = seeking sexually; *face* = buttocks. Notice that when you apply these second meanings, other words and phrases take on sexual nuance as well. Examples include *another benefice* (a sexual reward) and *ambuscadoes* (sexual attacks or rape). As Mercutio, feel free to relish your own cleverness and/or its shock value. Remember, however, that these are secondary meanings underlying the primary ones and that many of them are lost to today's audiences.

Although there are many sounds in this piece for you to find and use, the one that is most prevalent is the pervaSive Sexual, SenSuouS, Snide, Swept-away, Scatological S. Read the piece aloud, and these Ss will jump right out at you. Also, be sure to take advantage of Mercutio's use of onomatopoeia (*puffs*; *starts*; *gallops*). Using onomatopoeic sounds within the imagery helps bring the vision to life. Similarly, the invented word *atomies* describes through its sound the tinier-than-an-atom size of the creatures in Mab's employ. And for help exploiting the sound of the word *O* to its full advantage, see "O, No! An *O*!," page xxxiii.

SIGNIFICANT SCANS

The meter of this piece is quite regular, which supports its dreamlike flow. This heightens the contrast of line 88, where a new sentence begins in the middle of the line (*This is that very Mab*). Furthermore, the sentence begins with an inverted foot. Mercutio's thoughts seem to be accelerating, and the pitch of the nightmare is growing more intense.

When performing this monologue solo, use Romeo's lines as silent feet during which you will make the significant transition out of the nightmare and back into reality. Note that line 95 is headless:

```
    x       / x  /       x      /         x      /         x      /
(pause) This is she— (pause-pause) (pause-pause) (pause-pause)
```

x / x / x / x / x /
(pause-pause) (pause-pause) (pause) True, I talk of dreams

Here are some other variations to be aware of. There is an inverted foot in the middle of line 62 (*made of*), where the caesura is not marked by punctuation:

x / x / / x x / x /
Her wagon-spokes made of long spinners' legs

There is a crowded foot (*as he lies*), as well as an inverted first foot, in line 80:

/ x x / x / x- x / x /
Tickling a parson's nose as he lies asleep

Mercutio has been through so much by the end of this piece that his last line is a complete aberration in meter. The line provides a strong, startling, and memorable end to the monologue through its juxtaposition with the relatively even meter of the rest of the piece:

/ x x / x x / x x /
Turning his face to the dew-dropping South

Don't forget to elide: *chariot* (CHA-ryut) in line 59; *watery* (WAT-ree) in line 65; *courtiers'* in line 72 and *courtier's* in line 76 (both: KOR-tyurz); *being* (BEENG) and *prayer* (PRARE) in line 87; and *Even* (ee'en) or (eev'n) in line 101;

. . . and to expand: *carriage* (CA´-ree-ADJ) in line 94.

Note: in the Second Quarto (which is the authoritative source for most editions of the play) lines 59–61 appear after line 69, but we agree with those editors who have moved the lines up. They believe—and we agree—that there was a transcription error in that Quarto, since the piece makes more sense when the chariot is mentioned before it is described.

IRRELEVANT HISTORY: A *MIDSUMMER* TRAILER?

Does Mercutio's "Mab" speech remind you of anything? *A Midsummer Night's Dream* is believed to have been written on the heels of *Romeo and Juliet*. Whether he had already written some or all of *Midsummer* at the time he wrote "Mab" or was still just fiddling with the idea, Shakespeare clearly already had fairies on the brain.

ROMEO AND JULIET

ACT II, SCENE i

MERCUTIO

GENDER: M
PROSE/VERSE: blank verse
AGE RANGE: young adult to adult
FREQUENCY OF USE (1–5): 3.5

Mercutio, a relative of the Prince of Verona, was invited to a masked ball at the Capulets', and brought along his good friends, two cousins named Benvolio and Romeo. Mercutio is annoyed, though, because Romeo has been so listless and mopey lately, mooning over some piece of fluff named Rosaline whom he thinks he loves. Mercutio has tried repeatedly to snap him out of it—after all, love is a waste of emotion that gets in the way of having uncomplicated, good sex. After dragging his feet en route to the ball, Romeo had the nerve to ditch his buddies once they arrived. Mercutio and Benvolio have been looking everywhere for him, to no avail. Benvolio has said that he thought he saw Romeo run over here and leap over this orchard wall. He's just asked Mercutio to call for Romeo, and Mercutio says he'll do better than that:

Nay, I'll conjure, too:
Romeo! Humors! Madman! Passion! Lover!
Appear thou in the likeness of a sigh.
Speak but one rhyme and I am satisfied.
10 Cry but "ay, me!," pronounce but "love" and "dove,"
Speak to my gossip Venus one fair word,
One nickname for her purblind son and heir,
Young Abraham Cupid, he that shot so trim
When King Cophetua loved the beggar maid! . . .
15 He heareth not, he stirreth not, he moveth not—
The ape is dead, and I must conjure him:

6 *Nay* in response to Benvolio's urging to call for Romeo: not only will I do so, but . . . ; *conjure* summon up a spirit (here, Romeo) using magic (usually done by calling the spirit by different names until the conjurer has found one that the spirit will respond to—Mercutio is about to attempt this with Romeo); 7 *Humors* Whims, fancies, caprices; 10 *ay, me!* an interjection expressing woefulness (like a spoken sigh); 11 *gossip* (1) a female familiar acquaintance or friend; (2) a gossiping woman; *Venus* the Roman goddess of love and beauty; *fair* kind; auspicious; 12 *purblind* completely blind (with secondary meanings: shortsighted or dim-witted) [*her purblind son and heir* i.e., Cupid, Venus's son with Mars, the god of war. Cupid, the personification of love, caused people to fall in love by shooting them with love arrows. He was often depicted as blind (hence the term *love is blind*) because of the frequent occurrence of mismatched couples in the world]; 13 *Abraham* No one is quite sure why Mercutio bestowed upon Cupid the first name Abraham. One theory is that the term *Abraham-man* referred to a half-naked man who traveled the countryside begging, so Mercutio is emphasizing the common depiction of Cupid as clad in nothing but a scarf around his loins. Another theory is that Abraham also meant "auburn," which in Shakespeare's time meant "blond." Yet another is that Mercutio is referring to Cupid's agelessness by suggesting that he has been around as long as Abraham; *shot* i.e., shot his arrows; *trim* well (used with irony); 14 *maid* unmarried, virginal woman [*When King Cophetua loved the beggar maid* Mercutio refers to a ballad in which a fictional African monarch named Cophetua scorned marriage until he met and fell passionately in love with a young beggar woman, whom he married and with whom he lived happily ever after, despite the disparity in their social stations]; 16 *The ape is dead* an affectionate reference to

I conjure thee by Rosaline's bright eyes,
By her high forehead and her scarlet lip,
By her fine foot, straight leg, and quivering thigh,
20 And the demesnes that there adjacent lie,
That in thy likeness thou appear to us!

[BENVOLIO: *If he hear thee, thou wilt anger him.*]

This cannot anger him. 'Twould anger him
To raise a spirit in his mistress' circle
25 Of some strange nature, letting it there stand
Till she had laid it and conjured it down—
That were some spite. My invocation
Is fair and honest: in his mistress' name
I conjure only but to raise up him.

30 [BENVOLIO: *Come, he hath hid himself among these trees*
To be consorted with the humorous night.
Blind is his love, and best befits the dark.]

If love be blind, love cannot hit the mark.
Now will he sit under a medlar tree

Romeo, likening him to trained apes at fairs, who "played dead" until their handlers "revived" them with a "magic" word; 17 *Rosaline* Romeo's former love object—Mercutio does not know that Romeo has fallen in love with Juliet; 20 *demesnes* (dih-MAYNZ) regions [*the demesnes . . . lie* the regions that are adjacent to the thigh (i.e., her genitals and buttocks)]; 21 *in thy likeness thou appear to us* you appear before us in your own form, as yourself; 24 *spirit* supernatural being (with sexual double meaning: penis); *mistress* here, the woman Mercutio thinks Romeo loves, Rosaline; *circle* magical circle (in which seances were conducted to summon spirits) [*his mistress' circle* i.e., Rosaline's magical circle (if Romeo will not be conjured in Mercutio's circle, perhaps he will answer to Rosaline's), with sexual double meaning of *circle*, "vagina"]; 25 *strange* foreign [*Of some strange nature* i.e., belonging to someone other than Romeo]; *there stand* with sexual double meaning: be erect there; 26 *laid it* caused it to sink, caused it to return to the underworld where it came from (with sexual double meaning: had intercourse with it); *conjured it down* used magic to make the spirit return from whence it came (with sexual double meaning: made the erection disappear by giving him an orgasm); 27 *were* would be; *spite* outrage; 28 *In his mistress's name . . . to raise up him* I'm only conjuring Romeo in the name of his beloved (i.e., Rosaline) in order to bring him before us (with sexual double meaning: I'm only using his beloved's name because the thought of her will give him an erection); 31 *To be consorted with* to be associated with; *humorous* both (1) damp and (2) full of moodiness; 34 *medlar tree* a small tree, the fruit of which resembles a crab apple and is not eaten until in the early stages of decay (with a pun [frequently used in Shakespeare's time] on *meddler*, mean-

35 And wish his mistress were that kind of fruit
As maids call medlars when they laugh alone.
O, Romeo, that she were, O, that she were
An open-arse, and thou a poperin pear!
Romeo, good night. I'll to my truckle-bed;
40 This field-bed is too cold for me to sleep.
Come, shall we go?

1 minute, 45 seconds

ing one with a penchant for fooling around sexually); 36 *As* that; *when they laugh alone* i.e., when they are not in the company of males; 38 *open-arse* a nickname for the fruit of the medlar tree, given because of its appearance (used with its obvious sexual second meaning); *poperin pear* a pear from the Flemish town of Poperinghe (with sexual double meaning, "pop her in"). The fruit was thought to resemble the male genitalia; 39 *truckle-bed* a trundle bed, a bed with wheels or casters that may be pushed under another (normally slept in by a child or a servant); 40 *field-bed* a portable bed used by soldiers on military campaigns (Mercutio means "a bed in the open air," but uses the military term to imply that love is war, which he'll leave to Romeo to wage . . . Mercutio is going off to sleep in a small single bed, alone).

COMMENTARY

We know you enjoy performing . . . you wouldn't be preparing a monologue if you didn't. But here's your chance to play a character who himself enjoys the spotlight and has fun being theatrical. Mercutio does not merely call for Romeo, he tries to bait him out of his hiding place by putting on a show. And he does so in a way characteristic of guys horsing around with their guy friends: he lets off steam by playacting a "conjuring"; he affectionately (or not-so-affectionately) calls his friend an *ape*; and he then gets down and dirty (very dirty!) at Rosaline's expense. It's possible that he feels more than a little hostility toward Rosaline. After all, she's taken his friend's attention away from him. Romeo is off pining for her at this very moment (or so Mercutio thinks) instead of raising hell with his buddies on the streets of Verona where he belongs.

When performing this monologue on its own, don't worry about the first line being a response to a line the audience hasn't heard—your line contains the important information that you're going to pretend to "conjure" up Romeo, setting up the rest of the monologue. The audience will be caught up in what you do next and won't be worrying about what you might have been responding to. Be very specific about which lines Mercutio speaks directly to Benvolio and which ones he "performs."

Mercutio uses imagery to weave the magical aura in which he conducts his "seance." He starts right away by calling Romeo the personification of *Humors* and *Passion*, and by calling him a *Madman*. Not only does he invoke *Venus* and her son *Cupid*, he describes them in contemptuous terms, painting a humorous picture that no doubt delights Benvolio. And, since Mercutio hopes to lure Romeo out of whatever hiding place he's eavesdropping from, Mercutio is probably also trying to make Romeo laugh, which—if it doesn't draw him out of hiding—will at least reveal his hiding place.

Notice how Mercutio uses repetition of meter, words, and phrasing to create the sense that he is chanting an incantation to summon a spirit: *Romeo! Humors! Madman! Passion! Lover!* (all two-syllable words, with the accent on the first syllable); *Speak but . . . / Cry but . . . / pronounce but . . .* ; *He heareth not, he stirreth not, he moveth not*; *by Rosaline's . . . / By her / By her*). Using the guise of "invoking Rosaline" to conjure up Romeo, Mercutio steers the imagery toward one of his favorite topics: sex. Notice the progression from those features Rosaline presents to the outside world to those that she most certainly does not, starting with her eyes and forehead (ever visible) to the foot (hidden under her skirts, but peeking out to the world) to her leg, to her thigh, to her . . . um . . . other attributes.

Mercutio then delves into double entendre (see Annotation for sexual double meanings of his images). Unlike most double entendre, which is subtle and should not be played overtly, here the sexual content is blatant and intentional, and you should feel free to play it overtly. Perhaps Mercutio thinks that if he is outrageous enough, Romeo will have to emerge from hiding to defend his beloved's honor. Or perhaps Mercutio hopes that Romeo will return to his old self, and will emerge to join Mercutio in the fun. Other elements of the language support the decision to directly play the sexual content. One example is the use of the onomatopoeic *quivering*. Another example is Mercutio's use of the word *O* (*O, Romeo, that she were, O, that she were*)—Mercutio is mimicking the sounds of sex (also, *O* had the same sexual double meaning in Shakespeare's time as *circle*: "vagina"). See "O, No! An *O*!," page xxxiii, for help exploiting the sound of *O* to its best advantage. Line 38 is the culmination of Mercutio's verbal self-stimulation. There is a natural build in the monologue to that point of release. Notice how as soon as he's done, Mercutio's language becomes mundane, his imagery stark, his tone matter-of-fact: he's had his pleasure. He wraps up and is ready to leave.

SIGNIFICANT SCANS

As you can see, you share your first line with Benvolio, who speaks the first half of it. We recommend that when doing the monologue solo, you keep your words in their proper place at the end of the line and go straight on to the next line, rather than treating the line as though it is intentionally short.

Mercutio employs inverted feet several times, either at the beginnings of lines or following caesuras. This is particularly noticeable in lines 9–11, where he does so three lines in a row, starting the piece off with a punch and establishing its high energy. Likewise, Mercutio starts some sentences in the middle of lines, creating the feeling that he has just thought of some new thing to say and blurts it out.

For the stresses to fall properly in line 7, you must treat it as a headless line with a double ending. This gives you a brief pause (which Mercutio might take for dramatic effect, or in order to think up what on earth he'll say next):

x   / x   / x   / x   / x   /(x)
(pause) Romeo! Humors! Madman! Passion! Lover!

Notice that the line has the effect of being the exact opposite of iambic pentameter (trochaic pentameter). This is fitting for Mercutio, whose behavior does not comport with that expected of Italian royalty.

In line 15, you can either elide *moveth* (MOOVTH), so that the line is pentameter with a double ending, or you can deliver it as a six-footed line (hexameter):

x / x / x / x / x / x /
He heareth not, he stirreth not, he moveth not

When the line has six feet, the last *not* gets stressed, whereas when you elide *moveth* and make *not* a double ending, it doesn't receive a stress. Try both and see which delivery you prefer.

Lines 26 and 34 both contain inverted feet following caesuras that are not marked by punctuation (also note the inverted foot at the beginning of line 34):

x / x / x / / x x /
Till she had laid it and conjured it down

/ x x / / x x / x /
Now will he sit under a medlar tree

Consider the word *medlar*'s sexual double meaning, and then visualize where Mercutio is actually placing Romeo (not under "what," but under "whom"). No wonder he gives the sentence a little extra metrical "oomph."

Don't forget to elide: *Romeo* (ROME-yo) in lines 7, 37, and 39; *Abraham* (ABE-rum) in line 13; *Cophetua* (kuh-FETCH-wah) in line 14; *quivering* (QUIV-ring) in line 19; *mistress'* (MISS-tress not MISS-tress-ez) in lines 24 and 28; and *poperin* (POP-rin) in line 38;

. . . and to expand: *invocation* (IN-voh-CAY´-shee-UN) in line 27.

ROMEO AND JULIET

ACT II, SCENE II

ROMEO

GENDER: M
PROSE/VERSE: blank verse
AGE RANGE: young adult
FREQUENCY OF USE (1–5): 4

Romeo has just met the woman of his dreams at the party he crashed this evening. Her name is Juliet, and she's beautiful, smart, sassy, and really nice. He even managed to kiss her—twice—before she was called away. She's from the Capulet family, who are longtime enemies of Romeo's family, the Montagues, but he'll worry about that later. For now, he is thunderstruck with love and can think of nothing else. For that reason, he has ditched his friends, Benvolio and Mercutio, and has leapt the wall surrounding the Capulet property. Romeo has just overheard his buddies looking for him and griping teasingly about his lovesickness (although they think he's still in love with what's-her-name . . . Rosaline). As soon as they are safely gone, Romeo emerges from his hiding spot, and says:

He jests at scars that never felt a wound.
[*Enter Juliet, above*]
But soft! What light through yonder window breaks?
It is the East, and Juliet is the sun!
Arise, fair sun, and kill the envious moon,
5 Who is already sick and pale with grief
That thou, her maid, art far more fair than she.
Be not her maid, since she is envious;
Her vestal livery is but sick and green,
And none but fools do wear it—cast it off.
10 It is my lady. O, it is my love!
O that she knew she were!
She speaks, yet she says nothing. What of that?
Her eye discourses—I will answer it.
I am too bold—'Tis not to me she speaks.
15 Two of the fairest stars in all the heaven,
Having some business, do entreat her eyes
To twinkle in their spheres till they return.

1 *He* Romeo refers to his friend Mercutio; *jests at* laughs at, mocks [*He jests at scars that never felt a wound* Romeo has overheard his friends Benvolio and Mercutio mocking him for being lovesick and tells himself that they're mocking because they've never been wounded by love]; 2 *soft* stop; *yonder* term pointing out a specific item located at a distance; *breaks* dawns; 6 *maid* unmarried virginal woman (here, *her maid* means a vestal virgin devoted to serving Diana, the goddess of the moon, who was, herself, chaste); *fair* (1) beautiful; (2) unspotted, pure; (3) with a light complexion (which was considered beautiful in Shakespeare's time); 8 *Her vestal livery* (1) the robes worn by Diana's vestal virgins; and (2) the semblance of a virgin; *but sick and green* just sickly and green (the hue of the moon), with a play on "green-sickness," a sickness (possibly a form of anemia) thought in Shakespeare's time to afflict young women [*Be not her maid . . . sick and green* In a flowery way, Romeo is telling Juliet (though not to her face!) not to remain a virgin]; 9 *none but fools do wear it* the traditional costume of the court jester (a.k.a. the court "fool," was a pale green—Romeo cleverly suggests that only a fool would spurn love in favor of remaining chaste); 10 *my lady* In Shakespeare's time, people of rank referred to one another as "my lord" and "my lady." The term *my lady* would also be used by a servant to refer to his/her mistress (so Romeo could also be implying that as Juliet's suitor he is "at her service"). The term would also be used to mean "my wife" (so Romeo could also be implying that he intends Juliet to be his); 16 *Having some business* i.e., having to go attend to some business elsewhere; 17 *spheres* the Elizabethans still accepted the scientific theories of second-century Greek astronomer Ptolemy, who postulated that the sun, moon, and planets

What if her eyes were there, they in her head?
The brightness of her cheek would shame those stars
20 As daylight doth a lamp; her eyes in heaven
Would through the airy region stream so bright
That birds would sing and think it were not night.
See how she leans her cheek upon her hand.
O that I were a glove upon that hand,
25 That I might touch that cheek!

[JULIET: *Ay, me!*]

She speaks!
O, speak again, bright angel, for thou art
As glorious to this night, being o'er my head,
As is a wingèd messenger of Heaven
Unto the white-upturnèd wondering eyes
30 Of mortals that fall back to gaze on him
When he bestrides the lazy, puffing clouds
And sails upon the bosom of the air.

1 minute, 50 seconds

revolved around the earth in concentric spheres, and that the stars were fixed to the outermost sphere [*Two of the fairest stars . . . till they return* Two of the brightest/most beautiful stars in all the heavens, having some business to conduct elsewhere, ask her (Juliet's) eyes to stand in for them while they're gone and to twinkle in the stars' spheres until they return]; 18 *they in her head* i.e., and the stars were in her head; 21 *the airy region* i.e., the high altitudes of the sky [*Would through the airy region . . . it were not night* would issue such a bright stream of light high up in the sky that birds would think it was day and would sing]; 27 *being o'er my head* Romeo refers to Juliet, not to the sky; 28 *a wingèd messenger of Heaven* an angel; 29 *white-upturnèd* turned upward (by looking up) so high that the whites of the eyes are highly visible; 31 *bestrides* mounts (as onto a horse); *puffing* both (1) blowing and (2) swelling.

COMMENTARY

Before tonight, Romeo was in love with love. Now he's in love with Juliet, and he can't bring himself to part from her just yet.

Although this monologue begins a new scene, its first line contains a clue revealing that this scene continues immediately on the heels of the one that preceded it. The first line is a historic rhyme with the last line of the last scene, spoken by Benvolio (*. . . means not to be found / . . . never felt a wound*). This ties the two lines together to show that Romeo heard what his clueless friends just said about him in the preceding scene and is responding directly to it. Keeping the line gives you the opportunity to showcase your smooth transitions. On the other hand, you may cut the line if you wish and begin with *But soft . . .*

Juliet's entrance on her balcony shifts Romeo's focus and stops him from speaking further about his friends. His next line (*But soft! What light through yonder window breaks?*) is an embedded stage direction, indicating that Juliet comes and stands at a window or door, grabbing Romeo's attention. While this is obviously important information for Juliet when you're presenting the whole scene, it is also important to you when preparing the monologue solo—you must clearly visualize Juliet appearing above, and must react to the vision of perfection that has just blinded you with her radiance (to paraphrase Romeo himself).

Romeo's language conveys his excitement at the unexpected sight of Juliet. Unable to contain his joy, he repeats himself (not verbatim): *It is my lady. O, it is my love!* He then immediately builds upon his first expressive *O* with another: *O that she knew she were!*. Juliet *is* his love . . . she just doesn't know it yet—and Romeo can't stand the wait! The *O* is versatile, and perfectly captures the sounds of both excited utterances and moans of the lovesick. When one *O* is followed by another in rapid succession, they communicate a heightened intensity of emotion. Romeo has not one, but two such pairs of *O*s in this short monologue (see "O, No! An *O*!," page xxxiii).

Notice that Romeo employs the familiar *thou* when addressing Juliet (from afar). They are on intimate terms now that they've spoken and kissed at the party earlier in the evening.

It comes as no surprise that the chief device our love-struck puppy employs is imagery: he discusses his lovesickness as though it has left actual physical scars; he refers to *the bosom of the air* and says that Juliet's *eye* speaks; in one of the more clever arguments on record for losing one's virginity, he calls Juliet the *sun* and says she far outshines the *moon* (who, in turn, is jealous of Juliet's greater radiance)—likening all virgins to the devotees of Diana, the chaste goddess of the moon, Romeo argues that Juliet should cease serving a being she clearly surpasses (i.e., she should cease being a virgin); he personifies the stars, saying that even if two of them were to take the place of Juliet's eyes, they would be shamed by the brightness of her cheeks; he likens Juliet to an *angel* that *bestrides* (mounts) the *puffing* ([1] swelling; [2] fornicating) clouds while mortals *fall back to gaze* (*fall back* was a familiar term in Shakespeare's day for the position a woman assumed to invite sexual intercourse)—not entirely innocent images. It seems that Romeo can't get away from the idea of Juliet losing her virginity.

The spontaneous, excited quality of Romeo's imagery is enhanced by the pervasive references to light (*light / breaks / the East / sun / fair / the fairest stars / twinkle / brightness / daylight / lamp / so bright / not night / bright / glorious*) and to celestial bodies (*light . . . breaks / the East / sun / moon / the heaven / stars . . . in their spheres / daylight / the airy region / clouds / the bosom of the air*). Romeo is flying high! The radiance of these images, coming in such rapid fire, keeps the monologue effervescing.

The repetition of sounds and whole words creates a smooth path through the piece from start to finish, giving it the feeling of a love song: *jests / never / felt*; *But / What / light / It / Juliet*; *sun / sun*; *grief / far / fair*; *she / Be / she*; *envious / vestal*; *wear it / cast it / It is / It is*; *O / O*; *she knew she were / She / she*; *What of that?*; *eye / I / I*; *too / 'Tis / not / to / Two*; *me she speaks*; *heaven / Having*; *entreat / To / twinkle / till / return / What*; *her / there / they / her*; *daylight doth*; *stream so bright / That*; *bright / birds*; *bright / night*; *not / night*; *See / she / leans / cheek*; *how / her / her*; *that hand / That*; *I might*; *might / touch / that*; *As glorious / As is*; *eyes / mortals / gaze / bestrides / lazy / clouds / sails / bosom*; *lazy / sails / air.* Also note that the rhyming couplet that falls mid-monologue (lines 21–22) serves to wrap up Romeo's rhapsodic tangent. As indicated by the embedded stage direction to Juliet in line 23 (*See how she leans her cheek upon her hand*), her movement on the balcony has again attracted his attention. As with the first embedded stage direction, you must clearly visualize Juliet's actions, seeing that cheek touch that hand. And, finally, notice the extralong final sentence (lines 26–32). Its run-on nature suggests that Romeo is utterly swept off his feet.

SIGNIFICANT SCANS

As you can see, line 11 has only three feet:

/ x x / x / x / x /
O that she knew she were! (pause-pause) (pause-pause)

We recommend that you take the silent feet at the end of the line. Perhaps Romeo is considering how to tell Juliet that she is his love. Perhaps he's distracted by the fact that she appears to be speaking (which he muses on next) . . . You could decide, however, to take the pauses before speaking the line, to realize that although you've just declared that Juliet is your love, hey, wait a minute—she doesn't know it yet. Whatever you decide to do with the two-foot pause, the shortened line draws attention to itself, emphasizing how much Romeo wishes that Juliet knew how badly he wants her.

Line 25 is shared between yourself and Juliet. Don't worry that she's not there to say her piece of it (*Ay, me!*). Romeo does not react to what she says, but merely to the fact that she speaks at all. Take her one foot of dialogue as a silent foot, and use it to "hear" her. Then proceed.

Don't forget to elide: *Juliet* (JOOL-yet) in line 3; *envious* (EN-vyuss) in line 4 (but *not* in line 7!); and *heaven* (HEV'N) in lines 15 and 20;

. . . and to either elide *livery* (LIV-ree) or contract *livery is* (LI´-vu-REEZ) in line 8.

ROMEO AND JULIET

ACT II, SCENE ii

JULIET

GENDER: F
AGE RANGE: young adult
PROSE/VERSE: blank verse
FREQUENCY OF USE (1–5): 4.5

Earlier this evening, Juliet's dad hosted a big masquerade party at which he and her mother hoped she would get to know and like the man they want her to marry. Juliet was not impressed with the guy, but she did meet someone who is absolutely to die for. He's a great dancer and an even better kisser. But when she asked around to find out who he was, she discovered that he's Romeo Montague—the son of her family's hated enemies. The party is now over. Juliet has retreated to her room and is out on her balcony, alone with her thoughts. She soliloquizes:

O Romeo, Romeo, wherefore art thou Romeo?
Deny thy father and refuse thy name—
35 Or if thou wilt not, be but sworn my love
And I'll no longer be a Capulet.

'Tis but thy name that is my enemy:
Thou art thyself, though not a Montague.
40 What's Montague? It is nor hand, nor foot,
Nor arm, nor face, nor any other part
Belonging to a man. O, be some other name!
What's in a name? That which we call a rose
By any other name would smell as sweet;
45 So Romeo would, were he not Romeo called,
Retain that dear perfection which he owes
Without that title. Romeo, doff thy name,
And for thy name, which is not part of thee,
Take all myself.

1 minute

33 *wherefore* for what reason; why; 34 *Deny* Disown; *refuse* reject; disown; *name* i.e., family name; 35 *be but sworn* just swear to be; 38 *but* only; 39 *though not a Montague* i.e., even if you choose to go by a name other than Montague; 40 *nor* neither; 44 *By* if designated by, if identified by; 46 *owes* owns, possesses; 47 *doff* throw off; get rid of (a contraction of "do off").

COMMENTARY

Romeo and Juliet is *the* tragic love story of all time, and Juliet is the epitome of romantic ingenues. "Juliet and her Romeo" have become stock characters in the collective mental puppet box. So when performing this piece it is imperative that you take a cue from Juliet herself: *Deny*, *refuse*, and *doff* all your preconceived notions about these famous lines. Start with a clean slate and develop a character with real faults, real strengths, and real objectives.

Juliet is mature for her not-quite-fourteen years: in the space of one night she has worked through the problem that her family and Romeo's have not been able to resolve for generations, coming easily to the realization that Romeo the individual is a completely separate entity from his name and his family history, which have no real relevance to personal relationships. Yet maturity is not Juliet's sole defining characteristic. This piece reveals the two sides of Juliet that make her so interesting: the passionate teen and the levelheaded woman. She falls in love with the intensity and speed of a stereotypical teenager, but reacts to her love with surprisingly clearheaded ideas about how to handle it.

Juliet exhibits a directness and tendency toward action that are especially unusual for someone of her age and gender in Elizabethan times. These qualities are borne out in her manner of speech. In this monologue, Juliet—unlike her beloved (see Romeo's monologue, page 756)—does not use any of the poetic metaphors and sounds one expects to hear from the love-struck. The closest she comes to poetry is her indirect comparison of Romeo to a rose, and even then she does so primarily to support her argument and only secondarily (if at all) to rhapsodize about how sweet he smells.

Juliet has already made a decision about her intentions. She does not know that Romeo is listening, so she is able to say openly how she feels without fear of being improperly forward. Therefore her use of the familiar *thee* and *thou* are a sign that she already feels intimate with him. Juliet's use of repetition tells us where her energies are focused: she says the word *name* six times in this short piece. Not surprising, since her beloved's *name* is the main obstacle to her objective—snagging the boy for herself. She also says his name, *Romeo*, six times, and his last name, *Montague*, twice, repeatedly underscoring the irony that his name simulataneously represents the man she loves and the obstacle to her love. And in the first line, Juliet says Romeo's name twice in a row. Keep in mind that when Shakespeare uses a word twice, he does so for a reason. There should be a difference between the first and second times you say the name. Perhaps Juliet thinks first of Romeo himself, and then of his name (or vice versa); maybe she's testing his name out different ways to see how it sounds; or maybe she calls it out loudly, then reins herself in, fearing she'll wake someone in the house . . . it's up to you.

Also, note that Juliet's solutions include denying her own name. This takes courage in a world where women are dependent on parents or husbands for survival—Juliet's love for Romeo (or her conviction of his love for her) is that strong. You can interpret her offer, *be but sworn my love / And I'll no longer be a Capulet*, in one or both of two ways. Perhaps she simply means her love for him is so strong that she will risk everything by denying her own name even if he insists on retaining his. Or maybe she's punning rather sweetly on the fact that if Romeo marries her, Juliet's last name will be the same as his anyway, and she'll *no longer be a Capulet*.

All of Juliet's ideas—from the romantic to the radical—are substantiated by well-argued reason. In line 40, for example, she poses a half-line rhetorical question (*What's Montague?*), which she immediately begins to answer in the second half of the line. She then repeats the question-answer structure in line 43 (*What's in a name?*). Is Juliet speaking from true conviction here? Is she trying to rationalize her remaining doubts? Or is she perhaps rehearsing how to explain all of this to the outside world?

SIGNIFICANT SCANS

The meter of this piece scans quite evenly, which highlights three particular variations. The first of these is the *O* with which the piece begins, which gets a stress on the first, usually unstressed, syllable of the piece. Take full advantage of this *O*. Juliet is in quite a bind, and this may be the first moment she's had to focus on her love or on the problem at hand. The second variation falls in lines 40–42. The list Juliet begins in 40 carries through 41 and on into 42, enhancing and extending the build, which is abruptly cut off in the middle of line 42 by another *O*. You can use this sudden change in cadence to interrupt yourself with the sudden exclamation *O, be some other name!* (Note: it is important that you see "O, No! An O!," page xxxiii, for help with using the sound of *O* to its best advantage.) The third variation is another sentence that starts mid-line: in line 47, Juliet begins her concluding sentence (*Romeo, doff thy name . . .*), which continues through 48 and ends in 49, a short line. The mid-line start and the short line ending draw attention to the important statement Juliet is making—if Romeo will throw off his name, she is ready to give her whole self to him.

Don't forget to elide: *Romeo* (ROME-yo) in lines 33, 45, and 47.

P.S.

For more on Juliet, see "What's in a Name?," page 741.

ROMEO AND JULIET

ACT II, SCENE II

JULIET

GENDER: F
AGE RANGE: young adult
PROSE/VERSE: blank verse
FREQUENCY OF USE (1–5): 5

Earlier this evening, Juliet Capulet fell in love with Romeo, whom she met at a party thrown by her father. The catch: her beloved is a Montague—his family and hers are mortal enemies. The party's over, and Juliet has gone out on her balcony to think about him, expressing aloud her love for him, her wish that he was not a Montague, and her desire to be his. To her utter mortification, he actually answered her back with his own words of love! He was in the orchard below her window the whole time and heard every word! Beyond embarrassed, Juliet says:

JULIET

85 Thou knowest the mask of night is on my face,
Else would a maiden blush bepaint my cheek
For that which thou hast heard me speak tonight.
Fain would I dwell on form—fain, fain deny
What I have spoke. But farewell, compliment!
90 Dost thou love me? I know thou wilt say "Ay,"
And I will take thy word. Yet, if thou swearest,
Thou mayst prove false. At lovers' perjuries
They say Jove laughs. O gentle Romeo,
If thou dost love, pronounce it faithfully.
95 Or if thou thinkest I am too quickly won,
I'll frown and be perverse and say thee nay
So thou wilt woo; but else, not for the world.
In truth, fair Montague, I am too fond,
And therefore thou mayst think my 'havior light,
100 But trust me, gentleman, I'll prove more true
Than those that have more cunning to be strange.
I should have been more strange, I must confess,
But that thou overheardest ere I was ware
My true-love passion; therefore pardon me,
105 And not impute this yielding to light love,
Which the dark night hath so discoverèd.

1 minute, 15 seconds

86 *maiden* maidenly, virginal, modest; *bepaint* dye, stain [*Else would a maiden blush bepaint my cheek* i.e., or else you would see me modestly blushing]; 88 *Fain* willingly, gladly; *dwell on form* observe formal niceties, stick to formal behavior; 89 *compliment* polite conventions, outward shows of compliance with socially acceptable behavior; 92 *false* unfaithful, inconstant; *perjuries* i.e., infidelities; 93 *Jove* the supreme god of the Romans (here used to personify God) [*At lovers' perjuries / They say Jove laughs* They say that Jove laughs at the lies and infidelities of lovers (a proverbial expression that originated in Ovid's *Art of Love*)]; *gentle* used as an endearment: sweet, dear, kind, etc.; 94 *pronounce* declare; *faithfully* from the heart, earnestly; 97 *So* so that; *else* otherwise; 98 *fair* good, kind, lovely, etc. (used as a courteous term of address); *too fond* too doting, acting too foolishly in love; 99 *'havior* behavior; *light* wanton, "easy" (for acquiescing too quickly); 101 *strange* reserved, distant [*more cunning to be strange* more skill than I at being reserved]; 103 *But that* except that; *ere* before; *ware* aware (of your presence); 104 *My true-love passion* the passionate expression of my true love for you; 105 *not* do not; *this yielding* i.e., this quick agreement to be your love; *light love* love that is of little value (i.e., not true and deep, but shallow and of no moment); 106 *so* in this manner; *discoverèd* uncovered, revealed, betrayed [*so discoverèd* revealed in this manner (by hiding you, so that I thought I was alone and could speak freely of my love for you)].

COMMENTARY

Despite her mortification at being overheard by Romeo, Juliet handles the situation with aplomb in this wonderful piece. She wishes she could take back what she said (note her use of the word *fain* three times in one little line, line 88), but since she can't, so be it—she'll make her unwitting candor work for her and stay on the forthright path she's carved. So forthright is she that she even owns up to her embarrassment (by admitting to blushing) rather than attempt to appear nonchalant. Shakespeare gave Juliet a tendency to blush—she herself mentions blushing again in Act III, Scene ii (see monologue, page 774), and her Nurse remarks on her blushing in Act II, Scene v.

Juliet is eager to know Romeo's mind, and to explain her own. This is no time for nonsense. And so this piece is very straightforward (although she can't help one bit of wordplay on lines 90–91: *I* / *Ay* / *I*). There is very little imagery. The most notable image is *night*, which makes two appearances in this monologue and which is a master at cover-ups: first, by being a mask that hides Juliet's blush from Romeo, and later by being a turncoat that betrays Juliet by hiding Romeo, thus revealing Juliet's heart to him. The monologue contains almost no other imagery. Juliet paraphrases a proverbial reference to Jove, but tires of it practically before she's finished uttering it, interrupting herself midline with an exclamatory *O* and a whole new sentence. Be sure to see "O, No! An *O*!," page xxxiii, for help using the sound of *O* to its best advantage.

Proof of how much she's rattled by this unexpected turn of events, Juliet keeps abruptly alternating between two goals: (1) to ascertain whether Romeo's love is true; and (2) to assure Romeo of her faithfulness even while feeling obligated to put on the modest aloofness expected of young ladies in her day (well-bred, virtuous young ladies were supposed to act modest and reserved, and the pursuit of such a young lady supposedly fueled a man's ardor). These two related goals are evident in the overwhelming number of words and phrases about promises: *fain deny what I have spoke*; *thy word*; *thou swearest*; *prove false*; *perjuries*; *pronounce it faithfully*; *I'll prove more true*; *true-love passion*. Juliet's frequent and rapid switching between the subject of Romeo's pledge of love and that of her own are marked by the repeated use of the word *but* (bolstered by *yet* and *or*), as well as by the frequency with which she begins new sentences in the middles of lines (more on that below). These frequent shifts lend the piece a distinctly adolescent energy and tone.

Juliet uses antithesis (*thou mayst think my 'havior light* versus *I'll prove more true*; *light love* versus *the dark night*) to convince Romeo that if he does not *prove false* she will *prove . . . true*. No doubt she fears that Romeo believes the admonitions she's been taught about "easy" girls and is truly worried that Romeo will think ill of her for having professed her love prematurely. The stakes, therefore, are quite high at this moment.

SIGNIFICANT SCANS

While line 90 can be scanned as perfectly regular iambic pentameter (thereby stressing *thou* and *me*, which indicates that since she's just professed her love, she now seeks reciprocity), you also have the option of delivering it as a headless line, with a double ending before the caesura:

x / x / (x) x / x / x /
(pause) Dost thou love me? I know thou wilt say "Ay"

This option gives you a tiny pause, which Juliet would probably want to take before biting the bullet and asking Romeo whether he loves her—although notice that before she lets him answer, she jumps in and answers herself, thus protecting herself from the possibility of an answer she might not expect. We like both options—take your pick.

Speaking of not letting Romeo get a word in edgewise, we mentioned above how often Juliet jumps in and begins an entirely new sentence in the middle of a line. This has the obvious and important effect of never giving Romeo an opportunity to speak. Juliet is being very candid without having had any chance to rehearse, and so she keeps qualifying what she's just said until she's gotten it just right, has said all she needs to say, and is ready to give Romeo the mike. She is not going to give him the opportunity to interrupt her before she's good and ready.

Don't forget to elide: *knowest* (KNOW'ST) in line 85; *swearest* (SWEAR'ST) in line 91; *thinkest* (THINK'ST) in line 95; and *overheardest* (O-ver-HEARD'ST´) in line 103;

. . . and to expand: *discoverèd* (dis-CUH´-vur-EHD) in line 106.

P.S.

For more on Juliet, see "What's in a Name?," page 741.

ROMEO AND JULIET

ACT II, SCENE v

JULIET

GENDER: F
PROSE/VERSE: blank verse
AGE RANGE: young adult
FREQUENCY OF USE (1–5): 4

Juliet Capulet and Romeo Montague met last night, fell heads over heels in love, and decided to marry—in secret, because their families are sworn enemies. As per their agreement, Juliet has sent her Nurse to meet with Romeo to find out when and where Juliet is to go to marry him this afternoon. Nurse left at nine in the morning. It is now noon, and Juliet can't stand to wait any longer. She frets:

1 The clock struck nine when I did send the Nurse;
In half an hour she promised to return.
Perchance she cannot meet him. —That's not so.
O, she is lame! Love's heralds should be thoughts,
5 Which ten times faster glides than the sun's beams,
Driving back shadows over louring hills.
Therefore do nimble-pinioned doves draw Love,
And therefore hath the wind-swift Cupid wings.
Now is the sun upon the highmost hill
10 Of this day's journey, and from nine till twelve
Is three long hours, yet she is not come.
Had she affections and warm youthful blood,
She would be as swift in motion as a ball—
My words would bandy her to my sweet love,
15 And his to me.
But old folks, many feign as they were dead:
Unwieldy, slow, heavy and pale as lead.

1 minute

1 *the Nurse* Juliet refers to the servant who was her wet nurse and has been a sort of nanny to her ever since; 2 *In half an hour she promised to return* she promised to return in half an hour; 3 *cannot meet him* could not meet with him (i.e., with Romeo); 4 *lame* hobbled with age; *heralds* messengers; 6 *louring* (rhymes with SOUR-ing) darkly threatening; frowning; 7 *nimble-pinioned* quick-winged; *Love* i.e., Venus, the goddess of love [*Therefore do . . . Love* i.e., that's why Venus has quick-winged doves to pull her chariot]; 8 *wind-swift* swift as the wind; *Cupid* the son of Venus and, like her, a representation of love itself; 9 *Now is the sun . . . journey* The sun is now on the highest hill it will climb today (the sun's zenith), i.e., it is now noon; 11 *is not come* is not back yet, has not yet returned; 12 *affections* feelings, passions, the ability to experience emotions; 14 *bandy* strike or throw back and forth (a tennis term: Juliet continues the analogy about the ball that she began in line 13); *my sweet love* i.e., Romeo; 16 *feign as* act as if, pretend; 17 *pale* lackluster, wan.

COMMENTARY

We absolutely love this piece. Its clear language, clear imagery, and clear intent (are we making ourselves clear?) make it a natural first piece for anyone who has ever wanted to play Juliet but didn't want to leap straight into the *Gallop apace* monologue (to compare, see page 774).

Mature as Juliet has shown herself to be at other times in the play, in this monologue she has an unmistakably (and charmingly) adolescent tone, which is no doubt brought out by her impatience, and possibly by the fact that the Nurse is her surrogate mother, with whom she feels comfortable regressing. She petulantly complains that the Nurse hasn't returned yet (*O, she is lame!*; *But old folks, many feign as they were dead . . .*) and abruptly banishes the unwelcome thought that perhaps the Nurse couldn't meet Romeo. Her frequent references to the Nurse's advanced age are coupled with the misguided assumption that older people have no sexual desires (*Had she affections and warm youthful blood*). And she uses long, flyaway sentences in lines 9–11 and lines 12–15, chattering energetically.

Juliet contrasts the Nurse's slow pace (*she is lame*; *Unwieldy, slow, heavy and pale as lead*) with lovely images of *Love's* speed (*thoughts, / Which ten times faster glides than the sun's beams*; *nimble-pinioned doves*; *the wind-swift Cupid*; *as swift in motion as a ball*; *My words would bandy her to my sweet love, / And his to me*). Your own mental images of Juliet's *wind-swift* imagery will help you convey its breathtaking speed to your audience. Juliet uses sound to illustrate this contrast. For example, some of the sounds she employs enhance her descriptions of speed by creating a flow from one sound to the next: *nimble-pinioned doves draw Love*; *wind-swift Cupid wings*; *ball / bandy*. The rhyming couplet at the end contains several hEAvy EHs and thuDDing, ploDDing Ds, conveying the ponderous slowness she ascribes to the Nurse: *many / dead / Unwieldy / heavy / lead*. This couplet neatly sums up the cause of Juliet's frustration. Also, see "O, No! An *O*!," page xxxiii, for help with using the sound of the word *O* to its best advantage.

SIGNIFICANT SCANS

There are several lines with inverted first feet, as well as an inverted foot in the middle of line 17, following a caesura (*heavy*). Her punching of those first syllables creates the sense that each additional minute Juliet must wait is excruciating, and also suggests that she is letting off steam. Similarly, the inverted feet in lines 6 and 7 create a sense of the speed and momentum Juliet is describing there.

In line 15, Shakespeare has given you only two feet of spoken words, leaving three feet of silence to work with. These are in marked contrast to the quick pace of the rest of the monologue. Since the line's words complete the sentence begun on line 12, the pause should probably follow them:

x / x / x / x / x /
And his to me (pause-pause) (pause-pause) (pause-pause)

The silent feet give Juliet a chance to think: maybe for a moment she worries that the Nurse hasn't returned because Romeo has changed his mind, but then she quickly dismisses that notion (as she dismissed the notion that the Nurse couldn't meet Romeo, in line 3) and pins the fault for the delay squarely back on the Nurse. Or perhaps Juliet gets caught up in a reverie for a moment, remembering her sweet love's words from the night before. Maybe she eagerly checks the window to see if the Nurse is approaching. Whatever you decide, enjoy playing with the silence.

Don't forget to elide: *hour* (OWR) in line 2 (but not *hours* in line 11); and *louring* (rhymes with SOUR-ing) in line 6;

. . . and to contract: *She would* (She'd) in line 13.

P.S.

For more on Juliet, see "What's in a Name?," page 741.

ROMEO AND JULIET

ACT III, SCENE ii

JULIET

GENDER: F
PROSE/VERSE: blank verse
AGE RANGE: young adult
FREQUENCY OF USE (1–5): 5

Juliet was secretly married less than three hours ago to Romeo Montague, the son of her family's hated enemies. Now Juliet is desperate for nightfall, when Romeo will use a rope ladder (her nurse has just gone to get one) to climb up to her bedroom so they can take advantage of their newlywed status. Juliet can hardly contain her excitement as she soliloquizes:

Gallop apace, you fiery-footed steeds
Towards Phoebus' lodging. Such a wagoner
As Phaeton would whip you to the West
And bring in cloudy night immediately.
5 Spread thy close curtain, love-performing night,
That runaway's eyes may wink, and Romeo
Leap to these arms, untalked-of and unseen.
Lovers can see to do their amorous rites
By their own beauties; or, if Love be blind,
10 It best agrees with night. Come, civil night,
Thou sober-suited matron all in black,
And learn me how to lose a winning match,
Played for a pair of stainless maidenhoods.
Hood my unmanned blood, bating in my cheeks,

1 *apace* at a fast pace, quickly; *fiery-footed steeds* the chariot horses of Phoebus Apollo (see *Phoebus* below), described in Ovid's *Metamorphoses* as fiery-footed; 2 *Phoebus* (FEE-bus) Phoebus Apollo, god of the sun in Greek mythology, who pulls the sun across the sky each day in his chariot; *Phoebus' lodging* the place where Phoebus and his steeds pass the night, below the western horizon; *wagoner* chariot driver; 3 *Phaeton* (FAY´-ih-TUHN) son of Phoebus. (Phaeton was allowed to drive his father's chariot across the sky for one day, but lost control of the horses and drove them off their course, scorching part of the earth [the Sahara Desert]. To stop him from doing any more damage, Zeus killed him with a thunderbolt); *whip you to the West* i.e., whip you, causing you to run faster toward the west; 4 *cloudy* both (1) overcast; (2) obscuring; 5 *close* secretive, concealing; *love-performing* aiding and abetting the acts of lovers; 6 *That* so that; *wink* (1) close, as in sleep; (2) be hoodwinked; (3) make a sign of duplicity, by winking the eye; [*runaway's eyes may wink* There is much debate over the meaning of this phrase. The most likely possibilities are: (1) the eyes of the "runaway" sun and his horses may close in sleep (when the sun sleeps, darkness will allow Romeo to visit her); (2) (changing the punctuation to *runaways'*) vagabonds or nighttime ramblers may be hoodwinked (so as not to see Romeo on his way to her); or (3) Cupid's eyes may wink (signaling his approval of their rendezvous)]; 8 *do their amorous rites* perform their solemn ceremonies of love (i.e., make love); 9 *By their own beauties* by the light of the qualities they possess, which make them beautiful; *Love* Cupid, a.k.a. Eros, the god of love in Greek and Roman mythology [*if Love be blind* if love is blind (Cupid has long been represented as blind, due to his tendency to let loose his arrows almost at random, causing mismatches)]; 10 *It best agrees with* it is best suited to; *civil* solemnly decent, respectable; 11 *sober-suited* modestly dressed; 12 *learn* teach; *match* (1) marriage; (2) game or competition (here, a game of love); (3) a joining together (here, a sexual double entendre) [*lose a winning match* i.e., Juliet will lose her virginity in her match with Romeo, but will win a husband]; 13 *maidenhoods* virginities (male or female) [*Played for a pair of stainless maidenhoods* i.e., the untarnished virginities of Romeo and Juliet]; 14 *Hood*

15 With thy black mantle, till strange love grow bold,
Think true love acted simple modesty.
Come night, come Romeo, come thou day in night;
For thou wilt lie upon the wings of night
Whiter than new snow upon a raven's back.
20 Come gentle night, come loving black-browed night,
Give me my Romeo; and when he shall die,
Take him and cut him out in little stars,
And he will make the face of heaven so fine
That all the world will be in love with night,
25 And pay no worship to the garish sun.
O, I have bought the mansion of a love
But not possessed it, and though I am sold,
Not yet enjoyed. So tedious is this day
As is the night before some festival
30 To an impatient child that hath new robes
And may not wear them. O, here comes my nurse,
And she brings news, and every tongue that speaks
But Romeo's name speaks heavenly eloquence.
Now, Nurse, what news? What hast thou there, the cords
35 That Romeo bid thee fetch?

2 minutes

Cover with a hood (in falconry, covering the bird with a hood was often used as a training method); *unmanned* (1) untrained (also a term from falconry); (2) as of yet without a husband; *bating* (1) nervous flapping or fluttering of a falcon's wings (another term from falconry); 15 *mantle* cloak [*Hood . . . cheeks* i.e., cover my blushing cheeks with your darkness]; *strange* reserved, shy; 16 *true love acted* the physical act of true love; *simple* plain, harmless [*Think true love acted simple modesty* and thinks the physical act of true love is harmless, chaste propriety]; 17 *night* Juliet puns on *knight*, i.e., Romeo, her knight in shining armor; *day in night* i.e., Romeo; 20 *gentle* kind; amiable, full of endearing qualities; *black-browed* black-faced; 23 *face of heaven* surface of the sky; 26 *mansion of a love* i.e., Romeo's body; 27 *not possessed it* not enjoyed it; *sold* i.e., married; 28 *Not yet enjoyed* I have not yet been enjoyed (by my husband); *So tedious is this day / As is* This day is as tedious as; 31 *my nurse* the servant who nursed Juliet as a baby, and has cared for her all her life; 33 *But* only, simply; *eloquence* oratory, forceful and persuasive discourse; 34 *Now* often used to address another person, especially when expressing curiosity, impatience, or surprise; *cords* ropes (here, the rope ladder by which Romeo will climb to Juliet's bedchamber that night).

COMMENTARY

Juliet just can't stand it. The minutes are passing like eons and night just won't fall. If only she could just drag that sun across the sky herself . . .

There's no getting around it: Juliet just can't wait to get into Romeo's pants. She says it outright, with *Come, civil night . . . / And learn me how to lose a winning match, / Played for a pair of stainless maidenhoods* and *I have bought the mansion of a love / But not possessed it, and though I am sold, / Not yet enjoyed*. But she also says it through double entendre, which adds a sexual counterpoint to the remainder of the piece. Shakespeare's audience was familiar with the second meanings of the words Juliet uses, so for them this soliloquy was quite bawdy. See for yourself: *Spread* = to open one's legs for sexual intercourse; *close* = lecherous, indulging excessively in sex; *night* = knight (Romeo) [*love-performing night* = sexually "performing" knight]; *Leap* = copulate; *amorous rites* = rights of the marriage bed, i.e., sexual intercourse; *Come* = experience a sexual orgasm [*Come night* speaks for itself]; *sober* = chaste; *Hood* = either (1) the fold of skin covering the clitoris or (2) the foreskin; *unmanned* = not yet possessed sexually by a man ("manned"); *lie upon* = have sexual intercourse with; *wings* = may refer either to male or female genitalia; *Whiter* = More chaste; *raven's* = to copulate with a woman roughly; *back* = for Elizabethans this word evoked the image of a woman "falling on her back"—a common way of saying she was inviting intercourse; *Give* = surrender sexually [*Give me* = either (1) Give to me, sexually, or (2) Give me to, sexually]; *die* = experience a sexual orgasm. With these second meanings in mind, Juliet's repetition of the words *night* (nine times) and *come* (six times) make the topic on her one-track mind absolutely clear: she wants *night* to *come* so that she and her knight can . . . well . . . It's difficult to be delicate when the young lady puts it so bluntly herself.

It is nevertheless imperative that you keep Juliet's perspective on these second meanings! Remember that although she may know the words and be eager to experience their meanings firsthand, Juliet is not yet personally familiar with the acts she describes. You will have to carefully consider how many (if any) of these double meanings Juliet intends, and why: is it exciting to her to talk and think about these forbidden things that she is soon to experience? Is she trying to imagine what sex will be like? Whatever you decide, we strongly urge you not to sacrifice Juliet's innocence and sincerity—don't cheapen her experience. Shakespeare may have put in all these double entendres to get a reaction from his audience, but if you play for that reaction, you will miss out on Juliet's vulnerability, honesty, and freshness.

Juliet chooses wonderful metaphors to describe her desires. Alluding to ancient Greek mythology (*Phoebus*; *Phaeton*; *Love* [Cupid]) elevates her story to mythic proportions. But she quickly moves on to describe love as a game (*learn me how to lose a winning match, / Played for a pair of stainless maidenhoods*), then to imagine herself as an untrained falcon (*Hood my unmanned blood, bating in my cheeks*). Her metaphors for the acts of love are equally evocative: she refers to sex as lying on a *raven's back* and to orgasm as literally seeing *stars* (those made of your lover, that is). It will be helpful to decide why Juliet uses so many different metaphors. Perhaps she is trying to find the one that seems to fit, but since she doesn't really know the thing she is describing, none of them is satisfying. Or maybe it's her way of communicating the wild pictures that are flooding her imagination. Perhaps she thinks of herself as a poet, and is trying to turn her experience into art . . . It's up to you to find something that makes sense. Other questions arise from the change from these grand metaphors of mythology and nature to the rather domestic ones she uses at the end: *I have bought the mansion of a love* and *an impatient child that hath new robes / And may not wear them*. What is the reason for this shift? Is she trying to bring her thoughts down to earth? Has she run out of ideas? Or is she beginning to see her situation more realistically and thus using metaphors that more closely resemble her own life (e.g., Juliet *is* an *impatient child*).

Juliet uses sounds to bring her metaphors to life and effectively communicate her desires. She does this at the beginning of the piece with onomatopoeia (*Gallop*; *whip*). She also uses alliteration and consonance, which twine themselves through this soliloquy. Some examples: Fast-Flying Fs (*fiery-footed / Phoebus' / Phaeton*); Wishful Ws (*wagoner / would / whip / West / wink*; *wilt / wings / Whiter*; *world / will / worship*); Sensuous Ss (*Spread / close / runaway's eyes*; *civil / sober-suited / lose / stainless*); Beating Bs (*By / beauties / be blind / best*; *blood / bating / black / bold*); and Moaning Ms (*maidenhoods / unmanned / mantle / modesty / mansion*). In addition to the major sounds repeated throughout, you will find little pairings of alliteration, such as *close / curtain*; *learn / lose*; *Played / pair*. Be sure to make full use of the assonance in this piece. For instance, the lAnguishing As (*unmanned / black / mantle / acted*) and pIning Is (*lie / night / night / night / die / fine / night*). These vowel sounds are ideal vehicles for expressing Juliet's yearnings and frustration. In the last few lines, you can make use of the Needling, Nagging Ns to nudge the Nurse for her news (*nurse / news / name / Now / Nurse / news*). And for help using the sound of the word *O* to its best advantage, see "O, No! An *O*!," page xxxiii.

In addition to repeated sounds there are repeated parts of words. The use of *Hood* just after *maidenhoods* carries Juliet from virginity to blatant sexuality; the image brought up by *unmanned* is kept vivid in the mind of the listener by the echoes of "man" in *mantle* and *mansion*.

Of course, the sense of sexuality in the piece is clearly conveyed by its meter. About one third of the lines in this soliloquy have inverted first feet, which creates a sense of driving urgency throughout. The words *Gallop apace* start you right off in that galloping rhythm. In addition, Juliet uses an unusual number of imperatives, many of which appear at the beginnings of those lines with the inversions: *Gallop*; *Spread*; *Come*; *Hood*; *Come*; *Come*; *Give*; *Take*). Together, these elements provide a relentless, pulsating course from one idea to the next, as Juliet tries to think of the perfect way to frame her case for the immediate arrival of night.

Note that line 6 has a crowded foot (—*away's eyes*):

x / x - x / x / x / x/
That runaway's eyes may wink, and Romeo

Line 14 is tricky to scan. It's headless, and the first foot after the caesura is inverted and crowded (*bating in*):

x / x / x / / x - x x /
(pause) Hood my unmanned blood, bating in my cheeks

Don't forget to elide: *Phoebus'* (FEE-bus) in line 2; *immediately* (i-MEE´-djet-LEE) in line 4; *amorous* (AM-russ) in line 8; *Romeo* (ROME-yo) in lines 17, 21, 33, and 35 (but *not* in line 6); *upon* ('PON) in line 19; *heaven* (HEV'N) in line 23; *tedious* (TEE-dyuss) in line 28; and *heavenly* (HEV'N-lee) in line 33;

. . . and to expand: *Phaeton* (FAY´-ih-TUN) in line 3.

P.S.

For more on Juliet, see "What's in a Name?," page 741.

ROMEO AND JULIET

ACT III, SCENE ii

JULIET

GENDER: F
AGE RANGE: young adult
PROSE/VERSE: blank verse
FREQUENCY OF USE (1–5): 3

Juliet was secretly married just three hours ago to Romeo Montague, the son of her family's hated enemies. Juliet has been waiting impatiently for nightfall, when she and Romeo were to secretly take advantage of their new marital status. Juliet's nurse has just arrived with the rope ladder Romeo was to use that night—but the Nurse has also brought news that Romeo killed Juliet's cousin Tybalt in a street fight less than an hour ago, for which he has been banished. On hearing this, Juliet lashed out, calling Romeo every name in the book. But when the Nurse agreed with her, she quickly regretted her words, and once past her initial shock, she staunchly defends Romeo. When the Nurse protests, "Will you speak well of him that killed your cousin?" Juliet responds:

JULIET

Shall I speak ill of him that is my husband?
Ah, poor my lord, what tongue shall smooth thy name
When I, thy three-hours' wife, have mangled it?
100 But wherefore, villain, didst thou kill my cousin?
That villain cousin would have killed my husband.
Back, foolish tears, back to your native spring;
Your tributary drops belong to woe,
Which you, mistaking, offer up to joy.
105 My husband lives, that Tybalt would have slain,
And Tybalt's dead, that would have slain my husband.
All this is comfort—wherefore weep I then?
Some word there was, worser than Tybalt's death,
That murdered me. I would forget it, fain.
110 But, O, it presses to my memory
Like damnèd guilty deeds to sinners' minds.
"Tybalt is dead and Romeo banishèd."
That "banishèd," that one word, "banishèd,"
Hath slain ten thousand Tybalts. Tybalt's death
Was woe enough, if it had ended there.

97 *Shall I* Should I; 98 *poor my lord* my poor husband; *smooth thy name* speak your name kindly; 99 *three-hours' wife* wife of only three hours; 100 *wherefore* why; *villain* i.e., Romeo: here, a combination of the two ways it was most commonly used: (1) as a term of reproach; and (2) as a term of endearment; 101 *villain cousin* vile, wicked wretch of a cousin; *would have* wanted to; 102 *native spring* i.e., natural source; 103 *tributary drops* teardrops that pay tribute (with a play on a second meaning of *tributary*, "stream," continuing the "spring" metaphor of the line above) [*tributary . . . woe* teardrops are the appropriate tribute paid to grief]; 104 *you* she addresses her tears; *offer up to* offer as a tribute to [*Which you . . . joy* that you mistakenly offer at a joyous time]; 105 *that* whom; 107 *comfort* joy, happiness; 109 *fain* gladly; 110 *presses to*

115 Or if sour woe delights in fellowship,
And needly will be ranked with other griefs,
Why followed not, when she said, "Tybalt's dead,"
"Thy father," or "thy mother," nay, or both,
Which modern lamentation might have moved?
120 But with a rear-ward following Tybalt's death,
"Romeo is banishèd"—to speak that word,
Is father, mother, Tybalt, Romeo, Juliet,
All slain, all dead. "Romeo is banishèd."
There is no end, no limit, measure, bound,
125 In that word's death; no words can that woe sound.
Where is my father and my mother, Nurse?

1 minute, 45 seconds

pushes forcefully to the forefront of; 115 *sour* gloomy, sorrowful; *woe* here, woe is personified; *delights in fellowship* takes pleasure in companionship [*if sour . . . fellowship* i.e., literally, if misery loves company]; 116 *needly will be ranked* absolutely needs to be in the company of; 117 *she* refers to the Nurse [*Why followed . . . dead* when the Nurse said, "Tybalt's dead," why didn't she follow with]; 118 *nay* no (often, as here, used to correct that which was just said); 119 *modern* ordinary, commonplace [*Which modern . . . moved* that might have provoked ordinary mourning (because a parent's death is a grief one expects at some point to experience)]; 120 *rear-ward* the rearguard of an army [*But with a rear-ward following Tybalt's death* But following the news of Tybalt's death with the rearguard (bringing the news that)]; 124 *measure* limited extent; *bound* boundary; 125 *that word's death* i.e., the death contained in the word *banishèd*; *sound* (1) express; (2) measure the depth of [*no words . . . sound* no words can express or measure the depth of that grief].

COMMENTARY

In an instant, Juliet's entire world has changed. Moments ago she was an excited young bride whose biggest worry was how she would live through the endless afternoon until her new husband came to her bedchamber that night. Now, suddenly, she is a woman whose husband has murdered her cousin—a woman who might never see her husband again. It's hard to imagine the enormity of that shock. But that is what you must do, in order to understand this monologue and interpret the progression of Juliet's thoughts.

This monologue has two distinct parts. In the first eleven lines, Juliet comes to grips with the horrible reality of her cousin's death at Romeo's hand. Juliet tries her best to analyze the situation calmly and, more important, to rationalize her feelings of joy that it was her husband who killed her cousin, rather than the reverse. She uses antithesis to convince herself to be glad that Romeo killed Tybalt (*what tongue shall smooth thy name* versus *When I . . . have mangled it*; *woe* versus *joy*) and antithetical chiasmus (the inversion of the second of two parallel phrases) to bolster her argument (*But wherefore, villain, didst thou kill my cousin? / That villain cousin would have killed my husband* and *My husband lives, that Tybalt would have slain, / And Tybalt's dead, that would have slain my husband*). This section contains two embedded stage directions: in line 102, Juliet says *Back, foolish tears*—she has clearly been crying and is now trying to stop. But five lines later, in 107, she says *wherefore weep I then?*, indicating that her attempts to squelch the tears have not been successful.

Lines 108–12 provide a transition in which Juliet tries to block out the worst part of Nurse's news but eventually can't hold out against the thought of it—she remembers that *Romeo* [*is*] *banishèd*, which throws her into the second section of the piece. Now that this concept has taken root, she can't get past it. She repeats *banishèd* five times, twice uttering the same phrase: *Romeo is banishéd*. Each time it appears, *banishèd* is used in its expanded form, drawing even more attention to it. This is not the only example of word repetition: in fact, the monologue centers on it. Juliet uses *woe* four times, *Tybalt's death* three times, and *Tybalt is dead* or *Tybalt's dead* three times. These three thoughts—*Tybalt's dead*, *Romeo is banishèd*, and *woe*—repeated so many times give one the feeling that they are swimming around in Juliet's head in an endless, nerve-racking cycle. Many of these repetitions appear at the ends of lines, where there is a natural emphasis provided by the meter that makes them even more prominent.

Overall, the meter of this monologue is quite regular, except that it has many double endings to soften line endings, creating a gentle backdrop against which other variations are even more noticeable. There are four lines that begin with inverted feet. The first words of these lines receive additional force, highlighting the important points in the monologue: first, Juliet tries to force herself to stop crying and get a grip on herself (*Back, foolish tears*); next, she works through her cousin's death at Romeo's hand (*Tybalt is dead*); third, she focuses on the most important problem created by Tybalt's death (*Romeo is banishèd*); and finally, she decides to take action. She begins by turning to Nurse for information (*Where is my father and my mother, Nurse?*).

Juliet uses two obscured metaphors in the piece. She alludes to military rank as a way of comparing griefs (*ranked with other griefs*) and likens Nurse's news to a military attack, comparing the news of Romeo's banishment to the *rear-ward*, or rearguard, arriving after the initial bad news of Tybalt's death to strike the final blow. She also plays on another meaning of the word *ranked* ("overgrown") to present *woe* as a cultivator of excessive grief. In the early texts, *sour* was spelled (and was probably pronounced) the same as *sower*, one who plants a crop, and the words *ranked with* in Shakespeare's time also meant "overgrown with," or "rotted with." Although today's audience will probably not catch these metaphors, they provide a glimpse into Juliet's devastation. The most interesting and active of the images Juliet uses is the simile *Like damnèd guilty deeds to sinners' minds*. This, unlike the others, will be quite accessible to your audience, so it is particularly important to decide why Juliet uses it. Does she subconsciously feel some guilt over her secret marriage—which would have been seen as a transgression in her parents' eyes? Does she have a twinge of fear that God is punishing her? Maybe she wishes that she had let her cousin in on the secret, which might have prevented the fight. Or is she thinking of Romeo's guilt, and how the heavens might punish him—or of Tybalt's guilt, and how she hopes he will be punished? The possibilities are numerous and complex.

Shakespeare has provided many expressive vowel sounds. Some are as simple as the built-in O sound in the repeated word *woe*. Others appear in assonant groups: Incredulous IHs (*ill / him / is / villain / didst / kill / cousin / villain / cousin / killed*); tORtured ORs (*poor / lord*); injURed URs (*word / worser / murdered*); and hOrrified short Os (*followed / not*). Notice the dEAdened EHs strung throughout the piece (*presses / memory / dead / banishèd / banishèd / banishèd / ten / death / ended / when / said / dead / lamentation / death / banishèd / Juliet / dead / banishèd / end / measure / death*).

There are also pockets of consonance, particularly Mournful Ms (*modern / lamentation / might / moved*) and Woeful, Weepy Ws (*wherefore / weep / word / was / worser*). The string of soft Ws is followed on the next line by the harder Ms of *murdered me*, which not only contrast with the Ws, but also end a sentence in mid-line, enhancing their harshness with abruptness. Juliet wraps up her thoughts with a rhyming couplet in lines 124–25 (*bound / sound*), which emphasizes her conclusion and marks the transition from the body of the monologue to the last line of the piece, in which she shifts her focus from processing information to taking action, and seeks the Nurse's help.

Notice that the repeated O sound in *woe* echoes the word *O* found in line 110. During this mid-line *O*, you can recall the memory that causes Juliet the pain she expresses with the *O* (see "O, No! An *O*!," page xxxiii).

SIGNIFICANT SCANS

Line 123 has a pause at the caesura (the first half of the third foot is silent) and the elision and contraction of *Romeo is* (ROME-yo's):

x / x / x / x /x /
All slain, all dead. (pause) "Romeo is banishèd"

Don't forget to elide: *three-hours'* (THREE-owrz) in line 99; *Romeo* (ROME-yo) in lines 112, 121, and 122; *sour* (sowr) in line 115, and *following* FOLL-wing) in line 120;

. . . to elide and contract: *Romeo is* (ROME-yo's) in line 123;

. . . and to expand: *damnèd* (DAM-ned) in line 111; *banishèd* (BA´-nih-SHED) in lines 112, 113, 121, and 123; and *Juliet* (JOOL-yet) in line 122.

P.S.
For more on Juliet, see "What's in a Name?," page 741.

ROMEO AND JULIET

ACT III, SCENE iii

ROMEO

GENDER: M
AGE RANGE: young adult
PROSE/VERSE: blank verse
FREQUENCY OF USE (1–5): 3

Romeo's life has spiraled out of control over the last twenty-four hours. Last night he met Juliet and fell instantly in love. Unfortunately, his beloved turned out to be the daughter of his family's hated enemies, but in spite of their families' feud the two were secretly married by Friar Lawrence earlier today, and arranged to meet in her bedroom tonight for a secret conjugal rendezvous. In the meantime, Romeo ran into Juliet's cousin Tybalt on the street. Tybalt wanted to duel, but Romeo (not wanting to fight his new kinsman) refused without explanation. Romeo's friend Mercutio decided to fight for him. When Romeo tried to break it up, Tybalt saw an opening and killed Mercutio. Romeo then avenged his friend's death, killing Tybalt. Not knowing where to turn, Romeo has come to Friar Lawrence, whom he knows well and trusts. The Friar has just told Romeo the "good news" that the Prince has mercifully decided to override the usual death sentence, and to banish Romeo instead. Romeo responds:

'Tis torture and not mercy. Heaven is here,
30 Where Juliet lives; and every cat and dog
And little mouse, every unworthy thing,
Live here in Heaven and may look on her,
But Romeo may not. More validity,
More honorable state, more courtship lives
35 In carrion-flies than Romeo. They may seize
On the white wonder of dear Juliet's hand
And steal immortal blessing from her lips,
Who even in pure vestal modesty
Still blush, as thinking their own kisses sin.
40 But Romeo may not, he is banishèd.
Flies may do this, but I from this must fly—
They are free men, but I am banishèd.
And say'st thou yet that exile is not death?
Hadst thou no poison mixed, no sharp ground knife,
45 No sudden mean of death, though ne'er so mean,
But "banishèd" to kill me? Banishèd?
O Friar, the damnèd use that word in Hell.
Howling attends it. How hast thou the heart,
Being a divine, a ghostly confessor,
50 A sin-absolver, and my friend professed,
To mangle me with that word, "banishèd"?

1 minute, 20 seconds

33 *validity* value; 34 *state* rank, status; *courtship* elegant manners suitable both in the royal court and when courting or wooing a lady; 35 *carrion-flies* flies that feed on carrion (dead, rotting flesh); *seize / On* take hold of; 36 *white* (1) pale; (2) chaste; 37 *blessing* cause of happiness (i.e., kisses); 38 *Who* refers to Juliet's lips; *vestal* virginal [*even in . . . modesty* even though they are purely and virginally chaste]; 39 *Still* always; *as thinking . . . sin* i.e., as if thinking that the kisses each lip gives the other when they touch are sinful; 41 *do this* i.e., see and touch Juliet; *fly* flee; 42 *They* i.e., the flies; 43 *yet* still; 44 *mixed* prepared; *sharp ground* finely sharpened; 45 *sudden mean* quick means; *ne'er so* in the highest degree; *mean* base, sordid [*though ne'er so mean* though it may be of the most sordid, base kind]; 46 *banishèd* i.e., the word *banishèd* [*Hadst thou no . . . to kill me?* Didn't you have any poison prepared, any sharpened knife, any quick means of death, however supremely sordid, except the news of my banishment, with which to kill me?]; 48 *attends* accompanies [*Howling attends it* in the Elizabethan concept of Hell, one of the most prominent characteristics was the anguished howling of the tortured inmates]; 49 *divine* representing God; *ghostly* holy, spiritual; *confessor* (KON´-fess-OR) Christian priest who listens to the confessions of sinners; 50 *my friend professed* one who claims to be my friend; 51 *mangle me* reduce me to nothing.

COMMENTARY

Romeo's entire life has changed since last night . . . He's gone from mooning about some abstract ideal of love to actually *being* desperately in love. He's taken huge risks to marry Juliet, and just when things seemed to be going well, he got caught up in a senseless brawl, saw his friend die for no good reason, and actually killed someone himself. Now he is suddenly a fugitive. When performing this piece, it's essential to remember that Romeo has just taken refuge at Friar Lawrence's cell, hoping to be guided by a wise and understanding mentor. It is equally important to notice that Romeo's all-consuming passion for Juliet still overrides all other considerations, no matter how earthshaking.

Accordingly, this monologue is dominated by a single extended metaphor focusing on the object of Romeo's passion: *Heaven* is wherever Juliet is (*Heaven is here, / Where Juliet lives*); a kiss from her is an *immortal blessing*; and to be away from her is to be banished from Heaven, and tortured *in Hell*. The two halves of this long metaphor create an extended contrast between the Heaven of being with Juliet and the Hell of being banished from her, which is complemented by the use of antithesis: *torture* versus *mercy*; *every unworthy thing . . . may look on her* versus *Romeo may not*; *Flies may do this* versus *I from this must fly*; *They are free men* versus *I am banishèd*.

Romeo's harping on the unfairness of his sentence makes him sound like a petulant little boy. This petulance is enhanced by his repetition of the phrase *But Romeo may not*, and the repetition of the word *banishèd*. Remember that repetition is always there for a reason; if you decide what the reasons for these repetitions are, you will naturally deliver each one differently, imbuing the piece with an overall build. Perhaps Romeo is reiterating because the Friar isn't getting it. Maybe he's still trying to come to grips with the reality of his situation, and repeating it to himself to get it into his brain. Maybe he's working himself into an ever-greater frenzy over the injustice of his fate.

Romeo uses sounds to complement the ideas he communicates. Notice the Wistful, Worshipful Ws and Soft, Soothing Ss he uses when speaking of Juliet (*white wonder*; *Still / blush / as / kisses / sin*); the Horrified Hs when he confronts the Friar (*Howling / How / hast / heart*); and the Miserable Ms when he describes what the word *banishèd* does to him (*mangle me*). And for help exploiting the sound of the word *O* to its best advantage, see "O, No! An *O*!," page xxxiii.

Romeo's language reveals his depth. Twice in this short piece (in lines 41 and 45), Romeo uses a combination of chiasmus (reversed construction of the second of two parallel phrases) and puns, with *Flies* and *fly* in line 41, and again with *mean* and *mean* in line 45. Rather than punning two meanings of a single word, Romeo uses one version of the word in the first part of the parallel, and the other version (the pun) in the second. This combination of structure and pun is not exactly everyday speech. It is surprising to hear such language from a very young man who is, at the moment, in Big Trouble. It implies that Romeo is well educated, intelligent, and sincere: he wasn't just putting on fancy language to win Juliet in the balcony scene—this is really the way he talks!

Another clue to Romeo's inner life lies in his comparison of himself with the flies. Romeo is not only troubled by their luckier, i.e., unbanished status. He also sees them as having more value (*validity*), being of more *honorable* rank, and being more suitable to court Juliet. What has caused Romeo to have such a low opinion of himself? Be specific: Is he feeling guilty about the rash act of revenge he took just minutes ago, or about his role in Mercutio's death? Is he sorry to have pulled Juliet into this mess? Or is Romeo the sort of person who kicks himself when he's down?

SIGNIFICANT SCANS

This monologue contains many lines with inverted first feet, which give it an agitated tone. There are also several sentences that end and begin mid-line, creating the impression that Romeo is running on or rushing from one sentence to the next. Perhaps he is still in running mode from his dash to the safety of Friar Lawrence's cell. Maybe it's nervous energy. Or maybe he needs to release his distress, and goes on without stopping to avoid interruption by the long-winded Friar . . . In two of the lines with these mid-line breaks you'll find a crowded foot, as well as a silent pause during the unaccented half of the first foot after the caesura (in both, elide *Romeo* [ROME-yo]). Here's line 33 (and line 40 scans the same way):

x / x - x / x / x / x /
But Romeo may not. (pause) More validity

Line 41 is headless and has a double ending before the caesura:

x / x / (x) x / x / x /
(pause) Flies may do this, but I from this must fly

Don't forget to elide: *Heaven* (HEV'N) in line 29 (but *not* in line 32); *Juliet* (JOOL-yet) in lines 30 and 36; *Romeo* (ROME-yo) in lines 33, 35, and 40; *carrion* (CAR-yon) in line 35; *Friar* (FRIRE) in line 47; and *Being* (BEENG) in line 49;

. . . and to expand: *honorable* (HON´-er-UH-bl) in line 34; *banishèd* (BA´-nih-SHED) in lines 40, 42, and 46; and *damnèd* (DAM-ned) in line 47.

Carrion Flies, Corrupted

The various early texts of *Romeo and Juliet* contain different variations of lines 40–43, and it's not clear which is correct and which are corrupt. We have chosen the version that is most commonly accepted by today's editors and makes the most sense for the actor in performance.

ROMEO AND JULIET

ACT III, SCENE iii

FRIAR LAWRENCE

GENDER: M
PROSE/VERSE: blank verse
AGE RANGE: mature adult to older adult
FREQUENCY OF USE (1–5): 2

The Friar is having a heck of a day. He secretly married Romeo Montague and Juliet Capulet (whose families are sworn enemies), only to have a distraught, bedraggled Romeo reappear on his doorstep in the afternoon. It seems that after the newlyweds parted (intending to rendezvous that night), Romeo killed Juliet's cousin Tybalt in a duel. Only yesterday, the Prince had issued an edict ordering the execution of any Montague or Capulet caught fighting in the streets of Verona, but, upon learning that Tybalt had provoked the fighting, he commuted Romeo's death sentence to one of banishment. Juliet's nurse has just arrived at the Friar's, bearing news that Juliet is crying hysterically over the turn of events. At this news, Romeo draws a dagger to kill himself. The Friar stops him, saying:

Hold thy desperate hand!
Art thou a man? Thy form cries out thou art.
110 Thy tears are womanish; thy wild acts denote
The unreasonable fury of a beast.
Unseemly woman in a seeming man,
And ill-beseeming beast in seeming both!
Thou hast amazed me. By my holy order,
115 I thought thy disposition better tempered.
Hast thou slain Tybalt? Wilt thou slay thyself?—
And slay thy lady that in thy life lives,
By doing damnèd hate upon thyself?
Why railest thou on thy birth, the Heaven, and Earth,
120 Since birth and Heaven and Earth all three do meet
In thee at once, which thou at once wouldst lose?
Fie, fie, thou shamest thy shape, thy love, thy wit,
Which, like a usurer, aboundest in all

108 *Hold* Restrain, stop; *desperate* hopeless [*desperate hand* i.e., the hand with which Romeo was about to stab himself]; 109 *form* external appearance; 111 *unreasonable* not endowed with reason (considered that which distinguishes humans from beasts), with play on: not agreeable to reason; 112 *a seeming man* one who seems outwardly to be a man; 113 *ill-beseeming* unbecoming, unnatural, inappropriate; *beast* inhuman creature (as opposed to "animal," as in line 111); *in seeming both* i.e., by seeming to be both genders; 114 *By my holy order* an oath (from another comment he makes later, it seems that Friar Lawrence was a Franciscan, and is swearing here by the order of St. Francis); 115 *tempered* a baking term meaning "mixed together"—the Friar refers to a mixing together of the four "humours" Elizabethans believed to make up a person's constitution—see "Elizabethan Anatomy 101," page 558 [*better tempered* having a better balance of the four humours, which would yield better character]; 117 *thy lady* here, your wife; *in thy life lives* lives for you; 118 *doing damnèd hate upon thyself* i.e., killing yourself ("damned" because he believes suicide to be a mortal sin leading to damnation); 119 *thy birth* the circumstances of your birth, your parentage (i.e., being a Montague, hated by the Capulets); 120 *Heaven* here, Romeo's immortal soul; *Earth* here, Romeo's corporeal body [*birth and Heaven and Earth all three do meet / In thee at once* i.e., all three elements that make you a person—your human origin, your immortal soul, and your corporeal body—unite in your living self at one time]; 121 *at once wouldst lose* i.e., would end in a single moment (by killing yourself); 122 *Fie* a scolding exclamation of disapproval; *shape* your physical form, i.e., your male body [*thou shamest thy shape* i.e., by acting like you have a weak, female mind]; *love* capacity to love; *wit* intelligence; 123 *usurer* a moneylender who collects interest (considered a sin in

And usest none in that true use indeed
125 Which should bedeck thy shape, thy love, thy wit.
Thy noble shape is but a form in wax,
Digressing from the valor of a man;
Thy dear love sworn but hollow perjury,
Killing that love which thou hast vowed to cherish;
130 Thy wit—that ornament to shape and love—
Misshapen in the conduct of them both,
Like powder in a skilless soldier's flask
Is set afire by thine own ignorance,
And thou dismembered with thine own defense.
135 What—rouse thee, man! Thy Juliet is alive
For whose dear sake thou wast but lately dead—
There art thou happy. Tybalt would kill thee,
But thou slewest Tybalt—there art thou happy.
The law that threatened death becomes thy friend

Christianity, and therefore a hateful practice in Shakespeare's time—see "There Are Things in This Comedy . . . That Will Never Please," page 945); *aboundest in all* have an abundance of all (of the above, i.e., of shape, love, and wit); 124 *usest none to that true use indeed* (you) do not put these gifts to their proper use (with pun on usury image of not lending money honorably, i.e., without charging interest) [*thou shamest thy shape, thy love, thy wit, / Which . . . thy love, thy wit* you shame your male body, your capacity to love, and your intelligence, all of which you have in abundance, but like a moneylender who uses his abundant resources dishonorably, you do not use your attributes (body, love, and intelligence) as you should]; 126 *but a form in wax* merely a wax figure of a man; 127 *Digressing from the valor of a man* i.e., deviating from a man in that he has no valor; 128 *Thy dear love sworn* i.e., the precious love you swore you feel for Juliet; *but* is merely; 130 *ornament to* that which embellishes and adorns; 131 *Misshapen* has gone awry; *conduct* guidance [*Misshapen in . . . both* has gone awry in the guiding of both your shape and your love]; 132 *flask* powder horn (a case in which gunpowder is held); *Like powder . . . thine own defense* (Your intelligence [*Thy wit*]), like gunpowder in an inexpert soldier's powder horn, is set on fire through your own ignorance and you are dismembered by what should be used in your own defense (i.e., you are being destroyed by your own intellect, which you should be using right now to defend yourself). It was easy for an inexperienced soldier to dismember himself in Shakespeare's day: to fire a matchlock gun required both a flask of gunpowder and a lit matchcord—it was not uncommon for a soldier to inadvertently blow up the entire flask as he held it in his hand; 135 *What* an interjection expressing impatience; 136 *but lately dead* i.e., just recently wishing to die (rather than be banished from her)—see monologue, page 786; 137 *There* i.e., in that respect, on that front; *happy* lucky [*There art thou happy*

140 And turns it to exile—there art thou happy.
A pack of blessings light upon thy back;
Happiness courts thee in her best array;
But like a misbehaved and sullen wench
Thou pouts upon thy fortune and thy love.
145 Take heed, take heed, for such die miserable.
Go, get thee to thy love as was decreed,
Ascend her chamber—hence and comfort her.
But look thou stay not till the watch be set,
For then thou canst not pass to Mantua,
150 Where thou shalt live till we can find a time
To blaze your marriage, reconcile your friends,
Beg pardon of the Prince, and call thee back
With twenty hundred thousand times more joy
Than thou wentst forth in lamentation.
155 Go before, Nurse. Commend me to thy lady,
And bid her hasten all the house to bed,
Which heavy sorrow makes them apt unto.—
Romeo is coming.

3 minutes

i.e., you're lucky for that]; *would* wanted to; 140 *it* i.e., death; 141 *pack* tied-up bundle, bale; *light upon* alight, fall on (in a good sense—i.e., bestow themselves upon); 142 *courts* endeavors to win the favor of; *array* clothing; 143 *wench* a contemptuous term for a woman; 144 *fortune* good fortune; 145 *such* such people, people who behave in such a manner; 146 *decreed* decided, arranged beforehand; 147 *hence* be gone, scram; 148 *look thou stay not* see to it that you do not remain; *the watch* walled cities such as Verona would lock their gates at night and post watchmen to guard the entrance; *be set* be sent to assume their posts; 149 *Mantua* a city approximately twenty miles from Verona, where Romeo was to remain in exile; 151 *blaze* make public; *your friends* your two families; 152 *Beg pardon* request (and obtain) a pardon; 153 *With twenty hundred thousand times . . . lamentation* i.e., feeling two million times more joy than the grief with which you left town; 155 *Go before* i.e., go on ahead of him; *Commend me to* Give my regards to; *thy lady* here, the woman you serve (i.e., Juliet); 156 *bid her . . . to bed* direct her to hurry everyone in the household to bed; 157 *apt unto* inclined toward [*Which heavy . . . apt unto* which heavy sorrow (over the death of Tybalt) makes them inclined to do.

COMMENTARY

If Friar Lawrence thought that the monastic life would afford him serenity, he can forget it. At the moment, he's got a histrionic nurse babbling in the background and a hysterical teenager in the foreground poised to vivisect himself (we know this because the Friar's first line's *Hold thy desperate hand!* is an embedded stage direction for Romeo to make a move to stab himself and for the Friar to stop him). The Friar didn't know what he was setting in motion by marrying Romeo and Juliet earlier in the day. It is therefore entirely possible that in his attempt to calm Romeo, he's also trying to calm himself.

The Friar leaps right into this monologue with the command *Hold thy desperate hand!* He then chooses a tough-love strategy he hopes will succeed with an adolescent male: challenge his masculinity. He uses a string of images to describe Romeo in quite unflattering terms, the first and most notable image being that of a lowly, weak female (*Thy tears are womanish*; *Unseemly woman*; and, later, *a misbehaved and sullen wench*). He also likens Romeo to a *beast* (meaning both a wild animal, because of Romeo's unreasoning fury, and an unnatural monster—a man in appearance and a woman in temperament); an immoral moneylender who squanders his wealth; a wax figure (which looks like a man but does not have his valor); and a novice soldier who blows himself up with his means of defense. Be sure to specifically visualize these images, as well as the others he uses: *A pack of blessings* lands on Romeo's back, and *Wit* is depicted as an ornament adorning *shape* and *love*. [*B*]*irth*, *Heaven* and *Earth*, *perjury*, *love*, *The law*, and *Happiness* are all personified, and each is given its own specific action.

The Friar likes groupings of three (*woman / man / beast*; *birth, Heaven and Earth*; *thy shape, thy love, thy wit*)—a trinity, after all, has religious significance to the Friar. You'll also notice his tendency to use the same (or related) word(s) to mean different things at different times: *beast* (defined two ways, above); *Unseemly woman / a seeming man / ill-beseeming beast / in seeming both*; *thy love* (meaning both your capacity to love and Juliet); and *usurer / usest none / that true use*. The difference in meanings naturally leads to a difference in delivery.

Friar Lawrence also repeats words and phrases (some of the many examples: *woman*; *man*; *thy shape*, *thy love*, *thy wit*; *There art thou happy*; *Fie*; *Take heed*)—perhaps he's being emphatic, to drum certain points into Romeo's thick skull. And/or perhaps he's trying to be rhythmic and soothing, to calm a frantic Romeo and get the dagger out of the youngster's clutches.

In different sections of the monologue, the Friar alternates between imagery and logic to make his points. In one of the logical sections (lines 135–40 for example), the Friar provides a list of reasons Romeo is lucky. The phrase *There art thou happy* falls first at the beginning of a line, and then twice in the middles of lines, and the length of the preceding sentences changes each time. Try taking only a very short pause at the sentence breaks mid-line, and a whole new breath only at the end of each line, and you'll hear the build of that segment naturally materialize.

It's interesting that Friar Lawrence uses the image of gunpowder and the word *blaze* in this monologue (two very combustible word choices), since the Friar himself is playing with fire by aiding and abetting Romeo and Juliet. We also notice that he is not above indulging his own imagination and vicariously enjoying the romance a wee bit—he's more colorful than he needs to be when he instructs Romeo to *Ascend her chamber* (i.e., scale the walls of the house to enter Juliet's bedroom). His attempt to cajole Romeo by suggesting that he will return triumphantly to Verona *With twenty hundred thousand times more joy / Than thou wentst forth in lamentation* is likewise endearing—this is the type of description one might use to cheer a child. Perhaps the Friar, sensing that Romeo's suicidal urge has passed, can shed his stern approach in favor of his usual kindly demeanor.

You'll find that the many sounds Friar Lawrence employs support his intentions, as well as the progression of the piece. For example, the repeated use of thrEAtening EHs in lines 139–40 (*threatened / death / friend / exile*) creates the feeling of the menace (*death*) that has been deflected, although not altogether perfectly—the menace of *exile* remains. The Heaving Hs at the end of the monologue (*hasten / house / heavy*) suggest, perhaps, that by the end the Friar's exertion has exhausted him.

Finally, do note the humor in how Friar Lawrence assures Romeo all will be well: "all we have to do is sneak you into Juliet's bedroom, sneak you back out, sneak you off to Mantua, and keep you there until we obtain a full pardon from the Prince for the murder you committed, break the news of your elopement to the long-feuding Capulets and Montagues, bury the hatchet between them, and bring you back . . . it'll be a snap, you'll see. Cheer up." But we recommend that you not play the humor for obvious laughs. The more earnestly the Friar attempts to reassure Romeo, the more effective the piece will be, humor and all.

SIGNIFICANT SCANS

It's impossible not to notice the two-and-a-half-foot first line (the first two and a half feet of which are spoken by a maddened Romeo wielding a dagger). Because of the Friar's urgency, it may be best not to take the silent feet at the end of the line. Once the Friar begins the piece, he's got a life to save, and is off and running (don't forget to elide *desperate* [DES-prit]):

x / x / x / x / x /
(pause-pause) (pause-pause) (pause) Hold thy desperate hand!

This monologue is full of inverted feet, caesuras, double endings, and new sentences beginning mid-line, all of which combine to create a sense of urgency—the Friar is trying desperately to cram some sense into the boy and prevent him from killing himself. When the monologue is done in a scene, most directors have the Friar and Romeo grapple for the knife, which also comports with the choppy meter. Later, after Romeo's panic subsides, the Friar relaxes and the meter grows more regular, although irregular meter reappears at the end, when the Friar mobilizes both Romeo and the Nurse into action.

Line 110 can be scanned two ways: with a crowded fifth foot (*acts denote*)—

x / x / x / x / x - x /
Thy tears are womanish; thy wild acts denote

or as a six-footed line (hexameter), expanding *wild* (WIE-uld)—

x / x / x / x /x / x /
Thy tears are womanish; thy wild acts denote

Line 140 is tricky and can be scanned two different ways, depending on your pronunciation of *exile*. You could pronounce it with the accent on the first syllable (EK-sile) and give the line a crowded second foot (*it to ex*—), a silent half foot at the caesura, an inverted foot after the caesura (*there art*), and a double ending:

x / x-x /x / / x x / (x)
And turns it to exile (pause)—there art thou happy

Or you could use the historic pronunciation for *exile* (ek-SILE) and avoid the crowded foot and pause at the caesura:

x / x / x / / x x / (x)
And turns it to exile—there art thou happy

The irregular meter of line 140 underscores the fact that this line contains the Friar's most important point: your life has been spared. We'll work out the details later and everything will be all right, as long as you don't now throw away the life that has just been reprieved!

Line 138 has the same pause at the caesura as line 140 (scanned the first way), but doesn't have a crowded foot.

And finally, the last line, with its dramatic proclamation (*Romeo is coming*), has fewer than five feet of text (indicating that there is supposed to be silence after the Friar concludes): you can either elide *Romeo* (ROME-yo) and invert the first of the two and a half spoken feet:

/ x x / x
Romeo is coming

or don't elide the name and treat the line as a headless line, with a half foot of silence before you begin speaking. This would set up the line's momentousness:

x / x / x / x
(pause) Romeo is coming

Your listeners will be expecting to hear a full line, so your shortened line will surprise their ears, giving the line extra resonance. Stay with the scene for the silent part of the line and give the line the moment it deserves.

Don't forget to elide: *railest* (RAILST) and *Heaven* (HEV'N) in lines 119 and 120; *shamest* (SHAYMST) in line 122; *aboundest* (a-BOUNDST) in line 123; *slewest* (slewst) in line 138; and *miserable* (MIZ´-ra-BLE) in line 145;

. . . to either elide *Juliet* (JOOL-yet) *or* contract *Juliet is* (JOO´-lee-YET'S) in line 135;

. . . to both contract *and* expand: *The unreasonable* (Th'un-REE´-zun-A-ble) in line 111;

. . . and to expand: *lamentation* (LA-men-TAY´-shee-UN) in line 154.

ROMEO AND JULIET

ACT III, SCENE v

LORD CAPULET

GENDER: M
PROSE/VERSE: blank verse
AGE RANGE: mature adult
FREQUENCY OF USE (1–5): 2

Capulet has arranged the perfect marriage for his only child, Juliet, to Count Paris, a wealthy, landed gentleman of noble birth. Paris is quite a catch, and Capulet has spent a lot of time, effort, and money securing the deal. Capulet's nephew Tybalt was killed in a street fight yesterday, sending Juliet into fits of grief over her cousin (or so Capulet thinks). He hopes the good news of his daughter's upcoming wedding to Paris will cheer her up and put an end to her excessive melodramatics, and has sent his wife to tell Juliet the news. But when he arrives at Juliet's room, he finds her pale and miserable, rather than blushingly aglow as a bride should be. Capulet's wife has just told him—did he hear that right?—that Juliet "will none" of Paris, thank you very much. Capulet responds:

Soft, take me with you, take me with you, wife—
How? Will she none? Doth she not give us thanks?
Is she not proud? Doth she not count her blessed,
145 Unworthy as she is, that we have wrought
So worthy a gentleman to be her bridegroom?

150 How, how, how, how! Chopped logic! What is this?
"Proud" and "I thank you" and "I thank you not"
And yet "not proud"? Mistress minion you,
Thank me no thankings, nor proud me no prouds,
But fettle your fine joints 'gainst Thursday next
155 To go with Paris to Saint Peter's Church,
Or I will drag thee on a hurdle thither.
Out, you green-sickness carrion! Out, you baggage!
You tallow-face!

Hang thee, young baggage! Disobedient wretch!
I tell thee what; get thee to church a' Thursday
Or never after look me in the face.
Speak not, reply not, do not answer me.
165 My fingers itch—wife, we scarce thought us blessed

142 *Soft* Hold on; wait a minute; *take me with you* i.e., let me understand you correctly; 143 *How* an exclamation used to express surprise; 144 *proud* i.e., of the excellent match he has arranged; *count her blessed* consider herself blessed; 146 *gentleman* (1) a man of high social rank; (2) an honorable, well-bred man; 150 *Chopped logic* deceptive argumentation, which is logical only in appearance (in Shakespeare's time a "chop-logic" referred to a sophist, a deceptively false reasoner); 152 *Mistress* a courteous term used when speaking of or to a woman, regardless of her marital status; sometimes, as here, used with contempt to a woman one formerly loved; *minion* spoiled darling (used here contemptuously) [*Mistress minion you* he now addresses Juliet]; 154 *fettle* dress; prepare; *'gainst* i.e., in expectation of; 156 *hurdle* wooden sledge on which criminals were drawn through the streets to the place of execution; 157 *Out* often used as an interjection expressing anger or abhorrence; *green-sickness* (1) anemic; (2) foolish, immature (anemia was thought by Elizabethans to affect young women at puberty; "green-sickness" was used as an adjective and implied foolishness and immaturity); *carrion* lump of dead, rotting flesh; *baggage* worthless woman (a term of contempt); 158 *tallow* animal fat used to make candles (and which is pale yellowish-white in color) [*tallow-face* pale face]; 161 *Hang thee* i.e., may you be hanged; *wretch* often, as here, expressing contempt; 162 *a'* on; 165 *My fingers itch* i.e., Capulet's fingers itch to strike Juliet; *scarce thought us blessed* thought ourselves scarcely

That God had lent us but this only child,
But now I see this one is one too much,
And that we have a curse in having her.
Out on her, hilding!

God's bread, it makes me mad!
Day, night, hour, tide, time, work, play,
Alone, in company—still my care hath been
180 To have her matched. And having now provided
A gentleman of noble parentage,
Of fair demesnes, youthful and nobly ligned,
Stuffed, as they say, with honorable parts,
Proportioned as one's thought would wish a man—
185 And then to have a wretched puling fool,
A whining mammet, in her fortune's tender
To answer "I'll not wed. I cannot love.
I am too young. I pray you, pardon me."
But an you will not wed, I'll pardon you!
190 Graze where you will, you shall not house with me.
Look to't, think on't, I do not use to jest.
Thursday is near. Lay hand on heart, advise:
An you be mine, I'll give you to my friend;
An you be not, hang, beg, starve, die in the streets,
195 For by my soul, I'll ne'er acknowledge thee,
Nor what is mine shall never do thee good.
Trust to't, bethink you, I'll not be forsworn.

1 minute, 30 seconds (Sections 1 and 4)

Total: 2 minutes, 30 seconds

blessed; 166 *lent us* given us; 169 *hilding* (HILL-ding) good-for-nothing wretch; 177 *God's bread* the wafer used in the Communion service of the Catholic and English Churches (used here as an expletive); 178 *tide* season; 179 *in company* in the company of others; *still* always, constantly; *care* concern; 180 *To have her matched* i.e., to match her with an appropriate husband; 182 *fair* (1) beautiful; (2) honorable; (3) in good order; *demesnes* (dih-MAYNZ) landholdings; estates; *nobly ligned* (LINED) of noble lineage or descent; 183 *Stuffed . . . with* full . . . of; *parts* qualities; 184 *thought* imagination, expectations [*Proportioned . . . a man* as well proportioned as one would hope a man to be]; 185 *wretched* contemptible; *puling* (PYOOL-ing) whimpering; 186 *mammet* doll, puppet; *tender* an offer [*in her fortune's tender* i.e., when she is offered good fortune]; 189 *an* if; *I'll pardon you* I'll dismiss you from my company; I'll give you leave to go (punning on Juliet's request for forgiveness); 190 *Graze where you will* i.e., eat wherever you like; 191 *Look to't* i.e., be on your guard; take heed; *on't* i.e., about it; *I do not use to* it is not my habit to; 192 *Lay hand on heart* i.e., think seriously about this; *advise* consider; ponder; 193 *An you be* if you are; 195 *acknowledge thee* i.e., as my child; 196 *Nor what . . . thee good* nor will anything of mine ever do you good (in Shakespeare's time a double negative was often used for emphasis); 197 *Trust to't* i.e., depend on it; believe me; *bethink you* think it over; *forsworn* made a liar by breaking an oath [*I'll not be forsworn* I will not break my word].

COMMENTARY

If you're in the mood to blow off some steam, consider working on this piece. You'll have the fun of flying off the handle, and will also get to unravel the mystery of Capulet's motivation. As we know, earlier in the play Capulet told Paris that he would not marry Juliet off without her willing consent (which he assumed his dutiful daughter would give without question). Here, Capulet goes ballistic when Juliet refuses to give that consent. Was he just putting on a liberal and loving show earlier, and is he now showing his true colors? Is the match such a good deal on her side (Juliet would be marrying into nobility, since Paris is a count) that her stupidity in refusing it drives him to fury? Is he already so fed up with Juliet's excessive mourning (which he believes to be for her cousin Tybalt) that this foolishness is simply the last straw? Does Capulet often lose his temper this way, or is this an unusual event? These decisions are all yours to sort through.

This monologue has a long, progressive build and requires several transitions, allowing you to showcase your versatility and range. Be sure to examine the different sections of the piece to discover where the transitions take place, and to start the piece at a level that leaves room to build. Remember that Capulet has just heard the news, so there is shock and surprise to get over first before he tries different tactics to change Juliet's mind and gets carried away by his own fury (a very human tendency). Capulet's building outrage results in a clear progression in his perspective on and treatment of his daughter, which is evident in the language he uses throughout the piece: at the start he simply calls her *unworthy*; several lines later, he is sarcastic about her (*Mistress minion*; *fettle your fine joints*); a few lines later still, she has become a disobedient, rotting lump of worthless flesh (*green-sickness carrion*; *baggage*; *tallow-face*; *Disobedient wretch*); by line 165, he can barely keep from striking her (*My fingers itch*); by 168, he is *cursed in having her*; finally, Juliet becomes a *wretched puling fool* and a *whining mammet*, whom he will gladly disown and leave to *hang, beg, starve, die in the streets* if she does not obey him. Capulet invites her to *Graze where* [*she*] *will*, reducing her to the level of a farm animal. Notice that the violence in his language escalates as he fuels his own fire and as Juliet is progressively degraded. Capulet's style of communication is about as far from poetic sentimentality as it could be, but he does manage to come up with little pockets of sound repetitions to drive home some of his most biting insults, for example: *Mistress minion*; *fettle your fine*; *puling fool*.

You'll want to go through the piece and determine whom you are addressing with each group of lines: Capulet's speech is directed partly to his wife and partly to Juliet. In addition, he sometimes addresses his wife, but the message is clearly intended for his daughter.

This monologue is packed with helpful clues for you to interpret: In line 154 Capulet says to Juliet, *fettle your fine joints*, addressing her with "you." Two lines later, he tells her, *I will drag thee thither*, and then continues to address her as *thee* and *thou* throughout the piece. Although it is appropriate for an adult to use the familiar form with a child, Juliet is considered a marriageable adult, and until this moment her parents have both addressed her as such. Thus, the switch in form of address pinpoints the moment when Capulet demotes his daughter to a child. Another clue is found in line 164, which seems needlessly repetitive until one considers what Juliet is doing. The line *Speak not, reply not, do not answer me* implies the embedded stage direction for Juliet to try to speak. The impertinent little thing has no respect for her elders and keeps trying to interrupt, requiring Capulet to silence her each time. And in lines 185–86, Capulet describes Juliet as a *wretched puling fool* and a *whining mammet*. It follows that in lines 187–88, when Capulet mimics Juliet, he derisively exaggerates his daughter's whining and whimpering pleas. The words *I'll pardon you* in the following line (189) are a pun on Juliet's sincere request for forgiveness. Capulet makes his daughter the butt of a nasty joke, revealing the extent to which his esteem for her has been degraded.

Capulet uses antithesis throughout the piece: *Unworthy as she is* versus *So worthy a gentleman*; *scarce thought us blessed* versus *have a curse*; *but this only child* versus *this one is one too much*; *Day* versus *night*; *work* versus *play*; *Alone* versus *in company*; Paris (*A gentleman of noble parentage, / Of fair demesnes, youthful and nobly ligned, / Stuffed . . . with honorable parts, / Proportioned as one's thought would wish a man*) versus Juliet (*a wretched puling fool, / A whining mammet*). With this device, Capulet is able to make his points crystal clear. His use of one antithetical example after another gives the monologue an aggressive, confident tone. The parallels in Capulet's antitheses are complemented (and in some cases supported) by parallel phrasal structures: *Thank me no thankings, nor proud me no prouds*; *this one is one too much*; *have a curse in having her*; *An you be mine . . . An you be not*; *Look to't . . . Trust to't*. These phrases all use repeated words, which often appear in a positive form in one half of the parallel, and in a negative form in the other half. Sometimes the repetition simply reinforces the point being made.

These repetitions are echoed in other parts of the speech by Capulet's tendency to repeat words as he thinks matters through or has new ideas. The monologue opens with one example of this (*take me with you, take me with you, wife*). Keep in mind that Shakespeare always repeats for a reason, and finding that reason here will enable you to deliver the phrase differently the second time. In the first line, perhaps Capulet is repeating himself to stall for time as he assimilates the unthinkable information his wife has just given him. Maybe she has not clarified her statement quickly enough. Or possibly he's taking his anger out on her a little bit before he turns to his daughter. Or maybe it's for effect, to make Juliet anxious before he turns on her. Similarly, the repetition of *How, how, how, how!* in line 150 should be used to full advantage, by making each *how* bigger than and distinct from the next, as Capulet's anger increases. Does Capulet say some of them to his wife and some to Juliet? Does he start out bewildered and work his way to outraged? Or maybe he works his way from denial to astonished laughter . . . Experiment to find the combination that works for you.

SIGNIFICANT SCANS

There are three places in the monologue where lines are short; lines 158 and 169 would have been shared with other characters in the scene, and line 177 is written that way. These silent feet all occur at important transition points, so you will be able to make your transitions or move to the next level in your build during the pauses.

There are also a few tricky lines to scan, but they're well placed and add dimension to the cadence of the piece. The variations will help you capture Capulet's manner of speech, as well as his agitation. Two of the lines with variations are consecutive. First, there's line 152, which is headless:

x / x / x / x / x /
(pause) And yet "not proud"? Mistress minion you

Next, in line 153, two inverted feet (one following a caesura that has not been marked by punctuation) create an unusual departure from the regular iambic rhythm, which makes this mockingly nasty line stand out:

/ x x / x / / x x /
Thank me no thankings, nor proud me no prouds

The most difficult line to scan in this piece is line 178. One option is to use the first syllable of each of the first two feet as a silent pause, which creates an interesting build in the pace of the line:

x / x / x / x / x /
(pause) Day, (pause) night, (pause) hour, tide, time, work, play

Note that this requires the elision of *hour* (OWR), as does the next option: you can read the line as hexameter (a line with six feet). The beginning of the line is the same as above, but you take an additional pause during the first syllable of each of the last two feet. This creates an interesting balance in the line (an antithetical pair at the beginning; a quicker-paced triplet of similar things in the middle; and another pair of opposites at the end). It helps if you alter the punctuation a bit, putting semicolons after *night* and *time*, to see how this reads:

x / x / x / x / x / x /
(pause) Day, (pause) night; (pause) hour, tide, time; (pause) work, (pause) play

Don't forget to elide: *carrion* (CAR-yon) in line 157; *Disobedient* (DIS-oh-BEED′-yent) in line 161; *hour* (OWR) in line 178; and *company* (CUMP-nee) in line 179;

. . . to contract: *worthy a* (WORTH-yuh) in line 146; *and nobly* (N'NO-blee) in line 182; and *the streets* (TH'STREETS) in line 194;

. . . and to expand: *honorable* (ON′-er-UH-bl) in line 183.

ROMEO AND JULIET

ACT IV, SCENE iii

JULIET

GENDER: F
AGE RANGE: young adult
PROSE/VERSE: blank verse
FREQUENCY OF USE (1–5): 3

Juliet secretly eloped with Romeo yesterday, despite the fact that her family and his are sworn enemies. Later that afternoon, Romeo fought and killed Juliet's cousin Tybalt, to avenge Tybalt's murder of Romeo's close friend Mercutio. As punishment, Romeo has been banished. Juliet's parents, meanwhile, have arranged her marriage to Count Paris . . . to be held tomorrow morning! In a panic, Juliet went to Friar Lawrence (who performed her marriage ceremony to Romeo) for help. The Friar constructed a plan: he gave Juliet a potion that, if taken tonight, will make her appear dead tomorrow morning. Instead of a wedding ceremony, her parents will hold a funeral and will place her in the family crypt. Meanwhile, the Friar will send for Romeo, who will sneak back into town and be in the crypt when she awakes. He will take her away with him and the two will live together in exiled bliss until the day comes when they can return safely to Verona. It is now nightfall. Juliet has just sent away her mother and her servant, the Nurse, so that she might be alone in her bedroom to drink the potion. As soon as they are gone, Juliet says:

Farewell. God knows when we shall meet again.
15 I have a faint cold fear thrills through my veins
That almost freezes up the heat of life.
I'll call them back again to comfort me—
Nurse! —What should she do here?
My dismal scene I needs must act alone.
20 Come, vial.
What if this mixture do not work at all?
Shall I be married then tomorrow morning?
No! No—this shall forbid it. Lie thou there.
[*She lays down a knife*]
What if it be a poison which the Friar
25 Subtly hath ministered to me to have me dead,
Lest in this marriage he should be dishonored
Because he married me before to Romeo?
I fear it is. And yet methinks it should not,
For he hath still been tried a holy man.
30 How if, when I am laid into the tomb,
I wake before the time that Romeo
Come to redeem me? There's a fearful point!
Shall I not then be stifled in the vault,

15 *faint cold* causing faintness and coldness; 18 *should* would; 19 *needs must* need to, must; *act* carry out (with pun on "playacting"); 20 *vial* i.e., the vial containing the sleeping potion; 23 *this* it is widely accepted that Juliet refers to the knife she wields in Act IV, Scene i, when she tells the Friar she will commit suicide before she will commit bigamy by marrying Paris; *forbid* prevent; 25 *Subtly* craftily, slyly; *ministered* administered, prescribed; 26 *this marriage* i.e., the marriage to Paris that her parents have arranged to be held in the morning; 28 *it should not* it isn't, it wouldn't be; 29 *hath still been tried a holy man* has already proved himself to be a holy

To whose foul mouth no healthsome air breathes in,
35 And there die strangled ere my Romeo comes?
Or, if I live, is it not very like
The horrible conceit of death and night,
Together with the terror of the place,
As in a vault, an ancient receptacle
40 Where for this many hundred years the bones
Of all my buried ancestors are packed;
Where bloody Tybalt, yet but green in earth,
Lies festering in his shroud; where, as they say,
At some hours in the night spirits resort—
45 Alack, alack, is it not like that I,
So early waking, what with loathsome smells,
And shrieks like mandrakes torn out of the earth,
That living mortals, hearing them, run mad—
O, if I wake, shall I not be distraught,
50 Environèd with all these hideous fears,
And madly play with my forefathers' joints,
And pluck the mangled Tybalt from his shroud,
And, in this rage, with some great-kinsman's bone,
As with a club, dash out my desperate brains?
55 O look! Methinks I see my cousin's ghost
Seeking out Romeo, that did spit his body
Upon a rapier's point! Stay, Tybalt, stay! —
Romeo, Romeo, Romeo, here's drink: I drink to thee!
[*She drinks and falls upon her bed*]

2 minutes, 40 seconds

man; 34 *To* into; *whose* i.e., the vault's; 35 *strangled* suffocated; *ere* before; 36 *like* likely that; 37 *conceit* conception, image in the mind; 39 *As in* to wit, namely; 40 *this many hundred years* these many centuries past; 42 *yet but green in earth* newly planted in the earth (i.e., very recently dead); 44 *resort* frequent, go to habitually; 46 *So* in this manner, thus; 47 *mandrakes* narcotic herbs with purple or white flowers, short stems, and two-pronged, fleshy roots long held to resemble the human body [*mandrakes torn . . . run mad* It was believed that the mandrake plant would shriek when it was dug up. According to some, this shriek would bring either madness or death (or both) to any human that heard it]; 50 *Environèd with* surrounded by; 53 *rage* raving madness; *great-kinsman* an ancestor of several generations ago; 54 *As* as though, like; 56 *that* who; *his body* i.e., Tybalt's body; *spit his body . . . point* impaled Tybalt's body on his rapier's point as though on a spit; 57 *Stay* both (1) stop and (2) stay where you are (Juliet is imagining Tybalt rising from the dead).

COMMENTARY

In this soliloquy Shakespeare perfectly captures how one might feel facing the loss of home and family, the terror of impending interment with dozens of corpses (in a time when people genuinely accepted the existence of ghosts), and the potential loss of life; he has Juliet express these feelings in a uniquely adolescent manner and he effectively shows his audience her mettle as she confronts and overcomes her fears.

First, after bidding her mother and her nurse what might be a final farewell (waiting until after they've departed . . . she never intended for them to actually hear her), Juliet acknowledges her fright: she aptly describes just how she feels as she prepares to undertake a frightening course of action (*I have a faint cold fear thrills through my veins / That almost freezes up the heat of life*). The sounds she uses—shiVering Fs and Vs: *have / faint / fear / veins / freezes / life*; and the onomatopoeic (as well as alliterative) *thrills through*—help her convey this fear to the audience. It's interesting to note that the body's natural response to fear mimics the physical reaction Juliet will soon have to the potion she is to take . . . which, in turn, mimics death itself.

Almost succumbing to her fear, Juliet calls for her nurse. The line in which she does so (line 18) has only three feet of spoken words, which gives you an additional two feet of silence (we recommend taking them right after the word *Nurse*) during which to realize that she hasn't heard you and that she can't help you this time around anyway:

/ x x / x / x / x /
Nurse! (pause pause pause pause)—What should she do here?

Line twenty is an embedded stage direction: *Come, vial*. Obviously, Juliet now takes up the vial containing the potion she received from the Friar. Again you have a shortened line. This time, you have three and a half or four whole feet of silence (depending on whether you pronounce the word *vial* with one or two syllables) to play with, which you can take before and/or after her words: perhaps Juliet merely contemplates the vial. Perhaps she goes so far as to open it and almost drink before she gets cold feet. Make a choice that works for you.

Notice the progression of Juliet's fears from the realistic to the fantastic as her imagination begins to carry her away. First she fears that the Friar might be trying to poison her, then that she might suffocate in the vault, then that the horror of being alone in a crypt with the remains—and the spirits—of her relatives might drive her so mad that she'll take her own life in a frenzy. Many of us have had the experience of letting our imaginations run rampant and frighten us "to death" (convincing ourselves, for example, that we hear footsteps in an empty hall, a burglar downstairs, etc.). Juliet uses color, smell, sound, and texture to describe the crypt, her ancestors' bones, Tybalt's newly dead corpse, and her own various death scenarios (through poisoning, suffocation, or self-braining) and scares herself silly. You'll notice that lines 36–54, in which she describes the terror of the crypt, very fittingly comprise one long sentence! The fantasy Juliet spins becomes more and more intense and vividly horrific until it actually transports her and she believes that she sees her dead cousin, Tybalt, coming at her. Notice the Petrified and Terrified—and, again, onomatopoeic—Ps and Ts she employs to describe how Romeo killed Tybalt: *spit* / *Upon* / *rapier's point*. Also notice her use of repetition—*stay!* —/ *Romeo*. She twice tells Tybalt to stay, perhaps indicating that in her vision, Tybalt does not listen to her the first time. She calls Romeo three times, perhaps at first to save her from Tybalt, perhaps to replace the terrifying vision of Tybalt with a calming image of her beloved, or perhaps to span the physical distance she feels lies between them.

Note: be sure to see "O, No! An *O*!," page xxxiii, for help with using the sound of the word *O* to its best advantage.

SIGNIFICANT SCANS

There is a crowded foot (——*cient recep*——) in line 39:

x / x / x / x - x / x /
As in a vault, an ancient receptacle

Or, you may use the historic pronunciation of *receptacle* (REE´-sep-TUH-kl) and scan the line as regular iambic pentameter with a double ending, but this pronunciation may be difficult for your audience to comprehend.

Aside from many other trochaic (inverted) feet at beginnings of lines and after caesuras (which lend the piece an agitated tone), there is also one in the middle of line 44 following a caesura that is not marked by punctuation (*hours* is elided [owrs]):

x / x / x / / x x /
At some hours in the night spirits resort

This inversion where it's not expected draws extra attention to the word *spirits*, highlighting Juliet's fear.

And finally, scholars disagree about the last line of this soliloquy. We have printed the line as it appears in the First Folio, as well as the Second, Third, and

Fourth Quartos of this play. If you choose this version, the line is hexameter (a rare six-footed line), with an unusual variation—three inverted feet (note that *Romeo* is elided [ROME-yo]):

/ x /x / x x / x / x /
Romeo, Romeo, Romeo, here's drink: I drink to thee!

The line's extra length and inversions may convey Juliet's agitation, or the extent to which she has now lost control, or the extent of her longing for Romeo (she says his name three times, even though this extends the line), or the extra time she needs to psych herself up to drink the potion . . . there are numerous strong choices you can make.

The First Quarto's version of the line is *Romeo, I come! This do I drink to thee!* This line has two inverted feet, one at the beginning of the line and the other following the caesura (again, *Romeo* is elided):

/ x x / / x x / x /
Romeo, I come! This do I drink to thee!

If you want to wrap up the soliloquy with a less carried away and more determined tone, you may prefer this ending. Both are accepted and valid choices. Regardless of which you choose, note the macabre toast (the first version lends itself to a more wry interpretation, with *here's drink*).

Don't forget to elide: *vial* (VILE) in line 20 (optional); *Friar* (FRIRE) in line 24; *ministered* (MIN-sterd) in line 25; *Romeo* (ROME-yo) in lines 27, 35, 56, and the three *Romeos* in line 58 (but *not* in line 31); *festering* (FEST-ring) in line 43; *hideous* (HID-yuss) in line 50; *desperate* (DES-prit) in line 54; and *rapier's* (RAY-pyerz) in line 57;

. . . to contract: *if it* (IFT) in line 24; *to me* (T'MEE) in line 25; and *methinks it* (me-THINKS'T) in line 28;

. . . and to expand: *Environèd* (en-VIE´-roh-NEHD) in line 50.

P.S.

For more on Juliet, see "What's in a Name?," page 741.

TIMON OF ATHENS

ACT IV, SCENE iii

TIMON

GENDER: M
AGE RANGE: mature adult
PROSE/VERSE: blank verse
FREQUENCY OF USE (1–5): 1

In financial ruin and betrayed by his friends, Timon has abandoned his home in Athens and has been scrounging in the woods. The cynical, curmudgeonly old Apemantus has come to persuade him to return home. Timon has refused and now lashes out at Apemantus.

250 Thou art a slave, whom Fortune's tender arm
With favor never clasped, but bred a dog.
Hadst thou like us from our first swath proceeded
The sweet degrees that this brief world affords
To such as may the passive drugs of it
255 Freely command, thou wouldst have plunged thyself
In general riot, melted down thy youth
In different beds of lust, and never learned
The icy precepts of respect, but followed
The sugared game before thee. But myself,
260 Who had the world as my confectionary,
The mouths, the tongues, the eyes, and hearts of men
At duty more than I could frame employment;
That numberless upon me stuck, as leaves
Do on the oak, have with one winter's brush
265 Fell from their boughs and left me open, bare
For every storm that blows: I to bear this,
That never knew but better, is some burden.
Thy nature did commence in sufferance; time

250 *slave* hopeless wretch; *Fortune* Timon personifies fortune; 251 *favor* benevolence [*whom Fortune' . . . never clasped* who was never treated kindly by fortune]; *bred a dog* created as lowly as a dog (see "It's Greek to Us," page 816); 252 *us* me; *swath* swaddling clothes; *proceeded* followed the course of; 253 *degrees* steps in a progression; *brief world* short life [*Hadst thou like us . . . affords* If you had progressed as I did, from infancy through the sweet steps that this short life gives]; 254 *such* such people; *passive drugs* submissive servants (drudges); also drugs, symbolizing all things that could be exploited for either good or bad purposes [*To such . . . Freely command* to those (of us) who have people (and things) at our command (i.e., who "have the world on a string")]; 256 *general riot* all-around debauchery; *melted down* wasted; 259 *sugared* sweetly tempting; *game* animal pursued in the hunt; 260 *confectionary* place where sweets or sweetmeats are kept; 262 *At duty* at (my) command; *frame* devise, come up with [*At duty . . . employment* more (servants) at my command than I could devise tasks for]; 263 *numberless upon me stuck* countless (servants) stuck to me; 264 *brush* stripping off; 266 *I to bear . . . some burden* for me, who knew only better things, bearing this is a great burden; 268 *Thy nature did com-*

Hath made thee hard in't. Why shouldst thou hate men?
270 They never flattered thee. What hast thou given?
If thou wilt curse, thy father (that poor rag)
Must be thy subject, who in spite put stuff
To some she-beggar, and compounded thee
Poor rogue hereditary. Hence, be gone!
275 If thou hadst not been born the worst of men,
Thou hadst been a knave and flatterer.

1 minute, 30 seconds

mence in sufferance Your life started with suffering; 269 *Hath made thee hard in't* has hardened you; 271 *If thou wilt curse* If you're going to curse; *rag* shabby, beggarlike person; 272 *put stuff / To* had sex with (crude slang derived either from cooking or upholstery); 273 *she-beggar* he means both (1) female beggar and (2) whore (slang); *compounded* made; 274 *rogue hereditary* rascal by heredity; *Hence* Go away from here; 275 *worst* lowest in social stature; 276 *Thou hadst been* you would have been; *knave* villain, rascal.

COMMENTARY

Timon just can't get over it: all his life he thought the best of others, but now they've proved to be a bunch of worthless, deceitful users who didn't give a fig for him. And although Apemantus has never accepted his gifts or asked for favors, Timon is sure that under different circumstances, Apemantus would turn out to be just like the rest of them.

The piece is structured around one overarching concept: the contrast between the nobility of Timon's essential nature and the baseness of Apemantus's. Had Apemantus been given Timon's privileged birth, upbringing, and opportunity, his base nature would have led him to behave recklessly and immorally and ultimately to become a *knave and flatterer* like the "friends" who betrayed Timon.

Notice the imagery woven throughout of a dog licking something sweet—a metaphor Shakespeare often employed for a fawning flatterer buttering up a patron in order to receive treats: *dog*; *sweet*; *melted*; *icy*; *sugared game*; *confectionary*; *mouths*; *tongues*; *flattered*.

The scarce punctuation reveals the quickening pace of Timon's rant, and the sounds he uses match the various tones he employs: for example, when he speaks of his privileged upbringing, he uses soft Fs and EEs (*Fortune's / favor*; *proceeded / sweet / degrees*). He carries these soft sounds to the genteel *icy precepts of respect* that he admires, but shifts to harsh Gs to describe the *sugared game* for which he has contempt. We love the repeated use of aBrasive Bs as the speech builds toward the end (*numberless / brush / boughs / bare / blows / bear / but / better / burden*), and the SPiTTing sounds of the Ss, SPs, and STs as he hits his most contemptuous note (*curse / Must be thy subject, who in spite put stuff / some*).

In the final two lines, the antithesis between what Apemantus is and what he would have been if well-born is emphasized by the similarity in phrasing (*If thou hadst not been* versus *Thou hadst been*).

SIGNIFICANT SCANS

Don't forget to elide: *general* (JEN-rul) in line 256; *confectionary* (con-FEC′-shun-REE) in line 260; and *sufferance* (SUFF-rance) in line 268.

And this monologue concludes with one of the rare, the few, the special headless lines:

x / x / x / x / x /
(pause) Thou hadst been a knave and flatterer

It's Greek to Us

Since most of us don't speak Greek, haven't studied etymology, and are not up on our ancient schools of philosophy, the little joke embedded in this monologue may go right over our heads: Shakespeare has drawn Apemantus as quite a cynic—he might even have been one of the Cynics, subscribers to the eponymous ancient Greek school of philosophy. Well, as the origin of the word *cynic* is *kynikos*, which means "doglike," Shakespeare must have been oh-so-amused at himself for making Timon call Apemantus a dog throughout this scene.

TITUS ANDRONICUS

ACT III, SCENE ii

TITUS ANDRONICUS

GENDER: M
AGE RANGE: mature adult
PROSE/VERSE: blank verse
FREQUENCY OF USE (1–5): 2

Titus Andronicus, the beloved Roman general, has been repaid for his military feats and his support of the current emperor, Saturninus, with cruelty: his daughter, Lavinia, was jilted by the Emperor, and then two of his three remaining sons (most of his twenty-five sons gave their lives fighting for their country) were falsely accused of murder and sentenced to death. When told that he could ransom his sons' lives by cutting off one of his hands and sending it to the Emperor, Titus did so—only to have his hand sent right back to him along with his sons' heads. Meanwhile, his last living son was banished. Furthermore, his daughter, Lavinia, was mutilated, her tongue cut out and hands cut off, rendering her unable to identify her assailants. Some time has passed. Titus sits down to dinner with his brother, Marcus, and the mute, handless Lavinia. Titus encourages Lavinia to mourn, and even to die of sorrow. When Marcus says, "Teach her not thus to lay / Such violent hands upon her tender life," Titus replies:

How now! Has sorrow made thee dote already?
Why, Marcus, no man should be mad but I.
25 What violent hands can she lay on her life?
Ah, wherefore dost thou urge the name of hands,
To bid Aeneas tell the tale twice o'er,
How Troy was burnt and he made miserable?
O, handle not the theme, to talk of hands,
30 Lest we remember still that we have none.
Fie, fie, how franticly I square my talk,
As if we should forget we had no hands
If Marcus did not name the word of hands.
Come, let's fall to; and gentle girl, eat this.
35 Here is no drink! Hark, Marcus, what she says—
I can interpret all her martyred signs—
She says she drinks no other drink than tears
Brewed with her sorrow, meshed upon her cheeks.
Speechless complainer, I will learn thy thought;
40 In thy dumb action I will be as perfect
As begging hermits in their holy prayers.
Thou shalt not sigh, nor hold thy stumps to Heaven,
Nor wink, nor nod, nor kneel, nor make a sign,
But I of these will wrest an alphabet,
45 And by still practice learn to know thy meaning.

1 minute, 20 seconds

23 *How now* a common phrase, used here to mean "what's the matter?"; *dote* act or speak irrationally; 24 *Why* an interjection, often used when a new thought comes to mind; *mad* insane; *but I* except me; 26 *wherefore* why; *dost thou urge* do you mention; *name of* the word; 27 *To bid* to ask; *Aeneas* In classical legend, a hero of the Trojan War who escaped after the fall of Troy, and whose descendants eventually founded Rome. Aeneas is the hero of Virgil's epic poem the *Aeneid* [*To bid . . . burnt* to ask Aeneas to recount the story of the burning of Troy and how miserable it made him—a reference to lines in Virgil's *Aeneid*: when Aeneas's lover, the Carthaginian Queen Dido, asks him to recount the story of the end of the Trojan War, he says that the retelling will renew his grief]; 28 *How* of how; *he* i.e., Aeneas; *made* was made; 29 *handle not* do not speak of; 30 *we* he refers to himself and Lavinia; *remember still* be reminded again and again; 31 *Fie* an exclamation of contempt or dislike; *franticly* madly, insanely; *square* shape [*I square my talk* i.e., I speak]; 32 *should* would; 33 *name the word of* mention the word; 34 *fall to* begin to eat; *gentle* good, dear, sweet [*gentle girl* i.e., Lavinia]; 35 *Here is no drink* There is no drink here; *Hark* Listen and hear; 36 *martyred signs* i.e., signs made by the tortured girl; 37 *no other drink than tears* a reference to Psalm 80: "Thou . . . givest them tears to drink in great measure"; 38 *meshed* archaic form of *mashed*: mixed with warm water to form wort, the substance that, after fermentation, becomes mash, or beer; 40 *dumb action* silent gesture; *perfect* well versed; perfectly knowledgeable; 41 *begging hermits* beadsmen, who were indentured to pray for their benefactors; 43 *wink* blink; 44 *wrest* pull, twist or get with effort [*Thou shalt not . . . alphabet* Every time you sigh, or hold your stumps up to Heaven, or blink, or nod, or kneel, or make a gesture, I will make these signs into an alphabet]; 45 *still* continual.

COMMENTARY

At some unpleasant point in our lives, we all feel like saying, "Why does *everything* happen to *me*?" Most of us then realize that there are others whose suffering exceeds our own. In Titus's case, however, that's just not true—things in the Andronicus household can't get much worse.

Titus makes allusions to the *Aeneid* (*bid Aeneas tell the tale twice o'er, / How Troy was burnt*) and the Bible (*drinks no other drink than tears*), putting the Andronici's sufferings on a grand scale by association. The confidence with which he does so reveals the enormity of his righteous indignation, which inspires him to assert that only *he* has a right to be insane. The most important task you have in preparing this piece is deciding exactly what is going on in Titus's mind, and why he speaks and acts so oddly. Is he insane or not? First look at the clues in the monologue, which may help you decide:

- The subject of madness does not come up naturally. Titus brings it up himself, arriving at his reference to Marcus as *doting* in a rather circuitous way.
- Although Titus asks his brother not to speak of *hands*, he himself repeats the word *five* times in this short piece, using it in a prominent position at the end of a line four of those five times, and punning on it with *handle not the theme, to talk of hands*.
- He alludes to the possibility that he is mad by saying, *Fie, fie, how franticly I square my talk*.
- Right after harping on the amputation of their hands, Titus abruptly encourages everyone to eat up, saying, *Come, let's fall to*.
- He "interprets" Lavinia's thoughts in a strangely aggressive, weirdly detailed, and almost callous way, insisting he will *wrest* meaning from her signs. The word *wrest* implies both violent action and an intention to find meaning in her signs whether *she* intends it or not. The word *wrest* also has a second definition: "misinterpret." While ostensibly claiming to understand his daughter and promising to be her mouthpiece, Titus is also saying in a veiled way (consciously or not) that he will purposely misinterpret her.

Does Titus want to appear insane, in preparation for his scheme of revenge, or for some other reason? Is he so shocked by the horrible violence done to his family that he actually is a little off-balance? Is he trying very hard to become mad, so as to escape the pain of what has happened to him? There are many possible interpretations.

The answers to these questions will determine how you use the aggressive alliterative spurts in the first half of the monologue: Leering Ls (*lay on her life*); Tackling Ts (*tell / tale / twice / Troy*); Maddened Ms (*Marcus / man / mad*; *made miserable*); Fitful Fs (*Fie, fie, how franticly*); and of course, Hysterical Hs—sprinkled throughout, but anchored by the repeated word *hands* (*How / Has / hands / hands / How / handle / hands / had no hands / hands / Here / Hark*). Also, see "O, No! An *O*!," page xxxiii, for help with exploiting the sound of the word *O* to its best advantage.

Notice that Titus appropriates Lavinia's suffering as his own. You must decide why that is. Perhaps he loves her so much that he suffers her pain as parents often do. On the other hand, men of his time viewed their daughters as their property: Titus would see her mutilation as a violation of his goods, and evil done to her as having been done to him. The piece itself seems to suggest some balance between these two attitudes. For example, in the second half of the monologue, where Titus focuses on Lavinia, we find a strange dichotomy. On one hand, Titus's speech becomes gentler as the driving alliteration disappears, and several double endings (*perfect*; *prayers*; *Heaven*; *meaning*) soften his words. Also, Titus seems sincere about his intent. He doesn't just say, "Don't worry, Lavinia, I'll put you in a really *nice* institution." Instead, he says he will interpret every detail of her gestures, listing each one particularly. It seems like fatherly concern, and yet at the same time this concern has a bizarre quality to it: first, he irrationally says he will interpret certain gestures that are involuntary, such as blinking or sighing; second, as we mentioned, the way Titus phrases his promise has an almost menacing double meaning. You may wish to explore whether he suspects (again, either consciously or not) that she has been raped (and thus "ruined"). If so, perhaps Titus is trying to keep himself from knowing the truth, is trying to prevent Lavinia from communicating the secret to others (to avoid shaming the family), or is blaming the victim, as was even more common in his time than it is today. Or you may decide to play it straight—sane or insane, he may simply be a heartbroken father determined to help his suffering child.

The metaphors Titus uses for himself might help you define him. First, he refers to Aeneas retelling the story of the fall of Troy—it takes some ego to compare yourself to a legendary Trojan hero. In his lifetime, Aeneas fought valiantly for Troy; escaped when it fell, carrying his aged father on his back; had a torrid afair with the Queen of Carthage; and journeyed bravely into the infernal regions and to Elysium—and that's just the headline! But there are similarities: Titus has done great service for Rome; Aeneas's descendants founded it. And Titus and Aeneas are both famous and beloved warriors. In contrast, consider the second metaphor Titus uses for himself: a begging hermit, a "beadsman," who would be required to pray for his benefactors in return for meager food and lodging. The third metaphor for Titus is more subtle, but he seems to see himself as a young student, learning the language of his daughter's gestures as if it were an alphabet, and continually practicing to perfect his lessons. These last two metaphors, contrasted with the first, reflect how low the once mighty Titus has been brought by the massacre, the mutilation, and, most important, the disgrace of his family (keep in mind that this is a man who—when he learns that she was raped—will soon be slitting his daughter's throat because her honor was lost).

There is one very odd metaphor—that of the brewing of Lavinia's tears on her cheeks as if they were beer. What can one make of this? Titus's other metaphors may not be poet laureate material, but they're certainly respectable. Perhaps this is yet another sign of his "madness," whether intended by him or not. Maybe he does suspect what has happened to Lavinia, or is just disgusted by the disfigurement of her beauty, and beer on her face expresses the unsavory way she has been sullied . . . or maybe you will choose another explanation for the metaphor, equally bizarre. Nothing is too weird or grotesque for *Titus Andronicus*.

Be sure to make clear choices about the physical problems in the piece. Both Marcus and Lavinia are at the table with Titus throughout the monologue. If you don't have other actors onstage with you, do your work on this in detail. Who is where, doing what, and when? Pay close attention to the most difficult moment, the embedded stage direction *and gentle girl, eat this*. Many directors have Titus feeding Lavinia here. That could get sticky in a monologue. You may decide to simply place the food in front of her, or to offer it and imagine that she refuses. Also be sure you know exactly whom you are addressing at all times.

Don't forget to elide: *violent* (VIE-lent) in line 25.

Appearing on the Scene, an Additional Scene

The scene that incorporates this monologue is not included in any of the three Quarto versions of the play: it appears for the first time in the First Folio, decades after *Titus* was first performed. Although there is some disagreement over its authorship, most scholars agree that the scene is Shakespeare's, and was probably added while the play was in production. After all, why would Heminge and Condell, Shakespeare's colleagues and the compilers of the Folio, have included it if they knew it to be someone else's?

TITUS ANDRONICUS

ACT IV, SCENE ii

AARON

GENDER: M
PROSE/VERSE: blank verse
AGE RANGE: adult to mature adult
FREQUENCY OF USE (1–5): 2

Aaron the Moor (i.e., "Blackamoor," an archaic term for a West African) is the personal servant—and lover—of Tamora, Queen of the Goths, who was imprisoned by the Romans and then wed to their new emperor, Saturninus. She has just given birth to a child that, by its skin tone, is evidently *not* her husband the Emperor's. She has sent a nurse to bring the newborn to Aaron, with orders to kill it. Aaron is with Tamora's grown sons, Demetrius and Chiron, when the nurse arrives with his son. Tamora's sons are distraught at the ruin this baby will cause their mother, and they wish to kill it themselves immediately. Demetrius says, "I'll broach the tadpole on my rapier's point: / Nurse, give it me—my sword shall soon dispatch it." Aaron snatches the baby from the nurse, draws his sword, and replies, "Sooner this sword shall plough thy bowels up!" He then goes on to say:

Stay, murderous villains! Will you kill your brother?
Now, by the burning tapers of the sky
90 That shone so brightly when this boy was got,
He dies upon the scimitar's sharp point
That touches this my first-born son and heir!
I tell you, younglings, not Enceladus,
With all his threatening band of Typhon's brood,
95 Nor great Alcides, nor the god of war,
Shall seize this prey out of his father's hands.
What, what—ye sanguine, shallow-hearted boys!
Ye white-limed walls! Ye alehouse painted signs!
Coal-black is better than another hue
100 In that it scorns to bear another hue;
For all the water in the ocean
Can never turn the swan's black legs to white,
Although she lave them hourly in the flood.
Tell the Empress from me I am of age
105 To keep mine own, excuse it how she can.

1 minute

88 *Stay* Stop; 89 *tapers* slender candles [*the burning tapers of the sky* i.e., the stars]; 90 *was got* was conceived; was fathered; 91 *He* i.e., anyone who attacks my child; *scimitar* a curved, single-edged Arabian sword; 92 *That* who; 93 *younglings* striplings, novices, duffers; *not* not even; *Enceladus* (En-SELL´-uh-DUSS) In Greek mythology, one of a brood of giants with one hundred arms and serpents for legs, created by Mother Nature to war with the gods. He was finally killed by the goddess Athena, who flattened him under Mount Etna; 94 *band of Typhon's brood* Typhon was the largest and most fearsome monster in Greek mythology, who battled Zeus (king of the gods) and nearly defeated him. Here, Aaron wrongly suggests that Typhon fathered Enceladus and his siblings—according to mythology, however, he was born after Enceladus was destroyed; 95 *Alcides* (Al-SIE-deez) i.e., Hercules, superstrong hero of classical Greek legend; *the god of war* i.e., Mars, the Roman god of war; 96 *this prey* i.e., the baby; 97 *What* an exclamation, used here to express anger; *sanguine* red-faced; 98 *white-limed walls* whitewashed walls, coated in white lime but darker beneath it—i.e., hypocrites (Aaron may, anachronistically, be alluding to either [1] the "whited sepulchres" of Matthew 23:27 or [2] "a wal whit-lymed" from William Langland's allegorical poem "Piers Plowman"); *alehouse painted signs* i.e., mere crude representations of men; 100 *In that* because; *scorns* disdains; *bear* to have; to present (with play on second meaning, "give birth to"—people of his ethnicity would not bear white children); 101 *For* because; 103 *lave* (LAYV) wash; 104 *the Empress* i.e., Tamora; *of age* an adult, one who has reached majority [*of age / To keep mine own* i.e., old enough to decide that I wish to keep my own child (no longer a minor who must obey others and who might have to relinquish a child born out of wedlock)]; 105 *excuse it how she can* i.e., and she'll just have to explain it (the child's racial makeup) however she can.

COMMENTARY

We feel it's only fair to apprise you that in reading this monologue you have stumbled upon one of Shakespeare's three greatest villains, the other two being Iago and Richard III—the three are examples of the "Machiavel," the cynical, clever, lewd, and humorous Elizabethan character type who delights in evil for its own sake, and uses reason and intelligence to achieve his own selfish ends. In other scenes in *Titus*, Aaron expresses the sheer delight he takes in committing acts of evil. By his own admission, he'd do more were there more hours in the day, and he regrets only those days in which he could have committed nasty acts but didn't. In this monologue, however, Aaron reveals a great deal more complexity.

Here, Aaron asserts pride in things other than villainy—in fatherhood, in life experience, and, chiefly, in ethnicity. He is fiercely protective of his newborn child, although we do not doubt that he would skewer another man's child at the drop of a hat. It is doubtful that he thinks of the child as an individual, but, rather, as an extension of himself (he says later that he will raise the boy to be a fierce warrior). Of course, you are free to decide otherwise. (We'll take this opportunity to remind you, as you put this piece on its feet, that to protect his son Aaron has grabbed the baby and drawn a sword. Have fun juggling the two . . . just don't hurt the baby!)

It is interesting that Aaron asks *Will you kill your brother?*, as though fratricide would violate the moral code of someone who has recently helped mastermind the plot by which a man is murdered, two others are framed and executed, and a woman is raped and mutilated. It is yours to decide whether he considers this an abominable act or whether this is an expedient moral position to take now that the brother in question is his own son.

Many of the sounds in this piece support its content. For example, in lines 91–92 (*He dies upon the scimitar's sharp point / That touches this my first-born son and heir!*), notice the preponderance of curt, crisp one-syllable words in a row. Aaron wants to get the message across quickly, and so he is blunt and to the point. Also, when one word ends with the same letter that begins the next word, it is important to enunciate the letter separately each time. This occurs twice in these two lines (*sharp point / That touches*), lending the lines a particularly menacing tone.

The sneering term *younglings* sums up Aaron's contempt for Chiron and Demetrius. He emphasizes their puniness by contrasting them with the awesome might of mythological monsters. He has considered himself their mentor in evil, but they have been less than star pupils. No matter . . . he now has his own flesh and blood to rear and train.

Notice that he repeats the exclamation *What*. It is important that you decide why he does so, in order to differentiate between your two deliveries. Perhaps

Aaron does not like the response he gets (or lack thereof) from Chiron and Demetrius after the first *What*. Or perhaps he is so furious that he needs the extra *what* to collect his thoughts before blurting out his string of insults . . . or maybe he just wasn't done exclaiming yet.

The most momentous part of the piece is Aaron's assertion of his pride in his ancestry and race. This piece affords a wonderful opportunity to respond to the racism Aaron must have encountered since leaving his homeland for Europe (the circumstances of which we can only imagine—when we first meet him, he is already a servant to the Queen of the Goths, a Teutonic people). We see evidence of such racism throughout the play. It is for you to decide what makes Aaron tick. One question to consider is to what extent relentless racism contributed to his hatred of everyone and everything, and his commitment to evil.

SIGNIFICANT SCANS

The meter of the verse sheds light on Aaron's intentions. The first two lines of the piece have inverted first feet, which start the piece off with a bang: Aaron has drawn a sword—he will use deadly force, if necessary, to defend his young. Punching the beginnings of those lines energizes the lines and emphasizes his seriousness.

Line 104 can be scanned two ways: with a headless first foot (*Tell*) and crowded third foot (——*press from me*)—

x / x / x - x /x / x /
(pause) Tell the Empress from me I am of age

Or with a headless first foot (*Tell*) and a contraction (*I am*)—

x / x / x / x / x /
(pause) Tell the Empress from me I am of age

This is an important line—here Aaron defies a direct order from the Empress of Rome. Granted, she is his mistress, and the audience has already learned from him (and seen evidence from her) that Tamora is completely in love with him, but the fact remains that she is the Empress, and he is her servant. Disobeying her command could mean more than the end of the affair . . . it could get a guy killed. Perhaps Aaron chooses to pause at the beginning of the line to compose himself before issuing a direct refutation of the Empress's command, or perhaps he needs a moment to decide how he wishes to word it—it's up to you to decide why he pauses. This line's departures in meter from the rest of the lines in the piece draw attention to it, making the audience sit up and take notice.

Don't forget to elide: *murderous* (MUR-druss) in line 88 and *hourly* (OWR-lee) in line 103;

. . . and to expand: *ocean* (OH´-shee-AN) in line 101—expanding the word to fit the meter emphasizes the point Aaron is trying to make about the hugeness of the ocean.

Renaissance Rationalization of Racism

Elizabethans and Jacobeans, who were fearful of all foreigners, reserved their greatest suspicion for people of color, whose outward appearance immediately identified them as aliens. More than a bit muddled about ethnic distinctions, the English tended to label any person of color a "Moor," a term that originated with the ancient Greeks, who referred to their darker neighbors in North Africa as "mauros" ("dark"). From this the Romans coined the Latin name Maurus (also the root of Mauritania). Arabs and Berbers invaded the Iberian Peninsula in the eighth and ninth centuries, ruling and inhabiting it until they were driven out by Ferdinand and Isabella in 1492. The Spanish called the invaders "Moros" and the French called them "Maures"; in England they came to be known as "Moors."

When Portuguese slave traders began lining their coffers by abducting and selling inhabitants of the west coast of Africa in the fifteenth century, the English were introduced to West Africans, whom they labelled "black Moors," or "blackamoors." But in general, the English made no distinction among Arabs, West Africans, and even western Asians, calling anyone with darker skin than theirs, simply, a "Moor."

The insidious combination of xenophobia and nationalism swelled under the Tudor dynasty, to the enormous misfortune of people of color. Lightness was considered emblematic of godliness and moral righteousness, while darkness, or "blackness," was associated with the devil and evil. Queen Elizabeth's naturally fair complexion, which she enhanced with makeup, was celebrated as representing God's favor toward England; the nation's defeat of the swarthier Spanish and its colonization of Africa, Asia, and North America were perceived as the triumph of good over evil. And simply by virtue of his skin color, the "Moor"—whether Arab or West African—came to be represented as a natural villain in all forms of popular culture, from literature to theatre. Shakespeare's contemporaries made ample use of the stock character type. The Bard used it himself, overtly with the Machiavellian Aaron in *Titus Andronicus*, with greater nuance in the complex title character of *Othello*, and to a lesser degree with the bombastic and unpleasant, but essentially harmless, Prince of Morocco in *The Merchant of Venice*.

THE ROMANCES

In the final years of his career, Shakespeare began exploring a new genre, the romance. His last four plays carry a sense of grave sadness at the state of mankind and have plots that could easily have developed in the direction of tragedy, but which end instead with a patient acceptance of humankind's failings, focusing as they do on the theme of reconciliation. His Romances combine elements of tragedy and comedy, and depict such themes and motifs as separation, long journeys to exotic locales, perceived loss and ultimate reunification of family, the restoration of nobility, and magic and the supernatural. The Romances were written several years into the Jacobean era when the court masque—an extravagant entertainment with mythological or philosophical themes—was in vogue, which influenced Shakespeare to insert similar attractions into his plays. Unlike in prior years, performances were often held indoors at the Blackfriars Theatre, so when devising his settings, characters, and plots, Shakespeare took advantage of the opportunity to use artificial light and elaborate sets. The evolution of the Romances can be seen in the chronological progression of the four plays: Shakespeare first tried his hand at the genre when collaborating on *Pericles*, ventured out quasi-successfully with *Cymbeline*, improved with *The Winter's Tale*, and perfected the form with his glorious *Tempest*.

CYMBELINE

ACT II, SCENE ii

IACHIMO

GENDER: M
AGE RANGE: young adult to adult
PROSE/VERSE: blank verse
FREQUENCY OF USE (1–5): 2

Iachimo delights in braggadocio and mischief, and when his new pal Posthumus boasted of the faithfulness of his beautiful wife, Princess Imogen of Britain, Iachimo sensed a challenge: he instantly bet his entire estate that he could seduce her. Iachimo traveled from Rome to Britain's royal palace, where he found Imogen to be not only beautiful, but also utterly devoted to Posthumus. Rather than lose the bet, Iachimo decided to win it by trickery: he will gather evidence to convince Posthumus that he has slept with Imogen. Iachimo convinced Imogen to safeguard a trunk containing "valuables" by keeping it in her bedchamber overnight. He then stowed himself in the trunk, planning to take a detailed inventory of the items in her room while she is asleep. The trunk has been delivered to Imogen's bedroom, Iachimo has waited for hours within its cramped walls for the household to fall asleep, and he can now finally emerge from the trunk to carry out his plan.

The crickets sing, and man's o'erlabored sense
Repairs itself by rest. Our Tarquin thus
Did softly press the rushes ere he wakened
The chastity he wounded. Cytherea,
15 How bravely thou becomest thy bed! Fresh lily,
And whiter than the sheets! That I might touch!
But kiss—one kiss! Rubies unparagoned,
How dearly they do't! 'Tis her breathing that
Perfumes the chamber thus. The flame o' th' taper
20 Bows toward her and would underpeep her lids
To see th' enclosèd lights, now canopied
Under these windows, white and azure-laced
With blue of Heaven's own tinct. But my design
To note the chamber. I will write all down:
25 Such and such pictures; there the window; such
The adornment of her bed; the arras, figures,
Why, such and such; and the contents o' the story.
Ah, but some natural notes about her body
Above ten thousand meaner moveables
30 Would testify, t'enrich mine inventory.

11 *The crickets sing* Iachimo refers to the crickets chirping outside; *o'erlabored* tired out, weary; *sense* spirit, mind; 12 *rest* resting [*man's . . . rest* i.e., everyone is asleep]; *Our Tarquin* Iachimo refers to the Roman prince Sextus Tarquinius, who, according to legend, invaded the bedroom of Lucrece, the virtuous and beautiful wife of his cousin, while her husband was away, and raped her. Iachimo uses the term *Our* because he, like Tarquin, is from Rome; 13 *press* i.e., flatten by stepping on; *the rushes* floors in England in Shakespeare's time were commonly covered in rushes as we now cover them in carpets; *ere* before; 14 *Cytherea* (SIH-thuh-REE´-uh) a.k.a. Aphrodite or Venus, the ancient Greek/Roman goddess of love and beauty; 15 *bravely* splendidly; *thou becomest* you grace [*How bravely thou becomest thy bed* how splendidly you grace your bed, i.e., how attractive you look in your bed (suggesting that Iachimo would like to join Imogen there)]; *lily* in Shakespeare's time, the lily was an emblem of chastity; 16 *That* If only; I wish; 17 *But* Merely; *Rubies unparagoned* Matchless rubies (Iachimo refers to Imogen's lips); 18 *How dearly they do't* Editors suggest a few possible meanings: (1) how well Imogen's lips imitate perfect rubies; (2) how well Imogen's lips kiss each other; or, a choice less favored by scholars; (3) how well Imogen's lips kiss me (if Iachimo risks discovery by faintly kissing the sleeping Imogen); 20 *would underpeep her lids* would like to peek under her eyelids; 21 *th' enclosèd lights* i.e., Imogen's eyes; 22 *these windows* these shutters, i.e., Imogen's eyelids; *azure-laced* (A-zhur) blue-laced (referring to the veins visible in Imogen's eyelids); 23 *tinct* color, hue; *design* plan, intention; 24 *note* commit to memory; 25 *such* of that kind is/are; 26 *adornment* decoration; *arras* tapestry (hung on a wall of Imogen's bedchamber); *figures* the figures of people carved into the fireplace (Iachimo will later describe these figures to Posthumus); 27 *the contents o' the story* Tapestries often depict scenes from well-known stories. Iachimo refers to the story woven on Imogen's tapestry; 28 *natural notes* natural marks, such as birthmarks or scars; 29 *meaner* lesser; *moveables* furnishings [*Above ten thousand meaner moveables / Would testify* i.e., would be better proof than ten thousand details remembered about the less important furni-

O sleep, thou ape of death, lie dull upon her!
And be her sense but as a monument,
Thus in a chapel lying. Come off, come off . . .
[*Taking off her bracelet*]
As slippery as the Gordian knot was hard!
35 'Tis mine; and this will witness outwardly,
As strongly as the conscience does within,
To the madding of her lord. On her left breast
A mole cinque-spotted, like the crimson drops
I' th' bottom of a cowslip. Here's a voucher
40 Stronger than ever law could make. This secret
Will force him think I have picked the lock and ta'en
The treasure of her honor. No more. To what end?
Why should I write this down that's riveted,
Screwed to my memory? She hath been reading late
45 The tale of Tereus—here the leaf's turned down
Where Philomel gave up. I have enough.

ture]; 31 *ape* mimic, imitator; *dull* heavy [*lie dull upon her* i.e., keep Imogen in a deep sleep]; 32 *her sense* that which experiences through the senses, i.e., her body; *monument* the recumbent figure of a person, carved of stone (in Shakespeare's time these were commonly placed on tombs); 34 *the Gordian knot* According to Greek legend, a peasant named Gordius became King of Phrygia and tied his wagon to a post in a public place using an intricate knot, to serve as a reminder of Zeus's greatness. It was said that he who could untie the "Gordian knot" would rule all Asia. For centuries all were unsuccessful, until Alexander the Great arrived, cut the rope with his sword, and proceeded to conquer the continent; 35 *witness* give testimony; *outwardly* externally; 36 *the conscience* scholars disagree: (1) consciousness, knowledge; or (2) inner conviction [*this will witness . . . conscience does within* Four possible meanings: (1) telling Posthumus of the mole on Imogen's breast will prove externally (i.e., to anyone who listens) that Imogen has been unfaithful as surely as it will convince Posthumus internally; (2) it will be external evidence of something Posthumus will surely then know internally; (3) this will prove Imogen's faithlessness to the outside world as strongly as Imogen's own conscience proves her innocence to herself; or (4) Iachimo's knowledge of the mole will be evidence of Imogen's infidelity that is as strong as Posthumus's current inner conviction of her faithfulness (and hence it will turn his thoughts around and convince him that she has cheated)]; 37 *To the madding . . . lord* driving her husband crazy; 38 *cinque-spotted* (sink-SPOT-tehd) having five spots; 39 *cowslip* an English primrose, bearing yellow flowers (the spots he refers to are actually a deep orange, but this does not reflect faulty observation by Iachimo: Shakespeare occasionally interchanged his use of the terms *crimson* and *golden*); *voucher* a piece of evidence; 41 *think* to think; 42 *The treasure of her honor* i.e., Imogen's chastity [*I have picked . . . her honor* i.e., I have slept with her]; *No more* Possibly an embedded stage direction: Iachimo may have been writing down the details of the birthmark and now stops himself. Can also mean "I don't need any more details about Imogen"; 45 *Tereus* (TEER-yuss) Surpassing Tarquin in villainy, the Thracian King Tereus raped his wife's sister Philomela, and then cut out her tongue so that she could not identify her attacker. This myth is famously recounted in Ovid's *Metamorphoses*, which Imogen apparently has on her bedside table; *the leaf's turned down* the page is dog-eared; 46 *Philomel* (FILL´-oh-MELL) The young woman raped and mu-

To the trunk again, and shut the spring of it.
Swift, swift, you dragons of the night, that dawning
May bare the raven's eye! I lodge in fear:
50 Though this is a heavenly angel, Hell is here.
[*Clock strikes*]
One, two, three. Time, time!
[*Exits into the trunk*]

2 minutes, 30 seconds

tilated by her brother-in-law, Tereus. According to the legend, the gods then turned her into a nightingale, whose nightly song recounts her tragedy; *gave up* yielded, succumbed; 48 *you dragons of the night* according to ancient mythology, Hecate, the goddess of the dark side of the moon, pulled night across the sky in her chariot drawn by dragons; 49 *bare the raven's eye* i.e., wake the raven. (The raven supposedly roosted facing the sunrise and awoke at dawn. The bird was also associated with nighttime: Iachimo may be likening himself to the raven, thus indicating how badly he wants day to come so that the trunk he'll be hiding in will be taken from Imogen's room and he can get out of it); 50 *this* i.e., Imogen.

COMMENTARY

Iachimo (pronounced YAH-kih-moh) is a minor example of a "Machiavel"—the cynical, clever, lewd, and humorous classical character type who delights in evil for its own sake, and uses reason and intelligence to achieve his selfish ends. Unlike Shakespeare's great tragic and historical Machiavels (Iago—from whose name Iachimo, or "little Iago," is derived—Richard III, and Aaron the Moor), Iachimo is relatively benign, more mischief maker than evildoer, as befits a romance; his comic emergence from the trunk in the beginning of this monologue confirms that he is a limited threat to Imogen. Although this is a very active piece, Iachimo himself is all talk—gorgeous talk, at that—and no action. His references to the villains Tarquin and Tereus are pure conceit: Iachimo has no intention of raping Imogen . . . merely of winning a bet.

Iachimo's observation that *The crickets sing* suggests that it is so quiet in Imogen's bedchamber that one can hear the crickets outside. Yet dramatic license allows Iachimo to speak a forty-one-line monologue without shattering that silence or waking Imogen before he's accomplished his task. According to the convention of soliloquy, the audience has entered Iachimo's mind. There are an uncommon number of Ss and similar sounds (Zs, Shs, and Ths) in this piece, which subtly assist the actor in maintaining the illusion of quiet: they create the sense of whispering without your having to actually do so. Do *not* succumb to the temptation to stage-whisper the entire monologue—no one will understand you. Shakespeare further emphasizes the S sounds by placing several of them back to back, at the end of one word and the beginning of the next (*crickets sing*; *As slippery*; *As strongly*; *This secret*), which calls for separate enunciation of each word so that the adjacent Ss do not slur together. Also, for help exploiting the sound of the word *O* to its best advantage, see "O, No! An *O*!," page xxxiii.

Notice the rapid progression of actions in this monologue, as Iachimo sets the scene for the audience; revels in his likeness to the evil Tarquin; is sidetracked by Imogen's beauty; recalls and begins the task at hand; hits paydirt by noting Imogen's mole and removing her bracelet; peeks at her bedside reading just in case; gloats; and finally takes his leave of the audience, locking himself back in the trunk. The urgency of his mission is reflected in the meter: many of the lines contain double endings, both at line ends and mid-line before caesuras, suggesting that Iachimo is compressing a lot of thought into a brief space. Likewise, he speaks with an unusual number of contractions and many elisions, which also create the sense that he is operating swiftly. Many new sentences begin and end mid-line, where you do not take as long a pause as you would at a full stop occurring at the end of a line. This is also a signal not to pause too long for any of the business in the scene.

The monologue is rich in literate, apt, sensuous imagery, indicating that Iachimo is educated and intelligent, astute and even somewhat artistic, and sensitive to the beauty of the world. Imagery comes quickly and naturally to Iachimo, as though he thinks metaphorically. For example, he instantly notices the *crickets* and uses them to convey that it is late at night and very quiet in Imogen's room. He then immediately draws the analogy between himself and *Tarquin* stealing up on the sleeping Lucrece. Using metaphor, he then quickly refers to Imogen as *Cytherea* and *Fresh lily* in rapid succession. Observing her fair complexion, he notes the contrast of her crimson lips, which he instantly calls *Rubies unparagoned*. A moment later he says that her breath *Perfumes* her bedchamber. And on he goes, from image to image, engaging all the senses. Iachimo's descriptions are minutely detailed, from the observation that Imogen's eyelids are *white and azure-laced*, as indeed the eyelids of the fair-skinned often are, to his later observation that her *cinque-spotted* mole is reminiscent of the *crimson drops / I' th' bottom of a cowslip* (which implies that he has given the same attention to such flowers as he does to the mole). He even notes exactly which page of her book Imogen has dog-eared.

Note the shift from Iachimo's image-laden speech of the first thirteen lines to his tone of brisk efficiency when he inventories the items in Imogen's bedchamber. But also notice that he loses this businesslike crispness when he returns his attention to Imogen to inventory her body. Once he notices the mole on her breast, he reverts to his image-rich language.

Words are repeated throughout the monologue, for instance: *Such*; *kiss*; *lie / lying*; *Come off*; *Swift*; and *Time*. Where a word is repeated, be sure to give each successive use a distinct delivery. For example, Iachimo utters *Come off, come off* as he is removing the bracelet from Imogen's wrist, much like the diamond thief on a heist who carefully extracts the diamond without triggering the alarm. The second *come off* may indicate that Iachimo is having trouble removing it (despite his later comment to the contrary); that he is worried that he may wake Imogen before he's finished removing the bracelet; or that he is excited at the prospect of having this proof that he's slept with her. Or he may feel completely in control of the situation, even having fun as he delicately coaxes the bracelet in a singsongy way off Imogen's wrist. With *Time, time*, Iachimo may either be continuing to count the chimes (suggesting that the clock chimes five times); or if the clock strikes only three times, he may be admonishing "time" to hurry up; or he may be wearily sighing over how slowly time moves; or he may be admonishing himself that he's dawdled enough and the time has come to return to the trunk, etc.

Iachimo uses antithesis to talk himself through the actions he must take (*As slippery as the Gordian knot was hard*; *this will witness outwardly, / As strongly as the conscience does within*; *Though this is a heavenly angel, Hell is here*). There is also an unspoken overarching contrast to play with: the tension between Iachimo's self-assuredness and his fear of detection. Despite his self-association with the villains Tarquin and Tereus and with Alexander the Great (who undid the Gordian knot), Iachimo begins the monologue with a comment about how quiet it is (and hence, how quiet he'd better be!) and wraps up with a rhyming couplet (*fear / here*), in which he expresses that—for all his swaggering—he is nervous about being caught.

Several bawdy sexual innuendos and double entendres convey Iachimo's attraction to Imogen. For example, with *The flame o' th' taper / Bows toward her*, Iachimo refers to the heat Imogen is generating in his loins, and the erection he is getting. *Arras* had the double meaning "ass" in Shakespeare's time, suggesting that although Iachimo is ostensibly inventorying the tapestry, he is simultaneously noticing Imogen's fine figure. And several of the images Iachimo uses—of unlocking, untying, breaking into, etc.—are frankly sexual as well.

Do not worry if you don't have a trunk to emerge from and return to. When performing this monologue as an audition piece, you may emerge from behind a chair, or simply enter and exit the stage. You may begin and end in a crouch, or may decide that the monologue begins the moment after you've climbed from the trunk and ends the moment before you reenter it. Whatever you decide, commit to it fully and you'll be fine.

SIGNIFICANT SCANS

Line 18 has a one-syllable pause at the caesura (as well as a crowded second foot:——*ly they do't*), permitting you to take a moment to watch Imogen sleep:

x /x - x / x / x / x /
How dearly they do't! (pause) 'Tis her breathing that

Note that the scansion of this line requires the contraction of *do't* (DOOT). If you find the contraction awkward you may choose to expand the word and replace the pause with the word "it."

Line 42 is a bit tricky to scan, until you realize that there is a double ending before the first caesura, and that you are to contract *To what* (t'wut):

x / x / x /(x) x / x /
The treasure of her honor. No more. To what end?

So is line 50, in which you must crowd the second foot (*is a heaven*——) and elide *heavenly* (HEV'N-lee):

x / x-x / x / x / x /
Though this is a heavenly angel, Hell is here

In fact, many of the lines may seem difficult to scan until you consult the lists of elisions and contractions, below.

We recommend that you scan line 51 as follows:

x / x / x / x / x /
(pause) One, (pause) two, (pause) three. (pause) Time, (pause) time!

or, if he pauses slightly longer to listen for a fourth bell before hurrying himself into the trunk:

x / x / x / x / x /
(pause) One, (pause) two, (pause) three. (pause-pause) Time, time!

Don't forget to elide: *o'erlabored* (ore-LAY-burd) in line 11; *Our* (owr) in line 12; *becomest* (bee-KUMST) in line 15; *toward* (tord) in line 20; *Heaven's* (HEV'NZ) in line 23; *natural* (NATCH-rul) in line 28; *slippery* (SLIP-ree) and *Gordian* (GORD-yun) in line 34; *ta'en* (TAIN) in line 41; *memory* (MEM-ree) in line 44; *Tereus* (TEER-yuss) in line 45; and *heavenly* (HEV'N-lee) in line 50;

. . . to contract: *do't* (DOOT) in line 18; *o' th' taper* (oth-TAY-pur) in line 19; *The adornment* (Thu-DORN-ment) in line 26; *the contents* (TH'CON-tents) in line 27; *t'enrich* (ten-RICH) in line 30; *the madding* (TH'MAD-ding) in line 37; *I' th' bottom* (Ith-BOT-tom) in line 39; *I have* (I've) in line 41; *To what* (t'wut) in line 42; and *the trunk* (TH'TRUNK) in line 47;

. . . and both to contract *and* expand: *th' enclosèd* (then-CLO-sehd) in line 21.

CYMBELINE

ACT III, SCENE ii

IMOGEN

GENDER: F
AGE RANGE: young adult
PROSE/VERSE: blank verse and prose
FREQUENCY OF USE (1–5): 3

As the only child of Cymbeline, King of Britain, Imogen was expected to follow her father's wishes and marry her stepbrother. Instead, she secretly married Posthumus Leonatus, a poor but honorable gentleman who was brought up at court after his father died in service to the King. When he learned of the marriage, Cymbeline immediately banished Leonatus, who left behind his servant Pisanio to serve as go-between for the couple. Pisanio has just brought Imogen a letter from his master. She is thrilled to receive it, and even more thrilled when she discovers what's inside.

Who, thy lord? That is my lord Leonatus?
O, learn'd indeed were that astronomer
That knew the stars as I his characters;
He'd lay the future open. You good gods,
30 Let what is here contained relish of love,
Of my lord's health, of his content—yet not
That we two are asunder, let that grieve him.
Some griefs are med'cinable; that is one of them,
For it doth physic love. Of his content,
35 All but in that. Good wax, thy leave. Blest be
You bees that make these locks of counsel. Lovers
And men in dangerous bonds pray not alike;
Though forfeiters you cast in prison, yet
You clasp young Cupid's tables. Good news gods!
[*She reads*]
40 *Justice and your father's wrath (should he take me in his dominion) could not be so cruel to me as you, O the dearest of creatures, would even renew me with your eyes. Take notice that I am in Cambria at Milford Haven. What your own love will out of this advise you,*
45 *follow. So he wishes you all happiness that remains loyal*

26 *thy lord* your master; *my lord* my husband; 27 *learn'd* educated, well versed in science; *were* would be; *astronomer* astrologer; 28 *as I* as well as I know; *characters* handwriting (with a possible allusion to astrological "characters" or constellations); 30 *relish of* taste pleasingly of; 31 *content* happiness, contentment; *not* i.e., not content; 33 *med'cinable* of medicinal value, curative; *that* refers to the grief of being parted from a loved one; 34 *doth physic* cures; makes strong and healthy; *of his content, / All but in that* i.e., may he be content in all but the fact that we are apart; 35 *Good wax* she addresses the wax seal on Posthumus's letter; *thy leave* i.e., pardon me for breaking you; 36 *counsel* secrets [*locks of counsel* wax seals (which in Shakespeare's time validated legal documents [much as a signature does today] and secured confidential letters)]; 37 *in dangerous bonds* who are bound by legal documents that impose stringent penalties; *pray not alike* i.e., do not share the same prayers with regard to waxen seals: lovers welcome them while contract breakers fear and hate them; 38 *forfeiters* those who break contracts; *you* she addresses either the wax seals or the bees; 39 *tables* writing tablets or notebooks [*Cupid's tables* i.e., love letters]; *Good news gods* i.e., please let this be good news, gods; 40 *take* capture; 41 *as* but that [*as you . . . renew me with your eyes* that one glance from you, O dearest of creatures, could not restore me]; 43 *Cambria* (KAM´-bree-UH) (the Latin name for the portion of Great Britain now known as Wales); *Milford Haven* a seaside town in Wales (*haven* meaning harbor or port); 44 *What your own love . . . follow* i.e., follow what your heart leads you to do upon reading this letter; 45 *So he wishes you all happiness that remains loyal to his vow, and your increasing in love* Two possibilities: (1) So he that remains loyal to his vow wishes you all

to his vow, and your increasing in love.
—Leonatus Posthumus.

O, for a horse with wings! Hear'st thou Pisanio?
He is at Milford Haven. —Read, and tell me
50 How far 'tis thither. If one of mean affairs
May plod it in a week, why may not I
Glide thither in a day? Then, true Pisanio,
Who long'st like me to see thy lord, who long'st—
O, let me bate—but not like me, yet long'st,
55 But in a fainter kind—O, not like me,
For mine's beyond beyond; say, and speak thick—
Love's counselor should fill the bores of hearing,
To th' smothering of the sense—how far it is
To this same blessèd Milford. And by th' way
60 Tell me how Wales was made so happy as
T'inherit such a Haven. But first of all,
How may we steal from hence, and for the gap
That we shall make in time from our hence-going
And our return, to excuse. But first, how get hence?
65 Why should excuse be born or ere begot?
We'll talk of that hereafter. Prithee speak,
How many score of miles may we well rid
'Twixt hour and hour?

1 minute, 50 seconds

2 minutes, 30 seconds

happiness and advancement or prosperity in love; or (2) So he that remains loyal to his vow and to the advancement of his love for you wishes you all happiness; 47 *Leonatus Posthumus* note that Posthumus signs his surname before his given name; 50 *thither* to that place; *mean affairs* ordinary business; 54 *bate* lessen, i.e., modify my statement; 55 *fainter kind* weaker, less zealous sort; 56 *mine's* i.e., my longing is; *speak thick* speak many words quickly; 57 *Love's counselor* i.e., one who counsels a lover; *bores* holes [*bores of hearing* i.e., ears]; 58 *To th' smothering of the sense* i.e., until the sense of hearing is overwhelmed; 59 *by th' way* on the way, as we go; 61 *T'inherit such a Haven* To possess such a haven (with a play on *haven*, meaning "refuge"); 62 *steal from hence* sneak away from here; *for the gap . . . to excuse* how will we explain our absence from the time we leave until we return; 64 *how get hence* i.e., how will we get away from here; 65 *Why should excuse be born or ere begot* i.e., why should we invent an excuse before we have even done the thing that needs explanation; 66 *hereafter* at a later time; *Prithee* I entreat you (from "I pray thee"); 67 *well rid* dispose of expediently (to "rid ground" means to cover ground); 68 *'Twixt hour and hour* between one hour and the next.

COMMENTARY

This charming piece has a wonderful progression to work with. First, Imogen is elated to receive Posthumus's letter. Notice that she does not tear it open right away, but instead savors the moment. She takes the time to think of how well she knows his handwriting (after all, they grew up together at court, and unlike many newlyweds of the time, probably knew each other quite well). She prolongs the delicious anticipation of opening the letter, fervently hoping for its contents to be exactly what she wants to hear. Next, she reads the letter aloud, switching from verse to prose. It is important not to anticipate the letter's contents—keep in mind that Imogen never expects to hear that Posthumus is back in Britain. Finally, she grasps the wonderful news and begins planning an adventurous trip to see her beloved.

Imogen's growing excitement is evident in the meter of the piece. There are many variations in both of the verse sections, including double endings both at the ends of lines and before caesuras, inverted (trochaic) feet both at the beginnings of lines and after caesuras, quite a few elisions and contractions, and many thoughts beginning and ending mid-line. Especially in the last section of the piece, these variations contribute to the chaotic flow of Imogen's ideas and to her high energy. Notice that although she asks Pisanio many questions (even telling him he should *speak thick*) she never pauses for a second, or lets him get a word in edgewise.

The audience, meanwhile, is having a very different experience from Imogen's, knowing that the letter is a setup for Imogen's unjust murder. The language of the letter is intentionally ambiguous, so that the audience can hear the first sentence both as Imogen interprets it and as "Justice and your father's wrath (should he take me in his dominion) could not be so cruel to me as you!" The focus on wax also offers a foreboding allusion: Imogen wishes for a *horse with wings* so she can fly to Milford Haven, which is on the sea. Those familiar with classical mythology (as Shakespeare's audiences were) will link Imogen's journey with the story of Icarus, whose father made him a pair of wax-and-feather wings with which to escape captivity. When Icarus ignored his father's warning and flew too close to the sun, the wax melted; Icarus fell from the sky and was drowned in the sea below. This is all good to know, but you must not actively play any of it. The monologue's success depends on Imogen's complete trust in Pisanio and Posthumus, and her joy at the prospect of traveling to Wales.

You can't miss Imogen's charming manner. Her endearingly girlish and optimistic character is defined by such phrases as *Good wax, thy leave*; *Blest be / You bees*; *beyond beyond* and *how Wales was made so happy as / T'inherit such a Haven*. What sets her apart from heroines with similar qualities is her sheer spunk. The moment she finishes reading the letter, she cries *O, for a horse with wings!* Without a second thought, she begins making plans that would have cowed most young women of her time. For help using the sound of the word *O* to its best advantage, see "O, No! An *O*!," page xxxiii.

Note: in line 67, we have retained the First Folio's use of the word *rid*, which, according to the OED, was commonly used to mean "dispose of expediently," as it is here. The Second Folio, however, "corrects" the word, changing it to "ride," which also makes sense, and which may be easier for today's audiences to understand. Since we will never know which word Shakespeare intended, feel free to choose whichever works best for you.

Also note that while we have followed the First Folio's punctuation of line 26 (*Who, thy lord? That is my lord Leonatus?*), editors have punctuated the line in many different ways (e.g., *Who, thy lord that is my lord Leonatus?* or *Who, thy lord? That is my lord, Leonatus!*). As with all of Shakespeare's text, you should feel free to mentally repunctuate the line to suit your own interpretation, since your guess is as good as anyone's as to how the Bard himself might have punctuated it (see "The Lowdown on Punctuation . . . ," page lvii).

SIGNIFICANT SCANS

Although inverted feet normally appear at the beginnings of lines or following caesuras that are marked by punctuation, the second inversion in line 30 does not:

/ x x / x / /x x /
Let what is here contained relish of love

Line 33 is a bit tricky to scan. The word *med'cinable* has not one but two syllables that are elided. Try saying MED´-sin-BL. If you also contract *that is* (that's), you get a line of regular iambic pentameter:

x / x / x / x /x /
Some griefs are med'cinable; that is one of them

Or you may read —*cinable* as a crowded foot:

x / x / x-x/ x / x /
Some griefs are med'cinable; that is one of them

When read as regular iambic pentameter, line 64 becomes quite expressive, placing emphasis on *get*: i.e., Imogen's next thought is, how will she even *get* to the point of needing an excuse for being away? Notice you'll need to elide *our*, and contract *to excuse*, and that *hence* is a double ending:

x / x / x / x / x / (x)
And our return, to excuse. But first, how get hence?

Don't forget to elide: *med'cinable* (MED′-sin-BL or MED′-sin-uh-BL) in line 33; *dangerous* (DAIN-jruss) in line 37; *Pisanio* (Pih-ZAHN-yo) in lines 48 and 52; *our* (OWR) in line 64; and *hour* (OWR) in line 68;

. . . to contract: *that is* (that's) in line 33 and *to excuse* (tex-KYOOZ) in line 64;

. . . to elide *and* contract: *th' smothering* (THSMU-thring) in line 58;

. . . and to expand: *blessèd* (BLESS-ehd) in line 59.

CYMBELINE

ACT III, SCENE vi

IMOGEN

GENDER: F
AGE RANGE: young adult
PROSE/VERSE: blank verse
FREQUENCY OF USE (1–5): 3

Imogen, the daughter of King Cymbeline of Britain, married the noble but poor Posthumus against the wishes of her father, who subsequently banished the young man. Posthumus fled to Rome, where he was tricked into believing that Imogen has recently been unfaithful to him. Furious, he sent a letter home to his servant, Pisanio, ordering him to take her to Wales and kill her there. En route, Pisanio revealed the order to Imogen, but proposed a plan to set matters aright: Imogen is to disguise herself as a boy and go to the port town of Milford Haven, where she can obtain employment with the Roman ambassador Lucius, who is about to return to Rome. She can thus be near Posthumus until Pisanio can convince him of her innocence and the couple can be reunited. Taking Pisanio's suggestion, Imogen has donned men's clothing and headed for Milford Haven, but has lost her way and has been wandering in the woods for two days. Exhausted and starved, she has just arrived at the mouth of a dark, foreboding cave, but does not yet see it. She says:

I see a man's life is a tedious one.
I have tired myself and for two nights together
Have made the ground my bed. I should be sick
But that my resolution helps me. Milford,
5 When from the mountaintop Pisanio showed thee,
Thou wast within a ken. O Jove! I think
Foundations fly the wretched—such, I mean,
Where they should be relieved. Two beggars told me
I could not miss my way. Will poor folks lie,
10 That have afflictions on them, knowing 'tis
A punishment or trial? Yes. No wonder,
When rich ones scarce tell true. To lapse in fullness
Is sorer than to lie for need, and falsehood
Is worse in kings than beggars. My dear lord,
15 Thou art one o' th' false ones. Now I think on thee
My hunger's gone, but, even before, I was
At point to sink for food. —But what is this?
Here is a path to 't. 'Tis some savage hold.
I were best not call; I dare not call. Yet famine,
20 Ere clean it o'erthrow nature, makes it valiant.

1 *tedious* both (1) physically tiresome and (2) full of annoyance, odious; 2 *together* in a row; 4 *But* except; *my resolution* my resolve (to reach Milford Haven); *helps* cures; 6 *within a ken* within view; *Jove* a.k.a. Jupiter, the supreme god of the ancient Romans; 7 *Foundations* safe refuge, security (with play on second meaning, "charitable hospitals," which are needed by the "afflicted" beggars she will mention next); *fly* flee from; *the wretched* the unfortunate, the downtrodden, those suffering hardship (such as poverty or disability); 8 *relieved* given help when in distress [*such . . . relieved* i.e., just when they (the wretched) should be provided relief from distress]; 9 *miss my way* lose my way; 10 *That have afflictions on them* i.e., that are suffering (e.g., from poverty or disability or both); 11 *trial* a test of faith or virtue [*A punishment or trial* Imogen refers to the belief that poverty and ailments were tests of faith or virtue, or were punishments for lack thereof] [*Will poor folks lie . . . trial* Imogen suggests that if the beggars who directed her toward Milford Haven were lying, they are courting disaster by lying while being tested by God]; 12 *scarce* scarcely, hardly ever; *tell true* tell the truth; *To lapse in fullness* i.e., to lie when one is prosperous; 13 *sorer* a greater crime; 14 *lord* husband; 15 *Now I think on thee* now that I think about you; 16 *but* and yet; *even before* i.e., only a moment ago; 17 *At point to sink for food* i.e., on the verge of fainting from hunger; *this* Imogen refers to the mouth of the cave; 18 *hold* stronghold; 19 *I were best not* I'd better not; *call* (1) attract notice of those within, upon arriving for a visit (e.g., by knocking or calling out); or (2) visit, enter; 20 *Ere* before; *clean* entirely; *o'erthrow* defeat, bring to nothing; *nature* a person's physical and moral constitution [*Yet famine . . . valiant* yet hunger, before completely destroying a person's constitution,

Plenty and peace breeds cowards; hardness ever
Of hardiness is mother. Ho! Who's here?
If anything that's civil, speak; if savage,
Take or lend. Ho! No answer? Then I'll enter.
25 Best draw my sword, and if mine enemy
But fear the sword like me, he'll scarce look on 't.
Such a foe, good Heavens!

1 minute, 50 seconds

first makes it courageous]; 21 *hardness* hardship; *ever* always [*hardness ever . . . mother* hardship has always bred endurance and courage]; *Ho!* an exclamation used to draw attention; 23 *If anything that's civil* i.e., if anyone civilized is within the cave; *if savage, / Take or lend* if you are a savage, either take my life or my money, or go ahead and give me blows; 25 *if mine enemy . . . like me* if whatever lurks within this cave ("mine enemy") is just as afraid of a drawn sword as I am; 26 *scarce look on't* scarcely look at it (i.e., be too afraid to even look at it, never mind challenge me); 27 *Such a foe, good Heavens!* May the Heavens grant me such a foe!

COMMENTARY

Imogen has been a beloved heroine since she first took center stage in the early seventeenth century. If you're looking to delight your audience with a charming, forthright, strong, yet vulnerable character, this monologue fits the bill. It's also a wonderful opportunity for an actor to work on obstacles: Imogen is dressed as a man and has been passing herself off as one for two days, but here her words contrast with her physicality as she gives the audience a woman's-eye view of the world of men. Upon discovering the cave, however, she must fight her impulse to remain in woman mode and must commit to carrying through what she has begun.

This is a very active monologue. Imogen shares her experience of the past two days, reflects upon it, reacts to her surroundings, reflects further, and takes decisive action in the face of grave danger. In doing so, she shows tremendous mettle. Remember that she was raised in the sheltered environment of the royal court. And yet this young woman had the courage to defy her royal father's wishes and marry for love, to defy him again by heading off to meet her husband (or so she thought), and then to navigate the wilderness alone, intending to pose as a boy, obtain a job, and travel to a foreign land. Although she faces daunting circumstances, Imogen does not succumb to the fear and physical burnout she acknowledges feeling. Instead she treats the whole experience as a test of faith (not unlike the suffering of the beggars she mentions) and is determined to pass with flying colors.

Imogen is delightfully candid. Her blend of interrogative and declarative sentences supports her candor, as she shares with her audience the connections she strives to make between the experience she is undergoing and the lessons it provides her. She also shares intimate responses, such as her instant loss of appetite at the thought of her husband. The monologue contains several exclamations (*O Jove!*; *Ho!*; *Such a foe, good Heavens!*) that provide insight into her state of mind. See "O, No! An *O*!," page xxxiii, for help using the word *O* to its best advantage. The monologue has a clear progression, moving from Imogen's initial commentary on the hardships of a man's life to her ultimate embodiment of the role she has assumed, when she summons her courage to "act like a man" and enter the cave. But keep in mind that although Imogen may believe she is adopting a man's courage, she is actually displaying her own innate courage.

Imogen's language is straightforward. Only toward the end of the monologue is there any imagery at all, and it falls neatly into two categories: the first pair of images (in which she personifies *famine* and *nature*) pits the two against each other in combat, with *nature* proving courageous but *famine* proving the ultimate victor. This image aptly reflects Imogen's inner struggle as she gathers the courage to face the unknown inhabitant of the cave. Her other images (*Plenty and peace breeds cowards*; *hardness ever* / *Of hardiness is mother*) are of maternal relationships; perhaps the frightened Imogen either consciously or unconsciously pines for her mother, long since dead. Or maybe she is reassuring herself that having grown up without a mother has bred hardiness in her.

SIGNIFICANT SCANS

The monologue contains many double endings, softening line endings and giving it a slightly hesitant tone, as well as one befitting a person who is exhausted. Sentences begin and end mid-line, suggesting that Imogen's thoughts are coming to her quickly.

Note that the word *trial* is correctly pronounced with either one or two syllables (TRILE or TRIE-ul). In line 11 you may pronounce it with two syllables (in which case the line scans as regular iambic pentameter) or pronounce it as one and take a one-syllable pause before the word *Yes*.

The final line has only six syllables of spoken text. You may treat the line as headless, and take the rest of the silent feet at the end (probably to draw your sword and march into the cave):

x / x / x / x / x /
(pause) Such a foe, good Heavens! (pause) (pause-pause)

Or you may take more of the silent feet before the line, if you wish to draw your sword and shore up your courage before speaking. The choice is yours.

Don't forget to elide: *tedious* (TEE-dyuss) in line 1; *Pisanio* (Pih-ZAHN-yo) in line 5; *even* (EEN) in line 16; and *o'erthrow* (ORE-throw) in line 20;

. . . and to contact: *I have* (I've) in line 2; *Thou art* (Th'art) and *o' th'* (oth) in line 15; *to 't* (toot) in line 18; *I were* (I're) in line 19; and *on 't* (ONT) in line 26.

PERICLES

ACT IV, SCENE iii

DIONYZA

GENDER: F
PROSE/VERSE: blank verse
AGE RANGE: adult to mature adult
FREQUENCY OF USE (1–5): 1

Dionyza, First Lady of Tarsus, was displeased that her foster child, Marina, outshone her own daughter. So she has (as far as she knows) had Marina killed by her servant Leonine. Her husband, Cleon, Governor of Tarsus, has just learned of her actions, and is distraught. They are in mid-argument. Cleon has just asked her how they will explain Marina's death to her father, Pericles.

16 She died at night; I'll say so. Who can cross it,
Unless you play the impious innocent
And for an honest attribute cry out,
"She died by foul play"?

Be one of those that thinks
The petty wrens of Tarsus will fly hence
And open this to Pericles. I do shame
To think of what a noble strain you are
25 And of how coward a spirit.

Yet none does know but you how she came dead,
30 Nor none can know, Leonine being gone.
She did distain my child and stood between
Her and her fortunes. None would look on her,
But cast their gazes on Marina's face,
Whilst ours was blurted at and held a mawkin,
35 Not worth the time of day. It pierced me through;
And though you call my course unnatural—
You not your child well loving—yet I find
It greets me as an enterprise of kindness
Performed to your sole daughter.

40 And as for Pericles,
What should he say? We wept after her hearse,
And yet we mourn. Her monument
Is almost finished, and her epitaphs
In glitt'ring golden characters express
45 A general praise to her, and care in us,
At whose expense 'tis done.

1 minute, 30 seconds

16 *cross* contradict; 18 *attribute* reputation; 22 *petty* little, insignificant; *wrens* referring to the old superstition that birds will reveal crimes (this is where we get the phrase "a little birdie told me"); *hence* from here; 23 *open* disclose; 24 *of* from; *strain* lineage; 25 *coward* cowardly; 29 *Yet* As of right now; *none does know* no one knows; *came* became; 30 *can know* has any way of knowing; *Leonine* (LEE´-uh-NINE); 31 *distain* sully, dishonor (by comparison); 32 *on* at; 33 *But* but instead; 34 *Whilst* while; *blurted at* scorned, pooh-poohed at; *mawkin* slovenly woman; kitchen wench; slut (variant of *malkin*); 36 *course* course of action; *unnatural* violating the ways of nature (here, unwomanly, not as a foster mother should treat a child in her care); 37 *not your child well loving* not loving your child well enough; 38 *greets* gratifies, pleases; presents itself to; 41 *should* could; 42 *yet* still; 44 *characters* letters; 45 *general* (1) in all respects (praising all her attributes); (2) public; or (3) run-of-the-mill (not particular to Marina [see Commentary]); *to* of; *care* grief and sorrow; watchful regard; *in us* on our part.

COMMENTARY

How do you solve a problem like Marina? Dionyza had found the perfect solution, which her shortsighted husband fails to appreciate. Cleon's criticism of Dionyza forces her to defend her actions, and her tactic is to take the offensive against him. You can hear this in the sarcastic language of the first two sections (note her tone: *play the impious innocent*; *The petty wrens*; and her mimicry of him: *She died by foul play*).

Dionyza uses antithesis to turn the tables on him: She contrasts his *noble strain* with his so *coward a spirit*; she justifies killing Marina by contrasting the public's perception and disparate treatment of the two young women; and, in a final twist of logic, she characterizes her unkindness toward Marina as an act of maternal love for her birth child and Cleon's kindness toward Marina as an act of paternal indifference.

In the last section, she dismisses Cleon's concern about Pericles, using imagery and alliteration (*What / We wept*; *her hearse*; *mourn / monument*; *glitt'ring golden*; *characters / care*) to be grandiose and overblown in her description of the showy funeral rites they'll give Marina. There are many interesting choices for the delivery of the last two lines. Is Dionyza still trying to persuade Cleon (especially with the phrase *a general praise*), or is she already laughing about how easily they'll dupe Pericles with their display? Or is she callously dismissing the whole matter?

SIGNIFICANT SCANS

Cleon's responses to Dionyza have been excised to create this monologue, giving it lines that have fewer than five feet of text. Use the resulting silent feet in these lines to make your transitions from one section to the next (two at the end of line 19 plus two at the beginning of line 21; one and a half at the end of line 25; one and a half at the end of line 39 plus two at the beginning of line 40). Also note that line 46 has two silent feet at the end that you can use to your advantage: perhaps Dionyza stares down her husband, or gauges his response, or decides it is pointless to continue, etc.

Dionyza's forcefulness is reflected in the meter, which contains several inverted feet at beginnings of lines (and one in line 30 mid-line after the caesura), as well as double endings. New thoughts often begin mid-line, indicating that they follow fast on the heels of their predecessors. The variations occur most frequently in the third section, suggesting Dionyza's geniune distress at the affront to her daughter.

Shakespeare built a pause into line 42, which has only four feet of spoken text. Although you may put the pause wherever you choose, we think it works best at the caesura, where the pause occurs naturally anyway:

x / x / x / x / x /
And yet we mourn. (pause-pause) Her monument

Don't forget to elide: *Pericles* (PEHR-kleez) in line 23 (but not in line 40); *coward* (COWRD) in line 25; *glitt'ring* (GLIT-ring) in line 44; and *general* (JEN-rull) in line 45;

. . . to contract: *the impious* (th'im-PIE-uss) in line 17;

. . . and to expand: *foul* (FOW-l) in line 19.

THE TEMPEST

ACT I, SCENE ii

ARIEL

GENDER: M
PROSE/VERSE: blank verse
AGE RANGE: young adult to adult
FREQUENCY OF USE (1–5): 3

Ariel, a spirit, was imprisoned in a tree by a witch who formerly inhabited his island home. He languished there until the island's current master, the magician Prospero, freed him in exchange for his service. Ariel has served Prospero loyally ever since, and hopes that he will soon have paid his debt and will be free to go. Prospero has just magically roused a storm to ensnare a passing ship, whose passengers include the King and Prince of Naples. He sent Ariel to stage a shipwreck in which the ship's passengers would be brought ashore unharmed (albeit terrified). Ariel has just returned and briefs his master on his successful mission.

ARIEL

All hail, great Master! Grave sir, hail! I come
190 To answer thy best pleasure, be 't to fly,
To swim, to dive into the fire, to ride
On the curled clouds: to thy strong bidding task
Ariel and all his quality.

I boarded the King's ship. Now on the beak,
Now in the waist, the deck, in every cabin,
I flamed amazement. Sometime I'd divide,
And burn in many places; on the topmast,
200 The yards, and boresprit would I flame distinctly,
Then meet and join. Jove's lightnings, the precursors
O' th' dreadful thunderclaps, more momentary
And sight-outrunning were not; the fire and cracks
Of sulphurous roaring the most mighty Neptune
205 Seem to besiege, and make his bold waves tremble,
Yea, his dread trident shake.

Not a soul
But felt a fever of the mad and played

189 *All hail* a greeting implying the wish of good fortune and happiness; *Grave* worthy, venerable, reverend; 190 *To answer thy best pleasure* i.e., to fulfill whatever you wish me to do; *be 't* whether it is; 192 *task* employ, command to perform; 193 *quality* (1) powers, skills; and/or (2) colleagues (cospirits); 196 *beak* the forecastle (the foremost part of a ship's upper deck); 197 *waist* the middle part of a ship (between the quarterdeck and the forecastle, usually sunken, with steps leading into it from both sides); 198 *flamed amazement* struck terror by appearing as fire (scholars agree that Ariel's feat imitates the real-world phenomenon known as Saint Elmo's fire, in which the luminous electrical discharge from heavy storms makes tall objects such as church steeples, ship mastheads, tops of skyscrapers, and sometimes even cattle horns or heads of people appear to glow); 199 *the topmast* the mainmast (the principal mast, located second from the ship's bow); 200 *yards* pieces of timber by which sails are extended; *boresprit* bowsprit (the large spar projecting forward from the bow of a ship); *distinctly* separately [*flame distinctly* manifest myself as a separate flame in each of these places]; 201 *Jove* the supreme god of the ancient Romans (a.k.a. Jupiter), believed to cause lightning by throwing his weapon, the lightning bolt; 203 *sight-outrunning* swifter than sight; 204 *sulphurous* made of brimstone (in Shakespeare's time, thunder and lightning were thought to contain brimstone) [*sulphurous roaring* i.e., the roaring of the "fire"]; *Neptune* the ancient Roman god of the sea; 205 *Seem* seemed (Ariel may be using the present tense colloquially) [*the fire and cracks . . . to beseige* i.e., the sight and sounds of the "raging fire" seemed to overtake the whole sea]; 206 *dread* greatly feared, terrible; *trident* three-pronged spear (Neptune's weapon, which he would use for such purposes as smashing rocks, stirring up or calming storms, and raising waves with which to pound the seashore); 208 *Not a soul / But felt* i.e., every single person felt; 209 *fever of the mad* i.e., the type of fit that insane people experience; *played / Some tricks of desperation* ex-

210 Some tricks of desperation: all but mariners
Plunged in the foaming brine, and quit the vessel,
Then all afire with me; the King's son, Ferdinand,
With hair up-staring—then like reeds, not hair—
Was the first man that leaped, cried, "Hell is empty,
215 And all the devils are here!"

Not a hair perished.
On their sustaining garments not a blemish,
But fresher than before; and as thou bad'st me,
220 In troops I have dispersed them 'bout the isle.
The King's son have I landed by himself,
Whom I left cooling of the air with sighs
In an odd angle of the isle, and sitting,
His arms in this sad knot.

Safely in the harbor
Is the King's ship, in the deep nook where once
Thou called'st me up at midnight to fetch dew
From the still-vexed Bermooths—there she's hid;
230 The mariners all under hatches stowed,
Who, with a charm joined to their suffered labor,
I have left asleep. And for the rest o' th' fleet,
Which I dispersed, they all have met again,
And are upon the Mediterranean flote,
235 Bound sadly home for Naples,
Supposing that they saw the King's ship wracked,
And his great person perished.

2 minutes, 30 seconds

perienced the tricks on their minds that desperate people undergo; 210 *all but mariners* everyone except for the sailors; 212 *all afire with me* i.e., seeming to be completely ablaze with the "fire" I am posing as; 213 *up-staring* standing on end; 218 *sustaining garments* either (1) enduring clothing, clothing that bore up under the duress of the storm or (2) the clothing that buoyed its wearers in the sea; 219 *bad'st* commanded; 220 *troops* groupings of people; 222 *cooling of the air* cooling the air; 223 *odd* lonely, desert; *angle* corner; 224 *in this sad knot* Ariel illustrates by folding his arms; 229 *still-vexed* ever-agitated; *Bermooths* Bermudas (see "The Americas: A Magical Mystery Tour," page 858); 230 *under hatches* below the ship's deck; 231 *with a charm joined to their suffered labor* with a magic spell added to the agonizing trials they've just endured; 232 *for* as for; *the rest o' th' fleet* only the ship carrying the King, the Prince, their attendant nobles, and their personal servants was shipwrecked; the rest of the fleet accompanying them was unharmed; 234 *flote* sea; 236 *wracked* shipwrecked; 237 *his great person* i.e., King Alonso.

COMMENTARY

The role of the amorphous Ariel presents a unique and exciting challenge to an actor. There is much in the play by which to define the character. Ariel proves highly intelligent, creative and competent, diligent and loyal. He expresses true care and concern for Prospero alongside the fear that Prospero will reimprison him should he fail to perform well. Ariel also articulates a fervent yearning to be free, which adds a bittersweet quality to all that he does, however good-humored he appears. We learn that he can transform himself at will, appearing as fire, as a harpy, or even under a cloak of invisibility. Beyond that, however, he is yours to create. When he appears before Prospero in his natural state, is he earthbound or does he continue to fly (and what physical choices would you make to manifest this)? Though Ariel refers to himself with the male possessive pronoun in line 193 (and so we have followed suit), is Ariel male, female, some other amalgam of both . . . or somehow of neither? You have carte blanche to create the spirit of your wildest imagination. As this piece is very active, we urge you to explore physicality that will support Ariel's animated storytelling.

This monologue is notably high-energy right from the onset. Notice the repetition of *hail* in the first line—Ariel wouldn't repeat the word without reason: is Ariel exuberant because he's just done such a great job, or is he being overly effusive to butter up his master and put him in a good mood? (An angry Prospero is a dangerous Prospero.) You must make a decision that distinguishes the two *hail*s. The whole first paragraph is a show of deference, Ariel-style. He asks Prospero which delightful pastime Prospero wishes him to perform next (*to fly, / To swim, to dive into the fire, to ride / On the curled cloud*). As the monologue makes clear, however, he would actually be performing one of these activities in order to accomplish some larger task, like the mock shipwreck he has just staged. Perhaps Ariel distills such tasks to their enjoyable components because he truly loves to perform them . . . or perhaps it behooves him to give Prospero this impression.

Ariel is re-creating an event for Prospero, and uses imagery to paint the scene in detail. Though much of the imagery is fantastical (Ariel outblazes Jove's lightning bolts and seems to besiege *the most mighty Neptune*, making his *dread trident shake*), it is possible to play Ariel as being completely literal: Ariel is of the world of the supernatural and may actually know these gods personally. He may likewise be literal when he likens the ship's passengers to madmen he has actually driven insane with fear. The accuracy with which he recounts the "fire" and "shipwreck" indicates that he replicated these disasters perfectly. And so most, if not all, of the images in this monologue are not metaphoric, but literal representations of actual events. The more clearly you picture the details for yourself, the better you will be able to convince your listeners that you actually brought these events to pass and are now recalling them from memory.

Enjoy playing with the sounds of the monologue, such as the onomato poeic *cracks*, *roaring*, and *sighs*, and the near-onomatopoeic *flamed* and *wracked*, for example. The consonance and assonance woven through the piece give it a magical quality, and keep the pace flowing briskly. Some of the many examples include: *All hail / hail; great / Grave; to fly, To swim, to dive . . . to ride / to thy; Ariel and all / quality; flamed amazement; I'd divide; more momentary; Of sulphurous; most mighty; Seem to beseige; felt a fever; mad and played; all afire / Ferdinand; hair up-staring; Hell / empty / devils.* Notice the half rhyme of lines 217–18: *perished / blemish*.

You may wish to know that a few editors prefer to put a period at the end of line 211 and to change the semicolon in line 212 to a comma. Doing so changes the meaning—*all afire with me* then describes *Ferdinand* instead of the *vessel* or the *mariners*. You are free to choose whichever interpretation you prefer.

SIGNIFICANT SCANS

This monologue's meter gives it its inherently quick, dynamic pace. The piece contains a great number of full or partial stops occurring mid-line, where one doesn't take a long pause, suggesting that Ariel's thoughts are pouring out, each rapidly landing on the heels of the thought preceding it. More than a third of the lines contain double endings (notice how many of these lines occur in a row), creating the sense that Ariel is excited and trying to fit a lot of information into a brief report. This excitement is emphasized by the many inverted feet, both at beginnings of lines and mid-line following caesuras, as well as by several unusual variations in the last section of the monologue, as Ariel triumphantly wraps up his report, clearly proud of a job well done.

There are four places where Prospero's lines have been excised to create one long monologue. You don't want to take too long to make transitions at these places, lest you drain the high energy of the monologue. Don't worry about Prospero's missing lines—they are mere interjections and their absence does not affect the progression of the story. The lines immediately preceding and following the first break are perfect iambic pentameter, but the lines immediately preceding and following the remaining three breaks are short (206–8, 215–17, and 224–26). We recommend that you combine each pair of short lines into one line of iambic pentameter, as follows.

Take only a half-foot pause between lines 206 and 208, where parts of each line as well as all of line 207 have been excised (also, note that the first foot is inverted):

/ x x / x / x / x /
Yea, his dread trident shake. (pause) Not a soul

The half-foot pause gives you enough time to make your transition to the next marvelous event you describe, while maintaining the monologue's lively pace.

Lines 215 and 217 combine perfectly, creating an iambic line with an inverted foot after the caesura (note the elision of *devils* (DEV'LZ) and the line's double ending):

x / x / x / / x x / (x)
And all the devils are here!" Not a hair perished

And, finally, we would do the same for lines 224 and 226 (note the contraction of *the harbor* [TH'HAR-bor] and the double ending):

x / x / x / / x x / (x)
His arms in this sad knot. Safely in the harbor

Notice the crowded foot in line 203 (—*ning were not*) and the half-foot pause at the caesura in line 229 (which has an inverted first foot):

/ x x / x / x / x /
From the still-vexed Bermooths— (pause) there she's hid

Also notice that line 235 has only three and a half feet of text, leaving you a foot and a half of silence to play with. Perhaps you illustrate the remaining ships and their passengers sadly heading home. Or perhaps you share a grin with Prospero at the joke of it all—the passengers were brilliantly duped! Likewise, your last line has only three feet of text—we urge you to use your final two feet of silence. Ariel may wish to see how Prospero likes the work he's done. Or he may be sure of approval and use the pause to collect his due. Whether you opt for any of these choices or for other ideas, be sure to use these pauses actively.

Don't forget to elide: *fire* (FYR, as opposed to FIE-ur) in lines 191 and 203, and *afire* (a-FYR) in line 212; *sulphurous* (SUL-fruss) in line 204; *mariners* (MAR-ners [retain the short "a" sound of *manners*]) in line 210 (but *not* in line 230); *Ferdinand* (FERD-nand) in line 212; *devils* (DEV'LZ) in line 215; *isle* (ILE) in lines 220 and 223; and *Mediterranean* (MEH-dih-TRANE´-yin) in line 234;

. . . and to contract: *be 't* (BEET) in line 190; *O' th' dreadful* (oth-DRED-ful) in line 202; *the harbor* (TH'HAR-bor) in line 226; and *I have* (I've) and *o' th' fleet* (oth-FLEET) in line 232.

The Americas: A Magical Mystery Tour

Though the English had long been exploring the Americas by the turn of the seventeenth century, at that time the "brave new world" recaptured the nation's fancy, as tales of the English colonization of this wild and mysterious place began trickling back to the old country—tales that offered the imagination an embarrassment of riches. And whose imagination would be more engaged than that of the professional tall-tale teller William Shakespeare? Shakespeare most certainly plumbed accounts of the explorers Ferdinand Magellan and Sir Francis Drake, as well as Richard Rich's 1610 *Newes from Virginia*, for source material for *The Tempest*. But he hit paydirt with the fascinating firsthand accounts of a miraculous shipwreck-that-wasn't in Sylvester Jourdain's *A Discovery of the Bermudas, Otherwise Called the Isle of Devils* (1610) and William Strachey's *A True Repertory of the Wreck and Redemption . . . from the Islands of the Bermudas*, written in 1610 but not published until much later (it is believed that Shakespeare knew Strachey personally, since he must have read the account in manuscript form). These writings describe the Bermuda isles in detail as places of untamed beauty, inhabited by spirits and devils. Both also recount a vicious storm that separated the *Sea-Venture* from the rest of her fleet of settlers bound for Virginia and tossed the ship about, certain to wreck it. Those aboard the remaining ships believed the *Sea-Venture* lost and continued on to Virginia. Both accounts describe the prolonged terror of the crew and passengers, the violence of the weather, and the ship's miraculous escape from destruction . . . Sounds like our Ariel at work.

Ariel + Caliban = (Your Name Here)

According to Aristotle, each human being is composed of four elements: the two "higher," more spiritual elements of fire and air, and the two "lower," more bodily elements of earth and water. In *The Tempest*, Shakespeare, who adhered to this theory, created two creatures who have divided the four elements between them: Ariel the spirit is of fire and air, representing the soul unencumbered by the corporeal, while the coarse Caliban (who tried to rape Miranda) is of earth and water, suggesting the body unendowed with loftier elements. Was Shakespeare suggesting that there is a little Ariel and a little Caliban in each of us?

THE TEMPEST

ACT II, SCENE ii

TRINCULO

GENDER: M
AGE RANGE: young adult to mature adult
PROSE/VERSE: prose
FREQUENCY OF USE (1–5): 4

Trinculo was the court jester for King Alonso of Naples and was traveling with him by sea when, as far as Trinculo knows, the ship was wrecked and he alone survived, washing ashore this seemingly desert isle. (Unbeknownst to him, the ship's "wreck" was staged by one of the island's few inhabitants, the magician Prospero, and all its passengers were safely brought ashore and set in different locations.) The misshapen Caliban, another islander, just saw Trinculo approaching. Fearing that Trinculo was a spirit sent by Prospero to torment him, Caliban threw himself facedown on the ground in a sorry attempt to hide. Trinculo, who does not yet see Caliban, says:

Here's neither bush nor shrub to bear off any
weather at all, and another storm brewing—I hear
20 it sing i' th' wind. Yond same black cloud, yond
huge one, looks like a foul bombard that would
shed his liquor. If it should thunder as it did before,
I know not where to hide my head; yond same
cloud cannot choose but fall by pailfuls. What have
25 we here? A man or a fish? Dead or alive? A fish; he
smells like a fish—a very ancient and fishlike smell,
a kind of not-of-the-newest poor-John. A strange
fish! Were I in England now, as once I was, and
had but this fish painted, not a holiday fool there
30 but would give a piece of silver; there would this
monster make a man—any strange beast there
makes a man: when they will not give a doit to relieve a lame beggar, they will lay out ten to see a
dead Indian. Legged like a man . . . and his fins like
35 arms . . . warm, o' my troth! I do now let loose my

18 *bear off* ward off; 19 *weather* i.e., bad weather, storm; *at all* refers to the foliage, not the weather; 20 *Yond same black cloud* That particular black cloud over there; 21 *bombard* a large leather liquor container [*foul bombard* both (1) a leather liquor container made of a stormy cloud and (2) a rotting leather liquor container (which is about to fall apart and lose its contents)]; *would* will; wants to; 22 *shed* pour, cause to flow out; *his* its; *liquor* In Shakespeare's time, *liquor* meant both "alcoholic beverage" and, more generally, "liquid." Thus, Trinculo intends both definitions simultaneously]; 24 *What have we here* Trinculo notices the prone Caliban; 27 *poor-John* the colloquial name for salted and dried hake, an inexpensive fish related to cod, eaten especially during Lent; 29 *had but* only had; *painted* i.e., on a sign hanging outside his booth at a fair; Trinculo imagines exhibiting the "strange fish" for money; *holiday fool* gullible holiday customer [*not a holiday fool . . . piece of silver* i.e., there isn't a gullible customer there who could help but fork over some money]; 31 *make a man* i.e., make a man rich, make his fortune (with a humorous secondary meaning, that in England any monster can "make" [pass himself off as] a man); 32 *they* i.e., members of the general public; *doit* coin of very small value; 33 *lay out* spend; *a dead Indian* A Native American was brought as a captive to England by Sir Martin Frobisher in the 1570s to be displayed for money as a specimen of a "savage." The man died in Bristol, but his corpse was brought to London and nonetheless displayed. This paved the way for subsequent displays of captive Native Americans throughout Shakespeare's life; 34 *Legged* Having legs; 35 *o' my troth* on my honor, in truth (here, an exclamation of sur-

TRINCULO

1 minute, 30 seconds

opinion, hold it no longer: this is no fish, but an islander that hath lately suffered by a thunderbolt. [*Thunder*] Alas, the storm is come again. My best way is to creep under his gaberdine; there is no
40 other shelter hereabout. Misery acquaints a man with strange bedfellows. I will here shroud till the dregs of the storm be past.

prise); *let loose* set forth, release (unintentionally carrying the connotation: release vomit, urine, excrement, or a fart); 37 *hath . . . suffered* i.e., has . . . been killed; 38 *My best way* My best plan of action, my best option; 39 *creep* hide myself; *gaberdine* a long and loose cloak; 41 *shroud* take shelter; 42 *dregs* the last residue (i.e., of the storm, although usually the residue of a beverage—Trinculo clings to his "bombard" simile from above).

COMMENTARY

Trinculo is described in the character list as a "jester" (a.k.a. a fool), but if you wish to present a real Shakespearean fool, you must move on. In Shakespeare's day, a fool was anything but: he was a skilled professional with a keen wit, a highly developed sense of irony, and a well-honed talent for mimicry and song. The fool would comment trenchantly for his employer(s) on issues of the day, offering insightful criticism with the objectivity of an outsider and the bitingly targeted humor of an insider. In employing Trinculo, King Alonso seems to have hired the least-qualified man for the job. Trinculo's traits better befit Shakespeare's "clown," the simple, unsophisticated, and bumbling (yet also oddly astute) type who draws laughs only inadvertently, through his mishaps and malapropisms as well as through charming, candid, and funny asides. This monologue is just such an aside, introducing and establishing Trinculo's character.

It is fitting that Trinculo speaks in prose here and throughout the play. Though, as this monologue illustrates, he believes he has much upon which to expound, Trinculo is clearly not the cleverest of men, perhaps too fatuous for the elevated language of verse. The use of prose suggests a simplicity that better suits him.

But of course Trinculo doesn't have the self-awareness to recognize his limitation. His two hasty and faulty forensic assessments of Caliban, his tangential discourse on the ways of England (which this Neapolitan onetime tourist has no problem "expertly" summing up), his unintentional double meaning of *let loose* (which perfectly describes the worth of his revelation—see Annotation), and his belabored, not-of-the-aptest comparison of a raincloud to a leather alcohol jug seem to reveal a person who is secure in his intellect. Yet despite his shortcomings, Trinculo is immensely likeable. His irrational fear of the storm is childlike and sweet, as is his charming way of sharing his thought process as it progresses: the audience fairly sees the wheels turning in his mind as he confronts the storm and Caliban, and—eureka!—figures out what to do about both.

There is much in the language to enjoy exploring. Notice the preponderance of Blubbering Bs in the beginning of the monologue (*bush / bear / brewing / black / bombard*), where Trinculo is afraid of the storm, the Caught Cs, which give that section a stammering quality (*black cloud*; *cloud cannot*), the Manly Ms when he waxes on about the English (*monster make a man*), and the Loquacious Ls (*lame / lay out / Legged like / let loose / longer / lately*) when he generously shares his insights. He repeats those words that convey the key concepts of the monologue, such as *yond*, *cloud*, *fish*, *strange*, *make a man*, *storm*, *thunder(bolt)*. Trinculo's colloquial tone and choice of terms are inherently funny (we can't explain why the word *doit* in line 32 is funny, it simply is, as are the words *creep* in line 39 and *dregs* in line 42).

You may decide that Trinculo is not being at all poetic when he says *I hear it sing i' th' wind*. Remember that the storm that caused the "shipwreck" was conjured by Prospero with Ariel's help, and that both Prospero and Ariel incorporate music into their magical work. It is entirely possible that the storm Trinculo fears is being wrought by Prospero with the aid of musical incantations, and that when Trinculo says he hears it sing, he is being literal.

Trinculo forgets all about the storm while discoursing about the English, but remembers and scares himself silly with his "realization" that the *islander* was killed by a thunderbolt (a conclusion that then seems confirmed, with impeccable timing, by actual thunder). That's the thought that drives him to hide under Caliban, pronto. Yet Trinculo just can't help but pause a moment to share one final pithy observation: *Misery acquaints a man with strange bedfellows*. Thanks for the insight, Trinculo.

THE TEMPEST

ACT III, SCENE ii

CALIBAN

GENDER: M
PROSE/VERSE: blank verse
AGE RANGE: young adult to adult
FREQUENCY OF USE (1–5): 2.5

Caliban has been enslaved on his own island ever since the magician Prospero and his daughter, Miranda, arrived years ago. Now he has a chance to retaliate. Two new gods, or so he perceives them to be, have arrived on the island, bringing with them a delicious and mind-bending elixir (actually just booze), which they have shared with him. Caliban hopes to convince one of them to kill Prospero, take Miranda for his mate, and accept him as his loyal servant. He tells the god how to kill Prospero, and explains the importance of destroying his books, the source of his power.

95 Why, as I told thee, 'tis a custom with him
I' th' afternoon to sleep. There thou mayst brain him,
Having first seized his books; or with a log
Batter his skull, or paunch him with a stake,
Or cut his weasand with thy knife. Remember
100 First to possess his books, for without them
He's but a sot, as I am, nor hath not
One spirit to command—they all do hate him
As rootedly as I. Burn but his books.
He has brave utensils—for so he calls them—
105 Which, when he has a house, he'll deck withal.
And that most deeply to consider is
The beauty of his daughter. He himself
Calls her a nonpareil. I never saw a woman
But only Sycorax my dam, and she;
110 But she as far surpasseth Sycorax
As great'st does least.

1 minute

95 *Why* used as an interjection, sometimes much like an expletive; *custom with him* a habit of his; 96 *There* On that occasion (often used with reference to time in Shakespeare); *brain him* knock his brains out; 97 *his books* refers to the books that contain Prospero's magical spells; 98 *paunch* stab in the belly; eviscerate; 99 *weasand* (WEE-znd) windpipe; 100 *possess* i.e., get possession of; 101 *sot* fool, ignoramus; *nor hath not* and has not (Shakespeare often uses the double negative for emphasis); 102 *spirit* supernatural being (such as a fairy, ghost, etc.); 103 *rootedly* deeply; *Burn but his books* (1) Just make sure you burn his books; and/or (2) Burn only his books; 104 *brave* splendid, impressive; *utensils* (YOO´-ten-SLZ) household furnishings; 105 *deck withal* decorate it with; 106 *that* that which is; *to consider* to be considered; 108 *a nonpareil* (NON-puh-RELL´ or NON-puh-RAY´) i.e., a beauty without equal; 109 *But* except; *Sycorax* (SIK´-or-AX) Caliban's mother was a witch whom the people of Algiers would have executed but for the fact that she was pregnant with him (little did they know the father was a devil). Instead, she was banished to the island, where Caliban was then born. The name is perhaps a combination of two Greek words: *sys* ("cow") and *korax* ("raven"); *dam* mother.

COMMENTARY

Caliban's monologue may seem short and simple, but the role requires quite a bit of physical and mental homework. First, Caliban is not human. As the son of a witch and a devil, he could take almost any form you choose. In addition to deciding what his appearance, movements, and voice are like, you'll want to consider the conditions under which he's lived thus far. After his mother died he was alone on the island for twelve years, probably living much like an animal. Then Prospero arrived. Caliban took him on a tour of the island and showed him the ropes, and Prospero taught Caliban to speak. Unfortunately, the magician did not take it kindly when Caliban put the moves on Prospero's daughter, Miranda. Now Caliban is a slave to Prospero, living under a rock while Prospero rules the island that should be his. This backstory raises many questions about Caliban, such as: How "human" is he, both in mind and body? How well does he understand the foreign culture and language Prospero has brought to the island? Answering questions such as these will help you develop Caliban's physicality.

Unlike many of Shakespeare's uneducated characters, who speak in plain prose but reveal their intelligence through clever turns of phrase, Caliban, who is more beast and less cerebellum, has clearly mastered the technical aspect of language. He speaks easily and effectively in verse, but his limited understanding of abstract concepts and of the culture that created the language undermines his speech. Much of Caliban's humor arises from his naïveté.

Twice Caliban betrays the fact that he is merely mimicking Prospero's use of words. For instance, the *utensils* he speaks of can only be the few things Prospero managed to bring with him in his trunk, which was filled mostly with books. What does Caliban imagine a house looks like, and what is it filled with? Blankets, perhaps, and books, candles, a simple kettle or pan, baby clothing . . . and not much else! The archaic pronunciation of *utensils* works well here. Today's audience may not know that this was the correct pronunciation in Shakespeare's time (and even long thereafter); perhaps they will think that in trying to imitate his master, Caliban has merely pronounced the word incorrectly. In a second example, Caliban calls Miranda a *nonpareil*, although he admits that he's never seen another woman aside from her and his mother, the witch.

SIGNIFICANT SCANS

Caliban is eager to get rid of Prospero, and the meter supports this urgency with several inverted feet, especially when Caliban speaks of the actual murder or of Prospero's books. In line 100, one such inversion stresses *First*, highlighting the most critical step in Caliban's plan—seizing the books, an idea that is reinforced by the emphasis on *them* at the end of the line. Caliban clearly has no doubts about how this must be done. Your interpretation of line 103 will determine whether or not there is an inversion after the caesura (see Annotation). Also, line 108 is hexameter—a rare six-footed line—with a double ending. Notice that after this long, eleven-syllable line, the piece winds down: two regular lines of blank verse follow, and the piece ends with a short line, which provides three silent feet in which to let your statement sink in. Or, you can insert two of the silent syllables into the text to drive home your point:

x / x / x /
As great'st (pause) does (pause) least

(An ingenious simile—Caliban must be proud of his masterful use of the English language!)

Shakespeare's Native American Studies 101

The Tempest is one of Shakespeare's most original plays. As far as we know there was no principal source for the plot. There were, however, many minor sources, the most significant of which relate to the colonization of the New World. Shakespeare was very interested in the questions this raised about the relationship between the colonizers and the native people. In representing Caliban as a beast with little or no morality, Shakespeare expresses the common view of his time (note that *Caliban* is a near anagram of *cannibal*). But he also explores the complexities of the situation, portraying Caliban as: one who helped the newcomers survive their environment, only to be enslaved by them; a character with a poetic appreciation for the natural beauty of his surroundings and an innate sense of his rights to personal liberty and cultural freedom; and a naïve victim of one of the colonists' most damaging imports—alcohol.

P.S.

For an additional interesting tidbit about Caliban, see "Ariel + Caliban = (Your Name Here)," page 858.

THE TEMPEST

ACT IV, SCENE i

PROSPERO

GENDER: M

AGE RANGE: mature adult to older adult

PROSE/VERSE: blank verse

FREQUENCY OF USE (1–5): 2

Prospero, the former duke of Milan, has been living with his daughter, Miranda, on a nearly deserted island ever since he was ousted from power years ago by his younger brother, with the help of King Alonso of Naples. When a ship bearing Prospero's brother, King Alonso, and Alonso's son, Ferdinand, passed by the island, Prospero, an accomplished sorcerer, magically "wrecked" the ship, bringing all its passengers safely ashore to different parts of the island. Prince Ferdinand and Miranda met and fell in love. After testing Ferdinand's devotion to Miranda, Prospero consented to their engagement. In honor of their betrothal, Prospero arranged for spirits to entertain them with a masque. Suddenly recalling that his slave, Caliban, is about to implement a plot against his life, Prospero has just abruptly dispersed the spirits. Noticing Ferdinand's concerned reaction to his outburst, Prospero says:

PROSPERO

You do look, my son, in a movèd sort,
As if you were dismayed—be cheerful, sir.
Our revels now are ended: these our actors,
As I foretold you, were all spirits, and
150 Are melted into air, into thin air;
And, like the baseless fabric of this vision,
The cloud-capped towers, the gorgeous palaces,
The solemn temples, the great globe itself,
Yea, all which it inherit, shall dissolve,
155 And, like this insubstantial pageant faded,
Leave not a rack behind. We are such stuff
As dreams are made on, and our little life
Is rounded with a sleep. Sir, I am vexed.
Bear with my weakness; my old brain is troubled.
160 Be not disturbed with my infirmity.
If you be pleased, retire into my cell
And there repose. A turn or two I'll walk
To still my beating mind.

1 minute

146 *a movèd sort* a troubled or agitated state; 148 *revels* entertainment (the masque just presented for Miranda and Ferdinand); 150 *into thin air* Jacobeans firmly believed in the existence of spirits, which they believed to be composed of air; spirits became visible through the thickening of air and would become invisible when the air thinned again (see "Ariel + Caliban = (Your Name Here)," page 858); 151 *baseless* without foundation, without substance (with play on second meaning: "not base," i.e., not vile, lowly, or evil); *fabric* structure; *this vision* i.e., the masque; 152 *cloud-capped* having a summit so tall it reached the clouds; 153 *the great globe itself* the earth (with a play on the Globe Theatre, built for Shakespeare's acting company, in which many of his plays [including *The Tempest*] were first publicly performed); 154 *it inherit* occupy it; 156 *rack* a wisp of cloud (with play on secondary meaning: a stage cloud, used in Jacobean court masques to "dissolve" a scene); 157 *made on* both (1) built upon and (2) composed of; 158 *rounded* (1) surrounded; (2) completed (with possible additional meaning, "crowned") [*rounded with a sleep* This difficult passage has been interpreted by scholars to mean: (1) life comes full circle, ultimately ending back at the sleep (lack of consciousness) that preceded it (our lives are thus the dreams that emerge from that sleep); or, more literally, (2) life is surrounded (pervaded) by sleep (out of which may come the dreams we experience)]; 159 *my old brain is troubled* i.e., Prospero is vexed at the conspiracy plot of Caliban, Stephano, and Trinculo, though the words he has just spoken may have added to his distress; 160 *with* by; 161 *If you be pleased* i.e., if it would please you to do so; 162 *repose* lie down to rest; 163 *To still* to calm; *beating* agitated, troubled by thoughts.

COMMENTARY

This is one of the most famous monologues in Shakespeare's canon, and for good reason: though short, it runs deep. When taken on three different levels, the monologue seems to give voice to three people: the character Prospero, the actor playing Prospero, and Shakespeare himself, who was about to retire. Prospero's assurance to Miranda and Ferdinand that the spirits were merely performing in a pageant is also the actor's reminder to the audience that he is merely performing the role of Prospero in *The Tempest* (and that all such plays are merely visions), and the aging playwright's philosophical observation that we are all likewise temporary performers on this earth. In preparing the monologue, however, you will want to focus on Prospero's situation and objectives. The other layers of meaning will become manifest on their own.

It is important to understand the setting of this monologue: Prospero is nearing the completion of his grand scheme to regain the dukedom of Milan and set his daughter on the throne of Naples. And yet upon its fruition, Prospero will be setting aside his beloved sorcery (his lifelong passion) forever (see monologue, page 874). His presentation of the masque for the delight of his daughter and Ferdinand was thus his last joyous act of magic; he may have conjured it for his own benefit as much as for theirs, and it may have been quite bittersweet to do so. This may be in the back of his mind when he tells Ferdinand that *Our revels now are ended*. Being forced to end this final pageant before its conclusion because of Caliban—whose irksome plot against him could yet undo all of his careful work—must have been more than a bit upsetting (notice that he digs at the "base" Caliban by calling the beautiful pageant *baseless* in comparison). Ending the pageant prematurely to contend with Caliban must also have reminded Prospero that the pageant he had just created was frivolous when compared with the real-world concerns to which he must soon reluctantly return.

All this might prompt a man approaching the end of his life to consider such real-world concerns. How real are our concerns? Our daily dramas? What are their sources, and, ultimately, of what lasting consequence are they? Or we? After all, just as the *spirits* in the pageant have vanished into nothingness, so too, someday, shall we all. Prospero contrasts *our little life* with grand images of man-made structures, all of lofty heights (*cloud-capped towers*; *gorgeous palaces*; *solemn temples*; and the second meaning of *great globe itself*—Shakespeare's own theater), to demonstrate that as important as we fancy ourselves and as enduring as we fancy the monuments we build to ourselves, to our royalty, our religions, and our art, everything we construct will ultimately return to dust. In the end, what will it all have meant?

When Prospero says that Ferdinand looks *in a movèd sort, / As if . . . dismayed*, he ostensibly speaks to calm Ferdinand, but is, of course, really seeking to regain his own composure. After baring his soul in the existential middle section of his monologue, Prospero is at last ready to acknowledge that it is in fact he who is upset. Notice that he uses the adjectives *vexed*, *troubled*, *disturbed*, and *beating* in a short space of six lines. Likewise, he uses the words *weakness*, *old*, and *infirmity* in those lines, suggesting, perhaps, that he fears he will become an infirm and ineffectual old man upon retiring his powers.

Throughout the piece, Shakespeare uses patterns of sound—especially assonance—to great effect. For example, the surprising number of sOOthing OOs at the beginning of the piece (*You do look / movèd / you*) echo the natural sound of concern that people voice instinctively, helping convey the concerned tone Prospero adopts toward Ferdinand. Other examples of assonance include: *be cheerful*; *Our / now / our*; *revels / ended*; *into / into thin / fabric / this vision*; *cloud-capped towers*; *which it inherit / dissolve*; *this insubstantial*; *disturbed / with / infirmity*; *be pleased*; *I'll / my / mind*. Some examples of alliteration are *cloud-capped*, *great globe*, *such stuff*, *little life*, *with my weakness*, *A turn or two*, and *my / mind*; and some examples of consonance are *my / movèd / dismayed*, *retire / there repose*, and *I'll / still*. These sound patterns build on one another, elevating the tone of the piece to match the import of its content, and helping to cast the monologue's powerfully dreamlike spell.

SIGNIFICANT SCANS

The first line of this monologue is headless, with a crowded fourth foot (*in a mov*——):

```
           x    /  x   /   x   /  x-x   / x   /
(pause) You do look, my son, in a movèd sort
```

Because it is headless, the line sounds as though all of its feet are inverted, starting off the monologue with a big punch, which is fitting considering that Prospero is in fact agitated. He quickly regains his composure—the monologue has only one other inversion (following the caesura on line 150) until its final few lines. Only after Prospero admits that he is *vexed* do lines 159–61 each begin with an inverted foot. Prior to that point the monologue has many double endings, both at line ends and mid-line before caesuras, which soften the tone, contributing to the hypnotic quality of the majority of the piece (also fitting, given that its subject is a *vision*). In addition, when Prospero discusses the elements of this *vision* (lines 151–54), the lines are smooth, flowing without any full stops mid-line to jar the listeners out of their reverie. In contrast, when Prospero gets to the philosophical heart of the matter (lines 156–58) sentences begin and end mid-line, drawing attention to the point he is making. These mid-line full stops continue throughout the rest of the monologue, as Prospero admits that it is he who is perturbed, and as he seeks to put the matter to rest quickly and deflect attention from his state of mind.

Don't forget to expand *movèd* (MOO-vehd) in line 146, which highlights the word as Prospero tries unsuccessfully to pretend it is Ferdinand and not himself who is distressed. Not one word of this monologue is elided, which suggests that Prospero is choosing his words and speaking quite carefully. Is this because what he says pains him? Is he picking his words and thoughts carefully because he is holding back from saying more, for fear of frightening his child and her betrothed? Or is he speaking carefully because he considers the message so very important? You will surely enjoy the exciting challenge of exploring Prospero's motivations for not just why but also how he delivers this philosophical piece.

If You Can't Beat 'Em, Join 'Em

Though not a huge fan of plays, King James loved a good court masque like some people love an Andrew Lloyd Webber musical (he'd laugh, he'd cry . . .). In this newly developed form of entertainment, royals were honored and their special occasions celebrated with extravaganzas containing elaborate sets, costumes, music, dance, and characters usually either drawn from classical mythology or representing well-known philosophical ideals. Knowing Jame's predilection, Shakespeare included mini-masques in all his final plays. Just as the masque of which Prospero speaks in this monologue is presented to celebrate the upcoming wedding of Miranda and Ferdinand, *The Tempest* itself was performed in 1613 in honor of the real-life impending nuptials of King James's daughter, Elizabeth, and Frederick, Elector Palatine (later the King of Bohemia), from whose grandson King George I today's English royal family is directly descended. Some scholars believe that the masque scene was added for that performance, since records reflect a prior performance of *The Tempest* before the King two years earlier.

Swan Song

Since *The Tempest* was the last play written entirely by Shakespeare—penned shortly before his retirement and only five years before his death—this speech has often been called his swan song. As such, it is a modest yet gorgeous acknowledgment of the many fully realized worlds Shakespeare was able to create onstage out of little more than mere words, which do [*melt*] *into air* . . . and *Leave not a rack behind*, almost as quickly as they are spoken. Shakespeare little realized, however, that his ode to the ephemeral nature of plays would so long endure.

THE TEMPEST

ACT V, SCENE i

PROSPERO

GENDER: M
PROSE/VERSE: blank verse
AGE RANGE: mature adult to older adult
FREQUENCY OF USE (1–5): 2.5

Many years ago, Prospero, the Duke of Milan, was deposed and set adrift with his toddler daughter. They landed on a near-desert island, where they have lived ever since. Prospero managed to bring his books, from which he has learned powerful magic. He recently discovered that those who deposed him were sailing through nearby waters, and he magically raised a storm that shipwrecked them on the island. After putting them through several ordeals to test and punish them, Prospero cast a spell of madness over them. He has now decided to release them from this enchantment, forgive the wrongs done him, renounce his magic, and sail back to Milan with the others, whose vessel he has not actually harmed. He calls upon his agents in the spirit world one last time:

Ye elves of hills, brooks, standing lakes, and groves,
And ye that on the sands with printless foot
35 Do chase the ebbing Neptune, and do fly him
When he comes back; you demi-puppets that
By moonshine do the green sour ringlets make,
Whereof the ewe not bites; and you whose pastime
Is to make midnight mushrooms, that rejoice
40 To hear the solemn curfew; by whose aid,
Weak masters though ye be, I have bedimmed
The noontide sun, called forth the mutinous winds,
And 'twixt the green sea and the azured vault
Set roaring war; to the dread rattling thunder
45 Have I given fire, and rifted Jove's stout oak
With his own bolt; the strong-based promontory
Have I made shake, and by the spurs plucked up
The pine and cedar; graves at my command
Have waked their sleepers, oped, and let them forth
50 By my so potent art. But this rough magic
I here abjure, and when I have required

PROSPERO

33 *standing* stagnant; 34 *printless* leaving no footprint; 35 *ebbing Neptune* i.e., retreating waves (in ancient Greek mythology, Neptune is the god of the sea); *fly* flee from; 36 *When he comes back* i.e., when the next wave comes; *demi-puppets* i.e., fairies half the size of puppets; 37 *green sour ringlets* fairy circles (circles of darker green, taller, sourer grass caused by the underground parts of toadstools, which affect the roots of the grass); 38 *Whereof the ewe not bites* i.e., which the sheep will not eat; 39 *midnight mushrooms* mushrooms that appear overnight; 40 *solemn curfew* evening bell, usually rung at nine o'clock (ushering in the time when spirits are out and their power is potent); 41 *masters* i.e., ministers; 42 *noontide* midday; 43 *'twixt* between; *the azured vault* i.e., the blue sky; 44 *Set* incited; *dread* terrible, fear-inspiring; 45 *given fire* i.e., added lightning; *Jove* a.k.a. Jupiter, ruler of the gods in ancient Roman mythology, whose weapon of choice was a lightning bolt [*rifted Jove's stout oak / With his own bolt* split the stout oak—the symbol of Jove's strength—with Jove's own lightning bolt]; 47 *spurs* roots; 49 *their sleepers* i.e., the corpses they contained; *oped* (rhymes with "hoped") opened; 50 *art* magic [*By my so potent art* by my magic, which is potent enough to do all these things]; *rough* harsh, crude (i.e., involving powers over the material world, rather than powers of the mind or spirit); 51 *here* now, on this occasion; *when* i.e., after; *required* (1) requested; (2) demanded;

Some heavenly music—which even now I do—
To work mine end upon their senses that
This airy charm is for, I'll break my staff,
55 Bury it certain fathoms in the earth,
And deeper than ever did plummet sound
I'll drown my book.

1 minute, 30 seconds

52 *heavenly music* celestial music (in Shakespeare's time it was believed that each planet produced a particular tone, and together the sounds created a beautiful harmony inaudible to the human ear); 53 *work* produce by means of magic; *mine end* my purpose; *their senses that* the senses of those whom; 54 *airy* (1) of the air; (2) of music; *charm* (1) magic spell; (2) song; *staff* i.e., magic wand; 55 *certain* a particular number of; *fathom* unit of measurement, equal to six feet of depth; 56 *plummet* plumb line used to sound (measure) the depth of water [*deeper than ever did plummet sound / I'll drown my book* I'll submerge my book in water deeper than any plummet ever measured (with a play on "sound plunging downward" [reading plummet as the verb and sound as the noun], another allusion to music).

COMMENTARY

The poetic language and imagery of this piece are as enchanting as a magic spell. Prospero's striking poetic gifts and his reverence for his books suggest that language is the very key to Prospero's magic. Powerful language is certainly the outstanding feature of this piece. This is not normal spoken language by any stretch of the imagination, even within the construct of dramatic verse. Prospero's final invocation to the spirits that serve him is differentiated from regular conversation in verse plays by its extraordinary poetic grammatical construction, its meter, and its sounds, which combine to give it a flowing, melodic, and incantatory feel. Notice that Prospero's use of the emphatic verb from (*Do chase*; *do fly*; *do the green sour ringlets make*), complex, formal grammar (*ye that on the sands with printless foot / Do chase*; *Whereof the ewe not bites*; etc.), and the word *Ye*—already an archaic form in Shakespeare's time—have the combined effect of making his words sound like an ancient and beautiful ritual.

Through this invocation to his ministers, Prospero gives his audience a glimpse into his magical world. The images he conjures in the listener's mind are not imagery to him, but rather the very real supernatural forces he has learned to control, and the actual magical feats he has been able to perform. If you take the time to visualize each of the creatures he commands and each of the acts he describes, you will be able to approach Prospero's world from his perspective. Imagine actually having the power to create a roaring hurricane, to split an oak in two with a thunderbolt, to pull trees out by their roots, and even to make the dead rise out of their graves! The possession of such power (and the wisdom to renounce it) will necessarily affect Prospero's bearing and demeanor. He is a mortal, but no ordinary mortal: he is one of those people whose power and wisdom are manifest in his mere presence.

Prospero weaves his spell chiefly through sound and meter. Sounds saturate the piece with a sense of the music to which Prospero alludes in his puns (the double meaning of *airy charm*, and the clever play on *plummet sound*, in which noun and verb are interchangeable). Notice the many assonant and consonant links between words that carry you through the piece: Ls and Vs/Fs (*elves of hills*); EHs (*ebbing Neptune*); OOs (*moonshine do / ewe*); Ms (*make midnight mushrooms*); EEs and Bs (*Weak / ye be / bedimmed*); IHs (*bedimmed / winds*); EEs (*green sea*); As (*And / and / azured*); Rs and ORs (*roaring war*); OHs (*Jove's / oak / own / bolt*); AWs (*strong-based / promontory*); AYs (*made shake*); UHs (*plucked up*); Ns (*mine end upon / senses*); Rs (*airy charm / for / break*); and D, ER, EE, and OW sounds (*And deeper / ever did / sound / drown*). When the same sound appears at the end of one word and the beginning of the next (*sour ringlets*; *Jove's stout*; *And deeper*), be sure to separate them and see what this does to your interpretation of the line. Also, take advantage of the striking onomatopoeic sounds that convey their own meanings (*fly*; *roaring*; *rattling*; *rifted*; *break*). Notice how many of these use Rumbling R sounds.

The meter in this piece is remarkably even, and it flows easily and continuously from line to line, since all thoughts begin and end at caesuras, mid-line. Even more strikingly, there is no full stop in the first seventeen and a half lines! Prospero's call to his ministers and his litany of magical feats is one long, continuous statement, further enhancing the monologue's incantatory quality. He doesn't pause until he reaches the crux of the issue: all of this has been accomplished *By my so potent art*. An important transition takes place here, in which Prospero changes his perspective on his magic: at the beginning of the line his magic is a *potent art*; by the end, it is only *rough magic*. Prospero sums up in this line the two faces of his magic, and with the single word *rough* he is able to toss away all his majestic powers, dismissing them as mere material, earthly, insignificant tricks. Be sure to consider whether he does so with enthusiasm or reluctance, and to define his motivation for renouncing what has been the focus of his life for so long. It seems clear from the play that Prospero's magic has kept him isolated from society—his preoccupation with his books made him vulnerable to his brother's coup all those years ago, indirectly causing his banishment, and now that he has waylaid his countrymen's ship, his magic is the principal obstacle to his return to normal life in Milan. Thus it is easy to imagine that this decision is a sacrifice Prospero makes—even though he may feel vulnerable—so that he can finally travel home: perhaps because he is homesick, because he finds that magical powers are no substitute for the comfort society brings to loneliness and old age, and, as he states in the play, because he wants to provide a normal, happy life for his daughter. Perhaps Prospero has tired of his life as a big, powerful fish in small, lonely pond, and now feels that his magic is not so important after all. And/or perhaps he has decided that although his *potent art* can be used for good, the unnatural imbalance of power it creates is an evil result that must be rejected. As you explore the different possibilities, you will discover that they are numerous, complex, and interrelated. Look for a set of ideas that resonates for you.

Following this crucial transition, the phrase *But this rough magic* begins the second continuous statement in the piece, which takes you all the way to its end. Each of the two sections contains its own build: in the first, the greatness of Prospero's powers is brought to a peak at *By my so potent art*, preparing us for the shock of the second, which builds to the profound and irrevocable destruction of that art. The scarcity of metrical variation aids both builds, while the few double endings that do appear in the piece serve to soften line endings and enhance the flowing feeling of the first. These softening endings no longer appear after Prospero switches perspective to *this rough magic*. There is, however, a single trochaic inversion in line 55, which stands out against the flow of the piece and drives home Prospero's final line, which has only two feet of spoken text. Following the long, rolling wave of engulfing sound in this monologue, the silence of the three-foot pause after *I'll drown my book* is profound.

It's easy to get caught up in the poetry of this piece, so don't forget to act! Sometime before, during, or just after this speech, Prospero makes a circle on the ground, into which his victims are led by Ariel. The circle was often used in ceremonial magic, and Prospero creates this one as the locus for his final enchantment—restoring his countrymen to their right minds. You'll have to decide why he has called forth all his helpers and listed all his magical achievements before doing so. Does he wish to ritualize the renunciation of his craft? To relinquish his power over his helpers "in person" and say goodbye? Perhaps he is also preparing himself and his helpers to carry out his final act of magic—remember, this ending is also a beginning.

Don't forget to elide: *mutinous* (MYOOT-nuss) in line 42; *rattling* (RAT-ling) in line 44; *given* (giv'n) in line 45; *promontory* (PRAW′-mun-TREE) in line 46; *required* (re-KWIERD) in line 51; and *heavenly* (HEV'N-lee) and *even* (een) in line 52.

METAMORPHOSES' MEDEA, MORPHED

Scholars believe that Shakespeare studied Ovid's *Metamorphoses* both in the original Latin and in the English translation by Golding. Drawing from *Metamorphoses*, Shakespeare based this monologue on a passage in which Medea calls on her gods for assistance, using white magic. He also based his description of Sycorax's black magic on Medea herself. This deliberate distinction between white magic and black is an important motif in the play that served to ensure the approval of King James, a staunch opponent of witchcraft and self-proclaimed expert on the subject (see "Wasn't This a Dainty Dish to Put Before the King," page 993).

THE WINTER'S TALE

ACT III, SCENE ii

HERMIONE

GENDER: F
PROSE/VERSE: blank verse
AGE RANGE: adult
FREQUENCY OF USE (1–5): 5

Queen Hermione's husband, King Leontes of Sicilia, has recently become uncharacteristically consumed by jealousy: he has wrongly accused her of having an affair with his lifelong friend King Polixenes of Bohemia and, furthermore, of carrying Polixenes' child (she in fact was pregnant with Leontes' second). After Polixenes fled for his life, Leontes arrested Hermione for treason and imprisoned her, forbidding her to see their son. While in prison she gave birth to their daughter, whom the King promptly ordered killed. Leontes has sent two courtiers to travel to the oracle of Apollo to obtain the guidance of the god. The courtiers have returned, but the answer they carry has not yet been revealed. Hermione has now been brought to public trial, where she has just reiterated her innocence. When Leontes, enraged at her denial, threatens her with death, she replies:

HERMIONE

Sir, spare your threats:
The bug which you would fright me with I seek;
To me can life be no commodity.
95 The crown and comfort of my life, your favor,
I do give lost, for I do feel it gone,
But know not how it went. My second joy,
And first-fruits of my body, from his presence
I am barred like one infectious. My third comfort
100 (Starred most unluckily) is from my breast,
The innocent milk in it most innocent mouth,
Haled out to murder; myself on every post
Proclaimed a strumpet; with immodest hatred
The childbed privilege denied, which 'longs
105 To women of all fashion; lastly, hurried
Here to this place, i' th' open air, before
I have got strength of limit. Now, my Liege,
Tell me what blessings I have here alive,
That I should fear to die? Therefore proceed.
110 But yet hear this—mistake me not: no life—
I prize it not a straw—but for mine honor,

93 *bug* bogey, bugbear (any source, real or imagined, of needless fear); *fright* frighten; 94 *commodity* asset; comfort; 95 *favor* kind regard, affection; 96 *give* consider; 97 *My second joy* i.e., Hermione's son, Mamillius; 98 *first-fruits of my body* i.e., my firstborn; 99 *like one infectious* i.e., as though I were a person infected with a contagious disease; 100 *Starred most unluckily* i.e., most ill-fated (Jacobeans believed that a person's fate was predetermined by the stars); 101 *innocent milk* i.e., mother's milk; *it* its; 102 *Haled* Dragged [*Haled out to murder* dragged out to be murdered]; *post* In Shakespeare's time, public notices were tacked up on posts outside sheriffs' offices; 103 *strumpet* prostitute; *immodest* immoderate, beyond reason; 104 *The childbed privilege denied* denied the privilege of bed rest after childbirth; *'longs* belongs; 105 *of all fashion* of all sorts, of all ranks (Hermione points to the irony of a queen being denied a privilege afforded to even a woman of the lowest status in society); 106 *i' th' open air* fresh air was believed by Jacobeans to be unhealthy for invalids, including women recovering from childbirth; 107 *strength of limit* strength regained by resting for a prescribed time after giving birth; *my Liege* i.e., your Majesty; 108 *here alive* i.e., here on this earth while I remain alive; 110 *no life* i.e., not to save my life; 111 *I prize it not a straw* proverbial: i.e., I don't even value it as highly as a

Which I would free, if I shall be condemned
Upon surmises, all proofs sleeping else
But what your jealousies awake, I tell you
115 'Tis rigor and not law. Your Honors all,
I do refer me to the oracle.
Apollo be my judge.

1 minute, 30 seconds

straw; *for mine honor* i.e., for the sake of my honor and reputation; 112 *would free* wish to clear and restore; 113 *surmises* suspicion; conjecture; *all proofs sleeping . . . your jealousies awake* i.e., there being no evidence except for what your jealous mind has been able to come up with; 115 *rigor and not law* tyranny, not justice; *Your Honors all* Hermione now addresses the court; 116 *refer me to* direct my appeal to; *the oracle* In ancient Greece, mortals would bring inquiries to the gods at designated shrines; they would receive answers through a priest who served as the god's medium. The term *oracle* could refer to the god's answer, the medium, or the shrine—here, Hermione refers to the answer that has been brought back to Leontes from the oracle at Delphos; 117 *Apollo* in ancient Greek mythology, the god of the sun [*Apollo be my judge* May Apollo be my judge].

COMMENTARY

If you're searching for a high-stakes, straightforward, elegant, yet gut-wrenching monologue, you've found it. Hermione's inherent dignity and integrity and her utter guiltlessness radiate from her words, as do a sense of confidence and power born of her lack of fear. She knows that she is innocent and believes in the oracle's power to vindicate her. And should it fail to do so, she would welcome death, since, as she explains, Leontes has already stripped her of all that makes life worth living.

Hermione wisely presents an emotional statement rather than a legal argument. Better than anyone, Leontes should know her to be incapable of committing the transgression of which he accuses her. Since he is clearly being irrational, rational arguments based on evidence and logic would be futile. So Hermione turns the tables and illustrates how *Leontes* has wronged *her*. Hermione contrasts herself, a queen who gave birth in a cold stone cell, with women of all walks of life who are able to give birth and remain in their own beds. She contrasts the love Leontes once bestowed upon her with his current withholding of it; the *blessings* of her former life with her current lack of blessings; the common fear of death with her own welcome of it; the worthlessness of her life with the high value of her honor; *surmises* with *proofs*; and Leontes as judge with *Apollo*; and she uses the antithesis of *rigor* versus *law*. Don't forget that although she addresses almost all of this speech to Leontes, Hermione is speaking in an outdoor public forum before throngs of interested subjects and therefore appeals to them from the onset as surely as she appeals to her husband. Yet she is not being calculating: Hermione's deep-felt hurt and betrayal emerge clearly.

Hermione's straightforward manner is reflected in strings of short, direct words, which in turn highlight those that are longer. For example, *commodity*, *infectious*, *innocent*, *honor*, and *condemned* conspicuously contrast with the stretches of one-syllable words that precede or surround them. Hermione's clipped words, her use of pointed attention-getting phrases (*yet hear this*; *mistake me not*; *I tell you*), and her colloquial use of the proverbial *I prize it not a straw* also communicate her scorn for the proceedings against her. Precision is also important in two instances where one word ends and the next begins with the same letter (*out to* in line 102 and *proofs sleeping* in line 113). Be careful to enunciate each word separately, rather than slurring the abutting letters together. Similarly, many words end in the letter *t*—it is important to sound them rather than dropping them as we do in common speech. Notice what this does to Hermione's defiant delivery. In line 101, Hermione's repetition of *innocent* hammers home the egregiousness of Leontes' act—not only against Hermione, but also against his blameless newborn daughter. Remember that Hermione is most likely still lactating. Imagine the mental and physical pain she must feel at producing milk to nourish a murdered child. This is supported by the Incredulous IHs and Mourning Ms of *The innocent milk in it most innocent mouth*.

Where Hermione does use images, they are simple, unliterary, and perfect. Her sparing imagery (such as *The bug which you would fright me with*; *The crown and comfort of my life*; *like one infectious*; *all proofs sleeping else / But what your jealousies awake*) contrasts poignantly with her stark descriptions of her situation (such as *is from my breast . . . to murder*; *myself . . . Proclaimed a strumpet*; *with immodest hatred . . . denied*; *hurried / Here . . . before / I have got strength of limit*; *no life . . . but for mine honor*; etc.). She appeals to her audience's reverence for motherhood with visceral images that remind her listeners that she has literally given of her self for her children (*first-fruits of my body*; *milk*). These images also remind those present of the harm Leontes has done to their children. Hermione has demonstrated her commitment to her children's welfare; as she has expressed earlier in the scene, she wishes to preserve her honor not for her own sake, but to prevent her son from being tainted by association.

Hermione's use of the emphatic form (*I do give lost, for I do feel it gone* and *I do refer me to the oracle*) at the beginning and at the end of the monologue underscores her important final point to Leontes: because you have turned against me without provocation or justification, you are unqualified to judge me and I turn to the oracle for the final word. Her declaration illustrates a pervasive theme of the romance: human dependence upon fate.

SIGNIFICANT SCANS

Hermione's first line is shared with Leontes; his three feet of text have been excised. She jumps right in on the heels of his line, and moves decisively forward from there.

The monologue contains many double endings, both at line ends and midline before caesuras. There are not as many inverted feet, causing the few there are to stand out (such as the atrocious crime *Haled out* to *murder* or Hermione's forceful *Tell me*).

The final line has only three feet of spoken text. Own and use the remaining two feet of silence . . . perhaps to stare down Leontes, perhaps to establish eye contact with the court officers and your subjects, or perhaps for a private prayer to Apollo to set matters aright.

Don't forget to elide: *innocent* (INN-cent) both times it appears in line 101;

. . . and to contract: *I am* (I'm) in line 99 and *i' th' open* (ith-O-pen) in line 106.

Note: this monologue is the heart of Hermione's passionate and eloquent "defense" speech from the trial scene. It stands beautifully on its own, but if you're interested in performing an even longer piece, more material is there for the taking.

THE WINTER'S TALE

ACT III, SCENE ii

PAULINA

GENDER: F
PROSE/VERSE: blank verse
AGE RANGE: mature adult
FREQUENCY OF USE (1–5): 3

As a lady of the Sicilian court and a close companion to Queen Hermione, Paulina (Paw-LIE-nuh) has been dismayed and outraged by King Leontes' recent behavior. He foolishly allowed his unfounded jealousy to rule him, accusing his devoted and virtuous wife of an adulterous relationship with his childhood friend King Polixenes. He asked the honorable Lord Camillo to murder Polixenes, causing both of them to flee. He threw his very pregnant, innocent wife in jail and refused to let her see their little boy, Mamillius. When Hermione gave birth to a healthy girl, he called the baby a bastard and had her deserted in the wilderness. At his wife's trial, he ignored the words of the Delphic oracle, which exonerated her, and was just about to convict her when news arrived that Mamillius had died, which caused poor Hermione to faint. Paulina has just taken her friend from the courtroom, and has now returned. She exclaims:

Woe the while!
O cut my lace, lest my heart, cracking it,
175 Break too!

What studied torments, tyrant, hast for me?
What wheels? Racks? Fires? What flaying? Boiling?
In leads or oils? What old or newer torture
Must I receive, whose every word deserves
180 To taste of thy most worst? Thy tyranny,
Together working with thy jealousies—
Fancies too weak for boys, too green and idle
For girls of nine—O think what they have done,
And then run mad indeed, stark mad! For all
185 Thy bygone fooleries were but spices of it.
That thou betrayed'st Polixenes, 'twas nothing;
That did but show thee of a fool, inconstant
And damnable ingrateful. Nor was't much,
Thou would'st have poisoned good Camillo's honor,
190 To have him kill a king; poor trespasses—
More monstrous standing by: whereof I reckon
The casting forth to crows thy baby daughter
To be or none or little, though a devil
Would have shed water out of fire ere done't.

173 *Woe the while* The present time is full of woe (an exclamation of grief); 174 *lace* a cord that laces the bodice of a dress together (much like a shoelace) [*cut my lace* a common exclamation for an agitated woman in Shakespeare's time: dresses were tightly laced, restricting breathing]; *lest . . . Break too* i.e., so that my heart (which is beating wildly and needs more room) will not break the lace and itself as well; 176 *studied* carefully practiced; *hast* do you have; 177 *wheels* The wheel was a torture and execution device: after the victim's body was repeatedly smashed so that all the limbs were broken, he or she was laid out on the wheel with the limbs "braided" through the spokes. The wheel was then hoisted up on a pole and the victim died a long, slow death while being picked at by crows and leered at by crowds; *Racks* torture victims were often stretched on racks until their limbs were dislocated; 178 *In leads or oils* i.e., in cauldrons of molten lead or boiling oil (two common medieval and Renaissance torture mediums); 180 *most worst* Shakespeare often uses double superlatives for emphasis; 182 *Fancies* thoughts founded on imagination, rather than reason; *weak* (1) foolish, stupid; (2) base, contemptible; *green* simpleminded, as of an inexperienced youth; *idle* foolish, silly; 183 *they* i.e., Leontes' tyranny and jealousies; 185 *but* only; *spices* slight tastes, small samples; 187 *did but show thee of a fool* only showed you to be a fool; *inconstant* fickle, not to be relied on; 188 *damnable* damnably; 189 *Thou* that thou; 190 *poor trespasses— / More monstrous standing by* small, insignificant sins, in comparison with the monstrous ones you've committed; 192 *to crows* i.e., to be eaten by crows; 193 *or none or little* either nothing or little; 194 *shed water out of fire* (1) shed tears out of burning eyes; (2) shed tears while engulfed by hellfire; *ere done't* before he would have done it [*a devil . . . ere done't* i.e., a devil would have shed tears for the damned before

PAULINA

195 Nor is't directly laid to thee the death
Of the young Prince, whose honorable thoughts,
Thoughts high for one so tender, cleft the heart
That could conceive a gross and foolish sire
Blemished his gracious dam. This is not, no,
200 Laid to thy answer; but the last—O lords,
When I have said, cry "woe!"—the Queen, the Queen,
The sweet'st, dear'st creature's dead, and vengeance for't
Not dropped down yet.

But, O thou tyrant,
Do not repent these things, for they are heavier
210 Than all thy woes can stir. Therefore betake thee
To nothing but despair. A thousand knees
Ten thousand years together, naked, fasting,
Upon a barren mountain, and still winter
In storm perpetual, could not move the gods
215 To look that way thou wert.

2 minutes

committing such an action]; 195 *Nor is't directly . . . young Prince* two possible nuances: (1) Nor are you directly responsible for the death of the young Prince; (2) Nor can the young Prince's death be directly blamed on you; 197 *high* noble; *tender* i.e., young; *cleft* split apart; 198 *conceive* understand that; *gross* base; coarse; *sire* father; 199 *Blemished* stained the reputation of; dishonored; *dam* mother; 200 *Laid to thy answer* brought as a charge against which you must defend yourself; 201 *said* finished speaking; 203 *Not dropped down yet* i.e., has not yet been handed down from Heaven; 210 *woes can stir* remorseful lamentations can remove [*they are heavier . . . can stir* i.e., they are so heavy that repentance is impossible]; *betake thee* think of, address yourself to; 211 *knees* i.e., prayers recited while kneeling; 212 *together* without intermission; 213 *still winter* continuous winter; 215 *To look that way thou wert* i.e., even to glance in your direction; to take any notice of you.

COMMENTARY

Paulina has let the King know her opinions before, but in the past she was trying to change his mind and his actions. Now it's too late for that, and Paulina has new objectives, which, depending on your interpretation, may range from making the King realize the enormity of his errors to causing him pain for what he has done. She may even wish to teach him a lesson. Until now, Paulina has been bold and defiant but in control; now she can no longer hold back her rage. With the help of this monologue's meter, it all comes pouring out. Almost every new accusation Paulina makes begins and ends mid-line, where the pause taken is slightly shorter than at line ends. In combination with many agitated double endings and several inverted feet, the mid-line breaks propel Paulina's words in a forceful, continuous tirade.

This brings us to the most important question: what does Paulina hope to accomplish with this monologue? The answer hinges on whether Paulina believes that Hermione is alive or dead. It is important to know that at the end of the play Hermione will reappear: Paulina will present her as a statue that comes to life. The play leaves this decision up to the director—or, if you're preparing this piece independent of the play, to *you*. The more common interpretation is that Paulina seizes this opportunity to fake Hermione's death and get her friend out of Leontes' abusive clutches while punishing him for his abuses. Another widely accepted choice is that Paulina truly believes Hermione is dead—that everything she says to Leontes now is absolutely true, and only later does she discover that Hermione has recovered. But there are many other options as well: Hermione could truly be dead and be brought back to life later in the play by an act of God, magic, witchcraft, or some other supernatural means (perhaps by Paulina—in which case, you must decide whether she already knows that she has this ability). Whatever you decide, keep in mind that Paulina's pent-up rage is absolutely genuine.

Paulina expresses herself well, even in this agitated state. Her aggressive use of sarcasm establishes her disdain for Leontes (*I . . . whose every word deserves / To taste of thy most worst*), then creates a build in her description of the crimes for which he is "not" responsible. The build allows Paulina to deliver the news of the Queen's death much more powerfully than had she simply rushed in and announced it. In this manner, she makes Leontes' guilt in his wife's death devastatingly clear. But Paulina is also subtle: she implies an antithetical comparison between Leontes, whose *Fancies* are *green and idle* (and thus low-minded for one as old and experienced as he), and his dead son, whose *Thoughts* were *high for one so tender*. Also notice the unusual meter of the word *honorable* (ON′-er-UH-bl) in line 196—a word that is usually crowded or elided. Paulina's pronunciation emphasizes this quality of the Prince's, further shaming the King. And for help exploiting the expressive word *O* to its best advantage, see "O, No! An *O*!," page xxxiii.

The text also raises the question of how Paulina knows that the King has asked Camillo to poison Polixenes. It is possible that she overheard Leontes speaking of it in his regretful monologue just before her entrance, which is only likely in the case that she knows Hermione to be alive: she would not pause outside the door to eavesdrop if she were rushing in with *Woe the while!* in genuine response to Hermione's death. It is also possible that Camillo himself confided in Paulina before he left. The connection between them is not unlikely, as he is the King's most trusted lord at court and she is the Queen's most trusted lady.

Paulina has a privileged position in the court: the Queen entrusts her newborn to Paulina and the King allows her to go unpunished after she admonishes him for rejecting his daughter in Act II. This special relationship is borne out by the text, where she mentions Leontes' *bygone fooleries*, apparently referring to behavior that predates his irrational jealousy of Hermione. This suggests that Paulina's anger toward him began long before he went off his rocker a month ago. She also uses the familiar *thou*, inappropriate and disrespectful when directed toward one's sovereign. Paulina does switch to the more formal "you" just after this piece, when one of the lords points out that she has gone too far, and she relents. If you have the opportunity to perform a longer monologue, you could consider adding this additional text.

SIGNIFICANT SCANS

Because it is shared with Leontes, Paulina's first line has only one and a half feet. When performing the piece solo, you may either jump right in, moving on to the second line without a pause, or you may use the three and a half silent feet after the words, to collect yourself, to cry, to gauge the effect of your dramatic entrance on Leontes and the court, etc. Line 175 is also shared with Leontes. Here, however, the words complete the sentence begun on the preceding line, so you must use the four silent feet at the end of the line, to make the transition from lamentation to accusation.

Line 177 scans quite easily as iambic pentameter with a double ending. Note that the first syllables of the second and third feet are silent, as sometimes happens at caesuras:

x / x / x / x / x / (x)
What wheels? (pause) Racks? (pause) Fires? What flaying? Boiling?

Lines 203 and 208 are both short, due to lines that have been omitted. You may either take the six combined feet in between as a silent pause in which to make a transition, or you may combine the two lines, creating one neat line of iambic pentameter that has a silent third foot at the caesura and a double ending. We prefer this quicker transition:

x / x / x / x / x / (x)
Not dropped down yet. (pause-pause) But, O thou tyrant

Don't forget to elide: *fooleries* (FOOL-reez) in line 185; *betrayed'st* (be-TRAIDST) in line 186; *sweet'st* (SWEETST) and *dear'st* (deerst) in line 202; *heavier* (HEV-yer) in line 209; and *perpetual* (per-PEH-tchwul) in line 214;

. . . and to contract: *was't* (wazt) in line 188; *done't* (DUNT) in line 194; *is't* (IZT) in line 195; and *for't* (FORT) in line 202.

THE WINTER'S TALE

ACT III, SCENE iii

SHEPHERD

GENDER: M
AGE RANGE: mature adult to older adult
PROSE/VERSE: prose
FREQUENCY OF USE (1–5): 1

The old Shepherd was minding his own business—and his own sheep—when two of his best animals were scared off by noisy young hunters. He would like nothing better than to find his missing sheep and get in out of the storm that has just begun to blow. He complains to himself as he searches:

60 I would there were no age between ten and three-and-twenty, or that youth would sleep out the rest; for there is nothing in the between but getting wenches with child, wronging the ancientry, stealing, fighting—Hark you now! Would any but these
65 boiled-brains of nineteen and two-and-twenty hunt this weather? They have scared away two of my best sheep, which I fear the wolf will sooner find than the master. If anywhere I have them, 'tis by the seaside, browsing of ivy. Good luck and't be Thy
70 will! What have we here? Mercy on's, a barne, a very pretty barne! A boy or a child, I wonder? A pretty one, a very pretty one: sure, some scape! Though I am not bookish, yet I can read waiting-gentlewoman in the scape. This has been some
75 stair-work, some trunk-work, some behind-door work. They were warmer that got this than the poor thing is here. I'll take it up for pity; yet I'll tarry till my son come. He halloed but even now. Whoa, ho, hoa!

1 minute, 15 seconds

60 *would* wish; 61 *sleep out the rest* i.e., sleep through the intervening years; 62 *in the between* i.e., between those ages; 63 *ancientry* old age (here, i.e., old people); 64 *Hark you* Listen; *any but* anyone except; 65 *boiled-brains* conveys both (1) addle-brained youths and (2) hotheaded youths; 66 *this* in this; 68 *If anywhere I have them* If I find them anywhere; 69 *browsing of* nibbling at; *ivy* i.e., sea ivy (which could mean either seaweed or sea holly [which grows in sand dunes and was used as an aphrodisiac in Shakespeare's time]); *Good luck and't be Thy will* Send me good luck if it is Your will; 70 *Mercy on's* from "God have mercy on us"; here, an exclamation of surprise; *barne* (pronounced barn or bairn) small child (northern dialect, only used by uneducated characters in Shakespeare); 71 *child* baby girl (a term from English West Country dialect); 72 *sure* surely, certainly; *scape* escapade (often, as here, a sexual transgression); 73 *bookish* fond of books and reading, literary (here, literate); *waiting-gentlewoman* gentlewoman who attends a lady in her chamber [*yet I can read . . . scape* the Shepherd surmises that an unmarried waiting-gentlewoman has become pregnant, and has had to deliver her child in secret and get rid of it to avoid losing her reputation and livelihood]; 75 *trunk-work* a pun on *trunk* meaning (1) secret place and (2) part of the body; 76 *that got this* who begot this baby; 77 *for* out of; 78 *tarry* wait; *halloed* shouted; *but even now* just now.

COMMENTARY

The word *teenager* may have been invented in the twentieth century but as the Shepherd can tell you, the shenanigans of adolescence are centuries old.

You will need to consider whether the Shepherd addresses his complaints about these hooligans to himself (or perhaps his sheepdog) or whether he directly addresses the audience for part or all of the monologue. Pay particular attention to the phrase *Hark you now*, which can be used very effectively to engage the audience, drawing their attention either to the raucous sounds of the hunters (which prove your previous point) or to your next comment.

It is essential to address the physicality both of the character and his circumstances. First, the Shepherd is, by his own count, an old man. Although he is only sixty-seven (and will see eighty-three by the play's end), he already counts himself as one of the *ancientry* who are wronged by youth. In Shakespeare's day, people—especially the hardworking poor—aged much more quickly than they do today. Thus, scrambling around after his sheep is probably not easy for the Shepherd. To make matters worse, a bad storm has begun to blow—as this scene is taking place, a ship is being wrecked just off shore.

Shakespeare's use of some well-placed words from rural dialects conveys the Shepherd's parochial quality, which is enhanced by the old man's mild misuse of words like *bookish* and *ancientry*, as well as euphemisms like *scape*, *stair-work*, *trunk-work*, and *behind-door work*. There's no need to try to pin down a particular accent, as none is really intended—this is Bohemia, where no one speaks English anyway.

The string of euphemisms in lines 75–76 (*stair-work*, *trunk-work*, and *behind-door work*) have two possible meanings. Some believe they refer to the manner in which "ze lovair" gained access to "ze beloved" (i.e., using the back stairs or hiding in trunks and behind doors). Others insist that the phrases refer more specifically to the sites of "ze rendezvous" themselves. Feel free to interpret them as you like. Another question that is often raised is that of the wide spread in ages mentioned by the Shepherd. Some even go so far as to replace the word *ten* with "sixteen." Surely this is unnecessary. The Shepherd is a comic character; maybe it's supposed to be funny! Perhaps he's using a wide age range to be sure he's covered both the precocious and the late bloomers. Also, the juxtaposition of *ten* and *three-and-twenty* is much funnier (both in how the words sound and in the images they conjure up) than "sixteen" and "three-and-twenty."

One last note: some editors have added a stage direction indicating that the Shepherd picks up the baby when he finds it. Conversely, you could interpret the words *yet I'll tarry* to mean not only that he'll wait for his son before going home, but also that he'll wait until then to do anything about the child. It's possible that he's initially nervous about touching or lifting the baby. Be sure to make a choice about exactly how *you* react to the child, and what you see or hear of it.

Synopses

WE'VE ALL BEEN THERE BEFORE . . .

Your agent has just called at the last minute with the audition of a lifetime. You have two hours to prepare your audition for a role in *Henry VIII*. You've got your all-purpose Shakespearean monologue prepared, but you'll probably also be asked to read sides from the play—and you've never read it! Well, we've included these synopses to help you out on just such an occasion, and also to help you wend your way through the more difficult-to-understand scenes and plot twists in the plays as you read them. In no way are these synopses intended to replace your reading the plays, however, when you're not under the gun. We cannot stress enough how helpful and important it is when preparing your monologues to *read the play*.

THE HISTORIES

KING JOHN

Shakespeare's audience had an advantage over us when watching *King John*—and all of the Histories. Elizabethans were as familiar with the succession of past kings to the English throne as Americans were more recently with the succession of Elizabeth Taylor's husbands. So we'll set the scene for you: following the death of King Richard I (Richard the Lion-Hearted), his younger brother John took the throne with the help of their mother, Queen Elinor of Aquitaine, thwarting the claim of John's nephew Arthur (son of John's dead older brother Geoffrey). Arthur's mother, Constance, Duchess of Brittany (a region in France controlled by the English at the time), wants to overthrow King John and instate her son as king. She has secured the backing of King Philip of France, who would be more than happy to see the young, malleable, half-French Arthur on the throne. (Still confused? See "Genealogical Chart for *King John*," page 231.) Now on to the play:

King John and his mother Queen Elinor receive a demand from King Philip of France that they relinquish the throne to Arthur or else King Philip's forces will attack. King John ups the ante: not only will he keep his throne, but he'll invade France too.

Then Robert Faulconbridge and his illegitimate half-brother Philip (known affectionately as "the Bastard") arrive at the court to ask the King to settle a dispute over which of them should inherit their late father's land. Although their father raised Philip as his son, Philip is rumored to be the love child of the deceased King Richard. Queen Elinor notes that the Bastard looks and acts *exactly* like Richard, and she offers her newfound grandson a position in her court if he will relinquish the land to Robert. The Bastard jumps at the opportunity, and is knighted on the spot—goodbye, small town; hello, big leagues! He's glad his mother fooled around with a king.

Cut to the French city of Angiers, occupied by the English. Outside the city walls, King Philip of France, his son Lewis (known affectionately as "the Dauphin," the title given to the heir to the French throne), Constance, little Arthur, and their troops, supported by the Archduke of Austria (known affectionately as "Austria") and his troops, are all met by King John, his Spanish niece Blanch (don't ask us why), Queen Elinor, the Bastard, and their forces. Each side demands to be admitted as the rightful ruler of Angiers, but the citizens tell them to fight it out among themselves, and they'll give allegiance to whoever wins. The women leave; the men skirmish. No winner—the city gates remain barred. The Bastard suggests that the two sides gang up on the city. They easily agree and are preparing to do so when it is proposed that instead they marry off Blanch and Lewis, who are happy to oblige. Again, self-interest prevails and they broker a deal in which King John gives France some land as Blanch's dowry, and in exchange France recognizes John as the rightful English king. As for little Arthur, he'll get to rule over little Angiers. Everyone heads into the city for the wedding, but the Bastard stays behind to soliloquize his view of the self-serving kings.

When Constance learns that King Philip has sold out her son, she is naturally fit to be tied. She rants. In a big way. And when the kings and the newlyweds return, she rants at them. Now the plot thickens: Pandulph, an ambassador from the Pope, has tracked down King John with a message from Rome. John reiterates his refusal to let the Pope choose the next archbishop of Canterbury, and is promptly excommunicated by Pandulph, who then threatens to excommunicate King Philip as well, unless he renounces the brand-new treaty and mobilizes his army against King John immediately. Philip is an obedient Catholic, so—it's war! Poor Blanch is torn between her uncle and her new husband.

A battle ensues. The Bastard has decapitated Austria (who he believes was responsible for his father, King Richard's, death) and enters carrying Austria's head. King John sends the Bastard back to England to loot the churches to finance the war. Little Arthur has been captured by the English. John turns him over to his adviser Hubert for safekeeping, hinting that were Hubert truly loyal, he would kill the boy.

In the French camp, King Philip, the Dauphin, and Pandulph bemoan the fact that King John has taken Angiers. Constance, grief-stricken and almost mad over her son's capture, arrives ranting, rants, and leaves ranting. King Philip follows, to make sure she doesn't do anything drastic. Pandulph urges Lewis to seek the English throne for himself, since his marriage to Blanch gives him a valid claim. The English will be receptive to Lewis, since they'll be angry at John for killing Arthur (as everyone assumes he'll do) and for looting the churches (always an unpopular move). They head off to get King Philip's go-ahead.

Back in England, in the play's most gut-wrenching scene, Hubert prepares to put out Arthur's eyes with hot irons. Arthur can't believe that his beloved Hubert would do such a thing to him after the loving rapport they've established, and poignantly entreats him to reconsider. After a harrowing exchange Hubert relents, but explains that he must pretend to King John that he has carried out his orders.

Two earls urge King John to free Arthur, as England's nobles are growing increasingly disgruntled about the boy's imprisonment. Hubert enters with the "news" of Arthur's death and the earls storm out in anger, leaving King John to repent having Arthur killed. His day goes from bad to worse: he learns that the French have attacked, Constance has died "in a frenzy," and his beloved mother, Elinor, is also dead. He is devastated. The day gets worse yet: the Bastard, arriving with the loot he's extorted from the churches, reports growing uneasiness across the land and fury among the nobles over Arthur's death. John sends the Bastard to gather the noblemen together, then turns on Hubert, blaming him for Arthur's death. When Hubert reveals the truth, King John is thrilled and sends him to get the boy, so he can display him and appease the angry nobles.

Meanwhile, Arthur, attempting to escape, jumps off the castle walls to his death. Outside the castle, three discontented English nobles are planning their defection to the invading French when they encounter the Bastard. The four discover little Arthur's broken body. The noblemen blame Hubert, who coincidentally arrives. Hubert is genuinely surprised and horrified by the sight of the dead boy, but the nobles don't believe him. They move to kill him, but are prevented by the Bastard. Arthur's death has deeply distressed the Bastard, who feels that events are spiraling out of control.

To appease the Pope, King John makes England a papal fief, in a ceremony in which he surrenders his crown to Pandulph and receives it back. As part of the bargain, Pandulph agrees to stop the French attack and goes off to do so. The Bastard arrives, reporting that the regions of Kent and London have surrendered to the French; furthermore, Arthur's death has provoked the English nobles to defect to the French. The Bastard is vexed to learn of King John's deal with the Pope—he wants to fight the French. King John agrees and places the campaign in the Bastard's hands.

At the French camp, the English nobles wrap up their deal with the French, although they regret that circumstances have forced them to turn against their own country. Pandulph enters and orders a cease-fire, but Lewis couldn't care less about some deal between the Pope and King John—he defiantly refuses to give up his push for the English throne. The Bastard arrives and, upon learning that the Dauphin will not back down, says that King John will be delighted to tear the Dauphin's troops to shreds. Both sides prepare to fight.

On the battlefield: King John tells Hubert that he's sick with a fever. He receives good news that the Dauphin's reinforcements have been shipwrecked crossing the Channel, and the French are retreating. King John leaves for Swinstead Abbey, to rest.

Meanwhile, Melun, a mortally wounded French noble, confesses to the defected English nobles that the Dauphin has deceived and used them—if he wins today, he intends to put them to death tonight. The nobles are glad for the excuse to switch their allegiance back to their own king.

A messenger briefs Lewis on the day's bad news (Melun dead; English lords vamoosed; reinforcements drowned). The one silver lining is King John's flight to Swinstead. Yippee!

Speaking of King John, he's dying. In Swinstead, Hubert tells the Bastard that John has been poisoned by a monk. His son, Prince Henry, is with him, and at the young man's request, John has pardoned the traitorous nobles. Hubert and the Bastard hurry to join the King.

In the abbey, the young Prince and the newly repentant nobles mourn his father's imminent death. As John writhes in pain, the Bastard rushes to his side and reports that most of his own troops have drowned in a flood, and that the Dauphin's troops are advancing. On that note, King John dies. The nobles update the Bastard: within the last hour, Pandulph has brought an acceptable offer of peace from the Dauphin, and the truce will be finalized that afternoon. The Bastard swears fealty to Prince Henry (soon to be

King Henry III), as do the nobles. The Bastard patriotically wraps up the play, proclaiming that England can never be conquered as long as its people remain loyal and united.

Dramatic Damage Control

Shakespeare seems to have interrupted his sequence of plays about the kings involved in the "Major Tetralogy" (*Richard II*; *Henry IV, Parts One* and *Two*; and *Henry V*) to write about a much earlier English monarch—King John. What caused him to shift his focus temporarily? Perhaps he was seeking to appease his Queen, Elizabeth I. After all, his last History play, *Richard II*—whether intentionally or not—drew rather uncomplimentary parallels between Richard and Elizabeth (see "The History of a History," page 905). *King John* draws very different parallels between John and Elizabeth (which would have been obvious to the Elizabethans, who all knew their English history as well as they knew their ABCs): both were designated as heirs to the English throne by reigning siblings who were on their deathbeds, the legitimacy of both reigns was challenged, and both were excommunicated by the Catholic Church. Shakespeare used these similarities to loyal and supportive ends in *King John*, which champions the importance of a strong reign over that of a "legitimate" one. Phew! Queen pleased, Shakespeare could now turn back to completing his tetralogy.

Revisionist History: The Theme Justifies the Means

The historical King John and the events of his life are mere jumping-off points for Shakespeare's play. In *King John*, the events of many years are condensed into a much shorter period and the legend of John's poisoning by a monk is reported as fact. In addition, although the historical John was despised by nobles and commoners alike, Shakespeare's audience sees the play—and John—through the eyes of the Bastard, who is loyal to John through thick and thin. Most significantly, Shakespeare altered the context of the conflict between John and little Arthur. Although Richard I initially chose Arthur (the next in line according to primogeniture) as his heir, he changed his mind on his deathbed, asking his barons to swear fealty to John as their next king. The concept of primogeniture was fairly new to England in the twelfth century, having been recently introduced by the Normans, while the tradition of monarchs designating their heirs, and that of brothers inheriting the right to rule, had been accepted for centuries. So although they may not have liked him much, John's subjects generally accepted him as the rightful heir to the English throne, and saw Arthur's challenge as an attempt to usurp his power. Shakespeare manipulated this situation to create the thematic conflict for his play, taking advantage of his sixteenth-century audience's unquestioning acceptance of the concept of primogeniture.

Magna Carta: No Ado About Something

By the way, you may have noticed that Shakespeare has basically ignored the incident for which King John is most famous today—the signing of the Magna Carta. That's because the Magna Carta was originally intended and understood as a document giving limited rights to a small number of English nobles. It wasn't until four hundred years later, during the century after Shakespeare's death, that lawyers began to interpret the Magna Carta as an important document granting to all English citizens the essential rights of trial by jury, habeas corpus, and parliamentary government to control taxation.

RICHARD II

Although King Richard II reigned for twenty-two eventful years, Shakespeare's play focuses on the King's action-packed final year in power and his inevitable downfall.

Lights up on the court of King Richard II. The King's first cousin, Henry Bolingbroke, Duke of Hereford, brings charges of treason against Thomas Mowbray, Duke of Norfolk. Bolingbroke accuses Mowbray of the murder of Thomas of Woodstock, Duke of Gloucester, uncle of both Bolingbroke and the King. Mowbray denies the allegations and challenges Bolingbroke to a duel to defend his honor. King Richard consents to let them duke it out in mortal combat and sets the date.

Later, the Duchess of Gloucester urges Bolingbroke's father, John of Gaunt, to avenge the murder of his brother, her late husband the Duke. Gaunt refuses because he believes that it was the King, not Mowbray, who was responsible for the murder, and since kings are God's deputies, only God may punish them (see "Riding Shotgun with God," page 235).

The Day of the Big Fight: trumpets sound; the crowds go wild. Mowbray and Bolingbroke face off, but King Richard suddenly cancels the duel to avoid bloodshed. To prevent further conflict on English soil, both men are banished: Mowbray for life and Bolingbroke for ten years, reduced to six 'cause they're kin. Gaunt is despondent, knowing he's too old and feeble to live until his son returns. Before departing, Mowbray warns that the King may trust Bolingbroke now, but he'll be sorry soon enough. Left alone, Gaunt and Bolingbroke bid each other a touching adieu.

Edward, Duke of Aumerle (another first cousin of both Bolingbroke and the King), has pretended to support Bolingbroke, but now visits King Richard and speaks disparagingly of their banished cousin. The King confides in Aumerle that he fears Bolingbroke's popularity with the commoners and doesn't look forward to his return. The conversation shifts to talk of squashing rebellions in Ireland: Richard plans to go fight in person, and will fund the war effort by leasing royal lands and squeezing the rich. He is therefore delighted to receive the news that Uncle Gaunt is near death, and looks forward to seizing his estate to further supplement the royal treasury.

Gaunt, at home on his deathbed, tells his brother, Edmund, Duke of York (Aumerle's dad), that before he dies he hopes to impart some wisdom to King Richard. He feels that Richard's financial misdealings weaken his beloved England. York thinks he's wasting his dying breath. To prove him right, along comes King Richard, accompanied by the Queen, Aumerle, and a batch of nobles. When Gaunt admonishes King Richard to rule more honorably in the future, Richard says he'd cut off Gaunt's head for such words were he not Richard's uncle. Gaunt retorts that Richard shouldn't let that stop him, as he's already killed another uncle, Gloucester. Gaunt dies minutes later and King Richard immediately orders the confiscation of his uncle's property to pay for his expeditions in Ireland. York is horrified at this illegal seizure and tells him so, to no avail. After King Richard leaves with his entourage, Henry Percy, Earl of Northumberland, remains behind with two other nobles to gripe about the King's unjust taxes, his banishment of Bolingbroke, and his confiscation of the property Bolingbroke should have inherited. Northumberland confides that Bolingbroke has raised an army and will land in England as soon as the King has left for Ireland. The three plan to throw their lots in with him.

At the castle, Queen Isabel experiences one of those Shakespeareo-wifely moments, in which she bemoans King Richard's departure and has a premonition of impending disaster. Lo and behold, news arrives that Bolingbroke has returned to England and a gang of nobles has defected to him, including Northumberland and his son, the junior Henry Percy. York, who has been left in charge, is in a pickle: the King has left behind no armed forces and no money. Furthermore, York is torn between his two nephews: he owes duty to Richard, his king, but feels morally obliged to assist the wronged Bolingbroke. Confounded, he departs with the Queen.

Meanwhile, Bolingbroke and Northumberland meet up with Northumberland's son, the junior Henry Percy (referred to in later plays as "Hotspur"), who informs them that York and a pack of nobles are camped out with an army nearby. York arrives to chastise Bolingbroke for traitorously disobeying the royal order of banishment. Bolingbroke explains that since the right to sue has been denied him, the King left him no choice but to come in person to reclaim his confiscated property. York declares neutrality, and invites Bolingbroke and his supporters to spend the night in the castle.

King Richard, meanwhile, has not returned from Ireland, and his forces in Wales have received no word from him. They disperse, and, watching them go, the Earl of Salisbury experiences one of those Shakepeareo-bit-partly moments, in which he foresees the fall of his king.

When Richard finally returns to England, he is met by Aumerle and the Bishop of Carlisle. The King is an emotional yo-yo, believing one moment that God will defend His chosen sovereign, and despairing the next that Bolingbroke will prevail. Salisbury arrives and reports that Richard's troops in Wales have dispersed. News arrives that Richard's subjects are flocking to Bolingbroke, who has executed two of Richard's courtiers. Richard is despondent. The specters of his death and the demise of his reign haunt him. The news of York's defection is the last nail in the coffin—Richard admits his defeat, dismisses his troops, and retreats to Flint Castle.

Bolingbroke arrives outside Flint Castle, where he learns that King Richard is holed up inside. Bolingbroke sends Northumberland in to relay his terms to the King: if Richard will return his property and rescind his banishment, Bolingbroke will lay down his arms and swear his allegiance. Otherwise, it's war. Northumberland delivers the message, and Richard agrees to the terms. After Northumberland returns to Bolingbroke, Richard has a wee breakdown over the indignity of submitting to his own subject. Bolingbroke and Richard meet face to face. Although Bolingbroke has promised allegiance, Richard knows the score: he gives himself up into his more powerful cousin's custody, and they head for London.

In her garden, Queen Isabel overhears the gardeners discussing Richard's capture and likely deposition. She's always the first to suspect, and the last to know.

Bolingbroke has taken over Parliament. York arrives with the news flash that Richard has relinquished his crown. When Bolingbroke moves to take the throne, the Bishop of Carlisle calls him a traitor, condemns his supporters for substituting their choice of king for God's, predicts that this will result in civil war, and begs them to reconsider. No dice. The Bishop is arrested for treason and placed into the custody of the Abbot of Westminster. Richard is called for, to surrender in public. He arrives and hands over his power to Bolingbroke, and then is carried off to the Tower of London (where all of England's elite offenders were detained while awaiting their fates). After the court is cleared, Westminster, Carlisle, and Aumerle stay behind and begin to plot against Bolingbroke.

Isabel is comforting Richard when Northumberland arrives with the order that Richard be taken to Pomfret Castle, while Isabel is banished to France. Their pleas to stay together are ignored, and they bid each other a touching adieu.

Over at the Yorks' house, the Duke tells the Duchess that while he feels for Richard, his allegiance is to Bolingbroke, who is now King Henry IV. When the Duke discovers that his own son, Aumerle, is conspiring against the new king, he immediately sets out for London to inform on him. The Duchess urges her son to rush to the King, and to beg his pardon before the Duke arrives. Aumerle is the first to reach King Henry. He begs for a pardon, but before he can explain why he needs one, his father arrives and accuses him of treason. His mother comes in and begs mercy for her son, which the King grants.

Sir Pierce Exton, a noble, believing that King Henry wishes someone would knock off Richard, resolves to be the guy to do it. While Richard sits in prison ruing his situation, Exton rushes in with other murderers. A scuffle ensues: Richard kills a few of his assailants before being killed by Exton, who instantly regrets the deed.

Back at the palace, Northumberland reports the deaths of rebel leaders and the conspiring Abbot of Westminster. The Bishop of Carlisle is brought before King Henry, who pardons him for his speech in Parliament, wishing him well. Exton has borne Richard's coffin from Pomfret, and proudly presents the corpse to Henry. The King says that he's not pleased: although he benefits from the result of the deed, he loves neither the deed itself nor its doer. He banishes Exton and pledges to lead a crusade to the Holy Land to cleanse his conscience. The stage is set for *Henry IV, Part One*.

THE HISTORY OF A HISTORY

While all ten of Shakespeare's Histories recount parts of England's history, only *Richard II* actually plays a role in it. In 1601, Robert Devereux, Earl of Essex, one of Queen Elizabeth's longtime favorites, planned a coup against his aging sovereign. For inspiration, a few of Essex's supporters commissioned Shakespeare's company to perform *Richard II* the day before the coup. The play was already several years old and probably wouldn't draw much of a crowd, but the noblemen were willing to pay in advance, so how could the actors refuse? The day after the performance, Essex and his two hundred men rode into London, spurred on by the play's theme of a monarch deposed. Alas for Essex, his coup was defeated and he was tried, convicted, and beheaded. The players feared for their own heads, but fortunately for Shakespeare, for the Lord Chamberlain's Men, and for us, the players were absolved of any wrongdoing in the matter, and went on to produce many more of Shakespeare's plays.

HENRY IV, PART ONE

Shakespeare considered Henry IV important enough to name two plays after him . . . but not important enough to make him the star of either one (he played a much bigger role in *Richard II*, in which he deposed King Richard). *Henry IV, Part One* focuses on his wayward son and heir Prince Henry (a.k.a. "Harry," a.k.a. "Hal"), the young and rash Harry "Hotspur" Percy, and the old and dissolute Sir John Falstaff.

King Henry and his second son, John, are planning a crusade to the Holy Land. Sadly, it will have to be postponed: news arrives that the Welsh rebel lord Owen Glendower has captured Edmund Mortimer, Earl of March, and slain many of his troops. Furthermore, young Henry (a.k.a. "Harry," a.k.a. "Hotspur") Percy has successfully led English troops to victory against Scottish rebels in the north and has captured their leader, the fierce Archibald, Earl of Douglas (a.k.a. "the Douglas"). It disappoints King Henry to compare Hotspur's valor with his own Harry's profligacy. The King is also upset that Hotspur refuses to turn over the prisoners he has taken.

At Prince Hal's, the Prince and his drinking buddy, old Sir John Falstaff, are joined by their cohort Edward (a.k.a. "Yedward," a.k.a. "Ned") Poins, who invites them to participate in a little highway robbery masterminded by his crony, Gadshill. Falstaff jumps at the chance. Hal declines, but after Falstaff leaves, Poins convinces him to play a prank on Falstaff: Hal and Poins will accompany the others to the robbery site, but at the last minute will disguise themselves, ambush Falstaff and the others right after the heist, and steal the loot from them. They look forward to hearing Falstaff's spurious version of the events later on. When Poins leaves, Hal soliloquizes that when the time comes, he will throw off his dissolute ways and prove an excellent ruler, believing that he will be all the more appreciated when his reformation is contrasted with his present debauchery.

Back at the palace, King Henry meets with Hotspur, Henry Percy, Earl of Northumberland (Hotspur's father), and Thomas Percy, Earl of Worcester (Northumberland's brother). Hotspur explains that he never refused to relinquish his Scottish prisoners to the King. When the King's emissary arrived at the battlefield to claim them, he insulted the nearby wounded and dead English soldiers. He then mistook Hotspur's angry response for a refusal to yield the prisoners. In fact, Hotspur would be happy to turn them over . . . as soon as the King ransoms his brother-in-law, Edmund Mortimer, Earl of March, who was taken prisoner by Owen Glendower. But since Mortimer has married Glendower's daughter, King Henry believes he has defected. Henry refuses to ransom Mortimer and leaves in a huff. Left alone, the three Percys rail against the King's lack of gratitude for the aid they lent him when he deposed Richard II. Worcester proposes a rebellion. They agree on a plan in which Hotspur will free his Scottish prisoners and obtain Scotland's help in raising an army, while Northumberland secures the aid of Richard Scroop, the Archbishop of York (who hates King Henry for killing his brother). Worcester will go to Wales to secure the backing of Glendower and Mortimer.

At a roadside inn outside London, Gadshill confirms that the travelers he and his buddies plan to rob are, indeed, setting out for London shortly, carrying gobs of gold. Gadshill doesn't fear being hanged if caught, since he has friends in high places. Later, Prince Hal, Poins, Gadshill, Falstaff, and two others, Peto and Bardolph, prepare to waylay their victims. At the last minute, Hal and Poins discreetly duck out and disguise themselves. The others successfully ambush and rob their targets, after which Hal and Poins, unrecognized by their associates, ambush and rob them. The four thieves run for their lives.

At the Percy estate, Hotspur is annoyed that one of the nobles has R.S.V.P.-ed that he will not be attending the rebellion. Hotspur's wife, Lady Percy (a.k.a. "Kate"), has noticed that he's been agitated lately, and asks him to confide in her. He demurs, saying he must leave immediately, but will send for her.

Later, in the Boar's Head Tavern, a pub and inn in the slummy Eastcheap neighborhood of London, Prince Hal and Poins meet up with their cronies. Falstaff accuses Hal and Poins of chickening out before the robbery. True to form, he concocts an outlandish story of his bravery when attacked by a dozen—no, make that fifty—thieves, who robbed him of the loot and left him alive only because he single-handedly, swashbucklingly fought his way to safety. Prince Hal reveals that it was he and Poins, disguised, who robbed them, and they've got the loot to prove it. Falstaff retorts that he knew it all along, and only feigned ignorance because he could never harm the heir to the throne. A messenger arrives summoning Hal to King Henry's court first thing in the morning, because Hotspur, Glendower, and others have sparked a rebellion. Falstaff and Hal conduct a mock interview between Hal and the King. They are interrupted by the arrival of the Sheriff, who is looking for the robbers. Falstaff hides, while Hal gets rid of the Sheriff.

At a summit meeting in Wales, Hotspur, Worcester, Glendower, and Mortimer finalize the terms of their alliance and plan to join forces at Shrewsbury. Glendower and Hotspur can't stand each other—their sniping almost breaks the deal. Lady Mortimer and Lady Percy are brought in to bid their husbands farewell, and the men depart to initiate the rebellion.

Back at the palace, King Henry chews out Prince Hal for being a disgrace. Hal claims he's not as much of a disgrace as rumor would have him, but sincerely apologizes for the wrongdoing he has committed. He vows to redeem himself and make his father proud by defeating Hotspur at Shrewsbury. The King assigns him to lead some of the forces.

Later, at the Boar's Head Tavern, Falstaff has a dispute with the Hostess (the tavern's proprietor). He refuses to pay the money he owes her, and accuses her of having picked his pocket. Happily for her, Prince Hal arrives and discloses that Falstaff had no money in his pocket to pick. Hal has assigned Falstaff a command in the infantry; he will receive his orders when they meet the next day.

At Shrewsbury, Hotspur, Worcester, and the Douglas are dismayed to hear that Northumberland is too sick to bring his troops. Hotspur is not deterred by the absence of his father's troops—if they can win this battle without him, they will seem invincible when he joins them. News arrives of the King's large and powerful forces advancing from three directions. Hotspur can't wait to fight them, particularly Prince Hal. He doesn't even flinch when he hears that Glendower and his troops have been detained. They'll just have to win without Northumberland and Glendower, or die trying.

On the march toward Shrewsbury, Falstaff soliloquizes about having accepted payoffs to exempt men from the draft, pressing beggars and prisoners into service instead. Prince Hal meets up with him and urges him to hurry to the battlefield with his men. Falstaff secretly hopes he'll arrive when the battle is over.

In the rebel camp, Hotspur and the Douglas are chomping at the bit to fight, while Worcester wants to wait for reinforcements, since they are vastly outnumbered by the King's forces. Their dispute is interrupted when an emissary arrives from the King. Henry asks for a list of the rebels' grievances. If they're reasonable, he will address them and pardon the rebels. Hotspur doesn't trust the King to keep his word, since he has already broken many vows to those who helped him in the past. Nevertheless, he agrees to send his uncle Worcester to speak with the King in person.

In York, the Archbishop worries that the rebels are seriously outnumbered at Shrewsbury, and are likely to be defeated.

The next morning in the King's camp, Worcester reiterates the rebels' grievances. Hal suggests saving the lives of thousands of soldiers by resolving the conflict in a single bout of hand-to-hand combat between Hotspur and himself. The King rejects this solution. He sends Worcester back with an ultimatum; either they accept his gracious offer to be pardoned, or they fight. After the meeting breaks up, Falstaff asks Hal to protect him in the battle, but Hal says he's on his own, and leaves. Falstaff soliloquizes that honor is not worth dying over.

Worcester decides not to tell Hotpsur of the King's offer, fearing that if Hotspur were to accept the deal, the King would eventually punish them all anyway. He tells his nephew that the battle's on, and relates Hal's challenge to single combat. Hotspur looks forward to the rendezvous, and urges all to prepare for battle.

Battle scene: the rebels are fighting well. Falstaff has led his ragamuffin troops to their demise. He encounters Prince Hal, who needs to borrow a weapon and is furious to discover a bottle of booze in Falstaff's pistol case instead. Later in the battle, King Henry encourages his sons to quit fighting for the day, but they refuse and reenter the fray. The Douglas arrives and attacks the King, but Hal returns and fights him off, forcing him to flee. The King tells his son that he has redeemed himself. After he leaves Hotspur enters, and he and Hal finally cross swords. As they fight, Falstaff enters, followed shortly by the Douglas, and they spar as well. Falstaff feigns death, and the Douglas leaves him. Prince Hal kills Hotspur and pauses to speak kindly of his fallen foe. He then discovers Falstaff on the ground, and says a few words about him as well. After he leaves, Falstaff gets up, dusts himself off, spies Hotspur's corpse, and decides to take credit for killing him. He stabs the corpse in the thigh to bloody his sword, slings the body over his shoulder, and is about to walk off when the two princes return. They are surprised to see him alive, and even more surprised by his claim to have killed Hotspur. When Hal asserts the truth, Falstaff explains that both he and Hotspur were simply "down and out of breath"—after Hal left, they got up and fought each other, and Falstaff killed Hotspur with this serious wound to his thigh. Hal says he'll go along with the story if it will benefit his friend.

Victory for the King's forces! Worcester has been captured and is to lose his head, and King Henry grants Hal's request to be permitted to dispose of the Douglas as he sees fit. He sees fit to pardon and release him for the valor he has shown in the battle. The rebels Northumberland, the Archbishop of York, and Glendower remain at large. King Henry prepares to face them . . .

HENRY IV, PART TWO

As the title suggests, the saga continues: when last we met our hero King Henry (who, as we said on page 906, isn't actually the main character of the play), he was fighting against a group of English, Scottish, and Welsh rebels. His forces had just won a battle at Shrewsbury, defeating the Scots and the English nobleman Henry "Hotspur" Percy, leaving Hotspur's dad (the Earl of Northumberland), the Archbishop of York, and the Welsh leader Owen Glendower still to be dealt with. *Henry IV, Part Two* takes up the story where *Part One* left off.

False reports that Hotspur's rebel forces were victorious at Shrewsbury have spread and have reached Hotspur's father, Northumberland, in his castle, where rumor has it he lies feigning illness. Northumberland is very excited for about two seconds, until conflicting news arrives that the rebels have been defeated and that Hotspur is dead. This report is confirmed by the arrival of Morton, who was an eyewitness. He reports that the King has sent his son Prince John of Lancaster and the Earl of Westmoreland with troops to capture Northumberland—whose illness suddenly improves. He throws away his crutch and resolves to fight. Morton tells him that the Archbishop of York is also preparing to fight the King.

Sir John Falstaff, a longtime crony of Prince Hal, heir to the throne (who, until recently, has been notoriously debauched), meets up with his long-standing nemesis, the Lord Chief Justice, the highest-ranking judicial officer in England. The Chief Justice complains that Falstaff repeatedly ignored a summons concerning a robbery he is accused of, and Falstaff makes the excuse that he couldn't answer the summons because he had to go fight against the rebels. He then tries to borrow money from the Chief Justice, which prompts the Justice's hasty exit. Falstaff (no spring chicken) then remarks that his limp, caused by gout, will appear to be from a war injury, which will get him a bigger pension.

Rebel strategy meeting at the Archbishop's palace: the Archbishop, Lord Hastings, Lord Thomas Mowbray, and Lord Bardolph discuss whether they should wait for Northumberland's troops before fighting the King. Hastings says that they should have no trouble, even without Northumberland, since the King's forces are divided into three parts: one group must fight the French, who have attacked England's coast; King Henry and Prince Hal lead their troops against Owen Glendower in Wales; which leaves only the forces of Prince John and the Earl of Westmoreland to fight with them. They decide to spread the word about their cause and secure the support of the populace, who are already weary of Henry's reign.

Mistress Quickly (a.k.a. the Hostess), proprietor of the Boar's Head Tavern in London's slummy Eastcheap neighborhood, has entered a suit against Falstaff, who has incurred a sizable debt at her establishment and refuses to pay her. She and some officers approach Falstaff on the street, but he resists arrest with the help of his friend Bardolph (not to be confused with the rebel *Lord* Bardolph). As luck would have it, the Lord Chief Justice happens by and restores order. Mistress Quickly explains that Falstaff not only owes her money, but also promised to marry her. Despite Falstaff's claim that she is insane, the Chief Justice orders him to pay the debt and apologize. Falstaff promptly sweet-talks her and borrows more money, while the Chief Justice is distracted by a messenger who tells of King Henry and Prince Hal's return to London.

On another street, Prince Hal (just returned from Shrewsbury, where his valiant military service redeemed his terrible reputation in his father's eyes) cracks jokes to his buddy Poins, who remarks that such jests are inappropriate at a time when Hal's father, the King, is seriously ill. Hal explains that though he "bleeds inwardly" over his father's illness, his bad-boy reputation would make expression of his feelings seem hypocritical.

Bardolph arrives and says that Falstaff is to dine at the Boar's Head Tavern that evening with Mistress Quickly and Doll Tearsheet, a prostitute. Hal and Poins plan to disguise themselves as waiters and spy on Falstaff for their own amusement.

Back at his castle, Northumberland is preparing to fulfill his promise to join the rebel forces. His wife has given up trying to dissuade him, but his daughter-in-law, Lady Percy (widow of his son, Hotspur), shames him out of going by reminding him that he broke that same promise when it was made to his own son, leaving Hotspur's forces unsupported at Shrewsbury, where he was killed in battle. Northumberland acquiesces to the women's request that he flee to Scotland.

Slapstick interlude: at the Boar's Head Tavern, Mistress Quickly, Doll Tearsheet, and Falstaff have had a few too many. Enter Pistol, a blowhard friend of Falstaff's, also drunk, who picks a fight with Doll, draws his sword on her, and is ejected by Falstaff. When Doll asks about Prince Hal and Poins, Falstaff describes them so insultingly that Hal and Poins drop their waiter disguises, reveal themselves, and confront him. Falstaff explains that he disparaged them out of friendship, to protect them from being sought out by "the wicked" who are present. Peto, another crony, arrives with news that the King is amassing his troops at Westminster Palace. Hal feels terrible that he has been goofing off, and hurries to his father.

King Henry soliloquizes that the burdens of the monarchy keep him up at night, while his subjects enjoy a peaceful sleep. Two nobles arrive and try to comfort him. Henry worriedly reminds them that his predecessor, King Richard II, once prophesied that Northumberland would turn on him, and now he fears the rest of his ominous prophecies will come true as well. Warwick and Surrey reassure him, saying that Northumberland is a weasel, and anyone could have "foretold" his rebellion. Furthermore, the rebels will be easily defeated—Owen Glendower is already dead!

In Gloucestershire, Justice Silence and Falstaff's old friend Justice Shallow have gathered the local men for draft selection. Falstaff selects several men, releasing the two most able-bodied when they offer him bribes. He has noticed that Shallow is an easy mark, and as he leaves with his pathetic new recruits, he makes a mental note to come back and swindle the man.

In the Forest of Gaultree, the Archbishop of York tells Lords Hastings and Mowbray of Northumberland's desertion. Westmoreland arrives as emissary from Prince John, who is authorized to negotiate on behalf of his father, the King. Despite their misgivings, the rebels give Westmoreland a list of grievances and agree to meet with Prince John to discuss them. At the meeting, Prince John butters up the rebels, promises to address their grievances, and convinces them to disband their armies. As soon as their troops disband, the Prince arrests the rebels for treason and sentences them to execution. The stunned rebels are led away to the block.

In yet another part of the forest, Falstaff encounters a fleeing rebel officer who surprises Falstaff by surrendering. Falstaff turns him over to Prince John, who sentences the officer to execution. John upbraids Falstaff for hiding until the rebels were defeated. After the Prince departs, Falstaff soliloquizes that John is utterly humorless, while his brother Hal is valiant. If you ask Falstaff, Hal's superior nature is due to his steady diet of good sherry. He plans to return home via Gloucestershire, so he can "visit" Justice Shallow.

At Westminster Palace, King Henry is very ill and very worried that Prince Hal, who is partying with Poins at this very moment, will make a terrible king. Even Westmoreland's arrival with news of the rebels' defeat can't cheer him up. He wearily hears further news of Northumberland's downfall in the north, and feels so faint that he asks to be carried off.

Later, Prince Hal arrives and is left alone with his dying father. Since the King doesn't appear to be breathing, Hal believes he is dead. Hal addresses the crown, which lies on the King's pillow, blaming it for overburdening his father. He places the crown on his own head to signify his reluctant and dutiful acceptance of the burdens of the monarchy. After he leaves the room, the King revives and is distraught to discover that Hal has taken the crown—it seems as though Hal can't wait for him to die, so he can be king. When Hal returns, his father berates him. Hal abjectly apologizes, expressing the devastation he felt when he thought that his father was dead, and the resignation with which he approached the crown. Hal's words appease the King, who lovingly imparts some final advice to his son and heir: to keep peace within the kingdom, engage in some foreign quarrel that will unite England against a common foe.

In London, news spreads of King Henry's death. Prince Hal assures everyone that he has turned over a new leaf, and will prove a mature, responsible, and merciful monarch. The Lord Chief Justice is worried that Hal will take revenge on him for having once imprisoned him during his lawless youth. Prince Hal surprises everyone by agreeing that the Chief Justice was right to imprison him and inviting him to keep his position and to serve as his adviser.

Meanwhile, Falstaff, who has returned to Gloucestershire to swindle Justice Shallow, learns that Hal has become King Henry V. Falstaff sets off for London with Shallow in tow, expecting to cash in on his relationship with the new king—foremost in his mind is revenge on the Lord Chief Justice.

On a street in London, Mistress Quickly and Doll Tearsheet, who have been arrested for participating in a deadly brawl, are dragged off to prison.

Near Westminster, Falstaff waits with Shallow and Pistol for the new king's procession to pass. When King Henry arrives, he is cold to his old friend. He forbids Falstaff to come within a ten-mile radius of him. Adding insult to injury, he assigns the Lord Chief Justice to carry out his order. In a small gesture of kindness, he grants Falstaff a pension to live on (so he won't resort to thievery). After King Henry departs, Falstaff immediately claims that this was all a show, and that Hal will surely send for him privately later on. The Lord Chief Justice has Falstaff taken away. Prince John tells the Lord Chief Justice that he bets they'll be at war with France within a year (Shakespeare's way of saying "Stay tuned for the next episode—*Henry V*").

HENRY V

Shakespeare opens *Henry V* with a prologue, in which he apologizes in advance with false modesty for the play's inadequate representation of its epic events: when last we left our hero at the end of *King Henry IV, Part Two*, he had just been crowned. Heeding his father's deathbed advice, Henry—with the go-ahead of his advisers—now plans to assert his claim to the French throne (see "Genealogy of French Monarchs, and the English Claim to the French Throne . . . ," page 232). *Voilà!* Enter the French ambassador, with a condescending gift of tennis balls, offered deliberately to suggest that Henry is still a dissolute youth, courtesy of the Dauphin (the French crown prince). Henry turns the insolent joke around, promising to "play a set / Shall strike his father's [the French King's] crown into the hazard," and declaring war. While the English prepare for war, three noblemen plot—with the aid of the French—to overthrow Henry.

Meanwhile, two of Henry's former cronies in London's slummy Eastcheap neighborhood are at odds: Pistol has married the Hostess of the Boar's Head Tavern, who was formerly engaged to marry Nym—they nearly duel, but another crony, Bardolph, convinces them to reconcile. Their houseboy (hereinafter "the Boy") reports that Falstaff is terribly ill, and they rush off to his bedside.

As Henry and his men are about to board ship for France, he mentions to the three traitors his intention to pardon a drunken soldier who spoke out against him, but they urge zero tolerance. He then exposes the three traitors and sentences them to death in accordance with their own advice.

At the Boar's Head, the Hostess touchingly describes Falstaff's death to his cronies. Pistol, Nym, Bardolph, and the Boy bid her a loving adieu and depart for France.

Meanwhile, in France, King Charles VI discusses the upcoming English invasion with advisers and the Dauphin, who denigrates Henry as a foolish, inconsequential youth. Henry's ambassador arrives and delivers an ultimatum: surrender the crown or it's war.

Henry invades France and is offered marriage to the French Princess Katharine and a dowry that includes several dukedoms. No thanks, he'd rather fight for the crown. At the gates of Harfleur, he urges his soldiers forward with a battle cry. Among the troops, Bardolph echoes Henry's battle cry, but his friends wish they were back home. The Boy remarks, aside, that his masters are a thieving, cowardly lot whose service he hopes soon to leave. In a humorous Battle of the Dialects, soldiers from Wales, Scotland, Ireland, and England converge and chat until they hear the sounding of a parley—at Harfleur's gates, the Governor is "persuaded" by King Henry to surrender.

Back at the French palace, Princess Katharine receives an English lesson from her attendant, Alice. Their conversation is studded with humorous mispronunciations and unwitting sexual double entendre. Elsewhere in the palace, her father, the King, discusses the success of the English forces despite the fact that their rapidly dwindling numbers are weary, underfed, and diseased. He is surprised but unfazed, and confidently orders a full-blown attack.

En route to Agincourt, Bardolph has been caught stealing a small item from a church and is sentenced to death. The Welsh commander Fluellen refuses Pistol's pleas to intercede, and although Bardolph is Henry's old friend, Henry upholds the sentence to show what will happen to any soldier who mistreats French civilians on the march to battle. Montjoy, the French herald, arrives with an offer of truce from the King in exchange for a ransom from Henry. Henry refuses and marches on.

In the French camp at Agincourt on the night before the battle, the cocky French nobles can't wait to trounce the outnumbered English. Meanwhile, in the English camp, the weak and weary soldiers anticipate defeat. Henry circulates, bolstering their spirits. He then dons a cloak and moves among the troops incognito, listening to his men. When he encounters Pistol, Pistol blesses his king and speaks insultingly of Fluellen. The King then overhears a conversation that reveals Fluellen's valor. He then encounters Williams, a soldier who insults the King. They argue, and Williams challenges "the stranger" to a duel after the battle. They exchange gloves, which they will wear in their caps by which to recognize each other. Left alone in the wee hours before the battle, Henry soliloquizes about the heavy burdens of kingship.

In both camps, the soldiers arm for battle: the French are confident, while the English are nervous—they are outnumbered five to one by the well-fed and -rested French. Henry bolsters them brilliantly, asserting brotherhood with them, assuring them of God's aid and of lasting fame at home in England. The men are heartened. Montjoy returns, repeating King Charles's previous offer, which Henry proudly rejects.

The battle rages: Pistol captures a French soldier and demands ransom; the Boy translates and the two men go off to make the exchange. The Boy remarks that only Pistol's cowardice has saved him from death.

The French are losing the battle (see "Medieval Maccabees," page 136). They order reinforcements be sent in; when Henry learns of this, he orders all French prisoners killed (in express violation of the laws of war). He is then outraged to learn that the French have slaughtered all the English boys who were left to guard the luggage (also a violation of the laws of war). Before he can implement revenge, Montjoy arrives, conceding defeat and requesting permission for the French to gather their dead.

Henry asks Fluellen to wear Williams's glove, explaining that he took it from a French soldier, and that any man who challenges it is the King's enemy. Fluellen is delighted by this honor. He soon encounters Williams, who sees the glove and challenges him. They are intercepted before they can duel, and Henry gives Williams a glove filled with coins for his mettle.

Henry sails triumphantly to England, regroups, and then returns to continue the war in France (see "The Ruin of Rouen," page 121). In the English camp, Pistol's dispute with Fluellen persists. He insults the leek (a symbol of Wales) that Fluellen wears in his helmet. Fluellen beats him and makes him eat the leek. The bitter Pistol—who has also received news that his wife has died—resolves to go home to England where he will become a thief and pretend that his scars from the beating are war wounds.

Some time later, at the French royal palace, Henry discusses with King Charles and a bevy of noble advisers the terms of a peace treaty, which include marriage to Princess Katharine. Henry is left alone to woo her for four minutes, during which he attempts to break the language barrier. She eventually consents to the marriage. The others return, the wedding is arranged, and the audience is told of the ensuing short-lived peace and the birth of Henry's son . . . the title character of *Henry VI, Parts One*, *Two*, and *Three*.

HENRY VI, PART ONE

Most scholars agree that *Henry VI, Part One* was among the first plays that Shakespeare wrote. What they can't agree on is whether he wrote most, all, or only segments of it—some argue that its uneven quality is a sign of the playwright's developing talent, while others believe that better-written sections are Shakespeare's, with the rest attributable to one or more other author(s). Like his other Histories, it contains double time (see "Double Double Time and Trouble," page 998), as well as the telescoping of long periods into much shorter ones to achieve dramatic effect. The play also corresponds with Shakespeare's other works thematically: it is less concerned with battle scenes and war strategies than with the idea that a weak monarchy and moral flaws among the aristocracy will cause social disorder.

Order has already been lost at the opening of the play. Henry V, the beloved king who united England in an all-out campaign against France, has just died, leaving behind an infant son as his heir. As the curtain goes up on King Henry V's funeral, his brothers and uncles learn that France has rebelled against English rule, and Charles the Dauphin (the French heir to the throne that the English have claimed) has been crowned King Charles VII. Furthermore, England's greatest knight, Lord Talbot, has been captured. John, Duke of Bedford (the late king's brother), who is the Regent of France, vows to reclaim the French crown for England. The nobles prepare to join their countrymen, who are struggling to keep Orléans under seige.

Cut to Orléans. The overconfident Charles and his leaders decide to attack the English. They are quickly and decisively beaten back, even though they outnumber the English ten to one. Just as they are about to abandon the town, a noble known as the Bastard of Orléans arrives with a young woman called Joan la Pucelle (you guessed it—Joan of Arc), who claims that the Virgin Mary appeared to her in a vision and instructed her to save her country. She proves herself in hand-to-hand combat with Charles, easily defeating him. Charles is delighted with (and more than a little enamored of) his new little helper, and decides to stick it out at Orléans.

Meanwhile, back in Merry Old England, all is not so merry. Young Henry VI's great-uncle the Bishop of Winchester has taken control of the Tower of London and will not allow the Duke of Gloucester (Henry VI's uncle, who is Protector of both the realm and the young King) to enter. They and their men begin to fight in the street, but are restrained by the Mayor of London.

Meanwhile, Lord Talbot has been released in exchange for a French prisoner, and is strategizing on a tower outside Orléans when a cannonball from inside the city strikes the tower, killing his fellow commander. Talbot is still mourning the loss of this great warrior when he learns that Charles the Dauphin and Joan la Pucelle are about to attack.

Outside the gates of Orléans, the battle rages. Englishmen run from Joan. Talbot meets her in hand-to-hand combat, but neither prevails. To Talbot's utter mortification, Joan succeeds in taking the city and driving the English back into their trenches. Charles applauds her victory.

The English forces, led by Talbot and joined by the Duke of Burgundy (who is French), attack the French at night, taking them by surprise. The French quickly abandon the city, and then fall to bickering over whose fault it was that they were unprepared. Joan urges them all to shut up and plan a fresh attack on the English. They are all scared off by an Englishman calling the battle cry "a Talbot!"

The victorious Talbot is invited to visit a French countess who lives nearby. During his visit, she ridicules him. He turns to leave and she says that he is her prisoner. Talbot politely explains that he chooses not to be imprisoned—his hidden soldiers enter and the Countess concedes that Talbot is just as great as he was rumored to be.

Back in England, things are less merry than ever. In London's Temple Garden, a dispute has arisen between Richard Plantagenet, a cousin of the King, and the Duke of Somerset, another cousin. The Earl of Warwick and most of the other nobles back Plantagenet, while the Earl of Suffolk sticks up for Somerset. During the argument, Plantagenet plucks a white rose to represent his cause, while Somerset chooses a red one for himself. Their supporters follow suit. Somerset denigrates Plantagenet, whose title was forfeited when his father was executed for treason. Plantagenet claims that his father's execution was illegal, and Warwick assures him that his title (Duke of York) will be reinstated. The civil wars known as the Wars of the Roses have just been hatched (see "The Red Rose and the White . . . the Fatal Colors of Our Striving Houses," page 238).

Plantagenet now visits his dying uncle, Edmund Mortimer, long imprisoned in the Tower of London. Mortimer explains his imprisonment and the execution of Plantagenet's father: Mortimer has a valid claim to the English throne, stemming from the time when Henry VI's grandfather, Henry IV, usurped it from Richard II (for more on this, see the synopses of *Richard II* and *Henry IV, Part One*). During Henry V's reign, Richard, Earl of Cambridge (Richard Plantagenet's father and Mortimer's brother-in-law—if confused, see "Genealogical Chart—the Wars of the Roses," pages 236–37), raised an army and tried to install Mortimer as king, for which he was beheaded. Mortimer has no sons of his own, and names Plantagenet as his heir, but warns him against trying to usurp the throne from the Lancasters. He dies, and Plantagenet vows to himself to become king.

Winchester and Gloucester continue their bickering at Parliament House, ignoring the pleas of the now-adult King Henry VI to stop. Their supporters brawl in the streets, some overflowing into Parliament. Finally, the young King and the Mayor of London convince the two men to shake hands in a reluctant truce. Warwick then brings before the King the matter of Plantagenet's lost title. King Henry restores his title and inheritance, and Plantagenet—hereinafter known as York—pledges his humble service to the King. Gloucester then announces that Henry will travel to Paris to be crowned King of France.

The French, meanwhile, have not been sitting around on their *derrières* twiddling their *pouces*. Joan la Pucelle has disguised herself and several soldiers as commoners, and is thus able to sneak into Rouen, which is held by the English. Once inside, Joan climbs to the top of a tower and signals to the French army, who seize the city, driving out the English. Joan and Charles taunt the English from the city walls. Talbot and Burgundy launch a counterattack, and succeed in retaking the city. Reassured, the ailing Bedford, who had refused to leave the battle, can now die peacefully. Talbot and Burgundy celebrate their victory and mourn Bedford.

At the French camp outside Rouen, Burgundy agrees to speak with the French. Joan points out to him the plight of his countrymen and of his beautiful homeland, and persuades him to defect.

King Henry arrives in Paris, where he knights Talbot. After the King is crowned, news arrives of Burgundy's defection and Talbot heads off to march against Burgundy. The conflict between York and Somerset, which has been gaining momentum among their supporters, surfaces. Attempting to show equal favor to both sides, King Henry comes up with the brilliant idea of dividing his forces in France between the two men. He takes the red rose of Somerset, but appoints York as Regent of France to replace the late Bedford.

Before the city gates, Talbot demands the surrender of Bordeaux. The French refuse, since the Dauphin's forces are on their way to defend the city. Sensing the imminent danger, Talbot cheers on his troops.

Sir William Lucy rides to York's camp and entreats him to send reinforcements to

Bordeaux. York puts him off, blaming the delay on Somerset. When Lucy rides on to Somerset's camp and makes the same request, Somerset blames the delay in reinforcements on York. Somerset agrees to send them now, but Lucy fears it is too late.

Back at Bordeaux, Talbot urges his son John to leave, fearing he will die in the battle, but John refuses to so dishonor his family name. In the middle of the battle, John is cornered and Talbot rescues him. Once again, he entreats his son to leave and once again his son refuses. They head back into the fray together. Talbot reenters, fatally wounded and searching for his son, who is soon brought in, dead. Talbot mourns his son and then dies. The French leaders arrive and admire Talbot's valor.

Back home in England, Gloucester explains to King Henry that a treaty has been drawn up for peace between the two countries, and that one of the provisions is Henry's marriage to the daughter of the Earl of Armagnac. The King reluctantly agrees.

In Anjou, Charles and his supporters are delighted to hear that the Parisians have rebelled against the English. They are less delighted to hear that the English army has been reunited, and is on its way.

The battle rages outside Angiers. Joan, distressed at the English success, calls on a group of evil spirits to come to her aid. The spirits appear, but then silently abandon her, and she realizes her beloved France will be defeated. Burgundy and York fight. Later, Suffolk enters with Margaret of Anjou as his prisoner. In love with her but already married, he devises a plan to marry her off to King Henry and have her as his mistress. He makes the marriage offer to Margaret's father, Reignier, who promises to consent if his lands are returned. Suffolk agrees to get Anjou and Maine for him. As he takes his leave of Margaret, she makes it clear that he is the reason the offer interests her.

At the English camp, the Duke of York, who has captured Joan, prepares to burn her at the stake. Her shepherd father has sought her out, but she denies him, saying she is of noble blood. She tells the English that she is chosen by God, and that they will be damned for killing her; then, in a last-ditch effort to save her life, she denies the virginity she has so long touted, saying that she is pregnant. The English mock her, and then send her off to her fiery death. The French arrive to negotiate the peace. Under the terms offered by the English, Charles will retain his title, but will rule subject to the greater authority of King Henry. Charles balks, but his advisers persuade him to sign, saying he can break his word later.

In London, Suffolk's description of Margaret has convinced King Henry that she's the gal for him. Against Gloucester's wishes, Henry ignores his earlier marriage contract, and sends Suffolk back to France to arrange a marriage to Margaret. Gloucester fears that this will result in some very, very unmerry days for England. Aside, Suffolk schemes that when Margaret is queen, he will rule England through her. Stay tuned for *Henry VI, Part Two*.

HENRY VI, PART TWO

As the saga of the sensitive King Henry VI continues, the Earl of Suffolk presents the King's bride, Margaret of Anjou, to the royal court. The King is mighty pleased with her, and the terms of the marriage contract are read aloud: Margaret's father is to receive the territories of Anjou and Maine (French territories held by the English, who currently rule much of France) and is to pay no dowry. King Henry VI grants Suffolk a dukedom, temporarily suspends the Duke of York's position as Regent of France, and departs with Margaret and Suffolk to prepare for Margaret's coronation.

The King's uncle the Duke of Gloucester (who is still the Lord Protector though King Henry is no longer a minor) is distressed by the marriage, fearing that with the loss of England's stronghold in Normandy, England will lose France altogether. Gloucester leaves to avoid a confrontation with his nemesis, Cardinal Beaufort, the Bishop of Winchester. Once he's gone, the Cardinal unfairly asserts that Gloucester, who is next in line for the throne, is eager to get it and is no friend to the King or the realm. The other nobles agree to remove Gloucester as lord protector, and the Cardinal departs to bring the matter to Suffolk's attention. Somerset and Buckingham agree that the Cardinal is too full of himself and should not become the next lord protector. They depart. Left behind, the Earl of Warwick, the Earl of Salisbury, and the Duke of York concur that Somerset and Buckingham are no better than the Cardinal, and agree to support Gloucester. After Warwick and Salisbury take off, York soliloquizes that Henry VI's forefathers have usurped the throne, which is rightfully his (he's right—see "Genealogical Chart—the Wars of the Roses," pages 236–37). He plans to back Gloucester's supporters and then seize the throne when he gets the chance.

At the Gloucesters' home, Eleanor, the Duchess of Gloucester, nags her husband to seek the throne. Gloucester tells her to banish her ambitious thoughts, and leaves to go hawking with the King and Queen. The Duchess then soliloquizes that she intends to make her husband king. A priest arrives to finalize arrangements for a seance. When the Duchess leaves, the priest soliloquizes that he is a spy for the Duke of Suffolk and the Cardinal, who plan to bring about Gloucester's downfall by taking advantage of his wife's ambition.

At the palace, Queen Margaret is sick of listening to the commoners' petitions. She complains to Suffolk that her new husband (unlike Suffolk) isn't the powerful man she had expected him to be, that the other nobles seem to be ruling him, and that their wives treat her with contempt. Suffolk assures her that he will do away with the King's rivals.

Along comes King Henry with the whole gang of nobles, who are squabbling over who should be regent of France—Somerset or York. Gloucester and the Queen exchange unpleasant words over his protectorship and he takes a walk around the quadrangle to cool off. The Queen accidentally-on-purpose strikes the Duchess of Gloucester, and the Duchess takes a walk around the quadrangle to cool off. Gloucester returns and again nominates York for the regency. When Suffolk claims York is unfit, Gloucester switches his support to Somerset, and Henry follows Gloucester's advice, granting Somerset the regency.

Later, the priest returns to the Duchess with a witch and a conjurer. In a seance, they raise a spirit whom the Duchess questions about the futures of King Henry, Suffolk, and Somerset (thus betraying her ambition to be queen). The spirit reveals that a duke will depose Henry but then die a violent death, that Suffolk shall die by water, and that Somerset should shun castles. As the spirit disappears, York and Buckingham break in and arrest the Duchess and her spiritualists.

The royal couple are out hunting with Gloucester, the Cardinal, and Suffolk. Insults escalate between Gloucester and the Cardinal. News arrives of the Duchess's arrest. Gloucester affirms his loyalty to the King, pledging to renounce his wife if the allegations prove true.

At the York estate, York explains his claim to the English throne to Salisbury and

Warwick, who pledge their support. They plan to wait until Gloucester and, in turn, his opponents are brought down before staging their coup.

Fast-forward to the Duchess's sentencing: she is to be publicly shamed for three days and then banished to the Isle of Man for life. The others who participated with her are to be put to death. Henry revokes Gloucester's protectorship. The Duchess of Gloucester is paraded through the streets of London, barefoot and clad in a white sheet, to the jeers of onlookers. She encounters her husband and pauses for one gut-wrenching monologue, in which she describes her pain and shame and warns him to beware of his enemies. With stunning lack of foresight, Gloucester assures her that he cannot be brought down as long as he does no wrong. Tearful adieus are exchanged.

The King, the Queen, and the usual pack of nobles (sans Gloucester) have assembled at Parliament. The Queen alleges that Gloucester is plotting against the King. Her yes-men (Suffolk et al.) concur, but the King refuses to believe it. Somerset brings news that England has lost all its territories in France. The King is resigned, accepting the defeat as God's will. Gloucester finally arrives, and is promptly arrested by Suffolk for high treason. Gloucester proclaims his innocence. The King believes Gloucester but is resigned, entrusting the matter to the nobles and hoping that Gloucester will be able to prove his case. After Henry leaves and Gloucester is led away to prison, Margaret and her yes-men plot Gloucester's murder. News arrives of a rebellion in Ireland, and York is assigned to suppress it. Left alone, he soliloquizes that he will soon seize the throne: he will stir up a rebellion to be led by a certain Jack Cade, creating an excuse to bring his army from Ireland into England, ostensibly to put down Cade's rebellion.

Gloucester's murderers report their success to Suffolk, who sends them off to be paid. The King and Queen arrive with the Cardinal and Somerset. Suffolk is sent to check on Gloucester, and returns with the news that he is dead. The King faints; the Queen wails melodramatically that she will be blamed. Warwick and Salisbury hurry in and report that the commoners are angered by Gloucester's murder, and want revenge against Suffolk and the Cardinal. Warwick accuses Suffolk and the Cardinal of the murder. Suffolk challenges Warwick to a duel. He accepts, and they go out to fight but rush back in, pursued by a bunch of commoners who demand that Suffolk be killed or banished. Henry is not sure who killed Gloucester, but he is resigned, and banishes Suffolk. The Queen pleads for Suffolk, to no avail. The King departs with Warwick and the others, leaving Margaret alone with Suffolk. Devastated, they bid each other a passionate adieu. They are interrupted by the news that the Cardinal is dying. When the King, Warwick, and Salisbury visit the Cardinal, he admits his guilt and dies.

En route to banishment, Suffolk is captured by pirates. A pirate named Walter Whitmore is permitted to deal with Suffolk as he wishes. Because Whitmore lost an eye in the attack on Suffolk's ship, he decides to kill Suffolk. Suffolk recalls with a shock that he was to die "by Water" (Walter was pronounced "Water" in Shakespeare's time). Whitmore leads him off to be beheaded and returns with his severed head and body, which are to be sent back to the King and Queen.

Meanwhile, in Kent, the cavalierly brutal Jack Cade is gathering support for his rebellion, claiming to be John Mortimer (a cousin of York's who would have been heir to the throne had he not died). After a brief skirmish with the King's forces, he leads his followers on toward London.

Back at the palace, Queen Margaret grieves, carrying Suffolk's head. The King jokes that if he died, Margaret would not mourn so for him. The King, Buckingham, and Lord Say, Treasurer of England, discuss the approach of Cade, who has almost reached London and has support among the citizens. The King and Queen decide to leave town, but Lord Say insists on staying behind so as not to further endanger them, since Cade particularly despises him.

Cade, who has taken London Bridge, declares himself "Lord of the City" and decrees that henceforth he shall be called Lord Mortimer under penalty of treason. A soldier arrives calling "Jack Cade" and is immediately killed. Cade sets off to burn down London Bridge and the Tower. A while later, the captured Lord Say is brought before Cade. He is sentenced to beheading for such crimes as speaking Latin, building a school, and appointing justices of the peace. He is executed and his head paraded through London on a spike.

Buckingham appears before a crowd of commoners with Lord Thomas Clifford, who offers them the King's pardon in exchange for their allegiance. The frenzied commoners enthusiastically endorse Clifford and then Cade, before returning their allegiance to the King. Cade, abandoned, takes to his heels and Buckingham announces a hefty reward for his head.

The King bemoans his lot in life, but is resigned. Buckingham and Clifford arrive to announce the end of the rebellion, and the King pardons the now-repentant rebels. News arrives that York has returned from Ireland with a mighty army and is marching toward London to unseat his chief rival, Somerset, who he claims is a traitor. Henry sends Buckingham to meet with York, and sends Somerset to the tower until York's troops are dismissed.

Cade hides in a garden. He is discovered by its owner, Alexander Iden. In the ensuing scuffle, Iden kills Cade. Iden bears Cade's head to the King and is duly knighted and rewarded.

On the road to London with his troops, York is met by the King. Learning that Somerset is in the Tower, York pretends loyalty to Henry and makes a show of dismissing his troops. When Somerset arrives, York is enraged—he accuses the King of lying and claims the throne for himself. Somerset arrests York for treason, but York summons two of his sons, Edward and Richard, for bail. They arrive, as do Clifford and his son, John, creating a standoff. Warwick and Salisbury come to York's defense. The King is resigned: a battle must take place.

The battle rages on the fields of St. Albans: York kills Old Clifford; Young Clifford vows to kill York's children in revenge. Richard and Somerset enter fighting, and Somerset is killed under the sign of an alehouse called The Castle, fulfilling another part of the spirit's prophecy. As Richard exits, the King and Queen enter. The Queen insists that they flee to avoid capture.

The King's troops flee. York, Richard, Warwick, and Salisbury congratulate one another and plan to pursue the King's retreating forces. Warwick imagines that the Battle of St. Albans will be eternally remembered (surely some playwright, sometime in history, will write about it . . .).

P.S.

For an overview of the Wars of the Roses, see "The Red Rose and the White . . . the Fatal Colors of Our Striving Houses," page 238.

The Contention and *The Whole Contention*: A Lot to Contend With, and No One Is Content

In 1594 a shorter, inferior version of *Henry VI, Part Two* was published under the title *The First Part of the Contention betwixt the two famous houses of Yorke and Lancaster, with the death of the good Duke Humphrey: And the banishment and death of the Duke of Suffolke, and the tragicall end of the proud Cardinall of Winchester, with the notable rebellion of Iacke Cade: And the Duke of Yorkes first claim unto the crown*. Today's scholars have nicknamed this version *The Contention*. Scholars still hotly contend whether *The Contention* is a Bad Quarto edition of Shakespeare's play (a pirated version reconstructed by actors or observers from memory for a greedy publisher) or is an earlier play by another author, revised by Shakespeare for performance as *Henry VI, Part Two*. A similarly inferior version of *Henry VI, Part Three*, called *The True Tragedy*, was originally published in 1595. In 1619, the two shoddy plays were published together. This new concoction, known today as *The Whole Contention*, was published under the title *The Whole Contention between the two Famous Houses, Lancaster and Yorke. With the tragicall ends of the good Duke Humphrey, Richard Duke of Yorke, and King Henrie the sixt*. Having earned a pretty penny for their moneygrubbing Elizabethan publishers, *The Contentions* are now fodder for feuding scholars of sixteenth-century literature.

HENRY VI, PART THREE

Having sowed the seeds for the English Wars of the Roses in *Richard II* and cultivated them in *Henry VI, Parts One* and *Two*, we are up to our necks in thorns by now (for an overview, see "The Red Rose and the White . . . the Fatal Colors of Our Striving Houses," page 238). The Lancaster branch of the royal family has ruled England since poor sensitive King Henry VI's grandfather took the throne. When last we left our title character, his troops had just been defeated in battle at St. Albans by Richard, Duke of York, who claims the English throne for himself and his branch of the family (and rightfully so—see "Genealogical Chart—the Wars of the Roses," pages 236–37). The Duke of York, his sons Edward and Richard, and their followers the Earl of Warwick, the Duke of Norfolk, and Lord Falconbridge have taken over Parliament, where they are recounting their victory. Richard throws down the head of the Duke of Somerset, which speaks for itself of his triumph (not literally!). Warwick then encourages York to take a seat on the throne, which he does.

King Henry enters with his entourage, who are outraged at York's insolence, but Henry tells them to be patient. York asserts his claim that Henry's grandfather usurped the crown from Richard II. Henry replies that Richard resigned the crown to his grandfather, but in an aside he privately worries that his own claim is weak. Northumberland declares that Henry will not be deposed, and Warwick declares that he will. Clifford vows to fight in his king's defense, whether his title is right or wrong. Warwick signals to his soldiers, who come out of the woodwork and look menacing. Henry asks York to allow him to rule in peace for the remainder of his lifetime. York agrees and promises not to rebel, provided that Henry bequeath the crown to York and his heirs. Henry is unhappy but resigned, and does so. York and his entourage depart. King Henry's followers are incensed on behalf of his heir, Prince Edward, England, and themselves, and three of them, Northumberland, Clifford, and Westmoreland, storm out.

News travels fast: Queen Margaret rushes in with Prince Edward (who is already a young adult—if you've read *Henry VI, Part Two*, and are confused, see "Double Double Time and Trouble," page 998). She is livid! When Henry apologizes, claiming that he was forced to disinherit Edward, she rails at him for his cowardice and renounces both his bed and their marriage until he reinstates his son as heir to the throne. She tells him that she has the support of the northern lords Northumberland, Clifford, and Westmoreland, and plans to fight York. The Prince says he'll go along with Mom.

In Yorkshire, York's sons convince him that he should not wait for King Henry to die, but should fight and take the throne now. York prepares for battle. News arrives that Queen Margaret is approaching with the forces of the northern lords. York decides to fight her, even though his troops are outnumbered four to one.

The Battle of Wakefield ensues. York's young son, Rutland, is captured by Clifford while trying to escape with his tutor. York killed Clifford's father in battle (in *Henry VI, Part Two*), and Clifford has vowed to kill York's children in revenge. Rutland pleads piteously for his life, but Clifford kills him.

The Queen is winning the battle. She, Clifford, Northumberland, and Prince Edward corner York. Margaret taunts him viciously, standing him on a molehill to illustrate his pathetic failure to seize greatness, showing him a handkerchief stained with his young son's blood, and placing a paper crown on his head. She then orders him beheaded. York condemns Margaret in a vitriolic reply and mourns his son. Northumberland pities him, but Clifford and Margaret gleefully stab York to death.

York's sons, Edward (not to be confused with King Henry's son, *Prince* Edward) and Richard (not to be confused with his now-deceased father, Richard, Duke of York), see three suns in the sky (keep in mind they have been fighting hard all day in that heavy armor, and could probably use a glass of water and an aspirin) and take it as a good omen. A messenger brings news of their father's horrible death, followed by Warwick, who tells them that the Queen has won the day. Warwick encourages the boys to keep fighting until Edward (York's oldest son) is crowned, and they agree. Richard vows revenge on Clifford for the death of Rutland.

Queen Margaret, King Henry, Clifford, Northumberland, and Prince Edward gather before the city of York. Margaret points out York's head, which has been raised on a spike on the city walls. King Henry fears God's revenge. Clifford tells Henry to toughen up and urges him to defend his crown for the sake of his son. The King replies that evil actions do not produce good results. Margaret tells him to toughen up and knight his son, which he does. The York faction arrives. Edward demands that Henry kneel and recognize him as king. Margaret and Clifford tell him to buzz off. Clifford and Richard exchange bitter words. Henry tries to interject, but is cut off by Margaret and Clifford. The bickering escalates, finally reaching an impasse.

The war continues, now at Towton. Richard and Clifford square off in hand-to-hand combat, but before either can prevail, Warwick appears and Clifford flees.

Meanwhile, all by his lonesome, poor King Henry describes the ever-shifting battle. He has been chased away by Margaret and Clifford, who say they are more successful without him around. He wishes first that he were dead, and then that he were a carefree shepherd. He witnesses a soldier who discovers that he has slain his own father, and another who discovers that he has slain his own son. Henry feels terrible about the whole war. Queen Margaret and the Prince rush in. Their forces are in retreat, and they urge the King to flee with them.

Clifford enters, an arrow protruding from his neck. He fears that without him the Queen's forces will be defeated. York's sons arrive with Warwick, and are delighted to see Clifford take his final breath. Warwick decides that Clifford's head shall replace York's on the city walls. Then it's off to London to crown Edward King of England and to arrange his marriage to Lady Bona (King Lewis of France's sister-in-law). His brother George shall become Duke of Clarence and Richard shall be Duke of Gloucester. Warwick shall be Edward's chief adviser.

King Henry, meandering through the forest in disguise, is recognized by two gamekeepers, who capture him. He is dismayed by the loyalty they pledge to the new King Edward but is resigned and goes with them to be turned over to the authorities.

In London, King Edward hears the petition of Lady Elizabeth Grey, whose husband's lands were seized when he died in battle fighting for the Yorks at St. Albans. King Edward agrees to return the lands on the condition that she become his mistress. Scandalized, she refuses, which fuels his ardor: he proposes marriage. The news arrives of Henry's capture and all but Richard go to investigate. Alone, Richard soliloquizes that he hopes there are no offspring, because he fully intends to become king, and will be killing all who stand between him and the crown. Meanwhile, he will convincingly play the role of loyal brother.

Margaret and her son, Edward, have gone to France to seek King Lewis's assistance. He agrees to help her, but when Warwick arrives with King Edward's proposal of marriage to Lady Bona, King Lewis consents, much to Margaret's chagrin. News then arrives of Edward's marriage to Lady Elizabeth Grey. Warwick is incensed that Edward has made a liar of him, besmirching his honor. He defects to Margaret, vowing to avenge the wrong done to Lady Bona and to reinstate Henry on the throne. King Lewis also pledges his support to Margaret. They plan their attack.

In London, Edward and his brothers hear of the upcoming invasion. They also learn of Warwick's defection and his elder daughter's engagement to Margaret's son, Edward. George, who is engaged to Warwick's younger daughter, leaves to join Warwick. In an aside, Richard states that he is staying, but for love of the crown rather than for love of his brother the King. Aloud, he assures his brother that he stands by him. Edward feels sure of victory, and they go to prepare for battle.

Warwick arrives at Warwickshire with his French soldiers. He is met by George and welcomes his support, reaffirming his promise of his daughter's hand in marriage. Later, Warwick and his men sneak into the English camp and capture King Edward. Warwick takes the crown from Edward's head and announces that he will return to London and restore the crown to Henry. Back in London, the pregnant Queen Elizabeth learns of her husband's capture and seeks religious sanctuary to protect his heir. Shortly thereafter, Edward is rescued by Richard.

Speaking of rescues, King Henry has finally been released from the Tower of London by Warwick and George and others. The grateful Henry says that he will wear the crown, but assigns to Warwick the authority to govern. When he notices that young Henry Tudor, Earl of Richmond, the last Lancastrian male, is present, Henry prophesies that Richmond will one day rule over a peaceful England. News arrives of Edward's escape.

Richmond will be sent to Brittany for his safety while the rest go to prepare for the rocky road ahead.

Meanwhile, Edward has returned home to York with Richard, to find the city gates closed against him by its citizens, who claim allegiance to King Henry. He gains entry by promising that he claims nothing but his original dukedom of York. A noble arrives with troops to support Edward. Edward would like to wait to reclaim the throne until he is more powerful, but the noble threatens to withdraw his troops, so Edward agrees to re-assert his claim now.

Having learned that Edward is marching toward London, Warwick meets with King Henry to strategize. After Warwick departs for Coventry to assemble his troops, Henry is captured suddenly by Edward and Richard, who carry him off to the Tower.

In Coventry, Warwick is besieged by Richard and Edward. Noblemen arrive with reinforcements for Warwick. The last of these nobles is George, who is taken aside by his brother Richard and persuaded to return his allegiance to his brother Edward.

The Battle of Barnet rages: mortally wounded by Edward, Warwick realizes that his prior power and riches have amounted to nothing. His supporters plan to join Margaret's forces, which have just arrived from France.

On another part of the field, Edward, Richard, and George celebrate their victory and plan to march to Tewksbury to fight Margaret before her forces have time to regroup.

At Tewksbury, Margaret gives a rousing pep talk to her son, Edward (henceforth Edward L.), their noble supporters, and the troops. The Yorks arrive, and their Edward (Edward Y.) and Margaret each launch their troops into battle.

After the battle, during which Margaret and Edward L. have been captured by the Yorks, Edward L. insultingly and defiantly demands that Edward Y. recognize him as king. Instead, Edward Y. stabs him. Richard and George follow suit, killing him. Margaret cries, "O, kill me, too!" Richard is about to do so, but Edward Y. stops him, and Richard leaves for London and the Tower, "on a serious matter." As Margaret laments, the Yorks head back to London, where Edward Y. hopes his wife has given birth to a son.

In London, Richard pays a little visit to Henry in the Tower. Henry recognizes that Richard has come to kill him, recalls the bad omens that accompanied Richard's birth, and makes his second prophecy: Richard shall make a great many people miserable. In the middle of the prophecy, Richard decides he has heard enough, and stabs Henry to death. Richard again soliloquizes about his intention to ascend the throne using whatever ruthless means he must.

Later, at the palace, King Edward celebrates his resumption of the throne and the birth of his son, the newest Edward, Prince of Wales. While Richard pretends to rejoice at the family's advancement and prosperity, his nasty asides set the stage for the next episode in England's historical miniseries . . . *Richard III*.

P.S.

For some irrelevant silliness about *Henry VI, Part Three*, see "*The Contention* and *The Whole Contention*: A Lot to Contend With, and No One Is Content," page 920.

RICHARD III

For the moment, it seems that the York branch of the royal family has beaten out the Lancaster branch for the English throne (see synopses of *Henry VI, Parts One, Two,* and *Three* and "The Red Rose and the White . . . the Fatal Colors of Our Striving Houses," page 238, to learn more about the intra-family feud that pitted cousin against cousin and tore the nation apart). At the close of *Henry VI, Part Three*, the three York brothers, Edward, Earl of March; George, Duke of Clarence; and Richard, Duke of Gloucester, took up residence in the royal palace—Edward, the eldest, has been crowned King Edward IV.

In the most famous opening soliloquy of all time, the youngest brother, Richard, remarks that now that the York victory has brought peace to England, his eldest brother, King Edward, is living the high life, but that he himself, being deformed, is not cut out for such an existence. Richard wants the throne, and explains that he has laid plots to set his older brothers "in deadly hate, the one against the other." There is a prophecy that "G" will be the murderer of King Edward's children, and the superstitious King should be arresting their other brother, George, any minute now.

In fact, along comes George now (referred to as "Clarence"—see "Imagine Being Known as '415 South Street,' " page 235), in custody and being led away to the dreaded Tower of London (where England's elite offenders were detained while awaiting their fates). Richard pretends to be shocked and upset, and promises to convince the King to release him. After George is led away, Richard soliloquizes that he loves his brother so much he plans to send him off to enjoy the delights of Heaven without delay. Lord William Hastings, the Lord Chamberlain, arrives, fresh from his own imprisonment in the Tower, and tells Richard of the King's sickly condition. When Hastings departs, Richard again soliloquizes, musing that he will encourage King Edward to kill Clarence, and that he intends to marry Lady Anne Neville, despite the fact that he personally killed both her husband and her father-in-law (the Lancastrian Prince Edward and King Henry VI).

Speak of the devil (figuratively): on a London street, Lady Anne is escorting King Henry's corpse to its final resting place. She mourns him and curses his murderer. Speak of the devil (literally): along comes Richard, who wooes her, saying that he killed her husband and father-in-law out of love for her. He offers her the opportunity to kill him, which she cannot bring herself to do. Incredibly, he manages to talk her into wearing his ring and considering his suit. After Anne leaves, he gloats at his adroit manipulation of her.

King Edward's wife, Queen Elizabeth, speaks with her brother and her two young adult sons from her first marriage. She is worried because, after Edward's death, Richard will be appointed Protector of the Realm (one who rules while a sovereign is a minor or is incompetent) since her son Edward, Prince of Wales, is still a boy. Other nobles arrive, followed by Richard, who exchanges angry words with Queen Elizabeth. As if everyone's blood pressure weren't high enough already, Margaret, widow of the late King Henry VI, enters, dramatically curses all assembled—particularly Richard (who, as we mentioned, killed her husband)—and leaves, with a parting warning to Henry Stafford, Duke of Buckingham, to beware Richard. Everyone's hair "doth stand on end." A messenger arrives to summon all to the King's side. Richard stays behind and makes final arrangements with two murderers he's hired to kill his brother Clarence.

Speaking of Clarence, he's just had a nightmare in which he drowned. The murderers arrive at his cell in the Tower to kill him. When he begs them to spare him, promising that Richard will reward them for it, they reveal that it is actually Richard who has hired them. Clarence refuses to believe it. One of the murderers has a pang of conscience and hesitates, but the other stabs Clarence and drags him off to drown him in a vat of wine.

At the King's command, his relatives and other noblemen gather at his bedside to end their infighting and make peace among themselves. They all profess great love for one another. King Edward's self-congratulations are marred by Richard's arrival with the news of Clarence's death. The King protests that his order of execution had been reversed, but Richard claims that the countermand did not arrive in time to stop the order. The King is distraught. When Lord Thomas Stanley, Earl of Derby ("Stanley"), requests the King's pardon for one of his servants, the King reproaches all present for failing to request just such a pardon for his poor departed brother.

Shortly thereafter, the King up and dies. His aged mother, Cicely Neville, Duchess of York, and Queen Elizabeth try to outlament each other over the deaths of Edward and Clarence. Richard and Buckingham arrive and tell Elizabeth her son Edward will be brought to London. Left alone, the men plot to separate the young Prince from his mother and her relatives.

On London's streets, citizens discuss the precarious state of the realm, given the Prince's youth and the inevitable power struggle between Richard and the Queen's relatives.

In the palace, Queen Elizabeth, her youngest son, Richard, Duke of York ("York"), the old Duchess of York, and the Archbishop of York await Prince Edward's arrival. News arrives that Richard and his cronies have seized Prince Edward, and have imprisoned his escorts—Elizabeth's brother and oldest son. The terrified Queen rushes off to sanctuary with little York.

Prince Edward arrives in London and is surprised that his mother, brother, and uncles are not there to meet him. At Richard's command, the Prince's brother is fetched from sanctuary, and—for their "best health and recreation"—the two brothers are sent to enjoy the accommodations at the Tower. Left alone, Richard and Buckingham discuss their next step: they decide that if Lord Chamberlain Hastings does not back Richard's bid for the throne, he must die. Richard promises Buckingham an earldom for helping him become king.

In the wee hours of the morning, Hastings receives a message from Stanley, expressing fear of Richard and urging Hastings to flee with him. Hastings dismisses Stanley's concerns. To ascertain whether Hastings would support his bid for the throne, Richard sends a plant to casually mention the idea to him and gauge his response. Hastings disagrees vehemently.

Meanwhile, Richard has ordered the summary executions of the Queen's brother and her eldest son. En route to the block, they recall old Margaret's curse, which prophesied their fate.

Later that day at a council meeting, Prince Edward's coronation is discussed. Buckingham takes Richard aside to report Hasting's opposition to Richard as king. They return to the meeting, where Richard deftly corners Hastings, spins a web of lies about him, and has him led off to his prompt execution for treason. Hastings belatedly understands Stanley's warning, and recalls old Margaret's curse, which prophesied his fate.

Later, Richard justifies his immediate execution of the "dangerous" Hastings, and the Mayor of London takes him at his word. Richard then instigates a rumor that the late King Edward and his sons in the Tower are all illegitimate.

Later still, Buckingham reports to Richard that people have accepted the rumor of the princes' illegitimacy. He informs Richard that the Mayor of London is about to ask Richard to reign, and suggests that Richard feign piety and a reluctance to assume the throne. The Mayor arrives with his officials, and Richard carries out Buckingham's plan. After much urging, Richard graciously agrees to rule.

Outside the Tower, the old Duchess, Lady Anne (now Richard's wife), Queen Elizabeth, and Elizabeth's remaining adult son are barred from entering to visit the young princes. Boy, are they all surprised when Stanley arrives to inform them that Richard has been declared king, and to escort Anne to her coronation as Richard's queen. Anne goes unwillingly, regretting the ease with which she was manipulated into her marriage, and sure that he will soon be rid of her. Elizabeth sends her son abroad to safety and returns to sanctuary.

The newly crowned King Richard III suggests to Buckingham that he conveniently dispose of the two little nuisances in the Tower. Buckingham balks, angering the King. After Buckingham leaves, Richard hires a thug to do the deed. He also initiates a rumor that Anne is deathly ill—he wishes to cement his rule by marrying Elizabeth's daughter (yes, his own niece), also named Elizabeth. Buckingham returns and demands the earldom he was promised. Richard is not in a giving mood. He stalks out. Buckingham decides to flee before he meets the same fate as Hastings.

The boys have been murdered. Their deaths, along with Anne's recent death (never explained . . .), please Richard immensely. On the other hand, he is concerned about Henry Tudor, Earl of Richmond (who is next in line for the throne on the Lancastrian side and has been living abroad in safety; in *Henry VI, Part Three*, unbeknownst to Richard, King Henry prophesied that Richmond would one day rule England). Like Richard, Richmond wants to marry Richard's niece Elizabeth to strengthen his claim to the throne. Rumor has it that he's raising troops to attack Richard, and noblemen are defecting to Richmond's side. Furthermore, Buckingham has raised troops against Richard as well.

In another wing of the palace, the womenfolk lament their numerous dead. Margaret relishes watching them suffer at the hands of Richard what she suffered at the hands of all their menfolk—what comes around, goes around. After she and the old Duchess leave, Richard arrives to ask Elizabeth for her daughter's hand. Horrified, she at first rebuffs him, but then pretends to acquiesce, buying time to get her daughter away to safety. Receiving word of Richmond's invasion, Richard issues panicked, disorganized commands. When Stanley departs to muster his forces, Richard suspects that he will defect to Richmond, and demands Stanley's son as hostage. He learns that his own forces have defeated Buckingham's. This lifts his spirits and he leads his troops off to fight Richmond at Bosworth Field. Stanley was, in fact, intending to defect, but sends news to Richmond that he must now delay the defection to protect his hostage son.

En route to his execution, Buckingham recalls old Margaret's curse, which prophesied his fate (notice a pattern here?).

Back on English soil after many years, Richmond happily encourages his troops to fight heartily, to bring lasting peace to England.

On Bosworth Field, both sides prepare for the next day's battle. That night, both Richard and Richmond dream: Richard is visited by the ghosts of all the family members and loyal supporters he has murdered, who tell him to "despair and die." He wakes up panicked and disoriented, and soliloquizes about the evil he's wrought, realizing that he is hated by all, including himself. Richmond, on the other hand, has been assured of victory by the same ghosts, and awakes refreshed and invigorated. He once more assures his troops of God's aid in their just cause. Richard's go-get-'em speech to his troops, on the other hand, merely bad-mouths his foe's troops. The march into battle begins. Stanley has not brought his troops to Richard's aid. Richard orders Stanley's hostage son beheaded, but there is no time to do so—Richmond's forces approach too quickly.

Later, mid-battle, Richard's horse has been killed, but he forges forward on foot, seeking out Richmond (and shouting in desperation for another horse). He and Richmond come face to face. They fight, and Richmond kills Richard. He then praises his troops for their victory. Stanley offers Richmond the crown, and he delivers a speech announcing his marriage to the young Elizabeth, which will unite both branches of the royal family, ushering in a new age of peace for England.

HENRY VIII

Henry VIII was written in late 1612 or early 1613—long enough after the demise of Queen Elizabeth to write a play about her father without fear of repercussions. No one argues that Shakespeare wrote certain sections of it, but some scholars insist that Shakespeare was the sole author while others are convinced that the play's episodic nature, nonevolving characters, and inconsistent writing reflect the fact that half the play was written by the up-and-coming John Fletcher. What we do know is that although this play is counted among Shakespeare's Histories, it behaves more like a romance (which makes sense, since it was written right after his Romances): its plot is episodic, it is studded with pageantry, and it explores the role of divine providence in human affairs. The play's Prologue wastes no time in establishing its themes, informing the audience it is about to witness a play about matters of grave consequence.

As the play opens, the Duke of Buckingham, his son-in-law Lord Abergavenny, and the Duke of Norfolk discuss the recent peace summit in France between King Henry VIII and the French king. They worry that the terms of peace greatly compromise England, and complain that Cardinal Wolsey, who has been seizing too much political power of late, influenced King Henry's decision to sign the peace agreement. Norfolk, who knows that Buckingham and Wolsey have been feuding, warns his friend to beware Wolsey. Speak of the devil, the Cardinal himself arrives and states that he is to meet with Buckingham's surveyor, the overseer of the Duke's estate, to scrutinize his affairs for signs of wrongdoing, then departs. Buckingham vents his anger, asserting that the Cardinal is a traitor who was bribed by the Holy Roman Emperor to create a weak peace with France. He is still railing when an officer arrives to arrest him and Abergavenny for high treason—clearly the work of Cardinal Wolsey, who must have bribed Buckingham's overseer to bring false evidence against him.

At a council meeting, King Henry thanks Wolsey for quelling Buckingham's conspiracy. Queen Katherine arrives and petitions the King on behalf of his subjects to ease the stiff taxes Wolsey has imposed upon them without the King's knowledge, but Wolsey lies to the King, claiming he is not responsible for the taxation. The King orders Wolsey to repeal the unfair taxes. Out of earshot of the King, Wolsey instructs his secretary to do so, but to make it seem as though this benevolent act is due to his intercession on the people's behalf. Queen Katherine is expressing her dismay about Buckingham's arrest when Buckingham's surveyor arrives and testifies falsely that his employer planned to take the throne if Henry died without a male heir and that he spoke of assassinating both Henry and Wolsey. Katherine doesn't believe the surveyor but Henry does—he's furious and calls for Buckingham to be tried for treason.

En route to a banquet at Wolsey's, the Lord Chamberlain and others joke about the current fad among the nobility to imitate the ridiculous manners of the French. At Wolsey's, the party is in full swing. Male guests joke lewdly about female ones. A group of masquers dressed as shepherds (the King among them) arrives and they dance with the women. The King, who finds himself powerfully attracted to Anne Bullen, one of Queen Katherine's ladies-in-waiting, selects her as his dance partner; after the dance, he elicits her identity from Wolsey.

Although all of London knows that Wolsey framed him, Buckingham has been tried and convicted of treason. He is brought out to a public square to be executed, and delivers a speech in which he forgives his executioners, swears his everlasting fealty to the King, and notes that his father, too, was betrayed and executed in a miscarriage of justice. As he is led away, two gentlemen discuss a rumor that Wolsey's next target will be the Queen: because her nephew, the Holy Roman Emperor, denied Wolsey a prestigious archbishopric he sought, Wolsey hopes to convince the King to divorce her and thus deeply embarrass the Emperor.

The Lord Chamberlain, Norfolk, and another noble discuss the rumblings of the King's divorce; Henry claims to be troubled by the sacrilege of having married his brother's widow. They know Wolsey has planted this seed of discontent and hope that the King will remember his virtuous wife's twenty years of devotion and will recognize Wolsey's treachery before it's too late. When they visit the King's private chamber to speak with him he is angered by the interruption, but is tickled when Wolsey and a cardinal from Rome, Campeius, do the same. The nobles are sent away, and the King and cardinals confer: the King is convinced that he has no choice but to divorce Katherine—he sends her a message and announces that a hearing will be held on the matter.

News travels fast. Anne Bullen talks with an old woman about the Queen's plight, expressing pity for her and saying she'd rather be a happy poor woman than a miserable queen. The old lady accuses her of hypocrisy, and, through double entendre, suggests that if given the chance, Anne would sleep her way to the top. The Lord Chamberlain arrives and tells Anne that having sized her up favorably, the King has chosen to bestow upon her a title, estate, and yearly stipend. The Lord Chamberlain is impressed by Anne's modest response. After he leaves, the old lady exults for Anne, but Anne is dismayed on the Queen's behalf.

At the divorce proceedings, Katherine asks on what grounds Henry is divorcing her. She speaks eloquently of her devotion to her husband, of her attention to his well-being, of their years and children together, and of her royal lineage. When Wolsey has the temerity to suggest that she be patient, she tells him exactly what she thinks of him and demands to go over his head, directly to the Pope, to settle the matter. After she storms out, the King praises her virtues, but declares Wolsey blameless of her accusations. When Campeius adjourns the hearing until Katherine agrees either to be present or to give up her appeal to the Pope, King Henry wishes Bishop Cranmer were present to expedite matters.

Wolsey and Campeius visit Katherine and attempt to convince her to abandon her suit, professing to be her friends. Outraged, she accuses them of orchestrating her undeserved downfall. They urge her to permit them to assist her while the King still feels favorably toward her. Realizing that she is to be divorced whether she likes it or not, and that the displeasure of these two powerful men could worsen her plight, she apologizes for her outburst and thanks them for their counsel.

Norfolk, the Lord Chamberlain, and others discuss recent events: a letter from Wolsey to the Pope was inadvertently routed to the King. In it, Wolsey asked the Pope to oppose the King's divorce to prevent his marriage to the Protestant Anne Bullen. Wolsey was unsuccessful in thwarting the marriage, however, since the Pope never received his letter, and the marriage has already taken place in secret. Furthermore, Wolsey's nemesis, Cranmer, has been made Archbishop of Canterbury. Wolsey himself arrives, clearly disgruntled, and mutters, aside, that he plans to have the King marry a French noblewoman and not Anne. The King arrives, far more disgruntled than Wolsey. It seems that in addition to Wolsey's letter to the Pope, the King also accidentally received an accounting of the Cardinal's property, which indicates that he has accumulated considerably more wealth than a cardinal should. The King sarcastically thanks Wolsey for placing his religious and patriotic duties above his own personal gain, hands him the sheaf of papers, and stalks off, followed by the nobles. Wolsey examines the packet and realizes that the jig is up—he's finished. The Lord Chamberlain, Norfolk, and the rest shortly return, and Norfolk is only too happy to place Wolsey under arrest for treason. The nobles recite with gusto the long list of charges against him. After they leave, Wolsey soliloquizes that his downfall has opened his heart to the error of his ways, and he will face whatever awaits him with equanimity. When Cromwell arrives, Wolsey urges him to serve the King loyally.

Anne's coronation is described in detail by a gentleman who was present. As he and his cronies watch the coronation procession, they admire Anne and discuss the hatred Gardiner, the Bishop of Winchester, bears the good Archbishop Cranmer. They aren't worried, though, because Cranmer has an ally and protector in Cromwell, who has become King Henry's adviser.

Meanwhile, news of Wolsey's death reaches Queen Katherine, who is near death herself. She's bitter about him, but relents when reminded that Wolsey also did much good in his life, and that he died repentant and at peace with his Maker. Katherine naps and has a vision, a pageant in which six dancing figures present her with garlands. She sends a message to King Henry, asking, among other things, that he raise their daughter lovingly and well for her sake, and that he compensate her attendants appropriately for their loyal service to her. She returns to her bed to die.

Time has flown: Anne is in difficult labor and may die. Bishop Gardiner tells a nobleman that it would be best for the country if she does, since she is a heretical Protestant. He also accuses Archbishop Cranmer, as well as Cromwell, of heretical beliefs, and says that he's had Cranmer summoned before the council the next morning for interrogation. Later that night, King Henry meets with Cranmer and warns him that he will have enemies at the council meeting who may attempt to slander him. Henry gives him a ring with which to prove he has the King's protection in the event that Gardiner attempts to charge and jail him. An old lady arrives with good news and bad news: Anne and her baby are fine . . . but the baby is a girl. Henry rushes off to see mother and child.

The next day, Cranmer is kept waiting outside the council meeting. When he is finally admitted, he is accused of spreading heresies, and Gardiner suggests that swift punishment is needed to quell further damage. Though Cranmer asserts his innocence and asks to hear the witnesses against him, Gardiner declines and states that it is the King's wish that Cranmer be imprisoned in the Tower of London. When the council unanimously backs Gardiner, Cranmer produces the King's ring, proving Gardiner a liar. Moments later, the King arrives; he has been watching the proceedings from a balcony, unobserved. Cranmer's enemies realize that the King has trapped them. After raging at them, the King honors Cranmer by asking him to baptize his infant daughter.

At the infant Elizabeth's christening, Cranmer delivers a speech in which he predicts that the child, herself destined for greatness, will bring times of peace, prosperity, and greatness to the whole nation. King Henry thanks him and declares the day a national holiday. The Epilogue charmingly urges the audience to admit that the play was good.

P.S.

The Globe Theatre, home of Shakespeare's company, burned to the ground in 1613 when a misfired cannon set the roof ablaze during a performance of *Henry VIII*. See "A Firsthand Account of the Globe Fire," page lv.

THE COMEDIES

AS YOU LIKE IT

With *As You Like It*, Shakespeare decided to try his hand at the "pastoral," a popular Elizabethan comedic genre that painted an idyllic portrait of rural life and the quaint and amorous shepherds who typified its simple existence. Shakespeare was not content merely to adopt the form: *As You Like It*, which draws heavily from Thomas Lodge's famous pastoral *Rosalynde*, is both a pastoral and a gentle parody of the genre. But the curtain does not rise on *As You Like It*'s wonderful forest of Arden, where the formal pastoral takes place; the action begins at the home of young Orlando de Boys, near the all-too-"civilized" court of Duke Frederick.

Orlando complains to his trusted elderly servant Adam that ever since his father died, his oldest brother, Oliver, who was entrusted with his care and education, has sent their middle brother to school but has kept him home and treated him like a stable hand, forcing him to live among the farmworkers and to labor with the livestock. Orlando is at the end of his rope. When Oliver arrives and strikes him, Orlando seizes Oliver by the neck, refusing to release him until he promises to treat Orlando as their father wished. Oliver agrees, but secretly plans to be rid of him. His chance presents itself: the famed wrestling champion Charles comes to visit. He and Oliver discuss the fact that Duke Frederick has usurped the dukedom from his elder brother, Duke Senior, who now camps out in the Forest of Arden with his band of supporters. Duke Senior's only daughter, Rosalind, remained at the court at the insistence of Duke Frederick's only daughter, Celia, with whom she has shared a deep bond of sisterhood since infancy. Charles then confides that Orlando has signed up to wrestle him in an upcoming bout before Duke Frederick, and Charles fears he will hurt the lad. Oliver says that Orlando is a villain who will try every which way to kill Charles in the ring; he exhorts Charles to beat Orlando to the punch. Charles thanks him for the tip.

In Duke Frederick's palace, Rosalind grieves for her banished father as Celia tries to cajole a smile from her. Touchstone, the court fool, arrives, and the three learn that

Charles the wrestler has killed several of his challengers, and the match's venue is about to resume right here. In come Duke Frederick, his retinue, and the wrestlers—Orlando's bout is next. Rosalind and Celia attempt to dissuade him from wrestling, to no avail. Lo and behold, Orlando defeats Charles! But when he identifies himself, Duke Frederick refuses to give him the promised prize, because Orlando's late father had opposed his seizure of the dukedom. After Frederick leaves, Celia and Rosalind remain behind to congratulate Orlando. Rosalind, who has fallen in love at first sight, gives him her necklace to keep. Orlando, who has fallen every bit as hard, accepts it. As soon as the young women leave, Orlando finds out Rosalind's identity. He is warned that Duke Frederick intends to harm him and flees the court.

Rosalind and Celia are discussing Orlando when Duke Frederick suddenly appears and banishes Rosalind: she is too popular with the citizenry, who may back her should she seek to regain her father's dukedom. The Duke leaves as abruptly as he arrived, and Celia reassures her reeling cousin that by banishing her, the Duke has banished them both. The two decide to find Rosalind's father in the Forest of Arden. To ensure their safety en route, Rosalind will disguise herself as a boy named Ganymede and they'll travel as brother and sister. They will also ask Touchstone to accompany them.

Cut to the Forest of Arden, where Duke Senior and his band of noblemen extol the virtues of the bucolic life they've carved for themselves in the forest. They mock an absent member of their company, Jaques, for his melancholy, and Duke Senior requests that they fetch him.

Back at Duke Frederick's court, Frederick has discovered Celia's absence. Suspecting that she and Rosalind have teamed up with Orlando, he sends his men to arrest the young man. If Orlando has already fled, the men are to arrest Oliver instead. Meanwhile, Orlando is at home, poised to flee. Adam insists on accompanying him, dismissing Orlando's concern for his well-being, and they head for the woods.

In the woods, Rosalind (now Ganymede), Celia (now Aliena), and Touchstone are exhausted. They encounter a shepherd named Corin, from whom they learn of a cute little cottage they can purchase, along with a plot of land and a flock of sheep that they can hire Corin to tend . . . perfect!

At Duke Senior's forest enclave, Jaques lampoons a song sung by another nobleman, poking fun at the nobles' idealization of this life in the forest that has been foisted upon them.

Orlando and Adam have been trekking through the underbrush for too long: Adam collapses, weak with exertion and hunger. Orlando sets off to find him some sustenance. He stumbles across Duke Senior's enclave and, drawing his sword, interrupts dinner just as Jaques was describing an encounter he had with "a Fool" (actually Touchstone). Duke Senior realizes that Orlando has hijacked their meal out of desperation, and invites him to eat. Orlando explains about Adam and goes to fetch him. While he is gone, Jaques remarks quasi-existentially on the seven stages of a man's life. But when Orlando returns with Adam, Duke Senior treats the old man with kind reverence, in direct refutation of Jaques's condescending assessment of Adam's advanced stage of life.

Meanwhile, Oliver has been hauled before Duke Frederick, who doesn't believe that Oliver is ignorant of his brother's whereabouts. Oliver's possessions are confiscated and he is given one year to produce Orlando or be killed or banished.

Speaking of Orlando, he is busy writing bad love poems to Rosalind (whom he believes is still in Duke Frederick's court and lost to him forever), which he tacks up on trees throughout the forest. Touchstone twits Corin about his simple existence, but Corin, sans idealization, points out the lifestyle's benefits. Rosalind enters reading one of Orlando's odes, followed by Celia, who is reading another, even worse than the first. Celia knows who has written them and, after teasing Rosalind awhile, finally reveals that the author is Orlando, who is here in the forest with Rosalind's father, Duke Senior. Speak of the devil, along comes Orlando, exchanging barbs with Jaques. Rosalind and Celia hide and observe the interchange. After Jaques leaves, "Ganymede" swaggers out and introduces himself to Orlando, stating that he is expert at curing people of love—if Orlando will come by his cottage every day and woo him as he would woo his love, he will pose as this Rosalind whom Orlando is so smitten by, and will cure him. Orlando eagerly agrees.

Touchstone has taken up with a simple young goatherd named Audrey. Jaques overhears the Fool's remarks on love and marriage, which go right over the rather thick young woman's head. When a priest arrives to marry the couple, Jaques interrupts, objecting that they are not in a church, and breaks up the ceremony.

Orlando is late for his first appointment with "Ganymede," to Rosalind's chagrin. She and Celia then witness an interesting exchange between Silvius, a young shepherd, and Phebe, the shepherdess who spurns his love. Rosalind (as Ganymede, of course) intercedes, berating Phebe for her cruel rejection of a decent suitor and urging her to grab the offer while she can, since she is no bargain and it may be her only one. Phebe is smitten by this cute and edgy newcomer to the forest. After Rosalind and Celia leave, Phebe denies having fallen for the "lad," but softens toward Silvius, agreeing to grace him with her company provided he'll deliver letters she will write to Ganymede.

Rosalind has met up with Jaques, whom she chastises for his melancholy. Orlando then finally shows up, and Rosalind (as Ganymede-posing-as-Rosalind) chastises him for being late. In true boy-imitating-girl style, she overacts, pretending to sulk and act coquettish, and derailing each of Orlando's advances. After a mock wedding ceremony, Orlando leaves to meet Duke Senior, promising to return at two o'clock that afternoon for his next session. After he leaves, Rosalind tells Celia that she is more in love with him than ever.

That afternoon, Orlando is late again. While Rosalind and Celia await him, Silvius delivers a letter from Phebe, and when "Ganymede" reads it aloud, the shepherd is crushed to hear that it is a love letter. "Ganymede" sends him back to Phebe with instructions to love Silvius instead of "him." Orlando's brother Oliver suddenly arrives, with apologies from Orlando and a strange tale to tell: Orlando was returning to meet with Ganymede when he saw a lioness, poised waiting to pounce on a sleeping man. Upon closer examination, Orlando realized that the man was his evil older brother. He considered leaving his brother to his bloody fate, but could not. He wrestled and defeated the lioness, but was injured in the attempt. Orlando's kindness prompted a complete change of heart in Oliver, and the brothers buried the hatchet. Orlando is now recuperating and Oliver has come bearing a bloody handkerchief as proof of the tale. Upon seeing the bloody handkerchief, Rosalind faints. She is quickly resuscitated and is led into the cottage by "her sister, Aliena," and Oliver . . . who have fallen in love at first sight.

Meanwhile, Touchstone and Audrey bump into Audrey's other suitor, William.

Touchstone talks circles around the young man, who, bewildered, gives up his suit and wanders away.

Oliver tells Orlando of his love for "Aliena": choosing to remain in the forest with her and tend sheep, he relinquishes their father's estate to Orlando. Orlando will invite Duke Senior et al. to the wedding, which will be held tomorrow. When Rosalind arrives, Orlando tells "Ganymede" that seeing his brother's happiness makes him pine for the real Rosalind even more. "Ganymede" assures him that "he" can conjure up the real Rosalind—Orlando can marry her the following day, at the same time as Oliver and "Aliena." Phebe strides in, with Silvius in her wake. She is furious that Ganymede has shared her love letter aloud. "Ganymede" strikes a deal with her: she should arrive tomorrow at the double wedding. If Ganymede can marry her at the time, he will. If he can't, she must promise to marry Silvius. Phebe consents.

The wedding day arrives. Duke Senior and his entourage keep Orlando, Oliver, and "Aliena" company as they await "Ganymede," who soon arrives with Silvius and Phebe. After receiving assurances from all parties that they will wed the appropriate people (and from Duke Senior that he consents that his daughter and Orlando be wed), "Ganymede" and "Aliena" depart . . . and return later as the two beautiful brides Rosalind and Celia. Phebe realizes instantly that Ganymede will never marry her. Touchstone and Audrey have arrived as well, and Hymen, the god of marriage, arrives and blesses the unions of all four couples. This is followed by the sudden arrival of the middle de Boys brother, who bears the news that Duke Frederick, fearing that Duke Senior was raising an army against him, had come to the forest to fight him, but met "an old religious man" and was converted, bequeathing the dukedom back to his brother, the rightful duke. There is much to celebrate, and all go off to do so except Rosalind, who remains behind to deliver a brief, charming epilogue.

As Anyone Likes It

It has been suggested that the title *As You Like It* is a sexual double entendre that refers to the play's variety of sexual pairings: Orlando's unquestioning and ardent courtship of (and Phebe's inexplicable attraction to) the sexually ambiguous "Ganymede"; the cerebral Touchstone's lust for the animalistic Audrey; and the seeming gender-role reversal of Phebe and Silvius. Because each couple is unique, the play truly offers "something" for everyone.

Forest of Mom

Although there is a wooded area on the French-Belgian border known as the Ardennes, and there was also an ancient forest in Shakespeare's home county of Warwickshire by the name of Arden, the Forest of Arden in *As You Like It* is an invention of Shakespeare's own. The general consensus is that Shakespeare named his delightful setting in honor of his mother, Mary Arden Shakespeare (whose ancestors took their name from the Warwickshire forest) . . . and perhaps it amused him to name the forest's most tongue-tied progeny "William."

THE COMEDY OF ERRORS

Some scholars claim that *The Comedy of Errors* is Shakespeare's first play, perhaps written even before he hit London. We can't verify that it is his first, only that it is his shortest. Don't be misled by the fact that it is sidesplittingly hilarious farce: though it lacks the depth of the Bard's later plays, this one is far from shallow. It grapples with issues of individuality and identity and how they are defined by one's relationships and one's place in society. It also tackles, and ultimately affirms, love in many forms: maternal, paternal, fraternal, intimate, compassionate, spiritual. With *The Comedy of Errors*, the young playwright was off to a running start.

Upon arriving in Ephesus, Egeon, a merchant of Syracuse, was promptly arrested and brought before the Duke, who now explains that according to Ephesian law, any Syracusan found on Ephesian soil must be put to death . . . unless, of course, said Syracusan can pay a hefty fine on the spot. Egeon cannot. He tells the tragic tale that has brought him to the shores of Ephesus. (Pay attention: this is very important exposition!) More than two decades ago, his wife gave birth to twin sons so identical that even their parents could not tell them apart. At the same time, identical twin sons were born to an impoverished woman and Egeon purchased them to be raised with his sons as their servants. Egeon and his wife were aboard a ship with the four babes when a storm struck. Egeon lashed himself and one pair of master/servant babies to one end of a mast while his wife did the same for herself and the other pair. They floated in this fashion until the mast split in two, separating Egeon and his two charges from his wife and hers. Egeon witnessed his wife and the babies picked up by what seemed to be a boatful of Corinthian fishermen, who sailed out of sight. Egeon, his remaining son, and the remaining servant baby were saved too, but they never saw Mrs. Egeon and the other babies again. Egeon raised his remaining son and his son's servant until they were eighteen, at which time they set off into the world to find their brothers; the two have not been heard from since. Egeon has been desperately seeking them lo these past five years; his search has unluckily landed him in Ephesus. Taking pity on the poor man, the Duke gives him until sunset to secure the outrageously large sum that will spare his life. In the interim, he is taken into custody.

By amazing coincidence, Egeon's son, Antipholus of Syracuse (hereinafter Antipholus S.), arrives in Ephesus shortly thereafter with his trusty servant, Dromio of Syracuse (hereinafter Dromio S.). Giving Dromio S. all of their money and luggage, Antipholus S. sends him ahead to check them into an inn while he checks out the town. Only moments later, he sees Dromio of Ephesus (hereinafter Dromio E.) approach. Yes, you've guessed correctly: the long-lost twins reside right here in Ephesus, unaware that they even have twin brothers. And yes, each parent thought s/he had the pair named Antipholus and Dromio.) Mistaking Dromio E. for his own Dromio S., Antipholus S. asks why he's returned so quickly. Dromio E. (who, in turn, mistakes Antipholus S. for his own master, Antipholus E.) responds with the seeming nonsequitur that Antipholus is late for the midday meal and his wife is furious. Antipholus S. asks Dromio E. what he's done with the money he gave him. Miscommunication ensues: Dromio E. rightfully claims he has none of his master's money, Antipholus S. denies he's married, and Antipholus S. eventually boxes Dromio E.'s ears. Poor Dromio E. flees, leaving behind an outraged Antipholus S., who is convinced that his servant has stolen his money.

Meanwhile, back at Antipholus E.'s abode, the stew has grown cold and Antipholus E.'s wife, Adriana, is stewing. Her sister, Luciana, tries in vain to calm her. When Dromio E. returns and relates the bizarre conversation he has just had, Adriana sends him back to fetch his master. She is beside herself that her husband has denied being married: she believes he has lost interest in her because her looks are fading with age.

On the streets of Ephesus, Antipholus S. is perplexed: he's just gone to the inn, and his money and luggage are safely stowed there . . . Dromio must have been jesting. Dromio S. arrives and, when asked, denies that he ever denied having his master's money. In fact, he denies having seen his master at all since he was sent to check into the inn. He thinks his master is jesting with him, until Antipholus S.—certain that Dromio S. is lying—beats him, to Dromio S.'s understandable indignation. Adriana and Luciana appear to summon them to lunch. Adriana is understandably indignant that Antipholus has denied—and continues to deny—being married to, or even knowing her. She tells him that she had sent Dromio to fetch him, which furnishes Antipholus S. with seeming proof that Dromio just lied to him when he denied fetching him to this woman's home earlier, and shocks poor Dromio S., who did no such thing. Both men are thoroughly perplexed (Dromio thinks he is in Fairyland, being tormented by sprites), but Antipholus S. decides to humor the clearly insane woman (with the cute sister) who insists on feeding him. Adriana believes the men are performing a practical joke to torment her. As she leads Antipholus S. into the house, she posts Dromio just inside the gate, with strict instructions to permit no one to enter. And she means no one.

Antipholus E. arrives at home shortly thereafter with Dromio E., bringing a goldsmith and a merchant to dine with him. The door is locked against them and Dromio S. (who cannot see who stands outside the gate) keeps it so. Antipholus E. is understandably indignant at being barred entry to his own home and suspects that Adriana is entertaining a lover; furious, he departs to dine with the Courtesan, who runs an establishment known as the Porpentine. He sends the goldsmith to fetch the gold chain he had commissioned for Adriana: he will give it to the Courtesan instead.

Inside Antipholus E.'s home, Luciana gives Antipholus S. a stern talking-to about his husbandly duties. Enchanted, he falls hopelessly in love with her. When he declares as much, Luciana is horrified and assumes her brother-in-law has gone insane. She rushes off to fetch her sister. Dromio S. runs in, traumatized. He has just encountered a most unattractive kitchen wench who claims they are betrothed. This wacky town is bewitched, and he and his master want out of it, pronto . . . though Antipholus will miss the delightful Luciana. Moments after Dromio goes off to make travel arrangements, the goldsmith returns with the gold chain for Antipholus E. Saying he'll return later to be paid for it, he leaves it with the bewildered Antipholus S., who dons it and heads out to meet Dromio S.

Later that afternoon, the goldsmith invites a merchant, to whom he is in debt, to accompany him to the home of Antipholus E., where he'll collect the money he's owed for the gold chain and will turn it over to the merchant. As they set out for the house, Antipholus E. and Dromio E. approach them, coming from lunch with the Courtesan. Antipholus E. sends Dromio E. to purchase a length of rope, with which he intends to beat Adriana for locking him out of his home. When the goldsmith asks to be paid for the chain he delivered earlier, Antipholus E. truthfully denies having received a chain from him. The goldsmith has Antipholus E. arrested for refusing to pay for the chain.

Antipholus E. is outraged. Dromio S. approaches and tells Antipholus E. that he's made arrangements for them to depart on a ship that will be leaving port shortly. Antipholus E. thinks his servant has gone mad: he sent him to buy rope, not book passage. He sends a confused Dromio S. to Adriana to retrieve a purse full of gold coins for bail.

At the home of Antipholus E., Luciana and Adriana are discussing his apparent sudden love for Luciana when Dromio S. arrives, tells the women about Antipholus's arrest, and retrieves the purse of money, departing in haste to post bail for the man he thinks is his master so that they can skip town.

Back on the street, Dromio S. encounters Antipholus S. Dromio S. presents his master with the purse full of gold (*more* free gold?!). Yet another confusing conversation ensues, in which Antipholus S. baffles Dromio S. by asking whether he's made arrangements for their departure, and Dromio S. baffles Antipholus S. by asserting that he already informed Antipholus S. of the ship they are to board, then further baffles him by reminding him of his arrest and by insisting that Antipholus ordered him to fetch the gold. To complicate matters further, the Courtesan from the Porpentine arrives, demanding the gold chain that she maintains Antipholus promised her at lunch in exchange for a ring he took from her at that time. Antipholus S. and Dromio S. can only conclude that she must be a sorceress sent from Satan to condemn their souls. They attempt to "unconjure" the spirit to make her vanish. The Courtesan thinks that Antipholus has lost his mind, and hurries to his abode to tell Adriana so. To get her ring back, the Courtesan plans to tell Adriana that in a fit of madness Antipholus took it from her by force.

Meanwhile, Antipholus E., still under arrest, awaits the return of Dromio S. with the bail money. Instead, he gets the return of Dromio E. with a length of rope. Antipholus E. beats Dromio E. with the rope. Adriana, Luciana, and the Courtesan arrive with one Dr. Pinch, whom they've employed to exorcise the demons they believe are making Antipholus mad. Furious, Antipholus E. strikes Dr. Pinch. He asserts that he is not insane and that his wife is playing a cruel trick on him, much like the one she played at lunchtime when she shut him out of his home. This confirms to the women that he is insane (after all, they are certain that they dined with him themselves). Dr. Pinch concurs with their assessment, and has Antipholus and Dromio bound and carted off to a dark room at home. The women remain behind and are shocked when Antipholus S. and Dromio S. suddenly arrive, rapiers drawn (their only remaining recourse in a town of sorcerers). The terrified women think that the madmen have escaped from Dr. Pinch, and run, screaming. Antipholus S. and Dromio S. are pleased to see that "these witches are afraid of swords." They depart, to board ship and be gone from this wild, witchy place.

En route to their ship, Antipholus S. and Dromio S. encounter the goldsmith and the merchant, who wrongly deduce that Antipholus E. must have escaped arrest. Worse, he is wearing the gold chain he earlier denied having received! They scuffle and swords are drawn, just as Adriana, Luciana, and the Courtesan approach with others. When Adriana insists that the two be bound up, Antipholus S. and Dromio S. escape into the nearby priory, where they seek sanctuary. The Abbess of the priory, a gracious and reverend middle-aged woman, emerges. She forbids anyone to seize the two men and returns within. By amazing coincidence, the Duke happens by, reluctantly bringing to the chopping block Egeon (remember Egeon?), to whom he has taken a shining, but who has failed while incarcerated to raise the funds needed to ransom his life. As the Duke passes by, Adriana intercepts him, asking him to hand down justice against the Abbess for failing to relinquish Adriana's husband. The Duke sends for the Abbess, and while they await her return, a messenger arrives in a lather, announcing that Adriana's husband and servant have broken loose and are about to kill Dr. Pinch. Adriana contradicts the messenger about Dr. Pinch; after all, her husband is in the priory. Suddenly, Antipholus E. and Dromio E. arrive . . . *from a different direction than that of the priory*. Adriana is shocked. Antipholus E. is distraught, begging justice of the Duke. Egeon is amazed, for he believes he is looking at his son Antipholus S. and his servant Dromio S. Confusion mounts as Adriana, the goldsmith, the Courtesan, the merchant, Antipholus E., and Dromio E. each tell his or her contradictory version of events. Egeon thinks he can clear the matter up: he turns to Antipholus E. for acknowledgment that he is his father, which Antipholus E. denies. The situation can get no screwier; the time has come for a deus ex machina to set them aright. And so, along comes the Abbess, along with Antipholus S. and Dromio S. The townspeople are shocked. Adriana is shocked. The twins are shocked. Egeon is the most shocked of all . . . it turns out that the Abbess is his long-lost wife! All the confusion is smoothed over, Egeon's life is spared, Antipholus E. and Adriana are reconciled, Antipholus S. and Luciana are free to love each other, and, after everyone has repaired to the priory for a celebratory feast, the two Dromios stay behind to bask in the sight of each other. Since they cannot ascertain which twin is the elder, they resolve to treat each other with equal respect, and enter the priory hand in hand.

ERRORS' ESCAPADES IN EPHESUS EMANATE FROM EPHESIANS

Shakespeare deviated from his source for *Errors—Menaechmi*, an ancient Roman play by Plautus—in several aspects, including the setting. Shakespeare replaced Plautus's Epidamnus with Ephesus, which was better known to his audience because of its prominence in the New Testament. Ephesus was a notorious center of witchcraft and magic, which made it an ideal setting for the bewildering events of the play, which are repeatedly attributed to supernatural forces by the out-of-towners. Shakespeare also drew heavily from St. Paul's Epistle to the Ephesians throughout this play, especially in Luciana's and the Abbess's admonitions to Adriana for her jealousy.

LOVE'S LABOUR'S LOST

Love's Labour's Lost is the only one of Shakespeare's comedies in which none of the characters is ever faced with any real danger. In fact, not much happens. Instead, the play consists mostly of witty repartee and philosophical discourse. And yet in the midst of all the sparkling banter and gorgeous poetry, the characters manage to evolve.

When we first meet them, the young King Ferdinand of Navarre and his courtier friends Longaville, Dumaine, and Berowne have taken an oath to give up partying and forsake the company of women for three years and to spend the time in scholarly pursuits. Longaville and Dumaine sign on more readily than Berowne, who points out that (1) it's unnatural, (2) three years is a long time to live without women, and (3) the Princess of France is already on her way, and you can't blow off the Princess of France. The King agrees to make an exception for the Princess.

Constable Dull arrives with a letter from Don Adriano de Armado, a pretentious Spaniard. The letter accuses Costard, a country swain, of having spoken to Jaquenetta, a country maid, thus breaking the King's edict against consorting with women. The King sentences Costard to a weeklong bran-and-water fast, with Don Armado as his keeper.

Meanwhile, Don Armado is at home chatting with his young and clever servant, Mote, whose mocking responses are too sophisticated for his verbose but dull-witted master. Don Armado confides to Mote that he's surprised to find himself in love with the socially inferior Jaquenetta. Constable Dull brings in Costard and Jaquenetta, and turns Costard over to Don Armado's keeping. Don Armado takes Jaquenetta aside and confesses his love. She's unimpressed, and leaves with the Constable. Don Armado sends Costard to be locked up by Mote, and then grandiloquently soliloquizes his love for the lowly Jaquenetta.

The Princess of France has arrived in Navarre. Having heard of the King's boycott of women, she sends her adviser Boyet to tell him that they must meet to discuss serious business. She and her waiting-gentlewomen gab about the King's courtiers, whom they've met before. They're not sorry to be visiting: Maria says Longaville is esteemed for having many—ahem—talents. Katharine thinks Dumaine is incredibly hot; and Rosaline likes Berowne because he makes her laugh.

Boyet returns, totally put out. He tells the Princess that she and her entourage will be staying in tents in the fields, so that the King won't have to break his oath by letting women into his palace. When the King arrives with his courtiers, the Princess lets him know that she's not pleased with the accommodations. She then delivers a message from her father, the King of France, while Berowne and Rosaline flirt shamelessly with each other. After the King apologizes for the inconveniences his oath has caused, he and his buddies return to the palace. One by one, each courtier sneaks back out to ask Boyet the name of the particular lady in whom he is interested (and who, in each instance, just happens to be the one who is interested in him).

Back in Don Armado's neck of the woods, Armado has written a glorious love letter to Jaquenetta. He sends Mote to fetch Costard, and when they return Don Armado orders Costard to deliver the letter to Jaquenetta. (What is he thinking, we wonder, sending his rival to be his representative?)

Berowne also has a love letter for Costard to deliver—this one, of course, is for Rosaline. Two letters, one illiterate messenger. Can you tell where this is heading? Left alone, Berowne takes this opportunity to expound upon his love in perfect verse.

The women are out hunting. Along comes Costard, with a letter for Rosaline. Oops! He's delivered the wrong letter! The Princess has Boyet read Don Armado's fustian, hyperbolic, sesquipedalian verbiage aloud. Much amusement ensues, for characters and audience alike.

Meet two new characters: Holofernes, a nearly incomprehensible Latin-spouting schoolteacher, and Nathaniel, a curate, discuss the women's hunt using pseudo-academic language. Constable Dull, who can't understand them, is trying to participate. Along come Jaquenetta and Costard, looking for someone literate to read Jaquenetta's letter. Nathaniel reads it aloud. Oops! It's the other letter—a love sonnet from Berowne to Rosaline. Holofernes tells Jaquenetta to deliver the letter to the King, as it may be important. She goes, taking Costard with her.

Berowne wanders the grounds alone, pining over Rosaline. He sees the King approaching and hides. The King enters, pining over the Princess, and reads a love poem he's composed to her. He sees Longaville approaching, and hides. Longaville enters, pining over Maria, reads his love poem, sees Dumaine approaching, and hides. Dumaine enters, pines, reads poem; doesn't get a chance to hide. Longaville jumps out and hypocritically accuses Dumaine of breaking his vow. The King jumps out and hypocritically accuses Longaville of breaking his vow. Berowne jumps out, hypocritically accuses them all, and is on a roll about "no women for three years" when Jaquenetta and Costard appear with his love poem. Berowne tears it up, but the others recognize his writing. He sheepishly admits his guilt and rationalizes all of their behavior, stating that their vow contradicted the nature of young men—if they want to study for three years, they should be studying love. The others agree! They go off to make plans to woo their sweeties.

Don Armado feels very important because he's been asked to prepare a pageant to entertain the Princess. He and Holofernes decide to enact a tableau of the Nine Worthies (a dramatic lineup of legendary heroic warriors: Joshua, David, Judah Maccabee, Hector of Troy, Julius Caesar, Alexander the Great, King Arthur, Charlemagne, and our favorite, Godfrey of Bouillon).

The Princess and her friends are discussing the gifts they have received from their respective suitors when Boyet arrives to warn them that the men plan to visit them disguised as Russians. The Princess comes up with a plan: she and her women will be masked when the men arrive. To confuse the men, each woman will wear the gift given to one of the others. In come the costumed men, with music and revelry. Each man takes aside the woman wearing the token he has given (i.e., the wrong woman), and professes his love in insultingly drippy language. Each woman responds mockingly. After the men leave, the women laugh that each man has sworn undying love to the wrong woman. Boyet tells them that the men will be back, in their own attire.

The men soon return, and the women tease them by describing the goofy "mess of Russians" that visited them earlier. The men try to keep up the pretense but quickly realize that they've been had, and confess. When the King swears that his earlier words of love to the Princess were true, he's shocked to discover that those words were sworn to Rosaline. Berowne figures out that the women had switched identities, and upbraids Boyet for tipping them off about the Russian disguises.

In comes Costard, who announces that the pageant is about to begin. Throughout the pageant, the nobles mercilessly heckle the performers. In the middle of Don Armado's performance of "Hector," Costard decides to announce to all that Jaquenetta is pregnant and accuses Don Armado of being the father. Don Armado challenges him to a duel, but when it seems he may actually have to fight, he squirms out of it.

Everything comes to an abrupt halt with the sudden arrival of Monsieur Marcade, a messenger who brings the sobering news that the Princess's father is dead. The Worthies are sent away, and the Princess prepares to return to France that night. With Berowne's help, the King candidly tells the Princess that he loves her. The Princess apologizes for the light treatment the women gave the men's prior advances—she explains that they believed the men were only filling time with pleasant diversions. She tells the King that she will accept his suit on the condition that he live in ascetic seclusion while she mourns her father's death throughout the coming year. The King agrees. Katherine and Maria exact similar promises from Dumaine and Longaville. Rosaline insists that Berowne spend the following year using his wit to comfort the terminally ill. Against his better judgment, Berowne pledges to do so.

Don Armado returns and announces that he has pledged to work as a farmer for three years to prove his love to Jaquenetta. He asks the nobles if they will hear the pageant's concluding song. They agree. The song is sung. The play is done.

Inconsequential Courtly Capers and Incomprehensible Courtly Commentary

Although the earliest version of *Love's Labour's Lost* dates from 1598, there is evidence that some draft of it was first presented in the late 1580s or early 1590s in a private court performance. Such plays, called Court Comedies, were written for courtly audiences and often centered on witty, refined dialogue, topical and scholarly references, and in-jokes. With *Love's Labour's Lost*, the twenty-nine-year-old fledgling writer created a lovelier piece of froth than had any of his colleagues and developed the form further by giving its characters depth and its content meaning. Nevertheless, the play's pervading topical and scholarly references and dated in-jokes make much of *Love's Labour's Lost* difficult for today's audiences to understand: many of its conversations and jokes refer to political and philosophical disputes of the time. In particular, Shakespeare mercilessly shreds George Chapman's stoic philosophy as set forth in his epic poem *The Shadow of Night* (Chapman may have been the model for the pedantic schoolmaster, Holofernes). Actors preparing roles in this play nowadays are bound to say "What the . . . ?" now and again.

Making Fun of the French: An English National Pastime

In *Love's Labour's Lost*, Shakespeare turned prominent French nobles of the day into objects of humor. Henri, the real King of Navarre (later King of France), and the Renaissance-style academy he founded are lampooned in the figure of Ferdinand and his ill-conceived stoical curriculum; prominent men in Henri's court become Ferdinand's rash and frivolous courtiers. The French are great lovaires, *non*? Not Shakespeare's courtiers, whose ludicrous wooing methods get them in hot water with their lady friends.

King Henri did receive a visit from a French princess, Margaret of Valois (a.k.a. Queen Margot), to discuss—among other things—the fate of Aquitaine, as in the play, but far from wooing her, he was actually (1) already married to her and (2) estranged from her. Since the long-standing French-English rivalry was well under way by the sixteenth century, Shakespeare's courtly audience would have reveled in this parody of their counterparts across the Channel.

THE MERCHANT OF VENICE

The Merchant of Venice revolves around two ancient folktales familiar to Elizabethan audiences. The fable of the pound of flesh derives from ancient Roman law, and is one of the many details Shakespeare drew from *Il Pecorone* ("The Simpleton"), an Italian story published in 1558 that was his primary source for the play. The tale of the three caskets first appears in a ninth-century romance, but Shakespeare based his version of it on a popular collection of Latin stories called *Gesta Romanorum*, published six hundred years later. Shakespeare wove these tales together, adding an element that had recently become popular in secular theatre, the Jewish villain. Here's how he did it.

Antonio, a Venetian merchant, has invested all his money in trading expeditions, but he insists to his friends that he is not worried—he's sure his business ventures will be successful. His best friend, Bassanio, is flat broke, but has his own scheme to get rich quick: he plans to woo and win a wealthy heiress named Portia, who is also reputedly beautiful and brilliant. All he needs is a little loaner so he can court the lady properly. Antonio has no cash at the moment, but gallantly offers to let his friend borrow against his credit.

Over at the grand estate of Belmont, the aforementioned heiress has her own troubles. She discusses with her waiting-gentlewoman, Nerissa, her frustration with her late father's will, which requires that Portia marry whichever man chooses correctly among three caskets, one of which contains his written approval and a portrait of Portia. Luckily, all the suitors who have come courting thus far have declined to take the risk, as choosing the wrong casket carries grave consequences: the suitor must vow never to marry at all. Portia is extremely relieved to see them go, as none of the suitors has appealed to her in the least. She and Nerissa share a good laugh as they review the sorry lot. There is, however, one gentleman Portia has met in the past whom she wouldn't mind having as a suitor. His name is . . . Bassanio.

Back in Venice, Antonio and Bassanio visit Shylock, a Jewish moneylender, to apply for a loan. Shylock hates Antonio, who lends money without interest, thus bringing down the rate, and who spits on Shylock, kicks him, and hurls anti-Semitic epithets when he sees him in public. Antonio admits that Shylock must view this as a loan made to an enemy. But Shylock offers a "friendly" deal to Antonio, who would prefer to borrow without interest: he will make the three-month loan interest-free—but if Antonio cannot pay it back in full when it comes due, Shylock may take payment in a pound of Antonio's flesh. Despite Bassanio's objections, Antonio agrees, confident that his investments will pay off with plenty of time to spare.

In the meantime, Shylock's servant, Launcelot Gobbo, debates with himself whether he should leave his Jewish master and seek employment elsewhere. Launcelot asks his old, blind father to entreat Bassanio to employ his son. When Bassanio arrives, old Gobbo does so, and Bassanio hires Launcelot. Bassanio next encounters his friend Gratiano, who asks if he may accompany him to Belmont. Bassanio agrees, on the condition that Gratiano behave himself properly.

Over at Shylock's house, his daughter, Jessica, says goodbye to Launcelot and asks him to deliver a letter to her secret suitor, Lorenzo, who will be dining with Bassanio that evening. Left alone, she briefly soliloquizes her desire to leave her father, become a Christian, and marry Lorenzo.

Launcelot finds Lorenzo with Gratiano and their friends, planning a masque for Bassanio's dinner. He delivers Jessica's letter, and Lorenzo asks him to return to her with a message that he will not fail her. When the others depart, Lorenzo confides in Gratiano that he and Jessica plan to elope that night. Launcelot, meanwhile, returns to Shylock's house with an invitation to dine at Bassanio's, which Shylock grudgingly accepts, warning Jessica to guard the house while he is gone. Before he departs, Launcelot manages to convey to Jessica that Lorenzo will soon arrive.

Later that night, Lorenzo's friends accompany him as he comes to collect Jessica, who is disguised, to her embarrassment, as a page. The two go off together to be married. Antonio arrives with news that the wind has shifted and the masque has been cancelled—Bassanio is about to sail for Belmont. Gratiano hurries off to join him.

In the meantime, the Prince of Morocco has arrived at Belmont and is eager to try his luck for Portia's hand in marriage, despite the risk involved. He and Portia review the inscriptions on the caskets together. The first is gold, and offers "what many men desire"; the second is silver, and promises he who chooses it "as much as he deserves"; and the third is of lead and warns, "Who chooseth me must give and hazard all he hath." The Prince chooses the golden casket and is disappointed to find a reproachful message that "All that glisters is not gold." His hopes dashed, he quickly departs, after which Portia remarks, "a gentle riddance . . . Let all of his complexion choose me so."

Back in Venice, Antonio's friends worry over him. Shylock was infuriated by the loss of his daughter—as well as the gold and jewels she took with her—and they fear he will take his anger out on Antonio if the debt is not paid on time. This is a distinct possibility, as rumor has spread that a Venetian vessel recently went down in the English Channel. They can only hope that the vessel was not Antonio's.

In Belmont, the Prince of Arragon has arrived and now makes his choice among the caskets. He opens the silver one, only to find a portrait of a fool and a rhyme urging him to "Be gone." He soon complies—Portia has once again narrowly escaped lifelong misery. A visitor from Venice is announced, and Portia hopes it is Bassanio.

Antonio's friends in Venice have learned that one of his ships has definitely sunk. They run into Shylock, who is still furious over his daughter's elopement and is glad to hear of Antonio's misfortune. Denigrated repeatedly throughout the conversation for his heritage, Shylock insists that a Jew is just as human as any Christian both physically and psychologically, and asserts his intention to take revenge on Antonio just as a Christian would. Shylock's friend Tubal reports to him that he has not been able to track down Jessica. Shylock is distressed, but is somewhat consoled when he learns that yet another of Antonio's ships has been wrecked.

Bassanio has been courting Portia at Belmont, and the two have fallen in love. Portia is reluctant to let Bassanio try his hand at the caskets, lest he fail. Bassanio, however, can't stand the uncertainty. He examines the caskets and rejects the showy gold and silver. Portia is overjoyed when he opens the leaden casket and finds her portrait inside, with a scroll inviting Bassanio to "claim her with a loving kiss." Portia gives Bassanio a ring which—at her behest—he vows never to part with. Conveniently, Nerissa and Gratiano have also fallen in love, and he vows to keep her ring as well. Just as the four begin to plan a double wedding, Lorenzo and Jessica arrive with one of Antonio's friends, bearing the news that all of Antonio's ships have been lost, that Antonio's debt has come due, and that Shylock intends to claim his payment of a pound of Antonio's flesh (which will certainly kill him). Portia urges Bassanio and Gratiano to depart for Venice right away, as soon as their marriage ceremony has been performed. She will provide them with twenty times the amount of the debt with which to pay Shylock and save their friend.

Meanwhile, Antonio visits Shylock, who refuses to listen to him, insisting that he will "have [his] bond." Antonio is resigned to dying, but hopes that Bassanio will come to see him through it.

Portia leaves her household in the charge of Lorenzo and Jessica, pretending that she and Nerissa will reside at a convent until their husbands return. She then sends a message ahead to her friend at Padua, Doctor Bellario, requesting certain garments and documents. Finally she lets Nerissa in on the plan: they will follow their husbands to Venice disguised as men.

In Venice, court is in session, with the honorable Duke of Venice presiding. The Duke suggests that Shylock show Antonio mercy, but Shylock demands that his bond be fulfilled, and turns down Bassanio's offer to double his money. The Duke reveals that he has sent to a learned scholar of law, Doctor Bellario, for judgment in this case. A messenger from Bellario is announced, and in come Portia and Nerissa, disguised as a brilliant young lawyer and his clerk, sent by Bellario. After interviewing Antonio and Shylock, Portia eloquently counsels Shylock to show mercy. When he refuses, demanding the exact terms of his bond and nothing else, Portia awards Shylock exactly that, but stops him before he can strike, warning that he must remove the pound of flesh without spilling a drop of Antonio's blood, as blood is not mentioned in the agreement. Shylock relents, and says he will accept the cash, but Portia rules that according to his own suit, he may only collect his bond or drop the case entirely. Shylock admits defeat, but Portia is not through punishing him. Citing Venetian law, she points out that as a foreigner who attempted to take a Venetian's life, Shylock is subject to the death penalty, and to the confiscation of his entire estate. The Duke decides to let Shylock live, and Antonio persuades him to take only half of Shylock's estate, to be held in trust for Jessica and Lorenzo. The Duke also follows Antonio's suggestion to require Shylock's conversion to Christianity.

As court is adjourned, Portia refuses to accept a fee from Bassanio and Antonio. When Bassanio presses her to take some token of their gratitude, she asks for his ring. Reluctantly, Bassanio tells the "lawyer" that he cannot give away the ring, as he vowed to his wife never to remove it from his finger. After Portia departs, Bassanio regrets his show of ingratitude and sends Gratiano after her with the ring. When he catches up with the women (still disguised), Portia graciously accepts the ring and asks that Gratiano show her "clerk" the way to Shylock's house, to deliver some documents he must sign. Nerissa tells Portia, aside, that she will try to get Gratiano's ring away from him, too.

Lorenzo and Jessica are enjoying a beautiful, moonlit night at Belmont when Portia and Nerissa arrive, just ahead of Bassanio, Gratiano, and Antonio. The women berate their husbands for relinquishing their rings. When the men have been sufficiently tortured, Portia reveals the truth, adding the good news that Antonio is not ruined after all—three of his ships are safe in harbor. She tells Lorenzo and Jessica of their inheritance, and the happy group repairs to the house to celebrate.

There Are Things in This Comedy . . . That Will Never Please

In the ongoing discussion about *Merchant*, the question of whether Shakespeare intended to focus on anti-Semitism or rather on the practice of usury is occasionally posed. A glimpse into Jewish history reveals that the two are inexorably linked.

In medieval and Renaissance Europe, the term *usurer* (moneylender who charges interest) was practically synonymous with *Jew*. Christian doctrine did not permit the practice of usury, and yet, as the basis of Europe's economy shifted from agriculture to commerce and the need for capital grew, usury became an "ugly" necessity. Jews, who had traditionally been merchants and artisans, were gradually forced into usury in more than one way: ever refugees, expelled from one locale after another (hence the term *Wandering Jew*), they had to resort to professions such as usury, which dealt in portable commodities; also, Jews were viewed as "aliens" and "infidels" and were progressively barred from their traditional professions and from owning land. In a vicious cycle, Christians pushed their Jewish neighbors into the usury they needed but could not themselves perform; the Jews' "sinful" profession then further confirmed the Christians' view of the Jew as anathema.

In countries from which the Jews had been banished, this view of them persisted in the public consciousness long after they were gone. This was true in England, from which all Jews had been banished in 1290 by King Edward I, who extorted their financial resources and confiscated their immovable properties. The few Jews who straggled back into England over the next centuries had either converted to Christianity or were posing as Christians, practicing Judaism in secret. Nevertheless, three centuries after the expulsion, the "Jewish moneylender" was still a commonplace. Whether despite or due to the Jews' absence, fallacies about them flourished, such as the Jews' descent from the Devil and their habitual use of the flesh or blood of Christians in ritual practice. One famous accusation of such blood libel was memorialized in enduring popular ballads blaming the accidental death of "little Hugh of Lincoln" on the town's Jewish population; for Elizabethans, the "pound of flesh" Shylock demands would have been reminiscent of this alleged practice. Thus, Shakespeare and his contemporaries had no contact (as far as they knew) with actual Jews and no first-hand knowledge of their culture, and were instead creating characters based on the demons of popular lore.

In the late sixteenth century, the Jewish villain became a popular feature on the London stage. The most famous predecessor of Shylock is, of course, Barabas, the central figure in Christopher Marlowe's *The Jew of Malta*. Barabas was a Machiavel nonpareil who mass-murdered Christians for the sheer joy of it, and who was ultimately boiled to death in hot oil, much to the Elizabethan audience's satisfaction. In fact, Barabas was considered so typical a Jew that a series of revivals of Marlowe's play was mounted immediately following the torturous execution of the Queen's physician (and spy for the Queen), a Spanish convert to Christianity named Rodrigo Lopez, who was falsely convicted of plotting to poison her. At his execution, when he stated on the scaffold that he loved the Queen even more than he loved his Savior, the crowd jeered, "He is a Jew! He is a Jew!" *The Merchant of Venice* was written in the anti-Semitic aftermath of Lopez's sensational killing (it is believed that when Gratiano calls Shylock's soul that of "a wolf . . . hanged for human slaughter," Shakespeare is punning on Lopez's name, the Latin root of which means "wolf"). Although he capitalized on a hot topic, Shakespeare also managed to create a Jewish character who transcended the stereotype and the stock characters on which he was based, and who would eloquently express the plight of the Jew—and all oppressed people—for centuries to come.

THE MERRY WIVES OF WINDSOR

According to tradition, Queen Elizabeth I so enjoyed the character of Falstaff in Shakespeare's *Henry IV, Part One* that she made a special request to see him in a comedy—and more specifically, to see him in love. Moreover, it is said that Shakespeare had only two weeks in which to comply! Here's what the Bard came up with:

Shallow, a local justice of the peace, his young cousin Slender, and Sir Hugh Evans, a Welsh parson, arrive at the home of Master Page in the small town of Windsor. Shallow intends to sue Master Page's guest, Sir John Falstaff, who has been poaching on his estate. Evans persuades him to focus instead on making a match between Slender and Page's daughter, Anne, whose dowry is impressive. Master Page emerges from the house, followed by Falstaff, who unrepentantly admits to poaching on Shallow's estate, assaulting his servants, and breaking into his lodge. Mistress Page and her friend Mistress Ford invite everyone inside, but Shallow and Evans stay behind to speak with Slender about whether he'd like to marry Anne Page. When Anne herself appears to call them in to dinner, they leave her alone with the nervous Slender, who babbles awkwardly at her until they, too, are called in to eat.

Falstaff's expenses at the Garter Inn, where he lodges, are too heavy for his pocketbook. Luckily, he has a plan to make some easy money: he believes that both Mistress Page and her friend Mistress Ford have the hots for him—since they control their husbands' money, he will seduce them both to obtain some of it. He has written letters to both women, which his followers Nym and Pistol refuse to deliver. He fires them and sends the letters with Robin, his page.

Meanwhile, Evans has sent Slender's servant Simple to the home of Dr. Caius. He is to ask Caius's housekeeper, Mistress Quickly, to promote Slender as a suitable match for her friend Anne Page. Just as Mistress Quickly agrees to help, Dr. Caius returns home, so she hides Simple in the closet. Dr. Caius soon discovers him there, and is alarmed by Simple's explanation for his visit since the doctor intends to marry Mistress Anne himself. He sends Simple packing, with a letter challenging Evans to a duel.

Mistress Page has received Falstaff's love letter and is outraged by its insulting implications. Mistress Ford comes to visit her friend, having received an identical letter. She is particularly distressed by Falstaff's communiqué because such a letter would surely provoke her husband's jealous nature, should he discover it. The two women plan their revenge: they will lead Falstaff on until he goes bankrupt courting them, and humiliate him in the process. They meet up with Mistress Quickly, and engage her as their messenger to Falstaff. Meanwhile, their husbands have been warned by Pistol and Nym that Falstaff plans to seduce their wives. Page found Nym to be a scoundrel, and dismisses his warning, but Ford judged Pistol to be sensible, and now begins to obsess jealously about his wife and Falstaff. The men run into Shallow and the Host of the Garter Inn, who are on their way to the duel between Evans and Dr. Caius. Ford takes the Host aside and bribes him to introduce him to Falstaff as "Master Brooke."

Mistress Quickly visits the Garter Inn, where she delivers the wives' responses to Falstaff. Both letters are encouraging, and Mistress Ford invites him to visit her that very morning at eleven. After Mistress Quickly departs, Falstaff is visited by "Master Brooke" (Ford in disguise), who claims that he is in love with Mistress Ford, but that she rejects him, claiming to be completely chaste. "Brooke" pays Falstaff to seduce Mistress Ford, so that he can catch her committing adultery, thus paving the way for his own advances. Falstaff assures "Brooke" that he has an appointment with Mistress Ford that very morning. After Falstaff departs for the rendezvous, Ford soliloquizes that he intends to be revenged.

Dr. Caius waits in a field outside Windsor where he believes the duel is to take place. Evans seems to be a no-show. Shallow, Slender, Page, and the Host arrive and try to convince the hotheaded Dr. Caius that it's all for the best that the duel is off. They persuade him to accompany the Host to Frogmore to see Anne Page. The others then proceed to a field outside Frogmore, where Evans has been waiting to duel Dr. Caius. The Host soon steers Caius that way, and the intended duelists argue over the location of the meeting place. Finally, the Host reveals that he deceived them both, so as not to lose either his doctor or his priest in the duel. He encourages them to befriend each other. They do so, united by the mutual desire to get revenge on the Host, who has made fools of them both.

Master Ford encounters Mistress Page, who is on her way to visit his wife, accompanied by Robin. As she heads toward his house, he soliloquizes that his suspicions are confirmed by seeing Mistress Page with John Falstaff's page: both she and his own wife are obviously unfaithful. He resolves to catch his wife in action with Falstaff at the eleven o'clock rendezvous. To this end, he invites the group just returning from the canceled duel back to his house (planning to have them all witness his wife's shame and Falstaff's punishment). Shallow and Slender excuse themselves, as they have an appointment with Mistress Anne Page. Page assures Slender that he supports his love suit to Anne, although his wife prefers Dr. Caius as a future son-in-law. The Host suggests a third suitor, young Master Fenton, but Page rejects him—he feels Fenton is too high-born for Anne and suspects that having squandered away his own fortune, Fenton is probably interested only in her dowry.

Meanwhile, the wives have plotted their revenge. Falstaff arrives and subjects Mrs. Ford to his inept wooing techniques until Mistress Page interrupts them with news that an irate Master Ford is on his way home to search out his wife's lover. The women hide Falstaff in a huge laundry basket which the servants carry out just as Ford arrives with his friends. The men search the house but find nothing, and Ford admits to his unreasonable jealousy.

While Master Page is busy reproaching his friend, his daughter, Anne, is at home urging Fenton to continue seeking her father's approval as her suitor. When Shallow and Mistress Quickly arrive with Slender, Anne steps aside to hear Slender court her and learns that he's perfectly happy to marry her since his cousin wishes it, but has no particular feelings for her himself. Anne's parents arrive, and encourage Slender. Page then invites Shallow and Slender into the house, and orders Fenton away. Fenton entreats Mistress Page to support his suit, as he sincerely loves Anne. Mistress Page says she will consult with her daughter, whom she ushers inside. Before departing, Fenton pays Mistress Quickly to ingratiate him with Mistress Page. Left alone, Mistress Quickly soliloquizes that having promised to help all three suitors, she will do just that (although she herself prefers Fenton).

After his narrow escape in the laundry basket, Falstaff was unceremoniously dumped into a muddy ditch adjoining the Thames. He has made his way back to his rooms at the Garter Inn, mortified and indignant, not to mention filthy, soaked, and shivering with cold. But when Mistress Quickly arrives with an apology for the mishap and a second invitation from Mistress Ford, Falstaff greedily accepts. His next visitor is "Master Brooke," to whom he relates the details of his adventures, emphasizing the great hardship he has undergone for Brooke's sake. He promises to triumph at his upcoming second rendezvous with her. Ford is more determined than ever to get revenge on Falstaff.

Once again, Falstaff visits Mistress Ford, and once again they are interrupted by the arrival of Mistress Page with a warning of Master Ford on the warpath. This time the two women conceal Falstaff by disguising him as a local old woman who is reputed to be a witch and whom Ford detests (he has threatened to beat her if she ever returned to his home). Ford arrives with his friends, tears through all the dirty laundry, and is once again confounded by the absence of Falstaff. Further angered at finding the old witch in his home, he drives "her" away, beating "her" mercilessly. Delighted by the success of their plot, the wives now decide to let their husbands in on it, and to engage their help in a third round of Con the Con Man. With the help of Evans, the two couples devise a scheme whereby Falstaff will meet the wives by an ancient oak in Windsor Forest. He is to come disguised as Herne the Hunter, a folkloric figure who wears stag's antlers. They will use this setup to publicly humiliate Falstaff. Secretly, Master Page plans to take this opportunity to have Anne elope with Slender, while Mistress Page makes a similar plan for Anne and Dr. Caius.

Yet again, Mistress Quickly visits Falstaff at the Garter Inn. She tells him of the wives' invitation to a threesome in the forest. Falstaff sends Mistress Quickly off to get his costume, and then receives a visit from "Master Brooke." This time, he promises, he will succeed with Mistress Ford.

Meanwhile, Anne and Fenton have learned of her parents' respective plots, and have concocted a plot of their own. Fenton bribes the Host to assist them.

At midnight, all the plotters hide in the forest awaiting the night's events: Shallow, Slender, and Page in one location; the wives and Dr. Caius in another; and Evans in a third, escorting Anne and the town's children, who are dressed as fairies and elves. Falstaff arrives at the ancient oak in his disguise and is delighted when the wives appear. To his dismay, however, the women soon hear a noise and run away. Suddenly Falstaff finds himself accosted by fairies and elves, who harass him under the guidance of the Fairy Queen (Anne in disguise). During the hubbub, Slender and Caius each sneak off with the disguised fairy he believes to be Anne. Meanwhile, Anne herself sneaks off with Fenton. Finally, the Pages and the Fords call a halt to the chaos and reveal the whole plot to the humiliated Falstaff. Slender and Caius then return, each having come *this* close to marrying a boy. Fenton and Anne appear and announce that they are married. The Pages accept Fenton into the fold and the Fords invite everyone—including the chastened Falstaff—back to their house for a conciliatory celebration.

A MIDSUMMER NIGHT'S DREAM

The "Ancient Athens" in which Shakespeare set this play is actually Elizabethan England, loosely disguised by a whimsical concoction of history, mythology, and fantasy.

As the play opens, Theseus, the Duke of Athens, and his bride-to-be, Hippolyta, Queen of the Amazons, are at the palace discussing their upcoming wedding. They are interrupted by Egeus, a nobleman whose daughter, Hermia, refuses to marry the man he has chosen for her.

OK, pay attention: Hermia and Lysander are in love, but Egeus has promised her to Demetrius, who also loves her. Demetrius was formerly engaged to and in love with Hermia's best friend, Helena. Helena still loves Demetrius madly.

Egeus wants Theseus to enforce the Athenian law according to which Hermia must obey her father's wishes, or choose between being put to death and becoming a nun. Theseus gives Hermia time to weigh her options.

Hermia decides to run away with Lysander. Along comes Helena. Hermia and Lysander confide in her that they are escaping to the other side of the forest, beyond the jurisdiction of Athenian law, where they can be married and live with his aunt. After they leave, Helena soliloquizes that she can score brownie points with Demetrius by telling him where Hermia and Lysander have gone.

The action now shifts to the forest . . . the domain of the fairies. Puck, who serves Oberon, King of the Fairies, encounters a fairy from the court of Titania, the Fairy Queen. Puck tells the fairy that Oberon is furious because Titania will not give him a little human boy she has been raising. Oberon and Titania arrive, and continue their argument. Titania refuses to give up the boy. After she leaves, Oberon tells Puck his plan to humiliate Titania and get the boy from her. He orders Puck to fetch him a flower with magical properties. The juice of this flower, when dribbled into sleeping eyes, will cause the victim to fall madly in love with the first creature he or she sees upon waking. Oberon plans to dose Titania that night in her forest nest.

After Puck leaves, Oberon watches as Demetrius charges through the forest, seeking to kill Lysander and "rescue" Hermia. Helena follows close at his heels. He tells her that she makes him sick, and threatens to harm her if she follows him further. He takes off. She follows him further.

Puck returns with the magical flower. Oberon, who feels bad for Helena, sends Puck to find Demetrius and dose him with part of the flower, so that he will fall in love with her. Oberon then goes to Titania's forest bed, where her fairies are lulling her to sleep. After she drops off, he doses her.

Meanwhile, Lysander and Hermia have been trudging through the forest and are exhausted. They go to sleep on the ground. Puck discovers them lying there and thinks that Lysander is the Athenian whom Oberon told him to find, so he doses him. After Puck leaves, Demetrius charges by, with Helena following close at his heels. Out of breath, Helena pauses for a brief monologue. She sees Lysander and wakes him up. Having been dosed, he immediately falls in love with her. He begins wooing Helena, but she thinks he is mocking her. Hurt and upset, she leaves. Lysander follows close at her heels. Hermia wakes up from a bad dream, discovers that Lysander is gone, freaks out, and goes to look for him.

Meanwhile, the Mechanicals, a group of bumbling laborers from Athens, have been in the woods rehearsing a play that they hope to perform at Theseus and Hippolyta's wedding. Puck comes across them and watches the rehearsal, invisible. When the lead actor, Bottom, finishes his scene and "exits" behind a bush, Puck can't resist a little mischief—he entertains himself by giving Bottom the head of an ass. Bottom reenters the scene, oblivious to his condition, and scares the pants off his fellow actors. They scatter, willy-nilly, leaving him alone to ponder out loud their strange behavior.

Titania, who has been asleep nearby, is awakened by Bottom and, having been dosed, immediately falls in love with him. Titania dotes on Bottom. She orders her fairies to wait on him and bring him to her bed.

Puck rushes back to Oberon and reports his multiple successes: not only did he dose the Athenian as ordered (or so he thinks), but he also helped to humiliate Titania beyond Oberon's wildest expectations. Just then, Hermia charges in, Demetrius following close at her heels. She accuses Demetrius of having harmed Lysander, while Demetrius professes his love for her. She says that she hates him and storms off. Demetrius, worn out, goes to sleep on the ground. Oberon is furious that Puck has dosed the wrong Athenian. He takes this opportunity to remedy the situation by dosing Demetrius. He then orders Puck to find Helena and bring her back, so that she will be in Demetrius's sight when he wakes up.

Puck quickly returns with Helena, Lysander following close at her heels. Demetrius wakes, sees Helena, and immediately falls in love with her. When he and Lysander begin to compete for her love, Helena thinks they have teamed up to mock her. Hermia arrives, and when both men reject her, Helena thinks that Hermia is playing along in this cruel mind game. Meanwhile, Hermia can't understand why Lysander no longer loves her. She thinks that Helena has stolen him with her greater height. A catfight ensues. The men defend Helena until their machismo mandates that they go off to duel over her. Helena, afraid, runs away, after which Hermia exits.

Oberon wants the situation corrected right away. He instructs Puck to surround the young men with a fog and then lead them away from each other by imitating their voices. When he has exhausted them, and they have fallen asleep, Puck is to dose Lysander with a new herb which will lift the spell and restore his love for Hermia. Puck does as he is told. Exhausted, Helena and Hermia each wander in and fall asleep on the ground.

Later, at her forest lair, Titania and her fairies entertain Bottom before bedtime. Puck and Oberon arrive to find Titania and Bottom asleep in each other's arms. Oberon explains to Puck that a short while ago, he encountered Titania and demanded the boy. Dosed and infatuated with Bottom, she happily turned over the child. Now Oberon pities her and lifts the spell. Titania wakes and is horrified at the sight of her bedfellow. Reunited, Titania and Oberon dance.

Early morning: Theseus, Hippolyta, and Egeus are hunting in the forest. They stumble across the four lovers, asleep on the ground. The lovers explain what little they can remember of the previous night. Since Demetrius no longer wants to marry Hermia, Theseus overrides Egeus's wishes, and authorizes Hermia and Lysander to marry. He invites the two couples to be wed alongside Hippolyta and himself. As the nobles all go off toward Athens, Bottom wakes up with his own head. He is amazed by his "dream" and thinks it would make a good play. He goes off and finds his pals. Happy to see one another, they head toward Athens to prepare for their performance.

Back at the palace, the triple-wedding ceremony has taken place, the couples have dined, and the entertainment is about to begin. Theseus and Hippolyta discuss the strange story the young lovers have told them. The lovers then join them and Theseus's servant, Philostrate, brings the list of entertainment options. He discourages Theseus from selecting the Mechanicals' play, but Theseus insists. The actors enter. Quince, the director, presents a prologue, but is so nervous that he garbles its meaning. The actors introduce their characters and proceed to mutilate a beautiful and tragic love story. The newlyweds weep . . . with laughter. The Mechanicals conclude their performance with a dance, after which the lovers retire.

Out come the fairies. Puck explains that this is the hour when fairies frolic. The fairies sing and dance. Oberon blesses the newlywed couples. After the other fairies leave, Puck remains onstage to persuade the audience to think of the play as nothing more than a dream.

MUCH ADO ABOUT NOTHING

Much Ado About Nothing is the first of Shakespeare's three late Comedies, crafted on the eve of the period in which he wrote his great Tragedies; and, like *As You Like It* and *Twelfth Night*, the play is hilarious even as it poses darker moral issues. And yet, unlike the later Problem Plays, these three Comedies never depart from the comedic format, and their endings are unambiguously joyful. But let's start at the beginning:

Don Pedro, Prince of Aragon, has been victorious in battle; he now arrives at the estate of Leonato, Governor of Messina, accompanied by Claudio and Benedick, two young gentlemen who have fought heroically, and Don Pedro's younger brother, Don John, a surly sort who has only lately been back in his older brother's good graces. Leonato greets them with his daughter, Hero, and his niece, Beatrice, inviting them to be his houseguests for a month. Beatrice and Benedick once shared a romance that didn't pan out and the two dislike each other; they exchange witty barbs deriding love in general and each other in particular. After everyone departs, leaving Claudio and Benedick alone, Claudio confides that he has fallen desperately in love with Hero and wants to marry her. Benedick denigrates marriage, but when Don Pedro returns, Benedick tells him of Claudio's wish. Don Pedro teasingly suggests that Benedick, too, shall fall in love someday. In the interim, Don Pedro will help secure Hero for Claudio by posing as him at that evening's masked ball and wooing the young woman. Once he's sure of her affections for Claudio, he will approach her father on the young man's behalf. Eavesdropping, Governor Leonato's brother overhears this conversation incorrectly, and mistakenly reports to Leonato that Don Pedro wishes to marry his daughter.

Meanwhile, Don John's follower Borachio tells him of the Prince's plan to woo Hero on behalf of Claudio. A self-described malcontent and villain who is envious of both his brother and Claudio, Don John decides to find a way to foil the plan.

Later that evening, just prior to the masked ball, Beatrice jokes disparagingly about marriage while Leonato coaches his daughter to respond positively to Don Pedro's anticipated love suit. Their houseguests arrive in masks, and the ball begins: Don Pedro and Hero dance and talk, as other masked couples pair up. Benedick dances with Beatrice, who recognizes him despite his mask and, feigning ignorance of his identity, gossips about that fellow Benedick, saying—among other things—that he is *the Prince's jester* and *a very dull fool*. Benedick is flabbergasted; he is also deeply hurt. Don John tells Claudio that Don Pedro is wooing Hero for himself; Claudio believes him and leaves, upset, telling Benedick on his way out. Benedick then confronts Don Pedro on Claudio's behalf, and is assured that Claudio is mistaken. Benedick confides in the Prince that he is rattled by Beatrice's harsh comments about him and flees when he sees her approaching with Claudio, whom Don Pedro had sent her to fetch. Don Pedro announces that Leonato has consented to the marriage of Claudio and Hero. Claudio is thrilled and the wedding date is set for the following week. After Beatrice leaves, Don Pedro enlists everyone's help in implementing a plan to bring Beatrice and Benedick together.

Borachio approaches Don John with a scheme to undermine the marriage between Claudio and Hero: Hero's waiting-woman, Margaret, is hot for Borachio and would gladly meet him for a tryst. He will instruct her to do so in Hero's bedchamber the night before the wedding, wearing Hero's clothing. Don John need only bring Claudio past Hero's window and Claudio will believe he is seeing Hero and a lover in flagrante delicto. Claudio will surely then call off the wedding.

Alone in the orchard a few days later, Benedick muses that Claudio has betrayed his soldierly spirit by falling in love and becoming a simpering idiot. Benedick doesn't think himself capable of doing so, unless the many qualities he seeks in a mate could ever all be rolled up in one woman . . . impossible! Suddenly he sees Don Pedro, Leonato, and Claudio who, unbeknownst to him, have come to implement phase one of Don Pedro's plan to dupe him and Beatrice. They stage a conversation for him to overhear, in which they loudly discuss the fact that Beatrice is tormented by unrequited love for Benedick, but will maintain her facade of crossness toward him and will never reveal her love. After they leave, Benedick soliloquizes his amazement, acknowledges to himself that he is hopelessly in love with Beatrice, and, in utter refutation of everything he said a few minutes earlier, determines to marry her. Speak of the devil, along comes Beatrice, who crossly states that she has been sent against her wishes to summon him to dinner. Sure that her words carry a double meaning of love, he thanks her gently for taking the time and effort to do so.

Later, phase two of Don Pedro's plan is implemented: Hero and Margaret stage a conversation for Beatrice to overhear, in which they sing Benedick's praises and remark that the poor man is deeply in love with Beatrice, but that Beatrice must not know, lest she exploit the fact as an opportunity to be cruel to him. After the women depart, Beatrice soliloquizes her astonishment, as well as her determination to set aside her prior contemptuous behavior and return Benedick's love.

Don Pedro and Claudio can't help but notice a change in Benedick and they tease him that he must be in love, but he blames any such changes on a toothache and goes off to speak with Leonato. Don John arrives to tell Claudio and Don Pedro that if they accompany him that night he will prove that Hero is having a fling with someone.

Cut to the night watch. The malapropism-prone Constable Dogberry and his men are patrolling the area when they overhear Borachio telling another of Don John's cronies of his success in duping Claudio and Don Pedro into believing that Hero has spent the night with a man. He further confides that Claudio intends to publicly humiliate Hero at their wedding the next day. Though befuddled, Dogberry and his men have enough good sense to arrest Borachio and his comrade.

Back at the *palazzo* on the morning of the wedding, Beatrice claims to be ill, but Hero and Margaret tease her that it is lovesickness for Benedick.

Dogberry and his partner have come to inform Leonato of the treachery against Hero, but as he is late for the wedding and the lawmen are inarticulate, he shoos them away, telling them to interrogate their prisoners and write a report that he will review after the wedding.

During the wedding ceremony, Claudio refuses Hero's hand in marriage, publicly denouncing her as unchaste. Don Pedro supports the allegation, explaining that he, Don John, and Claudio saw her at her window with a man the night before. Hero falls to the ground, unconscious, and only Beatrice moves to help her. Claudio, Don Pedro, and Don John leave, and Leonato bewails the shame his daughter has brought upon him, ignoring the assurances of the Friar, Beatrice, Benedick, and the revived Hero herself that she is innocent. The Friar suggests that they publicize that Hero has died, which will move people to pity rather than condemn her. Her "death" will also quell Claudio's anger and rekindle his love for her. If Hero cannot be exonerated, she will be smuggled to a convent to pass the rest of her days, but if her innocence is proved, all will then be set aright. Leonato agrees and departs with the Friar and Hero to implement the plan, leaving Beatrice and Benedick alone together. They acknowledge their love for each other, and Benedick promises to challenge Claudio to a duel, since Beatrice wants to avenge Hero's honor but cannot, as she is a woman.

After a hilariously incomprehensible interrogation of Borachio and his comrade, Dogberry has them bound to be brought before Leonato. Meanwhile, Leonato and his brother tell Don Pedro and Claudio of Hero's death; the two elderly men challenge the Prince and the young soldier to a duel, which the younger men refuse to fight. Benedick arrives and challenges Claudio to a duel, to be fought later, and departs. Just then, Dogberry arrives with his prisoners, and Don Pedro elicits a full confession from Borachio. Now the Prince and Claudio are sorry, and Claudio loves the deceased Hero more than ever. Leonato (who has been apprised of Borachio's confession) arrives while Claudio is expressing his remorse, and instructs Claudio to right the wrong done to Hero by publicly mourning her, proclaiming her innocence, and marrying her lookalike "cousin." Claudio tearfully agrees to do so.

Meanwhile, Benedick tells Beatrice that he has challenged Claudio. The two are bantering flirtatiously when news arrives of Borachio's confession.

Claudio visits what he believes is Hero's burial site, where he reads an epitaph to his lost love. Upon returning to Leonato's estate to wed "Hero's cousin," he is presented

MUCH ADO ABOUT *WHAT*?!?

Shakespeare was a shrewd marketer, who knew that sex meant big box office: Elizabethans—a bawdy bunch—used the slang term *thing* to mean "penis." Thus, the slang term for the vagina was *no thing*, or "nothing" (represented by a zero, which is the same shape as an *O*, another slang term for "vagina"). The word *nothing* is also a pun on *noting*, which, to Elizabethans, was synonymous with *pricking* (playing the notes of a song), which in turn was slang for "having sex." And so Elizabethan audiences were tipped off in advance that the plot of this play would concern the undue fuss made about the alleged removal of a young woman's maidenhead and maidenhood . . . in short, *Much Ado About Nothing*.

with a veiled bride, whom he is delighted to discover is . . . Hero herself! Beatrice and Benedick slip into their old mode of sparring, but when love poems they've written about each other are produced by those around them, they admit their love and agree to marry. Plans for a proper double wedding are discussed and news arrives that Don John has been apprehended. He will be punished, but meanwhile there is merrymaking to attend to. The happy ensemble join in a celebratory dance.

THE TAMING OF THE SHREW

Did you ever have one of those days . . . You've tinkered hard all over Warwickshire, you stop in for a well-deserved brew or three, get thrown out of the local alehouse, take a short nap on the curb, and the next thing you know, you wake up in a sumptuous bed in a palatial mansion with a zillion servants and a gorgeous wife who tell you you're a nobleman? That's the kind of day Christopher Sly is having in the Induction (Introduction) of *The Taming of the Shrew*. What he doesn't know is that while he lay asleep in the gutter, a nobleman came by and decided to play an elaborate practical joke on him. The gentleman took him home and instructed his servants to pretend that Sly is a nobleman who has been suffering from a strange illness that caused him to imagine he was only a poor tinker. A young male servant is ordered to play the role of Sly's wife. When he awakes, the bewildered Sly happily accepts the explanation of his circumstances and is eager to "reacquaint" himself with his "wife." Stalled by the warning that sex so soon upon recovery will cause a relapse of his malady, Sly agrees to watch a comedy performed just for him.

Act I: *Benvenuto a* Padua! Lucentio, a young nobleman, has just arrived with his trusty manservant, Tranio. The two overhear a conversation in which Baptista Minola tells the two suitors of his younger daughter, Bianca, that she will not be wed before her older sister, Katherina. The suitors, Gremio and Hortensio, protest that Katherina is too "shrewish" to find a husband. They humiliate Katherina, joking at her expense until she lashes back at them. Baptista sends Bianca into their house, and she modestly obeys. (Lucentio, watching from the sidelines, immediately falls in love.) Baptista asks Gremio and Hortensio to find tutors to instruct Bianca and he and Katherina then exit. After agreeing to set aside their rivalry temporarily and team up to find a husband for Katherina, Hortensio and Gremio go off together.

Lucentio now implores Tranio to help him get Bianca. Tranio suggests that Lucentio pose as a schoolmaster and tutor Bianca so that he can secretly woo her. Lucentio switches clothes with Tranio, who will pose as Lucentio around town (simple, since no one in Padua has met them yet). When his other servant, Biondello, arrives, Lucentio fills him in on the plan. He then orders Tranio to become one of Bianca's suitors (posing as "Lucentio," *naturalmente*).

(Sly has dozed off. A servant wakes him and his "wife" asks how he is enjoying the play. He finds it excellent and he wishes it was over—he still looks forward to the other pleasures the evening may afford him). This is the last we hear from Sly.)

Still Act I: Petruchio, a gentleman of Verona, arrives in Padua with his servant, Grumio (not to be confused with Bianca's elderly suitor Gremio), to visit his good friend Hortensio and to find a rich wife. Hortensio suggests Katherina, but warns Petruchio that she's "intolerable curst." No problem, says Petruchio, as long as her father has a good reputation . . . and she's rich. Petruchio knows of Katherina's father, and determines—sight unseen—to wed her. Hortensio decides to pose as a music teacher for Bianca, so that he can secretly woo her. Off they go to Baptista's house. Along the way, they come across Gremio and Lucentio, who is disguised as Cambio the schoolmaster. They overhear Gremio hire "Cambio" to tutor Bianca and plead for Gremio as her suitor. Hortensio then greets Gremio and introduces Petruchio as a suitor for Katherina. Tranio (as Lucentio) comes along and asks the way to Baptista's house, acknowledging that he, too, is a suitor of Bianca. They all decide to go off to the tavern to share a bottle of Chianti before getting down to the business of wooing the Minola sisters.

Act II: Katherina has tied Bianca's hands together and torments her, until Dad enters and makes her stop. Katherina caustically expresses her envy and hurt at his favoritism toward Bianca. After she storms out, the suitors and tutors arrive. Petruchio presents himself to Baptista as a suitor for Katherina, and introduces the now-disguised Hortensio as Litio the music teacher, brought to tutor his prospective bride. Baptista tries to warn Petruchio of Katherina's temperament, but Petruchio is resolved. Gremio then presents "Cambio" as a Latin tutor for Bianca. Baptista is tickled. Next, Tranio (as Lucentio) introduces himself as a new suitor to Bianca and presents a lute and some books he has brought as a gift for the daughters. Baptista sends the new "tutors" off to instruct his daughters, and takes Petruchio aside to negotiate Katherina's dowry, warning Petruchio that the deal is contingent on his ability to win Katherina's *amore*. "Litio" then returns with a head injury, announcing that Katherina has used his head to break the lute in half. Petruchio is enchanted: he can't wait to meet her. Baptista sends Katherina out to meet Petruchio. Petruchio teases her flirtatiously, and she rebuffs him, setting off a verbal sparring match. Petruchio declares that he will tame her. Before Kate can reply, Baptista returns with Gremio and Tranio/Lucentio. Petruchio claims to have won Katherina's love, and when she protests, he explains that they have privately agreed that she will continue to act like a shrew in public. Against Katherina's will, the wedding date is set for the following Sunday.

Mamma mia! Bianca's suitors are ecstatic! Baptista will now auction off Bianca to the highest bidder. Gremio is loaded, but Tranio/Lucentio consistently outbids him and is promised Bianca's hand. They are to marry one week after Katherina's wedding, on the condition that Lucentio's father guarantees his net worth. Otherwise, Bianca will be given to Gremio. Baptista and Gremio leave, and Tranio plots to hire someone to pose as Lucentio's father, Vincentio.

Act III: Lucentio (as Cambio) and Hortensio (as Litio) are vying for Bianca's undivided attention so that each can give her a "lesson." Bianca sends Hortensio off to tune his instrument while she studies Latin with Lucentio, who "translates" the Latin passage into phrases that reveal his identity and declare his love. Bianca repeats the phrases, "translating" them to mean that Lucentio should not presume . . . but should not despair. Hortensio's music lesson follows: he uses it to communicate his love to Bianca, but is rejected by her. Each "tutor" is suspicious of the other's intentions.

Katherina's wedding day arrives, but her groom—Petruchio—doesn't. Katherina is humiliated. When he finally does show up, Petruchio is dressed in clownish, moth-eaten, mismatched clothing. Baptista implores him *per favore* to change into something befitting the occasion, but he refuses. As the others go off to the ceremony, Tranio informs Lucentio of his plan to hire a faux Vincentio. Gremio returns and describes the ceremony, in which Petruchio was even more shrewish than Katherina. The wedding party returns, and Petruchio announces that he can't stay for the feast. Despite Katherina's entreaties, and to her utter mortification, he drags her away with him.

Act IV: Grumio, sent ahead to Petruchio's house to prepare for the newlyweds' arrival, tells another servant of their horrible four-hour journey: When Katherina's horse stumbled, she fell under it, into the mud. Rather than helping his bride, Petruchio began beating Grumio for letting the horse stumble. Katherina extracted herself and waded through the mud to pull Petruchio off of Grumio, after which the horses ran away. Grumio warns that Petruchio is in quite a state. The servants experience this themselves—when Petruchio arrives with Katherina in tow, he sends them scurrying and demands that supper be served immediately. He then rails that the food is burnt and inedible (although it looks delicious to the *molto* famished Katherina), and throws it at the servants before his new wife can eat a bite. He decides that he and Katherina will go straight to bed without eating, and leads her off. He returns shortly, and soliloquizes his strategy for taming his shrew: he will deprive her of food and sleep, continuously finding fault with the food and accommodations, all the while professing that he does so for her sake.

Back in Padua, Hortensio (as Litio) has tattled to Tranio/Lucentio that the other tutor is behaving inappropriately toward his betrothed, and brings him to spy on them and see for himself. When Lucentio and Bianca walk by, talking of love, Tranio declares that he will give her up. Hortensio reveals his true identity to Tranio, and says that he, too, has suddenly lost all interest in Bianca, and plans to marry a wealthy widow instead. Hortensio leaves, and Lucentio and Bianca approach. Lucentio and Bianca (who has fallen in love with Lucentio and is now in on his plan) are delighted to learn that Hortensio is out of the picture. Biondello rushes in saying that he has found an old merchant to pose as Lucentio's father, Vincentio. Tranio sends the lovers off, and proceeds to con said merchant: when Tranio learns that the merchant is from Mantua, he says that there is a new law in Padua condemning to death any Mantuans found on Paduan soil. Luckily for the merchant, Tranio is willing to protect him; he will pretend the merchant is his ("Lucentio's") Pisan father, Vincentio. The merchant gratefully agrees.

Back at the ranch in Verona, Petruchio finally brings Katherina some food, but withholds it until he has extracted a *grazie* from her. Just as she is about to eat, a tailor and a haberdasher arrive with a gorgeous hat and gown for her. True to form, Petruchio claims the garments are ill-fitting and cheap and refuses them. He tells Katherina that it is seven o'clock and if they leave now for her father's house, they will arrive by lunchtime. When she corrects him, saying that it is already two in the afternoon and they won't be there until supper, he imperiously declares that it is whatever time of day he says it is, and that she must stop contradicting him.

In Padua, Tranio/Lucentio has dressed the merchant as Vincentio, and introduces him to Baptista as such. Baptista accepts "Vincentio's" guarantee, and sends "Cambio" (the real Lucentio) to inform Bianca. Baptista, Tranio/Lucentio, and "Vincentio" go off to finalize the marriage agreement. When Lucentio returns from his errand to Bianca, Biondello tells him that arrangements have been made for his elopement with Bianca.

As Petruchio and Katherina set out for Padua at midday, Petruchio remarks that the moon is shining brightly. When she contradicts him, he threatens to cancel their trip unless she agrees that the sun is the moon. As soon as she complies, he says it is the sun.

Katherina suddenly gives in: she concurs with his opinion of the sun, and assures him that whatever he calls it, she'll call it. An old man crosses their path. Petruchio points him out to Katherina as a *bellissima* young maiden, and instructs Katherina to greet "her" as such. When she complies, Petruchio says she's gone mad, as this is clearly an old man. Katherina immediately apologizes for her mistake—the sun was in her eyes. The man turns out to be the real Vincentio (the real Lucentio's real father). He, too, is en route to Padua, to surprise his son with a visit. Happy to be the bearer of good news, Petruchio tells the real Vincentio of his son's betrothal to Katherina's sister. Off they go together.

Act V: Lucentio and Bianca sneak off to be married. Petruchio, Katherina, and the real Vincentio arrive at Lucentio's *pensione*. When the real Vincentio knocks and asks to see his son, the merchant comes to his window and insists that he is Lucentio's father. Their argument causes a disturbance, and Baptista arrives with Tranio, who tries to keep up the game. The real Vincentio recognizes his son's servant, but no one believes him. He is about to be arrested as an impostor when Lucentio and Bianca arrive, newly married. Lucentio throws himself at his father's feet and begs his pardon. He explains the whole situation. Baptista is furious that Lucentio has eloped with his favorite daughter, until the real (and really wealthy) Vincentio promises to appease him, and they all go indoors, leaving Petruchio and Katherina in the street. Petruchio demands a kiss, which Katherina is embarrassed to give him in public. He threatens to take her home, and she gives in.

Some time later, all the nobles and their servants are gathered for a banquet at Lucentio's house. After dinner, the ladies withdraw to the parlor, and the men tease Petruchio about his shrewish wife. Petruchio challenges Lucentio and Hortensio to a wager over which of their wives is most obedient. Biondello is sent to fetch Bianca, but returns with the message that—*scusi*—she is too busy to come. Next, Biondello is sent to fetch Hortensio's new wife, the widow, but returns with the message that she suspects her husband is up to some prank, and refuses to come. Finally, Grumio is sent to fetch Katherina, who immediately appears. Petruchio sends her back to get the other two wives, and

A Tale of Two *Shrews*

Once upon roughly the same time, two plays were born. The beautiful and clever play *The Taming of* the *Shrew* was written by Shakespeare and beloved by all (this was before feminism—long before), while the ugly and ill-favored play *The Taming of* a *Shrew* was performed to no acclaim at all, and was soon forgot. This was because *A Shrew* (as it is unaffectionately called) was really an impostor! Most scholars now believe that *A Shrew* was a Bad Quarto, pirated from *The Shrew* without Shakespeare's permission by mnemonically challenged individuals, although some believe it was either the source for *The Shrew* or that both *The* and *A* were developed from the same, earlier source.

A Shrew departs from *The Shrew* in its inferior language and plotline, which includes not two but three sisters (thereby eliminating the rivalry between the suitors), and a continuation and conclusion of Christopher Sly's frame. Directors have occasionally used *A Shrew*'s additional Sly material in their productions of *The Shrew*, to tie Sly's story into a neat little package. Even so, only *The Shrew* got to live happily ever after.

All Shrews Beshrewed

Today, the word *shrew* is used as a derogatory term for a shrill-voiced nag (usually female but sometimes male), but four hundred years ago it might have referred to any woman who defied the patriarchal society in which she lived. In Shakespeare's time, a married woman did not have the status of an individual person; she was merely chattel, owned by her husband, and she had no right to express her own opinions. Because women who did speak out were seen as a threat to male power, being labeled a "shrew" or "scold" also came to have legal ramifications: not just a sharp-tongued or nagging woman, but any woman who spoke her mind could be convicted of being a "shrew" in a court of law, and brutally punished. The intent of the punishment was primarily to make an example of the "shrew" through public humiliation, but the methods used were usually physically abusive as well. While punishments varied, and could include being pilloried, whipped, or dunked (in any weather), the most common sanction was being paraded through the streets wearing a torture device called a brank or scold's bridle, an iron cage in which the woman's head was padlocked. The bridle included a piece of metal that was forced into the woman's mouth; this part of the bridle often had spikes that dug into the tongue and soft palate, or was so large it could cause her to vomit. The victim was led through the streets by a rope attached to this device, so that every tug would jar the bridle, causing further pain and disfigurement, possibly even shattering the jawbone. Because such reinforcement of the status quo was commonplace in Elizabethan society, the subject matter and events in *The Taming of the Shrew* were unremarkable to its original audience.

when the three return he proves how easily he has won the wager by ordering Katherina to give the other women a lesson in wifely "virtue and obedience." She complies in a long speech in which she chastises the other two women and outlines the proper roles and behavior of husbands and wives. Petruchio kisses her, says *ciao!* to his buddies, and takes her off to bed.

TWELFTH NIGHT, OR WHAT YOU WILL

The complexity of *Twelfth Night*, the last of Shakespeare's Comedies, betrays the playwright's eagerness to get on to the weightier matters of the Tragedies.

As is fitting for a comedy with a dark side, the action is set in an exotic place that inspired an uneasy fear in Elizabethans. Illyria, a region on the Adriatic coast, was known to be a hotbed of piracy but was also remote enough to seem romantic: just the sort of place where one might find a fellow such as Orsino, Duke of Illyria, whose love for a local countess has rendered him utterly useless, as he woefully observes at the top of the play. Olivia, the lady in question, has determined to spend seven years in secluded mourning for her late brother.

Meanwhile, there's been a shipwreck on the coast. A young noblewoman named Viola has survived, but fears that her twin brother did not. She meets a local captain, who agrees to help her disguise herself as a man so that she can seek employment with the Duke, since the shipwreck left her almost destitute.

At the home of the lovely Olivia, her servant Maria (Muh-RYE-uh) admonishes Olivia's uncle, Sir Toby Belch, and his visiting friend, Sir Andrew Aguecheek, for their excessive carousing. They ignore her and continue to plan Sir Andrew's courtship of Olivia (which Toby knows is futile, but which will keep Sir Andrew in town, picking up Toby's bar tab).

Viola works fast: she is already in the Duke's employ, disguised as a boy called Cesario, and has become Orsino's favorite. To her dismay, he asks her to court Olivia on his behalf—not such a disagreeable task if she hadn't already fallen head-over-tea-kettle in love with Orsino herself.

Olivia's jester, Feste, is in the doghouse for staying away from court too long, but easily regains her goodwill with his jokes, despite the efforts of Olivia's disgruntled steward, Malvolio, to discredit him. Olivia is told that "Cesario" is at the door and refuses to leave until he speaks with her directly. Olivia reluctantly admits Cesario; she hears his poetic pleas on Orsino's behalf, and falls giddily in love . . . with Cesario. After "the youth" leaves, Olivia sends Malvolio after "him" with a ring that she claims Cesario gave her from the Duke and with an entreaty to return tomorrow.

Miraculously, Viola's brother, Sebastian, also survived the shipwreck! Unaware that his sister is alive, he sets off for Orsino's court. His devoted rescuer, Antonio, decides to follow him, despite his many enemies there.

When Malvolio delivers the ring to Cesario, Viola realizes that Olivia has fallen in love with "him," and soliloquizes her predicament.

Late that night, Sir Toby, Sir Andrew, and Feste awaken Maria and then Malvolio with their loud, drunken reveling. Malvolio berates them all. After he departs, Maria plots their revenge on him: she will forge an ambiguous love letter in Olivia's handwriting which Malvolio will find and believe is meant for him.

Orsino wallows in his lovesickness and wonders if Cesario, too, has been in love. "The youth" confesses to loving someone very much like him. The Duke is too preoccupied to catch on, and sends Cesario off for a second attempt at wooing Olivia on his behalf.

Maria, meanwhile, has planted the forged letter, and she and her cohorts spy on Malvolio as he discovers it. Elated to think that Olivia loves him, he eagerly plans to follow its instructions: he will wear yellow cross-gartered stockings and smile constantly to indicate to his mistress that he received the message and returns her affections. The conspirators are gleeful at their success.

When Cesario pleads Orsino's case with Olivia, she confesses her love for "the youth." Viola rejects her as gently as possible, and Olivia tells "him" to visit again, saying that perhaps she will come to love the Duke. Meanwhile, Sir Andrew decides to give up his suit to Olivia, since she has been favoring Cesario. Sir Toby claims that Olivia was only trying to make Sir Andrew jealous, and convinces him to challenge Cesario to a duel.

On the streets of Illyria, Antonio has caught up with Sebastian. Since this is a dangerous place for him, he entrusts Sebastian with his purse. He goes off to book rooms for them at an inn, where they will meet up later.

Back in Olivia's garden, Malvolio wears an outlandish getup and smiles his face off at a bewildered Olivia. Thinking he is mad, she instructs Maria to take care of him. When Olivia leaves, Maria and Sir Toby plan to tie Malvolio up in a dark room, as though he were truly insane. Sir Andrew arrives with his written challenge to Cesario, and Sir Toby reads it aloud: it is comically unmenacing. When Sir Andrew departs, Sir Toby determines not to deliver his ridiculous letter, but to make the challenge in person instead. He and his friends clear out as Olivia and "Cesario" arrive, still debating whom Olivia should love. Olivia tells Cesario to come again tomorrow. When she heads back to the house, Sir Toby corners Cesario and terrifies "him" with claims of Sir Andrew's deadly skill at swordplay. He then fetches Sir Andrew, giving him the same song and dance about Cesario. The two cringing duelists are about to begin when Antonio, having mistaken the disguised Viola for Sebastian, rushes to his friend's rescue. Antonio is arrested by two officers and turns to Viola, whom he assumes has his purse. When Viola denies knowing him, Antonio accuses "Sebastian" of betrayal as he is led away. Viola hopes this means her brother is alive. As she departs, Sir Toby points out that Cesario is a coward, and Sir Andrew decides to challenge him again.

Later, Feste runs into Sebastian and, thinking he is Cesario, is surprised when he acts as though they are strangers. Sir Andrew arrives with Sir Toby. He, too, is in for a surprise: when Sir Andrew attacks, Sebastian fights back skillfully. Sir Toby draws his sword, but Olivia arrives in time to break up the fight. Sending the others away, she entices a very confused but not unhappy Sebastian to join her in the house.

Feste visits Malvolio disguised as Sir Topas, a clergyman. He insists that the room is not dark at all, and that Malvolio is mad. Sir Toby fears that they have gone too far, and sends Feste back in as himself, to see if he can discover a way to end the prank.

Back in Olivia's garden, Sebastian's mind is boggled. A beautiful, rich lady he's never met before has fallen instantaneously in love with him. When Olivia arrives with a priest, Sebastian readily agrees to marry her.

In front of the house, Antonio is brought before the Duke. He tells the story of his adventures with Sebastian and of his betrayal, all the while pointing out Cesario as the culprit. Olivia comes out and when she persists in rejecting Orsino, he decides to kill Cesario, whom both he and Olivia love, to spite her. Viola says she will willingly die to comfort him. Olivia calls out to her "husband," and Orsino stops in his tracks. The priest arrives and confirms that he married them just hours ago. Sir Andrew and Sir Toby are close on his heels. They are wounded and accuse Cesario. Finally, Sebastian arrives. Everyone is astounded. Sebastian and Viola are reunited, Viola reveals her identity, and all mysteries are resolved. Feste arrives with a letter from Malvolio, claiming he has been misused. He is sent for, and shows Olivia the forged letter. Olivia agrees not to punish Maria for forging it, since Sir Toby set her on to the plot, and has now married her in return. Feste teases Malvolio, who stalks off, vowing revenge. The Duke has decided to marry Viola. All go off to celebrate as Feste wraps up with a droll and somewhat disconcerting little song.

THE TWO GENTLEMEN OF VERONA

Shakespeare's early comedy *The Two Gentlemen of Verona* focuses on two popular themes in Renaissance theatre, both derived from classical drama: romantic love gone awry and male friendship disrupted by romance.

At the start of *Two Gents*, one such male friendship is about to be disrupted. Valentine, a young gentleman, is leaving Verona to see a bit of the world. His best buddy, Proteus, refuses to join him, as he has fallen in love with a local lady named Julia. Although she has made no reply to the love letter he sent, he is determined to win her love.

Meanwhile, Julia is at home questioning Lucetta, her waiting-woman, as to which of Julia's suitors she prefers. Lucetta chooses Proteus, and teases her mistress with the letter he sent, which she has received from his messenger. Julia feigns disinterest, impetuously tearing the letter to pieces and dismissing Lucetta. As soon as she is alone, however, she regrets her action and quickly tries to piece the letter back together, admitting that she returns Proteus's love.

Proteus soon receives a love letter from Julia in return, but his delight is short-lived, for his father has just decided to ship him off to Milan. He is to join Valentine at the court of the Duke of Milan, where he will be "tried and tutored" in the ways of the world.

In Milan, meanwhile, Valentine has fallen in love with Silvia, the daughter of the Duke. Silvia has asked Valentine to write a love letter for her (ostensibly for her to send to someone else), but when he gives her the letter, she nervously gives it back to him without explaining why. After she is gone, Valentine's servant, Speed, explains that this was Silvia's way of letting him know that she loves him.

Back in Verona, Proteus and Julia sadly say their goodbyes and exchange rings. Proteus swears that he will be faithful to his love. Proteus's servant, Launce, is distraught at having to leave his family to join his master in his travels. He complains at length that his hard-hearted dog, Crab, couldn't care less about his troubles.

When Valentine hears of his friend's imminent arrival at court, he praises Proteus to the Duke. Proteus then arrives, and is greeted warmly by Valentine and Silvia. Silvia soon leaves the two friends alone, and Valentine confides in Proteus that he and his beloved are planning to elope. Claiming that he must retrieve his belongings from his ship, Proteus stays behind as his friend goes off to prepare for the elopement. He soliloquizes that he has suddenly fallen in love with Silvia, and that he is willing to betray both Valentine and Julia to win her. Later, Proteus soliloquizes again, convincing himself that his love for Silvia outweighs the loyalty he owes Julia and Valentine. He decides to reveal the lovers' elopement plans to the Duke.

Little does Proteus know that Julia is not patiently pining away in Verona. She has decided to travel to Milan disguised as a page. Lucetta warns her that Proteus may have forgotten her, but Julia is confident that her beloved remains faithful.

Proteus, meanwhile, discloses to the Duke his daughter's imminent elopement, then makes himself scarce as Valentine approaches. The Duke tricks Valentine into revealing the rope ladder he has hidden under his cloak, with which he had intended to climb to Silvia's window that night. Valentine's ingratitude and betrayal infuriate the Duke, who plans to marry his daughter to Thurio (a suitor whom Silvia hates). The Duke banishes Valentine from Milan on pain of death, and leaves him to bemoan his fate until Proteus arrives with Launce. Proteus offers to see his friend off safely, and the two go off together. Launce soliloquizes his own love for a local milkmaid. He has compiled a list of her virtues, and when Speed arrives the two discuss the list.

Thurio and the Duke are distressed to find that Silvia despises Thurio more than ever since Valentine's banishment. They turn to Proteus, who advises slandering Valentine, and "reluctantly" agrees to be the one to do so, since the words of Valentine's close friend will be most effective.

Meanwhile, Valentine and Speed have been wandering in the forest near Mantua, where they are suddenly captured by a band of outlaws who turn out to be gentlemen who were all banished for minor offenses. Admiring Valentine's education and breeding, the outlaws invite him to be their leader. He agrees, on the condition that they promise not to harm women or poor travelers.

Back in Milan, Proteus miserably soliloquizes that his betrayal and deceit have only encouraged Silvia to reject him. He encounters Thurio below Silvia's window, where Thurio has brought musicians to serenade her. During the serenade, the disguised Julia enters, unnoticed by the others. After Thurio and the musicians depart, Julia listens while Proteus woos Silvia, who has emerged on her balcony. When Silvia rebukes Proteus for betraying his beloved back home as well as Valentine, Proteus claims that both are dead. Silvia continues to refuse him, but agrees to give him a picture of herself, since such a false lover as he is well suited to worship the empty shadow of a picture. The hidden Julia is stunned and saddened by what she has seen.

The next day, Silvia is visited by her trusted friend Sir Eglamour, whom she has summoned to help her escape Milan and seek out Valentine. Eglamour gallantly agrees to accompany her on the journey.

Outside the Duke's palace, Launce complains bitterly of Crab's disgraceful behavior: the dog has rewarded Launce's friendship by urinating in the Duke's dining chamber, for which Launce protectively took the blame. Proteus and the disguised Julia come along in mid-conversation. He has agreed to employ this "youth" as his page, and now sends her off to retrieve the promised picture from Silvia and to give her a ring—the very ring Julia had given him when they parted. Though it pains her to do so, Julia dutifully delivers the ring to Silvia and receives the portrait. She is comforted to find that Silvia knows the ring belonged to Proteus's betrayed love, and that she pities her. After Silvia departs, Julia examines the portrait she has received, comparing herself (not unfavorably) with Silvia's image before setting off to deliver it to Proteus.

That evening, Silvia meets up with Sir Eglamour, and makes her escape. When the Duke discovers that his daughter has fled, he immediately goes after her, followed by Thurio, Proteus, and the disguised Julia.

Silvia is captured in the forest by several outlaws, who plan to bring her to their captain. Back at the outlaws' den, Valentine soliloquizes that his lonely forest existence is the perfect setting for his misery over losing Silvia. Hearing a noise in the brush, he hides just as Proteus, Silvia, and Julia approach. Proteus has rescued Silvia from the outlaws, and demands her love as his reward. When she refuses, he threatens to rape her. Valentine leaps forward to defend her. He scathingly disowns Proteus, who is filled with shame and remorse and begs Valentine to forgive him. Valentine not only forgives his friend, but in a show of chivalric friendship, he offers Proteus his beloved Silvia as well. This is all too much for Julia, who falls to the ground in a faint. The others revive her, and she reveals her true identity. Proteus's love for Julia is instantly restored. The outlaws now arrive with the Duke and Thurio as captives. Valentine releases them, and Thurio immediately claims Silvia as his. Valentine fiercely threatens Thurio, who backs down in a pathetic display of cowardice. This convinces the Duke that Valentine is the worthier fellow. He promises Valentine his daughter's hand, and pardons all of the outlaws. The whole ensemble heads back to Milan, where they will soon celebrate the double wedding of the two gentlemen of Verona.

THE PROBLEM PLAYS

ALL'S WELL THAT ENDS WELL

All's Well takes first prize for Most Ironic Title in the Canon. From beginning to end, all is most certainly not well in this play, which is based on a story from Boccaccio's *Decameron*.

As the play opens, its main characters are in mourning. The Countess of Rossillion (a region of southern France) mourns the recent loss of her husband, as well as the imminent departure of her schmuck of a son, Bertram, who is headed for the court of the King of France. Helena, the Countess's ward, is in mourning for her recently deceased father. They both fear that they may presently be mourning the death of the King himself, who is ill. The Countess tells her elderly friend, Lord Lafew, that Helena's father was a famously skilled doctor who could possibly have cured the King. Bertram takes off for the court, accompanied by Lafew. After everyone departs, Helena soliloquizes that she is helplessly and hopelessly in love with Bertram. She bemoans the fact that she's not of noble birth and thus not a suitable match for Bertram. Bertram's lying, cowardly fool of a friend, Parolles, arrives, and although she sees right through him, Helena is pleasant with him for Bertram's sake. After Parolles leaves to join Bertram at court, Helena begins to muse on how she might be able to help the King, and help herself in the bargain.

At court, the King announces that France will remain neutral in the current conflict between Italy and Austria, but that he will allow French noblemen to fight voluntarily for either side. He welcomes the newly arrived Bertram, Lafew, and Parolles. Remembering Bertram's father fondly, the King grieves over his lost youth and his current illness.

Meanwhile, back in Rossillion, the Countess discovers that Helena—whom she adores—is in love with Bertram. She sends for Helena, who confesses her love and also confides her plan to go to the King with rare medicinal potions her father left to her. The Countess sends her off with her full blessing and support.

At the King's court, several young nobles head for the battlefields in Italy, while Bertram looks on and gripes to Parolles that he's been commanded to stay put. Unbeknownst to him, Helena has arrived at court. Lafew brings her to the King, who listens skeptically to her proposal: she is willing to bet her life that her prescription will cure him within twenty-four hours. If it works, she asks only that she be permitted to select her own mate from among the young frat boys . . . oops, we mean nobles, lounging around the palace. They shake on it.

One miraculous twenty-four-hour recovery later, the noblemen are lined up against the wall, and Helena chooses Bertram for her prize. Bertram refuses to marry Helena because of her lower social status, but the King commands him to do so, and Bertram grudgingly acquiesces. As the others head for the ceremony, Parolles impudently insults Lafew, who puts him in his place with scathing retorts, and leaves. The newly married Bertram rushes back in to tell Parolles he has concocted a plan: he will run off to the wars in Italy without consummating his marriage. Parolles will take a message to Helena, instructing her to return to Rossillion.

Later the same day, Lafew tries to warn the obtuse Bertram that Parolles is a jerk, to no avail. Helena comes in and tells Bertram she is all packed and ready to go, and that she is his humble servant. Bertram dodges a goodbye kiss. Helena heads home, while Bertram and Parolles take off for Italy.

Later, the Countess receives a petulant letter from Bertram, explaining what happened and declaring that he will never treat Helena like a wife. The Countess is terribly disappointed in her son's disobedience to the King and his miserable treatment of the worthy and wonderful Helena. Helena has received her own petulant letter, in which Bertram says that until she has his ring, which he will never give her, and is pregnant with his child, which he'll also never give her, he won't be her husband. He tops it off with "Til I have no wife, I have nothing in France." Helena is distraught that she has caused her beloved to risk his life on the battlefield. She soliloquizes her intention to leave so that Bertram can return home. Soon the Countess receives another letter, this one from Helena, explaining that she has become a pilgrim of St. Jaques, and asking the Countess to write to Bertram about it. The Countess does so, hoping that her son will return, and that news of this will eventually bring Helena back as well.

Meanwhile, although she is dressed as a pilgrim, Helena is *not* on her way to the tomb of St. Jaques. She has made great time traveling to Florence, where she meets the Widow Capilet and her daughter, Diana. They just happen to be discussing the new French general (Bertram), who is rumored to have abandoned his wife and has been attempting to seduce Diana. The Widow Capilet just happens to be housing pilgrims, and Helena agrees to stay with her.

In the French camp, two lords tell Bertram that they can prove Parolles to be a coward. Parolles arrives, boasting of his plan to recapture a drum from the enemy, and Bertram eggs him on. Helena, meanwhile, has settled in at the Widow's house and has confided in her, revealing that she is Bertram's wife. She now pays the Widow to participate in a scheme: Diana will agree to let Bertram come to her bedchamber, but will demand his ring first. Helena will then take Diana's place in the darkened bedchamber to fulfill Diana's end of the bargain.

Back at the French camp, Parolles—true to form—has been too cowardly to recapture the drum. Pretending to be foreign mercenaries, the lords and their soldiers rush out speaking gibberish, grab Parolles, and quickly blindfold him. One of the soldiers pretends to interpret the gibberish as they "interrogate" him. Parolles instantly surrenders and says he will reveal everything he knows in exchange for his life.

Meanwhile, Bertram is busy trying to get into Diana's bloomers. Diana obtains his ring in exchange for her promise to sleep with him later that night. He is told he will have only one hour, and is not to speak with her during the visit. (These are restrictions? Bertram's in heaven!)

After the Big Date, Bertram returns to camp, where a rumor has spread that he's scored with Diana, as has word that his wife died on a pilgrimage. Bertram is brought into a tent where Parolles, still blindfolded, reveals military secrets and speaks disparagingly of Bertram as he begs for his own life. Parolles's blindfold is removed and, realizing what a fool he's been, he resolves to become a professional fool. Bertram and the other officers depart for France, as the war has ended.

Helena is also setting out toward France, bringing along the Widow Capilet and Diana, who can corroborate her claim to have slept with Bertram. In Rossillion, meanwhile, the Countess and Lafew mourn Helena's death and decide to marry Bertram to Lafew's daughter. They await the arrival of Bertram and the King, who is coming to visit. Later, outside the palace, Lafew runs into Parolles, who has skulked his way back to Rossillion. Lafew forgives Parolles and agrees to employ him. Back inside the palace, they join the newly arrived King and the Countess in mourning Helena.

When Bertram enters, he is forgiven by the King and told yet again that he is soon to be married, this time to Lafew's daughter (poor Bertram). Bertram gives Lafew a ring for his daughter, but the King recognizes it as one he had given to Helena himself. Bertram denies it was the King's, claiming it was thrown to him from a window in Florence. The King suspects that Bertram may have murdered Helena and has him arrested. With perfect timing, Diana enters and claims that Bertram deflowered her in Florence, showing the ring he gave her as proof. She claims to have given him the ring that the King has just taken from Bertram. Bertram admits that he received it from her. He also admits that he gave her his ring but says that he did so as payment to a prostitute. Parolles, honest for the first time, jumps in to corroborate Diana's version of the story, adding that Bertram had promised to marry her.

Finally, Helena arrives and explains the whole matter. She claims Bertram as her husband, now that she has met the impossible terms he had set out in his letter to her: she has the ring he had given Diana, and she is pregnant with his child. Bertram accepts his fate and the happy King lets Diana pick out a husband and promises to pay her dowry. As far as he can see, all has ended well, so he wraps up the play with a neat little epilogue.

Bed-Tricking Bertram

The implausible bed trick—an old theatrical convention—is a comedic device in which one character takes the place of another in bed, duping a lover under the cover of darkness. Although the device is inherently sordid, Shakespeare has two of his most virtuous and respected heroines use it to achieve honorable and respectable (not to mention expedient) ends. In Helena's case it is the only method she can devise to validate her holy bond of matrimony while preserving Diana's chastity.

Today's audiences may find the bed trick difficult to accept at face value, but it fits the dark tone of *All's Well That Ends Well*. Helena strives alone in a world that demands she adapt to it. As we see in her cure of the King and her use of the bed trick,

Helena has the power to harness potent elements such as drugs and sex—elements that can harm or heal—but because of her admirable nature her actions always yield harmonious and ameliorative results.

MEASURE FOR MEASURE

Here's the recipe for Jacobean tragicomedy: throw one measure of tragedy into the pot, simmer until Act V, remove from fire, add a measure of comedic resolution. To make it a dish fit for a king, set the tragicomedy in Vienna, garnish liberally with zest of sex and death, serve on a bed of moral ambiguity—and *bon appétit*! You've got *Measure for Measure*.

Duke Vincentio (not Italian—don't let the name fool you), ruler of Vienna, decides to take a sabbatical, and leaves Lord Angelo (also not Italian) to govern in his absence, with old Lord Escalus (not from ancient Rome) as Angelo's second-in-command.

On a Viennese street, Mistress Overdone, madam of a local bordello, informs one of her regulars, a gentleman named Lucio (he's not Italian either), that Signor Claudio (born and bred in Vienna) has been arrested and is to be executed in three days for getting his fiancée, Juliet (also *von* Vienna), in the family way. It seems that Angelo has asserted his new powers by enforcing a long-ignored Viennese statute under which extramarital sex is punishable by death. Mistress Overdone's pimp, Pompey (not from Pompeii), arrives with news that Angelo is shutting down brothels citywide. He suggests that they move the business to a new location.

Claudio is being paraded through the streets en route to prison. When he sees his friend Lucio, he explains the mitigating circumstances of his "crime": he and Juliet were engaged, and were to be married as soon as they could afford it. Claudio tells Lucio that he has a sister, Isabella (not Spanish), who is about to take her vows as a nun and doesn't know of his arrest. He entreats Lucio to seek Isabella out and send her to plead with Angelo for his life.

Meanwhile, the Duke is in hiding at a monastery. He explains to one of the friars that over the years his failure to enforce many of the city's statutes has caused his people to grow wayward. He wants the codes obeyed, but he knows his citizens would resent him for cracking down on behavior he's permitted for so long. He prefers to have Angelo reinstate the rules for him. Angelo's a puritanical guy, though, and might act overzealously: to keep tabs on him, the Duke plans to roam Vienna disguised as "Friar Lodowick."

Cut from monastery to convent: Lucio breaks the bad news to Isabella, who agrees to visit Angelo and plead for her brother's life.

The Duke had his deputy pegged: Angelo is determined to execute Claudio, despite Escalus's attempts to persuade him to temper his judgment with mercy. He orders the Provost (jailer) to execute Claudio in the morning. Constable Elbow then arrives with Pompey, who has tried to procure Mrs. Elbow's "services." Annoyed by Elbow's malapropism-laden accusal and Pompey's evasive rebuttal, Angelo assigns the case to Escalus, who merely lectures Pompey and his customer.

Later that day, the Provost returns to see if Angelo has relented; Angelo confirms his order. Lucio ushers in Isabella, who pleads eloquently for her brother's life. Angelo says he'll think about it—Isabella should return the next morning for his decision. After everyone leaves, Angelo, rattled, soliloquizes his intense desire for this young woman.

The Duke, as Friar Lodowick, visits the Provost. When the pregnant Juliet arrives to see Claudio, the Provost explains the couple's plight and the Duke offers Juliet "friarly" advice (repent, etc.).

The next morning, Angelo is still pacing and muttering to himself about Isabella. When she arrives, he insinuates that she can buy her brother's life with her virginity. When she refuses (fearing that she'll burn in Hell for the sin), he ups the stakes: if she rejects the deal, her brother's death will be long and painful. He gives her a day to think it over and leaves her. With nowhere to turn for help against Angelo, she resolves to go to her brother and help him prepare for death.

Meanwhile, "Friar Lodowick" advises Claudio to accept his impending death and has just convinced him to do so when Isabella's arrival renews Claudio's hopes of rescue. She quickly dashes them. When she tells him of Angelo's vile offer, he is outraged and agrees that she couldn't possibly comply, but backpedals as the fear of death overtakes him. He describes his terror and begs Isabella to yield to Angelo. She is horrified. The disguised Duke, who has been eavesdropping, intercepts Isabella on her way out and proposes a plan: Angelo had contracted to marry Mariana, a gentlewoman, but broke the contract when her dowry was lost. Since Mariana still pines for her beloved, the Duke suggests that Isabella accept Angelo's offer, but substitute Mariana at the time of the tryst, under cover of darkness. Thus, Claudio's life will be saved, Mariana will get her man, and Isabella's honor and soul will be spared. Isabella agrees to the plan.

Constable Elbow has arrested Pompey yet again. They run into Lucio, and Pompey hopes he'll post bail, but Lucio refuses, so Pompey is carted off to jail. Lucio encounters the "Friar" and tells him that Angelo is a cold fish. He claims to know the absent Duke personally and insists that the Duke would never have been so harsh on these sex crimes because he was plenty familiar with pleasures of the flesh himself. As Lucio leaves, Escalus and the Provost bring in Mistress Overdone, who was arrested after Lucio informed on her. She complains to the "Friar" that Lucio fathered a child that she has been raising, but is taken away to the prison. Escalus comments to the "Friar" that Angelo is too severe, and the "Friar" replies that if Angelo's own behavior does not meet the standards he sets for others, he'll be judged as severely as those he now judges.

Later that day, the Duke, still disguised, introduces Mariana to Isabella, who has just arranged a rendezvous with Angelo for later that night. Mariana agrees to participate in the plot.

Back at the prison, the Provost offers to release Pompey if he will assist Abhorson, the executioner, at the beheadings of Claudio and a murderer named Barnardine the following day. Pompey is game, and goes off with Abhorson for training. "Friar Lodowick" arrives, holding out hope of a pardon for Claudio, but they soon receive just the opposite: an order for Claudio's execution by four o'clock that afternoon, no matter what. The Provost is to send the head to Angelo by five.

The "Friar" tells the Provost that in a few days he will be able to prove that Angelo himself has committed the same offense for which he has condemned Claudio. He asks the Provost to spare Claudio until then, and suggests that he fulfill Angelo's order by executing Barnardine and substituting his bloody, shaved, and unrecognizable head for Claudio's. The "Friar" assures the Provost that the Duke himself will return to Vienna in two days to set things right. The Provost agrees to the plan.

Pompey and Abhorson try to execute Barnardine, but he declines to be killed, as he has a terrible hangover. Luckily, another prisoner has died, and his head is sent to Angelo instead. When Isabella arrives, the "Friar" tells her that Claudio has been executed but urges her to take heart: when the Duke returns to Vienna tomorrow, Angelo's actions will be avenged. The "Friar" then encounters Lucio, who boasts of his sexual escapades and dishes more dirt about that womanizer, the Duke.

Angelo has received a letter commanding him to greet the Duke at the city gates when he arrives, and to proclaim throughout Vienna that all who wish to complain of injustices should present their cases publicly at that time. Angelo is now guilt-ridden and anxious over his actions.

Shortly before the Duke arrives, Isabella and Mariana prepare to address him. Isabella explains that the "Friar" has warned her that to help her prevail in her suit, he must first pretend to denounce her.

Finally, the Big Convoluted Dénouement. At the city gate, the Duke "returns from his journey" and praises Angelo for a job well done. Isabella accuses Angelo of murdering Claudio and violating her chastity. Refusing to believe her, the Duke has her arrested. Isabella claims that a friar named Lodowick will corroborate her story. Lucio pipes in that he knows this friar—he's the one who was insulting the Duke in his absence. Mariana steps forward and reveals that unbeknownst to Angelo, she went to his bed in Isabella's place the night before. Since they are still contracted to be married and have now consummated the union, she claims Angelo as her husband in all but ceremony. Angelo accuses the women of lying and suspects that someone else has put them up to it. The Duke suggests it might be this Friar Lodowick fellow and orders that he be sent for. He leaves Angelo to judge his own accusers. Moments later he reappears, disguised once more as Friar Lodowick. Lucio accuses him of having slandered the Duke and pulls off his friar's hood to shame him, revealing to all . . . the Duke himself! Lucio and Angelo realize that they're in hot water.

The Duke orders the Provost to take Angelo and Mariana to the nearest church, marry them, and bring them right back. Off they go. Moments later they reappear, married. Having made a respectable (and wealthy) woman of Mariana, the Duke now orders Angelo's death for Claudio's. Mariana begs the Duke's mercy for her husband, and persuades Isabella to do so as well, but to no avail. The Provost brings forth the prisoner Barnardine, Juliet, and Claudio, with his face covered. The cover is removed, revealing to all . . . Claudio, alive! The Duke pardons Barnardine. Then he pardons Claudio. Next, the Duke asks Isabella to marry him. Finally, he pardons Angelo, warning him that he had better love his wife. The Duke can't get past Lucio's slanderous tongue, however: Lucio will be forced to marry the mother of his illegitimate child, after which he will be whipped and hanged (the Duke then relents on the whipping and hanging). After ordering Claudio to marry Juliet right away, the Duke takes Isabella off to his palace, to propose properly to her in private.

The Bed-Trick Shtick

The bed trick is an old theatrical convention in which one character takes the place of another in bed, duping a lover under the cover of darkness. Despite its inherent sordidness, Shakespeare has two of his most virtuous and respected heroines use it to achieve honorable and respectable (not to mention expedient) ends. In Isabella's case it is the only way she can save her brother's life while preserving her Christian soul and her good reputation.

While today's audiences may find the bed trick implausible, it fits the dark tone of *Measure for Measure*, and underscores an important theme in the play: do not judge without mercy, lest ye be judged harshly yourself. To achieve a noble end, Isabella must engage in a dishonest, sordid plot the likes of which she would have condemned not two days earlier.

Tabloid Tales of Trysts and Betrayal

Shakespeare was a crowd pleaser, and he knew what pleased the crowd best—a titillating, real-life shocker. He must have been delighted to come across his source for *Measure for Measure*, a novella by the Italian author Cinthio published in 1565 that retold a true story which took place in 1547: an Italian judge promised the wife of a condemned murderer to spare her husband in exchange for sex, but executed the man as soon as he received his payment. As punishment, the judge was forced to marry the woman (thus making her rich), after which he was executed.

Irrelevant History: New King on the Block

This play was written soon after the coronation of King James I in 1603, and was performed for him at court in 1604 by Shakespeare's acting company, the King's Men (formerly the Chamberlain's Men). Although it was probably not written specifically for the court performance, *Measure for Measure* seems to have been written with the King in mind. The play explores issues in which he was particularly interested, such as the divine right of rulers (see "Riding Shotgun with God," page 235) and the nature of the monarch's role in government. Its title and theme derive from an oft-quoted tenet from the Bible—"Judge not, that ye be not judged . . . with what measure ye mete, it shall be measured to you again"—which was sure to please Shakespeare's new patron . . . the man who went on to commission the King James Bible.

With *Measure*, Shakespeare could at once flatter and guide the new king. To flatter, he need only model the Duke after James by making him reputedly wise (as James was), disguising him as a friar (James was deeply religious), and inserting plot points reminiscent of James's own actions (for instance, the King once waited until a group of condemned prisoners were on the scaffold, about to be executed, before pardoning them). To instruct, Shakespeare made the Duke a model for James to follow: while James luxuriated in exaggerated praise, the Duke is sickened by it; where James was crude and impolite about the commoners, the Duke is concerned about and kind toward them; where James meted out harsh discipline, the Duke tempers his judgments with mercy.

TROILUS AND CRESSIDA

All's fair (more or less) in love and the Trojan War. (For a Who's Who of the Trojan War, see "The Trojan War: Back to Haunt You," page 973.)

We're in Troy, in the midst of the war. The Greeks are camped just outside the city walls. Troilus, one of the Trojan princes, is so head over heels in lust with a lovely young woman named Cressida that he can't concentrate on fighting and has left the battlefield. To his frustration, he can woo Cressida only by sending messages via her shifty uncle, Pandarus. When Troilus hears that his brother, Prince Paris, has just been wounded, he feels guilty and rejoins the battle.

Pandarus visits Cressida and the two find a good vantage point from which they can observe the Trojan warriors as they return from battle. Cressida is impressed by many of them, but Pandarus says that they are all nothing compared to Troilus. When Pandarus is summoned away, Cressida soliloquizes that she thinks Troilus is kind of cute, but she is determined not to let him know—that would be the fastest way to lose his interest.

Out in the Greek camp, Agamemnon, the Greek general, gives his commanders a pep talk. He tells them not to sweat the fact that they've been fighting for seven years with little result: it's just a test from the gods. Ulysses puts in his two cents, claiming that disorder and disrespect for authority among the troops is the problem. He singles out Achilles as an example, and describes how Achilles encourages his buddy Patroclus to parody each of the commanders for his amusement. Nestor adds that Ajax and Thersites have been following in Achilles' insubordinate footsteps. Just then, Aeneas arrives and makes an elaborate announcement (trumpets included) that Hector challenges the Greeks to send out their best contender to fight with him in single combat tomorrow. The commanders then take Aeneas off to the mess tent, leaving behind Ulysses and Nestor, who agree that while Hector's challenge is obviously meant for Achilles, it is not in the Greeks' best interest for Achilles to fight: if he wins, his already fat head will swell unbearably; if he loses, the Trojans will take heart in Hector's victory over the Greeks' renowned best warrior. Ulysses concocts a plan: the Greeks will arrange to choose their combatant by lottery . . . which will be rigged so that Ajax pulls the short straw. Nestor loves the plan. They go off to tell Agamemnon.

Thersites mocks the dull-witted Ajax, who tops the jokester's clever gibes with several sharp blows to the head. Achilles and Patroclus arrive and pull Ajax off Thersites, who thanks them by turning his witty insults on them. Achilles tells Ajax about Hector's challenge and the lottery.

Meanwhile, a family squabble erupts at the Trojan palace over Hector's suggestion that they release Helen and thereby end the bloodshed. Hector is eventually persuaded by his brothers that in order to preserve their honor, they must not do so.

Back at the Greek camp, Thersites complains to himself about the miserable treatment he receives from Ajax and Achilles. He insults them behind their backs, and when Achilles and Patroclus arrive he insults them to their faces. Achilles sees the other commanders approaching, and ducks into his tent. Ulysses goes in to speak with him, and soon returns to report that Achilles won't fight the next day and won't say why.

In Troy, Pandarus arranges for Troilus and Cressida to meet in his orchard, and leaves them alone there. Troilus tells Cressida of the "monstruosity" of his love. Pandarus returns, and is surprised that his niece has not yet promised her love, so he does it for her, prompting a reluctant confession of love from Cressida herself. The lovers vow to be faithful to each other, and Pandarus seals the bargain, saying that if one of the lovers should ever prove false to the other, then let all unfaithful men be called "Troiluses," all unfaithful women "Cressids," and all pitiful goers-between "Pandars." Pandarus clinches the deal by showing the happy couple to a bedchamber.

What does Cressida's dad, Calchas, think of all this? He doesn't even know about it. Calchas has deserted the Trojans to help the Greeks. Over at the Greek camp, Calchas asks the commanders to exchange his daughter for one of their Trojan POWs. Agamemnon agrees and sends one of the commanders, Diomedes, to make the trade.

Ulysses lectures Achilles, warning him that past deeds are soon forgotten, and that Ajax is quickly achieving Mythological Proportions, since Achilles hasn't been fighting lately. After Ulysses leaves, Thersites arrives. He cracks up Achilles and Patroclus with his description of Ajax, whose arrogance has rocketed out of control in anticipation of his certain defeat of Hector in the big fight. Achilles wants Patroclus to ask Ajax to bring Hector to meet him. When Patroclus rehearses his request with Thersites, who plays the role of a dumb-headed, incompetent Ajax, Achilles decides to send a letter instead.

Meanwhile, Diomedes brings the POW to Troy and meets with Paris, who sends Aeneas ahead to Cressida's home to break the news of the swap to Troilus.

At Cressida's, Troilus is up early, preparing for battle. Although he is very sweet to Cressida, she complains petulantly about his leaving so soon. Pandarus intrudes and cracks lewd jokes about the night the two have spent. Aeneas then arrives at the house and tells Troilus about the impending exchange. Troilus is upset and heads outside to meet up with Paris. Pandarus is left behind to break the news to Cressida. She melodramatically declares that she will not leave Troy(lus). Outside the house, Paris tells Troilus to go inside and tell Cressida to hurry up and pack her bags. By the time Troilus returns to Cressida, her lamentations are full blown. He tries to calm her down by promising to sneak into the Greek camp to visit her, and admonishes her repeatedly to be true to him. They vow to be true and exchange tokens: he gives her a sleeve; she gives him a glove. Troilus then hands Cressida over to Diomedes, telling him to treat her well. Diomedes ignores him and flirts with Cressida. The two men spar testily, until Troilus vows to make Diomedes run for cover on the battlefield.

Back at the Greek camp, the commanders are awaiting Hector's arrival for the big fight when Diomedes returns with Cressida. The men tease Cressida in a sexually suggestive way. After Diomedes takes Cressida to her father's tent, Nestor admires her intelligent sense of humor, but Ulysses calls her a wanton slut.

Hector arrives and the big fight begins, but Hector refuses to fight to the death with Ajax because they're kin. The commanders come forward: introductions all around. Achilles and Hector exchange insults and arrange to fight each other the next day. As the crowd disperses, Troilus stays behind to ask Ulysses for directions to Calchas's tent. Ulysses promises to show him the way, warning him that Diomedes has taken a shine to Cressida.

In another part of the camp, Achilles tells Patroclus that he plans to get Hector drunk tonight in order to defeat him more easily in battle tomorrow. Thersites delivers a letter for Achilles from his little Trojan love, Polixena. While Achilles reads the letter, Thersites and Patroclus exchange nasty insults. Achilles interrupts them to announce that he'll have to back out of tomorrow's combat: Polixena's letter entreats him to stay out of combat as he vowed he would. Achilles and Patroclus go off to prepare for the evening's festivities.

Along come the rest of the commanders, bringing Hector and Troilus to the feast. Diomedes excuses himself and slips away, in the direction of Calchas's tent. Ulysses and Troilus follow after him. Thersites, who mistrusts Diomedes, follows out of curiosity.

Arriving at Calchas's tent, Diomedes calls out for Cressida. Troilus and Ulysses (and Thersites, farther off) watch from the darkness as Cressida joins Diomedes. She flirts with him and plays hard to get, just as she once did with Troilus. Diomedes tells her to stop playing games with him. She gives him the sleeve she received from Troilus, and Diomedes promises to wear it on his helmet in battle the following day. They plan to tryst later that night and Diomedes leaves, whereupon Cressida blames her weakness on her gender before retreating into her tent. Shocked and furious, Troilus resolves to find the helmet with the sleeve and kill its wearer in tomorrow's battle.

Back at the palace in Troy, Hector's wife, Andromache, and his sister, Cassandra, beg him not to fight—his sister has seen bad omens in her dreams. Of course, he ignores them. Troilus bounds in, primed for battle. Pandarus arrives with a letter for Troilus from Cressida, which Troilus promptly tears up.

Outside the city walls, the battle has now begun. Thersites looks on and describes how the warriors are "clapper-clawing" one another. He himself avoids fighting by branding himself a cowardly rascal. The Trojans—especially Hector and Troilus—have killed many Greeks, including Patroclus. Ulysses reports that Achilles' grief and anger over Patroclus's death has moved him to arm for battle, vowing to kill Hector, and that Ajax is in deadly pursuit of Troilus. On another part of the battlefield, Ajax and Diomedes are both looking for Troilus; Troilus arrives and rushes at Diomedes. Ajax jumps in, and the three exit fighting. Hector enters, with Achilles close on his heels. Although he is exhausted, Achilles attacks Hector, who chivalrously offers to allow Achilles to rest. Achilles disdains this courteous offer and leaves, promising they'll meet again. Hector takes on another opponent, and they exit, fighting.

Achilles instructs his soldiers, the Myrmidons, to surround Hector and attack him, and then leads them off in search of him. Thersites avoids battle once again, telling his latest challenger that since they are both bastards, they shouldn't fight.

On another part of the field, Hector decides he's put in a good day's work, and takes off his armor to rest. Just then Achilles and his Myrmidons arrive. Hector asks Achilles not to use this unfair advantage, but Achilles orders his Myrmidons to attack the unprotected prince. Hector is killed, and Achilles plans to drag his body around the battlefield behind his horse. When the Greek commanders hear the report that Hector has been slain by Achilles, they are cautiously optimistic—if the report is accurate and Hector is dead, the war is as good as won.

Behind Trojan lines, Troilus announces that Hector has been killed, and his body dragged in shame through the field. He urges the Trojan warriors not to give up, but to avenge Hector's death by defeating the Greeks. Pandarus enters, and Troilus denounces him. Left alone on the stage, Pandarus bemoans his fate, sings a little song, and then, in a brief epilogue, addresses the pimps and prostitutes among the audience members, asking for their empathy, as they will end up like him sooner or later.

The Trojan War: Back to Haunt You

In case you haven't thought of the Trojan War since seventh-grade Greek Mythology class, here's a refresher course:

Young Prince Paris of Troy (one of King Priam's fifty sons) was minding his own business atop Mount Ida, tending his sheep (how that came about is another story), when the goddesses Hera, Athena, and Aphrodite appeared and demanded that he arbitrate a dispute for them. Each claimed rightful possession of a golden apple inscribed, "To the fairest." Being goddesses, each offered incentives for selecting her: Hera offered him royalty and wealth; Athena offered military prowess; but Paris chose Aphrodite's offer of the most beautiful woman on earth, and he awarded the apple to the goddess of love.

The most beautiful woman on earth at the time was Helen, and here's the catch: she was already married to Menelaus, ruler of Sparta. Another catch: Aphrodite didn't ship overnight. She did, however, help him steal Helen away from Menelaus. He carried her back to Troy and installed her in a wing of the palace.

Menelaus didn't enjoy being robbed of the most beautiful woman on earth (who does?). He and his brother, Agamemnon, rustled up the greatest Greek warriors, including Achilles, Ajax, Diomedes, Ulysses, and Nestor (why they were all willing to sail across the Aegean and fight a ten-year war is another story). Then he rustled up some wind (by sacrificing his daughter Iphigenia, which is yet another story) and they all sailed happily on toward Troy.

When they arrived, they discovered that the Trojan army was playing with a powerful defense, led by Prince Hector (Paris's brother), who was not only a great warrior, but also a really stand-up guy (in fact, reputed to be the single kindest, noblest, most ethical and chivalrous fictional character in antiquity). The two powers were so well matched that the fighting went on for ten years (*Troilus and Cressida* occurs at year seven), and they might be fighting still if the Trojans hadn't fallen for the old Trojan Horse ploy (but that's another story).

THE TRAGEDIES

ANTONY AND CLEOPATRA

We last encountered Mark Antony at the end of *Julius Caesar*, in which he and his partners, Octavius Caesar and Marcus Lepidus, defeated the forces of Marcus Brutus and Caius Cassius. As *Antony and Cleopatra* begins, Antony, Caesar, and Lepidus are ruling the Roman Empire jointly as a triumvirate. Antony governs the easternmost third of the empire, which includes Egypt. Having fallen hard for Egypt's Queen Cleopatra, he has tucked his wife, Fulvia, away in Rome and has taken up residence in Alexandria, where the passionate lovers are enjoying a hedonistic lifestyle. Back in Rome, Caesar is less than pleased that Antony is not devoting his full attention to the Triumvirate's expansionist international policy.

Messages arrive for Antony from Rome, and Cleopatra persuades him to ignore them. Meanwhile, a soothsayer tells Cleopatra's waiting-women, Charmian and Iras, that they will outlive their queen, but the women laugh at him. Antony finally listens to the messengers from Rome and learns that his wife and brother had teamed up to fight against Caesar but were defeated; Antony fears that Caesar will think he masterminded the attack. Furthermore, lands conquered by Rome have been lost while Antony has been otherwise engaged with Cleopatra; Antony feels remiss for having let the territories slip away. More news arrives: Antony's wife has died; Antony feels guilty for having wished her dead while he dallied with Cleopatra. When he learns that Pompey (whose father, Pompey the Great, was defeated years earlier by Julius Caesar) has just rebelled, Antony tells Cleopatra he must return to Rome to help Octavius Caesar. Realizing that her pouting is failing to change his mind, Cleopatra earnestly wishes him a successful trip.

Back in Rome, Octavius Caesar is disgusted by Antony's dissolute behavior in Egypt and hopes that he will return to Rome to help fight Pompey. Meanwhile, in Alexandria, Cleopatra pines for her magnificent Antony. When Charmian reminds her that she once felt the same for Julius Caesar, Cleopatra dismisses those feelings as puppy love from her "salad days, when [she] was green in judgment."

Pompey initially chose this time to rebel because Antony was busy with Cleopatra; when he learns that Antony has returned to Rome, he is nervous. He's not the only one: Lepidus and Caesar worry about Antony's intentions. At a meeting of the Triumvirate and their supporters, Antony assures the others that he was not responsible for the rebellion of his wife and brother and apologizes for slacking his duties while in Alexandria. Antony agrees to marry Caesar's sister Octavia to cement the amity between the two men. After the Triumvirs leave, one of their supporters expresses relief that Antony has given up Cleopatra. Antony's lieutenant Enobarbus describes Cleopatra's spectacular first impression on Antony and explains that Antony will never manage to give her up permanently.

At Caesar's home, Antony pledges faithfulness to his new wife, Octavia. But the Egyptian soothsayer warns him to return to Egypt, as Caesar is dangerous to him. Meanwhile, a messenger has arrived in Egypt with news of Antony's marriage; Cleopatra, devastated, beats the messenger and threatens his life.

The Triumvirs meet with Pompey and his supporter, the powerful pirate Menas, and negotiate a peace settlement. As they go off to celebrate, Enobarbus speculates that Octavia is too frigid for Antony and he will soon return to "his Egyptian dish," which will anger Caesar. Later, amid the reveling on Pompey's ship, Menas urges him to kill the drunken Triumvirs, but Pompey considers the suggestion dishonorable and declines. Disgusted, Menas decides to desert him.

Antony and Octavia bid Caesar an emotional farewell and depart for Athens. Meanwhile, in Alexandria, Cleopatra grills a messenger about Octavia and rewards him for his unflattering description of her rival.

In Athens, Antony is angry with Caesar for waging war against Pompey in violation of their truce and for denigrating Antony to others. Octavia begs to be permitted to return to Rome to serve as an intermediary between her brother and her husband. Antony agrees.

When Enobarbus learns that Caesar has defeated Pompey and arrested Lepidus for treason, he correctly foresees civil war between Caesar and Antony. In Rome, Caesar is furious to learn that Antony has returned to Egypt and has crowned Cleopatra and her children rulers of Egypt and nearby territories. Caesar has sent a messenger demanding that Antony yield various territories, though he knows that Antony will refuse and they will go to war. Octavia arrives in Rome and is apprised of her husband's return to Cleopatra.

It's war! Antony's army has set up camp near Actium, in southern Greece. Enobarbus expresses frustration that Cleopatra insists on being there when her presence distracts Antony and makes his forces a laughingstock in Rome. Caesar has challenged Antony to a naval battle. To Enobarbus's chagrin, Antony ignores his advice and agrees to the sea battle, even though his ships are no match for Caesar's.

After the battle, Enobarbus learns that Cleopatra's ship fled at a critical moment. Antony's ship turned to follow hers, and the battle was lost to Caesar. Enobarbus is despondent yet determined to remain loyal to Antony, despite the obvious folly of doing so. Back at Cleopatra's palace, Antony is ashamed of his retreat and urges his followers to desert him and join Caesar. He tells Cleopatra of his despair. She apologizes, insisting that she never thought he'd follow her fleeing ship, and he replies that her love is worth all that he has lost.

Caesar receives Antony's request that he be permitted to live as a civilian in Egypt and Athens, and Cleopatra's request that she and her heirs continue to govern Egypt. Caesar denies Antony's request and replies to Cleopatra that she may have whatever she likes, provided she either drive Antony from Egypt or kill him.

When Caesar's messenger arrives, Cleopatra pledges allegiance to Caesar and the messenger kisses her hand. Antony arrives in time to witness this; he orders the messenger whipped and rails against Cleopatra. He then sends the whipped messenger back to Caesar with a challenging message. Cleopatra then assures Antony of her love and loyalty. Appeased and encouraged, Antony determines to fight Caesar and win.

Caesar's troops, which have arrived in Alexandria, outnumber Antony's twenty to one; he refuses Antony's challenge to fight him in hand-to-hand combat. The night before the battle, Antony moves his listeners to tears with the suggestion that this meal may be his last, then hastily seeks to reassure them that he shall prevail against Caesar.

The next day, Cleopatra helps Antony into his armor amid love patter, and he leaves for battle feeling optimistic. He takes in stride the news that Enobarbus has deserted to Caesar because he knows that he has driven Enobarbus to do so; and he graciously sends Enobarbus's belongings to him. When Enobarbus receives them, he is remorse-ridden and, vowing not to fight Antony, repairs to a ditch where he literally dies of a broken heart.

Antony is victorious and returns triumphantly to Cleopatra, praising the valor of his men. While he prepares to battle further both on land and at sea, Caesar makes plans to fight at sea only.

When Cleopatra's navy deserts to Caesar, Antony accuses her of betraying him and threatens her. After she flees, he determines to kill her for causing his downfall. Cleopatra, who is ignorant of her navy's actions, believes Antony has gone mad. She takes refuge in her burial monument and sends him word that she has committed suicide with his name on her lips. When the despondent Antony is told that Cleopatra committed suicide, he resolves to do so as well. His servant refuses to kill him, so Antony falls on his sword, wounding himself. Cleopatra, fearing Antony will harm himself, has sent word to Antony that she is alive, but the messenger arrives moments too late. Antony is carried to the monument on a litter and is hoisted up to her. They reconcile, and Antony says he is proud that he dies by his own hand rather than Caesar's. He dies, and Cleopatra vows to die proudly as well.

When Caesar learns of Antony's death, he mourns the loss of a great man. He sends word to Cleopatra that he will treat her kindly and honorably. Though Cleopatra professes allegiance to Caesar, she draws a dagger to kill herself, but is disarmed by Caesar's men. She vows to do what she must to rob Caesar of a victory over her. Dolabella, one of Caesar's officers, arrives to guard her until she can be brought alive to Rome. She tells him of Antony's greatness. Smitten, he confides that despite Caesar's assurance to the contrary, Cleopatra is to be paraded through the streets of Rome in humiliation and defeat. Caesar arrives and assures Cleopatra that he will treat her with mercy. She gives him an accounting of her possessions, and is embarrassed when her accountant points out that she has "forgotten" to list half of them. After Caesar leaves, Dolabella warns her that he intends to bring her to Rome within three days. A basket of figs is delivered for Cleopatra. Hidden inside are poisonous snakes. Cleopatra's waiting-women dress her in her crown and royal robes. Iras is the first to be bitten, and dies. Cleopatra bids the world farewell and, lifting two snakes to bite her, dies as well. Charmian is the last to be bitten, dying right after the guards return. Caesar appears, and decrees that Cleopatra shall be buried with full pomp beside her Antony.

P.S.
For information about the historical Antony and Cleopatra, see "Antony A-Go-Go," page 619, and "Athenian Arrogator/Egyptian Empress/Drama Queen," page 465.

CORIOLANUS

Coriolanus is an enigma: through the years, scholars and audiences have been trying to figure out exactly what this play is, and what its message is. It's been classified as pro-aristocracy, pro-democracy; pro-Communism, pro-Fascism. It's been glorified, it's been banned. Today's audiences will have a very different reaction to the play and its characters than Elizabethan audiences did. We'll never know *what* Shakespeare intended the story to mean—we know only the story itself.

The citizens of Rome are rioting against the city's aristocratic leaders. The crowd begins by attacking Caius Martius—although he fought fearlessly for Rome, Martius's pride and his contempt for the commonfolk have kept corn (i.e., grain) prices too high, causing famine among the commoners. Menenius Agrippa, a congenial nobleman, addresses the rioters, using allegory to explain that the commoners need the aristocrats, who work hard at governing and protecting them. Caius Martius enters spewing invectives at the "rabble," and angrily informs Menenius that the commoners have been granted the right to elect five tribunes (judges). Generals Cominius and Lartius, accompanied by Roman senators and two of the new tribunes, Junius Brutus and Sicinius Velutus, arrive to ask Martius to help fight the Volscians, who are currently preparing to attack Rome. Martius would be delighted—he has often fought (and bested) his nemesis, the mighty Volscian general Tullus Aufidius, and would love to do so again.

Cut to the Senate House in Corioles, where the Volscian general Aufidius meets with the Volscian senators. Volscian intelligence has learned that the Romans have assembled armed forces. Aufidius is sure that the Romans know of the Volscians' attack plans and are headed toward Corioles—the Volscians must move swiftly. Aufidius will lead troops to the field (where he hopes to encounter his nemesis, Caius Martius), and the senators will remain within the city to defend it.

Back in Rome, at Martius's abode, his mother, Volumnia, chastises his wife, Virgilia, for not rejoicing that he is away in battle, and reminisces that when Martius was a boy, she could barely wait until he was grown so she could send him off to battle to accrue honor. His honorable death would bring her indescribable joy. She hopes he returns from this battle with bloody wounds, and considers Virgilia a silly fool for hoping that Martius returns unharmed.

The battle at Corioles: at the entrance to the city, senators of Corioles stave off the attacking Roman troops, who retreat. Caius Martius curses them, and when the city's gates are opened to readmit the Volscian troops, Martius charges in after them alone. The gates close, shutting him in—the Romans are sure he's a goner. Amazingly, he suddenly emerges from the city, chased by Volscian soldiers. The Romans rally to his aid and win the battle. Once Corioles has been taken by the Romans, the bleeding Martius finds Cominius, who has retreated from the enemy's powerful forces. Martius obtains permission (and troops) from Cominius to seek out and fight his nemesis, Aufidius. On the battlefield, as Martius and Aufidius square off, Aufidius's soldiers shame him by running from Martius.

Not surprisingly, the Romans have defeated the Volscians. General Cominius lavishly praises Martius's heroism, much to Martius's discomfort. Soldiers cheer. Martius squirms. To honor Martius for his role in capturing Corioles, he is given a new surname, Coriolanus.

In Corioles, Aufidius is beside himself. This is his fifth military defeat (and his twelfth in hand-to-hand combat) at the hands of Caius Martius (Coriolanus). He vows that next time he shall be the victor, even if he must resort to dishonorable methods.

Back in Rome, when Brutus and Sicinius talk disparagingly of Coriolanus's excessive pride, Menenius lambastes the two tribunes, criticizing their performance as judges and belittling the commoners whose cases they adjudicate. A crowd gathers to hail the returning heroes. Coriolanus leads the triumphal march, crowned with a victory wreath and flanked by the generals. All hail Coriolanus, who is uncomfortable and asks everyone to please cut it out. He heads off to the Capitol with his mother, his wife, and Menenius to be further honored. Brutus and Sicinius, left behind, fear that Coriolanus will now be elected consul, but hope that his pride will keep him from exhibiting his scars to the commoners—a prerequisite for holding the position—and that they can then incite the people to reject him as consul.

At the Capitol, Coriolanus is nominated to the consulate. He asks to be excused from displaying his wounds to the commoners, but the tribunes insist that he do so. Menenius persuades Coriolanus to comply.

Out on a public street, a group of citizens discuss Coriolanus's nomination, which they'll support if he asks them to and shows his wounds. Coriolanus arrives and does so rather ungraciously. The citizens grant their support of Coriolanus's nomination—all that remains is that he be formally inducted. After Menenius and Coriolanus leave, Brutus and Sicinius express shock that the citizens could support the elitist, commoner-hating Coriolanus, and convince the citizens to rescind their approval before his formal induction.

Coriolanus hears that Aufidius is in Antium, amassing new troops for an attack on Rome, and that he hates Coriolanus more than anything in the world. Coriolanus is positively itching for an excuse to fight him again. When Brutus and Sicinius come to announce that the citizenry have rescinded their approval of Coriolanus for consul (citing his opposition to the people's corn subsidies), he loses his temper, calling the citizenry a multiheaded monster unfit to select its consul. Brutus and Sicinius pronounce this sentiment treasonous, and call for aediles (peacekeeping officials) to arrest Coriolanus. Commoners arrive, and the tribunes incite them against Coriolanus, who draws his sword to keep from being thrown off a cliff. In the ensuing group fight scene, Cominius whisks Coriolanus away to safety, and Menenius convinces the tribunes not to kill Coriolanus, but to try him properly.

Back at home, Coriolanus vents his outrage at the people's ingratitude. Menenius arrives to implore him to apologize to the tribunes. Coriolanus won't hear of it until his mother tells him to do so; she says that the apology need not be sincere, but merely convincing. He grudgingly bows to her wishes.

At the Forum, Brutus and Sicinius plan to provoke Coriolanus's not-so-mild temper during the trial. Sure enough, Coriolanus is calm and pseudo-contrite until Sicinius charges that he is a traitor, whereupon he loses control and insults the commoners. This seals Coriolanus's fate: banishment from Rome under penalty of death should he return.

At the city gates, Coriolanus rejects offers of help, promises to write, and bids his loved ones adieu. Volumnia then encounters Sicinius and Brutus on the street, where she rants and raves at them.

Some time passes. Coriolanus has made his way to Antium where, dressed as a poor man, he asks directions to Aufidius's home. A feast is being held there that night. He enters and, after insulting all the servants, reveals himself to Aufidius, explaining what has befallen him and pledging to help Aufidius lead the Volscians against Rome. Aufidius says he's happier than he was on his wedding day. He invites Coriolanus to join the feast and meet the Volscian senators.

Back in Rome, ignorant of their impending doom, the tribunes and citizens are enjoying peacetime. They reminisce about the bad old days when Coriolanus hung around being obnoxious. An aedile breaks their reverie with the news that the Volscians are advancing on Rome. Further reports pour in that Coriolanus has joined forces with Aufidius. Cominius arrives and blames the tribunes for Rome's impending ruin. A group of citizens contend that they banished Coriolanus only reluctantly and have felt since then that it was wrong to have done so.

At a camp outside Rome, Aufidius and a lieutenant confer. The lieutenant doesn't like Coriolanus's growing popularity among the troops; he fears Aufidius's power wanes as a result. Aufidius tells him not to worry: first they'll sack Rome, which will surely fall to Coriolanus. Then Coriolanus will fall to him.

At a strategy meeting in Rome, Menenius at first refuses to go seek an audience with Coriolanus, because Coriolanus has already turned away General Cominius. The tribunes implore Menenius to go; he finally acquiesces and heads off to the Volscian camp. When Menenius arrives, he explains to the watch that he is an old friend of Coriolanus's—like a father, really—and that Coriolanus will surely agree to speak with him. The soldiers are rude to Menenius, and when Coriolanus appears, so is he. He coldly orders Menenius away.

Coriolanus and Aufidius speak: Aufidius assures Coriolanus that he will tell the Volscian senators how true Coriolanus is to the Volscian cause. Coriolanus points out that he even rejected Menenius, who loved him as a father does. Coriolanus believes that sending Menenius to him was the Romans' last-ditch effort to soften him. He is shocked, therefore, to see his mother, wife, and son approaching with their friend Valeria. Coriolanus is resolved not to be swayed by them.

Virgilia addresses Coriolanus first, and he is moved, but not enough. Volumnia presents his son, Martius Jr., at whose words Coriolanus grows more agitated. Volumnia argues that it would not be weak to shape a peace with Rome—the Volscians can claim the greater strength by saying they showed Rome mercy, and both sides can hail Coriolanus as a hero. When Coriolanus remains unmoved, Volumnia turns to go. She tells the others that the guy she's pleading with has a Volscian for a mother and a wife in Corioles, and that the similarity between him and Martius Jr. is pure coincidence. This shatters Coriolanus, who can withstand anything but his mother's rejection. Faced with the decision to destroy Rome (including his mother, wife, and child) or himself (for he will surely be killed if he now betrays the Volscians), he opts to forfeit himself. Aufidius, who has heard the entire exchange, is secretly pleased: now he has a reason to destroy Coriolanus.

When the ladies return to Rome, they are publicly thanked by the senators amid drums, trumpets, and shouts of welcome.

Aufidius now has Coriolanus right where he wants him. Since Coriolanus has just returned to Antium, Aufidius fetches that city's patricians to the marketplace, where he will lodge a formal complaint against Coriolanus. He then speaks with a band of assassins, who agree to assist him. The city's patricians arrive just moments before Coriolanus, who presents himself as the Volscians' loyal soldier and his treaty with Rome as their victory. Aufidius speaks out against Coriolanus, urging the patricians to consider him a traitor and calling him "Martius" instead of the honored "Coriolanus"—Coriolanus is shocked. Aufidius calls him a "boy of tears" (a mama's boy)—now Coriolanus is angry. Exhibiting his famous temper, Coriolanus calls Aufidius a liar, threatens to beat him, and reminds him of his past single-handed victories over the Volscians in Corioles. Aufidius incites the crowd to rise up against Coriolanus, and the people call out to have him torn to pieces for killing their loved ones in past attacks on the city. The assassins quickly attack and kill Coriolanus. Aufidius announces that although all should be glad that the dangerous Coriolanus is dead, he is to be given the noble funeral befitting a heroic warrior. A death march sounds, as Coriolanus's body is solemnly borne away.

The Great Corn Riots of '07

Today the word *corn* is most often identified with maize, but before the discovery of the New World the term was applied more broadly to the seeds of various small grains, including wheat, rye, barley, and oats.

Although a corn shortage is mentioned in Plutarch's *Lives* (a translation of which was the primary source for *Coriolanus*), Shakespeare makes much more of it than his ancient predecessor did, using it to frame the class struggle at the heart of the play. Theories that he loved corn have been supplanted by historical evidence that he wrote the play shortly after the Midlands Insurrection of 1607, in which rioting swept the English countryside over the scarcity and pricing of corn. Shakespeare may have eluded the dangers of censorship or arrest by disguising this contemporary social issue in wreaths and togas.

HAMLET

Shakespeare's most famous play, *Hamlet*, is technically a "revenge play," and contains many of the genre's basic elements: a character or characters who avenge a wrong or wrongs (and whose actions are often avenged in turn); insanity (whether feigned or real); the appearance of a supernatural being; and several bloody killings (see " 'Revenge Is Profitable . . . ,' " page 1006, for more about revenge plays). With *Hamlet*, Shakespeare utterly transcended the genre, exploring the psychological and emotional complexities surrounding revenge, rather than simply exploiting its gory aspects. The result is considered by many to be the greatest play ever written in any language: a play in which every line is of the most exquisite quality; the characters reveal an intriguing depth and complexity; and questions about the human condition are infinitely layered and never exhausted. Thus it is no surprise that *Hamlet* is always fresh and interesting, always a play into which actors and audience alike are eager to delve.

Shortly before dawn, Horatio joins the night watchmen on the walls of Elsinore Castle, to investigate their reports of visitations by what appears to be the ghost of Hamlet, the recently deceased King of Denmark. After seeing the ghost himself, Horatio decides to tell his friend, Prince Hamlet, the late king's son.

In the castle, the recently crowned King Claudius and his new wife, Queen Gertrude, hold court. Claudius thanks those present for their support of his recent marriage to his late brother's widow. He sends ambassadors to the King of Norway to urge him to restrain his nephew Fortinbras, who is advancing on Denmark to recover lands taken from his late father. Claudius then grants permission to Laertes, son of his valued adviser Polonius, to return to his studies in France. Claudius and the Queen chastise her son, Hamlet, for continuing to mourn his father, and Claudius denies Hamlet permission to return to his studies in Wittenberg. He and Gertrude depart with their retinue, leaving Hamlet alone to express suicidal thoughts and air his disgust at his mother's hasty marriage to his uncle (incestuous according to the mores of the time). Horatio and the watchmen arrive and tell Hamlet about the Ghost. Determined to speak to it, Hamlet says he'll join them on the watch that night.

Laertes, about to sail for France, bids his sister, Ophelia, farewell and warns her not to let Hamlet woo her; the Prince's intentions can't be honorable because his marriage will be arranged to another royal. When their father, Polonius, arrives, he gives Laertes long-winded and clichéd advice, and then bids him adieu. After his son departs, Polonius forbids Ophelia to see Hamlet, and she promises to obey.

That night, on the castle walls, the Ghost appears to Hamlet and identifies himself as the late king. Revealing that he was murdered by his brother, Claudius, the Ghost urges his son to avenge the deed, and Hamlet vows to do so.

Ophelia, shaken, reports to her father that Hamlet has just burst into her room, looking and acting like a lunatic. Polonius believes that Ophelia's recent rejection of Hamlet has driven him mad, and he takes Ophelia off to tell the King.

Meanwhile, Claudius and Gertrude greet Rosencrantz and Guildenstern (hereinafter, R & G), Hamlet's childhood friends, whom they have summoned to Elsinore hoping that they will elicit from Hamlet the reason for his mad behavior. The young men agree to spy on their friend. News arrives that the King of Norway has diverted Fortinbras's efforts toward Poland. Polonius comes forward with his hypothesis about Hamlet's madness, producing a love letter from the Prince to Ophelia as proof. Claudius is unconvinced, but agrees to spy on a meeting between Hamlet and Ophelia. When Hamlet meanders in, Polonius sends the others away and tries to communicate with him, but Hamlet pointedly insults Polonius in a way that seems mad to him, so he leaves. Hamlet then greets his old friends R & G in the same "crazy" manner, easily extracting a confession that they were sent for by the King.

A group of players arrives, and one performs a monologue. Hamlet hires the players to perform the next night. He dismisses everyone, and then soliloquizes: a player has just expressed stronger emotions about a fabrication than Hamlet has shown about his own father's murder. He condemns his own cowardice and weakness for not yet having avenged the deed. He will have the players perform *The Murder of Gonzago*, which mimics his uncle's crime: if the Ghost's story is true, Claudius's reaction to the play will confirm his guilt, and Hamlet will take action.

The next day, R & G report that they have nothing to report. Polonius and Claudius place Ophelia where they can spy on her and Hamlet. Hamlet enters, pondering whether it is better to suffer through life or to die and face the unknown—and possibly horrible—existence of the afterlife. Ophelia walks by, as instructed. At first kind to her, Hamlet suddenly turns on Ophelia, saying he never loved her, railing against all women, and telling her, "Get thee to a nunnery." Ophelia laments Hamlet's ruin. Their exchange convinces Claudius that love is not the root of Hamlet's problems, and that he must get rid of Hamlet before Hamlet gets rid of him. He tells Polonius that he will send Hamlet with R & G to England on a state visit. Polonius, still sure that Hamlet suffers from unrequited love, suggests that Hamlet speak with his mother after the play that night.

That night, before the show, Hamlet gives the players pointers on acting technique. As the royal court arrives to see the play, Hamlet sits by Ophelia and embarrasses her with crude and bitter sexual banter. The play unfolds: its plot is strikingly similar to Claudius's alleged seduction of Gertrude and murder of his brother. At the moment in the play when the murderer pours poison into the king's ear, Claudius stops the play and rushes out of the room, followed by all except Hamlet and Horatio. Hamlet has his proof. R & G return to report that the King is very angry and that the Queen requests Hamlet's presence in her chamber before he goes to bed that night. Left alone, Hamlet soliloquizes his resolve and readiness to take action.

Meanwhile, Claudius asks R & G to accompany Hamlet to England, and they dutifully agree. Polonius announces that he is on his way to spy on Hamlet's meeting with his mother, and then hurries off. Left alone, Claudius tries to pray, but is unable to do so because he is still enjoying the results of his crime: the crown and the Queen. En route to his mother's chamber, Hamlet sees Claudius kneeling; here is the perfect chance to avenge his father's death. But as he draws his sword, Hamlet realizes that if he kills Claudius at prayer, his uncle's soul will go straight to Heaven, so he decides to wait and kill Claudius while the King is committing a sin. As Hamlet goes off to see his mother, Claudius rises, regretting aloud that try as he might, he has still been unable to truly repent his crime and pray.

In Gertrude's room, Polonius hides behind an arras (a tapestry). Hamlet arrives, and after an angry exchange between mother and son, Gertrude becomes frightened and calls for help. This frightens Polonius, who also cries out, prompting Hamlet to stab the intruder hiding behind the arras, killing him. He is sorry to learn that it was Polonius he stabbed and not the King. He compares his father's virtue to Claudius's evil, and berates his mother for marrying Claudius. Hamlet is mid-diatribe when his father's ghost appears, and he asks if it has come to chide him for delaying the revenge. The Ghost exhorts Hamlet to remember his obligation and to care for his confused mother. When Gertrude exclaims that he is mad, Hamlet realizes that she does not see the Ghost. He now gently urges his mother to confess her sins and to avoid Claudius's bed. He insists that he is not mad and leaves, dragging Polonius's body out with him.

Gertrude tells her husband that Hamlet is mad and has killed Polonius. Claudius sends R & G to fetch Hamlet and to bring Polonius's body to the chapel. Hamlet taunts R & G, but willingly goes with them to see Claudius. When Claudius questions him, Hamlet continues his teasing before revealing that he has stashed the body under the lobby stairs. Claudius tells Hamlet that for his own safety he is being sent to England that very night. Hamlet goes off to pack and board his boat. Left alone, Claudius considers his plan: he will send sealed letters to the English king, instructing him to kill Hamlet immediately.

Remember Fortinbras of Norway? En route to the boat, Hamlet passes him and his troops on their way to Poland. Hamlet contrasts Fortinbras's determination to regain his father's lands with his own inaction on behalf of his father, and is disgusted with himself. He renews his commitment to revenge.

Gertrude learns that Ophelia has been acting insane since her father's death. Ophelia makes a brief appearance, babbling incoherently and singing bawdy ditties, horrifying the King and Queen. Claudius tells Gertrude that Laertes has secretly returned from France. Speak of the devil, Laertes forces his way in, demanding to know how his father was killed and vowing revenge. Claudius is about to brief him when Ophelia reenters. Laertes is shocked and dismayed at her condition. The King takes him off to confer.

Meanwhile, Horatio receives a letter from Hamlet, reporting that he was captured by pirates but released, and is now returning to Denmark. Horatio heads off to meet him.

Claudius and Laertes are interrupted by the arrival of a letter from Hamlet, telling Claudius of his return to Denmark. His plot foiled, Claudius devises a new one: he will arrange a fencing match between Hamlet and Laertes, in which Laertes will poison the tip of his foil. Hamlet's inevitable death will be deemed accidental. And, as a backup, Claudius will have a cup of poisoned wine on hand. Gertrude arrives with the tragic news that Ophelia has drowned. Laertes is devastated.

Trekking back to Elsinore, Hamlet and Horatio come upon two grave diggers preparing a new grave. After joking about the skulls in the graveyard, they see a funeral procession approaching that includes the King, the Queen, and Laertes, so they hide. When Laertes mourns his sister extravagantly, Hamlet realizes that the funeral is for Ophelia. Laertes leaps into the grave for one final embrace, and Hamlet comes forward, expressing his own grief. Laertes attacks him, and the two grapple. They are pulled apart, and Hamlet leaves angrily. Aside, the King reminds Laertes that he shall shortly have his revenge.

Later, in the castle, Hamlet tells Horatio of his recent adventure at sea: unable to sleep one night, he looked at the letter R & G were carrying from Claudius to the King of England and discovered that it called for his immediate execution. He replaced it with a letter calling for the execution of R & G. The next day his ship was attacked by the pirates who brought him home. A courtier interrupts with a message: the King is wagering on Hamlet's skill in a fencing match with Laertes—will he oblige? Hamlet agrees. He suspects that he will die, but he is now prepared. The courtier goes off and soon returns with the King, the Queen, Laertes, and the rest of the royal court.

The fencing match begins. Hamlet wins the first round, and Claudius toasts his nephew, placing a (poisoned) pearl in Hamlet's cup, but Hamlet declines to drink and the fencing resumes. When Hamlet wins round two, the Queen takes his cup to drink to him. Dismissing the King's objection, she drinks. Hamlet, however, again declines to drink and the match continues. Laertes wounds Hamlet, and a scuffle ensues, in which their weapons are switched. In the next round, Hamlet wounds Laertes. Suddenly, the Queen swoons, and the fighting is halted. Crying out that she has been poisoned, the Queen dies. Hamlet leaps into action, seeking the villain. Laertes immediately confesses the whole plot and blames the King. Hamlet stabs Claudius with the poisoned sword, then forces him to drink the poisoned wine, and Claudius dies. Laertes asks Hamlet to exchange forgiveness, and dies as well; Hamlet forgives the dead Laertes. As Hamlet himself dies, he asks Horatio to reveal the true story behind these events, and designates Fortinbras as successor to the Danish throne. As though on cue, Fortinbras arrives and surveys the carnage. An English ambassador brings news that R & G are dead. Horatio promises to tell Fortinbras the whole story and Fortinbras orders a stately funeral for Hamlet.

Dramatic Grammaticus: From Amleth to Hamlet in Several Complicated Steps

Much of the legendary history of Denmark was recorded for the first time in C.E. 1200 by the Danish historian Saxo Grammaticus. Saxo's *Historiae Danicae* was written in Latin and included the story of a prince named Amleth, from which the title character and many of the story elements of *Hamlet* are derived (Amleth, by the way, means "dim-witted" in Old Norse, reflecting the character's feigned madness). The story was retold in French in 1580 by François Belleforest, in his *Histoires Tragiques*. Belleforest's work is believed to be the source for the mysterious *Ur-Hamlet*, a now-lost play (possibly written by Thomas Kyd) on which most scholars agree Shakespeare's masterpiece was based.

Irrelevant History: The Demon Barber of Urbino

The poison-in-ear method of murder in *Hamlet* was inspired by a real-life murder that took place in Italy in 1538, in which the famed Duke of Urbino died under mysterious circumstances. It was later revealed that a man named Luigi Gonzaga had paid the Duke's barber to (literally) rub him out by putting poisoned lotion into his ears. Shakespeare used the murderer's name in his play-within-a-play, *The Murder of Gonzago*.

JULIUS CAESAR

Julius Caesar was written just after Shakespeare completed nine of his ten History plays. It builds on the political themes of those plays (power struggle among the elite, civil war, and the resultant societal disorder) but presents these themes according to the formal conventions of early modern tragedy. In the tragic genre, the fatal flaw of a powerful individual is the catalyst both for social upheaval and the individual's eventual downfall.

Thus, *Julius Caesar*, written in 1599, is a bridge from Shakespeare's plot-driven Histories to his character-driven Tragedies of the 1600s.

Speaking of fatally flawed powerful individuals, the great Julius Caesar has just returned to Rome, quite pleased with himself for having defeated his rivals in battle. As Caesar parades triumphantly through the streets with his entourage, a soothsayer approaches with a warning: beware the ides of March (March 15, which is the next day). Caesar dismisses the warning, and departs with his followers. Caius Cassius and Marcus Brutus, two patricians (members of the Roman nobility), stay behind. Cassius sounds Brutus out about Caesar, and learns that Brutus shares his concern that the people will crown Caesar their emperor, destroying Rome's republican system of government, in which all the nobles have an equal voice. Cassius tries to persuade Brutus that the ambitious Caesar—who is no better than either of them—must be stopped. Brutus agrees to think it over.

Caesar returns with his entourage and confides to his protégé, Mark Antony, that he fears Cassius's "lean and hungry look." As they depart, Cassius and Brutus hold back Casca (another patrician), who reports that Antony offered Caesar the crown three times, to the cheers of the people. Each time Caesar "modestly" refused. After Casca and Brutus depart, Cassius soliloquizes that he will use Brutus's honorable nature to manipulate him into taking action against Caesar.

Late that night: a strange storm has struck the capital. Casca and another patrician, Cicero, bump into each other in the street and Casca tells of passing a lion in the square, which left him unharmed. He also encountered a hundred terrified women, who claimed to have seen men walking through the rain on fire. Casca fears these bizarre encounters in the storm are portents of evil. Cicero, however, is unfazed—it's just a bad storm. Casca next encounters Cassius and informs him that Caesar is to be crowned emperor at the Senate the following day; Cassius persuades Casca to join him in assassinating Caesar to prevent it. Another patrician joins them and the three decide to send Brutus forged messages "from the commoners" stating that they fear Caesar's ambition.

Brutus has been pacing in his garden all night. At dawn, he receives one of Cassius's "anonymous" letters, which convinces him that Caesar must die for the good of the republic. Cassius arrives with five coconspirators, and they plan Caesar's murder. When Cassius suggests that Antony be killed as well, Brutus insists that only Caesar need be killed, since Antony is of no danger without him. The conspirators depart and Brutus's wife, Portia, enters and entreats him to confide in her, since theirs is a marriage of equals and he wrongs himself and her by refusing to share what's troubling him. Brutus agrees to tell her all. Another conspirator arrives to accompany Brutus to the Senate and they depart.

Meanwhile, Caesar's wife, Calphurnia, has had nightmares in which his statue gushed blood from a hundred spouts. She urges him to stay home from the Senate, citing the bad omens of the past night's storm. Humoring her, Caesar agrees to stay home. When Decius (one of the conspirators) arrives to escort Caesar to the Senate, Caesar shares his wife's dream, which Decius "reinterprets" to mean that Rome will be revived by Caesar's new blood. Furthermore, the senators intend to crown Caesar emperor today. It would not look good for Caesar to stay home because of a woman's fears. Caesar changes his mind and heads for the Senate, joined by the conspirators and Antony.

Back at Brutus's home, Portia, who knows of the plot, is worried to death. She sends her houseboy, Lucius, to the Senate to bring her an update.

At the Senate, Caesar dismisses warnings from both the soothsayer he encountered yesterday and a teacher who has learned of the plot. While one of the conspirators diverts Antony, the others gather around Caesar, pretending to present a petition they know he will refuse. At his denial (their prearranged signal), they stab him. Caesar, amazed that Brutus is among the conspirators, asks *"Et tu, Brute?"* before he dies. Brutus has the conspirators wash their hands and swords in Caesar's blood, as a symbol of "peace, liberty, and freedom" that they will later show the people. Antony, who has fled to his house, sends word to the conspirators that he respects Brutus and will align with him if Brutus explains the conspirators' deed. Despite Cassius's misgivings, Brutus promises to do so and summons Antony. When Antony arrives and sees Caesar's corpse, he offers the conspirators the chance to kill him, too, but Brutus declines. Antony shakes each man's bloody hand. Brutus grants his request to deliver a eulogy at Caesar's funeral. When the conspirators leave, Antony mourns the loss of Caesar, begging forgiveness of his mentor for appearing to befriend his murderers, but vowing that their deed will be avenged in war. With uncanny timing, a message arrives from Caesar's adopted son and heir, Octavius, who is approaching Rome. Antony sends a message in return, warning Octavius to stay away until it is safe to approach.

At Caesar's funeral, Brutus delivers a dispassionate and rational oration, in which he explains that Caesar was ambitious and was killed to protect the people's freedom. They are persuaded, but miss the point completely and now clamor to have Brutus crowned emperor. Antony then delivers an impassioned and manipulative oration, in which he turns the crowd against Brutus, presenting evidence that Caesar was not ambitious and suggesting that Brutus's motives in murdering Caesar were less than honorable. The people are moved by his tears. He then uncovers Caesar's corpse, and reveals its many stab wounds, calling the conspirators traitors and subtly inciting the crowd to riot. He tells them that Caesar's will bequeathes his estate to the public. Antony then heads off to join Octavius and prepare to fight Brutus and Cassius, who have fled Rome.

The people riot, seeking to kill the conspirators. Incensed, they brutally murder the innocent poet Cinna, mistaking him for the conspirator of the same name.

In the aftermath, Antony, Octavius, and their crony, Lepidus, rule Rome. After sending Lepidus on an errand, Antony contemptuously belittles him to Octavius. The two strategize for the upcoming war against Brutus and Cassius, who are raising troops.

Meanwhile, Brutus and Cassius have been squabbling. Cassius arrives at Brutus's camp, where the two square off, airing their grievances over money matters. After a series of "did toos" and "did nots," Cassius hands Brutus his dagger and dares Brutus to kill him. This breaks the tension and they bury the hatchet. Brutus then confides to Cassius the reason for his irritability: Portia, distressed by Octavius and Antony's power in Rome, has killed herself by swallowing fire. Messala, one of Cassius's commanders, brings the news that Octavius and Antony are advancing and have executed one hundred of Brutus and Cassius's supporters in the Senate. Refusing to entertain Cassius's objections, Brutus insists that their forces march on Philippi, where Octavius and Antony are camped. They all hit the hay. While Brutus sleeps, the ghost of Caesar appears to him and says he'll visit him again at Philippi. Brutus awakes, disturbed.

At Philippi, Octavius and Antony are pleased that their opponents have left an advantageous position in the hills. They are bickering over battle positions when they are interrupted by the arrival of Brutus and Cassius, who have arrived to parley. The opposing parties exchange insults and Octavius and Antony depart. Cassius confides in Messala that it is his birthday, and that he has seen portents of disaster and fears they will lose the day's battle. Before parting to lead their troops into battle, Cassius and Brutus bid each other farewell and agree that if they are defeated they will both commit suicide rather than be taken captive.

In battle, Brutus orders additional troops to attack Octavius's forces, which he believes are weakening. Meanwhile, on another part of the field, Cassius learns that Brutus unnecessarily brought additional forces against Octavius, leaving Cassius at a disadvantage against Antony. Cassius's friend Titinius reports that their forces are surrounded, and Cassius sends him to determine whether the approaching troops are friend or foe. Cassius's slave, Pindarus, then reports that Antony's forces are in his camp and that Titinius has been surrounded by the approaching troops. Cassius, despairing, orders Pindarus to stab him, in exchange for which Pindarus is freed. Titinius and Messala then arrive—it was Messala's friendly army that Pindarus saw surrounding Titinius—with the good news that Octavius's forces were defeated by Brutus, but they find only Cassius's corpse. After Messala leaves to inform Brutus of Cassius's death, Titinius stoicly kills himself with Cassius's sword. Brutus arrives to find the two bodies. He delivers a brief eulogy to the two men and decides to launch a second attack later that day.

In the ensuing battle, Brutus's forces are defeated. Brutus asks one devoted follower after another to run him through with his sword, but one after another they decline. Finally, he persuades Strato, an honorable soldier, to hold his sword and divert his face while Brutus runs on it and dies. Octavius and Antony arrive and discover Brutus's body. They praise the slain man's nobility and virtue and plan to bury him with full honors.

KING LEAR

The aging King Lear is ready to retire. He has decided to divide up his kingdom into three parts, awarding each of his three daughters a portion equal to her love for him. To that end he commands each in turn to declaim publicly on the topic. Goneril and Regan, Lear's two older daughters, perform masterful orations to dear old Dad and are each awarded a lovely third of the kingdom, which they will rule with their respective husbands, the Dukes of Albany and Cornwall. But Lear's plans are foiled when his youngest (and favorite) daughter, Cordelia, refuses to take part in his forensics competition, saying only that she loves her father as duty requires and that she will also love her future husband. Lear immediately disinherits the ungrateful little snippet, despite protests from his trusted adviser, Kent, whom Lear then banishes for his pains. Luckily for Cordelia, one of her suitors—the King of France, no less—values her honesty and offers to marry her even without a dowry. As she leaves for France, her power-hungry sisters plot to keep their aged father under control.

Edmund, the bastard son of the Earl of Gloucester, soliloquizes about his illegitimacy and plots to get his brother Edgar's inheritance. When Gloucester arrives, Edmund uses a forged letter to trick him into believing that Edgar wants him dead so that he can receive his inheritance. Gloucester buys it hook, line, and sinker, and goes off in a state, leaving Edmund to soliloquize again, this time on the folly of believing in a predetermined destiny. Now Edgar arrives, and Edmund "warns" him that his father is furious with him, and that he'd better arm himself.

As king emeritus, Lear has arranged to spend alternate months at his daughters' homes, bringing his fool and his band of one hundred rowdy knights along with him. The loyal Kent has disguised himself as one of these men. When Lear and his retinue arrive for their first stint at Goneril's castle, Kent gets into a terrible scrap with Oswald, a servant whom Goneril has secretly instructed to instigate a fight. Furthermore, the hundred knights have been partying recklessly. Using these excuses, Goneril demeans her father, demanding that he dismiss half his men. Insulted, Lear refuses, electing instead to go and stay with Regan. Goneril sends Oswald ahead with a letter updating her sister.

Meanwhile, under the guise of helping him regain their father's love, Edmund tricks Edgar into "fighting" with him. He then uses this "assault" to convince Gloucester that Edgar attacked him for refusing to help murder their father. Gloucester vows to catch and punish Edgar and to make Edmund his heir. Regan and Cornwall arrive for a visit, and corroborate Edmund's claims.

Outside Gloucester's castle, Kent runs into Oswald and gets into another scrap, for which Cornwall puts him into the stocks. With time on his hands, Kent peruses a letter from Cordelia, who has heard of her father's mistreatment.

In the nearby countryside, Edgar is being hunted down. After a narrow escape, he decides to disguise himself as a crazy, wandering beggar, calling himself Tom o' Bedlam.

Lear and his retinue arrive at Gloucester's castle in search of Regan. Lear is angered to find one of his men (whom he still fails to recognize as Kent) in the stocks. When Regan and Cornwall appear, Kent is freed. Lear complains to Regan about Goneril's behavior, but Regan defends her. Goneril then arrives, and the two demand that Lear dismiss most—no, all—of his train. Lear is outraged! Although a terrible storm is brewing, he prefers its assault to this humiliation and heads off into the storm with his loyal Fool while his daughters take shelter in the castle.

Out on the heath, Lear's sanity begins to fray, and he rages at the storm. Kent catches up with him and steers him toward shelter in a nearby hovel. At first, Lear will not enter the hovel, since the storm helps him forget his daughters' betrayal. By coincidence, Edgar (as the crazy Tom o' Bedlam) has holed up in the same hovel. Lear—now mad himself—tries to comfort the babbling "madman." Gloucester arrives to offer shelter to Lear, despite having been forbidden by Cornwall to do so. He warns Kent that Lear's daughters wish him dead.

Meanwhile, Edmund informs Cornwall that Cordelia and her husband are planning an attack with Gloucester's support.

Now sheltered by Gloucester, Lear et al. enact a mock trial of his daughters. Gloucester returns with news of a plot against Lear and warns them to flee to Dover, where help awaits. Edgar/Tom remains behind, and laments the former king's misfortune.

Cornwall and Regan have had Gloucester arrested. He is brought before them, and they put out his eyes for his "treason." An outraged servant attacks Cornwall, fatally wounding him before being killed himself. The blinded Gloucester is tossed out of his own home. He is found by "Tom o' Bedlam" who—distraught at his father's condition—helps him, promising to lead him to Dover.

Meanwhile, Cordelia's forces have invaded. In a loving adieu, Goneril sends Edmund to Regan for troops (hinting that they should murder Albany so that they can marry). Albany arrives and berates his wife for her cruelty to her father. When news arrives of Gloucester's blinding, Albany privately vows to avenge him.

In Dover, Cordelia hears of Lear's madness but is assured that it can be alleviated with bed rest and drugs. She sends a search party to find him.

Back at Gloucester's castle, Regan learns that Oswald has a letter from Goneril for Edmund and jealously tries to persuade him to replace it with her own declaration of love. She also promises a reward if Oswald finds and kills Gloucester.

Gloucester is determined to leap from the cliffs of Dover to his death. Edgar/Tom tricks him into thinking that he has leaped and survived. Edgar then pretends to be a passerby who witnessed Gloucester's "fall." Granted a new lease on life, Gloucester tells the "stranger" that henceforth he will accept his disability. Coincidentally, along comes Lear, completely crackers. He rages about the evil and hypocrisy of mankind, until a messenger arrives to take him to Cordelia. Oswald now arrives and attempts to kill Gloucester, but Edgar kills him instead. Edgar finds Goneril's letter to Edmund urging him to do away with Albany.

When Lear awakes in Cordelia's camp, he thinks she is a spirit. As his madness then lifts, he recognizes his daughter and asks her forgiveness.

In Goneril and Regan's camp, Edmund leads Regan on, denying any romantic involvement with her sister. When Goneril arrives with husband and troops in tow, she stews in an aside that she would rather lose the war than lose Edmund to Regan. Edgar arrives in a new disguise, and gives Albany Goneril's letter. Alone, Edmund soliloquizes, musing over which sister to dally with, and determining that after the battle Lear and Cordelia will be executed, despite Albany's intentions to spare them.

In the battle, Cordelia and Lear are captured, but Edgar has helped Gloucester escape. Edmund sends Lear and Cordelia off to prison with secret instructions to have them killed. Albany arrives with Goneril and Regan. He takes command and arrests Goneril and Edmund. Regan feels ill and goes off, followed soon thereafter by her sister. Edgar arrives in yet another disguise and duels Edmund, fatally wounding him. The sisters' bodies are now brought in: Regan had been poisoned by Goneril, who has just stabbed herself. Edmund admits that he has ordered the deaths of Lear and Cordelia. As an officer is sent to save them, Edgar reveals his identity and reports his father's death. Too late—Lear enters howling, carrying Cordelia's body. Alternately grieving and thinking she is alive, he dies. Albany will rule the wounded state with Edgar's help.

His Tragic Fate: Tainted by Fate; Restored of Late

Old King Lear's kids were causing him grief long before Shakespeare wrote of the fact. The earliest Lir, or Llyr, was a Celtic sea god whose four children were transformed into swans. While the story of an ancient British king with nasty children may already have existed as folklore, the earliest recorded version is that of twelfth-century pseudo-historian Geoffrey of Monmouth, who recounted it as history in his *Historia Regum Britanniae* (or *Story of the British Kings*), circa 1135. Geoffrey's version was retold by historian Raphael Holinshed, who accepted it as fact, and whose *Chronicles of England, Scotlande, and Irelande* served as the source for Shakespeare and his contemporaries. Jacobeans were acquainted with dozens of versions of the tale, the most famous of which is found in Edmund Spenser's *The Faerie Queene*. Shakespeare's play is based on an anonymous play called *The True Chronicle History of King Leir*, written around 1590. It is thought that Shakespeare may have acted in *Leir*, playing the role on which Kent is based, since the lines in his own play that correspond most closely to those in *Leir* are spoken when Kent is onstage. Shakespeare was the first to end the story tragically, which did not go over well with audiences: his play was replaced by the very successful adaptation by Nahum Tate, *History of King Lear*, which was performed between 1681 and 1843 with varying amounts of Shakespeare's text incorporated, but which retained its happy ending until the 1820s. Shakespeare's original text began to be recognized as one of his great Tragedies in the nineteenth century, but was not widely performed until the twentieth.

LEAR'S LETTERS LINKED TO LIVE-AMMO LAWLESSNESS

Although it isn't a Gunpowder Play to the letter, *King Lear* does contain many of the elements of one (see "Explosive Material: The Gunpowder Plays," page 708), the most notable of which is the play's dependence on letters to reveal the many secret plots in its plot. It's no accident that the word *letter* appears in the play a whopping thirty-three times.

MACBETH

On a dark and stormy night in Scotland, three witches plan an encounter with Macbeth, Thane of Glamis, who recently defeated the rebel Thane of Cawdor in battle with the help of his good friend and commander, Banquo. This heroic victory has pleased the elderly King Duncan, who decides to reward his kinsman Macbeth by giving him Cawdor's title; he sends a messenger to inform Macbeth.

En route home from battle, Macbeth and Banquo run into the three Witches, who hail Macbeth not only by his title, Thane of Glamis, but also as Thane of Cawdor and as "king hereafter." They tell Banquo that he will father kings, and then depart. Immediately, King Duncan's messenger arrives and informs Macbeth of his new title. Realizing that part of the Witches' prophecy has come true, Macbeth is eager for the rest to be fulfilled as well and considers killing the King to bring it about.

Macbeth visits King Duncan's castle, where he is lavishly praised for his valor. After the King announces his appointment of his son Malcolm as heir, Macbeth departs to ready his home for an upcoming visit by the King. He is now convinced that he must kill Duncan to acquire the throne.

Lady Macbeth reads a letter from her husband telling of the latest events. Thrilled, she too begins to scheme, and when Macbeth arrives she urges him on. King Duncan and his sons are then welcomed to the Macbeth abode by Lady M. While she entertains the King, Macbeth frets about the fate of his everlasting soul should he go through with the murder. Lady Macbeth catches him ruminating and helps him make up his mind—he will proceed.

Later that night, after pretending to Banquo that he has forgotten all about the Witches' prophecies, Macbeth has a weird vision of a bloody dagger levitating before him. He is terrified but determined to commit the murder. Later yet, after killing the King, Macbeth returns to his wife. Overwhelmed, he has brought the bloody daggers back with him, instead of leaving them with Duncan's sleeping servants as planned. He is too freaked out to return them, and Lady M. does so herself. She then tells him to snap out of it and go wash up.

In the wee hours of the morning, the Macbeth family porter hears loud knocking at the front door. Drunk and pretending to be a porter at the gate of Hell, he admits Macduff, a neighboring noble who has come to give the King his wake-up call. Macduff discovers the murder, whereupon Macbeth feigns innocence and runs to see for himself. He returns, announcing that he has just killed the servants who committed the crime. When he is questioned further, Lady Macbeth calls for help and faints, creating a diversion. Duncan's sons decide to flee the country for their lives.

Time passes. Although everyone has taken the flight of Duncan's sons as a sign of their guilt, Banquo has his suspicions about Macbeth. Meanwhile, Macbeth—now king—fears that the Witches' prophecy about Banquo's heirs will unseat him. After seeing Banquo off on a ride with his son, Fleance, and reminding him to return in time for that evening's banquet, he elaborates on his fear and sends assassins to rub out father and son. He then hints of the deed to Lady M.

The assassins intercept the riders. They succeed in killing Banquo, but Fleance escapes.

At the banquet that evening, the murderers take Macbeth aside to report their partial success. When he returns to the table, Macbeth is surprised and not altogether pleased to find the ghost of Banquo in his chair, invisible to all but him (after all, he promised to be there!). Macbeth's reaction is explained away to the guests by Lady M., and when the ghost disappears Macbeth regains his composure, but not for long. Over soup, the ghost returns and Macbeth begins shouting at it, effectively ending the party despite Lady M.'s attempts at damage control. After the guests (and Banquo) leave, Macbeth recovers and tells Lady M. he will return to the Witches for a consultation.

The Witches know of Macbeth's impending visit and plan to manipulate him further. When he arrives, they raise gruesome apparitions, which warn him against Macduff, and tell him that "none of woman born / Shall harm Macbeth" and that he'll be King "until / Great Birnam Wood to high Dunsinane Hill / Shall come against him." He takes their words as a positive sign (if no man of woman born can harm him, he need not fear Macduff; and how could a forest ever climb a hill?), but when he insists on knowing whether Banquo's heirs will ever reign, the Witches show him a vision of eight kings, presented by Banquo's proud ghost. When the Witches disappear, the rattled Macbeth receives news that Macduff has deserted to Duncan's son Malcolm, who is gathering strength in England. Macbeth decides to punish Macduff. He sends murderers to Macduff's castle, where they slaughter his wife and children.

In England, Malcolm tests Macduff's loyalty and finds him sincere. He reveals that the King of England has agreed to provide military support against Macbeth. News arrives of the slaying of Macduff's family. The grief-stricken Macduff vows revenge on Macbeth.

Meanwhile, back at the palace, Lady Macbeth has taken to sleepwalking, during which she mumbles and repeatedly makes handwashing motions.

A group of Scottish rebels plan to rendezvous with Malcolm's approaching army at

Birnam Wood . . . Macbeth learns of the amassing troops, but because of the Witches' prophecies he remains unconcerned. He is concerned, however, that Lady Macbeth's doctor is unable to cure her hallucinations.

At Birnam Wood, Malcolm has joined forces with the rebels. He orders the soldiers to cut and carry boughs of wood to camouflage their numbers.

Macbeth sits in the castle atop Dunsinane Hill, still unafraid of Malcolm's impending attack. News of his wife's death is followed by word that Birnam Wood appears to be moving toward Dunsinane! He now realizes that his kingship is in deep trouble, and hurriedly moves to arm himself.

Malcolm, Macduff, and their forces approach the castle. Macbeth enters the fray with confidence, knowing he can't be harmed by any man "of woman born." Meanwhile, many of Macbeth's soldiers desert to Malcolm and Dunsinane Castle is surrendered. Macduff finds Macbeth and they fight. When Macbeth boasts of his "charmed life," Macduff reveals that he was "untimely ripped" (removed surgically) from his mother's womb. He kills Macbeth and ceremoniously presents his head to Malcolm, hailing him as the new king. Malcolm's first act as king is to bestow new titles of honor upon his loyal and valiant nobles.

Wasn't This a Dainty Dish to Put Before the King

When King James VI of Scotland became King James I of England, things Scottish became all the rage in London. Ever the crowd pleaser, Shakespeare delivered a Scottish play that would cater to popular demand and, more important, would be certain to curry favor with his new patron. *Macbeth* was probably written to be performed before King James, possibly on the occasion of the state visit by his brother-in-law, King Christian IV of Denmark, in 1606. Whatever Shakespeare may have thought of the supercilious, egotistical, preachy King James, he took pains to make the new monarch look good from all angles, playing to the King's pride in his fine lineage, absolute right to rule, and vast knowledge. Since it was believed that the King was descended from both Duncan and Banquo, Shakespeare altered history to present them glowingly (particularly Banquo: see "Buttering Up Banquo's Blood," page 716). He included blistering allusions to the Gunpowder Plot to overthrow the King, which the King had publicly credited himself with foiling (see "Explosive Material: The Gunpowder Plays," page 708). Finally, Shakespeare capitalized on the King's fascination with witchcraft, a topic on which James considered himself an expert. In 1597, the King had published a treatise entitled *Daemonology*, in which he revealed that the devil lured ignorant women into witchcraft and used them as his servants. The historical account of Macbeth included his consultations with witches, providing the perfect vehicle for Shakespeare to pander to the King's intellectual pretensions.

OTHELLO

Most Elizabethan tragedies followed the formula developed by the ancient Greeks, focusing on larger-than-life heroes whose actions had long-ranging, dramatic effects on those around them. One exception was the genre called Domestic Tragedy, of which

Othello is Shakespeare's only example. Far-reaching issues and philosophies are left behind, and the focus is on a highly personal drama. Perhaps this keen focus on the characters is what enabled Shakespeare to so finely hone *Othello*: every moment is relevant to the main action of the story. *Othello* is thus considered by many to be Shakespeare's most perfectly constructed work.

Poor Roderigo is the most miserable guy in Venice. His friend Iago has just tipped him off that Desdemona, the woman of his dreams, has eloped with Iago's employer, Othello the Moor, a general who's considered a war hero throughout Venice. Iago tells Roderigo that he, too, has reason to hate Othello, who recently passed him over for promotion to lieutenant, giving the job to the less experienced and less deserving Cassio. He confides that he serves Othello for his own purposes, and not out of loyalty. He convinces Roderigo to wake up Desdemona's father, Brabantio, and tell him about the elopement. When they do so, Brabantio organizes a search party.

Iago rushes to the inn where Othello is staying, and warns his boss that Brabantio is headed this way. Just as Cassio brings Othello an urgent summons from the Duke of Venice, Brabantio arrives and swords are drawn. Othello remains calm, refusing to fight. He explains that he has been called to the Duke's council, where Brabantio is probably also expected. They all head off to the council meeting.

The Duke has convened this emergency meeting because a Turkish fleet is about to attack Cyprus, which belongs to Venice. He orders Othello to sail for Cyprus immediately. Brabantio brings up his grievance, accusing Othello of using magic to enchant Desdemona. Othello insists that Desdemona married him of her own free will. She is sent for, and while the council awaits her arrival, Othello tells the moving story of how they fell in love. When Desdemona appears, she confirms Othello's story, and her father renounces her. Now the council can get down to business: Othello is to depart immediately, and Desdemona will be allowed to join him. All depart to make ready for the trip, while Iago and Roderigo wait behind.

Poor Roderigo is disconsolate. He considers drowning himself, but Iago has a better suggestion: Roderigo should come with him to Cyprus. Iago claims that Desdemona will soon be sorry she married Othello, and with Iago's help, Roderigo can have her for his lover yet. Iago is just about the best friend a guy could ask for. Roderigo goes happily off to sell all his land to finance the trip. Iago stays behind to ruminate on the ease with which he uses fools such as Roderigo and on his hatred for Othello, whom he suspects has cuckolded him. He concocts a plan to make Othello think that Desdemona is fooling around with Cassio, neatly killing two birds with one stone: he'll get revenge on Othello and simultaneously ruin Cassio so that he can have the lieutenantship.

What luck! On its way to attack Cyprus, the entire Turkish fleet is destroyed by a storm. The Venetians arrive safely and are greeted by Montano, the retiring governor, who leads them into the castle. Iago and Roderigo wait behind once more. Iago tells Roderigo that Desdemona has the hots for Cassio, and convinces him to pick a fight with Cassio that night, so that Cassio will be fired from his post. With Cassio out of the way, Roderigo will be next in line for Desdemona's affections. This seems reasonable to Roderigo, so he agrees.

Othello issues a proclamation: the people are to feast and make merry to celebrate the smiting of the Turks and his marriage to Desdemona. This will continue until eleven o'clock sharp, after which it's back to the grindstone.

That night, Othello leaves Cassio to command the watch. Cassio intends to start the watch early, but Iago pressures him to have a drink first. Cassio declines—he knows he can't hold his liquor—but Iago insists. By the time Cassio goes off to the watch, he is utterly inebriated. Iago sends Roderigo after him, as planned. The two soon return, fighting, and a brawl ensues, during which the drunken Cassio is tricked into injuring the retired governor, Montano. Iago sends Roderigo out to sound an alarm, which brings Othello running. Iago relates the story of the fight, claiming all the while that he loves Cassio, and that there must have been some extenuating circumstance. Othello fires Cassio and goes off to tend Montano's wounds. Cassio is crushed; his reputation is ruined. As usual, friend extraordinaire Iago is standing by with good advice: Cassio should ask Desdemona to plead his case for him—maybe Othello will reinstate him. Cassio's hopes are somewhat restored, and he goes off to bed, leaving Iago alone to contemplate the successful progress of his dastardly plan until Roderigo returns.

Poor Roderigo. He's moved to Cyprus, spent almost all his money, been beaten in a fight, and suspects that nothing will come of his efforts. He plans to return to Venice, but Iago helps him change his mind.

The next morning, Iago arranges a meeting between Desdemona and Cassio in the castle garden, where Desdemona promises to do what she can for Cassio. When they spot Othello and Iago coming toward them, Cassio quickly leaves. Iago points out to Othello that Cassio is slinking away guiltily from Desdemona. When they approach her, she immediately brings up Cassio's cause. After she departs, Iago "reluctantly" makes comments about Cassio and Desdemona that provoke Othello's jealous suspicion. He then suggests that Othello test Desdemona by putting off Cassio's reinstatement, and then watching to see how urgently she presses him about it. Iago leaves, and Othello grapples with the idea that Desdemona may have been unfaithful to him.

Desdemona returns with Iago's wife, Emilia, who serves as her attendant. When Desdemona asks Othello what is wrong, he says he has a pain in his head. She tries to bind it with her handkerchief, but he pushes it away and goes off, with Desdemona following. Emilia stays behind to pick up the handkerchief, which has dropped to the ground. She delights in having found it, for her husband has been trying to get her to steal it for him, but Desdemona never let the treasured hanky out of her sight, as it was her first gift from Othello. Along comes Iago, who grabs the handkerchief away from Emilia. She asks to have it back, suddenly realizing how upset Desdemona will be to have lost it, but Iago dismisses her, saying he has use for it. After she goes, he schemes to drop the hanky in Cassio's lodgings. Othello returns. His suspicions have thrown him into a frenzied state of angst, and he demands that Iago back up his allegations with proof. Iago claims that one night he heard Cassio talk of Desdemona in his sleep, and that Cassio has the beloved handkerchief. Othello is convinced, and swears to be revenged. Iago swears to help him.

Later, Desdemona is distraught over the lost handkerchief. When Othello arrives, she renews her appeal for Cassio, but all Othello wants to hear about is the hanky. He says that an Egyptian woman had given it to his mother, with a warning that as long as she kept it, her husband would love her, but if she lost it, he would look on her with loathing. Desdemona won't admit that the hanky is lost. When she tries to speak again of Cassio, Othello repeatedly demands the handkerchief, and when she does not produce it, he storms out. Iago and Cassio arrive, and Desdemona tells them she regrets that she has not been able to help Cassio. Iago says that he will go to Othello and try to cool his anger, and the men go off together. Cassio is soon tracked down by Bianca, a courtesan who is upset with him for ignoring her lately. Cassio gives her Desdemona's handkerchief and asks her to copy the embroidery on it before he returns it to whoever lost it in his lodgings.

In another part of the garden, Iago tells Othello that Cassio has confided in him that he slept with Desdemona. This puts Othello into such a fit of rage that he actually passes out. Just then, Cassio approaches. Iago stops Cassio from reviving Othello, and tells him to go off and hide until Othello is gone. Cassio goes, and Iago revives Othello. He tells him to hide in the brush and listen while he questions Cassio about Desdemona. Othello hides, and Cassio returns. When Iago asks him about Bianca, Cassio laughs and makes disparaging remarks about her. Othello overhears and, thinking he refers to Desdemona, becomes more enraged with each comment. Bianca arrives, throws the famous hanky in Cassio's face, and refuses to have anything to do with a bauble given him by another woman. That clinches it for Othello: Desdemona has obviously given his token of love to Cassio, who turned around and gave it to this harlot. Bianca stomps off, and Cassio follows after her. Othello comes out of hiding, and declares that Desdemona must die that night. Iago promises to dispose of Cassio that night as well.

Lodovico, a Venetian nobleman, is escorted to the garden by Desdemona. Lodovico has been sent to retrieve Othello, who is needed in Venice. Cassio is to stay behind as governor of Cyprus. When Desdemona says she is glad to hear this, Othello strikes her, much to Lodovico's surprise. After the two depart, Iago tells Lodovico that Othello's abuse of Desdemona is usually even worse than what they have just seen.

Meanwhile, Othello calls Desdemona a whore and ignores her claims that she is innocent. He leaves Desdemona alone with Emilia, heartbroken and bewildered. Emilia fetches Iago and explains to him what happened, saying she thinks that some "insinuating rogue" has slandered Desdemona. Desdemona swears that she is innocent and asks Iago to convince Othello of it. He tells her not to worry, and the women go in to supper.

Roderigo arrives. Poor, poor Roderigo feels that Iago has misled him. He says the jewels he has given Iago to deliver to Desdemona could have corrupted a nun. He has decided to give up: if she will simply return the jewels, Roderigo will be on his way. Otherwise, he intends to hold Iago responsible for his losses. Iago informs Roderigo that Cassio will be taking over as governor, and that Othello will leave the next day, taking his wife with him. He suggests that the best course of action is for Roderigo to kill Cassio that night, so that Othello will have to stay in Cyprus. He promises that if this is accomplished, Roderigo will have Desdemona the following night. This sounds like a good idea to Roderigo, so they go off together to plan the deed.

Inside the castle, Othello orders Desdemona to go straight to bed and to dismiss Emilia, as he will return shortly. He goes off with Lodovico, leaving the two women alone. Desdemona is confused and afraid. She tells Emilia that she can't believe there are women who would commit the sin of adultery: she would not do so for all the world. Emilia says that it's the husband's fault if his wife is unfaithful—that's what he gets for mistreating her, and ignoring the fact that she is a human being with feelings.

On a street in Cyprus, Iago sets up an ambush: Roderigo is to hide and attack Cassio when he appears. Iago is hoping they will kill each other in the fight, since either one of them could get him into big trouble. As Iago watches, Cassio arrives and Roderigo attacks, but Cassio's coat of mail protects him. Cassio wounds Roderigo, but then Iago sneaks up from behind and wounds Cassio in the leg. Cassio falls as Iago hides himself. Othello comes along and sees Cassio wounded. Inspired by this evidence that Iago has fulfilled his promise, Othello rushes off toward the castle to kill Desdemona.

Lodovico arrives with Gratiano, another Venetian noble. Iago rushes in, pretending he has just heard the noise of the fight. "Discovering" that the wounded man is his friend Cassio, Iago pretends to be outraged by the deed, and looks around for the culprit. Roderigo is lying wounded nearby. Iago dashes over and stabs him fatally before he can reveal Iago's treachery. Cassio is carried off by the noblemen as Bianca and Emilia each arrive at the scene. Iago accuses Bianca of plotting against Cassio and arrests her. He sends Emilia to the castle to tell Othello what has happened.

Meanwhile, Othello kisses the sleeping Desdemona. He is moved by her beauty and decides to kill her without marring it. When she wakes, he tells her to say her prayers, so her soul will be prepared. He claims that Cassio's possession of the handkerchief is proof of her guilt. She denies it, and suggests that he send for Cassio and question him. He tells her that Cassio is dead, and takes her distress at this news as further evidence of her guilt. Although she begs for mercy, he smothers her.

Emilia pounds at the door. When Othello lets her in, she reports Cassio's injury and Roderigo's death. Desdemona revives, asserts her innocence once more, and then dies. Othello admits that he killed her, and claims that she was a whore—in fact, it was Emilia's husband who proved Desdemona false. Montano, Gratiano, and Iago arrive, and Emilia turns to Iago hoping he'll deny that he ever said Desdemona was unfaithful. Iago says he did say so. When Othello mentions the handkerchief, Emilia realizes what has happened, and tries to tell the others. Iago orders her to be quiet, and when she refuses, he draws his sword on her. Emilia reveals the truth about the handkerchief. When Othello hears it, he lunges for Iago, but is held back by the others. Meanwhile, Iago fatally stabs Emilia, and then escapes. Montano goes after him.

Othello shares his grief and regret with Gratiano, who has stayed to guard him. Lodovico and Montano arrive with the captured Iago and the injured Cassio. Othello wounds Iago, but does not kill him, for death now seems desirable to him and he doesn't want Iago to enjoy it. Othello insists that everything he did was for honor's sake, but he admits that Cassio never gave him cause to kill him, and asks his pardon. He demands to know why Iago did it, but Iago refuses to speak. When the details of the plot are finally revealed, Lodovico appoints Cassio governor of Cyprus and takes Othello prisoner. Othello asks that when the nobles return to Venice they tell his full story, so that he will be remembered as "one that loved not wisely, but too well." He then stabs himself, and kisses Desdemona as he dies. Lodovico leaves Cassio to torture and punish Iago, while he departs for Venice to report what has passed.

IRRELEVANT HISTORY: SUFFRAGETTE OF THE SIXTIES

Desdemona was the first female role ever acted by an Actual Female Person in Britain. The honor went to Margaret Hughes, who played the part in 1660. Brava, Margaret!

> **A Real-Life, Real-Wife Murder**
> Shakespeare was a crowd pleaser, and he knew what pleased the crowd best—a titillating, real-life shocker. He must have been delighted to come across his source for *Othello*, a novella by the Italian author Cinthio. Cinthio's tale, published in 1565, retold a true story that took place that same year: an Italian diplomat heard false reports of his wife's infidelity, and while he believed her denial of it, he strangled her anyway to preserve his honor.

> **Double Double Time and Trouble**
> Double time is the dramatic device whereby the action of a play unfolds in two different time frames simultaneously. Shakespeare used it in many of his plays, but most noticeably and to greatest effect in *Othello*. In the play, the action clearly takes place over the course of only one or two days, yet the characters consistently behave as if a period of two or three weeks passes. The feeling of immediacy created by the short time frame engages the audience in the play's intensity and passion, and increases its tension; while the more realistic parameter of the long time frame disguises the shorter one and allows the audience to feel that the development of the action is probable. Because the play so actively captivates the audience members, the contradictions that result from double time pass unnoticed while they watch it.

ROMEO AND JULIET

Romeo and Juliet—oft proclaimed the greatest love story of all time—opens, appropriately, with an introductory sonnet (the poetic form of choice for the lovesick), in which Chorus presents an overview of the play, which takes place over five days.

Sunday: in the streets of Verona, servants of the feuding Capulet and Montague households brawl. Lords Capulet and Montague join in the fracas. The Prince of Verona intercedes, threatening them with death if they fight again. After they disperse, melancholy young Romeo Montague arrives and confides in his cousin, Benvolio, that he is pining away for the love of a sweetie named Rosaline.

Later, at the Capulet *palazzo*, Lord Capulet negotiates with Count Paris for the hand of Capulet's daughter, Juliet, in marriage, and invites the young Count to a masked ball he's hosting that night. He dispatches a servant to deliver the rest of the invitations. Out on the street, the illiterate servant asks Romeo and Benvolio to read the invitation list to him. Learning that his beloved Rosaline is invited, Romeo determines to attend the ball.

Back at the Capulets', Lady Capulet breaks the news to Juliet of her impending engagement to Paris. Juliet's nurse fondly recalls Juliet's babyhood. Juliet unenthusiastically agrees to obey her parents and marry Paris.

That night, en route to the ball, Romeo tells Benvolio and their friend, Mercutio (the Prince's kinsman), that a dream has left him with a sick, ominous feeling. Sick of Romeo's lovesickness, Mercutio descants on the insidiousness of dreams.

Meanwhile, the masque has begun! Capulet grandiosely welcomes his guests. Romeo and his friends arrive at the ball, masks in place. Romeo is thunderstruck by Juliet's beauty and waxes rhapsodic. Overhearing him, Juliet's cousin, Tybalt, recognizes his voice and sends for his rapier, but Capulet chastizes him for his willingness to start a riot at the masque. Tybalt departs, but vows to exact revenge on Romeo at a later date.

Romeo and Juliet meet, fall instantly in love, speak to each other in sonnet form, and kiss. After she is called away, Romeo discovers that Juliet is a Capulet. Oh, no! He departs, dejected. Juliet inquires and learns that Romeo is a Montague. Oh, no! She goes off to bed, dejected. In another sonnet, Chorus reassures the audience that the young lovers will not give up so easily . . .

Romeo has ditched his friends (who are annoyed) and has scaled the Capulets' garden wall. He spots Juliet on her balcony, and overhears her sighing for him. He reveals himself and the two confess their love for each other in highly elevated language. They kiss and agree to be wed the following day: Romeo will make arrangements and Juliet will send a messenger for the details.

Monday: Romeo can barely wait—at dawn, he visits a local friar, Friar Lawrence, who agrees to marry the lovebirds, hoping that this will bury the enmity between their families.

Benvolio and Mercutio learn that Tybalt—who is a highly skilled swordsman—has challenged Romeo to a duel. Romeo meets up with them. When Juliet's nurse appears, Romeo's friends heckle her and leave. Romeo tells the Nurse to send Juliet to Friar Lawrence in the afternoon to be married.

Meanwhile, Juliet waits impatiently at home. Finally, the Nurse returns, and after teasingly withholding the message, she delivers it. Juliet heads off to church immediately. Romeo and Juliet meet at the Friar's, reaffirm their love, and depart with the Friar to be wed.

Later that day, Benvolio and Mercutio encounter Tybalt on the street. Romeo arrives, and Tybalt challenges him. Romeo does not wish to fight his new kinsman, though he will not divulge why—he merely declines to fight. Disgusted, Mercutio takes the challenge on himself—he and Tybalt duel. Romeo steps in to break up the duel, unwittingly giving Tybalt the opening to fatally stab Mercutio. Tybalt flees. With his dying breath, Mercutio curses the houses of Montague and Capulet. Tybalt returns and, to avenge Mercutio's death, Romeo duels Tybalt and kills him. Romeo then flees. The Prince arrives and Benvolio explains what happened. Although the Capulets seek Romeo's death, the Prince recognizes Tybalt as the instigator and merely banishes Romeo, under penalty of death should he ever be found in Verona.

At the Capulets', Juliet waits impatiently for her secret wedding-night rendezvous with Romeo. Her nurse arrives and reports the death of Tybalt and Romeo's banishment. Juliet is distraught. The Nurse promises to bring Romeo to Juliet that night.

Friar Lawrence is harboring the fugitive Romeo. He informs Romeo that his punishment is banishment rather than death. Romeo would rather be put to death than be banished from Juliet. The Nurse arrives and tells Romeo that Juliet can't stop crying, at which Romeo draws his dagger to kill himself. The Friar admonishes him to pull himself together: Romeo should spend the night with Juliet, and flee to Mantua early in the morning. Friar Lawrence will keep him apprised until they can secure him a pardon from the Prince. Romeo is heartened, and heads off to see Juliet.

Meanwhile, Capulet is vexed by Juliet's extreme grief, which he believes to be for Tybalt's death. He decides to marry Juliet to Paris on Thursday, three days hence.

Tuesday: at dawn in Juliet's chamber, Romeo and Juliet bid each other a bittersweet adieu. After Romeo slides down the rope ladder, the Capulets arrive and tell Juliet that she is to be wed to Paris. Juliet refuses, claiming that it is too soon after Tybalt's death. Lord Capulet, infuriated by his daughter's disobedience and ingratitude, threatens to disown her if she does not comply. Out storm the Capulets, leaving the Nurse to comfort Juliet. She recommends that Juliet disregard her marriage to Romeo and marry Paris. Juliet thanks her for her advice but is privately horrified and resolved not to commit bigamy. She heads off to ask Friar Lawrence for help.

When Juliet arrives, she encounters Paris, whom Friar Lawrence is attempting (unsuccessfully) to dissuade from being wed so hastily. Juliet deflects Paris's attempts to flirt. After he departs, Juliet confides that she is considering suicide. This sparks an idea in the Friar—he will give her a potion to drink the night before her wedding, which will make her appear dead the next morning. While she is being interred in the Capulet crypt, he will get word of the plan to Romeo, who will be there when she revives—the two will then flee Verona together.

Back at the Capulets', Capulet is excitedly preparing for Juliet's wedding when she returns from the Friar. Juliet "apologizes" to her father, "promising" to be obedient and marry Paris. Capulet is so delighted with the results of his parenting that he moves the wedding up a day (to tomorrow!) and sets off to give Paris the good news. That evening, alone in her room, a terrified Juliet drinks the potion and goes to sleep.

Wednesday: early in the morning, the Nurse discovers Juliet's seemingly lifeless form as the wedding party arrives. Massive hysteria breaks out, and Friar Lawrence makes arrangements for her interment in the family crypt.

Meanwhile, in Mantua, Romeo receives news of Juliet's death. Believing it to be true, he purchases poison from an apothecary and sets off for Verona, where he intends to join his beloved in death.

Later that day, Friar Lawrence learns that his messenger has been unable to deliver the details of the plan to Romeo. Friar Lawrence heads to the crypt, to retrieve Juliet and hide her until Romeo can be found.

That night, Paris visits the Capulet crypt with flowers for his dead betrothed. Romeo arrives and encounters Paris; they duel and Paris is slain. Romeo enters the crypt, goes to Juliet (still "dead"), pledges eternal devotion, takes the poison, and dies kissing her. Friar Lawrence arrives seconds too late and discovers the dead youths just as Juliet awakes. Hearing the night watchman's approach, he urges her to flee. Juliet will not leave Romeo, so the Friar, spooked, leaves her there. Juliet takes Romeo's dagger and kills herself to join him in death. Meanwhile, the watchman has caught Friar Lawrence and sounded an alarm. In come the Prince, the Capulets, and Lord Montague. Friar Lawrence explains the whole story, and, as a gray day dawns (Thursday), the feuding families bury the hatchet for their children's sake.

A Recipe for Love

The story of the lovers Romeo and Juliet was originally folklore, and was told in *novelle* form by many fifteenth- and sixteenth-century writers in Europe. Its first translation into English, by Arthur Brooke in 1562, was Shakespeare's major source. Brooke's version, which is written in poem form, is introduced by three sonnets, thus emphasizing the similarities between the sonnet form and this story: both use thematic motifs and poetry to discuss an emotion as it functions both in the intimacy of private life and in the broader context of societal dynamics; both also end in a twist that leaves the listener pondering the central theme. Shakespeare took this idea a step further, incorporating sonnets into his play and using sonnetlike language throughout. He was also influenced by Chaucer's use of recurring leitmotifs and his deeper exploration of his characters' emotional lives in his poem *Troilus and Criseyde*. Shakespeare's recipe for *Romeo and Juliet*, which combines his predecessors' ingredients with the spice of his own genius, has become a staple in the diet of lovers the world over.

TIMON OF ATHENS

Timon of Athens is set in the fifth century B.C.E.—the Golden Age of Greece. As the play opens life is golden for our hero, Timon, but since this is, after all, a Shakespearean tragedy, it doesn't stay golden for long.

Timon is a generous guy, the host with the most; his pad (i.e., huge marble mansion) is the hub of the Athenian social scene. Need a loan? He's your man. Your favorite birthday present? Came from him. In fact, there's a party going on at his place tonight. You should stop by—he won't mind.

Speaking of Timon, a poet, a painter, a jeweler, and a merchant have met, and are speaking of Timon. They've all created products especially for him, for which they expect to be well compensated. Look! Here comes Timon himself. A messenger tells him that his friend Ventidius has been placed in debtors' prison, and Timon agrees to pay the five talents (about $55,000 today) to free him. Then he promises his servant Lucilius three talents ($33,000 today) plus more to come, so that Lucilius can marry the daughter of an aristocrat. Hey, there's Apemantus. Now, don't be put off by his gruff ways. He's a curmudgeon, but underneath he's really a quality guy—he tells it like it is. Apemantus grumbles that the artisans who have been making things for Timon are a bunch of flatterers and sycophants. Timon's friend Alcibiades has just arrived. Timon is happy to see him and is inviting him and all the rest of us to dinner. Why not? Free food!

Check out Timon's place. He's gone all out. He always does—that's Timon for you. Ventidius, already freed, is trying to repay his debt to Timon, but Timon won't hear of it. Apemantus just can't enjoy himself—he's still muttering that all the guests are using Timon, although Timon insists that they're true friends and would help him out of a jam. This party must have cost a fortune. Not only a band, but costumed performers—a guy in a Cupid suit! Amazons! And now Timon is handing out expensive gifts. Apemantus won't take one. Timon's steward, Flavius, is worried that Timon is going bankrupt. Not our problem. Have you tried the foie gras?

The next day Timon's generosity has his creditors worried . . . how long can his funds hold out? These guys (who had no problem accepting his hospitality last night) have sent their servants to collect their debts from him. Flavius regretfully reminds Timon that he has refused to balance his checkbook, and tells him he is now seriously in the red. Timon isn't worried, though. He knows his friends will help him out. He sends his servants to Lucius, Lucullus, Sempronius, and Ventidius to ask for money.

All of Timon's friends have refused him! Lucullus told the servant to pretend he never found him; Lucius claimed he'd help, but he's out of funds; Ventidius denied him outright; and Sempronius acted insulted to have been the last one asked.

Meanwhile, more and more of Timon's debts are called in. We've never seen Timon in such a state. He's shouting that he'll have to pay them in blood—they can hack him up and divvy up the pieces. Now Timon's servants are leaving, since he can't pay them (Flavius gave them what little he could from his own pocket). Good old Flavius is the only one left. Can you believe it—Timon is sending him out to invite everyone to dinner again! What will we wear?

Also, have you heard that Alcibiades went to the Senate to seek mercy for this one guy who had killed this other guy, and he wouldn't take no for an answer, so the senators got miffed at him and now he's banished? He took his private army, vowed revenge, and left town.

The banquet's about to be served, and we're all brought covered dishes. Chateaubriand? Pheasant? Knowing Timon, he's spared no expense. Drumroll, please . . . What's this? Rocks? In water? Timon has lost his mind. Now he's raving at all of us, calling us parasites and fools, cursing us! Look out—he's throwing the rocks at us—we're outta here!

So, apparently, is Timon. Now he's left Athens. We can hear him out there, cursing at the city walls. Flavius is worried and is going after him.

OK, here's what happens to Timon after he leaves (we've got our sources):

First, Timon wanders around the woods, cursing humanity and digging for roots. Wouldn'tcha know, Timon digs up a big pile of gold, but what does he do? Does he come back to Athens? No, he goes on cursing and eating roots.

Meanwhile, Alcibiades is on his way to attack Athens, with his troops and his two lady friends in tow. He bumps into Timon, who eggs him on and gives him some gold to pay his soldiers. He even gives the hookers gold and tells them to go spread venereal disease in Athens.

After Alcibiades and his crowd leave, Apemantus shows up. Apemantus tells Timon to go home and live by flattering others the way they flattered him—Timon won't do it. Apemantus offers Timon food—Timon rejects it. You know what it's like when two curmudgeons get together: pretty soon they're exchanging insults, and Apemantus leaves.

A bunch of bandits have heard that Timon has gold, and they find him. And listen to this: Timon praises them, gives them gold, and tells them to keep up the good work. They take off.

Poor Flavius finally finds his master. He offers Timon his life savings. Looking at Flavius, Timon has to acknowledge that there is one decent human being on this cold, lonely planet (but he curses the rest of us). Although Flavius wants to stay and help him, Timon pushes gold on him and forces him to leave.

The painter and the poet have also heard about Timon's gold and drop in on him. He's on to their tricks: he curses them and drives them away.

Now a group of senators trek out to the forest, led by Flavius. They offer Timon wealth and honor if he returns to Athens to lead its forces—as he had once before—this time against Alcibiades. He tells them he hopes that Alcibiades sacks Athens, kills its aged, and rapes its virgins . . . in other words, no thanks. He suggests that the senators hang themselves and offers them a tree.

Back in Athens, we soon hear the bad news: Timon is dead. One of Alcibiades' soldiers went to Timon's cave with a message and found a grave with a strange epitaph. He took a wax impression of it back to Alcibiades to decipher.

Alcibiades and his troops are right outside Athens—we're doomed. The senators have gone up onto the city's walls to negotiate with him. We can hear them from here: the senators are saying that those who offended Alcibiades are no longer living—they died of shame. If he attacks Athens now, he'll be killing innocent people. Alcibiades relents, provided that the senators turn over to him any remaining enemies of his and Timon's, to be killed. Here comes the soldier, with the news of Timon's death and the epitaph. Alcibiades reads it—it's a farewell curse by Timon from the grave. Alcibiades is clearly stricken. He promises to use his military strength to create a lasting peace in Athens.

PICTURING THE PLAYWRIGHT'S PROCESS

Scholars have figured out (and almost all of them agree) that *Timon of Athens* is the only existing unfinished play by Shakespeare. What's cool about this is that parts of the text provide a glimpse into his writing process. There are certain sections of text that are clearly drafts of blank verse: while the content of each line is in place, the meter of many lines is still extremely irregular. Why didn't he finish it? Did he get bored? Did his mates read a draft and pan it? And most of all, if it's unfinished, why is it included in the canon at all? See "A Narrow Escape from Oblivion," below.

A NARROW ESCAPE FROM OBLIVION

The compilers of the First Folio did not originally intend to include *Timon of Athens* in the collection. They were about to go to press when they encountered a copyright problem with *Troilus and Cressida*. Floundering around for something to put in its place, they came across the draft of *Timon* and stuck it in (and, obviously, they worked out that little *Troilus and Cressida* problem after all, since it was included as well). The compilers' legal headache was our gain: without it, *Timon* would not have squeaked its way into posterity.

TITUS ANDRONICUS

Everyone loves a good horror flick. The gorier, the better. But this human thirst for mayhem didn't start with the advent of the moving picture . . . movies are just the latest in a tradition of mutilation entertainment that spans millennia. The Elizabethans in particular relished a Saturday afternoon beheading, or a double-feature hanging. If an actual execution wasn't playing, they turned to the theatre, which served up some graphically gruesome fare. *Titus Andronicus* was one of the top-grossing box-office horror hits of its time. Break out the popcorn . . . if you have the stomach for it:

The Roman emperor has just died and his two sons, Saturninus and Bassianus, both want the job. Luckily, Titus Andronicus, Rome's beloved warrior, has returned from vanquishing the Goths just in time to decide which of the two should rule. But first, the gods must be thanked for the Roman victory with a human sacrifice. Titus has captured Tamora, the Queen of the Goths, and brought her and her three sons back to Rome with him. He decides that Tamora's oldest son, Alarbus, will make a nice juicy sacrifice, and ignores her desperate pleas for mercy. Titus's four remaining sons (most of his twenty-five sons died in battle), Lucius, Quintus, Martius, and Mutius (yes, those are their real names), drag Alarbus off to be chopped up and burned.

Now to the business at hand: Titus chooses Saturninus (the elder of the brothers) as emperor, and in return Saturninus declares that he will make Titus's daughter, Lavinia, his empress. Titus is pleased, but Bassianus is not—he is already betrothed to Lavinia and refuses to relinquish her. With the support of Titus's sons, Bassianus seizes Lavinia. In the ensuing skirmish, Titus, mortified by his own sons' treason, kills Mutius. Bassianus and the others escape with Lavinia. Saturninus (who is actually hotter for Tamora than he was for Lavinia, and who is also unnerved by Titus's popularity) takes the opportunity to denounce Titus and his boys for the junior Andronici's treasonous behavior. He declares that he will marry Tamora, and the two go off to be wed immediately. They return, married, as do Bassianus and Lavinia. Publicly, Tamora urges Saturninus to forgive Titus, but privately she tells him that they will seek revenge on Titus later, so that the citizenry, who love Titus, will not turn against their new emperor. As they all repair to a double wedding feast, Titus invites them to join him on a hunt the next day.

Tamora's lover Aaron, a Moor whom all believe to be her servant, soliloquizes about his great turn of fortune—he has long held Tamora in his spell, and will certainly benefit from her new status as the Roman Empress. Her sons, Chiron and Demetrius, enter arguing over who shall win Lavinia (they're unfazed by her new marital status). Aaron sees no need to win her—he suggests that the fellows team up to rape her at tomorrow's hunt, and the three go off to seek Tamora's help in planning the deed.

The next day, the hunting party gathers. Aaron, alone in the woods, buries a bag of gold in a big pit. He's joined by Tamora, and together they eagerly anticipate the violence to come. Bassianus and Lavinia come upon them, followed soon after by Chiron and Demetrius, who stab Bassianus to death at their mother's instruction and dump his body in the pit with the gold. Despite Lavinia's pleas that Tamora kill her to save her honor, Tamora leaves, and Chiron and Demetrius drag Lavinia off to rape her. Meanwhile, Aaron has lured Lavinia's brothers Martius and Quintus to the pit, into which they both fall. Aaron goes off and returns with Saturninus, who sees the brothers in the pit with Bassianus's body and the gold. Aaron shows him a forged letter framing Martius and Quintus for the death of Bassianus, and despite Titus's pleas for mercy, Saturninus has the two arrested.

Nearby, Chiron and Demetrius have raped Lavinia, and have cut out her tongue and cut off her hands so that she can't identify her assailants. She is found by her uncle (Titus's brother), Marcus Andronicus, who poetically laments her misfortune.

Later, Titus pleads in vain for his sons' lives as they are led to their execution. His remaining son, Lucius, tells him to spare his breath—Lucius himself has just been banished for making such pleas. Marcus enters with the mutilated Lavinia—more lamentation ensues. Aaron enters and claims that Titus's sons will be spared in exchange for the severed hand of either Titus, Marcus, or Lucius. The men squabble over who gets to make the sacrifice. Titus has Aaron chop off his hand while the other two are off searching for an axe. The hand is soon returned to him . . . along with his sons' heads. Tricked! Titus vows revenge. He sends Lucius to raise an army among the Goths. They exit, Marcus bearing one head, Titus the other (in his remaining hand), and Lavinia carrying her father's severed hand in her teeth.

At home, the grief-stricken Titus dines with Marcus and Lavinia. He feeds his daughter and says he can interpret her thoughts. He claims that he—and only he—has a right to be insane due to what he has suffered, but it is clear to the audience that his mind is painfully lucid. Nevertheless, Marcus believes that grief has made his brother mad.

Later, Lavinia gets her stumps on a copy of Ovid's *Metamorphoses*, and shows her father and uncle the story of the rape of Philomela (whose tongue was cut out so that she could not reveal her rapist). They realize what she is trying to tell them, and have her write the names of her rapists in the dirt, with a stick held between her stumps. Marcus and Titus vow revenge.

Chiron, Demetrius, and Aaron receive a veiled message from Titus, which only Aaron understands to mean that Titus knows of their guilt and will avenge it. A nurse enters, bringing Aaron the biracial child Tamora has just borne him, with orders from Tamora that he kill it. Chiron and Demetrius want to get rid of it quickly, before this evidence of her affair can ruin her. Aaron grabs the child from the nurse, defiantly threatening to kill anyone who touches his beautiful son. He plans to switch the baby with his friend's lighter-skinned biracial newborn, thus neatly averting disaster. He kills the nurse to prevent her from spilling the beans.

In downtown Rome, Titus, appearing mad, makes his family shoot arrows into the air, bearing petitions to the gods to bring justice against Saturninus. Marcus suggests that they shoot the arrows into the Emperor's courtyard to annoy him, which they do. Along comes a clown, carrying two pigeons. Titus hires the clown to give the two pigeons to the Emperor, along with a message from Titus, wrapped around a dagger.

Saturninus is already annoyed by the arrows landing in his courtyard when the clown arrives with Titus's delivery. After reading the message, he has the poor clown hanged. Saturninus wants Titus dragged to him so that he can kill him personally, but news arrives that Titus's son Lucius is marching on Rome with an army of Goths. Tamora suggests that she go speak with Titus; she will be able to persuade him to intercede with his son. Saturninus agrees.

Aaron has been captured outside Rome, en route to the baby swap, and is brought to Lucius's military camp. Lucius is about to have both father and baby hanged, but a plea bargain is reached instead: the baby will be spared in exchange for Aaron's information about the murder-rape-mutilation-and-framing scheme. Aaron is not sorry—his only regret is that he did not do more evil in his life. A messenger from the Emperor requests a parley with Lucius at Titus's house.

Tamora believes that Titus is mad and intends to use that fact to capture Lucius. Arriving at Titus's house disguised as "Revenge" (with her sons dressed as "Rape" and "Murder"), she tells Titus that they have come to his aid. She encourages him to arrange a banquet for the Emperor, at which she will avenge his wrongs. Titus sees through the disguise but pretends not to, and agrees to host the banquet and to invite Lucius to attend. When Revenge bids Titus adieu, he asks her to leave Rape and Murder with him, which she does. As soon as she's gone, he has the two tied up. As Lavinia holds a basin in her stumps to catch their blood, Titus slits the throats of Chiron and Demetrius. He plans to grind their bones into powder, mix it with their blood into a paste, and with it cook their heads into a pie to serve their mom at dinner.

That night, Lucius, Saturninus, and Tamora arrive for the banquet. After welcoming and seating his guests, Titus explains to the assembled company that his daughter has been ruined, and he promptly kills her. Next, Titus encourages Tamora to eat more of the pie he slaved over all afternoon. Tamora asks for her sons, and as she takes another bite of the pie, Titus reveals that she has just eaten them. He then promptly kills her. Saturninus calls Titus a "frantic wretch" and promptly kills him. Lucius promptly kills Saturninus for killing his dad. Marcus and Lucius then report to the citizens of Rome the whole sordid tale. The people declare Lucius emperor. Aaron is brought in, and Lucius sentences him to be buried up to his neck and starved to death. Aaron is still not sorry for his evil deeds. Emperor-elect Lucius orders dignified burials for all except Tamora. The end.

P.S.

This play is a prime example of double time at work. For information on this device, see "Double Double Time and Trouble," page 998.

"REVENGE IS PROFITABLE . . ." —EDWARD GIBBON, 1737–94

Titus Andronicus is Shakespeare's purest example of a revenge play, an extremely popular genre among Elizabethan audiences. In revenge plays, a character or characters avenge a wrong or wrongs (and their actions are often then avenged in return). Spectacular by nature, a revenge play usually contains insanity (whether feigned or real), the appearance of supernatural beings, and several outrageously bloody killings and mutilations. The genre was developed in Elizabethan times by Thomas Kyd, who wrote its most famous example, *The Spanish Tragedie*. Kyd, Shakespeare, and their fellow playwrights modeled the genre on the work of the Roman tragedian Seneca. Having no other classical plays available to them, the Elizabethan playwrights erroneously believed that Seneca's gory horror plays were typical examples of classical theatre. Scholars generally have very little respect for *Titus Andronicus*, and have tried every which way to attribute the play to someone other than Shakespeare, to no avail. Shakespeare wrote *Titus* early in his career. The fledgling playwright was catering to his market, and although rough around the edges, the play clearly shows traces of brilliance to come . . .

THE ROMANCES

CYMBELINE

Cymbeline was Shakespeare's second Romance, and scholars generally believe that he hadn't yet worked out all the kinks in his complex interpretation of the developing genre. *Cymbeline* comprises a jarring conglomeration of elements, which prompted J. C. Maxwell to write, in his introduction for the New Cambridge edition, that the play "has somewhat the air of a cumbrous and over-elaborate mechanism that one feels ought not to work and that none the less does work." As *Cymbeline* opens, its action-packed plot has already been set in motion.

King Cymbeline of Britain's daughter, Imogen, has gone behind her father's back and married a worthy but poor gentleman, Posthumus Leonatus, whom the outraged King has therefore banished. The King (not a little influenced by Imogen's stepmom, the Queen) had his own plans for his daughter. Since his two little sons were kidnapped many years ago, she is his only heir, and he had intended to marry her to her good-for-nothing stepbrother, Cloten.

The Queen pretends to be an ally to Imogen and Posthumus, helping them steal a few last moments together. She then heads straight for the King, to tip him off that the two are together. As they say their goodbyes, the newlyweds exchange love tokens—a ring for Posthumus and a bracelet for Imogen—which they vow never to part with. The King then descends upon the lovers and sends Posthumus packing. Posthumus leaves behind his servant, Pisanio, to serve as go-between: in this way Imogen learns that shortly after leaving the castle, Posthumus was attacked by Cloten, but after brief swordplay, Posthumus let him off easy.

In no time at all, Posthumus arrives in Rome, where he boasts to his new friends that Imogen is the most beautiful and virtuous of women. Iachimo, one of the Italians, baits Posthumus relentlessly and offers a wager on Imogen's virtue: Iachimo's whole estate against Posthumus's diamond ring—the one Imogen gave him—that Iachimo can seduce Imogen and bring back proof of the deed. Posthumus accepts the wager.

Back in Britain, the Queen is plotting and scheming. She acquires what she believes is poison from a doctor who suspects her motives and has substituted a strong sleeping potion in its place. The Queen gives the potion to Pisanio, claiming it has great "restorative" powers. If he'll only help convince Imogen to marry Cloten, she promises, Pisanio will have more rewards in store for him. Secretly, she hopes he will die from the poison, leaving Imogen with no link to Posthumus.

Iachimo arrives at court, where he tells Imogen that Posthumus is living it up in Rome. He suggests that she retaliate by means of a dalliance with him. When Imogen is horrified, Iachimo backpedals, claiming that he was only testing her fidelity to his good friend Posthumus. Imogen believes his story, and agrees to let him store a trunk of valuables in her bedchamber during his visit, falling right into his trap. Iachimo has devised a new plan to win the bet: if he cannot seduce Imogen, he will gather evidence to convince Posthumus that he has done so.

That night, while Imogen lies sleeping in her bed, Iachimo pops out of the trunk. He memorizes the details of the room's decor, notes a mole on her breast, and steals the bracelet Posthumus gave her right off her wrist without waking her.

The next day, Cloten, now boiling with resentment at Imogen's persistent preference for the lowly Posthumus, approaches Imogen. She rejects him, saying that even Posthumus's shabbiest clothes are more valuable than Cloten is. Cloten goes off vowing revenge while Imogen frets over her missing bracelet.

Meanwhile, Iachimo has returned to Rome. He convinces Posthumus that he has won the wager; the bracelet is strong evidence, and the mole on her breast is the clincher. Posthumus decries all women and vows revenge on Imogen.

Back at Britain's royal court, Lucius, an ambassador from the Roman Emperor, demands the overdue tribute money that Britain owes to Rome. The Queen and Cloten refuse to pay it, and King Cymbeline goes along with them. Lucius responds by regretfully declaring war in the name of Augustus Caesar.

Meanwhile, Pisanio is dismayed by a letter from Posthumus that instructs him to kill Imogen for being unfaithful. Pisanio is sure that his master has been deceived, but nonetheless he gives Imogen a second letter from Posthumus which asks her to meet him at Milford Haven. She is thrilled and prepares for the trip.

And now for something completely different: in a cave someplace in Wales, an old man lives with two young men who believe they are his sons. The boys regret their limited status and long to get out in the world and accomplish something. As they go off to hunt, the old man reveals that he is Belarius, a lord banished by Cymbeline years ago on a false charge of treason, and that his "sons" are the two Princes, whom he kidnapped at that time.

As he and Imogen near Milford Haven, Pisanio can't keep quiet any longer—he shows her Posthumus's letter instructing him to kill her. Thinking her husband must have been seduced by some Roman *signorina*, Imogen hands Pisanio his own sword and urges him to obey his master. Pisanio refuses, and tells her he has a plan: he will report to Posthumus that the deed is done, and meanwhile Imogen will disguise herself as a young man and seek out employment with Lucius, who will be departing for Rome from Milford Haven the next day. That way she can be near Posthumus until he is proven wrong about her and they can be reunited. Before they part, Pisanio gives Imogen the "restorative potion" he received from the Queen, in case of emergency.

Back at court, news of Imogen's disappearance is out. Cloten threatens Pisanio, who reluctantly shows him Posthumus's letter asking Imogen to meet him at Milford Haven. Cloten orders Pisanio to bring him some of Posthumus's clothing, and then soliloquizes his plan for revenge—he will kill Posthumus and rape Imogen, wearing the very clothes she used to insult him.

Remember that cave in Wales? Well, after wandering in the wilderness for two days, the lost, famished, and exhausted Imogen stumbles upon it. Belarius and his boys welcome Imogen, who introduces herself as "Fidele," a page on his way to Milford Haven. The boys find themselves strangely drawn to the young man and invite him to rest for the night in their cave. Imogen gratefully accepts. Little does she know Cloten is hot on her heels in Posthumus's clothes.

The next day, Imogen isn't feeling so hot. She drinks the potion Pisanio gave her and enters the cave to rest. Just then, Cloten arrives. Belarius recognizes him, fears he's been found out, and urges the boys to flee. When the older boy stands his ground, however, Cloten attacks and they fight. Cloten is known for losing his head; but now he literally does so. Belarius is distressed, sure now that they're done for. The boys, on the other hand, toss the head into the creek and are quite satisfied—until they come across the drugged "Fidele," who appears to be dead. Devastated, they plan a beautiful funeral, laying her body near Cloten's while they go off to prepare. Imogen now awakes and, seeing Cloten's body in her husband's clothes, believes that Posthumus is dead. She collapses onto the body in grief, just as Lucius is passing by on his way to Milford Haven. Claiming to be a page whose master has been slain, "Fidele" gets a job with Lucius.

Back at the palace, Cymbeline is distressed. Not only is his daughter gone, but his stepson has followed, throwing his wife into a fit of madness, and to top it off, the Roman legions have landed in Britain.

Meanwhile, back at the Welsh cave, Belarius and the boys decide to join the fighting in defense of their country.

Posthumus has arrived at Milford Haven with the Roman forces. He grieves remorsefully over a bloody cloth that Pisanio sent as proof of Imogen's death. He decides to disguise himself as a British peasant and join the fighting, hoping to die while defending Imogen's country.

The battle rages. Iachimo, fighting for Rome, is disarmed by the disguised Posthumus, but not killed. He believes that his military skill is dampened by his own guilty conscience. Elsewhere on the battlefield, Cymbeline is captured. Belarius and his boys, with Posthumus's help, rally the British troops and rescue the King. Lucius realizes his forces are in trouble and orders "Fidele" to retreat to safety.

After the battle, Posthumus is still determined to get himself killed. He changes back into his Roman uniform and is captured, just as he hoped. He is thrown in prison, where he prays for death. He falls asleep and has a vision in which his long-dead parents beseech Jupiter to help him. Jupiter decrees that Posthumus will live and be reunited with Imogen. But when Posthumus awakes a jailer arrives to lead him to his execution. Before they leave, Posthumus is summoned to the King.

At court, Cymbeline knights Belarius and his boys, and regrets that the fourth peasant who rescued him cannot be found. News arrives that the Queen is dead. What's more, she has confessed to terrible crimes on her deathbed. The Roman prisoners, including Lucius, Iachimo, Posthumus, and "Fidele," are led in. Lucius begs for mercy for Fidele, and Cymbeline grants it. He is strangely drawn to the boy, and grants him a boon. Fidele asks that Iachimo be made to explain where he got his diamond ring. Iachimo makes a remorseful confession. Hearing the truth, Posthumus rushes forward in dismay and reveals that he ordered Imogen's murder. "Fidele" rushes to him, and he strikes the boy down. Pisanio hurries to Imogen's aid, and step by step the complications of the plot are revealed. The lovers are reunited, as are the King and his long-lost sons. Cymbeline forgives Belarius for the kidnapping and frees the Roman prisoners, deciding that Britain will pay its tribute to Rome after all. All is forgiven and a great celebration begins.

> CHARACTER QUITE CONTRARY TO CELTIC CUNOBELINUS
> The historical figure whose name Shakespeare borrowed for King Cymbeline was a powerful Celtic chieftain called Cunobelinus by the Romans, of whom very little is known. He was an ally of the Romans (who did not actually invade his territory until after his death) and he bears no other resemblance to Shakespeare's king than his name, which the historian Holinshed recorded as "Kymbeline." Shakespeare's sources for the central plotline of *Cymbeline* were not history books, but fictional texts—mainly two versions of an old and well-known story: Boccaccio's *Decameron* (one of Shakespeare's favorites) and *Frederyke of Jennen*, an anonymous English translation from the Dutch.

PERICLES

When Shakespeare's first Romance, *Pericles*, opened in London (circa 1607–8) it was a big hit. Not only were English theatregoers on a tragicomedy kick, but this was a familiar and beloved story complete with evil king, wicked stepmother, pristine princesses, long sea voyages, and miraculous resurrections and reunions. Fasten your seat belts:

Valiant Prince Pericles of Tyre has traveled to Antioch to try for the hand of King Antiochus's babe-a-licious daughter in marriage. To win her he must solve a riddle; if he fails, he will be put to death. Unlike former suitors, Pericles understands the riddle, which, to his horror, reveals that the King is committing incest with his daughter. Pericles does not answer the riddle outright, but makes it clear that he knows the secret. The King says he'll give Pericles an extra forty days to answer, but Pericles knows the King will kill him to protect his secret, so he flees.

Back home in Tyre, Pericles fears that King Antiochus will wage war against his people to silence him. He leaves his trusted adviser Helicanus in charge and sets sail for Tarsus, bringing food to relieve its famine. He is gratefully received by Cleon, Governor of Tarsus, and his wife, Dionyza. Pericles is well loved in Tarsus, but sets sail once again when Helicanus sends word that Antiochus has sent an assassin after him.

Shipwrecked! Sole survivor Pericles washes ashore in Pentapolis, where amiable fishermen happen to have caught his armor in their nets, and happen to know that King Simonides happens to be holding a tournament for his daughter Thaisa's hand in marriage. Not one to learn from past experiences, Pericles dons the rusty armor and heads for the palace.

Pericles participates anonymously and, of course, wins. Thaisa is smitten and her father won over by Pericles' sterling character. The fact that he turns out to be a prince doesn't hurt either, and Pericles and Thaisa are wed. Happy ending . . . *not*.

Helicanus summons Pericles home to rule. He and a very pregnant Thaisa set sail for Tyre. Thaisa goes into labor. Storm at sea! In the midst of the storm, Pericles is informed that Thaisa has died giving birth to a daughter, whom he names Marina. Sailors insist that Thaisa's body be buried at sea to appease the gods.

Storm over. Thaisa's coffin/trunk washes ashore in Ephesus and is found by Cerimon, a physician and sorcerer. Opening the trunk, he recognizes that Thaisa is not completely dead and revives her. Since she figures she'll never see her beloved husband again, she decides to become a nun of the goddess Diana's temple in Ephesus.

Distraught at having lost his beloved wife, and fearing that his infant daughter will not survive the journey, Pericles stops off at Tarsus and leaves her in the care of Cleon and Dionyza, then continues on to Tyre.

Time passes. Marina is now a beautiful and virtuous teen. Dionyza hates her for overshadowing her own daughter, who is the same age, and arranges for her servant Leonine to murder Marina. Reluctantly, he takes her to the beach and is about to do the deed when some pirates come ashore and seize her. Leonine returns to Dionyza, claiming that he has killed Marina. She poisons him to cover her tracks. Her husband is not pleased.

The pirates bring Marina to Mytilene, where they sell her to a brothel. She wreaks havoc on business there by speaking so virtuously to customers that they leave reformed, while Marina remains chaste. One such customer is Lysimachus, Governor of Mytilene. She persuades her keepers to permit her to earn them money by tutoring young women in the arts.

Meanwhile, Pericles has gone to retrieve his daughter and has learned of her death. Grief-stricken, he has once again taken to the seas. His ship arrives in Mytilene, where Lysimachus comes aboard to greet him. As the Fates would have it, someone suggests bringing Mytilene's newest phenom (Marina) on board to cheer up Pericles, who is speechless with sorrow.

Joyful reunion! This so exhausts Pericles that he needs a nap. The goddess Diana appears to him in a dream, and instructs him to hie himself hence to her temple in Ephesus, make a sacrifice, and tell his life story to all assembled there. Off he goes, with Marina, Lysimachus, et al.

Cut to Ephesus: Pericles tells his tale, upon which Thaisa, now the abbess of Diana's temple, faints. Joyful reunion! Pericles announces that Marina and Lysimachus will be married and will rule in Tyre, while he and Thaisa will govern her native Pentapolis, since her father has just died. Finally, we learn that Cleon and Dionyza have been burned in their palace by an angry mob, avenging Marina's supposed death. Happy ending!

You Can Only Do So Much . . .

It is generally accepted that Shakespeare either collaborated on *Pericles* or was brought in as a script doctor. Most scholars believe that the last three acts are mostly his, and that, if anything, he just tinkered with the inferior first two acts. We have selected a little piece of wickedness that is widely considered to be his.

THE TEMPEST

The Tempest is the last Romance Shakespeare wrote, and the last play that he wrote alone. Many consider it his farewell to the theatre, and it is often hailed as his greatest accomplishment. The play was written at a time when accounts of the colonization of the Americas were trickling back to England. These reports depicted a strange, wondrous, and intriguingly exotic place, both ominous and hopeful. Though Prospero's island is set in the Mediterranean, it is clearly inspired by this "brave new world." The Americas were the perfect setting for a romance, a genre noted for combining such elements as long journeys to exotic locales, magic, the supernatural, and the triumph of optimism over despair (see "The Americas: A Magical Mystery Tour," page 858). These elements emerge spectacularly right from the start.

The Tempest opens with . . . a full-blown tempest. A ship carrying King Alonso of Naples, his son, Ferdinand, and other Italian nobles home from Tunisia is wrecked in the storm. Watching the shipwreck from the nearby shore of a small island, a young woman named Miranda begs her father, a magician named Prospero, to use his powers to quiet the storm and save the hapless ship. He assures her that not one passenger has been harmed. Prospero then exposits the circumstances that brought him and Miranda to the island and led him to stage today's shipwreck: Prospero was once the rightful Duke of Milan, but was more interested in magic than governance and was deposed by his younger brother, Antonio. He and Miranda (who was then not quite three years old) were cast out to sea in a leaky, rotting boat, with a few provisions and Prospero's books of sorcery, slipped to him by a loyal noble named Gonzalo. The boat came to rest on this exotic isle, where they have lived ever since. Now Fortune has brought Antonio and his coconspirators, who include King Alonso and his brother, Sebastian, as well as Gonzalo, within arm's reach of the island, and Prospero has magically raised the storm to bring them all ashore so that he can right the wrongs they have done to him. He now casts a spell to make Miranda sleep, and calls for his spirit servant, Ariel.

Ariel arrives instantly, reports that he carried out the shipwreck as commanded, and describes it in detail. He has separated and scattered the ship's passengers about the island and has restored and hidden the ship and its crew, who are under a sleeping spell. He reminds Prospero that he desires his freedom. Prospero reminds Ariel that he freed the spirit from imprisonment by the island's former inhabitant, the evil witch Sycorax, and that Ariel's service is rendered in exchange. Before he gains his freedom, Ariel must work for two more days, invisible to all but Prospero. Off Ariel goes, and Prospero wakes Miranda and brings her to visit his slave, Caliban (the savage and deformed son of Sycorax), the only other inhabitant of the island. When Caliban complains about his enslavement, Prospero angrily reminds Caliban that he educated him and treated him well until Caliban tried to rape Miranda. Caliban is sent to gather wood.

Ariel returns, leading Prince Ferdinand of Naples by singing mesmerizing tunes. Believing himself the sole survivor of the wreck, Ferdinand mourns the loss of his father. Miranda is enchanted by the handsome young man who, upon seeing her, is equally enchanted and wishes to marry her. Prospero is secretly delighted, but lest Ferdinand take Miranda for granted by winning her too quickly, Prospero calls him a spy and, ignoring Miranda's entreaties, takes him prisoner.

Meanwhile, King Alonso, Sebastian, Antonio, and the kindly and now elderly Gonzalo, who have been deposited by Ariel on another part of the island, believe themselves to be the sole survivors of the wreck. When Gonzalo suggests to the grieving King that his son may have survived, he is mocked by Antonio and Sebastian. Ariel arrives and casts a sleeping spell on all but Antonio and Sebastian. Antonio convinces Sebastian to kill the King and Gonzalo while they sleep and to seize the throne of Naples, but just as they draw their swords to do so, Ariel returns and wakes the rest of the party. They all depart to search for Ferdinand.

On another part of the island, Caliban sees the approaching Trinculo, King Alonso's jester. Caliban thinks Trinculo is a spirit sent by Prospero to torment him, and he tries to hide. Trinculo sees him and at first believes him to be a fish, then an islander killed by lightning in the tempest. He hides himself under Caliban to seek shelter from the impending storm. Along comes Stephano, King Alonso's drunken butler, who thinks Caliban and Trinculo are a two-headed, four-legged monster. He shares his wine with Caliban and discovers Trinculo, and the two are joyfully reunited. They believe themselves to be the sole survivors of the wreck. Caliban offers to serve the two men as gods in exchange for more wine.

Meanwhile, Ferdinand cheerfully hauls logs for Prospero—thoughts of Miranda's sympathy lighten his load. Miranda arrives and offers to help. To the delight of the eavesdropping Prospero, the two pledge to marry.

Elsewhere, Trinculo, Stephano, and Caliban have gotten drunk. Ariel arrives and, impersonating Trinculo, baits Caliban and Stephano, who angrily respond to the bewildered Trinculo. Caliban proposes that Stephano kill Prospero and rule the island, with Miranda as his queen. Mightily pleased, Stephano agrees. Ariel plans to inform Prospero and, mesmerizing them with a tune, leads the three off.

In the interim, the hungry and tired Alonso, Gonzalo, Antonio, and Sebastian have not found Ferdinand, and they stop to rest. Prospero looks on, invisible. He causes a magical banquet to appear, but before the hungry men can eat, Ariel materializes, dressed like a harpy (a mythological creature with the head of a woman, the body of a bird, and digestive problems of, well, mythic proportions). He tells the astonished Antonio, Sebastian, and Alonso that they sinned by usurping Prospero years ago, in exchange for which the sea has now swallowed up Alonso's son. After Ariel and the banquet disappear, the men babble in fear.

Prospero frees Ferdinand, giving him his blessing to marry Miranda. A masked pageant ensues in which Ceres, the goddess of the earth, her rainbow messenger, Iris, and Juno, the Queen of the Gods, shower blessings on the betrothed couple. The spirits of nymphs and reapers dance for the pair. Prospero explains that the goddesses and dancers were merely spirits acting roles—that in fact we are all merely "such stuff as dreams are made on."

To disarm the still-drunk Caliban, Trinculo, and Stephano, Ariel strings a clothesline of enticingly beautiful clothing for them to find. They do, and despite Caliban's warnings, the other two are momentarily distracted from their murder plot and dress themselves up in the "frippery." Suddenly, they are beset by spirit hounds, who chase them off.

Prospero is ready to wrap up the show: Ariel reports that King Alonso, Sebastian, and Antonio have gone crazy, and that Gonzalo is grieving about it. Ariel expresses pity for them, and Prospero promises to treat them with mercy. He sends Ariel to fetch them and release them from the insanity spell. While Ariel does so, Prospero describes the magic he has performed in the past, and says that once all has been set aright, he will renounce his powers. Ariel brings on the Italian nobles, and while their spell is gradually lifted, Prospero changes from his sorcerer's robes to those he wore as duke and presents himself to the men. He forgives them for having wronged him, takes his dukedom back from Antonio (who unrepentantly says nothing), and then reveals Miranda and Ferdinand, playing chess. The King and Prince are each amazed to find the other alive and well. The King joyfully accepts Miranda as his daughter-in-law. Ariel brings on the ship's crew, who report that the boat is in perfect condition to sail. Ariel then leads in the drunken, nattily dressed Caliban, Stephano, and Trinculo, who are dressed down by the royals and commanded to return the frippery to Prospero. The royals all repair to Prospero's home, where he will share the story of his years on the island. They will then embark for Italy, where Miranda and Ferdinand will be wed and Prospero restored to power. Prospero gives Ariel one final command—to generate calm seas and auspicious winds for the sail home, after which the spirit is finally set free.

THE WINTER'S TALE

Shakespeare's third Romance, *The Winter's Tale*, is widely considered his first fully successful attempt at the genre. Like many romances, *The Winter's Tale* is also an example of tragicomedy, which usually consists of a tragic plot with a comedic (i.e., happy) ending. Although its structure departs from the norm, *The Winter's Tale* perfectly exemplifies the dual nature of tragicomedy. The play is neatly divided into antithetical halves: the first is a tragedy; and the second a romantic comedy. Shakespeare's structural innovation is surprisingly effective onstage. The outcome of the tragedy depends on the oracle, while the resolution of the comedy relies on the virtues of its lovers; the two halves of the play dovetail to reflect the prevailing theme of Shakespearean Romance: although humanity is dependent on fate for its survival, it also requires active virtue, particularly forgiveness and mercy. As the curtain rises on *The Winter's Tale*, such virtues are far from the mind of Bohemia's reigning king.

Leontes, King of Sicilia, has been enjoying the company of his childhood friend, Polixenes, King of Bohemia, who has been visiting for several months. As Polixenes is taking his leave, Leontes entreats him to stay a bit longer, and asks his very pregnant wife, Hermione, to persuade him. When she politely does so, Leontes becomes irrationally jealous. He takes aside his most trusted lord, Camillo, and confides his suspicions. Unmoved by Camillo's attempts to reason with him, Leontes orders him to kill Polixenes. Camillo pretends to agree, but instead reports the plot to Polixenes, and the two flee for Bohemia.

While Hermione is off playing with her little son, Mamillius, Leontes learns of Polixenes' escape, which only confirms his suspicions. He charges Hermione with adultery and treason, and has Mamillius taken from her. Although Hermione denies any wrongdoing, Leontes sends her to prison. The lords of the court, led by Antigonus, try to reason with the King, but he stubbornly insists that Apollo's oracle at Delphos will prove him right—he has sent messengers to relay the story and ask for advice.

Antigonus's wife, Paulina, tries to visit Hermione in prison. She is allowed to see Hermione's attendant, who reports that the Queen has given birth to a baby girl. Paulina brings the child to Leontes, hoping the sight of it will soften him. Her attempt backfires: Leontes is enraged by the sight of the baby, and orders Antigonus to abandon it beyond the borders of his kingdom.

Hermione is brought to trial. She defends herself, Polixenes, and Camillo, but is unafraid of the threat of death, since Leontes has already stripped her of all that made her life worth living. The oracle's reply proclaims her innocent, but Leontes decides that the oracle is false. Just then news arrives that little Mamillius has died of fear for his mother's fate. Hermione faints. Leontes finally realizes that he was mistaken. As Hermione is taken off by Paulina, he plans to apologize and make everything as good as new. But it's not that easy: Paulina returns to report that Hermione, too, has died. She lambastes Leontes for his foolishness and cruelty, and he accepts her judgment. He vows to spend the rest of his life mourning his wife and son.

Antigonus has dreamed that Hermione asked him to leave the baby in Bohemia, and to name her Perdita. He sadly carries out his task, leaving the baby with a bundle and a box of gold, just as a storm begins. He hears the sound of hunters and exits (famously) pursued by a bear. An old Shepherd enters, complaining that adolescent hunters have scared off his sheep, and stumbles upon Perdita. His son, the Clown, rushes in and tells of seeing poor Antigonus eaten by the bear and his ship wrecked in the storm. The Shepherd shows his son the child and they discover the gold. The Shepherd takes the baby home while the Clown heads off to bury what's left of Antigonus.

As we shift from tragedy to comedy, time passes . . . sixteen long years of it. At the Bohemian castle, Camillo now seeks permission to go home to Sicilia and comfort the grief-stricken Leontes, who has shut himself away. Polixenes tells Camillo that he is too essential to the Bohemian government to be spared. Besides, Polixenes needs Camillo's help handling his son, Prince Florizel, who has been spending altogether too much time at the home of a poor shepherd. The shepherd, by the way, happens to have a rather attractive sixteen-year-old daughter.

Meanwhile, the annual sheep-shearing festival is under way. On his way to market to prepare for the celebration, the Clown is conned by Autolycus, a petty thief and former servant to Florizel. As the mistress of the feast, Perdita wears festival garb and flowers, and Florizel finds her goddesslike. Perdita worries that Florizel's father will learn of their love, but Florizel says he will forfeit his birthright if he must, to marry her. Perdita was right to worry: Polixenes and Camillo arrive in disguise, to monitor Florizel. Autolycus, dressed as a wandering peddler, also joins the party, and leads the merrymakers in song. Flirting and joking, the party-goers eventually depart. Polixenes prods Florizel and Perdita into declaring their love, and then reveals his identity. He threatens Perdita and the Shepherd with a torturous death and his son with disinheritance should the lovers ever meet again. Polixenes then storms off, and the terrified Shepherd flees. Florizel refuses to forsake Perdita, so Camillo suggests that they escape to Sicilia while Polixenes cools down. They agree, and when Autolycus returns (having emptied all the celebrants' pockets) Camillo pays him to change clothes with Florizel. Perdita is to disguise herself as well. As they depart, Camillo hopes to himself that Polixenes will ask him to pursue them. He would then get his wish to return to Sicilia.

Autolycus runs into the Shepherd and the Clown and, gathering the gist of the situation, sees a possibility for profit. They are planning to approach the King with proof that they are not really related to Perdita. Autolycus offers to bring them to the King for a small fee. In truth, however, he plans to lead them to Florizel, who, he hopes, will reward him.

Sicilia hasn't changed much after all these years. Paulina is still letting the King know her mind: she makes him promise not to remarry without her approval. Florizel and Perdita arrive, claiming that Polixenes has sent them, and that they are married. Leontes is delighted—but news soon arrives that Polixenes is in Bohemia looking for his son, and the lovers are forced to reveal the truth. Leontes promises to help them if he can.

Later, after conducting the Shepherd and the Clown to Florizel, Autolycus hears the word on the street: Perdita's identity has been revealed by the papers that the Shepherd carried with him. There has been a joyful reunion between the kings and their children, who are now engaged to be married. Autolycus is miffed: he's done a good deed by mistake and doesn't get a penny for it. He encounters the Shepherd and the Clown, now dressed to the nines, and they promise that if he mends his ways they will help restore him to Florizel's good graces.

Paulina has gathered everyone at her home to witness the unveiling of a statue of Hermione. The statue is so lifelike that it renews Leontes' grief and provokes Perdita to kneel for her mother's blessing. Paulina commands the statue to come down from its pedestal, and as it does, the others realize that they have been admiring Hermione herself—she is alive. Only Paulina is left without a mate, and Leontes rectifies this by giving Camillo her hand. Subdued happiness reigns in the land.

This Is the *Winter* of Greene's Discontent

Shakespeare's source for *The Winter's Tale* was *Pandosto*, a romantic novel by Robert Greene, one of the University Wits (the playwrights who developed Elizabethan drama in the 1580s). Shakespeare followed *Pandosto* closely—in places his language repeats Greene's almost word for word. He did, however, add new material and deviate from Greene on two important points: in *Pandosto*, Bellaria (Hermione) dies at the end of the trial and Pandosto (Leontes) commits suicide at the end of the story. Greene considered the young Shakespeare an "upstart crow" who rode the coattails of his elders. Surely any vindication he might have felt to learn that Shakespeare had imitated one of his own works would have been outweighed by chagrin at the success of *The Winter's Tale*, had he lived to witness it (for more on Greene, see "Irrelevant History: Greene's Groatsworth of Gripe," page 178).

GLOSSARY OF COMMON ARCHAIC WORDS, VERB FORMS, ELISIONS, AND CONTRACTIONS

COMMON ARCHAIC WORDS

alack: an interjection expressing sorrow
alas: an interjection expressing sorrow or pity
ay: yes
bid: (1) ask; (2) command; (3) invite
his/her: its
lest: for fear that
methinks: I think
mine: my
oft: often
perchance: perhaps
spake: spoke
thence: from there
thither: to that place
wherein: in which
whiles: while
whilst: while
withal: with it; with them
ye: you
yon (xxx): that (xxx) over there
yonder: over there; or, that (xxx) over there

ARCHAIC PERSONAL PRONOUNS

These pronouns are used to connote intimacy or to address a peer or a social inferior:

thee: you (singular only; used as the object of a sentence or clause)
thine: yours (singular only; also used in place of *thy* before words beginning with vowels)
thou: you (singular only; used as the subject of a sentence or clause)
thy: your (singular only)

ARCHAIC VERB FORMS

The following conjugations are used in conjunction with *thou*:
art: are (second person singular only)
dost: do (second person singular only)
wast: were (second person singular, past tense)
wert: were (second person singular, past or past subjunctive tense)
And —*est* or —*st* used as a suffix with verbs to form the second person singular indicative (e.g., mayst, canst, didst, carriest).
You will often find the words *art thou* used to mean "you are" rather than "are you," i.e., as part of a statement rather than a question.

OTHER UNUSUAL CONJUGATIONS

be: is (used in place of both *am* and *are*)
As well as —*eth*, —*th*, or —*ith* used as a suffix with verbs to form the third person singular indicative (e.g., maketh, thinketh, doth, hath, saith).
Also, Shakespeare made more frequent use of the emphatic form than we do today, using such phrases as *didst go*, *does make*, and *doth speak*, where we would simply use *went*, *makes*, or *speaks*.

COMMON ELISIONS

e'er: ever
'em: them
o'er: over
ta'en: taken
Verbs ending in —*en* often drop the E sound (e.g., *stol'n* for "stolen").
Verbs ending in —*est* often drop the E sound (e.g., *know'st* for "knowest").

COMMON CONTRACTIONS

i' th': in the
o' th': of the
thou'dst: thou shouldst or thou wouldst
'tis: it is
'twas: it was
'twere: it were
Words followed by *it* are often contracted with *'t* (e.g., *is't* for "is it"; *on't* for "on it");
Words that follow *to* (most often words beginning with vowels) are sometimes contracted with *t'* (e.g., *t'assume* for "to assume"; *t'make* for "to make").

INDEX TO THE MONOLOGUES

Please note that although we have divided the monologues by gender, many monologues lend themselves to be played by either sex (and not only the obvious Puck and Ariel, but also the likes of Snug, Gobbo, and Jaques, to name a few). Furthermore, we encourage gender-blind casting of even those roles that are overtly gendered. Also note that each monologue is categorized below by its own particular timbre, rather than by the genre of the play from which it is taken (e.g., the Nurse's monologue is listed under "Monologues for Women—Comedic" even though *Romeo and Juliet* is one of the Tragedies).

MONOLOGUES FOR WOMEN—DRAMATIC

ALL'S WELL THAT ENDS WELL

Helena	(Act III, Scene ii)	young adult to adult	blank verse	433

ANTONY AND CLEOPATRA

Cleopatra	(Act I, Scene v)	adult to mature adult	blank verse	461
Cleopatra	(Act IV, Scene xv)	adult to mature adult	blank verse	474
Cleopatra	(Act V, Scene ii)	adult to mature adult	blank verse	481
Cleopatra	(Act V, Scene ii)	adult to mature adult	blank verse	485
Cleopatra	(Act V, Scene ii)	adult to mature adult	blank verse	491

CORIOLANUS

Volumnia	(Act V, Scene iii)	mature adult to older adult	blank verse	512

HAMLET

Ophelia	(Act II, Scene i)	young adult	blank verse	529
Ophelia	(Act III, Scene i)	young adult	blank verse	559
Gertrude	(Act IV, Scene vii)	mature adult	blank verse	582

HENRY IV, PART TWO

Lady Percy	(Act II, Scene iii)	young adult to adult	blank verse	91

HENRY V

Chorus	(Prologue)	any age	blank verse	116

HENRY VI, PART ONE

Joan la Pucelle	(Act V, Scene iii)	young adult to adult	blank verse	143

HENRY VI, PART TWO

Queen Margaret	(Act I, Scene iii)	young adult to adult	blank verse	149
Eleanor	(Act II, Scene iv)	adult to mature adult	blank verse	158

HENRY VI, PART THREE

Queen Margaret	(Act I, Scene iv)	adult to mature adult	blank verse	164

HENRY VIII

Queen Katherine	(Act II, Scene iv)	mature adult	blank verse	223

JULIUS CAESAR

Portia	(Act II, Scene i)	mature adult	blank verse	602
Calphurnia	(Act II, Scene ii)	adult to mature adult	blank verse	610

KING JOHN

Constance	(Act III, Scene i)	adult to mature adult	blank verse	17
Constance	(Act III, Scene iv)	adult to mature adult	blank verse	23
Constance	(Act III, Scene iv)	adult to mature adult	blank verse	29

KING LEAR

Goneril	(Act I, Scene iv)	young adult to adult	blank verse	648

MACBETH

Lady Macbeth	(Act I, Scene v)	adult to mature adult	prose and blank verse	671
Lady Macbeth	(Act I, Scene v)	adult to mature adult	blank verse	677
Lady Macbeth	(Act I, Scene vii)	adult to mature adult	blank verse	691

MEASURE FOR MEASURE

Isabella	(Act II, Scene ii)	young adult to adult	blank verse	438

THE MERCHANT OF VENICE

Portia	(Act IV, Scene i)	young adult to adult	blank verse	308

A MIDSUMMER NIGHT'S DREAM

Titania	(Act II, Scene i)	adult	blank verse	342

OTHELLO

Emilia	(Act IV, Scene iii)	adult to mature adult	blank verse	731

PERICLES

Dionyza	(Act IV, Scene iii)	adult to mature adult	blank verse	848

RICHARD II

Duchess of Gloucester	(Act I, Scene ii)	mature adult to older adult	blank verse	46

RICHARD III

Lady Anne	(Act I, Scene ii)	young adult to adult	blank verse	191
Lady Anne	(Act IV, Scene i)	young adult to adult	blank verse	208
Margaret	(Act IV, Scene iv)	mature adult to older adult	blank verse	212

ROMEO AND JULIET

Juliet	(Act II, Scene ii)	young adult	blank verse	762
Juliet	(Act II, Scene ii)	young adult	blank verse	766
Juliet	(Act III, Scene ii)	young adult	blank verse	774
Juliet	(Act III, Scene ii)	young adult	blank verse	780
Juliet	(Act IV, Scene iii)	young adult	blank verse	806

THE WINTER'S TALE

Hermione	(Act III, Scene ii)	adult	blank verse	880
Paulina	(Act III, Scene ii)	mature adult	blank verse	885

MONOLOGUES FOR WOMEN—COMEDIC

AS YOU LIKE IT

Phebe	(Act III, Scene v)	young adult	blank verse	254
Rosalind	(Act III, Scene v)	young adult	blank verse	258
Phebe	(Act III, Scene v)	young adult	blank verse	264

THE COMEDY OF ERRORS

Adriana	(Act II, Scene ii)	adult	blank verse	270
Luciana	(Act III, Scene ii)	young adult to adult	rhymed iambic pentameter	276

CYMBELINE

Imogen	(Act III, Scene ii)	young adult	blank verse and prose	837
Imogen	(Act III, Scene vi)	young adult	blank verse	843

HENRY IV, PART TWO

Mistress Quickly	(Act II, Scene i)	mature adult	prose	87

THE MERCHANT OF VENICE

Portia	(Act III, Scene iv)	young adult to adult	blank verse	302

THE MERRY WIVES OF WINDSOR

Mistress Page	(Act II, Scene i)	mature adult	prose	313

A MIDSUMMER NIGHT'S DREAM

Helena	(Act I, Scene i)	young adult	rhymed iambic pentameter	333
Helena	(Act I, Scene i)	young adult	rhymed iambic pentameter	336

ROMEO AND JULIET

Nurse	(Act I, Scene iii)	mature adult	blank verse	735
Juliet	(Act II, Scene v)	young adult	blank verse	770

TROILUS AND CRESSIDA

Cressida	(Act III, Scene ii)	young adult	blank verse	454

TWELFTH NIGHT

Viola	(Act II, Scene ii)	young adult	blank verse	386
Olivia	(Act III, Scene i)	young adult to adult	blank verse	401

THE TWO GENTLEMEN OF VERONA

Julia	(Act I, Scene ii)	young adult	blank verse	406
Julia	(Act IV, Scene iv)	young adult	blank verse	425

MONOLOGUES FOR MEN–DRAMATIC

ANTONY AND CLEOPATRA

Enobarbus	(Act II, Scene ii)	mature adult	blank verse	466

AS YOU LIKE IT

Duke Senior	(Act II, Scene i)	mature adult	blank verse	243
Jaques	(Act II, Scene vii)	adult to mature adult	blank verse	248

CORIOLANUS

Menenius	(Act II, Scene i)	mature adult to older adult	prose	497
Coriolanus	(Act IV, Scene v)	adult to mature adult	blank verse	501
Aufidius	(Act IV, Scene v)	adult to mature adult	blank verse	506

HAMLET

Hamlet	(Act I, Scene ii)	young adult to adult	blank verse	517
Hamlet	(Act II, Scene ii)	young adult to adult	blank verse	542
Hamlet	(Act III, Scene i)	young adult to adult	blank verse	552
King Claudius	(Act III, Scene iii)	mature adult	blank verse	570
Hamlet	(Act III, Scene iii)	young adult to adult	blank verse	576

HENRY IV, PART ONE

Hotspur	(Act I, Scene iii)	young adult to adult	blank verse	72
Hotspur	(Act II, Scene iii)	young adult to adult	prose	78

HENRY IV, PART TWO

King Henry IV	(Act III, Scene i)	mature adult	blank verse	98
Prince Hal	(Act IV, Scene v)	young adult to adult	blank verse	110

HENRY V

Chorus	(Prologue)	any age	blank verse	116
King Henry V	(Act I, Scene ii)	adult	blank verse	122
King Henry V	(Act IV, Scene iii)	adult	blank verse	129
King Henry V	(Act V, Scene ii)	adult	mostly prose	137

HENRY VI, PART THREE

Richard, Duke of York	(Act I, Scene iv)	mature adult	blank verse	171
King Henry VI	(Act II, Scene v)	mature adult	blank verse	179

JULIUS CAESAR

Cassius	(Act I, Scene ii)	mature adult	blank verse	588
Brutus	(Act II, Scene i)	mature adult	blank verse	597
Antony	(Act III, Scene i)	adult to mature adult	blank verse	615
Brutus	(Act III, Scene ii)	mature adult	prose	620
Antony	(Act III, Scene ii)	adult to mature adult	blank verse	625
Antony	(Act III, Scene ii)	adult to mature adult	blank verse	630

KING JOHN

Philip the Bastard	(Act I, Scene i)	adult to mature adult	blank verse	5
Philip the Bastard	(Act II, Scene i)	adult to mature adult	blank verse	11
Lewis	(Act V, Scene ii)	young adult to adult	blank verse	35
Philip the Bastard	(Act V, Scene ii)	adult to mature adult	blank verse	40

KING LEAR

Edmund	(Act I, Scene ii)	young adult to adult	blank verse	637
Edmund	(Act I, Scene ii)	young adult to adult	prose	642
King Lear	(Act II, Scene iv)	older adult	blank verse	654
King Lear	(Act III, Scene ii)	older adult	blank verse	660
King Lear	(Act III, Scene iv)	older adult	blank verse	665

MACBETH

Macbeth	(Act I, Scene vii)	mature adult	blank verse	683
Macbeth	(Act II, Scene i)	mature adult	blank verse	697
Macbeth	(Act III, Scene i)	mature adult	blank verse	710

MEASURE FOR MEASURE

Claudio	(Act III, Scene i)	young adult to adult	blank verse	443

THE MERCHANT OF VENICE

Character	Scene	Age	Form	Page
Shylock	(Act I, Scene iii)	mature adult to older adult	blank verse	285
Shylock	(Act III, Scene i)	mature adult to older adult	prose	296

A MIDSUMMER NIGHT'S DREAM

Character	Scene	Age	Form	Page
Theseus	(Act I, Scene i)	adult to mature adult	blank verse	326

OTHELLO

Character	Scene	Age	Form	Page
Iago	(Act I, Scene i)	adult to mature adult	blank verse	717
Othello	(Act I, Scene iii)	adult to mature adult	blank verse	722
Iago	(Act I, Scene iii)	adult to mature adult	blank verse	727

RICHARD II

Character	Scene	Age	Form	Page
John of Gaunt	(Act II, Scene i)	mature adult to older adult	blank verse	50
King Richard	(Act III, Scene ii)	adult to mature adult	blank verse	55
King Richard	(Act III, Scene iii)	adult to mature adult	blank verse	60
Bishop of Carlisle	(Act IV, Scene i)	mature adult to older adult	blank verse	66

RICHARD III

Character	Scene	Age	Form	Page
Richard	(Act I, Scene i)	adult to mature adult	blank verse	185
Richard	(Act I, Scene ii)	adult to mature adult	blank verse	197
King Edward IV	(Act II, Scene i)	adult to mature adult	blank verse	203
King Richard	(Act V, Scene iii)	adult to mature adult	blank verse	218

ROMEO AND JULIET

Character	Scene	Age	Form	Page
Mercutio	(Act I, Scene iv)	young adult to adult	blank verse	742
Romeo	(Act II, Scene ii)	young adult	blank verse	756
Romeo	(Act III, Scene iii)	young adult	blank verse	786
Friar Lawrence	(Act III, Scene iii)	mature adult to older adult	blank verse	791
Lord Capulet	(Act III, Scene v)	mature adult	blank verse	799

THE TEMPEST

Character	Scene	Age	Form	Page
Prospero	(Act IV, Scene i)	mature adult to older adult	blank verse	868
Prospero	(Act V, Scene i)	mature adult to older adult	blank verse	874

TIMON OF ATHENS

Character	Scene	Age	Form	Page
Timon	(Act IV, Scene iii)	mature adult	blank verse	812

TITUS ADRONICUS

Character	Scene	Age	Form	Page
Titus Andronicus	(Act III, Scene ii)	mature adult	blank verse	817
Aaron	(Act IV, Scene ii)	adult to mature adult	blank verse	822

MONOLOGUES FOR MEN—COMEDIC

CYMBELINE				
Iachimo	(Act II, Scene ii)	young adult to adult	blank verse	829
HAMLET				
Polonius	(Act I, Scene iii)	mature adult to older adult	blank verse	524
Polonius	(Act II, Scene ii)	mature adult to older adult	blank verse and prose	534
Hamlet	(Act III, Scene ii)	young adult to adult	prose	564
HENRY IV, PART ONE				
Falstaff	(Act V, Scene i)	older adult	prose	83
HENRY IV, PART TWO				
Falstaff	(Act IV, Scene iii)	older adult	prose	104
LOVE'S LABOUR'S LOST				
Berowne	(Act V, Scene ii)	young adult to adult	rhymed iambic pentameter	282
MACBETH				
Porter	(Act II, Scene iii)	mature adult to older adult	prose	704
THE MERCHANT OF VENICE				
Launcelot Gobbo	(Act II, Scene ii)	young adult to adult	prose	291
THE MERRY WIVES OF WINDSOR				
Falstaff	(Act III, Scene v)	older adult	prose	318
A MIDSUMMER NIGHT'S DREAM				
Lysander	(Act I, Scene i)	young adult	blank verse	330
Oberon	(Act II, Scene i)	adult	blank verse	348
Puck	(Act III, Scene ii)	young adult to adult	rhymed iambic pentameter	354
Bottom	(Act IV, Scene i)	adult to mature adult	prose	359
Snug	(Act V, Scene i)	any age	rhymed iambic pentameter	364
MUCH ADO ABOUT NOTHING				
Benedick	(Act II, Scene iii)	young adult to adult	prose	368
Benedick	(Act II, Scene iii)	young adult to adult	prose	373
ROMEO AND JULIET				
Mercutio	(Act II, Scene i)	young adult to adult	blank verse	749

THE TAMING OF THE SHREW

Petruchio	(Act IV, Scene i)	adult	blank verse	377

THE TEMPEST

Ariel	(Act I, Scene ii)	young adult to adult	blank verse	852
Trinculo	(Act II, Scene ii)	young adult to mature adult	prose	859
Caliban	(Act III, Scene ii)	young adult to adult	blank verse	864

TROILUS AND CRESSIDA

Ulysses	(Act I, Scene iii)	mature adult	blank verse	447

TWELFTH NIGHT

Orsino	(Act I, Scene i)	adult	blank verse	381
Malvolio	(Act II, Scene v)	adult to mature adult	prose (with some verse)	392

THE TWO GENTLEMEN OF VERONA

Launce	(Act II, Scene iii)	young adult to adult	prose	413
Launce	(Act IV, Scene iv)	young adult to adult	prose	420

THE WINTER'S TALE

Shepherd	(Act III, Scene iii)	mature adult to older adult	prose	891